Organisational Behaviour

Fifth Edition

Organisational Behaviour

Fifth Edition

Knud Sinding and Christian Waldstrom

McGraw Hill Education

London Boston Burr Ridge, IL Dubuque, IA Madison, WI New York San Francisco
St. Louis Bangkok Bogotá Caracas Kuala Lumpur Lisbon Madrid Mexico City
Milan Montreal New Delhi Santiago Seoul Singapore Sydney Taipei Toronto

Organisational Behaviour, Fifth Edition
Knud Sinding and Christian Waldstrom
ISBN-13 9780077154615
ISBN-10 0077154606

Published by McGraw-Hill Education
Shoppenhangers Road
Maidenhead
Berkshire
SL6 2QL
Telephone: 44 (0) 1628 502 500
Fax: 44 (0) 1628 770 224
Website: www.mcgraw-hill.co.uk

British Library Cataloguing in Publication Data
A catalogue record for this book is available from the British Library

Library of Congress Cataloguing in Publication Data
The Library of Congress data for this book has been applied for from the Library of Congress

Acquisitions Editor: Peter Hooper
Production Editor: James Bishop
Marketing Manager: Alexis Gibbs

Cover design by Adam Renvoize
Printed and bound in Singapore by Markono Print Media Pte Ltd

ISBN-13 9780077154615
ISBN-10 0077154614

Dedication

For Paul Christian and Martin Andreas,
and for Julie and Jonathan – our kids.

Brief Table of Contents

Detailed Table of Contents

Case Grid

Part 1: The World of Organisational Behaviour		
1 Foundations of organisational behaviour	Opening Case Study: Christmas snow in the Channel Tunnel	
	OB in Real Life: No one best way of managing organisations	
Part 2: Individual Process		
2 Personality Dynamics	Opening Case Study: Narcissist Personality Leaders	
	OB in Real Life: Culture dictates the degree of self-disclosure in Japan and the USA	
3 Values, attitudes and emotions	Opening Case Study: Why insensitivity is a vital managerial trait	
4 Perception and Communication	Opening Case Study: Wobbly Wheels: Rabobank, cycling and drugs	
	OB in Real Life: Happy feet, beautiful shoes	
5 Content and Motivation Theories	Opening Case Study: Société Générale and the motivation of Jerome Kerviel	
6 Process Motivation Theories	Opening Case Study: Bonuses for bankers	
	OB in Real life: Students at FedEx	
	OB in Real Life: The nuances of feedback: performance reviews and culture	
	OB in Real Life: Pay practices in Britain	
	OB in Real Life: Rewards in China	
Part 3: Group and Social Processes		
7 Group Dynamics	Opening Case Study: A retrospective of the Challenger Space Shuttle disaster: was it groupthink?	
	OB in Real Life: Managing groups in the World of Warcraft	
8 Teams and teamwork	Opening Case Study: Miracle on the Hudson	
	OB in Real Life: The Israeli tank-crew study	
	OB in Real Life: This London company has turned corporate team building into a circus	
	OB in Real Life: Liverpool FC	
	OB in Real Life: Stage Co	
	OB in Real Life: Texas Instruments	
	OB in Real Life: BP Norge	
9 Organisational climate: conflict, diversity and stress	Opening Case Study: Real partners simply do not get sick	
	OB in real life: Fritz the Boss	
	OB in Real Life: Stress and death at France Telecom	

Part 4: Organisational Processes		
10 Organisation structure and types	Opening Case Study: Siemens – scandal and restructuring	
	OB in Real Life: Keeping Opel independent – maybe	
	OB in Real Life: The Mogamma, bureaucracy Egyptian style	
11 Organisational design: structure, technology and effectiveness	Opening Case Study: Keeping Nokia fit or shooting in the dark	
	OB in Real Life: Sir Stelios and the battle for EasyJet	
	OB in Real Life: Strategically choosing social responsibility at Patagonia	
	OB in action: Royal Dutch Shell	
	OB in Real Life: Lego's second coming	
12 Organisation and international culture	Opening Case Study: Seoul machine	
	OB in Real Life: Dress code at Apple	
13 Decision making	The Gulf of Mexico oil spill	
	OB in Real Life: 'Put jam in your pockets, you are going to be toast'	
	OB in Real Life: Incrementally creating the sick note	
14 Power, politics and conflict	Opening Case Study: The Stanford prison experiment	
	OB in Real Life: Ferdinand and Wolfgang – and Wendelin	
	OB in Real Life: Nasty people at work	
	OB in Real Life: Being social at work	
	OB in Real Life: Winning moves	
15 Leadership	Opening Case Study: Sweaty feet – with style, no stink	
	OB in Real Life: Ernst & Young	
	OB in Real Life: Hewlett-Packard	
	OB in Real Life: Richard Branson	
	OB in Real Life: Saatchi and Saatchi	
16 Diagnosing and Changing Organisations	Opening Case Study: Oh, no! First place	
	OB in Real Life: Asda	
	OB in Real Life: Boehringer Ingelheim	
	OB in Real Life: Bang & Olufsen	

Preface

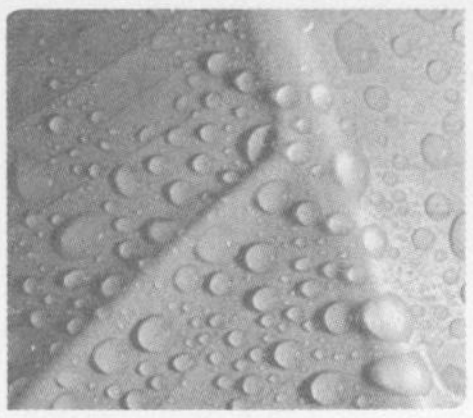

This is the second time we've been involved with *Organisational Behaviour*. Working on the previous edition was an honour and, whilst we did make a large number of changes and replaced a lot of cases, we felt that we should stick closely to the existing structure. Revisiting the text to prepare this fifth edition, however, has been a different experience altogether. With the benefit of hindsight, and invaluable feedback from our colleagues and students, we've been able to take a more objective look at what was working and what wasn't.

As before, our main challenges has been how to strike a balance between keeping the core of the text true to what our readers have come to expect and how to adapt to review feedback. With this in mind we have streamlined the chapter that used to be on Change and Knowledge to make it easier to understand and use – but the core content that students need remains. We have removed the focus from Knowledge Management to allow room to explore how students can analyse and implement change and this is reflected in the new chapter title 'Diagnosing and Changing Organisations'. While we appreciate the importance of Knowledge Management, this is a topic usually covered in more specialised courses and rarely in the introductory level courses on organisations for which this book is designed.

This change to Chapter 16 also reflects one of the ways we've enhanced the application of material. This chapter now has diagnosis in the title and it begins with a long section that deals with analytical or diagnostic challenges related to each of the main chapters (or sets of chapters). The logical progression is that it makes no sense to consider any aspect of organisational change if it is not preceded by a diagnosis. It's a long version of 'if it ain't broke, don't fix it': managers or leaders must be able to pinpoint where the organisation is broken before they start changing it.

We also found that the chapter on corporate responsibility wasn't widely used so it has been removed from this edition to allow a focus on more key topics.

It's also worth noting that we have moved coverage of Conflict from Chapter 9 'Organisational Climate' to Chapter 14 'Power, Politics and Conflict' where we feel it has a more logical fit.

As you would expect, this edition of *Organisational Behaviour* retains a strong European focus with full acknowledgement that many of the theories within the field are American, thus striving for a balance between theories from both sides of the Atlantic.

For this edition, as in the fourth, we've focused strongly on updating cases throughout the book in order to put theories into contemporary perspectives that are more likely to resonate with students and enhance their engagement with the subject. Cases now include The Gulf of Mexico oil spill, Royal Dutch Shell, and FedEx to name a few.

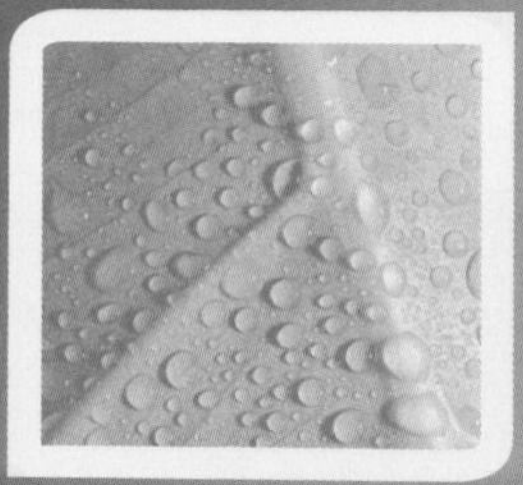

Acknowledgements

Our thanks go to the following reviewers for their comments at various stages in the text's development:

Joost Bücker, Radbound University, Nijmegen
Conny Droge-Pott, Hanze University of Applied Sciences, Groningen
John Hassard, University of Manchester
Anni Hollings, Stafforshire University
Kent Wickstrøm Jensen, University of Southern Denmark
David Spicer, Bradford University

Every effort has been made to trace and acknowledge ownership of copyright and to clear permission for material reproduced in this book. The publishers will be pleased to make suitable arrangements to clear permission with any copyright holders whom it has not been possible to contact.

Guided Tour

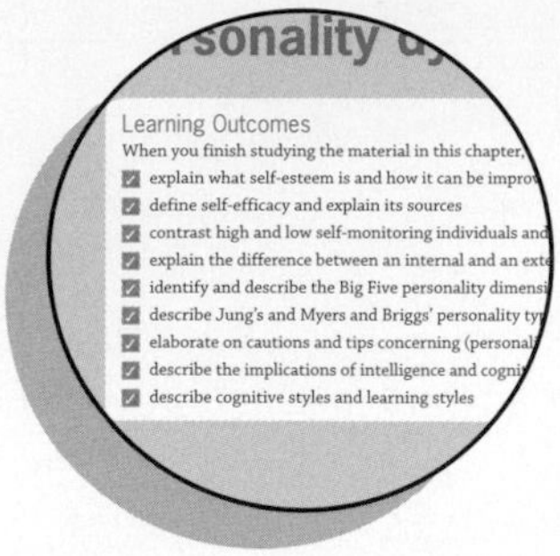

Learning Outcomes

When you finish studying the material in this chapter,

☑ explain what self-esteem is and how it can be improv
☑ define self-efficacy and explain its sources
☑ contrast high and low self-monitoring individuals and
☑ explain the difference between an internal and an exte
☑ identify and describe the Big Five personality dimensi
☑ describe Jung's and Myers and Briggs' personality ty
☑ elaborate on cautions and tips concerning (personal
☑ describe the implications of intelligence and cogni
☑ describe cognitive styles and learning styles

Learning Outcomes

Each chapter opens with a set of learning outcomes that pinpoint the key concepts introduced.

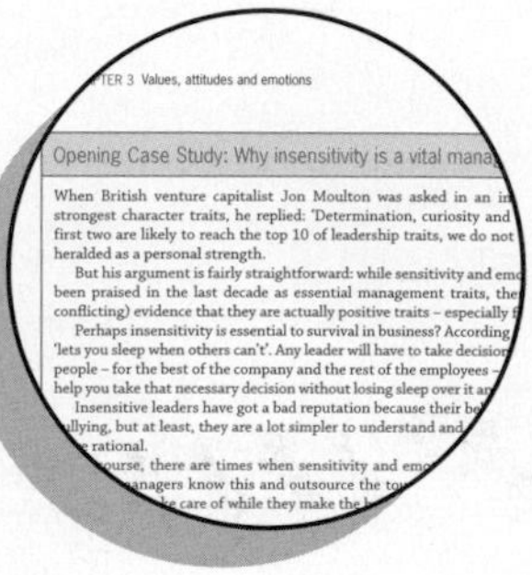

Opening Case study

Each chapter opens with an interesting and relevant case study to introduce and apply key theories in OB. Each case study contains questions to encourage discussion.

Opening Case Study: Why insensitivity is a vital mana

When British venture capitalist Jon Moulton was asked in an i
strongest character traits, he replied: 'Determination, curiosity and
first two are likely to reach the top 10 of leadership traits, we do not
heralded as a personal strength.

But his argument is fairly straightforward: while sensitivity and em
been praised in the last decade as essential management traits, the
conflicting) evidence that they are actually positive traits – especially f
Perhaps insensitivity is essential to survival in business? According t
'lets you sleep when others can't'. Any leader will have to take decision
people – for the best of the company and the rest of the employees
help you take that necessary decision without losing sleep over it an
Insensitive leaders have got a bad reputation because their be
bullying, but at least, they are a lot simpler to understand and b
e rational.

course, there are times when sensitivity and em
managers know this and outsource the to
take care of while they make the

Glossary

A

Ability Stable characteristic responsible for a person's maximum physical or mental performance.

Accommodator Learning style preferring learning throug ing and feeling.

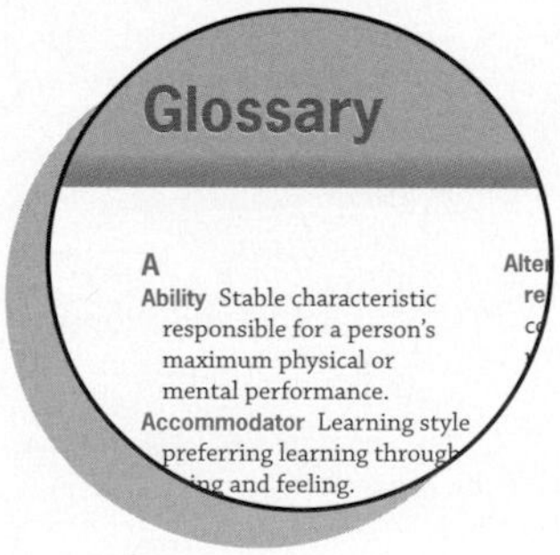

Key Terms

Each new term introduced in the book is defined in the text and highlighted to indicate this. A complete list of key terms is provided in the glossary at the end of the book.

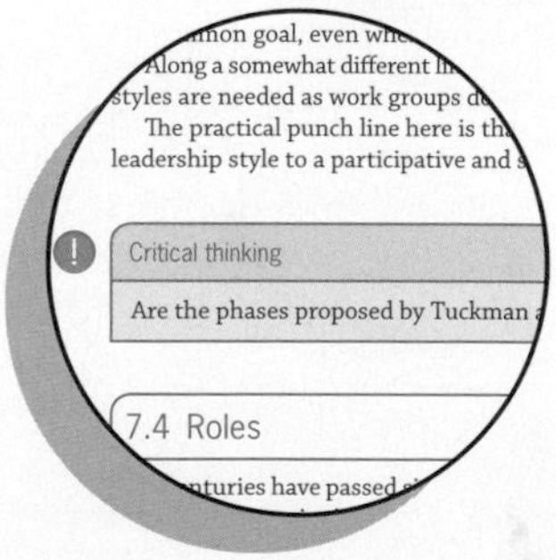

Critical thinking questions

Critical thinking boxes have been added throughout the chapters to encourage debate and discussion among students and to foster critical thinking skills.

mon goal, even whe
Along a somewhat different li
styles are needed as work groups d
The practical punch line here is th
leadership style to a participative and

ⓘ Critical thinking

Are the phases proposed by Tuckman a

7.4 Roles

nturies have passed s

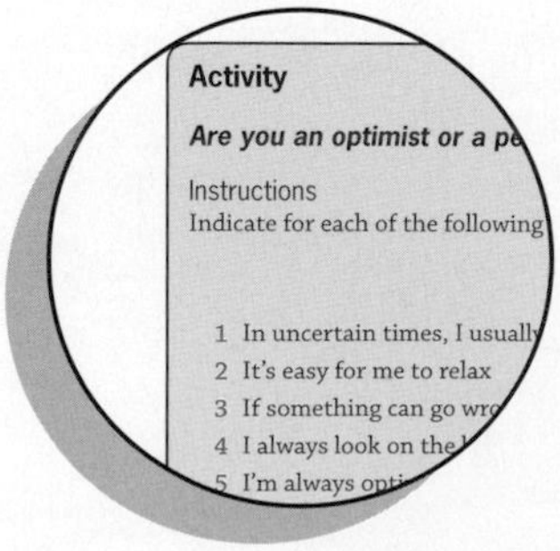

Activities

Activities are interspersed throughout the text to encourage analytical thinking and to develop skills through interactive tasks.

Activity

Are you an optimist or a pe

Instructions
Indicate for each of the following

1 In uncertain times, I usuall
2 It's easy for me to relax
3 If something can go wro
4 I always look on the
5 I'm always opti

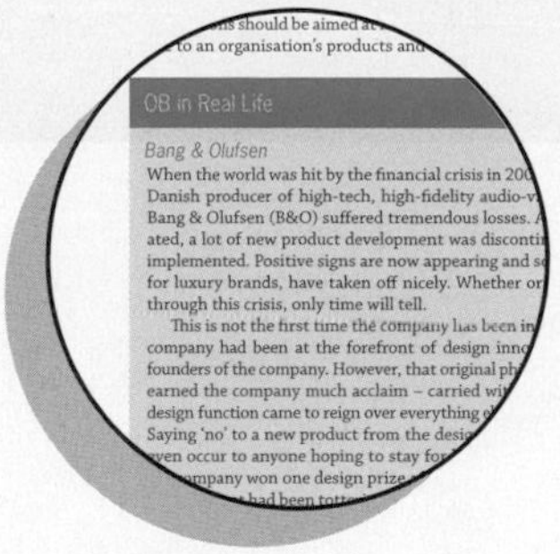

OB in Real Life boxes

These mini cases provide examples from around the globe, focusing on the differences in perceptions, cultures and beliefs that affect behaviour in the workplace, providing relevant and interesting insights and an international outlook on OB.

'HR' icons

Look out for 'HR' icons which appear in the margin of the page whenever there is a link to HR in the text. This acknowledges the relationship between the two closely-related disciplines and demonstrates where they overlap.

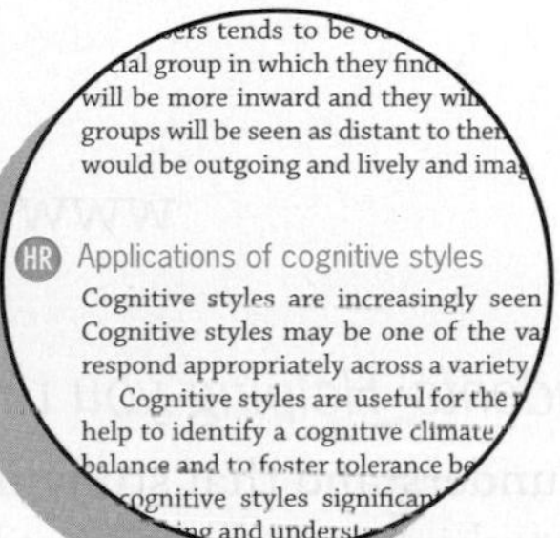

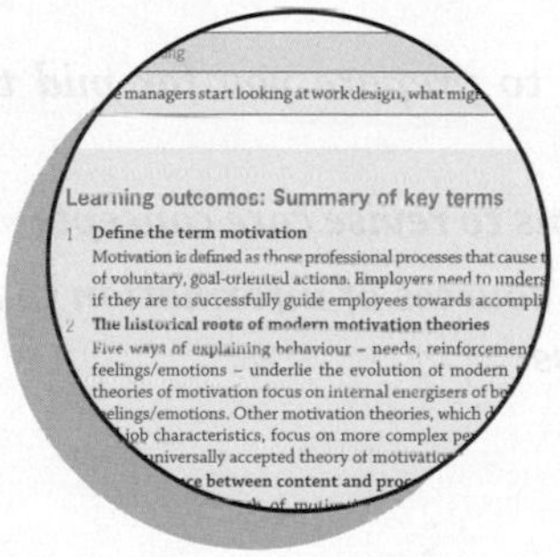

Learning Outcomes: Summary of Key Terms

At the end of each chapter, a short recap reinforces and clarifies the chapter learning outcomes.

Review Questions

These end of chapter exercises test understanding of core theories and can be used in class or as an assessment. As well as checking comprehension, the exercises require you to demonstrate your analytical abilities by citing examples and applications of the concepts in the chapter.

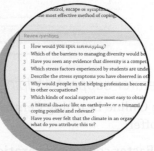

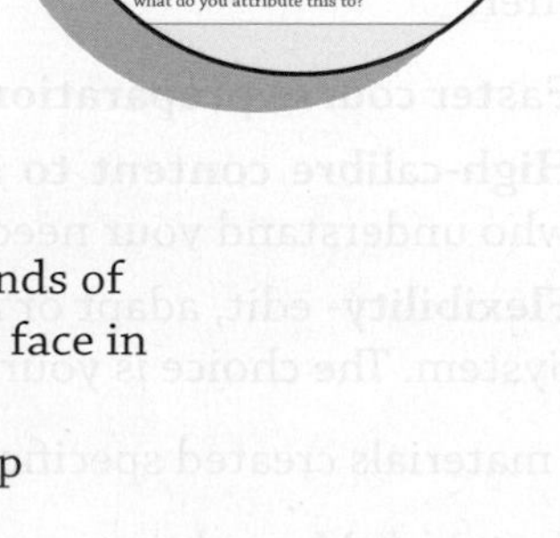

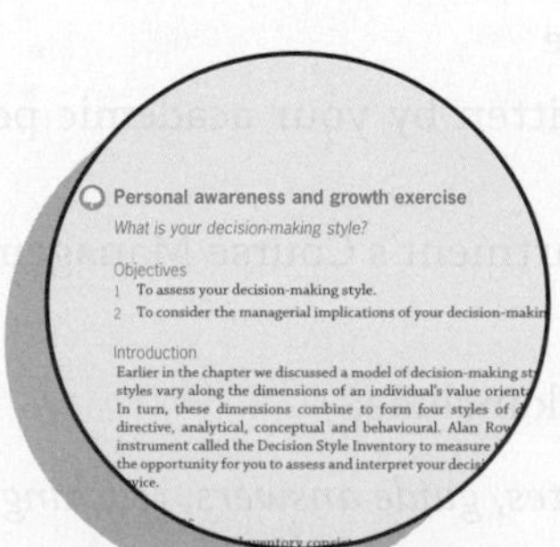

Exercises

A variety of different exercises at the ends of chapters illustrate decisions one might face in the workplace. They develop ethical awareness, transferable skills and group discussion.

Technology to enhance learning and teaching

Online Learning Centre
www.mcgraw-hill.co.uk/textbooks/sinding

Students- Helping you to Connect, Learn and Succeed

We understand that studying for your module is not just about reading this textbook. It's also about researching online, revising key terms, preparing for assignments, and passing the exam. The website above provides you with a number of **FREE** resources to help you succeed on your module, including:

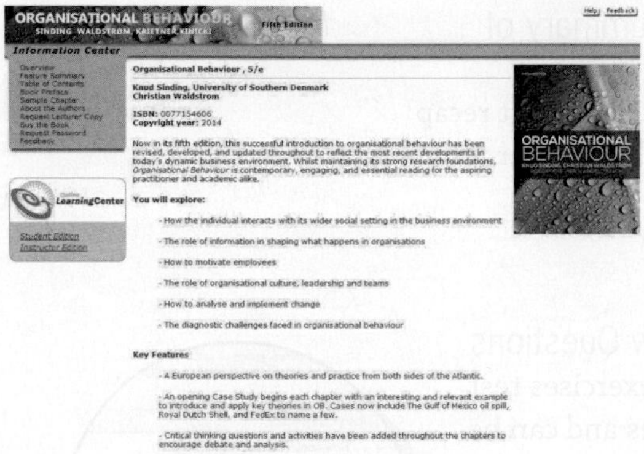

- ***Self-test questions to prepare you for mid term tests and exams***
- ***Glossary of key terms to revise core concepts***
- ***Web links to online sources of information to help you prepare for class***
- ***Internet exercises***

Lecturer support- Helping you to help your students

The Online Learning Centre also offers lecturers adopting this book a range of resources designed to offer:

- **Faster course preparation**- time-saving support for your module
- **High-calibre content to support your students**- resources written by your academic peers, who understand your need for rigorous and reliable content
- **Flexibility**- edit, adapt or repurpose; test in EZ Test or your department's Course Management System. The choice is yours.

The materials created specifically for lecturers adopting this textbook include:

- *Lecturer's Manual to support your module preparation, with case notes, guide answers, teaching tips and more*
- *Lecture Outlines*

- *PowerPoint presentations to use in lecture presentations*
- *Image library of artwork from the textbook*
- *Chapter Summaries*
- *Case studies from previous editions*
- *Test Bank*
- *Essay Questions*
- *Supplementary Lecturettes*

To request your password to access these resources, contact your McGraw-Hill Education representative or visit www.mcgraw-hill.co.uk/textbooks/sinding

EZ TEST ONLINE

Test Bank available in McGraw-Hill EZ Test Online

A test bank of hundreds of questions is available to lecturers adopting this book for their module through the EZ Test online website. For each chapter you will find:

- A range of multiple choice, true or false, short answer or essay questions
- questions identified by type, difficulty, and topic to help you to select questions that best suit your needs

McGraw-Hill EZ Test Online is:

- **Accessible** anywhere with an internet connection – your unique login provides you access to all your tests and material in any location
- **Simple** to set up and easy to use
- **Flexible**, offering a choice from question banks associated with your adopted textbook or allowing you to create your own questions
- **Comprehensive**, with access to hundreds of banks and thousands of questions created for other McGraw-Hill titles
- **Compatible** with Blackboard and other course management systems
- **Time-saving**- students' tests can be immediately marked and results and feedback delivered directly to your students to help them to monitor their progress.

To register for this FREE resource, visit www.eztestonline.com

Make the grade!

Part 1

The world of organisational behaviour

Part content

Chapter 1

Foundations of organisational behaviour and research

Learning Outcomes

When you finish studying the material in this chapter, you should be able to:

- ✓ give an overview of the different views that were a source for the development of the organisational behaviour (OB) field
- ✓ explain Taylor's principles
- ✓ describe the five key tasks of a manager according to Fayol
- ✓ give Barnard's view on co-operation
- ✓ explain Simon's ideas about motivating workers and bounded rationality
- ✓ describe the four alternative views on organisation studies
- ✓ contrast McGregor's Theory X and Theory Y assumptions about employees
- ✓ describe Morgan's eight organisational metaphors
- ✓ define the term 'organisational behaviour'

Opening Case Study: Christmas snow in the Channel Tunnel

On 18 December 2009, just before the Christmas holidays, massive snowfall in southern England and northern France severely disrupted train services. One service, in particular, was affected, the Eurostar, which connects London to Paris, Lille and Brussels. Five trains broke down in the tunnel due to electrical failures and passengers had to be evacuated in various ways. The train service was suspended and many passengers were inconvenienced. The breakdowns and subsequent failures led to a media storm, which, in turn, led to an independent inquiry. This edited version of the executive summary tells the story:

Executive summary excerpts

On the night of 18 December 2009, snow fell in the UK, with even heavier snowfall in France. The M20 was closed, as were a number of roads and motorways in the north of France. In these conditions, five Eurostar trains travelling to the UK from Brussels, Paris and Marne-la-Vallée (Disneyland Paris) broke down in the Channel Tunnel.

The first train to fail was recovered relatively quickly. The subsequent four trains then broke down in rapid succession and passengers from two of them had to be evacuated onto Eurotunnel passenger shuttles within the Tunnel. This was the first time this had happened in 15 years of operation in the Tunnel.

Whilst the rescue operation was carried out safely, passengers on all trains were delayed for a very considerable period before they arrived at their destination.

Following the train failures on the Friday night (18th), Eurostar services were suspended for three days, causing severe disruption to thousands of passengers. Over the days that followed, before Eurostar resumed a limited service on Tuesday 22 December, over 90,000 passengers were due to travel to and from the UK by Eurostar.

With Eurostar now having over 65% of the passenger market, even if disruption were to occur in ideal weather conditions, it would be virtually impossible to make adequate alternative travel arrangements to accommodate all passengers. On this occasion, the adverse weather made provision of alternative transport all the more difficult. However, Eurostar should have been better prepared for this scale of disruption and reacted earlier to try to help passengers caught up in the delays. The fact remains that Eurostar did not have a plan in place and had to improvise, and its provision of information to customers was inadequate.

In the main, the evacuation of the trains was carried out efficiently and in some cases creatively by Eurotunnel and the authorities. However, the Review highlighted serious concerns about the procedures in the Tunnel for dealing with conditions that arise on Eurostar trains when they lose power and subsequently their air conditioning and lighting.

The Review found no reason why, even with five trains delayed in the Tunnel the passengers could not have been evacuated in an emergency situation (which was not the case here) in a totally safe manner.

Twenty-one recommendations were made in this report, including introduction of video links between the various control and operation centers, a better rehearsed evacuation procedure, more training for staff and, most notably, the following:

1. We recommend that key complementary measures should be taken before the coming winter.

18.2. We recommend that Eurostar should agree with SNCF that as a general rule trains should not be left in the middle of the countryside or in a small station overnight.

The first one is simple to the point of banality: another heavy snowfall may come along as soon as next winter. The other clearly intelligible recommendation is 18.2, which sends a very rich message in just a few words.

More generally, this is a case where trains broke down and thousands of passengers were stranded in trains in the tunnel or in the countryside between Calais and Paris, or in icy stations when they showed up for their Christmas holidays. Conditions were poor, trains overheated, toilets stopped working and food and water ran out. Many organisations were involved (Eurotunnel, SNCF, Network Rail, Eurostar) whose co-operation was based on contracts and agreements.

The train breakdown and all the derived effects highlight organisational problems in a broad number of areas, including communication and specific procedures for this type of emergency. From these overall failings follows the need for a cascade of organisational modifications required to address each and every one of the detailed problems identified in the report.[1]

For discussion

At which levels of the involved organisations is there a need for change – and how can those responsible ensure that similar situations do not recur?

Source: Executive summary of the independent review of the Eurostar Incident: www.icpem.net/LinkClick.aspx?Fileticket=Q6EG8pYFIeQ%3D&tabid=107&mid=588

1.1 The history of organisational behaviour

It is nearly a century since Henry Ford said: 'You can destroy my factories and offices, but give me my people and I will build the business right back up again.'[2] Every day, business magazines come up with new stories reporting famous chief executive officers' (CEOs') claims that their employees are their main source of competitive advantage. The founder of Virgin, Richard Branson, said: 'There is only one thing that keeps your company alive, that is: the people you work with. All the rest is secondary. You have to motivate people, and attract the best. Every single employee can make a difference [. . .] People are the essence of an organisation and nothing else.'[3]

However, Dilbert cartoonist Scott Adams, who humorously documents managerial lapses of sanity, sees it differently. Adams rates the often heard statement 'Employees are our most valuable asset' as top of his list of Great Lies of Management.[4] This raises serious questions. Is Branson an exception, a manager who actually acts on the idea that people are the most valuable resource? Does the typical manager merely pretend to acknowledge the critical importance of people? If so, what are the implications of this hypocrisy for organisational productivity and employee well-being?

A number of studies have been enlightening. Generally, they show that there is a substantial and rapidly expanding body of evidence – some of it based on quite sophisticated methodology – of the strong connection between how firms manage their people and the economic results they achieve.[5]

A study by the University of Sheffield's Institute of Work Psychology, based on extensive examination of over 100 medium-sized manufacturing companies over a seven-year period, revealed that people management is not only critical for business performance. It is also far more important than quality, technology, competitive strategy, and research and development in its influence on the bottom line. The study also showed that half the firms have no individual in charge of human resources and that more than two-thirds have no written personnel strategy. One researcher said: 'Managers placed considerable emphasis on strategy and technology, but our research suggests that these areas account for only a small part of the differences in financial performance.'[6]

Jeffrey Pfeffer and his colleagues from Stanford University reviewed evidence from companies in both the USA and Germany finding that 'people-centred practices' were strongly associated with much higher profits and significantly lower employee turnover. Further analysis uncovered the following seven people-centred practices in successful companies:

- Job security (to eliminate fear of losing a job).
- Careful hiring (emphasising a good fit with the company culture).
- Power to the people (via decentralisation and self-managed teams).
- Generous pay for performance.
- Lots of training.
- Less emphasis on status (to build a 'we' feeling).
- Trust-building (through the sharing of critical information).[7]

These factors form a package deal – they need to be installed in a co-ordinated and systematic manner rather than in bits and pieces.

Many organisations, however, tend to act counter to their declarations that people are their most important asset. Pfeffer and his colleagues blame a number of modern management trends and practices. For example, undue emphasis on short-term profit precludes long-term efforts to nurture human resources. Also, excessive job cuts – when organisations view people as a cost rather than an asset – erode trust, commitment and loyalty.[8] 'Only 12 per cent of the organisations', according to Pfeffer, 'have the systematic approaches and persistence to qualify as true people-centred organisations, thus giving them a competitive advantage.'[9] Thus, there seems to be a major opportunity for improvement in most organisations.

The aim of this book is to help the student of organisational behaviour to become aware of the potential in understanding the people-centred aspects of modern companies and organisations.

Some **organisational behaviour** issues are becoming even more challenging as the activities of organisations become increasingly global in reach, either because outsourcing and specialisation places activities where there is an operating advantage, or because organisations seek to pursue opportunities wherever they may arise. Globalisation does not in itself change the way organisational behaviour works, but anyone venturing away from a well-known and well-understood context needs to appreciate that the emphasis on OB may vary depending on location. Variations can essentially occur in any of the fields covered in this book, but some areas are more likely to be impacted than others. This applies to motivation, culture, climate, leadership and power. Other areas are somewhat less affected; for example, organisational design. This and other areas may, however, be indirectly affected. For example, if decentralisation is partly based on trust, culture and teamwork, this practice may not travel well to countries where the assumptions are different.

Sources of inspiration of organisation and organisational behaviour theories

We start our journey in the organisational behaviour field with a look at the history of the field. A historical perspective of the study of people at work helps in studying organisational behaviour (OB), because we can achieve a better understanding of where the field of OB stands today and where it appears to be heading by appreciating where it has been.

Throughout history, there has always been a need to organise the efforts of many people, whether in the case of armies, city states or even larger empires. The history of modern organisational behaviour began in the early years of the Industrial Revolution.

In the nineteenth century, sociologists such as Karl Marx, Emile Durkheim and Max Weber studied the implications of a shift from feudalism to capitalism and from an agriculture-based society to an industrial one. Karl Marx[10] studied the development of the working class,[11] while Emile Durkheim[12] studied the loss of solidarity in the new kind of society. Max Weber was the first to study the working of organisations and the behaviour of people within organisations.[13] He is especially known for his work on bureaucratic organisations (see Chapter 10). As a sociologist, he also studied the rise of rationality in the new society and the importance of legal authority and efficiency in industrial production in particular.

Organisation studies developed as a separate field with the birth of 'scientific management' (see the next section on Frederick Taylor). This happened around the beginning of the twentieth century with the founding of the first large corporations, such as Ford, General Motors and Standard Oil. Scientific management offered a rational and efficient way to streamline production. It is called 'scientific management' because the recommendations to companies were based on exact scientific studies of individual situations inspired by the advances in natural sciences.

In organisations, people were only elements in the production system. This scientific approach to organisations evolved in the second phase of industrialism,[14] when the factory system expanded from simple manufacturing processes, such as textile, to more complex manufacturing ones, such as food, engineering and iron. These complex processes required complex organisational procedures, including control mechanisms, routinisation and, especially, intense specialisation. Profound scientific study of the processes was required to develop complex but also highly efficient organisation structures (for more on organisation structures, see Chapters 10 and 11). As part of that evolution, the function of management and administrative tasks rose and expanded considerably in number.

From the late 1930s the human factor started receiving more attention but it took several decades before the organisational behaviour field became well developed. The different sequential and contemporary views have resulted in different ways of studying, evaluating and managing people and organisations. Organisational behaviour developed from this human relations view as a separate academic discipline. Below we will highlight the work of some of the major management thinkers and explain the different views on organisations.

Later, other theoretical lenses for the study of organisations were proposed, including conflict theory, critical complexity theory and emergence, symbolic interactionism and postmodernism.

There is sometimes confusion about the distinction between organisational behaviour and organisational theory. This is not surprising as there is substantial overlap and many of the concepts from one field are directly applicable in the other. Organisational behaviour is associated with the behaviour of individuals and groups in the organisation, sometimes also called a 'micro' perspective. Higher levels in the organisation are correspondingly referred to as 'macro' issues, and refer to the field of organisation theory. The behavioural or 'micro' approach is sometimes seen as more psychological in nature, whereas the 'macro' level is seen as more sociological. Both have a number of distinct theoretical approaches and methods. Gareth Morgan, an organizational theorist, for instance, has emphasised that there are numerous ways in which we can view organisations. He summarised these different views in eight 'lenses' or metaphors for looking at organisations.

This chapter concludes by presenting the ways in which we can learn more about organisational behaviour. In addition, a topical model for understanding and managing OB is introduced.

1.2 A rational-system view of organisations

We now focus on the early days of organisational behaviour in the beginning of the twentieth century, based on the works of Frederick Taylor, Henri Fayol and Chester Barnard.

Frederick Taylor

Frederick Taylor is one of the best-known figures in the rational-system view of organisations and is the founding father of **scientific management**, a scientific approach to management in which all tasks in organisations are analysed, routinised, divided and standardised in depth, instead of using rules of thumb. Taylor was born into a Quaker Philadelphia aristocratic family in 1856. At that time, Philadelphia was an important industrial region in the USA with several engineering companies – hence, providing the ideal location for the development of scientific management. The breakthrough for Taylor came when he started to work for the Midvale Steel Company in 1878.[15]

Taylor made the work of labourers more efficient by increasing the speed of work and by organising the work differently. He studied each task by comparing how different workers performed the same task. Each of the studied tasks was divided into as many subtasks as possible. The next step was eliminating the unnecessary subtasks and timing the fastest performance of each task. The whole task with its subtasks was then described in detail and an optimal time was attached to each task. Workers were asked to do the task in exactly this manner and time. Each task had to be performed in the 'one best way' allowing no freedom for workers to choose 'how' to do their tasks. Making the work in factories more efficient was an obsession. Taylor accused workers of deliberately working at a slower pace, known as 'soldiering'. Part of the slow working was due to the fact that there was no management to control the workforce, who were left entirely on their own to develop their own working methods and to use ineffective rules of thumb. Workers were also systematically soldiering so they could just take it easy. In fact, Taylor accused them of conspiring to work slower in order to hide how fast they really could work.

Applying the ideas of Taylor resulted in the following consequences for the factory owners and workers:

- Higher output.
- Standardisation.
- Control and predictability.
- The routine of the tasks allowed the replacement of skilled workers by non-skilled workers.
- Thinking is for the managers, workers only work.
- Optimisation of the tools for each worker (such as size and weight of the tools).

Taylor also analysed the work of foremen. Their jobs could be divided into subtasks and greater efficiency could be reached if different foremen specialised only in one of the subtasks, such as controlling the speed, inspecting the quality or allocating the work. Low-skilled, and thus cheaper, workers could replace high-skilled workers through the use of more machinery and specialisation.

One of the most famous examples of a factory that successfully applied Taylor's principles was the Ford Motor Company. Many managers tried to implement time studies and other elements of

Taylor's system but refused to pay the higher wages that are also part of Taylor's system. The Ford Motor Company doubled wages simultaneously with the implementation of assembly lines and scientific management to compensate workers for the dull work – and as a way of creating customers for the cars.[16] Henry Ford, the founder of the Ford Motor Company, changed the production of automobiles from custom-made to a product for the masses. The Ford T, only available in black with no factory options at all, was the first car produced in great numbers for the enormous segment of middle-income people for whom cars had so far been an unthinkable luxury. This model was in production from 1908 until 1927 and 15 million Ford Ts were produced. This lower cost could only be reached by highly efficient production based on standardised and interchangeable parts (all pieces of the cars are the same for all cars), continuous flow (making use of an assembly line), division of labour (each worker is specialised in one very particular task) and elimination of unnecessary efforts (by applying motion studies).

Car manufacturers, as well as many other factories, are still working according to many of Taylor's principles. The work on assembly lines in particular has hardly been changed. There is a strong incentive to keep the assembly line moving as fast as possible. However, there is an increasing focus on quality and flexibility, so now both productivity and quality must coexist, leading to even higher pressures on employees. Many workers resisted Taylor's methods because they feared the harder work and their skills becoming obsolete. Skilled jobs were turned into non-skilled ones that could be done by anyone. Hence, workers lost their value as skilled employees. They also lost any decision-making power regarding their work. Taylor selected workers and foremen on the basis of qualities other than their skills and ability to think about their job. He chose them on the basis of their physical condition and their ability to learn and cope with the standard methods. Although the workers regarded Taylor and his principles as a threat, in his way Taylor respected them by paying them more when they followed his methods and increased productivity. Nonetheless, he mainly saw workers as people who could be perfectly conditioned and trained. The application of Taylor's ideas in many factories led to resistance by the labour unions and even to a strike. On 21 August 1911, a special committee of the House of Representatives of the USA was assigned the task of investigating shop floor systems, including Taylor's system. From these investigations grew a general resistance towards Taylor's systems on grounds of inhumanity.

Taylor's systems were very useful in creating high levels of efficiency and productivity, not only for labour workers but also for office workers and those in service industries. However, Taylor's ideas have been misinterpreted and misused, giving him a bad (but unfair) reputation for pressurising workers by inhuman work methods and forcing them to work at speed to enrich management. Nonetheless, Taylor did neglect some important organisational behaviour aspects, such as the importance of job satisfaction (see Chapter 3), non-financial work incentives (see Chapter 6) and the positive role of groups and teams (see Chapters 7 and 8). Taylor saw groupings of workers as the basis of 'soldiering'. Furthermore, later critics have referred to the 'deskilling' of jobs because the systems and machinery replaced craftsmen's skills and destroyed work satisfaction. Deskilling was especially prevalent in the Ford Motor Company's production systems, also called 'Fordism'. Taylor optimised productivity around existing tools and machinery but did not strive for maximum replacement of skilled labour by machinery. It was a combination of Taylor's principle on specialisation by dividing the tasks and the use of new machinery (Fordism) that led to deskilling. Many researchers in the organisational behaviour field have reacted to job deskilling, the alienation of the workers from their work and the products they are making, and the negative human consequences of scientific management.

However, a study of UK call centres teaches us that the principles of scientific management and Frederick Taylor are still alive (see the activity).[17]

Activity

Are Taylor's principles still alive?

Call centres are subject to tight control on call handling time with standardisation of the way customers' queries are handled. However, this should not be generalised for all call centres. Some focus on quantity and apply Taylor's principles to maximise the number of calls, while others focus on quality and allow more flexibility in time and manner of call handling. Nonetheless, most call centres are intensively monitoring their operators, even if this reduces staff motivation.

Questions

1. Do you agree that tight control and intensive monitoring are necessary at work in general?
2. Do you agree that tight control and intensive monitoring are necessary in an environment such as a call centre?
3. Will people work more if they are paid more?
4. What else other than pay do people work for?

Henri Fayol

Henri Fayol is of the same period as Taylor but was born and lived in France where he worked as an engineer and manager in the mining industry. Fayol is known through his landmark work *General and Industrial Management* in which he described the basic principles of management.[18] His management principles were proposed as general principles and based on rationality, in a similar way to Taylor, who also took a fundamentally rational view on management. Fayol worked his whole career, first as an engineer and later as a manager, in a mining company. His famous book summarised the lessons he learned during his work as manager in that company. The reason for its success is that Fayol was the first to describe management as a separate profession and activity in companies, practically inventing the concept of management. This does not mean that companies had no leaders, directors or managers previously, but management as a separate task (i.e. different from military leadership, e.g. Sun Tzu's *The Art of War*, or government rule, e.g. Niccolò Machiavelli's *The Prince*) was not studied separately until Fayol.

Henri Fayol made management visible by defining it and describing in a normative way what managers should do. There are a number of general principles that managers should follow and basic tasks that they should execute. Table 1.1 describes the five main management tasks identified by Fayol.

To execute these five basic tasks of management well, 14 general management principles should be obeyed. These are:

1. Division of labour.
2. Authority and responsibility.
3. Discipline.
4. Unity of command.
5. Unity of direction.
6. Subordination of individual interest to the general interest.
7. Fair remuneration of personnel.

Table 1.1 The Five Basic Management Tasks According to Fayol

Planning	Predicting and drawing up a course of action to meet the planned goals. To plan is literally making written plans, for 10 years, one year, one month, one week, one day and special plans. The 10-year, one-year and special plans are the most important and form the general plan. The 10-year plan should be adapted slightly every year and totally reviewed every five years
Organising	This consists of allocating the materials and organising the people. Most organisations are very hierarchical but every employee and department can still take some initiative. Nonetheless, authority, discipline and control are major forces in the organisation. Fayol pays a lot of attention to the role of the Board of Directors, which is the hardest to compose and has the important task of selecting the general management
Leading (commanding)	Giving directions and orders to employees. Commanding consists of influencing and convincing others to make them accomplish the goals and plans. This involves not only giving orders but also motivating people
Co-ordinating	Co-ordinating mainly refers to meetings with the departmental heads to harmonise the different departments into one unit, working for the general interest of the company. Liaison officers can help to tune radically different ideas and goals between two departments
Controlling	Controlling to what extent the goals were met and if everyone is following orders rigorously. This should be carried out by an independent and competent employee

Source: Based on H. Fayol, *Administration Industrielle et Générale* (Paris: Dunol, 1916).

8 Centralisation.
9 Hierarchy.
10 Order.
11 Equity.
12 Stability of tenure of personnel.
13 Initiative by every employee.
14 Unity among the employees.

These principles clearly include some aspects that we would now consider part of organisation theory, organisational behaviour and human resource management fields. Authority cannot work without responsibility. Everyone needs to know his or her responsibilities and should be punished or rewarded by his or her boss. Discipline includes sanctions when the rules are broken. Although Fayol puts the stress on centralisation in the organisation, he recognises that we should not overreact but find an optimal balance between centralisation and decentralisation. The same goes for hierarchy, which should not be too strict since it makes the organisation inflexible. Direct communication between two persons of the same hierarchical level but from different departments should be possible with the permission of their two direct bosses. Fayol took a very mechanistic view of management and a lot of what he considers management refers to organising and structuring organisations. In Chapter 10, you will notice that the four basic elements of the organisation structure, namely a common goal, division of labour, co-ordination and hierarchy of authority, parallel the managerial tasks of Fayol.

Fayol's major concern was the lack of management teaching, although management is the most important task for directors. Lack of teaching had three causes. First, there was no management theory or management science and, therefore, this could not be taught like other sciences. Second, mathematics was considered for decades as the best and highest possible development for engineers who will run a company. Third, in France, the most highly regarded schools were the schools that educated engineers (broadly speaking, this is still the case today). Accordingly, the smartest students were stimulated to choose engineering studies and so would learn more mathematics than writing and social skills. Specific knowledge, such as mathematics, is only one of the many skills a director needs. Fayol identifies six important skills a good manager or director needs. These are physical qualities, mental qualities, moral qualities, general education, specific education and experience.

Fayol admired Taylor, although he disagreed with two very important aspects of Taylor's ideas. Fayol did not totally separate thinking and acting. Every employee has some management tasks and should be able to take initiatives within his or her area of responsibility and within the rules of the company. Unity of command (i.e. one employee should only receive orders from one boss – see Chapter 10) is a very important principle for Fayol but does not fit in with the principles of Taylor. According to Taylor, there should be functional management instead of military management. Functional management refers to the specialisation of managers and departmental heads in certain management fields, such as time study, planning, the way the task should be performed, and so on. Fayol accepts the importance of this daily guidance of the workers by specialised managers but this does not imply that unity of command disappears. This very normative approach in his work is often criticised. Not all organisations need to be very hierarchical, tightly controlled and mechanistically organised to be successful. In fact, applying such principles may even threaten the success of the organisation.

Chester Barnard

Chester Barnard is less well known than the other authors mentioned in this overview but his ideas are no less important. He found that previous organisation theories had underestimated the variability of individual behaviour and its effects on organisational effectiveness.[19] Barnard was the president of the New Jersey Bell Telephone Company and in 1938 published his ideas in *The Functions of the Executive*.

Barnard builds his theory and ideas on some general principles of co-operative systems. Co-operation involves individuals. He describes individuals as separate beings but not totally independent. They have individual behaviour and the power of choice but their freedom is bounded by two kinds of limitations, biological and physical. An individual has only limited possibilities when acting alone because of limited physical strength and the impact on his or her environment. Co-operative action in a formal organisation is therefore needed. However, co-operation is not obvious. There are several possible limitations to co-operative actions which Barnard categorises as either a lack of efficiency or a lack of effectiveness (see also Chapter 11). Efficiency exists when there is a contribution of resources for the use of material and for human effort in such a way that co-operation can be maintained. If the reward for one's efforts is too small, one will resign from co-operation. Effectiveness exists, according to Barnard, when the (personal) goals of the co-operative action are achieved. Barnard identifies three necessary elements for co-operative actions, namely the willingness to co-operate, a common purpose and communication (see Table 1.2).[20]

Furthermore, Barnard explains that every organisation consists of smaller, less formal groups with their own goals. Management needs to align those goals with the overall organisational goal. An informal organisation exists within formal organisations and formal organisations cannot exist without the informal organisation. The informal organisation is more invisible and its existence is too often denied. Barnard made a major contribution by including individual choice,

Table 1.2 Necessary Co-operation Elements According to Barnard

Willingness to co-operate	The will to co-operate is often very low. There are a lot of organisations and in only a few is people's willingness large enough to co-operate
A common purpose	Goals differ for each person but there has to be some consensus between the individual and organisational goals
Communication about actions	Communication should be interpreted very broadly; a signal can be enough but the communication needs to be clear
Specialisation	Specialisation refers to the way things are done, which things are done, who to contact, at what places and in what time period. Organisations should try to find new ways of specialisation to make the work more efficient
Incentives	Incentives are necessary to persuade people to join co-operative actions and to reduce the burden of the work. There are many types of incentives, some are objective and some are subjective (also see Chapter 6)
Authority	Authority is 'communication (to order) in a formal organisation by virtue of which it is accepted by a contributor of the organisation for governing the contributor's actions'. Authority does not work without the individual's will to accept the orders, however
Decision-making	Decision-making is determining what has to be done in what way and can be based on own initiatives or authority. The former should be limited. Opportunism is the counterpart of decision-making. It is only a reaction to the environment. For every action there are some limitations in the environment. To perform the action the limiting factors must be removed, but doing this leads to new limitations. Constantly eliminating the limitations requires experience and experiment. See Chapter 13 on decision-making

Source: Based on C. I. Barnard, *The Functions of the Executive* (Cambridge, MA: Harvard University Press, 1938).

power and informal groups into organisation theory. Managers do not only need to 'pull' the formal organisation but have to manage also the informal aspects of the organisation (see also Chapters 7 and 8). This informal aspect of management and organisations is the major difference of scientific management that was still very popular when Barnard wrote his ground-breaking book. Barnard also clearly rejects the idea that material incentives (wages) are sufficient to motivate workers.

! Critical thinking

Describe to yourself or others your own encounters with thinking linked to Taylor's, Fayol's or Barnard's approach to management.

Herbert Simon

The work of Herbert Simon[21] is far too comprehensive to be simply labelled as a rational-system view of organisations and is much broader than the work of Taylor and Fayol. He is also from a later period. Nonetheless, we categorise Herbert Simon under the rational view because of his rational approach to the working of organisations and because he tried to apply principles of the 'hard' sciences (such as physics and mathematics) to social sciences, in particular to administrative and decision-making processes.

Simon had no working experience in factories, but instead followed an academic career. From 1949, he worked at the Carnegie Mellon University. He started with research in administrative behaviour, but was also very interested in cognitive science and computer science. He did pioneering research in programming for computer applications. In his later years, he was especially active in research in computer science. One of the most important highlights of his career was winning the Nobel Prize in economics for his pioneering research into the decision-making processes of organisations.

His famous work *Administrative Behavior* describes the behaviour of managers and the process of decision-making by managers and individuals in organisations. Simon explains that an organisation is characterised by its communications, relations and its decision-making processes. A major concern in Simon's book is how one can motivate an employee to work in the organisation.

Simon identifies three ways. The first one is the loyalty of the employee to the organisation because the employee identifies him or herself with the organisation (see also Chapter 3 for work-related attitudes). This seems to be the best reason to work for an organisation, but there is a danger that the employee puts the organisational goals above those of society. Organisational goals should not go against the goals of society, which are at a higher level. Second, training can help to teach the employee to work according to the organisational goals and it reduces the need for authority and control. The third aspect is coercion, further divided into authority (via persuasion, leadership, formal hierarchy or informal authority relations), advisory and information. In the last two situations, the employee is not so much forced as convinced. Simon describes in depth the role of authority in organisation.

Simon is also very (or most) famous for challenging the idea that people always make decisions in a fully rational way. Rationality means taking into account all advantages and disadvantages and aspects like future positive and negative effects (both uncertain). Humans want to be rational but are limited in their possibilities to be rational. Simon indicates this limitation as 'bounded rationality'. Limitations are both physiological (limited brain capacity and the physical ability to speak and read) and social (physiological limits are determined by social factors). Chapter 13 elaborates on the implications of bounded rationality in decision-making in organisations. Most theories, especially in economics, were based on the idea that human beings would always make rational decisions. Nowadays, the bounded rationality concept is also taken into account in a number of economic theories.

Simon worked together with one of his former doctoral students, James March, on the rationality concepts. They published another classic, *Organisations*, in 1958. March is possibly the most famous living organisation theorist. He also wrote *A Behavioral Theory of the Firm* with Richard Cyert, which is equally as famous. The latter two books discuss decision-making processes in organisations and question the rational-economic view of the working of organisations. Bargaining, control and adjustment determine the objectives in the organisation. Bargaining occurs among all parties in the organisation. There are coalitions formed mostly with owners and managers and not with employees. Still, the latter have some bargaining power. March and Cyert further explain that decision-making in organisations is not only a political process but also heavily influenced by the existing situation and the decision-making rules being used, which can be considered as the organisation's memory. The authors create a more realistic model of decision-making in organisations but are still trying to develop general rules for decision-making in a very scientific way, similar to the approaches of the other organisation theorists taking a rational-system view on organisations.

1.3 The human relations movement

A unique combination of factors during the 1930s fostered the human relations movement. First, following legalisation of union–management collective bargaining in the USA in 1935, management began looking for new ways of handling employees. Second, behavioural scientists conducting on-the-job research started calling for more attention to be paid to the human factor. Managers who had lost the battle to keep unions out of their factories accepted the need for better human relations and improved working conditions.

Elton Mayo and the Hawthorne studies

The connection between improving productivity and treating workers with respect was not new. Elton Mayo was one of the well-known human relations theorists who focused attention on employees. He did research at Western Electric's Hawthorne plant and these studies (known as the Hawthorne studies) gave rise to the profession of industrial psychology, focusing on the human factor in organisations.[22]

To understand the value of the Hawthorne studies, it is important to bear in mind the situation of the workers at that time: time-and-motion studies were used as an efficient way to improve performance. Piecework wage incentive was also introduced to motivate workers and to increase productivity.

At first the scientific management approach was very successful as it provided an answer to the chaotic business atmosphere. Later on concern arose about its disregard of employees' needs. Trade unions rebelled against the principles and practices of scientific management. A public investigation followed. Time-and-motion studies were no longer allowed in any US government work programmes and projects. The same was true for piecework rate systems and bonuses.

Until then there were not enough empirical data to justify paying more attention to human factors. The Hawthorne studies, however, provided concrete evidence. The experiments took place at the Hawthorne plant of the Western Electric Company, the manufacturing subsidiary of the American Telephone and Telegraph Company (AT&T).

The first study was designed to study human factors in organisations and took place between 1924 and 1927. The purpose of this study was to find a relationship between the environment and worker efficiency. The original hypothesis was that improved lighting would increase productivity. Tests were done in three different departments and results indicated that productivity increased in all three departments. No relationship was found with the level of lighting. The conclusion of the researchers was that many different factors influence worker output.

The second study, which took place between 1927 and 1933, is known as the Relay Assembly Test Room. Six women (and their work) were put into a special test room. Researchers studied the influence of certain variables, like length of workday, temperature and lighting. After one year the researchers, however, had failed to find any correlation between working conditions and output. Researchers were convinced that not only money and working conditions had an influence on productivity. Increases in output of the six women were influenced by the motivating effect of the special status (being involved in the experiment), participation (they were consulted and informed by the experimenter), another type of supervision (they were not supervised by their own supervisor but by an experimenter) and the support and mutual dependence within their working group.

On the basis of the results of the second study, the researchers decided to interview all employees at the Hawthorne plant. Researchers learned about workers' attitudes towards company policies and management practices. Also, the existence of informal groups within the formal groups was revealed. The interviews provided workers with the opportunity to air grievances, but, in the meantime, they showed appreciation for management's interest in their output. Management really used the results of the interviews to change the way of working in the organisation, to improve working conditions, supervisory techniques and employee relations.

The last study (1931–2) took place in the Bank Wiring Observation Room. Fourteen men were organised into three subgroups (of three wirers and one supervisor). Two inspectors moved between the three groups. The study revealed two important findings with regard to the social organisation of employees. First of all, two informal groups existed within the three formal groups. Members of an informal group did not always belong to the same formal group. Second, these informal groups developed their own rules of behaviour, their own norms. Workers were more responsive to the social forces of their peer group than to the controls and incentives of management.

Ironically, many of the Hawthorne findings have turned out to be more myth than fact. Interviews conducted decades later with three subjects of the Hawthorne studies and a re-analysis of the original data using modern statistical techniques do not support the initial conclusions about the positive effect of supportive supervision. Specifically, money, fear of unemployment during the Great Depression, managerial discipline and high-quality raw materials – not supportive supervision – turned out to be responsible for high output in the relay assembly test room experiments.[23] Nonetheless, the human relations movement gathered momentum through the 1950s, as academics and managers alike made stirring claims about the powerful effect that individual needs, supportive supervision and group dynamics apparently had on job performance.

Mary Parker Follett

Another human relations researcher reacting against the lack of attention for the human side in scientific management was Mary Parker Follett. She stressed the importance of human relations in organisations. Crucial to her was improving the relationship between management and employees. According to Follett, this was very important for the effective functioning of an organisation. Mary Parker Follett was in favour of participatory decision-making and a decentralised power base. Employees, the human elements of the organisations, were the key parts. Paying attention to their needs was the way to improve productivity.

Mary Parker Follett's view[24] on management was the integration of the individual and the organisation. She focused on both the interests and needs of workers and managers. The self-development of employees was very important to her. Her work was rather philosophical and idealistic. She had no experience with organisations but she observed business leaders and translated their ideas into useful management concepts. Several of today's management concepts are based on her ideas. Important themes for today's managers that are discussed in Follett's work are dynamism, empowerment, participation, leadership, conflict and experience (several of these themes are addressed in later chapters of this book). Table 1.3 gives an overview of these six concepts as explained by Mary Parker Follett.

Mary Parker Follett has received significant attention for her early insights into the very modern complexities of administration.[25] Her philosophical and managerial arguments were idiosyncratic in her own time, injecting a humanistic element into the scientific and analytical approach to human relations.[26]

Douglas McGregor

In 1960, Douglas McGregor wrote a book entitled *The Human Side of Enterprise*, which has become an important philosophical base for the modern view of people at work.[27] Drawing on his experience

Table 1.3 Management Concepts of Mary Parker Follett

Dynamism	An organisation is a complex system of dynamic social relations. People influence each other and they react to each other. 'When we think we have solved a problem, well, by the very process of solving, new elements or forces come into the situation and you have a new problem on your hand to be solved'[28]
Empowerment	According to Mary Parker Follett, there are two types of power: 'power-over' is coercive power; 'power-with' is the co-active, jointly developed power. According to Follett, power is a self-developed capacity, not a 'pre-existing thing' given to someone. Power cannot be delegated but you have to give employees the opportunity to grow and develop their power. The concept of empowerment today is in accordance with Follett's ideas: employees are authorised to develop their power in the workplace (see further in Chapter 14)
Participation	Follett describes participation as the co-ordination of the contribution of each individual so that it becomes a working unit. The prerequisites for co-ordination are clear communication, openness and explicitness (see further in Chapter 13 about participative management)
Leadership	Follett does not see the leader as a commander but as someone who communicates and shares the vision of the organisation. A good leader inspires others to innovate and to achieve new goals (see further Chapter 15)
Conflict	According to Follett, a conflict is neither good nor bad. Conflict shows the differences between people. Differences can be solved through domination, compromise or integration. No one likes to be dominated and a compromise feels like a loss. Follett's idea is that integration is the best solution. People can talk about the differences and reach a solution that is accepted by all parties. Integration is not always possible but it stimulates creative problem-solving which is also today very important (see further in Chapter 14)
Experience	Follett's ideas are based on interviewing business people. She really has a lot of respect for experience. 'We should make use of all available present experience, knowing that experience and our learning from it should be equally continuous matters'[29]

as a management consultant, McGregor formulated two sharply contrasting sets of assumptions about human nature (see Table 1.4). His **Theory X** assumptions were pessimistic and negative and, according to McGregor's interpretation, typical of how managers traditionally perceived employees. To help managers break with this negative tradition, McGregor formulated his **Theory Y**, a modern and positive set of assumptions about people.

McGregor believed managers could accomplish more through others by viewing them as self-energised, committed, responsible and creative beings. Forty years ago, motivation at work tended to be tackled as single-issue psychology (see also Chapters 5 and 6). Typical advice was 'people will work harder if you give them more attention'. Today, research in Britain revealed that if, for example, a company gives its people a chance to express themselves, they might feel that the organisation is a safe environment in which they can become personally involved. This, in turn, might make them more committed to their work so that they produce a larger amount of better-quality work.[30]

Unfortunately, unsophisticated behavioural research methods caused the human relations theorists to embrace some naive and misleading conclusions. For example, they believed in the axiom 'A satisfied employee is a hard-working employee'. Subsequent research, as discussed later in this book (Chapter 3), shows the satisfaction–performance link to be more complex than originally thought.

Despite its shortcomings, the human relations movement opened the door to more nuanced, some would say more progressive, thinking about human nature. Rather than continuing to view employees as passive economic beings, organisations began to see them as active social beings and took steps to create more humane work environments.

Table 1.4 McGregor's Theory X and Theory Y

Outdated (Theory X) assumptions about people at work	Modern (Theory Y) assumptions about people at work
1 Most people dislike work; they avoid it when they can 2 Most people must be coerced and threatened with punishment before they will work. People require close direction when they are working 3 Most people actually prefer to be directed. They tend to avoid responsibility and exhibit little ambition	1 Work is a natural activity like play or rest 2 People are capable of self-direction and self-control if they are committed to objectives 3 People generally become committed to organisational objectives if they are rewarded. They are interested only in security for doing so 4 The typical employee can learn to accept and seek responsibility 5 The typical member of the general population has imagination, ingenuity and creativity

Source: Adapted from D. McGregor, *The Human Side of Enterprise* (New York: McGraw-Hill, 1960), Ch 4.

! Critical thinking

Have you ever encountered a manager holding pure Theory X views?

1.4 Alternative and modern views on organisation studies

The rational-system view was – and still is – very dominant in organisation studies. However, there are other views as well, approaching the working of organisations from a less mathematic, more subjective and often more realistic view. These alternative views are aimed less at developing general principles for all organisations but instead try to explain the variation in organisations, organisational forms and their working. We briefly introduce the alternative views of symbolic interactionism, postmodernism, conflict theory and critical theory.

One stream within the field of organisational studies is **symbolic interactionism** which is mainly concerned with analysing the individual's behaviour and interactions on a micro level. It studies our interaction and the symbols of this interaction, and this communication and the meaning we give to the elements in the communication.

One of the best-known theorists of symbolic interactionism within an organisational behaviour context is the American psychologist Karl Weick, who views organisations as sense-making systems. People, managers and employees in organisations make sense of their environment and are actually 'creating' a language to talk about their environment. Weick explains the enacted theory in his book *The Social Psychology of Organizing*, published in 1969. This theory states that we create a phenomenon, such as an organisation, by talking about it. Hence, our world is a world created or socially constructed by our minds. Therefore, the world is subjective and how the world and organisations look and work depends on our subjective reference frame. Peter Berger and Thomas Luckman are two German sociologists who explained in depth the idea of a socially constructed world.[31] Weick applied this to organisations. He explains, among other things, that organisational leaders are selectively absorbing information from the environment, interpreting this information and constructing, on the basis of that information, the environment in which they think they are operating. They then make decisions based on this constructed environment. The filtering is personal but heavily determined by the social and cultural context of individuals. Within a similar context, people can observe or interpret the environment equally and are convinced that they have an objective view of the environment. This enacted view is important because it explains why people can have very different reactions and make different decisions in similar situations. It also stresses the difficulty in developing general scientific and rational principles on the working of organisations.[32] Chapter 4 discusses in depth the concept of perception and the biases this might cause.

The way individuals interpret their world is also the topic of study in **postmodernism**. The postmodernist view on organisations takes an even stronger subjective approach to organisations and their working, making it impossible to develop general applicable theories of this world. There are many authors taking a postmodern view of the world but there are not many who applied it to the organisation studies field. A well-known postmodernist thinker is the Frenchman Jean-François Lyotard.

Furthermore, there are no uniform concepts within the postmodernist field because that field specifically rejects uniform concepts, general principles or any other statement about the truth or the true world. There is no such thing as 'the' world or 'the' truth. Postmodernist thinkers also question traditional boundaries that are placed between work and private life, between the organisation and the outside world, between different cultures, groups, and so on. They also agree on the fact that the boundaries of organisations, as far as boundaries exist or are interpreted by us as boundaries, will fade and that work will be more flexible, informal, decentralised and unpredictable.

It was no coincidence that postmodernism developed in a period of change with new information and communication technology and globalisation changing the way organisations can and must work. Changes fitting within this postmodernist world are: just-in-time, global product and financial markets, despecialisation, flexible working forms (such as teleworking), virtual organisations, interorganisational networks, temporary organisations and jobs, and many other new trends in working that seem to blur time and space in our work conditions (several of these changes are handled throughout the book). However, organisation theory and organisational behavioural theories will not help us much to predict and control these changes according to the postmodernist view.

Nonetheless, postmodernism provides us with a critical way of thinking and a deconstructive approach to organisational theories. Those theories should be deconstructed to their basic assumptions and analysed from the point of view or reference frame with which they are constructed. In fact, you need to clear your mind of all previously held assumptions when you want to study the working of organisations to allow yourself to see things really differently. The lack of general principles in this view has, however, meant that this view has had minimal impact on organisational behavioural theories.[33] Nevertheless, postmodernism deals with the new trends in the daily life of organisations and can, therefore, become more influential in the way we do research and how we organise work.[34]

Conflict theory states that all social structures and relationships are based on changes and conflicts between groups and social classes. This contradicts the rational-system view, which sees organisations primarily as stable with a clear order. According to the system view, change can occur but is simply a temporary phase between two periods of stability. According to conflict theory, there is never stability. People in society and in organisations are always in a state of conflict because they have different goals and worldviews based on the different social, religious, ethnic, occupational or regional classes to which people belong. Scarce resources in combination with different objectives and views create conflicts that can never be fully resolved. Viewing organisations as based on conflicts between people has major consequences for organisation theories. Power, conflict and politicking will dominate the principles of organisation theory and organisational behaviour (see Chapter 14). Conflict is a source of change. Hence, conflict views on organisations are also used to explain transformations of societies and organisations. The roots of conflict theory can be found in conflicts between workers and company owners in the capitalistic economic model. The worker class and the capitalist class fight over control of resources and the distribution of profits. Karl Marx's theories are, therefore, an important foundation of conflict theory.[35]

Critical theory also has a very different point of view to that of the rational-system view, strongly criticising the functional perspective, control and efficiency orientation of this view, accusing many of the other organisation views as supporting capitalistic thinking. The field of critical theory is dispersed and broad and, therefore, one definition or description of this view is difficult to find. However, all critical thinkers have in common the criticism of functionalism and capitalism. Critical theory is, like conflict theory, grounded in Karl Marx's theories, and similarly has an emphasis on power as the dominant system in organisations. Critical theory takes as its starting point in studying organisations the assumption that control over resources and the labour force is the major objective of owners, leaders and managers.

So far, the impact of both critical and conflict theories on established organisational behaviour theories has been limited. The functional view, originating from the rational-system view, is still very dominant.[36]

The **ecological approach** has nothing to do with being 'green' or with 'sustainable development'. One of the great organisation theorists of the past 40 years is undoubtedly Howard Aldrich. He has always been acutely interested in the organisation-environment interface and his advanced texts are excellent at synthesising the current state of the field. Although Aldrich favours an evolutionary perspective and an overarching or metatheoretical framework, his overview of six alternative approaches is comprehensive and should be familiar to anyone interested in organisation theory. For each approach, Aldrich and Ruef focus on how that approach can explain organisational outcomes.[37]

The ecology involved is the ecosystem of other organisations in which a specific one finds itself. Outcomes, such as success or failure, are determined by the characteristics of the population and the environment of the organisation. 'How many are there?' and 'What is the size-distribution?' are key questions. Organisations in a population are very similar and respond in a similar way to environmental contingencies. In this approach, organisations compete with similar organisations for the same resources, regardless of whether they are Finnish newspapers, Danish banks or Arizonian undertakers.

Strongly connected to the ecological approach is the institutional approach, which focuses on the idea that participants in organisational life perceive the nature of organisations and their environment as something to take for granted. The classic concept involves institutionalisation as a process of instilling values.[38] Something that has been institutionalised has a quality like a rule or a social fact, irrespective of a specific factor or situation. These qualities are closely connected to the notion of organisational isomorphism, which consists of coercive, mimetic and normative isomorphism. Most attention seems to have been given to mimetic isomorphism, the idea that organisations copy what other organisations do. The institutional approach is broad and very popular. One of the most cited articles in all of social science, by DiMaggio and Powell, is central to this approach.[39]

The **interpretive approach** focuses on meaning at a micro level of analysis. Organisational reality is constructed socially and meaning depends on negotiation with others. The interesting part is not specific individuals but types of individuals, as defined by a social category. There is no agreement within this approach about what to focus on. Some believe that collecting stories, myths, ceremonies and rituals will provide explanations for organisational outcomes. Others hold that observation of behaviour and job history is a better source of information. Much of the interpretive approach finds application when we study **organisational culture**. There are, however, differences in emphasis.

Adaptive learning and knowledge development are two strands of the **organisational learning** approach. The basic idea in both is that individuals – and by extension, also groups and organisations – notice, interpret and use information to adjust how they fit within their environment. The adaptive learning strand involves repeating (i.e. keeping) behaviours that are successful (or seemingly successful) while getting rid of those that are unsuccessful. In the knowledge development strand, organisations are sets of people with shared patterns of cognition and belief. When patterns of cognitive associations are communicated and institutionalised, learning takes place. In this version, learning is more than trial and error, being based on sense-making, enactment, inference and experience.

Resource dependence is an approach that looks very much to the ways in which organisations are interdependent of their environments. It is an approach that views managers' motives in political terms – they seek to secure resources by interacting with others, well aware that these interactions also constrain their autonomy. There is a degree of similarity between resource dependence and the interpretive approach, in the sense that both view organisations as places where incentives and competing interests meet. The definitive treatment of this approach is to be found in the work of Pfeffer and Salancik, drawing on political sociology, industrial economics and social psychology.[40]

The economist Ronald Coase is most famous for investigating the nature of the firm and developing what has become the **transaction cost** approach.[41] Organisational outcomes are here seen as determined by the choice between 'market or hierarchy'. The level of analysis is different from the others, where the focus ranges from organisations as a whole (the ecological and, to some degree, resource dependency) approach to individuals. The transaction cost approach takes each individual transaction as the starting point and, every single time, managers have to ask themselves: make or buy? The decision is not necessarily a simple rational one, nor are all transactions similar. Managers are both opportunists and suffer from bounded rationality problems (as described by Herbert Simon), while some transactions involve asset specificity that sets off strategic behaviour between parties.

1.5 Organisational metaphors and modern organisation theory

During the 1980s, organisation studies, including large parts of the organisation behaviour field, became influenced by a set of powerful metaphors. These were strongly influenced by Gareth Morgan who is known particularly for his *Images of Organization*. In this, he explains that each individual has a different 'image' of how organisations look in general. Each individual can view organisations through different lenses. Morgan explains that each lens or image only gives a partial view of how organisations work. The overview and evolution of views of organisation theory and organisational behaviour presented earlier in this chapter all take different lenses to view organisations and, therefore, all take a partial view. Hence, if we want to understand organisations, we need to combine different lenses. Morgan's 'images' are highly recognisable metaphors. (A metaphor is a figure of speech characterising an object in terms of another object, often a more common object that helps to explain a more complex object.)

The field of organisation theory has moved far since Morgan published his important work. One of the most thorough treatments of the massive number of contributions to organisation theory was published in 2006 by Howard Aldrich and Martin Ruef, building on earlier books by Aldrich from 1979 and 1999. Aldrich and Ruef identify six perspectives which are distinct from the 'evolutionary' approach they themselves favour.

Eight organisational metaphorical lenses

The eight lenses identified by Morgan are summarised in Table 1.5 and explained in some detail below. Even though new organisation theory has appeared since they were first published in 1986, they remain intellectually stimulating.

The machine metaphor is very similar to how bureaucratic organisations (see Chapter 10) are described and the way that rational-system thinkers view organisations. Machines represent a

Table 1.5 Morgan's Organisational Metaphors

Metaphor	Characterised by
Organisations as machines	Orderly relationships Clearly defined logical system with subsystems Predictability and controllability
Organisations as organisms	Adaptation to the environment Open system that transforms inputs in various outputs Dealing with survival
Organisations as brains	Think tanks, having information-processing capacity Strategy formulation, planning processes and management of the organisation Self-regulation of dispersed intelligence
Organisations as cultures	Constructed beliefs and interpretations Subjective reality Own language, shared values, norms and mental models
Organisations as political systems	Competition, conflict and influencing Power and politicking Own goals versus organisational goals
Organisations as physical prisons	Being controlled mentally by the organisation Constrained thinking Unconsciously getting trapped in web of own creation
Organisations as flux and transformation	Self-producing system Mutual causality Dialectic change
Organisations as instruments of domination	Ugly face External domination of environment and humans Dominating own people

Source: Based on G. Morgan, *Images of Organization* (Thousand Oaks, CA: Sage Publications, 1986).

number of relationships between elements that work together harmoniously. Each element, each component in the machine, is crucial and must work exactly as intended or the whole machine malfunctions. The machine metaphor thus represents a system with subsystems but does not take the point of view of single individuals. In a machine view, there is no space for creativity, individual thinking or change unless the whole system changes. Concepts such as hierarchy, authority, line of command, departments, work allocation and organisation charts are all crucial elements in the machine view of organisations (these concepts are all explained more thoroughly in Chapters 8 and 15).

Machines are built for automating repetitive work and so are organisations, which look like machines. Production lines, fast-food hamburger chains such as McDonald's and other kinds of organisations oriented towards efficiency and routine work can be viewed as machines. However, taking a machine view in the case of organisations that need to be creative will lead to the application of inappropriate principles. Furthermore, the machine metaphor is criticised for neglecting human aspects and for viewing people as instruments or parts of the machine. Nonetheless, many people still see organisations as logical systems with orderly relationships which are predictable and controllable.

The **organism metaphor** compares organisations with the human body. Human beings need resources to survive. In biological sciences, the survival of living beings through evolution and competition is an important topic. An organism metaphor thus considers that organisations must try to adapt to their environment to be able to survive. The organism model characterises the organisation as an open system that transforms inputs into various outputs. The outer boundary of the organisation is permeable. People, information, capital, goods and services move back and forth across this boundary. Feedback about such things as sales and customer satisfaction or dissatisfaction enables the organisation to self-adjust and survive despite uncertainty.

Adaptation is the key concept when we study organisations from this metaphor. Hence, principles of open systems (see Chapter 11), change (see Chapter 16) and life cycles fit within this view. Contrary to the machine, organisms thrive on change. Such a kind of metaphor is of particular interest when we study organisations that are in a highly turbulent and demanding environment, such as many e-business organisations today. Internally, the organisation is seen as flexible, open and creative with only loose structures. However, a disadvantage of this view is the too strong emphasis on change, since organisations need some structure as a backbone to establish and maintain outward legitimacy, and cannot change infinitely.

Organisations learn, make decisions and process information; in other words, they act and think like our brains do. For organisation theorists taking the brain metaphor view as a dominant paradigm, the information processing capacity is the most crucial aspect of the working of organisations. Our brains, however, do not process information in a linear cause-and-effect way or via a fixed set of relations between elements of our brains. Brains have a more complex and flexible way of processing information.

Considering organisations as brains, however, does not mean that we focus on the strategic decision-making unit, the planning processes or the management of the organisations. Viewing organisations as brains means that thinking is dispersed in organisations. They work because dispersed intelligence in the organisation works together in a self-regulating manner. The learning capacity of organisations is crucial in this metaphor. Everyone in the organisation is able to learn and has valuable knowledge. Frederick von Hayek explains that every worker holds valuable knowledge and discusses how organisations work with the 'problem of utilisation of knowledge not given to anyone in its totality'.[42] Furthermore, such organisations are characterised by self-regulation (instead of structure), flexibility, autonomy, openness, horizontal co-operation and empowerment.

In the machine view of organisations, there is a clear task differentiation with a clear distinction between the decision and thinking tasks and the acting and operational tasks. Hence, such a view clearly contradicts the brain metaphor.

This metaphor is described by the organisation theorists Richard Daft and Karl Weick as a move away from the mechanical and biological metaphors, where organisations are seen as more than just transformation processes or control systems. In order to survive, organisations must be capable of interpreting ambiguous events through interpretative meaning systems: 'Once interpretation occurs, the organisation can formulate a response.'[43] In fact, the concept of the learning organisation, which will be discussed in detail in Chapter 16, is very popular in management literature and among practitioners and builds on the brain metaphor.

Viewing organisations as cultures (**cultural metaphor**) means that we emphasise the development of norms, language, shared values and mental models among people during their interactions. Hence, organisations are social groups that interact, build intersubjectively shared meanings and reinforce this meaning and interpretations through further co-operation and interacting. Important in this view is the fact that the members of the organisation construct their subjective reality. Thus, constructed beliefs and interpretations bind the organisational members.

The culture metaphor relates to the symbolic interactionism view of organisations. However, it is not the development of this organisational view that led to the culture metaphor but the impression that Japanese organisations were much more successful than Western organisations in the 1960s and 1970s. Researchers found that culture was the only factor that could explain the differences in success. Chapter 12 discusses in depth the importance of culture in organisations. However, many organisational behaviour researchers studying culture are looking at culture as an element of organisations besides other elements, such as formal structures, decision-making processes, co-ordination systems, and so on.

The **political metaphor** is a model of competition. Organisations have scarce resources and everyone in the organisation takes part in the competition for these. Furthermore, each employee in the organisation has his or her own goals, which often do not match the organisational ones. Hence, politicking is used to achieve personal goals. This metaphor parallels the conflict view of organisations. Central values in such organisations are: power, conflict, coalitions, competition and influence. Politicking is actually the unjustified use of power. Power can originate from formal positions in the organisation (authority), expertise (the possession of unique knowledge), (charismatic) leadership, a position of control, having valuable information about the organisation (knowing how things work around here), dependency (hold-up positions) or from a powerful personality.[44] Interest groups and pressure groups, which try to influence decision-making, arise in the organisation.

The strength of the metaphor is in the fact that politicking is not neglected as in many other organisational views. Many, if not all, organisations face some degree of politicking, although most like to hide or deny that fact. However, viewing organisations as only political is for most organisations highly inaccurate. An organisation that is dominantly political will suffer from large dysfunctionality and may have difficulty surviving. Power is used in organisations to achieve personal goals or to get control of more of the resources than is appropriate.[45] Hence, the achievement of organisational goals is at risk. Chapter 14 teaches us more about how to deal with conflict, power and politicking in organisations.

People can become trapped in the organisation as in a kind of **psychic prison metaphor**. We spend a great deal of our time working in organisations and our thinking can be dominated by that organisation, its rules and way of working. Our identification with the organisation can become so great that it starts to control us mentally. Our thinking becomes constrained by our life in the organisation. In fact, the organisation becomes a prison for our mind and body, not just from nine to five but also when we are outside it. Organisations with a strong control system, requiring obedience to many rules and limiting individual creativity, for instance, will also limit our ability for creative thinking outside the organisation.

However, people themselves create the organisation, rules and social systems that become their prisons. Hence, people construct organisations based on their own beliefs shaped partly by their own personality, while the constructed organisation in turn shapes their beliefs and personality. As Morgan puts it: 'Human beings have a knack of getting trapped in webs of their own creation.'[46] Important in this metaphor is that the development of a psychic prison happens unconsciously. Hardly any organisational member is really aware of the impact that the organisation has on his or her life in general.

The **flux and transformation metaphor** views organisations as being in a continuous change process. Morgan compares the organisation with all other aspects of our universe that are in constant evolution. The organisation is permanent in the sense that it can exist for a long time, but it is constantly changing inside. We observe permanence and order, but underneath, there is a logic of change. Morgan further explains that 'the explicate reality of organisational life is formed and transformed by underlying processes with a logic of their own'.[47] He suggests three images of change to explain this underlying logic.

First, there is the logic of self-producing systems or autopoiesis systems. Such systems are closed and autonomously self-renewing. The organisation makes representations of its environment and organises this environment as part of itself. Note the similarity with the self-represented or constructed environment in the postmodernist view of organisations.

Second, there is the logic of mutual causality. There can be negative or positive feedback making the system change. Negative feedback loops prevent change and create stability, while positive feedback loops result in exponential change. The organisation consists of numerous feedback loops based on causal relationships between its elements. To understand organisations, we need to understand these loops.

Third, there is the logic of dialectical change. All phenomena have their opposites: cold and hot, order and disorder, and so on. One cannot exist without the other, meaning that there is no use talking about wrong when there is no right. The same logic counts for organisations. An organisation exists because of its opposite, disorder. This also goes for any other aspect of organisations. The two sides often include conflict. Hence, many aspects of organisations are based on conflict. Think back to the conflict view on organisations previously mentioned in this chapter, for instance, the conflict between capital and labour.

Finally, organisations can also be seen as **instruments of domination**, what Morgan calls the 'ugly face'. He means that organisations are able to create many good things for the world but can also be very destructive for humans and the environment. Think of environmental pollution, social disasters when thousands of people lose their jobs at once, the health effects of cigarettes, the production of arms, child labour, and so on. In fact, the organisation producing cigarettes obtains profits for its owners and creates jobs for its employees, but in the meantime destroys the health of many others. Hence, this organisation uses its dominance to gain benefits at the expense of others. It actually uses power, not internally as in the political organisation, but externally to dominate others in the environment. Think also of multinationals that escape control of local government or can even control these local governments. Hence, we view here again the conflict view of organisations with conflicts between different social classes.

However, the dominance of organisations, like the bureaucratic organisation forms (see Chapter 10), also has negative implications for employees of these organisations. This dominant form of organisations forces many people to work in such organisations and suffer from the disadvantage of control and alienation. Furthermore, some people dedicate most of their lives to one organisation, spending all their energy and emotions in the organisation and sacrificing their private lives. They are voluntarily or involuntarily abused and dominated by that organisation. In 2002, 143 people committed suicide because of overwork in Japan. 'Japan is the only country in the world that has a specific word that means death by overwork: Karoshi.'[48] Many researchers also investigated the exploitation of blue- and white-collar workers and the creation of organisation structures that favour workaholism. This metaphor found support in the critical view on organisations, criticising the capitalistic system.

Activity

Assessing your understanding of Morgan's organisational metaphors

Review Morgan's eight metaphors in Table 1.5. Think about an example for each of the images Morgan describes. It may help to use organisational characteristics such as:

- A recent merger.
- A strong mission statement.
- A lot of contact with stakeholders.
- Strict internal procedures.
- A high absenteeism and/or turnover rate.
- A strong CEO.

1.6 Learning about OB from theory, evidence and practice

As a human being with years of interpersonal experience to draw on, you already know a good deal about people at work. But more systematic and comprehensive understanding is possible and desirable. A working knowledge of current OB theory, evidence and practice can help you develop a tightly integrated understanding of why organisational contributors think and act as they do. In order for this to happen, however, prepare yourself for some intellectual surprises from theoretical models, research results or techniques that may run counter to your current thinking. For instance, one important reason why stress and satisfaction remain popular concepts is the belief that happy, satisfied workers are necessarily more productive workers (see also Chapters 3 and 9). Hence, improving the 'feel-good factor' is believed to produce improvements in work performance. This argument has great superficial appeal, but, on closer inspection, it makes less sense. For example, feeling particularly happy may make it difficult to concentrate on a complex task, while a person's performance in a repetitive, machine-paced job may not depend on how he or she feels. In addition, there is little research evidence that supports such links.[49]

Therefore, research surprises can not only make learning fun, they can also improve the quality of our lives both in and outside the workplace. Let us examine the dynamic relationship between, and the value of, OB theory, research and practice.

Figure 1.1 Learning about OB through a Combination of Theory, Research and Practice

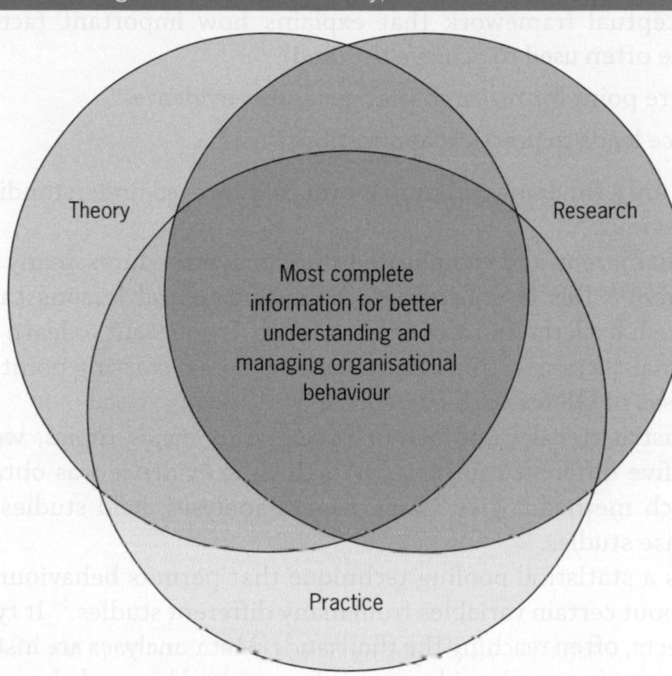

Figure 1.1 illustrates how theory, research and practice are related. Throughout the balance of this book, we focus primarily on the central portion, where all three areas overlap. Knowledge of why people behave as they do and what organisations can do to improve performance is greatest within this area of maximum overlap. For each major topic, we build a foundation for understanding with generally accepted theory. This theoretical foundation is then tested and expanded by reviewing the latest relevant research findings. After interpreting the research, we discuss the nature and effectiveness of related practical applications.

Sometimes, depending on the subject matter, it is necessary to venture into the large areas outside the central portion of Figure 1.1. For example, an insightful theory supported by convincing research evidence might suggest an untried or different way of managing. In other instances, an innovative management technique might call for an explanatory theoretical model and exploratory research. Each area – theory, research and practice – supports and, in turn, is supported by the other two. Each area makes a valuable contribution to our understanding of, and ability to manage, organisational behaviour.

Learning from theory and evidence

Theory is a story defining key terms, providing a conceptual framework and explaining why something occurs. A respected behavioural scientist, Kurt Lewin, once said there is nothing as practical as a good theory. According to one management researcher, a theory is a story that explains 'why'.[50] Another calls well-constructed theories 'disciplined imagination'.[51] A good OB theory, then, is a story that effectively explains why individuals and groups behave as they do. Moreover, a good theoretical model:

- Defines key terms.
- Constructs a conceptual framework that explains how important factors are interrelated (graphic models are often used to achieve this end).
- Provides a departure point for research that generates evidence.
- Theory and evidence leads to practical applications.

Indeed, good theories are a fundamental contributor to improved understanding and management of organisational behaviour.[52]

Because of unfamiliar jargon and complicated statistical procedures, many managers are put off by behavioural research.[53] This is unfortunate because practical lessons can be learned as OB researchers steadily push back the frontier of knowledge. If you want to learn more about research methods in OB, the final section in this chapter can be a good starting point. Let us examine the various sources and uses of OB research evidence.

To enhance the instructional value of our coverage of major topics, we systematically cite 'hard' evidence from five different categories. Worthwhile evidence was obtained by drawing on the prioritised research methodologies, namely meta-analyses, field studies, laboratory studies, sample surveys and case studies.

A **meta-analysis** is a statistical pooling technique that permits behavioural scientists to draw general conclusions about certain variables from many different studies.[54] It typically encompasses a vast number of subjects, often reaching the thousands. Meta-analyses are instructive because they focus on general patterns of research evidence, not fragmented bits and pieces or isolated studies.[55]

In OB, a **field study** probes individual or group processes in an organisational setting. Because field studies involve real-life situations, their results often have immediate and practical relevance for organisations.

In a **laboratory study**, variables are manipulated and measured in contrived situations. University students are commonly used as subjects. The highly controlled nature of laboratory studies enhances research precision, but generalising the results to organisational contexts requires caution.[56]

In a **sample survey**, samples of people from specified populations respond to questionnaires. The researchers then draw conclusions about the relevant population. Generalisability of the results depends on the quality of the sampling and questioning techniques.

A **case study** is an in-depth analysis of a single individual, group or organisation. Because of their limited scope, case studies yield realistic but not very generalisable results.[57]

Organisational scholars point out that organisations can put relevant research findings to use in three different ways.[58]

1 *Instrumental use*. This involves directly applying research findings to practical problems. For example, a manager experiencing staff motivation problems tries alternative approaches, such as goal-setting (see Chapter 6).

2 *Conceptual use*. Research is put to conceptual use when professionals derive general enlightenment from its findings. The effect here is less specific and more indirect than with instrumental use. For example, after reading a meta-analysis showing a negative correlation between absenteeism and age,[59] a manager might develop a more positive attitude towards hiring older people (see Chapter 9).

3 *Symbolic use*. Symbolic use occurs when research results are relied on to verify or legitimise stances that are already held. Negative forms of symbolic use involve self-serving bias, prejudice, selective perception and distortion (see Chapter 4). For example, tobacco industry spokespeople routinely deny any link between smoking and lung cancer because researchers are largely, but not 100 per cent, in agreement about the negative effects of smoking. A positive example would

be professionals maintaining their confidence in setting performance goals after reading a research report about the favourable impact of goal setting on job performance (see Chapter 6).

By systematically reviewing and interpreting research relevant to key topics, this book provides instructive insights about OB.

Learning from practice

Relative to learning more about how to effectively manage people at work, one might be tempted to ask, 'Why bother with theory and research; let's get right down to how to do it.' Scholars have wrestled for years with the problem of how to apply best the diverse and growing collection of management tools and techniques. Our answer lies in the contingency approach. The contingency approach calls for the use of management techniques, or specific theoretical models, in a manner which fits the situation at hand, instead of trying to rely on 'one best way'.

The contingency approach encourages professionals to view organisational behaviour within a situational context. According to this modern perspective, evolving situations, not hard-and-fast rules, determine when and where various management techniques are appropriate. For example, as will be discussed in Chapter 15, contingency researchers have determined that there is no single best style of leadership. In Chapter 11, contingency theory is applied to organisation design. Also, consider the next 'OB in Real Life' as an example of the contingency approach.

Fortunately, systematic research is available that tests our 'common-sense' assumptions about what works where. Management 'cookbooks' and many of the management books available in airport bookshops provide only 'how-to-do-it' and 'self-improvement' advice with no underlying theoretical models or supporting research, thereby virtually guaranteeing misapplication. As mentioned earlier, the three elements of theory, research and practice mutually reinforce one another.

The theory → research → practice sequence discussed in this section will help you better understand each of the major topics addressed later in the book. Attention now turns to a topical model that sets the stage for what lies ahead.

OB in Real Life

No one best way of managing organisations

One cross-cultural study of a large multinational corporation's employees working in 50 countries led the Dutch researcher Geert Hofstede to conclude that most made-in-America management theories and techniques are inappropriate in the context of other cultures.[60] Many, otherwise well-intentioned, performance improvement programmes based on American cultural values have failed in other cultures because of naive assumptions about transferability.

In France, the most common medical complaint is *crise de foie* (liver crisis), while in Germany, it is *Herzinsufficienz* (heart insufficiency). Prescriptions to soothe the digestive system are higher in France, while in Germany, digitalis is prescribed six times more frequently to stimulate the heart. These differences have been attributed to the French cultural obsession with food, and the German cultural quest for romanticism. In other words, different countries have very different approaches to medicine. If the practice of medicine is shaped by its cultural origins, why should the practice of management be any different?

Source: Based on C. Schneider and J. L. Barsoux, *Managing across Cultures* (London: Prentice-Hall, 1997).

A topical model for understanding and managing OB

By definition, organisational behaviour is both research- and application-oriented. The three basic levels of analysis in OB are the individual, the group and the organisation. OB draws on a very diverse array of disciplines – including psychology, management, sociology, organisation theory, social psychology, statistics, anthropology, general systems theory, economics, information technology, political science, vocational counselling, human stress management, psychometrics, ergonomics, decision theory and ethics. This rich heritage has spawned many competing perspectives and theories about human work behaviour. By the mid-1980s, one researcher had identified 110 distinct theories about behaviour within the field of OB.[61]

'Organisational behaviour' is an academic designation. With the exception of teaching and research positions, OB is not an everyday job category such as accounting, marketing or finance. Students of OB typically do not get jobs in organisational behaviour as such. This reality in no way demeans OB or lessens its importance in effective organisational management. OB is a horizontal discipline that cuts across virtually every job category, business function and professional specialty. Anyone who plans to make a living in a large or small, public or private, organisation needs to study organisational behaviour.

Figure 1.2 is a map for our journey through this book, indicating the topics through which we pass. Our destination is organisational effectiveness via continuous improvement. The study of OB can be a wandering and pointless trip if we overlook the need to translate OB lessons into effective and efficiently organised endeavour.

At the far left of our 'topical road map' are managers, those who are responsible for accomplishing organisational results with and through others. The three circles at the centre of the map correspond to the different parts of this book. Logically, the flow of topical coverage in this book

Figure 1.2 A Topical Model for What Lies Ahead

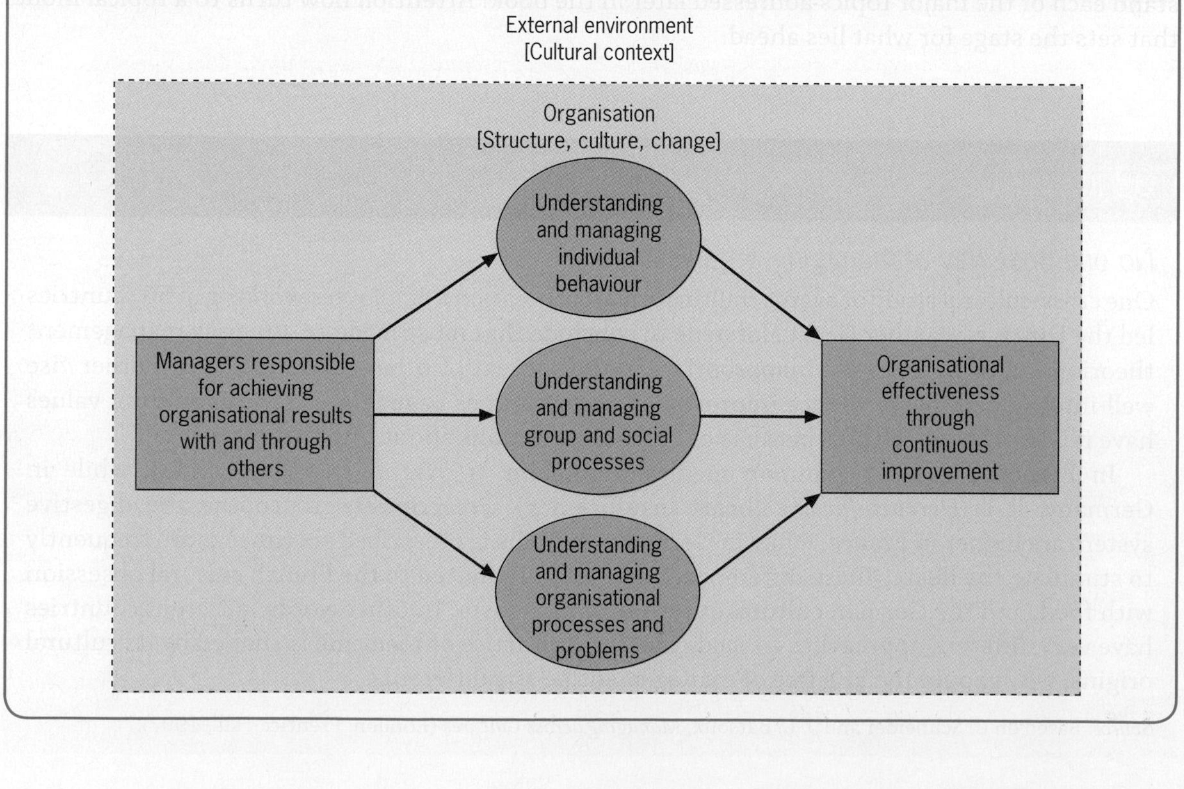

(following the introductory Part 1) goes from individuals to group processes, to organisational processes and problems. Around the core of our topical road map in Figure 1.2 is the organisation.

The broken line represents a permeable boundary between the organisation and its environment. Energy and influence flow both ways across this permeable boundary. Truly, no organisation is an island in today's highly interactive and interdependent world.

1.7 Research methods in organisational behaviour

In the future, you will probably be involved in developing and/or implementing programmes for solving business problems. You may also be asked to assess recommendations derived from in-house research reports or judge the usefulness of proposals from consultants. These tasks might entail reading and evaluating research findings presented both in scientific and professional journal articles. Thus, it is important for professionals to have a basic working knowledge of the research process. Moreover, such knowledge can help you critically evaluate research information encountered daily in newspaper, magazine and television reports.

Studies revealed that people often cannot judge the difference between good and bad research.[62] So, how do they know what to believe about research results pertaining to organisational or societal problems? This learning module presents a foundation for understanding the research process. Our purpose is not to make you a research scientist. The purpose is to make you a better consumer of research information.

Research on organisational behaviour is based on the scientific method. The scientific method is a formal process of using systematically gathered data to test hypotheses or to explain natural phenomena.

Measurement and data collection

Job satisfaction, turnover, performance and perceived stress are variables typically measured in OB research. Valid measurement is one of the most critical components of any research study because research findings are open to conflicting interpretations when variables are poorly measured.[63] Four techniques are frequently used to collect data: (1) direct observation, (2) questionnaires, (3) interviews and (4) indirect methods.

1 *Observation*. This technique consists of recording the number of times a specified behaviour is exhibited. For example, psychologist Judith Komaki developed and validated an observational categorisation of supervisory behaviour. She then used the instrument to identify behaviour differences between effective and ineffective managers from a large medical insurance firm. Managerial effectiveness was based on superior ratings. Results indicated that effective managers spent more time monitoring their employees' performance than did ineffective managers. Komaki also applied the same instrument to examine the performance of sailboat captains competing in a race. Similarly to her previous study, skippers finished higher in the overall race standings when they monitored and rewarded their crews.[64]

2 *Questionnaires*. Questionnaires ask respondents for their opinions or feelings about work-related issues. They generally contain previously developed and validated instruments and are self-administered. Given their impersonal nature, poorly designed questionnaires are susceptible to rate bias. Nevertheless, a well-developed survey can be an accurate and economical way to collect large quantities of data.[65]

3 *Interviews*. Interviews rely on either face-to-face or telephone interactions to ask respondents questions of interest. In a structured interview, interviewees are asked the same question in the same order. Unstructured interviews do not require interviewers to use the same questions or format. Unstructured interviews are more spontaneous. Structured interviews are the better of the two because they permit consistent comparisons between people. Accordingly, human resource management experts strongly recommend structured interviews during the hiring process to permit candidate-to-candidate comparisons.[66]

4 *Indirect methods*. These techniques obtain data without any direct contact with respondents. This approach may entail observing someone without his or her knowledge. Other examples include searching existing records, such as personnel files, for data on variables such as absenteeism, turnover and output. This method reduces rater error and is generally used in combination with one of the previously discussed techniques.

Evaluating research methods and conclusions

All research methods can be evaluated from three perspectives: (1) generalisability, (2) precision in control and measurement, and (3) realism of the context.[67] Generalisability, which is also referred to as 'external validity', reflects the extent to which results from one study are generalisable to other individuals, groups or situations. Precision in control and measurement pertains to the level of accuracy in manipulating or measuring variables. A realistic context is one that naturally exists for the individuals participating in the research study. In other words, realism implies that the context is not an artificial situation contrived for purposes of conducting the study. Table 1.6 presents an evaluation of the five most frequently used research methods in terms of these three perspectives.

In summary, there is no one best research method. Choosing a method depends on the purpose of the specific study.[68] For example, if high control is necessary, as in testing for potential radiation leaks in pipes that will be used in a nuclear power plant, a laboratory experiment is appropriate (see Table 1.6); in contrast, sample surveys would be useful if a company wanted to know the generalisable impact of a television commercial for light beer.

There are several issues to consider when evaluating the quality of a research study. The first is whether results from the specific study are consistent with those from past research. If not, it is helpful to determine why discrepancies exist. For instance, it is insightful to compare the samples, research methods, measurement of variables, statistical analyses and general research procedures across the discrepant studies. Extreme differences suggest that future research may be

Table 1.6 Assessment of Frequently Used Research Methods

Method	Generalisability	Precision in control and measurement	Realistic context
Case study	Low	Low	High
Sample survey	High	Low	Low
Field study	Moderate	Moderate	High
Laboratory experiment	Low	High	Low
Field experiment	Moderate	Moderate	Moderate

Source: Adapted in part from J. E. McGrath, J. Martin and R. A. Kulka, *Judgment Calls in Research* (Beverly Hills, CA: Sage Publications, 1982).

needed to reconcile the inconsistent results. In the meantime, however, we need to be cautious in applying research findings from one study that are consistent with those from a larger number of studies.

The type of research method used is the second consideration. Does the method have generalisability? If not, check the characteristics of the sample. If the sample's characteristics are different from the characteristics of your work group, conclusions may not be relevant for your organisation. Sample characteristics are very important in evaluating results from both field studies and experiments.

The level of precision in control and measurement is the third factor to consider. It is important to determine whether valid measures were used in the study. This can be done by reading the original study and examining descriptions of how variables were measured. Variables have questionable validity when they are measured with one-item scales or 'ad hoc' instruments developed by the authors. In contrast, standardised scales tend to be more valid because they are typically developed and validated in previous research studies. We have more confidence in results when they are based on analyses using standardised scales. As a general rule, validity in measurement begets confidence in applying research findings.

Finally, it is helpful to brainstorm alternative explanations for the research results. This helps to identify potential problems with research procedures.

Reading a scientific journal article

A vast volume of research, both empirical and theoretical, is published in scientific journals and professional magazines. Table 1.7 is a short list of journals relevant in some way to the OB field. This is a ranking based on how much papers from different journals are cited in other published papers.

These are indeed very scholarly. They are also often somewhat repetitive and, of course, since they are written by scholars and for scholars, a high level of prior knowledge is often implicitly assumed. All the material in these journals is potentially interesting, but not all published papers stand out or become classics. Those that do are often well worth the effort.

Reading a scholarly article is sometimes a matter of starting at the beginning. However, the vast volume of material needs selective navigation. Sorting based on key words or a quick reading of the abstract often helps when facing an overwhelming volume of material. Students using this book should look at a selection of papers from one or more of the journals listed in Table 1.7.

Table 1.7 The Most Important Management and Business Journals 2013, Ranked by Article Influence® Score

Management Information Systems Quarterly
Academy of Management Journal
Academy of Management Review
Organization Science
Administrative Science Quarterly
Strategic Management Journal
Academy of Management Annals
Personnel Psychology
Journal of Management
Journal of Applied Psychology

Source: Thomson Reuters, ISI Web of Knowledge.

Activity

Present the key points of any of the following articles, 'The collapse of sensemaking in organisations: the Mann Gulch disaster' by Weick, 'Toward a theory of stakeholder identification and salience: Defining the principle of who and what really counts' by Mitchell, Agle and Wood, or another paper from one of the journals listed in Table 1.7.

Scholars are not always focused on publishing in highly specialised journals. The list in Table 1.7, in fact, covers journals both broad and narrow in scope. None are well suited for the general reader, the manager or the management consultant. To serve these markets, a number of more accessible journals are available. The leader among these is probably *Harvard Business Review*. Other examples of this type of journal include *Business Horizons, HR Magazine, Sloan Management Review* and *California Management Review*. These publications are more accessible and essentially provide a window that allows a glimpse of research results, without the technical trappings.

Learning outcomes: Summary of key terms

1 **The early development of the organisational behaviour field**

First studies on organisational behaviour were made by the sociologists. However, studies of the working of organisations started at the very beginning of the twentieth century with the birth of scientific management in which a rational-system view of organisations is taken. The main researchers of this view were Taylor, Fayol, Barnard and Simon. Later, alternative views on the working of organisations developed, such as symbolic interactionism, postmodernism, conflict theory and critical theory. Around 1930, the human relations movement arose with more attention paid to the human factor in organisations. The Hawthorne studies, Mary Parker Follett and McGregor's Theory Y provided the most influential ideas in this movement.

2 **Taylor's principles**

Taylor increased productivity by studying work methods. He divided tasks into many small subtasks for which he determined the most optimal time and manner to do the task. All tasks should be standardised, controlled and routinised. The management of the tasks and the execution of the tasks should be clearly separated.

3 **The five key tasks of a manager according to Fayol**

The key tasks are: planning, organising, commanding, co-ordinating and controlling. Every person in the company has to do these tasks to some degrees but the higher in the hierarchy, the more time is spent on these five sequential tasks.

4 **Barnard's view on co-operation**

There are several conditions that need to be fulfilled to allow co-operation, such as a willingness to co-operate, a common purpose and communication. This needs to be accomplished with specialisation, incentives, authority and decision-making to allow efficient co-operation in organisations. Managers need to create the conditions for efficient co-operation but have to pay attention to informal aspects as well, such as the existence of informal groups and power.

5 **Simon's ideas about motivating workers and bounded rationality**

There are three ways in which employees can be motivated: identification with the organisation, training and coercion. To make the right decisions in organisations, we need to think rationally but humans are bounded, physically and socially in their ability to process information and to be rational.

6 **Four alternative views of organisation studies**

Symbolic interactionism explains that our world is subjectively created through interactions. Postmodernism questions the existence of any objective concept and principle. Conflict theory is based on the idea that all organisational structures are based on conflict. Critical theory reacts against the dominant capitalistic view of organisations, which is based on control over resources.

7 **McGregor's Theory X and Theory Y assumptions about employees**

Theory X employees, according to traditional thinking, dislike work, require close supervision and are primarily interested in security. According to the modern Theory Y, employees are capable of self-direction, seeking responsibility and being creative.

8 **Morgan's eight organisational metaphors**

The eight metaphors are: machines (a system view on organisations), organisms (organisations are like human organisms), brains (dispersed information-processing and knowledge-creating capacity), culture (organisation is a culture), political system (competition is the core of organisations), psychic prison (our lives are completely dominated by the organisation), flux and transformation (there are fundamental change processes in organisations) and instruments of domination (organisations dominate their internal and external environment).

9 **Why OB is a horizontal discipline**

Organisational behaviour (OB) is an interdisciplinary field dedicated to better understanding and managing people at work. It is both research- and application-oriented. Except for teaching and research positions, one does not normally get a job in OB. Rather, because OB is a horizontal discipline, its concepts and lessons are applicable to virtually every job category, business function and professional specialty.

Review questions

1 Why has Taylor been so strongly criticised?

2 What are the major differences between the ideas of Taylor, Fayol and Barnard?

3 What do you think are the functions of a manager?

4 Consider the alternative views and the rational view of organisations. Which of these views is, in your opinion, the most realistic view of the working of organisations? Why?

5 Why look at the typical employee as a human resource?

6 Why is it said that Mary Parker Follett was ahead of her time?

7 What is your personal experience of Theory X and Theory Y managers (see Table 1.4)? Which did you prefer? Why?

Personal awareness and growth exercise

What is your view of today's employees?

Objective

To identify whether you have a rather modern or a rather conservative view of today's employees.

Introduction

How we look at employees influences our behaviour towards them. Douglas McGregor identified two contrasting sets of assumptions of people at work, as described in Table 1.4. The rather positive, modern view is called Theory Y, the contrasting, negative one Theory X.

Instructions

Respond to the items below as they apply to your view of people at work today. On completion, compute your total score by adding up your responses. In the scoring key, you will find the interpretation of your results.

5 = strongly agree
4 = agree
3 = neither agree nor disagree
2 = disagree
1 = strongly disagree

1	Work is distasteful to most employees.	5	4	3	2	1
2	People are mainly motivated by extrinsic rewards, such as bonuses.	5	4	3	2	1
3	Most people dislike working.	5	4	3	2	1
4	People prefer to avoid responsibility.	5	4	3	2	1
5	People working in large companies show no interest in organisational goals. They only have their own interests in mind.	5	4	3	2	1
6	Most people have little innovative capacity and do not help to solve problems within their companies.	5	4	3	2	1
7	Most people desire to be directed.	5	4	3	2	1
8	Most people are not ambitious, prefer to stay where they are and do not want to work hard to get ahead in life.	5	4	3	2	1
9	Work is unnatural to most people.	5	4	3	2	1
10	Most employees show no interest in developing their full potential and abilities.	5	4	3	2	1

Your score: ___________

Scoring key and norms

Once you have added up your responses, you get a total between 10 and 50.

A score below 20? You have a very positive view of employees and they certainly enjoy working under your supervision!

A score above 40? Your view of employees is outdated and you are probably convinced that close direction is the only way to lead. We have serious doubts about the atmosphere in your team. This should certainly change!

A score between 20 and 40? You are characterised by both Theory X and Y. Ask yourself which points of view should be altered to enhance the relationship with your employees!

The lower your score, the more positive your view of people at work is. You are convinced that people have a natural need to work and you will do everything to create a climate to meet that need. The higher your score, however, the more negative your view of modern employees is. You are convinced that people only come to work to earn an income. You also think that people are inherently lazy.

Group exercise

Timeless advice

Objectives

1 To get to know some of your fellow students.

2 To put the management of people into a lively and interesting historical context.

3 To begin to develop your teamwork skills.

Introduction

Your creative energy, willingness to see familiar things in unfamiliar ways, and ability to have fun while learning are keys to the success of this warm-up exercise. A 20-minute, small-group session will be followed by brief oral presentations and a general class discussion. Total time required is approximately 40 to 45 minutes.

Instructions

Your lecturer will divide your class randomly into groups of four to six people each. Acting as a team, with everyone offering ideas and one person serving as official recorder, each group will be responsible for writing a one-page memo to your current class. Subject matter of your group's memo will be 'My advice for managing people today is . . .'. The fun part of this exercise (and its creative element) involves writing the memo from the viewpoint of the person assigned to your group by your lecturer.

Among the memo viewpoints your lecturer may assign are the following:

- Henry Ford (the founder of Ford Motor Company).
- A Japanese bank manager requiring full dedication of its employees.
- Mary Parker Follett.
- Douglas McGregor.
- A Theory X supervisor of a construction crew.
- The manager of an extremely competitive organisation where everyone is competing to be perceived as the best.
- Henri Fayol.
- The manager of a company operating in a communistic world.

- The owner of a company that developed a totally new kind of fast airway transportation in 2030.
- A Japanese auto company executive.
- The head of the world's largest call centre.

Use your imagination, make sure everyone participates and try to be true to any historical facts you have encountered. Attempt to be as specific and realistic as possible. Remember, the idea is to provide advice about managing people from another point in time (or from a particular point of view at the present time).

Make sure you manage your 20-minute time limit carefully. A recommended approach is to spend 2–3 minutes putting the exercise into proper perspective. Next, take about 10–12 minutes brainstorming ideas for your memo, with your recorder jotting down key ideas and phrases. Have your recorder use the remaining time to write your group's one-page memo, with constructive comments and help from the others. Pick a spokesperson to read your group's memo to the class.

Questions for discussion

1 How can each of the views and lenses from the different researchers help us to improve the working in organisations?

2 Suppose you have to work for one of the managers from the above list. For which one would you like to work? Why?

3 Which of the views is most accurate for the situation in which organisations operate today? Are the ideas of Taylor and Barnard of almost a century ago still useful today? Why (not)?

4 Which of the different views in this chapter on how to motivate people will be most effective?

Online Learning Centre

When you have read this chapter, log on to the Online Learning Centre website at ***www.mcgraw-hill.co.uk/textbooks/sinding*** to access test questions, additional exercises and other related resources.

Notes

1 C. Cooper, 'Management Blasted at Nuclear Plant', *People Management*, 16 March 2000.

2 P. Whiteley, 'Five Steps to Added Value', *The Times*, 19 October 2000.

3 Adapted and translated from D. Sheff, 'Richard Branson: Je mensen zijn het belangrijkst', *Vacature*, 28 June 1997.

4 Scott Adams, *The Dilbert Principle* (New York: Harper-Business, 1996), p. 51. Also see A. Bryant, 'Make That Mr. Dilbert', *Newsweek*, 22 March 1999, pp. 46–7.

5 J. Pfeffer and J. F. Veiga, 'Putting People First for Organizational Success', *Academy of Management Executive*, May 1999, p. 37.

6 J. West and M. Patterson, 'Profitable Personnel', *People Management*, 8 January 1998.

7 Adapted from J. Pfeffer and J. F. Veiga, see note 5.

8 See the brief report on lay-offs in the United States in G. Koretz, 'Quick to Fire and Quick to Hire', *Business Week*, 31 May 1999, p. 34. For the case against lay-offs, see J. R. Morris, W. F. Cascio and C. E. Young, 'Downsizing After All These Years:

Questions and Answers About Who Did It, How Many Did It, and Who Benefited from It', *Organizational Dynamics*, Winter 1999, pp. 78–87.

9 Data from J. Pfeffer and J. F. Veiga, 'Putting People First for Organizational Success', *Academy of Management Executive*, May 1999, p. 47.

10 K. Marx, *Economic and Philosophical Manuscripts of 1844* (New York: International Publishing, 1964).

11 E. Durkheim, *The Division of Labour in Society* (New York: Free Press, 1984 – first published in 1893).

12 E. Durkheim *De la division du travail social: étude sur l'organisation des sociétés supérieures* (Paris: Alcan, 1983 – translated 1933).

13 M. Weber, *Gesammelte Aufsätze zur Soziologie und Sozialpolitik* (Tübingen: Mohr, 1924).

14 T. Burns, 'The Sociology of Industry', in *Society: Problems and Methods of Study*, eds A. T. Walford, M. Argyle, D. V. Glass and J. J. Morris (London: Routledge, 1962).

15 R. Kanigel, *The One Best Way: Frederick Winslow Taylor and the Enigma of Efficiency* (London: Little Brown and Company, 1997).

16 H. Ford and S. Crowther, *My Life and Work* (London: William Heinemann, 1924); and P. Collier and D. Horowitz, *The Fords: An American Epic* (London: Futura Collins, 1987).

17 See P. Bain, A. Watson, G. Mulvey, P. Taylor and G. Gall, 'Taylorism, Targets and the Pursuit of Quantity and Quality by Call Centre Management', *New Technology, Work and Employment*, November 2002, pp. 170–72; and P. Taylor and P. Bain, 'An Assembly Line in the Head: Work and Employee Relations in the Call Centre', *Industrial Relations Journal*, June 1999, pp. 101–17.

18 H. Fayol, *Administration Industrielle et Générale* (Paris: Dunol, 1916).

19 C. I. Barnard, *The Functions of the Executive* (Cambridge, MA: Harvard University Press, 1948).

20 Ibid.

21 H. A. Simon, *Administrative Behavior* (New York: The Free Press, 1945). Discussion of the life and work of Simon (translated), see M. Buelens, *Managementprofeten* (Amsterdam: Uitgeverij Nieuwezijds, 2000), pp. 34–41.

22 Based on B. J. Rieger, 'Lessons in Productivity and People', *Training and Development*, October 1995, pp. 56–8.

23 Evidence indicating that the original conclusions of the famous Hawthorne studies were unjustified can be found in R. G. Greenwood, A. A. Bolton and R. A. Greenwood, 'Hawthorne a Half Century Later: Relay Assembly Participants Remember', *Journal of Management*, Fall–Winter 1983, pp. 217–31; and R. H. Franke and J. D. Kaul, 'The Hawthorne Experiments: First Statistical Interpretation', *American Sociological Review*, October 1978, pp. 623–43. For a positive interpretation of the Hawthorne studies, see J. A. Sonnenfeld, 'Shedding Light on the Hawthorne Studies', *Journal of Occupational Behaviour*, April 1985, pp. 111–30.

24 T. R. Miller and B. J. Vaughan, 'Messages from the Management Past: Classic Writers and Contemporary Problems', *S.A.M. Advanced Management Journal*, Winter 2001, pp. 4–12.

25 P. Graham, *Mary Parker Follett – Prophet of Management* (Boston, MA: Harvard Business School Press, 1995). Also see N. O. Morton and S. A. Lindquist, 'Revealing the Feminist in Mary Parker Follett', *Administration and Society*, no. 3, 1997, pp. 349–71.

26 R. L. Verstegen and M. A. Rutherford, 'Mary Parker Follett: Individualist or Collectivist? Or Both?', *Journal of Management History*, no. 5, 2000, pp. 207–23.

27 See D. McGregor, *The Human Side of Enterprise* (New York: McGraw-Hill, 1960).

28 See L. F. Urwick, *The Elements of Administration* (New York: Harper & Row, 1944), quoting Follet, p. 102.

29 E. M. Fox and L. F. Urwick, Dynamic Administration: The Collected Papers of Mary Parker Follett, second edition (London: Pitman Publishing, 1973).

30 R. McHenry, 'Spuring Stuff', *People Management*, 24 July 1997.

31 P. L. Berger and T. Luckmann, *The Social Construction of Reality: A Treatise in the Sociology of Knowledge* (Garden City, NY: Doubleday, 1966).

32 For an explanation of symbolic interactionism, see M. J. Hatch, *Organization Theory* (New York: Oxford University Press, 1997). The main works of Karl Weick on enacted theory are K. E. Weick, *The Social Psychology of Organizing* (Reading, MA: Addison-Wesley Publishing Company, 1969); and K. E. Weick, *Sensemaking in Organizations* (Thousand Oaks, CA: Sage Publications, 1995).

33 See M. J. Hatch, *Organization Theory* (Oxford: Oxford University Press, 1997), p. 387; and D. Jaffee, *Organization Theory* (New York: McGraw-Hill, 2001), p. 315. Also see S. R. Clegg, *Modern Organizations: Organization Studies in the Postmodern World* (Newbury Park, CA: Sage Publications, 1990); and D. Harvey, *The Conditions of Postmodernity* (Cambridge: Blackwell, 1989).

34 A. B. Thomas, *Controversies in Management, second edition* (London: Routledge, 2003), p. 260; and D. Jaffee, *Organization Theory: Tension and Change* (Boston, MA: McGraw-Hill, 2001), p. 315.

35 See G. Burrell and G. Morgan, *Sociological Paradigms and Organizational Analysis* (London: Heinemann, 1979); and D. Jaffee, *Organization Theory* (New York: McGraw-Hill, 2001), p. 315.

36 J. Pfeffer, *New Directions for Organization Theory* (New York: Oxford University Press, 1997), p. 264.

37 H. Aldrich, H. and M. Ruef, *Organizations Evolving* (Thousand Oaks: Sage Publications, 2006).

38 P. Selznick, *Leadership in Administration* (New York: Harper & Row, 1957).

39 P. J. DiMaggio and W. W. Powell, 'The Iron Cage Revisited: Institutional Isomorphism and Collective Rationality in Organizational Fields', *American Sociological Review*, no. 48, April 1983, pp. 147–160.

40 J. Pfeffer and G. Salancik, *The External Control of Organizations: A Resource Dependence Perspective* (New York, Harper & Row: 1978).

41 R. H. Coase, 'The nature of the firm', *Economica*, vol. 4, no. 16, 1937, pp. 386–405.

[42] F. von Hayek, 'The Use of Knowledge in Society', *American Economic Review*, no. 35, 1945, pp. 519–30.

[43] R. L. Daft and K. E. Weick, 'Toward a Model of Organizations as Interpretation Systems', *Academy of Management Review*, April 1984, p. 293.

[44] J. R. P. French and B. Raven, 'Bases of Social Power', in *Studies in Social Power*, ed. D. Cartwright (Ann Arbor, MI: University of Michigan, 1959); D. Krackhardt, 'Assessing the Political Landscape: Structure, Cognition, and Power in Organizations', *Administrative Science Quarterly*, June 1990, pp. 342–69; and J. Pfeffer, *Power in Organizations* (Cambridge, MA: Ballinger Publishing Company, 1981).

[45] H. Mintzberg, *The Structuring of Organizations* (Englewood Cliffs, NJ: Prentice Hall, 1979).

[46] G. Morgan, *Images of Organization* (Thousand Oaks, CA: Sage Publications, 1986), p. 199.

[47] Ibid., p. 235.

[48] D. Ibison, 'Asia-Pacific: Overwork Kills Record Number of Japanese', *Financial Times*, 29 May 2002.

[49] B. Briner, 'Feeling for the Facts', *People Management*, 9 January 1997.

[50] See R. L. Daft, 'Learning the Craft of Organizational Research', *Academy of Management Review*, October 1983, pp. 539–46.

[51] K. E. Weick, 'Theory Construction as Disciplined Imagination', *Academy of Management Review*, October 1989, pp. 516–31. Also see D. A. Whetten's article in the same issue, pp. 490–95.

[52] Theory-focused versus problem-focused research is discussed in K. E. Weick, 'Agenda Setting in Organizational Behavior: A Theory-Focused Approach', *Journal of Management Inquiry*, September 1992, pp. 171–82. Also see K. J. Klein, H. Tosi and A. A. Cannella, Jr, 'Multilevel Theory Building: Benefits, Barriers, and New Developments', *Academy of Management Review*, April 1999, pp. 243–8. (Note: The special forum on multilevel theory building in the April 1999 issue of *Academy of Management Review* includes an additional five articles.)

[53] For instance, see M. R. Buckley, G. R. Ferris, H. J. Bernardin and M. G. Harvey, 'The Disconnect between the Science and Practice of Management', *Business Horizons*, March–April 1998, pp. 31–8.

[54] Complete discussion of this technique can be found in J. E. Hunter, F. L. Schmidt and G. B. Jackson, *Meta-Analysis. Cumulating Research Findings across Studies* (Beverly Hills, CA: Sage Publications, 1982); and J. E. Hunter and F. L. Schmidt, *Methods of Meta-Analysis: Correcting Error and Bias in Research Findings* (Newbury Park, CA: Sage Publications, 1990). Also see R. Hutter Epstein, 'The Number-Crunchers Drugmakers Fear and Love', *Business Week*, 22 August 1994, pp. 70–71.

[55] Limitations of meta-analysis technique are discussed in P. Bobko and E. F. Stone-Romero, 'Meta-Analysis May Be Another Useful Tool, But It Is Not a Panacea', in *Research in Personnel and Human Resources Management*, vol. 16, ed. G. R. Ferris (Stamford, CT: JAI Press, 1998), pp. 359–97.

[56] For an interesting debate about the use of students as subjects, see J. Greenberg, 'The College Sophomore as Guinea Pig: Setting the Record Straight', *Academy of Management Review*, January 1987, pp. 157–9; and M. E. Gordon, L. A. Slade and N. Schmitt, 'Student Guinea Pigs: Porcine Predictors and Particularistic Phenomena', *Academy of Management Review*, January 1987, pp. 160–63.

[57] Good discussions of case studies can be found in A. S. Lee, 'Case Studies as Natural Experiments', *Human Relations*, February 1989, pp. 117–37; and K. M. Eisenhardt, 'Building Theories from Case Study Research', *Academy of Management Review*, October 1989, pp. 532–50. The case survey technique is discussed in R. Larsson, 'Case Survey Methodology: Analysis of Patterns across Case Studies', *Academy of Management Journal*, December 1993, pp. 1515–46.

[58] Based on discussion found in J. M. Beyer and H. M. Trice, 'The Utilization Process: A Conceptual Framework and Synthesis of Empirical Findings', *Administrative Science Quarterly*, December 1982, pp. 591–622.

[59] See J. J. Martocchio, 'Age-Related Differences in Employee Absenteeism: A Meta-Analysis', *Psychology & Aging*, December 1989, pp. 409–14.

[60] For complete details, see G. Hofstede, 'The Cultural Relativity of Organizational Practices and Theories', *Journal of International Business Studies*, Fall 1983. For related discussion, see G. Hofstede, 'Cultural Constraints in Management Theories', *Academy of Management Executive*, February 1993, pp. 81–94.

[61] See J. B. Miner, 'The Validity and Usefulness of Theories in an Emerging Organizational Science', *Academy of Management Review*, April 1984, pp. 296–306.

[62] This study is discussed in A. Finkbeiner, 'Some Science Is Baloney; Learn to Tell the Difference', *USA Today*, 11 September 1997, p. 15A.

[63] A thorough discussion of the importance of measurement is provided by D. P. Schwab, 'Construct Validity in Organizational Behavior', in *Research in Organizational Behavior*, eds B. M. Staw and L. L. Cummings (Greenwich, CT: JAI Press, 1980), pp. 3–43.

[64] See J. L. Komaki, 'Toward Effective Supervision: An Operant Analysis and Comparison of Managers at Work', *Journal of Applied Psychology*, May 1986, pp. 270–79. Results from the sailing study can be found in J. L. Komaki, M. L. Desselles, and E. D. Bowman, 'Definitely Not a Breeze: Extending an Operant Model of Effective Supervision to Teams', *Journal of Applied Psychology*, June 1989, pp. 522–9.

[65] A thorough discussion of the pros and cons of using surveys or questionnaires is provided by J. A. Krosnick, 'Survey Research', in *Annual Review of Psychology*, eds J. T. Spence, J. M. Darley, and D. J. Foss (Palo Alto, CA: 1999); pp. 537–67.

[66] See F. L. Schmidt and M. Rader, 'Exploring the Boundary Conditions for Interview Validity: Meta-Analytic Validity Findings for a New Interview Type', *Personnel Psychology*, Summer 1999, pp. 445–64; and M. A. McDaniel, D. Whetzel, F. L. Schmidt, and S. Maurer, 'Validity of Employment Interviews: a Comprehensive Review and Meta-Analysis', *Journal of Applied Psychology*, August 1994, pp. 599–616.

[67] A complete discussion of the guidelines for conducting good research methods is provided by T. D. Cook and D. T. Campbell, *Quasi-Experimentation: Design & Analysis Issues for Field Settings* (Chicago: Rand McNally, 1979).

[68] Ibid.

Part 2

Individual processes

Part content

Chapter 2

Personality dynamics

Learning Outcomes

When you finish studying the material in this chapter, you should be able to:

- ✓ explain what self-esteem is and how it can be improved
- ✓ define self-efficacy and explain its sources
- ✓ contrast high and low self-monitoring individuals and describe resulting problems each may have
- ✓ explain the difference between an internal and an external locus of control
- ✓ identify and describe the Big Five personality dimensions
- ✓ describe Jung's and Myers and Briggs' personality typology
- ✓ elaborate on cautions and tips concerning (personality) testing in the workplace
- ✓ describe the implications of intelligence and cognitive abilities
- ✓ describe cognitive styles and learning styles

Opening Case Study: Narcissistic personality leaders

Think about prominent leaders you are very familiar with and consider them in terms of their sense of self-importance, sense of being special and views on their own success. Then consider how they respond to admiration and how they expect to be treated. Do they take advantage of others without regard for their feelings and needs? Are they are arrogant? Are they envious of what others have? These traits briefly sum up people who are narcissists. Five of the seven traits are sufficient for a diagnosis of Narcissist Personality Disorder (NPD).

Without in any way suggesting that any of these traits are in evidence, it is instructive to consider a report about an obscure insurance company called Delphi Financial. According to a report in *The New York Times*, the CEO of Delphi, Robert Rosenkranz, had negotiated a sale of the company to a Japanese investor. As part of the deal, Mr. Rosenkranz was to be paid $60 million more than the other shareholders, despite company charter provisions that explicitly prohibited this. Naturally, the shareholders sued Delphi to prevent the extra payment going ahead. The trial judge was not impressed by what he heard, stating that 'Mr. Rosenkranz believed he was "morally" entitled to this money for building this company. Mr. Rosenkranz's apparent hubris led him to violate a bargain he had struck with shareholders at the time of Delphi's IPO.' Nor was this the only effort Mr. Rosenkranz made to extract additional money.

Court documents suggest that one director of Delphi 'thought that Mr. Rosenkranz had a "competitive" personality and a "great sense of entitlement"'. The documents also 'tell of Mr. Rosenkranz's response to the board's attempt to prevent him from obtaining a premium over other shareholders. They describe Mr. Rosenkranz as being "upset," "angry" and "depressed" and as thinking that he had been "treated harshly" at the negotiations.' The judge did not block the sale of Delphi, but was strongly critical of Mr. Rosenkranz.

The journalist writing this story thought it appropriate to speculate that the behaviour of CEOs in this and other cases resembled narcissism. While we could not possibly comment, it is clear that some executives are more willing than most to take on great risk. There is solid research to support this argument. CEOs scoring high on narcissism were also more avid pursuers of bold (i.e. large) deals – while their firms performed no worse or no better than firms on average.[1] Similarly, CEOs who borrow more on their private residences lead firms with higher levels of debt,[2] and CEOs who take on more risk in their personal lives are associated with riskier firms.[3]

For discussion

Well then, can you find someone who has at least five of the traits?

Source: Based on Steven A. Davidoff, 'A Mirror Can Be a Dangerous Tool for Some C.E.O.s', *Mergers & Acquisitions*, Deal Professor, 6 March 2012, http://dealbook.nytimes.com/2012/03/06/a-mirror-can-be-a-dangerous-tool-for-some-c-e-o-s/?ref=business

What makes you you? What characteristics do you share with others? Which ones set you apart? Perhaps you have a dynamic personality and dress accordingly, while a low-key friend dresses conservatively and avoids crowds. Some computer freaks would rather surf the Internet than eat; other people suffer from computer phobia. Sometimes students who skim their reading assignments at the last moment get higher grades than those who study for days. One employee consistently does

Figure 2.1 A Conceptual Model for the Study of Individual Differences in OB

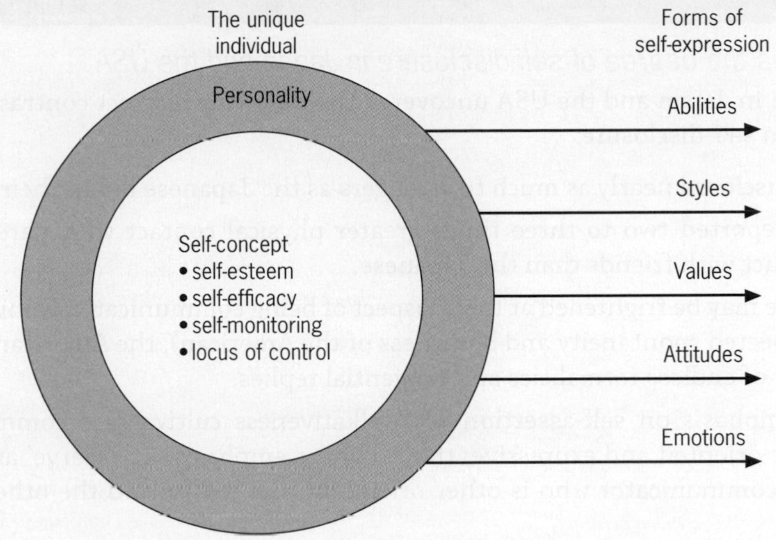

more than asked, while another equally skilled employee barely does the job. A vast array of individual differences such as these give modern organisations a rich and interesting human texture. Dealing with all these individual differences makes organisational life an ongoing challenge. If workforce diversity is growing, for example, due to immigration, organisations must view individual differences in a fresh way.

Figure 2.1 is a conceptual model showing the relationship between self-concept (how you view yourself), personality (how you appear to others) and key forms of self-expression. Self-concept, personality, abilities and styles are elaborated in this chapter. In the next chapter, we look at emotions, values and attitudes. Considered all together, these individual differences provide a foundation for understanding each employee better as a unique and special individual.

2.1 Self-concept: the I and me in OB

Self is the core of one's conscious existence. Awareness of self, how you view yourself or **self-concept** can be defined as: 'the concept the individual has of themself as a physical, social, and spiritual or moral being'.[4] Because you have a self-concept, you recognise yourself as a distinct human being. A self-concept would be impossible without the capacity to think. This brings us to the role of **cognitions**. Cognitions represent 'any knowledge, opinion or belief about the environment, about oneself or about one's behaviour'.[5] Among the many different types of cognitions, those involving anticipation, planning, goal setting, evaluating and setting personal standards are particularly relevant to organisational behaviour.[6]

OB in Real Life

Culture dictates the degree of self-disclosure in Japan and the USA

Survey research in Japan and the USA uncovered the following distinct contrasts in Japanese versus American self-disclosure:

- Americans disclosed nearly as much to strangers as the Japanese did to their own fathers.
- Americans reported two to three times greater physical contact with parents and twice greater contact with friends than the Japanese.
- The Japanese may be frightened at the prospect of being communicatively invaded (because of the unexpected spontaneity and bluntness of the American); the American is annoyed at the prospect of endless formalities and tangential replies.
- American emphasis on self-assertion and talkativeness cultivates a communicator who is highly self-oriented and expressive; the Japanese emphasis on 'reserve' and 'sensitivity' cultivates a communicator who is other-oriented (oriented toward the other person) and receptive.

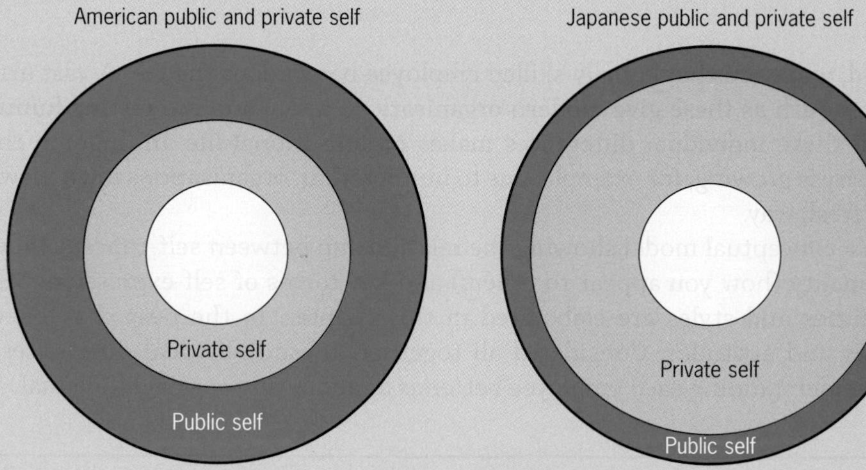

Source: Adapted from D. C. Barnlund, 'Public and Private Self in Communicating with Japan', *Business Horizons*, March–April 1989, pp. 32–40.

Several cognition-based topics are discussed in later chapters. Differing cognitive styles are introduced later on in this chapter and attitudes will be elaborated in Chapter 3. Cognitions play a central role in social perception, as will be discussed in Chapter 4. Also, as we will see in Chapters 5 and 6, modern motivation theories and techniques depends on cognitions. It is important to keep in mind that ideas of self and self-concept vary from one historical era to another, from one socio-economic class to another, and from one national culture to another.[7] How well one detects and adjusts to different cultural notions of self can determine success or failure in international dealings.

The above example of differences in Japanese and American conceptions of self suggests that communication and understanding is often hindered by significantly different degrees of self-disclosure. With a comparatively large public self, Americans pride themselves in being open, honest, candid and to the point (direct). Meanwhile, Japanese people, who culturally discourage self-disclosure, typically view Americans as blunt, prying and insensitive to formalities. For their part, Americans tend to see Japanese as distant, cold and evasive.[8] A key difference involves culturally rooted conceptions of self and self-disclosure. Related to these cultural differences in self and self-disclosure are also cultural differences in emotional display rules and norms (also see Chapter 3).

2.2 Self-esteem: a controversial topic

Self-esteem is a belief about one's own self-worth based on an overall self-evaluation.[9] It refers to the degree to which people like or dislike themselves. People with high self-esteem see themselves as worthwhile, capable and acceptable. People with low self-esteem view themselves in negative terms. They do not feel good about themselves and are hampered by self-doubts.[10] The subject of self-esteem is controversial, particularly among educators and those seeking to help the disadvantaged.[11] Both sides generally agree that positive self-esteem is a good thing for students and youngsters. The disagreement is about how self-esteem can be improved. A British study among students in sports schools reveals that after entry, the self-esteem and self-image of students at sport schools increased after a while relative to that of students in other secondary schools. Their academic results increased as well. Moreover, adolescents at a sport school have a more positive image of their body, something that is very important for a teenager. These results are clear for boys, less so for girls. A reason for this gender difference might be that boys are more sensitive to the way in which sport improves their image.[12]

Feelings of self-esteem are, in fact, shaped by circumstances and by how others treat us. Researchers who surveyed young adults over an eight-year period found higher self-esteem among those in school or working full time than among those with part-time jobs or unemployed.[13] Similarly there can be a difference in self-esteem between unemployed and re-employed people: higher self-esteem seemed to facilitate re-employment.[14]

Evidence about self-esteem

Is high self-esteem always a good thing? A pair of studies confirmed that people with high self-esteem (HSE) handle failure better than people with low self-esteem (LSE). Specifically, when confronted with failure, HSEs drew upon their strengths and emphasised the positive whereas LSEs focused on their weaknesses and had primarily negative thoughts.[15] In another study, however, HSEs tended to become egotistical and boastful when faced with pressure situations.[16] High levels of self-esteem may also be associated with aggressive and even violent behaviour. Indeed, contrary to the common belief that low self-esteem and criminality go hand in hand, youth gang members and criminals often score highly on self-esteem and become violent when their inflated egos are threatened.[17] Thus, high self-esteem can be a good thing, but only if – like many other human characteristics such as creativity, intelligence and persistence – it is nurtured and channelled in constructive and ethical ways.

From the organisation's point of view, high self-esteem can also be a mixed blessing. In stable or growing organisations, employees with lower self-esteem tend to leave, but during organisational lay-offs self-confidence and self-esteem have a positive direct effect on intent to leave.[18] Individuals with the capabilities and the confidence to perform well in other firms tend to leave first. In this way the downsizing companies are losing the wrong people as well as keeping the wrong people (low performers they had hoped would leave).

Self-esteem or the lack of it has far-reaching consequences. A study of all babies born in the UK in the first week of April 1970 started by interviewing the parents at the time of birth. The children were then questioned at ages 5, 10, 16, 26 and again as they reached their 30th birthday in April 2000. Self-esteem was monitored at the age of 10 by asking the children a series of questions. A very close correlation between childhood self-esteem and adult success was found. The study showed that there is clear evidence that children with higher self-esteem at age 10 get as much of a kick to their adult earning power as those with equivalent higher maths or reading ability. Childhood self-esteem can also outweigh academic disadvantage or social deprivation in determining future earnings power.[19]

Self-esteem is to some degree culture-bound. A survey of 13 118 students from 31 countries worldwide, found a moderate positive correlation between self-esteem and life satisfaction. However, the relationship was stronger in individualistic cultures (such as the USA, Canada, New Zealand and the Netherlands) than in collectivist cultures (such as Korea, Kenya and Japan). The analysis concluded that individualistic cultures socialise people to focus more on themselves, while people in collectivist cultures are socialised to fit into the community and to do their duty.[20] Global organisations need to remember to de-emphasise self-esteem when doing business in collectivist ('we') cultures, as opposed to emphasising it in individualistic ('me') cultures (for more on organisational and international culture, see Chapter 12).

HR Application: self-esteem enhancement

Can self-esteem be improved? The short answer is yes (also see Table 2.1), in the sense that having the person think of desirable characteristics he or she possesses raises self-esteem more than thinking about undesirable characteristics from which that person is free.[21] This approach can help to neutralise the self-defeating negative thoughts of people with low self-esteem (sometimes called LSEs). See also the related discussions of the self-fulfilling prophecy in Chapter 4.

Table 2.1 Six Pillars of Self-Esteem

What nurtures and sustains self-esteem in grown-ups is not how others deal with us but how we ourselves operate in the face of life's challenges – the choices we make and the actions we take.

This leads us to the six pillars of self-esteem:

1 *Live consciously*: be actively and fully engaged in what you do and with whom you interact.
2 *Be self-accepting*: do not be overly judgemental or critical of your thoughts and actions.
3 *Take personal responsibility*: take full responsibility for your decisions and actions in life's journey.
4 *Be self-assertive*: be authentic and willing to defend your beliefs when interacting with others, rather than bending to their will to be accepted or liked.
5 *Live purposefully*: have clear near-term and long-term goals and realistic plans for achieving them to create a sense of control over your life.
6 *Have personal integrity*: be true to your word and your values.

Between self-esteem and the practices that support it, there is reciprocal causation. This means that the behaviours that generate good self-esteem are also expressions of good self-esteem.

Source: Excerpted and adapted from N. Branden, Self-Esteem at Work: *How Confident People Make Powerful Companies* (San Francisco, CA: Jossey-Bass, 1998), pp. 33–6.

According to a study by the Society for Human Resource Management, organisations can build employee self-esteem in four ways:

- Be supportive by showing concern for personal problems, interests, status and contributions.
- Offer work involving variety, autonomy and challenges that suit the employee's values, skills and abilities (also see Chapters 5 and 6 on motivation).
- Strive for supervisor–employee cohesiveness and build trust. Trust, an important teamwork element, is discussed in Chapter 8.
- Have faith in each employee's self-management ability. Reward each success.[22]

2.3 Self-efficacy

Those who are confident about their ability seem to succeed, while those who are preoccupied with failing seem to fail. At the heart of this performance mismatch is a specific dimension of self-esteem called self-efficacy. **Self-efficacy** is a person's belief about his or her chances of successfully accomplishing a specific task. It arises from the gradual acquisition of complex cognitive, social, linguistic and/or physical skills through experience.[23] Self-efficacy refers to personal beliefs about your competencies, skills and abilities. To gain a better understanding of what this concept entails, consider the words of James Dyson, founder of Dyson Appliances.

> The key to success is failure. Not other people's failure, but how you respond to failure yourself. Everyone gets knocked back, no-one rises smoothly to the top without hindrance. The ones who succeed are the ones who say, right, let's give it another go. Who cares what others think? I believe in what I'm doing. I will never give up. Success is made up of 99 per cent failure. You galvanise yourself and you keep going.[24]

The relationship between self-efficacy and performance is cyclical. Efficacy performance cycles can spiral upward toward success or downward toward failure.[25] Studies of naval cadets (young aspiring officers) have shown a strong link between high self-efficacy expectations and success in widely varied physical and mental tasks, anxiety reduction, addiction control, pain tolerance, illness recovery and avoidance of seasickness.[26] In contrast, those with low self-efficacy expectations tend to have low success rates. Chronically low self-efficacy is associated with a condition called **learned helplessness**, the severely debilitating belief that one has no control over one's environment.[27] Although self-efficacy sounds like some sort of mental magic, it operates in a very straightforward manner.

The mechanisms of self-efficacy

A basic model of self-efficacy based on the work of Albert Bandura[28] is shown in Figure 2.2. Imagine you have been told to prepare and deliver a 10-minute talk to an OB class of 50 students on the workings of the self-efficacy model in Figure 2.2. Your self-efficacy calculation would involve cognitive appraisal of the interaction between your perceived capability and the situational opportunities and obstacles.

As you begin to prepare for your presentation, the four sources of self-efficacy beliefs come into play. Because prior experience is the most potent source, it is listed first.[29] Past success in public speaking would boost your self-efficacy. Bad experiences with delivering speeches, however, would

Figure 2.2 A Model of How Self-Efficacy Beliefs Can Pave the Way for Success or Failure

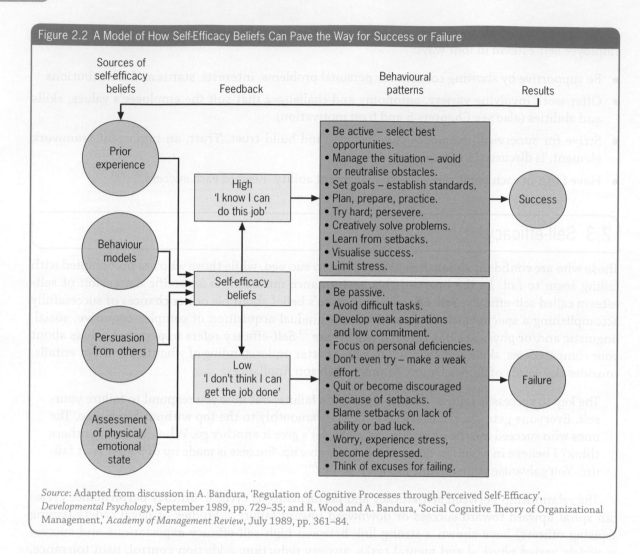

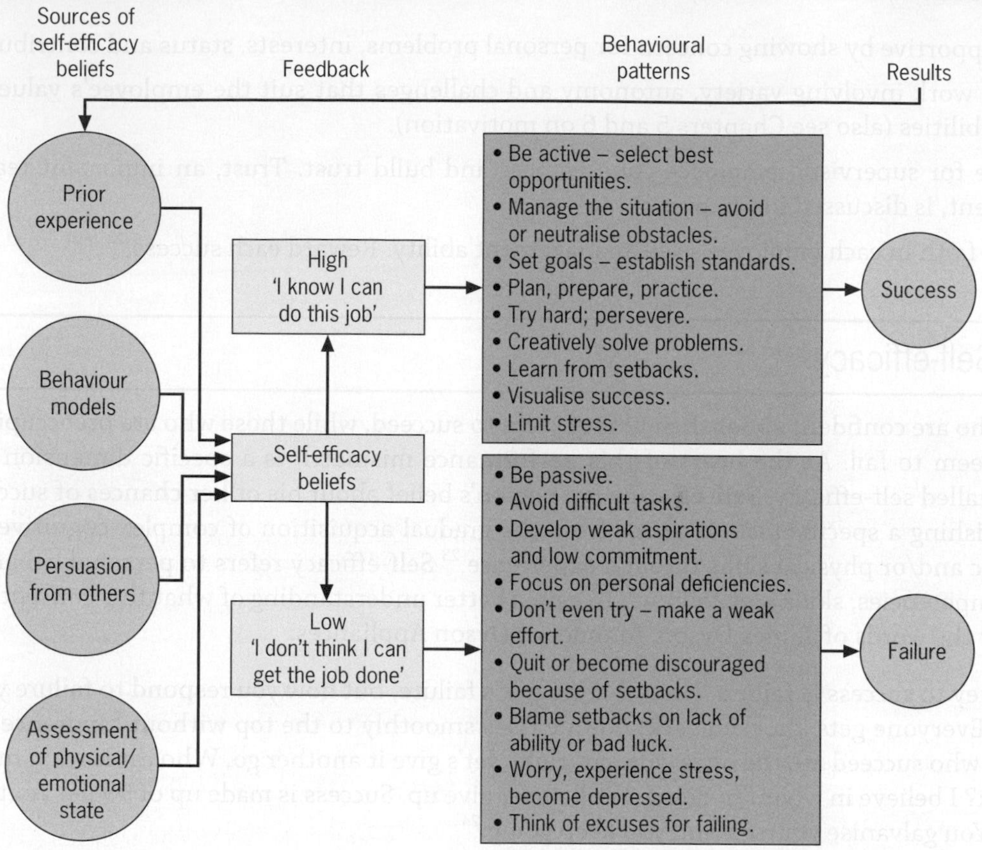

Source: Adapted from discussion in A. Bandura, 'Regulation of Cognitive Processes through Perceived Self-Efficacy', *Developmental Psychology*, September 1989, pp. 729–35; and R. Wood and A. Bandura, 'Social Cognitive Theory of Organizational Management,' *Academy of Management Review*, July 1989, pp. 361–84.

reduce it. Second, the success or failure of your classmates in delivering similar talks will influence you. Their successes would tend to increase your self-efficacy. Likewise, any supportive persuasion from your classmates that you will do a good job would enhance your self-efficacy. Physical and emotional factors might also affect your self-confidence. A sudden case of sore throat or a bout of stage fright could cause your self-efficacy expectations to decrease sharply. Your cognitive evaluation of the situation would then yield a self-efficacy belief. Significantly, self-efficacy beliefs are not merely boastful statements based on bravado; they are deep convictions supported by experience.

In the behavioural patterns portion of Figure 2.2, we see how self-efficacy beliefs are acted out. If you have high self-efficacy about giving the speech you will work harder, more creatively and longer when preparing for your talk than will your low self-efficacy classmates. Working harder, trying harder, seeing fewer obstacles, getting more innovative ideas is a great benefit of high self-efficacy. However, people with this characteristic may also get carried away, persisting beyond what is useful and exhibiting overconfidence in their own skills and abilities.[30]

HR

Evidence about self-efficacy

On-the-job research evidence encourages professionals to nurture self-efficacy, both in themselves and in others. A meta-analysis encompassing 21 616 participants found a significant positive correlation between self-efficacy and job performance.[31]

The evidence suggests further that organisational members with high self-efficacy are better at taking initiatives; they produce more innovative ideas, work harder and try more persistently to overcome problems.[32] In contrast, people with low self-efficacy do not do any of these things – and are less productive as a result.[33] The downside of high self-efficacy is that people who have this characteristic are at risk of becoming more confident about their abilities than these really warrant.[34]

Application of self-efficacy

Self-efficacy requires constructive action in each of the following eight organisational areas:

- Recruiting/selection/job assignments: interview questions can be designed to probe job applicants' general self-efficacy as a basis for determining orientation and training needs. Pencil-and-paper tests for self-efficacy are not in an advanced stage of development and validation. Care needs to be taken not to hire solely on the basis of self-efficacy, because studies have detected below-average self-esteem and self-efficacy among women and protected minorities (also see the 'Group exercise' at the end of this chapter).[35]
- Job design: complex, challenging and autonomous jobs tend to enhance perceived self-efficacy.[36] Boring, tedious jobs generally do the opposite (see Chapter 5).
- Training and development: employees' self-efficacy expectations for key tasks can be improved through guided experiences, mentoring and role modelling.[37] A recent study also found a positive influence of all kinds of group stimuli (like diversity, an open group climate and supportive leadership) on people's self-efficacy.[38]
- Self-management: systematic self-management training involves enhancement of self-efficacy expectations (see also Chapter 8).[39]
- Goal setting and quality improvement: goal difficulty needs to match the individual's perceived self-efficacy.[40] As self-efficacy and performance improve, goals and quality standards can be made more challenging (see also Chapter 6).
- Coaching: those with low self-efficacy, and employees victimised by learned helplessness, need lots of constructive pointers and positive feedback (see also Chapters 6 and 15).[41]
- Leadership: the necessary leadership talent surfaces when top management gives high self-efficacy professionals a chance to prove themselves under pressure (see also Chapter 15).[42]
- Rewards: small successes need to be rewarded as stepping-stones to a stronger self-image and greater achievements (see also Chapter 6).

!

Critical thinking

How confident do you feel about the skill at which you believe you are best (e.g. playing tennis or passing exams)?

2.4 Self-monitoring

Consider the following contrasting scenarios:

- You are rushing to an important meeting when a colleague pulls you aside and starts to discuss a personal problem. You want to break off the conversation, so you glance at your watch. He keeps talking. You say, 'I'm late for a big meeting.' He continues. You turn and start to walk away. The person keeps talking as if he never received any of your verbal and non-verbal signals that the conversation was over.
- Same situation. Only this time, when you glance at your watch, the person immediately says, 'I know, you've got to go. Sorry. We'll talk later.'

In the first scenario, you are talking to a 'low self-monitor'. The second scenario indicates a 'high self-monitor'. But more is involved here than an irritating situation (for you). **Self-monitoring** is the extent to which people observe their own self-expressive behaviour and adapt it to the demands of the situation. It refers to people's ability to adapt their behaviour to external factors. Experts on the subject suggest that individuals high in self-monitoring may regulate the way they present themselves in response to the demands of the situation. Individuals low in self-monitoring lack either ability or motivation to do so.[43]

In organisational life, both high and low self-monitors are subject to criticism. High self-monitors are sometimes called chameleons, who readily adapt their self-presentation to their surroundings. Low self-monitors, on the other hand, are often criticised for being on their own planet and insensitive to others. Remember, within an OB context, self-monitoring is like any other individual difference, not a matter of right or wrong or good versus bad but rather a source of diversity that needs to be adequately understood.

Self-monitoring is not an either–or proposition. It is a matter of being relatively high or low in terms of related patterns of self-expression. The following activity is designed to assess your self-monitoring tendencies. It can help you better understand yourself. Take a short break from your reading to complete the 10-item survey. Does your score surprise you in any way? Are you unhappy with the way you present yourself to others? What are the ethical implications of your score (particularly with regard to items 9 and 10)?

Activity

What are your self-monitoring tendencies?

Instructions

In an honest self-appraisal, mark each of the following statements as true (T) or false (F), and then consult the scoring key.

______ 1 I reckon I put on a show to impress or entertain others.

______ 2 In a group of people, I am rarely the centre of attention.

______ 3 In different situations and with different people, I often act like very different people.

______ 4 I would not change my opinions (or the way I do things) in order to please someone or win their favour.

______ 5 I have considered being an entertainer.

______ 6 I have trouble changing my behaviour to suit different people and different situations.
______ 7 At a party I let others keep the jokes and stories going.
______ 8 I feel a bit awkward in public and do not show up quite as well as I should.
______ 9 I can look anyone in the eye and tell a lie with a straight face (if for the right reason).
______10 I may deceive people by being friendly when I really dislike them.

Scoring key and norms

Score one point for each of the following answers: 1 T; 2 F; 3 T; 4 F; 5 T; 6 F; 7 F; 8 F; 9 T; 10 T

Score: ______
1– 3 = Low self-monitoring
4 – 5 = Moderately low self-monitoring
6 – 7 = Moderately high self-monitoring
8 – 10 = High self-monitoring

Source: Excerpted and adapted from M. Snyder and S. Gangestad, 'On the Nature of Self-Monitoring: Matters of Assessment, Matters of Validity', *Journal of Personality and Social Psychology*, July 1986, p. 137.

Evidence about self-monitoring

According to field research, there is a positive relationship between high self-monitoring and career success. Among 139 MBA graduates who were surveyed over five years, high self-monitors enjoyed more internal and external promotions than did their low self-monitoring classmates.[44] Another study of 147 managers and professionals found that high self-monitors had a better record of acquiring a mentor (someone to act as a personal career coach and professional sponsor).[45] These results are consistent with an earlier study that found managerial success (in terms of speed of promotion) tied to political savvy (knowing how to socialise, network and engage in organisational politics).[46] A study among 118 telecommunications employees and their colleagues investigated the moderating effects of self-monitoring on speaking-up behaviour. As predicted, low self-monitors, in comparison to high self monitors, spoke up more often as internal locus of control, self-esteem, top management openness and trust in supervisor increased.[47] A meta-analysis based on 23 191 people from 136 samples concluded that self-monitoring is a relevant and useful factor when dealing with job performance and emerging leaders.[48]

! Critical thinking

How do you feel you monitor yourself?

2.5 Locus of control: self or environment?

Individuals vary in terms of how much personal responsibility they take for their behaviour and its consequences. The **locus of control** concept helps explain these differences, in the sense that people tend to attribute the causes of their behaviour primarily either to themselves or to environmental factors.[49]

People who believe they control the events and consequences that affect their lives are said to possess an **internal locus of control** ('internals'). Internals see themselves as active agents. They trust in their capacity to influence the environment and assume that they can control events in their lives by effort and skill. For example, an internal tends to attribute positive outcomes, such as passing an exam, to her or his abilities. Similarly, an internal tends to blame negative events, such as failing an exam, on personal shortcomings (e.g. not studying hard enough). Many entrepreneurs eventually succeed because their internal locus of control helps them overcome setbacks and disappointments. They see themselves as masters of their own fate and not simply lucky.

On the other side of this personality dimension are those who believe their performance is the result of circumstances beyond their immediate control. These individuals are said to possess an **external locus of control** ('externals'). Externals see themselves as passive agents. They believe that events in their lives and things that they want to achieve are subject to uncontrollable forces, luck, chance and powerful others. Unlike someone with an internal locus of control, an external would attribute a pass in an exam to something external (e.g. an easy test or a good day) and attribute a failing grade to an unfair test or problems at home. Recent studies suggest that locus of control beliefs may vary across situations. This means that locus of control beliefs at work may differ from locus of control beliefs in other life areas.[50]

Evidence about locus of control

Internals and externals have different information-processing capabilities and learning strategies. Internals are more inclined to search for relevant information than externals, and seem to learn more from feedback and past experiences than externals. Since internals are more concerned with self-direction, they pay more attention to information that is relevant for attaining their goals and they recognise the relevance of information for goal attainment more quickly than do externals. They will also process this information more actively. Externals, on the other hand, more readily accept dependency on a more competent other and thus have less need for information.[51]

Another study found that an internal locus of control was positively related to the initiative dimension of performance, which means that internals engaged more frequently in innovative and spontaneous performance that goes beyond basic job requirements. External locus of control was related to the compliant dimension of performance, which means behaviour that complies with given role requirements. This relationship between an internal locus of control and performance is explained by the stronger motivation of employees with an internal locus of control. They place a higher value on goal attainment and feel more in control to attain these goals. The differential impact of locus of control on different performance dimensions is explained by the fact that internals look at themselves for direction, while externals depend on outside factors such as a supervisor or company rules.[52]

The high value placed on personal autonomy in Western culture implies that an internal locus of control is viewed more favourably than an external locus of control. In other cultures external locus of control beliefs are more widespread than in Europe and North America. Locus of control beliefs, like values and attitudes, tend to be formed early in life and are influenced by learning experiences, family and other sources (see Chapter 12 about socialisation). Taking cultural identity into account can thus be important for correctly interpreting someone's locus of control.[53] A study among 5185 managers from 24 countries, showed that the relationship between locus of control and well-being was found to be universal (i.e. consistent among all samples), although there may be other cross-cultural differences and similarities affecting locus of control beliefs.

HR Application: the location of control

Since internals have a tendency to believe they control the work environment through their behaviour, they will attempt to exert control over the work setting. This can be done by trying to influence work procedures, working conditions, task assignments or relationships with peers and supervisors. As these possibilities imply, internals may resist a boss's attempts to closely supervise their work. Accordingly, organisations may want to place internals in jobs requiring high initiative and low compliance. Internals seem to be more satisfied with supervision than externals under a participative leadership style, whereas externals are more satisfied than internals under a directive style. Externals might be more amenable to highly structured jobs requiring greater compliance. Routine and clearly structured tasks are found to increase the motivation of externals, while they decrease motivation among internals. Direct participation can also improve the attitudes and performance of externals. Externals who had been significantly involved in designing their organisation's computer information system had more favourable attitudes toward the system than their external-locus co-workers who had not participated.[54]

Locus of control has implications for motivation strategies used and reward systems (see Chapters 5 and 6). Given that internals have a greater belief that their effort leads to performance, internals would probably prefer, and respond more productively to, incentives such as merit pay or sales commissions and also to goal setting and feedback. Externals on the other hand seem unresponsive to incentives. They want them, but will not necessarily work harder for them.[55]

! Critical thinking

Examine some of your failures and successes at work or elsewhere in your life. How did you feel about those events at the time?

2.6 Personality

Individuals have their own way of thinking and acting, their own unique style or personality. **Personality** is defined as the combination of stable physical and mental characteristics that give the individual his or her identity.[56] These characteristics or traits – including how one looks, thinks, acts and feels – are the product of interacting genetic (nature) and environmental (nurture) influences. Nature refers to genetic factors you inherited from your parents. Research on twins that grew up apart from each other suggests that these genetic or hereditary factors may be responsible for roughly half of the variation in personalities.[57] Nurture refers to external influences from culture, social class, work environment, family, peers, and so on. Experiences, learning and socialisation in these different environments influence who we are. After a long-standing debate, most researchers now believe that both kinds of influences determine our personality. If our personality is completely determined by our genes it would be fixed from birth and not adaptable by, for instance, experiences or other external influences. On the other hand, if personality was solely determined by upbringing, no consideration would be given to the fact that a major part of personality is rather stable and consistent.

In this section we introduce two different ways of looking at personalities. One is concerned with personality dimensions or traits and the other is concerned with personality types. Both can be useful in organisations and both approaches are widely used in organisations.

Personality factor models

Personality is a concept that is used to refer to many characteristics of people. Characteristics of people that are shown in varying situations are called personality traits. Traits that are fairly consistent and that show up in many situations are important in describing someone's personality. Endless lists of personality dimensions and traits have been suggested (including Machiavellianism, authoritarianism, dogmatism, risk-taking propensity, type A and type B personality).

The early models of personality traits or factors attempted to define a set of traits that would cover the whole range of personality.[58] Over the years, people have tried to reduce the number of dimensions and traits. The work of Hans Eysenck (who identified two dimensions on which personality varies: the extroversion–introversion or 'E' dimension and the neuroticism–stability or 'N' dimension)[59] for instance, stimulated others to search for reduced models of personality, including Carl Gustav Jung (see below). The two best-known attempts to distinguish central personality dimensions and traits are Cattell's 16 personality factors and the Big Five personality model.

Cattell identified 16 personality factors (or source traits) that can be used as a framework for personality testing. Table 2.2 lists these 16 personality factors (**16 PF model**).

Sixteen factors are difficult to operationalise, and the most influential effort to reduce the long list of personality dimensions and traits led to the identification of five dimensions, known as the '**Big Five**' personality dimensions (or just 'Big Five'), that are assumed largely to describe human personality[60] (see Table 2.3).

Extroversion refers to people's comfort level with relationships. People scoring high on this dimension (extroverts) tend to be sociable, outgoing, assertive and talkative. They enjoy interacting with other people and are more open to establishing new relationships. People scoring low on this dimension (introverts) are rather reserved and quiet. They tend to be more reluctant to start new relationships. Introverts are more inclined to direct their interests to ideas than social events.

Table 2.2 Cattell's 16 Personality Factors

Factor	High score description	Low score description
A	Outgoing	Reserved
B	More intelligent (abstract thinker)	Less intelligent (concrete thinker)
C	Emotionally stable	Emotionally unstable
E	Dominant (assertive)	Submissive (humble)
F	Optimistic	Pessimistic
G	Conscientious	Expedient
H	Adventurous	Timid
I	Tender-minded	Tough-minded
L	Suspicious	Trusting
M	Imaginative	Practical
N	Shrewd	Forthright
O	Apprehensive (insecure)	Self-assured
Q1	Experimenting	Conservative
Q2	Self-sufficient	Group-dependent
Q3	Controlled	Undisciplined (casual)
Q4	Tense (frustrated)	Relaxed (tranquil)

Source: Based on Table 4.1 in R. B. Cattell and P. Kline, *The Scientific Analysis of Personality and Motivation* (London: Academic Press, 1977), pp. 44–5. Reprinted with permission from Elsevier.

Table 2.3 The Big Five Personality Dimensions

Dimension	High scorers are . . .	Low scorers are . . .
Extroversion	Outgoing, enthusiastic and active; seek novelty and excitement.	Aloof, quiet and independent; cautious and enjoy time alone.
Emotional stability	Prone to stress, worry and negative emotions.	Emotionally stable but can take unnecessary risks.
Conscientiousness	Organised, self-directed and successful, but controlling.	Spontaneous, careless, can be prone to addiction.
Agreeableness	Trusting, empathetic and compliant, slow to anger.	Uncooperative and hostile, find it hard to empathise with others.
Openness	Creative, imaginative, eccentric and open to new experiences.	Practical, conventional, sceptical and rational.

Agreeableness refers to people's ability to get along with others. Highly agreeable people are more forgiving, tolerant, co-operative, trusting, soft-hearted, understanding, gentle and good-natured in their interactions with others. People scoring low on this dimension are described as rude, cold, uncaring, unsympathetic, irritable and not co-operative.

Conscientiousness refers to the extent that people are organised, careful, responsible, dependable and self-disciplined. A highly conscientious person is dependable, responsible, achievement-oriented, reliable and persistent, while a low conscientious person tends to be careless, sloppy, inefficient, disorganised, irresponsible and easily distracted.

Emotional stability refers to the extent people can cope with stress situations and experience positive emotional states. People with high emotional stability are fairly relaxed, secure, unworried and self-confident. They are expected to cope better with stress, pressure and tension. People with low emotional stability tend to be nervous, anxious, depressed, indecisive and subject to mood swings.

Openness to experience refers to the extent people are open to new experiences and have a broad interest and fascination with novelty. People who are open to experience are curious, broad-minded, intellectual and imaginative. People who score low on this dimension tend to be resistant to change, conventional, habit-bound, closed to new ideas and unimaginative.

Standardised personality tests determine how people score on each of these dimensions. A person's scores on the Big Five reveal a unique personality profile. It is important to mention that each endpoint of these five dimensions has positive and negative sides. One endpoint is not more desirable than the other; everything depends on the situation and environment. For instance extroverts are sociable, assertive and talkative, but also easily bored with tasks that are uninteresting (to them) and time-consuming. This means people with extrovert traits will be more useful in sales jobs, while introverts will be better in, for instance, production management.

HR Evidence about personality

Organisations are interested in research linking these personality dimension models with organisational behaviour and job performance. Studies of the Big Five in an organisational context have found links between personality dimensions, organisational behaviour and performance.[61]

Big Five personality dimensions that correlate positively and strongly with job performance would be helpful in the selection, training and appraisal of employees. A meta-analysis of 117 studies involving 23 994 participants from many professions offers guidance. Among the Big Five, conscientiousness had the strongest positive correlation with job performance and training performance in the sense that 'those individuals who exhibit traits associated with a strong sense of purpose, obligation and persistence generally perform better than those who do not'.[62] In some cases, when jobs require social confidence, extroversion predicts performance, whereas this is not generally the case.[63]

Another study concluded that low emotional stability was associated with low career satisfaction.[64] People with high emotional stability, on the other hand, are found to work better in stressful situations than other people. People with high agreeableness, as well as the ones with high conscientiousness and emotional stability, tend to provide better customer services.[65] The Big Five dimensions have also found to be useful predictors for job search behaviour.[66]

One important question remains unanswered. Are personality models ethnocentric or unique to the culture in which they were developed? At least as far as the Big Five model goes, recent cross-cultural research points in the direction of 'no'. Specifically, the Big Five personality structure held up very well in several studies with men and women from different countries (e.g. Russia, Canada, Hong Kong, Poland, Germany, Finland, South Korea, Great Britain, the Netherlands, Norway, Spain and France).[67] One study even reviewed and compared several studies covering 15 nations of the European Union.[68]

We will return to personality traits at several points in later chapters, explicitly or not. For example there is evidence to suggest that in group settings extroverts initially tend to acquire high status, whereas neurotics are are easy to dismiss as valuable group members, resulting in low status. However, as time goes on, the extroverts show their true colours, poor listening skills, fomenting competition and losing status. The neurotics, at the same time, work to escape their initial low status, work hard and deliver more than initially expected, thus gaining status.[69]

HR Application: hiring the right people

When the available evidence suggests that traits such as conscientiousness and emotional stability predict high performance, the case for using testing to discover job applicant's traits should be clear. However, such arguments may not overcome the objections to testing held by the human resources (HR) department (which may be uncomfortable with the idea of testing as well as with the possible legal liabilities). This does not mean that traits, such as those of the Big Five model, cannot be used, only that the information must be obtained in some other way. The key to a practical solution in cases where testing is not available is to use references from previous jobs to provide a picture of the applicant, since past performance is the best predictor of future performance.[70]

Personality testing is in fact widely used by companies for selecting and promoting employees. In many instances such tests are not free, nor are they always reliable. The greatest problem, however, is not necessarily the tests themselves, but the people who buy them without understanding fully how they work and what information they produce.[71] Testing of personality traits should, if used at all, be part of a broader set of tests that also cover items such as those covered in this chapter, i.e. locus of control, self-monitoring, self-efficacy and cognitive ability.

2.7 Personality types

Whereas trait theories of personality aim to reduce the existing amount of personality traits in a smaller set of dimensions, a second stream of theories wants to identify different **personality types** of people based on common patterns of characteristics between people. The difference between these two approaches is that people belong to types, while traits belong to people. We focus here on the two most often mentioned type theories: Jung's and Myers and Briggs'.

Jung's personality types

Early in the twentieth century, the famous Swiss psychoanalyst Carl Gustav Jung worked on a personality typology.[72] He distinguished three dimensions: one related to how people perceive, one related to how people judge and one focusing on how people look at the world.

According to Jung, there are two ways of perceiving or taking in information: **sensing** (S), by which we become aware of things directly through our five senses, and **intuiting** (N), by which we comprehend ideas and associations indirectly, by way of the unconscious. Sensing types see things as they are and have great respect for facts. They have an enormous capacity for detail, seldom make errors and are good at close, demanding tasks. They typically want to focus on rules and regulations, standard operating procedures, step-by-step explanations and doing things the way they have always been done. People who prefer intuiting concentrate on possibilities. They are holistic in handling problems and impatient with details. They often 'intuit' solutions and fail to back them with data, having gone on to something else. Intuiting types tend to concentrate on outwitting rules and regulations, creating new procedures, supplying conceptual or theoretical explanations and trying new ways of doing things.

People do not only perceive differently, they also use different approaches to make judgements and draw conclusions from their perceptions: based on thinking (T) or feeling (F). **Thinking** implies a logical process that attempts to be objective and impersonal, while **feeling** is a process of appreciation that is subjective and personal. Thinking types are analytical, precise and logical. They are concerned with principles, laws and objective criteria. They may find it easy to critique the work and behaviour of others, but are often uncomfortable dealing with people's feelings. Thinking types prefer objective analysis and decisions based solely on standards and policies. Feeling types are interested in the feelings of others, dislike intellectual analysis and follow their own likes and dislikes. They enjoy working with people and want to maintain harmony in the workplace.

Jung also formulated two different ways people look at the world. People who get their energy from their environment, from interacting with people and things, are **extroverts** (E). Others get their energy from time spent alone, focusing their attention internally, on concepts and ideas. They are **introverts** (I). Extroverts tend to respond quickly to situations and are oriented toward action, rather than reflection and introspection. Introverts, on the other hand, respond slowly to situations or the demands of others, as they require time to integrate and assimilate outside information. When circumstances permit, extroverts prefer to direct perception and judgement outwards, while introverts like to base perception and judgement upon ideas.

According to Jung, thinking, feeling, sensing and intuiting are functional types, while extroversion and introversion are attitudinal orientations. Because functional types are considered to be most important in distinguishing one's personality type, Jung arrived at eight combined types based on these three dimensions.

Myers and Briggs' personality typology

Although Jung completed his landmark work on personality types in the 1920s, his ideas did not catch on in the research of personality until the 1940s. That was when the mother–daughter team of Katharine C. Briggs and Isabel Briggs Myers created the Myers–Briggs Type Indicator (MBTI),[73] a self-evaluation questionnaire that was developed to measure the dimensions identified in Jung's type theory. Today, the MBTI is a widely used (and abused) personal growth and development tool in further education and business. (The personal awareness and growth exercise at the end of this chapter, patterned after the MBTI, will help you determine your personality type.)

Katharine Briggs and Isabel Briggs Myers added a fourth dimension to the work of Jung, referring to the choices people make on how to allocate time priorities: either gathering information (relates to the **perceiving** dimension) or making decisions (relates to the **judging** dimension). Some people want a lot of information (based on either sensing or intuiting) before they make a decision; these are called the perceptive type (P). Perceptive types enjoy searching new information, can tolerate ambiguity and are more concerned with understanding life than controlling it. They prefer to stay open to experience, enjoying and trusting their ability to adapt to the moment. Others make decisions quickly despite the fact that they may have little data. Their priority is to reach a decision. They are called the judging type (J). Judging types like clarity and order, dislike ambiguity and are concerned with resolving issues. They tend to live in a planned, orderly way and want to regulate life and control it.

The MBTI classifies people according to their combination of preferences along four dimensions: extroversion–introversion, sensing–intuiting, thinking–feeling and judging–perceiving. Each of the four dimensions is independent of the other three, which leads to 16 personality types.

Keeping track of the types is no simple matter, and the distinctive elements separating adjacent types can seem blurred. As a result, often only the perceiving and judging dimensions are used and combined in four personality types or styles. An individual's personality type is then determined by the pairing of one's perceiving and judging tendencies. Characteristics of each type are summarised in Table 2.4.

An individual belonging to an ST type uses senses for perception and rational thinking for judgement. The ST-type person uses facts and objective analysis and develops greater abilities in

Table 2.4 Personality Types Based on Myers and Briggs' Personality Model

	ST Types	NT Types	SF Types	NF Types
Preferences	Sensing + Thinking	Intuiting + Thinking	Sensing + Feeling	Intuiting + Feeling
Focus of attention	Realities	Possibilities	Realities	Possibilities
Way of handling things	Objective analysis	Objective analysis	Personal warmth	Personal warmth
Tendency to become	Practical and matter-of-fact	Logical and analytical	Sympathetic and friendly	Enthusiastic and insightful
Expression of abilities	Technical skills with objects and facts	Theoretical and technical developments	Practical help and services to people	Understanding and communicating with people
Representative occupations	Applied science	Physical science	Health care	Behavioural science
	Business	Research	Community service	Research
	Administration	Management	Teaching	Literature
	Banking	Computers	Supervision	Art and music
	Law enforcement	Law	Religious service	Religious service
	Production	Engineering	Office work	Health care
	Construction	Technical work	Sales	Teaching

Source: Based on and adapted from I. Briggs-Myers, *A Description of the Theory and Applications of the Myers-Briggs Type Indicator* (California: Consulting Psychologists Press, 1990), p. 28.

technical areas involving facts and objects. A successful bank manager could be expected to belong to this type. In contrast, a person belonging to an NT type focuses on possibilities rather than facts and displays abilities in areas involving theoretical or technical development. This type can, for instance, be found within research scientists. Although an SF person is likely to be interested in gathering facts, he or she tends to treat others with personal warmth, sympathy and friendliness. Successful counsellors or teachers probably belong to this type. Finally, an NF-type person tends to exhibit artistic flair while relying heavily on personal insights rather than objective facts.[74]

Evidence about the MBTI

Many studies used Jung's typology and the MBTI to investigate the link between personality types and all kinds of organisational behaviour.[75] If the personality typologies are valid, then individuals who belong to different types should seek different kinds of information when making a decision. A study of 50 MBA students found that those belonging to different personality types did in fact use qualitatively different information while working on a strategic planning problem.[76] Individuals who make judgements based on 'thinking' have higher work motivation and quality of work life than 'feeling' types. In addition, sensing individuals have higher job satisfaction than intuiting people. Small business owners and managers belonging to a 'thinking' type made more money than their 'feeling' counterparts. But no correlation was found between the four personality types and small business owner/manager success.[77]

Correlation is not, however, evidence of causality and generally efforts to find links between type preferences and managerial effectiveness have been disappointing. 'Indeed, the findings are inconsistent and no definitive conclusions regarding these relationships can be drawn.'[78] Jung's typology and the MBTI are useful for diversity training and management development purposes but are inappropriate for making personnel decisions such as hiring and promoting.[79]

HR Application of the MB type indicator

Organisations can use the knowledge of these different personality types to enhance understanding between people and reduce miscommunication and conflicts. It is clear from the description of the different types that barriers and conflicts can easily arise given the big differences between them. For instance, thinking and feeling types may have difficulties in understanding each other's decision-making processes. Someone scoring high on thinking may have difficulty in understanding the lack of logic behind a decision of a feeling type. Someone scoring high on feeling may search for the opinion and values of a thinking type related to his or her logical decision.

Organisations can also use these types to stimulate co-operation between people. Opposite types can complement each other. This makes it possible for everyone to use his or her own strengths and balance his or her weaknesses. For instance, when people approach a problem from opposite sides, they see things which are not visible to the other and tend to suggest different solutions. Someone scoring high on thinking, for instance, can help a feeling type to analyse a problem thoroughly, while a feeling type can help a thinker to forecast how the other will feel about a solution.

These models measure preferences. People can act in opposition to their type if they have to, but they will not like it very much and they will not be that good at it. It is like being left- or right-handed: when you are, for instance, right-handed you can write with your left hand when you have to, but it is not easy or natural or pretty. Similarly, no one is, for instance, totally introverted or extroverted: we all have the ability to behave either way at various times. However, we all have a preference to relate more in one way than the other.

Critical thinking

Restate for yourself how personality types differ from personality factors

The problem with personality types is that the types are rigid and the boundaries between them unyielding. Inaccurate answers to test questions can send a person to the wrong box and stick the wrong label onto that person. This problem is less pronounced for the Big 5 traits model.

2.8 Abilities and styles

Individual differences in abilities, styles and accompanying skills are a central concern for organisations because nothing can be accomplished without appropriately skilled personnel. **Ability** represents a broad and stable characteristic responsible for a person's maximum – as opposed to typical – performance on mental and physical tasks. A **style** usually refers to a pattern or preferred way of doing something. A **skill**, on the other hand, is the specific capacity to manipulate objects physically.

Abilities and skills are receiving a good deal of attention in organisations these days. The more encompassing term 'competences' is often used. A **competence** is 'an underlying characteristic of an individual which is causally related to effective or superior performances'.[80] In other words, a competence is any individual characteristic that differentiates between superior and average performers or between effective and ineffective performers. Table 2.5 lists 20 competences that are mostly associated with success in technical and professional jobs, managerial jobs and senior executive jobs.[81]

The idea of specifying, assessing and possibly measuring competences are widely used in organisations, because they offer a common language to identify and describe the key attributes (be it skills, abilities, traits or styles) required for effective performance.[82] This common language makes it possible to use it in job advertisements, hiring and other job-related decisions.

There is one main difference between abilities and styles.[83] Ability is a 'unipolar' concept; this means that people can have more or less of an ability (e.g. verbal comprehension). Usually, having more of an ability is considered as being better. Style, on the other hand, is usually defined as a 'bipolar' concept; it represents a dimension that ranges from one extreme to another. The two extremes (poles) of various style dimensions present different preferences of people. No one style is inherently better than another style, they are just different. One researcher summarises it as follows: 'Both style and ability may affect performance on a given task. The basic distinction between them is that performance on all tasks will improve as ability increases, whereas the effect of style on performance for an individual will either be positive or negative depending on the nature of the task.'[84]

Intelligence and cognitive abilities

Although experts do not agree on a specific definition, **intelligence** represents an individual's capacity for constructive thinking, reasoning and problem-solving. A similar debate as in personality research can be found in the history of intelligence research: nature versus nurture, genes or environment. Historically, intelligence was believed to be an innate capacity, passed genetically

Table 2.5 Twenty Most Widely Used Competences in Organisations

Competence	Technical/professional job	Managerial job	Executive job
Achievement orientation	X	X	X
Concern for quality and order	X	X	
Initiative	X	X	X
Interpersonal understanding	X	X	X
Customer-service orientation	X	X	
Impact and influence		X	X
Organisational awareness			X
Relationship building (networking)		X	X
Directiveness		X	
Teamwork and co-operation	X	X	X
Developing others		X	
Team leadership			X
Technical expertise	X		
Information seeking	X		
Analytical thinking	X	X	
Conceptual thinking	X	X	X
Self-control; stress resistance	X	X	X
Self-confidence		X	
Organisational commitment; 'business-mindedness'	X	X	X
Flexibility		X	X

Source: L. M. Spencer, D. C. McClelland and S. M. Spencer, *Competency Assessment Methods: History and State of the Art* (Boston, MA: Hay/Ber Research Press, 1994).

from one generation to the next (nature). Research since has shown, however, that intelligence (like personality) is also a function of environmental influences (nurture). There is, for example, mounting evidence of the connection between alcohol and drug abuse by pregnant women and intellectual development problems in their children.[85]

Human intelligence has been studied by examining the relationship between measures of mental abilities and behaviour, allowing the isolation of the major components of intelligence. Using this empirical procedure, the pioneering psychologist Charles Spearman proposed that two types of ability determine all cognitive performance.[86] The first type is the general mental ability required for all cognitive tasks. This general factor, called 'g', influences all intellectual activities and accounts for a large proportion of the variance in intelligence scores. The second type of ability is unique to the task at hand. So, although people who do well on one type of task (e.g. spatial, verbal, numerical, memory or other tasks) tend to do well on other tasks also, a certain amount of variance is specific to each task.[87] For example, an individual's ability to complete crossword puzzles is a function of his or her general mental ability as well as the specific ability to perceive patterns in partially completed words. Through the years much research has been devoted to developing and expanding Spearman's ideas on the relationship between cognitive abilities and intelligence.

Attempts have been made to split the g-factor into specific abilities.[88] Table 2.6 contains definitions of the seven most frequently cited mental abilities.[89] Of these seven, personnel selection

Table 2.6 Mental Abilities Underlying Performance

Ability	Description
1 Verbal comprehension	The ability to understand what words mean and to readily comprehend what is read
2 Word fluency	The ability to produce isolated words that fulfil specific symbolic or structural requirements
3 Numerical reasoning	The ability to make quick and accurate arithmetic computations such as adding and subtracting
4 Spatial ability	Being able to perceive spatial patterns and to visualise how geometric shapes would look if transformed in shape or position
5 Memory	Having good rote memory for paired words, symbols, lists of numbers or other associated items
6 Perceptual speed	The ability to perceive figures, identify similarities and differences, and carry out tasks involving visual perception
7 Inductive reasoning	The ability to reason from specifics to general conclusions

Source: Adapted from M. D. Dunnette, 'Aptitudes, Abilities, and Skills', in *Handbook of Industrial and Organizational Psychology*, ed. M. D. Dunnette (Skokie, IL: Rand McNally, 1976), pp. 478–83.

researchers have found verbal ability, numerical ability, spatial ability and inductive reasoning to be valid predictors of job performance for both minority and mainstream applicants.[90]

Distinguishing different personality traits in people or assigning them to different types is, whether the Big Five, the MBTI or some other method is used, a sensitive area, but somehow acceptable and in any case widely used. One reason is that there is no obvious 'right' or 'wrong' personality. Intelligence or cognitive ability is more controversial, among other things, because the measures of intelligence are unipolar. Ranking people according to how bright they are makes many people uncomfortable. Ranking emphasises differences and this collides head on with deeply held cultural beliefs (at least in European and North American contexts) about equality between human beings. It would seem from ongoing debates in the US blogosphere that a major source of discomfort is the existence of a movement or group of people who believe that intelligence depends on inheritance rather than on environment (or nature rather than nurture). One rather extreme position in this debate is the view that black people (African Americans) and women, among others, are less intelligent than whites and males.[91]

Discomforting or not, the evidence is very strong that cognitive ability is the best predictor of performance regardless of what the job is. Cognitive ability is more than twice as good a predictor as the best personality factor (conscientiousness) and even better for jobs that require the ability to evaluate information and make judgements.[92]

Some research has concentrated on expanding the meaning of intelligence beyond mental ability. Gardner suggests that there are multiple intelligences.[93] Practical intelligence, for instance, is one of the more recent concepts, referring to all kinds of problem-solving strategies people use to arrive at solutions.[94] Another new, although already widely used, concept is emotional intelligence, which is further elaborated in Chapter 3.

Another recent study divides intelligence into cognitive, social, emotional and cultural components.[95] Cognitive intelligence refers to the mental abilities that are measured by the traditional intelligence tests. Social intelligence refers to the ability to relate effectively with others. Emotional intelligence refers to the ability to identify, understand and manage your own and other people's emotions. Cultural intelligence refers to the ability to recognise cross-cultural differences and to function effectively in cross-cultural situations.

Evidence about intelligence and abilities

Not all jobs demand the same level of intellectual ability. Jobs that demand more information processing will also require higher general intelligence and verbal abilities to perform successfully.[96] Other jobs require more routine and less of one's own intellectual input, so high intelligence may here be unrelated to job performance. A unique, five-year study documented the tendency of people to end up in jobs that fit their abilities.[97] This prompts the vision of the job market acting as a giant sorting machine, with employees tumbling into various ability bins.

A steady and significant rise in average intelligence among those in developed countries has been observed over the past 70 years (called the Flynn effect, after the psychologist James Flynn who first discovered this phenomenon in the 1980s).[98] Why? Experts at a recent conference concluded: 'Some combination of better schooling, improved socio-economic status, healthier nutrition and a more technologically complex society, might account for the gains in IQ scores.'[99]

All is not well with intelligence scores, or rather with their long uninterrupted rise. Danish males around 18–20 years of age seem to be growing less intelligent. Amongst this cohort, the best scores were in 1998. Since then scores, last measured for the 2003–4 intake of males assessed for military service, have deteriorated so that the last measurement was back at 1988 levels.[100] Whether the Flynn effect is real or not is of little use to the average person. What really matters is what each person believes about intelligence, for this in turn affects that person's ability to change. When people believe that their intelligence is fixed and unchangeable this causes them to think that there is no point in making the effort to become more intelligent (gain more cognitive ability). Conversely, when people think they can improve their cognitive abilities (get smarter), they do improve these abilities.[101]

HR Application of intelligence and cognitive abilities

The evidence suggests numerous avenues for application. Since intelligence is a better predictor of job performance than any single personality factor, the case for using intelligence testing as a tool for selecting new employees or for deciding promotions should be very clear. Aside from the more emotional objections to testing aside, personality testing cannot stand alone, neither can intelligence testing, since skills, motivation and many other factors also influence job performance.

Despite the objections to explicit intelligence testing, it is ironic that many if not most decisions on hiring and promotion depends to a large degree on indirect testing. The record of any applicant's educational achievement is a rough indicator of cognitive ability and probably more valuable than impressions gained through a job interview.

! **Critical thinking**

Which is fairer: hiring based on cognitive ability or personal interviews with job applicants?

2.9 Psychological tests in the workplace

Psychometrics is the term used to refer to all kinds of measurements, assessments and tests that are used to assess one's intelligence, abilities and personality. Psychological tests can be divided into two categories: the ones measuring typical performance (personality tests are an example here) and the ones measuring maximum performance (intelligence tests are an example of this category). Tests on typical performance try to identify people's preferences in certain situations, which implies that there are no right or wrong answers. By contrast, tests on maximum performance assess people's abilities under standard conditions and performance here is judged as right or wrong. Here, we specifically focus on personality tests.

HR Evidence about personality testing in the workplace

Organisations administer all kinds of personality and psychological tests. However, personality testing as a tool for hiring applicants or for other job-related decisions can be questioned for three main reasons. First is the issue of predictive validity. Can personality tests actually predict job performance? In the Big Five meta-analysis discussed earlier, conscientiousness may have been the best predictor of job performance but it was not a strong predictor. Moreover, the most widely used personality test, the Minnesota Multiphasic Personality Inventory (MMPI), does not directly measure conscientiousness. It is no surprise that the MMPI and other popular personality tests have, historically, been poor predictors of job performance.[102]

Second is the issue of differential validity, relative to race. Do personality tests measure people of different races differently? We still have no definitive answer to this important and difficult question, though the limited available evidence indicates that differential validity is not typically associated with personality measures.[103] It is not surprising that personality testing remains a matter of controversy in the workplace.

A third issue involves faking. Both those who are in favour of and those who disapprove of personality testing in the workplace generally agree that faking occurs. Faking involves intentionally misrepresenting one's true beliefs on a personality test. What matters is the extent to which faking alters a personality test's construct validity (this is the degree to which the test actually measures what it is supposed to measure)? Recent research suggests faking *is* a threat to the construct validity of personality tests.[104]

HR Application: why not just forget about personality?

The practical suggestions in Table 2.7 can help organisations avoid abuses and costly discrimination lawsuits when using personality and psychological testing for employment-related decisions.[105] Another alternative for employers is to eliminate personality testing altogether. The growing use of job-related skills testing and behavioural interviewing is an alternative to personality testing.[106]

Neither methodological problems with personality testing, nor unethical applications automatically invalidate the underlying concepts. Organisations need to know about personality traits and characteristics, despite the controversy over personality testing. Rightly or wrongly, the term 'personality' is routinely encountered both inside and outside the workplace.[107]

Regardless of these cautious remarks concerning (personality) tests, the fact remains that they can be useful for self-awareness and for awareness of individual differences. Learning their own styles, types and traits makes people stronger, in the sense that they are made more aware of their own and other people's strengths and weaknesses and can act accordingly. Of course, this implies that people complete these tests for their own benefit and development and not, for instance, in a rewarding or appraisal context.

Knowledge of the Big Five or other personality aspects encourages more precise understanding of diversity among employees. Professionals are encouraged to take time to get to know each employee's unique combination of personality, abilities and potential and to create a productive

HR Table 2.7 Advice and Words of Caution about Personality Testing in the Workplace

Researchers, test developers and organisations that administer personality assessments offer the following suggestions for getting started or for evaluating whether tests already in use are appropriate for forecasting job performance:

- Define objectives, in hiring and elsewhere, by developing job descriptions (this advice applies regardless of whether testing is used or not).
- Determine what you hope to accomplish. If you are looking to find the best fit of job and employee, analyse the aspects of the position that are most critical for it.
- Look for outside help to determine if a test exists or can be developed to screen employees for the traits that best fit the position. Psychologists, professional organisations and a number of Internet sites provide resources.
- Insist that any test recommended by a consultant or sales representative for a testing organisation be validated scientifically for the specific purpose that you have defined. Vendors should be able to cite some independent, credible research supporting a test's correlation with job performance.
- Ask the test seller to document the legal basis for any assessment. Is it fair? Is it job-related? Is it biased against any racial or ethnic group? Does it violate an employee's right to privacy?
- Make sure that every person who will be administrating tests or analysing results is educated about how to do so properly and keeps results confidential.
- Use the scores of personality tests in combination with other factors that you believe are essential to the job, such as skills or experience, to create a comprehensive evaluation of the merits of applicants for a job. Apply those criteria identically for every person.
- Do not make employment-related decisions simply on the basis of personality test results. Supplement any personality test data with information from reference checks, personal interviews, ability tests and job performance records.

Source: S. Bates, 'Personality Counts', *HR Magazine*, February 2003, p. 34.

and satisfying person–job fit based on that knowledge. Personality tests can help professionals to lead, motivate and manage their employees differently, through awareness of their unique traits and types.

! Critical thinking

Which forms of testing have you come across – and did you feel that their results were accurate (if you got any results?)

2.10 Cognitive styles

Cognitive styles are extensively studied in domains like education or experimental psychology. A **cognitive style** is the way an individual perceives environmental stimuli, and organises and uses information. A cognitive style influences how people look at their environment for information, how they organise and interpret this information, and how they use these interpretations for guiding their actions.[108] Interest in cognitive styles originated from the disappointment with the traditional psychometric research on abilities and intelligence, because it failed to uncover the processes that generate individual differences in abilities and IQ. We focus on two widely studied cognitive style theories: Kirton's adaption–innovation model and Riding's cognitive styles model.

Kirton's adaption–innovation model

Michael Kirton observed that 'people characteristically produce qualitatively different solutions to seemingly similar problems'.[109] Some people typically adapt, while others typically innovate when searching for a solution. He developed a cognitive style model that situates these two styles on a continuum, with the ends labelled 'adaptive' and 'innovative', respectively.[110] He further explored the sort of behaviour that might be related to these two cognitive styles. Characteristics of adaptors and innovators can be found in Table 2.8.

According to Kirton, the adaption–innovation dimension is a basic dimension that is relevant to the analysis of organisational change, because it focuses on the interaction between people and their often changing work environment. It gives organisations new information on, and insight into, the individual's aspects of change in organisations.[111] Knowledge of each other's style may also lead to mutual appreciation and co-operation between people with differing cognitive styles. It is clear from Table 2.8 that people with an **innovator** and **adaptor** style are necessary and useful for organisations as they can complement each other's weaknesses.

Kirton developed the Kirton adaption–innovation inventory (KAI), a self-report measure with 32 items to measure these cognitive styles.[112] Research indicates that cognitive style differences

Table 2.8 Kirton's Adaption–Innovation Model

Adaptor	Innovator
In general:	*In general:*
Characterised by precision, reliability, efficiency, prudence, discipline, conformity	Seen as undisciplined, thinking, tangentially, approaching tasks from unsuspected angles
Seen as sound, conforming, safe, dependable	Seen as unsound, impractical, often shocks his or her opposite
Seems impervious to boredom, seems able to maintain high accuracy in long spells of detailed work	Capable of detailed routine work for only short bursts
Is an authority within given structures	Tends to take control in unstructured situations
Challenges rules rarely, cautiously, when assured of strong support	Often challenges rules, has little respect for past custom
For problem definition:	*For problem definition:*
Tends to accept the problems as defined and generates novel, creative ideas aimed at 'doing things better'. Immediate high efficiency is the keynote of high adaptors	Tends to redefine generally agreed problems, breaking previously perceived restraints, generating solutions aimed at 'doing things differently'
For solution generation:	*For solution generation:*
Generates a few well-chosen and relevant solutions that the adaptor generally finds sufficient, but which sometimes fails to contain ideas needed to break the existing pattern completely	Produces numerous ideas, many of which may not be either obvious or acceptable to others. Such a pool often contains ideas, if they can be identified, that may crack hitherto intractable problems
For organisational 'fit':	*For organisational 'fit':*
Essential to the ongoing functions, but in times of unexpected changes may have some difficulty moving out of his or her established role	Essential in times of change or crisis, but may have trouble applying him or herself to ongoing organisational demands

Source: Based on Table 1 from M. J. Kirton, *Adaptors and Innovators, Styles of Creativity and Problem Solving* (London: Routledge/KAI Distribution Centre, 1994), p. 10; and Table 1 from M. J. Kirton, 'Adaptors and Innovators: A Description and Measure', *Journal of Applied Psychology*, October 1976, p. 623. Copyright © 1976 by the American Psychological Association. Adapted with permission.

seem to vary more by occupation and work function than by nation. The Kirton adaption–innovation dimension appears to be largely independent of national culture.[113]

Riding's cognitive styles model

A decade after the work of Kirton, Richard Riding and colleagues developed another cognitive styles model, based on two dimensions. After reviewing various existing dimensions on cognitive styles, Riding and Cheema concluded that they can be grouped into two basic dimensions: the wholist–analytic and the verbal–imagery dimension.[114] These two dimensions are independent of one another. This means that the position of people on one dimension of cognitive styles does not affect their position on the other dimension.

HR The wholist–analytic style dimension describes the habitual way in which people process information: some individuals retain a global or overall view of information ('wholists'), while others process information into its component parts ('analytics'). **Wholists** tend to see the whole of a situation, are able to have an overall perspective and appreciate the total context. **Analytics** see the situation as a collection of parts and will often focus on one or two of these parts at a time, while excluding other parts. People in the middle of the continuum tend to use either mode of processing information; they are called 'intermediates'.

The verbal–imagery style dimension concerns people's preferred mode of representing information: whether they are inclined to represent information through verbal thinking ('verbalisers') or in mental pictures ('imagers'). **Verbalisers** read, listen to or consider information in words. When **imagers** read, listen to or consider information they experience fluent, spontaneous and frequent mental pictures. People in the middle of the continuum tend to use either mode of representation; they are called 'bimodals'.

Riding developed the cognitive styles analysis (CSA) to measure people's position on both the wholist–analytic and the verbal–imagery dimension.[115] People's score on the CSA is indicated by means of a ratio (that ranges from 0.4 through to 4.0 with a central value around 1.0). Although the two cognitive style dimensions are continua, they may be divided into groupings and given descriptive labels.

Evidence about cognitive styles

Several studies have looked at the models of Kirton and Riding in organisational contexts. People within different occupations are inclined to have different cognitive styles. For instance, bankers, technical engineers and accountants tend to be more adaptive, while employees in research and development (R&D), personnel and marketing tend to be more innovative.[116] Of course, this does not mean that all people in these professions show these cognitive styles, but in comparison with the mean the chance to show a certain style in a certain occupation is greater.

Research also studied the link between Kirton's cognitive style model and personality models.[117] The innovator, for instance, is found to be more extrovert, flexible, tolerant of ambiguity, risk-taking and self-confident, but less dogmatic and conservative than the adaptor. The tendency to solve problems using a more innovative than adaptive approach, as measured by the KAI, is positively correlated with MBTI preferences for extroversion, intuition, feeling and perception.[118] Innovators also tend to show higher self-esteem and higher self-confidence than adaptors. Adaptors tend to be more self-critical and doubtful about their abilities and skills. Research also found that adaptors are more likely to underrate themselves compared with others' ratings, unlike innovators.[119]

Kirton studied the link between his theory and the 'cognitive climate' in organisations; this is the collective preferred style of the group's majority. People who find themselves in a cognitive climate that is not suited to their own style are likely to be unhappy and tend to leave the group. They also feel more pressure to conform or to leave and they experience more stress. Interestingly, it seems that adaptors in non-fit situations may be under more pressure than corresponding innovators, because they are more concerned with being in consensus than innovators. Therefore, adaptors are more likely to feel the discomfort of not fitting.[120] The problem of feeling out of place is related to the organisational climate, and is explored in Chapter 9.

Riding's model is especially being studied in relation to children and students in school contexts. However, this does not make the results less useful and relevant in an organisational context. Research found that the verbal–imagery style dimension is related to performance on cognitive tasks, which can be relevant for training and development contexts.[121] For instance, it was found that imagers learned better from the pictorial presentation of material, while verbalisers learned better from the written material.[122] Imagers did best on the material that was highly descriptive and contained very few unfamiliar terms. Verbalisers were superior on the understanding and recall of the information from the material that contained the unfamiliar and acoustically difficult terminology.[123] When there is a mismatch between cognitive style and material or mode of presentation, performance is reduced.[124]

Cognitive styles will also influence the focus and type of an individual's activity. The focus of verbalisers tends to be outward towards others. They prefer a stimulating environment and the social group in which they find themselves will be an extension of themselves. The focus of imagers will be more inward and they will be more passive and content with a static environment. Social groups will be seen as distant to themselves and they may be less socially aware. Socially, verbalisers would be outgoing and lively and imagers polite and restrained.[125]

HR Applications of cognitive styles

Cognitive styles are increasingly seen as a critical intervening variable in work performance. Cognitive styles may be one of the variables that determine whether or not people are able to respond appropriately across a variety of situations.[126]

Cognitive styles are useful for the manager who wants to build effective teams, because they can help to identify a cognitive climate within the organisation.[127] The challenge is to create the right balance and to foster tolerance between team members with different cognitive styles. Differences in cognitive styles significantly affect one-on-one and team interactions in the workplace.[128] Identifying and understanding each employee's unique cognitive style provides an excellent opportunity to enhance individual and team performance and productivity.

Cognitive styles may be used to inform and improve the quality of decision-making in relation to personnel selection and placement, task and learning performance, internal communication, career guidance and counselling, fitting in with the organisation climate, task design, team composition, conflict management, team building, management style, and training and development.[129] Human resource managers have a crucial role in fostering individual versatility and in facilitating innovation through the effective management of differences in cognitive style.[130]

In other words, knowing employees' cognitive styles implies that they can be placed in jobs they like and in which they are likely to succeed. It can explain why people with the same abilities, knowledge and skills perform differently in the organisation. Research found that people effectively tend to choose professions that reward their own style.[131] People have different mental processes and different mental preferences and these affect their choice of work and activities. Knowing cognitive styles will also improve respect for diversity. People understand each other better when they know their own and others' cognitive style and they will be able to build on their strengths and to balance their weaknesses.

! Critical thinking

Identify different cognitive styles among friends and colleagues.

2.11 Learning styles

Research on learning has a long history, dating back to the beginning of the twentieth century, and has its roots in the history of psychology.[132] The early theories on learning focused on rather simple learning situations and led to a research stream called 'behaviourism' (e.g. the work of Watson, Pavlov, Thorndike and Skinner). A second stream of research, called 'cognitivism', considered more complex learning situations and tried to understand individual differences in learning (e.g. the work of Piaget, Tolman, Bruner, Ausubel and Vygotsky). Learning styles belongs in this second stream of research.

HR The interest in learning styles arose at the end of the 1960s and the beginning of the 1970s. The style concept became popular among educators, because it was a useful concept to deal with individual differences in school contexts and classrooms.[133] David Kolb defines a **learning style** as 'the way people emphasise some learning abilities over others'.[134] It refers to people's preferences in acquiring and using information. Cognitive styles and learning styles are sometimes confused. Some researchers believe the two terms mean the same and use the terms interchangeably,[135] while others consider them to be different terms and attempt to define them as separate concepts,[136] and still others regard a learning style as a subcategory of cognitive style.[137] We focus here on the most well-known learning style models: the experiential learning cycle of David Kolb.

The experiential learning cycle

The ability to learn or adapt and master changing demands is, according to Kolb, a prerequisite for success, even more than having skills or knowledge. Kolb describes learning as a process whereby knowledge is created through the transformation of experience. Knowledge is continuously derived from and tested out in the experiences of the learner. This implies that all learning is actually relearning, in the sense that it is the forming and reforming of ideas through experiences. The job of a trainer is in this way not only passing on new ideas, but also modifying ideas already present. Learning involves a transaction between a person and the environment.[138]

Effective learners need four different kinds of abilities:

- Concrete experience: the ability to involve yourself fully, openly and without bias in new experiences (e.g. experiencing what it is to use a computer).
- Reflective observation: the ability to observe and reflect upon these experiences from many perspectives (e.g. about what happens when you are using a computer program).
- Abstract conceptualisation: the ability to create concepts that integrate these observations in logically sound theories (e.g. conceptualising principles that count when using a computer).
- Active experimentation: the ability to use these theories to make decisions and solve problems (e.g. applying these abstract computer principles in reality).

Figure 2.3 Kolb's Experiential Learning Cycle Model

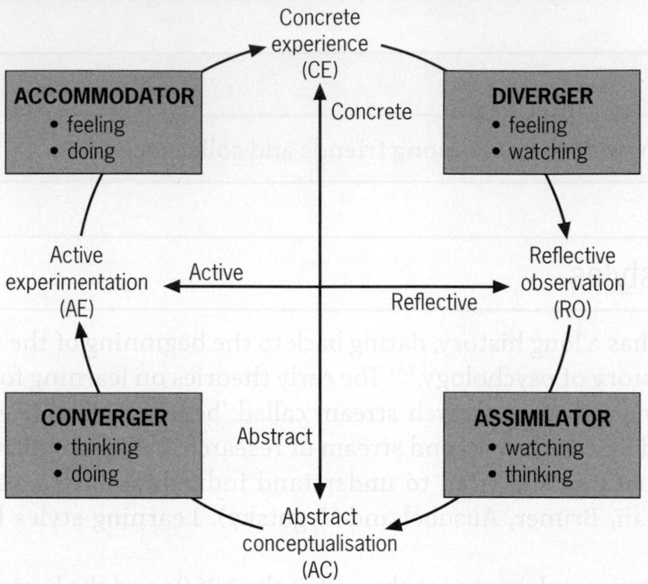

Source: Adapted from D. Kolb, *Experiential Learning: Experience as the Source of Learning and Development* (Upper Saddle River, NJ: Pearson Education, Inc., 1984).

These abilities are situated on two independent dimensions (see Figure 2.3) One ranges from concrete experience (CE) to reflective observation (RO) and the other from abstract conceptualisation (AC) to active experimentation (AE).

Effective learners will be equally good in all these abilities. However, in practice learners are rarely like this. As a result of heredity, past experiences and demands of the situation, people develop learning styles that emphasise some learning abilities over others. Each individual develops a preferred learning style that has some strengths and some weaknesses. Therefore, Kolb tries to identify people's location on both dimensions to determine their preferred learning style. He distinguishes four learning styles:

- **Divergers** prefer to perceive information concretely (CE) and process it reflectively (RO). They learn by concrete information that is given to them by their senses (feeling) and by watching. They like sharing ideas, working in groups, brainstorming and reflecting on consequences of ideas. Their greatest strength lies in their imaginative abilities. They can easily look at concrete situations and ideas from many perspectives. A potential weakness of people with this style is that they can sometimes be hindered by too many alternatives and become indecisive. Divergers are interested in and concerned with people. They tend to be emotional and value harmony. They are imaginative, often have broad interests and get their name because they perform best in situations in which they have to generate many ideas or many perspectives on one idea.
- **Assimilators** prefer to switch between reflection (RO) and conceptualisation (AC) and use inductive reasoning to develop new theory. They learn by watching and thinking. They value stability, order, accuracy, expert opinions, continuity, detailed information and certainty. They prefer to work alone. Their greatest strengths lie in the ability to create new theories. A potential weakness of people with this style is that they can be impractical and sometimes too cautious.

Assimilators are more concerned with abstract concepts than with the practical application of ideas. For them, it is more important that a theory is logically sound and precise. Assimilators are also less interested in people. These learners are called 'assimilators', because they are good at assimilating different observations into an integrated model.

- **Convergers** prefer to apply ideas, which means taking an idea (AC) and testing it out in practice (AE). They learn by doing and thinking. These learners value practicality, productivity, efficiency and punctuality. Convergers do not like ambiguity, working in groups and wasting time. Their greatest strength is the practical application of ideas. A potential weakness is that they sometimes may act too quickly without having enough data or missing important implications. Convergers tend to be rather unemotional and impersonal and prefer to work with things rather than people. These learners are called 'convergers', because they do best in situations where they have to find a single correct answer or solution to a problem.
- **Accommodators** prefer concrete experiences (CE) and active experimentation (AE). They learn by concrete information from their senses (feeling) and doing. They like to learn from talking with others and they also like to influence others. Accommodators do not like strict timetables, too many procedures and rules and too much structure. Accommodators tend to be more risk-takers than the other three styles. The greatest strength of accommodators lies in doing things, in experimenting and carrying out plans. A potential weakness is that their plans may sometimes be impractical (because they tend to overlook theory when it conflicts with their own experience or their view of the facts) and they also do not complete work on time. Accommodators tend to be at ease with people, but they are sometimes seen as being impatient or 'pushy'. These learners are called 'accommodators', because they are good at adapting themselves to different circumstances and are good at applying knowledge in new situations.

Kolb developed the learning style inventory (LSI) to measure people's learning styles.[139] It is a self-report instrument that forces people to rank four words for several items. Complete the next activity, based on Kolb's LSI, to discover what your learning style is.

Evidence about learning styles

The learning styles theories have been extensively studied in relation to other variables, such as learning strategies, performance outcomes, vocational choice, person–job fit and job satisfaction, problem-solving and decision-making.[140]

A study looked at the relationship between Kolb's learning styles and the MBTI.[141] People who score high on abstract conceptualisation (AC) also score high on thinking, while people who score high on concrete experience (CE) score high on feeling. People who score high on reflective observation (RO) tend to be introverts, while people who score high on active experimentation (AE) tend to be extroverts. The hypothesised relations between abstract conceptualisation (AC) and intuiting and between concrete experience (CE) and sensing were not confirmed in this study.

The learning styles can be linked with strengths in certain problem-solving aspects.[142] The problem-solving strengths of divergers lie in identifying possible problems and opportunities that exist in reality. Convergers are good at selecting solutions and evaluating the consequences of solutions. The problem-solving strengths of assimilators lie in building an abstract model that can help identify problem and alternative solutions. Accommodators are good at executing solutions and also at initiating problem findings based on some goal or model about how things should be. This research shows how people with different learning styles also perform better in different problem-solving phases.

Kolb's own research also shows that people's learning style indicates whether they perceive the characteristics of the learning environment to be a help or a hindrance for learning. For instance, the learning of people who score high on concrete experience seemed to be enhanced by personalised feedback, sharing feelings, applying skills to real-life problems and peer feedback. On the other hand, theoretical reading assignments hindered their learning.[143]

HR Application of learning styles thinking

The evidence shows the importance of taking into account people's learning style in organisations to enhance learning; for instance, by matching people's learning style and the learning environment or intentionally mismatching them to promote people's abilities to learn from a variety of learning perspectives (stylistic versatility). A study investigated the effect of both approaches on learning performance, which fits in with the discussion on whether learning styles are stable or not.[144] Empirical support was found in 12 of the 19 studies involved for the matching hypothesis. No empirical support was found so far for the mismatching hypothesis. However, some support suggests that it is possible to promote stylistic versatility through training.

The learning styles theory of Kolb can be very useful and relevant for organisations, certainly where change and innovation are viewed as ever-present requirements and where organisations seek to be 'learning organisations'.[145] People's learning style determines how they prefer to perceive and process information. Moreover, we tend to send information in the same way as we wish to receive it. Differences in learning styles can cause misunderstandings and conflicts when they are not addressed appropriately.

Learning styles can be used effectively in an organisational context when:[146]

- The strengths and weaknesses of one's own learning style are recognised.
- The learning styles of other people are respected – as all styles are equal. The most effective learning environments are those which respect differences in perspective.
- Use of the preferred style of others is made, for two reasons: to deliver the message quickly and easily and to avoid unnecessary misunderstanding.
- Teams are developed in a smart way, mixing or matching people with different styles appropriately to capitalise on strengths and compensate for weaknesses.
- Trainers communicate in a variety of ways, making sure to use different assignments, material and presentation skills to address all learning styles, at least part of the time.

There is, however, a caveat. In order to be effective, learning style inventories leads to tailor-fitted interventions based on the inventories. Both inventory and intervention depends on accurate data. Data, however, are never free.

Activity

What is your learning style?

Instructions

Rank order each set of four words below (from 4 to 1). Give 4 to the word which best characterises your learning style, 1 for the word which least describes you as a learner.

1	☐ Discriminating	☐ Tentative	☐ Involved	☐ Practical
2	☐ Receptive	☐ Relevant	☐ Analytical	☐ Impartial
3	☐ Feeling	☐ Watching	☐ Thinking	☐ Doing
4	☐ Accepting	☐ Risk-taker	☐ Evaluative	☐ Aware
5	☐ Intuitive	☐ Productive	☐ Logical	☐ Questioning
6	☐ Abstract	☐ Observing	☐ Concrete	☐ Active
7	☐ Present-oriented	☐ Reflecting	☐ Future-oriented	☐ Pragmatic
8	☐ Experience	☐ Observation	☐ Conceptualisation	☐ Experimentation
9	☐ Intense	☐ Reserved	☐ Rational	☐ Responsible

Scoring key

Sum up your scores in column one for items 2, 3, 4, 5, 7, 8 = ________ CE
Sum up your scores in column two for items 1, 3, 6, 7, 8, 9 = ________ RO
Sum up your scores in column three for items 2, 3, 4, 5, 8, 9 = ________ AC
Sum up your scores in column four for items 1, 3, 6, 7, 8, 9 = ________ AE

Scoring norms

Comparative norms for concrete experience (CE):
6 – 11 = Low
12 – 15 = Moderate
16 and above = High

Comparative norms for reflective observation (RO):
6 – 10 = Low
11 – 14 = Moderate
15 and above = High

Comparative norms for abstract conceptualisation (AC):
6 – 15 = Low
16 – 20 = Moderate
21 and above = High

Comparative norms for active experimentation (AE):
6 – 14 = Low
15 – 17 = Moderate
18 and above = High

Source: Based on and adapted from D. A. Kolb, I. M. Rubin and J. M. McIntyre, *Organizational Psychology: An Experiential Approach*, second edition (Englewood Cliffs, NJ: Prentice-Hall, 1974), pp. 23, 25, 27.

Learning outcomes: Summary of key terms

1 **Self-esteem and how it can be improved**

Self-esteem is a belief about one's own self-worth based on an overall self-evaluation. It refers to the degree to which people like or dislike themselves. People with high self-esteem see themselves as worthwhile, capable and acceptable. People with low self-esteem do not feel good about themselves and are hampered by self-doubts. Organisations can build employee's self-esteem in four ways, by: (1) being supportive and showing concern; (2) offering varying, autonomous and challenging work, related to one's abilities, values and skills; (3) striving for supervisor–employee cohesiveness and trust; and (4) having faith in one's self-management ability and rewarding successes.

2 **Self-efficacy and its sources**

Self-efficacy involves one's belief about one's ability to accomplish specific tasks. Those extremely low in self-efficacy suffer from learned helplessness. Four sources of self-efficacy beliefs are prior experience, behaviour models, persuasion from others and assessment of one's physical and emotional states. High self-efficacy beliefs foster constructive and goal-oriented action, whereas low self-efficacy fosters passive, failure-prone activities and emotions.

3 **High and low self-monitoring individuals and their problems**

A high self-monitor strives to make a good public impression by closely monitoring his or her behaviour and adapting it to the situation. Very high self-monitoring can create a 'chameleon' who is seen as insincere and dishonest. Low self-monitors do the opposite by acting out their momentary feelings, regardless of their surroundings. Very low self-monitoring can lead to a one-way communicator who seems to ignore verbal and non-verbal cues from others.

4 **Internal and external locus of control**

People with an internal locus of control ('internals') see themselves as active agents. They trust in their capacity to influence the environment and assume that they can control events in their lives by effort and skill. Internals see themselves as masters of their own fate. People with an external locus of control ('externals') see themselves as passive agents. They believe that events in their lives and things that they want to achieve are subject to uncontrollable forces, luck, chance and powerful others.

5 **Big Five personality dimensions**

The Big Five personality model is the most widely used of the trait theories of personality. It identifies five dimensions that are assumed to largely describe human personality. These five dimensions are extroversion (people's comfort level with relationships); agreeableness (people's ability to get along with others); conscientiousness (the extent to which people are organised, careful, responsible, dependable and self-disciplined); emotional stability (the extent to which people can cope with stress situations and experience positive emotional states); and openness to experience (the extent to which people are open to new experiences and have a broad interest in and fascination with novelty).

6 **Jung's and Myers and Briggs' personality typology**

Jung's personality typology is one of the type theories of personality. Jung identified three dimensions: one related to how people perceive and take in information (sensing versus intuiting), one related to how people judge and draw conclusions (thinking versus feeling) and one focusing on how people look at the world (extroversion versus introversion). Myers and Briggs' personality typology is an extension of Jung's work. The Myers–Briggs Type Indicator (MBTI) is primarily concerned with individual differences that result from where people like to focus their attention (extroversion–introversion), the way they like to take in information (sensing–intuiting), the way they like to decide (thinking–feeling) and the kind of lifestyle they adopt (judging–perceiving). The MBTI classifies people according to their combination of preferences along these four dimensions, which leads to 16 personality types.

7 **Personality testing in the workplace**

Personality testing as a tool for hiring applicants or for other job-related decisions (like promotions) can be questioned for three main reasons. First is the issue of predictive validity. Can personality tests actually predict job performance? Second is the issue of differential validity, relative to race. Do personality tests measure whites and other races differently? A third issue involves faking (this is intentionally misrepresenting one's true beliefs on a personality test). To what extent does faking alter a personality test's construct validity (this is the degree to which the test actually measures what it is supposed to measure)? The critical remarks and cautions concerning (personality) tests do not alter the fact that (personality) tests can be useful for self-awareness and for awareness of individual differences. Of course, this implies that people complete these tests for their own benefit and development and not for instance in a rewarding or appraisal context.

8 **Intelligence and abilities**

Human intelligence has been studied predominantly through the empirical approach. By examining the relationship between measures of mental abilities and behaviour, researchers have statistically isolated major components of intelligence. Spearman proposed that two types of abilities determine all cognitive performance: a general mental ability required for all cognitive tasks and abilities unique to the tasks at hand. Over the years much research has been devoted to developing and expanding Spearman's ideas on the relationship between cognitive abilities and intelligence. Several researchers also attempted to split the general factor g in a number of more specific abilities. The seven most frequently cited mental abilities are verbal comprehension, word fluency, numerical reasoning, spatial ability, memory, perceptual speed and inductive reasoning. Criticism has been levelled at the IQ concept. Opponents see it as too narrow-focused and failing to cover the full range of intellectual activity. So, researchers start to expand the meaning of intelligence beyond mental abilities.

9 **The cognitive styles of Kirton and those of Riding**

Kirton observed that some people typically adapt, while others typically innovate when searching for a solution. He developed a cognitive style model that situates these two styles on a continuum, with the ends labelled 'adaptive' and 'innovative', respectively. Characteristics of adaptors and innovators can be found in Table 2.8. Riding developed a cognitive style model based on two dimensions. The wholist–analytic style dimension describes the habitual way in which people process information: some individuals retain a global or overall view of information ('wholists'), while others process information into its component parts ('analytics'). The verbal–imagery style dimension concerns people's preferred mode of representing information: whether they are inclined to represent information through verbal thinking ('verbalisers') or in mental pictures ('imagers').

10 **The learning styles of Kolb and those of Honey and Mumford**

Kolb developed an experiential learning cycle that describes four stages, which each need other learning abilities. These abilities are situated on two independent dimensions: concrete experience (CE)–reflective observation (RO) and abstract conceptualisation (AC)–active experimentation

(AE). People develop learning styles that emphasise some learning abilities over others. Kolb distinguishes between divergers, assimilators, convergers and accommodators.

Honey and Mumford worked further on Kolb's experiential learning model. They kept the idea of learning as a four-stage process and also developed four learning styles, related to these four phases. The learning styles of Honey and Mumford are activist, reflector, theorist and pragmatist.

Critical thinking

Getting the data (personality testing, intelligence tests, even interviewing shortlisted candidates) for many of the models that describe personality and abilities is time-consuming and costly. However, the kind of data provided by a job applicant (CV, certificates, exam transcripts) can be of more help than first meets the eye. Think critically about how this may be the case.

Review questions

1 What is your personal experience with improving self-esteem?
2 How is someone you know with low self-efficacy, relative to a specified task, 'programming him or herself for failure'? What could be done to help that individual develop high self-efficacy?
3 What are the career implications of your self-monitoring score in the Activity?
4 How would you respond to the following statement: 'Whenever possible, organisations should hire people with an external locus of control'?
5 On scales of low = 1 to high = 10, how would you rate yourself on the Big Five personality dimensions? Is your personality profile suitable for a managerial position?
6 Which of the seven mental abilities mentioned in Table 2.6 are you good at? Which ones need some more improvement?
7 What is your learning style according to the Activity? How can this style help or hinder you to study this subject?

Personal awareness and growth exercise

What is your personality type?

Objectives

1 To identify your personality type, according to Jung's and Myers and Briggs' typology.[147]
2 To consider the practical implications of your personality type.

Instructions

Please respond to the 16 items on the next page. There are no right or wrong answers. After you have completed all items, go to the scoring key.

Questionnaire

Part I. Circle the response that comes closest to how you usually feel or act.

1 Are you more careful about:
A people's feelings?
B their rights?

2 Do you usually get along better with:
A imaginative people?
B realistic people?

3 Which of these two is the higher compliment:
A a person has real feeling?
B a person is consistently reasonable?

4 In doing something with many other people, does it appeal more to you:
A to do it in the accepted way?
B to invent a way of your own?

5 Do you get more annoyed at:
A fancy theories?
B people who do not like theories?

6 It is higher praise to call someone:
A a person of vision?
B a person of common sense?

7 Do you more often let:
A your heart rule your head?
B your head rule your heart?

8 Do you think it is worse:
A to show too much warmth?
B to be unsympathetic?

9 If you were a teacher, would you rather teach:
A courses involving theory?
B fact courses?

Part II. Which word in each of the following pairs appeals to you more? Circle A or B.

10 A compassion?
B foresight?

11 A justice?
B mercy?

12 A production?
B design?

13 A gentle?
B firm?

14 A uncritical?
B critical?

15 A literal?
B figurative?

16 A imaginative?
B matter of fact?

Scoring key

To categorise your responses to the questionnaire, count one point for each response on the following four scales, and total the number of points recorded in each column. Instructions for classifying your scores are indicated below.

SENSING		INTUITING		THINKING		FEELING	
2 B	______	2 A	______	1 B	______	1 A	______
4 A	______	4 B	______	3 B	______	3 A	______
5 A	______	5 B	______	7 B	______	7 A	______
6 B	______	6 A	______	8 A	______	8 B	______
9 B	______	9 A	______	10 B	______	10 A	______
12 A	______	12 B	______	11 A	______	11 B	______
15 A	______	15 B	______	13 B	______	13 A	______
16 B	______	16 A	______	14 B	______	14 A	______
Totals =	______	=	______	=	______	=	______

Classifying total scores

Write *intuiting* if your intuiting score is equal to or greater than your sensing score.
Write *sensing* if your sensing score is greater than your intuiting score.
Write *feeling* if feeling is greater than thinking.
Write *thinking* if thinking is greater than feeling.
When *thinking* equals feeling, you should write feeling if a male and thinking if a female.

Questions for discussion

1 What is your personality type?
  Sensing/Thinking (ST)
  Intuiting/Thinking (NT)
  Sensing/Feeling (SF)
  Intuiting/Feeling (NF)
2 Do you agree with this assessment? Why or why not?
3 Will your personality type, as determined in this exercise, help you achieve your career goal(s)?

Group exercise

Gender and self-efficacy

Objectives

1 To learn more about self-efficacy beliefs.
2 To think about possible ways organisations can increase people's – and especially women's – self-efficacy.

Introduction

Discussions about the leadership capacities and abilities of men and women, respectively, are centuries old. Women are often viewed as less effective leaders, while men are viewed as better suited for decision-making tasks. Women would lack the necessary leadership abilities, so is the belief. Nowadays, progress has been made and women find their way to higher positions. However, progress is rather small. Inequity remains, especially in upper-level managerial and executive positions. This has led researchers to search for reasons other than the existence of sex-based stereotypes to explain this inequity (see case below). We will deal with this topic in a group exercise. A 20-minute, small-group session will be followed by brief oral presentations and a general class discussion. Total time required is approximately 45 minutes to an hour (depending on how many groups there are).

Instructions

Your lecturer will divide the class into groups of four to six. You should first read the following case. Once all group members are finished, try to answer the discussion questions below. When your discussion is over, prepare a short presentation with your answers to the class group. These short presentations can be followed by a general class discussion.

Case: self-limiting behaviour in women[148]

Could it be that women internalise negative beliefs (related to sex-based stereotypes) and as a result lack confidence in their ability to perform non-traditional tasks successfully? If women indeed have a low self-efficacy concerning leadership tasks, they will show self-limiting behaviour, for instance, avoiding leadership roles. This in turn would influence their career advancement.

A recent study by Amy Dickerson and Mary Anne Taylor investigated this hypothesis. They first tested women's global self-esteem and their task-specific self-esteem (self-efficacy). In an experimental situation, women were then asked to choose between different tasks: a leadership task and a subordinate task.

The results of their study show that women with high self-efficacy (this means, women who believe they have the abilities needed to perform the leadership task) were more likely to choose this task and expressed more interest in performing it. However, women with low self-confidence in their leadership abilities (low self-efficacy) were more likely to self-select out of the leadership task and to choose the subordinate task. Global self-esteem measures were not useful to predict task choice.

These findings suggest that low self-efficacy may lead to self-limiting behaviour or self-selection out of leadership positions. This implicates that raising women's self-efficacy beliefs about leadership tasks may encourage women to take leadership roles. Useful tools hereto are modelling, mentoring, verbal persuasion, guided practice and feedback. Concretely, this means that women should have the opportunity to observe effective leaders and have the chance to talk with them about their strategies as leaders. Women should also be encouraged to accept leadership positions. Employing more women in leadership positions is a challenge for organisations, as diversity at all levels means enrichment and may lead to better results.

Questions for discussion

1. Do you agree with the findings of this study? Do you recognise forms of self-limiting behaviour of women in organisations? How can organisations become aware of this phenomenon?
2. Can the suggested solutions be effective ways to raise women's self-efficacy beliefs? Can you find some more useful tools to achieve the same result?
3. How can organisations stimulate people's self-efficacy beliefs in general.

Online Learning Centre

When you have read this chapter, log on to the Online Learning Centre website at ***www.mcgraw-hill.co.uk/textbooks/sinding*** to access test questions, additional exercises and other related resources.

Notes

1 A. Chatterjee and D. C. Hambrick, 'It's All about Me: Narcissistic Chief Executive Officers and Their Effects on Company Strategy and Performance', *Administrative Science Quarterly*, vol. 52, no. 3, 2007, pp. 351–86.

2 H. Cronqvist, A. K. Makhija and S. E. Yonker, 'Behavioral consistency in corporate finance: CEO personal and corporate leverage', *Journal of Financial Economics*, vol. 103, no. 1, 2012, pp. 20–40.

3 M. D. Cain and S. B. McKeon 'CEO Personal Risk-Taking and Corporate Policies', 2013. Available at SSRN: http://ssrn.com/abstract=1785413 or http://dx.doi.org/10.2139/ssrn.1785413.

4 V. Gecas, 'The Self-Concept', in *Annual Review of Sociology*, no. 5, eds R. H. Turner and J. F. Short, Jr (Palo Alto, CA: Annual Reviews, 1982), p. 3. Also see J. J. Sullivan, 'Self Theories and Employee Motivation', *Journal of Management*, June 1989, pp. 345–63; and L. Gaertner, C. Sedikides and K. Graetz, 'In Search of Self-Definition: Motivational Primacy of the Individual Self, Motivational Primacy of the Collective Self, or Contextual Primacy?', *Journal of Personality and Social Psychology*, January 1999, pp. 5–18.

5 L. Festinger, *A Theory of Cognitive Dissonance* (Stanford, CA: Stanford University Press, 1957), p. 3.

6 See J. Holt and D. M. Keats, 'Work Cognitions in Multicultural Interaction', *Journal of Cross-Cultural Psychology*, December 1992, pp. 421–43.

7 A Canadian versus Japanese comparison of self-concept can be found in J. D. Campbell, P. D. Trapnell, S. J. Heine, I. M. Katz, L. F. Lavallee and D. R. Lehman, 'Self-Concept Clarity: Measurement, Personality Correlates, and Cultural Boundaries', *Journal of Personality and Social Psychology*, January 1996, pp. 141–56.

8 See D. C. Barnlund, 'Public and Private Self in Communicating with Japan', *Business Horizons*, March–April 1989, pp. 32–40; and the section on 'Doing Business with Japan', in P. R. Harris and R. T. Moran, *Managing Cultural Differences, fourth edition* (Houston, TX: Gulf Publishing, 1996), pp. 267–76.

9 Based in part on a definition found in V. Gecas, 'The Self-Concept', in *Annual Review of Sociology*, vol. 8, eds R. H. Turner and J. F. Short, Jr (Palo Alto, CA: Annual Reviews Inc., 1982), p. 3. Also see N. Branden, *Self-Esteem at Work: How Confident People Make Powerful Companies* (San Francisco, CA: Jossey-Bass, 1998).

10 For related research, see R. C. Liden, L. Martin and C. K. Parsons, 'Interviewer and Applicant Behaviors in Employment Interviews', *Academy of Management Journal*, April 1993, pp. 372–86; M. B. Setterlund and P. M. Niedenthal, '"Who Am I? Why Am I Here?": Self-Esteem, Self-Clarity, and Prototype Matching', *Journal of Personality and Social Psychology*, October 1993, pp. 769–80; and G. J. Pool, W. Wood and K. Leck, 'The Self-Esteem Motive in Social Influence: Agreement with Valued Majorities and Disagreement with Derogated Minorities', *Journal of Personality and Social Psychology*, October 1998, pp. 967–75.

11 See S. J. Rowley, R. M. Sellers, T. M. Chavous and M. A. Smith, 'The Relationship between Racial Identity and Self-Esteem in African American College and High School Students', *Journal of Personality and Social Psychology*, March 1998, pp. 715–24.

12 'Sport "Improves Boys' Behaviour"', *BBC News*, 14 June 2004 (news.bbc.co.uk). Also see B. Debusschere, 'Uit het slop dankzij de sport', *De Morgen*, 16 June 2004, p. 33.

13 See J. A. Stein, M. D. Newcomb and P. M. Bentler, 'The Relative Influence of Vocational Behavior and Family Involvement on Self-Esteem: Longitudinal Analyses of Young Adult Women and Men', *Journal of Vocational Behavior*, June 1990, pp. 320–38.

14 L. E. Waters and K. A. Moore, 'Self-Esteem, Appraisal and Coping: A Comparison of Unemployed and Re-Employed People', *Journal of Organizational Behavior*, August 2002, pp. 593–604.

15 Based on P. G. Dodgson and J. V. Wood, 'Self-Esteem and the Cognitive Accessibility of Strengths and Weaknesses after Failure', *Journal of Personality and Social Psychology*, July 1998, pp. 178–97.

16 Details may be found in B. R. Schlenker, M. F. Weigold and J. R. Hallam, 'Self-Serving Attributions in Social Context: Effects of Self-Esteem and Social Pressure', *Journal of Personality and Social Psychology*, May 1990, pp. 855–63.

17 See R. F. Baumeister, L. Smart and J. M. Boden, 'Relation of Threatened Egotism to Violence and Aggression: The Dark Side of High Self-Esteem', *Psychological Review*, January 1996, pp. 5–33; and R. Vermunt, D. van Knippenberg, B. van Knippenberg

and E. Blaauw, 'Self-Esteem and Outcome Fairness: Differential Importance of Procedural and Outcome Considerations', *Journal of Applied Psychology*, August 2001, pp. 621–8.

18 M. A. Mone, 'Relationships between Self-Concepts, Aspirations, Emotional Responses, and Intent to Leave a Downsizing Organization', *Human Resource Management*, Summer 1994, pp. 281–98.

19 T. Apter, 'Confidence Tricks', *The Guardian*, 27 September 2000.

20 E. Diener and M. Diener, 'Cross-Cultural Correlates of Life Satisfaction and Self-Esteem', *Journal of Personality and Social Psychology*, April 1995, p. 662. For crosscultural evidence of a similar psychological process for self-esteem, see T. M. Singelis, M. H. Bond, W. F. Sharkey and C. S. Y. Lai, 'Unpackaging Culture's Influence on Self-Esteem and Embarrassability', *Journal of Cross-Cultural Psychology*, May 1999, pp. 315–41.

21 W. J. McGuire and C. V. McGuire, 'Enhancing Self-Esteem by Directed-Thinking Tasks: Cognitive and Affective Positivity Asymmetries', *Journal of Personality and Social Psychology*, June 1996, p. 1124.

22 Adapted from discussion in J. K. Matejka and R. J. Dunsing, 'Great Expectations', *Management World*, January 1987, pp. 16–17. Also see P. Pascarella, 'It All Begins with Self-Esteem', *Management Review*, February 1999, pp. 60–61.

23 M. E. Gist, 'Self-Efficacy: Implications for Organizational Behavior and Human Resource Management', *Academy of Management Review*, July 1987, p. 472. Also see A. Bandura, 'Self-Efficacy: Toward a Unifying Theory of Behavioral Change', *Psychological Review*, March 1977, pp. 191–215; M. E. Gist and T. R. Mitchell, 'Self-Efficacy: A Theoretical Analysis of Its Determinants and Malleability', *Academy of Management Review*, April 1992, pp. 183–211; and S. L. Anderson and N. E. Betz, 'Sources of Social Self-Efficacy Expectations: Their Measurement and Relation to Career Development', *Journal of Vocational Behavior*, February 2001, pp. 98–117.

24 A. Davidson, 'The Andrew Davidson Interview: James Dyson', *Management Today*, July 1999.

25 Based on D. H. Lindsley, D. A. Brass and J. B. Thomas, 'Efficacy-Performance Spirals: A Multilevel Perspective', *Academy of Management Review*, July 1995, pp. 645–78.

26 See, for example, V. Gecas, 'The Social Psychology of Self-Efficacy', in *Annual Review of Sociology*, no. 15, eds W. R. Scott and J. Blake (Palo Alto, CA: Annual Reviews, Inc., 1989), pp. 291–316; C. K. Stevens, A. G. Bavetta and M. E. Gist, 'Gender Differences in the Acquisition of Salary Negotiation Skills: The Role of Goals, Self-Efficacy, and Perceived Control', *Journal of Applied Psychology*, October 1993, pp. 723–35; D. Eden and Y. Zuk, 'Seasickness as a Self-Fulfilling Prophecy: Raising Self-Efficacy to Boost Performance at Sea', *Journal of Applied Psychology*, October 1995, pp. 628–35; and S. M. Jex, P. D. Bliese, S. Buzzell and J. Primeau, 'The Impact of Self-Efficacy on Stressor-Strain Relations: Coping Style as an Explanatory Mechanism', *Journal of Applied Psychology*, June 2001, pp. 401–9.

27 For more on learned helplessness, see M. J. Martinko and W. L. Gardner, 'Learned Helplessness: An Alternative Explanation for Performance Deficits', *Academy of Management Review*, April 1982, pp. 195–204; C. R. Campbell and M. J. Martinko, 'An Integrative Attributional Perspective of Empowerment and Learned Helplessness: A Multimethod Field Study', *Journal of Management*, March 1998, pp. 173–200; and S. B. Schepman and L. Richmond, 'Employee Expectations and Motivation: An Application from the "Learned Helplessness" Paradigm', *Journal of American Academy of Business*, September 2003, pp. 405–8.

28 A. Bandura, *Social Foundations of Thought and Action: A Social Cognitive Theory* (Englewood Cliffs, NJ: Prentice Hall, 1986); and A. Bandura, *Self-Efficacy: The Exercise of Control* (New York: W. H. Freeman, 1997).

29 Research on this connection is reported in R. B. Rubin, M. M. Martin, S. S. Bruning and D. E. Powers, 'Test of a Self-Efficacy Model of Interpersonal Communication Competence', *Communication Quarterly*, Spring 1993, pp. 210–20.

30 See G. Whyte, A. Saks, and S. Hook 'When Success Breeds Failure', *Journal of Organizational Behavior*, no. 18, 1997, pp. 415–32.

31 Data from A. D. Stajkovic and F. Luthans, 'Self-Efficacy and Work-Related Performance: A Meta-Analysis', *Psychological Bulletin*, September 1998, pp. 240–61.

32 See C. Speirer and M. Frese, 'Generalized Self-Efficacy as a Mediator and a Moderator between Control and Complexity at Work and Personal Initiative', *Human Performance*, no. 10, 1997, pp. 171–92.

33 See N. Kreuger and P. R. Dickson, 'Self-Efficacy and Perceptions of Opportunities and Threats, *Psychological Report*, no. 72, 1993, pp. 1235–40.

34 See S. M. Jex and P. D. Bliese, 'Efficacy Beliefs as a Moderator of the Impact of Work-Related Stressors,' *Journal of Applied Psychology*, no. 84, 1999, pp. 349–61.

35 Based in part on discussion in V. Gecas, 'The Social Psychology of Self-Efficacy', in *Annual Review of Sociology*, vol. 15, eds W. R. Scott and J. Blake (Palo Alto, CA: Annual Reviews, 1989), pp. 291–316.

36 See S. K. Parker, 'Enhancing Role Breadth Self-Efficacy: The Roles of Job Enrichment and Other Organizational Interventions', *Journal of Applied Psychology*, December 1998, pp. 835–52.

37 The positive relationship between self-efficacy and readiness for retraining is documented in L. A. Hill and J. Elias, 'Retraining Midcareer Managers: Career History and Self-Efficacy Beliefs', *Human Resource Management*, Summer 1990, pp. 197–217. Also see M. E. Gist, C. K. Stevens and A. G. Bavetta, 'Effects of Self-Efficacy and Post-Training Intervention on the Acquisition and Maintenance of Complex Interpersonal Skills', *Personnel Psychology*, Winter 1991, pp. 837–61; A. M. Saks, 'Longitudinal Field Investigation of the Moderating and Mediating Effects of Self-Efficacy on the Relationship between Training and Newcomer Adjustment', *Journal of Applied Psychology*, April 1995, pp. 211–25; and S. P. Brown, S. Ganesan and G. Challagalla, 'Self-Efficacy as a Moderator of Information-Seeking Effectiveness', *Journal of Applied Psychology*, October 2001, pp. 1043–51.

38 J. N. Choi, R. H. Price and A. D. Vinokur, 'Self-Efficacy Change in Groups: Effects of Diversity, Leadership, and Group Climate', *Journal of Organizational Behavior*, June 2003, pp. 357–72.

39 See A. D. Stajkovic and F. Luthans, 'Social Cognitive Theory and Self-Efficacy: Going Beyond Traditional Motivational and Behavioral Approaches', *Organizational Dynamics*, Spring 1998, pp. 62–74.

[40] See P. C. Earley and T. R. Lituchy, 'Delineating Goal and Efficacy Effects: A Test of Three Models', *Journal of Applied Psychology*, February 1991, pp. 81–98; J. B. Vancouver, C. M. Thompson and A. A. Williams, 'The Changing Signs in the Relationships among Self-Efficacy, Personal Goals and Performance', *Journal of Applied Psychology*, August 2001, pp. 605–20; and A. Bandura and E. A. Locke, 'Negative Self-Efficacy and Goal Effects Revisited', *Journal of Applied Psychology*, February 2003, pp. 87–99.

[41] See W. S. Silver, T. R. Mitchell and M. E. Gist, 'Response to Successful and Unsuccessful Performance: The Moderating Effect of Self-Efficacy on the Relationship between Performance and Attributions', *Organizational Behavior and Human Decision Processes*, June 1995, pp. 286–99; R. Zemke, 'The Corporate Coach', *Training*, December 1996, pp. 24–8; J. P. Masciarelli, 'Less Lonely at the Top', *Management Review*, April 1999, pp. 58–61; and S. Berglas, 'The Very Real Dangers of Executive Coaching', *Harvard Business Review*, June 2002, pp. 89–92.

[42] A model of 'leadership self-efficacy' can be found in L. L. Paglis and S. G. Green, 'Leadership Self-Efficacy and Managers' Motivation for Leading Change', *Journal of Organizational Behavior*, March 2002, pp. 215–35.

[43] M. Snyder and S. Gangestad, 'On the Nature of Self-Monitoring: Matters of Assessment, Matters of Validity', *Journal of Personality and Social Psychology*, July 1986, p. 125. Also see M. Snyder, *Public Appearances/Private Realities: The Psychology of Self-Monitoring* (New York: W. H. Freeman, 1987).

[44] Data from M. Kilduff and D. V. Day, 'Do Chameleons Get Ahead? The Effects of Self-Monitoring on Managerial Careers', *Academy of Management Journal*, August 1994, pp. 1047–60.

[45] Data from D. B. Turban and T. W. Dougherty, 'Role of Protege Personality in Receipt of Mentoring and Career Success', *Academy of Management Journal*, June 1994, pp. 688–702.

[46] See F. Luthans, 'Successful vs. Effective Managers', *Academy of Management Executive*, May 1988, pp. 127–32. Also see A. Mehra, M. Kilduff and D. J. Brass, 'The Social Networks of High and Low Self-Monitors: Implications for Workplace Performance', *Administrative Science Quarterly*, March 2001, pp. 121–46; and W. H. Turnley and M. C. Bolino, 'Achieving Desired Images while Avoiding Undesired Images: Exploring the Role of Self-Monitoring in Impression Management', *Journal of Applied Psychology*, April 2001, pp. 351–60.

[47] S. F. Premeaux and A. G. Bedeian, 'Breaking the Silence: The Moderating Effects of Self-Monitoring in Predicting Speaking Up in the Workplace', *Journal of Management Studies*, September 2003, pp. 1537–62.

[48] Data from D. V. Day, D. J. Schleicher, A. L. Unckless and N. J. Hiller, 'Self-Monitoring Personality at Work: A Meta-Analytic Investigation of Construct Validity', *Journal of Applied Psychology*, April 2002, pp. 390–401. Also see P. M. Caligiuri and D. V. Day, 'Effects of Self-Monitoring on Technical, Contextual, and Assignment-Specific Performance: A Study of Cross-National Work Performance Ratings', *Group & Organization Management*, June 2000, pp. 154–74; S. W. Gangestad and M. Snyder, 'Self-Monitoring: Appraisal and Reappraisal', *Psychological Bulletin*, July 2000, pp. 530–55; and I. M. Jawahar, 'Attitudes, Self-Monitoring and Appraisal Behaviors', *Journal of Applied Psychology*, October 2001, pp. 875–83.

[49] For an instructive update, see J. B. Rotter, 'Internal versus External Control of Reinforcement: A Case History of a Variable', *American Psychologist*, April 1990, pp. 489–93. A critical review of locus of control and a call for a meta-analysis can be found in R. W. Renn and R. J. Vandenberg, 'Differences in Employee Attitudes and Behaviors Based on Rotter's (1966) Internal-External Locus of Control: Are They All Valid?', *Human Relations*, November 1991, pp. 1161–77.

[50] See G. P. Hodgkinson, 'Development and Validation of the Strategic Locus of Control Scale', *Strategic Management Journal*, May 1992, pp. 311–18; and S. E. Hahn, 'The Effects of Locus of Control and Daily Exposure, Coping and Reactivity to Work Interpersonal Stressors: A Diary Study', *Personality and Individual Differences*, October 2000, pp. 729–48.

[51] See P. E. Spector, 'Behavior in Organizations as a Function of Employee's Locus of Control', *Psychological Bulletin*, May 1982, pp. 482–97; and H. M. Lefcourt, *Locus of Control: Current Trends in Theory and Research, second edition* (Hillsdale, NJ: Lawrence Erlbaum Associates, 1982).

[52] G. J. Blau, 'Testing the Relationship of Locus of Control to Different Performance Dimensions', *Journal of Occupational and Organizational Psychology*, June 1993, pp. 125–38.

[53] See L. I. Marks, 'Deconstructing Locus of Control: Implications for Practitioners', *Journal of Counseling & Development*, Summer 1998, pp. 251–60.

[54] See S. R. Hawk, 'Locus of Control and Computer Attitude: The Effect of User Involvement', *Computers in Human Behavior*, no. 3, 1989, pp. 199–206. Also see A. S. Phillips and A. G. Bedeian, 'Leader-Follower Exchange Quality: The Role of Personal and Interpersonal Attributes', *Academy of Management Journal*, August 1994, pp. 990–1001; and S. S. K. Lam and J. Schaubroeck, 'The Role of Locus of Control in Reactions to Being Promoted and to Being Passed Over: A Quasi Experiment', *Academy of Management Journal*, February 2000, pp. 66–78.

[55] These recommendations are from P. E. Spector, 'Behavior in Organizations as a Function of Employee's Locus of Control', *Psychological Bulletin*, May 1982, pp. 482–97.

[56] For a good overview, see L. R. James and M. D. Mazerolle, *Personality in Work Organizations* (Thousand Oaks, CA: Sage Publications, 2002). For evidence on the stability of adult personality dimensions, see R. R. McCrae, 'Moderated Analyses of Longitudinal Personality Stability', *Journal of Personality and Social Psychology*, September 1993, pp. 577–85. Adult personality changes are documented in L. Pulkkinen, M. Ohranen and A. Tolvanen, 'Personality Antecedents of Career Orientation and Stability among Women Compared to Men', *Journal of Vocational Behavior*, February 1999, pp. 37–58.

[57] T. J. Bouchard, Sr, 'Genetic and Environmental Influences on Intelligence and Special Mental Abilities', *American Journal of Human Biology*, April 1998, pp. 253–75; L. Wright, *Twins: And What They Tell Us about What We Are* (New York: John Wiley, 1999).

[58] For more information on this model, see R. B. Cattell, H. W. Eber and M. M. Tatsouka, *Handbook for the Sixteen Personality Factor Questionnaire 16PF* (Champaign, IL: IPAT, 1970); and R. B. Cattell and P. Kline, *The Scientific Analysis of Personality and Motivation* (London: Academic Press, 1977).

[59] H. J. Eysenck, *The Structure of Human Personality* (London: Methuen, 1960).

[60] The landmark report is J. M. Digman, 'Personality Structure: Emergence of the Five-Factor Model', in *Annual Review of Psychology*, vol. 41, eds M. R. Rosenzweig and L. W. Porter (Palo Alto, CA: Annual Reviews, 1990), pp. 417–40. Also see R. R. McCrae, 'Special Issue: The Five-Factor Model: Issues and Applications', *Journal of Personality*, June 1992; M. R. Barrick and M. K. Mount, 'Autonomy as a Moderator of the Relationships between the Big Five Personality Dimensions and Job Performance', *Journal of Applied Psychology*, February 1993, pp. 111–18; and C. Viswesvaran and D. S. Ones, 'Measurement Error in "Big Five Factors" Personality Assessment: Reliability Generalization across Studies and Measures', *Educational and Psychological Measurement*, April 2000, pp. 224–35.

[61] For research on the 'Big Five', see R. P. Tett, D. N. Jackson and M. Rothstein, 'Personality Measures as Predictors of Job Performance: A Meta-Analytic Review', *Personnel Psychology*, Winter 1991, pp. 703–42; P. H. Raymark, M. J. Schmidt and R. M. Guion, 'Identifying Potentially Useful Personality Constructs for Employee Selection', *Personnel Psychology*, Autumn 1997, pp. 723–42; G. M. Hurtz and J. J. Donavan, 'Personality and Job Performance: The Big Five Revisited', *Journal of Applied Psychology*, December 2000, pp. 869–79; D. B. Smith, P. J. Hanges and M. W. Dickson, 'Personnel Selection and the Five-Factor Model: Reexamining the Effects of Applicant's Frame of Reference', *Journal of Applied Psychology*, April 2001, pp. 304–15; and M. R. Barrick, G. L. Stewart and M. Piotrowski, 'Personality and Job Performance: Test of the Mediating Effects of Motivation among Sales Representatives', *Journal of Applied Psychology*, February 2002, pp. 43–51.

[62] For more studies on the 'conscientiousness' dimension, see O. Behling, 'Employee Selection: Will Intelligence and Conscientiousness Do the Job?', *Academy of Management Executive*, February 1998, pp. 77–86; H. Moon, 'The Two Faces of Conscientiousness: Duty and Achievement Striving in Escalation of Commitment Dilemmas', *Journal of Applied Psychology*, June 2001, pp. 533–40; and L. A. Witt, L. A. Burke, M. R. Barrick and M. K. Mount, 'The Interactive Effects of Conscientiousness and Agreeableness on Job Performance', *Journal of Applied Psychology*, February 2002, pp. 164–9.

[63] C. J. Thorensen, J. C. Bradley, P. D. Bliese and J. D. Thorensen (2004) 'The Big Five Personality Traits and Individual Job Performance Growth Trajectories in Maintenance and Transitional Jobs', *Journal of Applied Psychology*, 89, pp. 835–53.

[64] S. E. Seibert and M. L. Kraimer, 'The Five-Factor Model of Personality and Career Success', *Journal of Vocational Behavior*, February 2001, pp. 1– 21.

[65] M. Dalton and M. Wilson, 'The Relationship of the Five-Factor Model of Personality to Job Performance for a Group of Middle Eastern Expatriate Managers', *Journal of Cross-Cultural Psychology*, March 2000, pp. 250–58.

[66] J. W. Boudreau, W. R. Boswell, T. A. Judge and R. D. Bretz, Jr, 'Personality and Cognitive Ability as Predictors of Job Search among Employed Managers', *Personnel Psychology*, Spring 2001, pp. 25–50.

[67] For cross-cultural studies on the 'Big Five', see M. S. Katigbak, A. T. Church and T. X. Akamine, 'Cross-Cultural Generalizability of Personality Dimensions: Relating Indigenous and Imported Dimensions in Two Cultures', *Journal of Personality and Social Psychology*, January 1996, pp. 99–114; S. V. Paunonen et al., 'The Structure of Personality in Six Cultures', *Journal of Cross-Cultural Psychology*, May 1996, pp. 339–53; V. Benet-Martinez and O. P. John, 'Los *Cinco Grandes* Across Cultures and Ethnic Groups: Multitrait Multimethod Analyses of the Big Five in Spanish and English', *Journal of Personality and Social Psychology*, September 1998, pp. 729–50; N. N. McCraw and P. T. Costa, 'A Big Five Factor Theory of Personality', in *Handbook of Personality, second edition*, eds L. A. Pervin and O. P. John (New York: Guilford, 1999), pp. 139–53; and K. Yoon, F. Schmidt and R. Ilies, 'Cross-Cultural Construct Validity of the Five-Factor Model of Personality among Korean Employees', *Journal of Cross-Cultural Psychology*, May 2002, pp. 217–35.

[68] See J. F. Saldago, 'The Five Factor Model of Personality and Job Performance in the European Community', *Journal of Applied Psychology*, February 1997, pp. 30–43.

[69] C. Bendersky and N. Shah, 'The Downfall of Extraverts and Rise of Neurotics: The Dynamic Process of Status Allocation in Task Groups', *Academy of Management Journal,* Spring 2012, pp. 387–406

[70] W. F. Cascio, *Applied Psychology in Personnel Management* (Reston, VA: Prentice-Hall, 1982).

[71] A. Furnham, *Management Intelligence: Sense and Nonsense for the Successful Manager* (Basingstoke: Palgrave Macmillan, 2008).

[72] C. G. Jung, *The Collected Works of C. G. Jung, Vol. 6: Psychological Types* (translated by H. G. Baynes, revised by R. F. Hull, originally published in 1921) (Princeton, NJ: Princeton University Press, 1971).

[73] See I. Briggs Myers (with P. B. Myers), *Gifts Differing* (Palo Alto, CA: Consulting Psychologists Press, 1980); I. Briggs Myers and M. H. McCaully, *Manual: A Guide to the Development and Use of the Myers-Briggs Type Indicator* (Palo Alto, CA: Consulting Psychologists Press, 1985); and I. Briggs Myers, *A Description of the Theory and Applications of the Myers-Briggs Type Indicator* (Palo Alto, CA: Consulting Psychologists Press, 1990).

[74] I. Briggs Myers, *A Description of the Theory and Applications of the Myers-Briggs Type Indicator* (Palo Alto, CA: Consulting Psychologists Press, 1990), p. 4.

[75] See, for instance, A. Furnham and P. Stringfield, 'Personality and Occupational Behavior: Myers-Briggs Type Indicator Correlates of Managerial Practices in Two Cultures', *Human Relations*, July 1993, pp. 827–42; A. H. Church and J. Waclawski, 'The Effects of Personality Orientation and Executive Behavior on Subordinate Perceptions of Workgroup Enablement', *International Journal of Organizational Analysis*, January 1996, pp. 20–40; N. H. Leonard, R. W. Scholl and K. B. Kowalski, 'Information Processing Style and Decision Making', *Journal of Organizational Behavior*, May 1999, pp. 407–20; and S. A. Berr, A. H. Church and J. Waclawski, 'The Right Personality Is Everything: Linking Personality Preferences to Managerial Behaviors', *Human Resource Development Quarterly*, Summer 2000, pp. 133–57.

[76] See B. K. Blaylock and L. P. Rees, 'Cognitive Style and the Usefulness of Information', *Decision Sciences*, Winter 1984, pp. 74–91. Also see D. E. Campbell and J. M. Kain, 'Personality Type and Mode of Information Presentation: Preference, Accuracy, and Efficiency in Problem Solving', *Journal of Psychological Type*, January 1990, pp. 47–51.

[77] See G. H. Rice, Jr and D. P. Lindecamp, 'Personality Types and Business Success of Small Retailers', *Journal of Occupational Psychology*, June 1989, pp. 177–82. Also see S. Goldman and W. M. Kahnweiler, 'A Collaborator Profile for Executives of Nonprofit Organizations', *Nonprofit Management and Leadership*, Summer 2000, pp. 435–50.

[78] W. L. Gardner and M. J. Martinko, 'Using the Myers-Briggs Type Indicator to Study Managers: A Literature Review and Research Agenda', *Journal of Management*, January 1996, p. 77. Also see R. Zemke, 'Second Thoughts about the MBTI', *Training*, April 1992, pp. 42–7; and D. W. Salter and N. J. Evans, 'Test-Retest of the Myers-Briggs Type Indicator: An Examination of Dominant Functioning', *Educational and Psychological Measurement*, August 1997, pp. 590–97.

[79] For example, see P. R. Lindsay, 'Counseling to Resolve a Clash of Cognitive Styles', *Technovation*, February 1985, pp. 57–67; M. J. Kirton and R. M. McCarthy, 'Cognitive Climate and Organizations', *Journal of Occupational Psychology*, June 1988, pp. 175–84; F. Ramsoomair, 'Relating Theoretical Concepts to Life in the Classroom: Applying the Myers-Briggs Type Indicator', *Journal of Management Education*, February 1994, pp. 111–16; B. McPherson, 'Re-Engineering Your Office Environment: Matching Careers and Personality via the Myers-Briggs Type Indicator', *Office Systems Research Journal*, Fall 1995, pp. 29–34; S. Shapiro and M. T. Spence, 'Managerial Intuition: A Conceptual and Operational Framework', *Business Horizons*, January–February 1997, pp. 63–8; and D. Leonard and S. Straus, 'Putting Your Company's Whole Brain to Work', *Harvard Business Review*, July–August 1997, pp. 111–21.

[80] R. E. Boyatzis, *The Competent Manager: A Model for Effective Performance* (Chichester: Wiley, 1982).

[81] L. M. Spencer, D. C. McClelland and S. M. Spencer, *Competency Assessment Methods: History and State of the Art* (London: Hay/McBer Research Press, 1994).

[82] For interesting reading on competences, see C. Woodruffe, *Assessment Centres: Identifying and Developing Competence, second edition* (London: IPM, 1993); and D. Dubois, *Competency-Based Performance Improvement: A Strategy for Organizational Change* (Amherst, MA: HRD Press, 1993).

[83] See H. A. Witkin, C. A. Moore, D. R. Goodenough and P. W. Cox, 'Field-Dependent and Field-Independent Cognitive Styles and Their Educational Implications', *Review of Educational Research*, Winter 1977, pp. 1–64; J. P. Guilford, 'Cognitive Styles: What Are They?', *Educational and Psychological Measurement*, Fall 1980, pp. 517–35; and S. Messick, 'The Nature of Cognitive Styles: Problems and Promises in Educational Practice', *Educational Psychologist*, Spring 1984, pp. 59–74.

[84] R. J. Riding, *Cognitive Styles Analysis: Research Applications, revised edition* (Birmingham: Learning and Training Technology, 2000), p. 3.

[85] For excellent works on intelligence, including definitional distinctions and a historical perspective of the IQ controversy, see S. J. Ceci, *On Intelligence* (London: Harvard University Press, 1996); M. J. A. Howe, *I.Q. in Question: The Truth about Intelligence* (London: Sage Publications, 1997); R. J. Sternberg and E. Grigorenko, *Intelligence, Heredity and Environment* (Cambridge: Cambridge University Press, 1997); and C. Cooper and V. Varma, *Intelligence and Abilities* (London: Routledge, 1999).

[86] C. Spearman, *The Abilities of Man* (Oxford: Macmillan, 1927).

[87] For related research, see M. J. Ree and J. A. Earles, 'Predicting Training Success: Not Much More Than g', *Personnel Psychology*, Summer 1991, pp. 321–32; and M. J. Ree, J. A. Earles and M. S. Teachout, 'Predicting Job Performance: Not Much More than g', *Journal of Applied Psychology*, August 1994, pp. 518–24.

[88] P. E. Vernon, 'The Hierarchy of Abilities', in *Intelligence and Abilities*, 2nd edn, ed. S. Wiseman (New York: Penguin, 1973); and J. P. Guilford, 'The Three Faces of Intellect', in *Intelligence and Abilities*, ed. S. Wiseman (New York: Penguin, 1959).

[89] These seven abilities were first described by L. L. Thurstone, 'Primary Mental Abilities', *Psychometric Monographs*, no. 1, 1938.

[90] See F. L. Schmidt and J. E. Hunter, 'Employment Testing: Old Theories and New Research Findings', *American Psychologist*, October 1981, p. 1128. Also see W. M. Coward and P. R. Sackett, 'Linearity of Ability–Performance Relationships: A Reconfirmation', *Journal of Applied Psychology*, June 1990, pp. 297–300; F. L. Schmidt and J. E. Hunter, 'The Validity and Utility of Selection Methods in Personnel Psychology: Practical and Theoretical Implications of 85 Years of Research Findings', *Psychological Bulletin*, September 1998, pp. 262–74; and Y. Ganzach, 'Intelligence and Job Satisfaction', *Academy of Management Journal*, October 1998, pp. 526–39.

[91] This point is made in a blog entry by Malcom Gladwell, at www.gladwell.typepad.com/gladwellcom/2009/12/pinker-round-two-.html. (Accessed 4 March 2010)

[92] K. R. Murphy, B. E. Cronin and A. P. Tam 'Controversy and Consensus Regarding the Use of Cognitive Ability Testing in Organizations', *Journal of Applied Psychology*, no. 88, 2003, pp. 660–71.

[93] See H. Gardner, *Frames of Mind: The Theory of Multiple Intelligences, second edition* (New York: Basic Books, 1993); H. Gardner, M. C. Kornhaber and W. K. Wake, *Intelligence: Multiple Perspectives* (London: Harcourt Brace, 1996); and H. Gardner, *Changing Minds: The Art and Science of Changing Our Own and Other People's Minds* (Boston, MA: Harvard Business School Press, 2004).

[94] R. J. Sternberg and R. K. Wagner, *Practical Intelligence* (Cambridge: Cambridge University Press, 1986). Also see S. Fox and P. E. Spector, 'Relations of Emotional Intelligence, Practical Intelligence, General Intelligence, and Trait Affectivity with Interview Outcomes: It's Not all Just "g"', *Journal of Organizational Behavior*, April 2000, pp. 203–20.

[95] See R. E. Riggio, S. E. Murphy and F. J. Pirozzolo, *Multiple Intelligences and Leadership* (Mahwah, NJ: Lawrence Erlbaum Associates, 2002).

[96] D. Lubinski and R. V. Dawis, 'Aptitudes, Skills and Proficiencies', in *Handbook of Industrial and Organizational Psychology*, no. 3, eds M. D. Dunnette and L. M. Hough (Palo Alto, CA: Consulting Psychologists Press, 1992), pp. 30–33.

[97] S. L. Wilk, L. Burris Desmarais and P. R. Sackett, 'Gravitation to Jobs Commensurate with Ability: Longitudinal and Cross-Sectional Tests', *Journal of Applied Psychology*, February 1995, p. 79.

[98] J. R. Flynn, 'The Mean IQ of Americans: Massive Gains 1932 to 1978', *Psychological Bulletin*, January 1984, pp. 29–51; J. R. Flynn, 'Massive IQ Gains in 14 Nations: What IQ Tests Really Measure', *Psychological Bulletin*, March 1987, pp. 171–91; and J. R. Flynn, 'Searching for Justice: The Discovery of IQ Gains over Time', *American Psychologist*, January 1999, pp. 5–20.

[99] B. Azar, 'People Are Becoming Smarter – Why?', *APA Monitor*, June 1996, p. 20. Also see U. Neisser, 'Rising Scores on Intelligence Tests', *American Scientist*, September–October 1997, pp. 440–47; and U. Neisser, *The Rising Curve: Long Term Gains in IQ and Related Measures* (Washington, DC: American Psychological Association, 1998).

[100] T. Teasdale and D. Owen, 'Secular declines in cognitive test scores: A reversal of the Flynn effect', *Intelligence*, vol. 36, no. 2, 2008, pp. 121–6.

[101] C. Dweck, *Mindset* (New York: Random House, 2006).

[102] See the discussion in M. R. Barrick and M. K. Mount, 'The Big Five Personality Dimensions and Job Performance: A Meta-Analysis', *Personnel Psychology*, Spring 1991, pp. 21–2. Also see J. M. Cortina, M. L. Doherty, N. Schmitt, G. Kaufman and R. G. Smith, 'The "Big Five" Personality Factors in the IPI and MMPI: Predictors of Police Performance', *Personnel Psychology*, Spring 1992, pp. 119–40; M. J. Schmit and A. M. Ryan, 'The "Big Five"' in Personnel Selection: Factor Structure in Applicant and Nonapplicant Populations', *Journal of Applied Psychology*, December 1993, pp. 966–74; and C. Caggiano, 'Psychopath', *Inc.*, July 1998, pp. 77–85.

[103] M. K. Mount and M. R. Barrick, 'The Big Five Personality Dimensions: Implications for Research and Practice in Human Resources Management', in *Research in Personnel and Human Resources Management*, vol. 13, ed. G. R. Ferris (Greenwich, CT: JAI Press, 1995), p. 189. See J. M. Collins and D. H. Gleaves, 'Race, Job Applicants, and the Five-Factor Model of Personality: Implications for Black Psychology, Industrial/Organizational Psychology, and the Five-Factor Theory', *Journal of Applied Psychology*, August 1998, pp. 531–44.

[104] See G. M. Alliger and S. A. Dwight, 'A Meta-Analytic Investigation of the Susceptibility of Integrity Tests to Faking and Coaching', *Educational and Psychological Measurement*, February 2000, pp. 59–72; and S. Stark, O. S. Chernyshenko, K. Chan, W. C. Lee and F. Drasgow, 'Effects of the Testing Situation on Item Responding: Cause for Concern', *Journal of Applied Psychology*, October 2001, pp. 943–53.

[105] Other sources relating to Table 2.7 are D. Batram, 'Addressing the Abuse of Personality Test', *Personnel Management*, April 1991, pp. 34–9; C. Fletcher, 'Personality Tests: The Great Debate', *Personnel Management*, September 1991, pp. 38–42; R. Feltham, H. Baron and P. Smith, 'Developing Fair Tests', *The Psychologist*, January 1994, pp. 23–5; C. Jackson, *Understanding Psychological Testing* (Leicester: BPS Books, 1996); and B. Leonard, 'Reading Employees', *HR Magazine*, April 1999, pp. 67–73.

[106] See J. C. McCune, 'Testing, Testing 1 2 3', *Management Review*, January 1996, pp. 50–52; and C. M. Solomon, 'Testing at Odds with Diversity Efforts?', *Personnel Journal*, April 1996, pp. 131–40.

[107] For example, see J. C. Connor, 'The Paranoid Personality at Work', *HR Magazine*, March 1999, pp. 120–26; and 'Your Sleep Has a Personality', *Management Review*, May 1999, p. 9.

[108] J. Hayes and C. W. Allinson, 'Cognitive Style and the Theory and Practice of Individual and Collective Learning in Organizations', *Human Relations*, July 1998, pp. 847–71.

[109] M. Kirton, 'Adaptors and Innovators: A Description and Measure', *Journal of Applied Psychology*, October 1976, p. 622.

[110] For more information on this model, see M. Kirton, 'Adaptors and Innovators: A Description and Measure', *Journal of Applied Psychology*, October 1976, pp. 622–9; M. Kirton, 'Adaptors and Innovators in Organizations', *Human Relations*, April 1980, pp. 213–24; and M. Kirton, *Adaptors and Innovators: Styles of Creativity and Problem Solving, second edition* (London: Routledge, 1994).

[111] For more information on the organisational relevance of KAI, especially for change processes, see S. Mudd, 'Kirton Adaption-Innovation Theory: Organizational Implications', *Technovation*, April 1995, pp. 165–75; and A. D. Tullett, 'The Adaptive-Innovative (A-I) Cognitive Styles of Male and Female Project Managers: Some Implications for the Management of Change', *Journal of Occupational and Organizational Psychology*, December 1995, pp. 359–65.

[112] M. J. Kirton, *KAI Manual, second edition* (Hatfield: Occuptional Research Centre, 1985).

[113] A. D. Tullett, 'Cognitive Style: Not Culture's Consequence', *European Psychologist*, September 1997, pp. 258–67.

[114] For more information on this model, see R. Riding and I. Cheema, 'Cognitive Styles: An Overview and Integration', *Educational Psychology*, September 1991, pp. 193–215; S. Rayner and R. Riding, 'Towards a Categorisation of Cognitive Styles and Learning Styles', *Educational Psychology*, March–June 1997, pp. 5–27; and R. Riding and S. Rayner, *Cognitive Styles and Learning Strategies* (London: David Fulton, 1998).

[115] R. Riding, *Cognitive Styles Analysis Users' Guide* (Birmingham: Learning and Training Technology, 1991).

[116] G. R. Foxall, 'Managers in Transition: An Empirical Test of Kirton's Adaption-Innovation Theory and Its Implications for the Mid-Career MBA', *Technovation*, June 1986, pp. 219–32; I. G. R. Foxall, 'Managerial Orientations of Adaptors and Innovators', *Journal of Managerial Psychology*, no. 2, 1986, pp. 24–8; G. R. Foxall, 'An Empirical Analysis of Mid-Career Managers' Adaptive-Innovative Cognitive Styles and Task Orientations in Three Countries', *Psychological Reports*, December 1990, pp. 1115–24; and G. R. Foxall and P. M. W. Hackett, 'Styles of Managerial Creativity: A Comparison of Adaption-Innovation in the United Kingdom, Australia and the United States', *British Journal of Management*, June 1994, pp. 85–100.

[117] M. J. Kirton and S. M. De Ciantis, 'Cognitive Style and Personality: The Kirton Adaption-Innovation and Cattell's Sixteen Personality Factor Inventories', *Personality and Individual Differences*, February 1986, pp. 141–6. Also see R. E. Goldsmith, 'Creative Style and Personality Theory', in *Adaptors and Innovators: Styles of Creativity and Problem Solving, second edition*, ed. M. J. Kirton (London: Routledge, 1994), pp. 34–50.

[118] C. M. Jacobson, 'Cognitive Styles of Creativity: Relations of Scores on the Kirton Adaption-Innovation Inventory and the Myers-Briggs Type Indicator among managers in the USA', *Psychological Reports*, December 1993, pp. 1131–8; and A. H. Church and J. Waclawski, 'The Effects of Personality Orientation and Executive Behavior on Subordinate Perceptions of Workgroup Enablement', *International Journal of Organizational Analysis*, January 1996, pp. 20–40.

[119] E. H. Buttner, N. Gryskiewicz and S. C. Hidore, 'The Relationship between Styles of Creativity and Managerial Skills Assessment', *British Journal of Management*, September 1999, pp. 228–38.

[120] M. J. Kirton and R. M. McCarthy, 'Cognitive Climate and Organizations', *Journal of Occupational Psychology*, June 1988, pp. 175–84. Also see K. M. McNeilly and R. E. Goldsmith, 'The Moderating Effect of Sales Managers' Approach to Problem Solving on the Salesperson Satisfaction/Intention to Leave Relationship', *Journal of Social Behavior and Personality*, March 1992, pp. 139–50.

[121] R. Riding and M. Watts, 'The Effects of Cognitive Style on the Preferred Format of Instructional Material', *Educational Psychology*, March–June 1997, pp. 179–83; and E. Sadler-Smith and R. Riding, 'Cognitive Style and Instructional Preferences', *Instructional Science*, September 1999, pp. 355–71.

[122] R. Riding and G. Douglas, 'The Effect of Cognitive Style and Mode of Presentation on Learning Performance', *British Journal of Educational Psychology*, September 1993, pp. 297–307.

[123] R. Riding and L. Anstey, 'Verbal-Imagery Learning Style and Reading Attainment in Eight-Year-Old Children', *Journal of Research in Reading*, February 1982, pp. 57–66.

[124] R. Riding and E. Sadler-Smith, 'Type of Instructional Material, Cognitive Style and Learning Performance', *Educational Studies*, November 1992, p. 329.

[125] R. Riding, *Personal Style Awareness and Personal Development* (Birmingham: Learning and Training Development, 1994).

[126] S. Streufert and G. Y. Nogami, 'Cognitive Style and Complexity: Implications for I/O Psychology', in *International Review of Industrial and Organizational Psychology*, eds C. L. Cooper and I. Robertson (Chichester: Wiley, 1989).

[127] M. J. Kirton and R. M. McCarthy, 'Cognitive Climate and Organizations', *Journal of Occupational Psychology*, June 1988, pp. 175–84.

[128] R. P. Talbot, 'Valuing Differences in Thinking Styles to Improve Individual and Team Performance', *National Productivity Review*, Winter 1989, pp. 35–50.

[129] J. Hayes and C. W. Allinson, 'Cognitive Style and Its Relevance for Management Practice', *British Journal of Management*, March 1994, pp. 53–71.

[130] E. Sadler-Smith and B. Badger, 'Cognitive Style, Learning and Innovation', *Technology Analysis & Strategic Management*, June 1998, pp. 247–65.

[131] D. Leonard and S. Straus, 'Putting Your Company's Whole Brain to Work', *Harvard Business Review*, July–August 1997, pp. 111–21.

[132] D. A. Bernstein, E. J. Roy, T. K. Srull and L. D. Wickens, *Psychology, second edition* (Boston, MA: Houghton Mifflin, 1991).

[133] For more information on the origins of learning styles, see E. L. Grigorenko and R. J. Sternberg, 'Thinking Styles', in *International Handbook of Personality and Intelligence*, eds D. H. Saklofske and M. Zeidner (New York: Plenum Press, 1995), pp. 205–29. For other reviews on learning styles, see S. Rayner and R. J. Riding, 'Towards a Categorization of Cognitive Styles and Learning Styles', *Educational Psychology*, March–June 1997, pp. 5–27; E. Sadler-Smith, 'Learning Style: Frameworks and Instruments', *Educational Psychology*, March–June 1997, pp. 51– 63.

[134] D. A. Kolb, 'On Management and the Learning Process', in *Organizational Psychology: A Book of Readings, second edition*, eds D. A. Kolb, I. M. Rubin and J. M. McIntyre (Englewood Cliffs, NJ: Prentice-Hall, 1974), p. 29.

[135] See, for instance, N. J. Entwistle, *Styles of Learning and Teaching* (Chichester: Wiley, 1981).

[136] See, for instance, J. P. Das, 'Implications for School Learning', in *Learning Strategies and Learning Styles*, ed. R. R. Schmeck (New York: Plenum Press, 1988).

[137] See, for instance, J. Hayes and C. W. Allinson, 'Cognitive Style and Its Relevance for Management Practice', *British Journal of Management*, March 1994, pp. 53–71; and J. Hayes and C. W. Allinson, 'Cognitive Style and the Theory and Practice of Individual and Collective Learning in Organizations', *Human Relations*, July 1998, pp. 847–71.

[138] Characteristics of experiential learning are elaborated in D. A. Kolb, *Experiential Learning: Experience as the Source of Learning and Development* (Englewood Cliffs, NJ: Prentice-Hall, 1984), pp. 25–38.

[139] D. A. Kolb, *LSI Learning Style Inventory: Self-Scoring Inventory and Interpretation Booklet*, revised version (Boston, MA: McBer, 1985); and D. M. Smith and D. Kolb, *User's Guide for the Learning Style Inventory: A Manual for Teachers and Trainers* (Boston, MA: McBer, 1986).

[140] For references to these studies, see S. M. DeCiantis and M. J. Kirton, 'A Psychometric Re-Examination of Kolb's Experiential Learning Cycle Construct: A Separation of Level, Style and Process', *Educational and Psychological Measurement*, October 1996, p. 809.

[141] N. H. Leonard, R. W. Scholl and K. B. Kowalski, 'Information Processing Style and Decision Making', *Journal of Organizational Behavior*, May 1999, pp. 407–20.

[142] D. A. Kolb, 'Management and the Learning Process', *California Management Review*, Spring 1976, p. 26.

[143] D. A. Kolb, *Experiential Learning: Experience as the Source of Learning and Development* (Englewood Cliffs, NJ: Prentice-Hall, 1984).

[144] Both approaches are elaborated in J. Hayes and C. W. Allinson, 'The Implications of Learning Styles for Training and Development: A Discussion of the Matching Hypothesis', *British Journal of Management*, March 1996, pp. 63–73.

[145] For works on the importance of learning and learning styles for organisations, see E. Sadler-Smith and B. Badger, 'Cognitive Style, Learning and Innovation', *Technology Analysis & Strategic Management*, June 1998, pp. 247–65; J. Hayes and C. W. Allinson, 'Cognitive Style and the Theory and Practice of Individual and Collective Learning in Organizations', *Human Relations*, July 1998, pp. 847–71; S. Gherardi, D. Nicolini and F. Odella, 'Toward a Social Understanding of How People Learn in Organisations', *Management Learning*, September 1998, pp. 273–97; and E. Sadler-Smith, C. W. Allinson and J. Hayes, 'Learning Preferences and Cognitive Style: Some Implications for Continuing Professional Development', *Management Learning*, June 2000, pp. 239–56.

[146] Based on J. E. Sharp, 'Applying Kolb Learning Style Theory in the Communication Classroom', *Business Communication Quarterly*, June 1997, pp. 129–34.

[147] The questionnaire and scoring key are excerpted from J. W. Slocum Jr and D. Hellriegel, 'A Look at How Managers Minds Work', *Business Horizons*, July–August 1983, pp. 58–68.

[148] Based on A. Dickerson and M. A. Taylor, 'Self-Limiting Behavior in Women: Self-Esteem and Self-Efficacy as Predictors', *Group & Organization Management*, June 2000, pp. 191–210.

Chapter 3

Values, attitudes and emotions

Learning Outcomes

When you finish studying the material in this chapter, you should be able to:

- define values and explain their sources
- identify and describe Rokeach's instrumental and terminal values
- explain Schwartz's basic human values model and his related work values model
- explain how attitudes influence behaviour in terms of the model of planned behaviour
- describe three key work-related attitudes: organisational commitment, job involvement and job satisfaction
- discuss the determinants and consequences of job satisfaction
- distinguish between positive and negative emotions and explain how they can be judged
- define what emotional intelligence is and which components it implies
- focus on emotional contagion in the workplace
- describe what flow is and how it influences organisational behaviour

Opening Case Study: Why insensitivity is a vital managerial trait

When British venture capitalist Jon Moulton was asked in an interview about his three strongest character traits, he replied: 'Determination, curiosity and insensitivity.' While the first two are likely to reach the top 10 of leadership traits, we do not often hear the last trait heralded as a personal strength.

But his argument is fairly straightforward: while sensitivity and emotional intelligence have been praised in the last decade as essential management traits, there is still very little (or conflicting) evidence that they are actually positive traits – especially for top managers.

Perhaps insensitivity is essential to survival in business? According to Moulton, insensitivity 'lets you sleep when others can't'. Any leader will have to take decisions that will hurt individual people – for the best of the company and the rest of the employees – so being insensitive might help you take that necessary decision without losing sleep over it and postponing the inevitable.

Insensitive leaders have got a bad reputation because their behaviour is seen as arrogant or bullying, but at least, they are a lot simpler to understand and their actions will typically seem more rational.

Of course, there are times when sensitivity and emotional intelligence are called for, but good top managers know this and outsource the touchy-feely stuff to others in the management team to take care of while they make the hard decisions.

For discussion

Do you agree that insensitivity (to some degree) is a necessary leadership trait?

Source: Based on L. Kellaway, 'Why Insensitivity is a Vital Managerial Trait', 15 February 2010, *The Irish Times*.

As can be seen in this opening case study, people's feelings and emotions influence how they behave and perform in an organisation. Professionals who are aware of the importance of people's internal states can use this information to manage effectively the work environment and increase employee's job satisfaction.

The concepts of values, attitudes and emotions (see Chapter 2, Figure 2.1) are different from the concepts presented in the previous chapter. Research on values, attitudes and emotions is more recent and is not characterised by the same research traditions as research on personality, abilities and styles. First, we focus on personal and work values and their impact on organisational behaviour and performance. Second, we define attitudes and take a closer look at some key work-related attitudes: organisational commitment, job involvement and job satisfaction. Finally, we elaborate on emotions, which is a rather recent stream of research that broadens the focus of traditional abilities research. It also balances some of the weaknesses of the other concepts. Research on emotions and emotional intelligence became important in the study of individual differences and organisational behaviour only a few decades ago.

3.1 Values

In our modern society, characterised by individualisation and globalisation, a person's values are of relevance for organisational behaviour. Individualisation is the process by which individuals increasingly become a point of reference in the shaping of values and attitudes.[1] In premodern times, values were based upon, and legitimised by, tradition and religion. In contemporary society, however, values are an object of personal autonomy and characterised by an ethic of personal fulfilment. Nevertheless, modern society is not only individualised, but also differentiated. This means that the different life areas became 'self-referential in terms of values'.[2] In contrast, premodern, traditional societies are described as integrated and non-differentiated. All life domains and their values were strongly connected, mainly by religion and the extended family. As a consequence of the decreasing influence of religion and kinship, individuals are now freer to choose their values. 'Modernity confronts the individual with a diversity of choices and at the same time offers little help as to which options should be selected.'[3]

Furthermore, individuals presently live in a 'global village'.[4] Information about different cultures is disseminated rapidly throughout the world, thereby confronting individuals with more alternatives. Accordingly, the likelihood that people select similar values is reduced. In addition, people are also increasingly influenced by foreign events, resulting in value fragmentation (i.e. increased diversity of individual value systems).

We first focus on what values are and then elaborate on two different value models. We also look at work values. We conclude this section with research findings and practical implications. Organisational values are elaborated more thoroughly in the chapter on organisational culture (see Chapter 12). We confine our discussion here by focusing only on personal and work values (and not, for instance, on cultural or social values) and their relevance for organisational behaviour.

Several different definitions of and views on values exist. Researchers, for instance, have likened values to beliefs, needs, goals, criteria for choosing goals and attitudes. Some authors tried to distinguish values from other constructs, while others did not. So, what are values then? Despite the abundance of definitions, most authors agree that **values** are standards or criteria for choosing goals or guiding actions, and that they are relatively enduring and stable over time.[5] Even though values are relatively enduring and stable, they can change during our lifetime. Rokeach, the most cited author concerning values, states it as follows: 'If values were completely stable, individual and social change would be impossible. If values were completely unstable, continuity of human personality and society would be impossible.'[6]

We can make a distinction between content and an intensity aspect of values. People do not only vary in what values they find important (content aspect), they also differ in how important several values are (intensity aspect). An individual's values are not single entities; they can be ranked according to their intensity. In other words, values are integrated within a **value system**, which is 'an enduring organisation of beliefs concerning preferable modes of conduct or endstates of existence along a continuum of relative importance'.[7]

Most researchers on values also propose, explicitly or implicitly, that values develop through the influence of personality, society and culture.[8] People are not born with an internal set of values (although a study[9] with twins reared apart concluded that 40 per cent of variance in work values can be attributed to genetic factors). Values are acquired throughout our life from diverse sources (parents, teachers, peers, work environment, national culture etc.), through what is referred to as a process of socialisation (see Chapter 12 for organisational socialisation). The enduring nature of our values refers back to the way we acquire them initially.[10]

Values are taught and learned initially in isolation from other values in an absolute, all-or-none manner. We are taught that it is always desirable to be honest and to strive for peace. We are not taught that it is desirable to be just a little bit honest or to strive for peace sometimes and not at other times. This absolute learning of values more or less guarantees their endurance and stability. As we grow older, we are exposed to several values from diverse sources that sometimes might be in conflict with each other. Gradually, we learn through a process of maturation and experience to integrate the isolated, absolute values we acquired in different contexts into a hierarchically organised system wherein each value is ordered in importance relative to other values. This does not mean that values cannot change during our life. Certainly in the adolescence phase, values are questioned.

This questioning process might lead to the conclusion that our values are no longer adequate. More often, however, this questioning leads to reinforcing the values we have.

HR Instrumental and terminal values

Milton Rokeach developed a model that distinguishes between instrumental and terminal values.[11] **Instrumental values** refer to desirable ways or modes of conduct to reach some kind of desirable goal. Conversely, **terminal values** refer to the desirable goals a person wants to reach during his or her life. Instrumental and terminal values are connected with each other and work together to help people reach their desirable goals through desirable ways of conduct. There is not necessarily a one-on-one correspondence between an instrumental and a terminal value. One way of conduct, for instance, may be instrumental in reaching several terminal goals or several modes of conduct may be instrumental in reaching one terminal value.

Rokeach developed the Rokeach Value Survey (RVS) to measure instrumental and terminal values. The RVS contains two sets of values (instrumental and terminal). Each set has 18 individual value items that were composed after several years of research (see Table 3.1). Respondents are instructed to arrange the instrumental and terminal values in order of importance, as guiding principles in their life.

Table 3.1 Rokeach's Instrumental and Terminal Values

Instrumental values		Terminal values	
AMBITIOUS	Hard-working, aspiring	A COMFORTABLE LIFE	A prosperous life
BROADMINDED	Open-minded	AN EXCITING LIFE	A stimulating, active life
CAPABLE	Competent, effective	A SENSE OF ACCOMPLISHMENT	Lasting contribution
CHEERFUL	Light-hearted, joyful		
CLEAN	Neat, tidy	A WORLD AT PEACE	Free of war and conflict
COURAGEOUS	Standing up for your beliefs	A WORLD OF BEAUTY	Beauty of nature and the arts
FORGIVING	Willing to pardon others	EQUALITY	Brotherhood, equal opportunity for all
HELPFUL	Working for the welfare of others	FAMILY SECURITY	Taking care of loved ones
HONEST	Sincere, truthful	FREEDOM	Independence, free choice
IMAGINATIVE	Daring, creative	HAPPINESS	Contentedness
INDEPENDENT	Self-reliant, self-sufficient	INNER HARMONY	Freedom from inner conflict
INTELLECTUAL	Intelligent, reflective	MATURE LOVE	Sexual and spiritual intimacy
LOGICAL	Consistent, rational	NATIONAL SECURITY	Protection from attack
LOVING	Affectionate, tender	PLEASURE	An enjoyable, leisurely life
OBEDIENT	Dutiful, respectful	SALVATION	Saved, eternal life
POLITE	Courteous, well-mannered	SELF-RESPECT	Self-esteem
RESPONSIBLE	Dependable, reliable	SOCIAL RECOGNITION	Respect, admiration
SELF-CONTROLLED	Restrained, self-disciplined	TRUE FRIENDSHIP	Close companionship
		WISDOM	A mature understanding of life

Source: Based on Table 2.1 in M. Rokeach, *The Nature of Human Values* (New York: The Free Press, 1973), p. 28.

Rokeach distinguishes between two kinds of instrumental values and two kinds of terminal values. Terminal values can be divided into personal and social ones. This means, terminal values may be self-centred, intrapersonal (e.g. inner harmony) or society-centred, interpersonal (e.g. a world at peace). Instrumental values are divided into moral and competence values. Moral values refer to those kinds of instrumental values that have an interpersonal focus and that lead to feelings of guilt and wrongdoing when violated. Competence or self-actualisation values refer to intrapersonal instrumental values, which lead to feelings of shame and personal inadequacy when violated. For instance, when behaving honestly or responsibly, you will feel that you behave morally, while behaving logically, intelligently or imaginatively, you will feel that you behave competently. People differ in the extent to which they value personal or social values, as well as moral or competence values.

The basic human values model

Shalom Schwartz, another expert on value research, elaborated the model of Rokeach further and proposed a theory on basic human values based on two components.[12] First, he distinguished 10 types of values that are recognised by members of most societies. Second, he shows how these values are connected dynamically with each other by specifying which values are compatible and mutually supportive, and which values are conflicting and opposed.

The 10 value types of Schwartz are distinguished according to the type of motivational goal they express (see Table 3.2). They were developed by using the idea that values represent, in the form

Table 3.2 Schwartz's Motivational Types of Values

Value type	Definition	Values
POWER	Social status and prestige, control and dominance over people and resources	Social power – Authority – Wealth
ACHIEVEMENT	Personal success through demonstrating competence according to social standards	Successful – Capable – Ambitious – Influential
HEDONISM	Pleasure and sensuous gratification for oneself	Pleasure – Enjoying life
STIMULATION	Excitement, novelty and challenge in life	Daring – A varied life – An exciting life
SELF-DIRECTION	Independent thought and action, seeking, creating, experimenting and exploring	Creativity – Freedom – Independent – Curious – Choosing own goals
UNIVERSALISM	Equality, tolerance and justice for all, and respect for nature	Broadminded – Wisdom – Social justice – Equality – A world at peace – A world of beauty – Unity with nature – Protecting the environment
BENEVOLENCE	Welfare for all, forgiveness, honesty, loyalty and responsibility	Helpful – Honest – Forgiving – Loyal – Responsible
TRADITION	Respect for traditional culture	Accepting one's portion in life – Humble – Devout – Respect for tradition – Moderate
CONFORMITY	Restraint for actions, inclinations and impulses likely to upset or harm others and violate societal expectations and norms	Self-discipline – Obedient – Politeness – Honouring parents and elders
SECURITY	Safety, security and stability in a stable society	Family security – National security – Social order – Clean – Reciprocation of favours

Source: Based on Table 1 in S. H. Schwartz and G. Sagie, 'Value Consensus and Importance: A Cross-National Study', *Journal of Cross-Cultural Psychology*, July 2000, p. 468.

of conscious goals, three universal requirements of human existence to which all individuals and societies have to be responsive: the needs of individuals as biological organisms, the requirements for co-ordinated social interaction, and the survival and welfare needs of groups. In order to cope with reality in a social context, groups and individuals represent these requirements cognitively as specific values about which they can communicate. Schwartz started from and extended Rokeach's list of 36 values to determine his own basic human values model.

Schwartz also investigated the relationships between these value types. His value structure is based on the idea that every action to reach a value has psychological, practical and social consequences that can be in conflict or compatible with the pursuit of other values. It is, for instance, difficult to strive for achievement and for benevolence at the same time.[13] The dynamics between Schwartz's values can be situated on two underlying dimensions: self-transcendence versus self-enhancement and openness to change versus conservation (see Figure 3.1). The first dimension represents the tension between acceptance of others as equal and concern for their welfare (universalism and benevolence) versus the dominance over others and pursuit of own success (power and achievement). The second dimension opposes values that emphasise independent thought and action and readiness for change (self-direction and stimulation) to values of preserving traditional practices, protection of stability and submissive self-restriction (security, conformity and tradition).

Figure 3.1 Schwartz's Basic Human Values Model

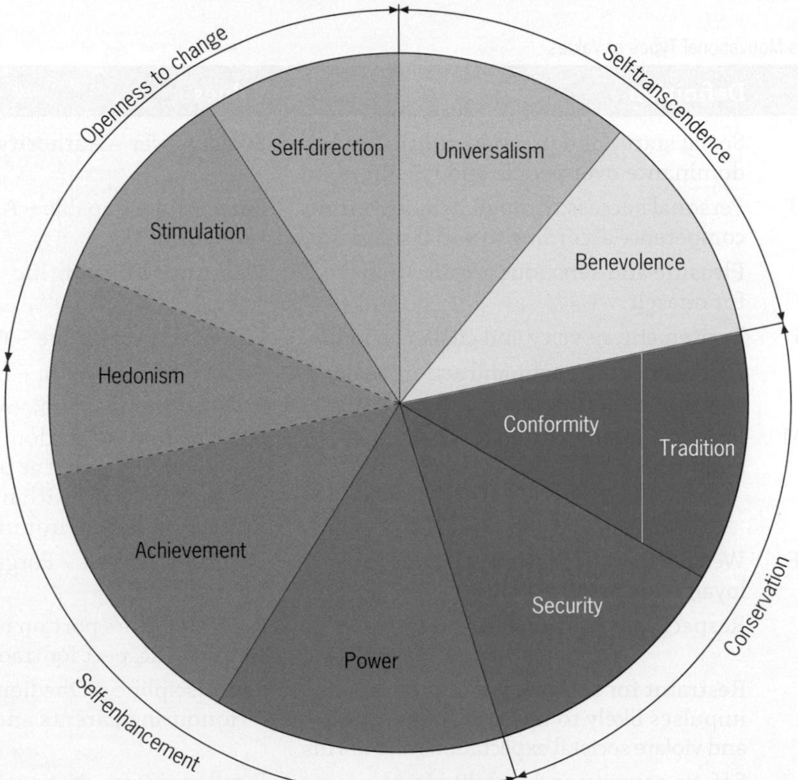

Source: S. H. Schwartz, 'Are There Universals in the Structure and Contents of Human Values?', *Journal of Social Issues*, Winter 1994, p. 24.

Work values

An important objective of research on values has been to study the link between individuals' value priorities and other aspects, such as social experiences and roles. Schwartz also adapted his basic values model to a work context, and he defines **work values** as expressions of basic values in the work setting. Like basic values, work values are ordered by their importance as guiding principles for evaluating work outcomes and settings, and for choosing among different work alternatives. Work values refer to what a person wants out of work in general, rather than to narrowly defined outcomes of particular jobs.

Parallel to the basic values model, Schwartz tried to identify general types of work values. Most researchers on work values identify the same two or three types of work values (i.e. intrinsic or self-actualisation values; extrinsic, security or material values; and social or relational values).[14] According to Schwartz, however, there should be four general types of work values, related to the four poles of his two-dimensional basic human values model.

The four types of work values that Schwartz identifies are intrinsic, extrinsic, social and prestige values. Intrinsic values express openness to change values (e.g. the pursuit of autonomy, interest, growth and creativity in work). Extrinsic values refer to conservation values (e.g. job security, income). Social or interpersonal work values express self-transcendence values (e.g. work as a vehicle for positive social relations or contribution to society). The prestige or power values, a type added to the work values research by Schwartz, imply values related to the self-enhancement values (e.g. authority, influence and achievement in work).

Schwartz developed the Work Value Survey (WVS) to measure people's work values. The following activity is based on the WVS. Which of the four work value types do you value most: intrinsic, extrinsic, social or prestige values?

Activity

Which work values are most important to you?

Indicate for each of the following work values how important it is for you.

		Not at all important				Very important
1	Good salary and work conditions	1	2	3	4	5
2	Job security (permanent job, pension)	1	2	3	4	5
3	Interesting and varied work	1	2	3	4	5
4	Work with people	1	2	3	4	5
5	Prestigious, highly valued work	1	2	3	4	5
6	Work in which you are your own boss	1	2	3	4	5
7	Contributing to people and society	1	2	3	4	5
8	Authority to make decisions over people	1	2	3	4	5
9	Social contact with co-workers	1	2	3	4	5
10	Opportunities for occupational advancement	1	2	3	4	5

Scoring key

Total your score:
Add questions 1 and 2 for the importance of extrinsic work values.
Add questions 3 and 6 for the importance of intrinsic work values.
Add questions 4, 7 and 9 for the importance of social work values.
Add questions 5 and 8 for the importance of prestige work values.

Scoring norms

Comparative norms for extrinsic, intrinsic and prestige work values:
2 – 4 = Low importance
5 – 7 = Moderate importance
8 and above = High importance
Comparative norms for social work values:
3 – 6 = Low importance
7 – 11 = Moderate importance
12 and above = High importance

Source: Excerpted and adapted from M. Ros, S. H. Schwartz and S. Surkiss, 'Basic Individual Values, Work Values and the Meaning of Work', *Applied Psychology: An International Review*, January 1999, pp. 58–9.

Evidence about values

A great deal of research on values exists, although the research field is very diverse. Some research investigates a single country or organisation, while other studies focus on a broader area. Many value studies distinguish different values according to life domains. However, a lot of these studies focus on only one life domain (e.g. work) and do not look at the interrelations between the values of several life domains (e.g. leisure time, private life, politics, family). We summarise some relevant research findings for organisational behaviour.

Both Rokeach and Schwartz studied relationships between their values model and other individual differences, such as voting behaviour, readiness for outgroup social contact, interpersonal cooperation. Schwartz, for instance, concluded from a study with 90 participants (a mixed-motive experimental game) that power, achievement and hedonism were strong predictors for non-co-operation, while people who attach importance to value types like benevolence, universalism and conformity were more likely to co-operate.[15]

Many studies focus on the relationship between work values and several aspects of organisational behaviour (e.g. organisational commitment, motivation, performance, etc.). One aspect of this research is, for instance, value congruence, which means the fit between people's work values and the job/organisation. Several studies found that people choose a job in accordance with their work values rather than the other way around.[16] Possible reasons for this finding are the fact that values have a relatively enduring and stable character and that many values are acquired very early in life.

Application of values

Individuals' values can explain a great deal regarding their interests and priorities, the choices they make and the goals for which they strive. Values are central to an individual because they serve as mechanisms that guide his or her life within society. The pervasive influence of values in all our life domains makes them an issue of utmost importance for organisations to take into account. Values influence employees' perception, motivation and performance and play a role in decision-making, ethics and evaluations. Differences in values can also cause conflicts and misunderstandings in organisations. Knowing, respecting and taking into account each other's values can be a good starting point for better co-operation and a nicer working sphere.

> **Critical thinking**
>
> In which situations might personal values conflict with work values or work requirements?

3.2 Attitudes and behaviour

Hardly a day goes by without the popular media reporting the results of another attitude survey. The idea is to take the pulse of public opinion. What do we think about euthanasia, the euro, refugees, legalisation of soft drugs or abortion? Meanwhile, organisations conduct attitude surveys to monitor such things as job and pay satisfaction. All this attention to attitudes is based on the assumption that attitudes somehow influence behaviour, such as voting for someone, working hard or quitting one's job. In this section, we examine the connection between attitudes and behaviour. We also look at job satisfaction as an important attitude that influences organisational behaviour.

An **attitude** is defined as a 'learned predisposition to respond in a consistently favourable or unfavourable manner with respect to a given object'.[17] In other words, attitudes are beliefs and feelings people have about specific ideas, situations and people, which influence their behaviour. Attitudes are often confused with values, because both are social abstractions. Attitudes, however, affect behaviour at a different level from values. While values represent global beliefs that influence behaviour across all situations, attitudes relate only to behaviour directed towards specific objects, persons or situations.[18] Attitudes are more directed towards specific goals or situations, while values are more abstract. Individuals usually have more attitudes than values. Values and attitudes are generally, though not always, in harmony. An employee who strongly values helpful behaviour may have a negative attitude towards helping an unethical co-worker. The difference between attitudes and values can be clarified further with a description of the three components of attitudes: a cognitive (cognition), affective (affect) and behavioural (intention) one.[19]

The **cognitive component of an attitude** refers to the beliefs, opinions, cognitions or knowledge someone has about a certain object, situation or person. For example, what is your opinion on bullying at work? Do you believe this behaviour is completely unacceptable or do you think it is not your problem?

The **affective component of an attitude** refers to the feelings, moods and emotions a person has about something or someone. Applied to the same example, how do you feel about someone who nags another colleague in the organisation? If you feel angry or frustrated about it, you will express negative feelings towards people who pester other people. If you feel indifferent about mobbing, the affective component of your attitude is neutral.

The **behavioural component of an attitude** refers to how a person intends or expects to act towards something or someone. For example, how do you intend to react to someone who pesters another colleague? Will you say or do something? Will you defend the victim? Attitude theory states that your ultimate behaviour in a certain situation is a function of all three attitudinal components. You will defend a victim of bullying at work if you feel angry about it (affective), if you believe bullying is completely unacceptable (cognitive) and when you have an intention of doing something about it (behavioural).

Stability of attitudes

In one landmark study researchers found the job attitudes of 5000 middle-aged male employees to be very stable over a five-year period. Positive job attitudes remained positive; negative ones remained negative. Even those who changed jobs or occupations tended to maintain their prior job attitudes.[20] More recent research suggests the foregoing study may have overstated the stability of attitudes because it was restricted to a middle-aged sample. This time, researchers asked: 'What happens to attitudes over the entire span of adulthood?' General attitudes were found to be more susceptible to change during early and late adulthood than during middle adulthood. Three factors accounted for middle-age attitude stability: (1) greater personal certainty; (2) perceived abundance of knowledge; and (3) a need for strong attitudes. Thus, the conventional notion that general attitudes become less likely to change as the person ages was rejected. Elderly people, along with young adults, can and do change their general attitudes because they are more open and less self-assured.[21]

Like values, attitudes are acquired and formed during our life from diverse sources (family, peer group, work environment, etc.) and from our own experiences and personality through a socialisation process. Although attitudes are relatively stable, they can change. Gaining new information, for instance, can lead people to change their attitudes. When you hear a certain car has been recalled for defective brakes, your beliefs about the quality of that car may change, possibly even when it is a Toyota. Attitudes can also change because the object of the attitude becomes less important or relevant to the person. You may, for instance, have a negative attitude towards your organisation's pension plans. When your private bank offers you a good pension plan, the attitude towards your organisation will be less negative because you no longer need to worry about it.

Another factor that might indicate that attitudinal change is necessary is cognitive dissonance.[22] **Cognitive dissonance** refers to situations where different attitudes are in conflict with each other or where people behave, for whatever reason, in a way inconsistent with their attitudes. In these situations, people will feel tension and discomfort and accordingly try to reduce these feelings (called 'dissonance reduction'). People like consistency between their attitudes and behaviour or among their attitudes. Possible ways to solve situations of dissonance are changing your attitudes, altering your behaviour or perceptually viewing the situation differently (this means developing a rationalisation for the inconsistency) (also see equity theory in Chapter 6).

Truthfulness can be a deep-seated value, yet some people decide to either bend the truth or be vague or economical about it. Some people even get away with it, telling 'lies' without blinking, feeling or showing the slightest discomfort.

HR Attitudes affect behaviour via intentions

Many have studied the relationship between attitudes and behaviour.[23] Early research assumed a causal relationship between attitudes and behaviour, implying that your attitudes determine what you do (often referred to as the A–B relationship). However, gradually, this relationship was criticised. Research found little or no relationship between attitudes and behaviour or that other aspects needed to be taken into account to explain the relationship between attitudes and behaviour.

Martin Fishbein and Icek Ajzen developed a comprehensive model of behavioural intentions used widely to explain attitude–behaviour relationships.[24] Over the years, they developed and refined this model that focuses on intentions as the key link between attitudes and actual behaviour.[25]

As shown in Figure 3.2, an individual's intention to engage in a given behaviour is the best predictor of that behaviour. Intentions are indicators of how hard people are willing to try and of how much effort they are planning to exert to use a certain type of behaviour. For example, the quickest and possibly most accurate way of determining whether an individual will quit his or her job is to have an objective third party ask if he or she intends to quit. A meta-analysis of 34 studies of employee turnover, involving more than 83 000 employees, validated this direct approach. The researchers found stated behavioural intentions to be a better predictor of employee turnover than job satisfaction, satisfaction with the work itself or organisational commitment.[26]

Although asking about intentions enables one to predict who will leave a job, it does not help explain why an individual would want to quit. Thus, to understand better why employees exhibit certain behaviours, such as quitting their jobs, one needs to consider their relevant attitudes and other related aspects. Three separate but interrelated determinants influence one's intention (planned behaviour) to do something (actual behaviour). As shown in Figure 3.2, behavioural intentions are influenced by one's attitude towards the behaviour, by perceived norms about exhibiting that behaviour and by perceived behavioural control.

The attitude towards the behaviour refers to the degree to which someone has a favourable or unfavourable evaluation or appraisal towards the behaviour in question. A person will have positive attitudes towards engaging in a given behaviour when he or she believes that it is associated with positive outcomes. An individual is more likely to leave a job when he or she believes it will result in a better position or in stress reduction. In contrast, negative attitudes towards quitting will

Figure 3.2 Ajzen's Theory of Planned Behaviour

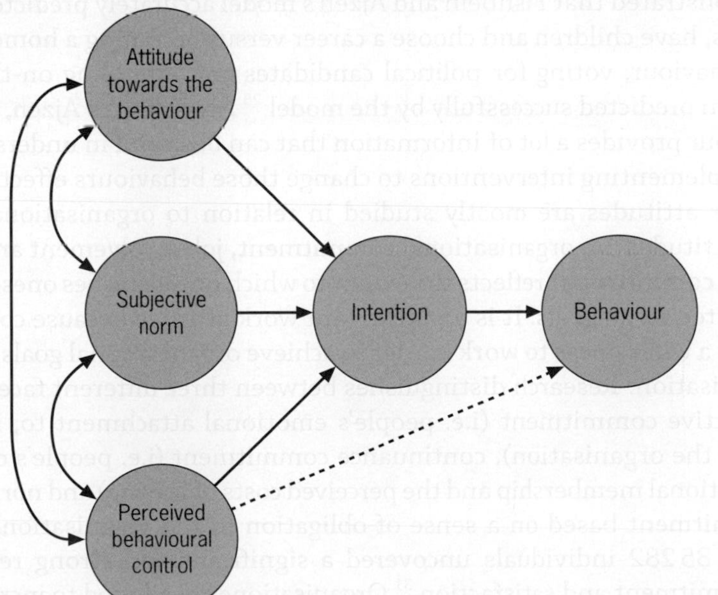

Source: Based on Figure 1 in I. Ajzen, 'The Theory of Planned Behaviour,' *Organizational Behavior and Human Decision Processes*, December 1991, p. 182.

be formed when a person believes quitting leads to negative outcomes, such as the loss of money and status.

The **subjective norm** refers to the perceived social pressure of whether or not to engage in the behaviour. Subjective norms can exert a powerful influence on the behavioural intentions of those who are sensitive to the opinions of respected role models. This effect was observed in a laboratory study of students' intentions to apply for a job at companies that reportedly tested employees for drugs. The students generally had a negative attitude about companies that tested for drugs. However, positive statements from influential persons about the need for drug testing tended to strengthen intentions to apply to companies engaged in drug testing.[27]

The perceived behavioural control refers to the perceived ease or difficulty in performing the behaviour. It is assumed that the degree of perceived behavioural control reflects past experiences as well as anticipated impediments and obstacles (such as lacking the necessary resources, unavailable opportunities, etc.). Perceived behavioural control varies across situations and actions. The theory of planned behaviour is an extension of Fishbein and Ajzen's model of reasoned action, made necessary by the limitations of the original model in dealing with behaviours over which people have incomplete volitional control.

As a general rule, Ajzen and Fishbein state that the more favourable the attitude and subjective norm and the greater the perceived behavioural control, the stronger an individual's intention will be to perform certain behaviour. The relative importance of attitudes, subjective norms and perceived behavioural control in the prediction of intention is, however, expected to vary across situations and actions. For instance, sometimes, only attitudes have a significant impact on intentions, while in another situation, two or all three determinants make independent contributions.

Evidence about attitudes

Research has demonstrated that Fishbein and Ajzen's model accurately predicted intentions to buy consumer products, have children and choose a career versus becoming a homemaker. Weight loss intentions and behaviour, voting for political candidates and attending on-the-job training sessions have also been predicted successfully by the model.[28] According to Ajzen, applying the theory of planned behaviour provides a lot of information that can be useful in understanding all kinds of behaviour or in implementing interventions to change those behaviours effectively.[29]

Three particular attitudes are mostly studied in relation to organisational behaviour. Those key work-related attitudes are organisational commitment, job involvement and job satisfaction.

Organisational commitment reflects the extent to which one identifies oneself with an organisation and is committed to its goals. It is an important work attitude because committed people are expected to display a willingness to work harder to achieve organisational goals and a greater desire to stay in an organisation. Research distinguishes between three different facets of organisational commitment: affective commitment (i.e. people's emotional attachment to, involvement in and identification with the organisation), continuance commitment (i.e. people's consideration of the benefits of organisational membership and the perceived costs of leaving) and normative commitment (i.e. people's commitment based on a sense of obligation to the organisation).[30] A meta-analysis of 68 studies and 35 282 individuals uncovered a significant and strong relationship between organisational commitment and satisfaction.[31] Organisations are advised to increase job satisfaction in order to elicit higher levels of commitment. In turn, higher organisational commitment can facilitate higher productivity.[32] Organisational commitment is also negatively related to absenteeism and turnover.[33] However, more commitment is not always better. For instance, very high commitment can lead to situations where people do not report unethical practices or, even worse, commit unethical and illegal acts themselves. Also, if low performers have very high organisational commitment, they will not easily leave the organisation.

Job involvement represents the extent to which an individual is personally involved with his or her work role. While organisational commitment refers to identification with one's organisation, job involvement refers to the extent one identifies with its specific job. A meta-analysis involving 27 925 individuals from 87 different studies demonstrated that job involvement was moderately related to job satisfaction.[34] High levels of job involvement also lead to lower absenteeism and turnover rates.[35] Another study also found a positive relationship between job involvement and performance.[36] Organisations are thus encouraged to foster satisfying work environments in order to fuel employees' job involvement. However, overly high levels of job involvement may not always be desirable. Workaholics neglect their family and private lives and may suffer from health problems.

We end this section on attitudes by elaborating further on job satisfaction as it is an important organisational variable and one of the most frequently studied attitudes by OB researchers. **Job satisfaction** is an affective or emotional response towards various facets of one's job and refers to the degree of fulfilment and pleasure one finds in one's job. In other words, job satisfaction is the general attitude one has towards one's job. Several factors may enhance job satisfaction (like need fulfilment, value attainment or met expectations). Job satisfaction in turn influences several aspects of organisational life (e.g. performance, motivation, organisational citizenship behaviour).

Application of attitudes

From an organisational point of view, the behavioural intention model we have just reviewed has important implications. First, organisations need to appreciate the dynamic relationships between beliefs, attitudes, subjective norms, perceived control and behavioural intentions when attempting to foster productive behaviour. Although attitudes are often resistant to change, they can be influenced indirectly through education and training experiences that change underlying beliefs. A case in point is a study documenting how men's beliefs about gender differences can be reduced by taking a women's studies course.[37] Another tactic involves redirecting subjective norms through clear and credible communication, organisational culture values and role models. Finally, regular employee-attitude surveys can let managers know whether their ideas and changes go with or against the grain of popular sentiment.

3.3 Job satisfaction

A person can be relatively satisfied with one aspect of his or her job and dissatisfied with another. Different people are also satisfied or dissatisfied with different aspects of their jobs. It seems that there is no general, comprehensive theory that explains job satisfaction so far.

It is also difficult to measure job satisfaction objectively. Researchers do not agree whether job satisfaction contains one single dimension or several. Researchers at Cornell University in the USA developed the Job Descriptive Index (JDI), the best-known scale to assess one's satisfaction, with the following job dimensions: work, pay, promotions, co-workers and supervision.[38] Researchers at the US University of Minnesota developed the Minnesota Satisfaction Questionnaire (MSQ) and concluded that there are 20 different dimensions underlying job satisfaction.[39] Other researchers use a single global rating to measure people's job satisfaction, like: 'all elements included, how satisfied are you with your job?' People are asked to indicate a number between one and five, ranging from 'very dissatisfied' to 'very satisfied'. Research indicates that both a questionnaire measuring several facets and one overall measure of job satisfaction seem to be valid and accurate.[40]

Job satisfaction is influenced by several individual, social, organisational and cultural variables. Five predominant models of job satisfaction specify its causes. The first four models support a situational perspective, which means they see job satisfaction largely as a function of environmental influences. The last model adheres to a dispositional perspective and sees job satisfaction as a function of individual factors. A brief review of these models will provide insight into the complexity of this seemingly simple concept:[41]

- *Need fulfilment.* These models propose that satisfaction is determined by the extent to which the characteristics of a job allow an individual to fulfil his or her needs (also see sources of motivation in Chapter 5). For example, a survey of 30 law firms revealed that 35–50 per cent of law-firm associates left their employers within three years of starting because the firms did not accommodate family needs. This example illustrates that unmet needs can affect both satisfaction and turnover.[42] Although these models generated a great degree of controversy, it is generally accepted that need fulfilment is correlated with job satisfaction.[43]
- *Discrepancies.* These models propose that satisfaction is a result of met expectations. Met expectations represent the difference between what an individual expects to receive from a job, such as good pay and promotional opportunities, and what he or she actually receives. When expectations are greater than what is received, a person will be dissatisfied. In contrast, this model predicts the individual will be satisfied when he or she attains outcomes above and beyond expectations. A meta-analysis of 31 studies, which included 17 241 people, demonstrated that met expectations were significantly related to job satisfaction.[44] Many companies use employee attitude or opinion surveys to assess employees' expectations and concerns.
- *Value attainment.* The idea underlying value attainment is that satisfaction results from the perception that a job allows for fulfilment of an individual's important work values.[45] In general, research consistently supports the prediction that value attainment is positively related to job satisfaction.[46] Organisations can thus enhance employee satisfaction by structuring the work environment and its associated rewards and recognition to reinforce employees' values.
- *Equity.* In this model, satisfaction is a function of how 'fairly' an individual is treated at work. Satisfaction results from one's perception that work outcomes, relative to inputs, compare favourably to those of a significant other. A meta-analysis involving 190 studies and 64 757 people supported this model. Employees' perceptions of being treated fairly at work related strongly to overall job satisfaction.[47] Chapter 6 explores this promising model in more detail (equity theory).
- *Dispositional/genetic components.* Have you ever noticed that some of your co-workers or friends appear to be satisfied across a variety of job circumstances, whereas others always seem dissatisfied? This model of satisfaction attempts to explain this pattern.[48] Specifically, the dispositional/genetic model is based on the belief that job satisfaction is partly a function both of personal traits and genetic factors. It suggests that stable individual differences are just as important in explaining job satisfaction as characteristics of the work environment. Although only a few studies have tested these propositions, results support a positive, significant relationship between personal traits and job satisfaction over time periods ranging from 2–50 years.[49] Genetic factors were also found to be significant in predicting life satisfaction, well-being and general job satisfaction.[50] Overall, researchers estimate that 30 per cent of an individual's job satisfaction is associated with dispositional and genetic components.[51]

Table 3.3 Correlates of Job Satisfaction

Variables related to job satisfaction	Direction of relationship	Strength of relationship
Motivation	Positive	Moderate
Organisational citizenship behaviour	Positive	Moderate
Absenteeism	Negative	Weak
Tardiness	Negative	Weak
Withdrawal cognitions	Negative	Strong
Turnover	Negative	Moderate
Heart disease	Negative	Moderate
Perceived stress	Negative	Strong
Pro-union voting	Negative	Moderate
Job performance	Positive	Moderate
Life satisfaction	Positive	Moderate
Mental health	Positive	Moderate

Job satisfaction has significant practical implications because thousands of studies have examined the relationship between job satisfaction and other organisational variables. It is impossible, however, to present them all, so we will consider a subset of the more important variables from the standpoint of practical relevance.

Table 3.3 summarises the pattern of results. The relationship between job satisfaction and these other variables is either positive or negative. The strength of the relationship ranges from weak to strong. Strong relationships imply that organisations can significantly influence that particular variable by increasing job satisfaction. Because of the complexity and broadness of the concept of job satisfaction, there is no one universal remedy for organisations to improve the job satisfaction of their employees. Rather, it is advised to make use of aspects in several chapters of this book to enhance facets of people's satisfaction (like feedback, reward systems, participation, coaching, etc.).

Let us now consider some of the key correlates of job satisfaction. Throughout the book, more research on job satisfaction will deal with:

- *Motivation.* A meta-analysis of nine studies and 2237 workers revealed a significant positive relationship between motivation and job satisfaction. Because satisfaction with supervision was also significantly correlated with motivation, supervisors are advised to consider how their behaviour affects employee satisfaction.[52]
- *Absenteeism.* Absenteeism is costly and organisations are constantly on the lookout for ways to reduce it. One recommendation has been to increase job satisfaction. If this is a valid recommendation, there should be a strong negative relationship (or negative correlation) between satisfaction and absenteeism. In other words, as satisfaction increases, absenteeism should decrease. A researcher investigated this prediction by synthesising three separate meta-analyses containing a total of 74 studies. Results revealed a weak negative relationship between satisfaction and absenteeism.[53] This result indicates that other factors also play an important role in explaining the relationship between absenteeism and job satisfaction. It is unlikely, therefore, that organisations will realise any significant decrease in absenteeism by increasing job satisfaction.

- *Withdrawal cognitions.* Although some people quit their jobs impulsively or in a fit of anger, most go through a process of thinking about whether or not they should quit.[54] **Withdrawal cognitions** encapsulate this thought process by representing an individual's overall thoughts and feelings about quitting. What causes an individual to think about quitting his or her job? Job satisfaction is believed to be one of the most significant contributors. For example, a study of managers, salespeople and auto mechanics from a national automotive retail store chain demonstrated that job dissatisfaction caused employees to begin the process of thinking about quitting. In turn, withdrawal cognitions had a greater impact on employee turnover than job satisfaction in this sample.[55] Results from this study imply that organisations can indirectly try to reduce employee turnover by enhancing job satisfaction.
- *Turnover.* Turnover is important to organisations because it both disrupts organisational continuity and is very costly. Although there are many things organisations can do to reduce employee turnover, many of them revolve around attempts to improve employees' job satisfaction.[56] This trend is supported by results from a meta-analysis of 67 studies covering 24 556 people. Job satisfaction obtained a moderate negative relationship with employee turnover.[57] Given the strength of this relationship, organisations are advised to try to reduce turnover by increasing employee job satisfaction. Other factors, however, also have a role in employees actually leaving an organisation, like labour-market conditions, expectations towards another job or organisational commitment.
- *Job performance.* One of the biggest controversies within organisational research centres on the relationship between satisfaction and job performance. Although researchers have identified seven different ways in which these variables are related, the dominant beliefs are either that satisfaction causes performance or that performance causes satisfaction.[58] A team of researchers attempted to resolve this controversy through a meta-analysis of data from 312 samples involving 54 417 individuals.[59] First, job satisfaction and performance are moderately related. This is an important finding because it supports the belief that job satisfaction is a key work attitude organisations should consider when attempting to increase employees' job performance. Second, the relationship between job satisfaction and performance is much more complex than was originally thought. It is not as simple as satisfaction causing performance or performance causing satisfaction. Instead, researchers now believe, both variables indirectly influence each other through a host of individual and work-environment characteristics.[60] There is one additional consideration to keep in mind regarding the relationship between job satisfaction and job performance.

Researchers believe that the relationship between satisfaction and performance is understated because of incomplete measures of individual-level performance. A team of researchers conducted a meta-analysis of 7939 business units in 36 companies. Results uncovered significant positive relationships between business-unit-level employee satisfaction and business-unit outcomes of customer satisfaction, productivity, profit, employee turnover and accidents.[61] It thus appears that organisations can positively affect a variety of important organisational outcomes, including performance, by increasing employee satisfaction.

! Critical thinking

How would you intervene in situations where negative attitudes and low job satisfaction were widespread?

Emotions

In the ideal world of organisation theory, employees pursue organisational goals in a logical and rational manner. Emotional behaviour seldom appears in the equation. The myth of rationality that reigned for a long time in organisations caused emotions to be long banished in organisational life.[62] However, creating emotion-free organisations is not possible. Day-to-day organisational life shows us how prevalent and powerful emotions can be. Anger and jealousy, both potent emotions, often push aside logic and rationality in the workplace. Professionals use fear and other emotions both to motivate and to intimidate.[63]

In this final section, our examination of individual differences turns to emotions. Several related terms and conceptualisations on this matter exist, like emotions, moods and affect.[64] **Emotions** are usually feelings directed to something or someone, so they are object-specific. For instance, you are angry at someone or happy about something. By contrast, moods are not directed to a certain object and are less intense. They are context-free, rather than general affective states. **Affect** refers to the broad range of feelings people experience, covering both emotions and moods.

We first define emotions by reviewing a typology of 10 positive and negative emotions and focus then on emotional intelligence. We conclude with three themes that are particularly relevant to deal with in organisational behaviour: emotional influencing, flow and the management of anger.

Richard Lazarus, a leading authority on the subject, defines emotions as 'complex, patterned, organismic reactions to how we think we are doing in our lifelong efforts to survive and flourish and to achieve what we wish for ourselves'.[65] The word 'organismic' is appropriate because emotions involve the whole person – biological, psychological and social. Significantly, psychologists draw a distinction between felt and displayed emotions.[66] **Felt emotions** are people's actual or true emotions, while **displayed emotions** refer to emotions that are organisationally desirable and appropriate in a given job. For example, a person might feel angry (felt emotion) at a rude co-worker but not make a nasty remark in return (displayed emotion). As will be discussed in Chapter 9, emotions play roles in both causing and adapting to stress and its associated biological and psychological problems. The destructive effect of emotional behaviour on social relationships is all too obvious in daily life.

Lazarus's definition of emotions centres on a person's goals. Accordingly, his distinction between positive and negative emotions is goal-oriented. Some emotions are triggered by frustration and failure when pursuing one's goals. Lazarus calls these negative emotions. They are said to be goal-incongruent. For example, which of the six negative emotions in Figure 3.3 are you likely to experience if you fail the final exam in a required course? Failing the exam would be incongruent with your goal of graduating on time. On the other hand, which of the four positive emotions in Figure 3.3 would you probably experience if you graduated on time and with honours? The emotions you would experience in this situation are positive because they are congruent (or consistent) with an important lifetime goal.

Of all the emotions in Figure 3.3, anger is the one most likely to be downright dangerous. It deserves special attention. Unchecked anger could be a key contributing factor to what one team of researchers calls organisation-motivated aggression.[67] Worse, uncontrolled anger is certainly a contributor to workplace violence. As awareness of workplace violence increases, employers are installing various security systems and training employees to avoid or defuse incidents. The European Commission's definition of workplace violence includes 'incidents where persons are abused, threatened or assaulted in circumstances relating to their work, involving an explicit challenge to their safety, wellbeing and health'.[68]

The individual's goals, it is important to note, may or may not be socially acceptable. Thus, a positive emotion, such as love/affection, may be undesirable if associated with sexual harassment (sexual harassment is discussed in Chapter 9). Conversely, slight pangs of guilt, anxiety and envy

Figure 3.3 Positive and Negative Emotions

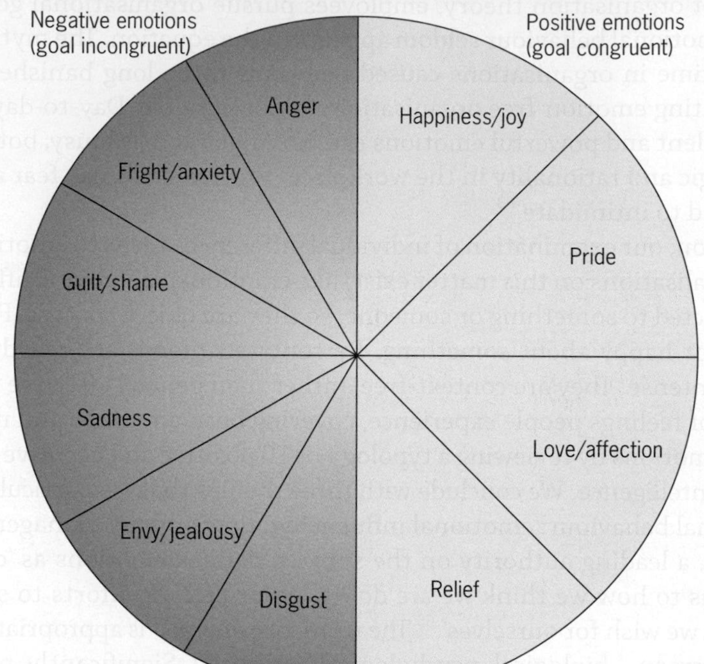

Source: Adapted from discussion in R. S. Lazarus, *Emotion and Adaptation* (New York: Oxford University Press, 1991).

can motivate extra effort. On balance, the constructive or destructive nature of a particular emotion must be judged in terms of both its intensity and the person's relevant goal.

Quotes like 'he is a real optimist, he sees everything in a positive way' or 'she is always negative, she is a pessimist' indicate that emotions are not changing from day to day. Although short-term variations and fluctuations occur, people seem to have underlying stable, fairly constant and predictable moods and emotional states.[69] Some people, often referred to as optimists, have a higher degree of **positive affectivity** which is a tendency to experience positive emotional states. These people are relatively optimistic and upbeat, see things usually in a positive light and have an overall sense of well-being. People with a higher degree of **negative affectivity** have a tendency to experience negative emotional states and are generally pessimistic and downbeat, usually see things in a negative way and seem to be in a bad mood all the time. Of course, negative events like being fired or missing a promotion may cause optimists to be in a bad mood. Or positive events like receiving positive feedback or being promoted may cause pessimists to be in a good mood. However, after the initial impact of these events, people generally seem to return to their normal positive or negative mood respectively.

People's moods and affectivity are expected to influence organisational behaviour and performance. Many studies, for instance, investigate the notion that happy workers are also productive workers. This means they study the relationship between affective states and work-related outcomes.[70] Results of these studies are not very clear and unequivocal. A study among 132 civil service employees shows that people scoring highly on optimism tend to be in jobs characterised by high levels of autonomy, variety, identity, feedback, significance and complexity.[71] People scoring highly on trait anxiety are found in jobs that have low levels of all these job characteristics. This indicates that people with certain personality traits can be found in certain types of jobs.

A recent study on the importance of leader happiness or sadness showed that this seemed to be contingent on the types of tasks. A leader's displays of happiness enhanced followers' creative performance, whereas a leader's displays of sadness enhanced followers' analytical performance. However, in subjective ratings leaders were perceived as more effective when displaying happiness rather than sadness irrespective of task type.[72]

The next activity helps you to find out whether you are an optimist or rather a pessimist.

Activity

Are you an optimist or a pessimist?

Instructions

Indicate for each of the following items to what extent you agree or disagree with them.

		Totally disagree				**Totally agree**
1	In uncertain times, I usually expect the best	1	2	3	4	5
2	It's easy for me to relax	1	2	3	4	5
3	If something can go wrong for me, it will	5	4	3	2	1
4	I always look on the bright side of things	1	2	3	4	5
5	I'm always optimistic about my future	1	2	3	4	5
6	I enjoy my friends a lot	1	2	3	4	5
7	It's important for me to keep busy	1	2	3	4	5
8	I hardly ever expect things to go my way	5	4	3	2	1
9	Things never work out the way I want them to	5	4	3	2	1
10	I don't get upset too easily	1	2	3	4	5
11	I'm a believer in the idea that 'every cloud has a silver lining'	1	2	3	4	5
12	I rarely count on good things happening to me	5	4	3	2	1
13	Overall, I expect more good things to happen to me than bad	1	2	3	4	5

Scoring key

Total your score:

Add the numbers you indicated for questions 1, 3, 4, 5, 8, 9, 11, 12 and 13.

Scoring norms

9 – 18 = Low optimism

19 – 35 = Moderate optimism

36 and above = High optimism

Source: Excerpted and adapted from Table 1 of M. F. Scheier and C. S. Carver, 'Optimism, Coping, and Health: Assessment and Implications of Generalized Outcome Expectancies', *Health Psychology*, May 1985, p. 225; and Table 1 of M. F. Scheier, C. S. Carver and M. W. Bridges, 'Distinguishing Optimism from Neuroticism (and Trait Anxiety, Self-Mastery, and Self-Esteem): A Reevaluation of the Life Orientation Test', *Journal of Personality and Social Psychology*, December 1994, p. 1066. Copyright © 1994 by the American Psychological Association. Adapted with permission.

Emotional intelligence

When we discussed intelligence and mental abilities (Chapter 2), criticisms of the IQ concept were already being levelled. Traditional models of intelligence (IQ) were too narrow, because they failed to consider interpersonal competence. One of the expansions of intelligence research beyond mental abilities is the concept of emotional intelligence. **Emotional intelligence** has its roots in the concept of 'social intelligence', first defined by Thorndike in the 1920s. In 1995, Daniel Goleman, a psychologist, created a stir in education and management circles with the publication of his book *Emotional Intelligence*.[73]

HR

What was an obscure topic among psychologists has become a popular topic among the general public. Emotional intelligence (referred to as EQ or EI) is according to Goleman more important in understanding people than general intelligence. His broader approach (emotional intelligence) includes 'abilities such as being able to motivate oneself and persist in the face of frustrations; to control impulse and delay gratification; to regulate one's moods and keep distress from swamping the ability to think; to empathise and to hope'.[74] In other words, emotional intelligence is the ability to manage your own emotions and those of others in mature and constructive ways. Emotional intelligence is said to have four key components: self-awareness, self-management, social awareness and relationship management. The first two components are referred to as 'personal' competence (those abilities that determine how we manage ourselves), while the last two are referred to as 'social' competence (those abilities that determine how we manage relationships) (see Table 3.4).

Table 3.4 Developing Personal and Social Competence through Emotional Intelligence

Personal competence	Social competence
Self-awareness • *Emotional self-awareness*: Reading one's own emotions and recognising their impact; using 'gut sense' to guide decisions • *Accurate self-assessment*: Knowing one's strengths and limits • *Self-confidence*: A sound sense of one's self-worth and capabilities	**Social awareness** • *Empathy*: Sensing others' emotions, understanding their perspective and taking active interest in their concerns • *Organisational awareness*: Reading the currents, decision networks and politics at the organisational level • *Service*: Recognising and meeting follower, client or customer needs
Self-management • *Emotional self-control*: Keeping disruptive emotions and impulses under control • *Transparency*: Displaying honesty and integrity; trustworthiness • *Adaptability*: Flexibility in adapting to changing situations or overcoming obstacles • *Achievement*: The drive to improve performance to meet inner standards of excellence • *Initiative*: Readiness to act and seize opportunities • *Optimism*: Seeing the upside in events	**Relationship management** • *Inspirational leadership*: Guiding and motivating with a compelling vision • *Influence*: Wielding a range of tactics for persuasion • *Developing others*: Bolstering others' abilities through feedback and guidance • *Change catalyst*: Initiating, managing and leading in a new direction • *Conflict management*: Resolving disagreements • *Building bonds*: Cultivating and maintaining a web of relationships • *Teamwork and collaboration*: Co-operation and team building

Source: Based on D. Goleman, R. Boyatzis and A. McKee, *Primal Leadership: Realizing the Power of Emotional Intelligence* (Boston, MA: Harvard Business School Press, 2002), p. 39.

The components listed in Table 3.4 constitute a challenging self-development agenda for each of us. Goleman and other researchers[75] believe a greater emotional intelligence can boost individual, team and organisational effectiveness. Of course, stimulating and enhancing people's emotional intelligence needs intensive coaching, feedback and practice. Emotional intelligence usually increases with age, as part of a maturity process. However, there are also some critical voices. Sometimes the validity and reliability of tests that are used to measure emotional intelligence are called into question.[76] Charles Woodruffe even questions the usefulness and newness of the emotional intelligence concept itself and states that its contribution to job performance has been exaggerated. He states that the concept 'emotional intelligence' is 'nothing more than a new brand name for a set of long-established competencies'.[77] Highly respected OB scholars, such as Edwin Loicke (of the Latham and Locke goal-setting approach to motivation), flatly declared that EI as proposed by Goleman was an invalid concept and that the addition of many different elements, such as trustworthiness, adaptability, innovation, communication, and team capabilities, was 'preposterously all-encompassing'.[78]

Although several theoretical models of emotional intelligence currently exist, Goleman's theory is the most widely known. Mayer and Salovey, for instance, developed another model of emotional intelligence.[79] They distinguish between four emotion-related abilities that move in their model from more basic towards more complex abilities: from perceiving and expressing emotion to assimilating emotion in thought, to understanding emotions and finally reflectively regulating emotions.

We conclude this section on emotions by elaborating on some emotional processes that can be particularly relevant to organisations. We focus on how people's emotions influence each other (emotional contagion and emotional labour), on how people can have optimal experience in their job (flow) and on how organisations can manage anger in the workplace.

Emotional influencing

Coinciding with the start of more research on emotions were studies on how emotions play a role in organisational life. We focus on two related concepts: emotional contagion and emotional labour.

One process through which people influence each other (un)consciously in organisations is emotional contagion.[80] **Emotional contagion** is defined as 'the tendency to automatically mimic and synchronise facial expressions, vocalisations, postures and movements with those of another person and, consequently, to converge emotionally'.[81] We can, quite literally, catch other people's bad/good moods or displayed negative/positive emotions. An illustrative image to clarify emotional contagion is 'the ripple effect'. As water ripples in a lake because of the wind, emotions can ripple through people, groups and organisations. Which mechanisms are involved in emotional contagion is not clearly known yet. Perceiving and (unconsciously) adopting other people's facial expressions seems to be important.[82] It seems that we, through the unconscious imitation of the facial expressions, gestures and other non-verbal signals of other people, internally also recreate the feelings they express. The person who expresses his or her emotion the strongest influences the emotions of the other(s) in the interaction.

More important than knowing how emotional contagion works exactly is being aware that it exists and understanding its influence on organisational life. Several studies investigate the influence of emotional contagion in organisations.[83] A study among 131 bank tellers and 220 exit interviews with their customers revealed that tellers who expressed positive emotions tended to have more satisfied customers.[84] Two field studies with nurses and accountants found a strong link between the work group's collective mood and the individual's mood.[85] Research also found that spreading positive feelings improved co-operation, decreased conflict and increased task performance in group work.[86] These findings indicate the importance of using emotional contagion effectively to improve organisational behaviour and performance. Goleman elaborates on five competences in which the effective use of the emotions of other people (or the principle of emotional contagion) is essential:[87]

- *Influencing.* The effective use of influencing tactics is based on inducing certain feelings in other people – for instance, enthusiasm for a project or the passion to outdo a competitor (see Chapter 14).
- *Communication.* Sending clear and convincing messages starts with the ability to know what others feel about something, how they will react and adapting your message accordingly (see Chapter 4).
- *Conflict management.*[88] Negotiating and solving conflicts is to a large extent a process of emotional influencing rather than a pure rational process (see Chapter 14).
- *Leadership.*[89] Inspiring and coaching employees is based on the effective communication of feelings in a two-way direction (see Chapter 15).
- *Change management.*[90] The effective communication and implementation of change processes requires a high level of emotional appeal and influence to break down people's resistance (see Chapter 16).

Related to the study of emotional contagion is the research field dealing with how people manage their emotions in the workplace, known as 'emotional labour'.[91] The research on emotional labour was first developed in relation to service jobs. **Emotional labour** refers to the effort, planning and control needed to express organisationally desired emotions during interpersonal interactions.[92] Emotional labour, for instance, implies expressing positive emotions, handling negative emotions, being sensitive to the emotions of clients and showing empathy. Organisations usually have certain (in)formal display rules. Display rules are norms that describe which emotions employees need to display and which emotions they need to withhold. Even when they feel bad, employees are told to 'smile, look happy for the customer'. This implies they sometimes have to fake and to mask their true feelings and emotions. Every employee has to undertake some emotional labour, for instance, being friendly to co-workers. However, not all jobs require the same amount of emotional labour. People in jobs that require frequent and long durations of contact with clients, customers, suppliers, co-workers and others experience more emotional labour than others. Because of the importance of emotional labour for organisations, they provide their employees with training in expressing the appropriate, organisationally required emotions. Moreover, some organisations believe that the best way to support emotional labour is to hire people with the right attitude and skills (e.g. good customer service skills).

However, people still have difficulty in hiding their true or felt emotions all the time; this is particularly the case for anger. True emotions tend to leak out – for instance, as voice intonations or body movements. This is called **emotional dissonance**, defined as the conflict between felt (true) and displayed (required) emotions.[93] Of course, cultural differences exist concerning which emotions may or may not be displayed.[94] For instance, Japanese people think it is inappropriate to show emotions and to become emotional in business, while Americans are more likely to accept or tolerate people displaying their true emotions at work. Research did not find any gender differences in felt emotions, but women were found to be more emotionally expressive than men.[95]

Evidence about emotional intelligence and emotions

Generally, the evidence about Goleman's concept is somewhat mixed and a heated debate reigns between enthusiastic supporters and somewhat more nuanced advocates. The latter were really the first to propose a model of EI. This model, briefly outlined above, has a narrowly defined meaning, whereas the enthusiasts add elements such as persistence, zeal, self-control, character as a whole, and other positive attributes.[96] Crowding additional elements into a model never simplifies the task of finding evidence to support it. From the case of the original (pre-Goleman) four-branch model of emotional intelligence, association or the lack thereof, between other measures of people's cognitive abilities and their personalities (Big Five or MBTI) lends support, albeit to a complex argument. The much broader set of elements included by Goleman and associates (Table 3.4) would make empirical evidence complex beyond measure.

This has not prevented claims about the power of the EI approach. According to his critics, Goleman himself has first claimed that 'nearly 90% of the difference' between star performers at work and average ones was due to EI.[97] Even if Goleman has since claimed that he was misunderstood'[98] the schism between an 'all-including' and a rigorous approach remains, while only limited evidence has so far become available for either view.

Application of emotion-related models

The research lessons regarding emotional labour have been summarised as follows:

> Emotional labour can be particularly detrimental to the employee performing the labour and can take its toll both psychologically and physically. Employees . . . may bottle up feelings of frustration, resentment and anger; which are not appropriate to express. These feelings result, in part, from the constant requirement to monitor one's negative emotions and express positive ones. If not given a healthy expressive outlet, this emotional repression can lead to a syndrome of emotional exhaustion and burnout.[99]

A study among several groups of service workers (employees of service institutions, of the hotel business and call centres) led to the conclusion that the analysis of emotional work is a neglected area in organisational stress research that needs more attention in the future (also see Chapter 9). The data of the study suggest that emotional work is not *per se* either positive or negative. Rather, 'emotion display and sensitivity requirements are related to emotional exhaustion but also to personal accomplishment'.[100]

Critical thinking

Describe from personal experience an incident where a co-worker has misbehaved (define that for yourself) under the influence of toxic emotions (illness, personal problems with partners, children, money, etc.).

3.4 Flow in the workplace

Mihaly Csikszentmihalyi, an American psychologist, has studied the optimal experience for more than 30 years.[101] He is looking for the answer to the question: 'What makes some actions or activities worth pursuing for their own sake, even without any rational compensation?' Csikszentmihalyi calls this optimal experience 'flow' (or 'autotelic enjoyment'). Research in sport contexts also calls this phenomenon 'peak performance'.[102]

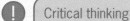

Table 3.5 Characteristics of Flow

- There are clear goals every step of the way.
- There is immediate feedback to one's actions.
- There is a balance between challenges and skills.
- Action and awareness merge.
- Distractions are excluded from consciousness.
- There is no worry of failure.
- Self-consciousness disappears.
- The sense of time becomes distorted.
- The activity becomes an end in itself.

Source: Based on M. Csikszentmihalyi, 'Happiness and Creativity', *The Futurist*, September–October 1997, pp. S8–S12.

According to Csikszentmihalyi, '**Flow** is a subjective psychological state that occurs when one is totally involved in an activity and feels simultaneously cognitively efficient, motivated and happy. It is the state in which people are so involved in an activity that nothing else seems to matter. The experience itself is so enjoyable that people will do it even at great cost, for the sheer sake of doing it.'[103] Time seems to stop; hours pass by as if it were only a few minutes.

Csikszentmihalyi studied people's flow experiences in order to understand more about their determinants and consequences. He developed the Experience Sampling Method (ESM) to measure people's quality of experience.[104] People receive an electronic pager (beeper) and a block of self-report forms with open-ended and scaled items (the Experience Sampling Form (ESF)). They keep this for a week and about 56 times at random intervals they are (by means of a signal) asked to describe their activity, feelings and experiences at that moment and to fill out some related questions. Csikszentmihalyi learned more about the characteristics of flow from people's descriptions. In interviews, people repeatedly mention certain key elements about their impressions of flow (Table 3.5).

A prerequisite to experience flow seems to be a match between people's perceived skills and the challenges they want to reach (i.e. attainable but challenging goals) (see also Chapter 6 on goal-setting theory).[105] In situations that are characterised by the simultaneous presence of high-perceived challenges and high-perceived skills, people may experience flow and the overall quality of the subjective experience is the highest. Challenges that are too low will lead to boredom and apathy, while too high challenges (in relation to people's perceived skills) may lead to stress and anxiety.

Flow is essentially a high level of concentration. The first step – being calm enough to start the activity – requires some discipline (think, for instance, about a top tennis player who has to play an important match or a professional who has to give an important presentation to the board of directors). Once the activity starts, attention tends to be focused and seems to take on a life of its own. For the moment, people forget everything else going on in their lives and in the world and become totally involved in their current activity. Even if we started an activity with another intention, a characteristic of flow is that it becomes a goal in itself that intrinsically motivates us. That is why flow activities are also called autotelic activities ('auto' means self and 'telos' is the Greek word for goal).

Evidence about flow

Experiences of flow are found in studies with artists, musicians, mathematicians, athletes, rock climbers, surgeons, chess players, factory managers and workers, as well as in middle- and high-level executives.[106] Flow seems to be a universal concept. It is found in all cultures, at all ages and in different social classes. People describe in a similar way how they felt during flow and also the reasons they give to explain their feelings are quite similar. Moreover, people's descriptions of flow during different kinds of activities seem to be fairly similar.

However, some people experience flow with a certain activity and others do not. Some people also experience more flow than others. Several researchers have studied the differences between people's flow experiences. They concluded that some people have characteristics or traits that stimulate the experience of flow, while others do not.[107] For instance, people who work primarily in order to be recognised and promoted will not experience flow. Paradoxically, people tend to do their best work and enjoy themselves in the process, when they forget about themselves and become involved in their current activity. People who do their job because they enjoy doing it, regardless of advancement, will be more likely to experience flow and achieve success. This is related to people's goal orientation: people who have a task goal orientation strive for learning and improvement, while people who have an ego goal orientation emphasise winning, outperforming others and demonstrating ability.[108] People who are intrinsically motivated also seem to have a higher opportunity to experience flow than the ones who are more extrinsically motivated. Some people tend to feel confident about their skills and spend more time in flow, while others feel less confident and spend more time in stress and anxiety.

HR Application of flow

Csikszentmihalyi formulates five 'Cs' that are essential to maximise people's flow at the workplace:[109]

- *Clarity.* Make sure people have clear goals. This also means that people should know what they want to do and reach in their work and where they are already in relation to these goals. Formulating goals in terms of progress and outcomes and appropriate feedback methods are useful tools to enhance 'clarity'. In Chapter 6, more tips concerning goal setting and feedback are formulated.
- *Centre.* People should have an ability to focus. This means that they should be able to attend what needs to be the object of attention and what they need to do if they want to achieve a goal. People should learn to focus only on the activity, on what they are doing here and now, and not, for instance, on themselves or what others might think of them.
- *Choice.* People need to believe they control their life, that they have choices. This means they do not act as if they are victims of their environment. People should also trust in their strengths to reach their goals.
- *Commitment.* This means that people should be able to commit themselves and their energy to whatever activity is needed to obtain their goals.
- *Challenge.* As flow happens when there is a balance between people's skills and their challenges, people continuously and constantly need to seek new challenges and set new goals. People learn to match their challenges with their skills and also to develop the necessary skills to reach their challenges.

Every activity may lead to flow if the right elements are present (like clear goals, concentration, task orientation, commitment, challenges, focus and control). We can enhance the quality of our (work)life if we make sure the required conditions for flow are constantly present.

! Critical thinking

Would a highly intelligent person working on very simple tasks be likely to experience flow – and vice versa for a person of medium (or low) intelligence working on very complex tasks?

Learning outcomes: Summary of key terms

1 **Values and their sources**

Values are standards or criteria for choosing goals or guiding actions that are relatively enduring and stable over time, although they can change during our life. Values develop through the influence of personality, society and culture. People are not born with an internal set of values. Values are acquired throughout our lives from diverse sources (e.g. parents, teachers, peers, work environment, national culture etc.).

2 **Rokeach's instrumental and terminal values**

Instrumental values refer to desirable ways or modes of conduct to reach some kind of desirable goal. Terminal values refer to the desirable goals a person wants to reach during his or her life. Instrumental and terminal values are connected with each other and work together to help people reach their desirable goals through desirable ways of conduct. Terminal values can be self-centred (personal) or society-centred (social). Instrumental values can be divided into moral and competence values. People differ in the extent to which they value personal or social values, as well as moral or competence values.

3 **Schwartz's basic human values model and his related work values model**

Schwartz developed a theory of basic human values. He distinguishes 10 types of values that are recognised by members of most societies and shows how these values are connected dynamically with each other by specifying which values are compatible and mutually supportive, and which values are conflicting and opposed. He situates the dynamics between these values in two underlying dimensions: self-transcendence versus self-enhancement and openness to change versus conservation. Parallel to the basic values model, Schwartz identified a model of work values. He distinguishes between intrinsic, extrinsic, social and prestige work values.

4 **Planned behaviour and how attitudes influence behaviour**

According to the model of planned behaviour, someone's intentions to engage in a given behaviour are the best predictor of that behaviour. Three separate but interrelated determinants influence one's intention (planned behaviour) to do something (actual behaviour). Behavioural intentions are influenced by one's attitude towards the behaviour, by perceived norms about exhibiting that behaviour and by perceived behavioural control. As a general rule, the more favourable the attitude and subjective norm and the greater the perceived behavioural control, the stronger an individual's intention to engage in certain behaviour. The relative importance of attitudes, subjective norms and perceived behavioural control in the prediction of intention is, however, expected to vary across situations and actions.

5 **Work-related attitudes: organisational commitment, job involvement and job satisfaction**

Organisational commitment reflects the extent to which an individual identifies themself with an organisation and is committed to its goals. It is an important work attitude because committed people are expected to display a willingness to work harder to achieve organisational goals and a greater desire to stay in an organisation. Job involvement represents the extent to which an individual is personally involved with his or her work role. While organisational commitment refers to identification with one's organisation, job involvement refers to the extent one identifies with a specific job. Job satisfaction is an affective or emotional response towards various facets of one's job. It refers to the degree of fulfilment and pleasure one finds in his or her job. Job satisfaction is the general attitude one has towards one's job.

6 **Determinants and consequences of job satisfaction**

Five models specify the sources of job satisfaction. They are need fulfilment, discrepancy, value attainment, equity and trait/genetic components. Job satisfaction has been correlated with hundreds of consequences. Table 3.3 summarises the pattern of results found for a subset of the more important variables. Because of the complexity and broadness of the concept of job satisfaction, there is no one panacea for organisations to improve the job satisfaction of their employees. Rather, it is advisable to make use of several aspects to enhance facets of people's satisfaction (feedback, rewards systems, participation, coaching, etc.).

7 **Positive and negative emotions and how they can be judged**

Positive emotions – happiness/joy, pride, love/affection and relief – are personal reactions to circumstances congruent with one's goals. Negative emotions – anger, fright/anxiety, guilt/shame, sadness, envy/jealousy and disgust – are personal reactions to circumstances incongruent with one's goals. Both types of emotions need to be judged in terms of intensity and the appropriateness of the person's relevant goal.

8 **Emotional intelligence and which components it implies**

Emotional intelligence is the ability to manage your own emotions and those of others in mature and constructive ways. It includes such abilities as being able to motivate oneself and persist in the face of frustrations; to control impulse and delay gratification; to regulate one's moods and keep distress from swamping the ability to think; to empathise and to hope. Emotional intelligence has four key components: self-awareness, self-management, social awareness and relationship management. The first two components are referred to as 'personal' competence, while the last two are referred to as 'social' competence.

9 **Emotional contagion in the workplace**

Emotional contagion refers to the process through which people catch the feelings of others. An illustrative image that clarifies emotional contagion is 'the ripple effect'. As water ripples in a lake because of the wind, emotions can ripple through people, groups and organisations. Which mechanisms are involved in emotional contagion is not clearly known yet. Perceiving and (unconsciously) adopting other people's facial expressions seems to be important. Research findings indicate the importance of effectively using emotional contagion to improve organisational behaviour and performance.

10 **Flow and how it influences organisational behaviour**

Flow is a subjective psychological state that occurs when one is totally involved in an activity. It is the state in which people are so involved in an activity that nothing else seems to matter. The experience itself is so enjoyable that people will do it even at great cost, for the sheer sake of doing it. In situations that are characterised by the simultaneous presence of high-perceived challenges and high-perceived skills, people may experience flow. Flow can be an important emotional process to stimulate in organisations as it has a positive influence on people's performance and well-being at work. Flow leads to higher productivity, motivation, creativity and satisfaction in people. People in flow also seem to be better 'equipped' to deal with stressful events.

Critical thinking

There is no doubt that there is much more focus on values, attitudes and emotions in current management education and management literature – but are they also becoming more and more important for managers and employees in organisations and companies?

Review questions

1. Can you give an example of how your values influenced a choice you made?
2. How would you respond to a person who made this statement: 'I'm only interested in behaviour. I've never seen an attitude, so why be concerned with attitudes'?
3. Do you believe that job satisfaction is partly a function of both personal traits and genetic factors? Explain.
4. Do you think job satisfaction leads directly to better job performance? Explain.
5. What are your personal experiences of negative emotions being positive; and of positive emotions being negative?
6. What is your personal experience with emotions being contagious?
7. Have you ever experienced flow? In what situation(s)? How can you describe this experience?

Personal awareness and growth exercise

How satisfied are you with your present job?

Objectives

1. To assess your job satisfaction towards your present or last (student) job.
2. To stimulate reflection on your job satisfaction and how to enhance it.

Introduction

As mentioned in the text, researchers at the US University of Minnesota developed the Minnesota Satisfaction Questionnaire (MSQ) to measure job satisfaction. Selected Minnesota Satisfaction Questionnaire items – measuring satisfaction with recognition, compensation and supervision – are listed in this exercise.[110]

Instructions

Relative to your present or most recent job, indicate how satisfied you are with the following aspects.

	Very dissatisfied				Very satisfied
1 The way I am noticed when I do a good job	1	2	3	4	5
2 The recognition I get for the work I do	1	2	3	4	5
3 The praise I get for doing a good job	1	2	3	4	5
4 How my pay compares with that for similar jobs in other companies	1	2	3	4	5
5 My pay and the amount of work I do	1	2	3	4	5
6 How my pay compares with that of other workers	1	2	3	4	5
7 The way my boss handles employees	1	2	3	4	5
8 The way my boss takes care of complaints brought to him or her by employees	1	2	3	4	5
9 The personal relationship between my boss and his or her employees	1	2	3	4	5

Scoring key

Total your score:
Add questions 1– 3 for satisfaction with recognition.
Add questions 4 – 6 for satisfaction with compensation.
Add questions 7 – 9 for satisfaction with supervision.

Questions for discussion

1 Compare your scores with the following comparative norms for each dimension of job satisfaction:
   3 – 6 = Low job satisfaction
   7 –11 = Moderate job satisfaction
   12 and above = High job satisfaction
2 Do you recognise your score for each of the job satisfaction dimensions?
3 List possible solutions or ways to enhance your job satisfaction for each of the job satisfaction dimensions. Can you personally add a lot to increasing your job satisfaction or are you mainly dependent on your work environment?

Group exercise

Anger control role play

Objectives

1 To demonstrate that emotions can be managed.
2 To develop your interpersonal skills for managing both your own and someone else's anger.

Introduction

Personal experience and research tells us that anger begets anger. People do not make their best decisions when angry. Angry outbursts often inflict unintentional interpersonal damage by triggering other emotions (such as disgust in observers and subsequent guilt and shame in the angry person). Effective professionals know how to break the cycle of negative emotions by defusing anger in themselves and others. The table below shows how anger can be controlled successfully:

Reducing chronic anger [in yourself]	Responding to angry provocation
Guidelines for action • Appreciate the potentially valuable lessons from anger • Use mistakes and slights to learn • Recognise that you and others can do well enough without being perfect • Trust that most people want to be caring, helpful family members and colleagues • Forgive others and yourself • Confront unrealistic, blame-oriented assumptions • Adopt constructive, learning-oriented assumptions	**Guidelines for action** • Expect angry people to exaggerate • Recognise the other's frustrations and pressures • Use the provocation to develop your abilities • Allow the other to let off steam • Begin to problem solve when the anger is at moderate levels • Congratulate yourself on turning an outburst into an opportunity to find solutions • Share successes with partners
Pitfalls to avoid • Assume every slight is a painful wound • Equate not getting what you want with catastrophe • See every mistake and slip as a transgression that must be corrected immediately • Attack someone for you getting angry • Attack yourself for getting angry • Try to be and have things perfect • Suspect people's motives unless you have incontestable evidence that people can be trusted • Assume any attempt to change yourself is an admission of failure • Never forgive	**Pitfalls to avoid** • Take every word literally • Denounce the most extreme statements and ignore more moderate ones • Doubt yourself because the other does • Attack because you have been attacked • Forget the experience without learning from it

Source: Reprinted with permission from D. Tjosvold, *Learning to Manage Conflict: Getting People to Work Together Productively*, pp. 127–9.

This is a role-playing exercise for groups of four. You will have a chance to play two different roles. All the roles are generic, so they can be played as either a woman or a man.

Instructions

Your lecturer will divide the class into groups of four. Everyone should read all five roles described. Members of each foursome will decide among themselves who will play which roles. All told, you will participate in two rounds of role playing (each round lasting no longer than eight minutes). In the first round, one person will play Role 1 and another will play Role 3; the remaining two group members will play Role 5. In the second round, those who played Role 5 in the first round will play Roles 2 and 4. The other two will switch to Role 5.

Role 1: The angry (out-of-control) shift supervisor

You work for a leading electronics company that makes computer chips and other computer-related equipment. Your factory is responsible for assembling and testing the company's most profitable line of computer microprocessors. Business has been good, so your factory is working three shifts. The day shift, which you are now on, is the most desirable one. The night shift, from 11 p.m. to 7.30 a.m. is the least desirable and least productive. In fact, the night shift is such a mess that your boss, the factory manager, wants you to move to the night shift next week. Your boss just broke this bad news as the two of you are having lunch in the company cafeteria. You are shocked and angered because you are one of the most senior and highly rated shift supervisors in the factory. Thanks to your leadership, your shift has broken all production records during the past year. As the divorced single parent of a 10-year-old child, the radical schedule change would be a major lifestyle burden. Questions swirl through your head. 'Why me?' 'What kind of reliable child care will be available when I sleep during the day and work at night?' 'Why should I be "punished" for being a top supervisor?' 'Why don't they hire someone for the position?' Your boss asks what you think.

When playing this role, be as realistic as possible without getting so loud that you disrupt the other groups. Also, if anyone in your group would be offended by foul language, please refrain from cursing during your angry outburst.

Role 2: The angry (under-control) shift supervisor

Although you will use the same situation as in Role 1, this role will require you to read and act according to the tips for reducing chronic anger in the left side of the table above. You have plenty of reason to be frustrated and angry, but you realise the importance of maintaining a good working relationship with the factory manager.

Role 3: The (hard-driving) factory manager

You have a reputation for having a 'short fuse'. When someone gets angry with you, you attack. When playing this role, be as realistic as possible. Remember, you are responsible for the entire factory with its 1200 employees and hundreds of millions of dollars of electronics products. A hiring freeze is in place, so you have to move one of your current supervisors. You have chosen your best supervisor because the night shift is your biggest threat to profitable operations. The night-shift supervisor gets a 10 per cent bonus. Ideally, the move will only be for six months.

Role 4: The (mellow) factory manager

Although you will use the same general situation as in Role 3, this role will require you to read and act according to the tips for responding to angry provocation in the right side of Table 3.6. You have a reputation for being results-oriented but reasonable. You are good at taking a broad, strategic view of problems and are a good negotiator.

Role 5: Silent observer

Follow the exchange between the shift supervisor and the factory manager without talking or getting actively involved. Jot down some notes (for later class discussion) as you observe whether or not the factory manager did a good job of managing the supervisor's anger.

1 Why is uncontrolled anger a sure road to failure?
2 Is it possible to express anger without insulting others? Explain.
3 Which is more difficult, controlling anger in yourself or defusing someone else's anger? Why?
4 What useful lessons have you learned from this role-playing exercise?

Online Learning Centre

When you have read this chapter, log on to the Online Learning Centre website at ***www.mcgraw-hill.co.uk/textbooks/sinding*** to access test questions, additional exercises and other related resources.

Notes

1 L. Halman and T. Petterson, 'Individualization and Value Fragmentation', in *Values in Western Societies*, ed. R. De Moor (Tilburg: Tilburg University Press, 1995), pp. 297–316.

2 M. Waters, *Modern Sociological Theory* (London: Sage Publications, 1994), p. 309.

3 A. Giddens, *Modernity and Self-Identity* (Stanford, CA: Stanford University Press, 1991), p. 80.

4 R. Robertson, *Globalization: Social Theory and Global Culture* (London: Sage Publications, 1992), p. 8.

5 J. J. Dose, 'Work Values: An Integrative Framework and Illustrative Application to Organizational Socialization', *Journal of Occupational and Organizational Psychology*, September 1997, pp. 219–40.

6 M. Rokeach, *The Nature of Human Values* (New York: The Free Press, 1973), pp. 5–6.

7 M. Rokeach, *The Nature of Human Values* (New York: The Free Press, 1973), p. 5.

8 J. J. Dose, 'Work Values: An Integrative Framework and Illustrative Application to Organizational Socialization', *Journal of Occupational and Organizational Psychology*, September 1997, pp. 219–40.

9 L. M. Keller, T. J. Bouchard, Jr, R. D. Arvey, N. L. Segal and R. V. Dawis, 'Work Values: Genetic and Environmental Influences', *Journal of Applied Psychology*, February 1992, pp. 79–88.

10 For a description of this process, see M. Rokeach, *The Nature of Human Values* (New York: The Free Press, 1973), p. 6.

11 For more information on Rokeach's ideas and model, see M. Rokeach, *Beliefs, Attitudes and Values* (San Francisco, CA: Jossey-Bass, 1968); M. Rokeach, *The Nature of Human Values* (New York: The Free Press, 1973); and M. Rokeach, *Understanding Human Values* (New York: The Free Press, 1979).

12 For more information on this basic human values model and its origins, see S. H. Schwartz and W. Bilsky, 'Toward a Universal Psychological Structure of Human Values', *Journal of Personality and Social Psychology*, September 1987, pp. 550–62; S. H. Schwartz and W. Bilsky, 'Toward a Theory of the Universal Content and Structure of Values: Extensions and Cross-Cultural Replications', *Journal of Personality and Social Psychology*, May 1990, pp. 878–91; S. H. Schwartz, 'Universals in the Content and Structure of Values: Theoretical Advances and Tests in 20 Countries', in *Advances in Social Psychology*, vol. 25, ed. M. Zanna (Orlando, FL: Academic Press, 1992), pp. 1–65; S. H. Schwartz, 'Are There Universal Aspects in the Structure and Contents of Human Values?', *Journal of Social Issues*, Winter 1994, pp. 19–45; and S. H. Schwartz and L. Sagiv, 'Identifying Culture-Specifics in the Content and Structure of Values', *Journal of Cross-Cultural Psychology*, January 1995, pp. 92–116.

13 For extension on the shared orientations, see S. Schwartz, 'Value Priorities and Behavior: Applying a Theory of Integrated Value Systems', in *The Psychology of Values: The Ontario Symposium*, no. 8, eds C. Seligman, J. M. Olson and M. P. Zanna (Mahwah, NJ: Lawrence Erlbaum Associates, 1996), p. 4. Also see S. H. Schwartz, 'Are There Universal Aspects in the Structure and Contents of Human Values?', *Journal of Social Issues*, Winter 1994, pp. 24–25.

14 For examples of studies that identified two or three work values, see L. Dyer and D. Parker, 'Classifying Outcomes in Work Motivation Research: An Examination of the Intrinsic-Extrinsic Dichotomy', *Journal of Applied Psychology*, August 1975, pp. 455–8; D. Elizur, 'Facets of Work Values: A Structural Analysis of Life and Work Values', *Journal of Applied Psychology*, August 1984, pp. 379–89; and D. Elizur, I. Borg, R. Hunt and I. M. Beck, 'The Structure of Work Values: A Cross-Cultural Comparison', *Journal of Organizational Behavior*, January 1991, pp. 21–38.

15 For more details on this study and other relevant research linking Schwartz's model with organisational behaviour, see S. Schwartz, 'Value Priorities and Behavior: Applying a Theory of Integrated Value Systems', in *The Psychology of Values: The Ontario Symposium, vol. 8*, eds C. Seligman, J. M. Olson and M. P. Zanna (Mahwah, NJ: Lawrence Erlbaum Associates, 1996), pp. 1–25.

16 T. A. Judge and R. D. Bretz, 'Effects of Work Values on Job Choice Decisions', *Journal of Applied Psychology*, June 1992, pp. 261–71; and J. J. Dose, 'Work Values: An Integrative Framework and Illustrative Application to Organizational Socialization', *Journal of Occupational and Organizational Psychology*, September 1997, pp. 219–40.

17 M. Fishbein and I. Ajzen, *Belief, Attitude, Intention, and Behavior: An Introduction to Theory and Research* (Reading, MA: Addison-Wesley, 1975), p. 6.

18 For a discussion of the difference between values and attitudes, see M. Rokeach, *The Nature of Human Values* (New York: The Free Press, 1973).

[19] For more information on the different aspects of attitudes, see A. P. Brief, *Attitudes In and Around Organizations* (Thousand Oaks, CA: Sage Publications, 1998), pp. 49–84.

[20] See B. M. Staw and J. Ross, 'Stability in the Midst of Change: A Dispositional Approach to Job Attitudes', *Journal of Applied Psychology*, August 1985, pp. 469–80. Also see J. Schaubroeck, D. C. Ganster and B. Kemmerer, 'Does Trait Affect Promote Job Attitude Stability?', *Journal of Organizational Behavior*, March 1996, pp. 191–6.

[21] Data from P. S. Visser and J. A. Krosnick, 'Development of Attitude Strength Over the Life Cycle: Surge and Decline', *Journal of Personality and Social Psychology*, December 1998, pp. 1389–410.

[22] L. Festinger, *A Theory of Cognitive Dissonance* (Stanford, CA: Stanford University Press, 1957). See also A. J. Elliot and G. Devine, 'On the Motivational Nature of Cognitive Dissonance: Dissonance as Psychological Discomfort', *Journal of Personality and Social Psychology*, September 1994, pp. 382–94; B. Burnes and H. James, 'Culture, Cognitive Dissonance and the Management of Change', *International Journal of Operations and Production*, no. 8, 1995, pp. 14–33; E. Harmon-Jones and J. Mills, *Cognitive Dissonance Progress on a Pivotal Theory in Social Psychology* (Washington, DC: Braum Brumfield, 1999); and A. H. Goldsmith, S. Sedo, W. Darity, Jr and D. Hamilton, 'The Labor Supply Consequences of Perceptions of Employer Discrimination During Search and On-the-Job: Integrating Neoclassic Theory and Cognitive Dissonance', *Journal of Economic Psychology*, February 2004, pp. 15–39.

[23] Several models and studies on the attitude–behaviour relationship exist, for instance S. J. Kraus, 'Attitudes and the Prediction of Behavior: A Meta-Analysis of the Empirical Literature', *Personality and Social Psychology Bulletin*, January 1995, pp. 58–75; M. Sverke and S. Kuruvilla, 'A New Conceptualization of Union Commitment: Development and Test of an Integrated Theory', *Journal of Organizational Behavior*, Special Issue 1995, pp. 505–32; and R. C. Thompson and J. G. Hunt, 'Inside the Black Box of Alpha, Beta and Gamma Change: Using a Cognitive Processing Model to Assess Attitude Structure', *Academy of Management Review*, July 1996, pp. 655–90.

[24] For information on the previous model of Fishbein and Ajzen, see M. Fishbein and I. Ajzen, *Belief, Attitude, Intention, and Behavior: An Introduction to Theory and Research* (Reading, MA: Addison-Wesley, 1975); and I. Ajzen and M. Fishbein, *Understanding Attitudes and Predicting Social Behavior* (Englewood Cliffs, NJ: Prentice-Hall, 1980).

[25] For a brief overview and update of the model, see I. Ajzen, 'The Theory of Planned Behaviour', *Organizational Behavior and Human Decision Processes*, December 1991, pp. 179–211; J. Doll and I. Ajzen, 'Accessibility and Stability of Predictors in the Theory of Planned Behavior', *Journal of Personality and Social Psychology*, November 1992, pp. 754–65; and I. Ajzen and M. Fishbein, 'Attitudes and the Attitude-Behavior Relation: Reasoned and Automatic Processes, in *European Review of Social Psychology*, eds W. Stroebe and M. Hewstone (New York: John Wiley, 2000), pp. 1–33.

[26] See R. P. Steel and N. K. Ovalle II, 'A Review and Meta-Analysis of Research on the Relationship between Behavioral Intentions and Employee Turnover', *Journal of Applied Psychology*, November 1984, pp. 673–86. Also see J. A. Ouellette and W. Wood, 'Habit and Intention in Everyday Life: The Multiple Processes by Which Past Behavior Predicts Future Behavior', *Psychological Bulletin*, July 1998, pp. 54–74; R. J. Vandenberg and J. B. Nelson, 'Disaggregating the Motives Underlying Turnover Intentions: When Do Intentions Predict Turnover Behavior?', *Human Relations*, October 1999, pp. 1313–36; and A. Kirschenbaum and J. Weisberg, 'Employee's Turnover Intentions and Job Destination Choices', *Journal of Organizational Behavior*, February 2002, pp. 109–25.

[27] Drawn from J. M. Grant and T. S. Bateman, 'An Experimental Test of the Impact of Drug-Testing Programs on Potential Job Applicants' Attitudes and Intentions', *Journal of Applied Psychology*, April 1990, pp. 127–31.

[28] For data on attitude formation research, see I. Ajzen and M. Fishbein, *Understanding Attitudes and Predicting Social Behavior* (Englewood Cliffs, NJ: Prentice-Hall, 1980); and I. Ajzen, *Attitudes, Personality and Behaviour* (Chicago, IL: Dorsey Press, 1988). Also see D. J. Canary and D. R. Seibold, *Attitudes and Behavior: An Annotated Bibliography* (New York: Praeger, 1984); S. Chaiken and C. Stangor, 'Attitudes and Attitude Change', in *Annual Review of Psychology*, eds M. R. Rosenzweig and L. W. Porter (Palo Alto, CA: Annual Reviews, 1987), pp. 575–630; and B. H. Sheppard, J. Hartwick and P. R. Warshaw, 'The Theory of Reasoned Action: A Meta-Analysis of Past Research with Recommendations for Modifications and Future Research', *Journal of Consumer Research*, December 1988, pp. 325–43.

[29] See I. Ajzen, 'The Theory of Planned Behaviour', *Organizational Behavior and Human Decision Processes*, December 1991, p. 206. For research on the theory of planned behaviour, see for instance M. Fishbein and M. Stasson, 'The Role of Desires, Self-Predictions, and Perceived Control in the Prediction of Training Session Attendance', *Journal of Applied Social Psychology*, February 1990, pp. 173–98; I. Ajzen and B. L. Driver, 'Application of the Theory of Planned Behavior to Leisure Choice', *Journal of Leisure Research*, Third Quarter 1992, pp. 207–24; J. Reinecke, P. Schmidt and I. Ajzen, 'Application of the Theory of Planned Behavior to Adolescents' Condom Use: A Panel Study', *Journal of Applied Social Psychology*, May 1996, pp. 749–72; and K. A. Finlay, D. Trafimow and A. Villarreal, 'Predicting Exercise and Health Behavioral Intentions: Attitudes, Subjective Norms, and Other Behavioral Intentions', *Journal of Applied Social Psychology*, February 2002, pp. 342–58.

[30] J. P. Meyer and N. J. Allen, 'A Three-Component Conceptualization of Organizational Commitment', *Human Resource Management Review*, Spring 1991, pp. 61–89; and J. P. Meyer and N. L. Allen, *Commitment in the Workplace: Theory, Research, and Application* (Thousand Oaks, CA: Sage Publications, 1997).

[31] See R. P. Tett and J. P. Meyer, 'Job Satisfaction, Organizational Commitment, Turnover Intention, and Turnover: Path Analysis Based on Meta-Analytic Findings', *Personnel Psychology*, Summer 1993, pp. 259–93.

[32] See J. E. Mathieu and D. Zajac, 'A Review and Meta-Analysis of the Antecedents, Correlates, and Consequences of Organizational Commitment', *Psychological Bulletin*, September 1990, pp. 171–94; and M. Riketta, 'Attitudinal Organizational Commitment and Job Performance: A Meta-Analysis', *Journal of Organizational Behavior*, May 2002, pp. 257–66.

[33] See R. T. Mowday, L. W. Porter and R. M. Steers, *Employee Organization Linkages: The Psychology of Commitment, Absenteeism, and Turnover* (New York: Academic Press, 1982); M. A. Huselid and N. E. Day, 'Organizational Commitment, Job Involvement, and Turnover: A Substantive and Methodological Analysis', *Journal of Applied Psychology*, June 1991, pp. 380–91; M. J.

Somers, 'Organizational Commitment, Turnover and Absenteeism: An Examination of Direct and Indirect Effects', *Journal of Organizational Behavior*, January 1995, pp. 49–58; M. Clugston, 'The Mediating Effects of Multidimensional Commitment on Job Satisfaction and Intent to Leave', *Journal of Organizational Behavior*, June 2000, pp. 477–86.

34 See S. P. Brown, 'A Meta-Analysis and Review of Organizational Research on Job Involvement', *Psychological Bulletin*, September 1996, pp. 235–55.

35 G. J. Blau and K. R. Boal, 'Conceptualizing How Job Involvement and Organizational Commitment Affect Turnover and Absenteeism', *Academy of Management Review*, April 1987, pp. 288–300; and A. Cohen, 'Organizational Commitment and Turnover: A Meta-Analysis', *Academy of Management Journal*, October 1993, pp. 1140–57.

36 M. Dieffendorp, D. J. Brown, A. M. Kamin and R. G. Lord, 'Examining the Roles of Job Involvement and Work Centrality in Predicting Organizational Citizenship Behaviors and Job Performance', *Journal of Organizational Behavior*, February 2002, pp. 93–108.

37 Based on evidence in C. J. Thomsen, A. M. Basu and M. Tippens Reinitz, 'Effects of Women's Studies Courses on Gender-Related Attitudes of Women and Men', *Psychology of Women Quarterly*, September 1995, pp. 419–26.

38 For a review of the development of the JDI, see P. C. Smith, L. M. Kendall and C. L. Hulin, *The Measurement of Satisfaction in Work and Retirement* (Skokie, IL: Rand McNally, 1969).

39 For norms on the MSQ, see D. J. Weiss, R. V. Dawis, G. W. England and L. H. Lofquist, *Manual for the Minnesota Satisfaction Questionnaire* (Minneapolis, MN: Industrial Relations Center, University of Minnesota, 1967).

40 See J. Wanous, A. E. Reichers and M. J. Hudy, 'Overall Job Satisfaction: How Good Are Single-Item Measures?', *Journal of Applied Psychology*, April 1997, pp. 247–52; and T. Oshagbemi, 'Overall Job Satisfaction: How Good Are Single versus Multiple-Item Measures?', *Journal of Managerial Psychology*, October 1999, pp. 388–403.

41 For a review of these models, see A. P. Brief, *Attitudes In and Around Organizations* (Thousand Oaks, CA: Sage Publications, 1998).

42 See A. R. Karr, 'Work Week: A Special News Report about Life on the Job – and Trends Taking Shape There', *The Wall Street Journal*, 29 June 1999, p. A1.

43 For a review of need satisfaction models, see E. F. Stone, 'A Critical Analysis of Social Information Processing Models of Job Perceptions and Job Attitudes', in *Job Satisfaction: How People Feel about Their Jobs and How It Affects Their Performance*, eds C. J. Cranny, P. Cain Smith and E. F. Stone (New York: Lexington Books, 1992), pp. 21–52.

44 See J. P. Wanous, T. D. Poland, S. L. Premack and K. S. Davis, 'The Effects of Met Expectations on Newcomer Attitudes and Behaviors: A Review and Meta-Analysis', *Journal of Applied Psychology*, June 1992, pp. 288–97; P. G. Irving and J. P. Meyer, 'Re-Examination of the Met-Expectations Hypothesis: A Longitudinal Analysis', *Journal of Applied Psychology*, December 1994, pp. 937–49; P. W. Hom, R. W. Griffeth, L. E. Palich and J. S. Bracker, 'Revisiting Met Expectations as a Reason Why Realistic Job Previews Work', *Personnel Psychology*, Spring 1999, pp. 97–112; and W. H. Turnley and D. C. Feldman, 'Re-Examining the Effects of Psychological Contract Violations: Unmet Expectations and Job Satisfaction as Mediators', *Journal of Organizational Behavior*, January 2000, pp. 25–42.

45 A complete description of this model is provided by E. A. Locke, 'Job Satisfaction', in *Social Psychology and Organizational Behavior*, eds M. Gruneberg and T. Wall (New York: John Wiley, 1984), pp. 93–117.

46 For a test on value attainment, see W. A. Hochwarter, P. L. Perrewe, G. R. Ferris and R. A. Brymer, 'Job Satisfaction and Performance: The Moderating Effects of Value Attainment and Affective Disposition', *Journal of Vocational Behavior*, April 1999, pp. 296–313.

47 Results can be found in J. Cohen-Charash and P. E. Spector, 'The Role of Justice in Organizations: A Meta-Analysis', *Organizational Behavior and Human Decision Processes*, November 2001, pp. 278–321.

48 A thorough discussion of this model is provided by T. A. Judge and R. J. Larsen, 'Dispositional Affect and Job Satisfaction: A Review and Theoretical Extension', *Organizational Behavior and Human Decision Processes*, September 2001, pp. 67–98.

49 Supportive results can be found in B. M. Staw and J. Ross, 'Stability in the Midst of Change: A Dispositional Approach to Job Attitudes', *Journal of Applied Psychology*, August 1985, pp. 469–80; and R. P. Steel and J. R. Rentsch, 'The Dispositional Model of Job Attitudes Revisited: Findings of a 10-Year Study', *Journal of Applied Psychology*, December 1997, pp. 873–9.

50 See R. D. Arvey, T. J. Bouchard, Jr, N. L. Segal and L. M. Abraham, 'Job Satisfaction: Environmental and Genetic Components', *Journal of Applied Psychology*, April 1989, pp. 187–92; E. Diener and C. Diener, 'Most People Are Happy', *Psychological Science*, May 1996, pp. 181–5; and D. Lykken and A. Tellegen, 'Happiness Is a Stochastic Phenomenon', *Psychological Science*, May 1996, pp. 186–9.

51 C. Dormann and D. Zapf, 'Job Satisfaction: A Meta-Analysis of Stabilities', *Journal of Organizational Behavior*, August 2001, pp. 483–504.

52 Results can be found in A. J. Kinicki, F. M. McKee-Ryan, C. A. Schriesheim and K. P. Carson, 'Assessing the Construct Validity of the Job Descriptive Index: A Review and Meta-Analysis', *Journal of Applied Psychology*, February 2002, pp. 14–32.

53 See R. D. Hackett, 'Work Attitudes and Employee Absenteeism: A Synthesis of the Literature', *Journal of Occupational Psychology*, 1989, pp. 235–48; and R. Steel and J. R. Rentsch, 'Influence of Cumulation Strategies on the Long-Range Prediction of Absenteeism', *Academy of Management Journal*, December 1995, pp. 1616–34.

54 A thorough review of the various causes of turnover is provided by T. R. Mitchell and T. W. Lee, 'The Unfolding Model of Voluntary Turnover and Job Embeddedness: Foundations for a Comprehensive Theory of Attachment', in *Research in Organizational Behavior*, eds B. M. Staw and R. I. Sutton (New York: JAI Press, 2001), pp. 189–246.

55 Results can be found in P. W. Hom and A. J. Kinicki, 'Toward a Greater Understanding of How Dissatisfaction Drives Employee Turnover', *Academy of Management Journal*, October 2001, pp. 975–87.

56 Techniques for reducing employee turnover are thoroughly discussed by R. W. Griffith and P. W. Hom, *Retaining Valued Employees* (Thousand Oaks, CA: Sage Publications, 2001).

[57] Results can be found in R. W. Griffeth, P. W. Hom and S. Gaertner, 'A Meta-Analysis of Antecedents and Correlates of Employee Turnover: Update, Moderator Tests, and Research Implications for the Next Millennium', *Journal of Management*, May 2000, pp. 463–88. Also see A. C. Glebbeek, 'Is High Employee Turnover Really Harmful? An Empirical Test Using Company Records', *Academy of Management Journal*, April 2004, pp. 277–86.

[58] The various models are discussed by T. Judge, C. Thoresen, J. Bono and G. Patton, 'The Job Satisfaction–Job Performance Relationship: A Qualitative and Quantitative Review', *Psychological Bulletin*, May 2001, pp. 376–407.

[59] Results can be found in T. Judge, C. Thoresen, J. Bono and G. Patton, 'The Job Satisfaction–Job Performance Relationship: A Qualitative and Quantitative Review', *Psychological Bulletin*, May 2001, pp. 376–407.

[60] T. C. Murtha, R. Kanfer and P. L. Ackerman, 'Toward an Interactionist Taxonomy of Personality and Situations: An Integrative Situational-Dispositional Representation of Personality Traits', *Journal of Personality and Social Psychology*, July 1996, pp. 193–207; and T. Judge, C. Thoresen, J. Bono and G. Patton, 'The Job Satisfaction–Job Performance Relationship: A Qualitative and Quantitative Review', *Psychological Bulletin*, May 2001, pp. 376–407.

[61] Results can be found in J. K. Harter, F. L. Schmidt and T. L. Hayes, 'Business-Unit-Level Relationship between Employee Satisfaction, Employee Engagement, and Business Outcomes: A Meta-Analysis', *Journal of Applied Psychology*, April 2002, pp. 268–79.

[62] L. L. Putnam and D. K. Mumby, 'Organizations, Emotions and the Myth of Rationality', in *Emotion in Organizations*, ed. S. Fineman (Thousand Oaks, CA: Sage Publications, 1993), pp. 36–57; B. E. Ashforth and R. H. Humphrey, 'Emotion in the Workplace: A Reappraisal', *Human Relations*, February 1995, pp. 97–125; and J. M. Kidd, 'Emotion: An Absent Presence in Career Theory', *Journal of Vocational Behavior*, June 1998, pp. 275–88.

[63] For works on emotions, see J. M. Jenkins, K. Oatley and N. L. Stein, eds, *Human Emotions: A Reader* (Malden, MA: Blackwell Publishers, 1998); T. A. Domagalski, 'Emotions in Organizations: Main Currents', *Human Relations*, June 1999, pp. 833–52; N. M. Ashkanasy, C. E. J. Härtel and C. S. Daus, 'Diversity and Emotion: The New Frontiers in Organizational Behavior Research', *Journal of Management*, May 2002, pp. 307–38; and F. Lelord and C. André, *La Force des Emotions* (Paris: Editions Odile Jacob, 2001).

[64] See N. H. Frijda, 'Moods, Emotion Episodes and Emotions', in *Handbook of Emotions*, eds M. Lewis and J. M. Haviland (New York: Guilford Press, 1993), pp. 381–403; J. M. George, 'Trait and State Affect', in *Individual Differences and Behavior in Organizations*, ed. K. R. Murphy (San Francisco: Jossey-Bass, 1996); H. M. Weiss and R. Cropanzano, 'Affective Events Theory: A Theoretical Discussion of the Structure, Causes and Consequences of Affective Experiences at Work', in *Research in Organizational Behavior, vol. 18*, eds B. M. Staw and L. L. Cummings (Greenwich, CT: JAI Press, 1996), pp. 1–74; and R. Kelly and S. G. Barsade, 'Mood and Emotions in Small Groups and Work Teams', *Organizational Behavior and Human Decision Processes*, September 2001, pp. 99–130.

[65] R. S. Lazarus, *Emotion and Adaptation* (New York: Oxford University Press, 1991), p. 6. Also see, D. Goleman, *Emotional Intelligence* (New York: Bantam Books, 1995), pp. 289–90; and J. A. Russell and L. F. Barrett, 'Core Affect, Prototypical Emotional Episodes, and Other Things Called Emotion: Dissecting the Elephant', *Journal of Personality and Social Psychology*, May 1999, pp. 805–19.

[66] Based on discussion in R. D. Arvey, G. L. Renz and T. W. Watson, 'Emotionality and Job Performance: Implications for Personnel Selection', in *Research in Personnel and Human Resources Management, vol. 16*, ed. G. R. Ferris (Stamford, CT: JAI Press, 1998), pp. 103–47. Also see L. A. King, 'Ambivalence Over Emotional Expression and Reading Emotions', *Journal of Personality and Social Psychology*, March 1998, pp. 753–62; and S. Mann, *Hiding What We Feel, Faking What We Don't* (Shaftesbury, Dorset, UK: Element, 1999).

[67] See A. M. O'Leary, R. W. Griffin and D. J. Glew, 'Organization-Motivated Aggression: A Research Framework', *Academy of Management Review*, January 1996, pp. 225–53; R. A. Baron and J. H. Neuman, 'Workplace Violence and Workplace Aggression: Evidence on Their Relative Frequency and Potential Causes', *Aggressive Behavior*, June 1996, pp. 161–73; and J. Fitness, 'Anger in the Workplace: An Emotion Script Approach to Anger Episodes between Workers and their Superiors, Co-Workers and Subordinates', *Journal of Organizational Behavior*, March 2000, pp. 147–62.

[68] E. Davies, 'How Violence at Work Can Hit Employers Hard', *People Management*, 12 September 1996, p. 50.

[69] For research in this area, see J. M. George and G. R. Jones, 'The Experience of Mood and Turnover Intentions: Interactive Effects of Value Attainment, Job Satisfaction, and Positive Mood', *Journal of Applied Psychology*, June 1996, pp. 318–25; and A. P. Brief and H. M. Weiss, 'Organizational Behavior: Affect in the Workplace', in *Annual Review of Psychology, vol. 53*, ed. S. T. Fiske (Palo Alto, CA: Annual Reviews, 2002), pp. 279–307.

[70] See, for instance, A. M. Isen and R. A. Baron, 'Positive Affect as a Factor in Organizational Behavior', in *Research in Organizational Behavior, vol. 13*, eds B. M. Staw and L. L. Cummings (Greenwich, CT: JAI Press, 1991), pp. 1–54; J. M. George and A. P. Brief, 'Feeling Good–Doing Good: A Conceptual Analysis of the Mood at Work-Organizational Spontaneity Relationships', *Psychological Bulletin*, September 1992, pp. 310–29; R. Cropanzano, K. James and M. A. Konovsky, 'Dispositional Affectivity as a Predictor of Work Attitudes and Job Performance', *Journal of Organizational Behavior*, November 1993, pp. 595–606; B. M. Staw, R. I. Sutton and L. H. Pelled, 'Employee Positive Emotion and Favorable Outcomes at the Workplace', *Organization Science*, February 1994, pp. 51–71; T. A. Wright and B. M. Staw, 'Affect and Favorable Work Outcomes: Two Longitudinal Tests of the Happy-Productive Worker Thesis', *Journal of Organizational Behavior*, January 1999, pp. 1–23; and T. A. Judge and R. J. Larsen, 'Dispositional Affect and Job Satisfaction: A Review and Theoretical Extension', *Organizational Behavior and Human Decision Processes*, September 2001, pp. 67–98.

[71] P. E. Spector, S. M. Jex and P. Y. Chen, 'Relations of Incumbent Affect-Related Personality Traits with Incumbent and Objective Measures of Characteristics of Jobs', *Journal of Organizational Behavior*, January 1995, pp. 59–65.

[72] V. A. Visser, D. V. Knippenberg, G. A. v. Kleef and B. Wisse, 'How leader displays of happiness and sadness influence follower performance: Emotional contagion and creative versus analytical performance', *Leadership Quarterly*, February 2013.

[73] See D. Goleman, *Emotional Intelligence* (New York: Bantam Books, 1995); D. Goleman, *Working with Emotional Intelligence* (New York: Bantam Books, 1998); and D. Goleman, R. Boyatzis and A. McKee, *Primal Leadership. Realizing the Power of Emotional Intelligence* (Boston, MA: Harvard Business School Press, 2002).

[74] D. Goleman, *Emotional Intelligence* (New York: Bantam Books, 1995), p. 34.

[75] See V. Dulewicz, 'Emotional Intelligence: The Key to Future Successful Corporate Leadership?', *Journal of General Management*, Spring 2000, pp. 1–14; J. M. George, 'Emotions and Leadership: The Role of Emotional Intelligence', *Human Relations*, August 2000, pp. 1027–55; H. Weisinger, *Emotional Intelligence at Work* (San Francisco, CA: Jossey-Bass, 2000); V. U. Druskat and S. B. Wolff, 'Building the Emotional Intelligence of Groups', *Harvard Business Review*, March 2001, pp. 80–90; G. Matthews, M. Zeidner and R. D. Roberts, *Emotional Intelligence: Science and Myths* (Cambridge, MA: The MIT Press, 2002); and R. J. Emmerling and C. Cherniss, 'Emotional Intelligence and the Career Choice Process', *Journal of Career Assessment*, May 2003, pp. 153–67.

[76] M. Davies, L. Stankov and R. D. Roberts, 'Emotional Intelligence: In Search of an Elusive Construct', *Journal of Personality and Social Psychology*, October 1998, pp. 989–1015; J. V. Ciarrochi, A. Y. C. Chan and P. Caputi, 'A Critical Evaluation of the Emotional Intelligence Construct', *Personality and Individual Differences*, March 2000, pp. 539–61; and R. D. Roberts, M. Zeidner and G. Matthews, 'Does Emotional Intelligence Meet Traditional Standards for an Intelligence? Some New Data and Conclusions', *Emotion*, September 2001, pp. 196–231.

[77] C. Woodruffe, 'Promotional Intelligence', *People Management*, 11 January 2001, pp. 26–9.

[78] The critique is in E. A. Locke, 'Why emotional intelligence is an invalid concept.' *Journal of Organizational Behavior*, 2005, no. 26, pp. 425–31.

[79] J. D. Mayer and P. Salovey, 'What is Emotional Intelligence?', in *Emotional Development and Emotional Intelligence: Implications for Educators*, eds P. Salovey and D. Sluyter (New York: Basic Books, 1997), pp. 3–34.

[80] For reviews on emotional contagion, see R. Neumann and F. Strack, 'Mood Contagion: The Automatic Transfer of Mood between Persons', *Journal of Personality and Social Psychology*, 2000, pp. 211–23; R. Kelly and S. G. Barsade, 'Mood and Emotions in Small Groups and Work Teams', *Organizational Behavior and Human Decision Processes*, September 2001, pp. 99–130; and J. M. George, 'Affect Regulation in Groups and Teams', in *Emotions in the Workplace: Understanding the Structure and Role of Emotions in Organizational Behavior*, eds R. G. Lord, R. Klimoski and R. Kanfer (San Francisco, CA: Jossey-Bass, 2002), pp. 183–217.

[81] E. Hatfield, J. T. Cacioppo and R. L. Rapson, *Emotional Contagion* (New York: Cambridge University Press, 1994), p. 4.

[82] The process of emotional contagion is explained more thoroughly in R. Kelly and S. G. Barsade, 'Mood and Emotions in Small Groups and Work Teams', *Organizational Behavior and Human Decision Processes*, September 2001, pp. 99–130.

[83] See, for instance, R. W. Doherty, L. Orimoto, T. M. Singelis, E. Hatfield and J. Hebb, 'Emotional Contagion: Gender and Occupational Differences', *Psychology of Women Quarterly*, December 1995, pp. 355–71; C. D. Fisher, 'Mood and Emotions While Working: Missing Pieces of Job Satisfaction', *Journal of Organizational Behavior*, March 2000, pp. 185–202; and A. Singh-Manoux and C. Finkenauer, 'Cultural Variations in Social Sharing of Emotions: An Intercultural Perspective', *Journal of Cross-Cultural Psychology*, November 2001, pp. 647–61.

[84] Data from S. D. Pugh, 'Service with a Smile: Emotional Contagion in the Service Encounter', *Academy of Management Journal*, October 2001, pp. 1018–27.

[85] Data from P. Totterdell, S. Kellett, K. Teuchmann and R. B. Briner, 'Evidence of Mood Linkages in Work Groups', *Journal of Personality and Social Psychology*, June 1998, pp. 1504–15. Also see P. Totterdell, 'Catching Moods and Hitting Runs: Mood Linkage and Subjective Performance in Professional Sport Teams', *Journal of Applied Psychology*, December 2000, pp. 848–59.

[86] S. G. Barsade, 'The Ripple Effect: Emotional Contagion and Its Influence on Group Behavior', *Administrative Science Quarterly*, December 2002, pp. 644–75. Also see C. A. Bartel and R. Saavedra, 'The Collective Construction of Work Group Moods', *Administrative Science Quarterly*, June 2000, pp. 197–231.

[87] D. Goleman, *Working with Emotional Intelligence* (New York: Bantam Books, 1998), pp. 163–97.

[88] For research on the role of emotional contagion in conflict management and negotiating, see R. Baron, 'Environmentally Induced Positive Affect: Its Impact on Self-Efficacy, Task Performance, Negotation and Conflict', *Journal of Applied Social Psychology*, March 1990, pp. 368–84; and J. P. Forgas, 'On Feeling Good and Getting Your Way: Mood Effects on Negotiator Cognition and Bargaining Strategies', *Journal of Personality and Social Psychology*, May 1998, pp. 565–77.

[89] For research on the role of emotional contagion in leadership, see J. M. George, 'Leader Positive Mood and Group Performance: The Case of Customer Service', *Journal of Applied Social Psychology*, May 1995, pp. 778–94; and K. M. Lewis, 'When Leaders Display Emotion: How Followers Respond to Negative Emotional Expression of Male and Female Leaders', *Journal of Organizational Behavior*, March 2000, pp. 221–34.

[90] For research on emotions and emotional contagion during change processes, see K. W. Mossholder, R. P. Settoon, A. A. Armenakis and S. G. Harris, 'Emotion during Organizational Transformations: An Interactive Model of Survivor Reactions', *Group & Organization Management*, September 2000, pp. 220–43; and S. Fox and Y. Amichai-Hamburger, 'The Power of Emotional Appeals in Promoting Organizational Change Programs', *Academy of Management Executive*, November 2001, pp. 84–94.

[91] The first researcher who focuses on emotional labour is A. Hochschild, *The Managed Heart: Commercialization of Human Feeling* (Berkeley, CA: University of California Press, 1983).

[92] J. A. Morris and D. C. Feldman, 'The Dimensions, Antecendents and Consequences of Emotional Labor', *Academy of Management Review*, October 1996, pp. 986–1010; J. A. Morris and D. C. Feldman, 'Managing Emotions in the Workplace', *Journal of Managerial Issues*, Fall 1997, pp. 257–74; and S. Mann, 'Emotion at Work: To What Extent Are We Expressing, Suppressing, or Faking It?', *European Journal of Work and Organizational Psychology*, September 1999, pp. 347–69.

[93] R. Abraham, 'Emotional Dissonance in Organizations: Antecedents, Consequences and Moderators', *Genetic, Social and General Psychology Monographs*, 1998, pp. 229–46.

[94] B. Mesquita and N. H. Frijda, 'Cultural Variations in Emotions: A Review', *Psychological Bulletin*, September 1992, pp. 179–204; and B. Mesquita, 'Emotions in Collectivist and Individualist Contexts', *Journal of Personality and Social Psychology*, September 2001, pp. 68–74.

[95] See A. M. Kring and A. H. Gordon, 'Sex Differences in Emotions: Expression, Experience, and Physiology', *Journal of Personality and Social Psychology*, March 1998, pp. 686–703.

[96] See J. D. Mayer, P. Salovey and D. R. Caruso, 'Emotional Intelligence: New Ability or Eclectic Traits?', *American Psychologist*, 2008, no. 63, pp. 503–17.

[97] D. Goleman, What makes a leader? *Harvard Business Review*, 1998, no. 76, pp. 93–102.

[98] See the preface in D. Goleman, *Emotional Intelligence* (10th anniversary edn) (New York: Bantam, 2005).

[99] N. M. Ashkanasy, 'Emotion in the workplace: The new challenge for managers', *The Academy of Management Executive (1993–2005)*, vol. 16, no. 1, 2002, pp. 76–86.

[100] D. Zapf, C. Vogt, C. Seifert, H. Mertini and A. Isic, 'Emotion Work as a Source of Stress: The Concept and Development of an Instrument', *European Journal of Work and Organizational Psychology*, September 1999, p. 396.

[101] For more information on flow, see M. Csikszentmihalyi, *Flow: The Psychology of Optimal Experience* (New York: HarperCollins, 1990); M. Csikszentmihalyi, *Creativity: Flow and the Psychology of Discovery and Invention* (New York: HarperPerennial, 1996); M. Csikszentmihalyi, *Finding Flow: The Psychology of Engagement with Everyday Life* (New York: Basic Books, 1997); and M. Csikszentmihalyi, *Good Business: Leadership, Flow and the Making of Business* (New York: Viking Books, 2003).

[102] C. Gilson, *Peak Performance: Business Lessons from the World's Top Sporting Organisations* (London: HarperCollins, 2000).

[103] M. Csikszentmihalyi, *Flow: The Psychology of Optimal Experience* (New York: HarperCollins, 1990).

[104] M. Csikszentmihalyi and R. Larson, 'Validity and Reliability of the Experience Sampling Method', *Journal of Nervous and Mental Disease*, June 1987, pp. 526–36.

[105] G. B. Moneta and M. Csikszentmihalyi, 'The Effect of Perceived Challenges and Skills on the Quality of Subjective Experience', *Journal of Personality*, June 1996, pp. 275–310.

[106] E. J. Donner and M. Csikszentmihalyi, 'Transforming Stress to Flow', *Executive Excellence*, February 1992, p. 16.

[107] For an overview, see S. A. Jackson, J. C. Kimiecik, S. K. Ford and H. W. Marsch, 'Psychological Correlates of Flow in Sport', *Journal of Sport and Exercise Psychology*, December 1998, pp. 358–78. Also see M. Csikszentmihalyi and I. Csikszentmihalyi, *Optimal Experience: Psychological Studies of Flow in Consciousness* (New York: Cambridge University Press, 1988).

[108] See J. L. Duda, 'Motivation in Sport Settings: A Goal Perspective Approach', in *Motivation in Sport and Exercise*, ed. G. Roberts (Champaign, IL: Human Kinetics, 1992), pp. 57–72; and S. A. Jackson and G. C. Roberts, 'Positive Performance States of Athletes: Toward a Conceptual Understanding of Peak Performance', *The Sport Psychologist*, March 1992, pp. 156–80.

[109] See M. Csikszentmihalyi, *Flow: The Psychology of Optimal Experience* (New York: HarperCollins, 1990). Also see H. L. Mills, 'Flow', 2001 (www.optimums.com).

[110] Adapted from D. J. Weiss, R. V. Dawis, G. W. England and L. H. Lofquist, *Manual for the Minnesota Satisfaction Questionnaire* (Minneapolis, MN: Industrial Relations Center, University of Minnesota, 1967). Used with permission.

Chapter 4

Perception and communication

Learning Outcomes

When you finish studying the material in this chapter, you should be able to:

- ✓ recognise what influences the perceptual process
- ✓ describe perception in terms of the social information processing model
- ✓ identify and explain two implications of social perception
- ✓ explain the central models explaining attribution
- ✓ discuss how the self-fulfilling prophecy is created and how it can be used to improve individual and group productivity
- ✓ describe the perceptual process model of communication
- ✓ describe the barriers to effective communication
- ✓ demonstrate your familiarity with oral, written and non-verbal communication skills
- ✓ discuss the primary sources of listener comprehension
- ✓ contrast the communication styles of assertiveness, non-assertiveness and aggressiveness
- ✓ discuss the patterns of hierarchical communication and 'the grapevine'
- ✓ explain the contingency approach to media selection
- ✓ elaborate on information overload and how to deal with it effectively

Opening Case Study: Wobbly Wheels: Rabobank, cycling and drugs

In October 2012, Rabobank, the Dutch mortgage lender, announced that it was ending its association with professional cycling at the end of that year. The reason given in the statement announcing the discontinuation of sponsorships was that 'we are no longer convinced that the international professional world of cycling can make this a clean and fair sport'.

Riding bicycles up and down mountains is hard work at the best of times. When practised by a professional cyclist as part of the vast entertainment event called 'Le Tour de France', the last thing a rider racing at 80–90 km/h downhill from an alpine summit needs is wobbly wheels. However, 'wobbly wheels' or 'clean sport' refers not to the equipment but to the possibility that cyclists themselves might be using drugs to enhance their performance.

Rabobank had waited some time before deciding to pull out, even though the Rabobank cycling team had a poor track record as far as drug use was concerned. The team was a separate business firm that used the Rabobank name as part of a long-running sponsorship arrangement. The cancellation of sponsorship came as little surprise to industry observers. Following the drama of the more or less unambiguous and forthright admissions in an interview with Oprah Winfrey by Lance Armstrong, the US winner of a record seven Tours and an iconic sports celebrity, that he had used various forms of doping, Rabobank decided to withdraw its sponsorship, which had begun in 1996. Since then a string of former riders in the Rabobank team have admitted that they too were heavy users of drugs for most of the period covered by the sponsorship.

There have always been concerns over the use of drugs of various kinds in professional cycling and other sports. Even in the first years of the Tour de France, which started in 1904, alcohol and cocaine were used. These concerns culminated in 1967 after the death of Tommy Simpson. Simpson was a veteran British cyclist whose career had started some 11 years before, when he won a bronze medal in the 1956 Melbourne Olympics. On 13 July 1967, Simpson was ascending Mont Ventoux, a gruelling incline over 21 km rising at an average of 7.43 per cent. One kilometre from the summit he collapsed and died. A post-mortem investigation indicated that his blood contained amphetamines and alcohol, and he had been suffering from a stomach condition. Added to this, it was an extremely hot day and the Tour organisers only permitted riders to take on 2 litres of water during the race.

For the Rabobank team and its Rabobank sponsor the really big scare came during the 2007 Tour. A member of the team, the Dane Michael Rasmussen, had advanced to lead the race and was wearing the famous yellow jersey. However, the team decided to withdraw Rasmussen and sent him home. The issue was inconsistencies in his reporting of his whereabouts in the training season of the spring of 2007. The team's failure to know Rasmussen's whereabouts led to the resignation of the team manager.

By 2007 doping was old news in the context of cycling. The sport had put stringent rules in place to prohibit the use of performance enhancing drugs and also the use of blood doping. These rules had evolved since the Tour was hit by a vast scandal in 1998. The entire Festina team had been excluded after the discovery that one of the Festina support cars was carrying a large cache of drugs.

One of the more curious facts to emerge from the 2007 Rabobank affair was a statement by Theo de Rooy, the team manager who resigned. Speaking in 2012 he said that 'if it happened, it was a deliberate decision by medical staff'. De Rooy always used the term 'medical care' and never the word 'drugs'.

Cyclists are employees of the various teams. Top riders are the stars, with salaries measured in millions of euros but the average cyclist is estimated to make a more modest €100,000 or so annually. However, in starting on a career in cycling and by signing a contract, cyclists also sign away far more personal liberties than most people would find reasonable. They have to report their whereabouts at all times and must be available for random drug screenings whenever an anti-doping official wishes to see them. Their food regime is regulated in all manner of ways. They cannot receive private visits from unauthorised individuals nor do many other things. Only a few organisations apply such drastic controls to their operating staff (these are typically found in other endurance sports such as cross-country skiing).

For discussion

How do information flows related to the whereabouts of professional cyclists make sense?

Source: Based on Cyclingnews.com, 19 October 2012 and F. Mercer 'Cycling's "Big Three" apologize to the peloton for skewing average salaries', http://www.cyclismas.com/biscuits/cyclings-big-three-apologize-to-the-peloton-for-skewing-average-salaries/ (Accessed 18 March 2013.)

In every social situation, we gather information about other people. We form a certain picture of them based on the signals we receive from them. We encode and store this information and use it every time we interact with each other or make a decision in our lives. We are constantly striving to make sense of our social surroundings, be it while watching a political debate on TV, having a romantic dinner or dealing with everyday tasks at work.

The resulting knowledge influences our behaviour and helps us navigate our way through life. For example, think of the perceptual process that occurs when meeting someone for the first time. Your attention is drawn to the individual's physical appearance, voice, language, mannerisms, actions and reactions to what you say and do. You ultimately arrive at conclusions based on your perceptions of this social interaction. That brown-haired, green-eyed individual turns out to be friendly and fond of outdoor activities. You further conclude that you like this person and then ask him or her to go to for coffee, calling the person by the name you stored in memory.

This reciprocal process of perception, interpretation and behavioural response also applies at work. Might employees' perceptions of how much an organisation valued them affect their behaviour and attitudes? Researchers asked samples of high school teachers, brokerage-firm clerks, manufacturing workers, insurance representatives and police officers to indicate their perception of the extent to which their organisation valued their contributions and their well-being. Employees who perceived that their organisation cared about them reciprocated with reduced absenteeism, increased performance, innovation and positive work attitudes.[1] This illustrates the importance of employees' perceptions.

Perception is not only important in organisational life. Perception theories are widely applied in politics, the media, by recruitment advertisements and in many other instances. Take bonuses for bankers. Following the financial crisis which began in 2008, and saw many large banks and insurance companies nationalised or bankrupted, the use of very large bonuses has become even more controversial than it was, with some politicians calling for an outright ban on the practice.[2] One perception associated with the bonuses is that they contributed to the crisis. Whether it is in fact correct is less important and the financial crisis is not the subject in any case.

Perception is about how individuals understand the information they receive or register using their eyes, nose, ears, fingertips or any other sensory organ. That information comes from somewhere. The state of nature is one thing, but more importantly, the information packages which arrive at the recipient or perceiver depends on how it gets there and thus on both the sender and on the transmission. These latter stages of the information process are often called communication.

Perception is just a starting point. What is perceived depends not just on the arriving information but also on the recipient's existing mental models and information that has arrived earlier.

This chapter deals with both sides of the information flow. On the perceiving side we focus on the antecedents of perception, on the social information processing model and some of the implications. On the communication side we focus on the process of communicating, the forms it takes and the barriers to making it work as intended. We integrate the two sides of the information flow in a discussion of how the distribution of information matters a great deal, i.e. whether it is asymmetric or not.

4.1 Factors influencing perception

Perception is a cognitive process that enables us to interpret and understand our environment. It involves the way we view the world around us and adds meaning to the information gathered via the five senses. The study of how people perceive one another is called social cognition. **Social perception** is the process by which people come to understand one another.[3]

We all perceive the world around us differently. These perceptions influence our current and future behaviour. For instance, running 4 km in 25 minutes is perceived as a piece of cake for somebody who is used to running marathons, while an untrained person is going to perceive it as a formidable task. Different sets of people may also diverge in perceptions. For example, entrepreneurial-minded people have lower risk perceptions associated with starting up new ventures compared to less entrepreneurial people.[4] Human behaviour and thus organisational behaviour are a function of how we perceive our surroundings.

To improve our insights in other people's behaviour we need to understand how perceptions operate. Understanding and studying the perceptions of other people improves our ability to understand the meaning of our own behaviour. For example, in a study about the perceived attractiveness of job ads, business students were asked to analyse job descriptions. The results showed that the combination of perceived proximity of work to home with challenging job features were the most attractive job characteristics influencing the readiness to apply for a job. The study recommended that organisations wishing to attract strong candidates from this labour pool should mention these features when drawing up job ads.[5]

In understanding the process of social perception we need first to learn which factors actually affect perception. These factors can be classified into three main categories as shown in Figure 4.1.

4.2 Features of perceived people, objects and events

The characteristics of perceived objects, people and events are of great importance in the formation of perceptions.[6] When a person looks at other people, objects or events, his or her interpretation is influenced by the features of the perceived target. A priest driving a Harley Davidson motorcycle will draw more attention than priest riding a pedal bike. First impressions about people are influenced in subtle ways by a person's skin colour, gender, hair colour, weight, clothes, and so on.[7] An inquiry found that criminal suspects were perceived as more violent and aggressive when dressed in black – a colour associated with the demonic, evil sects and death – than when they wore lighter clothing.[8] The answer is that our minds perceive objects, people and ideas as organised and meaningful patterns rather than as separate bundles of data. That objects are perceived as a whole

Figure 4.1 Antecedents Influencing Perception

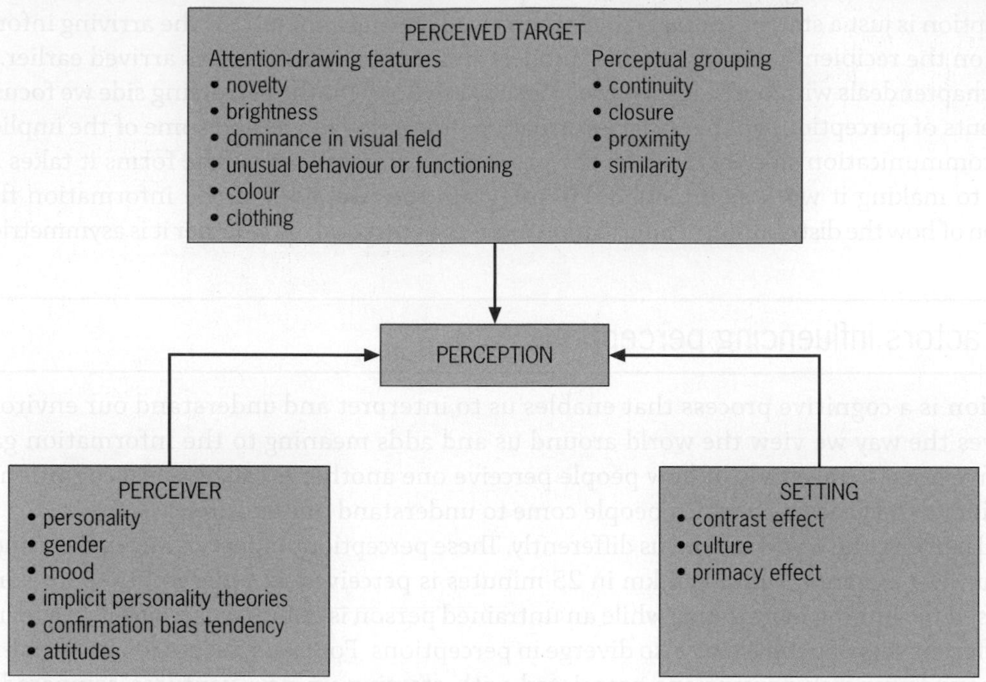

instead as the summation of their parts is well illustrated by Figure 4.2 and Figure 4.3. Even though the dots in the Figure 4.2 are not joined together we still perceive them it as a circle. In Figure 4.3 we perceive a dog instead of a large number of spots.

Several principles of perceptual grouping explain why we perceive objects as well-organised patterns rather than separate component parts. **Perceptual grouping** is the tendency to form individual stimuli into a meaningful pattern. The main factors that determine perceptual grouping are continuity, closure, proximity and similarity.[9]

Continuity is the tendency to perceive objects as continuous patterns. This principle, however, can have negative effects. An inflexible manager may demand that his employees follow strict procedures when doing their jobs, even though random activity may solve problems more imaginatively.

Closure is the tendency to perceive objects as a constant overall form. The dots looking like a circle in Figure 4.2 illustrate this organisation principle. Closure applies when we tend to see complete shapes even when a part of the information is missing. As a result, vital decisions are often taken on the basis of incomplete information.

Proximity is the organisation principle in which elements are grouped together on the basis of their nearness. People working in a department are often seen as a unit. When several people leave the department, however, for different unrelated reasons, the HR department may still perceive that there is a problem in that department and try to determine what it is.

Similarity is the tendency to group objects, people and events that look alike. In some organisations each department has its own colour to visually define separate functions. For instance, the sales department has yellow painted doors, while the marketing department has green painted doors, so they are clearly distinct.

Figure 4.2 Closure Principle

Figure 4.3 Perception of a Target as a Whole

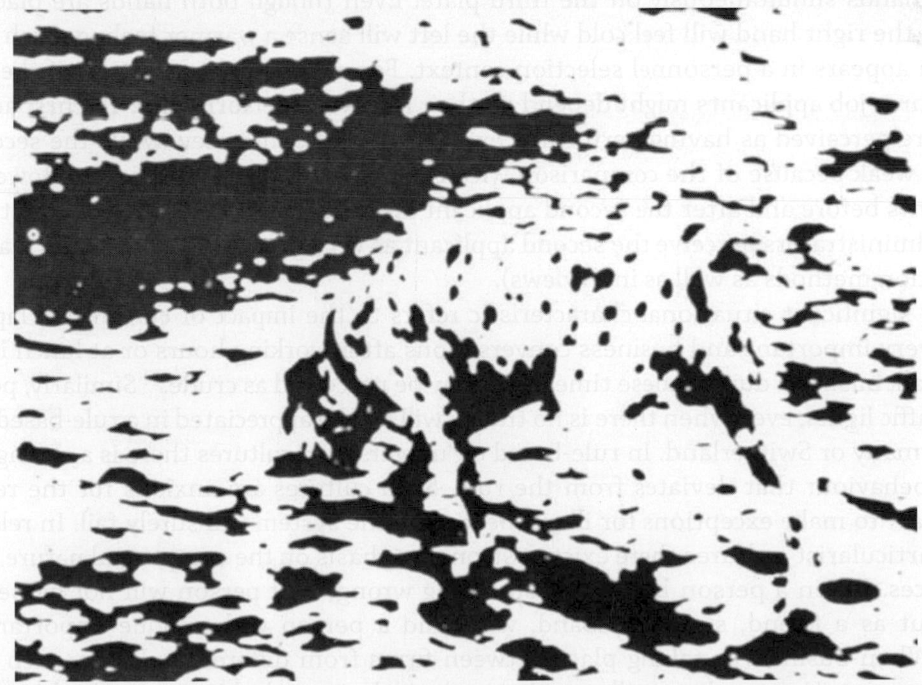

OB in Real Life

Symptoms in a row

Suppose you were presented with a list of six symptoms of thyroid cancer (fluctuations in weight, shortness of breath, feelings of being easily fatigued, pain in the throat or neck, difficulty breathing and a lump in the throat or neck). The first three are general symptoms, the last three are specific. Suppose further, that the list of symptoms was either short or long. Each of the three groups of symptoms is also known as a streak. Research shows that when a streak is presented, people are more likely to perceive that their risk is higher than if the common symptoms were presented with rarer symptoms in between.

The study showed that the sequence in which information is presented influences how much importance is attached to it. With a random sequence, risk may generally be perceived as lower than it would be if organised from high to low risk.[10]

The setting

The setting in which the interaction between perceiver and the perceived target (i.e. person, object or event) takes place, influences the perception. An important reason is that perceived targets are not looked at in isolation, the relationship of the target to its background or setting also influences perception.

A nice illustration of this phenomenon is the contrast effect. A **contrast effect** is the tendency to perceive stimuli that differ from expectations as being even more different than they really are.[11] Imagine that you have been presented with three iron plates – one cold, one warm and one at room temperature. After placing your left hand on the cold plate, and right hand on the hot plate, you place both hands simultaneously on the third plate. Even though both hands are placed on the same plate, the right hand will feel cold while the left will sense a warmer feeling. Such a contrast effect often appears in a personnel selection context. For example, the selection of the person to hire from three job applicants might depend on their interview performance. The first and the last applicant are perceived as having performed excellently in the interview while the second one is assessed as weak because of the comparison with the first and the last applicant. However, when the applicants before and after the second applicant are assessed as weak performers, these same selection administrators perceive the second applicant as very good (this is one more reason to use other selection methods as well as interviews).

Another significant situational characteristic refers to the impact of culture. In Japan, social context is very important and business conversations after working hours or at lunch is taboo. If you try to talk business during these times, you may be perceived as crude.[12] Similarly, pedestrians ignoring traffic lights, even when there is no traffic, will not be appreciated in a rule-based countries such as Germany or Switzerland. In rule-based or 'universalist' cultures there is a strong tendency to oppose behaviour that deviates from the rule. Such cultures are anxious for the reason that once you start to make exceptions for illegal behaviour the system will surely fail. In relationship-based or 'particularist' cultures there exists a strong emphasis on the exceptional nature of present circumstances. When a person has done something wrong, that person will not be perceived as a citizen but as a friend, sister, husband, wife, and a person with unique importance to the perceiver. When business is taking place between firms from different cultures, each will think the other corrupt. Universalists will perceive a particularist as lacking trustworthiness because they only help friends, while particularists perceive universalists as not trustworthy because of the perception that universalists do not even help friends.[13] Culture is further discussed in Chapter 12.

A third contextual factor distorting perceptions is the primacy effect. If you meet an individual for the first time and he is accompanied by someone you admire, your judgement of that person will probably be positive. This perception will however be reversed when someone you dislike accompanies that person. So the **primacy effect** is the effect by which the information first received often continues to colour later perceptions of individuals.[14] This effect is closely related to the cognitive bias or decision bias known as **anchoring.**[15]

The perceiver

The characteristics of the perceiver are also important. Factors inherent to the perceiver are sometimes the underlying reason why the same event, person or object is perceived differently. When people are asked to describe a group of target individuals, there is typically more overlap between the various descriptions provided by the same perceiver than there is between those provided for the same target. For example, listening to a friend describing the personality of a mutual acquaintance may tell us more about our friend's personality than the personality of the person being described. Part of the reason for these differences among perceivers is that we tend to use ourselves as a standard in perceiving others.[16]

HR

Besides personality (Chapter 2), gender could also be responsible for differences in perception. For example men and women seem to have a different perception of which social-sexual behaviours they consider to be harassment,[17] while women perceived greater gender inequity favouring males than did men.[18] Gender differences and sexual harassment influence the organisational climate (see Chapter 9).

A perceiver's mood can influence the impression formed about others. We think differently depending on whether we are in an optimistic or a pessimistic mood. When we are happy and an employee's task performance needs to be judged, we tend to assess this person's performance more positively than when we are in an unhappy state.[19]

Perception is also influenced when people have implicit personality theories about which physical characteristics, personality traits and behaviours are related to others. **Implicit personality theories** are a network of assumptions that we hold about relationships among various types of people, traits and behaviours. Knowing that someone has one trait leads us to infer that they have other traits as well.[20] For example knowing that someone is an entrepreneur leads us to infer that this person is a risk-taker, recognises opportunities and is full of confidence.

Previous learning and experience might influence the impressions formed about objects, people or events. We sometimes see what we expect to see based on previous learning and experience. As a consequence, formed perceptions are very powerful and resistant to non-corroborating information. Thus, people have the tendency to seek and interpret information that verifies existing beliefs.[21] This tendency is called the **confirmation bias.**

!

Critical thinking

Think about instances when your first impression of somebody turned out to be completely wrong. Which of the above-mentioned effects were at play?

4.3 A social information-processing model of perception

Social perception can be described as a four-stage information-processing sequence. Figure 4.4 illustrates the basic model. Three of the stages in this model – selective attention/comprehension, encoding and simplification, and storage and retention – describe how specific social information is observed and stored in memory. The fourth and final stage, retrieval and response, involves turning mental representations into real world judgements and decisions.

Keep the following everyday example in mind as you read about the four stages of social perception.

Stage 1: Selective attention/comprehension

People are constantly bombarded by physical and social stimuli. Since they do not have the mental capacity to fully comprehend all this information, they selectively perceive subsets of environmental stimuli. **Attention**, the process of becoming consciously aware of something or someone, plays a role. Attention can be focused on information either from the environment or from memory. When you sometimes find yourself thinking about totally unrelated events or people while reading a textbook, your memory is the focus of your attention. People tend to pay attention to salient stimuli.

Something is salient when it stands out from its context. For example, a competitor in the Scottish Highland Games caber (or pole) tossing event would certainly be salient in a women's aerobics class (even if he wears a kilt), but not at the annual 'Highland Games' in Edinburgh, Scotland. Social salience is determined by several factors (also see Figure 4.1), including:

- Novelty (the only person in a group of that race, gender, hair colour or age).
- Brightness (wearing a yellow shirt).
- Unusual for that person (behaving in an unexpected way, such as a person with a fear of heights climbing a steep mountain).
- Unusual for a person's social category (such as a company president driving a motorcycle to work).
- Unusual for people in general (driving 30 km/h in a 90 km/h zone).
- Extremely positive (a noted celebrity) or negative (the victim of a bad traffic accident).
- Dominant in the visual field (sitting at the head of the table).[22]

A person's needs and goals often dictate which stimuli are salient. For a driver whose petrol gauge shows empty, a Shell or BP sign is more salient than a McDonald's or Pepsi sign. The reverse would

Figure 4.4 Social Perception: A Social Information Processing Model

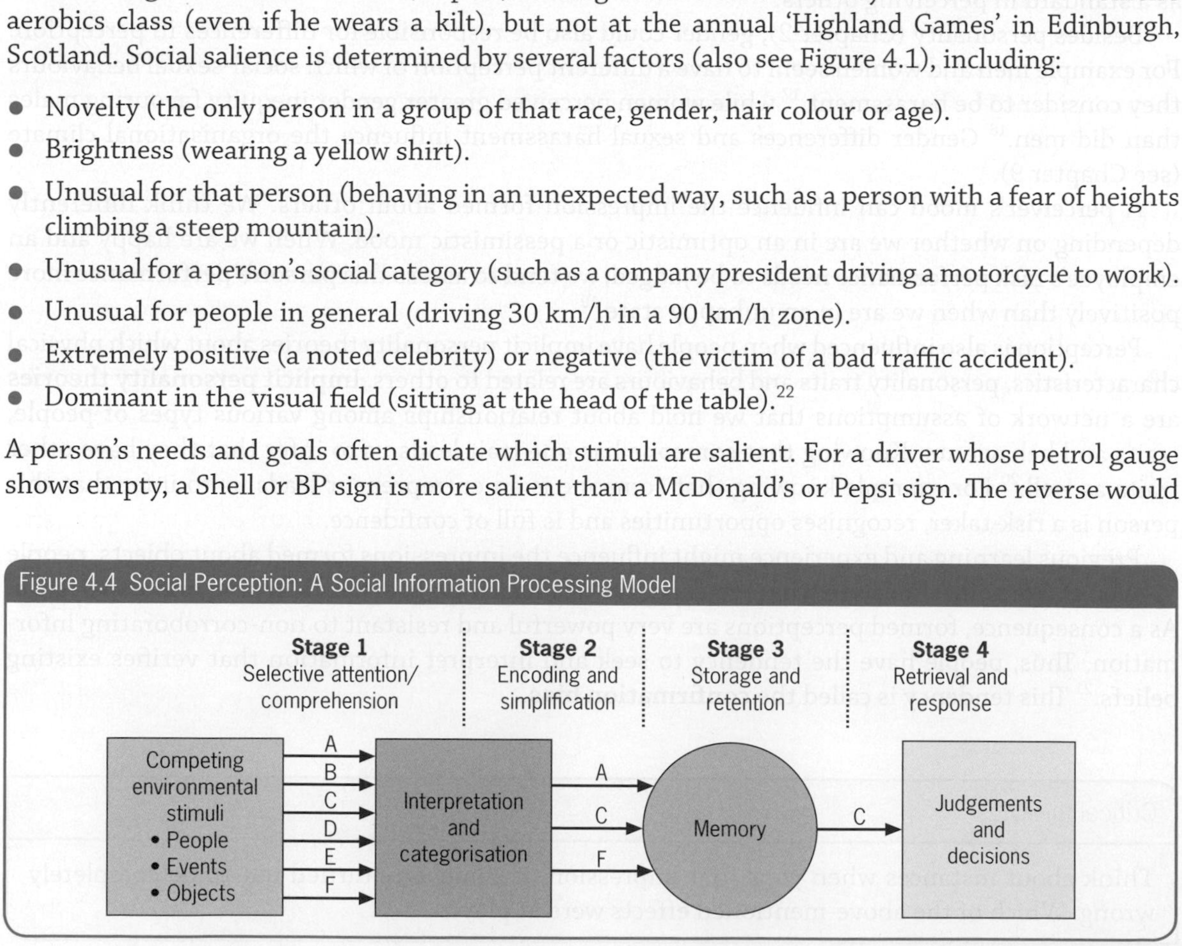

be true for a hungry and thirsty driver with a full tank of petrol. Moreover, people have a tendency to pay more attention to negative than to positive information. This leads to a negativity bias.[23] This bias helps explain the 'gawking factor' that slows traffic to a crawl following a car accident.

Stage 2: Encoding and simplification

Observed information is not stored in the memory in its original form. Encoding takes place; raw information is interpreted or translated into mental representations. To accomplish this, perceivers assign pieces of information to **cognitive categories**. By category we mean a number of objects that are considered equivalent. Categories are generally designated by names, such as dog or animal.[24] People, events and objects are interpreted and evaluated by comparing their characteristics with information contained in a schema (or, if plural, schemata).

According to social information processing theory, a **schema** represents a person's mental picture or summary of a particular event or type of stimulus. For example, your schema for restaurant meals might involve a number of distinct elements: you enter, and wait for a waiter to take you to your table. A menu is presented, food and drinks are ordered; drinks arrive, and food is served and eaten, in one or more rounds or courses. Eventually you signal to the waiter, with a hand signal that might indicate writing with a pen, and the bill is presented. For the regular restaurant eater, there are endless variations to the basic schema: ordering the wine; having it brought to the table and shown to the guest; and having the waiter uncork it and pouring a small sample for the customer to taste. Even the unspoken part of this ritual is a schema: if the wine does not taste as the customer thinks it should, the implicit assumption is that the bottle can be declared 'off', sent back and not paid for. For most eaters, this is a schema rarely used.

We use the **encoding** process to interpret and evaluate our environment. Interestingly, this process can result in differing interpretations and evaluations of the same person or event. Varying interpretations of what we observe occur for many reasons. First, people possess different information in the schemata used for interpretation. For instance, male chief executive officers (CEOs) and female executives disagree in their assessment of barriers preventing women from advancing to positions of corporate leadership. Second, our moods and emotions influence our focus of attention and evaluations (see Chapter 3).[25] Third, people tend to apply recently used cognitive categories during encoding. For example, you are more likely to interpret a neutral behaviour exhibited by a lecturer as positive if you were recently thinking about positive categories and events.[26] Fourth, individual differences influence encoding. Pessimistic or depressed individuals, for instance, tend to interpret their surroundings more negatively than optimistic and happy people (see Chapter 3).[27] The point is that we should not be surprised when people interpret and evaluate the same situation or event differently.

Stage 3: Storage and retention

This phase involves storage of information in long-term memory. Long-term memory consists of separate but related categories. The connected categories contain different types of information. Information also passes between these categories. Finally, long-term memory is made up of three compartments containing categories of information about events, semantic materials and people.

The **event memory** compartment is composed of categories containing information about both specific and general events. These memories describe appropriate sequences of events in well-known situations, such as going to a restaurant, going to a job interview, going to a food store or watching a football match.

Semantic memory refers to general knowledge about the world. In doing so, it functions as a mental dictionary of concepts. Each concept contains a definition (such as a good leader) and associated traits (outgoing), emotional states (happy), physical characteristics (tall) and behaviours (works hard). Just as there are schemata for general events, concepts in semantic memory are stored as schemata. Categories within the **person memory** compartment contain information about a single individual (your supervisor) or groups of people (managers).

Stage 4: Retrieval and response

People retrieve information from memory when they make judgements and decisions. Our ultimate judgements and decisions are either based on the process of drawing on, interpreting and integrating categorical information stored in long-term memory or on retrieving a summary judgement that was already made.[28]

Case: Processing information for selecting the best course instructor

Suppose you are thinking of taking a course in, say, personal finance. You can choose between three lecturers who teach parallel sections of the same course, using different types of instruction and testing procedures. Through personal experience, you have come to prefer good lecturers who rely on the case method of instruction and essay tests. According to social perception theory, you would be most likely to arrive at a decision regarding which lecturer to select in a way that reflects the four stages of the model.

Your search for the 'right' personal finance lecturer begins by asking friends who have taken classes from the lecturers. You may also interview the various lecturers who teach the class in order to collect more information. Returning to Figure 4.4, all the information you obtain represents competing environmental stimuli labelled A to F. Because you are concerned about the method of instruction, testing procedures and past grade distributions, information in those areas is particularly salient to you. You can then proceed to the second stage of information processing. Competing stimuli (e.g. represented by lines B, D and E in Figure 4.4) fail to get your attention and are discarded from further consideration.

Having collected the relevant information about the three personal finance lecturers and their approaches, you compare this information with other details contained in the schemata. This leads you to form an impression and evaluation of what it would be like to take a course with each lecturer. In turn, the relevant information is passed along to the third stage of information processing.

As the time draws near for you to decide which personal finance lecturer to select, your schemata are stored in the three categories of long-term memory. These schemata are available for immediate comparison and/or retrieval. It is course registration day and you have to choose which lecturer to select for your course. After retrieving from memory your schemata-based impressions of the three lecturers, you select the one who, in accordance with your preferences, uses the case method and gives essay tests. In contrast, you may choose your preferred lecturer by simply recalling the decision you made two weeks ago.

HR Evidence about social cognition

Social cognition is the window through which we observe, interpret and prepare our responses to people and events. A wide variety of activities, organisational processes and quality-of-life issues are thus affected by perception, including managerially crucial activities such as hiring and performance appraisal.

There is clear evidence that decisions are influenced by social cognition. For example, more attractive men and women were hired over less attractive applicants with equal qualifications.[29] Similarly, a study of the perception of diversity in the workplace revealed that people pretended to be rarely influenced by sex differences when hiring new employees. Age played a more important role: younger people preferred younger people; older respondents opted for their contemporaries. In traditional environments people chose more traditionally: ethnic minorities and (known) homosexuals had less chance of being recruited.[30]

Social cognition matters not only when hiring new people into an organisation. Evaluating or appraising the performance of existing staff is an integral part of management (Chapters 5 and 6 explains why it matters with respect to motivation). For example, a recent study of 166 production employees indicated that they had greater trust in management when they perceived that the performance appraisal process provided accurate evaluations of their performance.[31]

HR Application of social cognition

Some organisations hire new employees based on interviews, among other things (refer to Chapter 2 for information on personality and cognitive ability as hiring criteria). Sometimes much reliance is placed on interviews. This, however, is a risky approach which depends on two sets of perceptions. One is how the interviewer perceives the interviewee; the other is how the interviewer perceives the requirements of the position to be filled.

The information obtained by interview may be compromised by any number of mental models or schemata held by the interviewer; for example, notions about what a specific job involves and the skills or traits necessary to carry out the job. Some schemata related to characteristics such as sexual orientation, ethnic origin or political orientation may be totally irrelevant to hiring a good candidate and may also lead to illegal hiring decisions.

On the positive side, however, a recent study demonstrated that interviewer training can reduce the use of invalid schemata. Training improved interviewers' ability to obtain high-quality, job-related information and to stay focused on the interview task. Trained interviewers provided more balanced judgements about applicants than non-trained interviewers.[32] A supplement to training aimed at reducing the impact of irrelevant personal schemata is the use of clear and detailed job descriptions. This provides at least a preliminary specification of what knowledge, skills and abilities a candidate should possess. It also signals to the applicant about the properties of the job he or she is applying for.

Faulty schemata about what constitutes good as opposed to poor performance can lead to inaccurate performance appraisals, which erode work motivation, commitment and loyalty (see Chapter 6). Therefore, it is important for managers to identify accurately the behavioural characteristics and results indicative of good performance at the beginning of a performance review cycle. These characteristics can then serve as the benchmarks for evaluating employee performance.

The importance of using objective rather than subjective measures of employee performance was highlighted in a meta-analysis involving 50 studies and 8341 individuals. Results revealed that objective and subjective measures of employee performance were only moderately related. The researchers concluded that objective and subjective measures of performance are not interchangeable.[33] Managers are thus advised to use more objectively based measures of performance – as much as possible – because subjective indicators are prone to bias and inaccuracy. In those cases where the job does not possess objective measures of performance, however, professionals should still use subjective evaluations. Furthermore, because memory of specific instances of employee performance deteriorates over time, employers need a mechanism for accurately recalling employee behaviour.[34] Research shows that individuals can be trained to be more accurate raters of performance.[35] However, as was the case for hiring, detailed and accurate job descriptions are important. They are the backbone of the important objective side of performance evaluations. Job descriptions also contribute to organisational rigidity and inertia, which is not always a good thing (see Chapter 11 on organisational structure and Chapter 16 on organisational change).

> **Critical thinking**
>
> Your supervisor appears to be a wholly bad person, being inconsiderate, rude, insensitive and nasty. She may be allocated to the team you are managing. Apply the social information-processing model to your dealings with her to determine whether she is a bad boss or whether you yourself are having perceptual problems.

4.4 Attributions

Why did the plant manager not inform us earlier about the plans to outsource production to China? Why were some governments against arming Syrian rebels, whereas others supported such a policy? Why does Lionel Messi (a well-known football player) stand out from Christiano Ronaldo (another footballer)? And why was Dick Fuld, the former CEO of Lehman Brothers (a US bank that filed for bankruptcy in 2008) more preoccupied with staff wearing appropriate dress when his bank was moving towards disaster? Just like scientists, laymen try to answer why people are acting or behaving in a certain way, what the meaning is or underlying causes are of that unexpected behaviour. People want to make sense of the world by trying to find an explanation of other people's behaviour. The explanations they come up with for these 'why' questions are **attributions** or the inferred causes of why we behave in the way we do.

Attributions are cognitive evaluations that attempt to formulate explanations for an event, such as failure or success in an achievement-oriented task. Insight in the functioning of attributions is of great significance in understanding how decisions are made in the context of performance appraisal, and the capability of professionals to influence employees towards future performance achievement[36] and a great number of other decisions. As an example, two workers accomplish the same production level. The manager evaluates person A as displaying a lack of effort, while person B, who is achieving exactly the same productivity, is assessed as a hard worker. As a result of his evaluation the supervisor decides to give B a pay rise because of B's zeal at work seen by the supervisor. In contrast, A is reprimanded because of his lack of effort. These differences in attributed effort are really irrelevant: there is a failure to ask why they are observed or whether they really exist.

Types of attribution

Early work on attribution searched for location of causality, discerning internal and external causes of behaviour. Internal causes of behaviour concern factors within the actor (**internal factors**), while external causes are situated outside the actor (**external factors**).[37] Someone who fails a statistics exam can attribute this deficiency to misfortune, task difficulty (both external causes) or intelligence, mood or lack of preparation (internal causes).

Table 4.1 Attribution Dimensions

Locus of causality	Controllable		Uncontrollable	
	Stable	Unstable	Stable	Unstable
Internal	Typical effort	Intermediate effort	Ability	Mood
External	Supervisor	Co-workers	Task difficulty	Luck

Types of attributions: locus of causality, controllability and stability.

Source: D. Gioia and H. Sims, 'Cognitive-Behavior Connections: Attribution and Verbal Behavior in Leader–Subordinate Interactions', *Organizational Behavior and Human Decision Processes*, vol. 37, 1986, pp. 197–229. With permission from Elsevier.

The locus of causality classification was later expanded with a stability dimension,[38] which refers to whether the attribution is static or dynamic in time. A task failure resulting from a single instance of low effort is an unstable factor, while a lack of capability is considered a stable factor.

The controllability dimension underscores the significance of control over the causes of behaviour: are the events situated within or outside the command of a person? Low effort is a cause within the command of a person, while task difficulty is a less controllable cause. When a person is always facing a condition that he or she does not control and the outcome is negative, this could lead to learned helplessness (see Chapter 2).

The combination of the locus of causality, stability and controllability dimensions leads to eight categories of attributions as displayed in Table 4.1.

The generalisability dimension covers the specific character of a cause. This attribution dimension reveals information about whether an attribution or cause is generalisable between different situations. A nasty organisational climate attributed to the CEO's behaviour will have different implications from when this negative climate is explained by the existence of a culture that emphasises career advancement above all else (organisational culture is discussed in Chapter 12).

The desirability dimension mainly accentuates the features of attributions without considering the subjective appreciation and thus the social desirability of attributions. This dimension is essential for interpersonal attitudes. For example, Nicolas arrives at work half an hour late. The fact that he could not get out of bed is a less socially desirable attribution than being late at work because of trains being slow due to the wrong kind of snow.

The proximity dimension finally emphasises that behaviour can sometimes be explained by multiple causes in which different causes influence each other. For instance, job satisfaction at work is positively affected by organisational support, which in turn is influenced by the personality of organisational members. Burnout is influenced by perceived stress. However, this proximal cause of burnout can in turn be affected by optimism, a more distal cause of burnout.[39]

Attribution theories

Many theories have been developed connecting causes and behaviour. Three are particularly relevant to organisational behaviour: the correspondent inference theory; the co-variation theory; and the attribution theory and the related achievement motivation.

The **correspondent inference theory** describes how an alert perceiver infers another's intentions and personal dispositions from his or her behaviour. It is a theory of how we use other people's behaviour as a basic assumption for assessing the stability of their personalities. For example, your friend likes to help other people. Consequently you might infer that she has an altruistic personality because of her helpful behaviour. The extent to which a person's disposition (to help) is derived from a perceived slice of behaviour (what you observe) depends on three factors: non-common effects, social desirability of effects and degree of choice.

Non-common effects tell us more about a person's disposition than expected effects. Behaviour reveals more about a person when it diverges from what is known as typical expected behaviour. Socially undesirable behaviour leads to correspondent inference more than correct behaviour. A person making a strange noise and acting conspicuously while shopping in a supermarket reveals much information on that person's personality than does 'normal' or inconspicuous behaviour. A third factor is the person's degree of free choice. Behaviour that is freely chosen tells much more about personality than behaviour that is coerced.

In the correspondent inference theory behaviour is attributed to an underlying personality characteristic. However, behaviour can also be the result of situational factors. The **covariation principle** states that for a factor to be the cause of behaviour it must be present when the behaviour occurs and absent when it does not. This principle explains whether behaviour stems from internal or external causes. In this context people make internal or external inferences after gathering three types of information: the perceived stimulus object, other people who could be in a similar situation and the entire context surrounding the event (for instance, other time periods). These three types of information are also called distinctiveness, consensus and consistency.

Suppose your friend Helena is laughing all the way through the *Monty Python and the Holy Grail* (a 1975 cult movie). When you show her any other movie, even such comedy classics as *Life of Brian* or *The Meaning of Life* (two later Python movies, both arguably very funny, if you like that sort of humour), not a sound comes from her, which is behaviour very high in distinctiveness. If the pattern repeats itself at latter points in time Helena's behaviour is consistent. Finally, your friend Helena may be alone in not laughing at the other movies, a case of low consensus. If everyone fails to laugh, consensus is high – and you might start wondering how the others perceive you and your sense of humour.

Distinctiveness information is about whether the target person responds in the same way to other stimuli as well. Consensus information concerns whether only a few people respond in the same way as the target person. Finally, the consistency information answers the question: 'Does the target person always respond in the same way to other stimuli as well?'

The combination of high consensus (others behave in the same manner in this situation), high consistency (this person behaves in the same manner on other occasions when placed in the same situation) and high distinctiveness information (this person does not behave in this manner in other situations) is likely to lead to external attributions.[40] The combination of low consensus, high distinctiveness and low consistency will probably also result in external attributions.[41] However, the chance of making internal attributions is considerable when the perceived behaviour is low on consensus (others do not behave in the same manner in this situation), high on consistency (this person behaves in the same manner on other occasions when placed in the same situation) and low on distinctiveness (this person behaves in the same manner in other situations). This kind of information configuration leads to internal attributions of the perceived effects in 85 per cent of cases.[42] Figure 4.5 is an overview of which combinations of covariation information lead to internal or external attributions.

A third way of looking at attribution is a model designed to explain achievement behaviour and to predict subsequent changes in motivation and performance. Figure 4.6 presents a modified version of this model. According to this model, the attribution process begins after an individual performs a task. A person's performance leads him or her to judge whether it was successful or unsuccessful. This evaluation then produces a causal analysis to determine if the performance was due to internal or external factors. Figure 4.6 indicates that in this model, ability and effort are the primary internal causes of performance and task difficulty; luck and help from others are the key external causes. These attributions for success and failure then influence how individuals feel about themselves.

Figure 4.5 Covariation Information and Internal Versus External Attributions

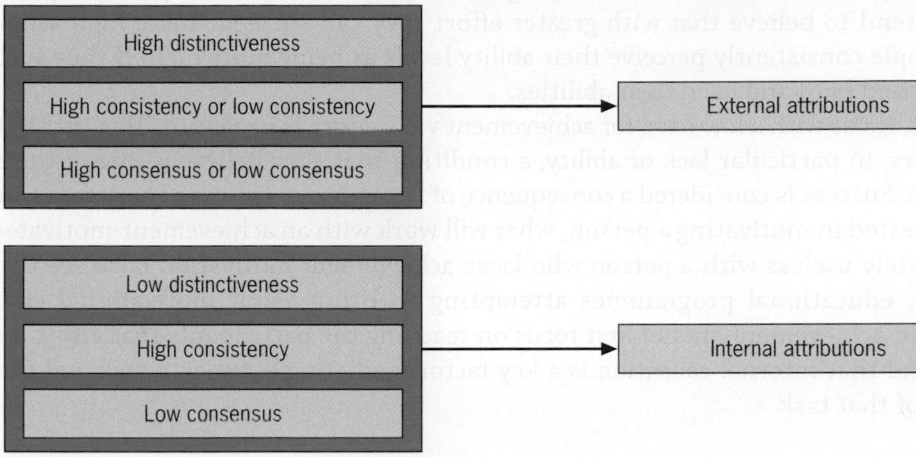

Figure 4.6 A Modified Version of Weiner's Attribution Model

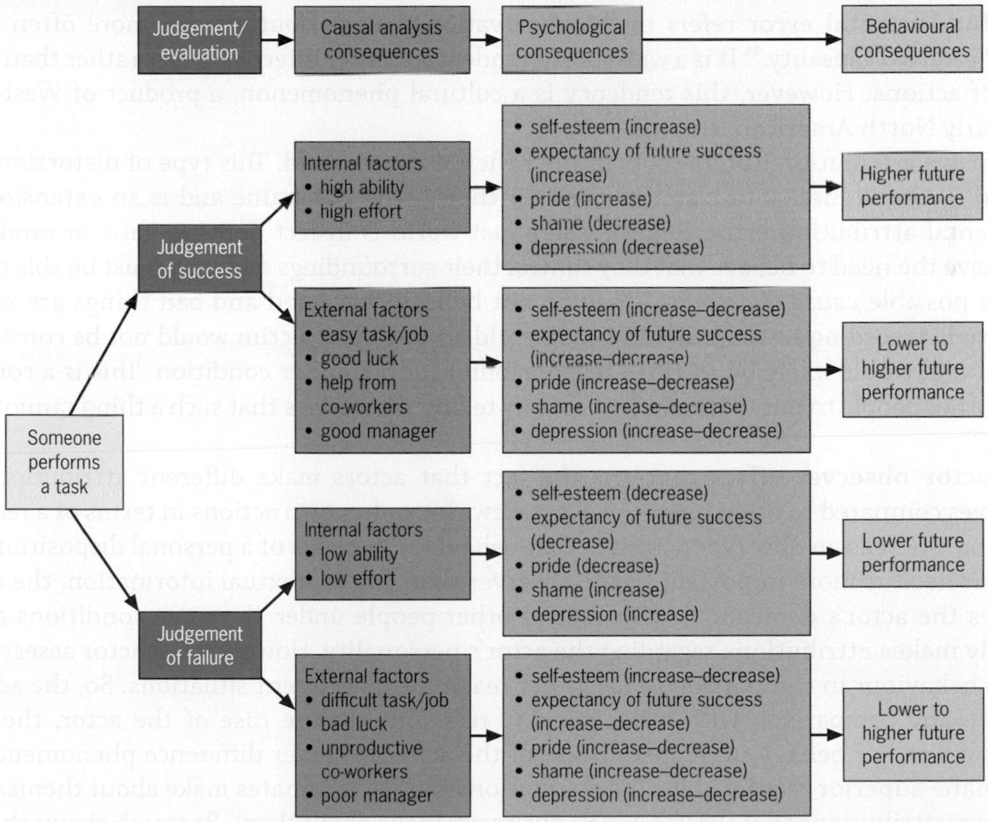

Source: Based in part on B. Weiner, 'An Attributional Theory of Achievement Motivation and Emotion', *Psychological Review*, October 1985, pp. 548–73; and T. S. Bateman, G. R. Ferris and S. Strasser, 'The "Why" behind Individual Work Performance', *Management Review*, October 1984, p. 71.

It has been pointed out that high achievement motivates people to attribute their successes to their own efforts and their failures to not trying hard enough. If they fail they are likely to try again because they tend to believe that with greater effort they can succeed. These high achievement-motivated people consistently perceive their ability levels as being quite high. If they succeed it is because they tried hard and used their abilities.

By contrast, those with a low need for achievement view effort as irrelevant. They attribute failure to other factors; in particular lack of ability, a condition that they believe is one of their general characteristics. Success is considered a consequence of the external factors of easy tasks and luck.[43] If we are interested in motivating a person, what will work with an achievement-motivated person may be absolutely useless with a person who lacks achievement motivation (also see Chapter 5). Consequently, educational programmes attempting to bring about motivational change and development in achievement should first focus on teaching the participants that effort does make a difference and that internal causation is a key factor mediating between a task and the level of performance of that task.

HR Attributional biases

Several tendencies or biases distort our interpretations of observed behaviour. Four important biases have been identified: the fundamental error, the defensive attribution, the actor–observer effect, self-serving bias and the fundamental attribution error.

The **fundamental error** refers to the observation that attributions are more often made in terms of internal causality.[44] It is a widespread tendency to infer internal causes rather than external causes of actions. However, this tendency is a cultural phenomenon, a product of Western, and particularly North American, culture.[45]

Defensive attribution has its roots in the belief in a just world. This type of distortion is characterised as the tendency to blame victims for their own misfortune and is an extension of the fundamental attribution error. Believing in a just world is in fact denying 'fate' or randomness. People have the need to believe that they control their surroundings and they must be able to reduce fate as a possible cause for events. They do not believe that good and bad things are randomly distributed. According to the belief in a just world an innocent victim would not be considered so innocent and would likely be ascribed responsibility for his or her condition. This is a convenient way for other people to put their minds at ease by telling themselves that such a thing cannot happen to them.[46]

The **actor–observer effect** concerns the fact that actors make different attributions about themselves compared to observers.[47] An actor views his or her own actions in terms of a reaction to a situation whereas an observer perceives that behaviour in terms of a personal disposition. As the behaviour itself is more important to the observer than the contextual information, the observer compares the actor's demeanour with that of other people under the same conditions and consequently makes attributions regarding the actor's personality. However, the actor assesses his or her own behaviour in comparison to his or her reactions in different situations. So, the actor does not make any comparison with other people's reactions. In the case of the actor, the context explains his or her behaviour. A special case of the actor–observer difference phenomenon is the subordinate–superior relationship. The attributions that subordinates make about themselves can differ from attributions that (professional) observers make about them. Research shows that actors and observers often perceive the same events in a totally different way. In a situation of failure a subordinate attributes the failure to external conditions, whereas the manager is likely to ascribe the failure to internal factors. This difference often leads to conflicts between the two.[48]

The **self-serving bias** is the tendency to attribute our positive outcomes to internal factors and to attribute our negative outcomes to external factors. People are inclined to accept personal responsibility for successful achievements but not for failures or problematic outcomes. In an organisational setting employees are likely to ascribe their successes to internal factors such as high ability and hard work, whereas failures or negative outcomes are attributed to uncontrollable external factors (difficult task, bad luck, unproductive co-workers or an unsympathetic boss).[49] Three explanations are possible for this. The first is a motivational explanation and is based on self-esteem (see Chapter 2). People want to keep or enhance their self-esteem. They will be resistant to negative explanations, such as lack of ability or effort, which attack their self-esteem. The second is an information-processing explanation. According to this process the self-serving bias tendency will occur because of an imbalance in the logical processing of available information. The third explanation refers to impression management. Self-serving bias will arise when individuals act to manage the impressions they make on others by taking credit for successes and denying responsibility for mistakes, errors or negative outcomes (see Chapter 14).[50]

The **fundamental attribution error** refers to the fact that desirable actions and behaviour are attributed to internal factors when it is made by in-group members and to external causes for out-group members. In the case of undesirable actions and behaviour, the attribution error is reversed. These are attributed to external factors when it is made by in-group members and to internal factors for out-group members.[51]

OB in Real Life

Why NOT wash hands?

Most readers of this book will have been taught by their parents to wash their hands regularly and that hygiene is important. Hand washing has also been considered important in hospitals for more than 175 years.

Yet, despite their upbringing, despite the legend of Ignaz Semmelweis, whose introduction of hand wash with chlorinated lime solution dramatically reduced the frequency of infections on maternity wards, healthcare professionals wash their hands only half as much as they should. This is unfortunate, particularly for those who end up with infections.

There are really two separate issues involved. One is about changing behaviour to increase hand washing, another is about understanding why the problem still exists. Here we concentrate on the latter, which contains part of the answer to the former.

In their study of how to motivate hand washing, Adam Grant and David Hoffman explain observed insufficient hand washing. They note in particular the possibility that health professionals may hold inaccurate notions of the risks facing them. Simply put, it is a matter of assessing whether *they* are at risk of being affected *and* believing that the risk will have serious consequences for *them*. It is as if medical people think about themselves as being somehow protected by magic.

Behind this sort of thinking lie perceptual errors. Individuals may overestimate (by discounting or even ignoring information indicating danger) their immunity partly because they have to do so in order to keep up a sense of security in an environment that is highly dangerous. Also, even if health professionals do get ill, the causal link to hand washing omissions may be weak. In essence many more instances of not getting sick are available – and it shows.

Source: Based on A. Grant and D. Hofmann, 'It's not all about me: Motivating hospital hand hygiene by focusing on patients', *Psychological Science*, vol. 22, 2011, pp. 1494–99.

HR Evidence about attribution

When you achieve high marks in an exam and you think this is the result of your intense preparation, then your self-esteem is likely to increase. However, the same grade can either increase or decrease your self-esteem if you believe that the test was easy. Over time, the feelings that people have about their past performance influence future performance. Figure 4.6 illustrates that future performance is likely to be higher when individuals attribute past success to internal causes in comparison with external attributions. Lower when failure is attributed to internal causes in comparison with external factors. Future performance is more uncertain when individuals attribute either their success or failure to external causes.

There is considerable evidence about the importance of attribution. A meta-analysis of 104 studies involving almost 15 000 individuals showed that people who attributed failure to their lack of ability (as opposed to bad luck) experienced psychological depression. The exact opposite attributions (good luck rather than high ability) tended to trigger depression in people experiencing positive events. In short, perceived bad luck took the sting out of a negative outcome, but perceived good luck reduced the joy associated with success.[52]

Similarly, a study of salesmen in the UK revealed that positive, internal attributions for success were associated with higher sales and performance ratings.[53] A second study examined the attribution processes of employees who were made redundant by a plant closing. The empirical evidence was consistent with the model: the explanation for job loss was attributed to internal and stable causes; so the life satisfaction, self-esteem and expectations for re-employment diminished. Furthermore, research shows that when individuals attribute their success to internal rather than external factors, they have higher expectations for future success, report a greater desire for achievement and set higher performance goals.[54]

Attribution models can be used to explain how professionals handle poorly performing employees. One study revealed that managers gave employees more immediate, frequent and negative feedback when they attributed their performance to low effort. This reaction was even more pronounced when the manager's success was dependent on an employee's performance. A second study indicated that professionals tended to transfer employees whose poor performance was attributed to a lack of ability. These managers also decided to take no immediate action when poor performance was attributed to external factors beyond an individual's control.[55]

HR Application of attribution models

The evidence presented in the previous section has several important implications for employers. First, employers tend to attribute behaviour disproportionately to internal causes.[56] This can result in inaccurate evaluations of performance, leading to reduced employee motivation. No one likes to be blamed for something caused by factors they perceive to be beyond their control. Further, because managers' responses to employee performance vary according to their attributions, attributional biases may lead to inappropriate actions, including promotions, transfers and lay-offs. This can weaken motivation and performance.

Attributional training sessions for managers are in order. Basic attributional processes can be explained and professionals can be taught to detect and avoid attributional biases. Finally, an employee's attributions for his or her own performance can have dramatic effects on subsequent motivation, performance and personal attitudes such as self-esteem. For instance, people tend to give up, develop lower expectations for future success and experience decreased self-esteem when they attribute failure to a lack of ability (see Chapter 2). Fortunately, attributional retraining can improve both motivation and performance. Research shows that employees can be taught to attribute their failures to a lack of effort rather than to a lack of ability.[57] This attributional realignment paves the way for improved motivation and performance.

Decision-makers and managers need to be aware of employee attributions if they are to make full use of the motivation concepts, explained in Chapters 5 and 6. The difficulty of doing so and of linking the pitfalls of attribution to the practical use of motivation theories may also explain the preference many students and managers have for simple, aged and also poorly supported theories, particularly those of Maslow and Herzberg (see Chapter 5).

Critical thinking

Use your accumulated experience (from work or school) to list stories of success and failure – then examine the factors to which those successes and failures were attributed.

4.5 Self-fulfilling prophecy

The essence of the **self-fulfilling prophecy**, also known as the Pygmalion, effect, is that people's expectations or beliefs determine their behaviour and performance, thus serving to make their expectations come true. It is also called the Galatea effect and it suggests that we strive to validate our perceptions of reality, no matter how faulty they may be. The notion of a self-fulfilling prophecy is an important perceptual outcome we need to understand better. Furthermore, this type of effect is not necessarily good. Negative expectations leads to poor outcomes, an effect sometimes called the Golem effect.

The Pygmalion and Golem effect

The self-fulfilling prophecy was first demonstrated in an educational environment. After giving a bogus test of academic potential to students from grades 1 to 6, researchers informed teachers that certain students had high potential for achievement. In reality, students were randomly assigned to the 'high potential' and 'control' (normal potential) groups. Results showed that children designated as having high potential obtained significantly greater increases in both IQ scores and reading ability than the control group.[58] The teachers of the supposedly high potential group got better results because their high expectations caused them to give harder assignments, more feedback and more recognition of achievement. Students in the normal potential group did not excel, because their teachers did not expect outstanding results.

Figure 4.7 presents a model of the self-fulfilling prophecy that helps explain how the Pygmalion effect works. As indicated, high supervisory expectation produces better leadership (link 1), which subsequently leads employees to develop higher self-expectations (link 2). Higher expectations motivate workers to exert more effort (link 3), ultimately increasing performance (link 4) and supervisory expectations (link 5). Successful performance also improves an employee's self-expectancy for achievement (link 6). The term the **set-up-to-fail syndrome** has been suggested to represent the negative side of the performance-enhancing process depicted in Figure 4.7.[59]

Assume that an employee makes a mistake, such as losing notes during a meeting, loses a valuable client or exhibits poor performance on a task by delivering a report a day late. An employer

Figure 4.7 A Model of the Self-Fulfilling Prophecy

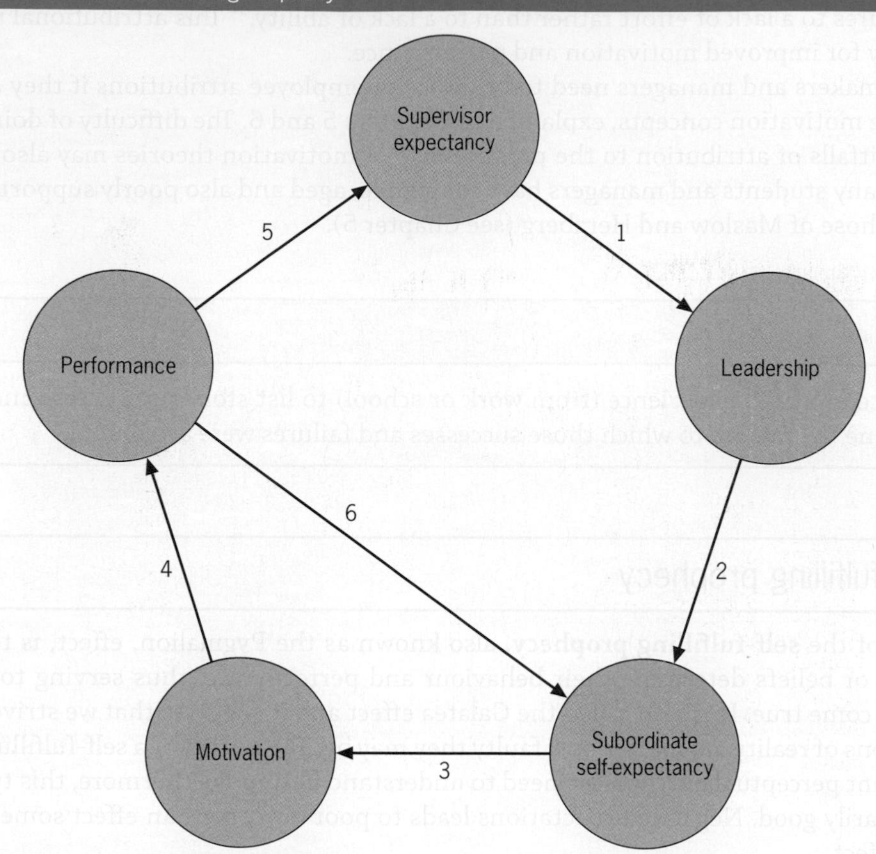

Source: D. Eden, 'Self-Fulfilling Prophecy as a Management Tool: Harnessing Pygmalion', *Academy of Management Review*, January 1984, p. 67. Used with permission.

then begins to wonder if this person has what it takes to be successful in the organisation. These doubts lead the employer to watch this person more carefully. The employee, of course, notices this and begins to sense a loss of trust. The employee then responds in one of two ways. She may doubt her own judgement and competence. This in turn leads the individual to become more averse to taking risk and to reduce the number of ideas and suggestions for review. The employer notices this behaviour and interprets it as an example of low initiative. Alternatively, the employee may do the opposite and take on more and more responsibility so that she can demonstrate her competence and worth. This is likely to cause her to fail, which in turn reinforces the employer's suspicions.[60] This process results in a destructive relationship fuelled by negative expectations, which is called the Golem effect, 'golem' meaning oaf in Hebrew and Yiddish. Expect an oaf and an oaf is what you get.[61]

HR Evidence about the self-fulfilling prophecy

By raising instructors' and professionals' expectations for individuals performing a wide variety of tasks, higher levels of achievement and productivity can be obtained.[62] Subjects in these field studies included airmen at the United States Air Force Academy Preparatory School, disadvantaged people in job-training programmes, electronics assemblers, trainees in a military command course,

US naval personnel and cadets in a naval officer course in the Israeli defence forces. However, these studies exclusively involved men.

To overcome this limitation, a recent team of researchers conducted two experimental studies on samples of female and male cadets in the Israeli defence forces. Results revealed that the Pygmalion effect was produced for both female and male cadets – but only when the leader was male. Female leaders did not produce a significant Pygmalion effect. This finding must be considered in the light of the fact that women were rated as better leaders than men in the Israeli defence forces. The researchers concluded that the Pygmalion effect clearly works on both women and men when the leader is male but not when the leader is female.[63] Recent evidence suggests, however, that the gender effect may not be as distinct as previously thought.[64]

A meta-analysis reviewed 13 studies regarding the Pygmalion effect in work organisations and had a closer look into the nature of the effect. Seventy-nine per cent of the people in the high expectancy groups outperformed the average people in the control groups. Furthermore, the meta-analysis revealed that the Pygmalion effect varied depending on the type of organisation. The effect was stronger in military settings than in business settings. The effect was also larger for those subordinates whose initial level of performance was low in comparison to those in which whole group expectations were induced.[65]

HR Application: the self-fulfilling prophecy at work

Largely due to the Pygmalion effect, expectations have a powerful influence on employee behaviour and performance. HR professionals can harness the Pygmalion effect by building a hierarchical framework that reinforces positive performance expectations throughout the organisation based on employees' self-expectations. In turn, positive self-expectations improve interpersonal expectations by encouraging people to work towards common goals. This co-operation enhances group-level productivity and promotes positive performance expectations within the work group.

As positive self-expectations are the foundation for creating an organisation-wide Pygmalion effect (and avoiding the negative side or Golem effect), let us then consider how employers can create positive performance expectations. This task may be accomplished by using various combinations of the following:

- Recognise that everyone has the potential to increase his or her performance.
- Instil confidence in your staff.
- Set high performance goals.
- Positively reinforce employees for a job well done.
- Provide constructive feedback when necessary.
- Help employees grow through the organisation.
- Introduce new employees as if they have outstanding potential.
- Become aware of your personal prejudices and any non-verbal messages that may discourage others.
- Encourage employees to visualise the successful execution of tasks.
- Help employees master key skills and tasks.

! Critical thinking

Relying on self-fulfilling prophecies might seem more than a little manipulative. What do you think?

4.6 Communication: the input to perception

The information we perceive sometimes comes to us without prompting and without any discernible sender. We observe the interior of our boss's office. The boss may or may not be aware of this. Our colleagues, superiors, subordinates and friends behave in certain ways, say things and do so in ways that convey to the perceiver a certain volume of information. From this section onwards we change focus from the recipients of information or the perceiver, to the sender or the communicator.

Even more than in the industrial age, communication is the central element in the information age or, as it is sometimes called, the information society. For example, the quality of student–faculty communication – in the professor's office, informally on campus, or before and after lectures – is positively related to student motivation. Similarly, employee satisfaction with organisational communication was positively and significantly correlated with both job satisfaction and performance.[66] Finally, note that many executives believe that written communication skills and interpersonal communication skills are critical competences that need enhancement via training. These executives believed the lack of communication skills had resulted in increased costs.[67] The following sections will help you understand better how communication processes work and how you can both improve your communication skills and design more effective communication programmes. We will discuss basic dimensions of the communication process, interpersonal communication, organisational communication patterns, the dynamics of modern communications and the distribution of information.

Communication is defined as 'the exchange of information between a sender and a receiver, and the inference (perception) of meaning between the individuals involved'.[68] Analysis of this exchange reveals that communication is a two-way process consisting of consecutively linked elements (see Figure 4.8). Anyone who understands this process can analyse their own communication patterns as well as design communication programmes that fit personal or organisational needs. This section reviews a perceptual process model of communication and discusses various barriers that can harm effective communication.

Figure 4.8 A Perceptual Process Model of Communication

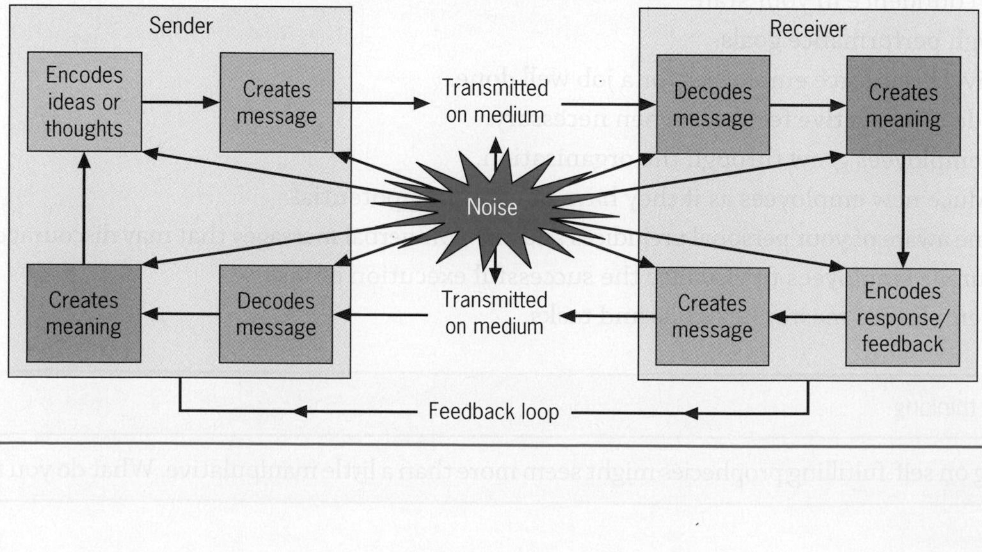

A perceptual process model of communication

Communicating is *not* like a pipe into which a message is placed at one end by a sender and retrieved at the other end by the receiver, unimpaired by passage, precise and perfectly understood. It is a process that is fraught with miscommunication. As a result, models of communication conceive it as a form of social information processing (recall the discussion earlier in this chapter) in which receivers interpret messages by cognitively processing information. This view led to the development of a **perceptual model of communication** in which communication as a process in which receivers create meaning in their own minds. The starting point (in Figure 4.8) is the sender, an individual, group or organisation that desires, or attempts, to communicate with a particular receiver. Receivers may be individuals, groups or organisations.

Communication begins when a sender encodes an idea or thought, translating them into a code or language that can be understood by others. People typically encode using words, numbers, gestures, non-verbal cues, such as facial expressions or pictures. Different methods of encoding can be used to portray similar ideas.

The output of encoding is a message. There are two important points to keep in mind about messages. First, they contain more than meets the eye. Messages may contain hidden agendas as well as trigger moods or emotional reactions. For example, comparisons of internal and external documents within the forest products industry, over a 10-year period, demonstrated that executives' private and public evaluative statements about events and situations were inconsistent. These executives apparently wanted to convey different messages to the public and to internal employees.[69] Similarly, a manager may discover that a complaint from someone about a lazy team member in reality reflected resentment about not being involved in that particular team.

Second, messages need to match the medium used to transmit information. How would you feel about being fired by a text message, or about being promoted by receiving orders that only implicitly indicate that you have in fact been promoted? These examples show thoughtless employers failing to consider the interplay between a message and the medium used to convey it.

People can communicate through a variety of **media**, including face-to-face conversations, telephone calls, email, voice mail, videoconferencing, written memos or letters, photographs or drawings, meetings, bulletin boards, computer output, and charts or graphs. Choosing the appropriate medium depends on many factors, including the nature of the message, its intended purpose, the type of audience, proximity to the audience, time horizon for disseminating the message and personal preferences.

All media have advantages and disadvantages. Face-to-face conversations are useful for communicating about sensitive or important issues and those requiring feedback and intensive interaction. Telephones are convenient, fast and private but non-verbal information is absent. Although writing memos or letters is time-consuming, it is a good medium when it is difficult to meet, when formality and a written record are important, and when face-to-face interaction is not necessary to enhance understanding. This ordering represents declining **media richness**.

Decoding is the receiver's version of encoding. Decoding consists of translating verbal, oral or visual aspects of a message into a form that can be interpreted. Receivers rely on social information processing to determine the meaning of a message during decoding (see the sections on perception in this chapter). Decoding is a key contributor to misunderstanding in interracial and intercultural communication because decoding by the receiver is subject to social and cultural values that may not be understood by the sender (see Chapter 12). Also, the growing popularity of email and the explosion in the use of social networking media such as Facebook, Twitter and blogging has brought about what some people refer to as a new language, one which is not always easily decoded by those unfamiliar with it.

In contrast to the simple conduit model's (the pipe at the beginning of this section) assumption that meaning is directly transferred from sender to receiver, the perceptual model is based on the belief that a receiver creates the **meaning** of a message in his or her mind. Often, a receiver's interpretation of a message will differ from what the sender intended. In turn, receivers act according to their own interpretations (not that of the sender). All the perceptual and attributional problems and effects can come into play in decoding an email.

Redundancy of communication is one way to reduce unintentionality in communication. Redundancy can be achieved by transmitting the message over multiple media. For example, a production manager might follow up a phone conversation about a critical schedule change with an email. Certainly for the communication of change processes it can be important to transmit your message over multiple media. This is necessary to reduce the resistance to change and to enhance acceptance of the announced changes (also see Chapter 16 on organisational diagnosis and change).

Communication is multidimensional and takes place at two separate but interrelated levels.[70] The **content level** ('what') covers basically factual or cognitive information, such as ideas, places, people and objects. The **relationship level** ('how') covers information on our emotional states or attitudinal reactions towards our environment. Consider the following example: 'Close the door!' and 'Would you mind closing the door, please?' The content of the messages is the same but different kinds of relationships are implicitly assumed.[71]

Much communication is actually an attempt to control a relationship. How can the angry reaction of a supervisor be explained when an employee indicates that the supervisor has made a mistake? On the content level the employee is right, but the supervisor has difficulty accepting that a subordinate corrects him. This example also illustrates that confusion between the two levels occurs frequently. Have you ever felt resistance from a colleague when you made remarks on his or her work? Criticising how a task is undertaken is quite often taken personally.

Communication is also influenced by the context in which it takes place (e.g. the space where the communication takes place or the temporal context). Difficulties with cross-cultural communication illustrate the importance of this context (see Chapter 12 on culture).

Feedback is the receiver's response to a message. Now the receiver becomes a sender. The receiver encodes a response and then transmits it to the original sender. This new message is then decoded and interpreted. Feedback is used as a comprehension check. It gives the initial senders an idea of how accurately their message has been understood. Feedback is influenced by perception and attribution and is a central element in process theories of motivation (see Chapter 6).

The distinction between sender and receiver is presented in a simple way to clarify the communication process. In real life, people are senders and receivers of messages simultaneously. When talking to someone, we are continuously looking at the effects of our words and, in doing so, receiving information from the so-called receiver. And vice versa: the receiver is reacting to the so-called sender's message while listening. The concept of communicators is proposed as an alternative to the distinction between sender and receiver.[72] The perceptual model of communication presents communication as a two-way process. A distinction can be made between one-way and two-way communication. One-way communication does not allow for immediate feedback, like sending a report to a colleague. Two-way communication has the opportunity to ask questions and to give feedback, as is possible in telephone calls or face-to-face conversations. One-way communication is usually faster but often less accurate than two-way communication.[73]

Noise represents anything that interferes with the transmission and understanding of a message. It affects all link in the communication process. Noise includes factors such as speech impairment, poor telephone connections, illegible handwriting, inaccurate statistics in a memo or report, poor hearing and eyesight and physical distance between sender and receiver and incompatible data formats.

Activity

Evaluate the following statements in terms of the encoding and decoding that may take place in creating and receiving them:

'This company imports and sells cars from exotic companies . . . Skoda, Daewoo, Isuzu.'
'This organisation faces some important challenges and opportunities. . . .'
'The organisation will be re-engineered to allow us to realise our full potential.'
'Have you noticed that the new vending machines are much smaller than the old ones?'

Barriers to effective communication

Communication noise is a barrier to effective communication as it interferes with the accurate transmission and reception of a message. Awareness of these barriers is a good starting point to improve the communication process. There are four key barriers to effective communication: process, personal, physical and semantic.

Every element of the perceptual model of communication shown in Figure 4.8 is a potential process barrier. Consider the following examples:

- *Sender barrier* A customer gets incorrect information from a customer service agent because he was recently hired and lacked experience.
- *Encoding barrier* An employee for whom English is a second language had difficulty explaining why a delivery was late.
- *Message barrier* An employee misses a meeting for which he or she never received a formal invitation.
- *Medium barrier* A salesperson gives up trying to make a sales call when the potential customer fails to return three previous phone calls.
- *Decoding barrier* An employee cannot respond to a supervisor's request to stop exhibiting 'passive aggressive' behaviour because the term is unknown to the employee.
- *Receiver barrier* A student who busy chatting on Facebook during a lecture asks the professor the same question as the one that has just been answered.
- *Feedback barrier* Nodding by an interviewer leads an interviewee to think that he or she is answering questions well.

Barriers in any of these process elements can distort the transfer of meaning. Reducing these barriers is essential for effective communication but is also a challenge in a world of considerable globalisation.

There are many **personal barriers** to communication. Eight of the more common ones are:

- People possess varying levels of communication skills.
- People use different frames of reference and experiences to interpret the world around them (see the previous sections on perception); people selectively attend to various stimuli. These differences affect both what we say and what we think we hear.

- The level of interpersonal trust between people can either prevent or enable effective communication. Communication is more likely to be distorted when trust is absent.
- The existence of stereotypes and prejudices can powerfully distort what we perceive about others (Chapter 9 on organisational climate discusses stereotypes).
- The egos of the people communicating can cause political battles, turf wars and the pursuit of power, recognition and resources. Egos influence how people treat each other as well as our receptivity to being influenced by others.
- The ability to listen varies.
- The natural tendency to evaluate or judge a sender's message from our own point of view or frame of reference. Strong feelings or emotions about the issue being discussed enhance our evaluation tendency.
- The inability to listen with understanding: seeing ideas and attitudes from the other person's point of view. Listening with understanding reduces defensiveness and improves accuracy in perceiving a message.

The distance between employees can be a physical barrier that interferes with effective communication. It is hard to understand someone who is speaking to you from 20 metres away. Noise is an additional barrier. Poor telephone lines or crashed computers represent physical barriers to effective communication through modern technologies. However, physical barriers can be reduced and walls can be torn down. This can create an open space office layout with easy communication – but lots of potential for noise problems. Making the optimum choice of medium and so reduce the physical barriers is a way to manage these barriers.

Semantics is the study of words. **Semantic barriers** show up as encoding and decoding errors because these phases of communication involve transmitting and receiving words and symbols. These barriers occur very easily. Consider the following brief statement: *crime is ubiquitous*.

Do you understand the statement? It might be simpler to say that 'crime is all around us' or 'crime is everywhere'. Choosing your words carefully is the easiest way to reduce semantic barriers. Avoiding jargon that is not familiar to the person you are talking to also helps avoiding miscommunication. This barrier can also be decreased by avoiding mixed messages and awareness of cultural diversity. Mixed messages occur when a person's words imply one message while his or her actions or non-verbal signals suggest something different.

Simple strategies may improve your personal communication skills. First, make sure your message is clear by using the following tips:

- *Empathy* Put yourself in the perspective of the receiver when you encode a message.
- *Redundancy* Repeat the major elements ('say what you are going to say, say it, and then say what you have said').
- *Effective timing* Choose a moment when it is less likely that the receiver is distracted by noise or other messages.
- *Descriptive* Focus on the problem instead of the person; give advice for improvement instead of blaming the receiver.
- *Feedback* Use feedback to check whether your message has been received and reached its response.
- *Ask questions.* Sum up meetings, explore the other side's ideas, objectives concerns, and so on.

Critical thinking

When a person tells you 'correct me if I'm wrong', it is a message encoded in words. Which different messages might this statement contain when it is encoded and decoded?

4.7 Interpersonal communication

The quality of interpersonal communication within an organisation is very important. People with good communication skills have been found to help groups make better decisions and to be promoted more frequently than individuals with less developed abilities.[74] Although there is no universally accepted definition of **communication competence**, it is a performance-based index of an individual's ability to use effectively the appropriate communication behaviour in a given context.[75]

Communication competence is determined by three components: communication abilities and traits, situational factors and the individuals involved in the interaction (see Figure 4.9). Cross-cultural awareness, for example, is an important communication ability or trait (Chapter 12). Communication competence also implies knowing which communication medium is most suitable in a given situation. Communication competence is also influenced by the individuals involved in the interaction. For example, people are likely to withhold information and react emotionally or defensively when interacting with someone they dislike or distrust. Communication competence can be improved by controlling one's communication skills.

Verbal and non-verbal communication

An important distinction in communication literature is the one between verbal (written and spoken) and non-verbal communication. Two major differences between verbal and non-verbal communication are commonly made.

Figure 4.9 Communication Competence Affects Upward Mobility

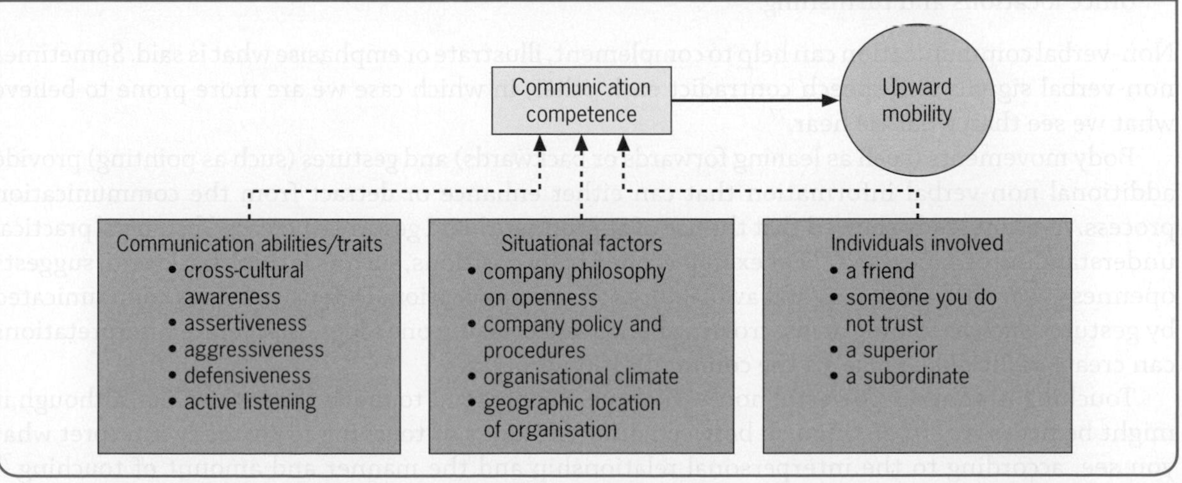

First, verbal communication is usually more conscious, while non-verbal signals are more automatic and unconscious. We rarely plan gestures and body movements during conversations, while we mostly do plan what to say or write. Second, non-verbal communication is not as clear and rule-bound as verbal communication. If your colleague looks at his watch, what does that mean? Are you boring him or does he have another appointment planned after this conversation? Consequently, non-verbal signals are more ambiguous and can be misinterpreted. Looking at the whole communication context might help to avoid misunderstandings. If your colleague is also leaning backwards and yawning while looking at his watch, there is a big chance you are indeed boring him.

Oral communication is the most frequent means of communication. Presentations, group discussions, face-to-face conversations, meetings, but also gossip and informal exchanges through the grapevine (which is the unofficial communication system of the informal organisation, as will be explained further in the chapter). Oral communication is fast and allows for immediate feedback. When an oral message is conveyed, rapid feedback is possible to check whether the receiver understands the message correctly. A major disadvantage of oral communication in organisations arises when a message has to pass through various people. Every receiver interprets the message differently and in the end, the content might be changed significantly. The more people are involved, the greater the chance that communication is distorted.

Writing is another way of verbal communication. Organisations typically use a lot of **written communication**: letters, emails, meeting minutes, manuals, organisational newsletters, reports. Written communication both has advantages and drawbacks. Writing leaves a record and can be easily verified. The message can be stored, which allows later reference to an existing written message (for instance, 'made a certain and eventually brilliant decision'). This implies that the message does not have to be repeated all over again. People can read it for themselves. Computers, networks and email have improved the efficiency of written communication significantly. Another advantage is that people usually think more carefully before writing something than before saying it. Consequently, a written message is probably clearer, more logical and better considered. These advantages come at a cost. Writing takes time, it is not very flexible and does not permit feedback, at least not instantaneously.

Non-verbal communication is any message, sent or received independently of the written or spoken word.

> [It] includes such factors as use of time and space, distance between persons when conversing, use of colour, dress, walking behaviour, standing, positioning, seating arrangement, office locations and furnishing.[76]

Non-verbal communication can help to complement, illustrate or emphasise what is said. Sometimes non-verbal signals and speech contradict each other, in which case we are more prone to believe what we see than what we hear.[77]

Body movements (such as leaning forwards or backwards) and gestures (such as pointing) provide additional non-verbal information that can either enhance or detract from the communication process. A recent study showed that the use of appropriate hand gestures increased listeners' practical understanding of a message.[78] For example, open body positions, such as leaning backward, suggests openness, warmth, closeness and availability for communication. Defensiveness is communicated by gestures such as folding arms, crossing hands and crossing one's legs. Inaccurate interpretations can create additional 'noise' in the communication process.

Touching is another powerful non-verbal cue. People tend to touch those they like, although it might be necessary to distinguish between different kinds of touching to correctly interpret what you see, according to the interpersonal relationship and the manner and amount of touching.[79]

Table 4.2 Norms for Touching Vary across Countries

China

- Hugging or taking someone's arm is considered inappropriate.
- Winking or beckoning with one's index finger is considered rude.

The Philippines

- Handshaking and a pat on the back are common greetings.

Indonesia

- Handshaking and head nodding are customary greetings.

Japan

- Business cards are exchanged before bowing or handshaking.
- A weak handshake is common.
- Lengthy or frequent eye contact is considered impolite.

Malaysia

- It is considered impolite to touch someone casually, especially on the top of the head.
- It is best to use your right hand to eat and to touch people and things.

South Korea

- Men bow slightly and shake hands, sometimes with two hands; women refrain from shaking hands.
- It is considered polite to cover your mouth while laughing.

Thailand

- Public displays of temper or affection are frowned on.
- It is considered impolite to point at anything using your foot or to show the soles of your feet.

Source: Guidelines taken from R. E. Axtell, *Gestures: The Do's and Taboos of Body Language Around the World* (New York: John Wiley & Sons, 1991).

A doctor who examines a patient touches only for professional reasons. More importantly, men and women interpret touching differently. It might be possible to diminish sexual harassment claims by keeping this perceptual difference in mind. Moreover, norms for touching vary significantly around the world (see Table 4.2).

Facial expressions convey a wealth of information. Smiling, for instance, typically represents warmth, happiness or friendship, whereas frowning conveys dissatisfaction or anger. However, the association between facial expressions and emotions varies across cultures.[80] One needs to be careful in interpreting facial expressions among diverse groups of employees. A smile, for example, does not convey the same emotion in different countries. In some cultures, people learn to suppress or hide their emotions. In Western countries; for instance, men are not supposed to cry, while women are not supposed to express anger in public.

Eye contact is a strong non-verbal cue that serves four functions in communication. First, eye contact regulates the flow of communication by signalling the beginning and end of conversation. There is a tendency to look away from others when beginning to speak and to look at them when done. Second, gazing (as opposed to glaring) facilitates and monitors feedback because it reflects interest and attention. Third, eye contact conveys emotion. People tend to avoid eye contact when discussing bad news or providing negative feedback. Fourth, gazing relates to the type of relationship between communicators. As is true for body movements, gestures and facial expressions, norms for eye contact vary across cultures. Westerners are taught at an early age to look at their parents when spoken to. In contrast, Asians are taught to avoid eye contact with a parent or superior in order to show obedience and subservience.[81]

OB in Real Life

Happy feet, beautiful shoes

Some people take great pride in their shoes, so much so that they cannot stop admiring them. However, for a small section of the populace, gazing at their own shoes has nothing to do with either shoes or feet. Nor does it happen all the time but only briefly and on select occasions.

Bob Sutton of Stanford University tells a story about an executive who one day was surprised and shocked when he was asked, 'When are the lay-offs?' The question came from an employee who simply took the ongoing communication amongst co-workers one step further and approached her boss. Amongst the employees, the expression 'the boss is wearing interesting shoes today' had become a standard code to indicate that when the executive paid his shoes a lot of attention, he would be relaying bad news. People who are unable to deliver bad news and look the recipient in the eye are probably quite common.

For discussion

Is it possible to change non-verbal communication patterns through training?

Active listening

A study showed that listening effectiveness was positively associated with success in sales and obtaining managerial promotions.[82] Estimates suggest that people typically spend about 9 per cent of a working day reading, 16 per cent writing, 30 per cent talking and 45 per cent listening.[83] Most people are not very good at listening. For example, communication experts estimate that people generally comprehend about 25 per cent of a typical verbal message. This problem is partly due to the fact that we can process information faster than most people talk. The average speaker communicates 125 words a minute while we can process 500 words a minute. Poor listeners use this information-processing gap to daydream and think about other things, thereby missing important parts of what is being communicated.[84]

Listening involves much more than hearing a message. Hearing is merely the physical component of listening. Listening is the process of *actively* decoding and interpreting verbal messages. Listening requires cognitive attention and information processing; hearing does not.

Listener comprehension represents the extent to which an individual can recall factual information and draw accurate conclusions and inferences from a verbal message. Factors that influence listener comprehension are the characteristics of the listener and the speaker, respectively. The character of the message and environmental conditions also play a role. Figure 4.10 illustrates the many influences on listening comprehension.

Assertiveness, aggressiveness and non-assertiveness

The saying 'You can attract more flies with honey than with vinegar' captures the difference between using an assertive communication style and an aggressive one. An **assertive style** is expressive and self-enhancing and is based on the 'ethical notion that it is not right or good to violate our own or others' basic human rights, such as the right to self-expression or the right to be treated with dignity and respect'.[85] An **aggressive style** is also expressive and self-enhancing but it tries to take

Figure 4.10 Listener Comprehension Model

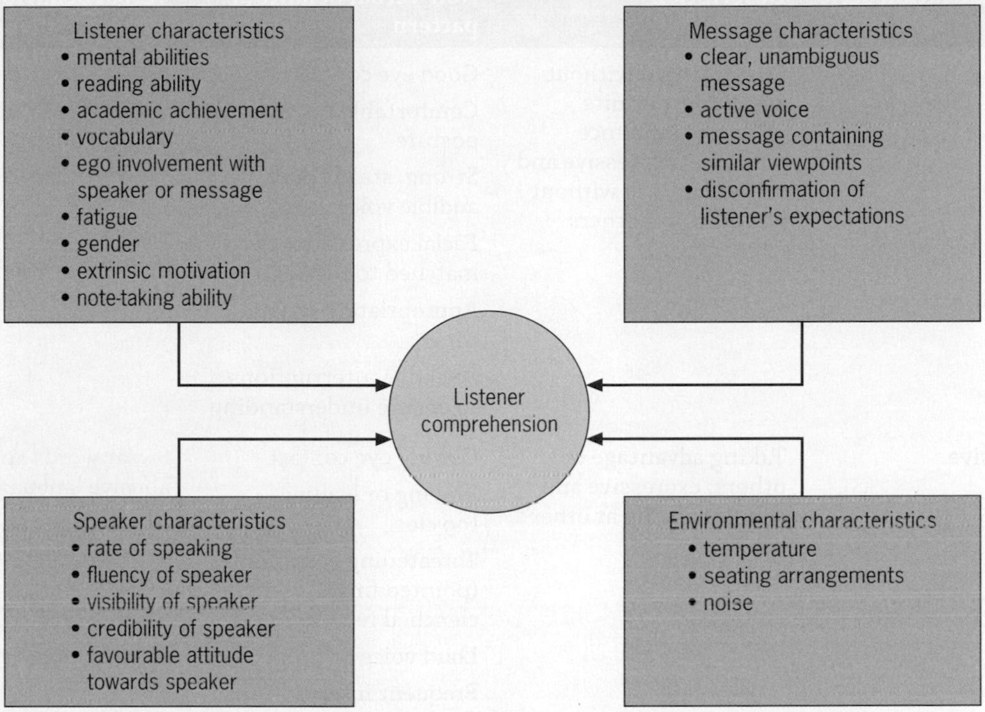

Source: Adapted from discussion in K. W. Watson and L. L. Barker, 'Listening Behavior: Definition and Measurement', in *Communication Yearbook 8*, ed. R. N. Bostrom (Beverly Hills, CA: Sage Publications, 1984), pp. 178–97.

unfair advantage of others. A **non-assertive style** is characterised by timid and self-denying behaviour. Non-assertiveness is ineffective because it gives the other person an unfair advantage. Non-assertiveness aims to appease others and avoid conflict at any cost.

It is possible to improve a person's communication competence by trying to be more assertive and less aggressive or non-assertive. This can be achieved by using the appropriate non-verbal and verbal behaviour listed in Table 4.3. Remember that non-verbal and verbal behaviour should complement and reinforce each other. One should attempt to use the non-verbal behaviour of good eye contact; a strong, steady and audible voice; and selective interruptions. Avoid non-verbal behaviour such as glaring or little eye contact; threatening gestures or a slumped posture; and a weak or whiny voice.

Appropriate verbal behaviour includes direct and unambiguous language and the use of 'I' messages instead of 'you' statements. For example, when you say, 'Mike, I was disappointed with your report because it contained spelling errors', rather than 'Mike, you made a bad report', then you reduce defensiveness. 'I' statements describe your feelings about someone's performance or behaviour instead of laying blame on the person. An alternative is the use of 'we' messages, as applied to the above example: 'Mike, we need to talk about your report, because there are some spelling errors. It is important that we deliver a good report.' 'We' messages help to convey an impression of partnership and joint responsibility for any problem to be discussed.[86] Of course, assertiveness implies more than reacting to behaviour of others. We distinguish between giving criticism, making clear requests and saying no.

Table 4.3 Communication Styles

Communication style	Description	Non-verbal behaviour pattern	Verbal behaviour pattern
Assertive	Pushing hard without attacking; permits others to influence outcome; expressive and self-enhancing without intruding on others	Good eye contact Comfortable but firm posture Strong, steady and audible voice Facial expressions matched to message Appropriately serious tone Selective interruptions to ensure understanding	Direct and unambiguous language No attributions or evaluations of other's behaviour Use of 'I' statements and co-operative 'we' statements
Aggressive	Taking advantage of others; expressive and self-enhancing at other's expense	Glaring eye contact Moving or leaning too close Threatening gestures (pointed finger, clenched fist) Loud voice Frequent interruptions	Swear words and abusive language Attributions and evaluations of other's behaviour Sexist or racist terms Explicit threats or put-downs
Non-assertive	Encouraging others to take advantage of us; inhibited; self-denying	Little eye contact Downward glances Slumped posture Constantly shifting weight Wringing hands Weak or whiny voice	Qualifiers ('maybe', 'kind of') Fillers ('uh', 'you know', 'well') Negaters ('It's not really that important', 'I'm not sure')

Source: Adapted in part from J. A. Waters, 'Managerial Assertiveness', *Business Horizons*, September–October 1982, pp. 24–9.

HR Evidence about non-verbal communication

Communication experts estimate that non-verbal communication is responsible for up to 60 per cent of a message being communicated. So, one's non-verbal signals should be consistent with one's intended verbal messages.

Women, in general, are more likely to focus on non-verbal signals when communicating, which explains why they are often better listeners than men. Men usually tend to focus more on words, both in conversations and written documents. The increase of impersonal communication through emails, faxes and documents favours male-oriented communication, while the rise of video-conferencing and other personal information technologies might be an advantage for women.[87]

Women nod their heads and moved their hands more than men. Leaning forward, large body shifts and foot and leg movements were exhibited more frequently by men.[88] Although it is both easy and fun to interpret body movements and gestures, it is important to remember that body-language analysis is subjective, easily misinterpreted and highly dependent on the context and cross-cultural differences.[89]

Application of interpersonal communication

To avoid confusion between the content and relationship levels of communication, it is important to give criticism in an appropriate way, focusing on the action and not on the person. Assertiveness implies being friendly towards the person, but being clear towards the task. The following advice can help to give criticism in an appropriate way, assuming that you have a higher rank than the other person:[90]

- Describe the situation or the behaviour of people to which you are reacting. Express your feelings and/or explain what impact the other's behaviour has on you.
- Give the other person the chance to react to your criticism. Empathise with the other person's position in the situation.
- Specify what changes you would like to see in the situation or in another person's behaviour and offer to negotiate those changes with the other person.
- Indicate, in a non-threatening way, the possible consequences if change does not occur.
- Summarise, after a two-way discussion, the agreed action, making sure the other person knows what is expected.
- Focus on 'the here-and-now': events from the past or old feelings may not influence your current interaction.

Making clear requests can help managers and others to avoid misunderstandings that lead to criticism. Clear requests can also help to fulfil unmet needs by simply asking for it. Some suggestions can help to make assertive requests:

- Decide what you want. This may not always be easy or clear-cut. First state what you do not want and then arrive at what you want through an elimination process.
- Decide whom to ask. This implies thinking about who can meet your request. Also prepare what to do when that person does not want to fulfil your request. It might be helpful to consider what impact your request may have on the other person.
- Decide when to ask. Timing is important when asking requests to someone.
- Decide how to ask. Do not speak in vague or ambiguous ways, because that makes it more difficult to understand clearly what you want.

Another important aspect of assertiveness implies saying 'no' to requests by other people. We often think that refusing a question will lead to anger or that the other person will not like us anymore. Or they may be hurt or think that we cannot cope with it. Accordingly, we often say yes while we want to say no, which may lead to an overload of work. We feel guilty saying no, although there is no reason for it. The following suggestions can help you to say no in an assertive way:

- Give reasons, not excuses.
- Keep it brief and simple, no long lists of reasons.
- Be clear and unambiguous that you refuse the request.
- Use appropriate non-verbal behaviour, which also fits with your verbal communication.
- Make use of the 'broken record' technique. This means calmly repeating the same message over and over again, without getting angry or changing your mind.

Activity

Estimate your potential for communication distortion

Instructions

Circle your response to each question by using the following scale:

1 = strongly disagree
2 = disagree
3 = neither agree nor disagree
4 = agree
5 = strongly agree

Supervisor's upward influence In general, my immediate supervisor can have a big impact on my career in this organisation.	1 2 3 4 5
Aspiration for upward mobility It is very important for me to progress upward in this organisation.	1 2 3 4 5
Supervisory trust I feel free to discuss the problems and difficulties of my job with my immediate supervisor without jeopardising my position or having it count against me later.	1 2 3 4 5
Withholding information I provide my immediate supervisor with a small amount of the total information I receive at work.	1 2 3 4 5
Selective disclosure When transmitting information to my immediate supervisor, I often emphasise those aspects that make me look good.	1 2 3 4 5
Satisfaction with communication In general, I am satisfied with the pattern of communication between my supervisor and I.	1 2 3 4 5

Arbitrary norms (to be considered per statement)

Low = 1–2
Moderate = 3
High = 4–5

Source: Adapted and excerpted in part from K. H. Roberts and C. A. O'Reilly III, 'Measuring Organizational Communication,' *Journal of Applied Psychology*, June 1974, p. 323.

4.8 Organisational communication patterns

Organisational communication implies both formal and informal communication, internal and external communication. Examining organisational communication patterns is a good way to identify factors contributing to effective and ineffective management. Employees seem not to receive enough information from their immediate supervisors. It is therefore no surprise to learn that many employees use unofficial, informal communication systems (the grapevine) as a source of information. This section promotes a working knowledge of two important communication patterns: hierarchical communication and the grapevine.

Hierarchical communication

Hierarchical communication is defined as 'those exchanges of information and influence between organisational members, at least one of whom has formal authority (as defined by official organisational sources) to direct and evaluate the activities of other organisational members'.[91] This communication pattern involves information exchanged downwards from supervisor to employee and upwards from employee to supervisor. Supervisors provide job instructions, job rationale, organisational procedures and practices, feedback about performances, official memos, policy statements and instillation of organisational goals. Employees communicate information upwards about themselves, co-workers and their problems, organisational practices and policies, and what needs to be done and how to do it. Timely and valid hierarchical communication can promote individual and organisational success.

In many companies hierarchical communication turns out to be highly problematic. Sometimes communication is non-existent, for example when it comes to telling employees about changes that are about to happen. When the information leaks (as it invariably will), such information can be damaging to morale, cause stress, as well as the departure of the most valuable people (and they are always the first to leave).

Another potential problem is **communication distortion** which occurs when an employee purposely modifies the content of a message, thereby reducing the accuracy of communication between managers and employees. Distortion tends to increase when supervisors have high upward influence or power (also see Chapter 14). However, these distortions come into a class of their own when used strategically. The standard organisational behaviour literature does not deal with this aspect of behaviour, but it is central in the field of organisational economics, which is concerned with incentives, payoffs, and the information flows associated with these concepts.

The grapevine

Even if supervisors communicate effectively with their employees, people will make use of the **grapevine**. The term originated from the US Civil War practice of stringing battlefield telegraph lines between trees. Today, the grapevine represents the unofficial communication system of the informal organisation (see also Chapter 7 on networks).[92] Information travelling along the grapevine supplements official or formal channels of communication. Although the grapevine can be a source of inaccurate rumours, it functions positively as an early warning sign for organisational changes, a medium for creating organisational culture, a mechanism for fostering group cohesiveness and a way of informally testing and discussing ideas. The grapevine is likely to be more active in organisations where people can communicate more easily and have similar backgrounds, because the grapevine is mainly based on informal social networks.

Contrary to general opinion, the grapevine is not necessarily counterproductive. It can help employees, managers and organisations alike to achieve desired results by helping employees to find the necessary information, particularly when it is not easily available through formal channels,[93] by relieving anxiety and by fulfilling the need for affiliation. This explains why the grapevine is far more active in times of uncertainty and ambiguity.[94] However, information in the grapevine is distorted by loss of detail and exaggeration, possibly adding to uncertainty and anxiety instead of reducing it. Moreover, when organisations fail to fill the gap between the official and unofficial messages quickly and effectively, employees will feel demotivated because it seems like management is not caring for them.

Communication in the grapevine follows predictable patterns (see Figure 4.11). The most frequent pattern is not a single strand or gossip chain but a cluster.[95] Although the probability and cluster patterns look similar, the process by which information is passed is very different. People gossip to others in a probability structure. For example, in the probability pattern in Figure 4.11 person A tells persons F and D a piece of information but ignores co-workers B and J. Person A may have done this simply because he or she ran into co-workers F and D in the corridor. In turn, persons F and D randomly discuss this information with others at work. In contrast, the cluster pattern is based on the idea that information is selectively passed from one person to another. People tend to communicate selectively because they know that certain individuals tend to leak or pass information to others, and they actually want the original piece of information to be spread around. For example the cluster pattern in Figure 4.11 shows that person A selectively discusses a piece of information with three people, one of whom – person F – tells two others, and then one of those two – person B – tells another. Only certain individuals repeat what they hear when the probability or cluster patterns are operating. People who consistently pass along grapevine information to others are called **liaison individuals** or 'gossips'.

Figure 4.11 Grapevine Patterns

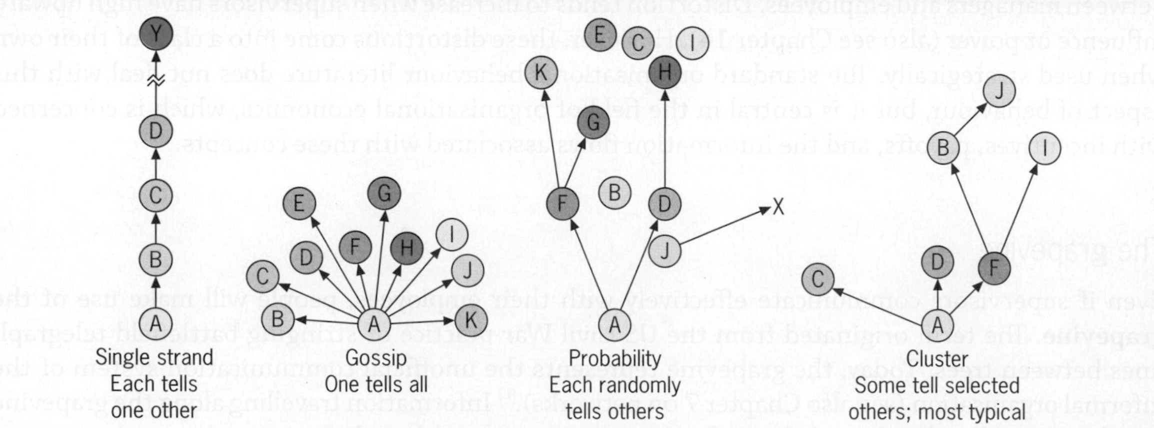

Source: K. Davis and J. W. Newstrom, *Human Behavior at Work: Organizational Behavior*, 7th edn (New York: McGraw-Hill, 1985), p. 317. Used with permission. Copyright © 1985. Reproduced with permission of the McGraw-Hill Companies.

Effective managers are able to monitor the pulse of work groups by regularly communicating with known liaison individuals. **Organisational moles**, however, use the grapevine for a different purpose. They obtain information, often negative, in order to enhance their power and status. They do this by secretly reporting their perceptions and hearsay about the difficulties, conflicts or failure of other employees to powerful members of management. This enables moles to divert attention away from themselves and to appear more competent than others. Organisations can counteract this behaviour and to try to create an open, trusting environment, since organisational moles can destroy teamwork, create conflict and damage productivity.

Communication differences between men and women

Differences in the way men and women communicate can create problems that undermine productivity and interpersonal communication. Five commonly observed (or claimed) communication problems between men and women are:

- Men are too authoritarian.
- Men do not take women seriously.
- Women are too emotional.
- Men do not accept women as co-workers or bosses.
- Women do not speak up enough.

Gender-based differences in communication are partly caused by the **linguistic styles** used by men and women, whether a person's characteristic speaking pattern or such features as 'directness or indirectness, pacing and pausing, word choice, and the use of such elements as jokes, figures of speech, stories, questions and apologies'.[96] These variations are culturally learned and are likely to vary with location (i.e. with national culture). Table 4.4 summarises the differences.

Differences in how men and women communicate may be caused by inherited biological (genetic) differences between the sexes. This perspective (the 'Darwinian' perspective or 'evolutionary psychology') attributes gender differences in communication to drives, needs and conflict associated with reproductive strategies used by men and women. Men communicate more aggressively, interrupt others more than women and hide their emotions because they have an inherent desire to possess features attractive to women in order to compete with other men for purposes of mate selection and cannot choose to turn off the biologically based determinants of their behaviour.[97]

In contrast, social role theory argues that girls learn conversational skills and habits that focus on rapport and relationships, whereas boys learn skills and habits that focus on status and hierarchies. Accordingly, women come to view communication as a network of connections in which conversations are negotiations for closeness. This orientation leads women to seek and give confirmation and support more so than men. Men, on the other hand, see conversations as negotiations in which people try to achieve and maintain the upper hand. Accordingly, it is important for men to protect themselves from others' attempts to put them down or push them around. This perspective increases men's need to maintain independence and avoid failure.[98]

The differences in how men and women communicate show some general tendencies, summarised in Table 4.4, even if there are men communicating in a feminine way – and vice versa. In any case, a person's linguistic style influences perceptions about their confidence, competence

Table 4.4 Communication Differences between Men and Women

Women are happy to ask for information in public situations	Men are less likely to ask for information or directions in public situations that would reveal their lack of knowledge
In decision-making, women are more likely to downplay their certainty	Men are more likely to downplay their doubts
Women tend to apologise even when they have done nothing wrong	Men tend to avoid apologies as signs of weakness or concession
Women tend to accept blame as a way of smoothing awkward situations	Men tend to ignore blame and place it elsewhere
Women tend to temper criticism with positive buffers	Men tend to give criticism directly
Women tend to insert unnecessary and unwarranted 'thank-yous' in conversations	Men may avoid thanks altogether as a sign of weakness
Women tend to ask 'What do you think?' to build consensus	Men often perceive that questions are a sign of incompetence and lack of confidence
Women tend to allow men to usurp their ideas without protest	Men tend to usurp [take] ideas stated by women and claim them as their own
Women use softer voice volume to encourage persuasion and approval	Men use louder voice volume to attract attention and maintain control
Women tend to give directions in indirect ways, a technique that may be perceived as confusing, less confident or manipulative by men	

Source: Excerpted from D. M. Smith, *Women at Work: Leadership from the Next Century* (Upper Saddle River, NJ: Prentice Hall, 2000), pp. 26–32.

and authority. These judgements may, in turn, affect their future job assignments and subsequent promotability.

Evidence about communication patterns

There is a vast literature on communication, some of it full of useful evidence. Here we provide a few samples. For example, an absence of job-related information causes unnecessary stress among employees.[99] Upward communication, on the other hand, provides bosses with necessary feedback concerning current organisational issues and problems and day-to-day operations to make effective decisions. It is also a source of feedback for the effectiveness of their downward communication.[100]

Employees tend to engage in communication distortion because of workplace politics, for strategic reasons or they are driven by a desire to manage impressions or fear of how a supervisor might respond to a message.[101] Employees also tend to modify or distort information when they aspire to move upwards and when they do not trust their supervisors.[102]

Past research about the grapevine has provided interesting insights. The grapevine is faster than formal channels; it is about 75 per cent accurate; people rely on it when they are insecure, threatened or faced with organisational changes; and employees use the grapevine to acquire the major part of their workplace information.[103] However, these findings may no longer be representative of the grapevine in an era of information and communication technologies.

Today, people are making use of email, instant message systems and social media to exchange informal messages besides traditional informal talks in the coffee corner of the organisation.

As a consequence, the informal social network of employees has expanded significantly, making it possible to gossip to anyone and not just to your own social network. It is even possible to post messages anonymously on certain websites so that everybody can see them. Electronic communication is easily misinterpreted. There is unfortunately, less room for subtleties of language or intonation, which makes it more difficult to see whether someone is making a joke, being sarcastic or telling the truth. If anything this places even greater weight on writing clear, unambiguous and readable text.

OB in Real Life

Men talk and talk; women speak with care

Men and women in the US senate who hold power (scored in the study along four dimensions: position, indirect influence, legislative activity and earmarks (legislative funding provisions)) were studied in terms of senators' speaking record on the senate floor.

The results were very distinct. Generally, power seems to be a licence to talk at length. This pattern is very clear for male senators, but it is absent for females. The volubility difference is not in question, since the data comes from the televised senate sessions. What is not clear is why there is a difference between the sexes.

To address this question, Victoria Brescoll set up a further experiment in which power could be varied. This confirmed the first result that women are less voluble (talking continuously) than men but it also points to an explanation. This is that women hold back in order to avoid being seen as too talkative. To further understand this effect a third experiment was carried out. Here the volubility of CEOs was assessed by 156 respondents and women who talked disproportionally longer were rated as being significantly less competent and less suitable for leadership than men who talked as much. Whether the rater was a man or a woman had no influence on the result.

Based on these results, women clearly seem to be better off if they stay relatively quiet. It is no coincidence that Brescoll ends her article by referring to Hilary Clinton's 'listening tour' that took place in the months before she was elected as a senator for the State of New York (she was, after all, from Chicago).

Source: Based on V. L. Brescoll 'Who takes the floor and why? Gender, power and volubility in organizations', *Administrative Science Quarterly*, vol. 56, no. 4, 2012, pp. 622–41.

Application: choosing communication patterns

The evidence suggests generally that timely and pertinent communication is a good idea. However, as we will see in Chapter 10, organisational structure strongly influences the volume and character of information that must be processed. Indeed the design of organisational structures is itself an exercise in creating (or removing) capacity to process information.

Lots of informal communication goes on alongside formal communication networks. The grapevine or informal communication networks supplement formal communications systems, sometimes being quicker and possibly also more accurate. The proliferation of digital communication can lead to formalisation, but the channels extend far beyond the reach of organisational systems. One aspect of informal systems is that they assist in the internal dissemination of hard to formalise information and knowledge, the kind that is full of causal ambiguity of the kind that is crucial to sustaining competitive advantage.[104]

Distortion is a fact of organisational life. Politics and strategic behaviour cannot be eradicated. However, one way to address distortion problems if they occur is to remove the factors that drive them – the chances for advancement through political gaming and the availability for financial gain from (distorted) communication and its companion, opportunistic behaviour.

One application of gender difference evidence is to recommend **genderflex**, the temporary use of communication behaviours typical of the other gender in order to increase the potential for influence.[105] For example, a woman might use sports analogies to motivate a group of males. This approach may increase understanding and sensitivity between the sexes.

Another approach is involving awareness of how linguistic styles work and how they influence our perceptions and judgements. Knowledge of linguistic styles may help ensure that people with valuable insights or ideas get a hearing.

Knowledge of differences in linguistic style can assist in devising methods to ensure everyone's ideas are heard and given fair credit in any organisational conversation. Similarly, this knowledge can remind members of either sex that the other side has another way of saying the same thing.

4.9 Strategic and asymmetric information

Two overarching perspectives have dominated in this chapter, that of the perceiver, who receives information in some form, and that of the communicator who sends information to a range of receivers. These views only indirectly allow for the possibility that either sender or recipient can be opportunistic, by using or manipulating the information in a way that gives the perceiver or communicator the greatest personal benefit. It is worth noting that if we are members of an organisation we will find ourselves in both roles, even without thinking about it.

The most explicit discussion of this type of issue appears in this chapter, under the heading of 'barriers to effective communication'. Communication can be wilfully distorted if trust is absent or when it is part of a political process in the organisation. The important element not covered in the section on communication distortion is that it may not be random or accidental, but may rather have a motive. Though usually the domain of economists and often part of a course on microeconomics, strategic use of information is an integral part of understanding how people behave in organisations.

This section briefly outlines the two core concepts of information economics as they apply to organisations. The first concept is 'hidden information' or **adverse selection**, which operates before a deal is made (remember that deals are made all the time inside organisations, even if there is no real market with defined prices and quantities). The second concept, 'hidden action' or **moral hazard**, refers to the actions of the parties after the deal has been made (deals made inside organisations must be implemented, just as any other deal).

The following OB in Real Life is a case of hidden information or adverse selection. This refers to the time before a contract is signed. The woman has private information about her reproductive plans. Even if the classic early work on hidden information concerned the market for used cars,[106] adverse selection can occur equally well in organisational settings, both when they engage in market transactions as in the example outlined here, and when internal deals are made. For example, you as a manager may be keen to sell your new idea and you might be tempted to downplay the negative sides of it.

OB in Real Life

Hidden information or adverse selection

A woman aged 30 years is applying for a job. Her educational background and experience makes her an outstanding candidate. Despite her obvious qualities, the organisation hesitates. One item of information about this woman is hidden; her reproductive plans. For all the hiring manager knows, she might already be pregnant. He would love to ask her about that particular part of her life, although she is unlikely to answer. In the interest of gender equality, many countries in fact ban this type of question. For her part, she is unlikely to reveal her plans, since she has reason to believe that it will reduce her prospects of getting the job if she does.

Organisations are interested in pregnancies because they remove the employee from circulation for extended periods (the latter stages of pregnancy, childbirth itself, maternity leave and subsequent sick leave when the child is sick). Even if the organisation is not required to pay the woman while she is not working, she represents an idle investment in terms of training, knowledge and skills.

Hidden action

People working in organisations are not monitored all the time. Monitoring is costly and constant monitoring is out of the question. Without monitoring, some of these workers could get away with doing no work and still get their regular salaries.

In most cases there is a little bit of monitoring; for example, a log of attendance. In addition, co-workers can act as additional informal monitors. If the workload is constant the absence of a person will increase the work the others have to do, making the absentee unpopular to some degree.

During the periods without monitoring, the worker can do his or her work (output monitoring is often used) but any spare time is unaccounted for – the managers may not even know there is any time left over. When the actions of subordinates (sometimes called agents) cannot be observed by superiors (sometimes principals), there is a case of hidden action (or inaction) or moral hazard. This expression comes from the insurance industry, where having insurance subtly changes behaviour to being more risky. However, the implications of hidden action have been known for centuries. For example, Adam Smith in *The Wealth of Nations* published in 1776 has little faith in joint stock companies (precursors for modern corporations)[107] because managers' actions were to a degree hidden from stock owners (shareholders).

The twin problems of hidden information and hidden action can be uncovered in endless organisational contexts. Both formal structure and organisational culture can moderate the effects. The use of steep performance incentives, on the other hand, can lead to unfortunate results that originate in information problems. This is discussed in the context of motivation in Chapters 5 and 6.

Evidence about asymmetric information

Evidence about adverse selection mechanisms at work inside organisations is rare. One study found that in an experimental setting the adverse selection model can be used to explain why projects are sometimes continued despite indications that they are failing.[108] However, the effects of adverse selection declined when project outcomes became strongly negative. Managers responsible for the failing project can also be viewed as being affected by the 'escalation of commitment' tendency discussed in Chapter 13.

Evidence about moral hazard, caused by 'hidden action' is almost as difficult to come by. One of the situations in which moral hazard is believed to exist is in the structure of top managers' pay. Managers can reduce shareholder value in a number of ways, including selling assets below their market value,[109] insufficient disclosure of pertinent information,[110] tolerating high costs,[111] and pursuing various personal objectives such as increased compensation, diversification and merger activity, that misuse free cash flow.[112] A study of situations where the interests of top manages had supposedly been aligned with those of shareholders, found that the commonly adopted instrument, stock options, can indeed work to reduce moral hazard, but that once these options can be exercised, they can lead to an overstatement of short-term financial performance of the firm they lead,[113] regardless of whether these statements are in fact fraudulent or not. This study relied on the concept of 'CEO duality', that is, when the CEO is also chair of the board and on the extent to which board members themselves received stock options. It showed (among other things) that a 'president and CEO' combined with a board holding stock options and no CEO stock options significantly increased the likelihood that fraudulent reporting would occur. Giving the CEO stock options then reduces the likelihood of fraud.

At its core both adverse selection and moral hazard is a question of information and communication. It might be described as an overlay of opportunism on top (or mixed into) the communication and perception process. The consequences of asymmetric information for motivation policies and instruments are discussed further in Chapter 6.

! Critical thinking

Is the economists' way of thinking about information consistent with that of OB scholars?

4.10 Dynamics of modern communication

Effective communication is the cornerstone of survival in today's competitive business environment. This is particularly true for companies that operate or compete worldwide or those undertaking significant organisational change. Those who use information technology effectively are more likely to contribute to organisational success. We conclude this chapter on communication with some relevant issues for modern communication. We also elaborate a contingency approach for choosing communication media and focus on how to deal with the huge amount of information that is available to us.

Choosing media: a contingency perspective

Media selection is a key component of communication effectiveness. If an inappropriate medium is used, decisions may be based on inaccurate information, important messages may not reach the intended audience and employees may become dissatisfied and unproductive. We propose a contingency model that is designed to help people select communication media in a systematic and effective manner. Media selection in this model is based on the interaction between information richness and the complexity of the problem or situation at hand.

Information richness has been defined as 'the information carrying capacity of data'. If the communication of an item of data, such as a wink, provides substantial new understanding, it would be considered rich. If the datum provides little understanding, it would be low in richness'.[114]

Information richness refers to the information-carrying capacity of a medium, which means the volume and variety of information that can be transmitted. As this definition implies, alternative media possess levels of information richness that vary from high to low.

Information richness is determined by four factors:

- Feedback (ranging from fast to very slow).
- Channel (ranging from the combined visual and audio characteristics of a video-conference to the limited visual aspects of a computer report).
- Type of communication (ranging from personal to impersonal).
- Language source (ranging from the natural body language and speech contained in a face-to-face conversation to the numbers contained in a financial report).

Face-to-face contact is the richest form of communication. It provides immediate feedback, which serves as a comprehension check and makes it possible to customise the information exchange to the situation. Moreover, multiple communication channels, like verbal and non-verbal ones, are used simultaneously. Although high in richness, telephone and videoconferencing are not as informative as the face-to-face medium. In contrast, newsletters, computer reports and emails possess the lowest richness. Feedback for these media is very slow, the channels involving only limited visual information and the information provided being generic or impersonal.

Organisational situations and problems range from low to high in complexity. Low complexity situations are routine, predictable and are managed by using objective or standard procedures. These situations are straightforward and have a minimum of ambiguity. Calculating an employee's pay is an example of low complexity. Highly complex situations, like a corporate reorganisation, are ambiguous, unpredictable, hard to analyse and often emotion-laden. Professionals spend considerably more time analysing these situations because they rely on more sources of information during their deliberations. There are no set solutions to complex problems or situations.

The contingency model for selecting media is graphically depicted in Figure 4.12 Effective communication occurs when the richness of the medium is matched appropriately with the complexity

Figure 4.12 A Contingency Model for Selecting Communication Media

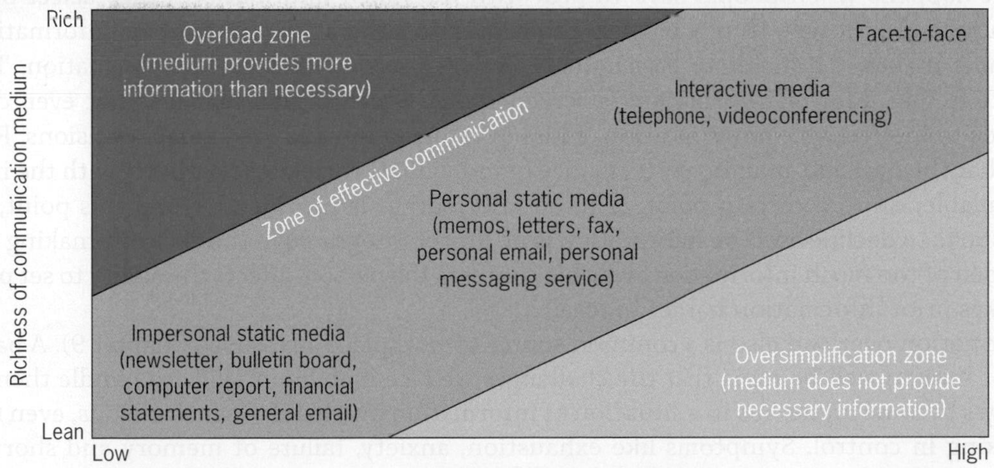

Sources: Adapted from R. Lengel and R. L. Daft, 'The Selection of Communication Media as an Executive Skill', *Academy of Management Executive*, August 1988, p. 226; and R. L. Daft and R. H. Lengel, 'Information Richness: A New Approach to Managerial Behavior and Organization Design', *Research in Organizational Behavior*, eds B. M. Staw and L. L. Cummings (Greenwich, CT: JAI Press, 1984) p. 199.

of the problem or situation. Media low in richness – impersonal static or personal static – are better suited to simple problems, while media high in richness – interactive media or face-to-face – are appropriate for complex problems or situations.

Conversely, ineffective communication occurs when the medium is either too rich or insufficiently rich for the complexity of the problem or situation. For example, a district sales manager would fall into the overload zone if he or she communicated monthly sales reports through face-to-face meetings or telephoning each salesperson (both rich media forms), would provide excessive information and would take more time than necessary to communicate monthly sales data. The oversimplification zone represents ineffective choice of communication medium used to communicate complicated problems. An example would be an executive who uses a letter or an email message to communicate news of a merger or a major reorganisation. This choice of medium is ineffective because employees are likely to be nervous and concerned about how a merger or reorganisation will affect their futures. Choosing the wrong medium in this situation will lead to misunderstanding and accordingly take a longer time to resolve things.

Helpful questions to select the most appropriate medium to deliver your message are for instance:

- How much information do I have to transmit?
- Is speed of importance?
- Is feedback needed?
- Does the message require deeper elaboration?
- Which media are certainly inappropriate for delivering the message?

Sometimes it can be necessary to use multiple media to convey your message effectively.

Evidence about the dynamics of communication

Information overload is a serious problem in many organisations, leading to a decrease in productivity. Managing information effectively within the organisation has become critically important because it provides a basis for gaining a competitive advantage.[115]

What happens when people have to deal with too much information? They select or ignore information; they forget things or pass them over to others. The amount of information that is available makes it difficult to discriminate between useless and useful information. The consequence is that a lot of information is screened out, which means that it is not even decoded. This leads to ineffective communication, a loss of information and inadequate decisions. Research shows that the decision-making performance of individuals correlates positively with the information available, up to a certain point. If more information is provided beyond this point, performance starts to decline and the information is no longer integrated in the decision-making process. The burden of too much information available confuses the person, affects the ability to set priorities and makes prior information harder to recall.[116]

Information overload also is a common source of workplace stress (see Chapter 9). A basic condition of human well-being is that the challenges we face match our skills to handle them. If the challenges become higher (as in a situation of information overload), we feel anxious, even fatigued and lacking in control. Symptoms like exhaustion, anxiety, failure of memory and shortness of attention are characteristic of this condition.[117]

Information overload also puts us under pressure to multitask, which means doing several tasks simultaneously: for example, talking on the phone while reading and writing emails. This leads to an inability to focus and makes us easily feel frustrated.

Application of communication dynamics

People do not have an infinite capacity to process information. Herbert Simon was the first to introduce the concept of bounded rationality, referring to the finding that people have limited cognitive abilities to process information (see Chapters 1 and 13).[118] When the information we have to work with exceeds our processing capacity, this results in information overload. The current diversity of communication media and technologies and the pressure to compete globally mean that more and more people feel overwhelmed by too much information and are unable to respond adequately to all the messages that reach them or to make adequate decisions with the available information.

Solutions to deal with information overload in organisations can be introduced both at the individual and organisational level.[119] Some organisations, for instance, encourage their employees to send fewer emails or discourage the use of the word 'urgent' when sending mails. Solutions to solve information overload can focus on two different aspects: increasing the information-processing capacity of people or reducing the information load that reaches people. Similarly, **netiquette rules** can help to develop an organisational policy for effective email writing and use; solutions to deal with information overload can be integrated in an organisational policy (see Table 4.5).

This also implies setting a time limit for how long you will search for information. It is easy to keep on searching and finding more and more information, even if you already have enough.

Table 4.5 Developing an Organisational Policy to Counter Information Overload

- Make use of an exception principle to regulate the information flow. This means that only exceptions or deviations from policies or procedures should be reported. Is it really necessary to email everyone in the department when reporting on the status of a project? Think twice before forwarding an article, interesting website or joke to colleagues. Do they really need this?
- Provide abstracts or summaries instead of entire documents if you want to inform a colleague of something. The entire document can be delivered later on when it is more useful.
- Make use of human interventions, like personal assistants, to select your messages. Only those documents or messages that are essential are forwarded.
- Install filters to banish unwanted junk mail (called spam) from mailboxes.
- Make use of intranet systems to store information that can be useful for multiple users. This will reduce the number of emails that are sent within organisations. Intranets also increase employees' access to information.
- Encourage people to use all kind of folders on their PCs or laptops to store information that they may need later on without having to consider it immediately. People often have the tendency to try to process all information that reaches them immediately, even if they cannot use it at that moment. This also means creating folders for low-priority emails that can be dealt with when there is time.
- Promote information literacy in individuals via appropriate training. Information literacy refers to the ability to access, evaluate and use information from a variety of sources. The key to information management is focusing on the quality of the data you receive.
  The necessary steps for information literacy are:
- To learn to articulate the information you need (this means, for instance, understanding your goals and priorities).
- To develop a sourcing strategy for finding the information you need (for instance, identifying potential sources, including books, articles, databases, people with expertise in that matter, and common keywords concerning the information you are looking for).

Learning outcomes: Summary of key terms

1 **Antecedents influencing the perceptual process**

Three groups of antecedents influence our perception. The first important group refers to the features of the perceived target. Some stimuli attract more attention than others. Novelty, brightness, dominance in the visual field, unusual behaviour and functioning of the target are attention-drawing characteristics. We perceive a target as a whole rather than the sum of its constituents. Perceptual grouping is the tendency which leads us to perceive objects as well-organised patterns rather than separate components. Four main factors determine perceptual grouping: continuity, closure, proximity and similarity. A second important group of antecedents affecting the perceptual process is labelled as 'setting'. The setting in which the interaction between perceiver and perceived target takes place influences the perception. Cultural context, for example, may be of great relevance in understanding the formation of perceptions. Finally, some features associated with the perceiver are an important group of antecedents (e.g. mood, gender, personality, attitudes etc.)

2 **Perception in terms of the social information processing model**

Perception is a mental and cognitive process that enables us to interpret and understand our surroundings. Social perception, also known as social cognition and social information processing, is a four-stage process. The four stages are selective attention/comprehension, encoding and simplification, storage and retention, and retrieval and response. During social cognition, salient stimuli are matched with schemata, assigned to cognitive categories and stored in long-term memory for events, semantic materials or people.

3 **Implications of social perception**

Social perception affects hiring decisions and performance appraisals. Inaccurate or racist and sexist schemata may be used to evaluate job applicants. Similarly, faulty schemata about what constitutes good versus poor performance can lead to inaccurate performance appraisals. Invalid schemata need to be identified and replaced with appropriate schemata through coaching and training. Further, professionals are advised to use objective rather than subjective measures of performance.

4 **Correspondent inference theory**

The correspondent inference theory describes how an alert perceiver infers another's intentions and personal dispositions from his or her behaviour. This theory explains how we use others' behaviour as a cornerstone for inferring their stable dispositions. The chance that a disposition is derived from a perceived slice of behaviour is dependent on three factors – non-common effects, social desirability of effects and degree of choice.

5 **Formulation of external and internal causal attributions**

Attribution theory attempts to describe how people infer causes for observed behaviour. According to Kelley's covariation model, external attributions tend to be made when consensus, consistency and distinctiveness are high or when consensus and consistency are low and distinctiveness high. Internal (personal responsibility) attributions tend to be made when consensus and distinctiveness are low and consistency is high.

6 **The self-fulfilling prophecy and its use**

The self-fulfilling prophecy, also known as the Pygmalion effect, describes how people behave so that their expectations come true. High expectations foster high employee self-expectations.

These, in turn, lead to greater effort and better performance, and yet higher expectations. Conversely, the set-up-to-fail syndrome represents the negative side of the self-fulfilling prophecy. Professionals are encouraged to harness the Pygmalion effect by building a hierarchical framework that reinforces positive performance expectations throughout the organisation.

7 **The perceptual process model of communication**

Communication is a process of consecutively linked elements. Historically, this process was described in terms of a conduit model. Criticisms of this model led to the development of a perceptual process model of communication that depicts receivers as information processors who create the meaning of messages in their own mind. Because receivers' interpretations of messages often differ from those intended by senders, miscommunication is a common occurrence. Noise refers to anything that interferes with the transmission and understanding of a message. Communication occurs on two separate but interrelated levels – the content and the relationship level – and needs to be interpreted in the context wherein it takes place.

8 **Barriers to effective communication**

Every element of the perceptual model of communication is a potential process barrier. There are eight personal aspects that commonly become a barrier for effective communication: (a) the ability to communicate effectively; (b) the way people process and interpret information; (c) the level of interpersonal trust between people; (d) the existence of stereotypes and prejudice; (e) the egos of the people communicating; (f) the inability to listen; (g) the natural tendency to evaluate or judge a sender's message; and (h) the inability to listen with understanding. Physical barriers pertain to distance, physical objects, time, and work and office noise. Semantic barriers show up as encoding and decoding errors because these phases of communication involve transmitting and receiving words and symbols. Cultural diversity is a key contributor to semantic barriers.

9 **Oral, written and non-verbal communication skills**

Oral communication refers to all verbal communication that is spoken. It is fast and allows for immediate feedback. Written communication refers to all kinds of verbal communication that is written. Written communication makes information distribution to a lot of people possible; it is tangible and can be verified easily. Body movements and gestures, touch, facial expressions and eye contact are important non-verbal cues. The interpretation of these nonverbal cues varies significantly across cultures.

10 **Listener comprehension and listening styles**

Listening is the process of actively decoding and interpreting verbal messages. Characteristics of the listener, speaker, message and environment influence listener comprehension. Communication experts identified three unique listening styles. A **results-style listener** likes to hear the bottom line or result of a message at the beginning of a conversation. **Reasons-style listeners** want to know the rationale for what someone is saying or proposing. **Process-style listeners** like to discuss issues in detail. Good listeners use the following 10 listening habits: (a) capitalise on thought speed by staying with the speaker and listening between the lines; (b) listen for ideas rather than facts; (c) identify areas of interest between the speaker and listener; (d) judge content and not delivery; (e) do not judge until the speaker has completed his or her message; (f) put energy and effort into listening; (g) resist distractions;

(h) listen to both favourable and unfavourable information; (i) read or listen to complex material to exercise the mind; and (j) take notes when necessary and use visual aids to enhance understanding.

11 **Communication styles**

An assertive style is expressive and self-enhancing but does not violate other people's basic human rights. In contrast, an aggressive style is expressive and self-enhancing but takes unfair advantage of others. A non-assertive style is characterised by timid and self-denying behaviour. An assertive communication style is more effective than either an aggressive or non-assertive style. Assertiveness is important when giving criticism, making clear requests and saying no to requests of others.

12 **Hierarchical communication**

Hierarchical communication patterns describe exchanges of information between supervisors and their employees. Supervisors provide five types of downward communication: job instructions, job rationale, organisational procedures and practices, feedback about performance, and indoctrination of goals. Employees communicate information upwards about themselves, co-workers and their problems, organisational practices and policies, and what needs to be done and how to do it. The grapevine is the unofficial communication system of the informal organisation. Communication along the grapevine follows four predictable patterns: single strand, gossip, probability and cluster. The cluster pattern is the most common.

13 **Asymmetric information**

When information about important decisions is unevenly distributed the opportunity for opportunistic exploitation of this asymmetry arises. Situations of asymmetric information can involve adverse selection (hidden information about one part to an agreement or contract) or moral hazard (hidden action by one part to an agreement after it has been made). Contracts, both formal ones and implicit ones, can be structured to reduce or avoid information asymmetries.

14 **The contingency approach to media selection**

Selecting media is a key component of communication effectiveness. Media selection is based on the interaction between the information richness of a medium and the complexity of the problem/situation at hand. Information richness ranges from low to high and is a function of four factors: speed of feedback, characteristics of the channel, type of communication and language source. Problems/situations range from simple to complex. Effective communication occurs when the richness of the medium matches the complexity of the problem at hand. Richer media need to be used as situations become more complex.

15 **Information overload**

Our 'Information Age' leads to an ever-increasing amount of information. When the information exceeds our information processing capacity, this results in information overload. Information overload leads to decreased productivity, ineffective communication, loss of information, inadequate decisions and workplace stress. Solutions to deal with information overload in organisations can be introduced at the individual level but also at the organisational level. These solutions can focus on two different aspects: increasing the information-processing capacity of people or reducing the information load that reaches people.

Review questions

1 Why is perception and attribution important?
2 When you are sitting in your course group, what stimuli are salient? What is your schema for course group activity?
3 A fellow student starts arguing in class with your lecturer. How would you formulate an attribution, according to Kelley's model?
4 In what situations do you tend to attribute your successes/failures to luck?
5 When did you last have trouble decoding a message – and what caused the problem?
6 Describe noises that interfere with communications you are trying to receive.
7 Explain which barrier to effective communication you think is most difficult to reduce?
8 Give some examples of non-verbal communication you have registered?
9 How would you describe your prevailing communication style?
10 Have you ever experienced gender differences concerning communication?
11 Is communication overload, effective communication or oversimplification most common in today's large organisations?
12 Have you ever felt overwhelmed with information?

Personal awareness and growth exercise

Assessing your listening skills

Objectives

1 To assess your listening skills.
2 To develop a personal development plan aimed at increasing your listening skills.

Introduction

Listening is a critical component of effective communication. Unfortunately, research and case studies suggest that many of us are not very good at actively listening. This is particularly bad in light of the fact that people spend more time listening than they do speaking or writing. This exercise provides you with the opportunity to assess your listening skills and develop a plan for improvement.

Instructions

The following statements reflect various habits we use when listening to others. For each statement, indicate the extent to which you agree or disagree with it by selecting one number from the scale provided. Circle your response for each statement. Remember, there are no right or wrong answers. After completing the survey, add up your total score for the 17 items and record it in the space provided.

Listening skills survey
1 = strongly disagree
2 = disagree
3 = neither agree nor disagree
4 = agree
5 = strongly agree

1	I daydream or think about other things when listening to others.	1	2	3	4	5
2	I do not mentally summarise the ideas being communicated by a speaker.	1	2	3	4	5
3	I do not use a speaker's body language or tone of voice to help interpret what he or she is saying.	1	2	3	4	5
4	I listen more for facts than overall ideas during classroom lectures.	1	2	3	4	5
5	I tune out dry speakers.	1	2	3	4	5
6	I have a hard time paying attention to boring people.	1	2	3	4	5
7	I can tell whether someone has anything useful to say before he or she finishes communicating a message.	1	2	3	4	5
8	I stop listening to a speaker when I think he or she has nothing interesting to say.	1	2	3	4	5
9	I get emotional or upset when speakers make jokes about issues or things that are important to me.	1	2	3	4	5
10	I get angry or distracted when speakers use offensive words.	1	2	3	4	5
11	I do not expend a lot of energy when listening to others.	1	2	3	4	5
12	I pretend to pay attention to others even when I'm not really listening.	1	2	3	4	5
13	I get distracted when listening to others.	1	2	3	4	5
14	I deny or ignore information and comments that go against my thoughts and feelings.	1	2	3	4	5
15	I do not seek opportunities to challenge my listening skills.	1	2	3	4	5
16	I do not pay attention to the visual aids used during lectures.	1	2	3	4	5
17	I do not take notes on handouts when they are provided.	1	2	3	4	5

Total score = ____________

Preparing a personal development plan

1 Use the following norms to evaluate your listening skills:
17–34 = good listening skills
35–53 = moderately good listening skills
54–85 = poor listening skills
How would you evaluate your listening skills?

2 Do you agree with the assessment of your listening skills? Why or why not?

3 The 17-item listening skills survey was developed to assess the extent to which you use the keys to effective listening. Ten keys to effective listening are presented in the following table:

Keys to effective listening	The bad listener	The good listener
1 Capitalise on thought speed	Tends to daydream	Stays with the speaker, mentally summarises the speaker, weighs evidence and listens between the lines
2 Listen for ideas	Listens for facts	Listens for central or overall ideas
3 Find an area of interest	Tunes out dry speakers or subjects	Listens for any useful information
4 Judge content, not delivery	Tunes out dry or monotone speakers	Assesses content by listening to entire message before making judgements
5 Hold your fire	Gets too emotional or worked up by something said by the speaker and enters into an argument	Withholds judgement until comprehension is complete
6 Work at listening	Does not expend energy on listening	Gives the speaker full attention
7 Resist distractions	Is easily distracted	Fights distractions and concentrates on the speaker
8 Hear what is said	Shuts out or denies unfavourable information	Listens to both favourable and unfavourable information
9 Challenge yourself	Resists listening to presentations of difficult subject matter	Treats complex presentations as exercise for the mind
10 Use handouts, overheads or other visual aids	Does not take notes or pay attention to visual aids	Takes notes as required and uses visual aids to enhance understanding of the presentation

Sources: Derived from N. Skinner, 'Communication Skills', *Selling Power*, July/August 1999, pp. 32–4; and G. Manning, K. Curtis and S. McMillen, *Building the Human Side of Work Community* (Cincinnati, OH: Thomson Executive Press, 1996), pp. 127–54.

Use the table and the development plan format to prepare your development plan. First, identify the five statements from the listening skills survey that received your highest ratings – high ratings represent low skills. Record the survey numbers in the space provided in the development plan. Next, compare the content of these survey items to the descriptions of bad and good listeners shown in the table above. This comparison will help you identify the keys to effective listening being measured by each survey item. Write down the keys to effective listening that correspond to each of the five items you want to improve. Finally, write down specific actions or behaviours that you can undertake to improve the listening skill being considered.

Development plan

Survey items	Key to effective listening I want to improve	Action steps required (what do you need to do to build listening skills for this listening characteristic?)

Group exercise

Practising different styles of communication

Objectives

1 To demonstrate the relative effectiveness of communicating assertively, aggressively and non-assertively.

2 To give you hands-on experience with different styles of communication.

Introduction

Research shows that assertive communication is more effective than either an aggressive or non-assertive style. This role-playing exercise is designed to increase your ability to communicate assertively. Your task is to use different communication styles while attempting to resolve the work-related problems of a poor performer.

Instructions

Form a group of three and read the 'poor performer' and 'store manager' roles provided here. Then decide who will play the poor performer role, who the managerial role, and who the observer. The observer will be asked to provide feedback to the manager after each role play. When playing the managerial role, you should first attempt to resolve the problem by using an aggressive communication style. Attempt to achieve your objective by using the non-verbal and verbal behaviour patterns associated with the aggressive style shown in Table 4.3. Take about four to six minutes to act out the instructions. The observer should give feedback to the manager after completing the role play. The observer should comment on how the employee responded to the aggressive behaviours displayed by the manager.

After feedback is provided on the first role play, the person playing the manager should then try to resolve the problem with a non-assertive style. Observers once again should provide feedback. Finally, the manager should confront the problem with an assertive style. Once again, rely on the relevant non-verbal and verbal behaviour patterns presented in Table 4.3, and take four to six minutes to act out each scenario. Observers should try to provide detailed feedback on how effectively the manager exhibited non-verbal and verbal assertive behaviours. Be sure to provide positive and constructive feedback.

After completing these three role plays, switch roles: manager becomes observer, observer becomes poor performer and poor performer becomes manager. When these role plays are completed, switch roles once again.

Role: poor performer

You sell shoes full time for a national chain of shoe stores. Over the past month, you have been absent three times without giving your manager a reason. The quality of your work has been slipping. You have a lot of creative excuses when your boss tries to talk to you about your performance.

When playing this role, feel free to invent a personal problem that you may eventually want to share with your manager. However, make the manager dig for information about this problem. Otherwise, respond to your manager's comments as you would normally.

Role: store manager

You manage a store for a national chain of shoe stores. In the privacy of your office, you are talking to one of your salespeople who has had three unexcused absences from work during the last month.

(This is excessive, according to company guidelines, and must be corrected.) The quality of the person's work has been slipping. Customers have complained that this person is rude and co-workers have told you this individual is not carrying a fair share of the work. You are fairly sure this person has some sort of personal problem. You want to identify that problem and get him or her back on course.

Questions for discussion

1 What drawbacks of the aggressive and non-assertive styles did you observe?

2 What were major advantages of the assertive style?

3 What were the most difficult aspects of trying to use an assertive style?

4 How important was non-verbal communication during the various role plays? Explain with examples.

Online
Learning Centre

When you have read this chapter, log on to the Online Learning Centre website at ***www.mcgraw-hill.co.uk/textbooks/sinding*** to access test questions, additional exercises and other related resources.

Notes

[1] Details may be found in R. Eisenberger, P. Fasolo and V. Davis-LaMastro, 'Perceived Organizational Support and Employee Diligence, Commitment, and Innovation', *Journal of Applied Psychology*, February 1990, pp. 51–9.

[2] British MP Vince Cable, in *The Times*, 8 February 2009. For a stunning example of how a few words can create an enduring perception of both the speaker's wit and the target's character (or lack thereof), see Cable's 'Stalin to Mr. Bean' comment on YouTube. Creating that perception in a few words takes less than 20 seconds.

[3] S. S. Brehm, S. M. Kassin and S. Fein, *Social Psychology* (Boston, MA: Houghton Mifflin Company, 1999).

[4] M. Simon, S. M. Houghton and K. Aquino, 'Cognitive Biases, Risk Perception, and Venture Formation: How Individuals Decide to Start Companies', *Journal of Business Venturing*, March 2000, pp. 113–34.

[5] R. McGinty and A. Reitsch, 'Using Student Perceptions and Job Characteristics to Recruit Recent Graduates', *Review of Business*, Summer–Fall 1992, pp. 38–42.

[6] J. R. Schermerhorn, J. G. Hunt and R. N. Osborn, *Organizational Behavior* (Oxford: John Wiley and Sons, 1997).

[7] T. R. Alley, 'Physionomy and Social Perception', in *Social and Applied Aspects of Perceiving Faces. Resources for Ecological Psychology*, ed. T. R. Alley (Hillsdale, NJ: Lawrence Erlbaum Associates, 1988), pp. 167–86.

[8] A. Vrij, 'The Existence of a Black Clothing Stereotype: The Impact of a Victim's Black Clothing on Impression Formation', *Psychology, Crime and Law*, no. 3, 1997, pp. 227–37.

[9] D. Hellriegel, J. W. Slocum, Jr and R. W. Woodman, *Organizational Behavior* (St. Paul, MN: West Publishing Company, 1976).

[10] V. S. Y. Kwan, S. P. Wojcik, T. Miron-Shatz, A. M. Votruba, and C. Y. Olivola, 'Effects of Symptom Presentation Order on Perceived Disease Risk', *Psychological Science*, vol. 23, no. 4, 2012, pp. 381–5.

[11] See S. S. Brehm, S. M. Kassin and S. Fein, *Social Psychology* (Boston, MA: Houghton Mifflin Company, 1999).

[12] J. E. Rehfeld, 'What Working for a Japanese Company Taught Me', *Harvard Business Review*, November–December 1990, pp. 167–76.

[13] F. Trompenaars and C. Hampden-Turner, *Riding the Waves of Culture* (New York: McGraw-Hill, 1998).

[14] S. Penrod, *Social Psychology* (Englewood Cliffs, NJ: Prentice Hall, 1983).

[15] Tversky, A. and Kahneman, D. (1974) Judgement Under Uncertainty: Heuristics and Biases, *Science*, no. 185, pp. 1124–130.

[16] S. Dornbush, A. H. Hastorf, S. A. Richardson, R. E. Muzzy and R. S. Vreeland, 'The Perceiver and the Perceived: The Relative Influence on the Categories of Interpersonal Cognition', *Journal of Personality and Social Psychology*, May 1965, pp. 434–40.

[17] M. Rotundo, D. H. Ngyuen and P. Sackett, 'A Meta-Analytic Review of Gender Differences in Perceptions of Sexual Harassment', *Journal of Applied Psychology*, October 2001, pp. 914–22.

[18] H. Ngo, S. Foley, A. Wong and R. Loi, 'Who Gets More of the Pie? Predictors of Perceived Gender Inequity at Work', *Journal of Business Ethics*, July 2003, pp. 227–41.

[19] J. P. Forgas, 'Mood and Judgement: The Affect Infusion Model', *Psychological Bulletin*, January 1995, pp. 39–66.

[20] C. Sedidikes and C. A. Anderson, 'Causal Perceptions of Intertrait Relations: The Glue That Holds Person Types Together', *Personality and Social Psychology Bulletin*, June 1994, pp. 294–302.

[21] See S. S. Brehm, S. M. Kassin and S. Fein, *Social Psychology* (Boston, MA: Houghton Mifflin Company, 1999).

[22] Adapted from discussion in S. T. Fiske and S. E. Taylor, *Social Cognition, second edition* (Reading, MA: Addison-Wesley Publishing, 1991), pp. 247–50.

[23] The negativity bias was examined and supported by O. Ybarra and W. G. Stephan, 'Misanthropic Person Memory', *Journal of Personality and Social Psychology*, April 1996, pp. 691–700; and Y. Ganzach, 'Negativity (and Positivity) in Performance Evaluation: Three Field Studies', *Journal of Applied Psychology*, August 1995, pp. 491–9.

[24] E. Rosch, C. B. Mervis, W. D. Gray, D. M. Johnson and P. Boyes-Braem, 'Basic Objects in Natural Categories', *Cognitive Psychology*, July 1976, p. 383.

[25] See J. P. Forgas, 'On Being Happy and Mistaken: Mood Effects on the Fundamental Attribution Error', *Journal of Personality and Social Psychology*, August 1998, pp. 318–31; and A. Varma, A. S. DeNisi and L. H. Peters, 'Interpersonal Affect and Performance Appraisal: A Field Study', *Personnel Psychology*, Summer 1996, pp. 341–60.

[26] See I. Ajzen and J. Sexton, 'Depth of Processing, Belief Congruence, and Attitude-Behavior Correspondence', in *Dual-Process Theories in Social Psychology*, eds S. Chaiken and Y. Trope (New York: The Guilford Press, 1999), pp. 117–38; and A. J. Kinicki, P. W. Hom, M. R. Trost and K. J. Wade, 'Effects of Category Prototypes on Performance-Rating Accuracy', *Journal of Applied Psychology*, June 1995, pp. 354–70.

[27] The relationship between depression and information processing is discussed by A. Zelli and K. A. Dodge, 'Personality Development from the Bottom Up', in *The Coherence of Personality*, eds D. Cervone and Y. Shoda (New York: The Guilford Press, 1999), pp. 94–126.

[28] A thorough discussion of the reasoning process used to make judgements and decisions is provided by S. A. Sloman, 'The Empirical Case for Two Systems of Reasoning', *Psychological Bulletin*, January 1996, pp. 3–22.

[29] Results can be found in C. M. Marlowe, S. L. Schneider and C. E. Nelson, 'Gender and Attractiveness Biases in Hiring Decisions: Are More Experienced Managers Less Biased?', *Journal of Applied Psychology*, February 1996, pp. 11–21.

[30] Adapted and translated from M. Buelens, F. Debussche and K. Vanderheyden, *Mensen en verscheidenheid* (Brussels: Vacature, 1997).

[31] See R. C. Mayer and J. H. Davis, 'The Effect of the Performance Appraisal System on Trust for Management: A Field Quasi-Experiment', *Journal of Applied Psychology*, February 1999, pp. 123–36.

[32] Details of this study can be found in C. K. Stevens, 'Antecedents of Interview Interactions, Interviewers' Ratings, and Applicants' Reactions', *Personnel Psychology*, Spring 1998, pp. 55–85.

[33] Results can be found in W. H. Bommer, J. L. Johnson, G. A. Rich, P. M. Podsakoff and S. B. Mackenzie, 'On the Interchangeability of Objective and Subjective Measures of Employee Performance: A Meta-Analysis', *Personnel Psychology*, Autumn 1995, pp. 587–605.

[34] See J. I. Sanchez and P. D. L. Torre, 'A Second Look at the Relationship between Rating and Behavioral Accuracy in Performance Appraisal', *Journal of Applied Psychology*, February 1996, pp. 3–10; and A. J. Kinicki, P. W. Hom, M. R. Trost and K. J. Wade, 'Effects of Category Prototypes on Performance-Rating Accuracy', *Journal of Applied Psychology*, June 1995, pp. 354–70.

[35] The effectiveness of rater training was supported by D. V. Day and L. M. Sulsky, 'Effects of Frame-of-Reference Training and Information Configuration on Memory Organization and Rating Accuracy', *Journal of Applied Psychology*, February 1995, pp. 158–67.

[36] H. Sims, Jr and P. Lorenzi, *The New Leadership Paradigm: Social Learning and Cognition in Organizations* (Newbury Park, CA: Sage Publications, 1992).

[37] See F. Heider, *The Psychology of Interpersonal Relations* (New York: Wiley, 1958).

[38] B. Weiner, I. H. Frieze, A. Kukla, L. Reed, S. Rest and R. M. Rosenbaum, *Perceiving the Causes of Success and Failure* (Morristown, NJ: General Learning Press, 1971).

[39] E. Chang, K. Rand and D. Strunk, 'Optimism and Risk for Job Burnout Among Working College Students: Stress as a Mediator', *Personality and Individual Differences*, August 2000, pp. 255–63.

[40] R. Baron and D. Byrne, *Social Psychology: Understanding Human Interaction* (Needham Heights, MA: Allyn & Bacon, 1987).

[41] See H. H. Kelly, 'The Processes of Causal Attribution', *American Psychologist*, February 1973, pp. 107–28.

[42] L. Z. McArthur, 'The How and What of Why: Some Determinants and Consequences of Causal Attributions', *Journal of Personality and Social Psychology*, January 1972, pp. 171–93.

[43] A. Kukla, 'Attributional Determinants of Achievement Related Behavior', *Journal of Personality and Social Psychology*, August 1970, pp. 166–74.

[44] L. Ross, 'The Intuitive Psychologist and His Shortcoming', in *Advances in Experimental Social Psychology*, ed. L. Berkowitz (New York: Academic Press, 1977).

[45] R. E. Nisbett and L. Ross, *Human Inference: Strategies and Shortcomings of Social Judgement* (Englewood Cliffs, NJ: Prentice Hall, 1980).

[46] K. G. Shaver, *An Introduction to Attribution Processes* (Cambridge, MA: Winthrop, 1975).

[47] E. E. Jones and R. E. Nisbett, 'The Actor and the Observer: Divergent Perceptions of the Causes of Behaviour', in *Attribution: Perceiving Causes of Behavior*, eds E. E. Jones, D. E. Kanouse, H. H. Kelly, R. E. Nisbett, S. Valins and B. Weiner (Morristown, NJ: General Learning Press, 1972).

[48] See H. Sims, Jr and P. Lorenzi, *The New Leadership Paradigm: Social Learning and Cognition in Organizations* (Newbury Park, CA: Sage Publications, 1992).

[49] C. Sedikides, W. K. Campbell, G. D. Reeder and A. J. Elliot, 'The Self-Serving Bias in Relational Context', *Journal of Personality and Social Psychology*, February 1998, pp. 378–86.

[50] See H. Sims, Jr and P. Lorenzi, *The New Leadership Paradigm: Social Learning and Cognition in Organizations* (Newbury Park, CA: Sage Publications, 1992).

[51] T. F. Pettigrew, 'The Ultimate Attribution Error: Extending Allport's Cognitive Analysis of Prejudice', *Personality and Social Psychology Bulletin*, October 1979, pp. 461–576.

[52] See P. D. Sweeney, K. Anderson and S. Bailey, 'Attributional Style in Depression: A Meta-Analytic Review', *Journal of Personality and Social Psychology*, May 1986, pp. 974–91.

[53] Results can be found in P. J. Corr and J. A. Gray, 'Attributional Style as a Personality Factor in Insurance Sales Performance in the UK', *Journal of Occupational Psychology*, March 1996, pp. 83–87.

[54] Supportive results can be found in J. Silvester, N. R. Anderson and F. Patterson, 'Organizational Culture Change: An InterGroup Attributional Analysis', *Journal of Occupational and Organizational Psychology*, March 1999, pp. 1–23; J. Greenberg, 'Forgive Me, I'm New: Three Experimental Demonstrations of the Effects of Attempts to Excuse Poor Performance', *Organizational Behavior and Human Decision Processes*, May 1996, pp. 165–78; and G. E. Prussia, A. J. Kinicki and J. S. Bracker, 'Psycho logical and Behavioral Consequences of Job Loss: A Covariance Structure Analysis Using Weiner's (1985) Attribution Model', *Journal of Applied Psychology*, June 1993, pp. 382–94.

[55] Details may be found in S. E. Moss and M. J. Martinko, 'The Effects of Performance Attributions and Outcome Dependence on Leader Feedback Behavior Following Poor Subordinate Performance', *Journal of Organizational Behavior*, May 1998, pp. 259–74; and E. C. Pence, W. C. Pendelton, G. H. Dobbins and J. A. Sgro, 'Effects of Causal Explanations and Sex Variables on Recommendations for Corrective Actions Following Employee Failure', *Organizational Behavior and Human Performance*, April 1982, pp. 227–40.

[56] See D. Konst, R. Vonk and R. V. D. Vlist, 'Inferences about Causes and Consequences of Behavior of Leaders and Subordinates', *Journal of Organizational Behavior*, March 1999, pp. 261–71.

[57] See M. Miserandino, 'Attributional Retraining as a Method of Improving Athletic Performance', *Journal of Sport Behavior*, August 1998, pp. 286–97; and F. Forsterling, 'Attributional Retraining: A Review', *Psychological Bulletin*, November 1985, pp. 496–512.

[58] The background and results for this study are presented in R. Rosenthal and L. Jacobson, *Pygmalion in the Classroom: Teacher Expectation and Pupils' Intellectual Development* (New York: Holt, Rinehart & Winston, 1968).

[59] See J.-F. Manzoni and J.-L. Barsoux, 'The Set-Up-to-Fail Syndrome', *Harvard Business Review*, March–April 1998, pp. 101–13.

[60] This example was based on J.-F. Manzoni and J.-L. Barsoux, 'The Set-Up-to-Fail Syndrome', *Harvard Business Review*, March–April 1998, pp. 101–13; and 'Living Down to Expectations', *Training*, July 1998, p. 15.

[61] E. Y. Babad, J. Inbar and R. Rosenthal, 'Pygmalion, Galatea, and the Golem: Investigations of Biased and Unbiased Teachers', *Journal of Educational Psychology*, 1982, no. 74, pp. 459–74.

[62] See D. Eden and Y. Zuk, 'Seasickness as a Self-Fulfilling Prophecy: Raising Self-Efficacy to Boost Performance at Sea', *Journal of Applied Psychology*, October 1995, pp. 628–35. For a thorough review of research on the Pygmalion effect, see D. Eden, *Pygmalion in Management: Productivity as a Self-Fulfilling Prophecy* (Lexington, MA: Lexington Books, 1990), Ch. 2.

[63] This study was conducted by T. Dvir, D. Eden and M. L. Banjo, 'Self-Fulfilling Prophecy and Gender: Can Women Be Pygmalion and Galatea?', *Journal of Applied Psychology*, April 1995, pp. 253–70.

[64] G. Natanovich and D. Eden, 'Pygmalion Effects Among Outreach Supervisors and Tutors: Extending Sex Generalizability', *Journal of Applied Psychology*, no. 93(6), November 2008, pp. 1382–89.

[65] N. M. Kierein and M. A. Gold, 'Pygmalion in Work Organizations: A Meta-Analysis', *Journal of Organizational Behaviour*, December 2000, pp. 913–28.

[66] See M. A. Jaasma and R. J. Koper, 'The Relationship of Student-Faculty Out-of-Class Communication to Instructor Immediacy and Trust and to Student Motivation', *Communication Education*, January 1999, pp. 41–7; and P. G. Clampitt and C. W. Downs, 'Employee Perceptions of the Relationship between Communication and Productivity: A Field Study', *Journal of Business Communication*, 1993, pp. 5–28.

[67] Results can be found in D. Fenn, 'Benchmark: What Drives the Skills Gap?', *Inc.*, May 1996, p. 111.

[68] J. L. Bowditch and A. F. Buono, *A Primer on Organizational Behavior, fourth edition* (New York: John Wiley & Sons, 1997), p. 120.

[69] Results of this study can be found in C. M. Fiol, 'Corporate Communications: Comparing Executives' Private and Public Statements', *Academy of Management Journal*, April 1995, pp. 522–36.

[70] P. Watzlawick, J. Beavin and D. Jackson, *Pragmatics of Human Communication* (New York: W. W. Norton, 1967).

[71] O. Hargie, C. Saunders and D. Dickson, *Social Skills in Interpersonal Communication, third edition* (London: Routledge, 1994), pp. 16–18.

[72] O. Hargie, C. Saunders and D. Dickson, *Social Skills in Interpersonal Communication, third edition* (London: Routledge, 1994), p. 11.

[73] H. J. Leavitt, *Managerial Psychology, revised edition* (Chicago: University of Chicago Press, 1964).
[74] Results can be found in B. Davenport Sypher and T. E. Zorn, Jr, 'Communication-Related Abilities and Upward Mobility: A Longitudinal Investigation', *Human Communication Research*, Spring 1986, pp. 420–31.
[75] Communication competence is discussed by J. S. Hinton and M. W. Kramer, 'The Impact of Self-Directed Videotape Feedback on Students' Self-Reported Levels of Communication Competence and Apprehension', *Communication Education*, April 1998, pp. 151–61; and L. J. Carrell and S. C. Willmington, 'The Relationship between Self-Report Measures of Communication Apprehension and Trained Observers' Ratings of Communication Competence', *Communication Reports*, Winter 1998, pp. 87–95.
[76] W. D. St John, 'You Are What You Communicate', *Personnel Journal*, October 1985, p. 40.
[77] S. F. Zaidel and A. Mehrabian, 'The Ability to Communicate and Infer Positive and Negative Attitudes Facially and Vocally', *Journal of Experimental Research in Personality*, September 1969, pp. 233–41.
[78] Results can be found in S. D. Kelly, D. J. Barr, R. B. Church and K. Lynch, 'Offering a Hand to Pragmatic Understanding: The Role of Speech and Gesture in Comprehension and Memory', *Journal of Memory and Language*, May 1999, pp. 577–92.
[79] L. Van Poecke, *Nonverbale communicatie* (Leuven: Garant, 1996).
[80] See J. A. Russell, 'Facial Expressions of Emotion: What Lies Beyond Minimal Universality?', *Psychological Bulletin*, November 1995, pp. 379–91.
[81] Norms for cross-cultural eye contact are discussed by C. Engholm, *When Business East Meets Business West: The Guide to Practice and Protocol in the Pacific Rim* (New York: John Wiley & Sons, 1991).
[82] See D. Ray, 'Are You Listening?', *Selling Power*, June 1999, pp. 28–30; and P. Meyer, 'So You Want the President's Job', *Business Horizons*, January–February 1998, pp. 2–6.
[83] Estimates are provided in both J. Hart Seibert, 'Listening in the Organizational Context', in *Listening Behavior: Measurement and Application*, ed. R. N. Bostrom (New York: The Guilford Press, 1990), pp. 119–27; and D. W. Caudill and R. M. Donaldson, 'Effective Listening Tips for Managers', *Administrative Management*, September 1986, pp. 22–3.
[84] See C. G. Pearce, 'How Effective Are We as Listeners?', *Training & Development*, April 1993, pp. 79–80; and G. Manning, K. Curtis and S. McMillen, *Building Community: The Human Side of Work* (Cincinnati, OH: Thomson Executive Press, 1996), pp. 127–54.
[85] J. A. Waters, 'Managerial Assertiveness', *Business Horizons*, September–October 1982, p. 25.
[86] O. Hargie, C. Saunders and D. Dickson, *Social Skills in Interpersonal Communication, third edition* (London: Routledge, 1994), p. 275.
[87] C. Harler, 'Electronic Communication May Accentuate Sex Differences', *Communications News*, April 1996, p. 4.
[88] Related research is summarised by J. A. Hall, 'Male and Female Nonverbal Behavior', in *Multichannel Integrations of Nonverbal Behavior*, eds A. W. Siegman and S. Feldstein (Hillsdale, NJ: Lawrence Erlbaum, 1985), pp. 195–226.
[89] A thorough discussion of cross-cultural differences is provided by R. E. Axtell, *Gestures: The Do's and Taboos of Body Language around the World* (New York: John Wiley & Sons, 1991). Problems with body language analysis are also discussed by C. L. Karrass, 'Body Language: Beware the Hype', *Traffic Management*, January 1992, p. 27; and M. Everett and B. Wiesendanger, 'What Does Body Language Really Say?', *Sales & Marketing Management*, April 1992, p. 40.
[90] Derived from P. McBride and S. Maitland, *The EI Advantage: Putting Emotional Intelligence into Practice* (London: McGraw-Hill, 2002), pp. 176–9; and J. A. Waters, 'Managerial Assertiveness', *Business Horizons*, September–October 1982, p. 27.
[91] C. Redding, *Communication within the Organization: An Interpretive Review of Theory and Research* (New York: Industrial Communication Council, 1972).
[92] See, for instance, N. B. Kurland and L. H. Pelled, 'Passing the Word: Toward a Model of Gossip and Power in the Workplace', *Academy of Management Review*, April 2000, pp. 428–38; and N. Nicholson, 'The New Word on Gossip', *Psychology Today*, June 2001, pp. 41–5.
[93] D. Krackhardt and J. R. Hanson, 'Informal Networks: The Company Behind the Chart', *Harvard Business Review*, July–August 1993, pp. 104–11; and H. Mintzberg, *The Structuring of Organizations* (Englewood Cliffs, NJ: Prentice Hall, 1979), pp. 43–9.
[94] M. Noon and R. Delbridge, 'News from Behind My Hand: Gossip in Organizations', *Organization Studies*, January–February 1993, pp. 23–36; R. L. Rosnow, 'Inside Rumor: A Personal Journey', *American Psychologist*, May 1991, pp. 484–96; and C. J. Walker and C. A. Beckerle, 'The Effect of State Anxiety on Rumor Transmission', *Journal of Social Behavior and Personality*, August 1987, pp. 353–60.
[95] See K. Davis, 'Management Communication and the Grapevine', *Harvard Business Review*, September–October 1953, pp. 43–9.
[96] D. Tannen, 'The Power of Talk: Who Gets Heard and Why', *Harvard Business Review*, September–October 1995, p. 139.
[97] For a thorough review of the evolutionary explanation of gender differences in communication, see A. H. Eagly and W. Wood, 'The Origins of Sex Differences in Human Behavior', *American Psychologist*, June 1999, pp. 408–23; and J. Archer, 'Sex Differences in Social Behavior: Are the Social Role and Evolutionary Explanations Compatible?', *American Psychologist*, September 1996, pp. 909–17.
[98] See H. Fisher, *The Natural Talents of Women and How They Are Changing the World* (New York: Ballantine Books, 1999); and D. Tannen, *You Just Don't Understand: Women and Men in Conversation* (New York: Ballantine Books, 1990).
[99] J. R. Carlson and R. W. Zmud, 'Channel Expansion Theory and the Experimental Nature of Media Richness Perceptions', *Academy of Management Journal*, April 1999, pp. 153–70.
[100] G. L. Kreps, *Organizational Communication* (New York: Longman, 1990), p. 203.

[101] For a thorough discussion of communication distortion, see E. W. Larson and J. B. King, 'The Systematic Distortion of Information: An Ongoing Challenge to Management', *Organizational Dynamics*, Winter 1996, pp. 49–61.

[102] For a review of this research, see J. Fulk and S. Mani, 'Distortion of Communication in Hierarchical Relationships', in *Communication Yearbook 9*, ed. M. L. McLaughlin (Beverly Hills, CA: Sage Publications, 1986), pp. 483–510.

[103] Earlier research is discussed by K. Davis, 'Management Communication and the Grapevine', *Harvard Business Review*, September–October 1953, pp. 43–9; and L. Festinger, D. Cartwright, K. Barber, J. Fleischl, J. Gottsdanker, A. Keysen and G. Leavitt, 'A Study of Rumor: Its Origin and Spread', *Human Relations*, September 1948, pp. 464–86. Recent research is discussed by G. Michelson and V. S. Mouly, 'You Didn't Hear it From Us But . . . Towards an Understanding of Rumour and Gossip in Organisations', *Australian Journal of Management*, September 2002, pp. 57–65; N. DiFonzo and P. Bordia, 'How Top PR Professionals Handle Hearsay: Corporate Rumors, Their Effects, and Strategies to Manage Them', *Public Relations Review*, Summer 2000, pp. 173–90; G. Michelson and S. Mouly, 'Rumor and Gossip in Organizations: A Conceptual Study', *Management Decision*, May 2000, pp. 339–46; and S. M. Crampton, J. W. Hodge and J. M. Mishra, 'The Informal Communication Network: Factors Influencing Grapevine Activity', *Public Personnel Management*, Winter 1998, pp. 569–84.

[104] S. A. Lippman and R. P. Rumelt, 'Uncertain Imitability: An Analysis of Interfirm Differences in Efficiency Under Competition', *Bell Journal of Economics*, 1982, no. 13, 418–38.

[105] This definition was taken from J. C. Tingley, *Genderflex: Men & Women Speaking Each Other's Language at Work* (New York: American Management Association, 1994), p. 16.

[106] G. Akerlof, 'The Market for Lemons: Qualitative Uncertainty and the Market Mechanism', *Quarterly Journal of Economics*, 1970, no. 84, pp. 488–500.

[107] In Book V, chapter 1, part III, article I.

[108] See P. D. Harrison and A. Harrell, 'Impact of "Adverse Selection" on Manager's Project Evaluation Decisions', *Academy of Management Journal*, 36(3), pp. 635–43.

[109] See A. Shleifer and R. W. Vishny, 'A Survey of Corporate Governance', *Journal of Finance*, 1997, no. 52, pp. 737–83.

[110] See A. A. Berle and G. C. Means, *The Modern Corporation* (New York: Commerce Clearing House, 1932).

[111] See M. C. Jensen and W. H. Meckling, 'Theory of the Firm: Managerial Behavior, Agency Costs and Ownership Structure', *Journal of Financial Economics*, 1976, no. 3, pp. 305–60.

[112] See M. C. Jensen, 'Agency Cost of Free Cash Flow, Corporate Finance and Takeovers', *American Economic Review*, 1986, no. 76, pp. 323–29.

[113] See J. P. O'Connor, R. L. Preim, J. E. Coombs and K. M. Gilley, 'Do CEO Stock Options Prevent or Promote Fraudulent Financial Reporting?', *Academy of Management Journal*, 2006, 40(3), pp. 483–500.

[114] R. L. Daft and R. H. Lengel, 'Information Richness: A New Approach to Managerial Behavior and Organizational Design', in *Research in Organizational Behavior*, eds B. M. Staw and L. L. Cummings (Greenwich, CT: JAI Press, 1984), p. 196.

[115] M. J. Tippins and R. S. Sohi, 'IT Competency and Firm Performance: Is Organizational Learning a Missing Link?', *Strategic Management Journal*, August 2003, pp. 745–61.

[116] M. J. Eppler and J. Mengis, 'A Framework for Information Overload: Research in Organizations', September 2003, www.knowledge-communication.org/wp10.pdf/.

[117] D. Lewis, *Information Overload: Practical Strategies for Surviving in Today's Workplace* (London: Penguin Books, 1999).

[118] H. A. Simon, 'Bounded Rationality and Organizational Learning', *Organization Science*, February 1991, pp. 125–34.

[119] For tips on dealing with information overload, see D. Lewis, *Information Overload: Practical Strategies for Surviving in Today's Workplace* (London: Penguin Books, 1999); D. Shenk, *Data Smog: Surviving the Information Glut* (New York: HarperCollins, 1997); C. W. Simpson and L. Prusak, 'Troubles with Information Overload: Moving from Quantity to Quality in Information Provision', *Journal of Information Management*, December 1995, pp. 413–25; and K. Alesandrini, *Survive Information Overload* (Homewood, IL: Business One Irwin, 1993).

Chapter 5

Content motivation theories

Learning Outcomes

When you have read this chapter, you should be able to:

- define the term motivation
- review the historical roots of modern motivation theories
- explain the difference between content and process approaches of motivation
- contrast Maslow's and McClelland's need theories
- describe Alderfer's theory and the frustration regression assumption
- explain the practical significance of Herzberg's distinction between motivators and hygiene factors
- describe how internal work motivation is increased by using the job characteristics model

Opening Case Study: Société Générale and the motivation of Jerome Kerviel

In 2008 a young French banker named Jerome Kerviel was discovered to have made a number of speculative transactions on behalf of his employer, the French bank Société Générale. The sums were enormous: Mr Kerviel had acquired investments worth €50 billion more than the entire value of the bank. Once discovered, Mr Kerviel was arrested and the bank lost a total of €4.9 billion selling the investments.

Large trading positions, which involve the bank buying and selling securities on its own account (and risking its own money), seem to have been common at Société Générale and many other banks. Mr Kerviel had earned significant sums for Société Générale since he was promoted to trader in 2005. His profits in 2007 had been €1.5 billion, although he had sought to carry much of this forward to 2008. Mr Kerviel admitted that some of his trading activities were unauthorised but claimed that during his trial in July 2010 these activities were known to his superiors and that they were tolerated as long as they were profitable. The bank, however, claimed that Mr Kerviel was a 'manipulator, a trickster, and a liar' who caused 'planetary trauma' which almost bankrupted one of the oldest banks in France.

On 5 October 2010 Mr Kerviel was convicted of fraud and sentenced to five years in prison. An appeal court later upheld the conviction. The case raised important questions about what motivates and about what individual organisations believe motivates. However, the case also raised important questions about who knew what and when. If Mr Kerviel's managers turned a blind eye as long as he made money from the unauthorised activities, the question is: Who knew about it? If highly placed managers did know what was going on then the information system worked well and the key issue concerns the ethics of those who allowed unauthorised trading to continue. If Mr Kerviel, as the bank claims, is a liar, then the question is about information. Essentially, why was the enormous trading activity not detected?

When thinking about this case and the question of 'unauthorised' trading activity, it is hard not to remember the drama that occurred in 1995, when a speculative bet was made by Nick Leeson, a trader with Barings Bank in Singapore. The bet was lost, the bank failed. Leeson fled but was extradited to Singapore. Convicted of various crimes, Leeson served time in prison, became ill with cancer and was eventually released.

For discussion

If profits from unauthorised trading activity are part of the performance assessment on which pay and bonuses are awarded, are they then really unauthorised?

Source: Based on Kim Willsher, 'Jérôme Kerviel Not a Fraudster but a "Creation" of Société Générale, Court Told', *The Guardian*, 25 June 2010, www.guardian.co.uk/world/2010/jun/25/societegenerale-jerome-kerviel.

Having a job, going to work and carrying out the tasks assigned is something people do because they receive something in return. That something is often money but can also, in varying degrees, involve experience, enjoyment and convenience. Whether a job provides enough of these elements to make someone stay in the job, makes him or her work hard and produce new ideas, depends on what effort is required and what the alternatives are; for example, offers from similar organisations.

In this chapter we concentrate on people's needs and the goals they want to attain, in the sense that attaining them allows them to meet their needs. The underlying logic is that meeting needs and attaining goals ensures that organisation members work hard. This type of thinking also implicitly assumes that the goals of individuals and the organisation they work for are aligned. This need not always be the case.

Effective employee motivation and satisfaction has long been one of management's most difficult and important duties. Success in this area is always a challenge. Even if many organisations think about 'downsizing', 'globalisation' and 're-engineering' and the challenges associated with managing a diverse workforce, none of this is really new. Businesses exposed to any form of competition must always seek to motivate as best they can, otherwise rivals will out-compete them. Companies are using a wide range of techniques to keep their staff happy and motivated, ranging from classical measures such as stimulating compensation schemes through signs of appreciation such as friendly and appreciative words from the boss. It is said that companies do not just want their employees to like their job; they want them to love their job. As a result, some innovative companies experiment with alternative, creative ways in which to create an overtly enthusiastic workforce. One executive cynically explains the rationale behind this trend: 'With the old techniques, we got their mind, now we've got their heart and soul too. . . .'[1] The motivation and values of modern-day workers differs from those of previous generations. These days people want significantly more than just a high salary and good career prospects. They want to experience autonomy, creativity and growth in their job. They rate meeting new challenges and finding self-expression higher than accruing status.[2]

These trends impose great challenges on contemporary employers who want to keep their people motivated. As mentioned in Chapter 1, Douglas McGregor presented two kinds of propositions regarding human motivation. Theory X implies that managers perceive that employees dislike work, are lazy, avoid responsibility and must be coerced to perform. As a result people have to be motivated by controlling their actions, with rewards and punishments. Theory Y assumes the managers hold the view that employees like work, are creative, seek responsibility and can exercise self-direction. So, in the eyes of Y-managers, people are motivated when they are treated as adults rather than as children. Giving responsibility and opportunities to develop self-direction and/or participation in decisions are important determinants to motivate people.[3]

The purpose of this chapter and the next is to give you the foundation for understanding the complexities of employee motivation. This chapter provides a definitional and theoretical foundation for the topic of motivation so that a rich variety of motivation theories and techniques can be introduced and discussed. Coverage of employee motivation continues in Chapter 6. After explaining what motivation involves, this chapter focuses on content theories of motivation and the job characteristics model of motivation. In the next chapter, attention turns to process-related theories of motivation. To get an encompassing view on what motivation implies and which theories exist, this chapter and Chapter 6 need to be considered together.

5.1 What does motivation involve?

The term 'motivation' derives from the Latin word *movere*, meaning 'to move'. No questions have been raised about the significance motivation plays in influencing performance at work.[4] However, job performance does not only depend on the motivation of employees. As illustrated in Figure 5.1, ability and opportunity are other factors that often play an important role in predicting job performance – and motivation alone is not enough. For example, a doctor may be highly motivated but without patients, drugs and equipment all that motivation is irrelevant. The capacity to perform refers to the ability, age, health, skills and level of education that individuals have. Having the

Figure 5.1 Determinants of Work Performance

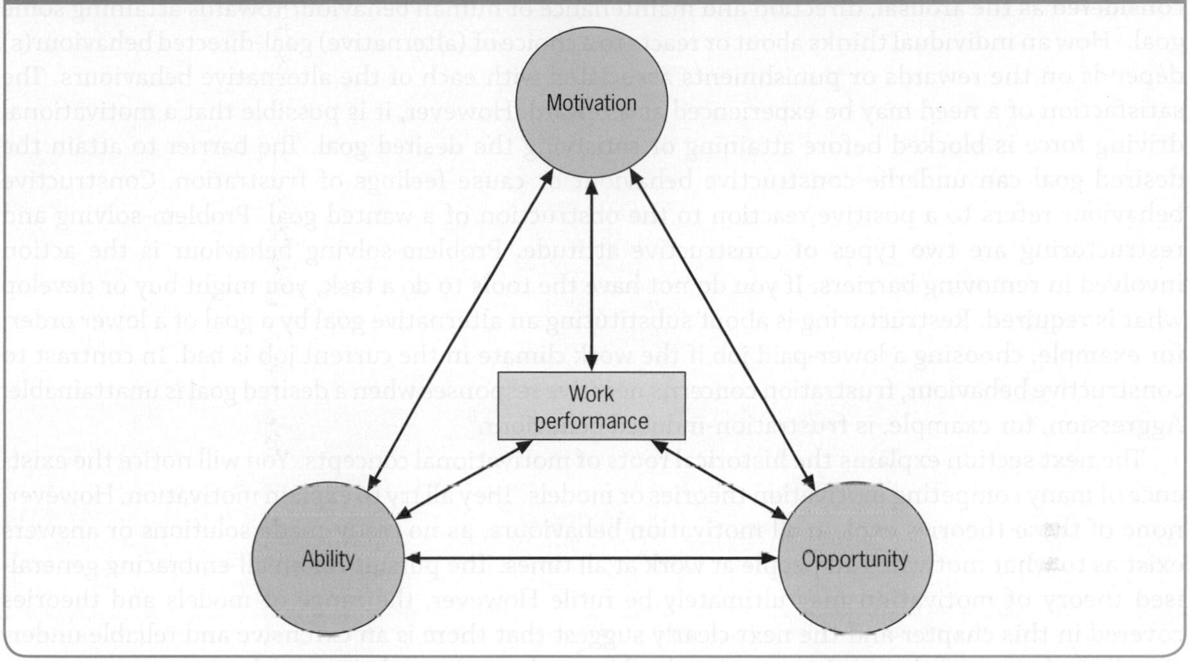

opportunity to perform is also a key factor for performance. Opportunity refers to the tools, equipment, materials, working conditions, leader behaviour, organisational politics, rules and procedures, time and pay.

Different combinations of these dimensions underlie different performance levels. A combination of favourable opportunities, higher capacity and higher motivation leads to very high performance, whereas a combination of low levels on the three dimensions should predict very low performance.[5] An important observation is that two people may claim that they are motivated, although their motivations may differ in direction, intensity and persistence. Direction refers to choices people make between different alternatives. The first employee, for example, may prefer intrinsic rewards (autonomy, self-growth etc.) over extrinsic rewards (like money, financial bonuses, relationship with colleagues), whereas the second one may prefer extrinsic over intrinsic rewards for the same work. The intensity component involves the strength of the response once the choice is made. Finally, persistence implies how long a person will continue to devote effort and energy.

Organisations and their managers need to understand the motivation process if they are to successfully guide employees towards accomplishing organisational objectives. The study of motivation is about the question: 'Why do people behave the way they do?'[6] If we want to learn about how motivation works we need at first to learn how motivation is induced. Needs can be considered as the starting point of motivations. Our needs concern something we want to attain. They refer to deficiencies individuals experience at some point in time, and function as triggers of behavioural responses. Deficiencies can have a physiological, psychological or relational nature. For example, if you are hungry while studying for your organisational behaviour exam, you might interrupt your reading and get something to eat. So needs direct behaviour aimed at satisfying those needs.

If needs stay unsatisfied or unmet they result in more intense feelings and more extensive behavioural modifications. Thus, a need deficiency usually triggers a search for ways to reduce this deficiency and this search in turn results in a choice of goal-directed behaviour. **Motivation** can be considered as the arousal, direction and maintenance of human behaviour towards attaining some goal.[7] How an individual thinks about or reacts to a choice of (alternative) goal-directed behaviour(s) depends on the rewards or punishments associated with each of the alternative behaviours. The satisfaction of a need may be experienced as a reward. However, it is possible that a motivational driving force is blocked before attaining or satisfying the desired goal. The barrier to attain the desired goal can underlie constructive behaviour or cause feelings of frustration. Constructive behaviour refers to a positive reaction to the obstruction of a wanted goal. Problem-solving and restructuring are two types of constructive attitude. Problem-solving behaviour is the action involved in removing barriers. If you do not have the tools to do a task, you might buy or develop what is required. Restructuring is about substituting an alternative goal by a goal of a lower order; for example, choosing a lower-paid job if the work climate in the current job is bad. In contrast to constructive behaviour, frustration concerns negative responses when a desired goal is unattainable. Aggression, for example, is frustration-induced behaviour.[8]

The next section explains the historical roots of motivational concepts. You will notice the existence of many competing motivation theories or models. They all try to explain motivation. However, none of these theories explain all motivation behaviours, as no ready-made solutions or answers exist as to what motivates all people at work at all times. The pursuit for an all-embracing generalised theory of motivation may ultimately be futile However, the range of models and theories covered in this chapter and the next clearly suggest that there is an extensive and reliable understanding of many of the mechanisms involved in motivating people in organisations.

Historical roots of modern motivation theories

Five methods of explaining behaviour – needs, reinforcement, cognition, job characteristics and feelings/emotions – underlie the evolution of theories of human motivation. As we explain the different theories and models, remember that the objective of them all is to explain and predict purposeful or goal-directed behaviour. The differences between theoretical perspectives lie in the causal mechanisms used to explain behaviour.

Needs theories are based on the premise that individuals are motivated by unsatisfied needs. Dissatisfaction with your social life, for example, should motivate you to participate in more social activities. Henry Murray, a 1930s psychologist, was the first behavioural scientist to propose a list of needs thought to underlie goal-directed behaviour. From Murray's work sprang a wide variety of needs theories, some of which remain influential today. Recognised needs theories of motivation are explored in the current chapter.

Reinforcement theorists, such as Edward L. Thorndike and B. F. Skinner, proposed that behaviour is controlled by its consequences, not by the result of hypothetical internal states such as instincts, drives or needs. This proposition is based on research data demonstrating that people repeat behaviours that are followed by favourable consequences and avoid behaviours that result in unfavourable consequences. Few would argue with the statement that organisational rewards have a motivational impact on job behaviour. However, behaviourists and cognitive theorists do disagree over the role, in motivation, of an individual's internal states and processes.

Uncomfortable with the idea that behaviour is shaped completely by environmental consequences, cognitive motivation theorists contend that behaviour is a function of beliefs, expectations, values and other mental cognitions. Behaviour is therefore viewed as the result of a process involving rational and conscious choices among alternative courses of action. In Chapter 6, we will discuss cognitive motivation theories involving equity, expectancies and goal setting.

The **job characteristics** or **job characteristic model** approach is based on the idea that the task itself is the key to employee motivation. Specifically, a boring and monotonous job stifles motivation to perform well, whereas a challenging job enhances motivation. Three ingredients of a more challenging job are variety, autonomy and decision-making authority. A popular way of applying this model involves adding variety and challenge to routine jobs in a process called 'job enrichment' (or 'job redesign'). This technique is addressed at the end of this chapter.

The most recent addition to the evolution of motivation theory is based on the idea that workers are 'whole people' who pursue goals other than that of becoming high performers.[9] For example, you may want to be a brilliant student, loving boyfriend or girlfriend, caring parent, good friend, responsible citizen or a happy person. Work motivation is thus thought to be a function of your feelings and **emotions** towards the multitude of interests and goals that you have.

Content or *process* approaches of motivation

Content theories try to explain the things that actually motivate people in their job. These theories emphasise the goals to which people aspire and focus on the factors within a person that direct, energise or stop behaviour. Consequently, content theories want to identify people's needs, and the goals they want to attain in order to satisfy these needs. Whereas content theories emphasise what motivates people, **process theories** attempt to explain the actual process of motivation. The difference is that process theories give individuals a cognitive decision-making role in selecting their goals and the means to achieve them. These theories are concerned with answering questions of how individual behaviour is stimulated, directed, maintained and stopped.[10] Table 5.1 provides an overview of the main content and process theories. The content theories, also labelled as 'needs' theories, are discussed in the remainder of this chapter. McGregor's content theory has already been addressed in Chapter 1. Process theories will be addressed in Chapter 6.

Critical thinking

Which types of motivation thinking have you encountered in real life?

Table 5.1 Content and Process Theories of Motivation

Theoretical classification	Main theories
Content theories Address the question of what motivates people	Maslow's hierarchy of needs model Alderfer's modified need hierarchy model McClelland's motivation theory Herzberg's two factor theory McGregor's Theory X and Y
Process theories Address the question of how people get motivated	Equity theory Expectancy theory Goal-setting theory

5.2 Needs theories of motivation

Needs theories attempt to pinpoint internal factors that stimulate behaviour. **Needs** are physiological or psychological deficiencies that arouse behaviour. They can be strong or weak and are influenced by environmental factors. Human needs vary over time and place. Three popular needs theories are discussed in this section: Maslow's need hierarchy theory, Alderfer's ERG (existence, relatedness and growth) theory and McClelland's need theory.

Maslow's need hierarchy theory

In 1943 an important humanistic psychologist, Abraham Maslow, published his now famous need hierarchy theory of motivation. Although the theory was based on clinical observation of a few neurotic individuals, it has subsequently been used to explain the entire spectrum of human behaviour. Maslow proposed that motivation is a function of five basic needs – physiological, safety, love, esteem and self-actualisation (the needs are frequently depicted in a pyramid-shaped diagram (see Figure 5.2), but the shape may overstate the lower needs and understate the higher ones). An advantage of this model is that it is based on human behaviour, whereas the reinforcement theories of motivation were inferred from laboratory rat experiments.

Maslow argued that these five need categories are arranged in a graduated hierarchy and that human needs generally emerge in a predictable stepwise fashion. Accordingly, once one's physiological needs are relatively satisfied, one's safety needs emerge, and so on up the need hierarchy, one step at a time. Once a need is satisfied it activates the need above in the hierarchy. This process continues until the need for self-actualisation is activated.[11] A description of the five basic needs is shown in Table 5.2.

Alderfer's ERG theory

Clayton Alderfer developed another important need motivation theory by reworking and refining Maslow's work.[12] The ERG theory extends Maslow's needs hierarchy theory in many respects. Although Maslow's need hierarchy theory is extremely popular among students and managers, it

Figure 5.2 Maslow's Need Hierarchy

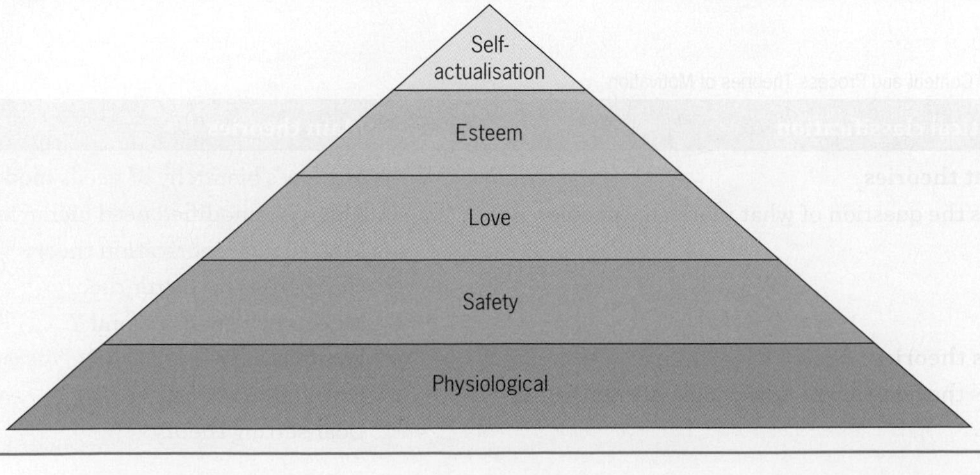

Table 5.2 Description of Five Basic Needs

Physiological needs	These needs are required to sustain life. In this category Maslow places chemical needs of the body such as sexual desire, hunger, sleepiness, activity needs and desired sensory satisfactions
Safety needs	Once the physiological needs are satisfied, one's needs are directed towards attaining a feeling of safety and security. It concerns the need for freedom from threat, that is, the security from threatening events or surroundings. So, people are motivated to avoid wild animals, extremes of temperature, assault, disease and the like. In this category the needs for living in a safe environment, medical insurance, job security and financial reserves are placed
Love needs	This category is used in a very comprehensive way as it includes the needs for affiliation and belongingness. It involves the need for friends, spouses, parents and group membership. Thus, typical love needs are friendship, belonging to a group, giving and receiving love
Esteem needs	This category falls into two broad categories. The first are internal esteem needs. They include desires for such feelings like power, achievement, confidence, freedom and independence. The second group refers to external esteem needs and is derived from reputation, prestige, recognition, attention and importance. Both groups of needs lead to higher self-confidence
Self-actualisation needs	These needs refer to the desire to realise or actualise one's full potential. This category includes needs such as truth, justice, wisdom, meaning, and so on.

lacks serious empirical evidence supporting its predictions.[13] The middle levels of Maslow's hierarchy are overlapping. Alderfer addressed this issue by reducing the five dimensions to three. The three letters of ERG theory represent three types of need. The first letter stands for **existence needs** and are comparable to Maslow's safety and physiological needs. This level involves the concern with basic material-existence requirements. The second group is **relatedness needs** and refers to the need to maintain significant relations. They are similar to Maslow's social and external esteem needs. Finally, the **growth needs** are concerned with the development of potential, and cover Maslow's self-esteem and self-actualisation needs. This third group represents an intrinsic desire for personal development. If you want to get an estimation of your growth need strength then complete the Activity below.

Activity

Assess your own growth need strength

Instructions

People differ in the kinds of jobs they would most like to hold. The descriptions and choices in Part A give you a chance to say just what it is about a job that is most important to you. For each entry, two different kinds of jobs are briefly described. Please indicate which of the two jobs you personally would prefer if you had to make a choice between them. For each pairing, pay attention only to the characteristics listed; assume that everything else about the job is the same. After circling each answer, use the scoring key in Part B.

Part A growth need strength scale

JOB A	Strongly prefer A	Slightly prefer A	Neutral	Slightly prefer B	Strongly prefer B	JOB B
1 A job where the pay is high	1	2	3	4	5	A job where there is considerable opportunity to be creative and innovative
2 A job where you are often required to make important decisions	1	2	3	4	5	A job with many pleasant people to work with
3 A job in which greater responsibility is given to those who do the best work	1	2	3	4	5	A job in which greater responsibility is given to loyal employees who have the most seniority
4 A job in a firm that is in financial trouble and might have to close down within the year	1	2	3	4	5	A job in a firm where you are not allowed to have any say whatever in how your work is scheduled or in the procedures to be used in carrying it out
5 A very routine job	1	2	3	4	5	A job where your co-workers are not very friendly
6 A job with a supervisor who is often very critical of you and your work in front of other people	1	2	3	4	5	A job that prevents you from using a number of skills that you have worked hard to develop
7 A job with a supervisor who respects you and treats you fairly	1	2	3	4	5	A job that provides constant opportunities for you to learn new and interesting things
8 A job where there is a real chance you could be laid off	1	2	3	4	5	A job with very little chance to do challenging work

JOB A	Strongly prefer A	Slightly prefer A	Neutral	Slightly prefer B	Strongly prefer B	JOB B
9 A job in which there is a real chance for you to develop new skills and advance in the organisation	1	2	3	4	5	A job that provides lots of vacation time and an excellent benefits package
10 A job with little freedom and independence to do your work in the way you best think	1	2	3	4	5	A job where working conditions are poor
11 A job with very satisfying team work	1	2	3	4	5	A job that allows you to use your skills and abilities to the fullest extent
12 A job that offers little or no challenge	1	2	3	4	5	A job that requires you to be completely isolated from co-workers

Part B scoring key and norms

Step one: Write down the circled numbers for the items indicated below, and add them to determine subtotal A.

___ + ___ + ___ + ___ + ___ + ___ = ________
(1) (5) (7) (10) (11) (12) **subtotal A**

Step two: The remaining items in the growth need strength scale need to be reverse-scored. To calculate a reverse score, subtract the direct score from 6. For instance if you circled 5 in item 2, the reverse score would be 1. If you circled 2 for item 9 the reverse score would be 4. Calculate the reverse scores for items 2, 3, 4, 6, 8, 9 and write them down in the formula below. Then make the sum of the reverse scores. This sum is subtotal B.

___ + ___ + ___ + ___ + ___ + ___ = ________
(2) (3) (4) (6) (8) (9) **subtotal A**

Step three: Make the sum of subtotal A and B. A total score below 30 is an indication that you have a relative low growth need strength, whereas a score above 42 indicates relative high growth need strength.

Source: See J. R. Hackman and G. Oldham, *Work Redesign* (Reading, MA: Addison Wesley, 1980), p. 275.

Beside these similarities, there are some major differences between both theories. Contrary to Maslow's need hierarchy model the ERG theory demonstrates that more than one need may motivate simultaneously. People can be motivated by money and self-development at the same time, according to the ERG theory. In the need hierarchy model, however, it is assumed that only one of the five needs can motivate at one point in time. For example, when someone's relatedness needs are completely satisfied, these needs cannot motivate as a higher level of esteem needs anymore. According to Alderfer the three groups of needs are more of a continuum. Maslow, in contrast, suggested that individuals progress through the hierarchy from existence needs, to relatedness needs, to growth needs, as the lower-level needs become satisfied.

A second significant difference is that when the gratification of a higher-order need is blocked, the desire to satisfy a lower-level need increases. This is also known as the **frustration-regression hypothesis**. According to this, individuals may also move down the hierarchy. The ERG theory acknowledges that this can happen, whereas the need hierarchy model does not. Suppose, for instance, that someone's basic needs are satisfied at relatedness level and he or she is now trying to satisfy their growth needs – that is, having many friends and social relationships and now trying to learn new significant skills, so as to make career advancement. However, because of a lack of opportunities to advance, those needs cannot be satisfied. No matter how hard he or she tries, a move upwards is blocked. According to the frustration-regression hypothesis, frustration of the growth needs will cause the relatedness needs to once again become dominant motivators. Henceforth, new energy will be put into making friends and building social relationships.

The ERG theory is more consistent with the knowledge of individual differences among people. This is a third major difference. Variables such as education, family background and cultural environment can alter the importance or driving force that a group of needs holds for a particular individual. This difference in hierarchy is not a problem for the ERG theory as it views the three groups of needs as a continuum and not a set of universal hierarchical levels. This is a significant problem with Maslow's hierarchy of needs model, which empirical research has shown is culture-bound. Japanese and Spanish people, for example, place social needs before their physiological requirements.[14] The hierarchy of needs in China is from low to high: physiological needs, self-actualisation through fitting in, esteem, sense of belongingness and love, safety and security.[15]

McClelland's need theory

David McClelland studied the relationship between needs and behaviour from the late 1940s to his death in 1998. Although he is mainly recognised for his research on the **need for achievement**, he also investigated the needs for affiliation and power. Before discussing each of these needs, let us consider the typical approach used to measure the strength of an individual's needs.

The thematic apperception test (TAT) is frequently used to measure an individual's motivation to satisfy various needs. In completing the TAT, people are asked to write stories about ambiguous pictures. These descriptions are then scored for the extent to which they contain achievement, power and affiliation imagery. A meta-analysis of 105 studies demonstrated that the TAT is a valid measure of the need for achievement.[16]

Activity

Assess your need strength with a thematic apperception test (TAT)

Instructions

The purpose of this exercise is to help you identify motivational themes expressed in the picture shown below. There are two steps. First, look at the picture briefly (10 to 20 seconds), and write the story it suggests by answering the following questions:

- What is happening? Who are the people?
- What past events led to this situation?
- What is wanted by whom?
- What will happen? What will be done?

Next, score your story for achievement, power and affiliation motivation by using the scoring guide and scales shown below. Score the motives from 1 (low) to 5 (high). The scoring guide identifies the types of story descriptions/words that are indicative of high motives. Give yourself a low score if you fail to describe the story with words and phrases contained in the scoring guidelines. A moderate score indicates that you used some of the phrases identified in the scoring guide to describe your story. Do not read the scoring guidelines until you have written your story.

	LOW	MODERATE			HIGH
• Achievement motivation	1	2	3	4	5
• Power motivation	1	2	3	4	5
• Affiliation motivation	1	2	3	4	5

Scoring key

Score achievement motivation high if:

- A goal, objective or standard of excellence is mentioned.
- Words such as good, better or best are used to evaluate performance.
- Someone in your story is striving for a unique accomplishment.
- Reference is made to career status or being a success in life.

Score power motivation high if:

- There is emotional concern for influencing someone else.
- Someone is actively striving to gain or keep control over others by ordering, arguing, demanding, convincing, threatening or punishing.
- Clear reference is made to a superior–subordinate relationship and the superior is taking steps to gain or keep control over the subordinate.

Score affiliation motivation high if:

- Someone is concerned about establishing or maintaining a friendly relationship with another.
- Someone expresses the desire to be liked by someone else.
- There are references to family ties, friendly discussions, visits, reunions, parties or informal get-togethers.

Achievement theories propose that motivation and performance vary according to the strength of one's need for achievement. For example, a field study of 222 life insurance brokers found a positive correlation between the number of policies sold and the brokers' need for achievement. McClelland's research supported an analogous relationship for societies as a whole. His results revealed that a country's level of economic development was positively related to its overall achievement motivation.[17]

The need for achievement is defined by the following desires:

- To accomplish something difficult.
- To master, manipulate or organise physical objects, human beings or ideas.
- To do this as rapidly and as independently as possible.
- To overcome obstacles and attain a high standard.
- To excel one's self.
- To rival and surpass others.
- To increase self-regard by the successful exercise of talent.[18]

This definition reveals that the need for achievement overlaps Maslow's higher-order needs of esteem and self-actualisation. One does not have to be a famous athlete, executive or personality to display high achievement. Achievement-motivated people share three common characteristics (see Figure 5.3).

Figure 5.3 Characteristics of High Need for Achievement People

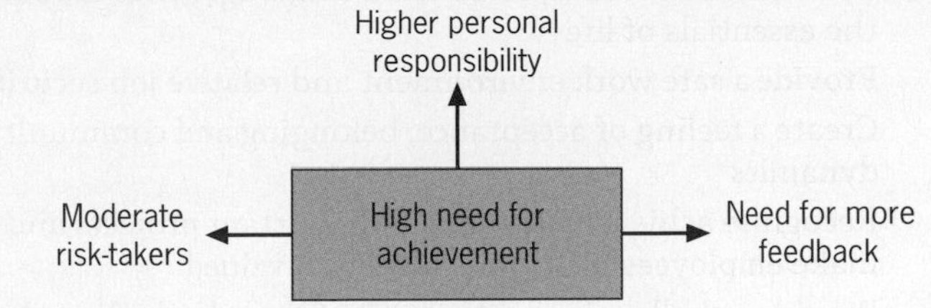

High achievers prefer to work on tasks of moderate difficulty. For example, when high achievers are asked to stand wherever they like while tossing rings at a peg on the floor, they tend to stand about 10 to 20 feet (3 to 6 metres) from the peg. This distance presents the ring tosser with a challenging but not impossible task. People with a low need for achievement tend to either walk up to the peg and drop the rings on or gamble on a lucky shot from far away. The high achiever's preference for moderately difficult tasks reinforces achievement behaviour by reducing the frequency of failure and increasing the satisfaction associated with successfully completing challenging tasks.

High achievers also like situations in which their performance is due to their own efforts rather than to other factors, such as luck. Personal satisfaction is derived from accomplishing the task. A third identifying characteristic of high achievers is that they desire more feedback from the outcome itself than do low achievers.[19] Feedback is a necessity, otherwise they cannot estimate failure or success in the accomplishment of their task, and derive satisfaction from their achievement. McClelland proposed that, given these characteristics, high achievers are more likely to be successful entrepreneurs – an idea subsequently confirmed.[20]

Researchers believe that people possess a basic desire to form and maintain a few lasting, positive and important interpersonal relationships. In addition, both psychological and physical health problems are higher among people who lack social attachments.[21] Just the same, not everyone has a high need to affiliate. People with a high **need for affiliation** prefer to spend more time maintaining social relationships, joining groups and wanting to be loved. Individuals high in this need are not the most effective employers or leaders because they have a hard time making difficult decisions without worrying about being disliked.

The **need for power** reflects an individual's desire to influence, coach, teach or encourage others to achieve. People with a high need for power like to work and are concerned with discipline and self-respect. There is a positive and negative side to this need. The negative face of power is characterised by an 'if I win, you lose' mentality. In contrast, people with a positive orientation to power focus on accomplishing group goals and helping employees obtain the feeling of competence. More is said about these two faces of power in Chapter 14.

Because effective employers must positively influence others, McClelland proposed that top managers should have a high need for power coupled with a low need for affiliation. He also believed that individuals with high achievement motivation are *not* best suited for top management positions. Several studies support these propositions.[22]

HR Evidence about needs theories

Students and managers seem to love the intuitively attractive ideas embodied in the needs hierarchies of Maslow and Alderfer. However, there is considerable evidence that they are largely barking

Table 5.3 Opportunities and Ways to Fulfil the Five Needs at Work

Physiological needs	Provide lunch breaks, rest breaks and wages that are sufficient to purchase the essentials of life
Safety needs	Provide a safe work environment and relative job security
Love needs	Create a feeling of acceptance, belonging and community by reinforcing team dynamics
Esteem needs	Recognise achievements, assign important projects and provide status to make employees feel appreciated and valued
Self-actualisation needs	Provide a challenging and meaningful work which enables innovation, creativity and progress according to the long term

up the wrong tree. The biological component makes some sense when seen in isolation: individuals will seek to meet the needs for survival and for security before seeking to meet higher needs. However even here there is a limit, since it may at times be a good idea to go hungry or thirsty if safety can be improved: people will try to escape volcanic eruptions (get to safety) even if thirsty and hungry. More importantly, the needs hierarchy thinking of Maslow and Alderfer may not work where organisational rewards are involved. These largely work through money payments (salary, bonuses, etc.) but the money medium may in fact work as a veil that obscures which need any given organisational member prioritises.

One further reason that the evidence does not support this theory may be that results from studies testing the need hierarchy are difficult to interpret given the complexity of the dynamics implied by the theory.[23] Maslow's theory seems to have important implications for an organisational setting. The five needs employees experience might be satisfied through compensation packages, company events, and so on. In Table 5.3 different opportunities are shown of how the five needs can be met.[24]

The hierarchy of needs models of Maslow and Alderfer are extremely popular with students and managers. Two reasons are that they are consistent with other theories of rational choice and because they ascribe freedom to individuals.[25] The assumption that people shape their actions to satisfy unfulfilled needs gives purpose and direction to individual behaviour. Thus, the popularity of these theories is embedded in their simplicity and transparency to explain human behaviour. However, a further reason is that these models are almost invariably among those that are taught before any other motivation theories, or at least appear early on in the textbook chapter on content motivation (this text is no exception). Further, Maslovian theory is frequently repeated in marketing texts and the combined effect of repetition and the appeal of simplicity may allow the ideas to stick in the student's mind to a greater degree than the evidence can support. The problems with the need theories are several, starting with the fact that Maslow himself provided no evidence to support his theory.[26]

People value the same needs differently. Maslow's theory, however, is a universalist theory which applies to everyone. As a result this theory cannot explain differences between people and between cultures. Employees do not always need to satisfy their needs through their work. It is possible that the higher level needs are satisfied through other life domains such as leisure. There is no conclusive evidence about how much time passes between the satisfaction of a lower-level need and the progress to a higher-order need.

Identical rewards may satisfy different needs. For instance, a high wage may satisfy the safety need and esteem need, because a high wage can be assessed as an important indicator for appraisal and recognition at work. Satisfaction in Maslow's theory is considered as the major motivational outcome of behaviour. However, job satisfaction does not necessarily improve work performance.

For employees with the same needs (same level in hierarchy), the motivational factors will be different because there are many diverse ways in which people may pursue satisfaction.

One possible explanation for the great staying power of needs theory may be that most people hold lay theories, or uninformed theories about motivation – and many other things besides. More importantly, the implicit distinction in the theory is that needs in the low part of the hierarchy are satisfied by extrinsic factors such as pay, promotions, whereas the upper needs are satisfied by intrinsic factors such as the enjoyment of work and the satisfaction associated with achieving one's potential. Evidence from laboratory and field studies in social psychology demonstrates that people are likely to hold lay theories containing an extrinsic incentives bias.[27] Quite apart from the asymmetric information problems (discussed in Chapter 4) in relations or contracts between principals (managers) and agents (employees), this bias may result in inappropriate (relative to the goals of the organisation) deals being offered to agents (employees), with an overly strong emphasis on extrinsic rewards.

Critical thinking

Do your own informal survey of motivation, asking friends or colleagues to identify five things that motivate people – and compare these to Maslow's needs to see if these individuals have any idea about motivation.

Application of needs-based motivation theories

Compared to the needs theories, the work of McClelland is better supported by evidence. Since adults can be trained to increase their achievement motivation,[28] providing achievement training for employees may increase motivation. It is also possible to base the selection of new employees on the achievement, affiliation and power needs of individuals. People with a high need for achievement are more attracted to companies that have a pay-for-performance environment than are those with a low achievement motivation.[29] After hiring, assignments or goals can be designed to be challenging because the need for achievement is positively correlated with goal commitment, which, in turn, influences performance.[30] (See Chapter 6 about goals as motivators.)

It is quite clear that the need for achievement as a higher-level need or an internal motivator has a North American bias. The assumption that high achievement works as an internal motivator underlies two cultural value dimensions: a willingness to accept moderate risks (which excludes countries with strong uncertainty avoidance) and concern with performance (which applies almost singularly to countries with strong quality-of-life characteristics). This combination, which is an integral part of the national cultural difference approach developed by Geert Hofstede (and presented at length in Chapter 12), is found in Anglo-American countries such as the USA, Canada and Great Britain.[31]

Herzberg's motivator-hygiene theory

The 'two-factor' theory, 'dual process' theory or Herzberg's theory is a job enrichment theory of motivation as it views motivation as social influence.[32] Frederick Herzberg's theory is based on

Figure 5.4 Herzberg's Motivator Hygiene Model

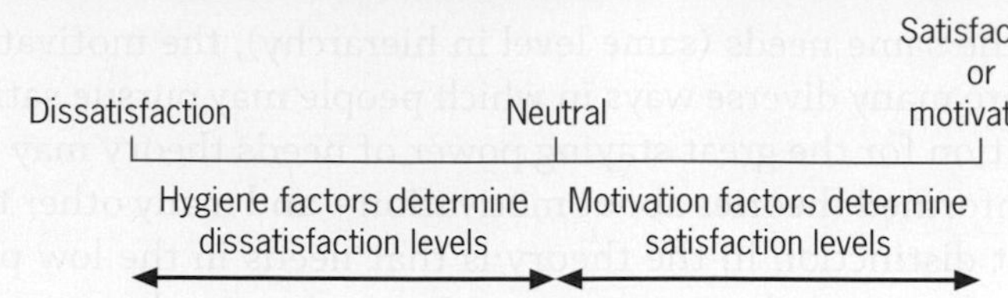

a study in which 203 accountants and engineers were interviewed. The interviews sought to determine the factors responsible for job satisfaction and dissatisfaction. Herzberg found separate and distinct clusters of factors associated with job satisfaction and dissatisfaction.

Job satisfaction was more frequently associated with achievement, recognition, characteristics of the work, responsibility and advancement. These factors were all related to outcomes associated with the content of the task being performed. Herzberg labelled these factors **motivators** because each was associated with strong effort and good performance. These factors concern all **intrinsic aspects of work**. He hypothesised that motivators cause a person to move from a state of no satisfaction to satisfaction (see Figure 5.4). Therefore, Herzberg's theory predicts that employers can motivate individuals by incorporating motivators into an individual's job.

Herzberg found job dissatisfaction to be associated primarily with factors in the work context or environment. Specifically, company policy and administration, technical supervision, salary, interpersonal relations with one's supervisor and working conditions were most frequently mentioned by employees expressing job dissatisfaction. These factors involve **extrinsic aspects of work**. Herzberg labelled this second cluster of factors **hygiene factors**. He further proposed that they were not motivational. At best, according to Herzberg's interpretation, an individual will experience no job dissatisfaction when he or she has no grievances about hygiene factors (see Figure 5.4).[33]

The key to adequately understanding Herzberg's motivator hygiene theory is to recognise that he believed that satisfaction is not the opposite of dissatisfaction. Herzberg concluded that 'the opposite of job satisfaction is not job dissatisfaction, but rather no job satisfaction; and similarly, the opposite of job dissatisfaction is not job satisfaction, but no dissatisfaction'.[34] Herzberg thus asserted that the dissatisfaction–satisfaction continuum contains a zero point, midway between dissatisfaction and satisfaction, where neither are present. The idea is that an organisation member who has good supervision, pay and working conditions but a tedious and unchallenging task with little chance of advancement would be at the zero midpoint. That person would have no dissatisfaction (because of good hygiene factors) and no satisfaction (because of a lack of motivators). Consequently, Herzberg warned employers that it takes more than good pay and good working conditions to motivate today's employees. It takes an 'enriched job' that offers the individual opportunity for achievement and recognition, stimulation, responsibility and advancement. Unfortunately, a study of 600 managers and 900 workers indicated that organisations may not be heeding Herzberg's advice. Results revealed that only 33 per cent felt that their managers knew what motivated them, and 60 per cent concluded that they did not receive any sort of recognition or rewards for their work.[35] Note, however, that such numbers may well be informative, but do not necessarily support Herzberg's theory.

Table 5.4 Comparison of Herzberg's Model with the Need Theories

Herzberg	Maslow	Alderfer	McClelland
Motivators	Self-actualisation	Growth	Achievement
	Esteem		Power
Hygiene factors	Love	Relatedness	Affiliation
	Safety	Existence	
	Physiological		

Source: Reprinted by permission of the *Harvard Business Review*. An exhibit from F. Herzberg, 'One More Time: How Do You Motivate Employees?', January/February 2003. Copyright © 2003 by the President and Fellows of Harvard College; all rights reserved.

Two different needs felt by human beings are assumed to underlie the observation that motivators are related to job satisfaction and hygiene factors to job dissatisfaction. The first set of needs stems from humankind's animal nature, that is the built-in drive to avoid pain from the environment, plus all the learned drives that become conditioned to the basic biological needs. For instance, hunger and thirst, basic biological drives, make it necessary to earn money, and then money becomes a specific drive. The second group of needs involves a unique human characteristic, the ability to achieve and, through achievement, to experience psychological growth. The stimuli for the growth needs are tasks that encourage growth in the work setting.[36] As a result, the motivators are situated among Maslow's higher order needs, such as esteem and self-actualisation needs. These motivators are also located at the same level of McClelland's need for achievement and need for power and Alderfer's growth need. Similarly, the hygiene factors correspond to Maslow's basic needs (physiological and safety needs), Alderfer's relatedness and existence needs, and McClelland's need for affiliation (see Table 5.4).

Evidence about the two-factor theory

A recent study among older engineers clearly demonstrates that a dissatisfying job experience usually results from inadequate hygiene factors. It appears that a significant change in the hygiene factors is required to produce a small change in job attitude. Analysis of these factors leads to the conclusion that significant changes in attitude using salary increases and changes in job environment appear to be very costly and are inefficient because their effects are short in duration. Additionally the data reveal that the effects of motivators on job attitudes are much longer lasting. These motivators also have a more profound impact on job attitudes.[37]

A recent job satisfaction poll among the 100 best employers according to *Fortune Magazine*, uncovered some striking findings not supporting the motivator-hygiene theory. The most conspicuous outcome concerned the difference between what was actually important to employees and what executives assumed was important to them. According to the employees, the top five job components contributing to job satisfaction were: job security, benefits, communication between employees and management, employee flexibility to balance work and life issues, and compensation/pay. So, hygiene factors like job security, benefits and salary were considered as major job components for the fulfilment of job satisfaction. The HR professionals rated communication between employees and management, and recognition by management as the most important determinants of job satisfaction followed by relationship with immediate supervisor, job security and compensation/pay.[38] In the activity below you can find out whether hygiene factors or motivator factors are more important to you.

Activity

Find out whether hygiene factors or motivator factors are more important to you

Instructions

Rate the following 12 job factors presented in Part A according to how important each is to you by ticking the corresponding number. Once done, mark your rating of each of the above factors in part A next to the corresponding numbers in part B. Add up each column in part B. If the total points in each column are equal this means that both factors are as important to you. A higher total number of points in one of the categories implies that you assess this category of factors as more important than the other category.

Part A

		Very important	Somewhat important		Not important	
		5	4	3	2	1
1	An interesting job					
2	A good boss					
3	Recognition and appreciation for the work I do					
4	The opportunity for advancement					
5	A satisfying personal life					
6	A prestigious job					
7	Job responsibility					
8	Good working conditions					
9	Sensible company rules, regulations, procedures and policies					
10	The opportunity to grow through learning new things					
11	A job I can do well and succeed at					
12	Job security					

Part B

Hygiene factors score	Motivator factors score
2 _____	1 _____
5 _____	3 _____
6 _____	4 _____
8 _____	7 _____
9 _____	10 _____
12 _____	11 _____
Total points:	Total points:

Source: R. Lussier, *Human Relations in Organizations: A Skill Building Approach*, 2nd edn (New York: The McGraw-Hill Companies, Inc, 1993).

Studies that have used the same methodology as Herzberg tend to support the theory. However, this methodology (critical incident technique) has itself been criticised. The descriptions of events (typical for this method) give rise to good and bad feelings. Afterwards, interviewers analyse these descriptions with an underlying risk of interviewer bias. So, the method-bound character of the theory makes its validity questionable. Another frequently mentioned critique is that the theory only applies to professionals and higher levels. The predictive power of this theory for people with unskilled jobs or repetitive work is limited. These people often are not interested in job growth-related opportunities. Furthermore, research has suggested that the model varies across cultures. A recent article on the cross-cultural applicability of the motivator-hygiene theory stated that US employees are more motivated by intrinsic factors such as growth and achievement while Japanese employees ascribe more importance to work context factors such as job security, work conditions and wages. Another study covering seven countries was more supportive for the universal character of intrinsic factors in the motivator-hygiene theory. Belgium, Britain, Israel and the USA rated 'interesting work' as the most important among 11 work goals. This factor was also ranked in the top three by Japanese, Dutch and German employees.

HR Application: Herzberg's model with vertical loading

Job enrichment is based on the application of Herzberg's ideas. Specifically, **job enrichment** entails modifying a job in such a way that an employee has the opportunity to experience achievement, recognition, stimulating work, responsibility and advancement. These characteristics are incorporated into a job through vertical loading. Rather than giving employees additional tasks of similar difficulty (horizontal loading), vertical loading consists of giving workers more responsibility. In other words, employees take on functions normally performed by their supervisors. Employers are advised to follow seven principles when vertically loading jobs (see Table 5.5).

Herzberg's theory generated a great deal of research and controversy. The controversy revolved around whether studies supporting the theory were flawed and thus invalid.[39] An assessment of the different views came to the conclusion that:

Table 5.5 Principles of Vertically Loading a Job

Principle	Motivators involved
A. Removing some controls while retaining accountability	Responsibility and personal achievement
B. Increasing the accountability of individuals for their own work	Responsibility and recognition
C. Giving a person a complete natural unit of work (module, division, area and so on)	Responsibility, achievement and recognition
D. Granting additional authority to an employee in their activity; job freedom	Responsibility, achievement and recognition
E. Making periodic reports directly available to the worker themself rather than to the supervisor	Internal recognition
F. Introducing new and more difficult tasks not previously handled	Growth and learning
G. Assigning individuals specific or specialised tasks, enabling them to become experts	Responsibility, growth and advancement

Source: Reprinted by permission of the *Harvard Business Review*. An exhibit from F. Herzberg, 'One More Time: How Do You Motivate Employees?', January/February 2003.

On balance, when we combine all of the evidence with all of the allegations that the theory has been misinterpreted, and that its major concepts have not been assessed properly, one is left, more than 20 years later, not really knowing whether to take the theory seriously, let alone whether it should be put into practice in organisational settings. There is support for many of the implications the theory has for enriching jobs to make them more motivating. But the two-factor aspect of the theory – the feature that makes it unique – is not really a necessary element in the use of the theory for designing jobs, per se.[40]

Critical thinking

The idea that 'more interesting jobs are more motivating' seems a no-brainer. But is it not possible that it may have exactly the opposite effect on employees?

5.3 Integration of need theories

All content theories have one internal weakness: they reveal nothing about the actual motivation process. People may be motivated by the same need, but choose different actions to satisfy these needs. Therefore, more complex theories have been developed and are described in the following chapter. However, despite the criticisms of the different theories, they do a great job in telling us what motivates people. Some general conclusions can be drawn from Table 5.4:

- People seem to seek security. Consequently, employers cannot neglect the security aspect in organisations.
- People also seek social systems. Regardless of whether you call this need relatedness, need for affiliation or belongingness, this sociability aspect is an important component of effective organisations (see Chapter 16).
- People seek personal growth. Whether we call it advancement, self-actualisation, need for achievement or growth, this self-development aspect is an important element of effective organisations. This development aspect is a key characteristic for learning organisations.

Other lessons to bear in mind after having reviewed the previous need theories are:

- It is better to presume that human needs operate within a flexible hierarchy or continuum. While most people focus first on existence needs when those needs are not satisfied, it is not possible to predict what the next most significant needs will be. As there is no fixed needs hierarchy, we should be cautious in predicting on which needs an employee will focus next.
- We should also be careful not to equate motivation with satisfaction. Satisfiers may demotivate. For instance, an employee whose wage is so high that he or she can afford anything they want may not be motivated to gain a financial incentive for reaching a particular performance goal.[41]
- Always keep in mind that needs theories were developed by American scholars and may be subject to cultural bias. Be aware of the literal application of these motivation theories to other cultures. For instance, Japanese or American employees are motivated by essentially the same needs, but conceptualisations of need satisfaction differs. Self-actualisation has a totally different significance for employees from individualistic countries than for employees from collectivistic countries (see also Chapter 12). American employees strive to attain self-growth by trying to improve themselves and their positions in life, whereas Japanese employees see self-actualisation in terms of success of the group as a whole.[42]

Critical thinking

What has been the most fulfilling experience in your life so far – and in your work life?

5.4 Job characteristics and the design of work

The job characteristics approach emerged as a reaction against Taylor's ideas about job design (see Chapter 1). Taylor's scientific management movement, with its emphasis on task specialisation and its simplistic view of human motivation, is blamed for the dehumanisation of work and the development of monotonous, routine jobs. Rather than motivating people in their jobs, the Taylorist approach yielded increased levels of absenteeism and turnover. The job characteristics approach, as a direct offshoot of job enrichment, attempts to tackle the dissatisfying and demotivating character of routine jobs through the modification of these jobs, so that employees get the opportunity to experience more recognition, stimulating work and responsibility.

The job characteristics model

This approach was developed by J. Richard Hackman and Greg Oldham. They tried to determine how work can be structured so that employees are internally (or intrinsically) motivated. **Internal motivation** occurs when an individual is 'turned on to one's work because of the positive internal feelings that are generated by doing well, rather than by being dependent on external factors (such as incentive pay or compliments from the boss) for the motivation to work effectively'.[43]

These positive feelings power a self-perpetuating cycle of motivation. As shown in Figure 5.5, internal work motivation is determined by three psychological states. In turn, these psychological states are fostered by the presence of five core job dimensions. The objective of this approach is to promote high internal motivation by designing jobs that possess the five core job characteristics.

The conditions under which individuals experienced the three critical psychological states can be described as follows:

- *Experienced meaningfulness*. The individual must perceive the work as worthwhile or important by some system of value he or she accepts.
- *Experienced responsibility*. He or she must believe in personal accountability for the outcomes of his or her efforts.
- *Knowledge of results*. He or she must be able to determine, on some fairly regular basis, whether or not the outcomes of the work are satisfactory.[44]

These psychological states generate internal work motivation. Moreover, they encourage job satisfaction and perseverance because they are self-reinforcing. If one of the three psychological states is short-changed, motivation diminishes.

The **core job dimensions** or characteristics are commonly found to a varying degree in all jobs. The five core job characteristics bring about the three psychological states (see Figure 5.5). Three of those job characteristics – skill variety, task identity and task significance – combine to determine experienced meaningfulness of work:

Figure 5.5 The Job Characteristics Model

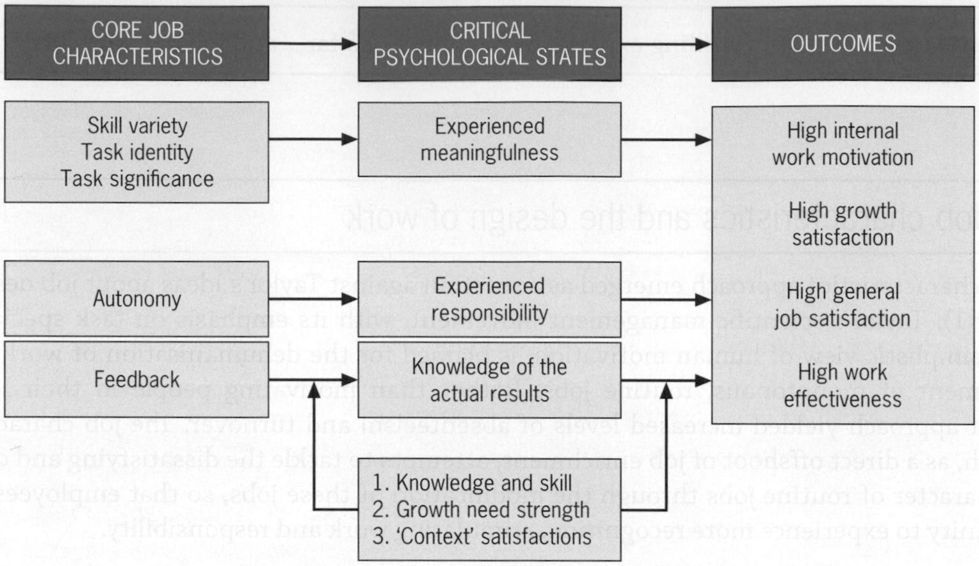

Source: J. R. Hackman and G. R. Oldham, *Work Redesign*, © 1980, Addison-Wesley Publishing Co., Reading, MA, p. 90. Reprinted with permission.

- *Skill variety*. The extent to which the job requires an individual to perform a variety of tasks that require him or her to use different skills and abilities.
- *Task identity*. The extent to which the job requires an individual to perform a whole or completely identifiable piece of work. In other words, task identity is high when a person works on a product or project from beginning to end and sees a tangible result.
- *Task significance*. The extent to which the job affects the lives of other people within or outside the organisation.

Experienced responsibility is elicited by the job characteristic of autonomy; whereas knowledge of results is fostered by the job characteristic of feedback, and these are defined as follows:

- *Autonomy*. The extent to which the job enables an individual to experience freedom, independence and discretion in both scheduling and determining the procedures used in completing the job.
- *Feedback*. The extent to which an individual receives direct and clear information about how effectively he or she is performing the job.[45]

Hackman and Oldham devised a tool for self-reporting in order to assess the extent to which a specific job possesses the five core job characteristics. With this tool (the job diagnostic survey), it is possible to calculate a motivating potential score for a job. The **motivating potential score** (MPS) is a summary index that represents the extent to which the job characteristics foster internal work motivation. Low scores indicate that an individual will not experience high internal work motivation from the job. Such a job is a prime candidate for job redesign. High scores reveal that the job is capable of stimulating internal motivation.

Arriving at an MPS involves two steps. First a job is rated on a scale from 1 (for not significant) to 7 (for very significant) in terms of its autonomy, task identity (an identifiable piece of work), variety (skills needed), significance (of the task) and feedback (from doing the work itself).

The second step is computing the MPS, as follows:

$$\text{MPS} = \frac{\text{skill variety} + \text{task identity} + \text{task significance}}{3} \times \text{autonomy} \times \text{feedback}$$

The maximum possible score is 343, the lowest 0. Jobs scoring above 200 are considered highly motivating; jobs below a score of 120 are low in motivation potential.

Judging from this equation, which core job characteristics do you think are relatively more important in determining the motivational potential of a job? Because autonomy and feedback are not divisible by another number, low scores on autonomy and feedback have a greater chance of lowering MPS than the job characteristics of skill variety, task identity and task significance. So, jobs that are high on MPS must be high on at least one of the three factors that lead to experienced meaningfulness, and they must be high on autonomy and feedback.

As previously discussed, not all people may want enriched work. Hackman and Oldham incorporated this conclusion into their model by identifying three attributes that affect how individuals respond to jobs with a high MPS. These attributes are concerned with the individual's knowledge and skill, need for strong growth (representing the desire to grow and develop as an individual), and context satisfactions (see Figure 5.5). Context satisfactions represent the extent to which employees are satisfied with various aspects of their job, such as pay, co-workers and supervision.

Hackman and Oldham proposed that people will respond positively to jobs with a high MPS when they have:

- The knowledge and skills necessary to do the job.
- High growth needs.
- An overall satisfaction with various aspects of the work context, such as pay and co-workers.

Although these recommendations make sense, several studies did not support the moderating influence of an employee's growth needs and context satisfaction.[46] The model worked equally well for employees with high and low growth needs and context satisfaction.

Evidence about the job characteristics theory

Organisations may want to use this model to increase employee job satisfaction. Research overwhelmingly demonstrates the existence of a moderately strong relationship between job characteristics and satisfaction.[47] A recent study of 459 employees from a glass manufacturing company also indirectly supported the job characteristics model. The company redesigned the work environment by increasing employees' autonomy and participation in decision-making and then measured employees' self-efficacy in carrying out a broader and more proactive role 18 months later. Job redesign resulted in higher self-efficacy.[48]

Unfortunately, job redesign appears to reduce the quantity of output just as often as it has a positive impact. Caution and situational appropriateness are advised. For example, one study demonstrated that job redesign works better in less complex organisations (small plants or companies).[49]

Nonetheless, employers are likely to find noticeable increases in the quality of performance after a job redesign programme. Results from 21 experimental studies revealed that job redesign resulted in a median increase of 28 per cent in the quality of performance.[50] Moreover, two separate meta-analyses support the practice of using the job characteristics model to help organisations reduce absenteeism and turnover;[51] and job characteristics were found to predict absenteeism over a six-year period. This latter result is very encouraging because it suggests that job redesign can have long-lasting positive effects on employee behaviour.

Considerable research has been done on the validity of the theory. Not all findings are supportive to the theory, although the positive results far outweigh the negative. Some queries exist about whether or not skill variety is redundant with autonomy, and whether or not task identity adds to the model's predictive ability.[52] Furthermore, it appears that calculating the motivating potential score by using a multiplicative relationship between core characteristics yields less optimal results. Simply adding the five scores works best.[53] Evaluation of the psychometric properties of the job diagnostic survey gives passing marks – probably even much better ones.[54] Several longitudinal studies have shown positive job enrichment effects on performance and on absenteeism.[55] The critical role of psychological states in the model has also gained support, although they may not operate in exactly the same manner *vis-à-vis* core characteristics and outcomes as originally hypothesised.[56] In summary, the current state of evidence supports the following statements:

- Overall analyses support the theory; people who work on enriched jobs are generally more motivated, productive and satisfied compared to those who are not.
- Job dimensions operate through the psychological states in influencing personal and work outcome variables rather than influencing them directly.
- The moderator effects of growth need strength, knowledge and context satisfactions are found to be very weak.

! Critical thinking

Is work design and work enrichment nothing more than cleverly disguised ways of making people work harder without paying them more?

HR Applications of the job characteristics theory

An advantage of the job characteristics theory is that Hackman and Oldham developed a reliable and valid instrument (job diagnostic survey) to measure the key variables of the theory.

A series of diagnostic steps and guidelines have been propounded on how to use the job diagnostic survey for the implementation of job enrichment.[57] These prescriptive steps and guidelines are presented in Table 5.6.

From the five core job characteristics of the theory, several hypotheses (action principles) have been inferred on how to achieve enriched jobs (see Figure 5.6). The principles for attaining higher motivating potential scores or for enriching jobs involve:

- Combining tasks. Give employees more than one part of the work in order to increase skill variety and task identity.
- Forming natural work units in order to increase task identity and task significance.
- Establishing client relationships in order to increase skill variety, autonomy and feedback.
- Implementing Herzberg's vertical loading principles (see above) in order to increase autonomy.
- Opening feedback channels in order to increase feedback.[58]

Table 5.6 Steps and Guidelines to Follow When Using Job Diagnostic Survey for Job Enrichment

Steps	Guidelines
Step 1: Check scores in the areas of motivation and satisfaction to see if problems exist in these areas. If they do, and the job outcomes are deficient, then job enrichment may well be called for	Guide 1: Diagnose the work system in terms of some theory of work redesign before introducing any change to see what is possible and what kinds of changes are most likely to work
Step 2: Check the motivating potential scores of the jobs to see if they are low. If they are not, job enrichment is not likely to be the answer	Guide 2: Keep the focus of the change effort on the work itself, rather than the other aspects of the work context, so that real job enrichment does occur
Step 3: Check scores for the five core dimensions to see what the basic strengths and weaknesses of the present job are. In this way it is possible to identify specific areas for change	Guide 3: Prepare in advance for any possible problems and side-effects, especially among employees whose jobs are not directly affected by the change; develop appropriate contingency plans
Step 4: Check to see what the growth need strength levels of job incumbents are. One can proceed with more confidence in enriching the jobs of employees with high growth needs since they are ready for the change	Guide 4: Evaluate the project on a continuing basis to see if anticipated changes actually are occurring and using as many and as objective measures as possible
Step 5: Check the scores for various aspects of job satisfaction and other information sources for roadblocks that might obstruct change or for special opportunities that might facilitate it	Guide 5: Confront difficult problems as early in the project as possible
	Guide 6: Design change processes in such a way as to fit the objectives of the job enrichment. Thus if autonomy in work is to be an objective, autonomy should be respected in designing the new jobs in the first place, in other words, be consistent with the theory in guiding the change effort throughout

Figure 5.6 Action Principles

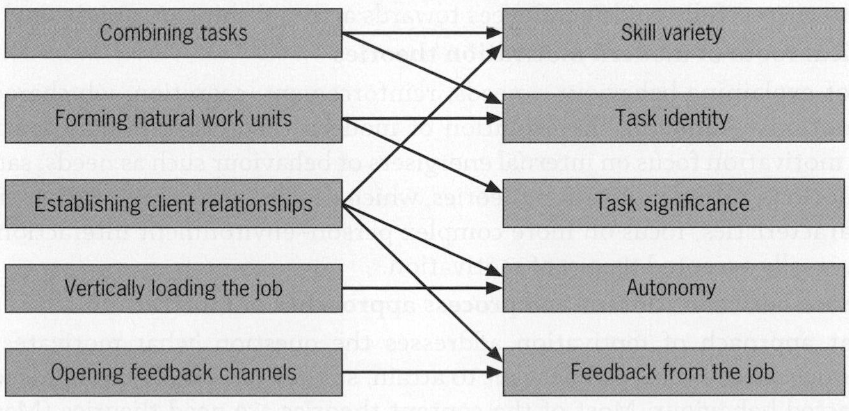

Source: J. R. Hackman and G. R. Oldham, *Work Redesign*, © 1980, Addison-Wesley Publishing Co., Reading, MA, p. 90. Reprinted with permission.

Job characteristics research also underscores an additional implication for companies undergoing re-engineering. Re-engineering potentially leads to negative work outcomes because it may increase job characteristics beyond reasonable levels. This occurs for two reasons:

- Re-engineering requires employees to use a wider variety of skills to perform their jobs, skills they may not have.
- Re-engineering typically results in downsizing and short-term periods of understaffing.[59]

The unfortunate catch is that understaffing was found to produce lower levels of group performance, and jobs with either overly low or high levels of job characteristics were associated with higher stress.[60] Employers are advised to consider carefully the level of perceived job characteristics when implementing re-engineering initiatives.

Job redesign is not a panacea for all employee satisfaction and motivation problems. To enhance the chances of success with this approach, managers need to remember that a change in one job or department can create problems of perceived inequity in related areas or systems within the organisation. Hackman and Oldham once noted: 'Our observations of work redesign programmes suggest that attempts to change jobs frequently run into – and sometimes get run over by – other organisational systems and practices, leading to a diminution (or even a reversal) of anticipated outcomes. . . . The "small change" effect, for example, often develops as managers begin to realise that radical changes in work design will necessitate major changes in other organisational systems as well.'[61]

Critical thinking

Once managers start looking at work design, what might they discover about their organisations?

Learning outcomes: Summary of key terms

1 **Define the term motivation**

Motivation is defined as those professional processes that cause the arousal, direction and persistence of voluntary, goal-oriented actions. Employers need to understand these psychological processes if they are to successfully guide employees towards accomplishing organisational objectives.

2 **The historical roots of modern motivation theories**

Five ways of explaining behaviour – needs, reinforcement, cognition, job characteristics, and feelings/emotions – underlie the evolution of modern theories of human motivation. Some theories of motivation focus on internal energisers of behaviour such as needs, satisfaction, and feelings/emotions. Other motivation theories, which deal in terms of reinforcement, cognitions, and job characteristics, focus on more complex person–environment interactions. There is no single, universally accepted theory of motivation.

3 **The difference between content and process approaches of motivation**

The content approach of motivation addresses the question 'what motivates people'. This approach concerns the goals people want to attain, so they can satisfy unmet needs, the drivers of goal-directed behaviour. Most of the content theories are need theories (Maslow, Alderfer and McClelland). Herzberg's job enrichment theory and McGregor's theory X and Y are also classified as content theories. The process approach includes much more complex theories (equity, expectancy and goal-setting theory) and was a reaction against the content theories. These latter theories have the internal weakness of saying nothing about the actual process of motivation. The former approach as the name conveys emphasises this actual process and tries to answer the question how people become motivated. Cognitive decisions people make between several choices are the key features of these theories.

4 **Maslow's and McClelland's need theories**

Two well-known need theories of motivation are Maslow's need hierarchy and McClelland's need theory. Maslow's notion of a graduated hierarchy of five levels of needs has not stood up well under research. McClelland believes that motivation and performance vary according to the strength of an individual's need for achievement. High achievers prefer moderate risks and situations where they can control their own destiny. Top managers should have a high need for power coupled with a low need for affiliation.

5 **Alderfer's theory and the frustration regression assumption**

Alderfer's need theory is in many ways a refinement of Maslow's hierarchy needs model. Clayton Alderfer determined that the middle levels in Maslow's model sometimes overlapped. He therefore reduced the five dimensions to three dimensions of needs. The existence needs refer to safety and physiological needs, whereas the relatedness needs refer to the need to maintain important relationships. Finally, the growth-related needs are concerned with the development of potential and cover Maslow's self-actualisation needs. According to the ERG theory people may regress down to a lower need level when a higher need is frustrated. For instance when people want to advance but the organisation does not give them opportunities to advance, people may become motivated by the level of pay. This is the frustration regression assumption.

6 **Herzberg's distinction between motivators and hygiene factors**

Herzberg believes job satisfaction motivates better job performance. His hygiene factors, such as policies, supervision and salary, erase sources of dissatisfaction. On the other hand, his motivators, such as achievement, responsibility and recognition, foster job satisfaction. Although Herzberg's motivator-hygiene theory of job satisfaction has been criticised on methodological grounds, it has practical significance for job enrichment.

7 **Internal work motivation and the job characteristics model**

The psychological states of experienced meaningfulness, experienced responsibility and knowledge of results, produce internal work motivation. These psychological states are fostered by the presence of five core job characteristics. People respond positively to jobs containing these core job characteristics when they have the knowledge and skills necessary to perform the job, high growth needs and high context satisfactions.

Review questions

1 Why should the average employer be well versed in the various motivation theories?

2 Give some examples of your own experience that support or disprove Maslow's hierarchy of needs model.

3 Are you a high achiever? How can you tell? How will this help or hinder your path to top management?

4 Do you agree or disagree that the need for achievement can be learned? Do you think it is easier to learn at an early or later age in life?

Personal awareness and growth exercise

What is your work ethic?

Objectives

1 To measure your work ethic.

2 To determine how well your work ethic score predicts your work habits.

Introduction

The work ethic reflects the extent to which an individual values work. A strong work ethic involves the belief that hard work is the key to success and happiness. In recent years, there has been concern that the work ethic is dead or dying. This worry is based on findings from observational studies and employee attitude surveys.

People differ in terms of how much they believe in the work ethic. These differences influence a variety of behavioural outcomes. What better way to gain insight into the work ethic than by measuring your own work ethic and seeing how well it predicts your everyday work habits?

Instructions

To assess your work ethic, complete the following eight-item instrument developed by a respected behavioural scientist.[62] Being honest with yourself, circle your responses on the rating scales following each of the eight items. There are no right or wrong answers. Add up your total score for the eight items, and record it in the space provided.

Following the work ethic scale is a short personal work habits questionnaire. Your responses to this questionnaire will help you determine whether your work ethic score is a good predictor of your work habits.

Work ethic scale

Agree completely **Disagree completely**

1 2 3 4 5

1 When the workday is finished, people should forget their jobs and enjoy themselves.	1	2	3	4	5
2 Hard work does not make an individual a better person.	1	2	3	4	5
3 The principal purpose of a job is to provide a person with the means for enjoying his or her free time.	1	2	3	4	5
4 Wasting time is not as bad as wasting money.	1	2	3	4	5
5 Whenever possible, a person should relax and accept life as it is, rather than always striving for unreachable goals.	1	2	3	4	5
6 A person's worth should not be based on how well he or she performs a job.	1	2	3	4	5
7 People who do things the easy way are the smart ones.	1	2	3	4	5
8 If all other things are equal, it is better to have a job with little responsibility than one with a lot of responsibility.	1	2	3	4	5

Total = ________

The higher your total score, the stronger your work ethic.

Personal work habits questionnaire

1 How many unexcused absences from classes did you have last term?
_______ absences
2 How many credit hours are you taking this term?
_______ hours
3 What is your overall grade point average?
_______ GPA
4 What percentage of your course expenses are you earning through full- or part-time employment?
_______ %
5 In percentage terms, how much effort do you typically put into your studies and/or work?
Studies = [?] _______ % Work = [?] _______%

Questions for discussion

1 How strong is your work ethic?
Weak = 8–18
Moderate = 9–29
Strong = 30–40
2 How would you rate your work habits/results?
Below average _______
Average _______
Above average _______
3 How well does your work ethic score predict your work habits or work results?
Poorly _______
Moderately well _______
Very well _______

Group exercise

Applying Maslow's hierarchy of needs model and Alderfer's ERG theory

Objectives

1 To correctly classify needs into the categories of Maslow's model and Alderfer's model.
2 To demonstrate that the use of Alderfer's theory is more straightforward and simple in comparison to Maslow's model.

Instructions

In the next exercise you will get a fragment in which the needs of the four main characters from the American sitcom *Seinfeld* (Elaine, George, Jerry and Kramer) are described. Read through the descriptions of the needs of the four individuals and identify the levels at which the characters would be placed on Maslow's hierarchy of needs and Alderfer's ERG theory. Also provide an explanation or rationale why you think a given level is most descriptive of an individual's dominant needs. Discuss afterwards the responses and the rationales in group.

Description

Jerry, George, Kramer and Elaine have different needs. Jerry is really dedicated to being the best stand-up comic he can, and he is very concerned about getting good reviews and being recognised in the entertainment industry. George just wants to be able to find a job he can hold on to so that he can move out of his parent's house into a place of his own. Kramer only cares about good food, having clothes on his back and a roof over his head. Elaine wants to have good, honest relationships with her friends, and find a stable, long-term romantic relationship.

At what level in his hierarchy of needs would Abraham Maslow place each of these four friends and why?

Please place a cross or tick in the correct need category and explain your rationale behind that choice.

	Maslow's need categories				
Character	Physiological	Safety	Love	Esteem	Self-actualisation
1. Jerry					
Rationale:					
2. George					
Rationale:					
3. Kramer					
Rationale:					
4. Elaine					
Rationale:					

How would Clayton Alderfer characterise their needs using ERG theory and why?

Please, place a cross or tick in the correct need category and explain your rationale behind that choice.

	Alderfer's need categories		
Character	Existence	Relatedness	*Growth*
1. Jerry			
Rationale:			
2. George			
Rationale:			
3. Kramer			
Rationale:			
4. Elaine			
Rationale:			

Source: C. S. Hunt, 'Must see TV: the timelessness of television as a teaching tool', *Journal of Management Education*, December 2001, pp. 631–47.

Online
Learning Centre

When you have read this chapter, log on to the Online Learning Centre website at ***www.mcgraw-hill.co.uk/textbooks/sinding*** to access test questions, additional exercises and other related resources.

Notes

1. K. Hilpern, 'Put a Little Spirit into your Work', *The Guardian*, 30 October 2000.
2. P. Ester, L. Halman and R. De Moor, *The Individualizing Society: Value Change in Europe and North America* (Tilburg: Tilburg University Press, 1994).

[3] D. McGregor, *The Human Side of Enterprise* (New York: McGraw-Hill, 1960).

[4] M. L. Ambrose and C. T. Kulek, 'Old Friends New Faces: Motivation Research in the 1990s', *Journal of Management*, Summer 1999, pp. 231–7. A recent number of the *Academy of Management Journal* (July 2004) is devoted to the future of work motivation theories.

[5] M. Blumberg and C. D. Pringle, 'The Missing Opportunity in Organizational Research: Some Implications for a Theory of Work Performance', *Academy of Management Review*, October 1982, pp. 560–69.

[6] T. R. Mitchell, 'Motivation: New Directions for Theory, Research and Practice', *Academy of Management Review*, January 1982, pp. 80–88.

[7] J. Greenberg and R. A. Baron, *Behavior in Organizations: Understanding and Managing the Human Side of Work* (Englewood Cliffs, NJ: Prentice Hall, 1997).

[8] L. J. Mullins, *Management and Organisational Behaviour, sixth edition* (Harlow: Prentice Hall, 2002).

[9] The effects of feelings and emotions on work motivation are discussed by J. M. George and A. P. Brief, 'Motivational Agendas in the Workplace: The Effects of Feelings on Focus of Attention and Work Motivation', in *Research in Organizational Behavior*, vol. 18, eds B. M. Staw and L. L. Cummings (Greenwich, CT: JAI Press, 1996), pp. 75–109.

[10] D. Buchanan and A. Huczynski, *Organizational Behaviour: An Introductory Text, fifth edition* (Harlow: Prentice Hall, 2004).

[11] For a complete description of Maslow's theory, see A. H. Maslow, 'A Theory of Human Motivation', *Psychological Review*, July 1943, pp. 370–96.

[12] C. P. Alderfer, 'An Empirical Test of a New Theory of Human Needs', *Organizational Behavior and Human Performance*, May 1969, pp. 142–75.

[13] A. K. Korman, J. H. Greenhaus, and I. J. Badin, 'Personnel Attitudes and Motivation', in *Annual Review of Psychology*, eds M. R. Rosenzweig and L. W. Porter (Palo Alto, CA: Annual Reviews, 1977), pp. 178–9.

[14] M. Haire, E. E. Ghiselli and L. W. Porter, 'Cultural Patterns in the Role of the Manager', *Industrial Relations*, February 1963, pp. 95–117.

[15] E. Nevis, 'Using an American Perspective in Understanding Another Culture: Toward a Hierarchy of Needs for the People's Republic of China', *Journal of Applied Behavioral Science*, no. 3, 1983, pp. 249–64.

[16] Results can be found in W. D. Spangler, 'Validity of Questionnaire and TAT Measures of Need for Achievement: Two Meta-Analyses', *Psychological Bulletin*, July 1992, pp. 140–54.

[17] Results can be found in S. D. Bluen, J. Barling and W. Burns, 'Predicting Sales Performance, Job Satisfaction, and Depression by Using the Achievement Strivings and Impatience–Irritability Dimensions of Type A Behavior', *Journal of Applied Psychology*, April 1990, pp. 212–16; and D. C. McClelland, *The Achieving Society* (New York: Free Press, 1961).

[18] H. A. Murray, *Explorations in Personality* (New York: John Wiley & Sons, 1983), p. 164.

[19] Recent studies of achievement motivation can be found in H. Grant and C. S. Dweck, 'A Goal Analysis of Personality and Personality Coherence', in *The Coherence of Personality*, eds D. Cervone and Y. Shoda (New York: The Guilford Press, 1999), pp. 345–71; and D. Y. Dai, S. M. Moon and J. F. Feldhusen, 'Achievement Motivation and Gifted Students: A Social Cognitive Perspective', *Educational Psychologist*, Spring–Summer 1998, pp. 45–63.

[20] A. Rauch and M. Frese, 'Psychological Approaches to Entrepreneurial Success: A General Model and Overview of Findings', in *International Review of Industrial and Organizational Psychology*, eds C. L. Cooper and I. T. Robertson (New York: Wiley, 2000); and K. G. Shaver, 'The Entrepreneurial Personality Myth', *Business and Economic Review*, April–June 1995, pp. 20–23.

[21] Research on the affiliative motive can be found in S. C. O'Connor and L. K. Rosenblood, 'Affiliation Motivation in Everyday Experience: A Theoretical Comparison', *Journal of Personality and Social Psychology*, March 1996, pp. 513–22; and R. F. Baumeister and M. R. Leary, 'The Need to Belong: Desire for Interpersonal Attachments as a Fundamental Human Motivation', *Psychological Bulletin*, May 1995, pp. 497–529.

[22] See D. K. McNeeseSmith, 'The Relationship between Managerial Motivation, Leadership, Nurse Outcomes and Patient Satisfaction', *Journal of Organizational Behavior*, March 1999, pp. 243–59; A. M. Harrell and M. J. Stahl, 'A Behavioral Decision Theory Approach for Measuring McClelland's Trichotomy of Needs', *Journal of Applied Psychology*, April 1981, pp. 242–7; and M. J. Stahl, 'Achievement, Power and Managerial Motivation: Selecting Managerial Talent with the Job Choice Exercise', *Personnel Psychology*, Winter 1983, pp. 775–89.

[23] C. C. Pinder, *Work Motivation: Theory, Issues, and Applications* (Glenview, IL: Scott, Foresman, 1984), p. 52.

[24] Retrieved from 'Maslow's Hierarchy of Needs', www.envisionsoftware.com/articles/Maslow_Needs_Hierarchy.html/, April 2004.

[25] G. R. Salancik and J. Pfeffer, 'An Examination of Need Satisfaction Models of Job Attitudes', *Administrative Science Quarterly*, September 1977, pp. 427–56.

[26] See L. J. Mullins, *Management and Organisational Behaviour, sixth edition* (Harlow: Prentice Hall, 2002).

[27] See C. Heath, 'On the Social Psychology of Agency Relationships: Lay Theories of Motivation Overemphasize Extrinsic Incentives', *Organizational Behavior and Human Decision Processes*, April 1999, pp. 25–62.

[28] For a review of the foundation of achievement motivation training, see D. C. McClelland, 'Toward a Theory of Motive Acquisition', *American Psychologist*, May 1965, pp. 321–33. Evidence for the validity of motivation training can be found in H. Heckhausen and S. Krug, 'Motive modification', in *Motivation and Society*, ed. A. J. Stewart (San Francisco, CA: Jossey-Bass, 1982).

[29] Results can be found in D. B. Turban and T. L. Keon, 'Organizational Attractiveness: An Interactionist Perspective', *Journal of Applied Psychology*, April 1993, pp. 184–93.

[30] See D. Steele Johnson and R. Perlow, 'The Impact of Need for Achievement Components on Goal Commitment and Performance', *Journal of Applied Social Psychology*, November 1992, pp. 1711–20.

[31] See S. P. Robbins, *Organizational Behavior: International Edition*, 10th edition (Harlow: Prentice Hall, 2003).

[32] See F. Herzberg, B. Mausner and B. B. Snyderman, *The Motivation to Work* (New York: John Wiley & Sons, 1959).

[33] Two tests of Herzberg's theory can be found in I. O. Adigun and G. M. Stephenson, 'Sources of Job Motivation and Satisfaction among British and Nigerian Employees', *Journal of Social Psychology*, June 1992, pp. 369–76; and E. A. Maidani, 'Comparative Study of Herzberg's Two-Factor Theory of Job Satisfaction among Public and Private Sectors', *Public Personnel Management*, Winter 1991, pp. 441–8.

[34] F. Herzberg, 'One More Time: How Do You Motivate Employees?', *Harvard Business Review*, January 2003, pp. 87–96.

[35] Results are presented in 'Are your Staffers Happy? They're in the Minority', *Supervisory Management*, March 1996, p. 11.

[36] See F. Herzberg, 'One More Time: How Do You Motivate Employees?', *Harvard Business Review*, January 2003, pp. 87–96.

[37] R. L. Lord, 'Traditional Motivation Theories and Older Engineers', *Engineering Management Journal*, September 2002, pp. 3–7.

[38] 'Motivation Secrets of the 100 Best Employers', *HR Focus*, October 2003, pp. 10–15.

[39] Both sides of the Herzberg controversy are discussed by N. King, 'Clarification and Evaluation of the Two-Factor Theory of Job Satisfaction', *Psychological Bulletin*, July 1970, pp. 18–31; and B. Grigaliunas and Y. Weiner, 'Has the Research Challenge to Motivation–Hygiene Theory Been Conclusive? An Analysis of Critical Studies', *Human Relations*, December 1974, pp. 839–71.

[40] C. C. Pinder, *Work Motivation: Theory, Issues, and Applications* (Glenview, IL: Scott, Foresman, 1984), p. 28.

[41] R. J. Aldag and L. W. Kuzuhara, *Organizational Behavior and Management: An Integrated Skills Approach* (Cincinnati, OH: Thompson Learning, 2002).

[42] See J. Di Cesare and G. Sadri, 'Do All Carrots Look the Same? Examining the Impact of Culture on Employee Motivation', *Management Research News*, no. 1, 2003, pp. 29–40.

[43] J. R. Hackman, G. R. Oldham, R. Janson and K. Purdy, 'A New Strategy for Job Enrichment', *California Management Review*, Summer 1975, p. 58.

[44] J. R. Hackman and G. Oldham, *Work Redesign* (Reading, MA: Addison Wesley, 1980), p. 58.

[45] Definitions of the job characteristics were adapted from J. R. Hackman and G. R. Oldham, 'Motivation through the Design of Work: Test of a Theory', *Organizational Behavior and Human Performance*, August 1976, pp. 250–79.

[46] A review of this research can be found in M. L. Ambrose and C. T. Kulik, 'Old Friends, New Faces: Motivation Research in the 1990s', *Journal of Management*, Summer 1999, pp. 231–92.

[47] See M. L. Ambrose and C. T. Kulik, 'Old Friends, New Faces: Motivation Research in the 1990s', *Journal of Management*, Summer 1999, pp. 231–92; C. Wong, C. Hui and K. S. Law, 'A Longitudinal Study of the Job Perception – Job Satisfaction Relationship: A Test of the Three Alternative Specifications', *Journal of Occupational and Organizational Psychology*, June 1998, pp. 127–46; and T. Loher, R. A. Noe, N. L. Moeller and M. P. Fitzgerald, 'A Meta-Analysis of the Relation of Job Characteristics to Job Satisfaction', *Journal of Applied Psychology*, May 1985, pp. 280–89.

[48] Results can be found in S. K. Parker, 'Enhancing Role Breadth Self-Efficacy: The Roles of Job Enrichment and Other Organizational Interventions', *Journal of Applied Psychology*, December 1998, pp. 835–52.

[49] Results can be found in M. R. Kelley, 'New Process Technology, Job Design, and Work Organization: A Contingency Model', *American Sociological Review*, April 1990, pp. 191–208.

[50] Productivity studies are reviewed in R. E. Kopelman, *Managing Productivity in Organizations* (New York: McGraw-Hill, 1986).

[51] Absenteeism results are discussed in Y. Fried and G. R. Ferris, 'The Validity of the Job Characteristics Model: A Review and Meta Analysis', *Personnel Psychology*, Summer 1987, pp. 287–322; and J. R. Rentsch and R. P. Steel, 'Testing the Durability of Job Characteristics as Predictors of Absenteeism Over a Six-Year Period', *Personnel Psychology*, Spring 1998, pp. 165–90. The turnover meta-analysis was conducted by G. M. McEvoy and W. F. Cascio, 'Strategies for Reducing Turnover: A Meta-Analysis', *Journal of Applied Psychology*, May 1985, pp. 342–53.

[52] Y. Fried and G. R. Ferris, 'The Dimensionality of Job Characteristics: Some Neglected Issues', *Journal of Applied Psychology*, August 1986, pp. 419–26.

[53] M. Hinton and M. Biderman, 'Empirically Derived Job Characteristics Measures and the Motivating Potential Score', *Journal of Business and Psychology*, Summer 1995, pp. 355–64.

[54] Y. Fried, 'Meta-Analytic Comparison of the Job Diagnostic Survey and Job Characteristics Inventory as Correlates of Work Satisfaction and Performance', *Journal of Applied Behavioral Science*, October 1991, pp. 690–97; and T. D. Taber and E. Taylor, 'A Review and Evaluation of Psychometric Properties of Job Diagnostic Survey', *Personnel Psychology*, Fall 1990, pp. 467–500.

[55] R. W. Griffin, 'Effects of Work Redesign on Employee Perceptions, Attitudes, and Behaviors: A Long-Term Investigation', *Academy of Management Journal*, June 1991, pp. 425–35; and J. R. Rentsch and R. P. Steel, 'Testing the Durability of Job Characteristics as Predictors of Absenteeism Over a Six-Year Period', *Personnel Psychology*, Spring 1998, pp. 165–90.

[56] R. W. Renn and R. J. Vandenberg, 'The Critical Psychological States: An Underrepresented Component in Job Characteristics Research', *Journal of Management*, no. 3, 1995, pp. 279–303.

[57] J. R. Hackman and G. Oldham, *Work Redesign* (Reading, MA: Addison Wesley, 1980), p. 275.

[58] J. R. Hackman and G. Oldham, *Work Redesign* (Reading, MA: Addison Wesley, 1980), p. 275.

[59] A thorough discussion of re-engineering and associated outcomes can be found in J. Champy, *Reengineering Management: The Mandate for New Leadership* (New York: Harper Business, 1995); and M. Hammer and J. Champy, *Reengineering the Corporation: A Manifesto for Business Revolution* (New York: Harper Business, 1993).

[60] See J. D. Jonge and W. B. Schaufeli, 'Job Characteristics and Employee Well-Being: A Test of Warr's Vitamin Model in Health Care Workers Using Structural Equation Modelling', *Journal of Organizational Behavior*, July 1998, pp. 387–407; and D. C. Ganster and D. J. Dwyer, 'The Effects of Understaffing on Individual and Group Performance in Professional and Trade Occupations', *Journal of Management*, no. 2, 1995, pp. 175–90.

[61] G. R. Oldham and J. R. Hackman, 'Work Design in the Organizational Context', in *Research in Organizational Behavior*, eds B. M. Staw and L. L. Cummings (Greenwich, CT: JAI Press, 1980), pp. 248–9.

[62] Adapted from M. R. Blood, 'Work Values and Job Satisfaction', *Journal of Applied Psychology*, December 1969, pp. 456–9.

Chapter 6

Process motivation theories

Learning Outcomes

When you finish studying the material in this chapter, you should be able to:

- ✓ discuss the role of perceived inequity in employee motivation
- ✓ explain Vroom's expectancy theory of motivation and Porter and Lawler's extension of the expectancy theory
- ✓ explain how goal setting motivates people and identify five practical lessons to be learned from goal-setting research
- ✓ discuss how a recipient's characteristics, perception and cognitive evaluation affect how he or she processes feedback
- ✓ list at least three practical lessons from feedback research
- ✓ list different types of organisational rewards
- ✓ describe practical recommendations to implement an organisational reward system
- ✓ specify issues that should be addressed before implementing a motivational programme

Opening Case Study: Bonuses for bankers

Bonuses on a grand scale have been blamed, among other things, for the financial crisis which began in earnest in 2008. Many banks were only saved from bankruptcy by large infusions of government support. In return, the state received shares, in some cases becoming majority owners of very large banks. The UK Treasury, for example, is estimated to have spent in the region of £850 billion and the average voter may, as an indirect shareholder, feel that paying bonuses to bankers who contributed to the arrival of the financial crisis is adding insult to injury.

In the case of the Royal Bank of Scotland, which is 70 per cent owned by the UK Treasury, the other side of the argument about bonuses, that they are needed to retain and attract the best people, was brought into the open when the Board of the bank threatened to resign if the bonuses were blocked by the major shareholder. The bank's chief executive, Stephen Hester, told a BBC radio programme that the thousands of people that had left the bank in 2009 might have added £1 billion to the bank's profits.

The story so far suggests that banking executives are eager to pay large bonuses to their employees and themselves. The argument used to support large bonuses is that they are driven by competition for good bankers The UK bonus payment practice must be seen in a historical perspective. Before the deregulation of the UK financial sector, often referred to the 'Big Bang', senior bankers were partners. The risks taken on the job were reflected in the profits made. However, after deregulation, risks were transferred to big institutions while the payment of bonuses remained.

The outcome of the RBS bonus debate was resolved when RBS changed the formula for paying the bonuses from pure cash payments to largely being made up of shares in the bank. Indeed, the CEO of Royal Bank of Scotland received no bonus payment for 2012, since he failed to meet the performance criteria in his contract. In an effort to set clear rules on bonuses, the European Banking Authority has proposed that anyone in a bank earning a salary of more than €500 000 annually will be allowed a bonus payment of 100 per cent of salary. In cases where a shareholder vote takes place on individual bonus payments, the limit is to be 200 per cent. The ideal would be to limit bonuses only to those employees who take material risk, but definitions of what that means are many and varied. The sum identified bypasses this problem but may extend the rules to many more employees at each bank.

For Barclays in 2012, the estimate is that 1338 employees received a total of more than £500 000 (note that this includes bonus payments). This bank claims to have 393 staff members who take or monitor risk.

All this carries the implicit suggestion that bonuses motivate. However, it is debatable whether bonuses actually motivate at all, or motivate only certain things. Dan Ariely, a behavioural economist, has run experiments to discover what different levels of bonus meant for performance in various tasks. First, medium-sized bonuses gave performance that was neither better nor worse than that of low bonuses. Further, those offered the biggest bonus (equivalent to five months' pay, instead of one day's worth of work for the low bonus and two weeks' work for the medium bonus) performed worse, regardless of the task they were given. Later replications of the study confirmed the result, as did a study where public scrutiny replaced the cash bonus. However, contrary to expectations that people would do better in public, they performed worse, despite having stated that they wanted to do better. Ariely concluded that money motivates, especially where effort rather than skill is required. But bonuses also create stress, which at some point overwhelms any motivational effect.

For discussion

Review your own personal experience with payments and bonuses.

Source: The interview was by Margaret Pogano and appeared in The *Independent*, 4 July 2010. Rest of case based on Jill Treanor, 'London "risk takers" to be hit by EU bank bonus cap', The *Guardian*, 17 May 2013; and Dan Ariely, 'What's the Value of a Big Bonus?', *New York Times*, 20 November 2008.

As may be seen in the case on bankers and bonuses, organisations can use different approaches to motivate people. Giving people rewards, whether or not related to their performance, is a widely used practice that fits in different motivation theories, as will be explained in this chapter. Another common practice to enhance people's motivation is giving people challenging, although reachable and specific goals. Striving for various goals motivates people. A long-distance runner, for example, who wants to take part in the Berlin Marathon, will probably train harder if he or she is in a competition. Even as soon as two weeks after the 2008 Olympics in Beijing, many athletes started their new training routines with the 2012 London games in mind. The goal-setting theory of motivation provides a good explanation for their behaviour.

This chapter explores five different aspects related to how people can be motivated and how their performance can be influenced. First, three process theories of motivation are elaborated: expectancy theory, equity theory and goal-setting theory. In contrast to the content theories of motivation discussed in the previous chapter, process theories help us explain why people behave the way they do by focusing on how people try to satisfy their needs.

Second, we focus on effective feedback and giving rewards as important tools to influence and enhance the performance of employees. Properly administered feedback and rewards can guide, teach and motivate people in the direction of positive change.

Finally, we return to bonuses and the many other practical issues upon which motivation initiatives depend for success – or failure.

6.1 Expectancy theory of motivation

The **expectancy theory** is the idea that people's actions are driven by expected consequences. Perception (Chapter 4) plays a central role in expectancy theory because it emphasises the cognitive ability to anticipate likely consequences of behaviour. One component of expectancy theory is the principle of hedonism. Hedonistic people strive to maximise their pleasure and minimise their pain. Generally, expectancy theory can be used to predict behaviour in any situation in which a choice between two or more alternatives must be made. Whether to resign or stay in a job; whether to put in substantial or minimal effort to do a task; or whether to choose business management, geology, accounting, marketing, civil engineering or communication as one's main field of study at university.

This section introduces and explores two expectancy theories of motivation: Victor Vroom's expectancy theory and Lyman Porter and Edward Lawler's extension of Vroom's theory. Understanding these cognitive process theories can help managers to develop organisational policies and practices that enhance rather than inhibit employee motivation.

Figure 6.1 Vroom's Expectancy Model

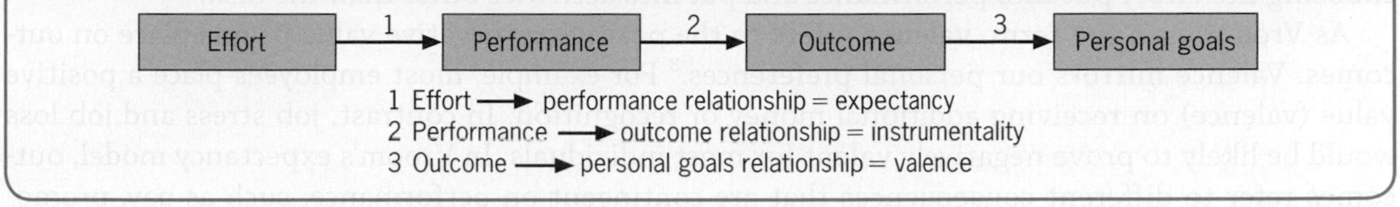

Vroom's expectancy theory

Motivation, according to Victor Vroom,[1] boils down to the decision about how much effort to exert in a specific task situation. This choice is based on a three-stage sequence of expectations (see Figure 6.1):

- First, motivation is affected by an individual's expectation that a certain level of effort will produce the intended performance goal. What can a person get from the organisation and what level of effort must that person put in to get the expected outcome?
- Motivation is also influenced by a person's perceived chances of getting various **outcomes** as a result of performing at a level which would result in the benefits.
- Individuals are motivated to the extent that they value the outcomes received. Only if the perceived value of the outcome is higher than the perceived value of the cost (or effort) will the effort be exerted.

The model shows that someone who attaches much value to an outcome, for example, getting a high mark in an exam will be more motivated to put extra effort to perform well and to reach this outcome. Someone else who values a high mark less will be less motivated to put in much effort in studying the exam and so the results will be correspondingly more modest. When the expected outcome (a high mark) fails to materialise, the motivation to study hard for future exams will be reduced (unless the outcome can be explained in some other way – bad luck, a nasty professor etc.).

An **expectancy**, according to Vroom's terminology, represents an individual's belief that a particular degree of effort will be followed by a particular level of performance. It is an effort → performance expectation. Expectancies take the form of subjective probabilities, where zero represents the perception that effort has no effort on performance (which is then random) and one represents the perception that everything depends on effort.

The following factors influence an employee's expectancy perceptions:

- Self-esteem.
- Self-efficacy.
- Previous success at the task.
- Help received from a supervisor and subordinates.
- Information necessary to complete the task.
- Good materials and equipment to work with.[2]

An **instrumentality** is a performance → outcome perception. It represents a person's belief that a particular outcome depends on performing at a specific level. Performance is instrumental when it leads to something else. For example, passing exams is instrumental to graduating from university. Instrumentalities can either directly link task performance to outcome, or not link it at all. However, instrumentality seen in this perspective excludes everything else. A more realistic model would include the possibility that task performance (and therefore the outcome as well) depends on choosing the effort put into performance and put into activities other than the task.

As Vroom used the term, **valence** refers to the positive or negative value people place on outcomes. Valence mirrors our personal preferences.[3] For example, most employees place a positive value (valence) on receiving additional money or recognition. In contrast, job stress and job loss would be likely to prove negatively valent for most individuals. In Vroom's expectancy model, outcomes refer to different consequences that are contingent on performance, such as pay, promotions or recognition. An outcome's valence depends on an individual's needs. Some perceive it as a symbol of success; for others it is something to reduce anxiety. Taking these different meanings into account when designing organisational reward systems can increase the effectiveness of the system and hence influence motivation accordingly. But it also makes the design more complex.

The sum of the valences of all relevant outcomes has to be positive. This means that some valences may be negative, although the positive valences must outweigh the negative ones. A stressful job (with negative valence) may still be highly valued and motivate to work hard, because it provides high pay and a great deal of recognition (both are positive valences). Many companies make use of alternative bonuses like extra holiday time, which is the most popular employee incentive after cash. There are, however, many other ways of putting together a 'motivation package'.[4]

Evidence about expectancy

Much research has tested expectancy theory, not just in business situations. In support of the theory, a meta-analysis of 77 studies indicated that expectancy theory significantly predicted performance, effort, intentions, preferences and choice.[5] Another summary of 16 studies revealed that expectancy theory correctly predicted occupational or organisational choice 63.4 per cent of the time; this was significantly better than chance predictions.[6] Further, components of expectancy theory accurately predicted task persistence, achievement, employment status of previously unemployed people, job satisfaction, decisions to retire (80 per cent accuracy), voting behaviour in union representation elections (over 75 per cent accuracy) and the frequency of drinking alcohol.[7]

Expectancy theory has been criticised for a variety of reasons. For example, the theory is difficult to test, and the measures used to assess expectancy, instrumentality and valence have questionable validity.[8] Nevertheless the theory has important practical implications for managers and organisations as a whole.

The expectancy theory can be useful for creating motivating working environments where people like to work and achieve high performance. In this model organisations cannot motivate their employees directly. Organisations can only try to establish a working environment which will lead to self-motivation. People want to feel productive, involved, useful and competent. Ideally, the personal goals people want to achieve are in line with the organisational expectations and vision. To enhance job satisfaction and motivation organisations have an important task in showing how people's efforts contribute to the organisational vision. Organisations can use various elements to enhance motivation by paying attention to the three important relationships of Vroom's theory. The checklist in Table 6.1 can both be used by organisations to create a motivational work climate and by individuals to get a better view to enhance self-motivation (replace 'the employee' with I).

HR Application of expectancy theory

Organisations can enhance expectancies of their employees by helping them to accomplish their performance goals. They can do this by providing support and coaching[9] and by increasing

Table 6.1 Organisational Implications of Expectancy Theory

Dealing with (effort–performance) expectancies
Is the employee's work reasonable, challenging, interesting and attainable?
Is the employee able to perform his or her work? Or is more education, training, experience, support or coaching needed?
Does the employee possess the necessary self-confidence and self-esteem to do his or her work? Or is time and effort needed to enhance his or her level of confidence?
Is it clear to the employee what acceptable levels of performance are? Do we agree on it? Can this performance easily be measured?
Does the work provide the employee with feelings of usefulness, involvement and competence? How can these feelings be reinforced?
Dealing with (performance–outcome) instrumentalities
Does the employee trust his/her superiors? Does the organisation keep promises made to employees? Does the organisation avoid lying to their employees?
Is the organisation fair and predictable in providing outcomes to employees? Is the organisation consistent in the application of giving rewards? While rewards may vary for different employees, are they perceived as being equitable?
Are the changes in outcomes large enough to motivate high effort?
Dealing with (outcome–personal goals) valences
Are the personal goals of the employee congruent with the organisational goals? How can a greater degree of alignment between these goals be accomplished?
Does the employee see the outcome as worth the expenditure of time and effort? What constraints on and off the job influence this employee? Do the employee and the organisation have realistic and mutual expectations?
Does the organisation reward the employee with something he or she really values? Does the organisation know which outcomes the employee values?
What kind of informal rewards can be used beside the more formal organisational rewards? How does the employee perceive these informal rewards?

Source: Adapted from R. G. Isaac, W. J. Zerbe and D. C. Pitt, 'Leadership and Motivation: The Effective Application of Expectancy Theory', *Journal of Managerial Issues*, Summer 2001, p. 221.

employees' self-efficacy. The evidence suggest that organisations have to provide employees with work that is reasonably challenging, in accordance with the employees' self-confidence, abilities, education, training, skills and experience.[10] Non-challenging work leads to boredom, frustration and low performance. Too difficult tasks, on the other hand, are rejected because they are not attainable and cause frustration. Paying attention to individual differences is crucial when trying to influence people's expectancies.[11] This fits well with the notion of psychological flow, (discussed in Chapter 3). Because the expectancy theory is based on perceptions, it is also important to base motivation decisions not simply on manager's views of abilities but also take into account people's own perceptions with regard to their abilities, self-confidence and self-esteem.

To enhance motivation, organisations also have to deal effectively with employees' instrumentalities. For organisations, it is, therefore, important to keep promises.[12] A promise – for instance that a certain level of performance will lead to a bonus – cannot be broken because economic conditions have become bad after the promise was made. Trust and honesty are certainly important aspects of organisations that are valued by employees. Treating employees fairly with regard to outcomes is another important aspect, as discussed in the section on equity theory. Fair treatment does not mean treating everyone the same. It implies treating people in the same way in similar situations (consistence) and in accordance with their needs.

As the last step, organisations have to monitor valences for various rewards. This raises the issue of whether organisations should use monetary rewards as the primary method to reinforce performance. Although money is certainly a positively valent reward for most people, individual differences (Chapters 2 and 3) and need theories (Chapter 5) tell us that people are motivated by different rewards. Motivation policy should therefore focus on linking employee performance to valued rewards, regardless of the type of reward used to enhance motivation.

The concept of instrumentality is applied very clearly in the concept of performance-related pay (PRP), also referred to as **pay-for-performance**, incentive pay or variable pay.[13] In this type of system, an employee's pay varies with the amount and the quality of the work carried out. The general idea behind pay-for-performance schemes – including, but not limited to, merit pay, bonuses and profit-sharing – is to give employees an incentive for working harder or smarter. Pay-for-performance is something extra, that is, compensation above and beyond basic wages and salaries. Advocates of this approach claim that variable pay schemes like PRP make employees understand better the connection between their performances and the rewards they receive.[14] Of course, this implies that high performance should be linked with high rewards, while low performance should be linked with low rewards. In practice, performance is complex to measure and ratings are subjective, causing the extra payments to be more or less decoupled from the effort put into a task. This might help explain why organisational reward systems often fail.

OB in Real Life

Students at FedEx

FedEx Corporation, the package distribution company, had problems keeping up the tempo in its operations. It was eventually realised that employees (many students in part-time jobs) worked slowly to increase the number of hours they were paid for. The solution was a guaranteed minimum wage, and the problem disappeared almost immediately.[15]

How did the FedEx Corporation get its student cargo-handlers to switch from low effort to high effort? According to Vroom's model, the student workers originally exerted low effort because they were paid on the basis of time, not output. It was in their best interest to work slowly and accumulate as many hours as possible. By offering to let the student workers go home early if and when they completed their assigned duties, FedEx prompted high effort. This new arrangement created two positively valued outcomes: guaranteed pay plus the opportunity to leave early. The motivation to exert high effort became greater than the motivation to exert low effort.

Judging from the impressive results, the student workers had both high effort → performance expectancies and positive performance → outcome instrumentalities. Moreover, the guaranteed pay and early departure opportunity evidently had strongly positive valences for the student workers. It is worth noting, however, that such an incentive structure may have perverse outcomes. If FedEx wants quick handling of packages that is precisely what it will get. But inappropriate handling that damages shipments, as well as errors in handling, may follow close on the heels of the productivity improvement. The skewed or even perverse incentive structure problems faced by FedEx could also be explained in terms of the agency theory outlined in Chapter 4.

Critical thinking

You are an executive of a power company that sells electricity to households and your bonus depends on how much power your customers actually consume through their meters. Why might this incentive structure not work well?

6.2 Equity theory of motivation

Equity theory is a model of motivation that explains how people strive for fairness and justice in social exchanges or give-and-take relationships. Equity theory is based on cognitive dissonance theory, developed by Leon Festinger in the 1950s. According to Festinger's theory, people are motivated to maintain consistency between their cognitive beliefs and their behaviour. Perceived inconsistencies create cognitive dissonance (or psychological discomfort) which, in turn, motivates corrective action (see also Chapter 3). For example, a cigarette smoker who sees a heavy-smoking relative die of lung cancer probably would be motivated to quit smoking if he or she attributed the death to smoking.

If we feel victimised by unfair social exchanges we experience discomfort and our resulting cognitive dissonance prompts us to correct the situation. Corrective action may range from a slight change in attitude or behaviour through to stealing or, in an extreme case, trying to harm someone. For example, people attempt to 'get even' for perceived injustices by using either direct (e.g. theft or sabotage) or indirect (e.g. intentionally working slowly, giving a co-worker the silent treatment) retaliation.[16] Figure 6.2 illustrates the equity theory. Three elements are important when applying this theory in a workplace or organisational setting:

- Awareness of the key components of the individual–organisation exchange relationship: inputs and outcomes. Employees expect a fair, just or equitable return (outcome) for what they contribute to their jobs.[17]
- This relationship is pivotal in the formation of employees' perceptions of equity and inequity. Employees decide what their equitable return should be by comparing their inputs and outcomes with that of comparison others (like colleagues).
- As a process theory of motivation, equity theory focuses on what people are motivated to do when they feel treated inequitably they try to reduce this inequity.

The individual–organisation exchange relationship

Two primary components are involved in the employee–employer exchange, inputs and outcomes. An employee's inputs, for which he or she expects a just return, include education, experience, skills and effort. On the outcome side of the exchange, the organisation provides such things as pay, fringe benefits and recognition. These outcomes vary widely, depending on one's organisation and rank. Table 6.2 presents a list of on-the-job inputs and outcomes that employees consider when making equity comparisons.

Negative and positive inequity

At work, feelings of inequity revolve around a person's evaluation of whether he or she receives adequate rewards in return for his or her contributive inputs. People perform these evaluations by

Figure 6.2 The Equity Theory of Motivation

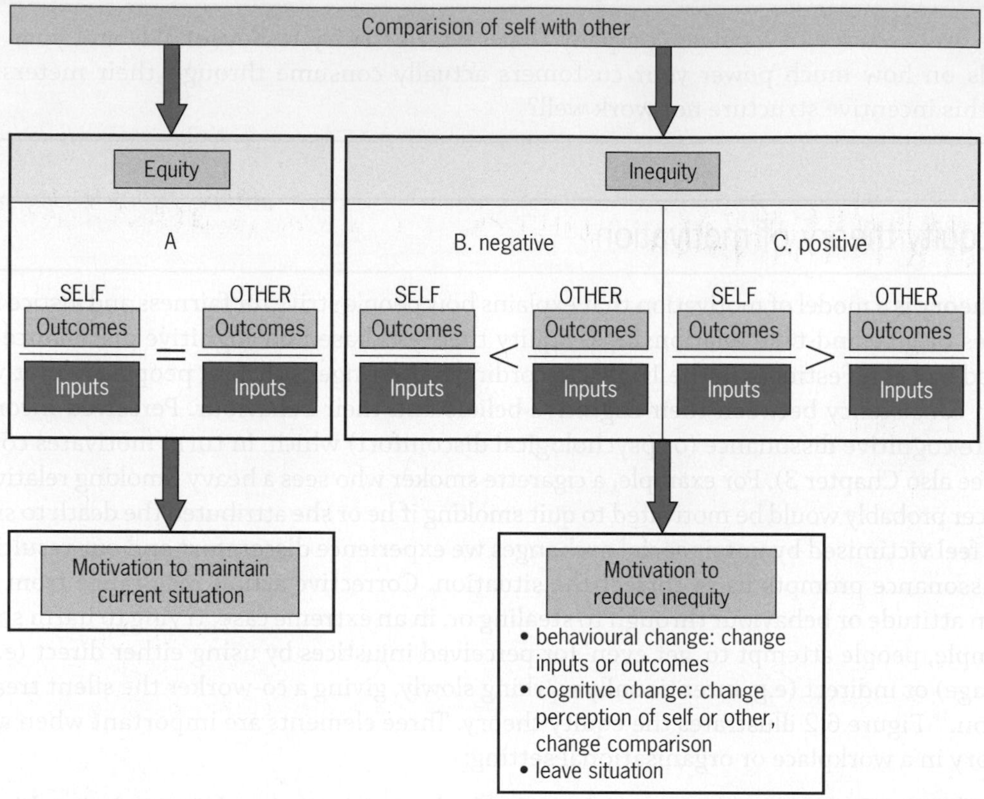

Table 6.2 Factors Considered When Making Equity Comparisons

Inputs	Outcomes
Time	Pay/bonuses
Education/training	Fringe benefits
Experience	Challenging assignments
Skills	Job security
Creativity	Career advancement/promotions
Seniority	Status symbols
Loyalty to organisation	Pleasant/safe working environment
Age	Opportunity for personal growth/development
Personality traits	Supportive supervision
Effort expended	Recognition
Personal appearance	Participation in important decisions

Source: Based in part on J. S. Adams, 'Toward an Understanding of Inequity', *Journal of Abnormal and Social Psychology*, November 1963, pp. 422–36.

comparing the perceived fairness of their employment exchange to that of relevant others. Three different equity relationships are illustrated in Figure 6.2: equity, negative inequity and positive inequity.

Assume the two people ('self' and 'other') in Figure 6.2 have equivalent backgrounds (equal education, seniority, and so on) and perform identical tasks. Only their hourly pay rates differ. Equity exists for an individual when his or her ratio of perceived outcomes to inputs is equal to the ratio of outcomes to inputs for a relevant (comparable job function and other attributes) co-worker (see part A in Figure 6.2). Since equity is based on comparing ratios of outcomes to inputs, inequity will not necessarily be perceived just because someone else receives greater rewards. If the other person's additional outcomes are due to his or her greater inputs, a sense of equity may still exist. However, if the comparison person enjoys greater outcomes for similar inputs, **negative inequity** or under-rewarding will be perceived (part B in Figure 6.2). On the other hand, a person will experience **positive inequity** or over-rewarding when his or her outcome to input ratio is greater than that of a relevant co-worker (part C in Figure 6.2). The example with pay and effort is a simple one, since pay is simple to measure. Effort is much harder to quantify as are other elements which can contribute to equity or inequity.

HR Dynamics of perceived inequity

Organisations can derive practical benefits from the equity theory of motivation by recognising two key findings: on the one hand, negative inequity is less tolerable than positive inequity and on the other that inequity can be reduced in a variety of ways. People have a lower tolerance for negative inequity than they do for positive inequity; they feel the discomfort more acutely. Those who are short-changed and feel a negative inequity are more powerfully motivated to correct the situation than those who are excessively rewarded. For example, if you have ever been overworked and underpaid – relative to comparable others – you know how feelings of negative inequity can erode your job satisfaction and performance. Perhaps you work less hard or quit the job to escape the negative inequity. Table 6.3 lists eight possible ways to reduce inequity. It is important to note that equity can be restored by altering one's equity ratios either behaviourally or cognitively or both. Equity theorists propose that the many possible combinations of behavioural and cognitive adjustments are influenced by the following tendencies:

- An individual will attempt to maximise the amount of positive outcomes he or she receives.
- People resist increasing inputs when it requires substantial effort or costs.
- People resist behavioural or cognitive changes in inputs important to their self-concept or self-esteem.
- Rather than changing cognitions about themselves, individuals are more likely to change cognitions about the comparison person's inputs and outcomes.
- Leaving the field (resigning) is chosen only when severe inequity cannot be resolved through other methods.[18]

HR Evidence about motivation and equity

Perhaps most importantly, equity cuts across national cultures, as the comparison process underlying the equity theory has been found to occur in different countries.[19] People tend to compare themselves with other individuals with whom they have close interpersonal ties (such as friends)

Table 6.3 Eight Ways to Reduce Inequity

Methods	Examples
1 Person can increase his or her inputs	Work harder
	Attend school or a specialised training programme
2 Person can decrease his or her inputs	Do not work as hard
	Take longer breaks
3 Person can attempt to increase his or her outcomes	Ask for a rise
	Ask for a new title
	Seek outside intervention
4 Person can decrease his or her outcomes	Ask for less pay
5 Person can leave the field	Absenteeism and turnover
6 Person can psychologically distort his or her inputs and outcomes	Convince self that certain inputs are not important
	Convince self that he or she has a boring and monotonous job
7 Person can psychologically distort the inputs or outcomes of comparison other	Conclude that other has more experience or works harder
	Conclude that other has a more important title
8 Person can change comparison other	Pick a new comparison person
	Compare self to previous job

Source: Adapted from J. S. Adams, 'Toward an Understanding of Inequity', *Journal of Abnormal and Social Psychology*, November 1963, pp. 422–36.

and/or to similar others (such as people performing the same job or of the same gender or educational level) rather than with dissimilar ones.[20] Several studies, for instance, have found that most part-time workers compare themselves to other part-time workers. Part-time workers who use full-time workers as referents tend to feel less satisfied, because they receive less pay and fewer benefits in comparison with full-time working colleagues.[21] The equity problem also cuts across genders: men and women have the same reactions to negative inequity. There were no gender differences in response to perceived inequity.[22]

Different insights have also been gained from laboratory studies that are relevant for organisations. The basic approach used in laboratory studies is to pay an experimental subject more (overpayment) or less (underpayment) than the standard rate for completing a task. The participants in the experiment are paid on either an hourly or piece-rate basis. Overpaid subjects on a piece-rate system lowered the quantity of their performance and increased the quality of their performance. In contrast, underpaid subjects increased the quantity and decreased the quality of their performance.[23] A study extended this stream of research by examining the effect of underpayment inequity on ethical behaviour. A total of 102 undergraduate students were either equitably paid or underpaid for performing a clerical task. Results indicated that underpaid students stole money to compensate for their negative inequity.[24]

Applying equity to motivation

Equity theory has at least eight important practical applications. Of course, applying equity theory directly in organisations is not that easy because people are different in their sensitivity to equity, which means that different people react differently in the same situation. They also value other inputs and outcomes than those easy to measure. Maintaining feelings of equity in organisations is certainly a challenge. Nevertheless:

- Equity theory provides organisations with another explanation of how beliefs and attitudes affect job performance (also see Chapter 3). According to this line of thinking, the best way to manage job behaviour is to understand properly underlying cognitive processes. Indeed, we are motivated powerfully to correct the situation when our ideas of fairness and justice are offended.
- One of the core elements of equity theory emphasises the need to pay attention to employees' perceptions of what is fair and equitable. No matter how fair organisations think their policies, procedures and reward systems are, each employee's perception of the equity of those factors is what counts (also see Chapter 4). People respond negatively when they perceive organisational and interpersonal injustices.
- A direct consequence is that hiring and promotion decisions based on merit-based, job-related information will be seen as relatively more equitable. Furthermore, justice perceptions are influenced by the extent to which decision-makers explain their decisions; the application of this evidence is to explain the rationale behind their decisions.
- Being able to appeal against a decision promotes the belief that organisations treat employees fairly and perceptions of fair treatment promote job satisfaction and organisational commitment and help reduce absenteeism and turnover (see Chapter 3).
- Employees are more likely to accept and support organisational change when they believe it is implemented fairly and when it produces equitable outcomes (also see Chapter 16).[25]
- Organisations can promote co-operation and teamwork among employees by treating them equitably. Research reveals that people are just as concerned with fairness in group settings as they are with their own personal interests.[26]
- Treating employees inequitably can lead to conflicts which may spill over into the outside world, with litigation and costly court settlements. Employees denied justice at work are more likely to turn to arbitration and the courts.[27]
- Organisations need to pay attention to their climate for justice. For example, an organisation's climate for justice was found to significantly influence employees' job satisfaction[28] and the type of customer service provided by employees. In turn, this level of service is likely to influence customers' perceptions of 'fair service' and their subsequent loyalty and satisfaction.[29]

Organisations can attempt to keep managers informed about equity issues by monitoring equity and justice perceptions through informal conversations, interviews or attitude surveys. For example, researchers have developed and validated a number of survey instruments that can be used to get a sense of equity perceptions. The activity below contains part of a survey that was developed to measure employees' perceptions of fair interpersonal treatment. If you perceive your work organisation as interpersonally unfair, you are probably dissatisfied and have contemplated quitting. In contrast, your organisational loyalty and attachment are likely to be greater if you believe you are treated fairly at work.

Activity

Measuring perceived fair interpersonal treatment

Instructions

Indicate the extent to which you agree or disagree with each of the following statements by considering what your organisation is like most of the time. Then compare your overall score with the arbitrary norms that are presented.

	Strongly disagree	Disagree	Neither	Agree	Strongly agree
1 Employees are praised for good work	1	2	3	4	5
2 Supervisors do not yell at employees	1	2	3	4	5
3 Employees are trusted	1	2	3	4	5
4 Employees' complaints are dealt with effectively	1	2	3	4	5
5 Employees are treated with respect	1	2	3	4	5
6 Employees' questions and problems are responded to quickly	1	2	3	4	5
7 Employees are treated fairly	1	2	3	4	5
8 Employees' hard work is appreciated	1	2	3	4	5
9 Employees' suggestions are used	1	2	3	4	5
10 Employees are told the truth	1	2	3	4	5

Total score = __________

Arbitrary norms

Very fair organisation = 38–50

Moderately fair organisation = 24–37

Unfair organisation = 10–23

Source: Adapted in part from M. A. Donovan, F. Drasgow and L. Munson, 'The Perceptions of Fair Interpersonal Treatment Scale: Development and Validation of a Measure of Interpersonal Treatment in the Workplace', *Journal of Applied Psychology*, October 1998, pp. 683–92.

! Critical thinking

Suppose you were employed as a supermarket manager. For a young person you get a significant monthly pay package. The working week in your country is 37½ hours but your colleagues and peers expect you to put in 60 to 80 hours. How do you feel about your actual wage rate and what does equity theory suggest your options could be?

6.3 Motivation through goal setting

Regardless of the nature of their specific achievements, successful people tend to have one thing in common. Their lives are goal-oriented. This is as true for politicians seeking votes as it is for rocket scientists probing outer space. In Lewis Carroll's tale of *Alice's Adventures in Wonderland*, the smiling Cheshire cat advised the bewildered Alice, 'If you don't know where you're going, any road will take you there.' Goal-oriented people tend to find the right road because they know where they are going. The idea that goals matter clearly has important implications for motivation and for management generally.

In the motivation context a **goal** is defined as 'what an individual is trying to accomplish; it is the object or aim of an action'.[30] The motivational impact of performance goals and goal-based reward plans has been recognised for a long time. At the turn of the century, Frederick Taylor attempted to establish scientifically how much work of a specified quality an individual should be assigned each day. He proposed that bonuses be based on accomplishing those output standards (see Chapter 1). More recently, goal setting has been promoted through a widely used technique called management by objectives (MBO).

Management by objectives is an approach that incorporates participation in decision-making, goal setting and objective feedback.[31] A meta-analysis of MBO programmes showed productivity gains in 68 out of 70 different organisations. Specifically, results uncovered an average gain in productivity of 56 per cent when top management commitment was high. The average gain was only 6 per cent when commitment from the top was low. A second meta-analysis of 18 studies further demonstrated that employees' job satisfaction was significantly related to top management's commitment to an MBO implementation.[32] These results highlight the positive benefits of implementing MBO and setting goals, but also hint at the mistakes which can undermine such policies.

The mechanics of goal setting

Despite abundant goal-setting research and practice, goal-setting theories are surprisingly scarce perhaps because it is more like a model or an approach than the basic model of goal setting (see Figure 6.3) that involves four motivational mechanisms.

Goals that are personally meaningful tend to focus one's attention on what is relevant and important. If, for example, you have a project deadline in a few days, your thoughts tend to revolve around completing that project before the deadline. Similarly, the members of a home appliance sales force who are told that one of them can win a trip to Hawaii for selling the most refrigerators will tend to steer customers towards the refrigerator display.

Not only do goals make us selectively perceptive, they also motivate us to act. The deadline for submitting your project would prompt you to complete it, rather than going out with friends, endlessly updating your Facebook profile or watching television. Generally, the level of effort expended is proportionate to the difficulty of the goal.

Within the context of goal setting, **persistence** represents the effort expended on a task over an extended period of time. It takes effort to run 100 metres; it takes persistence to run a 42-kilometre marathon. Persistent people tend to see obstacles as challenges to be overcome rather than as reasons to fail. A difficult goal that is important to an individual is a constant reminder to keep exerting effort in the appropriate direction. Astronaut Jim Lovell represents a great example of someone who persisted at his goals. Lovell commanded NASA's ill-fated Apollo 13 mission that almost did not return from its journey to the moon. Lowell persisted in many adverse situations,

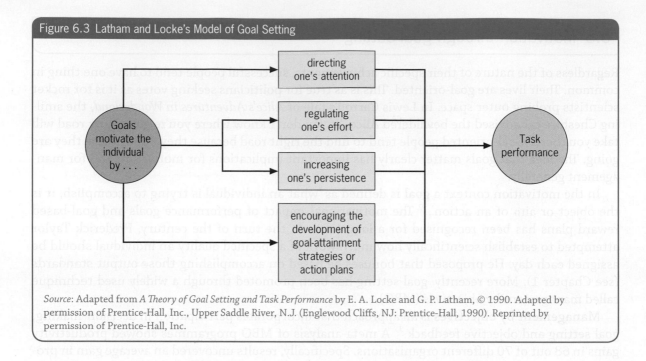

Figure 6.3 Latham and Locke's Model of Goal Setting

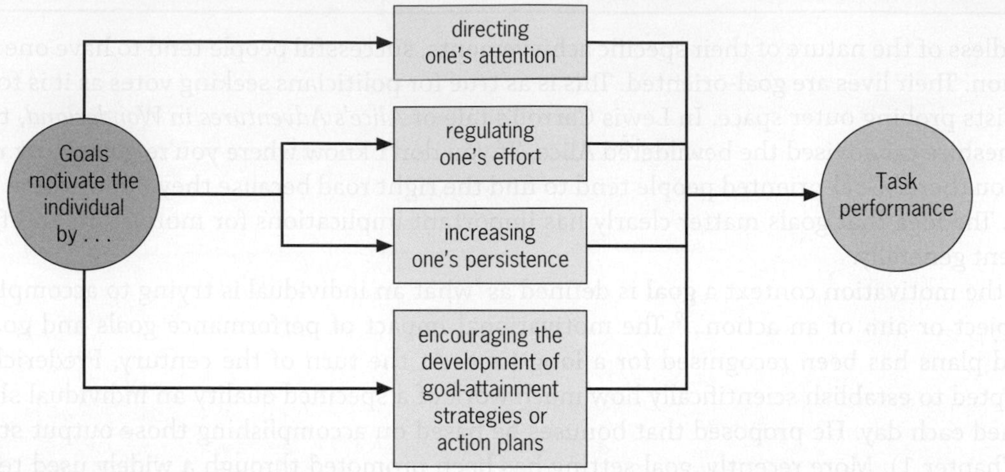

Source: Adapted from *A Theory of Goal Setting and Task Performance* by E. A. Locke and G. P. Latham, © 1990. Adapted by permission of Prentice-Hall, Inc., Upper Saddle River, N.J. (Englewood Cliffs, NJ: Prentice-Hall, 1990). Reprinted by permission of Prentice-Hall, Inc.

barely getting into the Naval Academy in his second attempt, and initially failing the physical test for entering the astronaut training programme.[33]

If you are here and your goal is out there somewhere, you face the problem of getting from here to there. An overweight person who has decided to lose 10 kilos must develop a plan for getting from 'here' (present weight) to 'there' (10 kilos lighter). Goals can help because they encourage people to develop strategies and action plans that enable them to achieve their goals.[34] By setting a weight-reduction goal, the overweight person may choose a strategy of exercising more, eating less or some combination of the two. It is worth noting that a person who publicly commits to a goal has an even stronger motivation. The overweight person who announces a weight loss goal to friends has a better chance of success than someone who keeps the goal quiet.

Feedback plays a key role in all areas of people's lives. For example, consider the role of feedback in bowling. Imagine going to the bowling lanes only to find that someone had hung a sheet from the ceiling to the floor in front of the pins. How likely is it that you would reach your goal score or typical bowling average? Not likely, given your inability to see the pins. Regardless of your goal, you would have to guess where to throw your second ball if you did not strike down all the pins with your first shot. The same principles apply at work. Feedback lets people know if they are heading towards their goals or if they are going in the wrong direction and need to redirect their efforts. Goals plus feedback is the recommended approach.[35] Goals inform people about performance standards and expectations so that they can channel their energies accordingly. In turn, feedback provides the information needed to adjust direction, effort and strategies for goal accomplishment. Feedback enhances the effect of specific, difficult goals.

How goals are best set remains a puzzle and no single approach seems consistently more effective than others in increasing performance.[36] Participative goals, assigned goals and self-set goals are equally effective. Managers are advised to use a **contingency approach** by picking a method that seems best suited to the individual and situation at hand. For example, employees' preferences for participation should be considered. Some employees desire to participate in the process of setting goals, but others do not. Employees are also more likely to respond positively to the opportunity to participate in goal setting when they have greater task information, higher levels of experience and training, and greater levels of task involvement. A participative approach may also help reducing employees' resistance to goal setting.

Because of individual differences (see Chapters 2 and 3), it may be necessary to establish different goals for employees performing the same job. For example, a study of 103 undergraduate business students revealed that individuals high in conscientiousness had higher motivation, greater goal commitment and obtained higher grades than students low in conscientiousness.[37] More generally, the absence of evidence on how goals are best set in a given organisational situation indicates that such evidence can be developed through a trial-and-error or experimental approach. This may allow managers an opportunity to identify which forms of setting goals works best in their organisation. However, while this is an admirable approach it gets the best results from careful planning and rigorous analysis of the whole process.

HR Evidence about the goal-setting model

Research has consistently supported goal setting as an effective motivational technique.[38] Setting performance goals increases individual, group and organisational performance. Further, the positive effects of goal setting were not only found in the USA but also in Australia, Canada, the Caribbean, England and Japan. Goal setting works in different cultures, although the effects of goal specificity and goal difficulty may vary between cultures.[39]

Difficult goals lead to higher performance. **Goal difficulty** reflects the amount of effort required to meet a goal. It is more difficult to sell nine cars a month than it is to sell three a month. A meta-analysis spanning 4000 people and 65 separate studies revealed that goal difficulty was positively related to performance.[40] As illustrated in Figure 6.4, however, the positive relationship between goal difficulty and performance breaks down when goals are perceived to be impossible. Figure 6.4 reveals that performance goes up when employees are given hard goals as opposed to easy or moderate ones. Performance then reaches a plateau and drops as the difficulty of a goal goes from challenging to impossible.[41]

Figure 6.4 Relationship Between Goal Difficulty and Performance

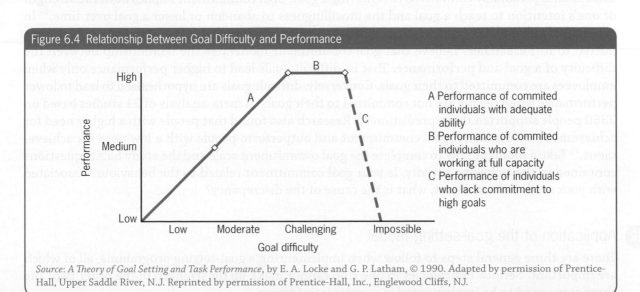

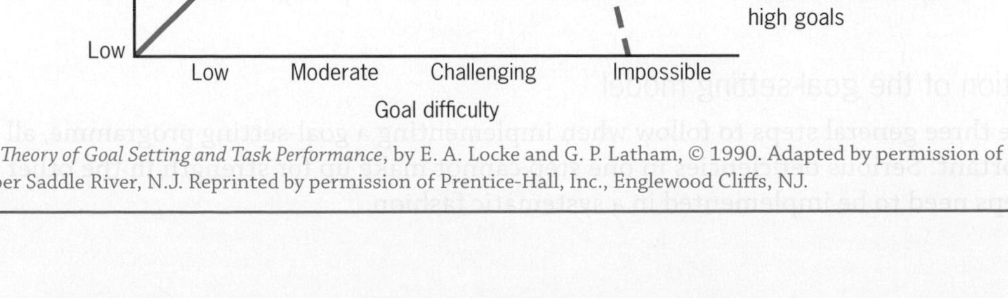

Source: *A Theory of Goal Setting and Task Performance*, by E. A. Locke and G. P. Latham, © 1990. Adapted by permission of Prentice-Hall, Upper Saddle River, N.J. Reprinted by permission of Prentice-Hall, Inc., Englewood Cliffs, NJ.

Research also found the same inverted-U relationship between goal difficulty and selling effort for US salespeople. Salespeople were less inclined to increase selling effort when the goals set by their sales managers were either easy or extremely difficult than when the goals were moderately difficult.[42] However, for Chinese salespeople this relationship was not found. One explanation can be a culturally ingrained relationship between effort and performance (a social norm embedded in China's culture that you can succeed if you try harder), which encourages the Chinese salespeople to keep on trying despite their difficult goals.[43] Another explanation could be that norms matter – an impossible goal leads to failure which is perceived, particularly in an East Asian context, as something very negative.

Specific, difficult goals lead to higher performance for simple rather than complex tasks. **Goal specificity** pertains to the quantifiability of a goal; this means it refers to the extent to which a goal is specifically stated and specified. For example, a goal of selling nine cars a month is more specific than telling a salesperson to do his or her best. In an early review of goal-setting research, 99 out of 110 studies found that specific, hard goals led to better performance than did either easy, medium, do-your-best goals or none. This result was confirmed in a meta-analysis of 70 studies conducted between 1966 and 1984, involving 7407 people.[44] In contrast to these positive effects, several later studies demonstrated that setting specific, difficult goals leads to poorer performance under certain circumstances. For example, a meta-analysis of 125 studies indicated that goal-setting effects were strongest for easy tasks and weakest for complex tasks.[45] There are two explanations for this finding.

First, employees are not likely to put forth increased effort to achieve complex goals unless they 'buy-into' or support them.[46] Thus, it is important for managers to obtain employee support for the goal-setting process, including the goals set by the process. Second, novel and complex tasks take employees longer to complete. This occurs because employees spend more time thinking about how to approach and solve these tasks. In contrast, employees do not have to spend much time thinking about solutions for easy tasks. Specific, difficult goals thus impair performance on novel, complex tasks when employees do not have clear strategies for solving these types of problems. On a more positive note, however, a recent study demonstrated that goal setting led to gradual improvements in performance on complex tasks when people were encouraged explicitly to solve the problem at hand.[47]

Goal commitment affects goal-setting outcomes. **Goal commitment** is the extent to which an individual is personally committed to achieving a goal. Goal commitment implies both the strength of one's intention to reach a goal and the unwillingness to abandon or lower a goal over time.[48] In general, an individual is expected to persist in attempts to accomplish a goal when he or she is committed to it. Researchers believe that goal commitment moderates the relationship between the difficulty of a goal and performance. That is, difficult goals lead to higher performance only when employees are committed to their goals. Conversely, difficult goals are hypothesised to lead to lower performance when people are not committed to their goals. A meta-analysis of 21 studies based on 2360 people supported these predictions.[49] Research also found that people with a higher need for achievement have a higher goal commitment and outperform people with a low need for achievement.[50] Take a moment now to complete the goal commitment scale and the study habits questions contained in the following activity. Is your goal commitment related to the behaviours associated with your study habits? If not, what is the cause of the discrepancy?

HR Application of the goal-setting model

There are three general steps to follow when implementing a goal-setting programme, all of which are important. Serious deficiencies in one step cannot make up for strength in the other two. The three steps need to be implemented in a systematic fashion.

Activity

Is your goal commitment for this course related to your behaviour?

Instructions

Begin by identifying your performance goal (desired grade) for this course. My desired grade is _____.

Next, use the rating scale shown below to circle the answer that best represents how you feel about each of the following statements. After computing a total score for the goal-commitment items, answer the questions related to your study habits for this course.

	Strongly disagree	Disagree	Neither	Agree	Strongly agree
1 I am trying hard to reach my performance goal.	1	2	3	4	5
2 I am exerting my maximum effort (100 per cent) in pursuit of my performance goal.	1	2	3	4	5
3 I am committed to my performance goal.	1	2	3	4	5
4 I am determined to reach my performance goal.	1	2	3	4	5
5 I am enthusiastic about attempting to achieve my performance goal.	1	2	3	4	5
6 I am striving to attain my performance goal.	1	2	3	4	5

Total score = __________

Arbitrary norms

Low goal commitment = 6–15
Moderate goal commitment = 15–23
High goal commitment = 24–30

Study habits

How many hours have you spent studying for this course? _____ hours
What is your grade at this point in the course? _____
How many times have you missed lectures? _____ absences

Source: Items were adapted from those presented in R. W. Renn, C. Danehower, P. M. Swiercz and M. L. Icenogle, 'Further Examination of the Measurement Properties of Leifer and McGannon's (1986) Goal Acceptance and Goal Commitment Scales', *Journal of Occupational and Organizational Psychology*, March 1999, pp. 107–13.

Goals must first be formulated somehow. A number of sources can be used as input during this goal-setting stage. Time and motion studies are one source. A second is the average past performance of employees. Third, the employee and his or her superior may set the goal participatively, through give-and-take negotiation. Fourth, goals can be set by conducting external or internal benchmarking. Benchmarking (also see Chapter 16) is used when an organisation wants to compare

Table 6.4 Guidelines for Writing Smart Goals

Specific	Goals should be stated in precise rather than vague terms. For example, a goal that provides for 20 hours of technical training for each employee is more specific than stating that a superior should send as many people as possible to training classes. Goals should be quantified when possible
Measurable	A measurement device is needed to assess the extent to which a goal is accomplished. Goals thus need to be measurable. It also is critical to consider the quality aspect of the goal when establishing measurement criteria. For example, if the goal is to complete a managerial study of methods to increase productivity, one must consider how to measure the quality of this effort. Goals should not be set without considering the interplay between quantity and quality of output
Attainable	Goals should be realistic, challenging and attainable. Impossible goals reduce motivation because people do not like to fail. Remember, people have different levels of ability and skill
Results oriented	Corporate goals should focus on desired end results that support the organisation's vision. In turn, an individual's goals should directly support the accomplishment of corporate goals. Activities support the achievement of goals and are outlined in action plans. To focus goals on desired end-results, goals should start with the word 'to', followed by verbs such as complete, acquire, produce, increase or decrease. Verbs such as develop, conduct, implement or monitor imply activities and should not be used in a goal statement
Time bound	Goals specify target dates for completion

Source: A. J. Kinicki, *Performance Management Systems* (Superstition Mt., AZ: Kinicki and Associates, Inc., 2009), pp. 2–9. Reprinted with permission; all rights reserved.

its performance or internal work processes with those of other organisations (external benchmarking) or other internal units, branches, departments or divisions within the organisation (internal benchmarking).[51] For example, a company might set a goal to surpass the customer service levels or profits of a benchmarked competitor (assuming reliable evidence on relevant benchmarks can be obtained). Finally, the overall strategy of a company (such as becoming the lowest-cost producer) may affect the goals set by employees at various levels within the organisation. In accordance with available research evidence, goals should be 'SMART'. SMART is an acronym that stands for specific, measurable, attainable, results oriented and time bound. These goals reflect the evidence presented above. Table 6.4 contains a set of guidelines for writing SMART goals.

When setting goals conflict may be introduced. **Goal conflict** refers to degree to which people feel that multiple goals are incompatible.[52] An externally imposed goal may be in conflict with a personal goal. Goal conflict may occur when people have to achieve multiple outcomes when performing a single task, like meeting a quantity quota and not making mistakes. In this case a trade-off between performance quality and quantity occurs: people make a lot of things with many mistakes (quantity at the expense of quality) or they make few things with no mistakes (quality at the expense of quantity). A third type of goal conflict occurs when several tasks or goals have to be accomplished (for instance, selling two different products, given a limited amount of time). In this case, people handle the conflict by prioritising one task at the expense of the other.

Goal commitment is important because employees are more motivated to pursue goals they view as reasonable, obtainable and fair. Goal commitment may be increased by using one or more of the following techniques:

- Explain why the organisation is implementing a goal-setting programme.
- Present the corporate goals and explain how and why an individual's personal goals support them.

- Have employees establish their own goals and action plans. Encourage them to set challenging, stretching goals. Goals should not be impossible.
- Train managers in how to conduct participative goal-setting sessions. Train employees in how to develop effective action plans.
- Be supportive. Do not use goals to threaten employees.
- Set goals that are under the employees' control and then provide them with the necessary resources.
- Provide monetary incentives or other rewards for accomplishing goals.

Goal setting will not work when people are not committed to the goals established. People have a higher goal commitment when they understand their goals, when they feel pressure from peers to perform well, when they perceive they can attain their goals and when they believe they will be recognised for their accomplishments.[53] One of the critical factors in cultivating goal commitment is demonstrating the relevance and importance of goals to individuals and organisations.[54]

Support and feedback in the form of resources and information required to get the job done must be provided. This includes ensuring that each employee has the necessary abilities and information to reach his or her goals. Appropriate goals without some degree of knowledge are not sufficient for successful performance.[55] Training is required to help employees achieve difficult goals. Moreover, managers should pay attention to employees' perceptions of effort → performance expectancies, self-efficacy and the valence of rewards (recall the elaboration of expectancy theory). This involves knowing whether employees expect the goal is attainable through effort, whether they believe they have the capacity and knowledge to reach the goal and which rewards they find important when reaching the goal.[56]

Finally, employees should be provided with timely, specific feedback (knowledge of results) on how they are doing. Research shows a complicated relationship between feedback and performance. Feedback did not affect the performance level of people who were already meeting expectations, but it significantly influenced performance levels of underachievers.[57] These findings indicate that feedback is not directly influencing performance. It rather serves as an essential condition of goal setting to work.[58] Because of the importance of feedback as a tool for reaching one's goals and for increasing motivation, we discuss key aspects of the feedback process in greater detail below.

Critical thinking

The manager of the passenger railway company has a bonus clause in his contract. If 95 per cent of trains arrive at their final destination on time he will receive a bonus of 30 per cent of his annual salary. Trains often do arrive on time without making timetabled stops at intermediate stations. Unfortunate passengers for these stations are told to take the next train. Give the arguments both for and against this bonus scheme.

6.4 Understanding feedback

Numerous surveys tell us employees have a hearty appetite for feedback.[59] So also do achievement-oriented students. Following a difficult exam, for instance, students want to know two things: how they performed and how their peers did. By letting students know how their work relates to grades and competitive standards, a teacher's feedback permits the students to adjust their study habits in order to reach their goals.

Managers in well-run organisations follow up goal setting with a feedback programme to provide a rational basis for adjustment and improvement. It seems that more and more organisations are formally installing feedback and appraisal procedures.

Although this sort of open-book management is becoming popular, feedback is often of inferior quality. In fact, 'poor or insufficient feedback' was the leading cause of deficient performance in a survey of US and European companies.[60] Although positive feedback is one of the most effective ways to reinforce good behaviour, people often feel that the only time they get feedback is when things go wrong.[61] As the term is used here, feedback is objective information about individual or collective performance. Subjective assessments such as, 'You're doing a poor job', 'You're too lazy' or 'We really appreciate your hard work' do not qualify as objective feedback. But hard data such as units sold, days absent, amount of money saved, projects completed, customers satisfied and products rejected are all suitable for objective feedback programmes.

Experts say feedback serves two functions for those who receive it; one is instructional and the other motivational. Feedback instructs when it clarifies roles or teaches new behaviour. For example, an assistant accountant might be advised to handle a certain entry as a capital item rather than as an expense item. On the other hand, feedback motivates when it serves as a reward or promises a reward.[62] Having the boss tell you that a gruelling project you worked on earlier has just been completed can be a rewarding piece of news. We expand on these two functions of feedback in this section by analysing a cognitive model of feedback and by reviewing the practical implications of recent feedback research.

A cognitive-processing model of performance feedback

Giving and receiving feedback at work are popular ideas. Conventional wisdom says the more feedback organisational members get the better. An underlying assumption is that feedback works automatically. Managers simply need to be motivated to give it. According to a recent meta-analysis of 23 663 feedback incidents, however, feedback is far from being automatically effective. While feedback did, in fact, have a generally positive impact on performance, performance actually declined in more than 38 per cent of the feedback incidents.[63] One possible explanation is that feedback is not always objective.

These results are a clear warning for those interested in improving job performance with feedback. Subjective feedback is easily contaminated by situational factors. Moreover, if objective feedback is to work as intended, professionals need to understand the interaction between feedback recipients and their environment.[64] A more complete understanding of how employees cognitively or mentally process feedback is an important first step, illustrated in Figure 6.5. A step-by-step exploration of the model in Figure 6.5 can help us better understand the feedback–performance relationship.

It almost goes without saying that employees receive objective feedback from others such as peers, supervisors, subordinates and outsiders. Perhaps less obvious is the fact that the task itself is a ready source of objective feedback.[65] Anyone who has spent hours on a 'quick' Internet search can appreciate the power of task-provided feedback. Similarly, skilled tasks such as computer programming, sailing a boat or landing an aircraft provide a steady stream of feedback about how well or poorly one is doing. A third source of feedback is oneself, even if self-serving bias and other perceptual problems can contaminate this source (see Chapter 4). Those high in self-confidence tend to rely on personal feedback more than those with low self-confidence. Although circumstances vary,

Figure 6.5 A Cognitive-Processing Model of Feedback

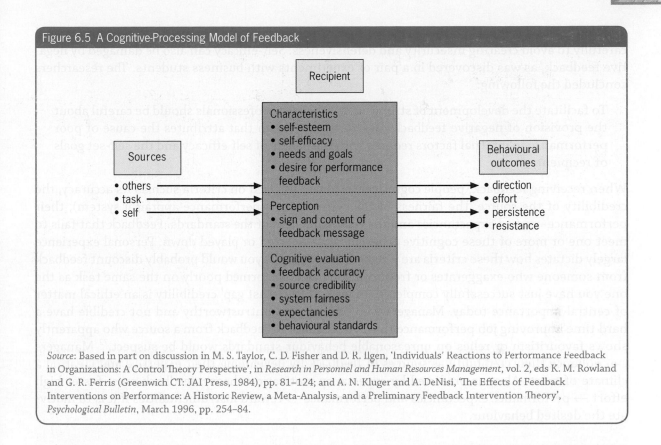

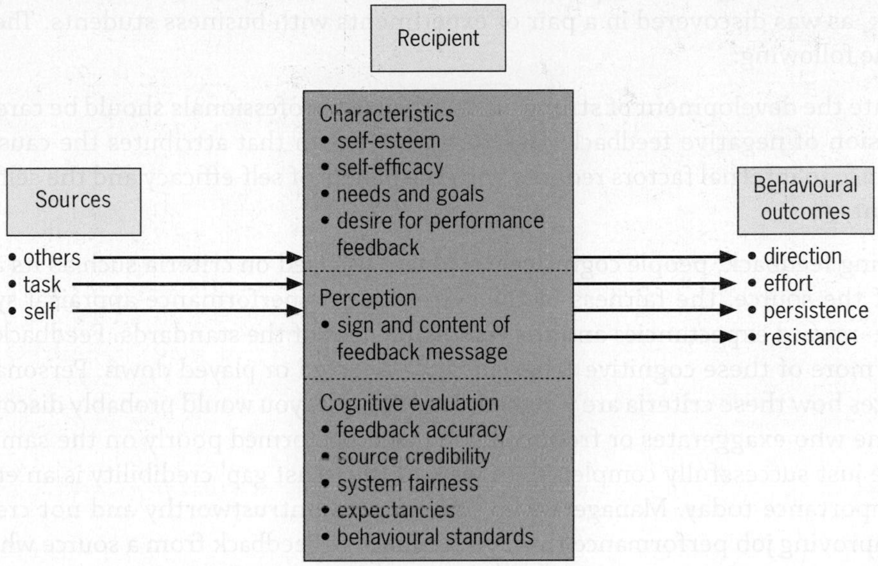

Source: Based in part on discussion in M. S. Taylor, C. D. Fisher and D. R. Ilgen, 'Individuals' Reactions to Performance Feedback in Organizations: A Control Theory Perspective', in *Research in Personnel and Human Resources Management*, vol. 2, eds K. M. Rowland and G. R. Ferris (Greenwich CT: JAI Press, 1984), pp. 81–124; and A. N. Kluger and A. DeNisi, 'The Effects of Feedback Interventions on Performance: A Historic Review, a Meta-Analysis, and a Preliminary Feedback Intervention Theory', *Psychological Bulletin*, March 1996, pp. 254–84.

an employee can be bombarded by feedback from all three sources simultaneously. This is where the 'gatekeeping functions' of perception and cognitive evaluation are needed to help sort things out.

Listed in the centre of Figure 6.5 are three aspects of the recipient requiring our attention. They are the individual's characteristics, perception and cognitive evaluation. Recipient characteristics such as self-esteem and self-efficacy (see Chapter 2) can help or hinder one's readiness for feedback.[66] Those having low self-esteem and low self-efficacy generally do not actively seek feedback. Needs and goals also influence one's openness to feedback. In a laboratory study, Japanese psychology students who scored high on the need for achievement responded more favourably to feedback than did their classmates who had a low need for achievement.[67] High self-monitors, those chameleon-like people we discussed in Chapter 2, are also more open to feedback because it helps them adapt their behaviour to the situation. Recall from Chapter 2 that high self-monitoring employees were found to be better at initiating relationships with mentors (who typically provide feedback). Low self-monitoring people, in contrast, are tuned into their own internal feelings more than they are towards external cues.

Perception of feedback depends on whether it is positive or negative. Generally, people tend to perceive and recall positive feedback more accurately than they do negative feedback.[68] However, feedback with a negative sign (such as being told your performance is below average) can have a positive motivational impact. In fact, in one study, those who were told they were below average on a creativity test subsequently outperformed those who were led to believe their results were above average. The subjects apparently took the negative feedback as a challenge and then set and pursued higher goals. Those receiving positive feedback were apparently less motivated to do better.[69]

Nonetheless, feedback with a negative sign or threatening content needs to be administered carefully to avoid creating insecurity and defensiveness. Self-efficacy can also be damaged by negative feedback, as was discovered in a pair of experiments with business students. The researchers concluded the following:

> To facilitate the development of strong efficacy beliefs, professionals should be careful about the provision of negative feedback. Destructive criticism that attributes the cause of poor performance to internal factors reduces both the beliefs of self-efficacy and the self-set goals of recipients.[70]

When receiving feedback, people cognitively evaluate it based on criteria such as its accuracy, the credibility of the source, the fairness of the system (e.g. a performance-appraisal system), their performance–reward expectancies and the reasonableness of the standards. Feedback that fails to meet one or more of these cognitive criteria will be rejected or played down. Personal experience largely dictates how these criteria are weighed. For example, you would probably discount feedback from someone who exaggerates or from someone who performed poorly on the same task as the one you have just successfully completed. In view of the 'trust gap' credibility is an ethical matter of central importance today. Managers who have proven untrustworthy and not credible have a hard time improving job performance through feedback.[71] Feedback from a source who apparently shows favouritism or relies on unreasonable behaviour standards would be suspect.[72] Managers can enhance their credibility as sources of feedback by developing their expertise and creating a climate of trust. Also, as predicted by expectancy motivation theory, feedback must foster high effort → performance expectancies and performance → reward instrumentalities if it is to motivate the desired behaviour.

OB in Real Life

The nuances of feedback – performance reviews and culture

Feedback is all well and good, especially in the context of goal setting. However, the way feedback is organised in a great many organisations, particularly those based in the USA may not meet many of the criteria for effective feedback. While this may not be a great problem in a culture where the annual performance-review-cum-pay rise session is deeply institutionalised, exporting the practice to other countries may be difficult, if not disastrous.

ITT's Industrial Products division was experiencing great problems with its system of performance ratings. Personnel turnover was very high and complaints that the system made people lose face in the organisation came from many places (in China, for example), the individualistic character of the ratings was in conflict with the collectivist ethos in southern Europe, while in Scandinavia, employees felt the rating system introduced a distance between bosses and workers that was out of place.

The effect appears to have been immediate and lasting. At one plant in China, the personnel turnover rate was cut in half. However, while the change seems to have been generally very well received, some operations in the USA have resisted it.[73]

We discussed earlier how goal setting gives behaviour direction, increases expended effort and fosters persistence. Because feedback is intimately related to the goal-setting process, it involves the same behavioural outcomes: direction, effort and persistence. However, while the fourth outcome

Table 6.5 Trouble Signs for Organisational Feedback Systems

1	Feedback is used to punish, embarrass or put down employees
2	Those receiving the feedback see it as irrelevant to their work
3	Feedback information is provided too late to do any good
4	People receiving feedback believe it relates to matters beyond their control
5	Employees complain about wasting too much time collecting and recording feedback data
6	Feedback recipients complain about feedback being too complex or difficult to understand
7	The positive acceptance of feedback is treated as a given
8	Feedback is given too infrequently

Source: Based on discussions in D. R. Ilgen, C. D. Fisher and M. S. Taylor, 'Consequences of Individual Feedback on Behavior in Organizations', *Journal of Applied Psychology*, August 1979, pp. 367–8; C. O. Longenecker and D. A. Gioia, 'The Executive Appraisal Paradox', *Academy of Management Executive*, May 1992, p. 18; C. Bell and R. Zemke, 'On-Target Feedback', *Training*, June 1992, pp. 36–44; and M. L. Smith, 'Give Feedback, Not Criticism', *Supervisory Management*, February 1993, p. 4.

of goal setting involves formulating goal-attainment strategies, the fourth possible outcome of feedback is resistance. Feedback schemes that either smack of manipulation, or fail on one or more of the perceptual and cognitive evaluation tests just discussed, breed resistance.[74]

Evidence about motivating through feedback

The notion that feedback is valuable and motivating was presented above. The arguments supporting the notion are clear: feedback motivates. As documented in one study, the motivational function of feedback can be significantly enhanced by pairing specific, challenging goals with specific feedback about results.[75] The long list of potential problems, starting with the difference between subjective and objective feedback noted above, is a strong reminder, however, that feedback is a difficult task. Table 6.5 lists some further problems researchers identified with regard to organisational feedback systems.[76]

Underlying all these problems is a more fundamental one relating to the concept of social facilitation. The essential point about social facilitation is the effect others have on performance. Since feedback and its related practices such as performance reviews (and the 360-degree feedback) by nature require the presence of others (and they do not have to be physically present if they are known to be watching) the effects of social facilitation are likely to be present. A meta-analysis of 241 studies indicated that the performance of simple tasks is facilitated whereas that of complex tasks is made slower and less accurate. This produces what is effectively an opposite effect, social inhibition.[77] Drawing on the quality guru above them all, W. Edwards Deming, Jeff Pfeffer and Bob Sutton made the point that feedback practices that involve ranking:

> 'breed internal competition are bad management because they undermine motivation and breed contempt for management'. . . . Deming maintained that when people get unfair negative evaluations, it can leave them 'bitter, crushed, bruised, battered, desolate, despondent, dejected, feeling inferior, some even depressed, unfit for work for weeks after receipt of the rating, unable to comprehend why they are inferior'.[78]

Application of feedback thinking

Keeping in mind these possible trouble signs and the following tips[79] can help managers to build credible and effective feedback systems:

- Relate feedback to existing performance goals and clear expectations.
- Give specific and concrete feedback tied to observable behaviour or measurable results. Focus on specific behaviours. Feedback needs to be tailored to the recipient.
- Channel feedback toward key result areas.
- Give feedback as soon as possible.[80]
- Give positive feedback for improvement, not just final results. Good feedback is future-oriented.
- Focus feedback on performance, not personalities. Feedback needs to be task-oriented and job-related instead of people-oriented.
- Base feedback on accurate and credible information.
- Keep in mind that feedback (certainly negative) is often perceived wrongly or rejected. This is especially true in cross-cultural exchanges.

360-degree feedback

Traditional top-down feedback programmes have given way to some interesting variations in recent years. Two newer approaches are upward feedback and so-called 360-degree feedback. Aside from breaking away from a strict superior-to-subordinate feedback loop, these newer approaches are different because they typically involve multiple sources of feedback. Instead of simply getting feedback from one boss, often during an annual performance appraisal, more and more employees receive structured feedback from superiors, subordinates, peers and even outsiders such as customers. Feedback that covers all relevant stakeholders in an employee's performance is frequently referred to as 360-degree, to indicate the comprehensiveness of this type of feedback. Even if some parts are impractical and costly (getting feedback from outsiders), this approach and also the special case where a subordinate gives 'upward' feedback to his or her boss has grown in popularity for at least six reasons:

- Traditional performance-appraisal systems have created widespread dissatisfaction.
- Team-based organisation structures are replacing traditional hierarchies. This trend requires professionals to have good interpersonal skills that are best evaluated by team members.
- Systems using 'multiple raters' are said to make for more valid feedback than single-source rating.[81]
- Internet and Intranet now facilitates multiple-rater systems.[82]
- Bottom-up feedback meshes nicely with the trend towards participative management and employee empowerment.
- Co-workers and subordinates are said to know more about a professional's strengths and limitations than the boss.[83]

Together, these factors suggest the wisdom of looking at other ways to give and receive performance feedback.

Upward feedback turns the traditional approach upside down by having subordinates provide feedback on a superior's style and performance. This type of feedback is generally anonymous. Most students are familiar with upward feedback programmes from years of filling out anonymous lecturer-evaluation surveys.

Superiors typically resist upward feedback programmes because they believe it erodes their authority. Other critics say anonymous upward feedback can become little more than a personality contest, or worse, the system can be manipulated by superiors making promises or threats.[84]

The concept of **360-degree feedback** involves letting individuals compare their own perceived performance with that of behaviourally specific (and usually anonymous) performance information supplied by their superior, subordinates and peers. Even outsiders, like customers, may be involved in what is sometimes called 'full-circle' feedback. Research, however, indicates that, even when 360-degree feedback is implemented it is often more accurate to describe it as 270-degree feedback, because often customers are not included as a data source.[85]

The idea is to let people know how their behaviour affects others, with the goal of motivating change. The 360-degree approach recognises that little change can be expected without feedback and that different sources can provide rich and useful information to professionals to guide their behaviour. In a 360-degree feedback programme, a given professional will play different roles, including focal person, superior, subordinate and peer. Of course, the focal person role is played only once. The other roles are played in relation to other focal individuals.[86] Looking at the practice of different companies, apparently 360-degree feedback can be used for a number of purposes. For example, the British Automobile Association uses a 360-degree feedback to screen employees to see whether they meet a set of new standards. Employees also receive a 'development guide', containing tips from supervisors, subordinates and colleagues to tackle certain weaknesses. This process is again guided by those who give the feedback. Similarly, the Avon Rubber Company uses 360-degree feedback as a team-building tool. Employees are evaluated by fellow team members on characteristics such as openness and co-operation and each is given behavioural comments that may help them improve their functioning within the team.[87]

Evidence about feedback practice

The question of whether upward feedback should be anonymous is tricky. One study showed that open feedback from (named) employees is viewed more positively by managers than anonymous feedback. However, employees felt less comfortable doing this and tended to be more lenient in their assessment.[88]

In another study, 83 supervisors were divided into three feedback groups: (a) group 1: feedback from both superiors and subordinates; (b) group 2: feedback from superiors only; and (c) group 3: feedback from subordinates only. Group 1 was most satisfied with the overall evaluation process and responded more positively to upward feedback. Group 3 expressed more concern that subordinate appraisals would undermine supervisors' authority and that supervisors would focus on pleasing subordinates.[89] In a field study of 238 corporate managers, upward feedback had a positive impact on the performance of low to moderate performers.[90] A longitudinal study of upward feedback found that repeated upward feedback from subordinates to their bosses had a lasting positive effect on performance.[91]

These research findings suggest the practical value of anonymous upward feedback used in combination with other sources of performance feedback and evaluation. Because of a superior's resistance and potential manipulation, using upward feedback as the primary determinant for promotions and pay decisions is not recommended. Carefully collected upward feedback is useful for setting up development programmes.[92]

Rigorous research evidence of 360-degree feedback programmes remains scarce. A review of multi-rater feedback systems concludes that there is ample evidence concerning the individual level, but little adequate research on the organisational conditions and effects.[93]

Because upward feedback is part of 360-degree feedback programmes, the evidence reviewed earlier applies here as well. As with upward feedback, the peer- and self-evaluations that are central to 360-degree feedback programmes are also a significant affront to tradition, but advocates insist that co-workers and superiors are appropriate performance evaluators because they are closest to the action.

Generally, research builds a strong case for using peer appraisals.[94] Self-serving bias (discussed in Chapter 4) can be a problem with self-ratings. However, it might be important to train people in how to observe, judge and record other people's behaviour because peer appraisals are also not free of certain biases.[95] Some people suggest supplementing the results of a 360-degree feedback process with feedback of other 'more objective' sources, obtained for instance with assessment centre methods.[96]

A two-year study of 48 managers given 360-degree feedback led to somewhat promising results: 'the group as a whole developed its skills but there was substantial variability among individuals in how much change occurred'.[97] Thus, as with any feedback, individuals vary in their response to 360-degree feedback.

Despite these positive results, they say little about the details of the process and very often only one round of 360-degree feedback is reported, with limited information available on any follow-up. However, using a psychometrically reliable instrument to conduct the 360-degree feedback process repeatedly with an 18-month cycle time in the management team assessed, the evidence suggests that improvements in managerial effectiveness are possible. However, in this case, the 360-degree feedback was coupled with follow-up support for those managers with identified needs.[98]

Application of feedback procedures

If feedback is formally required, based on anonymity, decoupled from pay and promotion decisions and combined with follow-up interventions where underperformance is detected, then both 360-degree and upward feedback may be a valuable motivational tool.

The main reason is that using 360-degree feedback for appraisal or for development affects the attitudes of the subordinates and the nature of the process itself. Developing effective 360-degree programmes is not a quick-and-easy fix, as some advocates would have us believe. It involves several interconnected steps, like describing and communicating the purpose of the 360-degree programme, developing a survey or other measuring method (survey is the most commonly used method, although alternative methods like focus groups are also used), writing a report, distributing the results and following up the improvement.[99] Table 6.6 summarises some conditions for the effective implementation of 360-degree feedback in organisations.

Table 6.6 Organisational Conditions for 360-Degree Feedback

1	Top management should be involved, both in the role of rater and in the role of focal person
2	Complement the results of peer- and self-appraisals with additional data from assessment centre methods
3	Involve the users in the design of the 360-degree process
4	Involve the users in the choice of peers and others who will be rating their skills, behaviour and outcomes
5	Anonymity and confidence of the feedback must be guaranteed, so the focal person remains the final owner of the data
6	Be careful in coupling multi-rater feedback systems with regular appraisal systems
7	Make sure the instrument is tested for coherence, and that it is scored, interpreted and reported following a research-based procedure

Source: Adapted from P. Jansen and D. Vloeberghs, 'Multi-Rater Feedback Methods: Personal and Organizational Implications', *Journal of Managerial Psychology*, October 1999, pp. 45–7; and R. Lepsinger, D. Antonioette and D. Lucia, *The Art and Science of 360° Feedback* (San Francisco, CA: Pfeiffer, 1997).

The difficulties are significant. Perhaps the most important single problem is the required combination of anonymity and decoupling from appraisal or performance review processes. While formal anonymity of respondents may be a possibility, it really only shifts the balance in terms of truth-telling. Anonymity may increase precision and honesty in feedback given, but any negative feedback (real or perceived) will make the person receiving feedback distrustful. Who gave me that negative feedback? Was it you or was it that snivelling little idiot down in accounting?

One curmodgeonly critic of performance reviews argues that they should be completely eliminated. While an objective evaluation is intended, this lofty ambition is rarely if ever fulfilled. The interested parties have different agendas (bosses want better performance, employees want better pay and promotions, roughly speaking). Pay is not really in the equation (only large rises have an impact as argued above), the procedure is rigid, and it affects personal development and disrupts teamwork.[100] To this we might add that such formalised feedback, especially if all the reservations outlined above are incorporated into the feedback process, are likely to be very costly indeed.

!

Critical thinking

If performance reviews were to be eliminated, what could managers do to let people know how they are doing?

6.5 Organisational reward systems

Rewards are an ever-present and always controversial feature of organisational life.[101] The large changes in compensation practices, combined with other factors like increased competition for the best employees, reduced employee loyalty, increased employee pay information and enhanced variability in pay practices in recent years, make compensation and organisational reward systems a matter of great interest to organisations and employees.[102]

Some employees see their jobs as the source of a pay cheque and little else. Others derive great pleasure from their jobs and association with co-workers. Even volunteers who donate their time to charitable organisations, such as the Red Cross, walk away with rewards in the form of social recognition and the pride of having unselfishly given their time. Hence, the subject of organisational rewards includes, but goes far beyond, monetary compensation.[103] This section examines key components of organisational reward systems. Despite the fact that reward systems vary widely, it is possible to identify and interrelate some common components. Figure 6.6 identifies the four important components.

Types of reward

The variety and magnitude of material organisational rewards is bewildering – from subsidised day care to education subsidies to stock options, from boxes of chocolates to golf club membership. In addition to the obvious pay and benefits, there are less obvious social and psychological rewards. Social rewards include praise and recognition from others both inside and outside the organisation. Psychological rewards come from personal feelings of self-esteem, self-satisfaction and accomplishment.

Figure 6.6 A General Model of Organisational Reward Systems

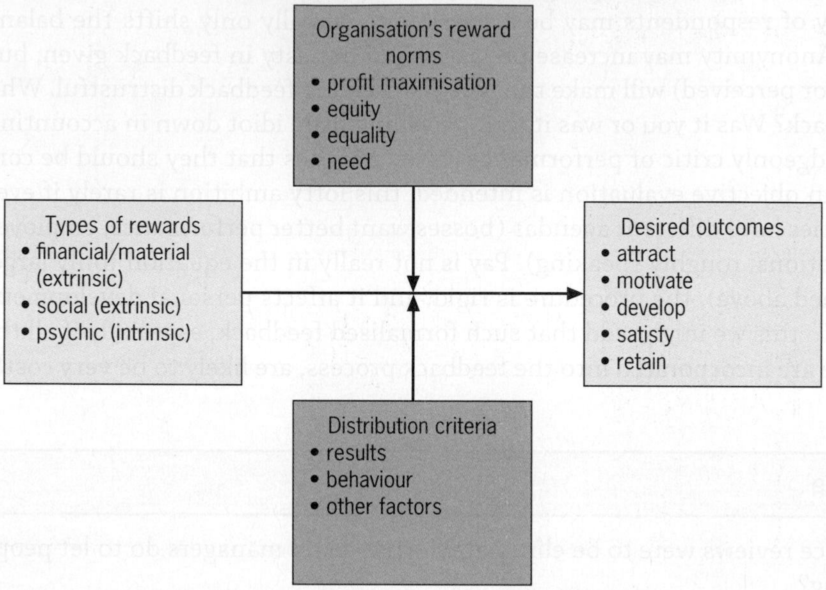

OB in Real Life

Pay practices in Britain

An annual large-scale national study from the [British] Chartered Institute of Personnel and Development (CIPD) on reward management (729 organisations took part in the 2010 survey) revealed that a wide range of rewards are used in British companies. Most employers have some form of pension plan. The survey also finds a widespread use of variable pay (although more in the private than in the public sector). Pay is composed of a base pay or salary level, mostly linked to market levels, with pay progression determined by individual performance (also market rates and competence). Bonuses are widely used, based on individual performance or business results. Just under half of British employers offer access to an employee share-ownership scheme. Other benefits, beside pensions, also are very important, but they vary from sector to sector and over time. The most recent data suggest that in manufacturing, the most widely used benefits are on-site parking, holidays and career development. In private sector services, the Christmas party and free soft drinks are more widespread than career development. In public services, extended maternity leave comes third, after holidays and career development. Special attention is paid to family-friendly benefits (like child-care vouchers, subsidised crèche facilities, enhanced maternity/paternity leave) and well-being benefits (like private health care, critical illness insurance, employee assistance). Another common practice is the use of flexible benefits (also known as cafeteria benefits or flex plans), which includes all kinds of arrangements that give employees a choice over the mix of cash and benefits they receive (like choosing between a car and additional cash).

An alternative typology for organisational rewards is the distinction between extrinsic and intrinsic rewards.[104] Financial, material and social rewards are defined as **extrinsic rewards** because they come from the environment. Psychological rewards, however, are **intrinsic rewards** because they are self-granted. An employee who works to obtain extrinsic rewards, such as money or praise, is said to be extrinsically motivated (**extrinsic motivation**). One who derives pleasure from the task itself or experiences a sense of competence or self-determination is said to be intrinsically motivated (**intrinsic motivation**). Intrinsically motivated behaviours are those that are performed without any apparent externally derived need.[105] The relative importance of extrinsic and intrinsic rewards is a matter of cultural context and personal tastes. In a large-scale study in a multinational manufacturing company (107 292 respondents from 49 countries) a relationship was found between valuing intrinsic or extrinsic rewards and cultural and socio-economic aspects.[106] Intrinsic job characteristics were valued higher (and led to higher job satisfaction) in richer countries, with better state-provided social welfare programmes and with a lower power distance and a more individualistic culture (see the national culture dimensions of Hofstede, Chapter 12), while they did not seem to work in countries with low social security and a large power distance culture. These findings contradict the conventional wisdom that intrinsic rewards are desirable for all employees. So, implementing organisational reward systems that overemphasise intrinsic rewards in countries with poor social security systems and a large power distance culture can be a serious mistake.

OB in Real Life

Performance pay in China

A recent study of performance pay in China found that generally performance pay is slightly over 17 per cent of total compensation for both men and women. Performance pay makes up a greater share of total pay among people with higher education, Han ethnicity, who work in skilled manual or professional occupations or in state-owned organisations. The share of performance pay is lower among workers who have long tenure and considerable general labour market experience, as well as for workers with children under the age of 6.

Relative to men, women receive a significantly lower share of wages as performance pay, largely because women are selected or attracted to ownership types, occupations and ranks that tend not to provide performance pay.

For discussion

Why might women be ending up in jobs with significantly lower shares of performance pay?

Source: Based on L. Xiu and M. Gunderson, M, 'Performance Pay in China: Gender Aspects', *British Journal of Industrial Relations*, vol. 51, no. 1, 2013, pp. 124–47.

Organisational reward norms

As discussed in the equity theory section of this chapter, the employer–employee linkage can be viewed as an exchange relationship. Employees exchange their time and talent for rewards. Ideally, four alternative norms dictate the nature of this exchange. In pure form, each would lead to a significantly different reward distribution system. These four **norms** – profit maximisation, equity, equality and need – are defined as follows.

- *Profit maximisation*. The objective of each party is to maximise its net gain, regardless of how the other party fares. A profit-maximising company would attempt to pay the lowest level of wages for maximum effort. Conversely, a profit-maximising employee would seek maximum rewards, regardless of the organisation's financial well-being, and leave the organisation for a better deal.
- *Equity*. According to the **reward equity norm**, rewards should be allocated in proportion to contributions. Those who contribute the most should be rewarded the most. A cross-cultural study of American, Japanese and Korean college students led the researchers to conclude: 'Equity is probably a phenomenon common to most cultures, but its strength will vary.'[107] Basic principles of fairness and justice, evident in most cultures, drive the equity norm.
- *Equality*. The **reward equality norm** calls for rewarding all parties equally, regardless of their comparative contributions. Because absolute equality does not exist in hierarchical organisations, the impact of pay inequality or pay dispersion (the pay gap between high-level and low-level employees) takes on special importance. It appears that the smaller the pay gap, the better the individual and organisational performance.[108] Thus, very large compensation packages of many of today's top executives is not only a widely debated moral issue, it is a productivity issue as well.[109]
- *Need*. This norm calls for distributing rewards according to employees' needs rather than their contributions.[110]

Conflict and ethical debates often arise over the perceived fairness of reward allocations because of disagreement about reward norms.[111] The existence of different reward allocation norms questions the generalisability of the equity theory. Individual differences and social and political-economic contexts might explain different reactions to inequity and different preferences for reward norms.[112] Stockholders, for instance, might prefer a profit-maximisation norm, while technical specialists would like an equity norm, and unionised hourly workers would argue for a pay system based on equality. A reward norm anchored to need might prevail in a family-owned and family-operated business.

Effective reward systems are based on clear and consensual exchange norms. Taking into account individual preference for reward-allocation norms and social, cultural and political-economic contexts when implementing a reward system might enhance people's job satisfaction and motivation. Pay and reward systems that are effective in motivating people in one context might be met with hostility, perceptions of inequity and dissatisfaction in an environment where other values and norms predominate.[113]

Reward distribution criteria

According to one expert on organisational reward systems, there are three general criteria for the distribution of rewards:

- *Performance in terms of results*. Tangible outcomes such as individual, group or organisation performance; quantity and quality of performance.
- *Performance in terms of actions and behaviours*. For example, teamwork, co-operation, risk taking, creativity.
- *Non-performance considerations*. Customary or contractual, where the type of job, nature of the work, equity, tenure, level in the hierarchy, and so on are rewarded.[114]

A review of recent studies on organisational compensation practices also revealed that factors other than individual productivity generally influence compensation decisions, such as own salary increases, performance of a whole group or organisational changes in business strategy.[115] As listed in Figure 6.6, a good reward system should attract talented people and motivate and satisfy them once they have joined the organisation.[116] It should also promote personal growth and development and keep talented people from leaving.

Despite huge investments of time and money in organisational reward systems, often the desired motivational impact is not achieved. The following eight reasons may help us understand:

- Too much emphasis on monetary rewards.
- Rewards lack an 'appreciation effect'.
- Extensive benefits become entitlements.
- Counter-productive behaviour is rewarded (e.g. a pizza delivery company related its rewards to the 'on-time' performance of its drivers, only to discover that it was inadvertently rewarding reckless driving).[117]
- Too long a delay between performance and rewards.
- Too many one-size-fits-all rewards.
- Use of one-shot rewards with a short-lived motivational impact.
- Continued use of demotivating practices such as lay-offs, across-the-board pay rises and cuts and excessive executive compensation.[118]

These persistent problems have fostered a growing interest in the available evidence about effective reward and compensation practices, like different pay-for-performance systems.[119]

Evidence about rewards

Many organisations, in both the private and the public sectors, expend significant resources trying to design performance-enhancing reward systems. Rewards can certainly increase performance but may not always turn out to be quite as attractive as was intended. Financial rewards can have impact on performance in three distinct ways. The first is motivational, in the sense that a reward makes people try harder (put in more effort). In the short run that is all they can do. Over time they might also learn and become better at doing a job, but not in the short run. This is the purpose in most reward systems, but it only works if the employees know what to do and if the outcome is under their control (i.e. there are no barriers to achieving high performance).[120]

The second effect of rewards is about the signals they send, for example to employees, about what is important to the organisation. An extra monthly payment of say €50 for each employee of a train company when the target for on-time services is reached is a very clear signal, even if the monetary amount is quite small.

The third effect of rewards is also indirect in its effect on performance. An organisation known to use rewards extensively will tend to attract people who value such rewards and at the same time believe that they have the skills required to actually earn the reward. It has been suggested that this selection or 'worker sorting' effect of rewards is as important to organisational performance overall as it is to motivation of individuals.[121]

There are several issues to consider when deciding on the relative balance between monetary and non-monetary rewards. First, some research shows that employees value interesting work and recognition more than money.[122] For instance, saying 'thank you' is a significant reward to many people. Second, extrinsic rewards can lose their motivating properties over time and may undermine intrinsic motivation.[123] This conclusion, however, must be balanced by the fact that performance is related to the receipt of financial incentives, although research found mixed results concerning the performance-enhancing effect of incentives.[124] A meta-analysis of 39 studies involving 2773 people showed that financial incentives were positively related to performance quantity but not to performance quality. Another study showed that the promise of a financial reward increased children's creativity when they knew that there was an explicit positive relationship between creative performance and rewards. Third, monetary rewards must be large enough to generate motivation.[125] For example, Steven Kerr, formerly chief learning officer at the Goldman Sachs Group, estimates that monetary awards must be at least 12–15 per cent above employees' base pay to truly motivate people.[126] Unfortunately, this percentage is well above the typical salary increase received by employees.

The use of monetary incentives to motivate employees is seldom questioned, despite much evidence on the accompanying difficulties. Unfortunately, recent research uncovered some negative consequences when goal achievement is linked to individual incentives. Case studies, for example, confirm the point made in the previous section, that pay should not be linked to goal achievement unless the following conditions are satisfied:

- Performance goals are under the employees' control.
- Goals are quantitative and measurable.
- Frequent, relatively large payments are made for performance achievement.[127]

Goal-based incentive systems are more likely to produce undesirable effects if these three conditions are not satisfied. Moreover, empirical studies demonstrated that goal-based bonus incentives produced higher commitment to easy goals and lower commitment to difficult goals. People were reluctant to commit to difficult goals that were tied to monetary incentives. People with high goal commitment also offered less help to their co-workers when they received goal-based bonus incentives to accomplish difficult individual goals. Individuals neglected aspects of the job that were not covered in the performance goals.

A shop worker paid in part by commission or a waiter paid in part by tips will, for example, tend to focus actions that maximise their own pay, at the expense of overall service quality. Anyone who has experienced a waiter who constantly asks 'How is everything?' while adding ice cold water to your glass may have observed an example of such thinking in action. As another case in point, several studies revealed that quality suffered when employees were given quantity goals.[128] These findings underscore some of the dangers of using goal-based incentives, particularly for employees in complex, interdependent jobs requiring co-operation. Organisations need to consider the advantages, disadvantages and dilemmas of goal-based incentives prior to their implementation.[129]

Application of reward mechanisms

How can employers improve the motivational impact of their current organisational reward plan? The fact is that most such plans are not pure types but hybrids. They combine features of several reward systems.[130] Organisational reward systems have to be complex, because they need to take several aspects into account. Reward systems simultaneously try to have strategic impact (this means leveraging motivation towards strategic actions) and to influence employee satisfaction and fairness.[131] Table 6.7 lists some practical recommendations that can help to build effective and fair organisational reward systems.

Table 6.7 Organisational Practices to Stimulate a Performance Culture

Mission and goals
• A well-articulated and clear mission and operating vision that is understood and accepted • Organisational goals that are credible, measurable and verifiable • Department, work unit and team goals that have a clear line of sight (connection) to the success of the organisation • Individual goals or work measures that are intuitively related to good performance
Communication and feedback
• A pay philosophy that is clearly specified and communicated to employees • Regular communication that keeps employees informed of performance results • Regular feedback to employees to guide and encourage their growth and career progression • Regular communication to recognise the importance of employee efforts and to make clear how their efforts contribute to the organisation's success
Organisational climate and culture
• An organisational climate that encourages people to look for new and better ways to accomplish goals • An organisational climate that stimulates people to pursue challenging goals • An organisational climate that encourages people to tackle new problems and new tasks to accomplish organisational goals • An organisational climate that emphasises the importance of the individual, his or her needs and aspirations • Training and development that is seen as an investment in people • An organisational climate where people have the opportunity to participate in the development of performance measures
Reward system
• A reward system that reinforces the importance of good performance at all levels, including both monetary and non-monetary rewards • A reward system that is implemented in a fair and objective way, including an appeal process for people who believe they have been treated unjustly • A reward system that encourages people to work together and co-operate, and that also creates opportunities to celebrate people's accomplishments

Source: Adapted from H. Risher, 'Pay-for-Performance: The Keys to Making it Work', *Public Personnel Management*, Fall 2002, pp. 326–7; and K. M. Bartol and E. A. Locke, 'Incentives and Motivation', in *Compensation in Organizations: Current Research and Practice*, eds S. L. Rynes and B. Gerhart (San Francisco, CA: Jossey-Bass, 2000), p. 124.

Critical thinking

Is regulation to make a large fraction of bonuses for bankers dependent on the long-term performance of the bank likely to change the risk taking that bankers engaged in?

Critical thinking

What kind of reward would motivate diligence and dedication in a public sector worker assigned to caring for elderly people in their homes, when the alternative is losing unemployment benefits?

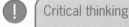

6.6 Putting motivational theories to work

It is clear from the previous and current chapter that motivating people is an important, although difficult to implement, issue for most organisations. Organisations cannot simply take one of the theories discussed in this book and apply it word by word. Dynamics within organisations interfere with applying motivation theories in 'pure' form. Moreover, although several theories exist that try to explain motivation; there are no ready-made and clear-cut solutions to deal effectively with employee motivation.[132] An all-including and ready-made motivation programme for organisations is also difficult to design. Because an all-encompassing theory of motivation does not exist (yet), organisations can try to create a stimulating and motivating work environment by implementing those aspects of existing theories that are useful and relevant for their particular work setting. We want to end the elaboration on motivation with raising some issues that need to be addressed before implementing a motivational programme. Our intent is not to discuss all relevant considerations but rather to highlight a few important ones.

The toughest job of managers is probably to turn around people who have lost their motivation to make a positive contribution to the organisation. Managers have an important task in creating an environment in which people can motivate themselves.[133] As implied by most of the process theories of motivation covered in this chapter, this does not need to be done with monetary incentives, bonuses and merit plans.[134] An important issue concerning organisational motivation is the distinction between motivation and recognition, although these concepts are often mixed up.[135] Recognition through open communication, the ability to make a difference at work and a career development plan are as effective and important to motivate people.[136] For example at Disneyland® Resort, Paris, an amusement park in France, a process called 'Small World', named after one of its attractions, relies on the idea of improving motivation through a process of decentralising power, cutting down hierarchy and creating internal competition between different parts of the park. Each 'small world' unit has 30–50 staff, led by a manager. The small worlds are given greater responsibility and flexibility to meet three goals: to achieve management targets, to improve visitor satisfaction and to get to know and motivate staff. One important incentive is that small world managers will receive up to 10 per cent of their salary in bonuses linked to performance. Ordinary staff will receive non-financial rewards, including improved promotion prospects.

It is clear from the description of several motivation theories that people are not motivated by the same aspects. Some people, for example, attach a lot of value to money, while others are mainly motivated by growth opportunities. People also vary in their intensity and persistence of motivated behaviour. Importantly, organisations should not ignore these individual differences, because they are an important input that influences motivation and motivated behaviour. Organisations are advised to develop employees so that they have the ability and job knowledge to perform their jobs effectively. In addition, attempts should be made to nurture positive employee characteristics, such as self-esteem, self-efficacy, positive emotions, a learning goal orientation and need for achievement.

Because motivation is goal-directed, the process of developing and setting goals should be consistent with our previous discussion. Moreover, the method used to evaluate performance also needs to be considered. Without a valid performance-appraisal system, it is difficult, if not impossible, to distinguish accurately between good and poor performers. Organisations need to keep in mind that both equity and expectancy theory suggest that employee motivation is crushed by inaccurate performance ratings. Inaccurate ratings also make it difficult to evaluate the effectiveness of any motivational programme, so it is beneficial for organisations to assess the accuracy and validity of their appraisal systems.[137]

In keeping with expectancy theory, organisations should make rewards contingent on performance.[138] In doing so, it is important that they consider the accuracy and fairness of the reward system, including the extent to which performance is under the control of those making the effort. The promise of increased rewards will not prompt greater effort and good performance unless those rewards are clearly tied to performance and they are large enough to gain employees' interest or attention. Moreover, equity theory tells us that motivation is influenced by employee perceptions about the fairness of reward allocations. Motivation is decreased when employees believe rewards are inequitably allocated. Rewards also need to be integrated appropriately into the appraisal system. If performance is measured at the individual level, individual achievements need to be rewarded. On the other hand, when performance is the result of group effort, rewards should be allocated to the group.

Feedback also needs to be linked to performance. Feedback provides the information and direction needed to keep employees focused on relevant tasks, activities and goals. Organisations should strive to provide specific, timely and accurate feedback to employees. Finally, the climate of an organisation (Chapter 9) and the organisation's culture significantly influences employee motivation and behaviour. A positive self-enhancing culture is more likely to engender higher motivation and commitment than a culture dominated by suspicion, fault finding and blame.

Learning outcomes: Summary of key terms

1 **Perceived inequity in employee motivation**

Equity theory is a model of motivation that explains how people strive for fairness and justice in social exchanges. At work, feelings of (in)equity revolve around a person's evaluation of whether he or she receives adequate rewards to compensate for his or her contributive inputs. People perform these evaluations by comparing the perceived fairness of their employment exchange with that of relevant others. Perceived inequity creates motivation to restore equity.

2 **The basic expectancy theory of motivation and its later extension of the expectancy theory**

Expectancy theory assumes motivation is determined by one's perceived chances of achieving valued outcomes. Vroom's expectancy model of motivation reveals how both the effort → performance expectancies and the performance → outcome instrumentalities will influence the degree of effort expended to achieve desired (positively valent) outcomes. Porter and Lawler developed a model of expectancy that enlarged upon the theory proposed by Vroom. This model specifies (a) the source of people's valences and expectancies and (b) the relationship between performance and satisfaction.

3 **How goal setting motivates people**

Goal-setting theory starts from the idea that people are motivated to reach goals. Goal setting provides four motivational mechanisms. It directs one's attention, regulates effort, increases persistence and encourages development of goal attainment strategies and action plans. Difficult goals lead to higher performance than easy or moderate ones. However, goals should not be impossible to achieve. Specific, difficult goals lead to higher performance for simple rather than complex tasks. Third, feedback enhances the effect of specific, difficult goals. Fourth, participative goals, assigned goals and self-set goals are equally effective. Fifth, goal commitment affects goal-setting outcomes.

4 **Recipient's characteristics, and how people process feedback**

Self-esteem, self-efficacy, needs, goals and desire for feedback determine the recipient's openness to feedback. The individual's perception determines whether feedback is viewed positively or negatively. Cognitively, the recipient will tend to act on feedback that is seen as accurate, from a credible source, based on a fair system and tied to reasonable expectations and behavioural standards.

5 **Practical lessons from feedback research**

Feedback is not automatically accepted as intended, especially negative feedback. A professional's credibility can be enhanced through expertise and a climate of trust. Feedback must neither be too frequent nor too scarce and must be tailored to the individual. Feedback accessed directly from computers is effective. Active participation in the feedback session helps people perceive feedback as more accurate.

6 **Types of organisational rewards**

A wide variety of organisational rewards exist, like pension plans, pay-for-performance systems or different types of benefit (e.g. childcare vouchers, private healthcare). In addition to the obvious pay and benefits, there are less obvious social and psychic rewards. Social rewards include praise and recognition from others both inside and outside the organisation. Psychic rewards come from personal feelings of self-esteem, self-satisfaction and accomplishment. An alternative typology for organisational rewards is the distinction between extrinsic and intrinsic rewards. Financial, material and social rewards qualify as extrinsic rewards because they come from the environment. Psychic rewards, however, are intrinsic rewards because they are self-granted.

7 **Recommendations on how to implement an organisational reward system**

Organisational reward systems usually combine several types of rewards to simultaneously try to have strategic impact (this means leveraging motivation toward strategic actions) and to influence employee satisfaction and fairness. To build an effective and fair organisational reward system, it is important to: (a) make the organisational reward system an integral part of the organisation's mission and goals; (b) communicate regularly and clearly about the system to all employees; (c) stimulate a performance culture; and (d) implement the system in a fair and objective way.

8 **Issues that should be addressed before implementing a motivational programme**

Successfully designing and implementing motivational programmes is not easy. Organisations cannot simply take one of the theories discussed in this book and apply it word for word. Dynamics within organisations interfere with applying motivation theories in 'pure' form. However, organisations need to understand the motivation process if they are to successfully guide employees towards accomplishing organisational objectives. Because an all-encompassing theory of motivation does not exist (yet), organisations can try to create a stimulating and motivating work environment by implementing those aspects of existing theories that are useful and relevant for their particular work setting. Professionals have an important task in creating an environment in which people can motivate themselves, through rewards and recognition. Also important to keep in mind is that motivation is only one of several factors that influence performance and that individual differences influence motivation and motivated behaviour.

Review questions

1 Is equal treatment of employees theoretically feasible or desirable?
2 Think about a job you have done and specify which elements were the most important to you.
3 An employee who reported to you seems to have a low expectancy for successful performance. What interventions would you suggest to address the problem – if it is a problem?
4 Do goals play an important role in your life? Explain.
5 Goal-setting research suggests that people should be given difficult goals. How does this prescription mesh with expectancy theory? Explain.
6 When students are given marks and general feedback for seminar presentations, they always compare (and sometimes complain about) their own outcome to that of others. What process is at work when this happens?
7 Which of the four organisational reward norms do you prefer? Why?
8 What is your personal experience with failed organisational reward systems and practices?

Personal awareness and growth exercise

What kind of feedback are you getting?

Objectives

1 To provide actual examples of on-the-job feedback from three primary sources: organisation/supervisor, co-workers and self/task.
2 To provide a handy instrument for evaluating the comparative strength of positive feedback from these three sources.

Introduction

A pair of researchers from Georgia Tech developed and tested a 63-item feedback questionnaire to demonstrate the importance of both the sign and content of feedback messages.[139] Although their instrument contains both positive and negative feedback items, we have extracted 18 positive items for this self-awareness exercise.

Instructions

Thinking of your current job (or your most recent job), circle one number for each of the 18 items. Alternatively, you could ask one or more employed individuals to complete the questionnaire for you. Once the questionnaire has been completed, calculate subtotal and total scores by adding the circled numbers. Then try to answer the discussion questions.

Instrument

How frequently do you experience each of the following outcomes in your present (or past) job?

Organisational/supervisory feedback

		Rarely		Occasionally		Very frequently
1	My supervisor complimenting me on something I have done.	1	2	3	4	5
2	My supervisor increasing my responsibilities.	1	2	3	4	5
3	The company expressing pleasure with my performance.	1	2	3	4	5
4	The company giving me a pay rise.	1	2	3	4	5
5	My supervisor recommending me for a promotion or pay rise.	1	2	3	4	5
6	The company providing me with favourable data concerning my performance.	1	2	3	4	5

Subscore = ________

Co-worker feedback

		Rarely		Occasionally		Very frequently
7	My co-workers coming to me for advice.	1	2	3	4	5
8	My co-workers expressing approval of my work.	1	2	3	4	5
9	My co-workers liking to work with me.	1	2	3	4	5
10	My co-workers telling me that I am doing a good job.	1	2	3	4	5
11	My co-workers commenting favourably on something I have done.	1	2	3	4	5
12	Receiving a compliment from my co-workers.	1	2	3	4	5

Subscore = ________

Self/task feedback

		Rarely		Occasionally		Very frequently
13	Knowing that the way I go about my duties is superior to most.	1	2	3	4	5
14	Feeling I am accomplishing more than I used to.	1	2	3	4	5
15	Knowing that I can now perform or do things that previously were difficult for me.	1	2	3	4	5
16	Finding that I am satisfying my own standards for 'good work'.	1	2	3	4	5
17	Knowing that what I am doing 'feels right'.	1	2	3	4	5
18	Feeling confident of being able to handle all aspects of my job.	1	2	3	4	5

Subscore = ________

Total score = ________

Questions for discussion

1 Which items on this questionnaire would you rate as primarily instructional in function? Are all of the remaining items primarily motivational? Explain.

2 In terms of your own feedback profile, which of the three types is the strongest (has the highest subscore)? Which is the weakest (has the lowest subscore)? How well does your feedback profile explain your job performance and/or satisfaction?

3 How does your feedback profile measure up against those of the other students? (Arbitrary norms, for comparative purposes, are: Deficient feedback = 18–42; Moderate feedback = 43–65; Abundant feedback = 66–90.)

4 Which of the three sources of feedback is most critical to your successful job performance and/or job satisfaction? Explain.

Group exercise

Rewards, rewards, rewards

Objectives

1 To tap the class's collective knowledge of organisational rewards.

2 To appreciate the vast array of potential rewards.

3 To contrast individual and group perceptions of rewards.

4 To practise your group creativity skills.

Introduction

Rewards are a centrepiece of organisational life. Both extrinsic and intrinsic rewards motivate us to join and continue contributing to organised effort. But not all rewards have the same impact on work motivation. Individuals have their own personal preferences for rewards. The best way to discover people's reward preferences is to ask them, both individually and collectively. This group brainstorming and class discussion exercise requires about 20 to 30 minutes.

Instructions

Your lecturer will divide your class randomly into teams of five to eight people. Each team will go through the following four-step process.

1 Each team will have a six-minute brainstorming session, with one person acting as recorder. The objective of this brainstorming session is to list as many different organisational rewards as the group can think of. Your team might find it helpful to think of rewards by category (such as rewards arising from the work itself, those you can spend, those you eat and drink, feel, wear, share, cannot see, and so on). Keep in mind that good brainstorming calls on you to withhold judgements about whether ideas are good or not. Quantity is what is wanted. Building on other people's ideas is encouraged too (see Chapter 13 for more on brainstorming).

2 Next, each individual will take four minutes to write down, in decreasing order of importance, 10 rewards they want from the job. *Note*: These are your personal preferences (your 'top 10' rewards that will motivate you to do your best).

3 Each team will then take five minutes to generate a list of 'today's 10 most powerful rewards'. List them in decreasing order of their power to motivate job performance. Voting may be necessary.

4 A general class discussion of the questions listed below will conclude the exercise.

Questions for discussion

1 How did your personal 'top 10' list compare with your group's 'top 10' list? If there is a serious mismatch, how would it affect your motivation? (To promote discussion, the lecturer may ask several volunteers to read their personal 'top 10' lists to the class.)

2 Which team had the most productive brainstorming session? (The lecturer may request each team to read its brainstormed list of potential rewards and 'top 10' list to the class.)

3 Were you surprised to hear certain rewards getting so much attention? Why?

4 How can organisations improve the incentive effect of the rewards most frequently mentioned in class?

Online Learning Centre

When you have read this chapter, log on to the Online Learning Centre website at ***www.mcgraw-hill.co.uk/textbooks/sinding*** to access test questions, additional exercises and other related resources.

Notes

[1] For a complete discussion of Vroom's theory, see V. H. Vroom, *Work and Motivation* (New York: John Wiley & Sons, 1964).

[2] R. G. Isaac, W. J. Zerbe and D. C. Pitt, 'Leadership and Motivation: The Effective Application of Expectancy Theory', *Journal of Managerial Issues*, Summer 2001, pp. 212–26; J. Chowdhury, 'The Motivational Impact of Sales Quotas on Effort', *Journal of Marketing Research*, February 1993, pp. 28–41; and C. C. Pinder, *Work Motivation* (Glenview, IL: Scott, Foresman, 1984), Ch. 7.

[3] The measurement and importance of valence was investigated by N. T. Feather, 'Values, Valences, and Choice: The Influence of Values on the Perceived Attractiveness and Choice of Alternatives', *Journal of Personality and Social Psychology*, June 1995, pp. 1135–51; and A. Pecotich and G. A. Churchill, Jr, 'An Examination of the Anticipated-Satisfaction Importance Valence Controversy', *Organizational Behavior and Human Performance*, April 1981, pp. 213–26.

[4] S. Trelford, 'Choice Rewards', *Marketing Week*, 24 June 1999, pp. 71–4.

[5] Results can be found in W. van Eerde and H. Thierry, 'Vroom's Expectancy Models and Work-Related Criteria: A Meta-Analysis', *Journal of Applied Psychology*, October 1996, pp. 575–86.

[6] J. P. Wanous, T. L. Keon and J. C. Latack, 'Expectancy Theory and Occupational/Organizational Choices: A Review and Test', *Organizational Behavior and Human Performance*, August 1983, pp. 66–86.

[7] These results are based on T. K. DeBacker and R. M. Nelson, 'Variations on An Expectancy-Value Model of Motivation in Science', *Contemporary Educational Psychology*, April 1999, pp. 71–94; R. M. Lynd-Stevenson, 'Expectancy-Value Theory and Predicting Future Employment Status in the Young Unemployed', *Journal of Occupational and Organizational Psychology*, March 1999, pp. 101–6; A. W. Stacy, K. F. Widaman and G. A. Marlatt, 'Expectancy Models of Alcohol Use', *Journal of Personality and Social Psychology*, May 1990, pp. 918–28; A. J. Kinicki, 'Predicting Occupational Role Choices for Involuntary Job Loss', *Journal of Vocational Behavior*, October 1989, pp. 204–18; E. D. Pulakos and N. Schmitt, 'A Longitudinal Study of a Valence Model Approach for the Prediction of Job Satisfaction of New Employees', *Journal of Applied Psychology*, May 1983, pp. 307–12; T. A. DeCotiis and J.-Y. LeLouarn, 'A Predictive Study of Voting Behavior in a Representation Election Using Union Instrumentality and Work Perceptions', *Organizational Behavior and Human Performance*, February 1981, pp. 103–18; P. W. Hom, 'Expectancy Prediction of Reenlistment in the National Guard', *Journal of Vocational Behavior*, April 1980, pp. 235–48; and D. F. Parker and L. Dyer, 'Expectancy Theory as A Within-Person Behavioral Choice Model: An Empirical Test of Some Conceptual and Methodological Refinements', *Organizational Behavior and Human Performance*, October 1976, pp. 97–117.

[8] For reviews of the criticisms of expectancy theory, see F. J. Landy and W. S. Becker, 'Motivation Theory Reconsidered', in *Research in Organizational Behavior*, vol. 9, eds L. L. Cummings and B. M. Staw (Greenwich, CT: JAI Press, 1987), pp. 1–38; and T. R. Mitchell, 'Expectancy Models of Job Satisfaction, Occupational Preference and Effort: A Theoretical, Methodological, and Empirical Appraisal', *Psychological Bulletin*, December 1974, pp. 1053–77.

[9] Components of coaching are discussed by M. Fleschner, 'The Winning Season: How Legendary Wrestling Coach Dan Gable Built Championships to Last', *Selling Power*, April 1998, pp. 14, 16; and S. R. Levine, 'Performance Coaching: Great Coaching Skills Help Build a Team of Champions', *Selling Power*, July–August 1996, p. 46.

[10] R. G. Isaac, W. J. Zerbe and D. C. Pitt, 'Leadership and Motivation: The Effective Application of Expectancy Theory', *Journal of Managerial Issues*, Summer 2001, pp. 217–18.

[11] For a meta-analysis on the relationship between personality and motivation, see T. A. Judge and R. Ilies, 'Relationship of Personality to Performance Motivation: A Meta-Analytic Review', *Journal of Applied Psychology*, August 2002, pp. 797–807. Also see F. Herrera, 'Demystifying and Managing Expectations', *Employment Relations Today*, Summer 2003, pp. 21–8.

[12] D. Daly and B. H. Kleiner, 'How to Motivate Problem Employees', *Work Study*, February 1995, pp. 5–7; and P. Karathanos, M. D. Pettypool and M. D. Troutt, 'Sudden Lost Meaning: A Catastrophe?', *Management Decision*, January 1994, pp. 15–19.

[13] P. S. Kim, 'Strengthening the Pay-Performance Link in Government: A Case Study of Korea', *Public Personnel Management*, Winter 2002, pp. 447–63; R. Plachy and S. Plachy, 'Rewarding Employees Who Truly Make a Difference', *Compensation & Benefits Review*, May–June 1999, pp. 34–9; R. Ganzel, 'What's Wrong with Pay for Performance?', *Training*, December 1998, pp. 34–40; R. P. Semler, 'Making a Difference: Developing Management Incentives That Drive Results', *Compensation & Benefits Review*, July–August 1998, pp. 41–8; D. Barksdale, 'Leading Employees through the Variable Pay Jungle', *HR Magazine*, July 1998, pp. 111–18; and S. T. Johnson, 'Plan Your Organization's Reward Strategy through Pay-for-Performance Dynamics', *Compensation & Benefits Review*, May–June 1998, pp. 67–72.

[14] For both sides of the 'Does money motivate?' debate, see B. Ettorre, 'Is Salary a Motivator?', *Management Review*, January 1999, p. 8; N. Gupta and J. D. Shaw, 'Let the Evidence Speak: Financial Incentives Are Effective!', *Compensation & Benefits Review*, March–April 1998, pp. 26, 28–32; and A. Kohn, 'Challenging Behaviorist Dogma: Myths about Money and Motivation', *Compensation & Benefits Review*, March–April 1998, pp. 27, 33–7.

[15] Excerpted from 'Federal Express's Fred Smith', *Inc.*, October 1986, p. 38.

[16] Retaliation in response to perceived injustice was investigated by D. P. Skarlicki and R. Folger, 'Retaliation in the Workplace: The Roles of Distributive, Procedural, and Interactional Justice', *Journal of Applied Psychology*, June 1997, pp. 434–43.

[17] J. S. Adams, 'Inequity in Social Exchange', in *Advances in Experimental Social Psychology, vol. 2*, ed. L. Berkowitz (New York: Academic Press, 1965), pp. 267–99.

[18] Adapted from a discussion in R. L. Opsahl and M. Dunette, 'The Role of Financial Compensation in Industrial Motivation', *Psychological Bulletin*, August 1966, pp. 94–118.

[19] The generalisability of the equity norm was examined by S. S. K. Lam, J. Schaubroeck and S. Aryee, 'Relationship between Organizational Justice and Employee Work Outcomes: A Cross-National Study', *Journal of Organizational Behavior*, February 2002, pp. 1–18; and J. K. Giacobbe-Miller, D. J. Miller and V. I. Victorov, 'A Comparison of Russian and US Pay Allocation Decisions, Distributive Justice Judgments, and Productivity Under Different Payment Conditions', *Personnel Psychology*, Spring 1998, pp. 137–63.

[20] The choice of a comparison person is discussed by P. P. Shah, 'Who Are Employees' Social Referents? Using a Network Perspective to Determine Referent Others', *Academy of Management Journal*, June 1998, pp. 249–68; and J. Greenberg and C. L. McCarty, 'Comparable Worth: A Matter of Justice', in *Research in Personnel and Human Resources Management, vol. 8*, eds G. R. Ferris and K. M. Rowland (Greenwich, CT: JAI Press, 1990), pp. 265–303.

[21] For more details, see D. C. Feldman and H. I. Doerpinghaus, 'Patterns of Part-Time Employment', *Journal of Vocational Behavior*, December 1992, pp. 282–94. See also T. J. Thorsteinson, 'Job Attitudes of Part-Time vs. Full-Time Workers: A Meta-Analytic Review', *Journal of Occupational and Organizational Psychology*, June 2003, pp. 151–77.

[22] C. Lee and J.-L. Farh, 'The Effects of Gender in Organizational Justice Perception', *Journal of Organizational Behavior*, January 1999, pp. 133–43; and L. A. Witt and L. G. Nye, 'Gender and the Relationship between Perceived Fairness of Pay or Promotion and Job Satisfaction', *Journal of Applied Psychology*, December 1992, pp. 910–17.

[23] Results can be found in R. W. Griffeth, R. P. Vecchio and J. W. Logan, Jr, 'Equity Theory and Interpersonal Attraction', *Journal of Applied Psychology*, June 1989, pp. 394–401; and R. P. Vecchio, 'Predicting Worker Performance in Inequitable Settings', *Academy of Management Review*, January 1982, pp. 103–10.

[24] J. Greenberg, 'Stealing in the Name of Justice: Informational and Interpersonal Moderators of Theft Reactions to Underpayment Inequity', *Organizational Behavior and Human Decision Process*, February 1993, pp. 81–103.

[25] The role of equity in organisational change is thoroughly discussed by A. T. Cobb, R. Folger and K. Wooten, 'The Role Justice Plays in Organizational Change', *Public Administration Quarterly*, Summer 1995, pp. 135–51.

[26] A comparison of individual and group perceptions of justice was conducted by E. A. Lind, L. Kray and L. Thompson, 'The Social Comparison of Injustice: Fairness Judgments in Response to Own and Others' Unfair Treatment by Authorities', *Organizational Behavior and Human Decision Processes*, July 1998, pp. 1–22.

[27] The legal issues of pay equity and employment at-will are discussed by M. Adams, 'Fair and Square', *HR Magazine*, May 1999, pp. 38–44; and B. B. Dunford and D. J. Devine, 'Employment At-Will and Employee Discharge: A Justice Perspective on Legal Action Following Termination', *Personnel Psychology*, Winter 1998, pp. 903–34.

[28] Results can be found in K. W. Mossholder, N. Bennett and C. L. Martin, 'A Multilevel Analysis of Procedural Justice Context', *Journal of Organizational Behavior*, March 1998, pp. 131–41.

[29] The relationship between organizational justice and customer service is discussed by D. E. Bowen, S. W. Gilliland and R. Folger, 'HRM Service Fairness: How Being Fair with Employees Spills Over to Customers', *Organizational Dynamics*, Winter 1999, pp. 7–23.

[30] E. A. Locke, K. N. Shaw, L. M. Saari and G. P. Latham, 'Goal Setting and Task Performance: 1969–1980', *Psychological Bulletin*, July 1981, p. 126.

[31] A thorough discussion of MBO is provided by P. F. Drucker, *The Practice of Management* (New York: Harper, 1954); and P. F. Drucker, 'What Results Should You Expect? A User's Guide to MBO', *Public Administration Review*, January–February 1976, pp. 12–19.

[32] Results from both studies can be found in R. Rodgers and J. E. Hunter, 'Impact of Management by Objectives on Organizational Productivity', *Journal of Applied Psychology*, April 1991, pp. 322–36; and R. Rodgers, J. E. Hunter and D. L. Rogers, 'Influence of Top Management Commitment on Management Program Success', *Journal of Applied Psychology*, February 1993, pp. 151–5.

[33] M. Fleschner, 'How High Can You Fly', *Selling Power*, November–December 1995, p. 15.

[34] Project planning is discussed by T. D. Conkright, 'So You're Going to Manage a Project . . .', *Training*, January 1998, pp. 62–7.

[35] Supportive results can be found in S. C. Selden and G. A. Brewer, 'Work Motivation in the Senior Executive Service: Testing the High Performance Cycle', *Journal of Public Administration Research and Theory*, July 2000, pp. 531–50; L. A. Wilk, 'The Effects of Feedback and Goal Setting on the Productivity and Satisfaction of University Admissions Staff', *Journal of Organizational Behavior Management*, Spring 1998, pp. 45–68; and K. L. Langeland, C. M. Johnson and T. C. Mawhinney, 'Improving Staff Performance in a Community Mental Health Setting: Job Analysis, Training, Goal Setting, Feedback, and Years of Data', *Journal of Organizational Behavior Management*, Spring 1998, pp. 21–43.

[36] See E. A. Locke and G. P. Latham, *A Theory of Goal Setting and Task Performance* (Englewood Cliffs, NJ: Prentice-Hall, 1990).

[37] J. A. Colquitt and M. J. Simmering, 'Conscientiousness, Goal Orientation, and Motivation to Learn During the Learning Process: A Longitudinal Study', *Journal of Applied Psychology*, August 1998, pp. 654–65.

[38] See, for instance, E. A. Locke and G. P. Latham, *Building a Practically Useful Theory of Goal Setting and Task Motivation* (Englewood Cliffs, NJ: Prentice Hall, 2002); and J. L. Austin and J. B. Vancouver, 'Goal Constructs in Psychology: Structure, Process and Content', *Psychological Bulletin*, November 1996, pp. 338–75. For a recent extension of the goal-setting theory with the role of time, see Y. Fried and L. H. Slowik, 'Enriching the Goal-Setting Theory with Time: An Integrated Approach', *Academy of Management Review*, July 2004, pp. 404–22.

[39] See, for instance, E. Fang, R. W. Palmatier and K. R. Evans, 'Goal-Setting Paradoxes? Trade-Offs between Working Hard and Working Smart: The United States versus China', *Journal of The Academy of Marketing Science*, Spring 2004, pp. 188–202.

[40] Results can be found in P. M. Wright, 'Operationalization of Goal Difficulty as a Moderator of the Goal Difficulty-Performance Relationship', *Journal of Applied Psychology*, June 1990, pp. 227–34.

[41] This linear relationship was not supported by P. M. Wright, J. R. Hollenbeck, S. Wolf and G. C. McMahan, 'The Effects of Varying Goal Difficulty Operationalizations on Goal Setting Outcomes and Processes', *Organizational Behavior and Human Decision Processes*, January 1995, pp. 28–43.

[42] J. Chowdbury, 'The Motivational Impact of Sales Quota on Effort', *Journal of Marketing Research*, February 1993, pp. 28–41.

[43] E. Fang, R. W. Palmatier and K. R. Evans, 'Goal-Setting Paradoxes? Trade-Offs between Working Hard and Working Smart: The United States versus China', *Journal of The Academy of Marketing Science*, Spring 2004, pp. 188–202.

[44] E. A. Locke, K. N. Shaw, L. M. Saari and G. P. Latham, 'Goal Setting and Task Performance: 1969–1980', *Psychological Bulletin*, July 1981, pp. 125–152; and A. J. Mento, R. P. Steel and R. J. Karren, 'A Meta-Analytic Study of the Effects of Goal Setting on Task Performance: 1966–1984', *Organizational Behavior and Human Decision Processes*, February 1987, pp. 52–83.

[45] Results from the meta-analysis can be found in R. E. Wood, A. J. Mento and E. A. Locke, 'Task Complexity as a Moderator of Goal Effects: A Meta-Analysis', *Journal of Applied Psychology*, August 1987, pp. 416–25.

[46] See the related discussion in L. A. King, 'Personal Goals and Personal Agency: Linking Everyday Goals to Future Images of the Self', in *Personal Control in Action: Cognitive and Motivational Mechanisms*, eds M. Kofta, G. Weary and G. Sedek (New York: Plenum Press, 1998), pp. 109–28.

[47] See R. P. DeShon and R. A. Alexander, 'Goal Setting Effects on Implicit and Explicit Learning of Complex Tasks', *Organizational Behavior and Human Decision Processes*, January 1996, pp. 18–36.

[48] J. W. Slocum, Jr, W. L. Cron and S. P. Brown, 'The Effect of Goal Conflict on Performance', *Journal of Leadership and Organizational Studies*, Summer 2002, p. 77.

[49] See J. J. Donovan and D. J. Radosevich, 'The Moderating Role of Goal Commitment on the Goal Difficulty-Performance Relationship: A Meta-Analytic Review and Critical Reanalysis', *Journal of Applied Psychology*, April 1998, pp. 308–15.

[50] D. S. Johnson and R. Perlow, 'The Impact of Need for Achievement Components on Goal Commitment and Performance', *Journal of Applied Social Psychology*, December 1992, pp. 1711–20; and M. C. Kernan and R. G. Lord, 'Effects of Valence, Expectations, and Goal-Performance Discrepancies in Single and Multiple Goal Environments', *Journal of Applied Psychology*, April 1990, pp. 194–203.

[51] The benefits of benchmarking were examined by L. Mann, D. Samson and D. Dow, 'A Field Experiment on the Effects of Benchmarking and Goal Setting on Company Sales Performance', *Journal of Management*, no. 1, 1998, pp. 73–96.

[52] E. A. Locke, K. G. Smith, M. Erez, D. Chuh and A. Schaffer, 'The Effect of Intra-Individual Goal Conflict on Performance', *Journal of Management*, Spring 1994, pp. 67–91.

[53] E. A. Locke and G. P. Latham, *A Theory of Goal Setting and Task Performance* (Englewood Cliffs, NJ: Prentice-Hall, 1990).

[54] G. P. Latham and T. H. Seijts, 'The Effects of Personal and Distal Goals on Performance on a Moderately Complex Task', *Journal of Organizational Behavior*, July 1999, pp. 421–9.

[55] E. A. Locke, 'Motivation, Cognition, and Action: An Analysis of Studies of Task Goals and Knowledge', *Applied Psychology: An International Review*, July 2000, pp. 408–29.

[56] Interesting reviews concerning the antecedents of goal commitment are H. Klein, M. Wesson, J. Hollenbeck and B. Alge, 'Goal Commitment and the Goal-Setting Process: Conceptual Clarification and Empirical Synthesis', *Journal of Applied Psychology*, December 1999, pp. 885–96; J. C. Wofford, V. L. Goodwin and S. Premack, 'Meta-Analysis of the Antecedents of Personal Goal Level and the Antecedents and Consequences of Goal Commitment', *Journal of Management*, September 1992, pp. 595–615.

[57] T. Matsui, A. Okada and R. Mizuguchi, 'Expectancy Theory Prediction of the Goal Setting Postulate: The Harder the Goal, the Higher the Performance', *Journal of Applied Psychology*, January 1983, pp. 54–8.

[58] E. A. Locke and D. Henne, 'Work Motivation Theory', in *Internal Review of Industrial and Organizational Psychology*, eds C. Cooper and I. Robertson (Chichester: Wiley, 1986), pp. 1–35.

[59] For instance, see 'Worker Retention Presents Challenge to U.S. Employers', *HR Magazine*, September 1998, p. 22; L. Wah, 'An Ounce of Prevention', *Management Review*, October 1998, p. 9; and S. Armour, 'Cash or Critiques: Which Is Best?', *USA Today*, 16 December 1998, p. 6B.

[60] Data from M. Hequet, 'Giving Feedback', *Training*, September 1994, pp. 72–7.

[61] P. McBride and S. Maitland, *The EI Advantage: Putting Emotional Intelligence into Practice* (London: McGraw-Hill, 2002), p. 215.

[62] Both the definition and the functions of feedback are based on discussion in D. R. Ilgen, C. D. Fisher and M. S. Taylor, 'Consequences of Individual Feedback on Behavior in Organizations', *Journal of Applied Psychology*, August 1979, pp. 349–71; and R. E. Kopelman, *Managing Productivity in Organizations: A Practical People-Oriented Perspective* (New York: McGraw-Hill, 1986), p. 175.

[63] Data from A. N. Kluger and A. DeNisi, 'The Effects of Feedback Interventions on Performance: A Historical Review, a Meta-Analysis, and a Preliminary Feedback Intervention Theory', *Psychological Bulletin*, March 1996, pp. 254–84.

[64] D. M. Herold and D. B. Fedor, 'Individuals' Interaction with Their Feedback Environment: The Role of Domain-Specific Individual Differences', in *Research in Personnel and Human Resources Management, vol. 16*, ed. G. R. Ferris (Stanford, CT: JAI Press, 1998), pp. 215–54.

[65] For relevant research, see J. S. Goodman, 'The Interactive Effects of Task and External Feedback on Practice Performance and Learning', *Organizational Behavior and Human Decision Processes*, December 1998, pp. 223–52.

[66] M. R. Leary, E. S. Tambor, S. K. Terdal and D. L. Downs, 'Self-Esteem as an Interpersonal Monitor: The Sociometer Hypothesis', *Journal of Personality and Social Psychology*, June 1995, pp. 518–30; M. A. Quinones, 'Pretraining Context Effects: Training Assignment as Feedback', *Journal of Applied Psychology*, April 1995, pp. 226–38; and P. E. Levy, M. D. Albright, B. D. Cawley and J. R. Williams, 'Situational and Individual Determinants of Feedback Seeking: A Closer Look at the Process', *Organizational Behavior and Human Decision Processes*, April 1995, pp. 23–37.

[67] T. Matsui, A. Okkada and T. Kakuyama, 'Influence of Achievement Need on Goal Setting, Performance, and Feedback Effectiveness', *Journal of Applied Psychology*, October 1982, pp. 645–8.

[68] B. D. Bannister, 'Performance Outcome Feedback and Attributional Feedback: Interactive Effects on Recipient Responses', *Journal of Applied Psychology*, May 1986, pp. 203–10.

[69] S. J. Ashford and A. S. Tsui, 'Self-Regulation for Managerial Effectiveness: The Role of Active Feedback Seeking', *Academy of Management Journal*, June 1991, pp. 251–80. For complete details, see P. M. Podsakoff and J.-L. Farh, 'Effects of Feedback Sign and Credibility on Goal Setting and Task Performance', *Organizational Behavior and Human Decision Processes*, August 1989, pp. 45–67.

[70] T. A. Louie, 'Decision Makers' Hindsight Bias after Receiving Favorable and Unfavorable Feedback', *Journal of Applied Psychology*, February 1999, pp. 29–41; and W. S. Silver, T. R. Mitchell and M. E. Gist, 'Responses to Successful and Unsuccessful Performance: The Moderating Effect of Self-Efficacy on the Relationship between Performance and Attributions', *Organizational Behavior and Human Decision Processes*, June 1995, p. 297.

[71] A. C. Wicks, S. L. Berman and T. M. Jones, 'The Structure of Optimal Trust: Moral and Strategic Implications', *Academy of Management Review*, January 1999, pp. 99–116; O. Harari, 'The TRUST Factor', *Management Review*, January 1999, pp. 28–31; K. van den Bos, H. A. M. Wilke and E. A. Lind, 'When Do We Need Procedural Fairness? The Role of Trust in Authority', *Journal of Personality and Social Psychology*, December 1998, pp. 1449–58; and J. McCune, 'That Elusive Thing Called Trust', *Management Review*, July–August 1998, pp. 10–16.

[72] S. E. Moss and M. J. Martinko, 'The Effects of Performance Attributions and Outcome Dependence on Leader Feedback Behavior Following Poor Subordinate Performance', *Journal of Organizational Behavior*, May 1998, pp. 259–74.

[73] Based on J. McGregor, 'Case Study: To Adapt, ITT Lets Go of Unpopular Ratings', *BusinessWeek*, 28 January 2008.

[74] S. H. Barr and E. J. Conlon, 'Effects of Distribution of Feedback in Work Groups', *Academy of Management Journal*, June 1994, pp. 641–55.

[75] P. C. Earley, G. B. Northcraft, C. Lee and T. R. Lituchy, 'Impact of Process and Outcome Feedback on the Relation of Goal Setting to Task Performance', *Academy of Management Journal*, March 1990, pp. 87–105.

[76] For a recent review of performance feedback in organisations, see A. M. Alvero, B. R. Bucklin and J. Austin, 'An Objective Review of the Effectiveness and Essential Characteristics of Performance Feedback in Organizational Settings (1985–1998)', *Journal of Organizational Behavior Management*, January 2001, pp. 3–29.

[77] See C. F. Bond and L. J. Titus, 'Social Facilitation: A Meta-Analysis of 241 Studies', *Psychological Bulletin*, September 1983, vol. 94, no. 2, pp. 265–92.

[78] The quote based on Deming is from J. Pfeffer and R. I. Sutton, *The Knowing-Doing Gap*, (Cambridge, MA: Harvard Business School Press, 2000).

[79] Practical tips for giving feedback can be found in M. Hequet, 'Giving Feedback', *Training*, September 1994, pp. 72–7; L. Smith, 'The Executive's New Coach', *Fortune*, 27 December 1993, pp. 126–34; T. Lammers, 'The Effective Employee-Feedback System', *Inc.*, February 1993, pp. 109–11; and E. Van Velsor and S. J. Wall, 'How to Choose a Feedback Instrument', *Training*, March 1992, pp. 47–52.

[80] For supporting evidence of employees' desire for prompt feedback, see D. H. Reid and M. B. Parsons, 'A Comparison of Staff Acceptability of Immediate versus Delayed Verbal Feedback in Staff Training', *Journal of Organizational Behavior Management*, Summer 1996, pp. 35–47.

[81] M. R. Edwards, A. J. Ewen and W. A. Verdini, 'Fair Performance Management and Pay Practices for Diverse Work Forces: The Promise of Multisource Assessment', *ACA Journal*, Spring 1995, pp. 50–63.

[82] G. D. Huet-Cox, T. M. Nielsen and E. Sundstrom, 'Get the Most from 360-Degree Feedback: Put It on the Internet', *HR Magazine*, May 1999, pp. 92–103.

[83] This list is based in part on a discussion in H. J. Bernardin, 'Subordinate Appraisal: A Valuable Source of Information about Managers', *Human Resource Management*, Fall 1986, pp. 421–39.

[84] B. P. Mathews and T. Redman, 'The Attitudes of Service Industry Managers Towards Upward Appraisal', *Career Development International*, January 1997, pp. 46–53.

[85] M. London and R. W. Beatty, '360-Degree Feedback as a Competitive Advantage', *Human Resource Management*, Summer 1993, p. 353.

[86] For a comprehensive overview of 360-degree feedback, see W. W. Tornow and M. London, *Maximizing the Value of 360-Degree Feedback* (San Francisco, CA: Jossey-Bass, 1998). Also see A. H. Church and D. W. Bracken, 'Advancing the State of the Art of 360-Degree Feedback: Guest Editors' Comment on the Research and Practice of Multirater Assessment Methods', *Group & Organization Management*, June 1997, pp. 149–61. For more information on 360-degree feedback, see further in this issue of *Group & Organization Management*, which is a special issue devoted to 360-degree feedback systems.

[87] Adapted and translated from 'Het oordeel van iedereen rondom je', *HRM Magazine*, 1 September 1997.

[88] Data from D. Antonioni, 'The Effects of Feedback Accountability on Upward Appraisal Ratings', *Personnel Psychology*, Summer 1994, pp. 349–56.

[89] H. J. Bernardin, S. A. Dahmus and G. Redmon, 'Attitudes of First-Line Supervisors Toward Subordinate Appraisals', *Human Resource Management*, Summer–Fall 1993, p. 315.

[90] Data from J. W. Smither, M. London, N. L. Vasilopoulos, R. R. Reilly, R. E. Millsap and N. Salvemini, 'An Examination of the Effects of an Upward Feedback Program Over Time', *Personnel Psychology*, Spring 1995, pp. 1–34.

[91] R. R. Reilly, J. W. Smither and N. L. Vasilopoulos, 'A Longitudinal Study of Upward Feedback', *Personnel Psychology*, Fall 1996, pp. 599–612.

[92] B. P. Mathews and T. Redman, 'The Attitudes of Service Industry Managers Towards Upward Appraisal', *Career Development International*, January 1997, pp. 46–53.

[93] P. Jansen and D. Vloeberghs, 'Multi-Rater Feedback Methods: Personal and Organizational Implications', *Journal of Managerial Psychology*, October 1999, pp. 45–7.

[94] G. W. Cheung, 'Multifaceted Conceptions of Self-Other Ratings Disagreement', *Personnel Psychology*, Spring 1999, pp. 1–36; J. D. Makiney and P. E. Levy, 'The Influence of Self-Ratings Versus Peer Ratings on Supervisors' Performance Judgments', *Organizational Behavior and Human Decision Processes*, June 1998, pp. 212–28; R. F. Martell and M. R. Borg, 'A Comparison of the Behavioral Rating Accuracy of Groups and Individuals', *Journal of Applied Psychology*, February 1993, pp. 43–50; J. R. Williams and P. E. Levy, 'The Effects of Perceived System Knowledge on the Agreement between Self-Ratings and Supervisor Ratings', *Personnel Psychology*, Winter 1992, pp. 835–47; J. Lane and P. Herriot, 'Self-Ratings, Supervisor Ratings, Positions and Performance', *Journal of Occupational Psychology*, March 1990, pp. 77–88; and M. M. Harris and J. Schaubroeck, 'A Meta-Analysis of Self-Supervisor, Self-Peer, and Peer-Supervisor Ratings', *Personnel Psychology*, Spring 1988, pp. 43–62.

[95] A. H. Church, 'Do I See What I See? An Exploration of Congruence in Ratings from Multiple Perspectives', *Journal of Applied Psychology*, June 1997, pp. 983–1020; K. L. Bettenhausen and D. B. Fedor, 'Peer and Upward Appraisals: A Comparison of Their Benefits and Problems', *Group & Organization Management*, June 1997, pp. 236–63; S. Salam, J. F. Cox and H. P. Sims, Jr, 'In the Eye of the Beholder: How Leadership Relates to 360-Degree Performance Ratings', *Group & Organization Management*, June 1997, pp. 185–209; J. W. Fleenor, C. D. McCauley and S. Brutus, 'Self-Other Agreement and Leader Effectiveness', *Leadership Quarterly*, Winter 1996, pp. 487–506; L. E. Atwater, P. Roush and A. Fischtal, 'The Influence of Upward Feedback on Self and Follower-Ratings of Leadership', *Personnel Psychology*, Spring 1995, pp. 35–59; and L. E. Atwater and F. J. Yammarino, 'Does Self-Other Agreement on Leadership Perceptions Moderate the Validity of Leadership and Performance Predictions', *Personnel Psychology*, Spring 1992, pp. 141–64.

[96] P. Jansen and D. Vloeberghs, 'Multi-Rater Feedback Methods: Personal and Organizational Implications', *Journal of Managerial Psychology*, October 1999, pp. 45–7; J. Francis-Smythe and P. M. Smith, 'The Psychological Impact of Assessment in a Development Center', *Human Relations*, February 1997, pp. 149–67; and A. S. Engelbrecht and A. H. Fischer, 'The Managerial Performance Implications of a Developmental Assessment Center Process', *Human Relations*, April 1995, pp. 387–404.

[97] M. K. Mount, T. A. Judge, S. E. Scullen, M. R. Sytsma and S. A. Hezlett, 'Trait, Rater and Level Effects in 360-Degree Performance Ratings', *Personnel Psychology*, Autumn 1998, pp. 557–76; and J. Fisher Hazucha, S. A. Hezlett and R. J. Schneider, 'The Impact of 360-Degree Feedback on Managerial Skills Development', *Human Resource Management*, Summer 1993, p. 42.

[98] See the work of Frank Shipper, particularly 'Investigating the Sustainability of a Sustained 360 Process', *Academy of Management Proceedings*, 2009, pp. 1–6.

[99] M. London and R. W. Beatty, '360-Degree Feedback as a Competitive Advantage', *Human Resource Management*, Summer 1993, pp. 356–7; D. W. Bracken, 'Straight Talk about Multirater Feedback', *Training & Development*, September 1994, p. 46; and D. Antonioni, 'Designing an Effective 360-Degree Appraisal Feedback Process', *Organizational Dynamics*, Autumn 1996, pp. 24–38.

[100] S. Culbert, *Get Rrid of the Performance Review*! Business Plus Books, 2010.

[101] S. Kerr, 'Risky Business: The New Pay Game', *Fortune*, 22 July 1996, pp. 94–5; and B. Filipczak, 'Can't Buy Me Love', *Training*, January 1996, pp. 29–34.

[102] S. L. Rynes and B. Gerhart, *Compensation in Organizations: Current Research and Practice* (San Francisco, CA: Jossey-Bass, 2000), p. xv.

[103] Strategic models of pay and rewards are discussed in C. Joinson, 'Pay Attention to Pay Cycles', *HR Magazine*, November 1998, pp. 71–8; M. Bloom and G. T. Milkovich, 'A SHRM Perspective on International Compensation and Reward Systems', in *Research in Personnel and Human Resources Management*, ed. G. R. Ferris (Stamford, CT: JAI Press, 1999), pp. 283–303; and J. Dolmat-Connell, 'Developing a Reward Strategy that Delivers Shareholder and Employee Value', *Compensation & Benefits Review*, March–April 1999, pp. 46–53.

[104] B. S. Frey and M. Osterloh, *Successful Management by Motivation: Balancing Intrinsic and Extrinsic Incentives* (New York: Springer-Verlag, 2002).

[105] For complete discussions, see A. P. Brief and R. J. Aldag, 'The Intrinsic-Extrinsic Dichotomy: Toward Conceptual Clarity', *Academy of Management Review*, July 1977, pp. 496–500; and E. L. Deci, *Intrinsic Motivation* (New York: Plenum Press, 1975), Ch. 2.

[106] For more details on this study, see X. Huang and E. Van de Vliert, 'Where Intrinsic Job Satisfaction Fails to Work: National Moderators of Intrinsic Motivation', *Journal of Organizational Behavior*, March 2003, pp. 159–79.

[107] C. C. Chen, J. R. Meindl and H. Hui, 'Deciding on Equity or Parity: A Test of Situational, Cultural, and Individual Factors', *Journal of Organizational Behavior*, March 1998, pp. 115–29; and K. I. Kim, H.-J. Park and N. Suzuki, 'Reward Allocations in the United States, Japan, and Korea: A Comparison of Individualistic and Collectivistic Cultures', *Academy of Management Journal*, March 1990, pp. 188–98.

[108] Based on M. Bloom, 'The Performance Effects of Pay Dispersion on Individuals and Organizations', *Academy of Management Journal*, February 1999, pp. 25–40.

[109] Good discussions can be found in A. Rappaport, 'New Thinking on How to Link Executive Pay with Performance', *Harvard Business Review*, March–April 1999, pp. 91–101; J. Kahn, 'A CEO Cuts His Own Pay', *Fortune*, 26 October 1998, pp. 56, 60, 64; and W. Grossman and R. E. Hoskisson, 'CEO Pay at the Crossroads of Wall Street and Main: Toward the Strategic Design of Executive Compensation', *Academy of Management Executive*, February 1998, pp. 43–57.

[110] List adapted from J. L. Pearce and R. H. Peters, 'A Contradictory Norms View of Employer–Employee Exchange', *Journal of Management*, Spring 1985, pp. 19–30.

[111] D. B. McFarlin and P. D. Sweeney, 'Distributive and Procedural Justice as Predictors of Satisfaction with Personal and Organizational Outcomes', *Academy of Management Journal*, August 1992, pp. 626–37.

[112] S. L. Mueller and L. D. Clarke, 'Political-Economic Context and Sensitivity to Equity: Differences between the United States and the Transition Economies of Central and Eastern Europe', *Academy of Management Journal*, June 1998, pp. 319–29.

[113] K. G. Wheeler, 'Cultural Values in Relation to Equity Sensitivity Within and Across Cultures', *Journal of Managerial Psychology*, October 2002, p. 612. Also see M. Brown and J. S. Heywood, *Paying for Performance: An International Comparison* (Armonk, NY: M. E. Sharpe, 2003).

[114] J. L. Pearce and R. H. Peters, 'A Contradictory View of Employer–Employee Exchange', *Journal of Management*, Spring 1985, pp. 19–30.

[115] S. L. Rynes and J. E. Bono, 'Psychological Research on Determinants of Pay', in *Compensation in Organizations: Current Research and Practice*, eds S. L. Rynes and B. Gerhart (San Francisco, CA: Jossey-Bass, 2000), pp. 3–31.

[116] Six reward system objectives are discussed in E. E. Lawler III, 'The New Pay: A Strategic Approach', *Compensation & Benefits Review*, July–August 1995, pp. 14–22. Also see A. E. Barber and R. D. Bretz, Jr, 'Compensation, Attraction, and Retention', *Compensation in Organizations: Current Research and Practice*, eds S. L. Rynes and B. Gerhart (San Francisco, CA: Jossey-Bass, 2000), pp. 32–60.

[117] D. R. Spitzer, 'Power Rewards: Rewards That Really Motivate', *Management Review*, May 1996, p. 47. Also see S. Kerr, 'An Academy Classic: On the Folly of Rewarding A, While Hoping for B', *Academy of Management Executive*, February 1995, pp. 7–14.

[118] List adapted from discussion in D. R. Spitzer, 'Power Rewards: Rewards That Really Motivate', *Management Review*, May 1996, pp. 45–50. Also see R. Eisenberger and J. Cameron, 'Detrimental Effects of Reward: Reality or Myth?', *American Psychologist*, November 1996, pp. 1153–66.

[119] See, for example, S. L. Rynes and B. Gerhart, *Compensation in Organizations: Current Research and Practice* (San Francisco, CA: Jossey-Bass, 2000); and T. P. Flannery, D. A. Hofrichter and P. E. Platten, *People, Performance, and Pay: Dynamic Compensation for Changing Organizations* (New York: The Free Press, 1996).

[120] These points are summed up eloquently by J. Pfeffer and R.I. Sutton in *Hard Facts, Dangerous Half-Truths and Total Nonsense*, Boston: Harvard Business School Press, 2000.

[121] See E. Lazear, 'The Power of Incentives', *American Economic Review*, May 2000, no. 90, pp. 410–14.

[122] Supportive results are presented in L. Morris, 'Employees Not Encouraged to Go Extra Mile', *Training & Development*, April 1996, pp. 59–60; and L. Morris, 'Crossed Wires on Employee Motivation', *Training & Development*, July 1995, pp. 59–60.

[123] E. L. Deci, R. Koestner and R. M. Ryan, 'A Meta-Analytic Review of Experiments Examining the Effect of Extrinsic Rewards on Intrinsic Motivation', *Psychological Bulletin*, November 1999, pp. 627–68; D. R. Spitzer, 'Power Rewards: Rewards That Really Motivate', *Management Review*, May 1996, pp. 45–50; and A. Kohn, *Punished by Rewards: The Trouble with Gold Stars, Incentive Plans, A's, Praise, and Other Bribes* (Boston, MA: Houghton Mifflin Company, 1993).

[124] See, for instance, L. W. Howard and T. W. Doughtery, 'Alternative Reward Strategies and Employee Reactions', *Compensation & Benefits Review*, January–February 2004, pp. 41–51; J. D. Shaw, N. Gupta and J. E. Delery, 'Pay Dispersion and Workforce Performance: Moderating Effects of Incentives and Interdependence', *Strategic Management Journal*, June 2002, pp. 491–512; S. E. Bonner, R. Hastie, G. B. Sprinkle and S. M. Young, 'A Review of the Effects of Financial Incentives on Performance in Laboratory Tasks: Implications for Management Accounting, *Journal of Management Accounting Research*, no. 1, 2000,

pp. 19–64; C. F. Camerer and R. M. Hogarth, 'The Effects of Financial Incentives in Experiments: A Review and Capital-Labor-Production Framework, *Journal of Risk and Uncertainty*, December 1999, pp. 7–42; and M. Bloom, 'The Performance Effects of Pay Dispersion on Individuals and Organizations', *Academy of Management Journal*, February 1999, pp. 25–40.

[125] For examples of research on pay rises, see A. Mitra, N. Gupta and G. D. Jenkins, Jr, 'A Drop in the Bucket: When is Pay Raise a Pay Raise?', *Journal of Organizational Behavior*, March 1997, pp. 117–37; and K. S. Teel, 'Are Merit Raises Really Based on Merit?', *Personnel Journal*, March 1986, pp. 88–94.

[126] S. Kerr, 'Organizational Rewards: Practical, Cost-Neutral Alternatives that You may Know, but Don't Practice', *Organizational Dynamics*, Summer 1999, pp. 61–70. Note that Kerr is famous for his very critical view on incentives, entitled 'On the Folly of Rewarding A, while Hoping for B', see note 146.

[127] See the related discussion in T. P. Flannery, D. A. Hofrichter and P. E. Platten, *People, Performance & Pay* (New York: The Free Press, 1996).

[128] Supporting results can be found in S. W. Gilliland and R. S. Landis, 'Quality and Quantity Goals in a Complex Decision Task: Strategies and Outcomes', *Journal of Applied Psychology*, October 1992, pp. 672–81.

[129] Potential pitfalls of goal setting and monetary incentives as well as guidelines to effectively deal with them are discussed in P. M. Wright, 'Goal Setting and Monetary Incentives: Motivational Tools That Can Work *Too Well*', *Compensation & Benefits Review*, May–June 1994, pp. 41–9.

[130] L. W. Howard and T. W. Doughtery, 'Alternative Reward Strategies and Employee Reactions', *Compensation & Benefits Review*, January–February 2004, pp. 41–51; H. Risher, 'Pay-for-Performance: The Keys to Making It Work', *Public Personnel Management*, Fall 2002, pp. 317–32; K. M. Bartol and E. A. Locke, 'Incentives and Motivation', in *Compensation in Organizations: Current Research and Practice*, eds S. L. Rynes and B. Gerhart (San Francisco, CA: Jossey-Bass, 2000), pp. 104–47; J. Igalens and P. Roussel, 'A Study of the Relationships between Compensation Package, Work Motivation and Job Satisfaction', *Journal of Organizational Behavior*, December 1999, pp. 1003–25; and D. O'Neill, 'Blending the Best of Profit Sharing and Gainsharing', *HR Magazine*, March 1994, pp. 66–70.

[131] L. W. Howard and T. W. Doughtery, 'Alternative Reward Strategies and Employee Reactions', *Compensation & Benefits Review*, January–February 2004, p. 45; and R. L. Heneman, G. E. Ledford, Jr, and M. T. Gresham, 'The Changing Nature of Work and Its Effect on Compensation Design and Delivery', in *Compensation in Organizations: Current Research and Practice*, eds S. L. Rynes and B. Gerhart (San Francisco, CA: Jossey-Bass, 2000), pp. 195–240.

[132] A recent issue of the *Academy of Management Review* (July 2004) is devoted to the future of work motivation theory. See, for instance, R. M. Steers, R. T. Mowday and D. L. Shaprio, 'The Future of Work Motivation Theory', *Academy of Management Review*, July 2004, pp. 379–87; and E. A. Locke and G. P. Latham, 'What Should We Do about Motivation Theory? Six Recommendations for the Twenty-First Century', *Academy of Management Review*, July 2004, pp. 388–404.

[133] N. Nicholson, 'How to Motivate Your Problem People', *Harvard Business Review*, January 2003, pp. 56–67; and H. Levinson, 'Management by Whose Objectives?', *Harvard Business Review*, January 2003, pp. 107–16.

[134] Useful and varied examples to reward people can be found in B. Fryer, 'Moving Mountains', *Harvard Business Review*, January 2003, pp. 41–7; and B. Nelson, *1001 Ways to Reward Employees* (New York: Workman Publishing, 1994).

[135] F. Hansen, M. Slith and R. B. Hansen, 'Rewards and Recognition in Employee Motivation', *Compensation & Benefits Review*, September–October 2002, pp. 64–72.

[136] P. Falcone, 'Motivating Staff Without Money', *HR Magazine*, August 2002, p. 105.

[137] Useful articles to help develop a performance appraisal system are F. Hansen, M. Slith and R. B. Hansen, 'Rewards and Recognition in Employee Motivation', *Compensation & Benefits Review*, September–October 2002, pp. 64–72; B. G. Mani, 'Performance Appraisal Systems, Productivity, and Motivation: A Case Study', *Public Personnel Management*, Summer 2002, pp. 141–59; and C. O. Longenecker and L. S. Fink, 'Creating Effective Performance Appraisals', *Industrial Management*, September–October 1999, pp. 18–23.

[138] This conclusion is consistent with research summarised in F. Luthans and A. D. Stajkovic, 'Reinforce for Performance: The Need to Go Beyond Pay and Even Rewards', *Academy of Management Executive*, May 1999, pp. 49–57.

[139] This exercise is adapted from material in D. M. Herold and C. K. Parsons, 'Assessing the Feedback Environment in Work Organizations: Development of the Job Feedback Survey', *Journal of Applied Psychology*, May 1985, pp. 290–305.

Part 3

Group and social processes

Part contents

Chapter 7

Group dynamics

Learning Outcomes

When you finish studying the material in this chapter, you should be able to:

- ☑ identify the four criteria of a group from a sociological perspective
- ☑ identify and briefly describe the five stages in Tuckman's theory of group development
- ☑ distinguish between role overload, role conflict and role ambiguity
- ☑ contrast roles and norms, and specify four reasons for norms being enforced in organisations
- ☑ distinguish between task and maintenance functions in groups
- ☑ summarise the practical implications for group size and group member ability
- ☑ describe groupthink, and identify at least four of its symptoms
- ☑ define social loafing, and explain how organisations can prevent it

Opening Case Study: A retrospective of the Challenger Space Shuttle disaster – was it groupthink?

The debate over whether to launch on 28 January 1986 unfolded as follows, according to the report of the Presidential Commission on the Space Shuttle Challenger Accident. Shortly after 1 p.m. ET on 27 January, NASA's (the National Aeronautic and Space Administration's) booster rocket manager in Cape Canaveral, Larry Wear, asks officials of rocket-maker Morton Thiokol in Utah whether cold weather on the 28th would present a problem for launch.

By 2 p.m., NASA's top managers are discussing how temperatures at the launch pad might affect the shuttle's performance. In Utah, an hour later, Thiokol engineer Roger Boisjoly learns of the forecast for the first time.

By late afternoon, mid-level NASA managers at the Cape are on the phone with Thiokol managers, who point out that the booster's rubbery O-rings, which seal in hot gases, might be affected by cold. That concern brings in officials from NASA's Marshall Space Flight Center in Huntsville, Alabama, who buy the rockets from Thiokol and ready them for launch. Marshall managers decide that a three-way telephone conference call is needed, linking NASA and Thiokol engineers and managers in Alabama, Florida and Utah.

The first conference call begins about 5.45 p.m., and Thiokol tells NASA it believes launch should be delayed until noon or afternoon, when the weather turns warmer. It is decided a second conference call would be needed later that evening. Marshall deputy project manager Judson Lovingood tells shuttle project manager Stan Reinartz at the Cape that if Thiokol persists, NASA should not launch. Top NASA managers at Marshall are told of Thiokol's concern.

At 8.45 p.m., the second conference call begins, involving 34 engineers and managers from NASA and Thiokol at the three sites. Thiokol engineers Roger Boisjoly and Arnie Thompson present charts showing a history of leaking O-ring joints from tests and previous flights. The data show that the O-rings perform worse at lower temperatures and that the worst leak of hot gases came in January 1985, when a shuttle launched with the temperature at 11.5°C. Thiokol managers recommend not flying Challenger at temperatures colder than that. NASA's George Hardy says he's 'appalled' at Thiokol's recommendation. Larry Mulloy, Marshall's booster rocket manager, complains that Thiokol is setting down new launch criteria and exclaims, 'My God, Thiokol, when do you want me to launch, next April?' Thiokol Vice President Joe Kilminster asks for five minutes to talk in private. The debate continues for 30 minutes. Boisjoly, Thompson, engineer Bob Ebeling and others are overruled by Thiokol management, who decide to approve the launch.

At 11 p.m., Kilminster tells NASA that Thiokol has changed its mind. Temperature is still a concern but the data are inconclusive. He recommends launch. Thiokol's concerns that cold weather could hurt the booster joints are not passed up NASA's chain of command beyond officials at the Marshall Space Flight Center. Challenger is launched at 11.38 a.m. 28 January in a temperature of 2.2°C.

Shortly after the launch, the Challenger was engulfed in a fiery explosion that led to the deaths of six astronauts and teacher-in-space Christa McAuliffe. As a shocked world was watching great billows of smoke trail over the Atlantic, it was clear to those involved that launching Challenger in 2.2°C weather was a catastrophic decision.

... Ten years later

Two who argued the longest and loudest against launch were Thiokol engineers Roger Boisjoly and Arnie Thompson. But their lives took widely differing paths after the accident. Boisjoly remembers the prelaunch debate this way: 'When NASA created the pressure, they all buckled.' He became known nationally as the primary whistle-blower. Thiokol removed Boisjoly from the investigation team and sent him home after he testified before a presidential commission that the company ignored evidence that the booster rocket seals would fail in cold weather. Boisjoly, 57, says he was blackballed by the industry and run out of town by Thiokol. For a time, he sought psychiatric help. 'It just became unbearable to function', says Boisjoly, who now lives with his wife and daughter in a small mountain town in Utah. He spoke on condition that the town is not named because he fears for his family's safety. Boisjoly is convinced he is a marked man because some former co-workers believe his testimony contributed to resulting lay-offs at Thiokol. After the accident, he says, drivers would try to run him off the road when he was out on a walk. He got threatening phone calls. Someone tried to break into his house. 'It became so uncomfortable for me that I went out and bought a .38 revolver', he says. Now retired, Boisjoly earns $1500 for speeches to universities and business groups. He also runs his own engineering company and teaches Sunday school in the Mormon Church, something he says he never would have dreamed of doing before the accident.

Thompson, the other voice against launch, says: 'There were the two of us that didn't want to fly and we were defeated. A lot of my top managers were not happy with me.' Yet, with longer ties to Thiokol than Boisjoly, Thompson was promoted to manager and stayed on through the shuttle's redesign. He retired three years ago at the end of a 25-year career. Now 66, he spends his time building a small office building in Brigham City, Utah. 'My attitude was, I wanted to stay on and redesign the bird and get back into the air', says Thompson. 'I had a personal goal to get flying again.'

Thiokol's Bob Ebeling was so sure that Challenger was doomed, he asked his daughter, Leslie, then 33, to his office to watch 'a super colossal disaster' unfold on live TV. When it exploded, 'I was in the middle of a prayer for the Lord to do his will and let all these things come to a happy ending and not let this happen', says Ebeling, who managed the rocket ignition system for Thiokol. 'We did our level best but it wasn't good enough.' The fact that he foresaw disaster and could not stop it has tortured him since.

Ebeling, 69, says that within a week of the accident, he suffered high stress and constant headaches, problems he still has today. After 40 years of engineering experience, Thiokol 'put me out to pasture on a medical' retirement, he says. Ebeling still feels 'the decision to recommend a launch was pre-ordained by others, by NASA leaning on our upper management. The deck was stacked.'

One of those who overruled Ebeling and the others was Jerry Mason, the senior Thiokol manager on the conference call. He took an early retirement from Thiokol five months after the disaster, ending a 25-year career in aerospace. 'I was basically responsible for the operation the day it happened', says Mason, 69. 'It was important to the company to put that behind them and get going on the recovery and it would be hard to do that with me sitting there. So I left.' In Mason's case, that meant going abruptly from corporate chieftain to unpaid volunteer. He helped set up a local economic development board and now chairs the Utah Wildlife Federation. 'I had a pretty successful career, and would have liked to have gone out with the feeling that I really had done very well all the time instead of having to go out feeling I'd made a mistake at the end.'

For Judson Lovingood, the loss was more personal. Formerly one of NASA's deputy managers for the shuttle project, he wonders still if Challenger contributed to the breakup of his marriage. 'I think (Challenger) had an effect on my personal life', says Lovingood, 'a long-term effect'. After the accident, he went to work for Thiokol in Huntsville and retired as director of engineering in 1993. Now remarried, he spends his time pottering in the yard of his Gurley, Alabama, home. 'Sometimes when I think about the seven people (aboard the shuttle), it's pretty painful', says Lovingood.

Besides McAuliffe, on board Challenger were Commander Dick Scobee, pilot Mike Smith and astronauts Ron McNair, Ellison Onizuka, Judy Resnik and Greg Jarvis. Their families settled with the government and Thiokol for more than $1.5 billion. Still, 'I think people should hold us collectively responsible as a group', Lovingood says. 'Every person in that meeting the night before the launch shared in the blame.'

Investigations of the Challenger explosion placed much of the blame on NASA's George Hardy, a senior engineering manager. By saying he was 'appalled' by Thiokol's fears of flying in cold weather, critics charged, Hardy pressured Thiokol into approving the launch. But Hardy refuses to shoulder the blame. 'If Thiokol had stuck to their position, there wasn't any way we were going to launch', he says. Hardy left NASA four months after the accident. Now 65, he runs a small aerospace consulting company in Athens, Alabama.

Whatever else the last decade brought, many of the recollections return to that pressure-packed conference call on the eve of launch.

For discussion

All things considered, who in this group was to blame for finally launching the Challenger?

Source: Based on G. Kranz, *Failure Is Not an Option* (New York: Berkley Publishing Group, 2001); P. Hoversten, 'Thiokol Wavers, Then Decides to Launch', *USA Today*, 22 January 1996, p. 2A. Copyright 1996, *USA Today*. Reprinted with permission; and P. Hoversten, P. Edmonds and H. El Nasser, 'Debate Raged before Doomed Launch', *USA Today*, 22 January 1996, *USA Today*. Reprinted with permission.

7.1 Groups

Because the management of organisational behaviour is above all else a social endeavour, professionals need a strong working knowledge of interpersonal behaviour. Research consistently reveals the importance of social skills for both individual and organisational success. Management involves getting things done with and through others. The job is simply too big to do it alone.

Let us begin by defining the term 'group' as a prelude to examining types of groups, functions of group members, the importance of social networks and the group development and formation process. Our attention then turns to group roles and norms, the basic building blocks of group dynamics. Impacts of group structure and member characteristics on group outcomes are explored next. Finally, three serious threats to group effectiveness are discussed. (Teams and teamwork are discussed in Chapter 8.)

Groups and teams are inescapable features of modern life. College students are often teamed with their peers for class projects. Parents serve on community advisory boards at their local high school. Professionals find themselves on product planning committees and productivity task forces. Productive organisations simply cannot function without gathering individuals into groups and teams.[1] But, as personal experience shows, group effort can bring out both the best and the worst in people. A marketing department meeting, where several people excitedly brainstorm and refine a creative new advertising campaign, can yield results beyond the capabilities of individual contributors. Conversely, committees have become the butt of jokes (e.g. a committee is a place where they take minutes and waste hours; a camel is a horse designed by a committee) because they all are too often plagued by lack of direction and by conflict. Organisations need a solid understanding of groups and group processes to both avoid their pitfalls and tap their vast potential.

Definitions

Although other definitions of groups exist, we draw from the field of sociology and define a **group** as two or more freely interacting individuals who share collective norms and goals and have a common identity.[2]

The size of a group is thus limited by the possibilities of mutual interaction and mutual awareness. Mere aggregates of people do not fit this definition because they do not interact and do not perceive themselves to be a group even if they are aware of each other as, for instance, a crowd on a street corner watching some event. A total department, a union or a whole organisation would not be a group in spite of thinking of themselves as 'we', because they generally do not all interact and are not all aware of each other. However, work teams, committees, subparts of departments, cliques and various other informal associations among organisational members would fit this definition of a group.[3]

OB in Real Life

Managing groups in the World of Warcraft

In this world his name is Jacob Theilgaard and he is a senior consultant in a Danish company. In the online computer role-playing game, *World of Warcraft*, he is called Saxodane and leads a guild of 445 creatures and has done so for more than five years. And he is actively promoting the use of online role play as a managerial learning tool.

In the last decade or so, computer games have gone from being primarily a solitary pastime to being social endeavours through online multiplayer aspects or MMORPGs (massive multiplayer online role-playing games). In the same period, gamers are no longer confined to the male teenage category, but now encompass all age groups and both men and women. However, there is still a while to go before online role-playing games become so mainstream and accepted that it will be a natural part of a conversation at the office lunch table. As more and more professionals, such as Jacob, go public with their gaming passion, however, several management researchers and companies are starting to sit up and take notice.

Leading a raiding party of sorcerers, warriors, axe-wielding dwarves and elves on an orc stronghold in a fantasy world might not seem like the type of training you would like your human resources (HR) manager to engage in, but underneath the surface a lot of similarities emerge.

One of the most intriguing aspects of studying online behaviour is the group dynamics that emerge over time. The most successful of the role-playing games have a strong focus on groups or teams of players banding together. All but the most trivial challenges cannot be overcome by one player alone, no matter how strong that character is. This means having to group together with other players, who have other competences (and weaknesses) and being able to co-ordinate the efforts of that group. And this often involves changing leadership of the group as situations change or simply as an organic change process.

The challenges facing the players are to be able to recruit, evaluate, reward, train and retain players that are likely very diverse on almost all imaginable dimensions and engage in collective decision-making based on limited information at very short notice, but with long-reaching consequences. Furthermore, this has to be done with a volunteer workforce with only intrinsic rewards.

Honing your interpersonal skills and group leadership might interestingly enough benefit from a detour into a fantasy environment where all the usual cues we pick up, such as gender, body language and age, are missing.

Jacob Theilgaard has started making management training seminars purely online, and it has already been a huge success with HR managers and top managers lining up to try this new 'group management simulator'.

Source: Based on N. Barfod, 'Computerrollespil godt for lederudvikling', *Børsen*, 8 June 2010; and B. Reeves, W. Thomas Malone and T. O'Driscoll, 'Leadership's Online Labs', *Harvard Business Review*, vol. 86, no. 5, 2010, pp. 58–66.

The Hawthorne studies of Elton Mayo (elaborated in Chapter 1) were one of the first studies that discovered the importance of group dynamics in organisations. Another psychologist who worked further on the idea that groups are important in organisations is Rensis Likert.[4] According to Likert, organisations should be viewed as a collection of groups rather than individuals. Work groups are important in satisfying individuals' needs. Groups in organisations that fulfil this psychological function are more productive. In addition to Likert, several authors promote the use of small groups as basic building blocks for an organisation.[5]

Formal and informal groups

Individuals join groups or are assigned to groups to accomplish various purposes. If the group is formed by a professional to help the organisation accomplish its goals (see also Chapter 10), then it qualifies as a **formal group** which is formed by the organisation. Formal groups typically wear such labels as work group, team, committee, quality circle or task force. According to the demand and processes of the organisation, different types of formal groups can be distinguished (for instance, the accounting department).

A command (or functional) group is fairly permanent and is usually specified by the organisation chart. A command group is characterised by functional reporting between subordinates and their group manager.

A task (or special-project) group contains employees who work together to complete a particular task. A task group is usually temporary and the group often dissolves when its task is finished. Employees mostly belong simultaneously to a command group and to one or several task groups.

An **informal group** exists when it is not deliberately created, but evolves naturally. Within the formal structure of organisations, there will always be an informal structure, often referred to as the distinction between the formal and the informal organisation (see also Chapter 14 about the grapevine and Chapter 10 about co-ordination mechanisms in organisations). Two specific types of informal groups are friendship groups and interest groups. Friendship groups arise mostly from some common characteristics of people, like their age, political beliefs or ethnic background that

Table 7.1 Groups Fulfil Organisational and Individual Functions

Organisational functions	Individual functions
1 Accomplish complex, interdependent tasks that are beyond the capabilities of individuals	1 Satisfy the individual's need for affiliation
2 Generate new or creative ideas and solutions	2 Develop, enhance and confirm the individual's self-esteem and sense of identity
3 Co-ordinate interdepartmental efforts	3 Give individuals an opportunity to test and share their perceptions of social reality
4 Provide a problem-solving mechanism for complex problems requiring varied information and assessments	4 Reduce the individual's anxieties and feelings of insecurity and powerlessness
5 Implement complex decisions	5 Provide a problem-solving mechanism for personal and interpersonal problems
6 Socialise and train newcomers	

Source: Adapted from E. H. Schein, *Organizational Psychology*, 3rd edn (Englewood Cliffs, NJ: Prentice Hall, 1980), pp. 149–51.

lead to relationships between people that often extend to off-the-job activities. Interest groups are organised around a common interest or activity, independent of the task or command groups they belong to. People group together to accomplish some common objective, although friendship may also develop between the members.

Although formal and informal groups often overlap, such as a team of corporate auditors heading for the tennis courts after work, some employees are not friends with their co-workers. The desirability of overlapping formal and informal groups is problematic. Some managers firmly believe personal friendship fosters productive teamwork on the job while others view workplace 'gossip' as a serious threat to productivity. It is the manager's job to strike a workable balance, based on the maturity and goals of the people involved.

Researchers point out that groups fulfil two basic functions: organisational and individual. The various functions are listed in Table 7.1. Complex combinations of these functions can be found in formal groups at any given time.

An important theory in explaining these mechanisms is social identity theory that states that we define ourselves by our social affiliations, making a distinction between the in-group and the out-group. We are motivated to belong to groups that are similar to ourselves, as this affiliation reinforces our social identity.[6]

7.2 Social networks

During the last decades of the twentieth century, the fascination with networks across almost all scientific fields led to a renewal in the interest of studying social networks. **Social networks** can be defined as social entities (individuals, groups, organisations etc.) and the relations (or lack thereof) between them.

Research in social networks in an organisational context draws on many of the findings and models from the field of group dynamics, but networks are very different from groups or teams in that there are typically no clear or obvious boundaries around networks. Unless, of course, one is imposed in order to study a particular context (a department or whole organisation) as a network.

Often, social networks have been likened to 'the shadow organisation' and the best way to understand it is to think of social networks in a given company as the emergent network (how people are really communicating, collaborating) – as opposed to the prescribed network (how people are linked to each other through the organisational diagram).

Figure 7.1 Sociogram

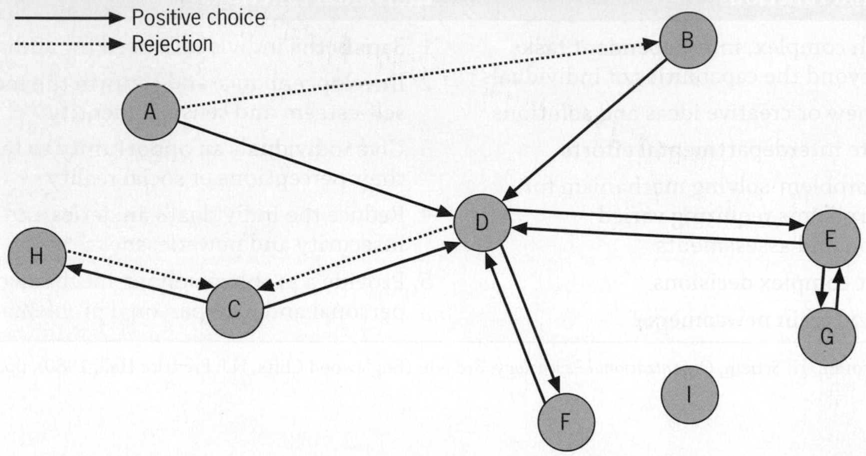

Source: Based on J. L. Moreno, *Who Shall Survive?* 2nd edn (New York: Beacon Press, 1953).

One could argue that groups or teams are also networks, but they typically consist of a number of individuals with relations between everyone in the group – thus making it a trivial network that could be described more precisely and correctly as groups or teams.

In order to illustrate and analyse those relations between individuals in the organisation, a separate field of research has developed: **social network analysis** is the systematic and quantifiable collection and analysis of social relations. This method emerged in the 1930s from the field of sociometry and has developed through the insights from various fields, such as graph theory, statistics, social-psychology and sociology.

One of the outputs of a social network analysis is sociograms, which are network maps, depicting types of relations between individuals (or groups), see Figure 7.1.

Social network analysis is concerned with the structure and patterning of these relationships and seeks to identify both their causes and consequences. Looking at a sociogram, different types of individuals can be identified:

- *Star*: a person who has got a large number of relations.
- *Isolate*: a person who has no relations.
- *Bridge builder*: a person connecting parts of the network not connected by others.

Social network analysis is applicable to a wide range of areas. For instance, at the organisational level, communication studies (see Chapter 14 about the grapevine) and work on power and political processes[7] can benefit from social network analysis. Also, to study careers[8] and socialisation, a better insight into networks of information and influence can be very useful. At the inter-organisational level, social network analysis can make the direct and indirect relationships between organisations more explicit.

Critical thinking

To what degree do you find it ethically questionable to map employees' social networks in order to improve knowledge sharing and communication?

7.3 Tuckman's group development and formation process

Groups and teams in the workplace go through a maturation process, such as one would find in any life-cycle situation (e.g. humans, organisations, products). While there is general agreement among theorists that the group development process occurs in identifiable stages, they disagree about the exact number, sequence, length and nature of those stages.[9]

An oft-cited model is the one proposed in 1965 by educational psychologist Bruce W. Tuckman. His original model involved only four stages (forming, storming, norming and performing). The five-stage model in Figure 7.2 evolved when Tuckman and a doctoral student added 'adjourning' in 1977.[10] A word of caution here. Somewhat akin to Maslow's need hierarchy theory (see Chapter 5), Tuckman's theory has been repeated and taught so often and for so long that many have come to view it as a documented fact, not merely a theory. Even today, it is good to remember Tuckman's own caution that his group development model was derived more from group therapy sessions than from natural-life groups. Still, many in the OB field like Tuckman's five-stage model of group development because of its easy to remember labels and common-sense appeal.[11]

Let us briefly examine each of the five stages in Tuckman's model. Notice in Figure 7.2 how individuals give up a measure of their independence when they join and participate in a group. Also, the various stages are not necessarily of the same duration or intensity. For instance, the storming stage may be practically non-existent or painfully long, depending on the goal clarity and the commitment and maturity of the members. You can make this process come to life by relating the various stages to your own experiences with work groups, committees, athletic teams, social or religious groups or class project teams. Some group happenings that surprised you when they occurred may now make sense or strike you as inevitable when seen as part of a natural development process.

Figure 7.2 Tuckman's Five-Stage Theory of Group Development

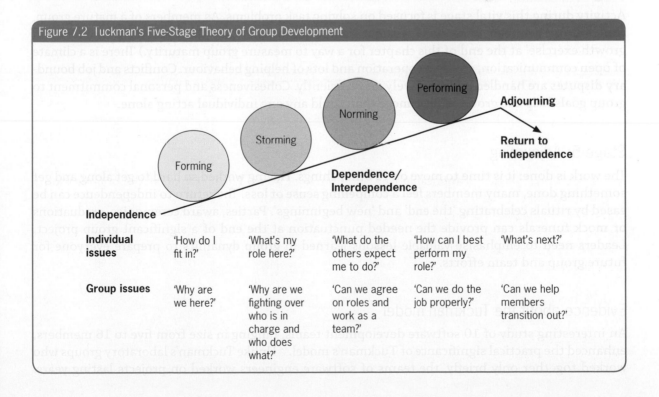

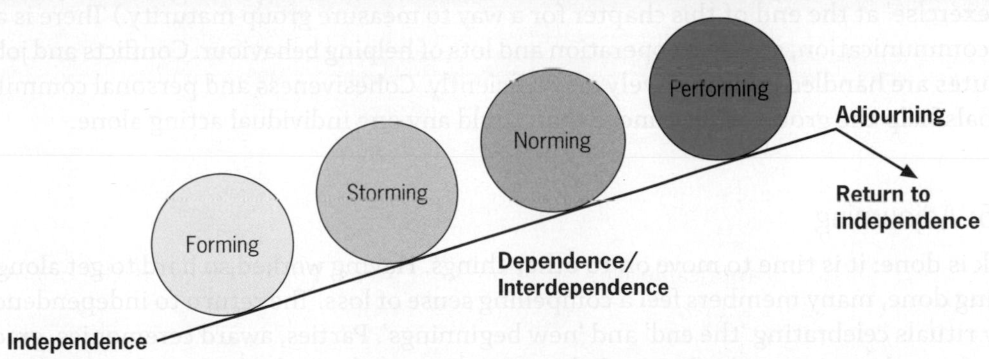

Individual issues	'How do I fit in?'	'What's my role here?'	'What do the others expect me to do?'	'How can I best perform my role?'	'What's next?'
Group issues	'Why are we here?'	'Why are we fighting over who is in charge and who does what?'	'Can we agree on roles and work as a team?'	'Can we do the job properly?'	'Can we help members transition out?'

Stage 1: Forming

During this 'ice-breaking' stage, group members tend to be uncertain and anxious about such things as their roles, who is in charge and the group's goals. Mutual trust is low, and there is a good deal of holding back to see who takes charge and how. If the formal leader (e.g. a supervisor) does not assert his or her authority, an emergent leader will eventually step in to fulfil the group's need for leadership and direction. Leaders typically mistake this honeymoon period as a mandate for permanent control. But later, problems may force a leadership change.

Stage 2: Storming

This is a time of testing. Individuals test the leader's policies and assumptions as they try to determine how they fit into the power structure. Subgroups take shape, and subtle forms of rebellion, such as procrastination, occur. Many groups stall in stage 2 because power politics (see also Chapter 14) erupts into open rebellion.

Stage 3: Norming

Groups that make it through stage 2 generally do so because a respected member, other than the leader, challenges the group to resolve its power struggles, so something can be accomplished. Questions about authority and power are resolved through unemotional, matter-of-fact group discussion. A feeling of team spirit is experienced because members believe they have found their proper roles.

Stage 4: Performing

Activity during this vital stage is focused on solving task problems. As members of a mature group, contributors get their work done without hampering others. (See the 'Personal awareness and growth exercise' at the end of this chapter for a way to measure group maturity.) There is a climate of open communication, strong co-operation and lots of helping behaviour. Conflicts and job boundary disputes are handled constructively and efficiently. Cohesiveness and personal commitment to group goals help the group achieve more than could any one individual acting alone.

Stage 5: Adjourning

The work is done; it is time to move on to other things. Having worked so hard to get along and get something done, many members feel a compelling sense of loss. The return to independence can be eased by rituals celebrating 'the end' and 'new beginnings'. Parties, award ceremonies, graduations or mock funerals can provide the needed punctuation at the end of a significant group project. Leaders need to emphasise valuable lessons learned in group dynamics to prepare everyone for future group and team efforts.

Evidence about the Tuckman model

An interesting study of 10 software development teams, ranging in size from five to 16 members, enhanced the practical significance of Tuckman's model.[12] Unlike Tuckman's laboratory groups who worked together only briefly, the teams of software engineers worked on projects lasting years.

Consequently, the researchers discovered more than simply a five-stage group development process. Groups were observed actually shifting into reverse once Tuckman's performing stage was reached, in what the researchers called *group decay*. In keeping with Tuckman's terminology, the three observed stages of 'group decay' were labelled 'de-norming', 'de-storming' and 'de-forming'. These additional stages take shape as follows:

- De-norming: as the project evolves, there is a natural erosion of standards of conduct. Group members drift in different directions as their interests and expectations change.
- De-storming: this stage of group decay is a mirror image of the storming stage. Whereas disagreements and conflicts arise rather suddenly during the storming stage, an undercurrent of discontent slowly comes to the surface during the de-storming stage. Individual resistance increases and cohesiveness declines.
- De-forming: the work group literally falls apart as subgroups battle for control. Those pieces of the project that are not claimed by individuals or subgroups are abandoned. 'Group members begin isolating themselves from each other and from their leaders. Performance declines rapidly because the whole job is no longer being done and group members little care what happens beyond their self-imposed borders.'

Another study hypothesised that interpersonal feedback would vary systematically during the group development process.[13] 'The unit of feedback measured was a verbal message directed from one participant to another in which some aspect of behaviour was addressed.' After collecting and categorising 1600 instances of feedback from four different eight-person groups, they concluded the following:

- Interpersonal feedback increases as the group develops through successive stages.
- As the group develops, positive feedback increases and negative feedback decreases.
- Interpersonal feedback becomes more specific as the group develops.
- The credibility of peer feedback increases as the group develops.

In general, it has been documented that leadership behaviour that is active, aggressive, directive, structured and task oriented seems to have favourable results early in the group's history. However, when those behaviours are maintained throughout the life of the group, they seem to have a negative impact on cohesiveness and quality of work. Conversely, leadership behaviour that is supportive, democratic, decentralised and participative seems to be related to poorer functioning in the early group development stages. However, when these behaviours are maintained throughout the life of the group, more productivity, satisfaction and creativity result.[14]

HR Practical implications of the Tuckman model

These findings hold important lessons for organisations. The content and delivery of interpersonal feedback among work-group or committee members can be used as a gauge of whether the group is developing properly. For example, the onset of stage 2 (storming) will be signalled by a noticeable increase in negative feedback. Effort can then be directed at generating specific, positive feedback among the members, so the group's development will not stall. The feedback model discussed in Chapter 6 is helpful in this regard.

Group leaders should not become complacent on reaching the performing stage, since it is not a static equilibrium and needs to be constantly maintained. Awareness is the first line of defence.

Beyond that, constructive steps need to be taken to reinforce norms, bolster cohesiveness and reaffirm the common goal, even when work groups seem to be doing their best.

Along a somewhat different line, experts in the area of leadership contend that different leadership styles are needed as work groups develop (see also Chapter 15).

The practical punch line here is that leaders are advised to shift from a directive and structured leadership style to a participative and supportive style as the group develops.[15]

Critical thinking

Are the phases proposed by Tuckman applicable in a classroom context?

7.4 Roles

Four centuries have passed since William Shakespeare had his character Jaques speak the following memorable lines in Act II of *As You Like It*: 'All the world's a stage, And all the men and women merely players: They have their exits and their entrances; And one man in his time plays many parts. . . .' This intriguing notion of all people as actors in a universal play was not lost on twentieth-century sociologists who developed a complex theory of human interaction based on roles. **Roles** are sets of behaviour that people expect of occupants of a position and role theory attempts to explain how these social expectations influence employee behaviour. This section explores role theory by analysing a role episode and defining the terms 'role overload', 'role conflict', 'role ambiguity' and 'task versus maintenance' roles.

A **role episode** consists of a snapshot of the ongoing interaction between two people (as illustrated in Figure 7.3). In any given role episode, there is a role sender and a focal person who is expected to act out the role. Within a broader context, one may be simultaneously a role sender and a focal person. For the sake of social analysis, however, it is instructive to deal with separate role episodes.

Role episodes begin with the role sender's perception of the relevant organisation's or group's behavioural requirements. Those requirements serve as a standard for formulating expectations for the focal person's behaviour. The role sender then cognitively evaluates the focal person's actual behaviour against those expectations. Appropriate verbal and non-verbal messages are then sent to the focal person to pressure him or her into behaving as expected.

Figure 7.3 A Role Episode

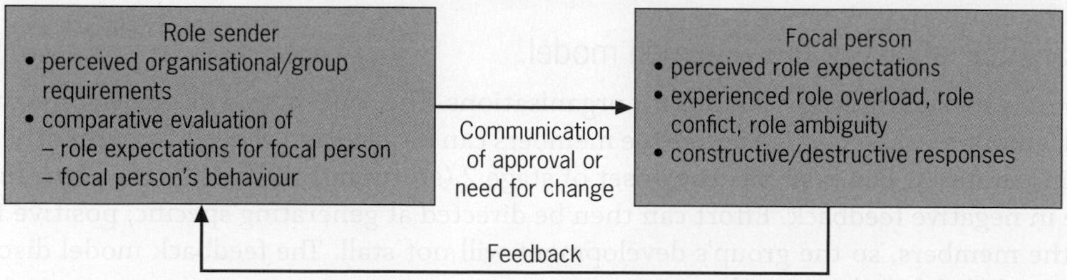

Source: Adapted in part from R. L. Kohn, D. M. Wolfe, R. P. Quinn, and J. D. Snoek, *Organizational Stress: Studies in Role Conflict and Ambiguity*, 1981 edn (Malabar, FL: Robert E. Krieger Publishing, 1964), p. 26.

On the receiving end of the role episode, the focal person accurately or inaccurately perceives the communicated role expectations. Various combinations of role overload, role conflict and role ambiguity are then experienced.[16] The focal person then responds constructively by engaging, for example, in problem-solving or destructively because of undue tension, stress and strain.

According to organisational psychologist Edgar Schein, **role overload** occurs when 'the sum total of what role senders expect of the focal person far exceeds what he or she is able to do'.[17] Students who attempt to handle a full-course load and maintain a decent social life while working 30 or more hours a week to support themselves know full well the consequences of role overload. As the individual tries to do more and more in less and less time, stress mounts and personal effectiveness slips (see also Chapter 9 on stress).

Have you ever felt like you were being torn apart by the conflicting demands of those around you? If so, you were a victim of role conflict. **Role conflict** is experienced when 'different members of the role set expect different things of the focal person'. Employees often face conflicting demands between work and family, for example. Interestingly, however, women experience greater role conflict between work and family than men, because women still perform the majority of the household duties and child-care responsibilities.[18]

Role conflict may also be experienced when internalised values, ethics or personal standards collide with others' expectations. For instance, an otherwise ethical production supervisor may be told by a superior to 'fudge a little' on the quality control reports, so an important deadline will be met. The resulting role conflict forces the supervisor to choose between being loyal but unethical or ethical but disloyal. Tough ethical choices, such as this, mean personal turmoil, interpersonal conflict and even resignation. Consequently, experts say business schools should do a better job of weaving ethics training into their course requirements (see also Chapter 17).

Those who experience role conflict may have trouble complying with role demands, but they at least know what is expected of them. Such is not the case with **role ambiguity**, which occurs when 'members of the role set fail to communicate to the focal person expectations they have or information needed to perform the role, either because they do not have the information or because they deliberately withhold it'.[19] In short, people experience role ambiguity when they do not know what is expected of them. Organisational newcomers often complain about unclear job descriptions and vague promotion criteria. According to role theory, prolonged role ambiguity can foster job dissatisfaction, erode self-confidence and hamper job performance.

Task roles enable the work group to define, clarify and pursue a common purpose. Meanwhile, **maintenance roles** foster supportive and constructive interpersonal relationships. In short, task roles keep the group on track while maintenance roles keep the group together. A fraternity or sorority member is performing a task function when he or she stands at a business meeting and says, 'What is the real issue here? We don't seem to be getting anywhere.' Another individual who says, 'Let's hear from those who oppose this plan', is performing a maintenance function. Importantly, each of the various task and maintenance roles may be played in varying combinations and sequences by either the group's leader or any of its members.

As described in Table 7.2, both task and maintenance roles need to be performed if a work group is to accomplish anything.[20]

HR The task and maintenance roles listed in Table 7.2 can serve as a handy checklist for supervisors and group leaders who wish to ensure proper group development. Roles that are not always performed when needed, such as those of co-ordinator, evaluator and gatekeeper, can be performed in a timely manner by the formal leader or assigned to other members. The task roles of initiator, orienter and energiser are especially important because they are goal-directed roles. Newer research studies on group goal setting confirm the motivational power of challenging goals. As with individual

Table 7.2 Functional Roles Performed by Group Members

Task roles	Description
Initiator	Suggests new goals or ideas
Information seeker/giver	Clarifies key issues
Opinion seeker/giver	Clarifies pertinent values
Elaborator	Promotes greater understanding through examples or exploration of implications
Co-ordinator	Pulls together ideas and suggestions
Orienter	Keeps group headed towards its stated goal(s)
Evaluator	Tests group's accomplishments with various criteria such as logic and practicality
Energiser	Prods group to move along or to accomplish more
Procedural technician	Performs routine duties (e.g. handing out materials or rearranging seats)
Recorder	Performs a 'group memory' function by documenting discussion and outcomes
Maintenance roles	**Description**
Encourager	Fosters group solidarity by accepting and praising various points of view
Harmoniser	Mediates conflict through reconciliation or humour
Compromiser	Helps resolve conflict by meeting others 'half way'
Gatekeeper	Encourages all group members to participate
Standard setter	Evaluates the quality of group processes
Commentator	Records and comments on group processes/dynamics
Follower	Serves as a passive audience

Source: Adapted from discussion in K. D. Benne and P. Sheats, 'Functional Roles of Group Members', *Journal of Social Issues*, Spring 1948, pp. 41–9.

goal setting (see Chapter 6), difficult but achievable goals are associated with better group results.[21] Also in line with individual goal-setting theory and research, group goals are more effective if group members clearly understand them and are both individually and collectively committed to achieving them. Initiators, orienters and energisers can be very helpful in this regard. International managers need to be sensitive to cultural differences regarding the relative importance of task and maintenance roles.

7.5 Norms

While roles involve behavioural expectations for specific positions, norms help organisational members determine right from wrong and good from bad. **Norms** are defined as shared attitudes, opinions, feelings or actions that guide social behaviour. Although norms are typically unwritten and seldom discussed openly, they have a powerful influence on group and organisational behaviour.

Non-conformists experience criticism and even rejection by group members. Anyone who has experienced the 'silent treatment' from a group of friends knows what potent social weapon exclusion can be. Norms can be put into a proper perspective by understanding how they develop and why they are enforced.

Elton Mayo during the Hawthorne experiments in the 1930s already noted the existence of group norms (see Chapter 1). The employees restricted their output to conform to a group-agreed norm or standard.

Generally speaking, experts say norms evolve in an informal manner as the group or organisation determines what it takes to be effective. Norms develop in various combinations of the following four ways:

- *Explicit statements by supervisors or co-workers*: for instance, a group leader might explicitly set norms about not drinking alcohol during work hours.
- *Critical events in the group's history*: these events can establish an important precedent. For example, a key recruit may have decided to work elsewhere because a group member said too many negative things about the organisation. Hence, a norm against such 'sour grapes' behaviour might evolve.
- *Primacy*: the first behaviour pattern that emerges in a group often sets group expectations. If the first group meeting is marked by very formal interaction between supervisors and subordinates, then the group often expects future meetings to be conducted in the same way (see Chapter 4).
- *Carry-over behaviours from past situations*: these behaviours from past situations can increase the predictability of group members' behaviours in new settings and facilitate task accomplishment.

Activity

Measuring role conflict and role ambiguity

Instructions

While thinking of your current (or last) job, circle one response for each of the following statements. Please consider each statement carefully because some are worded positively and some negatively.

		Very false				Very true		
1	I feel certain about how much authority I have.	7	6	5	4	3	2	1___
2	I have to do things that should be done differently.	1	2	3	4	5	6	7___
3	I know that I have divided my time properly.	7	6	5	4	3	2	1___
4	I know what my responsibilities are.	7	6	5	4	3	2	1___
5	I have to buck a rule or policy in order to carry out an assignment.	1	2	3	4	5	6	7___
6	I feel certain how I will be evaluated for a rise or promotion.	7	6	5	4	3	2	1___
7	I work with two or more groups who operate quite differently.	1	2	3	4	5	6	7___
8	I know exactly what is expected of me.	7	6	5	4	3	2	1___
9	I do things that are apt to be accepted by one person and not accepted by others.	1	2	3	4	5	6	7___
10	I work on unnecessary things.	1	2	3	4	5	6	7___

Role conflict score =

Role ambiguity score =

Scoring key and norms

In the space in the far right column, label each statement with either a 'C' for role conflict or an 'A' for role ambiguity. (See Note 22 for a correct categorisation.)[22]

Calculate separate totals for role conflict and role ambiguity and compare them with these arbitrary norms:

5–14 = low
15–25 = moderate
26–35 = high

Source: Adapted from J. R. Rizzo, R. J. House and S. I. Lirtzman, 'Role Conflict and Ambiguity in Complex Organizations', *Administrative Science Quarterly*, June 1970, p. 156.

Norms are not in themselves good or bad for individual and organisational performance but evolve due to psychological and sociological mechanisms. Norms tend to be enforced by group members when they:

- Help the group or organisation survive.
- Clarify or simplify behavioural expectations.
- Help individuals avoid embarrassing situations.
- Clarify the group's or organisation's central values and/or unique identity.[23]

Working examples of each of these four situations are presented in Table 7.3.

Evidence about roles and group norms

Both roles and norms are studied extensively in laboratory experiments and field research. Although instruments used to measure role conflict and role ambiguity have questionable validity,[24] two separate meta-analyses indicated that role conflict and role ambiguity affected employees negatively.

Table 7.3 Four Reasons Why Norms are Enforced

Norm	Reason for enforcement	Example
Make our department look good in top management's eyes	Group/organisation survival	After vigorously defending the vital role played by the human resources management department at a divisional meeting, a staff specialist is complimented by her boss
Success comes to those who work hard and do not make waves	Clarification of behavioural expectations	A senior manager takes a young associate aside and cautions him to be a bit more patient with co-workers who see things differently
Be a team player, not a star	Avoidance of embarrassment	A project team member is ridiculed by her peers for dominating the discussion during a progress report to top management
Customer service is our top priority	Clarification of central values/ unique identity	Two sales representatives are given a surprise Friday afternoon party for having received prestigious best-in-the-industry customer service awards from an industry association

Specifically, role conflict and role ambiguity were associated with job dissatisfaction, tension and anxiety, lack of organisational commitment, intentions to quit and, to a lesser extent, poor job performance.[25]

The meta-analyses results hold few surprises for organisations. Generally, because of the negative association reported, it makes sense for organisations to reduce both role conflict and role ambiguity. In this endeavour, organisations can use several practices explained throughout the book, like feedback (see Chapter 6), formal rules and procedures (see Chapter 14), directive leadership (see Chapter 15), setting of specific (difficult) goals (see Chapter 6) and participation (see Chapter 13).

7.6 Group size and composition

Work groups of varying size are made up of individuals with varying ability and motivation. Moreover, those individuals perform different roles, on either an assigned or voluntary basis. No wonder some work groups are more productive than others or that some committees are tightly knit while others wallow in conflict. In this section, we examine the importance of group size. We conclude with some general findings with regard to the use of homogeneous versus heterogeneous groups.

Evidence about ideal group size

How many group members are too many? The answer to this deceptively simple question has intrigued professionals and academics for years. Folk wisdom says 'two heads are better than one' but that 'too many cooks spoil the broth'. So where should an organisation draw the line when staffing a committee? At three? At five or six? At 10 or more? Researchers have taken two different approaches to pinpointing optimum group size: mathematical modelling and laboratory simulations. Let us briefly review findings from these two approaches.

The first approach involves building a mathematical model around certain desired outcomes of group action such as decision quality. Owing to differing assumptions and statistical techniques, the results of this research are inconclusive. Statistical estimates of optimum group size have ranged from three to 13.[26]

The second stream of research is based on the assumption that group behaviour needs to be observed first hand in controlled laboratory settings. A laboratory study by respected Australian researcher Philip Yetton and his colleague, Preston Bottger, provides useful insights about group size and performance.[27]

A total of 555 subjects (330 managers and 225 management students, of whom 20 per cent were female) were assigned to task teams ranging in size from two to six. The teams worked on the National Aeronautics and Space Administration moon survival exercise. This exercise involves the rank ordering of 15 pieces of equipment that would enable a spaceship crew on the moon to survive a 320-kilometre trip between a crash-landing site and home base.[28] After analysing the relationships between group size and group performance, Yetton and Bottger concluded the following: 'It would be difficult, at least with respect to decision quality, to justify groups larger than five members . . . Of course, to meet needs other than high decision quality, organisations may employ groups significantly larger than four or five.'[29]

Laboratory studies exploring the brainstorming productivity of various size groups (2–12 people), in face-to-face versus computer-mediated situations, proved fruitful. In the usual face-to-face brainstorming sessions (see also Chapter 13), productivity of ideas did not increase as the size of the group increased.

HR Application of group size

Within a contingency management framework, there is no hard-and-fast rule about group size. It depends on the organisation's objective for the group. If a high-quality decision is the main objective, then a three- to five-member group would be appropriate. However, if the objective is to generate creative ideas, encourage participation, socialise new members, engage in training or communicate policies, then groups much larger than five could be justified. Nonetheless, organisations need to be aware of qualitative changes that occur when group size increases. A meta-analysis of eight studies found the following relationships: as group size increased, group leaders tended to become more directive and group member satisfaction tended to decline slightly.[30]

Odd-numbered groups (e.g. three, five, seven members) are recommended if the issue is to be settled by a majority vote. Voting deadlocks (e.g. 2–2, 3–3) too often hamper effectiveness of even-numbered groups. A majority decision rule is not necessarily a good idea. One study found that better group outcomes were obtained by negotiation groups that used a unanimous as opposed to majority-decision rule. Individuals' self-interests were more effectively integrated when groups used a unanimous decision criterion.[31]

7.7 Homogeneous or heterogeneous groups?

Organisations increasingly search for selection methods to staff effective work groups and teams. Individual differences other than gender, abilities and roles are in that regard also studied in relation to group composition, like cognitive styles,[32] learning styles[33] and personality.[34]

A study among 182 employees of an insurance company led to the finding that in groups designed to achieve a balanced group learning process (based on the learning styles model of Honey and Mumford, see Chapter 2), the learning process model can predict group performance.[35]

A study among 298 graduate students performing in work teams for a course in 'Organisation Management' revealed that extraversion (one of the Big Five dimensions, see Chapter 2) is especially important to understand how personality traits influence team performance.[36]

As these research results reveal, group heterogeneity offers both opportunities and challenges with regard to group effectiveness. Does diversity in groups enhance or detract from its effectiveness? This depends on the diversity in question.[37]

Diversity with regard to task-related knowledge and skills is good as this implies that each group member has relevant and distinct skills that can contribute to accomplishing the task. Several studies confirm that task-related diversity can lead to greater effectiveness.[38] In Chapter 8, relevant teamwork skills are elaborated further.

However, relations-oriented diversity (meaning those characteristics that can cause differentiation between in-groups and out-groups,[39] like ethnicity, gender and age) can inhibit effectiveness, although studies found for each of these concepts mixed results.[40] For instance, age diversity in groups reflects differences in values, attitudes and perspectives, which might cause stereotypes and prejudices (see also Chapter 4). Risk-taking propensity is, for instance, related to age, which can cause conflicts over the degree of risk-taking to solve a certain problem. Earlier in the chapter we elaborated further on gender and group work and we pointed to some possible risks when using mixed-gender groups. Ethnocentrism (see Chapter 13) can be a problem in heterogeneous work groups.

HR

To conclude, diversity in groups can be seen as a double-edged sword: it is needed for innovation and creative solutions, but it can cause conflict and turnover. Neither extreme homogeneity nor heterogeneity is likely to be optimal when a series of compromises needs to be considered as groups are composed to meet multiple objectives (which are not always compatible, like striving for efficiency and for quality). On the one hand, heterogeneity or diversity increases the knowledge pool that is important for addressing team tasks. On the other hand, people generally prefer to be with others like themselves. Too much heterogeneity can also make it difficult to communicate and co-ordinate between team members.[41]

!

Critical thinking

Workplace diversity is almost universally praised in popular literature and among management consultants, even though evidence about the effect of diversity is more complex. Why do you think this is the case?

7.8 Threats to group effectiveness

Even when task groups are carefully staffed and organised, group dynamics can still go haywire. Forehand knowledge of three major threats to group effectiveness – the Asch effect, groupthink and social loafing – can help organisations take necessary preventive steps. Because the first two problems relate to blind conformity, some brief background is in order.

Very little would be accomplished in task groups and organisations without conformity to norms, role expectations, policies, and rules and regulations. After all, deadlines, commitments and product/service quality standards have to be established and adhered to if the organisation is to survive. However conformity is a two-edged sword:

> Social forces powerful enough to influence members to conform may influence them to perform at a very high level of quality and productivity. All too often, however, the pressure to conform stifles creativity, influencing members to cling to attitudes that may be out of touch with organisational needs.[42]

Moreover, excessive or blind conformity can stifle critical thinking, the last line of defence against unethical conduct. Almost daily accounts in the popular media of insider trading scandals, illegal dumping of hazardous wastes and other unethical practices make it imperative that professionals understand the mechanics of blind conformity.

The Asch effect

In the 1950s, social psychologist Solomon Asch conducted a series of laboratory experiments that revealed a negative side of group dynamics.[43] Under the guise of a 'perception test', Asch had groups of seven to nine volunteer college students look at 12 pairs of cards, such as the ones in Figure 7.4. The object was to identify the line that was the same length as the standard line. Each individual was told to announce his or her choice to the group. Since the differences among the comparison lines were obvious, there should have been unanimous agreement during each of the 12 rounds. But that was not the case.

Figure 7.4 The Asch Experiment

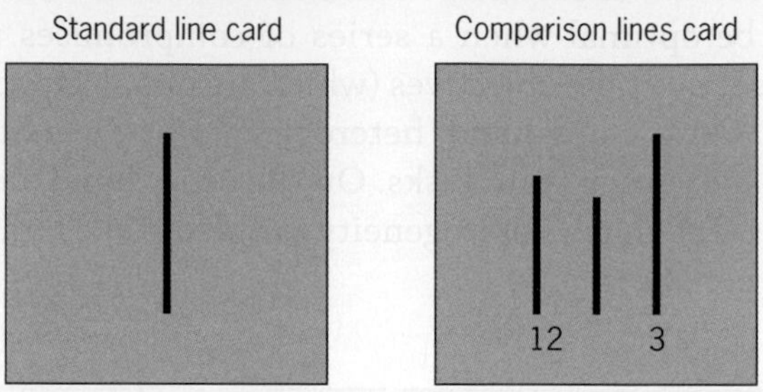

All but one member of each group were Asch's confederates who agreed to systematically select the wrong line during seven of the rounds (the other five rounds were control rounds for comparison purposes). The remaining individual was the naive subject who was being tricked. Group pressure was created by having the naive subject in each group be among the last to announce his or her choice. Thirty-one subjects were tested. Asch's research question was: 'How often would the naive subjects conform to a majority opinion that was obviously wrong?'

Only 20 per cent of Asch's subjects remained entirely independent; 80 per cent yielded to the pressures of group opinion at least once! Fifty-eight per cent knuckled under to the 'immoral majority' at least twice. Hence, the **Asch effect**, the distortion of individual judgement by a unanimous but incorrect opposition, was documented.

Groupthink

Why did President Lyndon B. Johnson and his group of intelligent White House advisers make some very unintelligent decisions that escalated the Vietnam War? How is it possible that, in 1995, Robert McNamara, US Secretary of Defense under Kennedy and Johnson, reflecting on the Vietnam War, had to admit 'We were wrong, terribly wrong'?[44] Those fateful decisions were made despite obvious warning signals, including stronger than expected resistance from the North Vietnamese and dwindling support at home and abroad. Systematic analysis of the decision-making processes underlying the war in Vietnam and other US foreign policy fiascos prompted Yale University's Irving Janis to coin the term 'groupthink'. Professionals nowadays can all too easily become victims of groupthink, just like President Johnson's staff, if they passively ignore the danger.

Janis defines **groupthink** as 'a mode of thinking that people engage in when they are deeply involved in a cohesive in-group, when members' strivings for unanimity override their motivation to realistically appraise alternative courses of action'.[45] He adds, '. . . groupthink refers to a deterioration of mental efficiency, reality testing and moral judgment that results from in-group pressures'.[46] Unlike Asch's subjects, who were strangers to each other, members of groups victimised by groupthink are tightly knit and cohesive. In short, policy- and decision-making groups can become so cohesive that strong-willed executives are able to gain unanimous support for poor decisions (see Figure 7.5).

Social loafing

Is group performance less than, equal to or greater than the sum of its parts? Can three people, for example, working together accomplish less than, the same as or more than they would working separately? An interesting study conducted more than a half century ago found the answer to

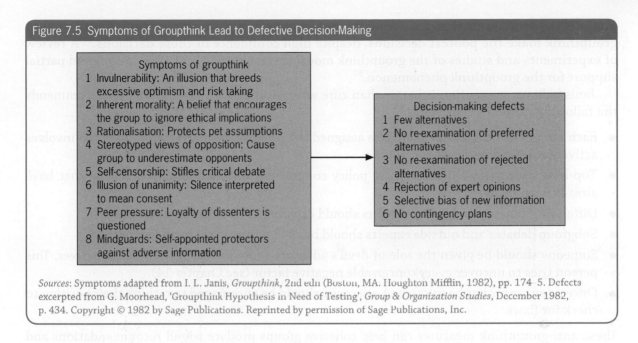

Figure 7.5 Symptoms of Groupthink Lead to Defective Decision-Making

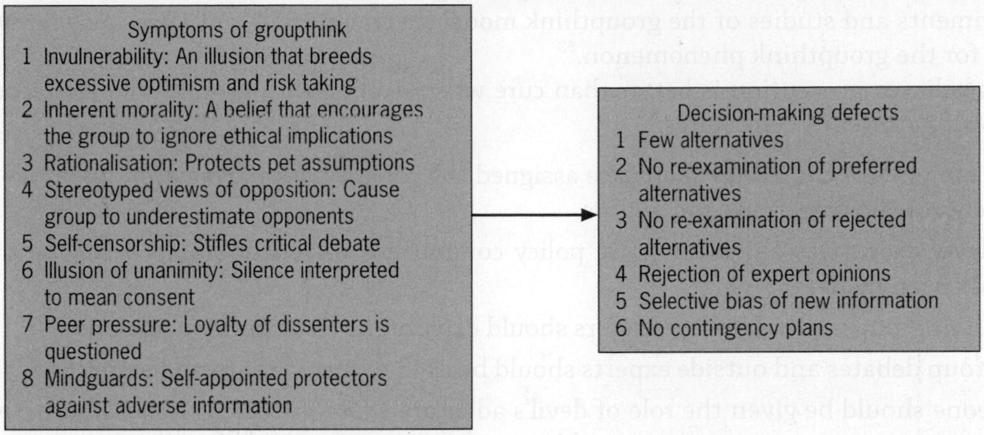

Symptoms of groupthink
1 Invulnerability: An illusion that breeds excessive optimism and risk taking
2 Inherent morality: A belief that encourages the group to ignore ethical implications
3 Rationalisation: Protects pet assumptions
4 Stereotyped views of opposition: Cause group to underestimate opponents
5 Self-censorship: Stifles critical debate
6 Illusion of unanimity: Silence interpreted to mean consent
7 Peer pressure: Loyalty of dissenters is questioned
8 Mindguards: Self-appointed protectors against adverse information
Decision-making defects
1 Few alternatives
2 No re-examination of preferred alternatives
3 No re-examination of rejected alternatives
4 Rejection of expert opinions
5 Selective bias of new information
6 No contingency plans

Sources: Symptoms adapted from I. L. Janis, *Groupthink*, 2nd edn (Boston, MA. Houghton Mifflin, 1982), pp. 174–5. Defects excerpted from G. Moorhead, 'Groupthink Hypothesis in Need of Testing', *Group & Organization Studies*, December 1982, p. 434. Copyright © 1982 by Sage Publications. Reprinted by permission of Sage Publications, Inc.

be 'less than'.[47] A rope-pulling exercise found that three people pulling together could achieve only two and a half times the average individual rate. Eight pullers achieved less than four times the individual rate. This tendency for individual effort to decline as group size increases has come to be called **social loafing.**[48]

Among the theoretical explanations for the social loafing effect are: (1) equity of effort ('Everyone else is goofing off, so why shouldn't I?'), (2) loss of personal accountability ('I'm lost in the crowd, so who cares?'), (3) motivational loss due to the sharing of rewards ('Why should I work harder than the others when everyone gets the same reward?') and (4) co-ordination loss as more people perform the task ('We're getting in each other's way').

Evidence about threats to group effectiveness

Asch's experiment has been widely replicated with mixed results. Both high and low degrees of blind conformity have been observed with various situations and subjects. Replications in Japan and Kuwait have demonstrated that the Asch effect is not unique to the USA.[49] A cross-cultural study using white British males and white American males showed no significant differences between them. The study confirmed the existence of the Asch effect, but remarked that the effect was significantly weaker than the results Asch reported in the 1950s.[50] Internationally, collectivist countries, where the group prevails over the individual, produced higher levels of conformity than individualistic countries.[51] The point is not precisely how great the Asch effect is in a given situation or culture, but rather, professionals committed to ethical conduct need to be concerned that the Asch effect exists. Even isolated instances of blind, unthinking conformity seriously threaten the effectiveness and integrity of work groups and organisations. Functional conflict and assertiveness can help employees respond appropriately when they find themselves facing an immoral majority. Ethical codes mentioning specific practices can also provide support and guidance.

Laboratory studies using college students as subjects validate portions of Janis's groupthink concept. Specifically, it has been found that groups with a moderate amount of cohesiveness produce better decisions than low- or high-cohesive groups. Highly cohesive groups victimised by groupthink make the poorest decisions, despite high confidence in those decisions.[52] A review of experiments and studies of the groupthink model (between 1974 and 1998) also found partial support for the groupthink phenomenon.[53]

Janis believes prevention is better than cure when dealing with groupthink. He recommends the following preventive measures:[54]

- Each member of the group should be assigned the role of critical evaluator. This role involves actively voicing objections and doubts.
- Top-level executives should not use policy committees to rubber-stamp decisions that have already been made.
- Different groups with different leaders should explore the same policy questions.
- Subgroup debates and outside experts should be used to introduce fresh perspectives.
- Someone should be given the role of devil's advocate when discussing major alternatives. This person tries to uncover every conceivable negative factor (see Chapter 14).
- Once a consensus has been reached, everyone should be encouraged to rethink their position to check for flaws.

These anti-groupthink measures can help cohesive groups produce sound recommendations and decisions.

Laboratory studies refined these theories by identifying situational factors that moderated the social loafing effect. Social loafing occurred when:

- The task was perceived to be unimportant, simple or not interesting.[55]
- Group members thought their individual output was not identifiable.[56]
- Group members expected their co-workers to loaf.[57]

But social loafing did not occur when group members in two laboratory studies expected to be evaluated.[58] Also, research suggests that self-reliant 'individualists' are more prone to social loafing than are group-oriented 'collectivists'. However, individualists can be made more co-operative by keeping the group small, by holding each member personally accountable for results and by fostering group cohesiveness.[59] A field investigation into social loafing also stresses the need to acknowledge the role that task interdependence might play in encouraging social loafing, especially given the trend in organisations towards interdependent work teams (see Chapter 8).[60]

HR Implications of threats to group effectiveness

These findings demonstrate that social loafing is not an inevitable part of group effort. Organisations can curb this threat to group effectiveness by making sure the task is challenging and perceived as important (see also Chapters 5 and 6). Additionally, it is a good idea to hold group members personally accountable for identifiable portions of the group's task. One way to do this is with the stepladder technique, a group decision-making process proven effective in some research. Compared with conventional groups, stepladder groups produced significantly better decisions in the same amount of time. 'Furthermore, stepladder groups' decisions surpassed the quality of their best individual members' decisions 56 per cent of the time. In contrast, conventional groups' decisions surpassed the quality of their best members' decisions only 13 per cent of the time.'[61] The stepladder technique could be a useful tool for organisations relying on self-managed or **total quality management** (TQM) teams (see Chapter 8).

Learning outcomes: Summary of key terms

1 **Identify the four criteria of a group from a sociological perspective**

Sociologically, a group is defined as (1) two or more (2) freely interacting individuals who (3) share collective norms and goals and (4) have a common identity.

2 **Identify and briefly describe the five stages in Tuckman's theory of group development**

The five stages in Tuckman's theory are forming (the group comes together), storming (members test the limits and each other), norming (questions about authority and power are resolved as the group becomes more cohesive), performing (effective communication and co-operation help the group get things done) and adjourning (group members go their own way).

3 **Distinguish between role overload, role conflict and role ambiguity**

Organisational roles are sets of behaviours people expect of occupants of a position. One may experience role overload (too much to do in too little time), role conflict (conflicting role expectations) or role ambiguity (unclear role expectations).

4 **Contrast roles and norms, and specify four reasons why norms are enforced in organisations**

While roles are specific to the person's position, norms are shared attitudes that differentiate appropriate from inappropriate behaviour in a variety of situations. Norms evolve informally and are enforced because they help the group or organisation survive, clarify behavioural expectations and the group's or organisation's central values and help people avoid embarrassing situations.

5 **Distinguish between task and maintenance functions in groups**

Members of formal groups need to perform both task (goal-oriented) and maintenance (relationship-oriented) roles if anything is to be accomplished.

6 **Summarise the practical implications for group size and group-member ability**

Laboratory simulation studies suggest decision-making groups should be limited to five or fewer members. Larger groups are appropriate when creativity, participation or socialisation are the main objectives. If majority votes are to be taken, odd-numbered groups are recommended to avoid deadlocks. Results of the Israeli tank-crew study (see Chapter 8) prompted researchers to conclude that it is better to concentrate high-ability personnel in separate groups. Within a contingency perspective, however, there are situations in which it is advisable to spread high-ability people around.

7 **Describe groupthink, and identify at least four of its symptoms**

Groupthink plagues cohesive in-groups that short-change moral judgement while putting too much emphasis on unanimity. Symptoms of groupthink include invulnerability, inherent morality, rationalisation, stereotyped views of opposition, self-censorship, an illusion of unanimity and peer pressure. Critical evaluators, outside expertise and devil's advocates are among the preventive measures recommended by Irving Janis, who coined the term 'groupthink'.

8 **Define social loafing, and explain how organisations can prevent it**

Social loafing involves the tendency for individual effort to decrease as group size increases. This problem can be contained if the task is challenging and important, individuals are held accountable for results and group members expect everyone to work hard. The stepladder technique, a structured approach to group decision-making, can reduce social loafing by increasing personal effort and accountability.

Review questions

1 Which of the following would qualify as a sociological group? A crowd watching a basketball game? One of the basketball teams? Explain.
2 What is your opinion about employees being friends with their co-workers (overlapping formal and informal groups)?
3 What is your personal experience with groups that failed to achieve stage 4 of group development? At which stage did they stall? Why?
4 Considering your current lifestyle, how many different roles are you playing? What sorts of role conflict and role ambiguity are you experiencing?
5 Which roles do you prefer to play in work groups: task or maintenance? How could you do a better job in this regard?
6 What norms do university students usually enforce in class? How are they enforced?
7 How would you respond to a manager who made the following statement: 'When it comes to the size of work groups, the bigger the better'?
8 Have you ever been a victim of either the Asch effect or groupthink? Explain the circumstances.
9 Have you observed any social loafing recently? What were the circumstances and what could be done to correct the problem?

Personal awareness and growth exercise

Is this a mature work group or team?

Objectives

1 To increase your knowledge of group processes and dynamics.
2 To give you a tool for assessing the maturity of a work group or task team as well as a diagnostic tool for pinpointing group problems.
3 To help you become a more effective group leader or contributor.

Introduction

Group action is so common today that many of us take it for granted. But are the groups and teams to which we contribute much of our valuable time mature and hence more likely to be effective?

Or do they waste our time? How can they be improved? We can and should become tough critical evaluators of group processes.

Instructions

Think of a work group or task team with which you are very familiar (preferably, one you worked with in the past or are currently working with). Rate the group's maturity on each of the 20 dimensions.[62] Then add your circled responses to get your total group maturity score. The higher the score, the greater the group's maturity.

	Very false (or never)				Very true (or always)
1 Members are clear about group goals.	1	2	3	4	5
2 Members agree with the group's goals.	1	2	3	4	5
3 Members are clear about their roles.	1	2	3	4	5
4 Members accept their roles and status.	1	2	3	4	5
5 Role assignments match member abilities.	1	2	3	4	5
6 The leadership style matches the group's developmental level.	1	2	3	4	5
7 The group has an open communication structure in which all members participate.	1	2	3	4	5
8 The group gets, gives and uses feedback about its effectiveness and productivity.	1	2	3	4	5
9 The group spends time planning how it will solve problems and make decisions.	1	2	3	4	5
10 Voluntary conformity is high.	1	2	3	4	5
11 The group norms encourage high performance and quality.	1	2	3	4	5
12 The group expects to be successful.	1	2	3	4	5
13 The group pays attention to the details of its work.	1	2	3	4	5
14 The group accepts coalition and subgroup formation.	1	2	3	4	5
15 Subgroups are integrated into the group as a whole.	1	2	3	4	5
16 The group is highly cohesive.	1	2	3	4	5
17 Interpersonal attraction among members is high.	1	2	3	4	5
18 Members are co-operative.	1	2	3	4	5
19 Periods of conflict are frequent but brief.	1	2	3	4	5
20 The group has effective conflict-management strategies.	1	2	3	4	5

Discussion questions

1 Compare your total score with the following arbitrary norms:

20–39 'When in doubt, run in circles, scream and shout!'

40–59 A long way to go

60–79 On the right track

80–100 Ready for group dynamics graduate school

2 Does your evaluation help explain why the group or team was successful or not? Explain.

3 Was (or is) there anything you could have done (or can do) to increase the maturity of this group? Explain.

4 How will this evaluation instrument help you be a more effective group member or leader in the future?

Group exercise

A committee decision

Objectives

1 To give you first-hand experience with work group dynamics through a role-playing exercise.[63]

2 To develop your ability to evaluate group effectiveness.

Introduction

Please read the following case before going on.

The Johnny Rocco case

Johnny has a grim personal background. He is the third child in a family of seven. He has not seen his father for several years, and his recollection is that his father used to come home drunk and beat up every member of the family; everyone ran when his father came staggering home.

His mother, according to Johnny, was not much better. She was irritable and unhappy, and she always predicted that Johnny would come to no good end. Yet, she worked when her health allowed her to do so in order to keep the family in food and clothing. She always decried the fact that she was not able to be the kind of mother she would like to be.

Johnny quit school in the seventh grade. He had great difficulty conforming to the school routine – he misbehaved often, truanted frequently and fought with schoolmates. On several occasions, he was picked up by the police and, along with members of his group, questioned during several investigations into cases of both petty and grand larceny. The police regarded him as 'probably a bad one'.

The juvenile officer of the court saw in Johnny some good qualities that no one else seemed to sense. Mr O'Brien took it on himself to act as a 'big brother' to Johnny. He had several long conversations with Johnny, during which he managed to penetrate, to some degree, Johnny's defensive shell. He represented to Johnny the first semblance of personal interest in his life. Through Mr O'Brien's efforts, Johnny returned to school and obtained a high school diploma. Afterwards, Mr O'Brien helped him obtain a job.

Now 20, Johnny is a stockroom clerk in one of the laboratories where you are employed. On the whole, Johnny's performance has been acceptable, but there have been glaring exceptions. One involved a clear act of insubordination on a fairly unimportant matter. In another, Johnny was accused, on circumstantial grounds, of destroying some expensive equipment. Though the investigation is still open, it now appears the destruction was accidental.

Johnny's supervisor wants to keep him on for at least a trial period, but he wants 'outside' advice as to the best way of helping Johnny grow into greater responsibility. Of course, much depends on how Johnny behaves in the next few months. Naturally, his supervisor must follow personnel policies that are accepted in the company as a whole. It is important to note that Johnny is not an attractive young man. He is rather weak and sickly, and he shows unmistakable signs of long years of social deprivation.

A committee is formed to decide the fate of Johnny Rocco. The chairperson of the meeting is Johnny's supervisor and should begin by assigning roles to the group members. These roles (shop steward (representing the union), head of production, Johnny's co-worker, director of personnel and social worker who helped Johnny in the past) represent points of view the chairperson believes should be included in this meeting. (Johnny is not to be included.) Two observers should also be assigned. Thus, each group will have eight members.

Instructions

After roles have been assigned, each role player should complete the personal preference part of the work sheet, ranking from 1 to 11 the alternatives according to their appropriateness from the vantage point of his or her role.

Once the individual preferences have been determined, the chairperson should call the meeting to order. The following rules govern the meeting: (1) The group must reach a consensus ranking of the alternatives; (2) the group cannot use a statistical aggregation, or majority vote, decision-making process; and (3) members should stay 'in character' throughout the discussion. Treat this as a committee meeting consisting of members with different backgrounds, orientation and interests who share a problem.

After the group has completed the assignment, the observers should conduct a discussion of the group process, using the group effectiveness questions here as a guide. Group members should not look at these questions until after the group task has been completed.

Group effectiveness questions

1 Referring to Table 7.2, what task roles were performed? By whom?
2 What maintenance roles were performed? By whom?
3 Were any important task or maintenance roles ignored? Which?
4 Was there any evidence of the Asch effect, groupthink or social loafing? Explain.

Questions for discussion

1 Did your committee do a good job? Explain.
2 What, if anything, should have been done differently?
3 How much similarity in rankings is there among the different groups in your class? What group dynamics apparently were responsible for any variations in rankings?

Worksheet Personal preference	Group decision
	Warn Johnny that at the next sign of trouble he will be fired.
	Do nothing, as it is unclear if Johnny did anything wrong. Create strict controls (do's and don'ts) for Johnny with immediate strong punishment for any misbehaviour.
	Give Johnny a great deal of warmth and personal attention and affection (overlooking his present behaviour) so he can learn to depend on others.
	Fire him. It's not worth the time and effort spent for such a low-level position.
	Talk over the problem with Johnny in an understanding way so he can learn to ask others for help in solving his problems.
	Give Johnny a well-structured schedule of daily activities with immediate and unpleasant consequences for not adhering to the schedule.
	Do nothing now, but watch him carefully and provide immediate punishment for any future behaviour.
	Treat Johnny the same as everyone else, but provide an orderly routine so he can learn to stand on his own two feet.
	Call Johnny in and logically discuss the problem with him and ask what you can do to help him.
	Do nothing now, but watch him so you can reward him the next time he does something good.

Online
Learning Centre

When you have read this chapter, log on to the Online Learning Centre website at ***www.mcgraw-hill.co.uk/textbooks/sinding*** to access test questions, additional exercises and other related resources.

Notes

1 For instructive research overviews, see K. L. Bettenhausen, 'Five Years of Group Research: What We Have Learned and What Needs To Be Addressed', *Journal of Management*, June 1991, pp. 345–81; R. T. Mowday and R. I. Sutton, 'Organizational Behavior: Linking Individuals and Groups to Organizational Contexts', in *Annual Review of Psychology*, vol. 44, eds L. W. Porter and M. R. Rosenzweig (Palo Alto, CA: Annual Reviews, 1993), pp. 195–229; R. A. Guzzo, 'Fundamental Considerations about Work Groups', in *Handbook of Work Group Psychology*, ed. M. A. West (Chichester: John Wiley, 1996), pp. 3–21; J. E. McGrath, 'Small Group Research, That Once and Future Field: An Interpretation of the Past With an Eye to the Future', *Group Dynamics: Theory, Research, and Practice*, no. 1, 1997, pp. 7–27; and S. G. Cohen and D. E. Baily, 'What Makes Teams Work: Group Effectiveness Research for the Shop Floor to the Executive Suite', *Journal of Management*, no. 3, 1997, pp. 239–90. A special issue of *Group Dynamics: Theory, Research, and Practice* (no. 1, 2000) is devoted to the history and future of group research. For instance, see E. Sundstrom, M. McIntyre, T. Halfhill and H. Richards, 'Work Groups: From the Hawthorne Studies to Work Teams of the 1990s and Beyond', *Group Dynamics: Theory, Research, and Practice*, no. 1, 2000, pp. 44–67.

2 This definition is based in part on one found in D. Horton Smith, 'A Parsimonious Definition of Group: Toward Conceptual Clarity and Scientific Utility', *Sociological Inquiry*, Spring 1967, pp. 141–67.

3 E. H. Schein, *Organizational Psychology*, 3rd edn (Englewood Cliffs, NJ: Prentice-Hall, 1980), p. 145. For more, see L. R. Weingart, 'How Did They Do That? The Way and Means of Studying Group Processess', in *Research in Organizational Behavior*, vol. 19, eds L. L. Cummings and B. M. Staw (Greenwich, CT: JAI Press, 1997), pp. 189–239.

4 R. Likert, *New Patterns of Management* (New York: McGraw-Hill, 1961).

5 See L. G. Bolman and T. E. Deal, *Reframing Organizations* (San Francisco, CA: Jossey-Bass, 1991), ch. 7; J. R. Katzenbach and D. K. Smith, *The Wisdom of Teams: Creating the High Performance Organization* (Boston, MA: Harvard Business School Press, 1993); and F. LaFasto and C. Larson, *When Teams Work Best: 6,000 Team Members and Leaders Tell What It Takes to Succeed* (Thousand Oaks, CA: Sage Publications, 2001).

6 For works on the social identity theory, see M. Hogg and D. Abrams, *Social Identifications: A Social Psychology of Intergroup Relations and Group Processes* (London: Routledge, 1988); B. E. Ashforth and F. Mael, 'Social Identity Theory and the Organization', *Academy of Management Review*, January 1989, pp. 20–39; M. A. Hogg and D. J. Terry, 'Social Identity and Self-Categorization Processes in Organizational Contexts', *Academy of Management Review*, January 2000, pp. 121–40; and J. C. Turner and K. J. Reynolds, 'The Social Identity Perspective in Intergroup Relations: Theories, Themes, and Controversies', in *Black well Handbook of Social Psychology: Intergroup Processes*, eds R. Brown and S. Gaertner (Oxford: Blackwell Publishing, 2001), pp. 133–52.

7 A. Pettigrew, 'Information Control as a Power Source', *Sociology*, 1972, pp. 187–204; and M. Zald, *Power in Organizations* (Nashville, TN: Vanderbilt University Press, 1970).

8 M. Grannovetter, *Getting a Job: A Study of Contacts and Careers* (Cambridge, MA: Harvard University Press, 1974).

9 For an instructive overview of five different theories of group development, see J. P. Wanous, A. E. Reichers and S. D. Malik, 'Organizational Socialization and Group Development: Toward an Integrative Perspective', *Academy of Management Review*, October 1984, pp. 670–83.

10 See B. W. Tuckman, 'Developmental Sequence in Small Groups', *Psychological Bulletin*, June 1965, pp. 384–99; and B. W. Tuckman and M. A. C. Jensen, 'Stages of Small-Group Development Revisited', *Group & Organizational Studies*, December 1977, pp. 419–27. An instructive adaptation of the Tuckman model can be found in L. Holpp, 'If Empowerment Is So Good, Why Does It Hurt?', *Training*, March 1995, p. 56.

11 Alternative group development models are discussed in L. N. Jewell and H. J. Reitz, *Group Effectiveness in Organizations* (Glenview, IL: Scott, Foresman, 1981), pp. 15–20; and R. S. Wellins, W. C. Byham and J. M. Wilson, *Empowered Teams: Creating Self-Directed Work Groups That Improve Quality, Productivity, and Participation* (San Francisco, CA: Jossey-Bass, 1991). Also see Y. Agazarian and S. Gantt, 'Phases of Group Development: Systems-Centered Hypotheses and Their Implications for Research and Practice', *Group Dynamics: Theory, Research, and Practice*, no. 3, 2003, pp. 238–52.

12 Based on J. F. McGrew, J. G. Bilotta and J. M. Deeney, 'Software Team Formation and Decay: Extending the Standard Model for Small Groups', *Small Group Research*, April 1999, pp. 209–34.

13 D. Davies and B. C. Kuypers, 'Group Development and Interpersonal Feedback', *Group & Organizational Studies*, June 1985, p. 194.

14 D. K. Carew, E. Parisi-Carew and K. H. Blanchard, 'Group Development and Situational Leadership: A Model for Managing Groups', *Training and Development Journal*, June 1986, pp. 48–9. For evidence linking leadership and group effectiveness, see G. R. Bushe and A. L. Johnson, 'Contextual and Internal Variables Affecting Task Group Outcomes in Organizations', *Group & Organization Studies*, December 1989, pp. 462–82.

15 For an excellent collection of readings on leadership, see F. Hesselbein, M. Goldsmith and R. Beckhard, *The Leader of the Future: New Visions, Strategies, and Practices for the Next Era* (San Francisco, CA: Jossey-Bass, 1996). See also C. Huxham and S. Vangen, 'Leadership in the Shaping and the Implementation of Collaboration Agendas: How Thing Happens in a (Not Quite) Joined-Up World', *Academy of Management Journal*, December 2000, pp. 1159–75; and N. Sivasubramaniam, W. D. Murry, B. J. Avolio and D. I. Jung, 'A Longitudinal Model of the Effects of Team Leadership and Group Potency on Group Performance', *Group & Organization Management*, March 2002, pp. 66–96.

16 E. H. Schein, *Organizational Psychology*, 3rd edn (Englewood Cliffs, NJ: Prentice-Hall, 1980), p. 198. The relationship between inter-role conflict and turnover is explored in P. W. Hom and A. J. Kinicki, 'Toward a Greater Understanding of How Dissatisfaction Drives Employee Turnover', *Academy of Management Journal*, October 2001, pp. 975–87.

17 E. H. Schein, *Organizational Psychology*, 3rd edn (Englewood Cliffs, NJ: Prentice-Hall, 1980), p. 198. See also E. Van De Vliert and N. W. Van Yperen, 'Why Cross-National Differences in Role Overload? Don't Overlook Ambient Temperature!', *Academy of Management Journal*, August 1996, pp. 986–1004.

18 See D. Moore, 'Role Conflict: Not Only for Women? A Comparative Analysis of 5 Nations', *International Journal of Comparative Sociology*, June 1995, pp. 17–35; and S. Shellenbarger, 'More Men Move Past Incompetence Defense to Share Housework', the *Wall Street Journal*, 21 February 1996, p. B1.

19 E. H. Schein, *Organizational Psychology*, 3rd edn (Englewood Cliffs, NJ: Prentice-Hall, 1980), p. 198. Four types of role ambiguity are discussed in M. A. Eys and A. V. Carron, 'Role Ambiguity, Task Cohesion and Self-Efficacy', *Small Group Research*, June 2001, pp. 356–73.

20 See K. D. Benne and P. Sheats, 'Functional Roles of Group Members', *Journal of Social Issues*, Spring 1948, pp. 41–9.

21 See H. J. Klein and P. W. Mulvey, 'Two Investigations of the Relationships among Group Goals, Goal Commitment, Cohesion, and Performance', *Organizational Behavior and Human Decision Processes*, January 1995, pp. 44–53; D. F. Crown and J. G. Rosse, 'Yours, Mine, and Ours: Facilitating Group Productivity through the Integration of Individual and Group Goals', *Organizational Behavior and Human Decision Processes*, November 1995, pp. 138–50; and A. L. Kristof-Brown and C. K. Stevens, 'Goal Congruence in Project Teams: Does the Fit Between Members' Personal Mastery and Performance Goals Matter?', *Journal of Applied Psychology*, no. 6, 2001, pp. 1083–95.

22 1 = A; 2 = C; 3 = A; 4 = A; 5 = C; 6 = A; 7 = C; 8 = A; 9 = C; 10 = C.

23 For more on norms, see K. L. Bettenhausen and K. J. Murnigham, 'The Development of an Intragroup Norm and the Effects of Intrapersonal and Structural Challenges', *Administrative Science Quarterly*, March 1991, pp. 20–35; R. I. Sutton, 'Maintaining Norms about Expressed Emotions; The Case of Bill Collectors', *Administrative Science Quarterly*, June 1991, pp. 245–68; R. D. Russell and C. J. Russell, 'An Examination of the Effects of Organisational Norms, Organizational Structure, and Environmental Uncertainty on Entrepreneurial Strategy', *Journal of Management*, December 1992, pp. 639–56; J. R. Hackman, 'Group Influences on Individuals in Organizations', in *Handbook of Industrial & Organizational Psychology*, vol. 3, 2nd edn, eds M. D. Dunnette and L. M. Hough (Palo Alto, CA: Consulting Psychologists Press, 1992), pp. 235–50; and T. Postmes, R. Spears and S. Cihangir, 'Quality of Decision Making and Group Norms', *Journal of Personality and Social Psychology*, no. 6, 2001, pp. 918–30.

24 See R. G. Netemeyer, M. W. Johnston, and S. Burton, 'Analysis of Role Conflict and Role Ambiguity in a Structural Equations Framework', *Journal of Applied Psychology*, April 1990, pp. 148–57; and G. W. McGee, C. E. Ferguson, Jr, and A. Seers, 'Role Conflict and Role Ambiguity: Do the Scales Measure These Two Constructs?', *Journal of Applied Psychology*, October 1989, pp. 815–18.

25 See S. E. Jackson and R. S. Schuler, 'A Meta-Analysis and Conceptual Critique of Research on Role Ambiguity and Role Conflict in Work Settings', *Organizational Behavior and Human Decision Processes*, August 1985, pp. 16–78. Also see L. A. King and D. W. King, 'Role Conflict and Role Ambiguity: A Critical Assessment of Construct Validity', *Psychological Bulletin*, January 1990, pp. 48–64.

26 For example, see B. Grofman, S. L. Feld and G. Owen, 'Group Size and the Performance of a Composite Group Majority: Statistical Truths and Empirical Results', *Organizational Behavior and Human Performance*, June 1984, pp. 350–59.

27 See P. Yetton and P. Bottger, 'The Relationships among Group Size, Member Ability, Social Decision Schemes, and Performance', *Organizational Behavior and Human Performance*, October 1983, pp. 145–59.

28 This copyrighted exercise may be found in J. Hall, 'Decisions, Decisions, Decisions', *Psychology Today*, November 1971, pp. 51–4, 86, 88.

29 P. Yetton and P. Bottger, 'The Relationships among Group Size, Member Ability, Social Decision Schemes, and Performance', *Organizational Behavior and Human Performance*, October 1983, p. 158.

30 Drawn from B. Mullen, C. Symons, L.-T. Hu and E. Salas, 'Group Size, Leadership Behavior, and Subordinate Satisfaction', *Journal of General Psychology*, April 1989, pp. 155–69. Also see P. Oliver and G. Marwell, 'The Paradox of Group Size in Collective Action: A Theory of the Critical Mass. II', *American Sociological Review*, February 1988, pp. 1–8.

31 Details of this study are presented in L. L. Thompson, E. A. Mannix and M. H. Bazerman, 'Group Negotiation: Effects of Decision Rule, Agenda and Aspiration', *Journal of Personality and Social Psychology*, January 1988, pp. 86–95.

32 See P. K. Hammerschmidt, 'The Kirton Adaption Innovation Inventory and Group Problem Solving Success Rates', *Journal of Creative Behavior*, First Quarter 1996, pp. 61–75; R. J. Volkema and R. H. Gorman, 'The Effect of Cognitive-Based Group

Composition on Decision-Making Process and Outcome', *Journal of Management Studies*, January 1998, pp. 105–21; S. G. Fisher, W. D. K. Macrosson and J. Wong, 'Cognitive Style and Team Role Preference', *Journal of Managerial Psychology*, no. 8, 1998, pp. 544–57; C. W. Allinson, S. J. Armstrong and J. Hayes, 'The Effects of Cognitive Style on Leader-Member Ex change: A Study of Manager-Subordinate Dyads', *Journal of Occupational and Organizational Psychology*, June 2001, pp. 201–20; K. W. Buffinton, K. W. Jablokow and K. A. Martin, 'Project Team Dynamics and Cognitive Style', *Engineering Management Journal*, September 2002, pp. 25–33; and M. M. Cheng, P. F. Luckett and A. K. D. Schulz, 'The Effects of Cognitive Style Diversity on Decision-Making Dyads: An Empirical Analysis in the Context of a Complex Task', *Behavioral Research in Accounting*, 2003, pp. 39–62.

33 See C. J. Jackson, 'Predicting Team Performance from a Learning Process Model', *Journal of Managerial Psychology*, no. 1/2, 2002, pp. 6–13; and D. A. Wyrick, 'Understanding Learning Styles to Be a More Effective Team Leader and Engineering Manager', *Engineering Management Journal*, March 2003, pp. 27–33.

34 See B. Barry and G. L. Stewart, 'Composition, Process, and Performance in Self-Managed Groups: The Role of Personality', *Journal of Applied Psychology*, no. 1, 1997, pp. 62–78; J. H. Bradley and F. J. Hebert, 'The Effect of Personality Type on Team Performance', *Journal of Management*, no. 5, 1997, pp. 337–65; S. L. Kichuk and W. H. Wiesner, 'Work Teams: Selecting Members for Optimal Performance', *Canadian Psychology*, no. 1/2, 1998, pp. 23–32; M. R. Barrick, G. L. Stewart, M. J. Neubert and M. K. Mount, 'Relating Member Ability and Personality to Work-Team Processes and Team Effectiveness', *Journal of Applied Psychology*, no. 3, 1998, pp. 377–91; G. A. Neuman, S. H. Wagner and N. L. Christiansen, 'The Relationship between Work-Team Personality Composition and the Job Performance of Teams', *Group & Organization Management*, March 1999, pp. 28–45; and A. E. M. van Vianen and C. K. W. De Dreu, 'Personality in Teams: Its Relationship to Social Cohesion, Task Cohesion, and Team Performance', *European Journal of Work and Organisational Psychology*, no. 2, 2001, pp. 97–120.

35 C. J. Jackson, 'Predicting Team Performance from a Learning Process Model', *Journal of Managerial Psychology*, no. 1/2, 2002, pp. 6–13.

36 B. Barry and G. L. Stewart, 'Composition, Process, and Performance in Self-Managed Groups: The Role of Personality', *Journal of Applied Psychology*, no. 1, 1997, pp. 62–78.

37 Based on a discussion in K. L. Unsworth and M. A. West, 'Teams: The Challenges of Cooperative Work', in *Introduction to Work and Organizational Psychology: A European Perspective*, ed. N. Chmiel (Oxford: Blackwell Publishers, 2000), pp. 327–46. Also see S. E. Jackson, K. E. May and K. Whitney, 'Understanding the Dynamics of Diversity in Decision-Making Teams', in *Team Effectiveness and Decision Making in Organizations*, eds R. A. Guzzo, E. Salas and Associates (San Francisco, CA: Jossey-Bass, 1995), pp. 204–61; S. E. Jackson, 'The Consequences of Diversity in Multidisciplinary Work Teams', in *Handbook of Work Group Psychology*, ed. M. A. West (Chichester: John Wiley, 1996), pp. 53–75; S. S. Webber and L. M. Donahue, 'Impact of Highly and Less Job-Related Diversity on Work Group Cohesion and Performance: A Meta-Analysis', *Journal of Management*, no. 2, 2001, pp. 141–62; A. Drach-Zahary and A. Somech, 'Team Heterogeneity and Its Relationship with Team Support and Team Effectiveness', *Journal of Educational Administration*, no. 1, 2002, pp. 44–66; and S. E. Jackson, A. Joshi and N. L. Erhardt, 'Recent Research on Team and Organizational Diversity: SWOT Analysis and Implications', *Journal of Management*, no. 6, 2003, pp. 801–30.

38 See, for instance, K. A. Bantel, 'Strategic Clarity in Banking: Role of Top Management Team Demography', *Psychological Reports*, December 1993, pp. 1187–201. An issue of *Journal of Organizational Behavior* (September 2004) is devoted to team diversity.

39 Based on the social identity theory, see M. Hogg and D. Abrams, *Social Identifications: A Social Psychology of Intergroup Relations and Group Processes* (London: Routledge, 1988); and J. C. Turner and K. J. Reynolds, 'The Social Identity Perspective in Intergroup Relations: Theories, Themes, and Controversies', in *Blackwell Handbook of Social Psychology: Intergroup Processes*, eds R. Brown and S. Gaertner (Oxford: Blackwell Publishing, 2001), pp. 133–52.

40 See for an overview, S. E. Jackson, A. Joshi and N. L. Erhardt, 'Recent Research on Team and Organizational Diversity: SWOT Analysis and Implications', *Journal of Management*, no. 6, 2003, pp. 801–30.

41 D. R. Ilgen, 'Teams Embedded in Organizations: Some Implications', *American Psychologist*, February 1999, p. 136.

42 R. R. Blake and J. Srygley Mouton, 'Don't Let Group Norms Stifle Creativity', *Personnel*, August 1985, p. 29.

43 For additional information, see S. E. Asch, *Social Psychology* (Englewood Cliffs, NJ: Prentice-Hall, 1952), ch. 16.

44 R. McNamara, *In Retrospect: The Tragedy and Lessons of Vietnam* (New York: Times Books, 1995).

45 I. L. Janis, *Groupthink, second edition* (Boston, MA: Houghton Mifflin, 1982), p. 9. Alternative models are discussed in K. Granstrom and D. Stwine, 'A Bipolar Model of Groupthink: An Extension of Janis's Concept', *Small Group Research*, February 1998, pp. 32–56; and A. R. Flippen, 'Understanding Groupthink from a Self-Regulatory Perspective', *Small Group Research*, April 1999, pp. 139–65.

46 I. L. Janis, *Groupthink, second edition* (Boston, MA: Houghton Mifflin, 1982), p. 9. For an alternative model, see R. J. Aldag and S. Riggs Fuller, 'Beyond Fiasco: A Reappraisal of the Groupthink Phenomenon and a New Model of Group Decision Processes', *Psychological Bulletin*, May 1993, pp. 533–52. Also see A. A. Mohamed and F. A. Wiebe, 'Toward a Process Theory of Groupthink', *Small Group Research*, August 1996, pp. 416–30.

47 Based on discussion in B. Latane, K. Williams and S. Harkins, 'Many Hand Make Light the Work: The Causes and Consequences of Social Loafing', *Journal of Personality and Social Psychology*, June 1979, pp. 822–32; and D. A. Kravitz and B. Martin, 'Ringelmann Rediscovered: The Original Article', *Journal of Personality and Social Psychology*, May 1986, pp. 936–41.

48 See J. A. Shepperd, 'Productivity Loss in Performance Groups: A Motivation Analysis', *Psychological Bulletin*, January 1993, pp. 67–81; R. E. Kidwell, Jr and N. Bennett, 'Employee Propensity to Withhold Effort: A Conceptual Model to Intersect Three Avenues of Research', *Academy of Management Review*, July 1993, pp. 429–56; and S. J. Karau and K. D. Williams, 'Social Loafing: Meta-Analytic Review and Theoretical Integration', *Journal of Personality and Social Psychology*, October 1993, pp. 681–706.

[49] See T. P. Williams and S. Sogon, 'Group Composition and Conforming Behavior in Japanese Students', *Japanese Psychological Research*, November 1984, pp. 231–4; and T. Amir, 'The Asch Conformity Effect: A Study in Kuwait', *Social Behavior and Personality*, July 1984, pp. 187–90.

[50] N. Nicholson, S. G. Cole and T. Rocklin, 'Conformity in the Asch Situation: A Comparison Between Contemporary British and US University Students', *British Journal of Social Psychology*, February 1985, pp. 59–63.

[51] Data from R. Bond and P. B. Smith, 'Culture and Conformity: A Meta-Analysis of Studies Using Asch's Line Judgment Task', *Psychological Bulletin*, January 1996, pp. 111–37.

[52] Details of this study may be found in M. R. Callaway and J. K. Esser, 'Groupthink: Effects of Cohesiveness and Problem-Solving Procedures on Group Decision Making', *Social Behavior and Personality*, July 1984, pp. 157–64. See also C. R. Leana, 'A Partial Test of Janis's Groupthink Model: Effects of Group Cohesiveness and Leader-Behavior on Defective Decision Making', *Journal of Management*, Spring 1985, pp. 5–17; G. Moorhead and J. R. Montanari, 'An Empirical Investigation of the Groupthink Phenomenon', *Human Relations*, May 1986, pp. 399–410; and J. N. Choi and M. U. Kim, 'The Organizational Application of Groupthink and its Limits in Organizations', *Journal of Applied Psychology*, April 1999, pp. 297–306.

[53] W. Park, 'A Comprehensive Empirical Investigation of the Relationships among Variables of the Groupthink Model', *Journal of Organizational Behavior*, December 2001, pp. 873–87.

[54] Adapted from discussion in I. L. Janis, *Groupthink, second edition* (Boston, MA: Houghton Mifflin, 1982), ch. 11.

[55] See S. J. Zaccaro, 'Social Loafing: The Role of Task Attractiveness', *Personality and Social Psychology Bulletin*, March 1984, pp. 99–106; J. M. Jackson and K. D. Williams, 'Social Loafing on Difficult Tasks: Working Collectively Can Improve Performance', *Journal of Personality and Social Psychology*, October 1985, pp. 937–42; and J. M. George, 'Extrinsic and Intrinsic Origins of Perceived Social Loafing in Organizations', *Academy of Management Journal*, March 1992, pp. 191–202.

[56] For complete details, see K. Williams, S. Harkins and B. Latane, 'Identifiability as a Deterrent to Social Loafing: Two Cheering Experiments', *Journal of Personality and Social Psychology*, February 1981, pp. 303–11.

[57] See J. M. Jackson and S. G. Harkins, 'Equity in Effort: An Explanation of the Social Loafing Effect', *Journal of Personality and Social Psychology*, November 1985, pp. 1199–206.

[58] Both studies are reported in S. G. Harkins and K. Szymanski, 'Social Loafing and Group Evaluation', *Journal of Personality and Social Psychology*, June 1989, pp. 934–41.

[59] Data from J. A. Wagner III, 'Studies of Individualism-Collectivism: Effects on Cooperation in Groups', *Academy of Management Journal*, February 1995, pp. 152–72. See also P. W. Mulvey and H. J. Klein, 'The Impact of Perceived Loafing and Collective Efficacy on Group Goal Processes and Group Performance', *Organizational Behavior and Human Decision Processes*, April 1998, pp. 62–87; P. W. Mulvey, L. Bowes-Sperry and H. J. Klein, 'The Effects of Perceived Loafing and Defensive Impression Management on Group Effectiveness', *Small Group Research*, June 1998, pp. 394–415; and L. Karakowsky and K. Mcbey, 'Do My Contributions Matter? The Influence of Imputed Expertise on Member Involvement and Self-Evalutions in the Work Group', *Group & Organization Management*, March 2001, pp. 70–92.

[60] R. C. Liden, S. J. Wayne, R. A. Jaworski and N. Bennett, 'Social Loafing: A Field Investigation', *Journal of Management*, June 2004, pp. 285–304.

[61] S. G. Rogelberg, J. L. Barnes-Farrell and C. A. Lowe, 'The Stepladder Technique: An Alternative Group Structure Facilitating Effective Group Decision Making', *Journal of Applied Psychology*, October 1992, p. 730. Also see S. G. Rogelberg and M. S. O'Connor, 'Extending the Stepladder Technique: An Examination of Self-Paced Stepladder Groups', *Group Dynamics: Theory, Research, and Practice*, no. 2, 1998, pp. 82–91.

[62] Twenty items excerpted from S. A. Wheelan and J. M. Hochberger, 'Validation Studies of the Group Development Questionnaire', *Small Group Research*, February 1996, pp. 143–70.

[63] D. A. Whetten and K. S. Cameron, *Developing Management Skills* (Glenview, IL: Scott, Foresman and Company, 1984). Copyright © 1984 by Scott, Foresman and Company. Reprinted by permission of Addison Wesley Educational Publishers, Inc.

Chapter 8

Teams and teamwork

Learning Outcomes

When you finish studying the material in this chapter, you should be able to:

- distinguish between a 'team' and a 'group'
- identify and describe the four types of work teams
- explain the ecological model of work team effectiveness
- discuss why teams fail
- list at least three things organisations can do to build trust
- distinguish two types of cohesiveness and summarise the related research findings
- define quality circles, virtual teams and self-managed teams

Opening Case Study: Miracle on the Hudson

There was only time for one clear order from the US Airways airplane pilot to the passengers: 'Prepare for impact!' Seconds later, he performed a successful emergency landing on the Hudson River off Manhattan, New York, just six minutes after taking off from La Guardia Airport.

During its initial climb, the plane hit a flock of geese, disabling both its engines. Unable to reach any of the nearby airports, an emergency landing on the Hudson was the pilot's only option.

Miraculously, all 155 passengers on board survived and apart from a few broken limbs, no one was seriously hurt. The fact that the pilot was able to land the plane on the river was a testament to his many years of training and dedication, but the great team of pilot, co-pilot and the rest of the crew played a significant part in this success.

When the emergency landing was inevitable, all parts of the team automatically started the necessary procedures – preparing the plane for a landing on water, calming passengers and helping passengers climb out of the plane, once it had landed on the river.

The flight crew had been widely praised for their actions during the incident, and then, President-elect Barack Obama invited the crew to attend his inauguration as President in Washington, D.C., five days later.

For discussion

Does the true value of teamwork most clearly show itself in times of crisis?

Sources: Based on NBC News, 'Miracle on the Hudson', available online at www.nbcnewyork.com/news/local-beat/Miracle-on-the-Hudson.html; www.msnbc.msn.com/id/28678669/.

Teams and teamwork are popular terms in organisations these days. Cynics might dismiss teamwork as just another fad or quick-fix gimmick. But a closer look reveals a more profound and durable trend. Following the economic recession in the 1980s, American and European companies did some introspection. Work redesign projects in work teams like Volvo in Sweden were the result. Also, errors of high visibility like airline accidents revealed a lack of teamwork. Moreover, the general movement towards flatter structures of organisation and reducing the layers of middle management (see also Chapter 14) increased the empowerment of employees and stressed the importance of effective teamwork. Lastly, teamwork was a solution to respond to the increased diversity in the marketplace.

There are some common traits at the heart of the most admired companies, and teamwork turned out to be a very important element.[1] According to management expert Peter Drucker, tomorrow's organisations will be flatter, information-based and organised around teams.[2] This opinion was bolstered by a survey of human resource executives in which 44 per cent called for more teamwork when asked what change employees need to make to achieve current business goals.[3] This means virtually all employees will need to polish their team skills. According to some managers, even scientists and information technology specialists, who are traditionally regarded as individualists and who rely mainly on technical skills to fulfil their jobs, will have to take on a broader role in the future.

Examples of the trend towards teams and teamwork abound. What are the advantages for organisations for implementing team-based working?

- Teams enable organisations to develop and deliver products and services speedily and cost-effectively, while retaining high quality.
- Teams enable organisations to learn and keep on learning more effectively.
- Innovation is promoted because of cross-fertilisation of ideas.
- Teams can integrate and process information in ways that individuals cannot.
- Teamwork can help to improve productivity.[4]

The emphasis in this chapter is on tapping the full and promising potential of teams. We will identify different types of work teams, introduce a model of team effectiveness, discuss keys to effective teamwork, review team-building techniques and explore applications of the team concept. One important approach to teams is not covered in this chapter, the team effectiveness model developed by J. Richard Hackman.[5] This model is also the foundation for the TDS (team diagnostic survey), which we discuss in Chapter 16.

Before moving on, it is necessary to make the distinction between the terms 'group' and 'team'. In some contexts the two words are used interchangeably, but in an organisational behavioural setting there is a difference. Guzzo[6] states that all teams are groups but not all groups are teams, as the word 'group' is used very extensively in general social sciences to even indicate social aggregates in which there is no interdependence of members (the latter being a crucial element to define a team).[7] Studies of many different kinds of teams – from athletic to corporate to military – concluded that successful teams tend to take on a life of their own. Thus, a **team** is defined as 'a small number of people with complementary skills who are committed to a common purpose, performance goals and approach for which they hold themselves mutually accountable'.[8] Relative to Tuckman's theory of group development (see Chapter 7) – forming, storming, norming, performing and adjourning – teams are task groups that have matured to the performing stage (but not slipped into decay).

Definitions of teams generally suggest a number of conditions which must be fulfilled before a group becomes a team:

- Members of the group have shared goals in relation to their work.
- They interact with each other to achieve those shared goals.
- All team members have well-defined and interdependent roles.
- They have an organisational identity as a team, with a defined organisational function.[9]

When Katzenbach and Smith refer to 'a small number of people' in their definition, they mean between two and 25 team members. Generally, they found effective teams to have fewer than 10 members, and other studies in the US and Canada have shown the average team size to be 10 with eight being the most common size.[10]

8.1 Team effectiveness

Imagine that you are a department head charged with making an important staffing decision amid the following circumstances. You need to form eight three-person task teams from a pool of 24 employees. Based on each of the employee's prior work records and their scores on ability tests, you know that 12 have high ability and 12 have low ability. The crux of your problem is how to assign the 12 high-ability employees. Should you spread your best talent around by making sure there are both high- and low-ability employees on each team? Then again, you may want to concentrate your best talent by forming four high-ability teams and four low-ability teams. Or should you attempt to find a compromise between these two extremes?

One field experiment provided an instructive and interesting answer.

OB in Real Life

The Israeli tank-crew study

Researchers from Tel Aviv University systematically manipulated the composition of 208 three-man tank crews. All possible combinations of high- and low-ability personnel were studied (high-high-high; high-high-low; high-low-low; and low-low-low). Ability was a composite measure of (1) overall intelligence, (2) amount of formal education, (3) proficiency in Hebrew and (4) interview ratings. Successful operation of the tanks required the three-man crews to perform with a high degree of synchronised interdependence. Tank-crew effectiveness was determined by commanding officers during military manoeuvres for the Israel defence forces.

As expected, the high-high high ability tank crews performed the best and the low-low-low the worst. But the researchers discovered an important interaction effect: each member's achievement was influenced by the performance of the other members.

The interaction effect also worked in a negative direction because the low-low-low ability crews performed far below expected levels. Moreover, as illustrated in Figure 8.1, significantly greater performance gains were achieved by creating high-high-high ability crews than by upgrading low-low-low ability crews with one or two high-ability members.

This brings us back to the staffing problem at the beginning of this section. Tziner and Eden recommended that the most productive solution would be to allocate six highs and all 12 lows to six teams of high-low-low ability and to assign the six remaining highs to two teams of high-high-high ability, thus avoiding the low-low-low combination with its extremely low performance and leaving a number of high-high-high performance teams. Their research showed that talent is used most efficiently when concentrated and not when spread around.[11]

Figure 8.1 Ability of Israeli Tank-Crew Members and Improvements of Effectiveness

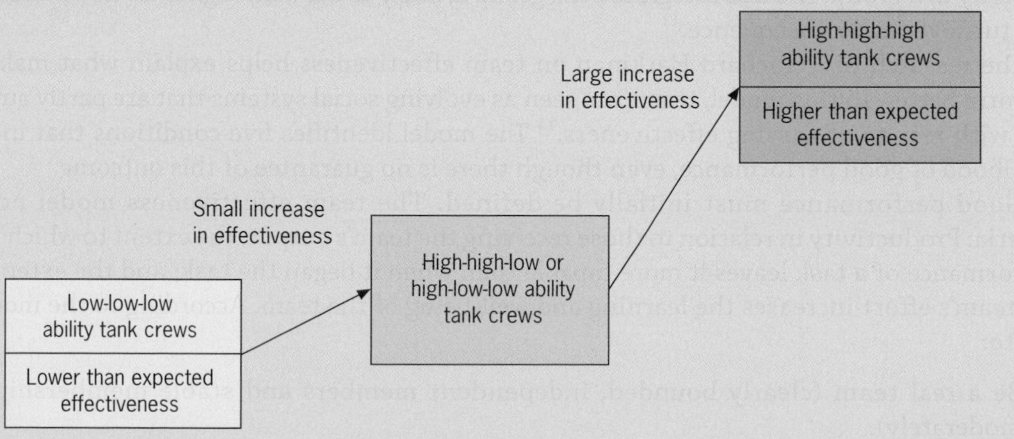

Figure 8.2 A Contingency Model for Staffing Work Teams: Effective Use of Available Talent

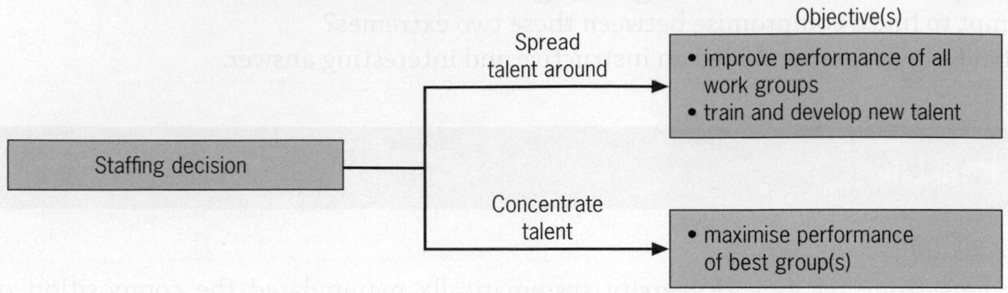

HR

While the real-life aspect of the tank-crew study makes its results fairly generalisable, a qualification is in order. Specifically, modern complex organisations demand a more flexible contingency approach. Figure 8.2 shows two basic contingencies. If organisations seek to improve the performance of all groups or train novices, high-ability personnel can be spread around. This option would be appropriate in a high-volume production operation. However, if the desired outcome is to maximise performance of the best group(s), then high-ability personnel should be concentrated. This second option would be advisable in research and development departments, for example, where technological breakthroughs need to be achieved. Extraordinary achievements require clusters of extraordinary talent.[12]

Critical thinking

Would you expect the results from the tank-crew experiment to change, if the team members were told their competence levels?

More diverse teams may be able to consider a broader range of perspectives and to generate more high-quality alternative solutions than less diverse groups. At the same time, the greater the diversity in a group, the less integrated the group is likely to be, with higher levels of dissatisfaction and turnover as a consequence.[13]

The research of J. Richard Hackman on team effectiveness helps explain what makes a team perform better. In this model, teams are seen as evolving social systems that are partly autonomous and with results of varying effectiveness.[14] The model identifies five conditions that increase the likelihood of good performance, even though there is no guarantee of this outcome.

Good performance must initially be defined. The team effectiveness model notes three criteria: Productivity in relation to those receiving the team's output, the extent to which the team's performance of a task leaves it more capable than when it began the task, and the extent to which the team's effort increases the learning and well-being of the team. According to the model a team has to:

- Be a real team (clearly bounded, independent members and stable membership, at least moderately).
- Have a compelling direction (with a clearly specified purpose).

- Have an enabling structure with clearly aligned task design and purpose (a small team with good diversity, not too much and not too little, and mutually agreed core norms of conduct).
- Have a supportive organisational context (in terms of positive rewards for excellent team performance, availability of upgrades of skills, knowledge and experience, and full access to any information the team needs to carry out its tasks).
- Have access to expert coaching (particularly in relation to the first three items).

Of course, ability is only one way in which people differ. In the next section, groups are composed based on personality differences. In that regard, it is better to create mixed groups.

8.2 Team roles and team players

Meredith Belbin developed a framework for understanding roles within a team.[15] His framework is very popular and widely used. People are typically chosen for functional roles on the basis of experience and not personal characteristics or aptitudes. Belbin's idea is that the most consistently successful groups comprise a range of different roles (based on personal characteristics) undertaken by various members. Belbin identified nine (initially eight) different roles (see Table 8.1).

Table 8.1 Different Roles in Teams

Team Role	Contribution	Allowable Weaknesses
Plant	Creative, imaginative, free-thinking. Generates ideas and solves difficult problems.	Ignores incidentals. Too preoccupied to communicate effectively.
Resource Investigator	Outgoing, enthusiastic communicative. Explores opportunities and develops contacts.	Over optimistic. Loses interest once initial enthusiasm has passed.
Co-ordinator	Mature, confident, identifies talent. Clarifies goals. Delegates effectively.	Can be seen as manipulative. Offloads own share of the work.
Shaper	Challenging, dynamic, thrives on pressure. Has the drive and courage to overcome obstacles.	Prone to provocation. Offends people's feelings.
Monitor Evaluator	Sober, strategic and discerning. Sees all options and judges accurately.	Lacks drive and ability to inspire others. Can be overly critical.
Teamworker	Co-operative, perceptive and diplomatic. Listens and averts friction.	Indecisive in crunch situations. Avoids confrontation.
Implementer	Practical, reliable, efficient. Turns ideas into actions and organises work that needs to be done.	Somewhat inflexible. Slow to respond to new possibilities.
Completer Finisher	Painstaking, conscientious, anxious. Searches out errors. Polishes and perfects.	Inclined to worry unduly. Reluctant to delegate.
Specialist	Single-minded, self-starting, dedicated. Provides knowledge and skills in rare supply.	Contributes only on a narrow front. Dwells on technicalities.

Source: Based on R. M. Belbin, Team Roles at Work (London: Butterworth-Heinemann, 1993).

In creative groups, there is a balance of all these roles. The different people fulfil roles that are complementary to one another. This does not mean that every group has to consist of nine people. A single person can play several roles. As can be seen in Table 8.1, the nine roles have their own characteristics, positive qualities and allowable weaknesses.

The nine roles can be classified into three broader categories: do-roles (the implementer, the shaper, the completer-finisher), think-roles (the specialist, the monitor-evaluator, the plant) and social roles (the resource investigator, the team worker, the co-ordinator). It is important that at least these three basic categories in your group are represented in order to be successful.

Evidence about Belbin's team roles

Belbin's theory has been studied extensively. Some of these studies were rather critical. There is little empirical evidence for the theory: it is difficult to find objective measures of team success that can be related to team composition. Moreover, Belbin uses a self-perception questionnaire to measure people's roles. The use of peer ratings, for instance, would be a more objective measure. Some research[16] into the reliability of the Belbin Self-Perception Inventory has concluded that internal consistency reliability is poor, raising concerns about the validity of the inventory as a selection and development tool. Swailes and McIntyre-Bhattty,[17] however, found that for a large data set results show that the internal consistency of item responses is better than previous research suggests and tends towards the boundary of which internal consistency is considered acceptable in social and psychological research.

Despite possible doubts about the value of Belbin's Self-Perception Inventory, it remains a popular method to examine teams and to compare the roles of individual team members. Balderson and Broderick state that in their 'experience, the very high face validity and acceptability of the measures . . . suggest that the . . . team roles proposed do have some validity even if aspects of their measurement may benefit from further scrutiny'.[18]

Identifying and developing good team players

Anyone who is familiar with wilderness hiking and camping knows the folly of heading for the wilds without proper gear and skills. One's life can depend on being able to conserve fluids, prevent hypothermia and avoid dangerous situations. So, too, organisations need to make sure teams are staffed with appropriately skilled people. Michael J. Stevens and Michael A. Campion developed a very useful model for assessing one's readiness for teamwork.[19] It lists the knowledge, skills and abilities (KSAs) needed for both team member and team success (see Table 8.2). Three of the KSAs are interpersonal: conflict resolution, collaborative problem-solving and communication. Two KSAs involve self-management: goal setting and performance management, and planning and task co-ordination. As an integrated package, these five KSAs are a template for the team players we need today. Professionals in team-oriented organisations need to be mindful of these KSAs when recruiting, hiring, staffing and training. How do you measure up? Where do you need improvement?

However, it is clear that staffing work teams on the basis of individual-task KSAs alone is not enough. Other characteristics of individual team members also facilitate team functioning, such as people's preferences, personality and interaction styles (see Chapter 7).[20]

Table 8.2 Good Team Players have the Right Knowledge, Skills and Abilities

Interpersonal KSAs

1 Conflict resolution KSAs

Recognising types and sources of conflict; encouraging desirable conflict but discouraging undesirable conflict; and employing integrative (win-win) negotiation strategies rather than distributive (win-lose) strategies.

2 Collaborative problem-solving KSAs

Identifying situations requiring participative group problem-solving and using the proper degree of participation; and recognising obstacles to collaborative group problem-solving and implementing corrective actions.

3 Communicative KSAs

Understanding effective communication networks and using decentralised networks where possible; recognising open and supportive communication methods; maximising the consistency between nonverbal and verbal messages; recognising and interpreting the non-verbal messages of others; and engaging in and understanding the importance of small-task and ritual greetings.

Self-management KSAs

4 Goal-setting and performance management KSAs

Establishing specific, challenging and accepted team goals; and monitoring, evaluating and providing feedback on both overall team performance and individual team-member performance.

5 Planning and task co-ordination KSAs

Co-ordinating and synchronising activities, information and tasks between team members, as well as aiding the team in establishing individual task and role assignments that ensure the proper balance of workload between team members.

Source: L. Miller, 'Reexamining Teamwork KSAs and Team Performance', Small Group Research, December 2001, Table I, p. 748, as adapted from M. J. Stevens and M. A. Campion, 'The Knowledge, Skill, and Ability Requirements for Teamwork: Implications for Human Resource Management', *Journal of Management*, Summer 1994, Table I, p. 505.

8.3 Work-team effectiveness: an ecological model

The effectiveness of athletic teams is a straightforward matter of counting the competitions you win against those you lose. Things become more complicated, however, when the focus shifts to work teams in today's organisations.[21] Figure 8.3 lists two effectiveness criteria for work teams: performance and viability. According to Sundstrom and his colleagues: 'Performance means acceptability of output to customers within or outside the organisation who receive team products, services, information, decisions or performance events (such as presentations or competitions).' While the foregoing relates to satisfying the needs and expectations of outsiders, such as clients, customers and fans, another team-effectiveness criterion arises – namely, **team viability** which is defined as team member satisfaction and continued willingness to contribute. Are the team members better or worse off for having contributed to the team effort?[22] A work team is not truly effective if it gets the job done but self-destructs in the process or burns everyone out.

Figure 8.3 is an ecological model because it portrays work teams within their organisational environment. In keeping with the true meaning of the word ecology – the study of interactions between organisms and their environments – this model emphasises that work teams need an organisational life-support system. Six critical organisational context variables are listed in Figure 8.3. Work teams have a much greater chance of being effective if they are nurtured and

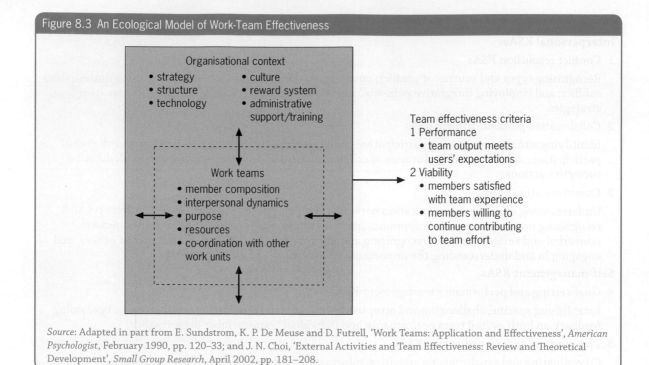

Figure 8.3 An Ecological Model of Work-Team Effectiveness

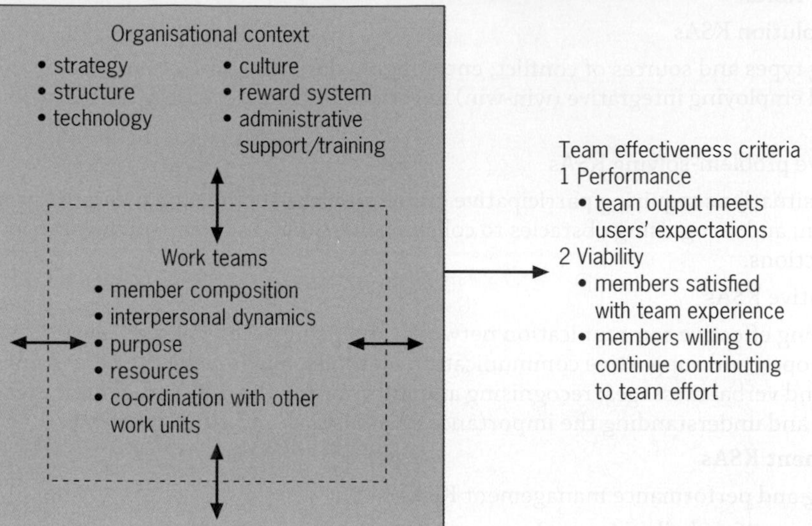

Source: Adapted in part from E. Sundstrom, K. P. De Meuse and D. Futrell, 'Work Teams: Application and Effectiveness', *American Psychologist*, February 1990, pp. 120–33; and J. N. Choi, 'External Activities and Team Effectiveness: Review and Theoretical Development', *Small Group Research*, April 2002, pp. 181–208.

helped by the organisation. The team's purpose needs to be in concert with the organisation's strategy. Similarly, team participation and autonomy require an organisational culture that values those processes. Team members also need appropriate technological tools and training. Teamwork needs to be reinforced by the organisational reward system (also see Chapter 6). Such is not the case when pay and bonuses are tied solely to individual output.

Five important factors of the internal processes of work teams are listed in Figure 8.3. Contained in Table 8.3 is an expanded list of team characteristics which can prove useful in evaluating task teams.[23]

Why do work teams fail? Pitfalls and stumbling blocks

Advocates of the team approach paint a very optimistic and bright picture, but teams are not a managerial cure all.[24] They are used for problems where technological change, radical decisions or individual excellence would be a better solution. No wonder that many managers express their disillusionment with the results of their team-working initiatives.

Often, the problems stem from the fact that teams are seen as an end rather than a means. When implemented unwisely, teamwork can turn into an organisational nightmare. For example, reflect on what probably happened at the European headquarters of Citrix Corporation in Shaffhausen, Switzerland, where a marketing executive quoted: 'Teamwork is a lot of people doing what I say.'[25]

Although these words sound extreme, teams can and often do fail. The American team specialist Richard Whitely speaks of a disease called teamitis.[26] Anyone contemplating the use of team structures in the workplace, therefore, needs a balanced perspective on their advantages and limitations. In their daily work with various companies, the British consultants Rob Yeung

Table 8.3 Characteristics of an Effective Team

1 Clear purpose	The vision, mission, goal or task of the team has been defined and is now accepted by everyone. There is an action plan
2 Informality	The climate tends to be informal, comfortable and relaxed. There are no obvious tensions or signs of boredom
3 Participation	There is much discussion, and everyone is encouraged to participate
4 Listening	The members use effective listening techniques such as questioning, paraphrasing and summarising to get out ideas
5 Civilised disagreement	There is disagreement, but the team is comfortable with this and shows no signs of avoiding, smoothing over or suppressing conflict
6 Consensus decisions	For important decisions, the goal is substantial but not necessarily unanimous agreement through open discussion of everyone's ideas, avoidance of formal voting or easy compromises
7 Open communication	Team members feel free to express their feelings on the tasks as well as on the group's operation. There are few hidden agendas. Communication takes place outside of meetings
8 Clear roles and work assignments	There are clear expectations about the roles played by each team member. When action is taken, clear assignments are made, accepted and carried out. Work is fairly distributed among team members
9 Shared leadership	While the team has a formal leader, leadership functions shift from time to time depending on the circumstances, the needs of the group and the skills of the members. The formal leader models the appropriate behaviour and helps establish positive norms
10 External relations	The team spends time developing key outside relationships, mobilising resources and building credibility with important players in other parts of the organisation
11 Style diversity	The team has a broad spectrum of team-player types, including members who emphasise attention to task, goal setting, focus on process and questions about how the team is functioning
12 Self-assessment	Periodically, the team stops to examine how well it is functioning and what may be interfering with its effectiveness

Source: G. M. Parker, Team Players and Teamwork: *The New Competitive Business Strategy* (San Francisco, CA: Jossey-Bass, 1990), p. 33.

and Sebastian Bailey encounter the following most frequently observed symptoms when implementing teamwork:[27]

- *Hidden agendas*: a belief that certain members of the team are secretly building their own empires or furthering their own careers rather than working for the good of the organisation.
- *Lack of understanding*: misconceptions about why the team has been brought together are common when a team is first formed.
- *Lack of leadership*: the team leader does not have the skills required to manage the team effectively. Sometimes, it may be that no one member is recognised by all as the leader.
- *Wrong mix of team members*: for example, there are 'creative types' who love to generate ideas but cannot focus on detail, while there are 'doers' who would rather not contribute to discussions and prefer to be given tasks to do. A team that is unevenly balanced could either generate ideas but fail to implement them, or alternatively, discover that it does not have any ideas to implement (also see Chapter 9).
- *Unhealthy team environment*: for example, the team is unable to cope under pressure.

Figure 8.4 Why Work Teams Fail

Mistakes typically made by management

- teams cannot overcome weak strategies and poor business practices
- hostile environment for teams (command-and-control culture; competitive/individual reward plans; management resistance)
- teams adopted as a fad, a quick fix; no long-term commitment
- lessons from one team not transferred to others (limited experimentation with teams)
- vague or conflicting team assignments
- inadequate team skills training
- poor staffing of teams
- lack of trust

Unrealistic expectations resulting in frustration

Problems typically experienced by team members

- team tries to do too much too soon
- conflict over differences in personal work styles (and/or personality conflicts)
- too much emphasis on results, not enough on team processes and group dynamics
- unanticipated obstacle causes team to give up
- resistance to doing things differently
- poor interpersonal skills (aggressive rather than assertive communication, destructive conflict, win-lose negotiation)
- poor interpersonal chemistry (loners, dominators, self-appointed experts do not fit in)
- lack of trust

Source: Adapted from discussion in S. R. Rayner, 'Team Traps: What They Are, How to Avoid Them', *National Productivity Review*, Summer 1996, pp. 110–15; L. Holpp and R. Phillips, 'When Is a Team Its Own Worst Enemy?', *Training*, September 1995, pp. 71–82; and B. Richardson, 'Why Work Teams Flop – and What Can Be Done About It', *National Productivity Review*, Winter 1994/95, pp. 9–13.

If teams are to be effective, both management and team members must make a concerted effort to think and do things differently. Figure 8.4 presents a useful summary of various stumbling blocks and pitfalls, which managers and team members must bear in mind if they want to avoid the above problems.

According to the centre of Figure 8.4, the main threats to team effectiveness are unrealistic expectations leading to frustration and lack of trust. Frustration, in turn, encourages people to abandon teams. Both managers and team members can be victimised by unrealistic expectations.[28] On the upper side of Figure 8.4 is a list of common management mistakes. These mistakes generally involve doing a poor job of creating a supportive environment for teams and teamwork. On the lower side of Figure 8.4 is a list of common problems for team members. Contrary to critics' Theory X contention (Chapter 1) that employees lack the motivation and creativity for real teamwork, it is common for teams to take on too much too quickly and to drive themselves too hard for fast results. Important group dynamics and team skills get lost in the rush for results. Consequently, team members' expectations need to be given a reality check by management and team members themselves. Also, teams need to be counselled against quitting when they run into an unanticipated obstacle. Failure is part of the learning process for teams, as it is elsewhere in life. Comprehensive training in interpersonal skills can prevent many common teamwork problems.

Critical thinking

With new generations (Generation Y, native to the Internet and mobile communication and networking) entering the workplace, how do you expect the nature of teamwork to change?

Evidence about teams

After conducting a meta-analysis of 122 studies encompassing a wide variety of subjects and settings, one team of researchers concluded the following:

- Co-operation is superior to competition in promoting achievement and productivity.
- Co-operation is superior to individualistic efforts in promoting achievement and productivity.
- Co-operation without intergroup competition promotes higher achievement and productivity than co-operation with intergroup competition.[29]

Given the size and diversity of the research base, these findings strongly endorse co-operation in modern organisations. Co-operation can be encouraged by reward systems[30] that reinforce teamwork as well as individual achievement (see also Chapter 6). Interestingly, co-operation can be encouraged by quite literally tearing down walls, or not building them in the first place.

There is a movement among architects and urban planners to design and build structures that encourage spontaneous interaction, co-operation and teamwork.[31] Research suggests that organisations can enhance equal employment opportunity and diversity programmes by encouraging voluntary helping behaviour in interracial work teams.[32] Accordingly, it is reasonable to conclude that voluntary helping behaviour could build co-operation in mixed-gender teams and groups as well. Remember Chapters 4 and 7 showed that 'diversity' should include more than just racial or gender differences.

8.4 Team building

Team building is a catch-all term for a whole host of techniques aimed at improving the internal functioning of work teams. Whether conducted by company trainers or outside consultants, team-building workshops strive for greater co-operation, better communication and less dysfunctional conflict. Experiential learning techniques, such as interpersonal trust exercises, conflict-handling role-play sessions and interactive games, are common. For example, Germany's Opel uses Lego® blocks to teach its car workers the tight teamwork necessary for just-in-time production. Meanwhile, Hamburg Mannheimer organised a three-day rafting trip in the French Alps: 15 staff who were performing well went on an adventure survival camp, including mountain climbing and bungee-jumping. Insurance company, Axa, sends its managers to a wine chateau in Bordeaux for management training, including team-building activities in the form of role play and simulations of business situations.

Complete coverage of the many team-building techniques would require a separate book. Consequently, the scope of our current discussion is limited to the goal of team building and the day-to-day development of self-management skills. This foundation is intended to give you a basis for selecting appropriate team-building techniques from the many you are likely to encounter in the years ahead.[33]

The goal of team building: high-performance teams

Team building allows team members to wrestle with simulated or real-life problems. Outcomes are then analysed by the team to determine what team processes need improvement. Learning stems from recognising and addressing faulty team dynamics. Perhaps, one sub-team withheld key information from another, thereby hampering team progress. With cross-cultural teams becoming commonplace in today's global economy, team building is more important than ever.

OB in Real Life

Turning corporate team building into a circus

Are you ready to take your corporate team to new heights? Prepare yourself, because the next departmental meeting may cover the flying trapeze, acrobatic balancing and tight-wire walking, that is, if the next meeting takes place at Circus Space.

Besides being one of Europe's top circus facilities, London's Circus Space offers programmes designed to help corporate groups learn the circus way when it comes to teamwork, leadership, communication and trust. While many companies claim these values, incorporating them into the workplace can be tricky.

'When an acrobatic or flying trapeze troupe works with a director on a new act for the show, they are inherently creating a successful team that trusts and relies on each other to create an end result', says Adult Programme Manager Rob Colbert. 'Likewise in business, you need a productive team that works well together.'

The tailor-made classes, which attempt to teach a different view of the simple goal, have attracted a word-of-mouth-based audience comprised of companies such as UBS Warburg, Disney, Microsoft, International Distillers and Unilever. Colbert attributes Circus Space's success to its unusual method of training.

'The main criticism of other team-building workshops from our clients is that they are either too dull or competitive, and this is where the circus training has come in', Colbert says. 'Our courses offer a shared physical experience where participants can directly gain new ways of learning and a real sense of achievement, develop a mutual support and respect for each other and have the opportunity to use the skills as a powerful management metaphor.'

Colbert says that just by coming to Circus Space, companies are stepping in the right direction. 'If companies employ us to be creative with their new recruits, then companies are sending a powerful message about their expectations and how they want their new employees to work', he explains. 'Whereas with managers and directors, the companies are saying: "We want you to open up and look at new possibilities, take risks and be creative."'[34]

According to Richard Beckhard, a respected authority on organisation development, the four purposes of team building are:

- To set goals and/or priorities.
- To analyse or allocate the way work is performed.
- To examine the way a group is working and its processes (such as norms, decision-making and communication).
- To examine relationships among the people doing the work.[35]

A nationwide survey of team members from many organisations undertaken by Wilson Learning Corporation provides a useful model or benchmark of what we should expect of teams. The researchers' question was simply: 'What is a high-performance team?'[36] The respondents were asked to describe their peak experiences in work teams. Analysis of the survey results yielded the following eight attributes of high-performance teams:

- *Participative leadership*: creating an interdependency by empowering, freeing up and serving others.
- *Shared responsibility*: establishing an environment in which all team members feel as responsible as the manager for the performance of the work unit.
- *Aligned on purpose*: having a sense of common purpose about why the team exists and the function it serves.
- *Good communication*: creating a climate of trust and open, honest communication.
- *Future focused*: seeing change as an opportunity for growth.
- *Focused on task*: keeping meetings focused on results.
- *Creative talents*: applying individual talents and creativity.
- *Rapid response*: identifying and acting on opportunities.[37]

These eight attributes effectively combine many of today's most progressive ideas on management,[38] among them being participation, empowerment, a service ethic, individual responsibility and development, self-management, trust, active listening and envisioning. But patience and diligence are also required. According to a manager familiar with work teams, 'high-performance teams may take three to five years to build'.[39] Let us keep this inspiring model of high-performance teams in mind as we conclude our discussion of team building.

Developing team members' self-management skills

A promising dimension of team building emerged in the 1980s: **self-management leadership** is the process of leading others to lead themselves. An underlying assumption is that self-managed teams are likely to fail if team members are not expressly taught to engage in self-management behaviours. This makes sense because it is unreasonable to expect employees who are accustomed to being managed and led to suddenly manage and lead themselves. Transition training is required and a key part of the transition to self-management involves current managers engaging in self-management leadership behaviours. This is team building in the fullest sense of the term.

Six aspects of self-management leadership behaviour were isolated in a field study of a manufacturing company organised around self-managed teams. The following leadership behaviours were observed:

- Encourages self-reinforcement (e.g. getting team members to praise each other for good work and results).
- Encourages self-observation/evaluation (e.g. teaching team members to judge how well they are doing).
- Encourages self-expectation (e.g. encouraging team members to expect high performance from themselves and the team).
- Encourages self-goal-setting (e.g. having the team set its own performance goals).
- Encourages rehearsal (e.g. getting team members to think about and practise new tasks).
- Encourages self-criticism (e.g. encouraging team members to be critical of their own poor performance).[40]

According to the researchers, Charles Manz and Henry Sims, this type of leadership is a dramatic departure from traditional practices, such as giving orders and/or making sure everyone gets along (see Chapter 15). Empowerment, not domination, is the overriding goal (see Chapter 14).

8.5 Effective teamwork through co-operation, trust and cohesiveness

As competitive pressures intensify, experts say organisational success will depend increasingly on teamwork rather than individual stars. For instance, Britain's Chartered Institute of Personnel and Development (CIPD) investigated seven European companies who were in the process of changing into what the researchers called 'lean and responsive organisations'. Teamwork and co-operation turned out to be the most important factors in this change process. A principal conclusion of the study was that employees have to work together and exchange experiences in order to succeed in the transformation process.[41] If this emphasis on teamwork has a familiar ring, it is because sports champions generally say they owe their success to it. Whether in the athletic arena or the world of business, three components of teamwork receiving the greatest attention are co-operation, trust and cohesiveness. Let us explore the contributions each can make to effective teamwork.

Co-operation

Individuals are said to be co-operating when their efforts are systematically integrated to achieve a collective objective. The greater the integration, the greater the degree of co-operation.

As early as the 1940s, Morton Deutch showed how people's beliefs are related to their interdependence. When acting in co-operation with each other, they believe that goal attainment by other people will also foster their own goals. When in competition, however, people believe that goal attainment by others ('competitors') will diminish their own: 'When others fail, I succeed.' Independent people see no relationship between their own results and the results of others.[42] In practice, most team members find themselves in a 'mixed motive' situation. Just think of the footballer who is in a position to score, yet sees a teammate even better placed to score the winner. John Kay – the British strategy specialist – illustrates this with the following analysis of Liverpool Football Club:

OB in Real Life

Liverpool FC

If we were to build a model of the game of football, it would recognise that every time a player has the ball he faces the alternative of shooting for goal or passing to a better placed player. If he passes to a player of similar calibre to himself, he will score fewer goals but the team will score more. If everyone in the team plays a passing game, every member of it can expect to score more goals than if their normal instinct is to shoot. That choice is repeated every few minutes in every match the team plays and there are two equilibria – a passing game or a shooting game. Liverpool is well known for its passing game. Many of its opponents adopt a more individualistic style.

Liverpool illustrates the principal ways in which architecture can form the basis of a distinctive capability. The club has created an intangible asset – the organisational knowledge of the club – which, although it is derived from the contributions of the individual members, belongs to the firm and not to the individual members and cannot be appropriated by them. There are organisational routines – complex manoeuvres, perfected through repeated trial – in which each player fulfils his own role without needing, or necessarily having, a picture of the whole. And there is the 'passing game', the co-operative ethic, in which the player's instinct is to maximise the number of goals the club scores rather than the number of goals he scores. Each of these sources of sporting success has its precise business analogies.[43]

However, it is not only managers and football trainers who have seen the benefits of cooperation. Many workers on the floor are delighted too by the team systems that are increasingly being implemented by Europe's largest companies.

A widely held assumption among American managers is that 'competition brings out the best in people'. From an economic viewpoint, business survival depends on staying ahead of the competition. However, from an interpersonal viewpoint, critics contend competition has been overemphasised, primarily at the expense of co-operation.[44]

Trust

Here we examine the concept of trust in teams and introduce six practical guidelines for building it.

Trust is defined as reciprocal faith in others' intentions and behaviour.[45] Experts on the subject explain the reciprocal (give-and-take) aspect of trust as follows: 'When we see others acting in ways that imply that they trust us, we become more disposed to reciprocity by trusting them more. Conversely, we come to distrust those whose actions appear to violate our trust or to distrust us.'[46]

In short, we tend to give what we get: trust begets trust; distrust begets distrust. A newer model of organisational trust includes a personality trait called **propensity to trust** which is a personality trait involving one's general willingness to trust others. Propensity might be thought of as the general willingness to trust others.

Trust involves 'a cognitive "leap" beyond the expectations that reason and experience alone would warrant'.[47] For example, suppose a member of a newly formed class project team works hard, basing this on the assumption that her teammates are also working hard. That assumption, on which her trust is based, is a cognitive leap that goes beyond her actual experience with her teammates. When you trust someone, you have faith in their good intentions. The act of trusting someone, however, carries with it the inherent risk of betrayal.[48] Progressive managers believe that the benefits of interpersonal trust far outweigh any risks of betrayed trust.

Management professor and consultant Fernando Bartolome offers the following six guidelines for building and maintaining trust:[49]

- *Communication*: keep team members and employees informed by explaining policies and decisions and providing accurate feedback. Be candid about your own problems and limitations. Tell the truth.
- *Support*: be available and approachable. Provide help, advice, coaching and support for team members' ideas.
- *Respect*: delegate real decision-making authority – it is the most important expression of managerial respect. Actively listening to the ideas of others is a close second. (Empowerment is not possible without trust, as will also be explained in Chapter 14.)

- *Fairness*: be quick to give credit and recognition to those who deserve it. Make sure all performance appraisals and evaluations are objective and impartial (also see Chapter 6).
- *Predictability*: as mentioned previously, be consistent and predictable in your daily affairs. Keep both expressed and implied promises.
- *Competence*: enhance your credibility by demonstrating good business sense, technical ability and professionalism.

Cohesiveness is a process whereby 'a sense of "we-ness" [togetherness] emerges to transcend individual differences and motives'.[50] Members of a cohesive team stick together. They are reluctant to leave the team. Cohesive team members stick together for one or both of the following reasons:

- They enjoy other team members' company.
- They need each other to accomplish a common goal.

Accordingly, two types of cohesiveness, identified by sociologists, are socio-emotional cohesiveness and instrumental cohesiveness.[51]

Socio-emotional cohesiveness is a sense of togetherness that develops when individuals derive emotional satisfaction from team participation. Most general discussions of cohesiveness are limited to this type. However, from the standpoint of getting things accomplished in task groups and teams, we cannot afford to ignore instrumental cohesiveness. **Instrumental cohesiveness** is a sense of togetherness that develops when team members are mutually dependent on one another because they believe they could not achieve the team's goal by acting separately. A feeling of 'we' is instrumental to achieving the common goal. Team advocates generally assume both types of cohesiveness are essential to productive teamwork. But is this really true?

Evidence and practical implications

What is the connection between team cohesiveness and performance? A landmark meta-analysis of 410 studies involving 8702 subjects provided the following insights:

- There is a small but statistically significant cohesiveness → performance effect.
- The cohesiveness → performance effect was stronger for smaller and 'real' teams (as opposed to contrived groups in laboratory studies).
- The cohesiveness → performance effect becomes stronger as one moves from (real) civilian groups to military groups to sports teams.
- Commitment to the task at hand (meaning that the individual sees the performance standards as legitimate) has the most powerful impact on the cohesiveness → performance linkage.
- The performance → cohesiveness linkage is stronger than the cohesiveness → performance linkage. Thus, the tendency for success to bind team members together is greater than the tendency for closely knit groups to be more successful.
- Contrary to the popular view, cohesiveness is not 'a 'lubricant' that minimises friction due to the human 'grit' in the system.[52]
- All this evidence led the researchers to the practical conclusion that: 'Efforts to enhance group performance by fostering interpersonal attraction or "pumping up" group pride are not likely to be effective.'[53]

A second meta-analysis found no significant relationship between cohesiveness and the quality of team decisions. However, support was found for Janis's contention that groupthink (see Chapter 7)

Table 8.4 Steps Managers Can Take to Enhance the Two Types of Cohesiveness

Socio-emotional cohesiveness
Keep the team relatively small
Strive for a favourable public image to increase the status and prestige of belonging
Encourage interaction and co-operation
Emphasise members' common characteristics and interests
Point out environmental threats (e.g. competitors' achievements) to rally the team
Instrumental cohesiveness
Regularly update and clarify the team's goal(s)
Give every team member a vital 'piece of the action'
Channel each team member's special talents towards the common goal(s)
Recognise and equitably reinforce every member's contributions
Frequently remind team members they need each other to get the job done

tends to afflict cohesive in-groups with strong leadership. Teams whose members liked each other a great deal tended to make poorer-quality decisions.[54]

Research tells us that cohesiveness is no 'secret weapon' in the quest for improved team performance. The trick is to keep task teams small, make sure performance standards and goals are clear and accepted, achieve some early successes and follow the tips in Table 8.4. A good example is Renault's restructured factory in Douai, France. A new production system was introduced for the construction of the Megane, based on strong employee involvement. Those who were involved in the project from the beginning were responsible for the training of 200 colleagues, who, in turn, instructed their peers. This training system enhanced employee co-operation.[55] Self-selected work teams (in which people pick their own teammates) and social events outside working hours can stimulate socio-emotional cohesiveness.[56] The fostering of socio-emotional cohesiveness needs to be balanced with instrumental cohesiveness. The latter can be encouraged by making sure everyone in the team recognises and appreciates each member's vital contribution to the team's goal. While balancing the two types of cohesiveness, professionals need to remember that groupthink theory and research cautions against too much cohesiveness.

HR

8.6 A general typology of work teams

Work teams are created for various purposes and, thus, face different challenges. Professionals can deal with those challenges more effectively when they understand how teams differ. A helpful way of sorting things out is to consider a typology of work teams developed by Eric Sundstrom and his colleagues.[57] Four general types of work teams listed in Table 8.5 are: advice, production, project and action teams. Each of these labels identifies a basic purpose. For instance, advice teams tend to make recommendations for managerial decisions and seldom make final decisions themselves. In contrast, production and action teams actually carry out the decisions of the management.

Four key variables in Table 8.5 deal with technical specialisation, co-ordination, work cycles and outputs. Technical specialisation is low when the team draws on members' general experience and problem-solving ability. It is high when team members are required to apply technical skills acquired through higher education or extensive training. The degree of co-ordination with other work units is determined by the team's relative independence (low co-ordination) or interdependence (high co-ordination). Work cycles are the amount of time teams need to discharge their missions. The

Table 8.5 Four General Types of Work Teams and Their Outputs

Types and examples	Degree of technical specialisation	Degree of co-ordination with other work units	Work cycles	Typical outputs
Advice Committees Review panels, boards Quality circles Employee involvement groups Advisory councils	Low	Low	Work cycles can be brief or long; one cycle can span team's life	Decisions Selections Suggestions Proposals Recommendations
Production Assembly teams Manufacturing crews Mining teams Flight attendant crews Data processing groups Maintenance crews	Low	High	Work cycles typically repeated or continuous process; cycles often briefer than team's lifespan	Food, chemicals Components Assemblies Retail sales Customer service Equipment repairs
Project Research groups Planning teams Architect teams Engineering teams Development teams Task forces	High	Low (for traditional units) or High (for cross-functional units)	Work cycles typically differ for each new project; one cycle can be team's lifespan	Plans, designs Investigations Presentations Prototypes Reports, findings
Action Sports team Entertainment groups Expeditions Negotiating teams Surgery teams Cockpit crews Military platoons and squads	High	High	Brief performance events, often repeated under new conditions, requiring extended training and/or preparation	Combat missions Expeditions Contracts, lawsuits Concerts Surgical operations Competitive Events

Source: Excerpted and adapted from E. Sundstrom, K. P. De Meuse and D. Futrell, 'Work Teams: Applications and Effectiveness', *American Psychologist*, February 1990, p. 125.

various outputs listed in Table 8.5 are intended to illustrate real-life effects. A closer look at each type of work team is required.[58]

Advice teams

As their name implies, advice teams are created to broaden the information base for managerial decisions. Quality circles, discussed later, are a prime example because they facilitate suggestions for quality improvement from volunteer production or service workers. Advice teams tend to have a low degree of technical specialisation. Likewise, co-ordination is low because advice teams generally work on their own. Ad hoc committees (e.g. the annual sports event committee) have shorter life cycles than standing committees (e.g. the grievance committee).

Production teams

This second type of team is responsible for performing day-to-day operations. Minimal training for routine tasks accounts for the low degree of technical specialisation. Generally, co-ordination is high, however, because work flows from one team to another. For example, track maintenance crews require fresh information from train crews about necessary repairs.

Project teams

Projects require creative problem-solving, often involving the application of specialised knowledge. For example, Boeing's 777 jumbo jet was designed by project teams consisting of engineering, manufacturing, marketing, finance and customer service specialists. State-of-the-art computer modelling programs allowed the teams to assemble three-dimensional computer models of the new aircraft. Design and assembly problems were ironed out during project team meetings before production workers started cutting any metal. Boeing's 777 design teams required a high degree of co-ordination between organisational sub-units because they were cross-functional.[59] A pharmaceutical research team of biochemists, on the other hand, would interact less with other work units because the projects are relatively self-contained.

Action teams

This last type of team is best exemplified by sports teams, airline cockpit crews, hospital surgery teams, mountain-climbing expeditions, film crews, management and trade union negotiating committees, and police special intervention teams, among others. A unique challenge for action teams is to exhibit peak performance on demand.[60]

OB in Real Life

Stage Co

For example, teams at Stage Co – a company that delivers technical stage crew to summer festivals such as Glastonbury in the UK, the Roskilde-Festival in Denmark, the Werchter festival in Belgium and 'Rock am Ring' in Germany – need to combine high specialisation with high co-ordination to ensure a good concert. Highly trained technicians build up the main stage, then they need to break it down immediately after the show, because the pieces are needed fast elsewhere, for the next festival. This requires immense speed and intense co-operation, so everybody in the crew needs to know exactly what to do. Moreover, co-ordination between the stage crew, the festival organisers, the sound engineers and the musicians has to be perfect. Also, some music groups bring their own crew along because of the specific needs of their performance, so a lot of topics have to be discussed with them too.[61]

This four-way typology of work teams is dynamic and changing, not static. Some teams evolve from one type to another. Other teams represent a combination of types.

8.7 Teams in action: quality circles, virtual teams and self-managed teams

All sorts of interesting approaches to teams and teamwork can be found in the workplace today. A great deal of experimentation is taking place as organisations struggle to become more flexible and responsive. This section profiles three different approaches to teams: quality circles, virtual teams and self-managed teams. We have selected these particular types of team for three reasons: they have recognisable labels; they have at least some research evidence; and they range from low to high degrees of empowerment.

As indicated in Table 8.6, the three types of teams are conceptually different but not mutually exclusive. For instance, virtual teams may or may not have volunteer members and may or may not be self-managed. Another point of overlap involves the fifth variable in Table 8.6, that is, the relationship to organisation structure. Quality circles are called parallel structures because they exist outside normal channels of authority and communication.[62] Self-managed teams, on the other hand, are integrated into the basic organisational structure. Virtual teams vary in this regard, although they tend to be parallel because they are made up of functional specialists (engineers, accountants, marketers etc.) who team up on temporary projects. Keeping these basic distinctions in mind, let us explore quality circles, virtual teams and self-managed teams.

Quality circles

Quality circles are small teams of people from the same work area who voluntarily get together to identify, analyse and recommend solutions for problems related to quality, productivity and cost reduction. Some prefer the term 'quality control' circles. With an ideal size of 10 to 12 members, they typically meet for about an hour to an hour and a half at a time on a regular basis. Some companies allow meetings during work hours; others encourage quality circles to meet after work on employees' time. Once a week or twice a month are common schedules. Management facilitates the quality circle programme through skills training and listening to periodic presentations of recommendations. Monetary rewards for suggestions tend to be the exception rather than the rule. Intrinsic motivation, derived from learning new skills and meaningful participation, is the primary reward for quality circle volunteers.

Table 8.6 Basic Distinctions Between Quality Circles, Virtual Teams and Self-Managed Teams

	Quality circles	Virtual teams	Self-managed teams
Type of team	Advice	Advice or project (usually project)	Production, project or action
Type of empowerment	Consultation	Consultation, participation or delegation	Delegation
Members	Production/service personnel	Managers and technical specialists	Production/service, technical specialists
Basis of membership	Voluntary	Assigned (some voluntary)	Assigned
Relationship to organisation structure	Parallel	Parallel or integrated	Integrated
Amount of face-to-face communication	Strictly face-to-face	Periodic to none	Varies, depending on use of information technology

American quality control experts helped introduce the basic idea of quality circles to Japanese industry soon after the Second World War. The idea eventually returned to the USA, Britain and many other countries and became a fad during the 1970s and 1980s. Proponents made zealous claims about how quality circles were the key to higher productivity, lower costs, employee development and improved job attitudes. At its zenith, during the mid-1980s, the quality circle movement claimed millions of employee participants around the world.[63] Hundreds of companies and government agencies adopted the idea under a variety of labels.[64] The dramatic growth of quality circles has been attributed to a desire to replicate Japan's industrial success; a penchant for business fads; and the relative ease of installing quality circles without restructuring the organisation.[65] All too often, however, early enthusiasm gave way to disappointment, apathy and despair.[66] Many quality circles failed because of insufficient preparation and management support, union opposition or other difficulties.[67] But quality circles, if properly administered and supported by management, can be much more than a management fad seemingly past its prime. According to researchers Edward E. Lawler and Susan A. Mohrman, 'quality circles can be an important first step toward organisational effectiveness through employee involvement'.[68]

Evidence and practical implications

There is a body of objective field research on quality circles. Still, much of what we know comes from testimonials and case histories from managers and consultants who have a vested interest in demonstrating the technique's success. Although documented failures are scarce, one expert concluded that quality circles have failure rates of more than 60 per cent.[69] Poor implementation is probably more at fault than the concept itself.[70]

To date, field research on quality circles has been inconclusive. Lack of standardised variables is the main problem, as is typical when comparing the results of field studies.[71] Team participation programmes of all sizes and shapes have been called quality circles. Here is what we have learned to date. A case study of military and civilian personnel found a positive relationship between quality circle participation and desire to continue working for the organisation. The observed effect on job performance was slight. A longitudinal study spanning 24 months revealed that quality circles had only a marginal impact on employee attitudes but had a positive impact on productivity. In another study, utility company employees who participated in quality circles received significantly better job performance ratings and were promoted more frequently than non-participants. This suggests that quality circles live up to their billing as a good employee development technique.[72] Overall, quality circles are a promising participative management tool, if they are carefully implemented and supported by all levels of management.

Virtual teams

Thanks to ubiquitous information technologies, you can be a member of a work team without really being there. These **virtual teams** consist of individuals who work across various boundaries, primarily space and time, using communication technology.[73] Traditional team meetings have a specific location. Team members are either physically present or absent. Virtual teams, in contrast, convene through information technology with members reporting in from different locations, different organisations, and different time zones.

As companies expand globally, face increasing time compression in product development, and use more foreign-based subcontracting labour, virtual teams promise flexibility, responsiveness, lower costs, and improved resource utilisation necessary to meet ever-changing task requirements in highly turbulent and dynamic global business environments.[74] On the negative side, lack of face-to-face interaction can weaken trust, communication and accountability. Other possible dysfunctions are low individual commitment, role overload, role ambiguity, absenteeism and social loafing.[75]

Remember from Chapter 4 that in face-to-face communication people rely on several cues: paraverbal (tone of voice, inflection, voice volume) and non-verbal (eye movement, facial expression, hand gestures, other body language). These cues provide feedback and help regulate the flow of conversation. These communication modalities are constrained to a varying extent in virtual teams. For example, electronic mail prevents both paraverbal and non-verbal cues, telephone conference calls allow the use of paraverbal cues (but not non-verbal cues) and videoconferencing provides both paraverbal and non-verbal cues.[76]

In virtual teams, it might be difficult to communicate contextual information (e.g. different perception of people from different organisations). Also unevenly distributed information, differences in speed of access to information, difficulty in communicating and understanding the salience of information (e.g. what is most important) and difficulty in interpreting the meaning of silence (e.g. is the other person absent or is he not eager to respond) can cause problems.[77] At last, in virtual teams, it is more difficult to exchange information. As a consequence, virtual teams are usually more task-oriented and exchange less social-emotional information. The development of relational links is slowed down. However, research had demonstrated the importance of strong relational links like enhanced creativity and motivation, increased morale, better decisions and fewer process losses.[78]

As shown previously in this chapter, trust is important for any team to function and excel, but its importance for virtual teams is even more critical.[79] So, in order to prevent geographical and organisational distances of virtual team members to become psychological distances, trust has to be established. Global virtual teams may experience 'swift' trust. 'Swift' trust is not based on strong interpersonal relationships (this is the traditional conceptualisation of trust) but on broad categorical social structures and, later on, action. Trust is imported into virtual teams rather than developed. Unlike face-to-face teams, where trust develops based on social bonds formed by informal chats around the water cooler, impromptu meetings or after work gatherings, virtual team members establish trust based on predictable performance.[80] Research results show some typical characteristics of virtual teams that started with low levels of trust: a lack of social introduction (e.g. family information), concern with technical uncertainties and a lack of enthusiasm. Teams that started with a high level of trust showed high initial enthusiasm and extensive social dialogue.

Teams that finished projects with low trust were characterised by negative leadership (e.g. complainers), lack of individual initiative and unpredictable communication (no regular pattern of communication). Teams finishing the project with a high level of trust showed predictable communication, substantive feedback, strong individual initiative and calm reaction to problems.[81]

Evidence about virtual teams

As one might expect with a new and ill-defined area, research evidence to date is a bit sparse. Here is what we have learned so far from studies of computer-mediated groups:

- Virtual teams formed over the Internet follow a group development process similar to that for face-to-face teams.[82]
- Internet chat rooms create more work and yield poorer decisions than face-to-face meetings and telephone conferences.[83]

Table 8.7 Recommendations for Leadership in Virtual Teams

• Provide training on participation in virtual teams, rather than assuming that best practices from traditional teams will transfer seamlessly to virtual environments.
• Start with team-building exercises, using face-to-face where possible to establish a basis for relationships.
• Make certain that both task and relational roles are provided for, either through team members or through software.
• Establish standards for communicating contextual cues with each message to reduce the potential for misinterpretations.
• Structure the process through appropriate process structuring tools, but remember to build flexibility where users can adapt tools to their own needs.
• Nurture emergent leadership and self-leadership that moves the team forward by frequent communication and feedback.
• Put special and continuous emphasis on relational development.
• Anticipate unintended consequences and debrief how the team dealt with those events.

Source: Reprinted from *Organizational Dynamics*, vol. 31, I. Zigurs, 'Leadership in Virtual Teams: Oxymoron or Opportunity?', pp. 339–51. Copyright 2003, with permission from Elsevier.

- Successful use of groupware (software that facilitates interaction among virtual group members) requires training and hands-on experience.[84]
- Inspirational leadership has a positive impact on creativity in electronic brainstorming groups.[85]
- Face-to-face groups reported a higher degree of cohesion, were more satisfied with the decision process followed by the groups and were more satisfied with the team's outcome.[86]
- While face-to-face teams reported greater satisfaction with the group interaction process, the exchange of information was no more effective than in virtual teams.[87]
- Conflict management is particularly difficult for asynchronous virtual teams (those not interacting in real time) that have no opportunity for face-to-face interaction.[88] A proactive effort to solve problems, however, strengthens relationships in virtual teams.[89]

Virtual teams may be in fashion but they are not a cure-all. Professionals who rely on virtual teams agree on one point: meaningful face-to-face contact, especially during early phases of the group development process, is absolutely essential. Virtual team members need 'faces' in their minds to go with names and electronic messages. Roy Harrison, training and development policy adviser at the UK's Chartered Institute of Personnel and Development, states that the main question surrounding virtual teams is indeed how to encourage positive interaction without face-to-face contact. 'Technology allows people to get in touch but where do you get the "soul" from?', he says.[90] Additionally, virtual teams cannot succeed without some old-fashioned factors, such as top management support, hands-on training, a clear mission and specific objectives, schedules, deadlines and effective leadership.[91] Table 8.7 lists eight recommendations for leadership in virtual teams (for more on leadership, see Chapter 15).

HR Practical implications of virtual teams

The following guidelines may help leaders of virtual teams:[92]

- Virtual teams need a clear objective for each meeting. To ensure success, the preparation is very important; for example, the right participants, the distribution of all appropriate documents beforehand and the establishment of the role of the leader.

- The psychological profile and the personality characteristics of team members in virtual teams are very important: in order to function well, participants have to be patient, persistent and they need a certain degree of flexibility, tolerance and understanding.
- In virtual teams, a clear definition of responsibilities is very important. This can prevent team members becoming confused and frustrated.
- Also helpful are clear guidelines on how often to communicate and a regular pattern of communication.

The way conflicts are handled in virtual teams is very important. As a team leader you should try to address discontent as quickly as possible and to focus on the concerned individual (do not involve the whole team when it is not necessary). To be most effective, team leaders need to do two things well: shift from a focus on time to a focus on results and recognise that virtual teams, instead of needing a fewer managers, require better supervisory skills among existing managers.

Self-managed teams

Something much more complex is involved than this apparently simple label suggests. The term 'self-managed' does not mean simply turning workers loose to do their own thing. Indeed, as we will see, an organisation embracing self-managed teams should be prepared to undergo revolutionary changes in management philosophy, structure, staffing and training practices, and reward systems. Moreover, the traditional notions of managerial authority and control are turned on their heads. Not surprisingly, many managers strongly resist giving up the reins of power to people they view as subordinates. They see self-managed teams as a threat to their job security.[93] Texas Instruments, for instance, has constructively dealt with this problem at its Malaysian factory by making former production supervisors part of the all-important training function. Also, specialists and support employees (such as engineers and HR professionals) may fear the introduction of self-managed teams. They will have to share their special knowledge with self-managed teams while this specific knowledge used to be a source of self-esteem and status.[94]

Self-managed teams are defined as groups of workers who are given 'administrative oversight' for their task domains. Administrative oversight involves delegating activities, such as planning, scheduling, monitoring and staffing. These are chores normally performed by managers. In short, employees in these unique work groups act as their own supervisor.[95] Self-managed teams are variously referred to as semi-autonomous work groups, autonomous work groups, self-directed work groups or super teams.

Self-managed teams are an offshoot of a combination of behavioural science and management practice.[96] Group dynamics research of variables, such as cohesiveness, initially paved the way. A later stimulus was the socio-technical systems approach in which researchers tried to harmonise social and technical factors. Their goal was to increase productivity and the quality of employees' working lives simultaneously.[97] The socio-technical systems approach is an integral approach that, in the 1950s, formed the basis for the principle of team-based organisations. It is an originally British approach (introduced in the 1940s at the Tavistock Institute in the UK) that finds worldwide implementation in organisational change processes and currently has an Australian, Scandinavian, Dutch and American variant.

The idea of self-managed teams has been given a strong boost by advocates of job design and participative management.[98] The job characteristics model of Hackman and Oldham, for example, outlined in Chapter 5, showed that internal motivation, satisfaction and performance can be

Figure 8.5 The Evolution of Self-Managed Work Teams

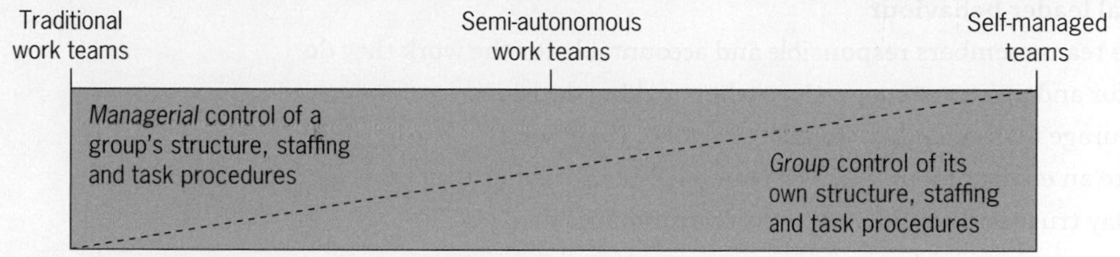

enhanced through five core job characteristics. In relation to members of self-managed teams, we can see that of those five core factors, increased autonomy is a major benefit. Autonomy itself comprises three types: method, scheduling and criteria (see the activity below on work group autonomy).

Members of self-managed teams score high on group autonomy. Autonomy empowers those who are ready and able to handle added responsibility.

The net result of this confluence is the continuum in Figure 8.5. The traditional clear cut distinction between manager and managed is being blurred as non-managerial employees are delegated greater authority and granted increased autonomy. It is important to note, however, that self-managed teams do not eliminate the need for all managerial control (see the upper right hand corner of Figure 8.5). Semi-autonomous work teams represent a balance between managerial and group control.[99]

Companies, such as Asea Brown Boveri, a Swedish-Swiss firm, 3M in the USA and BP Norge in Norway, successfully introduced self-managed teams. According to these companies, self-managed teams speed up decision-making and innovation. They also stimulate people to become self-motivated and they help employees to connect with the company's vision in a very personal way. Employees can affect important issues and they can develop their own skills such as leadership skills.[100]

Varying interpretations of 'self-managed' or 'self-directed' can lead to confusion and wrong steps. Essentially, the concept means that team members share or rotate leadership and hold themselves mutually responsible for a set of performance goals, an approach to their work and deliverables that reflect the company's mission, vision and business plan. The team members have a high responsibility: they decide how to organise themselves in order to get their work done and they are responsible for their own output as well as for that of others.[101]

What is the task of the former manager? Usually, the former manager starts as a team leader. He or she makes sure that every team member has the same information, understands the business vision and has clear goals (e.g. financial targets). The former manager is also responsible for keeping the project on track.

Once the team members have more experience with working in the team, they gradually take over some decision-making and conflict-resolution responsibilities from the team leader. As the team matures, the former manager acts more as a coach/adviser but always remains a member of the team, participating in decisions and supplying expertise, knowledge and resources. He or she has to teach the team members to cope with self-responsibility and self-accountability.

The team members must measure their progress against the agreed-upon goals and approach, as well as their skills and competences to determine where they require development, on-the-job training and coaching.[102]

HR Table 8.8 There Are Many Ways to Empower Self-Managed Teams

External leader behaviour
- Make team members responsible and accountable for the work they do
- Ask for and use team suggestions when making decisions
- Encourage team members to take control of their work
- Create an environment in which team members attempt to solve work-related problems
- Display trust and confidence in the team's abilities

Production/service responsibilities
- The team sets its own production/service goals and standards
- The team assigns jobs and tasks to its members
- Team members develop their own quality standards and measurement techniques
- Team members take on production/service learning and development opportunities
- Team members handle their own problems with internal and external customers
- The team works with a whole product or service, not just a part

Human resource management system
- The team gets paid, at least in part, as a team
- Team members are cross-trained on jobs within their team
- Team members are cross-trained on jobs in other teams
- Team members are responsible for hiring, training, punishment and firing
- Team members use peer evaluations to formally evaluate each other

Social structure
- The team gets support from other teams and departments when needed
- The team has access to and uses important and strategic information
- The team has access to and uses resources of other teams
- The team has access to and uses resources inside and outside the organisation
- The team frequently communicates with other teams
- The team makes its own rules and policies

Source: B. L. Kirkman and B. Rosen, 'Powering Up Teams', *Organizational Dynamics*, Winter 2000, Exhibit 3, p. 56.

As indicated in Table 8.8, self-managed teams can be empowered in many different ways, producing countless variations.

Among companies with self-managed teams, the most commonly delegated tasks are work scheduling and dealing directly with outside customers. The least common team chores are hiring and firing.[103] Most of today's self-managed teams remain bunched at the shop-floor level in factory settings. Experts predict growth of the practice in the managerial ranks and in service operations.[104]

Critical thinking

Are self-managed teams more or less demanding of managers than traditional teams? Explain.

Activity

Measuring work group autonomy

Think of your current (or past) job and work teams. Characterise the team's situation by circling one number on the following scale for each statement. Add your responses for a total score.

	Strongly disagree						Strongly agree
Work method autonomy							
1 My work team decides how to get the job done.	1	2	3	4	5	6	7
2 My work team determines what procedures to use.	1	2	3	4	5	6	7
3 My work team is free to choose its own methods when carrying out its work.	1	2	3	4	5	6	7
Work scheduling autonomy							
4 My work team controls the scheduling of its work.	1	2	3	4	5	6	7
5 My work team determines how its work is sequenced.	1	2	3	4	5	6	7
6 My work team decides when to do certain activities.	1	2	3	4	5	6	7
Work criteria autonomy							
7 My work team is allowed to modify the normal way it is evaluated so some of our activities are emphasised and some de-emphasised.	1	2	3	4	5	6	7
8 My work team is able to modify its objectives (what it is supposed to accomplish).	1	2	3	4	5	6	7
9 My work team has some control over what it is supposed to accomplish.	1	2	3	4	5	6	7

Total score ________

Norms

10–26 = low autonomy
27–45 = moderate autonomy
46–63 = high autonomy

Source: Adapted from an individual autonomy scale in J. A. Breaugh, 'The Work Autonomy Scales: Additional Validity Evidence', *Human Relations*, November 1989, pp. 1033–56.

Evidence about self-managed teams

As with quality circles and virtual teams, much of what we know about self-managed teams comes from testimonials and case studies. A review of three meta-analyses covering 70 individual studies concluded that self-managed teams had:

- A positive impact on productivity.
- A positive impact on specific attitudes relating to self-management (e.g. responsibility and control).
- No significant impact on general attitudes (e.g. job satisfaction and organisational commitment).
- No significant impact on absenteeism or turnover.[105]

Other research insights about self-managed teams include:

- Disciplinary actions should be handled by group consensus because individual team members tend to be too lenient.[106]
- Group cohesiveness is associated with higher performance ratings.[107]
- When implementing self-managed teams in multinational companies, societal values need to be taken into consideration because some cultures are more resistant to the practice than others. In fact, 'team-related resistance is apparently greater for employees in the United States than for those in Finland or the Philippines'.[108]

One of the most critical studies of self-managed teams is the often-cited paper by James Barker. This is based on an anthropological study of a manufacturing company making the transition from a traditional and hierarchical organisation towards more self-management. Barker finds that while on the surface the workers were free from the managers' control, the control was in fact transferred from the managers to the workers, making it less clear and ever-present. This *concertive control* 'resulted in a form of control more powerful, less apparent, and more difficult to resist than that of the former bureaucracy'.[109]

With mixed results from the evidence about self-managed teams, caution is in order. Nonetheless, it is likely that the the trend towards more self-managed work teams will continue in the future. Managers need to be prepared for the resulting shift in organisational administration.

The increasing use of self-managed teams in the workplace raises questions about how these teams need to be composed for best results. Little research evidence exists with regard to characteristics of successful self-managed team members. Given the specific context of laboratory studies, these results are not always generalisable to work teams in organisations. A study among 126 manufacturing and support personnel indicates that people's personality (Big Five) has an influence on their self-efficacy to participate in a self-managed team. This study's findings reveal the importance of taking into account people's personalities when deciding whether or not to implement self-managed teams and also to decide who to select to work in such teams.[110]

HR Practical implications about self-managed teams

Experience shows that it is better to build a new production or service facility around self-managed teams than to attempt to convert an existing one. The former approach involves so-called 'greenfield sites'. Greenfield sites give management the advantage of selecting appropriate technology and carefully screening job applicants likely to be good team players.

But the fact is most organisations are not afforded greenfield opportunities. They must settle for introducing self-managed teams into an existing organisation structure.[111] Extensive management training and socialisation are required to deeply embed Theory Y (Chapter 1) and participative management (Chapter 13) values into the organisation's culture. It is necessary for this new logic to start with top management and filter down; otherwise, resistance among middle- and lower-level managers will block the transition to teams.[112] Some turnover can be expected among managers who refuse to adjust to broader empowerment.

Both technical and organisational redesign are necessary for the transition to self-managed teams. The new teams may require special technology. Volvo's team-based car assembly plant, for example, relies on portable assembly platforms rather than traditional assembly lines. Structural redesign of the organisation must take place because self-managed teams are an integral part of the organisation, not patched onto it as in the case of quality circles.

OB in Real Life

Texas Instruments

For example, in one of Texas Instruments' computer chip factories, a hierarchy of teams operates within the traditional structure. Four levels of teams are responsible for different domains. Reporting to the steering team that deals with strategic issues are quality improvement, corrective action and effectiveness teams. Texas Instruments' quality-improvement and corrective-action teams are crossfunctional teams; and are made up of middle managers and functional specialists, such as accountants and engineers. Production workers make up the effectiveness teams. The corrective-action teams are unique because they are formed to deal with short-term problems and are disbanded when a solution is found. All the other teams are long-term assignments.[113]

In turn, systems for personnel, goal setting and rewards will need to be adapted to encourage the new self-managed teamwork. Staffing decisions may shift from management to team members who hire their own co-workers. A study of 60 self-managing teams involving 540 employees suggests how goal setting should be reoriented. Teams with highly co-operative goals functioned more smoothly and had better results than teams with competitive goals.[114] Accordingly, individual bonuses must give way to team bonuses. Supervisory development workshops are needed to teach managers to be facilitators rather than order givers.[115] Finally, extensive team training is required to help team members learn more about technical details, the business as a whole, and how to be team players.

OB in Real Life

BP Norge

The development of self-managed teams took place in three overlapping phases:

- *Discovery and agitation*: focusing; changing old thought patterns; recognising the differences between teamwork, groups and self-managed teams; linking the 'self-managed teams' concept to the BP Norge vision and business strategy; breaking the resistance.
- *Proliferation and dissemination*: exploring; establishing new ways of working; identifying teams and selecting team leaders; establishing specific teamwork products and measurable performance goals; transferring responsibility from the hierarchy to the self-managed teams; providing just-in-time training to develop specific competences and mental models.
- *Integration and institutionalisation*: having each group hold itself accountable as a team; aligning work processes, decision-making, information, measurement, performance management and organisation structure with the self-managed teams and business strategy; developing and rotating leadership; removing boundaries; and practising new competences at higher levels of proficiency.

All of these phases are necessary for long-term success of the self-managed teams. The first phase got the most attention because it is the most challenging one (e.g. overcoming resistance).

A two-day workshop was organised representing people from different levels in the organisation. First, a group of team leaders was trained to be facilitators and coaches for their own teams. Later on, other members would become team leaders.

Employees at BP Norge could decide themselves if they wanted to participate in self-managed teams. Therefore, management provided full information on self-managed teams. For instance, videos about self-managed teams were shown in which the concept was outlined both from the management perspective and the employee perspective. Examples of organisations which implemented self-managed teams successfully were also demonstrated.

There was deep scepticism but participants and facilitators talked about team development and they discussed the different stages through which any change project has to progress (denial, resistance, exploration and commitment). The use of humour also helped. During dinner on the first day, participants were asked: 'What hard questions do you have for senior management about self-managed teams – questions you or others have been the most embarrassed to ask?' Participants could be honest about their feelings and have an open dialogue. This way participants learned a lot about self-managed teams and, gradually, they started analysing the effectiveness of their current work groups.[116]

Learning outcomes: Summary of key terms

1 **Distinguish between a 'team' and a 'group'**

Definitions of teams generally suggest a number of conditions which must be fulfilled before a group becomes a team: members of the group have shared goals in relation to their work; they interact with each other to achieve those shared goals; all team members have well-defined and interdependent roles; and they have an organisational identity as a team, with a defined organisational function.

2 **Identify and describe the four types of work teams**

Four general types of work teams are advice, production, project and action teams. Each type has its characteristic degrees of specialisation and co-ordination, work cycle and outputs.

3 **Explain the ecological model of work team effectiveness**

According to the ecological model, two effectiveness criteria for work teams are performance and viability. The performance criterion is met if the team satisfies its clients/customers. A work team is viable if its members are satisfied and continue contributing. An ecological perspective is appropriate because work teams require an organisational life-support system. For instance, team participation is enhanced by an organisational culture that values employee empowerment.

4 **Discuss why teams fail**

Teams fail because unrealistic expectations cause frustration and failure. Common management mistakes include weak strategies, creating a hostile environment for teams, faddish use of teams, not learning from team experience, vague team assignments, poor team staffing, inadequate training and a lack of trust. Team members typically fail if they try too much too soon, experience conflict over differing work styles and personalities, ignore important group dynamics, resist change, exhibit poor interpersonal skills and chemistry, and display a lack of trust.

5 **List at least three things organisations can do to build trust**

Six recommended ways to build trust are through communication, support, respect (especially delegation), fairness, predictability and competence.

6 **Distinguish two types of cohesiveness and summarise the related research findings**

Cohesive groups have a shared sense of togetherness or a 'we' feeling. Socio-emotional cohesiveness involves emotional satisfaction. Instrumental cohesiveness involves goal-directed togetherness. There is a small but significant relationship between cohesiveness and performance. The effect is stronger for smaller teams. Commitment to task among team members strengthens the cohesiveness → performance linkage. Success can build team cohesiveness. Cohesiveness is not a cure-all for team problems. Too much cohesiveness can lead to groupthink.

7 **Define quality circles, virtual teams and self-managed teams**

Quality circles are small teams of volunteers who meet regularly to solve quality-related problems in their work area. Virtual teams are physically dispersed work teams that conduct their business via modern information technologies, such as the Internet, email and videoconferences. Self-managed teams are work teams that perform their own administrative chores, such as planning, scheduling and staffing.

Review questions

1 Why bother taking an ecological perspective of work team effectiveness?
2 Which of the factors listed in Table 8.3 is most crucial to a successful team? Explain.
3 In your personal friendships, how do you come to trust someone? How fragile is that trust? Explain.
4 Why is delegation so important to building organisational trust?
5 Why should a team leader strive for both socio-emotional and instrumental cohesiveness?
6 Are virtual teams likely to be just a passing fad? Why or why not?
7 Would you like to work on a self-managed team? Explain.
8 How would you respond to a manager who said, 'Why should I teach my people to manage themselves and work myself out of a job?'
9 Have you ever been a member of a high-performing team? If so, explain the circumstances and success factors.

Personal awareness and growth exercise

How trusting are you?

Objective

1 To introduce you to different dimensions of interpersonal trust.
2 To measure your trust in another person.
3 To discuss the managerial implications of your propensity to trust.

Introduction

The trend towards more open and empowered organisations where teamwork and self-management are vital requires heightened interpersonal trust. Customers need to be able to trust organisations producing the goods and services they buy, managers need to trust non-managers to carry out the organisation's mission, and team members need to trust each other in order to get the job done. As with any other interpersonal skill, we need to be able to measure and improve our ability to trust others. This exercise is a step in that direction.

Instructions

Think of a specific individual who currently plays an important role in your life (e.g. present or future spouse, friend, supervisor, co-worker, team member etc.), and rate his or her trustworthiness for each statement according to the following scale. Total your responses and compare your score with the arbitrary norms provided.

Overall trust	Strongly disagree									Strongly agree
1 I can expect this person to play fair.	1	2	3	4	5	6	7	8	9	10
2 I can confide in this person and know she or he desires to listen.	1	2	3	4	5	6	7	8	9	10
3 I can expect this person to tell me the truth.	1	2	3	4	5	6	7	8	9	10
4 This person takes time to listen to my problems and worries.	1	2	3	4	5	6	7	8	9	10
Emotional trust										
5 This person would never intentionally misrepresent my point of view to other people.	1	2	3	4	5	6	7	8	9	10
6 I can confide in this person and know that he or she will not discuss it with others.	1	2	3	4	5	6	7	8	9	10
7 This person gives constructive and caring responses to my problems.	1	2	3	4	5	6	7	8	9	10
Reliableness										
8 If this person promised to do me a favour, she or he would carry out that promise.	1	2	3	4	5	6	7	8	9	10
9 If I had an appointment with this person, I could count on him or her showing up.	1	2	3	4	5	6	7	8	9	10
10 I could lend this person money and count on getting it back as soon as possible.	1	2	3	4	5	6	7	8	9	10
11 I do not need a back-up plan because I know this person will come through for me.	1	2	3	4	5	6	7	8	9	10

Total score ________

Trustworthiness scale

63–88 = high (trust is a precious thing)
37–62 = moderate (be careful; get a rear-view mirror)
11–36 = low (lock up your valuables!)

Questions for discussion

1 Which particular items in this trust questionnaire are most central to your idea of trust? Why?
2 Does your score accurately depict the degree to which you trust (or distrust) the target person?
3 Why do you trust (or distrust) this individual?
4 If you trust this person to a high degree, how hard was it to build that trust? Explain. What would destroy that trust?
5 Based on your responses to this questionnaire, how would you rate your 'propensity to trust'? Low? Moderate? High?
6 What are the managerial implications of your propensity to trust?

Group exercise

Student team development project

Objectives

1 To help you understand better the components of teamwork.
2 To give you a practical diagnostic tool to assess the need for team building.
3 To give you a chance to evaluate and develop an actual group/team.

Introduction

Student teams are very common in today's college classrooms. They are an important part of the move towards co-operative and experiential learning. In other words, learning by doing. Group dynamics and teamwork are best learned by doing. Unfortunately, many classroom teams wallow in ambiguity, conflict and ineffectiveness. This team development questionnaire can play an important role in the life cycle of your classroom team or group. All members of your team can complete this evaluation at one or more of the following critical points in your team's life cycle: (1) when the team reaches a crisis point and threatens to break up, (2) about halfway through the life of the team, and (3) at the end of the team's life cycle. Discussion of the results by all team members can enhance the group's learning experience.

Instructions

Either at the prompting of your lecturer or by group consensus, decide at what point in your team's life cycle this exercise should be completed. Tip: Have each team member write their responses to the 10 items on a sheet of paper with no names attached. This will permit the calculation of a group mean score for each item and for all 10 items. Attention should then turn to the discussion questions provided in order to help any team development problems surface and to point the way towards solutions.

(An alternative to these instructions is to evaluate a team or work group you are associated with in your current job. You may also draw from a group experience in a past job.[117])

Questionnaire[118]

1 To what extent do I feel a real part of the team?

5	4	3	2	1
Completely a part all the time.	A part most of the time.	On the edge – sometimes in, sometimes out.	Generally outside except for one or two short periods.	On the outside, not really a part of the team.

2 How safe is it in this team to be at ease and relaxed, and to be myself?

5	4	3	2	1
I feel perfectly safe to be myself; they won't hold mistakes against me.	I feel most people would accept me if I were completely myself, but there are some I am not sure about.	Generally one has to be careful what one says or does in this team.	I am not a fool; I would never be myself in this team.	I am quite fearful about being completely myself in this team.

3 To what extent do I feel 'under wraps', that is have private thoughts, unspoken reservations or unexpressed feelings and opinions which I have not felt comfortable bringing out into the open?

5	4	3	2	1
Almost completely under wraps.	Under wraps many times.	Slightly more free and expressive than under wraps.	Quite free and expressive much of the time.	Almost completely free and expressive.

4 How effective are we, in our team, in getting out and using the ideas, opinions and information of all team members in making decisions?

5	4	3	2	1
We don't really encourage everyone to share their ideas, opinions and information with the team when making decisions.	Only the ideas, opinions and information of a few members are really known and used in making decisions.	Sometimes we hear the views of most members before making decisions, and sometimes we disregard most members.	A few are sometimes hesitant about sharing their opinions but we generally have good participation in making decisions.	Everyone feels his or her ideas, opinions and information are given a fair hearing before decisions are made.

5 To what extent are the goals the team is working toward understood, and to what extent do they have meaning for you?

5	4	3	2	1
I feel extremely good about goals of our team.	I feel fairly good but some things are not too clear or meaningful.	A few things we are doing are clear and meaningful.	Much of the activity is not clear or meaningful to me.	I really do not understand or feel involved in the goals of the team.

6 How well does the team work at its tasks?

5	4	3	2	1
Coasts, loafs, makes no progress.	Makes a little progress but most members loaf.	Progress is slow; spurts of effective work.	Above average in progress and pace of work.	Works well; achieves definite progress.

7 Our planning and the way we operate as a team are largely influenced by . . . ?

5	4	3	2	1
One or two team members.	A clique.	Shifts from one person or clique to another.	Shared by most of the members but some are left out.	Shared by all members of the team.

8 What is the level of responsibility for work in our team?

5	4	3	2	1
Each person assumes personal responsibility for getting work done.	A majority of the members assume responsibility for getting work done.	About half assume responsibility; about half do not.	Only a few assume responsibility for getting work done.	Nobody (except perhaps one) really assumes responsibility for getting work done.

9 How are differences or conflicts handled in our team?

5	4	3	2	1
Differences or conflicts are denied, suppressed or avoided at all costs.	Differences or conflicts are recognised but remain mostly unresolved.	Differences or conflicts are recognised, and some attempts are made to work them through by some members, often outside the team meetings.	Differences and conflicts are recognised, and some attempts are made to deal with them in our team.	Differences and conflicts are recognised, and the team usually works through them satisfactorily.

10 How do people relate to the team leader, chairperson or 'boss'?

5	4	3	2	1
The leader dominates the team, and people are often fearful or passive.	The leader tends to control the team, although people generally agree with the leader's direction.	There is some give and take between the leader and the team members.	Team members relate easily to the leader and usually they are able to influence leader decisions.	Team members respect the leader but they work together as a unified team, with everyone participating and no one dominant.

Total score__________

Questions for discussion

1 Have any of the items on the questionnaire helped you to understand better why your team has had problems? What problems?

2 Based on Table 8.1, are you part of a group or a team? Explain.

3 How do your responses to the items compare with the average responses from your group? What insights does this information provide?

4 What lasting lessons about teamwork have you learned from this exercise?

Online Learning Centre

When you have read this chapter, log on to the Online Learning Centre website at ***www.mcgraw-hill.co.uk/textbooks/sinding*** to access test questions, additional exercises and other related resources.

Notes

[1] E. Van Velsor and J. Brittain Leslie, 'Why Executives Derail: Perspectives Across Time And Culture', *Academy of Management Executive*, November 1995, p. 62. Also see S. A. Mohrman, S. G. Cohen and A. M. Mohrman, Jr, *Designing Team-Based Organizations* (San Francisco, CA: Jossey-Bass, 1995); P. MacMillan, *The Performance Factor: Unlocking the Secrets of Teamwork* (Nashville, TN: Broadman & Holman, 2001); and F. LaFasto and C. Larson, *When Teams Work Best: 6,000 Team Members and Leaders Tell What It Takes to Succeed* (Thousand Oaks, CA: Sage Publications, 2001).

[2] See P. F. Drucker, 'The Coming of the New Organization', *Harvard Business Review*, January–February 1988, pp. 45–53.

[3] Data from 'HR Data Files', *HR Magazine*, June 1995, p. 65.

[4] Based on S. A. Mohrman, S. G. Cohen and A. M. Mohrman, Jr, *Designing Team-Based Organizations* (San Francisco, CA: Jossey-Bass, 1995).

[5] J. R. Hackman, *Leading Teams* (Boston: Harvard Business School Press, 2002).

[6] R. A. Guzzo, 'Fundamental Considerations about Work Groups', in *Handbook of Work Group Psychology*, ed. M. A. West (Chichester: John Wiley, 1996), p. 9. Also see S. G. Cohen and D. E. Bailey, 'What Makes Teams Work: Group Effectiveness Research for the Shop Floor to the Executive Suite', *Journal of Management*, no. 3, 1997, pp. 239–90.

[7] See J. Arnold, *Work Psychology: Understanding Human Behavior in the Workplace*, 4th edn (Harlow: Prentice Hall, 2005), p. 449. Also see G. Van Der Vegt, B. Emans and E. Van De Vliert, 'Motivating Effects of Task and Outcome Interdependence in Work Teams', *Group & Organization Management*, June 1998, pp. 124–43; and H. van Vijfeijken, A. Kleingeld, H. van Tuijl, J. A. Algera and H. Thierry, 'Task Complexity and Task, Goal, and Reward Interdependence in Group Performance Management: A Prescriptive Model', *European Journal of Work and Organizational Psychology*, no. 3, 2002; pp. 363–83.

[8] J. R. Katzenbach and D. K. Smith, *The Wisdom of Teams: Creating the High-Performance Organization* (New York: HarperBusiness, 1993), p. 45. Sport teams are discussed in N. Katz, 'Sports Teams as a Model for Workplace Teams: Lessons and Liabilities', *Academy of Management Executive*, August 2001, pp. 56–67; R. Fusaro, 'The Big Comeback', *Harvard Business Review*, January 2002, p. 20; and G. Colvin, 'Think You Can Bobsled? Ha!', *Fortune*, 18 March 2002, p. 50.

[9] K. L. Unsworth and M. A. West, 'Teams: The Challenges of Cooperative Work', in *Introduction to Work and Organizational Psychology: A European Perspective*, ed. N. Chmiel (Oxford: Blackwell Publishers, 2000), p. 328.

[10] A Team's-Eye View of Teams', *Training*, November 1995, p. 16.

[11] Tziner, A. and Eden, D., 'Effects of Crew Composition on Crew Performance: Does the Whole Equal the Sum of its Parts?', *Journal of Applied Psychology*, vol. 70, no. 1, 1985, pp. 85–93.

[12] For related research, see R. Saavedra, C. P. Earley and L. Van Dyne, 'Complex Interdependence in Task-Performing Groups', *Journal of Applied Psychology*, February 1993, pp. 61–72; G. A. Neuman and J. Wright, 'Team Effectiveness: Beyond Skills and Cognitive Ability', *Journal of Applied Psychology*, no. 3, 1999, pp. 376–89; and J. A. LePine, 'Team Adaptation and Postchange Performance: Effects of Team Composition in Terms of Members' Cognitive Ability and Personality', *Journal of Applied Psychology*, no. 1, 2003, pp. 27–39.

[13] F. J. Milliken and L. L. Martins, 'Searching for Common Threads: Understanding the Multiple Effects of Diversity in Organizational Groups', *Academy of Management Review*, vol. 21, no. 2, 402–433.

[14] The best introduction to Hackman's body of work on teams is his book: J. R. Hackman, *Leading Teams* (Boston: Harvard Business School Press, 2002).

[15] R. M. Belbin, *Management Teams: Why They Succeed or Fail* (London: Butterworth-Heinemann, 1983); R. M. Belbin, *Team Roles at Work* (London: Butterworth-Heinemann, 1993); and R. M. Belbin, *The Coming Shape of Organizations* (London: Butterworth-Heinemann, 1996).

[16] A. Furnham, H. Steele and D. Pendleton, 'A Psychometric Assessment of the Belbin Team Role Self-Perception Inventory', *Journal of Occupational and Organizational Psychology*, September 1993, pp. 245–7; W. G. Broucek and G. A. Randall, 'An Assessment of the Construct Validity of the Belbin Self-Perception Inventory and Observer's Assessment from the Perspective of the Five-Factor Model', *Journal of Occupational and Organizational Psychology*, September 1996, pp. 389–405; S. G. Fisher, W. Macrosson and G. Sharp, 'Further Evidence Concerning the Belbin Team Role Self-Perception Inventory', *Personnel Review*, December 1996, pp. 61–7; B. Senior, 'Team Roles and Team Performance; Is There "Really" a Link?', *Journal of Organizational and Occupational Psychology*, September 1997, pp. 241–58; and S. G. Fisher, T. A. Hunter and W. D. K. Macrosson, 'A Validation Study of Belbin's Team Roles', *European Journal of Work and Organizational Psychology*, no. 2, 2001, pp. 121–44.

[17] S. Swailes and T. McIntyre-Bhatty, 'Research Note: The Belbin Team Inventory: Reinterpreting Reliability Estimates', *Journal of Managerial Psychology*, June 2002, pp. 529–36.

[18] S. J. Balderson and A. J. Boderick, 'Behavior in Teams: Exploring Occupational and Gender Differences', *Journal of Managerial Psychology*, no. 5, 1996, p. 33.

[19] See M. J. Stevens and M. A. Campion, 'The Knowledge, Skill, and Ability Requirements for Teamwork: Implications for Human Resource Management', *Journal of Management*, Summer 1994, pp. 503–30; M. J. Stevens and M. A. Campion, 'Staffing Work Teams: Development of a Selection Test for Teamwork Settings', *Journal of Management*, no. 2, 1999, pp. 207–28; and D. L. Miller, 'Reexamining Teamwork KSAs and Team Performance', *Small Group Research*, December 2001, pp. 745–66. Also see L. L. Thompson, *Making the Team: A Guide for Managers* (Upper Saddle River, NJ: Prentice Hall, 2000).

[20] R. Klimoski and R. G. Jones, 'Staffing for Effective Group Decision Making: Key Issues in Matching People and Teams', in *Team Effectiveness and Decision Making in Organizations*, eds R. A. Guzzo, E. Salas and Associates (San Francisco, CA: Jossey-Bass, 1995), pp. 308–9. Also see G. St. J. Burch and N. Anderson, 'Measuring Person-Team Fit: Development and Validation of the Team Selection Inventory', *Journal of Managerial Psychology*, no. 4, 2004, pp. 406–26.

[21] An instructive overview of team effectiveness models can be found in D. L. Gladstein, 'Groups in Context: A Model of Task Group Effectiveness', *Administrative Science Quarterly*, December 1984, pp. 499–517; P. S. Goodman, E. Ravlin and M. Schminke, 'Understanding Groups in Organizations', in *Research in Organizational Behavior*, vol. 9, eds L. L. Cummings and B. M. Staw (Greenwich, CT: JAI Press, 1987), pp. 121–73; M. A. Campion, G. J. Medsker and A. C. Higgs, 'Relations between Work Group Characteristics and Effectiveness: Implications for Designing Effective Work Groups', *Personnel Psychology*, Winter 1993, pp. 823–50; M. A. Campion, E. M. Papper and G. J. Medsker, 'Relations between Work Team Characteristics and Effectiveness: A Replication and Extension', *Personnel Psychology*, no. 2, 1996, pp. 429–52; D. E. Hyatt and T. M. Ruddy, 'An Examination of the Relationship between Work Group Characteristics and Performance: Once More into the Breech', *Personnel Psychology*, Autumn 1997; and S. G. Cohen and D. E. Bailey, 'What Makes Teams Work: Group Effectiveness Research for the Shop Floor to the Executive Suite', *Journal of Management*, no. 3, 1997, pp. 239–90.

[22] For more on team-member satisfaction, see M. A. Griffin, M. G. Patterson and M. A. West, 'Job Satisfacton and Teamwork: The Role of Supervisor Support', *Journal of Organizational Behavior*, August 2001, pp. 537–50; and C. M. Mason and M. A. Griffin, 'Group Task Satisfaction: Applying the Constructs of Job Satisfaction to Groups', *Small Group Research*, June 2002, pp. 271–312.

[23] Other team criteria are discussed in N. R. Anderson and M. A. West, 'Measuring Climate for Work Group Innovation: Development and Validation of the Team Climate Inventory', *Journal of Organizational Behavior*, May 1998, pp. 235–58; and M. J. Stevens and M. A. Campion, 'Staffing Work Teams: Development and Validation of a Selection Test for Teamwork Settings', *Journal of Management*, no. 2, 1999, pp. 207–28.

[24] For example, see C. O. Longenecker and M. Neubert, 'Barriers and Gateways to Management Cooperation and Teamwork', *Business Horizons*, September–October 2000, pp. 37–44; and M. D. Cannon and A. C. Edmondson, 'Confronting Failure: Antecedents and Consequences of Shared Beliefs about Failure in Organizational Work Groups', *Journal of Organizational Behavior*, March 2001, pp. 161–77.

[25] 'Managerial Wisdom: Real-life Dilberts – Did Managers Really Say That?', *Guardian*, 28 September 1999.

[26] Adapted and translated from R. Whitely and D. Hessan, *De klant als de kern van de zaak: vijf strategieën voor klantgerichte groei* (Amsterdam/Antwerpen: Contact Business Bibliotheek, 1997).

[27] R. Yeung and S. Bailey, 'Get It Together', *Accountancy*, June 1999.

[28] Team problems are revealed in S. Wetlaufer, 'The Team That Wasn't', *Harvard Business Review*, November–December 1994, pp. 22–38; L. Holpp, 'The Betrayal of the American Work Team', *Training*, May 1996, pp. 38–42; 'More Trouble with Teams', *Training*, October 1996, p. 21; and E. Neuborne, 'Companies Save, But Workers Pay', *USA Today*, 25 February 1997, pp. 1B–2B.

[29] D. W. Johnson, G. Maruyama, R. Johnson, D. Nelson and L. Skon, 'Effects of Cooperative, Competitive, and Individualistic Goal Structures on Achievement: A Meta-Analysis', *Psychological Bulletin*, January 1981, pp. 56–7. An alternative interpretation of the foregoing study that emphasises the influence of situational factors can be found in J. L. Cotton and M. S. Cook, 'Meta-Analysis and the Effects of Various Reward Systems: Some Different Conclusions from Johnson *et al.*', *Psychological Bulletin*, July 1982, pp. 176–83. Also see A. E. Ortiz, D. W. Johnson and R. T. Johnson, 'The Effect of Positive Goal and Resource Interdependence on Individual Performance', *Journal of Social Psychology*, April 1996, pp. 243–9; and S. L. Gaertner,

J. F. Dovidio, M. C. Rust, J. A. Nier, B. S. Banker, C. M. Ward, G. R. Mottola and M. Houlette, 'Reducing Intergroup Bias: Elements of Intergroup Cooperation', *Journal of Personality and Social Psychology*, March 1999, pp. 388–402.

30 See, for instance, S. T. Johnson, 'Work Teams: What's Ahead in Work Design and Rewards Management', *Compensation & Benefits Review*, March–April 1993, pp. 35–41; J. S. DeMatteo, L. T. Eby and E. Sundstrom, 'Team-Based Rewards: Current Empirical Evidence and Directions for Future Research', in *Research in Organizational Behavior, vol. 20*, eds B. M. Staw and L. L. Cummings (Greenwich, CT: JAI Press, 1998), pp. 141–83; and L. N. McClurg, 'Team Rewards: How Far Have We Come?', *Human Resource Management*, Spring 2001, pp. 73–86.

31 R. Lieber, 'Timex Resets Its Watch', *Fast Company Towns*, November 2001, p. 48; and F. Warner, 'He Builds Company Towns', *Fast Company Towns*, January 2002, pp. 46, 48.

32 S. W. Cook and M. Pelfrey, 'Reactions to Being Helped in Cooperating Interracial Groups: A Context Effect', *Journal of Personality and Social Psychology*, November 1985, p. 1243. Also see W. E. Watson, L. Johnson and D. Merritt, 'Team Orientation, Self-Orientation, and Diversity in Task Groups', *Group & Organization Management*, June 1998, pp. 161–88.

33 An excellent resource is W. G. Dyer, *Team Building: Current Issues and New Alternatives*, 3rd edn (Reading, MA: Addison-Wesley, 1995). Also see G. L. Stewart, C. C. Manz and H. P. Sims, Jr, *Team Work and Group Dynamics* (New York: John Wiley & Sons, 1999); and L. R. Offerman and R. K. Spiros, 'The Science and Practice of Team Development: Improving the Link', *Academy of Management Journal*, no. 2, 2001, pp. 376–92.

34 See A. B. Hollingshead, 'Group and Individual Training: Impact of Practice on Performance', *Small Group Research*, April 1998, pp. 254–80; and L. McDermott, B. Waite and N. Brawley, 'Putting Together a World-Class Team', *Training & Development*, January 1999, pp. 47–51.

35 R. Beckhard, 'Optimizing Team Building Efforts', *Journal of Contemporary Business*, Summer 1972, p. 24.

36 S. Bucholz and T. Roth, *Creating the High-Performance Team* (New York: John Wiley & Sons, 1987), p. xi. Also see J. R. Katzenbach and D. K. Smith, *The Wisdom of Teams: Creating the High-Performance Organization* (New York: HarperBusiness, 1993); and E. Salas, D. Rozell, B. Mullen and J. E. Driskell, 'The Effect of Team Building on Performance: An Integration', *Small Group Research*, June 1999, pp. 309–29.

37 S. Bucholz and T. Roth, *Creating the High-Performance Team* (New York: John Wiley & Sons, 1987), p. 14. Also see S. A. Wheelan, D. Murphy, E. Tsumura and S. F. Kline, 'Member Perceptions of Internal Group Dynamics and Productivity', *Small Group Research*, June 1998, pp. 371–93; M. F. R. Kets De Vries, 'High-Performance Teams: Lessons from the Pygmies', *Organizational Dynamics*, Winter 1999, pp. 66–77; G. Buzaglo and S. A. Wheelan, 'Facilitating Work Team Effectiveness: Case Studies from Central America', *Small Group Research*, February 1999, pp. 108–29; K. Maani and C. Benton, 'Rapid Team Learning: Lessons from Team New Zealand America's Cup Campaign', *Organizational Dynamics*, Spring 1999, pp. 48–62; J. Lipman-Blumen and H. J. Leavitt, 'Hot Groups "With Attitude": A New Organizational State of Mind', *Organizational Dynamics*, Spring 1999, pp. 63–73; M. J. Waller, 'The Timing of Adaptive Group Responses to Nonroutine Events', *Academy of Management Journal*, April 1999, pp. 127–37; V. U. Druskat and S. B. Wolff, 'Building the Emotional Intelligence of Groups', *Harvard Business Review*, March 2001, pp. 80–90; and A. Edmonson, R. Bohmer and G. Pisano, 'Speeding Up Team Learning', *Harvard Business Review*, October 2001, pp. 125–32.

38 See S. Caminiti, 'What Teamleaders Need To Know', *Fortune*, 20 February 1995, pp. 93–100; K. Labich, 'Elite Teams Got the Jobs Done', *Fortune*, 19 February 1996, pp. 90–96; and E. Hart, 'Top Teams', *Management Review*, February 1996, pp. 43–7.

39 P. King, 'What Makes Teamwork Work?', *Psychology Today*, December 1989, p. 17. A critical view of teams is presented in C. Casey, 'Come, Join Our Family: Discipline and Integration in Corporate Organizational Culture', *Human Relations*, February 1999, pp. 155–78.

40 Adapted from C. C. Manz and H. P. Sims, Jr, 'Leading Workers to Lead Themselves: The External Leadership of Self-Managing Work Teams', *Administrative Science Quarterly*, March 1987, pp. 106–29. Also see C. C. Manz, 'Beyond Self-Managing Work Teams: Toward Self-Leading Teams in the Workplace', in *Research in Organizational Change and Development*, vol. 4, eds R. W. Woodman and W. A. Pasmore (Greenwich, CT: JAI Press, 1990), pp. 273–99; C. C. Manz, 'Self-Leading Work Teams: Moving Beyond Self-Management Myths', *Human Relations*, no. 11, 1992, pp. 1119–40; C. C. Manz, *Mastering Self-Leadership: Empowering Yourself for Personal Excellence* (Englewood Cliffs, NJ: Prentice-Hall, 1992); M. Uhl-Bien and G. B. Graen, 'Individual Self-Management: Analysis of "Professional" Self-Managing Activities in Functional and Cross-Functional Work Teams', *Academy of Management Journal*, June 1998, pp. 340–50; G. E. Prussia, J. S. Anderson and C. C. Manz, 'Self-Leadership and Performance Outcomes: The Mediating Influence of Self-Efficacy', *Journal of Organizational Behavior*, September 1998, pp. 523–38; and P. Troiano, 'Nice Guys Finish First', *Management Review*, December 1998, p. 8.

41 Adapted and translated from 'Zuinige manier van werken', *Vacature*, 25 January 1999.

42 M. Deutsch, *The Resolution of Conflict* (New Haven, CT: Yale University Press, 1973).

43 J. Kay, *Foundations of Corporate Success* (New York: Oxford University Press, 1993), pp. 70–71.

44 See M. E. Haskins, J. Liedtka and J. Rosenblum, 'Beyond Teams: Toward an Ethic of Collaboration', *Organizational Dynamics*, Spring 1998, pp. 34–50; C. C. Chen, X. P. Chen and J. R. Meindl, 'How Can Cooperation Be Fostered? The Cultural Effects of Individualism-Collectivism', *Academy of Management Review*, April 1998, pp. 285–304; J. T. Delaney, 'Workplace Cooperation: Current Problems, New Approaches', *Journal of Labor Research*, Winter 1996, pp. 45–61; H. Mintzberg, D. Dougherty, J. Jorgensen and F. Westley, 'Some Surprising Things about Collaboration – Knowing How People Connect Makes It Work Better', *Organizational Dynamics*, Spring 1996, pp. 60–71; R. Crow, 'Institutionalized Competition and Its Effects on Teamwork', *Journal for Quality and Participation*, June 1995, pp. 46–54; and K. G. Smith, S. J. Carroll and S. J. Ashford, 'Intra- and Interorganizational Cooperation: Toward a Research Agenda', *Academy of Management Journal*, February 1995, pp. 7–23.

45 Also see D. M. Rousseau, S. B. Sitkin, R. S. Burt and C. Camerer, 'Not So Different After All: A Cross-Discipline View of Trust', *Academy of Management Review*, July 1998, pp. 393–404; and A. C. Wicks, S. L. Berman and T. M. Jones, 'The Structure of Optimal Trust: Moral and Strategic Implications', *Academy of Management Review*, January 1999, pp. 99–116.

[46] D. Lewis and A. Weigert, 'Trust as a Social Reality', *Social Forces*, June 1985, p. 971. Trust is examined as an indirect factor in K. T. Dirks, 'The Effects of Interpersonal Trust on Work Group Performance', *Journal of Applied Psychology*, June 1999, pp. 445–55.

[47] D. Lewis and A. Weigert, 'Trust as a Social Reality', *Social Forces*, June 1985, p. 970. Also see D. J. McAllister, 'Affect-and Cognition-Based Trust as Foundations for Interpersonal Cooperation in Organizations', *Academy of Management Journal*, February 1995, pp. 24–59; S. G. Goto, 'To Trust or Not to Trust: Situational and Dispositional Determinants', *Social Behavior and Personality*, no. 2, 1996, pp. 119–32; C. Gomez and B. Rosen, 'The Leader-Member Exchange as a Link between Managerial Trust And Employee Empowerment', *Group & Organization Management*, March 2001, pp. 53–69; M. Williams, 'In Whom We Trust: Group Membership as an Affective Context for the Trust Development', *Academy of Management Review*, July 2001, pp. 377–96; and S. Aryee, P. S. Budhwar and Z. X. Chen, 'Trust as a Mediator of the Relationship between Organizational Justice and Work Outcomes: Test of a Social Exchange Model', *Journal of Organizational Behavior*, May 2002, pp. 267–85.

[48] For an interesting trust exercise, see G. Thompson and P. F. Pearce, 'The Team-Trust Game', *Training & Development Journal*, May 1992, pp. 42–3.

[49] L. Kellaway, 'Welcome to the World of We', *Financial Times*, 11 September 2000. Adapted from F. Bartolome, 'Nobody Trusts the Boss Completely – Now What?', *Harvard Business Review*, March–April 1989, pp. 135–42. Also see P. Chattopadhyay, 'Beyond Direct and Symmetrical Effects: The Influence of Demographic Dissimilarity on Organizational Citizenship Behavior', *Academy of Management Journal*, June 1999, pp. 273–87; and R. Zemke, 'Can You Manage Trust?', *Training*, February 2000, pp. 76–83. For more on fairness, see K. Seiders and L. L. Berry, 'Service Fairness: What It Is and Why It Matters', *Academy of Management Executive*, May 1998, pp. 8–20. For support, see G. M. Spreitzer and A. K. Mishra, 'Giving Up Control without Losing Control: Trust and Its Substitutes' Effects on Managers' Involving Employees in Decision Making', *Group & Organization Management*, June 1999, pp. 155–87.

[50] W. Foster Owen, 'Metaphor Analysis of Cohesiveness in Small Discussion Groups', *Small Group Research*, August 1985, p. 416. Also see J. Keyton and J. Springston, 'Redefining Cohesiveness in Groups', *Small Group Research*, May 1990, pp. 234–54; S. A. Carless and C. De Paola, 'The Measurement of Cohesion in Work Teams', *Small Group Research*, February 2000, pp. 71–88; and A. V. Carron and L. R. Brawley, 'Cohesion: Conceptual and Measurement Issues', *Small Group Research*, February 2000, pp. 89–106.

[51] This distinction is based on discussion in A. Tziner, 'Differential Effects of Group Cohesiveness Types: A Clarifying Overview', *Social Behavior and Personality*, no. 2, 1982, pp. 227–39. Also see P. R. Bernthal and C. A. Insko, 'Cohesiveness without Groupthink: The Interactive Effects of Social and Task Cohesiveness', *Group & Organization Management*, March 1993, pp. 66–87.

[52] B. Mullen and C. Copper, 'The Relation between Group Cohesiveness and Performance: An Integration', *Psychological Bulletin*, March 1994, p. 224.

[53] B. Mullen and C. Copper, 'The Relation between Group Cohesiveness and Performance: An Integration', *Psychological Bulletin*, March 1994, p. 224. Additional research evidence is reported in T. Kozakaï, S. Moscovici and B. Personnaz, 'Contrary Effects of Group Cohesiveness in Minority Influence: Intergroup Categorization of the Source and Levels of Influence', *European Journal of Social Psychology*, November–December 1994, pp. 713–18; J. Henderson, A. E. Bourgeois, A. LeUnes and M. C. Meyers, 'Group Cohesiveness, Mood Disturbance, and Stress in Female Basketball Players', *Small Group Research*, April 1998, pp. 212–25; and A. Chang and P. Bordia, 'A Multidimensional Approach to the Group Cohesion-Group Performance Relationship', *Small Group Research*, August 2001, pp. 379–405.

[54] Based on B. Mullen, T. Anthony, E. Salas and J. E. Driskell, 'Group Cohesiveness and Quality of Decision Making: An Integration of Tests of the Groupthink Hypothesis', *Small Group Research*, May 1994, pp. 189–204. Also see L. D. Sargent and C. Sue-Chan, 'Does Diversity Affect Group Efficacy? The Intervening Role of Cohesion and Task Interdependence,' *Small Group Research*, August 2001, pp. 426–50; and D. I. Jung and J. J. Sosik, 'Transformational Leadership in Work Groups: The Role of Empowerment, Cohesiveness, and Collective-Efficacy on Perceived Group Performance,' *Small Group Research*, June 2002, pp. 313–36.

[55] Translated and adapted from P. Tranchart, 'Revolution Culturelle Chez Renault', *Entreprises Formation*, December 1995, pp. 10–11.

[56] See, for example, P. Jin, 'Work Motivation and Productivity in Voluntarily Formed Work Teams: A Field Study in China', *Organizational Behavior and Human Decision Processes*, 1993, pp. 133–55.

[57] See E. Sundstrom, K. P. DeMeuse and D. Futrell, 'Work Teams: Applications and Effectiveness', *American Psychologist*, February 1990, pp. 120–33.

[58] For an alternative typology of teams, see S. G. Cohen, 'New Approaches to Teams and Teamwork', in *Organizing for the Future: The New Logic for Managing Complex Organizations*, eds J. R. Galbraith, E. E. Lawler III and Associates (San Francisco, CA: Jossey-Bass, 1993), pp. 194–226; and S. G. Scott and W. O. Einstein, 'Strategic Performance Appraisal in Team-Based Organizations: One Size Does Not Fit All?', *Academy of Management Executive*, May 2001, pp. 107–16.

[59] For a good update, see A. Reinhardt and S. Browder, 'Boeing', *Business Week*, 30 September 1996, pp. 119–25. Also see G. Van der Vegt, B. Emans and E. Van de Vliert, 'Effects of Interdependencies in Project Teams', *Journal of Social Psychology*, April 1999, pp. 202–14.

[60] For a description of medical teams in action, see J. Appleby and R. Davis, 'Teamwork Used to Be a Money Saver, Now It's a Lifesaver', *USA Today*, 1 March 2001, pp. 1B–2B.

[61] Descriptions of action teams can be found in D. Field, 'Air and Ground Crews Team to Turn around Flights', *USA Today*, 17 March 1998, p. 10E; and K. S. Peterson, 'Minding the Patient: Teams Listen to Hearts, Minds', *USA Today*, 9 November 1998, p. 6D. Also see A. B. Drexler and R. Forrester, 'Interdependence: The Crux of Teamwork', *HR Magazine*, September 1998, pp. 52–62.

[62] Based on discussion in E. E. Lawler III and S. A. Mohrman, 'Quality Circles: After the Honeymoon', *Organizational Dynamics*, Spring 1987, pp. 42–54.

[63] For a report on 8000 quality circles in Mexico, see R. Carvajal, 'Its Own Reward', *Business Mexico*, Special Edition 1996, pp. 26–8.

[64] The historical development of quality circles is discussed by C. Stohl, 'Bridging the Parallel Organization: A Study of Quality Circle Effectiveness', in *Organizational Communication*, ed. M. L. McLaughlin (Beverly Hills, CA: Sage Publications, 1987), pp. 416–30; T. Li-Ping Tang, P. Smith Tollison and H. D. Whiteside, 'The Effect of Quality Circle Initiation on Motivation to Attend Quality Circle Meetings and on Task Performance', *Personnel Psychology*, Winter 1987, pp. 799–814; and N. Kano, 'A Perspective on Quality Activities in American Firms', *California Management Review*, Spring 1993, pp. 12–31. Also see the discussion of quality circles in J. B. Keys, L. T. Denton and T. R. Miller, 'The Japanese Management Theory Jungle – Revisited', *Journal of Management*, Summer 1994, pp. 373–402.

[65] Based on discussion in K. Buch and R. Spangler, 'The Effects of Quality Circles on Performance and Promotions', *Human Relations*, June 1990, pp. 573–82.

[66] See G. R. Ferris and J. A. Wagner III, 'Quality Circles in the United States: A Conceptual Reevaluation', *Journal of Applied Behavioral Science*, no. 2, 1985, pp. 155–67.

[67] B. Dale and E. Barlow, 'Quality Circles: The View from Within', *Management Decision*, no. 4, 1987, pp. 5–9.

[68] E. E. Lawler III and S. A. Mohrman, 'Quality Circles: After the Honeymoon', *Organizational Dynamics*, Spring 1987, p. 43. Also see E. E. Lawler III, 'Total Quality Management and Employee Involvement: Are They Compatible?', *Academy of Management Executive*, February 1994, pp. 68–76.

[69] See M. L. Marks, 'The Question of Quality Circles', *Psychology Today*, March 1986, pp. 36–8, 42, 44, 46.

[70] See A. K. Naj, 'Some Manufacturers Drop Effort to Adopt Japanese Techniques', *Wall Street Journal*, 7 May 1993, p. A1.

[71] See E. E. Adam, Jr, 'Quality Circle Performance', *Journal of Management*, March 1991, pp. 25–39.

[72] See M. L. Marks, P. H. Mirvis, E. J. Hackett and J. F. Grady, Jr, 'Employee Participation in a Quality Circle Program: Impact on Quality of Work Life, Productivity, and Absenteeism', *Journal of Applied Psychology*, February 1986, pp. 61–9; R. P. Steel and R. F. Lloyd, 'Cognitive, Affective, and Behavioral Outcomes of Participation in Quality Circles: Conceptual and Empirical Findings', *Journal of Applied Behavioral Science*, January 1988, pp. 1–17; and K. Buch and R. Spangler, 'The Effects of Quality Circles on Performance and Promotions', *Human Relations*, June 1990, pp. 573–82. Additional research is reported in T. Li-Ping Tang, P. Smith Tollison and H. D. Whiteside, 'Differences between Active and Inactive Quality Circles in Attendance and Performance', *Public Personnel Management*, Winter 1993, pp. 579–90; and C. Doucouliagos, 'Worker Participation and Productivity in Labor-Managed and Participatory Capitalist Firms: A Meta-Analysis', *Industrial and Labor Relations Review*, October 1995, pp. 58–77.

[73] See B. S. Bell and S. W. J. Kozlowski, 'A Typology of Virtual Teams: Implications for Effective Leadership', *Group Organization Management*, March 2002, pp. 14–49; A. M. Townsend, S. M. DeMarie and A. R. Hendrickson, 'Virtual Teams: Technology and the Workplace of the Future', *Academy of Management Executive*, August 1998, pp. 17–29; See W. F. Cascio, 'Managing a Virtual Workplace', *Academy of Management Executive*, August 2000, pp. 81–90; C. Joinson, 'Managing Virtual Teams', *HR Magazine*, June 2002, pp. 69–73; and D. Robb, 'Virtual Workplace', *HR Magazine*, June 2002, pp. 105–13.

[74] S. L. Jarvenpaa and D. E. Leidner, 'Communication and Trust in Global Virtual Teams', *Organization Science*, November–December 1999, pp. 791–815.

[75] Ibid.

[76] M. E. Warkentin, L. Sayeed and R. Hightower, 'Virtual Teams versus Face-to-Face Teams: An Exploratory Study of a Web-Based Conference System', *Decision Sciences*, Fall 1997, pp. 975–96. Also see J. Lipnack and J. Stamps, *Virtual Teams: People Working across Boundaries with Technology* (New York: John Wiley & Sons, 2001).

[77] C. Durnell Cramton, *Interaction Processes in Dispersed Teams* (George Mason University, School of Management, Working Paper, 1998).

[78] M. E. Warkentin, L. Sayeed and R. Hightower, 'Virtual Teams versus Face-to-Face Teams: An Exploratory Study of a Web-Based Conference System', *Decision Sciences*, Fall 1997, pp. 975–96.

[79] W. F. Cascio and S. Shurygailo, 'E-Leadership and Virtual Teams', *Organizational Dynamics*, January 2003, pp. 362–76.

[80] B. L. Kirkman, B. Rosen, C. B. Gibson, P. E. Tesluk and O. McPherson, 'Five Challenges to Virtual Team Success: Lessons from Sabre, Inc.', *Academy of Management Executive*, August 2002, pp. 67–79.

[81] S. L. Jarvenpaa and D. E. Leidner, 'Communication and Trust in Global Virtual Teams', *Organization Science*, November–December 1999, pp. 791–815.

[82] Based on P. Bordia, N. DiFonzo and A. Chang, 'Rumor as Group Problem Solving: Development Patterns in Informal Computer-Mediated Groups', *Small Group Research*, February 1999, pp. 8–28.

[83] See K. A. Graetz, E. S. Boyle, C. E. Kimble, P. Thompson and J. L. Garloch, 'Information Sharing in Face-to-Face, Teleconferencing, and Electronic Chat Groups', *Small Group Research*, December 1998, pp. 714–43.

[84] Based on F. Niederman and R. J. Volkema, 'The Effects of Facilitator Characteristics on Meeting Preparation, Set Up, and Implementation', *Small Group Research*, June 1999, pp. 330–60; and B. Whitworth, B. Gallupe and R. McQueen, 'Generating Agreement in Computer-Mediated Groups,' *Small Group Research*, October 2001, pp. 625–65.

[85] Based on J. J. Sosik, B. J. Avolio and S. S. Kahai, 'Inspiring Group Creativity: Comparing Anonymous and Identified Electronic Brainstorming', *Small Group Research*, February 1998, pp. 3–31; and B. Whitworth, B. Gallupe and R. McQueen, 'Generating Agreement in Computer-Mediated Groups', *Small Group Research*, October 2001, pp. 625–65.

[86] M. E. Warkentin, L. Sayeed and R. Hightower, 'Virtual Teams versus Face-to-Face Teams: An Exploratory Study of a Web-Based Conference System', *Decision Sciences*, Fall 1997, pp. 975–96.

[87] Ibid.

[88] Based on M. M. Montoya-Weis, A. P. Massey and M. Song, 'Getting It Together: Temporal Coordination and Conflict Management in Global Virtual Teams', *Academy of Management Journal*, December 2001, pp. 1251–62.

[89] R. K. Hart and P. L. McLeod, 'Rethinking Team Building in Geographically Dispersed Teams: One Message at a Time', *Organizational Dynamics*, January 2003, pp. 352–76.

[90] N. Merrick, 'Remote Control', *People Management*, 26 September 1996.

[91] For practical tips, see K. Kiser, 'Building a Virtual Team', *Training*, March 1999, p. 34.

[92] Derived from M. E. Warkentin, L. Sayeed and R. Hightower, 'Virtual Teams versus Face-to-Face Teams: An Exploratory Study of a Web-Based Conference System', *Decision Sciences*, Fall 1997, pp. 975–96; S. L. Jarvenpaa and D. E. Leidner, 'Communication and Trust in Global Virtual Teams', *Organization Science*, November–December 1999, pp. 791–815; and W. F. Cascio, 'Managing a Virtual Workplace', *Academy of Management Executive*, August 2000, pp. 81–90.

[93] See M. Moravec, O. J. Johannessen and T. A. Hjelmas, 'The Well-Managed Self-Managed Teams', *Management Review*, June 1998, pp. 56–8; and 'Case Study in C-Sharp Minor', *Training*, October 1998, p. 21.

[94] M. Moravec, O. J. Johannessen and T. A. Hjelmas, 'The Well-Managed Self-Managed Teams', *Management Review*, June 1998, pp. 56–8.

[95] For example, see M. Selz, 'Testing Self-Managed Teams, Entrepreneur Hopes to Lose Job', *Wall Street Journal*, 11 January 1994, pp. B1–B2; 'Even in Self-Managed Teams There Has to Be a Leader', *Supervisory Management*, December 1994, pp. 7–8; and R. M. Yandrick, 'A Team Effort', *HR Magazine*, June 2001, pp. 136–41.

[96] Good background discussions can be found in P. S. Goodman, R. Devadas and T. L. Griffith Hughson, 'Groups and Productivity: Analyzing the Effectiveness of Self-Managing Teams', in *Productivity in Organizations*, eds J. P. Campbell, R. J. Campbell and Associates (San Francisco, CA: Jossey-Bass, 1988), pp. 295–327; and C. Lee, 'Beyond Teamwork', *Training*, June 1990, pp. 25–32. Also see S. G. Cohen, G. E. Ledford, Jr and G. M. Spreitzer, 'A Predictive Model of Self-Managing Work Team Effectiveness', *Human Relations*, May 1996, pp. 643–76. See J. E. McGrath, 'Small Group Research, That Once and Future Field: An Interpretation of the Past With an Eye to the Future', *Group Dynamics: Theory, Research, and Practice*, no. 1, 1997, pp. 7–27. A special issue of *Group Dynamics: Theory, Research, and Practice* (no. 1, 2000) is devoted to the history and future of group research. For instance, see E. Sundstrom, M. McIntyre, T. Halfhill and H. Richards, 'Work Groups: From the Hawthorne Studies to Work Teams of the 1990s and Beyond', *Group Dynamics: Theory, Research, and Practice*, no. 1, 2000, pp. 44–67. See E. L. Trist, G. W. Higgin, H. Murray and A. B. Pollock, *Organizational Choice* (London: Tavistock, 1963); W. Niepce and E. Molleman, 'Work Design Issues in Lean Production from a Sociotechnical Systems Perspective: Neo-Taylorism or the next Step in Sociotechnical Design?', *Human Relations*, March 1998, pp. 259–87; and M. Moldaschl and W. G. Weber, 'The "Three Waves" of Industrial Group Work', *Human Relations*, March 1998, pp. 347–88. See E. L. Trist, G. W. Higgin, H. Murray and A. B. Pollock, *Organizational Choice* (London: Tavistock, 1963); W. Niepce and E. Molleman, 'Work Design Issues in Lean Production from a Sociotechnical Systems Perspective: Neo-Taylorism or the next Step in Sociotechnical Design?', *Human Relations*, March 1998, pp. 259–87; and M. Moldaschl and W. G. Weber, 'The "Three Waves" of Industrial Group Work', *Human Relations*, March 1998, pp. 347–88.

[97] See E. L. Trist, G. W. Higgin, H. Murray and A. B. Pollock, *Organizational Choice* (London: Tavistock, 1963); W. Niepce and E. Molleman, 'Work Design Issues in Lean Production from a Sociotechnical Systems Perspective: Neo-Taylorism or the next Step in Sociotechnical Design?', *Human Relations*, March 1998, pp. 259–87; and M. Moldaschl and W. G. Weber, 'The "Three Waves" of Industrial Group Work', *Human Relations*, March 1998, pp. 347–88.

[98] See G. Farias and A. Varma, 'Integrating Job Characteristics, Sociotechnical Systems, and Reengineering: Presenting a Unified Approach to Work and Organization Design', *Organization Development Journal*, Fall 2000, pp. 11–24; and S. K. Parker, T. D. Wall and J. L. Cordery, 'Future Work Design Research and Practice: Towards an Elaborated Model of Work Design', *Journal of Occupational and Organizational Psychology*, November 2001, pp. 413–40.

[99] For an instructive continuum of work team autonomy, see R. D. Banker, J. M. Field, R. G. Schroeder and K. K. Sinha, 'Impact of Work Teams on Manufacturing Performance: A Longitudinal Field Study', *Academy of Management Journal*, August 1996, pp. 867–90.

[100] M. Moravec, O. J. Johannessen and T. A. Hjelmas, 'The Well-Managed Self-Managed Teams', *Management Review*, June 1998, pp. 56–8.

[101] M. Moravec, O. J. Johannessen and T. A. Hjelmas, 'The Well-Managed Self-Managed Teams', *Management Review*, June 1998, pp. 56–8. Also see R. Wageman, 'How Leaders Foster Self-Managing Team Effectiveness: Design Choices versus Hands-on Coaching', *Organization Science*, no. 5, 2001, pp. 559–77.

[102] M. Moravec, O. J. Johannessen and T. A. Hjelmas, 'The Well-Managed Self-Managed Teams', *Management Review*, June 1998, pp. 56–8.

[103] Also see D. E. Yeats and C. Hyten, *High-Performing Self-Managed Work Teams: A Comparison of Theory to Practice* (Thousand Oaks, CA: Sage, 1998).

[104] See P. S. Goodman, R. Devadas and T. L. Griffith Hughson, 'Groups and Productivity: Analyzing the Effectiveness of Self-Managing Teams', in *Productivity in Organizations*, eds J. P. Campbell, R. J. Campbell and Associates (San Francisco, CA: Jossey-Bass, 1988), pp. 295–327.

[105] Drawn from P. S. Goodman, R. Devadas and T. L. Griffith Hughson, 'Groups and Productivity: Analyzing the Effectiveness of Self-Managing Teams', in *Productivity in Organizations*, eds J. P. Campbell, R. J. Campbell and Associates (San Francisco, CA: Jossey-Bass, 1988), pp. 295–327. Also see E. F. Rogers, W. Metlay, I. T. Kaplan and T. Shapiro, 'Self-Managing Work Teams: Do They Really Work?', *Human Resource Planning*, no. 2, 1995, pp. 53–7; and V. U. Druskat and S. B. Wolff, 'Effects and Timing of Developmental Peer Appraisals in Self-Managing Work Groups', *Journal of Applied Psychology*, February 1999, pp. 58–74.

[106] Based on R. C. Liden, S. J. Wayne and M. L. Kraimer, 'Managing Individual Performance in Work Groups', *Human Resource Management*, Spring 2001, pp. 63–72.

[107] See M. H. Jordan, H. S. Field and A. A. Armenakis, 'The Relationship of Group Process Variables and Team Performance: A Team Level Analysis in a Field Setting', *Small Group Research*, February 2002, pp. 121–50.

[108] B. L. Kirkman and D. L. Shapiro, 'The Impact of Cultural Values on Job Satisfaction and Organizational Commitment in Self-Managing Work Teams: The Mediating Role of Employee Resistance', *Academy of Management Journal*, June 2001, p. 565.

[109] J. R. Barker, 'Tightening the Iron Cage: Concertive Control in Self-managing Teams', *Administrative Science Quarterly*, vol. 38, no. 3, 1993, pp. 408–37.

[110] P. Thoms, K. S. Moore and K. S. Scott, 'The Relationship between Self-Efficacy for Participating in Self-Managed Work Groups and the Big Five Personality Dimensions', *Journal of Organizational Behavior*, July 1996, pp. 349–62. Also see B. Barry and G. L. Stewart, 'Composition, Process, and Performance in Self-Managed Groups: The Role of Personality', *Journal of Applied Psychology*, no. 1, 1997, pp. 62–78.

[111] For useful tips, see L. Holpp, 'Five Ways to Sink Self-Managed Teams', *Training*, September 1993, pp. 38–42; and P. Thoms, J. K. Pinto, D. H. Parente, and V. U. Druskat, 'Adaptation to Self-Managing Work Teams', *Small Group Research*, February 2002, pp. 3–31.

[112] See B. Dumaine, 'The New Non-Manager Managers', *Fortune*, 22 February 1993, pp. 80–4; and 'Easing the Fear of Self-Directed Teams', *Training*, August 1993, pp. 14, 55–6.

[113] See B. Dumaine, 'Who Needs a Boss?', *Fortune*, 7 May 1990, pp. 55, 58; and J. Hillkirk, 'Self-Directed Work Teams Give TI Lift', *USA Today*, 20 December 1993, p. 8B. A good contingency model for empowering teams is presented in R. C. Liden, S. J. Wayne and L. Bradway, 'Connections Make the Difference', *HR Magazine*, February 1996, pp. 73–9.

[114] Data from S. Alper, D. Tjosvold and K. S. Law, 'Interdependence and Controversy in Group Decision Making: Antecedents to Effective Self-Managing Teams', *Organizational Behavior and Human Decision Processes*, April 1998, pp. 33–52.

[115] For an instructive case study on this topic, see C. C. Manz, D. E. Keating and A. Donnellon, 'Preparing for an Organizational Change to Employee Self-Management: The Managerial Transition', *Organizational Dynamics*, Autumn 1990, pp. 15–26. Also see B. L. Kirkman and B. Rosen, 'Beyond Self-Management: Antecedents and Consequences of Team Empowerment', *Academy of Management Journal*, February 1999, pp. 58–74; and M. S. O'Connell, D. Doverspike and A. B. Cober, 'Leadership and Semiautonomous Work Team Performance: A Field Study', *Group & Organization Management*, March 2002, pp. 50–65.

[116] M. Moravec, O. J. Johannessen and T. A. Hjelmas, 'Thumbs Up for Self-Managed Teams', *Management Review*, July–August 1997, pp. 42–7.

[117] Questionnaire items adapted from C. Johnson-George and W. C. Swap, 'Measurement of Specific Interpersonal Trust: Construction and Validation of a Scale to Assess Trust in a Specific Other', *Journal of Personality and Social Psychology*, December 1982, pp. 1306–17; and D. J. McAllister, 'Affect- and Cognition-Based Trust as Foundations for Interpersonal Cooperation in Organizations', *Academy of Management Journal*, February 1995, pp. 24–59.

[118] Ten questionnaire items excerpted from W. G. Dyer, *Team Building: Current Issues and New Alternatives, third edition* (Reading, MA: Addison-Wesley, 1995), pp. 96–9.

Chapter 9

Organisational climate: diversity and stress

Learning Outcomes

When you finish studying the material in this chapter, you should be familiar with:

- ✓ stereotypes and the process of stereotype formation
- ✓ diversity and five reasons why managing diversity is a competitive advantage
- ✓ organisational practices used to effectively manage diversity
- ✓ the term 'stress'
- ✓ why the Karasek's Job Demand-Control (JD-C) model is so important
- ✓ the model of occupational stress
- ✓ what stressful life events are
- ✓ burnout and solutions to reduce it
- ✓ the mechanisms of social support
- ✓ coping with stress and burnout

Opening Case Study: Real partners simply do not get sick

Colin Tenner was a senior partner in the Northern Ireland office of PricewaterhouseCoopers (PwC), the accountancy firm. Mr Tenner was frequently ill from work-related stress and had, he has claimed at an employment tribunal, been bullied by a client. He had been with the firm for 23 years when he was fired in February 2010. In legal terms Mr Tenner was made 'redundant'.

At the employment tribunal, Mr Tenner said that his health had deteriorated in January 2009, following mismanagement by the firm and bullying by a client. He had told his managers that he was suffering from work-related stress caused by the bullying. A junior member of Mr Tenner's team had raised a formal complaint against the bully. Mr Tenner's complaints about the client had been made repeatedly over a six-month period. Despite the firm having an anti-bullying policy, Mr Tanner claims that nothing was done. Instead several senior managers had told him that he was not protected by the anti-bullying policy because he was a partner. As a result, Mr Tenner took two days' sick leave in January 2009. It is alleged that reactions by senior managers at the firm and their decision to make him redundant were discriminatory with respect to the disability he was suffering from at the time. The managing partner had declared in an email to another partner that he had heard that Mr Tenner was ill again and that the firm needed to point out that 'real partners do no not get ill'. According to Mr Tenner's claim, colleagues and partners in the firm believed that he was 'malingering' (i.e. exaggerating symptoms of illness for personal benefit or gain). A member of the firm's partner affairs team wrote to the firm's chief medical officer with the message that 'there was a strongly held view that [Mr. Tenner] was not as unwell' as he claimed.

The firm rejected this version of events, arguing that Mr Tenner's claim was 'completely without merit'. The firm faced a very large claim. Mr Tenner was 45 years old at the time of his redundancy and partners normally retire at 60. Mr Tenner claimed 15 years of lost earnings.

For discussion

The picture of the internal climate at this particular PwC office is not pretty. Are we missing parts of the story or should Mr Tenner's claim succeed?

Source: Based on two articles by Michael Herman, 'PwC manager said "real partners do not get sick"', *The Times*, 7 May 2010, and 'Bullying "did not apply" to PwC partner', *The Times*, 8 May 2010.

The traditional definition of organisational climate is that it is a shared perception in an organisation about what is important and what is appropriate.[1] The extensive research conducted on organisational climate suggests that it is highly important for the performance of individuals, teams and whole organisations.[2] Stress among employees, and conflict between them, whatever the reason, affect performance at all levels, as seen in product quality, safety performance and employee turnover. Conflict, stress and burnout are all factors that contribute to the quality of the overall climate in an organisation. In this chapter we explain first why and how the climate and the social life of the organisation can be understood and then go on to address two areas that affect the climate.

First of all, conflicts arise all the time. They can be about resources, structures, culture, power, money and many other things. Conflict is also closely linked to issues of power and politics in an organisation and we deal with all those issues in Chapter 14. Second, people are different. Men and women differ in a number of ways. People have different personalities, different ethnic backgrounds, subscribe to different spiritual beliefs (including none) and they can differ in sexual orientation. Each of these diversity factors can, on their own, create conflict and affect organisational climate. Third, work-related stress can arise for many reasons. Workload, poor supervision, bad bosses and any of these combined with any diversity issue can lead to stress. Stress rebounds as human resources lost to the organisation and can damage lives.

9.1 Organisational climate

In this chapter we use the term 'organisational climate' to present a series of issues that are of great practical importance for managers (and employees as well). Using the term 'climate' requires that a clear distinction is made between climate and the very closely related term 'culture', which is the subject of Chapter 12. In terms of popularity, culture seems to have pushed climate aside more than a decade ago. This, we argue, is fine as far as culture goes. However, conflict, diversity and stress are directly experienced and have immediate consequences. They do not fit well within the culture terminology and are better discussed in terms of organisational climate. These matters are often placed under headings such as perception (stereotypes and diversity) and power (conflict) or they get their own heading (most frequently in the case of stress).

Elements of climate – and culture

The distinction seems clear at first. **Climate** is about a situation and the feelings, reflections and behaviour of people in the organisation. In this sense climate is changing fairly rapidly over time, it depends on the observer and it can be shaped by individuals. In contrast, **culture** is a state or a context, determined by history and held by organisational members collectively. It lies deeper, it is resistant to change and any change happens slowly. The problem with climate and culture is that they not only overlap but affect each other. In a classic use of one meteorological analogy used to explain another, it has been suggested that organisational climate is like the wind chill factor, which is the subjective perception of two measurable characteristics, temperature and wind speed.[3] The problem is that climate and culture are two different ways of looking at something that is broadly similar. Culture examines underlying values and assumptions whereas climate examines surface level manifestations. In contrast to the importance of historical evolution, climate represents a cross-section or 'snapshot' made at a specific point in time. In this sense, both perspectives try to deal with the idea that the social context of an organisation is a *result* of social interaction and at the same time *shapes* that interaction.

In order to understand what climate means when it is encountered, a set of climate dimensions are helpful. The climate literature has a great multitude of measures. Aggregating and testing their validity is part of the research process. In this case the great number of variables in the literature can be reduced to eight dimensions, as indicated in Table 9.1.

The climate dimensions are a useful starting point for assessing the climate in any given organisation. Further, while they can be used systematically, for example to design a survey, even awareness of the eight dimensions will allow quick assessment of an organisational climate – only a few questions need to be asked.

Evidence about organisational climate

The studies of organisational outcomes in the context of climate indicate that this factor has implications for the financial performance of firms through employee involvement, well-being, innovation

Table 9.1 Eight Dimensions of the Universe of Psychological Climate Perceptions

Dimension name	Definition
Autonomy	The perception of self-determination with respect to work procedures, goals and priorities
Cohesion	The perception of togetherness of sharing within the organisation setting, including the willingness of members to provide material aid
Trust	The perception of freedom to communicate openly with members at higher organisational levels about sensitive or personal issues with the expectation that the integrity of such communications will not be violated
Pressure	The perception of time demands with respect to task completion and performance standards
Support	The perception of the tolerance of member behaviour by superiors, including the willingness to let members learn from their mistakes without fear of reprisal
Recognition	The perception that member contributions to the organisation are acknowledged
Fairness	The perception that organisational practices are equitable and non-arbitrary or capricious
Innovation	The perception that change and creativity are encouraged, including risk-taking into new areas or areas where the member has little or no prior experience

Source: D. Koys and T. DeCotiis, 'Inductive measures of organizational climate', *Human Relations*, no. 44, 1991, pp. 265–85.

and learning. For example climate factors have been found to explain variance in profits between firms, through a questionnaire method to assess climate in terms of how employees perceive the emphasis on human resources and perceived emphasis on goal accomplishment. These measures, while clearly simplifying a complex concept, are twice as powerful as economic factors (industry profitability and firm market share) in explaining why some firms are more profitable than others.[4]

The eight dimension identified in Table 9.1 are, as noted, useful descriptors. They may, however, be complex to work with in practice. A study of 245 Danish organisations showed that the eight dimensions could in fact be reduced to just one, called tension.[5] The idea that it is possible to discern a tense, as opposed to a 'relaxed', organisation is intuitively attractive. However, the ideal degree of tension is not likely to be the same for all organisations and at all times.

HR Application of organisational climate

The eight dimensions shown in Table 9.1 are closely linked to the application of climate thinking in an organisation. The items listed below are both suitable for assessing climate and for taking action to change climate:[6]

- *Communication*: how often and the types of means by which information is communicated in the organisation.
- *Values*: the guiding principles of the organisation and whether or not they are held by all employees, including leaders.
- *Expectations*: types of expectations regarding how managers and employees behave and make decisions.
- *Norms*: the normal, routine ways of behaving and treating one another in the organisation.
- *Policies and rules*: these convey the degree of flexibility and restriction of behaviours in the organisation.
- *Programmes*: programming and formal initiatives help support and emphasise a workplace climate.
- *Leadership*: leaders that consistently support the climate desired.

Four important factors that contribute to organisational climate are discussed in the following section, starting with conflicts generally and then moving on to some important sources of conflict and climate, stereotypes, diversity and stress.

> **Critical thinking**
>
> Think about two events or changes in an organisation you know. One should be instantaneous and the other gradual. What were the differences between them and the effects they had?

9.2 Stereotypes and diversity

The way people see one another is important for the climate in the organisation and for the occurrence and resolution of many conflicts. Seeing or perceiving those around you forms the starting point for understanding who others are and how we work and interact with them. The starting point in this section is that our perception of others is shaped by a set of beliefs about individuals and groups. These **stereotypes** can be the source of conflicts that influence the climate at any given time. Dealing with stereotypes, and the diversity of people (which is increasing with globalisation), which may contribute to stereotypes and other differences, is a way of managing the climate in an organisation.

Stereotypes

While it is often true that beauty is in the eye of the beholder, perception does result in some predictable outcomes. People aware of the perception process and its outcomes enjoy a competitive edge. The Walt Disney Company, for instance, takes full advantage of perceptual tendencies to influence customers' reactions to waiting in long lines at its theme parks. This is done by posting generously overestimated waiting times at each attraction, so that guests come away mysteriously grateful for having hung around only 20 minutes for a 58-second twirl in the Alice in Wonderland teacups.

Likewise, managers can use knowledge of perceptual outcomes and perception errors (see Chapter 4) to help them interact more effectively with employees. Since these perceptual errors often distort the evaluation of job applicants and employee performance, employers need to guard against them. This section examines one of the most important and potentially harmful perceptual outcomes associated with person perception: stereotypes. After exploring the process of stereotype formation and maintenance, we discuss **sex-role stereotypes**, age stereotypes, race stereotypes, and the challenge to avoid stereotypical biases.

Stereotype formation and maintenance

'A stereotype is an individual's set of beliefs about the characteristics or attributes of a group.'[7] This implies that people are judged on the basis of their membership of some known group. Stereotypes are not always negative. For example, the belief that engineers are good at maths is certainly part of a stereotype. In another example, it is known that women are most likely to be the possessors of the skills required to successfully design and develop information systems – a combination of technical and, crucially, social and communication skills. The information systems industry however, has been disproportionately populated by men. Male designers, developers and sales staff were often almost exclusively focused on the technology itself, rather than on the requirements of users or the commercial viability of the technical product.[8]

Stereotypes may be accurate, but very often this is not the case. For example, television coverage of football matches suggests that fans of the game are amiable, sometimes chubby and balding, working class and male. Hooligans, football fans given to violence before, during and after matches, are portrayed as males with clean-shaven heads, tattoos and beer bellies. Some hooligans, however, are ordinary-looking, lead boring and otherwise respectable lives and are very hard to spot.

Stereotyping is a four-step process. It begins by categorising people into groups according to various criteria, such as gender, age, race, religion, sexual orientation and occupation. Next, we infer that all people within a particular category possess the same traits or characteristics (e.g. all women are nurturing, older people have more job-related accidents, Africans are good athletes, all Muslims are fundamentalists, and all professors are absentminded). Then, we form expectations of others and interpret their behaviour according to our stereotypes. Finally, stereotypes are maintained by (1) overestimating the frequency of stereotypic behaviours exhibited by others, (2) incorrectly explaining expected and unexpected behaviours and (3) differentiating minority individuals from oneself.[9]

Although these steps are self-reinforcing, there are ways to break the chain of stereotyping. Research shows that the use of stereotypes is influenced by the amount and type of information available to an individual and his or her motivation to process information accurately.[10] People are less apt to use stereotypes to judge others when they encounter salient information that is highly inconsistent with a stereotype. People also are less likely to rely on stereotypes when they are motivated to avoid using them; that is, accurate information processing requires mental effort. Stereotyping is really a shortcut for information processing.

Gender stereotypes

A **gender stereotype** is the belief that differing traits and abilities make men and women particularly well suited to different roles. For example, gender stereotypes view women as more expressive, less independent, more emotional, less logical, less quantitatively oriented and more participative than men. Men, on the other hand, are more often perceived as lacking interpersonal sensitivity and warmth, less expressive, less apt to ask for directions, more quantitatively oriented and more autocratic and directive than women.[11]

Although research demonstrates that men and women do not systematically differ in the manner suggested by traditional stereotypes,[12] these stereotypes still persist. A study compared sex-role stereotypes held by men and women from five countries: China, Japan, Germany, the UK and the USA. Males in all five countries perceived that successful professionals possessed characteristics and traits more commonly ascribed to men in general than to women in general. Among the females, the same pattern of gender typing was found in all countries except the USA. American females perceived that males and females were equally likely to possess traits necessary for success.[13] Females are more often typed in terms of sexuality and sexual attractiveness, most types being negative (e.g. bimbo). Perceptions of male types were more differentiated in terms of occupation and that the 'typical' male has a job and a profession, whereas non-traditional males do not work. These results are consistent across multiple studies from different Western countries and we may conclude that they reflect current stereotypes of men and women in Western society.[14]

While gender stereotypes are not the only reason women have less than total equality, it may be a contributing factor. Perhaps the most important aspect of stereotypes, however, is that underlying trends change slowly. The legal industry has always been seen as male dominated. However, by 2009, more than 60 per cent of law students and trainee lawyers in England and Wales were women.[15]

HR Despite this positive trend women continue to encounter the glass ceiling.[16] The **glass ceiling** represents an invisible barrier that separates women and minorities from advancing into top management positions.

The number of women top managers is very low and the same applies to women board members. As in the case of professions, change is slow. Only where quotas have been introduced, as in Norway, do women have equal representation on corporate boards. Even neighbouring countries such as Denmark and Sweden, normally seen as culturally similar to Norway, lag behind, with women board members numbering between 20 per cent and 30 per cent.

Historically, female employment was concentrated in relatively low-paying and low-level occupation. The gender pay gap has narrowed a little in recent years and remains high – ranging from 5 per cent to 30 per cent in Europe. These variations are for national labour markets. More details from the UK show that the pay gap is greatest in skilled trades and narrowest in professional occupations.[17]

HR One of the reasons why women are unable to break the glass ceiling is the masculine culture typical for the highest corporate echelons. The glass ceiling may be constructed out of a culture which makes organisational life hard for women, leading to more stress and ultimately to more exits from management than is seen for men. Whether a male-dominated culture is to blame or whether women's career choices also play a role is not well known. In his book *The Leadership Mystique*, Manfred Kets de Vries argues that 'career advancement is not easy for women'. He gives a combination of explanations. 'Very often', he says, 'they centre on the anatomy-is-destiny theme: pregnancy and childrearing throw women off the career trajectory.' Another answer given is that women are more concerned about keeping a balanced lifestyle than men and therefore not prepared to make the kind of sacrifices that top management demands. A further possible explanation is that women are by nature more nurturing than men and therefore choose to focus on the needs of family and friends over career commitments. A more controversial answer sometimes given is that men, in their heart of hearts, are scared of women. And some are, really. Women, in contrast, are more likely to feel comfortable with both men and women.[18]

Age stereotypes

Age stereotypes reinforce age discrimination because of their negative orientation. The activity rate of 55–64-year-old employees in the European Union (EU) amounted to 40.1 per cent in 2002 and 47.4 in 2011, somewhat below the Union's objective of 50 per cent by 2010.[19] For example, long-standing age stereotypes depict older workers as less satisfied, not as involved with their work, less motivated, not as committed, less productive than their younger co-workers, and more apt to be absent from work. Older employees are also perceived as being more accident-prone. As with sex-role stereotypes, these age stereotypes are more fiction than fact. The business case for employing older workers seems more compelling than ever, as they are more likely to stay in their jobs for longer.[20]

HR The evidence does not support age stereotypes. Data from 185 different studies showed that as age increases so does employees' job satisfaction, job involvement, internal work motivation and organisational commitment. Moreover, older workers were not more accident-prone.[21]

HR Results are not as clear-cut regarding job performance. One meta-analysis (of 96 studies representing 38 983 people) revealed that age and job performance were unrelated.[22] Some propose that the relationship between age and performance changes as people grow older.[23] Data obtained from

24 219 individuals revealed that age was positively related to performance for younger employees (25–30 years of age) and then plateaued: older employees were not less productive. Age and experience also predicted performance better for more complex jobs, and job experience had a stronger relationship with performance than age.[24] Another study examined memory, reasoning, spatial relations and dual tasking for 1000 doctors, aged between 25 and 92, and 600 other adults. The researchers concluded 'that a large proportion of older individuals scored as well or better on aptitude tests as those in the prime of life'.[25]

HR What about turnover and absenteeism? A meta-analysis of 29 studies with 12 356 individuals revealed that age and turnover were negatively related: that is, older employees quit less often than younger employees. Similarly, another meta-analysis of 34 studies encompassing 7772 workers indicated that age was inversely related to both voluntary (a day at the beach) and involuntary (sick day) absenteeism.[26] Contrary to stereotypes, older workers are ready and able to meet their job requirements. Moreover these results suggest that managers should focus more attention on the turnover and absenteeism among younger workers than among older workers.

Ethnic and racial stereotypes

Research into people's attitudes towards migrants revealed that Sweden, Ireland, Norway, Finland and Denmark are most tolerant towards the entry of migrants. Hungary and Poland have the lowest score. Countries such as Spain, Slovenia, the Czech Republic and the Netherlands are in between.[27] Legislation banning headscarves and other religious symbols in schools and other public institutions and regulating correct wear in the workplace have been adopted or proposed in a number of countries. Denmark, for example, now has laws regulating the robes that judges must wear in court. This legislation was brought in to avoid the possibility that at some future point in time a woman would preside as a judge wearing a headscarf.

HR Unfortunately, three additional trends suggest that ethnic minorities are experiencing their own glass ceiling. First, ethnic minorities are advancing even less in the professional ranks than women. Applicants with foreign names are more likely to be rejected in job screening processes. In Belgium an increasing number of people originating from non-European countries are changing their names under pressure from their employers. The main reason is that a more familiar name sounds better; for example, when answering the phone.[28] Second, ethnic minorities also tend to earn less. Finally, a study into ethnic minorities in the boardroom among the 100 largest companies in Europe revealed a concrete ceiling instead of a glass one. Not one top company with a minority chief executive officer (CEO) could be found, and few with even one minority officer at any senior level. A spokesperson for a German chemicals company scanned his memory for a minority board member and recalled, 'We had a Belgian once.' These findings are consistent with previous studies that indicated that ethnic minorities have more negative career experiences, lower upward mobility, lower career satisfaction, decreased job involvement and greater turnover rates than their white counterparts.[29] It is, however, remarkable to notice that ethnic minorities are faced with obvious racism and fewer opportunities than their white colleagues, even though Europe is heading towards a labour shortage in the near future.

Evidence about stereotypes and diversity

Three different questions are involved when it comes to evidence: are there stereotypes out there; does that affect organisational performance; and does active pursuit of diversity give some organisations an advantage?

In general, stereotypic characteristics are used to differentiate a particular group of people from other groups.[30] The example highlights how people use stereotypes to interpret their environment and to make judgements about others. Unfortunately, stereotypes can lead to poor decisions and can create barriers for women, older individuals, ethnic minorities and people with disabilities. Stereotypes can also undermine loyalty and job satisfaction. For example, a study of 280 minority executives revealed that 40 per cent believed that they had been denied well-deserved promotions because of discrimination. Another sample of 2958 workers indicated that women and people of ethnic minorities perceived lower chances of advancement than white people. Finally, respondents who saw little opportunity for advancement tended to be less loyal, less committed and less satisfied with their jobs.[31]

There are compelling regulatory and institutional reasons to treat these areas seriously. Leaving stereotypes unchallenged may in some cases be illegal or it may create legal liabilities that appear as lawsuits with claims of harassment or discrimination. Leaving stereotypes unchallenged is also a sin of omission in that organisations failing to address stereotype issues reduce the pool of potentially valuable employees significantly.

HR

There is some evidence that effectively managing diversity is a competitive advantage. This advantage stems from the process in which the management of diversity affects organisational behaviour and effectiveness in a number of areas:

- *Lower costs and improved employee attitudes.* Turnover and absenteeism were found to be higher for women and ethnic minorities than for whites.[32] Diversity is also related to employee attitudes. Past research revealed that people who were different from most others in their work units in racial or ethnic background were less psychologically committed to their organisations, less satisfied with their careers and perceived less autonomy to make decisions on their jobs.
- *Improved recruiting efforts.* Attracting and retaining competent employees is a competitive advantage. Organisations that effectively manage diversity are more likely to meet this challenge, because women and minorities are attracted to such companies. Research at the University of Amsterdam showed that women compared themselves more with female than with male targets, and saw the situation of female targets as a more likely potential future for themselves.[33]
- *Increased sales, market share and corporate profits.* Workforce diversity is the mirror image of consumer diversity. It is thus important for companies to market their products so that they appeal to diverse customers and markets. For example, a study of over 1000 companies suggested that a diverse top management team can contribute to corporate profits. With a majority of women in senior management sales growth averaged 22.9 per cent. With ethnic minorities in senior management, sales grew 20.2 per cent, whereas an all-white male senior team managed only 13 per cent.[34] One reason for this may be that diversity promotes the sharing of unique ideas and a variety of perspectives, which in turn, leads to more effective decision-making.[35]
- *Increased creativity and innovation.* Preliminary research supports the idea that workforce diversity promotes creativity and innovation through sharing of diverse ideas and perspectives. Innovative companies deliberately used heterogeneous teams to solve problems, and they employed more women and ethnic minorities than less innovative companies. Innovative companies also did a better job of eliminating racism, sexism and class distinction. A recent summary of 40 years of diversity research supported the conclusion that diversity can promote creativity and improve a team's decision-making.
- *Increased group problem-solving and productivity.* Because diverse groups possess a broader base of experience and perspectives from which to analyse a problem, they can potentially improve

problem-solving and performance. Research based on experimental studies of short-term groups showed variation in terms of values, attitudes, educational backgrounds and experience supported this conclusion. Heterogeneous groups produced better-quality decisions and demonstrated higher productivity than homogeneous groups. In real organisational settings, the benefits of diversity for teams' process and outcomes only applied to highly outcome-interdependent (i.e. common goals) teams and teams low on longevity (i.e. short-term groups).[36]

Application: diversity management and stereotypes

Equality, broadly speaking, is about providing the same opportunities in an organisation and is often mandated by national or supranational laws. Affirmative action goes further, requiring that special opportunities are given to specific groups. The EU has significant influence on equality law and the development of best practice. However, Britain, along with Sweden, has more advanced legislation on racial discrimination than other EU member states.[37] The Treaty of Amsterdam adopted an important new provision enabling the EU to propose legislation to combat discrimination based on gender, racial and ethnic origin, religion, belief, disability, age or sexual orientation. Two important directives (one on racial and one on religious belief, age and sexual orientation) were agreed in 2000.[38] Member states were required to implement legislation outlawing discrimination in the workplace on grounds of sexual orientation and religion or belief by 2003, and age and disability by 2006.

Affirmative action or equal opportunities is an intervention aimed at giving management a chance to correct an imbalance, an injustice, a mistake, and/or outright discrimination. In some countries affirmative action is well accepted in the fight against gender based discrimination. Norway has, as already noted, recently adopted what is essentially affirmative action with respect to equal gender representation on corporate boards.

> **!** Critical thinking
>
> Think about affirmative action as if you were of the opposite sex or belonged to a minority: do you want a job because of your background or because you are the one who is best qualified?

An increasing number of people and institutions now question the positive action programmes. Although it creates tremendous opportunities for women and minorities, it does not foster the type of thinking that is needed to manage diversity effectively.[39] The law can help to mould behaviour. It is particularly important as a statement of values of society but it is not enough on its own and cannot be fully effective in changing attitudes which underlie behaviour.[40] **Diversity management** entails enabling people to perform up to their maximum potential. It focuses on changing an organisation's culture and infrastructure so that people provide the highest productivity possible. According to the UK's Institute for Personnel and Development, managing diversity and equal opportunities are not alternatives. They are interdependent.[41]

It is not surprising that organisations encounter significant barriers when trying to move forward with managing diversity. Table 9.2 identifies the most common barriers to implementing successful diversity programmes.

Many organisations are unsure of what it takes to effectively manage diversity. This is partly due to the fact that top management only recently became aware of the combined need and importance of this issue.

Table 9.2 Barriers to Diversity Management

Inaccurate stereotypes and prejudice	This barrier manifests itself in the belief that differences are viewed as weaknesses. In turn, this promotes the view that diversity hiring will mean sacrificing competence and quality
Ethnocentrism	The ethnocentrism barrier represents the feeling that one's cultural rules and norms are superior or more appropriate than the rules and norms of another culture (also see Chapter 12)
Poor career planning	This barrier is associated with the lack of opportunities for diverse employees to get the type of work assignments that qualify them for senior management positions
An unsupportive and hostile working environment for diverse employees	Diverse employees are frequently excluded from social events and the friendly camaraderie that takes place in most offices
Lack of political knowledge on the part of diverse employees	Diverse employees may not get promoted because they do not know how to 'play the game' of getting along and getting ahead in an organisation
Difficulty in balancing career and family issues	Women still assume the majority of the responsibilities associated with raising children. This makes it harder for women to work evenings and weekends or to frequently travel once they have children
Fears of reverse discrimination	Some employees believe that managing diversity is a smokescreen for reverse discrimination. This belief leads to very strong resistance because people feel that one person's gain is another's loss
Diversity is not seen as an organisational priority	This leads to subtle resistance that shows up in the form of complaints and negative attitudes. Employees may complain about the time, energy and resources devoted to diversity that could have been spent doing 'real work'
The need to revamp the organisation's performance appraisal and reward system	Performance appraisals and reward systems must reinforce the need to effectively manage diversity. This means that success will be based on a new set of criteria. Employees are likely to resist changes that adversely affect their promotions and financial rewards
Resistance to change	Effectively managing diversity entails significant organisational and personal change. As discussed in Chapter 16, people resist change for many different reasons.

So what are organisations doing to effectively manage diversity? Answering this question requires a framework for categorising organisational initiatives. Several relevant frameworks exist. One identifies eight generic action options that can be used to address any type of diversity issue:

HR

- *Include/exclude*. This choice is an extension of affirmative action programmes. Its primary goal is to either increase or decrease the number of diverse people at all levels of the organisations.
- *Deny*. People using this option deny that differences exist. Denial may manifest itself in proclamations that all decisions are colour-, gender- and age-blind and that success is solely determined by merit and performance. This may be combined with actions showing that this indeed the case.
- *Assimilate*. The basic premise behind this alternative is that all diverse people will learn to fit in or become like the dominant group. It only takes time and reinforcement for people to see the

light. Organisations initially assimilate employees through their recruitment practices and the use of company-orientation programmes. New employees generally are put through orientation programmes that aim to provide them with the organisation's preferred values and a set of standard operating procedures. Employees then are encouraged to refer to the policies and procedure manual when they are confused about what to do in a specific situation. These practices create homogeneity among employees. In France, for example, with its assimilationist culture all immigrants are expected to become French citizens rather than adopt dual nationality.[42]

- *Suppress.* Differences are quashed or discouraged by telling or reinforcing others to stop complaining about issues.
- *Isolate.* This option maintains the current way of doing things by setting the diverse person off to the side. In this way the individual is unable to influence organisational change. Employers can isolate people by putting them on special projects.
- *Tolerate.* Toleration entails acknowledging differences but not valuing or accepting them. It represents a live-and-let-live approach that superficially allows organisations to pay lipservice to the issue of managing diversity. Toleration is different from isolation in that it allows for the inclusion of diverse people. However, differences are not valued or accepted when an organisation uses this option.
- *Build relationships.* This approach is based on the premise that good relationships can overcome differences. It addresses diversity by fostering quality relationships – characterised by acceptance and understanding – among diverse groups.
- *Foster mutual adaptation.* In this option, people recognise and accept differences, and most importantly, agree that everyone and everything is open for change. Mutual adaptation allows the greatest accommodation of diversity because it allows for change even when diversity is being effectively managed. Areas such as flexible working to accommodate different religious holidays, traditional ways of dressing and accommodating other religious needs fall into this category.

Although the action options can be used alone or in combination, some are clearly better than others. Exclusion, denial, assimilation, suppression, isolation and toleration are among the least preferred options. Inclusion, building relationships and mutual adaptation are the preferred strategies. Mutual adaptation is the only approach that unquestionably endorses the philosophy behind managing diversity. In closing this discussion, it is important to note that choosing how to best manage diversity is a dynamic process that is determined by the context of the organisation. For instance, some organisations are not ready for mutual adaptation. The best one might hope for in this case is the inclusion of diverse people.

Another approach is based on the specific diversity initiatives used by 16 organisations that successfully managed diversity. Ann Morrison conducted a landmark study of the diversity practices used by 16 organisations that successfully managed diversity. She uncovered 52 different practices, 20 of which were used by the majority of the companies sampled. She classified the 52 practices into three main types: accountability, development and recruitment.[43] The top 10 practices associated with each type are shown in Table 9.3. The three types are discussed next in order of relative importance.

HR **Accountability practices** relate to a manager's responsibility to treat diverse employees fairly. Table 9.1 reveals that companies predominantly accomplish this objective by creating administrative procedures aimed at integrating diverse employees into the management ranks (practices number 3, 4, 5, 6, 8, 9 and 10). In contrast, work and family policies (practice 7) focuses on creating an environment that fosters employee commitment and productivity. A survey of workers in 13

Table 9.3 Common Diversity Practices

Accountability practices	Development practices	Recruitment practices
1 Top management's personal intervention	1 Diversity training programmes	1 Targeted recruitment of non-professionals
2 Internal advocacy groups	2 Networks and support groups	2 Key outside hires
3 Emphasis on employment statistics, profiles	3 Development programmes for all high-potential professionals	3 Extensive public exposure on diversity
4 Inclusion of diversity in performance evaluation goals, ratings	4 Informal networking activities	4 Corporate image as liberal, progressive, or benevolent
5 Inclusion of diversity in promotion decisions, criteria	5 Job rotation	5 Partnerships with educational institutions
6 Inclusion of diversity in management succession planning	6 Formal mentoring programme	6 Recruitment incentives such as cash supplements
7 Work and family policies	7 Informal mentoring programme	7 Internships
8 Policies against racism, sexism	8 Entry development programmes for all high-potential new hires	8 Publications or PR products that highlight diversity
9 Internal audit or attitude survey	9 Internal training (such as personal safety or language)	9 Targeted recruitment of professionals
10 Active employment committee, office	10 Recognition events, awards	10 Partnership with non-traditional groups

Source: Abstracted from Tables A.10, A.11 and A.12 in A. M. Morrison, *The New Leaders: Guidelines on Leadership Diversity in America* (San Francisco, CA: Jossey-Bass, 1992).

industrialised countries found that the desire for a decent balance between work and personal life was rated more highly than a good salary everywhere but in Russia.[44]

The use of **development practices** to manage diversity is relatively new compared with the historical use of accountability and recruitment practices. Development practices focus on preparing diverse employees for greater responsibility and advancement. These activities are needed because most non-traditional employees have not been exposed to the types of activity and job assignments that develop effective leadership and social networks.[45]

Recruitment practices focus on attracting job applicants at all levels that are willing to accept challenging work assignments. This focus is critical because people learn the leadership skills needed for advancement by successfully accomplishing increasingly challenging and responsible work assignments. Targeted recruitment of non-professionals (practice 1) and professionals (practice 9) are commonly used to identify and recruit women and ethnic minorities.

! Critical thinking

Notwithstanding that there may well be a sound business case for diversity, or no case against it, are there any types of people that organisations are still justified in keeping out at all costs?

9.3 Stress and burnout

Life at work in the twenty-first century can be hectic and stressful. Students must cope with tests, projects and competition when looking for a job after graduation. Couples must wrestle with the demands of managing careers and a family. Single parents encounter similar pressures. An estimate indicated that stress and mental illness causes more than half of all the working days lost in the UK during a year. In addition, mental illness (which is not always related to stress) was estimated in 2007 to cost UK companies a total of £26 billion every year.[46] Much of this cost (58 per cent) was caused by lower productivity at work, while the rest was attributed to absenteeism (32 per cent) and turnover (10 per cent). What is interesting is not when the study was conducted (around 2005) but the magnitude of the estimated costs.

The biggest contributor to work stress arises from fundamental changes that have been made in many organisations. As a result of increased competition, employees are being asked to deliver a better quality and a greater quantity of work in less time with fewer resources. Second, technological advancements make it harder for employees to completely disconnect from the office. Smartphones, apps, email and social media make it easy to disrupt people's free time while at home or on holiday. Third, the dynamics of modern life make it difficult to balance the demands of work and home: work stress tends to spill over into people's personal lives and vice versa.[47] Finally, motivation and stress are related. Striving for extrinsic goals, such as money, status, control over others, often requires stressful ego-involved activities.[48]

This section looks at the sources of stress, examines stressors and burnout, highlights four moderators of occupational stress and explores a variety of stress-reduction techniques.

Sources of stress

We all experience stress on a daily basis. Although stress is caused by many factors, researchers conclude that stress triggers one of two basic reactions: active fighting or passive flight, the so-called **fight-or-flight response**.[49] Stressors are environmental factors that produce stress. Physiologically, this stress response is a biochemical 'top gear' involving hormonal changes that mobilise the body for extraordinary demands. Imagine how our prehistoric ancestors responded to the stress associated with a charging sabre-toothed tiger. To avoid being eaten, they could stand their ground and fight the beast or run away. In either case, their bodies would have been energised by an identical hormonal change, involving the release of adrenaline into the bloodstream.

This fight-or-flight system still has a very visible consequence in the way we handle stress. Charging beasts have been replaced by problems such as deadlines, role conflict and ambiguity, financial responsibilities, information overload, technology, traffic congestion, noise and air pollution, family problems and work overload. Our response to stress may or may not trigger negative side-effects, including headaches, ulcers, insomnia, heart attacks, high blood pressure and strokes. The same stress response that helped our prehistoric ancestors survive has become a factor that can seriously impair our daily lives. Exhaustion, aching limbs, frequent infections, heart disease and depression are outward symptoms of stress.

To a horn player in a symphony orchestra, for whom the nature of the instrument means that the sound is either exactly right or terribly wrong, stress may be caused by playing a solo before a large audience. Similarly, while heat, smoke and flames may represent stress to a firefighter, delivering a speech or presenting a lecture may be stressful for those who are shy.

Formally defined, **stress** is 'an adaptive response, mediated by individual characteristics and/or psychological processes, that is a consequence of any external action, situation or event that places special physical and/or psychological demands upon a person'.[50] The key elements in this definition are environmental demands, referred to as 'stressors'; those that produce an adaptive response; and those that are influenced by individual differences.

Hans Selye, considered the father of the modern concept of stress, pioneered the distinction between stressors and the stress response and emphasised that both positive and negative events can trigger an identical stress response, which can be either beneficial or harmful. He referred to stress that is positive or produces a positive outcome as '**eustress**'. For example, an employee who has to make a presentation to a large audience can feel extra pressure, but the fact that he or she likes to do presentations very much will make him or her experience the pressure in a positive way – as very motivating and challenging – rather than in a negative way. Selye also noted that:

- Stress is not just nervous tension.
- Stress can have positive consequences.
- Stress is not something to be avoided.
- The complete absence of stress is death.[51]

All learning implies at least a moderate amount of stress. Regular exposure to a manageable amount of stress keeps us fit; too little stress makes us bored. An employee who really loved doing presentations would soon be bored by doing the same presentations many times. They would not have the time to recover between the presentations, and their regular tasks will keep on stacking up. If this situation continues, they might become very strained and exhausted.[52] Thus, a moderate amount of stress seems to be beneficial whereas excessive stress proves to be very detrimental. What conditions cause excessive stress and how can it be alleviated or even eliminated?

Robert Karasek developed and popularised the so-called 'job demand-control model' which emphasises the stress factors inherent in the work organisation, rather than the individual

Figure 9.1 Job Demand-Control Model

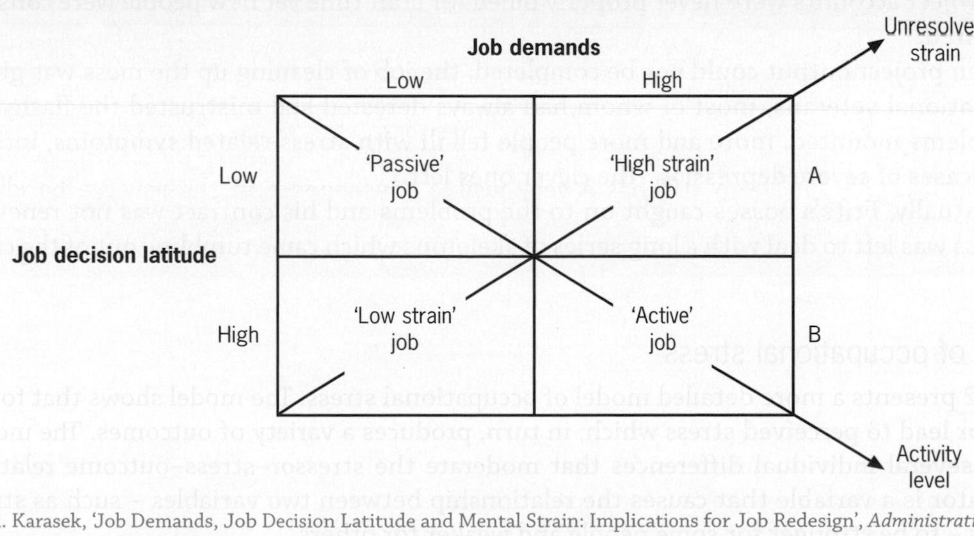

Source: R. Karasek, 'Job Demands, Job Decision Latitude and Mental Strain: Implications for Job Redesign', *Administrative Science Quarterly*, vol. 24, 1979, pp. 285–306.

characteristics. While studying the lack of success of stop-smoking programmes Karasek found that job stress is one cause of smoking. Individually oriented coping strategies such as stop-smoking campaigns were not very successful, because of work environment tensions.

The model consists of two dimensions.[53] Central to the model is the interaction between job demands and job control. The first dimension is the psychological demand of a job. The second dimension is the amount of autonomy, the control or 'decision latitude' permitted in deciding how to meet these demands.

Work stress becomes more likely when psychological demand is high and decision latitude is low. This means that high psychological demands or work pressure do not necessarily lead to work stress. The combination of high psychological demands and low autonomy to deal with these demands is more dangerous and can easily lead to depression, burnout and stress. The negative effects of this combination can be reinforced by a lack of social support.

OB in Real Life

Fritz the boss

Fritz was the boss. He had engineered a merger between three units and although initially the boss of a smaller unit, he had seen to it that he was appointed the boss of the merged unit. The majority of staff had come from the largest of the three original units. Having worked alongside Fritz they had a shrewd idea of his character, and they were unhappy.

The problem with Fritz was that he only really cared about himself and the advancement of his own career. He was very good at formulating grand schemes and brilliant at selling them to his bosses. Many of the people in his own unit were very happy working for him and on the exciting projects he attracted.

Notes of discord crept into the merged unit when it gradually became clear that many of the bright young people he had hired either left or were unable to deliver the project content they had promised. In addition, gossip had it on good authority that the unit's finances were in a mess, new project grants were being used to cover shortfalls and cost overruns in older projects. Project accounts were never properly billed for staff time yet new people were constantly being hired.

When project output could not be completed, the job of cleaning up the mess was given to organisational veterans, most of whom had always detested and mistrusted the flashy Fritz. As problems mounted, more and more people fell ill with stress-related symptoms, including several cases of severe depression. The clever ones left.

Eventually, Fritz's bosses caught on to the problems and his contract was not renewed. A new boss was left to deal with a long series of skeletons which came tumbling out of the closets.

A model of occupational stress

Figure 9.2 presents a more detailed model of occupational stress. The model shows that four types of stressor lead to perceived stress which, in turn, produces a variety of outcomes. The model also specifies several individual differences that moderate the stressor–stress–outcome relationship. A moderator is a variable that causes the relationship between two variables – such as stress and outcomes – to be stronger for some people and weaker for others.

HR **Stressors** are a prerequisite for stress. Figure 9.2 shows the four major types of stressors: individual, group, organisational and those outside the organisation (extra-organisational). The most

Figure 9.2 A Model of Occupational Stress

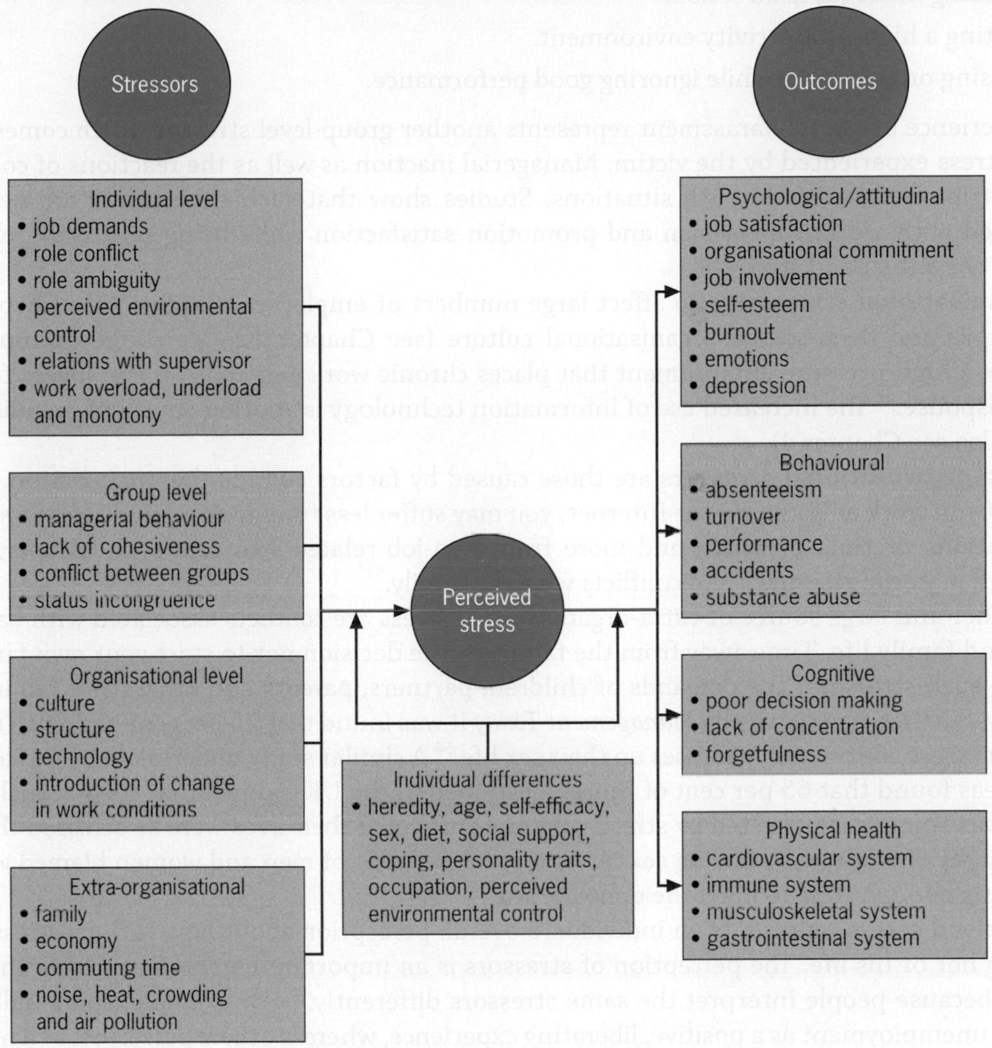

Source: Adapted from M. Koslowsky, *Modeling the Stress-Strain Relationship in Work Settings* (New York: Routledge, 1998); and M. T. Matteson and J. M. Ivancevich, 'Organizational Stressors and Heart Disease: A Research Model', *Academy of Management Review*, July 1979, p. 350.

common examples of stressors are job demands, work overload, role conflict, role ambiguity, everyday hassles, perceived control over events occurring in the work environment and job characteristics.[54]

HR **Individual-level stressors** are those directly associated with a person's work responsibilities. During the past few decades, a vast amount of research has been undertaken to determine the effect of these stressors. Messages received and replied to interrupt work, lack of control over how work is done and the degree of job security are all examples of stress at this level.

HR **Group-level stressors** are caused by group dynamics and managerial behaviour. Managers create stress for employees by:

- Exhibiting inconsistent behaviour.
- Failing to provide support.

- Showing lack of concern.
- Providing inadequate direction.
- Creating a high-productivity environment.
- Focusing on negatives while ignoring good performance.

The experience of sexual harassment represents another group-level stressor which comes on top of the stress experienced by the victim. Managerial inaction as well as the reactions of colleagues can contribute to stress in such situations. Studies show that such experiences are negatively associated with work, supervision and promotion satisfaction while being positively related to ambiguity, conflict and stress.[55]

Organisational stressors also affect large numbers of employees. Conflict (see Chapter 14), stereotypes and deep-seated organisational culture (see Chapter 12) are prime examples. For example, a high-pressure environment that places chronic work demands on employees fuels the stress response.[56] The increased use of information technology is another source of organisational stress (also see Chapter 4).

Extra-organisational stressors are those caused by factors outside the organisation. For example, if you work at home via the Internet, you may suffer less from task-related stressors such as interruptions or time pressure, and more from non-job-related stressors such as noisy home, restricted material resources and conflicts with the family.[57]

Another and large source of extra-organisational stress are conflicts associated with balancing career and family life. Time away from the family or the decision not to start your own family are just two such stressors. The demands of children, partners, parents and others also fall into this category. Further, in a survey by *Management Today* it was found that 25 per cent of British workers find that stress continuously messes up their sex life.[58] A similar study undertaken by the company Seven Seas found that 65 per cent of those questioned in the UK claimed that their sexual performance was sometimes affected by stress, and one-third said their lives were so stressed that they had thought of work while having sex. A total of 89 per cent of men and women blamed work for not having enough time to meet the opposite sex.[59]

HR

Perceived stress represents an individual's overall perception about how various stressors are affecting her or his life. The perception of stressors is an important component within the stress process because people interpret the same stressors differently.[60] For example, some individuals perceive unemployment as a positive, liberating experience, whereas others perceive it as a negative, debilitating one.[61]

Some researchers believe that stress has psychological/attitudinal, behavioural, cognitive and physical health consequences. However, people do not experience the same level of stress or exhibit similar outcomes for a given type of stressor. For example, the type of stressors experienced at work varied by occupation and gender. The stressor of low control (over one's job tasks) was higher in lower-level clerical jobs than professional occupations, while interpersonal conflict was a greater source of stress for women than men.[62] Perceived control was also a significant moderator of the stress process. People perceived lower levels of stress, and experienced more favourable consequences from stress, when they believed they could exert control over the stressors affecting their lives.[63]

In support of this finding, another study showed that employees had more negative physiological responses to perceived stress when they worked on an assembly line than in a more flexible work organisation.[64] Finally, people who are chronically angry, suspicious or mistrustful are twice as likely to have coronary artery blockages. We can all protect our hearts by learning to avoid such feelings.[65] In summary, even though researchers have been able to identify several important moderators, a large gap still exists in identifying relevant individual differences.

Important stressors and stress outcomes

Stressful life events such as experiencing the death of a family member, being assaulted, moving home, ending an intimate relationship, being seriously ill or taking a big test can create stress. These events are stressful because they involve significant changes that require adaptation and often social readjustment.

The next exercise allows you to assess your own exposure to stressful life events using a rating scale that consists of 51 life events. Each event has a corresponding value, called a life change unit, representing the degree of social readjustment necessary to cope with the event. The larger the value, the more stressful the event.

Research has revealed a positive relationship between the total score on the original Social Readjustment Rating Scale (SRRS) and subsequent illness. The interpretative norms reveal that low scores are associated with good health, and larger scores are related to increased chances of experiencing illness.

Activity

How much life stress do you experience?

Instructions

Place a tick next to each of the events you experienced within the past year. Then add the life change units associated with the various events to derive your total life stress score.

Life event	Life change unit
_____ Death of spouse/partner	87
_____ Death of close family member	79
_____ Major injury/illness to self	78
_____ Detention in prison or other institution	76
_____ Major injury/illness to close family member	72
_____ Foreclosure on loan/mortgage	71
_____ Divorce	71
_____ Being a victim of crime	70
_____ Being the victim of police brutality	69
_____ Infidelity	69
_____ Experiencing domestic violence/sexual abuse	69
_____ Separation or reconciliation with spouse/partner	66
_____ Being fired/laid-off/unemployed	64
_____ Experiencing financial problems/difficulties	62
_____ Death of close friend	61
_____ Surviving a disaster	59
_____ Becoming a single parent	59
_____ Assuming responsibility for sick or elderly loved one	56
_____ Loss of, or major reduction in, health insurance/benefits	56
_____ Self/close family member being arrested for breaking the law	56

______	Major disagreements over child support/custody/visiting rights	53
______	Experiencing/involved in a car accident	53
______	Being disciplined at work/demoted	53
______	Dealing with unwanted pregnancy	51
______	Adult child moving in with parent/parent moving in with adult child	50
______	Child develops behaviour or learning problem	49
______	Experiencing employment discrimination/sexual harassment	48
______	Attempting to modify addictive behaviour of self	47
______	Discovering/attempting to modify addictive behaviour of close family member	46
______	Employer reorganisation/downsizing	45
______	Dealing with infertility/miscarriage	44
______	Getting married/remarried	43
______	Changing employers/careers	43
______	Failure to obtain/qualify for a mortgage	42
______	Pregnancy of self/spouse/partner	41
______	Experiencing discrimination/harassment outside the workplace	39
______	Release from prison	39
______	Spouse/partner begins/ceases work outside the home	38
______	Major disagreement with boss/co-worker	37
______	Change in residence	35
______	Finding appropriate child care/day care	34
______	Experiencing a large, unexpected monetary gain	33
______	Changing positions (transfer, promotion)	33
______	Gaining a new family member	33
______	Changing work responsibilities	32
______	Child leaving home	30
______	Obtaining a home mortgage	30
______	Obtaining a major loan other than home mortgage	30
______	Retirement	28
______	Beginning /ceasing formal education	26
______	Being charged with breaking the law	22

Total score__________

Interpretation norms

Less than 150 = odds are you will experience good health next year
150–300 = 50% chance of illness next year
Greater than 300 = 70% chance of illness next year

Source: C. J. Hobson, J. Kamen, J. Szostek, C. M. Nethercut, J. W. Tiedmann and S. Wojnarowicz, 'Stressful Life Events: A Revision and Update of the Social Readjustment Rating Scale', *International Journal of Stress Management*, January 1998, pp. 7–8.

HR Burnout

Burnout is a stress-induced problem common among members of 'helping' professions such as teaching, social work, human resources, nursing and law enforcement. It does not involve a specific feeling, attitude or physiological outcome anchored to a specific point in time. Rather, burnout is a condition that occurs over time. Burnout can have a devastating impact on employee well-being. Typical characteristics are withdrawal, fatigue and less job involvement; the latter being mainly noticed in those who are normally highly involved. If you can answer 'yes' to several of the following questions, you are probably heading for, or already suffering from, a major burnout:

- Do you experience your work as an unbearable burden?
- Are you constantly worrying about your work?
- Do you consider every assignment an awful job?
- Are you constantly feeling empty and indifferent?
- Do you have to drag yourself out of your bed every morning?
- Is 'job satisfaction' a term you have only ever heard of (not experienced)?
- Do you hardly ever laugh at work?
- Do you find your colleagues immensely irritating?[66]

If you answer yes to one or more of these questions, Table 9.4 identifies some of the attitudes you are likely to exhibit in response.

A model of burnout is presented in Figure 9.3. The fundamental premise underlying the model is that burnout develops in phases. The three key phases are emotional exhaustion, depersonalisation and feeling a lack of personal accomplishment.[67] Figure 9.3 indicates how emotional exhaustion is due to a combination of personal stressors and job and organisational stressors.[68] People who expect a lot from themselves and the organisations in which they work tend to create more internal stress, which, in turn, leads to emotional exhaustion. Similarly, emotional exhaustion is fuelled by having too much work to do, by role conflict and by the type of interpersonal interactions encountered at work. Frequent, intense face-to-face interactions that are emotionally charged are associated with higher levels of emotional exhaustion. Over time, emotional exhaustion leads to depersonalisation, which is a state of psychologically withdrawing from one's job. This ultimately results in a feeling of being unappreciated, ineffective or inadequate. The additive effect of these three phases is a host of negative attitudinal and behavioural outcomes.

Table 9.4 Attitudinal Characteristics of Burnout

Attitude	Description
Fatalism	A feeling that you lack control over your work
Boredom	A lack of interest in doing your job
Discontent	A sense of being unhappy with your job
Cynicism	A tendency to undervalue the content of your job and the rewards received
Inadequacy	A feeling of not being able to meet your objectives
Failure	A tendency to discredit your performance and conclude that you are ineffective
Overwork	A feeling of having too much to do and not enough time to complete it
Nastiness	A tendency to be rude or unpleasant to your co-workers
Dissatisfaction	A feeling that you are not being justly rewarded for your efforts
Escape	A desire to give up and get away from it all

Source: Adapted from D. P. Rogers, 'Helping Employees Cope with Burn-out', *Business*, October–December 1984, p. 4.

Figure 9.3 A Model of Burnout

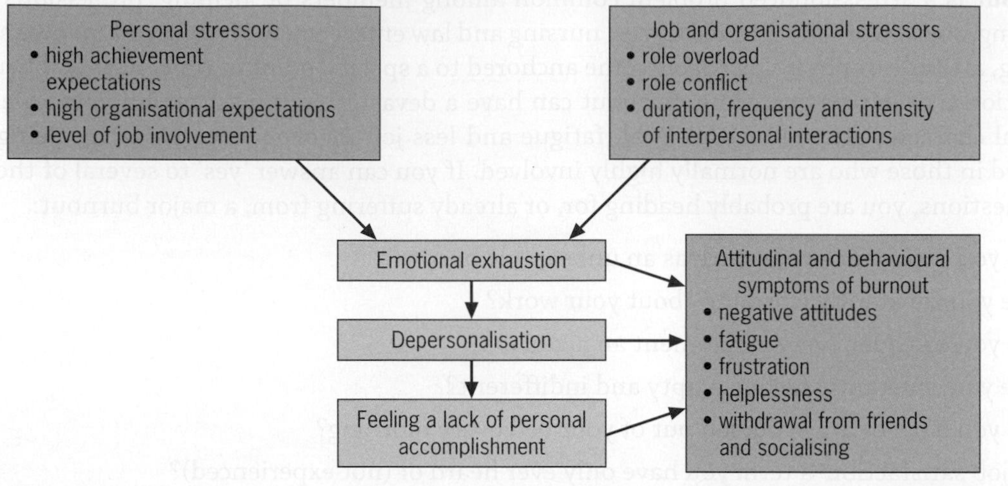

Source: Based in part on C. L. Cordes and T. W. Dougherty, 'A Review and an Integration of Research on Job Burnout', *Academy of Management Review*, October 1993, p. 641.

OB in Real Life

Stress and death at France Telecom

On 11 September 2009, a 32-year-old woman named Stephanie jumped to her death from an office window at France Telecom. She did it in front of colleagues at the end of a working day, leaving a note blaming unbearable working conditions and forced job changes. She thereby joined 33 other employees of the company who had also committed suicide since January 2008. At least a dozen others have tried to kill themselves. In many cases the dead have left notes indicating that the company was responsible for 'management by terror' and for bullying.

The chief executive of France Telecom, Didier Lombard, managed the incident with considerable clumsiness. A video showed Lombard telling managers that those who thought they could stick to routines and not worry about a thing were sorely mistaken and that staff outside Paris spent their time at the beach, fishing for mussels. However, poor communication skills at the top is not necessarily the main problem.

The company used to be state-owned, but after partial privatisation the state now holds only 27 per cent of the stock. The payroll has fallen by 15 000 over the past five years but further reductions are more difficult, since two-thirds of the remaining employees are protected from firing by their status as (former) civil servants. Not even outright staff cuts, however, can explain the loss of life. The story of Francis Le Bras may shed more light on the feelings of employees so stressed that they consider ending their lives.

His name simply disappeared from the organisational chart in his Paris office. France Telecom had cut his job as a software developer for Minitel, an early telephone-based information service unique to France. While Le Bras stayed on the payroll, he no longer had a title and his colleagues shunned him, averting their eyes. The humiliation continued when he was forced to write a CV and show up for job interviews, even though he had served the company for 20 years.

A similar story is told by Ludovic Nonclercq, a software engineer who was told that his job no longer existed even though he was not fired. He too considered ending his life but blames not so much the company but the system which allows people to remain in limbo, without a job but not fired. In his words, 'companies can't fire employees, so they brutalise them instead'. Job protection is very strong in France and getting hired in the first place is very difficult. For the same reason, getting fired is catastrophic. In Nonleclercq's view, this whole system is sick.

Management is also believed to have a large share of responsibility for the situation. Top managers in France are trained in elite schools, the *grandes écoles*. One commentator says that these managers or 'technocrats' have a sovereign contempt for ordinary employees. Workers are held to know nothing.

For discussion

Which stress factors are involved in this story?

Source: Based on 'France Telecom executive resigns after employee suicide tally rises to 24', *The Guardian*, 5 October 2009; and 'Suicides Inside France Telecom Prompting Sarkozy Stress Testing', *BusinessWeek*, 25 January 2010.

There also are two long-term strategies for reducing burnout that are increasingly being used by companies. Some use sabbaticals to replenish employees' energy and desire to work. These programmes allow employees to take a designated amount of time off from work after being employed a certain number of years. Companies in Canada, Australia and Israel also use sabbaticals to prevent stress and burnout, whereas Europe does not have a sabbatical culture. An employee retreat is the second long-term strategy. Retreats entail sending employees to an offsite location for three to five days. While there, everyone can relax, reflect or engage in team- and relationship-building activities. This is what PricewaterhouseCoopers does to help its employees cope with work stress. The firm has a two-day stress survival clinic where participants meet with a physician, nutritionist and psychiatrist. The retreat, held in such locations as Toronto and Captiva Island, Florida, includes Mediterranean-style cuisine served in candlelit dining rooms and time to focus on coping better with pressure.[69]

Evidence about stress and burnout

Numerous studies have examined the relationship between life stress on the one hand and illness and job performance on the other. Subjects with higher scores on the SRRS had significantly more problems with chronic headaches, sudden death from heart attack, pregnancy and birth complications, tuberculosis, diabetes, anxiety, depression and a host of minor physical ailments. Meanwhile, psychosocial problems and academic and work performance declined as scores on the SRRS increased.[70]

Negative personal life changes were associated with greater susceptibility to infections, job stress and psychological distress, and also lower levels of job satisfaction and organisational commitment.[71] Finally, recent studies revealed that women rated the life events contained in the SRRS as more stressful than men. Results also showed that there were no meaningful differences in life event ratings between various age groups and income levels.[72] The key implication is that employee illness and job performance are affected by extra-organisational stressors, particularly those that are negative and uncontrollable.

A meta-analysis of 61 studies covering several thousand people uncovered three important conclusions.[73] First, burnout was positively related to job stressors and turnover intentions and negatively associated with the receipt of supportive resources (e.g. social support and team cohesion), job enhancement opportunities, performance-contingent rewards, organisational commitment and job satisfaction. Second, the different phases of burnout, as shown in Figure 9.3, obtained differential relationships with a variety of behavioural and attitudinal symptoms of burnout. This supports the idea that burnout develops in phases. Nonetheless, researchers do not yet agree completely on the order of these phases.[74] Finally, burnout was more strongly related to employees' work demands than it was to the resources people received at work. This suggests that organisations should be particularly sensitive to employees' workloads. When they are unable or unwilling to treat their employees in a way that does not cause stress, loss of life can be an unintended consequence.

HR Application: avoiding, moderating and coping with stress

Because employees do not leave their personal problems at the office door or factory gate, organisations need to be aware of external sources of employee stress or, as the psychologist Professor Cary Cooper argues: 'Employers have a duty of care in respect of how they manage not only their equipment or physical environment but also their people, including their workload, their hours of work and perhaps their careers.'[75] Once identified, alternative work schedules, training programmes and counselling can be used to help employees cope with these stressors. This may not only reduce the costs associated with illnesses and absenteeism but may also lead to positive work attitudes, better job performance and reduced staff turnover.

In addition, by acknowledging that work outcomes are affected by extra-organisational stressors, professionals may avoid the trap of automatically attributing poor performance to low motivation or lack of ability. Such awareness is likely to engender positive reactions from employees and lead to a resolution of problems, not just symptoms. For individuals with a high score on the SRRS, it would be best to defer controllable stressors, such as moving house or buying a new car, until things settle down.

Removing personal, job and organisational stressors is the most straightforward way to prevent burnout. Organisations can also reduce burnout by buffering its effects. Potential **buffers** include extra staff or equipment at peak work periods, support from top management, increased freedom to make decisions, recognition for accomplishments, time off for personal development or rest and equitable rewards. Decreasing the quantity and increasing the quality of communications is another possible buffer. Finally, organisations can change the content of an individual's job by adding or eliminating responsibilities, increasing the amount of participation in decision-making, altering the pattern of interpersonal contacts or assigning the person to a new position.[76]

Moderators, as mentioned earlier, are variables that cause the relationship between stressors, perceived stress and outcomes to be weaker for some people and stronger for others. Managers with a working knowledge of important stress moderators can confront employee stress in the following ways:

- Awareness of moderators helps identify those most likely to experience stress and its negative outcomes. Then stress-reduction programmes can be formulated for high-risk employees.
- Moderators, in and of themselves, suggest possible solutions for reducing the negative outcomes of occupational stress.

Talking to a friend or getting together with 'mates' can be comforting during times of fear, stress or loneliness. For a variety of reasons, meaningful social relationships help people do a better job

Figure 9.4 A Flow Model of the Mechanisms of Social Support

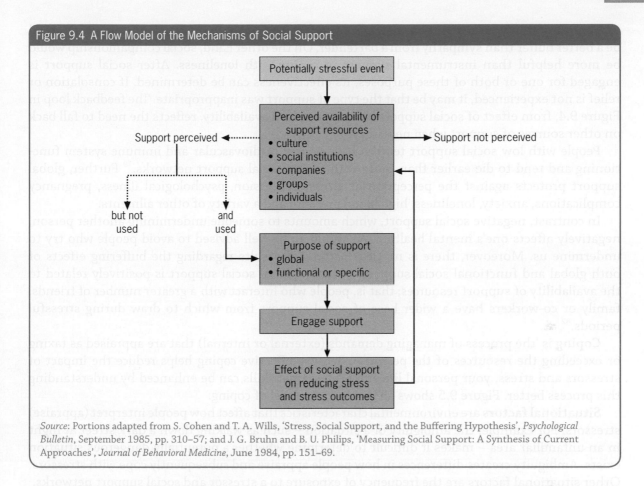

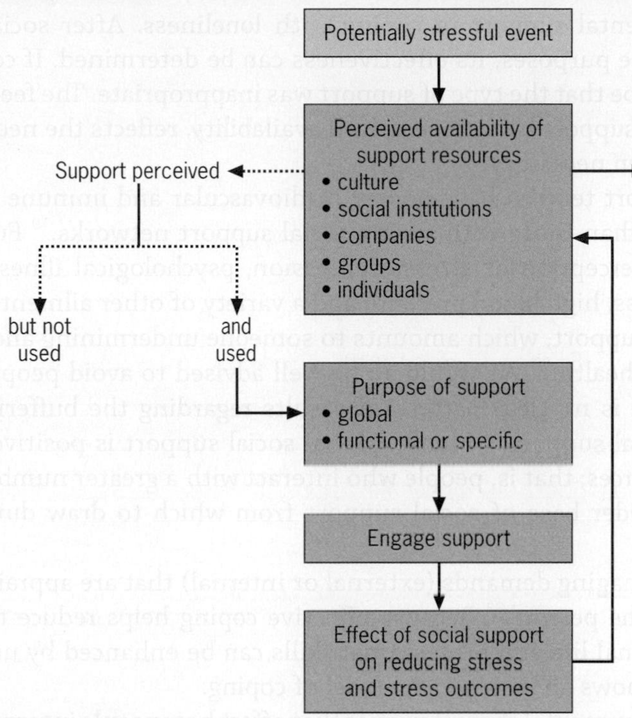

Source: Portions adapted from S. Cohen and T. A. Wills, 'Stress, Social Support, and the Buffering Hypothesis', *Psychological Bulletin*, September 1985, pp. 310–57; and J. G. Bruhn and B. U. Philips, 'Measuring Social Support: A Synthesis of Current Approaches', *Journal of Behavioral Medicine*, June 1984, pp. 151–69.

of handling stress. **Social support** is measured in terms of both the quantity and quality of an individual's social relationships. Figure 9.4 illustrates the mechanisms of social support.

A support network must be seen to exist by the person needing support before it can be used. Support networks evolve from any or all of five sources: cultural norms, social institutions, companies, groups or individuals. For example, there is more cultural emphasis on caring for the elderly in Japan than in Europe. Japanese culture is thus a strong source of social support for older Japanese people. Alternatively, individuals may fall back on social institutions such as social security services or the Red Cross, religious groups or family and friends for support. In turn, these various sources provide four types of support:

- *Esteem support*: providing information that a person is accepted and respected despite any problems or inadequacies.
- *Informational support*: providing help in defining, understanding and coping with problems.
- *Social companionship*: spending time with others in leisure and recreational activities.
- *Instrumental support*: providing financial aid, material resources or necessary services.[77]

If social support is perceived as available, an individual then decides whether to use it.[78] Generally, social support is used either as a global or a functional support but in some cases it is used as both. **Global social support** is very broad in scope, coming as it does from four sources, and is applicable to any situation at any time. **Functional social support** is narrower and, if relied on in the wrong situation, can be unhelpful.

For example, if you crashed your new car, a good insurance policy (instrumental support) would be a better buffer than sympathy from a bartender. On the other hand, social companionship would be more helpful than instrumental support in coping with loneliness. After social support is engaged for one or both of these purposes, its effectiveness can be determined. If consolation or relief is not experienced, it may be that the type of support was inappropriate. The feedback loop in Figure 9.4, from effect of social support back to perceived availability, reflects the need to fall back on other sources of support when necessary.

People with low social support tend to have poorer cardiovascular and immune system functioning and tend to die earlier than those with strong social support networks.[79] Further, global support protects against the perception of stress, depression, psychological illness, pregnancy complications, anxiety, loneliness, high blood pressure and a variety of other ailments.

In contrast, negative social support, which amounts to someone undermining another person, negatively affects one's mental health.[80] We would all be well advised to avoid people who try to undermine us. Moreover, there is no clear pattern of results regarding the buffering effects of both global and functional social support.[81] Finally, global social support is positively related to the availability of support resources; that is, people who interact with a greater number of friends, family or co-workers have a wider base of social support from which to draw during stressful periods.[82]

Coping is 'the process of managing demands (external or internal) that are appraised as taxing or exceeding the resources of the person'.[83] Because effective coping helps reduce the impact of stressors and stress, your personal life and professional skills can be enhanced by understanding this process better. Figure 9.5 shows an instructive model of coping.

Situational factors are environmental characteristics that affect how people interpret (appraise) stressors. For example, the ambiguity of a situation – such as walking down a dark street at night in an unfamiliar area – makes it difficult to determine whether a potentially dangerous situation exists. Ambiguity creates differences in how people appraise and subsequently cope with stressors. Other situational factors are the frequency of exposure to a stressor and social support networks.

Figure 9.5 A Model of the Coping Process

Source: Based in part on R. S. Lazarus and S. Folkman, 'Coping and Adaptation', in *Handbook of Behavioral Medicine*, ed. W. D. Gentry (New York: The Guilford Press, 1984), pp. 282–325.

Personal factors are personality traits and personal resources that affect the appraisal of stressors. For instance, because being tired or sick can distort the interpretation of stressors, an extremely tired individual may appraise an innocent question as a threat or challenge. Traits such as locus of control, self-esteem, optimism, self-efficacy (recall our discussion in Chapters 2 and 3) and work experience were also found to affect the appraisal of stressors.[84]

Cognitive appraisal reflects an individual's overall perception or evaluation of a situation or stressor. Cognitive appraisal results in a categorisation of the situation or stressor as either harmful, threatening or challenging. It is important to understand the differences between these appraisals because they influence how people cope. 'Harm (including loss) represents damage already done; threat involves the potential for harm; and challenge means the potential for significant gain under difficult odds.'[85] Coping with harm usually entails undoing or reinterpreting something that occurred in the past because the damage is already done. In contrast, threatening situations engage anticipatory coping. That is, people cope with threat by preparing for harm that may occur in the future. Challenge also activates anticipatory coping. In contrast with threat, an appraisal of challenge results in coping that focuses on what can be gained rather than what may be lost.

Critical thinking

Compare the classifications in Figure 9.2 to those in Figure 9.5 and assess whether the two classifications are consistent.

Coping strategies are characterised by the specific behaviours and cognitions used to cope with a situation. People use a combination of three approaches to cope with stressors and stress (see Figure 9.4).

The first, called a **control strategy**, has a 'take-charge' tone. For example, so-called 'downshifting', where someone moves to a less stressful job, is a possible coping strategy to gain more flexibility in your life. An **escape strategy** amounts to the opposite of tackling the problem head on. Individuals use this strategy when they passively accept stressful situations or avoid them by failing to confront the cause of stress (an obnoxious co-worker, for instance). Finally, a **symptom management strategy** uses methods such as relaxation, meditation, medication and exercise.

All told, it is estimated that almost 85 per cent of all illness and injury is the result of lifestyle choices.[86] Therefore, it is not surprising that, increasingly, organisations are implementing a variety of **stress-reduction programmes** to help employees cope with modern-day stress. Although this example is pretty striking, stress-prevention programmes in the UK tend to be confined to large organisations with 500 employees or more. However, a number of government initiatives have been introduced within the EU, including collaborative research programmes, new working regulations and published guidelines to help organisations reduce workplace stress and the formation of a European Health and Safety Agency located in Bilbao, Spain.[87]

Stress intervention can focus on the individual, the organisation (as in the above example) or on the interface between individual and organisation (e.g. through participation). There are many different individual stress-reduction techniques available. The most frequently used approaches are muscle relaxation, biofeedback, meditation and cognitive restructuring. Each method involves somewhat different ways of coping with stress (see Table 9.5). Most workplace stress initiatives focus on individual stress-management training and not on reducing the sources of organisational stress; for example, by redesigning tasks (also see Chapter 5). Some techniques deal almost exclusive with the bodily (or 'somatic') aspects; others concentrate on cognitive restructuring, while a third group concentrates on coping behaviour.

HR

Table 9.5 Stress-Reduction Techniques

Technique	Descriptions	Assessment
Muscle relaxation	Uses slow deep breathing and systematic muscle tension reduction	Inexpensive and easy to use; may require a trained professional to implement
Biofeedback	A machine is used to train people to detect muscular tension; muscle relaxation is then used to alleviate this symptom of stress	Expensive due to costs of equipment; however, equipment can be used to evaluate effectiveness of other stress-reduction programmes
Meditation	The relaxation response is activated by redirecting one's thoughts away from oneself; a four-step procedure is used	Least expensive, simple to implement, and can be practised almost anywhere
Cognitive restructuring	Irrational or maladaptive thoughts are identified and replaced with those that are rational or logical	Expensive because it requires a trained psychologist or counsellor
Holistic wellness approach	A broad, interdisciplinary approach that goes beyond stress reduction by advocating that people strive for personal wellness in all aspects of their lives	Involves inexpensive but often behaviourally difficult lifestyle changes

!

Critical thinking

The implicit message throughout this section is that stress is extremely costly for organisations. How can it be, then, that many organisations seem incapable of solving or even reducing the problem?

Learning outcomes: Summary of key terms

1 **Stereotypes and their formation**

Stereotypes represent grossly oversimplified beliefs or expectations about groups of people. Stereotyping is a four-step process that begins by categorising people into groups according to various criteria. Next, we infer that all people within a particular group possess the same traits or characteristics. Then, we form expectations of others and interpret their behaviour according to our stereotypes. Finally, stereotypes are maintained by overestimating the frequency of stereotypic behaviours exhibited by others, incorrectly explaining expected and unexpected behaviours and differentiating minority individuals from oneself. The use of stereotypes is influenced by the amount and type of information available to an individual and his or her motivation to accurately process information.

2 **Diversity and competitive advantage**

Diversity represents the host of individual differences that makes people different from and similar to each other. Diversity pertains to everybody. It is not simply an issue of age, race, gender or sexual orientation. Managing diversity can: (a) lower costs and improve employee attitudes; (b) improve an organisation's recruiting efforts; (c) increase sales, market share and corporate profits; (d) increase creativity and innovation and (e) increase group problem-solving and productivity.

3 **Effectively managing diversity**

There are many different practices that organisations can use to manage diversity. Eight basic responses for handling any diversity issue are: include/exclude, deny, assimilate, suppress, isolate, tolerate, build relationships and foster mutual adaptation. Exclusion, denial, assimilation, suppression, isolation and toleration are among the least preferred options. Inclusion, building relationships and mutual adaptation are the preferred strategies. Accountability practices relate to the organisation's responsibility to treat diverse employees fairly. Development practices focus on preparing diverse employees for greater responsibility and advancement. Recruitment practices emphasise attracting job applicants at all levels who are willing to accept challenging work assignments. Table 9.5 presents a list of activities that are used to accomplish each main type.

4 **Definition of stress**

Stress is an adaptive reaction to environmental demands or stressors that triggers a fight-or-flight response. This response creates hormonal changes that mobilise the body for extraordinary demands.

5 **Stress models**

The Karasek Job Demand-Control (JD-C) model has been highly influential in many European countries. Many work environment laws have been inspired by this model. The JD-C model emphasises the stress factors inherent in the work organisation, more than it stresses the individual characteristics.

6 **The occupational stress model**

Perceived stress is caused by four sets of stressors: individual level, group level, organisational level and extra-organisational. In turn, perceived stress has psychological/attitudinal, behavioural, cognitive and physical health outcomes. Several individual differences moderate relationships between stressors, perceived stress and outcomes.

7 **Stressful life events**

Stressful life events are changes that disrupt an individual's lifestyle and social relationships. Holmes and Rahe developed the SRRS to assess an individual's cumulative stressful life events. A positive relationship exists between the scores on the Social Readjustment Rating Scale (SRRS) and illness. Uncontrollable events that are negative create the most stress.

8 **Burnout**

Burnout develops in phases. The three key phases are emotional exhaustion, depersonalisation and feeling a lack of personal accomplishment. Emotional exhaustion, the first phase, is caused by a combination of personal stressors and job and organisational stressors. The total effect of the burnout phases is a host of negative attitudinal and behavioural outcomes. Burnout can be reduced by buffering its effects. Potential buffers include extra staff or equipment, support from top management, increased freedom to make decisions, recognition of accomplishments, time off, equitable rewards and increased communication from the top. The content of an individual's job can also be changed or the person can be assigned to a new position. Sabbaticals and employee retreats are also used to reduce burnout.

9 **Social support**

Social support, an important moderator of relationships between stressors, stress and outcomes, represents the amount of perceived helpfulness derived from social relationships. Cultural norms, social institutions, companies, groups and individuals are all sources of social support. These sources provide four types of support: esteem, informational, social companionship and instrumental.

10 **The coping process**

Coping is the management of stressors and stress. Coping is directly affected by the cognitive appraisal of stressors which, in turn, is influenced by situational and personal factors. People cope by using control, escape or symptom management strategies. Because research has not identified the most effective method of coping, a contingency approach to coping is recommended.

Review questions

1 How would you spot stereotyping?
2 Which of the barriers to managing diversity would be most difficult to reduce?
3 Have you seen any evidence that diversity is a competitive advantage?
4 Which stress factors experienced by students are under their control?
5 Describe the stress symptoms you have observed in others.
6 Why would people in the helping professions become burned out more readily than people in other occupations?
7 Which kinds of social support are most easy to obtain?
8 A natural disaster like an earthquake or a tsunami causes widespread stress. Is any kind of coping possible and relevant?
9 Have you ever felt that the climate in an organisation you visited was unpleasant and if so what do you attribute this to?

Personal awareness and growth exercise

How do diversity assumptions influence team member interactions?

Objectives

1 To identify diversity assumptions.
2 To consider how diversity assumptions affect team members' interactions.

Introduction

Assumptions can be so ingrained that we do not even know that we are using them. Negative assumptions can limit our relationships with others because they influence how we perceive and respond to those we encounter in our daily lives. This exercise is designed to help identify the assumptions that you have about groups of people. Although this exercise may make you uncomfortable because it asks you to identify stereotypical assumptions, it is a positive first step to facing and examining the assumptions we make about other people. This awareness can lead to positive behavioural change.

Instructions

Complete the diversity assumptions worksheet.[88] The first column contains various dimensions of diversity. For each dimension, the second column asks you to identify the assumptions held by the general public about people with this characteristic. Use the third column to determine how each assumption might limit team members' ability to effectively interact with each other. Finally, answer the questions for discussion.

Questions for discussion

1 Where do our assumptions about others come from?
2 Is it possible to eliminate negative assumptions about others? How might this be done?
3 What most surprised you about your answers to the diversity assumption worksheet?

Diversity Assumption Worksheet

Dimension of diversity	Assumption that might be made	Effect on team members' interactions
Age	Example: Younger people haven't had the proper experience to come up with good solutions.	Example: Input from younger employees is not solicited.
Ethnicity (e.g. Asian)		
Gender		
Race		
Physical ability (e.g. hard of hearing)		
Sexual orientation		
Marital/parental status (e.g. single parent with children)		
Religion (e.g. Muslim)		
Recreational habits (e.g. hikes on weekends)		
Educational background (e.g. college education)		
Work experience (e.g. union)		
Appearance (e.g. overweight)		
Geographic location (e.g. rural)		
Personal habits (e.g. smoking)		
Income (e.g. well-to-do)		

Personal awareness and growth exercise

Are you burned out?

Objectives

1 To determine the extent to which you are burned out.
2 To determine if your burnout scores are predictive of burnout outcomes.
3 To identify specific stressors that affect your level of burnout.

Introduction

An OB researcher named Christina Maslach developed a self-report scale measuring burnout. This scale assesses burnout in terms of three phases: depersonalisation, personal accomplishment and emotional exhaustion. To determine if you suffer from burnout in any of these phases, we would like you to complete an abbreviated version of this scale. Moreover, because burnout has been found to influence a variety of behavioural outcomes, we also want to determine how well burnout predicts three important outcomes.

Instructions

To assess your level of burnout, complete the following 18 statements development by Maslach.[89] Each item probes how frequently you experience a particular feeling or attitude. If you are currently working, use your job as the frame of reference for responding to each statement. If you are a full-time student, use your role as a student as your frame of reference. After you have completed the 18 items, refer to the scoring key and follow its directions. Remember, there are no right or wrong answers. Indicate your answer for each statement by circling one number from the following scale.

1 = a few times a year
2 = monthly
3 = a few times a month
4 = every week
5 = a few times a week
6 = every day

Burnout inventory

1	I've become more callous towards people since I took this job.	1 2 3 4 5 6
2	I worry that this job is hardening me emotionally.	1 2 3 4 5 6
3	I don't really care what happens to some of the people who need my help.	1 2 3 4 5 6
4	I feel that people who need my help blame me for some of their problems.	1 2 3 4 5 6
5	I deal very effectively with the problems of those people who need my help.	1 2 3 4 5 6
6	I feel I'm positively influencing other people's lives through my work.	1 2 3 4 5 6
7	I feel very energetic.	1 2 3 4 5 6
8	I can easily create a relaxed atmosphere with those people who need my help.	1 2 3 4 5 6
9	I feel exhilarated after working closely with those who need my help.	1 2 3 4 5 6
10	I have accomplished many worthwhile things in the job.	1 2 3 4 5 6

11 In my work, I deal with emotional problems very calmly. 1 2 3 4 5 6
12 I feel emotionally drained from my work. 1 2 3 4 5 6
13 I feel used up at the end of the working day. 1 2 3 4 5 6
14 I feel fatigued when I get up in the morning. 1 2 3 4 5 6
15 I feel frustrated by my job. 1 2 3 4 5 6
16 I feel I'm working too hard at my job. 1 2 3 4 5 6
17 Working with people directly puts too much stress on me. 1 2 3 4 5 6
18 I feel like I'm at the end of my tether. 1 2 3 4 5 6

Scoring

Compute the average of those items measuring each phase of burnout.
Depersonalisation (questions 1–4) ____________
Personal accomplishment (questions 5–11) ____________
Emotional exhaustion (questions 12–18) ____________

Assessing burnout outcomes

1 How many times were you absent from work over the last three months (indicate the number of absences from your course last term if using the student role)? ________ absences
2 How satisfied are you with your job (or role as a student)? Circle one.
Very dissatisfied Dissatisfied Neutral Satisfied Very satisfied
3 Do you have trouble sleeping? Circle one.
Yes No

Questions for discussion

1 To what extent are you burned out in terms of depersonalisation and emotional exhaustion?
Low = 1–2.99; moderate = 3–4.99; high = 5 or above
2 To what extent are you burned out in terms of personal accomplishment?
Low = 5 or above; moderate = 3–4.99; high = 1–2.99
3 How well do your burnout scores predict your burnout outcomes?
4 Do your burnout scores suggest that burnout follows a sequence going from depersonalisation, to feeling a lack of personal accomplishment, to emotional exhaustion? Explain.
5 Which of the unique burnout stressors illustrated in Figure 9.3 are affecting your level of burnout?

Group exercise

Using attribution theory to resolve performance problems

Objectives

1 To gain experience determining the causes of performance.
2 To decide on corrective action for employee performance.

Introduction

Attributions are typically made to internal and external factors. Perceivers arrive at their assessments by using various informational cues or antecedents. To determine the types of antecedents people use, we have developed a case containing various informational cues about an individual's performance. You will be asked to read the case and make attributions about the causes of performance. To assess the impact of attributions on behaviour, you will also be asked to recommend corrective action.

Instructions

Presented below is a case study that depicts the performance of Marie Martin, a computer programmer. Please read the case and then identify the causes of her behaviour by answering the question following the case. After completing this task, decide on the appropriateness of various forms of corrective action. A list of potential recommendations has been drawn up. The list is divided into four categories. Read each action, and evaluate its appropriateness by using the scale provided. Next, compute a total score for each of the four categories.

Causes of performance

To what extent was each of the following a cause of Marie's performance? Use the following scale:

		Very little			Very much	
a	High ability	1	2	3	4	5
b	Low ability	1	2	3	4	5
c	Low effort	1	2	3	4	5
d	Difficult job	1	2	3	4	5
e	Unproductive co-workers	1	2	3	4	5
f	Bad luck	1	2	3	4	5

The case of Marie Martin

Marie Martin, 30, received her degree in computer science from a reputable university in Europe. She also graduated with above-average grades. Marie is currently working in the computer support/analysis department as a programmer for a large organisation. During the past year, Marie has missed 10 days of work. She seems unmotivated and rarely completes her assignments on time. Marie is usually given the harder programs to work on.

Past records indicate that Marie, on average, completes programs classified as 'routine' in about 45 hours. Her co-workers, on the other hand, complete these routine programs in an average of 32 hours. Further, Marie finishes programs considered 'major problems' in about 115 hours on average. Her co-workers, however, finish these same assignments, in an average of 100 hours. When Marie has worked in programming teams, her peer performance reviews are generally average to negative. Her male peers have noted she is not creative in attacking problems and she is difficult to work with.

The computer department recently sent a questionnaire to all users of its services to evaluate the usefulness and accuracy of data received. The results indicate many departments are not using computer output because they cannot understand the reports. It was also determined that the users of output generated from Marie's programs found the output chaotic and not useful for decision-making.

Appropriateness of corrective action

	Very inappropriate				Very appropriate
Coercive actions					
a Reprimand Marie for her performance	1	2	3	4	5
b Threaten to fire Marie if her performance does not improve	1	2	3	4	5
Change job					
c Transfer Marie to another job	1	2	3	4	5
d Demote Marie to a less demanding job	1	2	3	4	5
Non-punitive actions					
e Work with Marie to help her do the job better	1	2	3	4	5
f Offer Marie encouragement to help her improve	1	2	3	4	5
No immediate actions					
g Do nothing	1	2	3	4	5
h Promise Marie a pay raise if she improves	1	2	3	4	5

Scoring key

Compute a score for the four categories:
Coercive actions a b
Change job c d
Non-punitive actions e f
No immediate actions g h

Questions for discussion

1 How would you evaluate Marie's performance in terms of consensus, distinctiveness and consistency?
2 Is Marie's performance due to internal or external causes?
3 What did you identify as the top two causes of Marie's performance? Are your choices consistent with Weiner's classification of internal and external factors? Explain.
4 Which of the four types of corrective action do you think is most appropriate? Explain. Can you identify any negative consequences of this choice?

Group exercise

Reducing the stressors in your environment

Objectives

1 To identify the stressors in your environment.
2 To evaluate the extent to which each stressor is a source of stress.
3 To develop a plan for reducing the impact of stressors in your environment.

Introduction

Stressors are environmental factors that produce stress. They are prerequisites to experiencing the symptoms of stress. As previously discussed in this chapter, people do not appraise stressors in the same way. For instance, having to complete a challenging assignment may be motivational for one person and threatening to another.

Instructions

Your lecturer will divide the class into groups of four to six. Once the group is assembled, the group should brainstorm and record a list of stressors that they believe exist in their environments. Use the guidelines for brainstorming discussed in Chapter 13. After recording all the brainstormed ideas on a piece of paper, remove redundancies and combine like items so that the group has a final list of unique stressors. Next, each group member should individually determine the extent to which each stressor is a source of stress in his or her life. For the purpose of this exercise, stress is defined as existing whenever you experience feelings of pressure, strain or emotional upset. The stress evaluation is done by first indicating the frequency with which each stressor is a source of stress to you. Use the six-point rating scale provided. Once everyone has completed their individual ratings, combine the numerical judgements to get an average stress score for each stressor. Next, identify the five stressors with the highest average stress ratings. Finally, the group should develop a plan for coping with each of these five stressors. Try to make your recommendations as specific as possible.

Rating scale

Answer the following question for each stressor: To what extent is the stressor a source of stress?

1 = never
2 = rarely
3 = occasionally
4 = often
5 = usually
6 = always

Questions for discussion

1 Are you surprised by the type of stressors that were rated as creating the most stress in your lives? Explain.
2 Did group members tend to agree or disagree when evaluating the extent to which the various stressors created stress in their lives? What is the source of the different appraisals?
3 Which form of coping did your plans include most, control or escape-oriented strategies? Explain.

Online
Learning Centre

When you have read this chapter, log on to the Online Learning Centre website at ***www.mcgraw-hill.co.uk/textbooks/sinding*** to access test questions, additional exercises and other related resources.

Notes

[1] W. H. Glick, 'Conceptualizing and Measuring Organizational and Psychological Climate', *Academy of Management Review*, no. 10, pp. 601–16, 1985.

[2] B. Schneider, J. J. Parkington and V. M. Buxton, 'Employee and Customer Perceptions of service in banks', *Administrative Science Quarterly*, no. 25, pp. 2252–267, 1980.

[3] R. Guion, 'A Note on Organizational Climate', *Organizational Behavior and Human Performance*, no. 9, pp. 120–25, 1973.

[4] See G. S. Hansen and B. Wernerfelt, 'Determinants of Firm Performance: The Relative Importance of Economic and Organizational Factors', *Strategic Management Journal*, no. 10, pp. 399–411.

[5] R. M. Burton, B. Obel and J. Lauridsen, 'Tension and Resistance to Change in Organizational Climate: Managerial Implications for a Fast Paced World', LOK working paper, www.lok.cbs.dk/images/publ/Burton%20og%20Obel%20og%20Lauridsen%20tension%202000.pdf.

[6] Based on D. Hellriegel, J. Slocum and R. Woodman, *Organizational Behavior*, Southwestern, 1998.

[7] C. M. Judd and B. Park, 'Definition and Assessment of Accuracy in Social Stereotypes', *Psychological Review*, January 1993, p. 110.

[8] R. Woodfield, 'Women and Information Systems Development: Not Just A Pretty (Inter)face?', *Information Technology & People*, no. 2, 2002, pp. 199–238.

[9] The process of stereotype formation and maintenance is discussed by S. T. Fiske, M. Lin and S. L. Neuberg, 'The Continuum Model: Ten Years Later', in *Dual-Process Theories in Social Psychology*, eds S. Chaiken and Y. Trope (New York: The Guilford Press, 1999), pp. 231–54.

[10] This discussion is based on material presented in G. V. Bodenhausen, C. N. Macrae and J. W. Sherman, 'On the Dialectics of Discrimination', in *Dual-Process Theories in Social Psychology*, eds S. Chaiken and Y. Trope (New York: The Guilford Press, 1999), pp. 271–90.

[11] See A. H. Eagly, S. J Karu and B. T. Johnson, 'Gender and Leadership Style among School Principals: A Meta-Analysis', *Educational Administration Quarterly*, February 1992, pp. 76–102; and I. K. Broverman, S. Raymond Vogel, D. M. Broverman, F. E. Clarkson and P. S. Rosenkrantz, 'Sex-Role Stereotypes: A Current Appraisal', *Journal of Social Issues*, 1972, p. 75.

[12] See B. P. Allen, 'Gender Stereotypes Are Not Accurate: A Replication of Martin (1987) Using Diagnostic vs. Self-Report and Behavioral Criteria', *Sex Roles*, May 1995, pp. 583–600.

[13] Results can be found in V. E. Schein, R. Mueller, T. Lituchy and J. Liu, 'Think Manager – Think Male: A Global Phenomenon?', *Journal of Organizational Behavior*, January 1996, pp. 33–41.

[14] R. Vonk and R. D. Ashmore, 'Thinking about Gender Types: Cognitive Organization of Female and Male Types', *British Journal of Social Psychology*, June 2003, pp. 257–80.

[15] Data from *The Report of the Advisory Panel on Judicial Diversity 2010*, at www.justice.gov.uk/publications/docs/advisory-panel-judicial-diversity-2010.pdf, (accessed 20 July 2010) and *Fact Sheet Women Solicitors 2009*. The Law Society, at www.lawsociety.org.uk/secure/file/185477/e:/teamsite-deployed/documents/templatedata/Publications/Research%20fact%20sheet/Documents/womensols09_v1.pdf.

[16] European Commision, *Employment in Europe* (Luxembourg: Office for Official Publications of the European Communities, 1997), p. 31.

[17] European data from www.ec.europa.eu/social/main.jsp?catId=685&langId=en and UK data from www.statistics.gov.uk/cci/nugget.asp?id=167.

[18] M. Kets de Vries, *The Leadership Mystique* (London: Pearson Education Limited, 2001).

[19] Translated from F. Latrive, '40,1%, Le Taux d'Activité des 55-64 and dans l'Union Européenne en 2002', *Libération*, 4 March 2004; http://epp.eurostat.ec.europa.eu/statistics_explained/index.php?title=File:Employment_rates_for_selected_population_groups,_2001-2011_%28%25%29.png&filetimestamp=20121030183007.

[20] 'Ageism Rife in UK Workplace', at www.peoplemanagement.co.uk/, 15 January 2004.

[21] For a complete review, see S. R. Rhodes, 'Age-Related Differences in Work Attitudes and Behavior: A Review and Conceptual Analysis', *Psychological Bulletin*, March 1983, pp. 328–67. Supporting evidence was also provided by G. Burkins, 'Work Week: A Special News Report about Life on the Job – and Trends Taking Shape There', *The Wall Street Journal*, 5 May 1996, p. A1.

[22] See G. M. McEvoy, 'Cumulative Evidence of the Relationship between Employee Age and Job Performance', *Journal of Applied Psychology*, February 1989, pp. 11–17.

[23] A thorough discussion of the relationship between age and performance is contained in D. A. Waldman and B. J. Avolio, 'Aging and Work Performance in Perspective: Contextual and Developmental Considerations', in *Research in Personnel and Human Resources Management*, vol. 11, ed. G. R. Ferris (Greenwich, CT: JAI Press, 1993), pp. 133–62.

[24] For details, see B. J. Avolio, D. A. Waldman and M. A. McDaniel, 'Age and Work Performance in Nonmanagerial Jobs: The Effects of Experience and Occupational Type', *Academy of Management Journal*, June 1990, pp. 407–22.

[25] D. H. Powell, 'Aging Baby Boomers: Stretching Your Workforce Options', *HR Magazine*, July 1998, p. 83.

[26] See P. W. Hom and R. W. Griffeth, *Employee Turnover* (Cincinnati, OH: SouthWestern, 1995), pp. 35–50; and J. J. Martocchio, 'Age-Related Differences in Employee Absenteeism: A Meta-Analysis', *Psychology and Aging*, December 1989, pp. 409–14.

[27] Translated from J. Billiet and K. Meireman, *Immigratie en asiel: de opvattingen en houdingen van Belgen in het Europeens sociaal survey. Onderzoeksverslag van het Departement Sociologie – Afdeling Dataverzameling en Analyse* (DA/2004-36), p. 25.

[28] Translated from D. De Coninck, 'Mohammed wordt Michaël, en dat is precies wat de wetgever wou', *De Morgen*, 4 September 2004.

[29] See Y. F. Niemann and J. F. Dovidio, 'Relationship of Solo Status, Academic Rank, and Perceived Distinctiveness to Job Satisfaction of Racial/Ethnic Minorities', *Journal of Applied Psychology*, February 1998, pp. 55–71; J. I. Sanchez and P. Brock, 'Outcomes of Perceived Discrimination among Hispanic Employees: Is Diversity Management a Luxury or a Necessity?', *Academy of Management Journal*, June 1996, pp. 704–19; and T. H. Cox, Jr and J. A. Finley, 'An Analysis of Work Specialization and Organization Level as Dimensions of Workforce Diversity', in *Diversity in Organizations*, eds M. M. Chemers, S. Oskamp and M. A. Costanzo (Thousand Oaks, CA: Sage Publications, 1995), pp. 62–88.

[30] For a thorough discussion of stereotype accuracy, see M. C. Ashton and V. M. Esses, 'Stereotype Accuracy: Estimating the Academic Performance of Ethnic Groups', *Personality and Social Psychology Bulletin*, February 1999, pp. 225–36.

[31] See C. Comeau-Kirschner, 'Navigating the Roadblocks', *Management Review*, May 1999, p. 8; and S. Shellenbarger, 'Work-Force Study Finds Loyalty Is Weak, Division of Race and Gender Are Deep', *The Wall Street Journal*, 3 September 1993, pp. B1, B9.

[32] D. R. Avery *et al.*, 'Unequal attendance: the relationships between race, organizational diversity cues, and absenteeism', *Personnel Psychology*, vol. 60, no. 4, 2007, pp. 875–902.

[33] B. P. Buunk and V. van der Laan, 'Do Women Need Female Role Models? Subjective Social Status and the Effects of Same-Sex Opposite-Sex Comparisons', *Revue Internationale de Psychologie Sociale*, December 2002, pp. 129–55.

[34] W. R. Thompson, 'Diversity among Managers Translates into Profitability', *HR Magazine*, April 1999, p. 10.

[35] For research into TMT demographics, see K. Y. Williams, 'Demography and Diversity in Organisations: A Review of 100 Years of Research' in *Research in Organizational Behavior*, vol. 20, eds B. M. Staw and L. L. Cummings (Greenwich, CT: JAI Press, 1998), pp. 77–140.

[36] M. C. Schipers, D. N. Den Hartog, P. L. Koopman and J. A. Wienk, 'Diversity and Team Outcomes: The Moderating Effects of Outcome Interdependence and Group Longevity and the Mediating Effect of Reflexivity', *Journal of Organizational Behavior*, September 2003, pp. 779–802.

[37] 'Managing Diversity. A IPD Position Paper', Institute of Personnel and Development, p. 7 (also see www.cipd.co.uk).

[38] www.cipd.co.uk/

[39] See R. R. Thomas, Jr, 'From Affirmative Action to Affirming Diversity', *Harvard Business Review*, March–April 1990, pp. 107–17.

[40] www.cipd.co.uk

[41] Ibid.

[42] R. Foroohar, S. Theil, S. Marias, T. Pepper, H. Wiedekind and B. Nadeau, 'Race in the Boardroom,' *Newsweek*, 18 February 2002, p. 34.

[43] For complete details and results from this study, see A. M. Morrison, *The New Leaders: Guidelines on Leadership Diversity in America* (San Francisco: Jossey-Bass, 1992).

[44] 'Balancing Act', *Financial Times*, 9 May 2000.

[45] Empirical support is provided by H. Ibarra, 'Race, Opportunity, and Diversity of Social Circles in Managerial Networks', *Academy of Management Journal*, June 1995, pp. 673–703; and P. J. Ohlott, M. N. Ruderman and C. D. McCauley, 'Gender Differences in Managers' Developmental Job Experiences', *Academy of Management Journal*, February 1994, pp. 46–67.

[46] 'Mental Health at Work: Developing the business case.' The Sainsbury Centre for Mental Health, Policy paper 8, 2007.

[47] See L. Grunberg, S. Moore and E. S. Greenberg, 'Work Stress and Problem Alcohol Behavior: A Test of the Spillover Model', *Journal of Organizational Behavior*, September 1998, pp. 487–502.

[48] D. Bouckenooghe, M. Buelens, J. Fontaine and K. Vanderheyden, 'The Prediction of Stress by Values and Value Conflict', *Journal of Psychology* (in press). Also see R. Knoop, 'Work Values and Job Satisfaction', *Journal of Psychology*, September 1994, pp. 683–90; and R. Knoop, 'Relieving Stress through Value Rich Work', *Journal of Psychology*, November 1994, pp. 829–36.

[49] The stress response is thoroughly discussed in H. Selye, *Stress without Distress* (New York: J. B. Lippincott, 1974).

[50] J. M. Ivancevich and M. T. Matteson, *Stress and Work: A Managerial Perspective* (Glenview, IL: Scott, Foresman, 1980), pp. 8–9.

[51] See H. Selye, *Stress without Distress* (New York: J. B. Lippincott, 1974).

[52] Adapted and translated from A. Giegas, 'Dossier: Stress', *Vacature*, published online only at www.vacature.com/scripts/index-page.asp?headingID_1103, 2000.

[53] See R. Karasek, 'Job Demands, Job Decision Latitude and Mental Strain: Implications for Job Redesign', *Administrative Science Quarterly*, 24, 1979, pp. 285–306; and R. Karasek and T. Theorell, *Healthy Work: Stress, Productivity and the Reconstruction of Working Life* (New York: Basic Books, 1990).

[54] See J. D. Jonge, G. J. P. Van Breikelen, J. A. Landeweerd and F. J. N. Nijhuis, 'Comparing Group and Individual Level Assessments of Job Characteristics in Testing the Job Demand Control Model: A Multilevel Approach', *Human Relations*, January 1999, pp. 95–122; and J. Schaubroeck and L. S. Fink, 'Facilitating and Inhibiting Effects of Job Control and Social Support on Stress Outcomes and Role Behavior: A Contingency Model', *Journal of Organizational Behavior*, March 1998, pp. 167–95.

[55] Supportive results can be found in V. J. Magley, C. L. Hulin, L. F. Fitzgerald and M. DeNardo, 'Outcomes of Self-Labeling Sexual Harassment', *Journal of Applied Psychology*, June 1999, pp. 390–402; and L. F. Fitzgerald, F. Drasgow, C. L. Hulin, M. J. Gelfand and V. J. Magley, 'Antecedents and Consequences of Sexual Harassment in Organizations: A Test of an Integrated Model', *Journal of Applied Psychology*, August 1997, pp. 578–89.

[56] The relationship between chronic work demands and stress was investigated by J. Schaubroeck and D. C. Ganster, 'Chronic Demands and Responsivity to Challenge', *Journal of Applied Psychology*, February 1993, pp. 73–85. Also see E. Demerouti, A. B. Bakker, F. Nachreiner and W. B. Schaufeli, 'The Job Demands-Resources Model of Burnout', *Journal of Applied Psychology*, June 2001, pp. 499–512.

[57] U. Konradt, G. Hertel and R. Schmook, 'Quality of Management by Objectives, Task-Related Stressors, and Non-Task-Related Stressors as Predictors of Stress and Job Satisfaction among Teleworkers', *European Journal of Work and Organizational Psychology*, March 2003, pp. 61–79.

[58] Anonymous, 'Het Britse seksleven is in gevaar', *Vacature*, 3 December 1999.

[59] Anonymous, 'Stress Causes One-Third to Think about Work While Having Sex', *The Guardian*, 5 November 1999.

[60] See R. Lazarus, *Stress and Emotion: A New Synthesis* (New York: Springer Publishing, 1999).

[61] Research on job loss is summarised by K. A. Hanisch, 'Job Loss and Unemployment Research from 1994 to 1998: A Review and Recommendations for Research and Intervention', *Journal of Vocational Behavior*, October 1999, pp. 188–220. Also see F. M. McKee-Ryan and A. J. Kinicki, 'Coping with Job Loss: A Life-Facet Perspective', in *International Review of Industrial and Organizational Psychology*, eds C. L. Cooper and I. T. Robertson (Chichester: John Wiley & Sons, 2002), pp. 1–30.

[62] Results can be found in L. Narayanan, S. Menon and P. E. Spector, 'Stress in the Workplace: A Comparison of Gender and Occupations', *Journal of Organizational Behavior*, January 1999, pp. 63–73.

[63] See M. E. Lachman and S. L. Weaver, 'The Sense of Control as a Moderator of Social Class Differences in Health and Well-Being', *Journal of Personality and Social Psychology*, March 1998, pp. 763–73.

[64] These findings are reported in B. Melin, U. Lundberg, J. Soderlund and M. Granqvist, 'Psychological and Physiological Stress Reactions of Male and Female Assembly Workers: A Comparison between Two Different Forms of Work Organization', *Journal of Organizational Behavior*, January 1999, pp. 47–61.

[65] Research on chronic hostility is discussed by 'Healthy Lives: A New View of Stress', *University of California, Berkeley Wellness Letter*, June 1990, pp. 4–5. Also see R. S. Jorgensen, B. T. Johnson, M. E. Kolodziej and G. E. Schreer, 'Elevated Blood Pressure and Personality: A Meta-Analytic Review', *Psychological Bulletin*, September 1996, pp. 293–320.

[66] Adapted and translated from A. Giegas, 'Dossier burnout', *Vacature*, at www.vacature.com/scripts/indexpage.asp? headingID_1477/, 2000.

[67] The phases are thoroughly discussed by C. Maslach, *Burnout: The Cost of Caring* (Englewood Cliffs, NJ: Prentice-Hall, 1982).

[68] The discussion of the model is based on C. L. Cordes and T. W. Dougherty, 'A Review and Integration of Research on Job Burnout', *Academy of Management Review*, October 1993, pp. 621–56.

[69] S. Armour, 'Employers Urge Workers to Chill Out Before Burning Out', *USA Today*, 22 June 1999, p. 5B.

[70] This research is discussed by K. S. Kendler, L. M. Karkowski and C. A. Prescott, 'Causal Relationship between Stressful Life Events and the Onset of Major Depression', *American Journal of Psychiatry*, June 1999, pp. 837–48; C. Segrin, 'Social Skills, Stressful Life Events, and the Development of Psychosocial Problems', *Journal of Social and Clinical Psychology*, Spring 1999, pp. 14–34; and R. S. Bhagat, 'Effects of Stressful Life Events on Individual Performance Effectiveness and Work Adjustment Processes within Organizational Settings: A Research Model', *Academy of Management Review*, October 1983, pp. 660–71.

[71] See D. R. Pillow, A. J. Zautra and I. Sandler, 'Major Life Events and Minor Stressors: Identifying Mediational Links in the Stress Process', *Journal of Personality and Social Psychology*, February 1996, pp. 381–94; R. C. Barnett, S. W. Raudenbush, R. T. Brennan, J. H. Pleck and N. L. Marshall, 'Change in Job and Marital Experiences and Change in Psychological Distress: A Longitudinal Study of Dual-Earner Couples', *Journal of Personality and Social Psychology*, November 1995, pp. 839–50; and S. Cohen, D. A. J. Tyrell and A. P. Smith, 'Negative Life Events, Perceived Stress, Negative Affect, and Susceptibility to the Common Cold', *Journal of Personality and Social Psychology*, January 1993, pp. 131–40.

[72] See C. J. Hobson, J. Kamen, J. Szostek, C. M. Nethercut, J. W. Tiedmann and S. Wojnarowicz, 'Stressful Life Events: A Revision and Update of the Social Readjustment Rating Scale (SRRS)', *International Journal of Stress Management*, January 1998, pp. 1–23; and R. H. Rahe, 'Life Changes Scaling: Other Results, Gender Differences', *International Journal of Stress Management*, October 1998, pp. 249–50.

[73] Results and conclusions can be found in R. T. Lee and B. E. Ashforth, 'A Meta-Analytic Examination of the Correlates of the Three Dimensions of Burnout', *Journal of Applied Psychology*, April 1996, pp. 123–33.

[74] See R. T. Lee and B. E. Ashforth, 'A Meta-Analytic Examination of the Correlates of the Three Dimensions of Burnout', *Journal of Applied Psychology*, April 1996, pp. 123–33; E. Babakus, D. W. Cravens, M. Johnston and W. C. Moncrief, 'The Role of Emotional Exhaustion in Sales Force Attitude and Behavior Relationships', *Journal of the Academy of Marketing Science*, no. 1, 1999, pp. 58–70; and R. D. Iverson, M. Olekalns and P. J. Erwin, 'Affectivity, Organizational Stressors, and Absenteeism: A Causal Model of Burnout and Its Consequences', *Journal of Vocational Behavior*, February 1998, pp. 1–23.

[75] S. Cartwright, 'Taking the Pulse of Executive Health in the UK', *Academy of Management Executive*, March 2000, pp. 16–24.

[76] Recommendations for reducing burnout are discussed by J. E. Moore, 'Are You Burning Out Valuable Resources', *HR Magazine*, January 1999, pp. 93–7; and L. Grensing-Pophal, 'Recognizing and Conquering On-the-Job Burnout: HR, Heal Thyself', *HR Magazine*, March 1999, pp. 82–8.

[77] Types of support are discussed in S. Cohen and T. A. Wills, 'Stress, Social Support, and the Buffering Hypothesis', *Psychological Bulletin*, September 1985, pp. 310–57.

[78] The perceived availability and helpfulness of social support was discussed by B. P. Buunk, J. D. Jonge, J. F. Ybema and C. J. D. Wolff, 'Psychosocial Aspects of Occupational Stress', in *Handbook of Work and Organizational Psychology, second edition*, eds P. J. D. Drenth, H. Thierry and C. J. D. Wolff (New York: Psychology Press, 1998), pp. 145–82.

[79] See R. A. Clay, 'Research at the Heart of the Matter', *Monitor on Psychology*, January 2001, pp. 42–5; B. N. Uchino, J. T. Cacioppo and J. K. Kiecolt-Glaser, 'The Relationship between Social Support and Physiological Processes: A Review with Emphasis on Underlying Mechanisms and Implications for Health', *Psychological Bulletin*, May 1996, pp. 488–531; and H. Benson and M. Stark, *Timeless Healing: The Power and Biology of Belief* (New York: Scribner, 1996).

[80] Supporting results can be found in L. L. Schirmer and F. G. Lopez, 'Probing the Social Support and Work Strain Relationship among Adult Workers: Contributions of Adult Attachment Orientations', *Journal of Vocational Behavior*, August 2001,

pp. 17–33; C. J. Holahan, R. H. Moos, C. K. Holahan and R. C. Cronkite, 'Resource Loss, Resource Gain, and Depressive Symptoms: A 10-Year Model', *Journal of Personality and Social Psychology*, September 1999, pp. 620–29; D. S. Carlson and P. L. Perrewe, 'The Role of Social Support in the Stressor–Strain Relationship: An Examination of Work–Family Conflict', *Journal of Management*, Winter 1999, pp. 513–40; and M. H. Davis, M. M. Morris and L. A. Kraus, 'Relationship-Specific and Global Perceptions of Social Support: Associations with Well-Being and Attachment', *Journal of Personality and Social Psychology*, February 1998, pp. 468–81.

81 See S. Aryee, V. Luk, A. Leung and S. Lo, 'Role Stressors, Interrole Conflict, and Well-Being: The Moderating Influence of Spousal Support and Coping Behaviors among Employed Parents in Hong Kong', *Journal of Vocational Behavior*, April 1999, pp. 259–78; and C. Viswesvaran, J. I. Sanchez and J. Fisher, 'The Role of Social Support in the Process of Work Stress: A Meta-Analysis', *Journal of Vocational Behavior*, April 1999, pp. 314–34.

82 For details, see B. P. Buunk, B. J. Doosje, L. G. J. M. Jans and L. E. M. Hopstaken, 'Perceived Reciprocity, Social Support, and Stress at Work: The Role of Exchange and Communal Orientation', *Journal of Personality and Social Psychology*, October 1993, pp. 801–11; and C. E. Cutrona, 'Objective Determinants of Perceived Social Support', *Journal of Personality and Social Psychology*, February 1986, pp. 349–55.

83 R. S. Lazarus and S. Folkman, 'Coping and Adaptation', in *Handbook of Behavioral Medicine*, ed. W. D. Gentry (New York: The Guilford Press, 1984), p. 283.

84 The antecedents of appraisal were investigated by G. J. Fogarty, M. A. Machin, M. J. Albion, L. F. Sutherland, G. I. Lalor and S. Revitt, 'Predicting Occupational Strain and Job Satisfaction: The Role of Stress, Coping, Personality, and Affectivity Variables', *Journal of Vocational Behavior*, June 1999, pp. 429–52; E. C. Chang, 'Dispositional Optimism and Primary and Secondary Appraisal of a Stressor: Controlling Influences and Relations to Coping and Psychological and Physical Adjustment', *Journal of Personality and Social Psychology*, April 1998, pp. 1109–20; and J. C. Holder and A. Vaux, 'African American Professionals: Coping with Occupational Stress in Predominantly White Work Environments', *Journal of Vocational Behavior*, December 1988, pp. 315–33.

85 R. S. Lazarus and S. Folkman, 'Coping and Adaptation', in *Handbook of Behavioral Medicine*, ed. W. D. Gentry (New York: The Guilford Press, 1984), p. 289.

86 See J. Rothman, 'Wellness and Fitness Programs', in *Sourcebook of Occupational Rehabilitation*, ed. P. M. King (New York: Plenum Press, 1998), pp. 127–44; and S. Shellenbarger, 'Work & Family: Rising Before Dawn, Are You Getting Ahead or Just Getting Tired?', *The Wall Street Journal*, 17 February 1999, p. B1.

87 S. Cartwright, 'Taking the Pulse of Executive Health in the UK', *Academy of Management Executive*, March 2000, pp. 16–24.

88 This exercise was modified from an exercise in L. Gardenwartz and A. Rowe, *Diverse Teams at Work* (New York: McGraw-Hill, 1994), p. 169.

89 Adapted from C. Maslach and S. E. Jackson, 'The Measurement of Experienced Burnout', *Journal of Occupational Behavior*, April 1981, pp. 99–113.

Part 4

Organisational processes

Part contents

Chapter 10

Organisation structure and types

Learning Outcomes

When you finish studying the material in this chapter, you should be able to:

- ✓ describe the four characteristics common to all organisations
- ✓ describe the balancing between differentiation and integration in organisations
- ✓ describe the organisation's parts and the way tasks can be grouped
- ✓ explain the different co-ordination mechanisms an organisation can use
- ✓ define and briefly explain the practical significance of centralisation and decentralisation
- ✓ discuss the bureaucratic organisation
- ✓ discuss the differences between mechanistic and organic organisations
- ✓ describe the seven organisation types of Mintzberg and discuss how they differ in the structural elements
- ✓ describe why new organisational forms developed and what the main differences are with the classical forms
- ✓ describe horizontal, hourglass and virtual organisations

Opening Case Study: Siemens – scandal and restructuring

Following the disappointment of Siemens 2 quarter results published in early May 2013, an influential observer noted that, as usual, something was not quite right. In this case, lower sales and higher costs were blamed. The note on Siemens concluded by calling for a cost-driven overhaul of the company, aimed at increasing the margins from core operating divisions to 12 per cent or more and added for good measure that everything could still go wrong.

None of this is very appreciative of the role played by the CEO of Siemens, Peter Löscher. In the summer of 2010, Siemens had announced that it would set up its own bank in order to finance future expansion in a world where banks seem less reliable than they used to be. Siemens is one of Germany's largest companies. Inventions such as the lift and the tram came from the company. Today Siemens is active in industrial solutions, energy and health care. Over the years, the company has experimented with other types of business, including the manufacture of mobile phone handsets and PCs. None of the latter have been very successful ventures.

However, a failing unit within a large company like Siemens must be routinely dealt with. The problem for Siemens has been that there have been many such units. Doing something about them requires tough decisions, something Siemens managers seemed reluctant to do. Instead of actually making decisions, Siemens managers had a reputation for referring difficult issues to committees to avoid making them themselves.

During 2005 and 2006, Klaus Kleinfeld, then the new chief executive officer (CEO), introduced a number of changes to make the company more profitable. This included selling off mobile phone operations, setting earnings goals for all units and making the company more customer-focused. Siemens was positioned to reap the benefits of its hard labour.

Things looked good until 15 November 2006, when it was revealed that the company had for years systematically been using bribes to win business deals. The sums were vast, reported as €420 million, spent since the early 1990s. These revelations were just a starting point. The chairman, Heinrich von Pierer, who had been CEO for most of the period in which bribes were standard procedure, was disgraced and resigned. Klaus Kleinfeld, who was not implicated, also resigned when the board did not unequivocally support a renewal of his contract. Eventually, the entire board was replaced and an outsider was hired for the top job, not a Siemens man, not even a German.

Austrian by birth, Peter Löscher came from the pharmaceutical company Merck and had worked for General Electric (also Siemens' biggest US competitor) and for the chemical company Hoechst. At Siemens, Löscher announced sweeping organisational changes. The organisation was at this time described as a 'grid' structure, with both products and geographical regions as dimensions in the grid. This was reorganised into three divisions: industry (with six subdivisions), energy (also six subdivisions) and health care (three subdivisions). Management layers were cut away, many administrative jobs were eliminated and incentives were tied to the long-term performance of the company.

Just as these radical changes were about to start paying off, the financial crisis hit Siemens. When worse than expected results hit Siemens in March 2008, Mr Löscher put the news down to three factors; the undeniable downturn in the economy, a greater transparency in the way the company interacted with its surroundings, and finally to costs following from the scandal, estimated to have been as high as €1.4 billion.

In 2013 Peter Löscher was again under pressure. This time Siemens' earnings were under pressure from a very sluggish recovery and disappointing earnings. Market observers want cost-cutting and better efficiency. However, this may be insufficient if the structure remains unchanged.

For discussion

Are further structural changes called for at Siemens – and if so, what should they be?

Source: Based on 'Siemens and it's demons', *The Economist*, 22 May 2007; L. Lionel, 'Cosmetic Change at Siemens', *Forbes*, 6 October 2007; J. Ewing, 'At Siemens the Loescher Regime Begins', *Business Week*, 22 July 2007; Daniel Schäfer, 'Siemens Plans to Set Up Own Bank', *Financial Times*, 28 June 2010; 'Siemens: revenge of the gremlins', *Financial Times*, 2 May 2013.

Virtually every aspect of life is affected at least indirectly by some type of organisation.[1] We look to organisations to feed, clothe, house, educate and employ us. Organisations attend to our needs for entertainment, police and fire protection, insurance, recreation, national security, transportation, news and information, legal assistance and health care. Many of these organisations seek a profit, others do not. Some are extremely large; others are tiny, family-run operations. Despite this vast diversity, modern organisations have one basic thing in common. They are the primary context for organisational behaviour, the chessboard on which the game of organisational behaviour is played.

This chapter explores the structural features and different types of mostly traditional and new organisations. We begin by defining the term 'organisation'. Our attention then turns to the main issues which determine organisation structure; namely, division of labour, hierarchy of authority and co-ordination of efforts. Next, we discuss how these different elements result in several organisation types. We conclude with a review of modern organisation types.

10.1 Organisation – defined, described and depicted

Chester Barnard defined an **organisation** as 'a system of consciously co-ordinated activities or forces of two or more persons'.[2] Organisations exist to allow groups of people to co-ordinate efforts to get things done. Embodied in the conscious co-ordination aspect of this definition are four factors common to all organisations: division of labour, hierarchy of authority, co-ordination of effort and common goal.[3] We will elaborate further on the first three later in this chapter. Effectively reaching common goals will be discussed in Chapter 11. Organisation theorists refer to these factors as the determinants of organisation 'structure'.[4] These are characteristic of all organisations but in terms of describing and categorising organisational structure a more precise set of terms is helpful. First, organisations can be given labels according to which type it belongs to. Common types, also frequently called forms or configurations, are simple, functional, divisional, matrix and ad hoc. The choice of form depends on how work is organised, as discussed below. In addition, when describing an organisation, three other dimensions or aspects provide important information about the nature of the organisation we face. The degree of centralisation tells us something about where decisions are made and where co-ordination occurs, while the degree to which formalisation is used tells us more about co-ordination; specifically, about how standardised co-ordination procedures are. Finally, organisational differentiation gives further information on division of labour and the specific organisation of everyday work activity.

Organisations are subject to norms of rationality,[5] meaning that organisations have goals and structures to achieve them. Common goals are what unite the organisation members and provide the organisation with a *raison d'être*. The goals are constantly evolving and organisations continue to reach for them. A few organisations have very clear and well-defined goals, such as the construction of a subway network in a city. Once the construction is finished, the common organisational goal is reached and the organisation can dissolve. Other organisations exist over long periods because their goals are infinite. For instance, organisations 'providing punctual, fast and cheap transportation to city inhabitants' as their goal exist as long as there are inhabitants in the city and they have sufficient support (users, subsidies etc.). In Chapter 11 we examine the different kinds of goals that organisations can have and their relatedness to organisational effectiveness and effectiveness criteria.

An **organisation chart** is a graphic representation of formal authority and division of labour relationships. To the casual observer, the term 'organisation chart' means the family-tree-like pattern of boxes and lines posted on workplace walls. Within each box one usually finds the names and titles of current position holders. To organisation theorists, however, organisation charts reveal much more. The partial organisation chart in Figure 10.1 reveals several of the structural dimensions discussed in the next paragraphs, hierarchy of authority, division of labour, departmentalisation, spans of control, and line and staff positions. However, organisation charts simplify the complexity of organisation structure, often running the risk of providing a partial view on the structure or even a misleading view. Organisation charts help understanding the organisation structure, but we need to dig deeper to fully understand the organisational structures and their implications.

Figure 10.1 Sample Organisation Chart for a Hospital (Upper Levels Only)

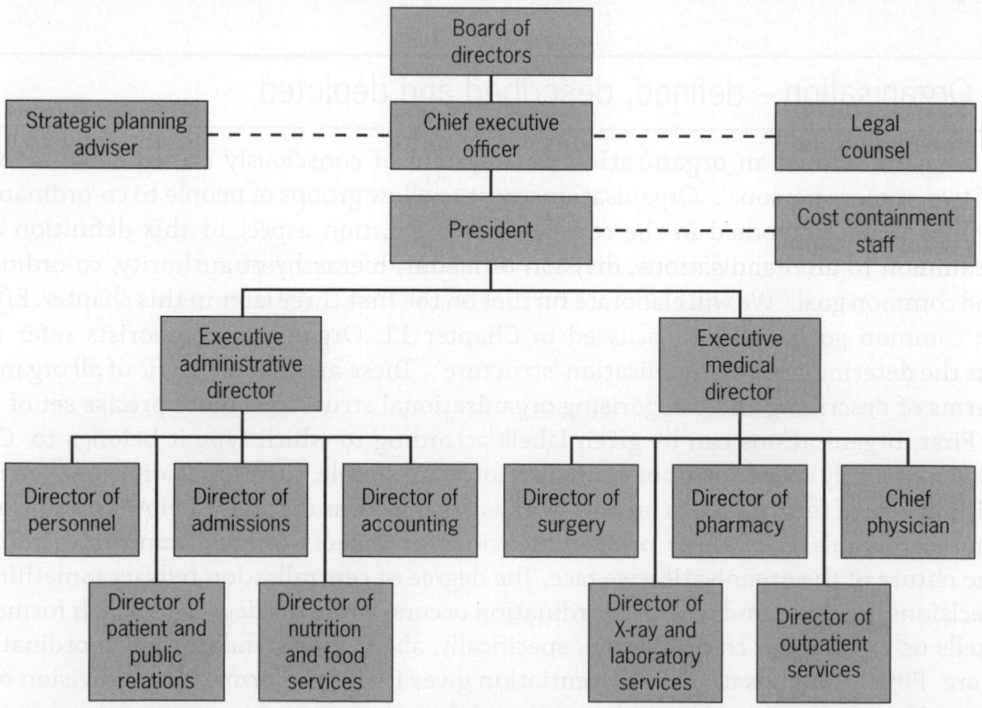

10.2 Elements of organisation structure

Organisational structure is about division of labour, co-ordination of effort, hierarchy of authority and common goals. Structure is also about a number of other elements such as boundaries, informal structure, political structure and the foundations of authority.

Each of these have important implications for the structure or configuration an organisation ends up having, and for the other design characteristics that are also part of any overall structure of an organisation.

Division of labour and responsibility

Organisations realise objectives and perform activities far beyond the possibilities of a single person. The construction of the Eurotunnel required the work of 15 000 people and lasted for seven years.[6] Each worker had his or her own task and responsibility for a very small part of the tunnel project. Getting the tunnel built required **division of labour** and responsibility. The purpose of dividing labour into smaller components is to have people specialise in one or a few well-defined tasks. Someone doing the same thing a great number of times becomes very good at it. This is the starting point for specialisation, but the implications are wide-ranging. Not only must each job be related to every other job, they must also fit together in a larger structure to get the work done (or, in other words, accomplish the organisation's everyday goals); for example, running the TRAM system in the French city of Strasbourg. An example of an overall plan is the functional organisation, where people are grouped according to the task they have been given. In the TRAM case, one function could be rail system maintenance; another could be maintenance of the trams themselves.

Specialisation involves both a horizontal and a vertical dimension. **Horizontal specialisation** refers to how many different activities are covered by a job. A machine operator who sits all day long at a big machine that punches holes in round metal discs has a job with very low horizontal specialisation. A person who works as a cleaner in a hospital carries out a number of different and distinct operations; cleaning floors, emptying waste bins, wiping surfaces, cleaning bathrooms, and so on. While the horizontal specialisation may seem small, it is considerably higher than the hole-punching machine operator. Several levels higher in terms of different activities one might find a doctor in an emergency room. While still limited, the range of different activities is considerable. All kinds of injuries and diseases may arrive in an emergency department; broken legs, allergic reactions, heart attacks and the plague and they all demand different skills, if only to stabilise patients before specialists arrive.

Vertical specialisation refers to how much one person is involved in the conception, execution and administration of activities. Thus, an organisation with many hierarchical levels has a high degree of specialisation.

Specialisation has a long history. The great economist Adam Smith was far from the first to notice specialisation but his case example, the manufacture of pins, remains as readable today as when it was first published in 1776. In it he estimates that a productivity increase between 240 times and 4800 times can be achieved through specialisation of labour.[7] Despite this and countless other examples of the benefits of specialisation, there are also limits to what specialisation can do. First of all, put yourself in the hole-punching machine operator's shoes for a bit. That job is intensely boring – which is also demotivating. More importantly, extreme specialisation is also very inflexible and requires lots of connections between all the specialised activities. In this sense, organising becomes a matter of balancing the benefits of specialisation or differentiation against the need to bind the various specialised units together.

Differentiation occurs through division of labour and technical specialisation. A behavioural outcome of differentiation is that technical specialists, such as computer programmers, tend to think and act differently from specialists in, say, accounting or marketing. Excessive differentiation can cause the organisation to become entrenched in miscommunication, conflict and politics. Thus, differentiation needs to be offset by an opposing structural force to ensure the necessary co-ordination. This is where **integration** enters the picture.

In their classic text, *Organization and Environment*, Paul Lawrence and Jay Lorsch studied successful and unsuccessful companies in three industries, concluding that as environmental complexity increased, successful organisations exhibited higher degrees of both differentiation and integration. In other words, an effective balance was maintained. Unsuccessful organisations, in contrast, tended to suffer from an imbalance of too much differentiation and not enough offsetting integration.

Managers need to maintain focus on the balance between growing and increasingly differentiated organisations and the evolution of ever better means of integration and co-ordination. They also discovered that 'the more differentiated an organisation, the more difficult it is to achieve integration'.[8] Managers of today's complex organisations need to strive constantly and creatively to achieve greater integration.[9]

Co-ordination of effort

Division of labour brings the need to co-ordinate the divided work in order to carry out the global organisation's activities. Galbraith presents **co-ordination** as an information-processing mechanism.[10] Co-ordination can only be achieved when information about the goals and the tasks is exchanged. However, to ensure that information flows as required, it is necessary to distinguish between the need for information processing in an organisation, and that same organisation's capacity to process information.

Co-ordination has, as did specialisation, both a horizontal and a vertical dimension. Vertical mechanisms include direct supervision, formal rules, plans and budgets. Mostly horizontal coordination involves committees of various kinds (many labels are possible here); liaison roles, co-ordinators, and so on. Some co-ordination tasks are routine in character. They occur regularly and involve a predictable set of actions. These can be set down in a set of standard procedures. More unusual situations can require mutual co-operation, meetings, task forces and committees. Each form of co-ordination has advantages, some of which are closely tied to communication. Meetings, for example, are a medium that allows very rich data to be exchanged. At the same time, meetings tend to take time and time spent in meetings is not always very productive.

Not all these co-ordination mechanisms work as intended and the list should also include informal groups that develop spontaneously to solve interdepartmental co-ordination without activating more costly formal procedures, while getting some of the benefits of richer communication.

Different forms of **standardisation** are some of the formal ways to co-ordinate tasks without additional information exchange. Henry Mintzberg identified four types of standardisation as co-ordination mechanisms.[11] Table 10.1 describes each of the four types.

Apart from specifying what employees should or should not do in specific situations, **formalisation** more generally indicates the level at which the rights and duties of the members of the organisation are fixed. The larger the organisation the more formalisation is used to keep control. The greater the use of informal groups and less use of hierarchy, rules, procedures and standardisation

Table 10.1 Four Types of Standardisation

Standardisation of work	This implies exactly specifying and programming the tasks in such a way that tasks are streamlined, without any deviation from the programme. This is especially possible when the tasks are routine, simple and easy to describe, such as the tasks in an assembly line
Standardisation of output	The results of the tasks are specified: what needs to be reached, not how. This approach is relevant when the way tasks are performed does not affect other units of the organisation or the overall objectives. The output is mostly determined by the number of pieces to be produced, number of customers to be visited or turnover to be realised
Standardisation of skills	By hiring people with the same skills, standardisation in the tasks is obtained, in a similar way to lawyers in law firms or doctors in hospitals. Standardisation of skills is also possible by making all employees go through the same training
Standardisation of norms	Hiring, training or influencing people to have them share the same norms. Those norms determine how they carry out the tasks. This way of achieving co-ordination is used widely in religious or radical organisations

Source: Based on H. Mintzberg, *Mintzberg on Management* (New York: The Free Press, 1989), p. 101.

of work, means lower formalisation in the organisation. In small organisations the manager is able to control and correct unacceptable behaviour directly. Formalisation covers not only the exact specification of what and how one should perform one's tasks but can be extended to all kinds of behaviour in the organisation, such as dress code, working hours, smoking regulations, use of office equipment or the Internet.

Decision rights

In any organisation, decisions have to be made somehow. Decision rights means that a hierarchy of authority determines the vertical distribution of responsibility and decision-making. As Figure 10.1 illustrates, there is an unmistakable hierarchy of authority.[12] The 10 directors report to the two executive directors who report to the president who reports to the CEO. Ultimately, the CEO answers to the hospital's board of directors. A formal hierarchy of authority also delineates the official communication network (Chapter 4).

The chart in Figure 10.2 also shows how unity of command up and down the line works. **Unity of command** indicates that each employee should report to only one manager. Otherwise, the argument goes, inefficiency would prevail because of conflicting orders and lack of personal accountability.[13] (Indeed, these are problems in today's more fluid and flexible organisations based on innovations such as cross-functional and self-managed teams (see Chapter 8).) The duality of command, which characterises the matrix form, with the resulting potential conflicts, is a situation that some organisations cannot afford. Military organisations, for example, maintain strict unity of command with a clear system of command and control. In a battle there is no time to discuss conflicting commands.[14]

Managers throughout an organisation must make **decisions**. However, the head of accounting is ill suited to make a marketing decision and the cleaner does not decide cleaning budgets or standards of required cleanliness. The right to make decisions, about initiating, approving, implementing and controlling activities must be distributed throughout the organisation. Such rights are almost invariably distributed along the vertical axis, which raises an ever present problem in organisations:

how much or how little decision-making authority should be decentral? The allocation of decision rights is not only a vertical or centralisation issue, there is also horizontal component. Even if a certain type of decision (measured for example in terms of value) must be made at a certain level, the organisation must also specify which individual at that level makes the decision. Big decisions about marketing are thus normally made by the head of the marketing department, not by the chief accountant or the head of engineering.

It is generally a good idea to leave decisions to those who are best informed. Production people know about factories and salespeople know about markets and customers. However, apart from the possibility that a department manager may look inward when making decisions, the most important issue is that information held by department managers may not show the whole picture. For example, while a certain level of production may be an excellent idea in terms of minimising unit costs, that same level of production may make little sense in terms of being able to sell that number of units. Similarly, goals can affect allocation of decision rights. If the production manager from the example could gain a bonus by achieving those low unit costs, that person would be tempted to disregard inconvenient information on the demand for the item.

The best place to locate a decision right also depends on the volume of information that must be processed for decisions to be made. Top managers have the broad overview of what goes on below but cannot handle all the information than an expert lower down commands. Finding the right balance between the need for detail and the limits of information processing is one of the enduring balancing acts for top managers.

Organisational boundaries

Just as organisational structure is a matter of specialising, co-ordinating and deciding, it is also a matter of **boundaries**. A supermarket chain does not manufacture a great many products itself, with the exception of certain food items such as bakery goods and similar products that are made in store. Most products, whether fresh spinach, chickens, cheese or soap, are supplied by other firms. It did not have to be like that. A national chain in a large country, for example, Carrefour of France or Tesco of the UK, probably have more than a sufficient volume of sales to justify producing many items themselves. They do in fact have lots of products carrying the name of the chain, but close reading of the small print is needed to discover if it was made by the chain or for the chain.

The dimensions involved in setting boundaries include **vertical integration** (how many stages of production do we want to be involved in) and **horizontal integration** (how many different businesses do we want to be involved in. This is sometimes referred to as the make-or-buy decision. Compared to elements such as division of labour, co-ordination and decision rights, which are determined for the organisation as a whole, the **make-or-buy decision** is one that allows each manager considerable discretion.

Other structural elements

Every organisation has **informal structures** in addition to the formal ones. People who work together or alongside each other develop ties that cross formal boundaries. Whether these are based on friendship or mutual interests within the firm means less than acknowledging their existence. Since opposition to decisions can be channelled through informal structures, decisions that do affect such structure – or can be expected to do so – are important elements when decisions about change are made.

In a related view, organisations are characterised by **politics**. People form coalitions and these can, but do not always follow organisational structure. Making decisions and getting them implemented needs to take political reality into account at all times. The matter of power in organisations is discussed further in Chapter 14, while the various techniques and models for making decisions are presented in Chapter 13.

The final element or structure that needs to be considered is bases of authority. Much authority is of the formal kind, closely linked to rank and title. The chief executive or the chairperson of the board are highly placed and can to a great extent dictate whatever they want. However, other factors such as expertise, personal charisma and social status, can be bases on which people can base their legitimacy. Bases of authority and the power any kind of authority gives is examined further in Chapter 14.

Evidence about structural elements

Specialisation that lowers costs is constantly sought, under the general heading of scale and scope economies. A detailed study of US mortgage banking shows that organisational structures in the industry change broadly in response to external changes. Over a 15-year period, integrated institutions, either banks or savings and loan associations, gradually broke up into smaller and more specialised organisations. In some segments of the market, specialisation allowed large firms able to obtain economies of scale, whereas in others there were diseconomies.[15] Ironically, this change in the way markets were organised and firm boundaries chosen may have contributed to the financial crisis that came much later.

There are other kinds of evidence about structural elements. For example, a lively scholarly debate is ongoing as to the impact of IT (information technology) on structural elements. IT allows more and cheaper information transmission and processing. However, this can enhance communication both within organisations (allowing larger and more complex organisations) and between organisations (allowing more outsourcing, even of complex tasks). A study focusing on the impact of IT on the use of so-called 'loosely coupled organisational forms' (essentially through alliances and loosely attached or 'contingent' workers) showed that IT does indeed lead to loose couplings. However, these outcomes depend on the level of uncertainty in the firm's environment – they only happen when uncertainty is low. In this study, institutional arrangements such as the establishment of industry standards and a low rate of technological development indicated stability.[16]

Application of structural elements

Putting structural elements to use requires considerable thinking about their nature, the consequences of applying them, and the relevancy in a specific case. This applies in particular to strategic and institutional considerations. Strategic considerations refer to industry structure and opportunities this offers for either narrow specialisation or broad integration of activities. Institutional considerations refer to the forces that apply pressure on organisations to do things in certain ways, whether it is called activity-based costing, quality management, social responsibility or something else.

Unless very strong forces dictate that an organisation must be structured in a certain way, we cannot yet be clear about what to do and which form to advocate. It is not simply a matter of choosing one of the forms we describe in the next section. Many factors influence the choice and before a meaningful decision can be made it is a good idea to conduct a thorough assessment which leads to a diagnosis, which may or may not indicate that something needs to be done. We return to the theme of diagnosis in Chapter 16 and also to some extent in Chapter 11.

Critical thinking

Your company's costs are out of control, managers do as they please, not just with money, but also with most other decisions. You are also now the chief executive, hired by the board to do something. . . . anything. What do you do?

10.3 Organisational forms

Whether simple or something more complicated, organisational form is what we see in most graphical representations. Any decent word processor has a built-in application that allows users to create organisation charts or diagrams of the kind shown in Figure 10.2. What such charts show is simply an organisational form. Only with supporting information and interpretation of what is in each box in a diagram can a more detailed picture be put together, one that is not easy to show graphically.

The simple form of organising

In small organisations one manager is enough. As soon as the number of members starts increasing, so does the number of relationships that the manager must keep track of. The challenge facing managers anywhere is to keep up with the management task as the number of relationships grows. Figure 10.2 shows how an increase in the number of subordinates from two to three increases the number of relations to be managed from three to six. Generally, the number of relationships grows much faster than the number of subordinates. Increasing subordinates to four gives ten relations. This goes on until the manager is no longer able to manage everything. The number of subordinates managed by someone is called the **span of control**. Since the fundamental issue is one of information processing it follows that subordinates doing simple and very predictable things can be managed in greater numbers by one manager.

Functional organisations

Most organisations never grow beyond the size where the simple form is the only one that makes sense. When organisations are successful and have outgrown the simple form, the functional form,

Figure 10.2 Management Spans of Control

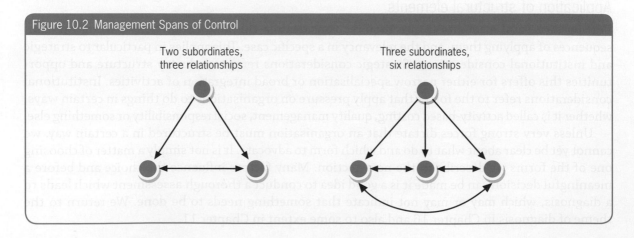

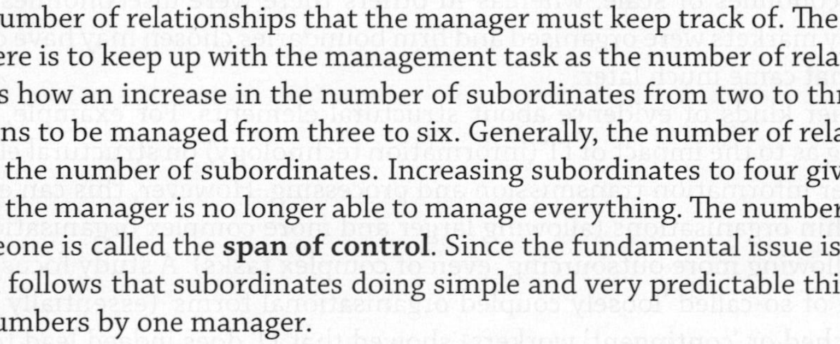

Figure 10.3 Functional Form

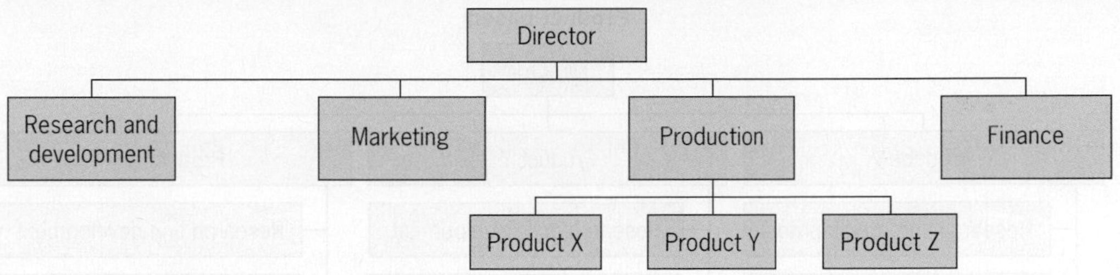

shown in Figure 10.3, is often the next choice. In a functional structure, all engineers or all marketing people are placed in the same department, headed by an engineering manager and a marketing manager, respectively. These departments are then responsible for all activities that have to do with engineering or marketing. Each of the departments has their own internal structure, a set of goals, a plan and a budget.

Functional organisations are well suited to activities where the fruits of specialisation are important, including functional expertise, efficiency and quality. These advantages are particularly attractive in a stable environment, where economies of scale, continual improvement in specialised skills and the establishment of career opportunities within the functional field are among the possible benefits. All of these advantages require investment of the kind that is hard to recover. This will only be forthcoming when the organisation operates in a relatively stable environment.

Grouping people with similar backgrounds and tasks together facilitates internal collaboration, efficiency and quality control. However, these advantages are inward-looking and each function may become focused on optimising within their own unit, resulting in **sub-optimisation**. Functional units are also ill suited when it is necessary to adjust to changes in the outside environment. Regardless of the reason the various co-ordination problems can be referred upwards in the hierarchy where they risk piling up on the desks of top managers. These managers may have too many problems to deal with and too much information coming through their door. This situation is sometimes called **information overload**. As a result, the functional form requires more co-ordination and co-operation between departments than did the simple organisation. The functional form differentiates and balancing integration is required. As soon as this form is adopted, conflicts between departments end up on the top manager's table. Managers have a number of co-ordination mechanisms, such as central staff (staff functions), planning systems and budgeting systems.

Divisional form variations

Some organisations have chosen (or have been told) to do things that have little to do with each other: container ships and supermarkets, plastic and medicines, for example. In a **divisional organisation**, sometimes called a departmentalised organisation, all organisational components, for example, those organised as engineering, production, marketing and sales, are contained within the boundaries of the division. These units report to the top division manager. Divisions can be organised according to what they make or by the region or country they operate in (see the two options in Figure 10.4). A third divisional form is one based on the clients served (e.g. consumers and industrial customers).

Figure 10.4 Product-based and Geographical Forms

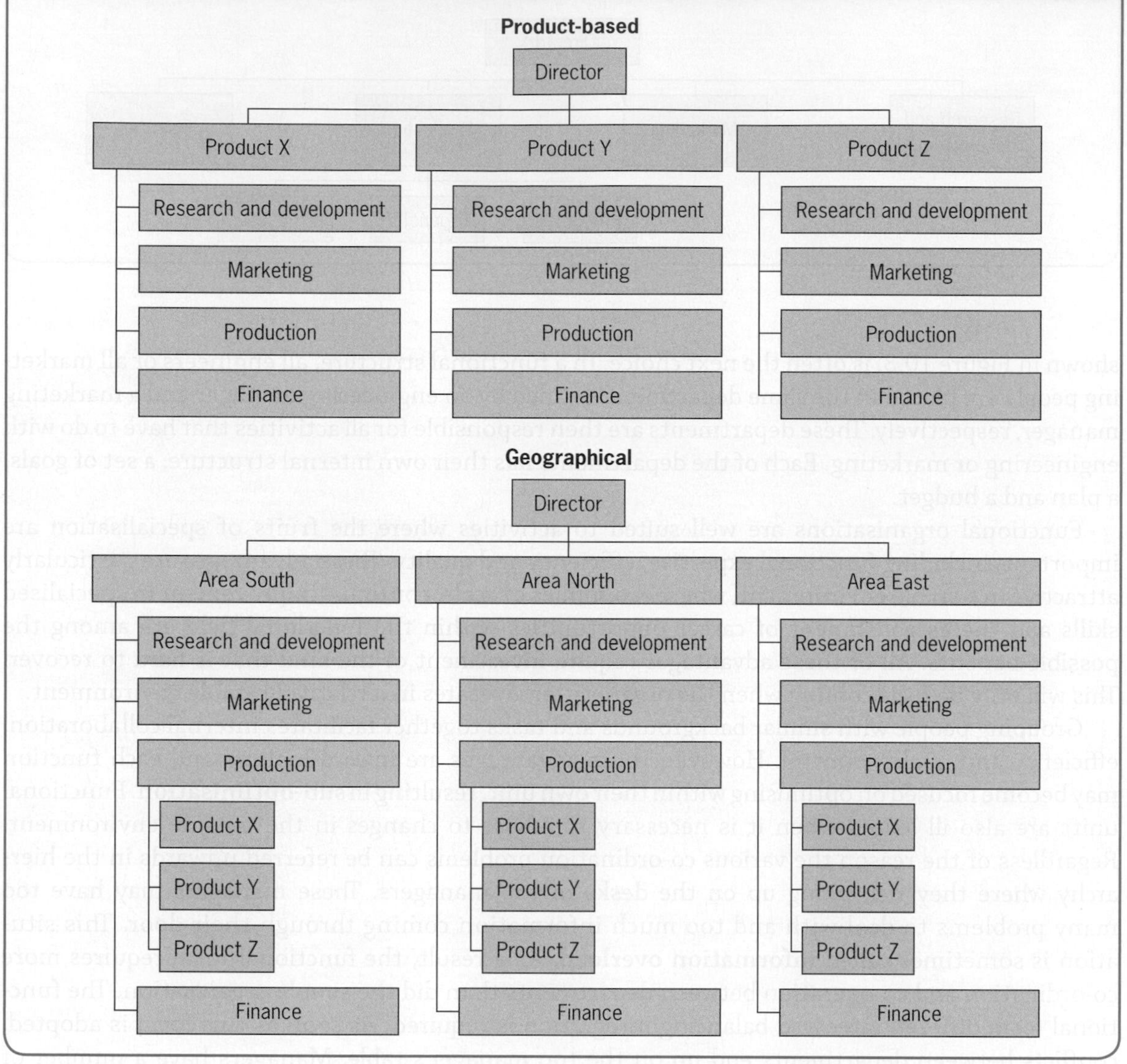

Each division can function as a **profit centre** and can, in principle, operate as a separate business. It can also easily be added to or taken away from the overall organisation – if it is truly independent. The divisional managers are powerful and if they are promoted to corporate headquarters it is because they have management and integration skills, and not, as in the case of the functional form, on the basis of functional expertise. The corporate headquarters set goals for divisions, determine overall strategy and decide how much autonomy divisions are given. They also allocate resources and have influence when large commitments are made by divisions; for example, the acquisition of other companies.

The advantages of the divisional form are several. Divisions are closer to the markets they serve and can better respond to uncertainty than can the corporate headquarters. Similarly, since budgeting and financial management takes place at the division level, accountability is clearly defined. The drawbacks are also significant, however. Economies of scale can be lost (unless divisions become so large that that they can be achieved anyway) and the economies of producing different things together (called economies of scope) may disappear. Divisions may also end up competing against each other or they may develop similar products for similar types of customers. Finally, they may duplicate internal services such as accounting, research and development (R&D) and finance.

OB in Real Life

Keeping Opel independent – at a cost

Among the firms seriously affected by the financial crisis that began in 2008, General Motors (GM) stands out for the depth and seriousness of its problems. GM has received substantial financial support from the US government and has been forced to sell or close a number of loss-making activities. One such sale was to have been the European car-making activities operating under the Opel and Vauxhall brands. A deal to sell these operations to Magna, a Canadian maker of car parts, had almost been completed when GM changed its mind and decided to keep Opel.

When this reversal was announced, Fritz Henderson, GM's president, promised more autonomy for Opel's operations. This had been a sore point for a long time. Opel did not even manage its own day-to-day cash position, but was wholly dependent on GM in Detroit. Similarly, decisions about models suitable for the European market were not necessarily taken at Opel headquarters. A popular MUV designed for European consumers was discontinued, and later replaced by a model from GM's Asian operations – with little or no input from Opel.

'We don't want entities to go their own way. But we want to reinvigorate the regional spirit', said Nick Reilly, the interim head of Opel/Vauxhall, who went on to say that 'regional entities will be given greater autonomy, but also greater accountability'.

These efforts managed to keep Opel autonomous. Calculating the cost of autonomy is difficult but Opel remains a loss-making part of General Motors, the loss of $1.8 billion for 2012 bringing losses since 1999 to $18 billion.

Source: Based on D. Schaeffer, 'Opel Fights to Keep Seat of Power', *Financial Times*, 14 November 2009; Tim Higgins 'Hannibal Inspires GM's Girsky to Slash at Opel's Culture', BloombergNews 26 March 2013 (http://www.bloomberg.com/news/2013-03-26/hannibal-inspires-gm-s-girsky-to-slash-at-opel-s-culuture.html).

The matrix form of organising

Some activities are not well suited to any of the three forms covered so far. They may benefit from having both the advantages of specialisation that comes with the functional form and from the benefits of strong co-ordination abilities. Developing a new product, designing a super tanker for the first time, or an offshore wind farm, or a vast iron ore mine in the high Arctic, are examples where different highly specialised skills are required at different times. The matrix form, shown in Figure 10.5, can be the solution when functional specialisation and cross-functional integration is required.

Most members of the organisation, top managers excepted, are affiliated with both a functional department and a project or a task. In an oil company engaged in exploration and production, for example, geologists, geophysicists and engineers may be affiliated with the exploration department and at the same time with active exploration projects, whether located in the Gulf of Mexico

Figure 10.5 Matrix Form

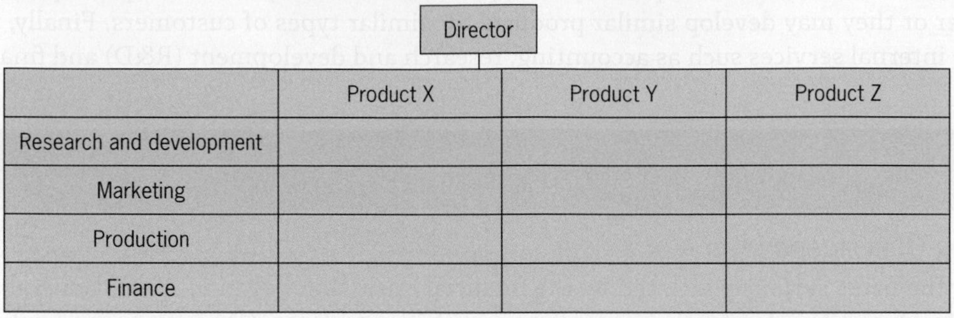

Table 10.2 Advantages and Disadvantages of the Matrix Structure

Advantages of the matrix structure	Disadvantages of the matrix structure
Combining the efficiency of the functional structure with the flexibility of the divisional (product) structure	Conflict due to dual lines of authority
Combining functional expertise with product (or project) expertise	Impossibility to combine the dual attention for functional and product/project demands
Dual attention for functional goals and product goals	Difficult allocation of functional experts over the different product groups
Flexibility to extend the number of products or to regroup	Imbalance between the two interests; resulting in the domination of one of the two and losing the advantages of the matrix
Maximising the value and use of individual experts	Confusion about responsibilities
	Costly co-ordination caused by the more complex structure

or on the Norwegian continental shelf. These functional specialists report to both their department and to the project(s) to which they are assigned.

In the matrix form, conflicts over resources are a natural consequence of the form. They must be settled by negotiation, which involves the employee and his or her bosses involved in the function and project(s). As a result, much time is spent in meetings. This is not always counterproductive, since these forced discussions allow complex issues to be examined from both or all perspectives. In this sense, a high degree of co-operation as well as sharing information and power is required for the form to work. Table 10.2 gives an overview of the advantages and disadvantage of the matrix structure.

Evidence about organisational form

The evidence associated with the classical organisation forms has accumulated over decades. Classic works such as that of Lawrence and Lorsch stand out. The work of Henry Mintzberg, also of great importance, is discussed below. The evidence about forms is also closely linked to the idea that form is determined by the situation in which any given firm finds itself. This is one way of referring to the 'contingency' perspective, which is the theme of Chapter 11. It is worth noting, however, that this extremely influential way of thinking has been challenged more or less continuously since 1989, when Mike Hannan and John Freeman published one of the first books to present the ecological or population approach to studying organisations. This approach, which is seen by some as being anti-management, is discussed further in Chapter 11.

One exception to a relative shortage of recent research on forms is a study of several large multi-nationals over four years and suggest that there is nothing fundamentally wrong with the matrix, as long as the cells in the matrix operate as semi-independent business units with a large degree of autonomy in decision-making and are combined with a hierarchy and processes that integrate these units and stipulate the horizontal co-ordination needs.[17]

Application of organisational forms

As noted, simple organisations are by far the most common, since little more than a simple form is needed when organisations are small. This form is by nature centralised, has little or no differentiation, specialisation or formalisation and relies on direct supervision.

Functional organisation is suited when the organisation outgrows the simple form. This happens at lower organisational sizes when the information content of relations between people in the organisation is high. If work is very simple it can be standardised and formalised and the change to the functional form becomes necessary at a larger organisational size. Given the underlying focus on specialisation and the weaknesses involved in co-ordination under uncertain conditions, it is a form suited to relatively small- and medium-sized organisations (the definition may vary between countries) producing a single or a small set of closely related products.

The divisional form (and hybrid forms that also have functional and matrix forms at lower levels) is suited for larger organisations operating under less certain environmental conditions and selling many different products or serving many different markets.

Despite its considerable drawbacks, the matrix form is suitable when the organisation needs technical specialisation in different areas and at the same time needs to bring these to bear on problem-solving a specific point in time during the completion of a project.

> **Critical thinking**
>
> There are only a handful of alternatives when it comes to forms. Why is it that organisations frequently still get it wrong? Alternatively, if they are not wrong about their choice of form, why do they still fail to prosper?

10.4 Organisation types

The notion of an organisational form is not the same as an organisation type. Types are based on the composition of previously elaborated structural elements: division of labour, hierarchy of authority and co-ordination. The type discussion is helpful because it allows a more complete understanding of complex issues. The use of overlapping terminology, is also, however, a source of confusion. Compare, for example, the four generic forms discussed in the previous section to the types identified in Table 10.4.

There is a clear evolution in the organisation types, an evolution that parallels business reality. The first large companies at the beginning of the twentieth century focused on efficiency and control, developing mechanistic and bureaucratic organisation types (also see Chapter 1). Later the shortcomings of very mechanistic organisations in terms of low flexibility were realised and more organic organisation types evolved. More organisation types appeared, operating in particular environments, such as in professional services or those combining a diversified range of activities. In the last quarter of the twentieth century, globalisation, high-speed technological evolution and the World Wide Web affected the development of new organisation types.

Furthermore, organisations can be categorised as do-organisations and think-organisations. The traditional organisation types were very much oriented towards acting or the pragmatic execution of the tasks with the emphasis on efficiency and effectiveness. Modern organisations often find themselves in more complex environments requiring an emphasis on 'thinking' or analysing the environment, seeking for opportunities and adapting to environmental changes through learning. The major classic and new organisation types will be described in the following paragraphs. Some organisation types will probably remind you of Morgan's organisational metaphors in Chapter 1. Keep in mind that the types described here are 'pure' types. In real life, such pure types are rarely found because many companies are hybrids that mix different elements, such as bureaucratic staff parts combined with a production core organised in some other way; for example, professional or organic.

Bureaucratic organisations

Max Weber's (1947) description of **bureaucracy** as the ideal organisation form inspired many organisation design theorists.[18] He based his ideal organisation after the much-vaunted Prussian army and called it 'bureaucracy'. 'Ideal' in the meaning 'perfect' is an abstraction, an ideal that must be distinguished from real life. Weber recognised three types of organisations depending on the use of authority and power. One type has a charismatic leader dominating the organisation; in another, standing (position in the hierarchy), precedents and habits determine power and authority; a third (ideal) organisational type bases authority and power on objective criteria: the bureaucratic organisation. Rules and procedures based on rationality and not on personality, habits or dominant leaders determine the bureaucratic organisation. In bureaucratic organisations the roles are very clearly defined and are focused on maximising efficiency. An organisation is not a group of people but a combination of roles and tasks. Power only originates from a certain role. Decision-making is fully rational. Such an organisation requires a huge number of rules, procedures and control mechanisms resulting in complexity, inefficiency and inflexibility. Human beings seem to find it difficult to operate in a perfect rational machine structure and start to 'use' the system. This has given Weber's bureaucracy a fairly poor reputation.

According to Weber's theory, the following four factors should make bureaucracies the models of efficiency:

- Division of labour: people become proficient when they perform standardised tasks over and over again.
- A hierarchy of authority: a formal chain of command ensures co-ordination and accountability.
- Framework of rules: carefully formulated and strictly enforced rules ensure predictable behaviour.
- Administrative impersonality: personnel decisions such as hiring and promoting should be based on competence not favouritism.

All this is wonderful if you need standardisation, accountability, uniform behavior and total fairness. All organisations possess varying degrees of the four characteristics listed above. Bureaucracies are typically associated with very large organisations. In terms of the ideal metaphor, a bureaucracy should run like a well-oiled machine and its members should perform with the precision of a highly trained military unit. But practical and ethical problems arise when bureaucratic characteristics become extreme or dysfunctional. For example, extreme specialisation, rule following and impersonality can cause a bureaucrat to treat a client as a number rather than as a person,[19] which may lead her to go elsewhere with her business.

Weber would probably be surprised and dismayed that his model of rational efficiency has become synonymous with inefficiency.[20] Today, bureaucracy stands for being put on hold, waiting in queues and getting shuffled from one office to the next (see the case study below on the Mogamma). This irony can be explained largely by the fact that organisations with excessive or dysfunctional bureaucratic tendencies become rigid, inflexible and resistant to environmental demands and influences.

OB in Real Life

The Mogamma, bureaucracy Egyptian style

In Cairo the bureaucracy is not just an engine of policy or even a state of mind. It is a semicircular concrete behemoth in the centre of this city's central square.

In this towering edifice – the Mogamma ('Uniting') Central Government Complex – office opens on to office, crumbling stairway on to crumbling stairway, and the circular corridors that surround a dimly lit inner courtyard seem to have no end.

The Mogamma holds 20 000 public employees in 1400 rooms. It is headquarters to 14 government departments. So deep is its reach into the everyday life of Cairenes that most adult city dwellers will find themselves forced to visit it several times a year. Upward of 45 000 people pass through its portals each day.

Perhaps unrivalled anywhere in the world as a symbol of governmental dithering and public despair, it is at once the most feared and hated structure in Egypt and the evolutionary product of millennia of bureaucracy on the shores of the Nile.

Twelve hapless clients of the Mogamma have hurled themselves from its broken windows or from the soaring circular balconies that ring the central lobby up to the thirteenth floor dome. A generation of Arab social engineers, who threw off a monarchy and seized Egypt in the name of its poor and unrepresented, planted their dreams in the Mogamma's corridors and largely watched them die there.

'The Mogamma is to Egypt generally a symbol of 4000 years of bureaucracy and for the average Egyptian, it means all that is negative about the bureaucracy routine, slow paperwork, complicated paperwork, a lot of signatures, impersonality. It is a Kafka building', said political sociologist Saad Eddin Ibrahim.

'You enter there, you can get the job done – the same job – in five minutes, in five days, in five months or five years', Ibrahim said. 'You can never predict what might happen to you in that building. Anybody who has dealt with that building for whatever reason knows the uncertainty of his affairs there.'

In Egypt, the legacy of bureaucracy dates back to the time of the pharaohs. Temple walls and statues depict countless scribes, papyrus and pen in hand, taking down for the files of posterity everything from the deeds of the Pharaoh to the tax man's inventory. Subsequent French, Turkish and British occupiers refined Egyptian red tape to a fine art.

Today, it takes 11 different permits for a foreign resident to buy an apartment in downtown Cairo. A bride wishing to join her husband working abroad in the Persian Gulf region must get stamps and signatures from the Foreign Ministry, the Ministry of Justice, the prosecutor general, the local court in her district, and the regional court, a process that one Cairo newspaper referred to as 'legalised torture'.

One young physician recently left the Mogamma in tears after three days of trying to resign from her government job. 'They told me finally it would be easier if I just took a long sick leave', she said with a sigh. 'But I'm leaving the country for a year!'

Following the Egyptian revolution of 2011, the Mogamma has become an arena for political fighting. It is located along one side of Tahir Square, where the revolution was centred. Many demonstrators still use the square to protest and have blocked entry to the Mogamma on a number of occasions.

Source: Kimberly Murphy, 'Woe Awaits in Tower of Babble', *Los Angeles Times*, 24 May 1993.

Mechanistic versus organic organisations

In the opening chapter we touched briefly upon the landmark study on organisation types that was reported by Tom Burns and G. M. Stalker. In the course of their research they made a very instructive distinction between what they called 'mechanistic' and 'organic' organisations. **Mechanistic organisations** are rigid bureaucracies with strict rules, narrowly defined tasks and top-down communication. Working in a McDonald's restaurant is a very mechanistic experience. Every job is broken down into the smallest of steps, and the whole process feels automated.[21] This sort of mechanistic structure is necessary at McDonald's because of the competitive need for uniform product quality, speedy service and cleanliness.

In contrast, organic organisations are flexible networks of multitalented individuals who perform a variety of tasks.[22] There tends to be centralised decision-making in mechanistic organisations and decentralised decision-making in **organic organisations**. Generally, centralised organisations are more tightly controlled while decentralised organisations are more adaptive to changing situations.[23] Each has its appropriate use.

It is important to note, as illustrated in Table 10.3, that each of the mechanistic–organic characteristics is a matter of degree. Organisations tend to be relatively mechanistic or relatively organic. Pure types are rare because divisions, departments or units in the same organisation may be more or less mechanistic or organic.

Table 10.3 Characteristics of Mechanistic and Organic Organisations

Characteristic	Mechanistic organisation	Organic organisation
1 Task definition and knowledge required	Narrow; technical	Broad; general
2 Linkage between individual's contribution and organisation's purpose	Vague or indirect	Clear or direct
3 Task flexibility	Rigid; routine	Flexible; varied
4 Specification of techniques, obligations, and rights	Specific	General
5 Degree of hierarchical control	High	Low (self-control emphasised)
6 Primary communication pattern	Top-down	Lateral (between peers)
7 Primary decision-making style	Authoritarian	Democratic; participative
8 Emphasis on obedience and loyalty	High	Low

Source: Adapted from discussion in T. Burns and G. M. Stalker, *The Management of Innovation* (London: Tavistock, 1961), pp. 119–25.

Activity

Do you prefer a mechanistic or an organic organisation?

This activity is designed to help you determine which organisation type you prefer. For example, you might prefer an organisation with clearly defined rules or no rules at all. You might prefer an organisation where almost any employee can make important decisions, or where important decisions are screened by senior executives.

Instruction

I would like to be in an organisation where

		Strongly agree		Neutral	Disagree strongly	
1	A person's career ladder has several steps toward higher status and responsibility	5	4	3	2	1
2	Employees perform their work with few rules to limit their discretion	1	2	3	4	5
3	Responsibility is pushed down to employees who perform the work	1	2	3	4	5
4	Supervisors have few employees, so they work closely with each employee	1	2	3	4	5
5	Senior executives make most decisions to ensure that the company is consistent in its actions	5	4	3	2	1
6	Jobs are clearly defined so there is no confusion over who is responsible for various tasks	5	4	3	2	1
7	Employees have their say on issues, but senior executives make most of the decisions	5	4	3	2	1
8	Job descriptions are broadly stated or non-existent	1	2	3	4	5
9	Everyone's work is tightly synchronised around top management's operating plans	5	4	3	2	1
10	Most work is performed in teams with close supervision	5	4	3	2	1
11	Work gets done through informal discussion with co-workers rather than through formal rules	1	2	3	4	5
12	Supervisors have so many employees that they cannot watch anyone closely	5	4	3	2	1
13	Everyone has clearly understood goals, expectations and job duties	5	4	3	2	1
14	Senior executives assign overall goals, but leave daily decisions to frontline teams	1	2	3	4	5
15	Even in a large company, the CEO is only three or four levels above the lowest position	1	2	3	4	5

Scoring key and norms

Add up your scores now. Scores range in a continuum from 15 to 75 with 15 representing the maximum preference for an organic structure and 75 representing the maximum presence for a maximum mechanistic structure. The statements are grouped under three factors.

Tall hierarchy: 1-4-10-12-15
Formalisation: 2-6-8-11-13
Centralisation: 2-5-7-9-14.

Source: Adapted from S. L. McShane and M. A. Von Glinow, *Organizational Behavior* (New York: McGraw-Hill, 2003), pp. 535–6.

Mintzberg's organisation types

A well-known overview of organisation types can be found in Henry Mintzberg's work, which covers seven organisation types.[24] These are configurations of co-ordination mechanisms, division of labour and hierarchy of authority, discussed earlier. We have already mentioned Mintzberg's emphasis on standardisation as a co-ordination mechanism (see Table 10.1) apart from informal mutual adjustment and direct supervision. Mintzberg, however, also emphasises that there are five parts in each organisation reflecting five types of tasks (see Figure 10.6):

Figure 10.6 Five Basic Parts of Organisations

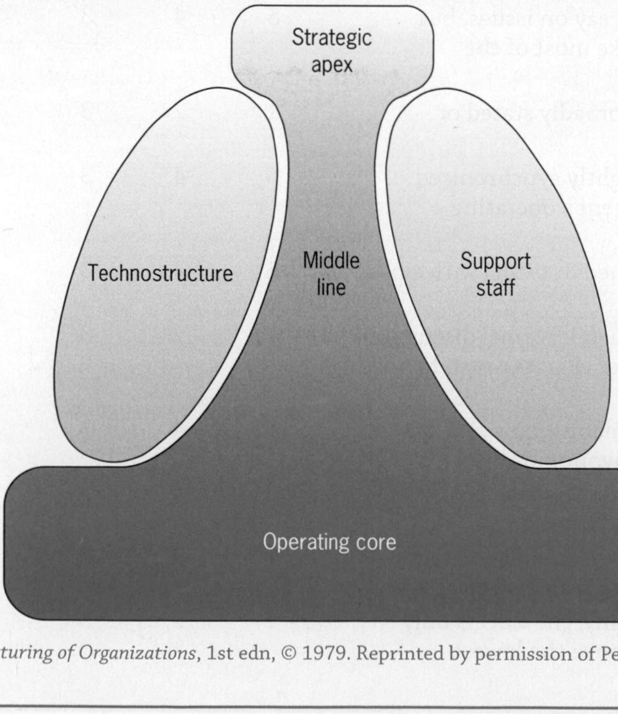

Source: H. Mintzberg, *Structuring of Organizations*, 1st edn, © 1979. Reprinted by permission of Pearson Education, Inc., Upper Saddle River, NJ.

- *Strategic apex* – managers and directors.
- *Middle line* – middle line managers having responsibility for sub-elements of the organisation's activity and authority over line personnel.
- *Operating core* – line personnel responsible for the core tasks of the organisation.
- *Technostructure* – **staff personnel** analysing and taking care of the administration of the work of the line personnel, such as accountants, control functions, human resource functions and planning functions.
- *Support staff* – staff functions who are not dealing with core tasks but who provide necessary support to allow the execution of the operational tasks, such as R&D, marketing, communication functions or the company's IT functions.

Each of Mintzberg's generic organisation types differs in the co-ordination mechanism that dominates and in the organisation part that is most important and most influential in the organisation. In Table 10.4, the seven types and their main features are listed.

The **entrepreneurial organisation** is a very simple organisation type, also likely to be simple in form. Its small size allows informality and the company leader is able to co-ordinate, control and manage the organisation on its own. Such type is often found with start-ups, small local firms, such as the local grocery store or companies led by owner-managers. The owner-managers try to maintain control of the organisation as long as possible even when the company is growing beyond the management limits of the owner-manager. Entrepreneurial organisations are often founded to introduce a new idea or product.

The **machine organisation** described by Mintzberg equals the mechanic organisation type of Burns and Stalker. It is a type found in larger organisations, often active in mass production. Control is the key word in this organisation and efficiency dominates effectiveness. The form is most likely to be functional.

The **diversified organisation** type, similar to the divisionalised organisation, arises because of companies that expanded their business through take-overs, exploiting new markets and products, acting globally or multinationally. These companies are always large with a diverse range of products or markets often unrelated. The size and diversity of operations makes it nearly impossible to integrate the business fully. Therefore, the organisation is divided in different semi-autonomous business units based on product, market or geography. The divisions are often large companies that can exist independently. This organisation distinguishes itself from other organisation types by the existence of headquarters that control business units and take over some divisions' support functions. Headquarters are heavily occupied in developing control structures for the divisions. The divisions themselves have generally few contacts with each other. Some form of divisionalisation is likely, combined with functional form at lower levels and possibly matrix in specialised areas.

Universities are an example of **professional organisations**. The professionals work in a functional structure but independently and with large decision-making power. Paradoxically, this does not lead to an informal flexible structure but to a kind of bureaucratic organisation with strict rules and procedures to control the highly skilled and complex tasks. Flexibility is low but the tasks are stable and often routine, allowing standardisation. There is very low co-operation and integration among the different groups of professionals. This leads to lack of innovation and a narrow outlook when it comes to interprofessional work. The difficulty in realising interdisciplinary research in universities is a consequence of the lack of integration in these kind of structures. As indicated, the form is functional, but not necessarily so. The matrix form is also widely used in a number of consulting firms.

Table 10.4 Mintzberg's Organisation Types

	Division of labour and key part of the organisation	Co-ordination	Hierarchy of authority
Entrepreneurial	Small, limited specialisation Strategic apex	Informal Direct supervision	Autocratic leader Centralisation
Machine	Strong specialisation Functional grouping Technostructure	Very formal Bureaucratic Rules and procedures as co-ordination – standardisation of processes	Centralised and hierarchic decision-making with unity of command
Diversified	Large, product-based structure Middle line	Formal Can be bureaucratic Full range of co-ordination mechanisms but emphasis on standardisation of output	Decentralised divisions, but centralisation and hierarchy at headquarters and divisions possible
Professional	Highly specialised with very autonomous workers Operating core	Bureaucratic Standardisation of skills in combination with a few rules as co-ordination mechanisms	Low hierarchy, decision-making power resides with the professionals Decentralised
Innovative	Lower specialisation through change but with experts able to innovate Operating core	Flexible and organic Co-ordination in formal and informal teams and through liaison personnel Informally – mutual adjustment	Decentralised with low levels of hierarchy Unity of command is violated
Missionary	Loosely organised small units, tasks and roles are clear and focused through the clarity of the mission	Co-ordination by standardisation of values and norms and often also strict explicit rules	Centralisation through charismatic leader and central mission but decentralisation in daily operations
Political	Different work deviations are possible but the choice will be political	Formal and mainly informal co-ordination by power	Decentralisation through politicking Enforcing or destroying hierarchy of authority

Source: Based on H. Mintzberg, *Mintzberg on Management* (New York: The Free Press, 1989).

The **innovative organisation** is organic and therefore opposite to the more bureaucratic forms just mentioned. Young R&D firms are characterised by this organisation type. The decentralisation, teamwork, limited authority, often matrix form, limited rules, procedures and standardisation and the bottom-up decision-making provide this organisation with the necessary flexibility and open character to be innovative and highly adaptable. However, efficiency is low and it is hard to keep control of the organisation.

A **missionary organisation** type is characterised by its very clear and strong mission about which the organisational members have strong beliefs. Médecins Sans Frontières is one example, but missionary organisations do also exist in the profit sector. However, this organisation type in the profit sector is often combined with other types, such as entrepreneurial or machine type. The values, norms and mission rule the organisation, enforced by a charismatic leader who keeps the mission and stories alive. Missionary organisations are decentralised in their operations but there is strong centralisation through the values and leadership that binds the members of the organisation and make sure tasks are co-ordinated. Many missionary organisations are not-for profit often with religious or ideological goals.

A **political organisation** is dominated by power and organisational politics (see also Chapter 14). Organisational politics can be so dominant that it rules out all other structural features. Political manoeuvring will then also become the only co-ordination mechanism. The same goes for decision-making, as the hierarchical power is undermined by playing politics. Some organisations, however, can be politicised without being fully dominated by organisational politics. Thus, the political organisation is often found in combination with one of the other organisation types, such as the machine organisation. Political intrigue thus destabilises the working of these organisation types.

New organisation types

Over the past decades several new organisation types and new forms have arisen. There is however uncertainty about what forms or types are involved and about their relative importance relative to the total stock of organisations in existence. One definition of form is helpful: 'Organisational forms, then, represent classes of organisations that audiences understand to be similar in their core features and distinctive from other classes of organisations.'[25]

All of the more recent forms are less hierarchical than the classic forms and try to achieve more flexibility in their structures. In the 1990s there were voices in the management literature whispering that small, lean and mean innovative firms could easily beat the big multinational corporations.[26] Large corporations try to prevent this from happening by creating divisions or subsidiaries, which were smaller, leaner and more innovative. Alternatives to making the whole organisation leaner are: more decentralisation, focus on core competences and products only, strategic alliances and network forms to create more flexibility. Flexibility can focus on many dimensions in the organisation, such as in the number of employees, divisions, products, markets, wages, costs, ability to quickly redefine tasks and functions, flexibility in production and the organisational form. The latter refers to new ways of grouping units and new kinds of alliances and co-operation between organisations. In these new forms, work division and co-ordination will require new mechanisms and is generally harder to achieve in a flexible organisation form. The relentless process of disembedding and recombining social relations and interactions in space and time makes the difference between the new organisations and their traditional counterparts.[27] However, flexibility is a threat to the integration of the organisation.[28] Strong integration cannot easily be combined with leanness.

New organisation types are also being developed because of a need to deal with more complexity. The classic organisation types are fairly simple and often unable to capture the complexity of business practices.[29] Choices between different organisational forms or between **centralisation** and **decentralisation** are not that straightforward in a complex business environment. However, more complex forms, such as the matrix structure, seem to complicate the working of the organisation even more.

Despite the fact that re-engineering became synonymous with job cuts and has been called a passing fad, it is likely to have a lasting effect on organisation design. It has helped refine the concept of a horizontally oriented organisation. Unlike traditional, vertically oriented organisations with functional units such as production, marketing and finance, **horizontal organisations** are flat and built around core processes aimed at satisfying customers.

Rather than focusing only on financial objectives or functional goals, the horizontal organisation emphasises customer satisfaction. Work is simplified and hierarchy flattened by combining related tasks – for example, an account-management process that subsumes the sales, billing and service functions – and eliminating work that does not add value. Information zips along an internal superhighway: the knowledge worker analyses it, and technology moves it quickly across the corporation instead of up and down, speeding up and improving decision-making.

Some of this is derived from something else; the obsession with process, for example, dates back to total quality management (see Chapter 11). Part of the beauty of the horizontal corporation is that it applies much of what we know about what works in managing today. Its advocates call it an actionable model. This is jargon for a plan you can work with – that allows companies to use ideas like teams, supplier–customer integration, and empowerment in ways that reinforce each other. A key virtue is that the horizontal corporation is the kind of company a customer would design. In most cases, a horizontal organisation requires some employees to be organised functionally where their expertise is considered critical, as in human resources or finance. But those departments are often pared down and judiciously melded into a design where the real authority runs along process lines.[30]

What is it like to work in a horizontal organisation?[31] It is a lot more interesting than traditional bureaucracies with their functional ghettos. Most employees are close to the customer (both internal and external) – asking questions, getting feedback, and jointly solving problems. Constant challenges come from being on cross-functional teams where co-workers with different technical specialties work side-by-side on projects. Sometimes people will find themselves dividing their time between several projects. Blurred and conflicting lines of authority break the traditional unity-of-command principle. Project goals and deadlines tend to replace the traditional supervisor role. Training in both technical and teamwork skills are a top priority. Multiskilled employees at all levels will find themselves working on different teams and various projects during the year. Self-starters and team players will thrive. Because of the flatness of the organisation, lateral transfers are more common than traditional vertical promotions. This might be a source of discontent for many of those who want to move upwards. Constant change will take its toll in terms of interpersonal conflict, personal stress and burnout. Furthermore, skill-based pay complements pay-for-performance (see Chapter 6).

While this is an extremely persuasive concept it has several drawbacks. In the rush to satisfy customers here and now, the focus on cost and efficiency of 'old' organisational forms, such as the functional, can be more or less lost. Similarly, there are a number of important issues related to conducting any type of business enterprise that are not easily addressed in a strongly horizontally oriented organisation. These include compliance with legal requirements, managing stakeholders and satisfying shareholders.

The **hourglass organisation** gets its name from the organisation's pinched middle. Thanks to modern information technology, a relatively small executive group is able to co-ordinate the efforts of numerous operating personnel who make goods or render services.[32] Multiple and broad layers of middle managers who served as conduits for information in old-style organisations are unnecessary in hourglass organisations. Competition for promotions among operating personnel is intense because of the restricted hierarchy. Lateral transfers are more common. Management will compensate for the lack of promotion opportunities with job rotation, skill training and pay-for-performance.

With few middle managers there will have to be cross-functional problem-solvers who also possess a number of technical skills. The potential for alienation between the executive elite and those at the base of the hourglass is great, thus giving trade unions an excellent growth opportunity.

A **network organisation** is similar to a horizontal organisation in being very flat. The links among the groups in the organisation are reciprocal communication patterns instead of hierarchical authority relationships.[33] The networks are formed around similar interests, tasks, products, know-how or any other goal to work together.

There exist informal networks in all types of organisations, even in the very bureaucratic ones, but a real network organisation is typified by the absence of unidirectional authority relationships and the presence of a complex web of relationships allowing direct, fast and flexible communication. In such network organisation the boundaries of the organisation become vague. The people involved in the internal organisational networks are also involved in networks with customers, suppliers, profession-related networks, non-professional private networks and networks with other (even competing) companies. The networks cross the traditional organisation boundaries, allowing more intense and flexible inter-organisational co-operation. The groups in the network organisation are loosely coupled instead of tied in a formal structure. However, there is no anarchy in the network organisation. Instead, there is self-organisation, self-control and self-responsibility in the network.

In the network organisation, trust and social control exist as forms of informal integration of the tasks. Some people take a facilitating role in the network and safeguard the integration of the tasks. Ronald Burt[34] uses the term 'structural holes' to indicate the people that have a boundary-spanning role between networks. Structural holes exist when two networks which are not related are nevertheless connected by one member who plays a brokerage role in connecting two separate networks. Burt uses this concept to explain the power and advantage that brokers have when they can link two separate networks. Take as an example a manager who changes jobs from one company to another, allowing her to link her previous network developed at the first company with her newly developed network in the second company. By bridging the two networks, a 'structural hole' exists and the manager can benefit from opportunities generated through linking the two networks.

Like virtual teams, discussed in Chapter 8, modern information technology allows people in **virtual organisations** to accomplish something despite being geographically dispersed.[35] Instead of relying heavily on face-to-face meetings, as before, members of virtual organisations send email and voicemail messages, exchange project information over the Internet, and convene videoconferences with far-flung participants using low-cost systems such as Skype. In addition, smartphones and tablet computers have made the dream of 'doing business from the beach' a reality

This disconnection between work and location is causing managers to question traditional assumptions about centralised offices and factories. Why keep offices for people who are never there because they are out finding and helping customers? Why have a factory when it is less expensive to contract out the work? Indeed, many so-called virtual organisations are really a network of several individuals or organisations hooked together contractually and electronically.

Commitment, trust and loyalty could erode badly if managers do not heed this caution by Charles Handy, the British management expert. According to Handy: 'A shared commitment still requires personal contact to make the commitment feel real. Paradoxically, the more virtual an organisation becomes the more its people need to meet in person.'[36]

Independent contractors, both individuals and organisations, participate in many different organisational networks and thus have diluted loyalty to any single one. Substandard working conditions and low pay at some smaller contractors make them little more than Internet-age sweat shops. Companies living from one contract to another offer little in the way of job security and benefits. Opportunities to start new businesses are numerous but prolonged success could prove elusive at Internet speed.

Some organisations have very particular activities that make the organisation types so far discussed unsuitable. Organisations that have just one or a few major large tasks, such as construction firms building entire motorways, or major bridges, need to adopt a **project organisation** type. All organisational resources are grouped around this one or these few projects. Each time a project stops or starts, the resources, such as the workers, need to be regrouped. There are project leaders and support staff for the administration of the projects. Traditional hierarchical layers and fixed structures would block the flexibility needed to complete the project. The projects are often also executed at the site of the customer. Hence, temporary offices (mostly office containers) are placed on the construction sites where engineers find their temporary bases. Teamwork in a project organisation is not only a way to co-ordinate interfunctionally but dominates the working of the organisation, hence, also the work deviation and decision-making. In project organisations the project groups work semi-autonomously resulting in a decentralised form of decision-making. The different project groups are loosely coupled and form a network of project groups. Parts of organisations often have a project structure while the rest of the company has a more functional one.

Finally, the **platform organisation** combines the new flexible types with the more classic organisation types.[37] It is a structure typically used in Japanese organisations with a hierarchical authority top structure, combined with flexible teams and a strong middle management that plays an important role in the integration of the organisation and combining the vertical and horizontal structure. Teams and autonomy should be complemented with hierarchical layers who co-ordinate the more routinely and stable parts of the activities in the organisation. The teams are then more loosely coupled and flexible in their tasks and composition. Systems and hierarchy are used to exploit efficiently innovations and new knowledge developed in these teams. Furthermore, hierarchy needs to set the rules and boundaries for the teamwork. Another precaution in the use of only horizontal organisations and self-regulation is based on the fact that middle management plays an important role in the organisation. This role is not substituted with an alternative in horizontal organisations. Middle managers translate goals in practical objectives, coach employees, communicate between units, take ad hoc decisions, solve conflicts, co-ordinate and plan tasks, measure output and provide expertise.[38] Providing expertise can be important in organisations where middle managers are former workers of the departments they are managing. Hierarchy should serve the organisation by transmitting information and knowledge in the organisation.

There are many new names floating around. The same goes for outsourcing, organised in different ways. Indeed, to add confusion to the plethora of terms to describe organisational types and forms, there are three additions: the hollow, the modular and the virtual structure. The hollow structure has only the core left, design, R&D and branding, leaving others, such as manufacturing and distribution, to do the actual work. The modular structure is more of a traditional outsourced organisation in that it focuses on the integration of modules from different competing firms. The virtual organisation works closely with its customers to optimise interfaces between components.[39] These terms are close to networked organisations and horizontal organisations.

Many of these novel forms are attractive in terms of solving various co-ordination problems. Decentralisation, for that is the core of all these types and forms, is great for innovation and customers' focus. However, lurking in the background is always the real or potential problem of control. Many organisations at various points in time find it necessary to tighten control. This is done by centralising decisions, increasing vertical information flows and scaling back various forms of autonomy. Some companies even experience repeated cycles where centralisation and decentralisation alternate over time. Decentralisation increases innovation, new products are brought to market and everyone is happy. But over time, costs rise as well, creating unsatisfactory performance. At some point, cost control through centralisation is applied, financial performance improves and everyone is happy – but only until low innovation or an absence of new products changes the mood. The cycle is now complete and a new one can begin with a period of decentralisation.

Learning outcomes: Summary of key terms

1 **Four characteristics common to all organisations**

They are co-ordination of effort (achieved through policies and rules, but also through standardisation and lateral mechanisms), a common goal (a collective purpose), division of labour (people performing separate but related tasks, choosing the right kind of departmentalisation) and a hierarchy of authority (the chain of command).

2 **Differentiation and integration in organisations**

Harvard researchers Lawrence and Lorsch found that successful organisations had found a proper balance between the two opposing structural forces of differentiation and integration. Differentiation forces the organisation apart. Through a variety of mechanisms – including hierarchy, rules, teams and liaisons – integration draws the organisation together.

3 **Organisational forms**

The basic forms include simple, functional, divisional and matrix. Organisations often combine forms to meet different types of organisational challenges.

4 **The organisation's parts and the way tasks can be grouped**

Mintzberg identified five parts that can be found in all kinds of organisation (strategic apex, middle line, operating core, technostructure, support staff). To group different tasks, organisations can choose between functional, product, market or project-based grouping, geographical groups and the matrix form.

5 **Co-ordination mechanisms an organisation can use**

Galbraith and Mintzberg identified a range of integration mechanisms which can be horizontal (integrators and formal groups), vertical (hierarchy, rules and procedures), informal (informal groups) or based on standardisation (standardisation of work, skills, output and norms).

6 **The significance of centralisation and decentralisation**

Because key decisions are made at the top of centralised organisations, they tend to be tightly controlled. In decentralised organisations, employees at lower levels are empowered to make important decisions. Contingency design calls for a proper balance.

7 **The bureaucratic organisation**

Weber proposed bureaucratic and mechanically working structures as the ideal way to create an efficient organisation. The extreme use of rules and procedures and the impersonal character of these rules conflict human nature resulting in dysfunctional behaviour. This might make a bureaucratic organisation highly inefficient.

8 **Burns and Stalker's findings regarding mechanistic and organic organisations**

Mechanistic (bureaucratic, centralised) organisations tended to be effective in stable situations. In unstable situations, organic (flexible, decentralised) organisations were more effective. These findings underscored the need for a contingency approach to organisation design.

9 **Mintzberg's seven organisation types**

The seven types are: entrepreneurial, machine, diversified, professional, innovative, missionary and political. These types differ in the kind of departmentalisation and the level of specialisation. They also differ in the co-ordination mechanisms used and the extent to which they have bureaucratic characteristics. The level of centralisation and decentralisation is another element that differentiates Mintzberg's seven types.

10 **Why new organisational forms develop and their differences with the classic forms**

There is a need for more flexibility, use of lateral co-ordination and organisations that can adapt very fast. The classic organisation types are too hierarchical, inflexible and seem to be able to operate only in stable environments requiring hardly any changing of the tasks and way of working.

11 **Horizontal, hourglass and virtual organisations**

Horizontal organisations are flat structures built around core processes aimed at identifying and satisfying customer needs. Cross-functional teams and empowerment are central to horizontal organisations. Hourglass organisations have a small executive level, a short and narrow middle-management level (because information technology links the top and bottom levels), and a broad base of operating personnel. Virtual organisations are normally families of interdependent companies. They are contractual and fluid in nature.

Review questions

1 Identify one real organisation from each form, as pure as possible.

2 Use your knowledge of any relevant organisation that does *not* have an organisation diagram to outlining what such a diagram would look like.

3 What is wrong with an organisation having too much differentiation and too little integration?

4 What are the advantages and disadvantages of more horizontal instead of vertical co-ordination?

5 When and under what assumption is a bureaucratic organisation a good choice?

6 If organic organisations are popular with most employees, why cannot all organisations be structured in an organic fashion?

7 Can you put labels on the different parts in your organisation – or one you know well (Mintzberg's organisation parts)?

8 Think of an existing example for each of Mintzberg's organisation types.

9 What are the disadvantages of many of the new organisational forms?

Personal awareness and growth exercise

Organisation design field study

Objectives

1 To get out into the field and talk to a practising manager about organisational structure.

2 To increase your understanding of the important distinction between mechanistic and organic organisations.

3 To broaden your knowledge of the differences between organisational forms and the evolution in those forms.

Introduction

A good way to test the validity of what you have just read about organisation design is to interview a practising manager. (*Note:* If you are a manager, simply complete the questionnaire yourself.)

Instructions

Your objective is to interview a manager about aspects of organisational structure, environmental uncertainty and organisational effectiveness. A manager is defined as anyone who supervises other people in an organisational setting. The organisation may be small or large and for-profit or not-for profit. Higher-level managers are preferred but middle managers and first-line supervisors are acceptable. If you interview a lower-level manager, be sure to remind him or her that you want a description of the overall organisation, not just an isolated subunit. Your interview will centre on the adaptation of Table 10.3, as discussed below.

When conducting your interview, be sure to explain to the manager what you are trying to accomplish. But assure the manager that his or her name will not be mentioned in lecture or group discussions or any written projects. Try to take brief notes during the interview for later reference.

Questionnaire

The following questionnaire, adapted from Table 10.3, will help you determine if the manager's organisation is relatively mechanistic or relatively organic in structure. *Note:* For items 1 and 2 on the following questionnaire, ask the manager to respond in terms of the average non-managerial employee. (Circle one number for each item.)

Characteristics

1 Task definition and knowledge required	Narrow; technical	1 2 3 4 5 6 7	Broad; general
2 Link between individual's contribution and organisation purpose	Vague or indirect	1 2 3 4 5 6 7	Clear or direct
3 Task flexibility	Rigid; routine	1 2 3 4 5 6 7	Flexible; varied
4 Specification of techniques, obligations and rights	Specific	1 2 3 4 5 6 7	General
5 Degree of hierarchical control	High	1 2 3 4 5 6 7	Low (self-control emphasised)
6 Primary communication pattern	Top-down	1 2 3 4 5 6 7	Lateral (between peers)
7 Primary decision-making style	Authoritarian	1 2 3 4 5 6 7	Democratic; participative
8 Emphasis on obedience and loyalty	High	1 2 3 4 5 6 7	Low

Total score__________

Questions for discussion

1 Using the following norms, was the manager's organisation relatively mechanistic or organic?
 8 – 24 = Relatively mechanistic
 25 – 39 = Mixed
 40 – 56 = Relatively organic
2 Which of all organisational forms discussed in this chapter comes closest to the manager's organisation?

Group exercise

Analysing a professional organisation's objectives

1 To continue developing your group interaction and teamwork skills.
2 To understand better how the abstract structural elements and organisational forms are used in a real situation.
3 To conduct an audit of an existing organisation and understand how hard the choices related to organisation structure are.
4 To establish priorities, deal with conflicting demands and consider trade-offs for modern managers.

Introduction

Choices about division of labour, co-ordination and hierarchy are much more complex in real life, even when the common goals are very clear. This exercise shows you how hard it is to apply this theory into practice.

It requires a team meeting of about one hour, several interviews, another meeting to bring the results together and a general class discussion for one hour. Total time required for this exercise is about one day.

Instructions

Your lecturer will randomly assign you to teams with about three members each. There needs to be at least four teams. In case there are more teams, the task of each team can be further split up.

1 Select your college or university as the case setting, but determine in advance which part you will audit. You might want to study the whole university or only the management department. It is most realistic to limit the exercise to one department if this exercise needs to be accomplished in one day.
2 Discuss with your instructor who you can interview. It might be necessary for your lecturer to inform a few people in the organisation about the fact that students pay them a short visit and ask some questions about the structure of their organisation.

It is the purpose to know for each of the topics discussed in this chapter how they are applied in the university or college. Start with a team brainstorming session to decide who will ask the questions and what questions you need to ask to obtain the required information. Each interview can be very brief, about 15 minutes. You can ask any employee in the organisation but you will need to interview several people (between three and 10, depending on the size of the organisation) to have a good view on the working of the organisation. Some interviewed might give you conflicting answers. Try to find out why and try to come to a consensus about each of the elements that you analyse.

The topics for the teams are:

Team 1: Identify the different groups in the organisation (i.e. management, middle managers, operating line personnel, supporting staff and technostructure staff) and the level of specialisation.

Team 2: Determine the division in decision-making tasks (i.e. hierarchy of authority, unity of command, span of control, level of centralisation).

Team 3: How do people work together to execute common tasks (i.e. which co-ordination mechanisms are used) and what is the level of formalisation?

Team 4: Look at the table below and try to decide whether the organisation is more an old type or new type organisation. Consider whether the organisation has enough flexibility.

New	Old
Dynamic, learning	Stable
Information rich	Information is scarce
Global	Local
Small and large	Large
Product/customer oriented	Functional
Skills oriented	Job oriented
Team oriented	Individual oriented
Involvement oriented	Command/control oriented
Lateral/networked	Hierarchical
Customer oriented	Job requirements oriented

Source: J. R. Galbraith and E. E. Lawler III, 'Effective Organizations: Using the New Logic of Organizing', p. 298 in *Organizing for the Future: The New Logic for Managing Complex Organizations*, eds J. R. Galbraith, E. E. Lawler III and Associates. Copyright 1993 Jossey-Bass Inc. Publishers. Reprinted by permission of Jossey-Bass, Inc., a subsidiary of John Wiley & Sons, Inc.

For each team: Ask if the interviewees are happy with the current state of these structural elements and why. Would they like to change anything?

Each team discusses its results and summarises the answers. Next, all teams bring their answers together by briefly presenting to the other teams in the classroom. Finally, during the general class discussion, try to confirm the organisation's type using Mintzberg's typology (see Table 10.4). Discuss also if this organisation has a good structure or if things can or should be changed.

Online Learning Centre

When you have read this chapter, log on to the Online Learning Centre website at ***www.mcgraw-hill.co.uk/textbooks/sinding*** to access test questions, additional exercises and other related resources.

Notes

[1] See P. F. Drucker, 'The New Society of Organizations', *Harvard Business Review*, September–October 1992, pp. 95–104; J. R. Galbraith, E. E. Lawler III, and Associates, *Organizing for the Future: The New Logic for Managing Complex Organizations* (San Francisco, CA: Jossey-Bass, 1993); and R. W. Oliver, *The Shape of Things to Come: Seven Imperatives for Winning in the New World of Business* (New York: McGraw-Hill, 1999).

[2] C. I. Barnard, *The Functions of the Executive* (Cambridge, MA: Harvard University Press, 1938), p. 73. Also see M. C. Suchman, 'Managing Legitimacy: Strategic and Institutional Approaches', *Academy of Management Review*, July 1995, pp. 571–610.

[3] Drawn from E. H. Schein, *Organizational Psychology, third edition* (Englewood Cliffs, NJ: Prentice-Hall, 1980), pp. 12–15.

[4] For interesting and instructive insights about organisation structure, see G. Morgan, *Images of Organization* (Newbury Park, CA: Sage, 1986); G. Morgan, *Creative Organization Theory: A Resource Book* (Newbury Park, CA: Sage, 1989); G. Hofstede, 'An American in Paris: The Influence of Nationality on Organization Theories', *Organization Studies*, no. 3, 1996, pp. 525–37; and J. G. March, 'Continuity and Change in Theories of Organizational Action', *Administrative Science Quarterly*, June 1996, pp. 278–87.

[5] W. R. Scott, *Institutions and Organizations, second edition* (Englewood Cliffs, NJ: Prentice-Hall, 1987).

[6] www.nationmaster.com/encyclopedia/Chunnel

[7] The pin factory example appears in the very first chapter of *An Inquiry into the Nature and Causes of the Wealth of Nations*. The book exists in numerous editions and is available online at www.gutenberg.org/files/3300/3300-h/3300-h.htm.

8 P. R. Lawrence and J. W. Lorsch, *Organization and Environment* (Homewood, IL: Richard D. Irwin, 1967), p. 157.

9 Pooled, sequential and reciprocal integration are discussed in J. W. Lorsch, 'Organization Design: A Situational Perspective', *Organizational Dynamics*, Autumn 1977, pp. 2–14. Also see J. E. Ettlie and E. M. Reza, 'Organizational Integration and Process Innovation', *Academy of Management Journal*, October 1992, pp. 795–827; and A. L. Patti and J. P. Gilbert, 'Collocating New Product Development Teams: Why, When, Where, and How?', *Business Horizons*, November–December 1997, pp. 59–64.

10 J. R. Galbraith, *Organization Design* (Reading, MA: Addison-Wesley Publishing Company, 1977).

11 H. Mintzberg, *Mintzberg on Management* (New York: Free Press, 1989).

12 For an interesting historical perspective of hierarchy, see P. Miller and T. O'Leary, 'Hierarchies and American Ideals, 1900–1940', *Academy of Management Review*, April 1989, pp. 250–65.

13 For related research, see S. Finkelstein and R. A. D'Aveni, 'CEO Duality as a Double-Edged Sword: How Boards of Directors Balance Entrenchment Avoidance and Unity of Command', *Academy of Management Journal*, October 1994, pp. 1079–1108.

14 Translated from H. Fischer, 'Die Artillerietruppe im Heer der Zukunft', *Bundesheer, Österreichische Militärische Zeitschrift*, 2/2004.

15 M. Jacobides, 'Industry Change through Vertical Disintegration: How and Why Markets Emerged in Mortgage Banking', *Academy of Management Journal*, 48(3), pp. 465–98, 2005.

16 A. Sahaym, H. K. Steensma and M. A. Schilling, 'The Influence of Information Technology on the Use of Loosely Coupled Organizational Forms: An Industry Level Analysis', *Organization Science*, 18(5), pp. 865–880, 2007.

17 M. Goold and A. Campbell, 'Structured Networks: Towards the Well-Designed Matrix', *Long Range Planning*, October 2003, pp. 427–39.

18 Based on M. Weber, *The Theory of Social and Economic Organization*, translated by A. M. Henderson and T. Parsons (New York: Oxford University Press, 1947). An instructive analysis of the mistranslation of Weber's work may be found in R. M. Weiss, 'Weber on Bureaucracy: Management Consultant or Political Theorist?', *Academy of Management Review*, April 1983, pp. 242–8.

19 For a critical appraisal of bureaucracy, see R. P. Hummel, *The Bureaucratic Experience, third edition* (New York: St. Martin's Press, 1987). The positive side of bureaucracy is presented in C. T. Goodsell, *The Case for Bureaucracy: A Public Administration Polemic* (Chatham, NJ: Chatham House Publishers, 1983).

20 See G. Pinchot and E. Pinchot, 'Beyond Bureaucracy', *Business Ethics*, March–April 1994, pp. 26–9; and O. Harari, 'Let the Computers Be the Bureaucrats', *Management Review*, September 1996, pp. 57–60.

21 K. Deveny, 'Bag Those Fries, Squirt That Ketchup, Fry Those Fish', *Business Week*, 13 October 1986, p. 86.

22 See D. A. Morand, 'The Role of Behavioral Formality and Informality in the Enactment of Bureaucratic versus Organic Organizations', *Academy of Management Review*, October 1995, pp. 831–72.

23 See G. P. Huber, C. C. Miller and W. H. Glick, 'Developing More Encompassing Theories about Organizations: The Centralization–Effectiveness Relationship as an Example', *Organization Science*, no. 1, 1990, pp. 11–40; and C. Handy, 'Balancing Corporate Power: A New Federalist Paper', *Harvard Business Review*, November–December 1992, pp. 59–72. Also see W. R. Pape, 'Divide and Conquer', *Inc. Technology*, no. 2, 1996, pp. 25–7; and J. Schmidt, 'Breaking Down Fiefdoms', *Management Review*, January 1997, pp. 45–9.

24 See H. Mintzberg, *Mintzberg on Management* (New York: Free Press, 1989); and H. Mintzberg, *The Structuring of Organizations* (Englewood Cliffs, NJ: Prentice Hall, 1979).

25 C. M. Fiol and E. Romanelli, 'Before Identity: The Emergence of New Organizational Forms', *Organization Science*, vol. 23, no. 3, 2012, pp. 597–611.

26 A reflection of the discussion going on in the 1990s can be found in D. M. Gordon, *Fat and Mean: The Corporate Squeeze of Working Americans and the Myth of Managerial 'Downsizing'* (New York: Free Press, 1996); and B. Harrison, *Lean and Mean: The Changing Landscape of Corporate Power in the Age of Flexibility* (New York: Basic Books, 1994).

27 H. Tsoukas, 'Re-Viewing Organization', *Human Relations*, January 2001, p. 7.

28 H. Kaufman, *Time, Change, and Organizations* (Chatman, NJ: Chatam House, 1985).

29 For research on organisational complexity, see S. L. Brown and K. M. Eisenhardt, 'The Art of Continuous Change: Linking Complexity Theory and Time-Paced Evolution in Relentlessly Shifting Organizations', *Administrative Science Quarterly*, no. 1, 1997, pp. 1–35; and J. Mathews, 'Holonic Organisational Architectures', *Human Systems Management*, no. 1, 1996, pp. 27–54.

30 R. Jacob, 'The Struggle to Create an Organization for the 21st Century', *Fortune*, 3 April 1995, pp. 91–2.

31 See S. Sonnesyn Brooks, 'Managing a Horizontal Revolution', *HR Magazine*, June 1995, pp. 52–8; and M. Hequet, 'Flat and Happy', *Training*, April 1995, pp. 29–34.

32 For related discussion, see B. Filipczak, 'The Ripple Effect of Computer Networking', *Training*, March 1994, pp. 40–47.

33 See the work of A. Grandori and G. Soda, 'Inter-Firm Networks: Antecedents, Mechanisms and Forms', *Organization studies*, no. 2, 1995, pp. 183–214; C. Hastings, *The New Organization: Growing the Culture of Organisational Networking* (London: McGraw-Hill, 1993); and W. W. Powell, 'Neither Market nor Hierarchy: Network Forms of Organization', in *Research in Organizational Behavior*, eds L. L. Cummings and B. M. Staw (Greenwich, CT: JAI Press, 1990), pp. 295–336.

34 R. S. Burt, *Structural Holes: The Social Structure of Competition* (Cambridge, MA: Harvard University Press, 1992).

35 See O. Harari, 'Transform Your Organization into a Web of Relationships', *Management Review*, January 1998, pp. 21–4; R. J. Alford, 'Going Virtual, Getting Real', *Training & Development*, January 1999, pp. 34–44; S. Greco, 'Go Right to the Outsource', *Inc.*, February 1999, p. 39; M. Minehan, 'Forecasting Future Trends for the Workplace', *HR Magazine*, February 1999, p. 176; and W. B. Werther, Jr, 'Structure-Driven Strategy and Virtual Organization Design', *Business Horizons*, March–April 1999, pp. 13–18.

36 Adapted from personal communication.

37 I. Nonaka and H. Takeuchi, *The Knowledge-Creating Company* (Oxford: Oxford University Press, 1995).

38 D. Keuning, T. H. Maas et al. *Delayering Organizations* (London: Pitman, 1994), p. 221.

39 R. Kreitner and A. Kinicki, *Organizational Behavior* (New York: McGraw-Hill, 2013).

Chapter 11

Organisational design: structure, technology and effectiveness

Learning Outcomes

When you finish studying the material in this chapter, you should be able to:

- describe the three general views on organisational fit: open systems, chaos theory and systems theory
- explain the contingency approach to organisations, including the benefits and shortcomings of such an approach
- describe the impact of environmental uncertainty on the organisation
- describe major strategy types and the relationship with organisation structure
- explain the role of size in the contingency view
- define technology as organisational element
- explain the effect of technology on the organisation structure and the four major studies that have explored the relationship between technology and structure
- describe the four generic organisational effectiveness criteria
- describe the resource-based view of organisations
- explain how professionals can prevent organisational decline

Opening Case Study: Keeping Nokia fit or shooting in the dark

Nokia was founded in 1865 as a paper mill. The name came along in 1871. It was a company of rather mixed fortunes. Paper was not a very profitable business for Nokia and the company only survived around 1920 because it was taken over by customers who bought electricity from Nokia's hydropower plant. Subsequently, Nokia became a rubber footwear company and a cable works – and eventually a widely diversified conglomerate. Gradually, in the 1960s and 1970s, the precursors for mobile phones evolved, partly to supply the Finnish armed forces. Over the years, Nokia became phenomenally successful as a maker of mobile phones, being the most sold brand of mobile phone for 14 years until 2012.

Nokia used to be the world's largest manufacturer of mobile phones (cell phones), with a 40 per cent market share. Smartphones, such as the Apple iPhone and various models based on Google's Android software platform, became Nokia's overriding problem. The essential concern was that since the iPhone was released in 2007, Nokia's alternatives in this market have been considered clunky.

Things were not well in Espoo, Finland. In April 2010, Nokia announced that the introduction of a new smartphone based on version 3 of the Symbian software had been delayed. In May 2010, the company announced a major restructure; in fact the second in just seven months. Problems in the smartphone side of the business were not the only problem facing Nokia. Basic but cheap alternatives started coming out of China.

Since 2010, the situation has moved from bad to worse. Even though Nokia announced a shift of focus to a Windows-based platform for smartphones, to be used in the Lumia models, sales started to fall and Nokia began losing money. This trend continued through to 2013, with Nokia trying to stem the losses by reducing staff in all parts of the organisation.

In September 2013, Nokia and Microsoft announced that Microsoft would acquire Nokia's phone business for €5.44 billion. According to several sources, this outcome was inevitable given the previous alliance to use the Windows Phone platform and given the rapid decline in Nokia's sales.

The future for Microsoft as a maker of mobile and smartphones is unclear, as it involves the competing systems of the iPhone and the Android software platform used by many other smartphones. The future for the remaining parts of Nokia is perhaps a little less uncertain. After the deal, Nokia will be half its previous size, with around 56 000 employees. The main business will be Nokia Solutions and Networks, which accounted for 90 per cent of Nokia's non-phone revenue in 2012. Other units left in Nokia will be a mapping service and a large portfolio of intellectual property.

For discussion

What makes the story of Nokia somewhat remarkable?

Sources:

A. Ward and A. Parker. Nokia's struggle over smartphone triggers fresh restructuring. *Financial Times*. 12 May 2010.

S.Schechner. Smaller Nokia to Focus on Network Gear, Mapping. *Wall Street Journal Europe*, 3 Sep 2013, http://en.wikipedia.org/wiki/Nokia (viewed 4 October 2013).

In the previous chapter, we described how organisations attempt to achieve their goals by division of labour, hierarchy of authority and co-ordination. Different combinations of these three structural features lead to different organisation types. Organisations have some freedom in choosing their form but this freedom is limited. To be an effective organisation, the elements of structure need to be appropriate for the situation (or context) in which the organisation operates. Part of the context is the internal climate (Chapter 9) and the organisation's culture (Chapter 12); aspects we come back to when discussing the contingency view of organisational design. However, the external context is almost always of great importance for the design of organisations.

First, we explain why the contextual factors are important and discuss the different views on a fit between external contextual and internal structural factors. Then, we look at the different contextual factors and their effect on the organisation structure. Next, the issue of organisational effectiveness and effectiveness criteria are described. We end the chapter by focusing on the threatening yet ultimately inevitable prospect of organisational decline, that vexing period all organisations face at some point.

11.1 Organisational fit

The notion of an interaction between the way an organisation is constructed and the situation in which it operates can be traced to the open systems view of organisations, and to the contingency view, both of which evolved in the 1950s and 1960s. This is the origin of the idea that there may be either a situation of 'fit' or 'misfit' between structure and context, structure here being quite broadly defined.

Systems theory

The **systems theory** approach states that each element, for example an individual, belongs as a subsystem to a system of higher order, for instance the organisation.[1] A hierarchy of systems goes from simplest to most complex and the working of the complex systems is based on the working of the lower subsystems. Applying this to organisations gives us the following subsystems: the organisation itself as an open system in interaction with its environment, the departments of the organisation as subsystems and the individuals in these departments also as a kind of subsystem with the procedures and control mechanisms as yet another kind of subsystem of a lower order.

The systems theory of organisations emerged from field studies by the London Tavistock Institute in the 1950s.[2] The systems theory in organisation theory is inspired by the general systems theory but focuses less on the organisation as a subsystem of the environment and more on the development of general abstract relations among organisational elements. Systems theory is important for analysing organisations, as it stresses the embeddedness of the different elements. Similar to the open-systems view, it emphasises that all elements are influencing each other and that the whole system should be taken into account when we try to build effective organisations.

Closed versus open systems

The distinction between a **closed system** and an **open system** is a matter of degree. Because every worldly system is partly closed and partly open, the key question is: how great a role does the environment play in the functioning of the system? For example, a battery-powered clock is a relatively closed system. Once the battery is inserted, the clock performs its time-keeping function hour after hour until the battery goes dead. The story might end here, as a perfect metaphor for a closed system. But batteries can be changed as most people are aware. Opening the lid to do so also changes the clock from a closed to an open system. The human body, on the other hand, is a very open system because it requires a constant supply of life-sustaining oxygen from the environment. Nutrients are also imported from the environment, while carbon dioxide and a variety of other waste products are discharged. Open systems are capable of self-correction, adaptation and growth, thanks to characteristics such as homeostasis and feedback control.

Organisations depend on the environment for their resources but are also influenced in several ways by their environment. There are no organisations that are fully closed but some depend more on their environment than others. The traditional mechanistic organisation discussed in the previous chapter is sometimes seen as a closed-system model because it largely ignores environmental influences. It gives the impression that organisations are self-sufficient entities. Conversely, the more organic and the newer organisation types emphasise interaction between organisations and their environments. These newer models are based on open-system assumptions. The distinction between open and closed systems is important because it illustrates how organisation theorists look at organisations. Organisations can be seen either as primarily closed – operating in a particular environment, in which the organisation adapts to this environment and creates a stable harmony with the environment – or as primarily open, which implies continuous interaction with the environment is preferred over stable harmony.

Even the most closed of organisations, however, still depends on buying inputs and selling outputs. Similarly, even the most closed organisations are made up of people who spend their entire working lives inside an organisation yet still spend their spare time elsewhere. This makes the closed-system metaphor somewhat imprecise, a problem that is not uncommon when metaphors are used.

! **Critical thinking**

Should managers spend time understanding complex models – and more generally spend time on keeping themselves informed about organisational theory research?

11.2 The contingency approach to organisation design

Those approaches to organisations which involve the notion of 'fit' between organisational design and the organisation's context do not generally offer a deterministic logic explaining how organisations must be designed but instead provide a systematic approach to look at variations in organisation structures in relation to contingency factors. The contingency approach, however, takes a normative view to organisational fit. According to the **contingency approach to organisation design**, organisations tend to be more effective when they are structured or designed to fit the demands of the situation.[3] The typical contingency variables are technology, environment, strategy, size, culture and structure.[4] A contingency-based design thus seeks a balanced fit among these variables as well as a fit between structural variables and external contingencies (also see Chapter 1).[5] According to this perspective, organisational problems are caused by a lack of such a fit, sometimes equated with the existence of one or more cases of 'misfit'. The contingency approach does not generate an unequivocal equation or algorithm that uses contingency factors as input and produces the one and only 'best' way of organising. It is merely concerned with finding or approaching the right or least inefficient combination of 'contingency factors'.[6]

A study comparing companies with and without bad fits in a sample of 224 Danish small- and medium-sized firms confirmed this performance loss. Any kind of bad fit could generate lower financial performance. However, more varieties of bad fits did not lead to greater losses. Hence, only the firms with no bad fits at all did better than companies suffering from one or more bad fits.[7] Another study of small firms in the USA indicated only very weak relationships between structural fit and performance. In fact, the researcher could not confirm that bad fits led to performance losses.[8] Mintzberg's models of ideal structures (discussed in the previous chapter) are examples of structures that have a perfect fit among the internal elements and the environment. However, a study categorising firms according to Mintzberg's typology does not indicate that firms which do not fit well in one of the ideal structures perform worse.[9] Nonetheless, the studies are all too limited in scope to fully reject the idea that organisations need a contingency fit to be successful.

Assessing and adapting to environmental uncertainty

The environment is a source of uncertainty. Most organisations are facing a range of influences from their environment, which they cannot control. Influences can come from changes in regulations from governments, changes in labour supply, in consumer incomes or expectations, changes in customer preferences, and so on. We will see later in this chapter that every organisation has many stakeholders (i.e. groups of people with an interest in the organisation), some of which can influence the organisation and are a source of uncertainty. Some are more powerful than others and the organisation tries to avoid conflict with its stakeholders by taking their interests and needs into account. The organisation is thus in interaction with its environment and can reduce uncertainty through this interaction. However, only very large organisations are able to reduce environmental uncertainty by having some measure of control of the environment instead of being wholly dependant on the environment.

Environmental uncertainty is caused by the fact that we cannot predict changes and that we cannot understand the complexity in that environment. Lawrence and Lorsch described uncertainty as the lack of clarity in information, cause-effect relationships and the time lag in information about the environment.[10] They mainly focus on the unpredictability aspect in environmental uncertainty. Different parts of the organisation can face different levels of uncertainty because they are influenced by different parts of the environment and have different levels of interaction with that environment. The sales department will interact more heavily with the environment than the accounting department.[11] Robert Duncan proposed a two-dimensional model for classifying environmental demands on the organisation[12] (see Table 11.1).

The horizontal axis is the simple → complex dimension. This dimension focuses on the number and the degree of similarity of factors in the environment. On the vertical axis of Duncan's model is the static → dynamic dimension. This dimension distinguishes between the factors that remain the same over time and those that change. When combined, these two dimensions characterise four situations that represent increasing uncertainty for organisations. According to Duncan, the complex–dynamic situation of highest uncertainty is the most common organisational environment today.

Few organisations are likely to view themselves as being in a simple and stable environment. Globalisation and climate change, as well as regional policies to strengthen competition and regulate externalities have, combined with technological shifts, made the environment seem more complex and more dynamic for all but a few organisations.

Several classic studies have focused on the environment itself as a contingency variable as well. Daft and Lengel have refined the understanding of uncertainty by distinguishing between the concepts *environmental uncertainty* and *equivocality*. The latter concept refers to uncertainty about cause and effect, and about multiple and conflicting interpretations of the environment, which cause confusion.[13]

Table 11.1 A Four-Way Classification of Organisational Environments

	Simple	Complex
Static	**Low perceived uncertainty** • Small number of factors and components in the environment • Factors and components are somewhat similar to one another • Factors and components remain the same and are not changing • Example: soft drink industry	**Moderately low perceived uncertainty** • Large number of factors and components in the environment • Factors and components are not similar to one another • Factors and components remain basically the same • Example: food products
	1	2
	3	4
Dynamic	**Moderately high perceived uncertainty** • Small number of factors and components in the environment • Factors and components are somewhat similar to one another • Factors and components of the environment are in continual process of change • Example: fast-food industry	**High perceived uncertainty** • Large numbers of factors and comp in the environment • Factors and components are not similar to one another • Factors and components of environment are in a continual process of change • Examples: commercial airline industry; telephone communications

Source: R. Duncan, 'What Is the Right Organization Structure? Decision Tree Analysis Provides the Answer', *Organizational Dynamics*, Winter 1979, pp. 59–80.

The static/dynamic distinction can also be refined by introducing environmental velocity to indicate organisations that are in an extremely volatile environment.[14] Information on how fast change is taking place may be inadequate, may be received too late and is often not available. Organisations then have no other choice than to react very quickly to the changes that occur and to take decisions based on limited information.

Besides the complexity and dynamism dimensions, Henry Mintzberg also added environmental diversity and hostility.[15] Organisational diversity exists when an organisation is active in many different products or markets. The more an organisation is specialised, the narrower its environment becomes. Reducing environmental diversity is a means to reduce complexity. Hostility exists when organisations have stakeholders who are not in co-operative relationships with the organisation. A polluting company will be in a hostile environment because government and a number of pressure groups will try to force the company to change its activities. Many companies also face uncertainty due to the sometimes unpredictable behaviour of stakeholders.

OB in Real Life

Sir Stelios and the battle for easyJet

Competition in the discount airline market is intense. Two of the main actors are Ryanair and easyJet. Both were founded by colourful personalities, Ryanair by Michael O'Leary and easyJet by Sir Stelios Haji-Ioannou.

While no longer involved in running the company, Sir Stelios and his family still owns 36.9 per cent of the shares and has very strong views on how the company should be run. His own words, in an open letter to shareholders and management, sums up the issues:

Since November 2008, I have been front and centre of a campaign to make the easyJet board more focused on shareholder value and less on top line growth. I had become increasingly concerned that our company had an expansion at any cost policy, built on ordering more overpriced aircraft from Airbus, a monopoly supplier. Back then the directors were arguing that other shareholders favoured a zero dividend policy and that it was normal to spend £300–£400m each year buying more aircraft – at the expense of profit margin.

Events since then have proven them wrong and following the replacement of certain directors, the rest of the board has now come round to my strategy of focusing on profit margin improvement rather than revenue growth.

I am delighted to say that my campaign has worked well for all easyJet shareholders. The share price has tripled within four years following the introduction of a dividend policy that pays out one third of post-tax earnings to shareholders. A more healthy 50% distribution ratio is now not too far away. While the board fought me tooth and nail, the market agreed with me by pushing the share price to an all time high.

There is still one major concern that could screw up this financial success story: another aircraft order. . . . The current fleet. . . . is also composed of brand new aircraft that will not need replacement for many years to come – certainly well beyond the tenure of the current directors.

If the board places another order for aircraft, it will destroy shareholder value into the future. If they place such an order now I will be looking to dispose of more of my stake before this happens.

It has always been my view since 2008, easyJet should have been run as a mature cash generative company in the current recessionary European environment. Instead of ordering new aircraft, easyJet should aim for a 10% profit margin, up from 1% four years ago and against the current level of 7%.

The alternative does not bear thinking about. A brief look back in aviation history shows a depressing trend of countless iconic airlines (once mighty names of the skies) going bust because their managements bought more aircraft than they had profitable routes to service.

Let's avoid this happening at easyJet! I will be a loyal shareholder for the long term provided management doesn't squander any more of our cash on new aircraft for at least the next 4–5 years.

For discussion

How significant are Sir Stelios's views for the managers running easyJet as a source of environmental dynamism and complexity?

Source: Based on 'Haji-Ioannou family: reduction in easyJet stake', http://easy.com/shareholder-news/3377-haji-ioannou-family-reduction-in-easyjet-stake.html. (Accessed 17 May 2013).

The structure of organisations is influenced by the above-mentioned characteristics. Certain structures are more or less effective and efficient under certain environmental conditions.[16] Figure 11.1 shows which structural factors relate to the two main dimensions of environmental uncertainty. High diversity and large equivocality will increase the complexity of the environment. Hostile environments mostly cause instability. To cope with a hostile environment all forces need to be concentrated within the organisation through centralisation.[17]

Figure 11.1 Structure Fitting the Environmental Characteristics

	Simple environment	Complex environment
Dynamic environment	**Low formalisation** • A need for many flexible co-ordination mechanisms (such as direct horizontal communication and direct supervision) • Organic • Large need for information about the environment • Simple structure (such as geographic) • Despecialisation	**Low formalisation** • A need for many flexible co-ordination mechanisms (such as direct horizontal communication, teams and integrators) • Organic • Large need for information about the environment • Divisional • Large differentiation • Decentralised
Stable environment	**High formalisation** • Limited use of co-ordination mechanisms (mainly: rules and procedures) • Simple structure (mostly functional) • Low differentiation • Centralisation	**High formalisation** • Limited use of co-ordination mechanisms (mainly: standardisation of procedures and skills) • Mechanic • Divisional • Large specialisation

Source: Based on T. Burns and G. M. Stalker, *The Management of Innovation* (London: Tavistock, 1961); P. R. Lawrence and J. W. Lorsch, *Organization and Environment* (Boston, MA: Harvard University Press, 1967); R. B. Duncan, 'Characteristics of Organizational Environments and Perceived Environmental Uncertainty', *Administrative Science Quarterly*, September 1972, pp. 313–27; and H. Mintzberg, *The Structuring of Organizations* (Englewood Cliffs, NJ: Prentice Hall, 1979).

Population ecology theory also seeks to explain the organisation in its environment but focuses on groups of similar organisations, active in similar markets or offering similar products and services. This area of organisation theory explains the birth, development and death of organisations in terms of their adaptiveness to their environment. Organisations that are able to adapt and consistently acquire crucial resources have the best chance to survive. Hence, the population ecology theory also emphasises the need for organisations to 'fit' their environment.[18] The connection between population and organisational decline is explored later in this chapter.

Overall, the contingency approach and the open-systems view have one important thing in common. They are based on an 'environmental imperative', meaning that the environment is said to be the primary determinant of effective organisational structure. Other organisation theorists disagree. They contend that factors such as the organisation's corporate strategy, size and core technology hold the key to organisational structure. The next sections examine the significance of these three additional contingency variables.

Strategy and organisation structure

Strategy is also a contingency variable. We mentioned in the previous chapter that organisations develop specialisation/differentiation and co-ordination to help them to achieve their goals. What those goals can be will be discussed in the section on organisational effectiveness. Strategy refers to the processes developed in the organisation to create value, seek for opportunities and to achieve its goals. Hence, strategy refers to the decision-making process to manage the organisation's relationships with its environment.

Alfred Chandler introduced the now famous phrase 'structure follows strategy'[19] indicating that structure is determined by the strategy of the organisation. Chandler based his statement on a study of about 100 large American companies. However, later researchers have found that structure can also affect strategy. Factors such as complexity, centralisation and formalisation have an impact on the decision-making process in the organisation and, hence, on the strategy that will emerge.[20] The kind of structure will also make the organisation more or less flexible, allowing more or less potential to see and grasp opportunities in the market. Although structure and strategy mutually influence each other, we can nevertheless make some statements about the kind of structure best fitting a particular strategy.

Michael Porter identified three generic strategies which will allow organisations to develop a competitive advantage over other organisations that are competing in the same markets.[21] These three strategies are 'cost leadership' (i.e. products offered at low prices based on efficient low-cost production), 'differentiation' (i.e. products offered at a premium price based on the uniqueness, image or brand of the product) and 'focus' (i.e. selecting a niche in the market where competition is low or even absent). The first strategy requires an organisation structure that is suited to realising economies of scale, while the other two strategies require a structure that allows close contact with the customers and the processing of information about the market.

Miles and Snow developed typology of strategy with four categories.[22] The first is 'defenders'; organisations that have few products or markets but are efficient in serving these markets. They can defend their market position by having low unit costs and can, if faced by entering competitors, lower prices to make entry very costly. Organisations with this strategy rarely make changes to their products, structure and operational goals. The second category refers to organisations with an 'analyser' strategy. Such organisations have their major business in a stable environment where they can emphasise efficiency and do not need to change their structure and products. However, they also have more turbulent products or areas in which they seek innovation and change, especially when they see that competitors are making important changes. This is a 'defender' strategy with an eye on the environment so as to be ready to change when this is necessary. The third category, the 'prospectors', refers to organisations which are very innovative and continually seeking change in their products, markets, structure and processes so as to be ahead of competition or to follow early trends in the environment. Efficiency is not a great priority in this type of organisation. Finally, there is the category of 'reactors'; organisations that are forced by their environment to change and to respond. However, their reactive character means that they only change when forced to, resulting in a poor fit between structure and strategy.

An organisation with a prospector's focus on innovation will require low formalisation, considerable decentralisation and extensive use of horizontal co-ordination mechanisms, such as teams and task forces. An organisation that focuses on differentiation towards different markets, or fits in the analyser category, will need a structure that allows it to capture a lot of customer information and should be moderately formalised and decentralised. Strategies that are stable over the long term, such as the defenders and cost leadership, allow high levels of formalisation and centralisation, in particular to achieve efficiency and cost control.[23]

Starting with John Child, some have rejected the notion that environment is the most important or 'imperative' factor for organisational structure in favour of a model based on behavioural rather than rational economic principles. Child believed structure resulted from a political process involving organisational power holders, with the outcome that the actual strategic choice is determined largely by the dominant coalition of top-management strategists.[24]

OB in Real Life

Strategically choosing social responsibility at Patagonia

Patagonia started as a manufacturer of mountaineering tools, under the name of 'Chouinard Equipment', named after the founder, Yvon Chouinard. The Patagonia name was introduced in the early 1970s, when the firm began selling clothing with an outdoor focus. The company, according to its own published history, was involved in a number of innovative activities. These were not always original, but built on the innovations of others. For example, by adopting products made of synthetics (polypropylene, polyester, and many others, developed to have specific properties) and introducing the concept of 'layering' – one layer for transporting moisture away from the skin, a middle layer for insulation and an outer shell for wind and rain protection – Patagonia had been part of a radical change in outdoor lifestyle.

At several points in the company's history, very explicit strategic choices had been made. The very first was driven by environmental concerns very narrowly defined. By 1970, Chouinard Equipment was the largest supplier of climbing equipment in the USA. Climbing mountains in the way it was then done, which involved hammering pitons (a specially shaped metal spike) into cracks in the rock face, had a significant environmental impact. In the company's history, how the decision to phase out the pitons, which were a very important product at the time, is described as follows: 'After an ascent of the degraded Nose route on El Capitan [a rock formation in Yosemite National Park in California], which had been pristine a few summers earlier, Chouinard and [Tom] Frost decided to phase out of the piton business.'

The replacement product, however, was on hand and Chouinard could produce it. This was the 'chock' or 'nut'. 'Nuts' were named after the primitive precursors to chocks used by British mountaineers as early as the 1920s; basically, old machine nuts. Placing these in cracks when climbing rocks was an alternative to pitons. Since the 1970s, chocks have broadly replace pitons in rock climbing.

The history of Patagonia provides another example of a strategic choice. In its 1992 fall/winter catalogue, the company, keenly aware that such catalogues are carefully read, argued as follows, when announcing a reduction in the number of items being offered: 'Well, last fall you had a choice of five ski pants; now you may choose between two. Two styles of ski pants are all anyone needs.' This and the broader interest in reducing environmental impact of Patagonia's operations can then be viewed as a strategic choice.

What is missing from these stories is some additional contextual details. The shift away from pitons happened at about the same time that the 'clean climbing' movement started growing. The early 1990s were a time of crisis for Patagonia. People were fired and banks withdrew credit.

For discussion

What was Patagonia doing? Was it strategic choice or adaptation to the environmental (in general, not just the 'green' environment) – and where exactly does one motive end and another take over?

Source: Based on S. Perlstein, 'Less Is More', *Business Ethics*, September–October 1993, p. 15, and Patagonia's history (www.patagonia.com/web/eu/patagonia.go?assetid=3351&ln=79).

Figure 11.2 The Relationship Between Strategic Choice and Organisational Structure

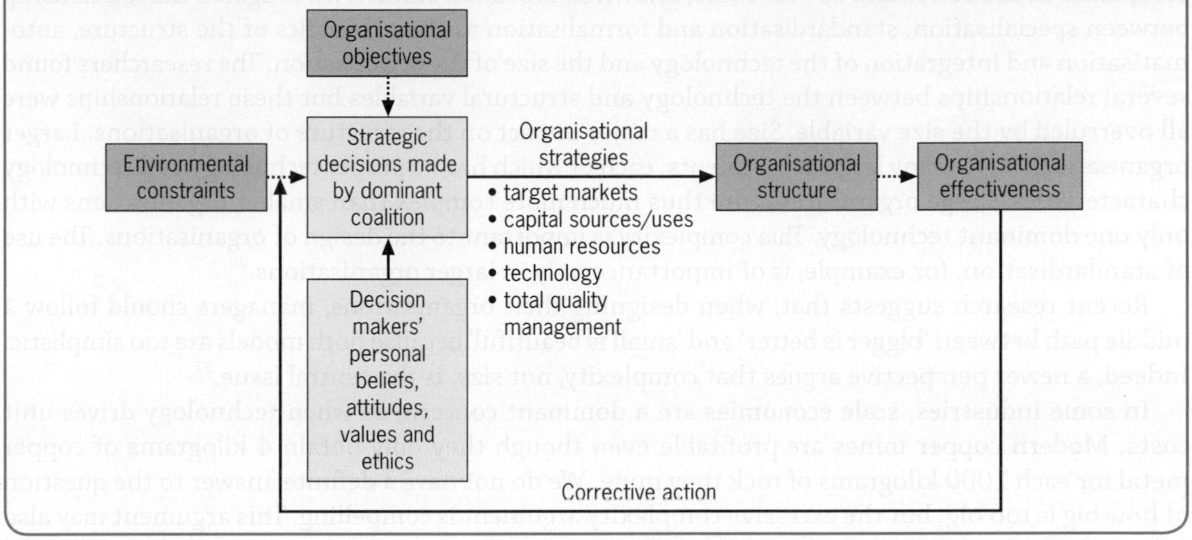

As Figure 11.2 illustrates, specific strategic choices or decisions reflect how the dominant coalition perceives environmental constraints and the organisation's objectives. These strategic choices are tempered by the decision-makers' personal beliefs, attitudes, values and ethics (see Chapters 2 and 3).[25] Consider the case of Patagonia, which more than a decade ago decided to change the way they thought about ethics and corporate strategy.

The choices Patagonia have made seem not to have affected its growth over the years, although general economic downturns have caused problems at times. Directing our attention once again to Figure 11.2, the organisation is structured to accommodate its mix of strategies. Ultimately, corrective action is taken if organisational effectiveness criteria are not met. In the case of Patagonia the strategic choice model is simple to apply. It is a privately held company, still controlled by its founder.

Organisational size and design

Another contingency variable is organisational size. It is an important structural variable subject to two schools of thought. Economists belonging to the first school have understood and argued the benefits of scale economies since the time of Adam Smith and his pin factory. This approach, often called the 'bigger is better' model, assumes the per-unit cost of production decreases as the organisation grows. In effect, bigger is said to be more efficient. For example, on an annual basis, Volkswagen can supposedly produce its hundred thousandth car less expensively than its tenth especially if all these 100 000 cars were completely identical.

The second school of thought is based on the notion of diminishing returns. Called the 'small is beautiful' model, this approach is based on the argument that large organisations and subunits tend to be plagued by costly behavioural problems. Large and impersonal organisations are said to breed apathy and alienation, with resulting problems such as staff turnover and absenteeism.

In the contingency literature, size is especially important because it affects the fit between the other structural and contingency elements. A group of researchers from the Tavistock Institute in

London did contingency-based research on the design of organisations on a large sample of British companies in the 1960s and 1970s. These, known as the Aston studies, investigated the relationship between specialisation, standardisation and formalisation as characteristics of the structure, automatisation and integration of the technology and the size of the organisation. The researchers found several relationships between the technology and structural variables but these relationships were all overruled by the size variable. Size has a major impact on the structure of organisations. Larger organisations have many large departments, each of which has its proper technology and technology characteristics. Large organisations are thus much more complex than smaller organisations with only one dominant technology. This complexity is important to the design of organisations. The use of standardisation, for example, is of importance only in larger organisations.[26]

Recent research suggests that, when designing their organisations, managers should follow a middle path between 'bigger is better' and 'small is beautiful' because both models are too simplistic. Indeed, a newer perspective argues that complexity, not size, is the central issue.[27]

In some industries, scale economies are a dominant concern, as when technology drives unit costs. Modern copper mines are profitable even though they only obtain 4 kilograms of copper metal for each 1000 kilograms of rock they mine. We do not have a definite answer to the question of how big is too big, but the excessive complexity argument is compelling. This argument may also help explain why many mergers have been disappointing in recent years. A meta-analysis by David King and others of a total of 93 studies of post-merger performance of firms have shown an almost universally poor outcome for the acquiring firm.[28]

OB in Real Life

Royal Dutch Shell

Some organisations become so large that top management loses sight of what is happening in the organisation. Large organisations need a structure that allows top management to receive all the crucial information about the workings of the organisation.

Royal Dutch Shell suffered from the consequences of such a faulty information system. In December 2003 it turned out that a claimed reserve of 2.3 billion barrels of oil did not qualify for inclusion in the category called reserves. Since the amount of oil in the ground is a strong indicator of future output, the impact on how the financial markets valued the company was severe. The Chairman, Sir Philip Watts, and the head of exploration and production, Walter van de Vijver, both lost their jobs. The question of who knew what and when remains unclear. What was clear even at the time was that Shell had an extremely convoluted organisational structure, both legally and operationally, a legacy of the dual British-Dutch origin of the company. The duality in the top decision-making structure contributed to poor supervision and is probably also the underlying cause of the long-term underperformance of the company.[29] The organisational structure has subsequently been radically simplified.

The effect of technology on structure

Technology is another contingency variable. Several of the classic organisation theorists have studied the relationship between technology and structure. **Technology** includes all the processes, means and instruments that are available in the organisation to allow the organisation to perform the tasks and reach its goals such as, procedures, skills, engineering techniques and working methods.

As one of the first theorists, Joan Woodward proposed a technological imperative in 1965, after studying 100 small manufacturing firms in Southern England. She found distinctly different structural patterns for effective and ineffective companies based on technologies. There are three broad levels of complexity based on the type of production, namely (in order of complexity):

- Single-piece production or small amounts.
- Mass production.
- Continuous or flow production.

The higher the complexity, the more specialisation and the more need for overhead functions. Co-ordination in single-piece production is based on autonomy and direct horizontal communication. In mass production, rules and procedures predominate. Finally, flow production requires direct supervision and direct contact with short communication lines. In this type of production there is also an extreme need for control requiring intensive use of diverse co-ordination mechanisms, such as hierarchy and rules. Effective organisations based on a technology of medium complexity tend to have a mechanistic structure (see Chapter 10). Effective organisations with either low- or high-complexity technology tend to have an organic structure. However, the focus on production is a limitation to the generalisation of Woodward's findings. Woodward concluded that technology was the overriding determinant of organisational structure.[30]

James Thompson also related technology to organisation design. He identified different types of interdependencies between units and tasks based on different technology in the organisation. The types of interdependencies shown in Figure 11.3 are: pooled, sequential and reciprocal.

In contrast to Woodward, Thompson also discusses service organisations. His types differ in the level of interdependency between the units and also in the level of standardisation of input, processes and output, and in the intensity of co-operation. When integrating these three criteria we can derive the following statements based on Thompson's work:

Figure 11.3 Task Interdependence and Technology

Task interdependence		Co-ordination	Examples
Pooled	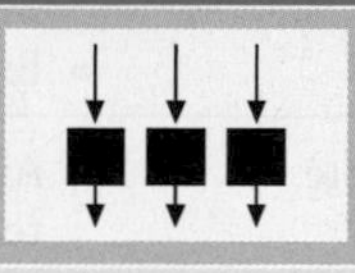	Standardisation (low cost)	Restaurant meals, craft manufacture
Sequential	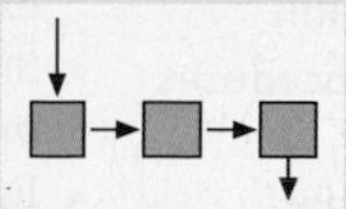	Planning and scheduling (medium cost)	Automaking, computers
Reciprocal	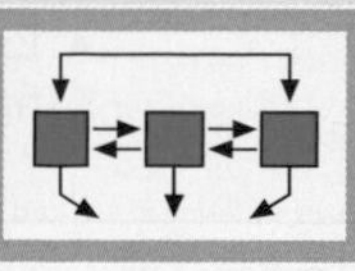	Mutual adjustment (high cost)	Medical treatment, restorations, product development

- In sequential and reciprocal technology, input, processes and output are fully standardised, while these are less standardised in the other two types.
- In pooled technology, there is only standardisation of processes.
- In intense technology (not shown in Figure 11.3), essentially a version of reciprocal interdependency, there is no standardisation possible. Therefore, co-ordination depends on the level of interdependency and standardisation.

Each type of technology is best organised by specific co-ordination mechanisms. Sequential technology needs rules and procedures. Pooled technology requires few co-ordination efforts and only a few rules, because there is no pressing need to integrate the tasks. Intense technology requires a lot of integration and, hence, the use of direct communication lines and continuous mutual adjustment. In this latter case integration must go so far that one unit becomes to a certain extent integrated in the other unit or organisation, even when the two parties are legally speaking not part of one organisation.

Charles Perrow developed a model to explain the structure of organisations by means of technology characteristics. While closely related to the standardisation of Thompson and production technologies of Woodward, Perrow has a more fine-grained description of complexity. He measures complexity along two dimensions, namely the level of change (or exceptions in the technology) and the level of analysability of the technology (or comprehensibility). Analysable technology can be divided into subtasks, which can then be automated or made more routine by standardised rules and procedures. Table 11.2 summarises these relationships between technology and structure.

Table 11.2 Technology and Structure

		Changes in the technology	
		Rare	**Very frequent**
Complexity of the technology	**High**	• Low analysability but routine • Low standardisation • Formalisation • Decentralisation • Continuous production flow • Non-routine production • Example: Nuclear plant	• Low analysability with many exceptions • Decentralisation • Low standardisation, except for standardisation of skills and low formalisation • Low span of control • Intense technology • Single-piece production • Example: Architect firm
	Low	• Analysable and understandable technology which is routine • Centralisation and formalisation • Standardisation, rules and procedures as co-ordination mechanisms • Mass production and sequential technology • Large span of control • Example: Car factory	• Analysable and understandable technology but with many exceptions • Standardisation of skills, rules and processes but low formalisation • Engineering-based production • Example: Software developing firms

Source: Based on C. Perrow, *Organizational Analysis: A Sociological View* (London: Tavistock Publications, 1970); J. D. Thompson, *Organizations in Action* (New York: McGraw-Hill, 1967); and J. Woodward, *Industrial Organization: Theory and Practice* (London: Oxford University Press, 1965).

The two technology dimensions can be combined to develop four categories of technology that each has particular characteristics and co-ordination needs:

- Few changes and high analysability result in routine technology with standard operating procedures.
- Many changes and low analysability allow no standardisation but require direct ad hoc communication.
- Many changes but also highly analysability is known as 'engineering technology' and can be standardised with specific rules and standards but not with routine procedures.
- Few changes but no analysability is to be found in craft work and does not allow procedures either.[31]

Finally, the central idea in Jay Galbraith's *Designing Complex Organizations* is that information can reduce uncertainty caused by the variability in the technology. When technology is uncertain, more information needs to be shared among decision-makers in order to co-ordinate the tasks in the organisation. Each mechanism for co-ordinating and structuring the organisation is different in the amount and type of information that can be shared.

The bottom line for Galbraith is that the need for processing information must at all times balance the capacity to process it. He basically identifies three ways in which the need for processing information can be reduced; exerting influence on the environment, create a buffer that reduces the need for processing information, and establishing independent units to handle information. Alternatively, the capacity to process information can be increased by expanding either vertical or horizontal information flows – or both.[32]

Leadership and organisational climate/culture as contingences

Both leadership and climate/culture are important contingences for organisational design. Climate, in the sense of the way organisation members experience a set of conditions, was covered in Chapter 9. The more deep-seated and less visible fundamental assumptions are discussed in detail in Chapter 12.

What is needed to treat these two variables as contingency factors is classifications of both that are operational in terms of the design elements available. Based on an extensive analysis of the literature, Richard Burton and Børge Obel come to two conclusions. First, that climate and culture can be treated as a variable for the purpose of design, and second that leadership preferences, again for the purposes of creating useful contingency variables, can similarly be reduced to a set of summary indicators.[33]

For climate and culture, Burton and Obel adapted the competing values framework of Cameron and Quinn (see Chapter 12), and arrived at what they called 'reduced climate indicators'. These are trust, conflict, morale, rewards, and resistance to change, leader credibility and scapegoating. For leadership, the contingency factors are based on a review of the literature that identifies leader decision-making, leader approach to risk, their information management, relations to other people and the way they choose to motivate and control others. This is transformed into operational terms (and thus measurable) as preference for delegation, level of detail in decision-making, reactive or proactive decisions, time horizon of decisions, preference for risk, and preference for motivating or controlling employees. Based on these, four types of leaders are distinguished: entrepreneurs, managers, leaders and producers.

Critics of the contingency approach

Criticisms of the contingency and fit approaches of organisation design are based on the fact that organisations consist of processes and not of stable structural elements. Moreover, those processes are continually evolving.[34] Critics also point out that neither the organisation nor its processes or the environment remain stable. Therefore, it is almost impossible to determine an optimal fit between the elements. We also need insight into the processes that lead to obtaining and maintaining fit and that enable us to explain the dynamism in organisations.[35]

Another criticism involves environmental determinism,[36] and states that organisations are shaped by their environment and have limited potential to influence that environment. The contingency approach, however, very much takes the same view. Criticism of this view is based on the resource-dependency perspective and in the 'enacted' view of organisations.

The resource-dependency perspective states that organisations depend on other organisations for acquiring their resources, which creates a natural source of uncertainty.[37] Outsourcing increases the dependency on others for resources, while vertical integration (i.e. taking over the organisation supplying one of the resources) puts more resources under the control of the organisation and therefore reduces uncertainty. However, the organisation is not completely dependent on the resource providers but can negotiate with them as well. Most organisations also have several alternative providers for each of their resources. The organisation will identify its most crucial resources and try to minimise the risk by obtaining a stable supply of the critical resources that are absolutely necessary to make the organisation able to achieve its goals.

Karl Weick introduced the concept of the enacted environment to explain that humans 'enact' or perceive our environment in a very personal and subjective way.[38] Key individuals in organisations, mostly the managers, 'construct' or 'enact' their environment and then react to it. Consequently, two managers can view the same environment as being very complex or fairly simple and will therefore react differently. The idea of an enacted view fits in with a broader sociological or interpretative view of the world. This view claims there is no world out there that we can observe. Instead, we only see the things we want to see from our very personal viewpoint. The enacted view also includes that we filter information based on our presuppositions about the world (see also symbolic interactionism in Chapter 1 and perception in Chapter 4).

However, as Drazin and Van de Ven[39] argue, although contingency theory is criticised, it is still useful. We need to make assumptions about relationships in organisations, knowing that the world is much more complex and that every assumption only holds good within certain boundaries. Thus, contingency theory offers a useful systematic way to study organisation structures.[40]

Evidence about the contingency approach

In a study of 97 small and mid-sized companies in Quebec, Canada, strategy and organisational structure were found to be highly interdependent. Strategy influenced structure and structure influenced strategy. This was particularly true for larger, more innovative and more successful firms.[41]

Many studies of the relationship between technology and structure have been conducted since these authors' landmark publications. Unfortunately, disagreement and confusion have prevailed. For example, a comprehensive review of 50 studies conducted between 1965 and 1980 found six technology concepts and 140 technology-structure relationships.[42]

The evidence about contingency is, however, problematic for different reasons. Apart from the ever-present problem of establishing causality between managerial actions (or interventions), and organisational outcomes, for example organisational performance, there is a deeper methodological problem involved. Even if we can find enough firms that have undertaken a change effort, we are likely to observe only those that lived to tell the tale. Many firms may have tried to change in some respect, but may have failed (and ceased to exist) in the process. Failure may be caused by the change effort or it may be unrelated. In any case these change efforts are often left out of studies of organisational change. The organisational ecology field of research traces many of its roots to the early work by Arthur Stinchcombe.[43]

Application of the contingency approach

Strategic choice theory and research teaches at least two practical lessons. First, the environment is just one of many determinants of structure. Second, like any other administrative process, organisation design is subject to the interplays of personal power and politics (see Chapter 14).

Some organisation theorists pay special attention to new technology and in particular to information technology (IT) in relation to the structure of organisations.[44] These theorists believe that IT has dramatically changed our way of working in organisations. On the one hand, IT allows organisations to routinise more of their processes. On the other hand, IT also allows more flexibility and complexity in the processes.

The benefits of the new technology can be summarised as:

- New opportunities for workers.
- New roles and communication lines cutting across traditional functional and vertical boundaries.
- New ways of horizontal co-operation.
- More communication, allowing more teamwork.

The negative aspects are:

- Dependency on technology and the risk of personal alienation.
- IT used by managers to reinforce their hierarchical power.
- Workers more extensively controlled and monitored, resulting in a climate of distrust.

Information technology has a much larger impact than other technological innovations because it not only automates our work but also 'informates' it. This has led to a major shift in the skills people need to do their job and in who has the power in organisations. Furthermore, IT has reduced personal interaction and rationalised and objectified work.[45]

Information technology is thus not only used in operations or to collect data but also to help in decision-making and managing the organisation. Customer relationship management (CRM) is one such IT-based management tool that is increasingly receiving attention. CRM goes further than merely collecting sales figures; it also analyses the data which is then ready for management to take decisions based on the CRM analyses.[46]

Critical thinking

Does contingency theory and all its practical implications apply when the national culture context is radically different?

11.3 Organisational effectiveness

We mentioned the need to define an organisational goal to give the members of the organisation their common goal and to allow the development of an organisation structure that supports the achievement of that goal. Organisational effectiveness refers to the degree that organisations are able to accomplish their goals. However, if someone asked you 'How effective are you?', you might find it difficult to answer. You might want to know if they were referring to your average marks, annual income, actual accomplishments, and ability to get along with others, public service or perhaps something else entirely. The same goes for modern organisations. Effectiveness criteria abound. Even when the overall organisational goal is clear, it remains difficult to determine what criteria will be used to measure if the organisation is moving towards its goal.

Assessing organisational effectiveness is an important topic for managers, stockholders, government agencies and OB specialists. The purpose of this section is to introduce a widely applicable and useful model of organisational effectiveness.

Generic organisational effectiveness criteria

A good way to understand this complex subject better is to consider four generic approaches to assessing organisational effectiveness (see Figure 11.4). These effectiveness criteria apply equally well to large or small and profit or not-for-profit organisations. Moreover, as indicated by the overlapping circles in Figure 11.4, the four effectiveness criteria can be used in various combinations. The key thing to remember is that 'no single approach to the evaluation of effectiveness is appropriate in all circumstances or for all organisation types'.[47] What do Coca-Cola and France Télécom, for example, have in common, other than being large profit-seeking corporations?

Goal accomplishment is the most widely used effectiveness criterion for organisations. Key organizational results or outputs are compared with previously stated goals or objectives. Deviations, either plus or minus, require corrective action. This is an organisational variation of the personal goal-setting process discussed in Chapter 6. Effectiveness, relative to the criterion of goal accomplishment, is measured by how well the organisation meets or exceeds its goals.[48]

Productivity improvement (e.g. of inputs) is a common organisation-level goal.[49] Additionally, goals may be set for organisational efforts such as minority recruiting, pollution prevention and quality improvement. Given today's competitive pressures and e-commerce revolution, innovation and speed are very important organisational goals worthy of measurement and monitoring.[50] Toyota gave us a powerful indicator of where things are going in this regard. The Japanese car manufacturer announced it could custom-build a car in just five days. A customer's new Toyota would roll off the Ontario, Canada, assembly line just five days after the order was placed. A 30-day lag was the industry standard at that time.[51]

The second criterion, resource acquisition, relates to inputs rather than outputs. An organisation is deemed effective in this regard if it acquires the necessary factors of production such as raw materials, labour, capital and managerial and technical expertise. Organisations such as Médecins Sans Frontières also have to judge their effectiveness in terms of how much money they raise from donations.

The **resource view** takes a different approach towards organisational effectiveness by emphasising the resources of the organisation.[52] The resources are all the instruments, machines, processes, knowledge, information, systems, skills or any kind of tangible and intangible assets that the

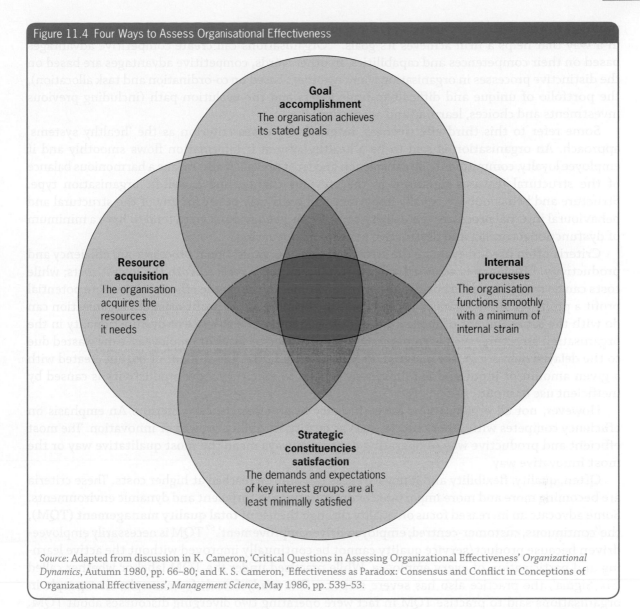

Figure 11.4 Four Ways to Assess Organisational Effectiveness

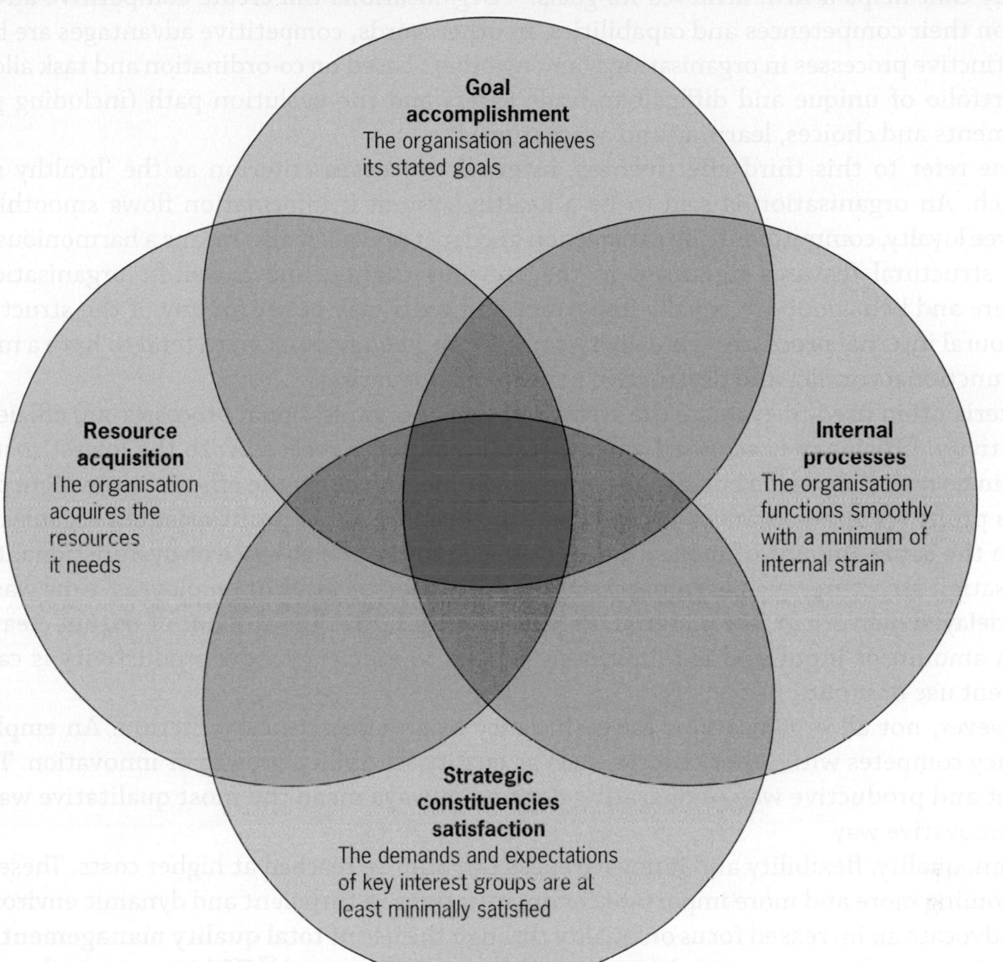
Goal accomplishment
The organisation achieves its stated goals
Resource acquisition
The organisation acquires the resources it needs
Internal processes
The organisation functions smoothly with a minimum of internal strain
Strategic constituencies satisfaction
The demands and expectations of key interest groups are at least minimally satisfied

Source: Adapted from discussion in K. Cameron, 'Critical Questions in Assessing Organizational Effectiveness' *Organizational Dynamics*, Autumn 1980, pp. 66–80; and K. S. Cameron, 'Effectiveness as Paradox: Consensus and Conflict in Conceptions of Organizational Effectiveness', *Management Science*, May 1986, pp. 539–53.

organisation possesses or can make use of. Unique and scarce resources can give some organisations an advantage over others. For organisations operating in a competitive environment, such advantages are very important. An organisation can thus be evaluated in terms of the scarce resources it has or can control. According to the resource-based view, the success and effectiveness of an organisation is based on the ability to develop and safeguard strategic valuable (scarce) resources. Strategic valuable resources can create value for the organisation by preventing the threat of decline or by allowing the exploitation of opportunities. They may also be scarce and hard to imitate or have no alternative that can replace the resource.[53]

On the basis of the resource-based view, several researchers have thoroughly studied the kind of organisational resources and introduced the terms 'capabilities' and 'competences' to indicate strategically valuable resources that help organisations to be competitive and create wealth. Capabilities are repeatable patterns of action in the use of assets to create, produce and/or offer products to a market.[54] A competence is the ability to sustain the co-ordinated deployment of assets in a way that helps a firm achieves its goals.[55] Organisations can create competitive advantages based on their competences and capabilities. In other words, competitive advantages are based on the distinctive processes in organisations (among others based on co-ordination and task allocation), the portfolio of unique and difficult-to-trade assets and the evolution path (including previous investments and choices, learning and adaptation).[56]

Some refer to this third effectiveness, **internal processes** criterion as the 'healthy systems' approach. An organisation is said to be a healthy system if information flows smoothly and if employee loyalty, commitment, job satisfaction and trust prevail. It also means a harmonious balance of the structural features discussed in the previous chapter and a well-fit organisation type. Structure and behaviour are equally important and goals may be set for any of the structural and behavioural internal processes. Healthy systems, from a behavioural view, tend to have a minimum of dysfunctional conflict and destructive political manoeuvring.

Criteria often used to evaluate the structural side of organisational processes are efficiency and productivity. **Efficiency** is achieved when a certain output is realised with the lowest costs; while costs can be monetary value but also resources and time. The larger the efficiency the more potential profit a profit-oriented organisation can make or the more a non-profit-oriented organisation can do with the same amount of money. Efficiency will require the absence of dysfunctionality in the organisation structure, such as unnecessary co-ordination of tasks or employees' time wasted due to the delayed delivery of raw material. **Productivity** indicates the amount of output created with a given amount of input and is thus closely related to efficiency. Low productivity is caused by inefficient use of input.

However, not all organisations have efficiency as an effectiveness criterion. An emphasis on efficiency competes with other criteria, such as quality, flexibility, growth or innovation. The most efficient and productive way of operating does not always mean the most qualitative way or the most innovative way.

Often, quality, flexibility and innovativeness can only be reached at higher costs. These criteria are becoming more and more important for organisations in turbulent and dynamic environments. Some advocate an increased focus on quality through the use of **total quality management (TQM)**, the 'continuous, customer-centred, employee-driven improvement'.[57] TQM is necessarily employee-driven because product/service quality cannot be continually improved without the active learning and participation of every employee. While practised under the TQM label or whether called 'Six Sigma', the practice also has severe sceptics. One study found, for example, that people in organisations said to practise TQM in fact were operating two diverging discourses about TQM. One was technical and rooted in the statistical analysis at the heart of TQM. The other discourse was very different, carried out by managers unable to understand the underlying principles and able to convince themselves that TQM could do many more things than it was designed or intended to.[58]

Organisations both depend on people and affect the lives of people. Consequently, many consider the satisfaction of key interested parties to be an important criterion of organisational effectiveness. A **strategic constituency** is any group of individuals who have some stake in the organisation – for example, resource providers, users of the organisation's products or services, producers of the organisation's output, groups whose co-operation is essential for the organisation's survival or those whose lives are significantly affected by the organisation.[59] We call these groups the 'stakeholders' of the organisation.

Strategic constituencies (or stakeholders) generally have competing or conflicting interests.[60] For example, shareholders who want higher dividends and consumers who seek lower prices would

Figure 11.5 A Sample US Stakeholder Audit Identifying Strategic Constituencies

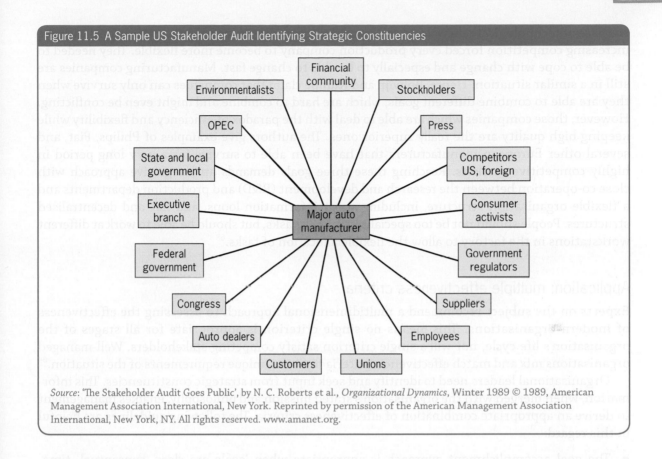

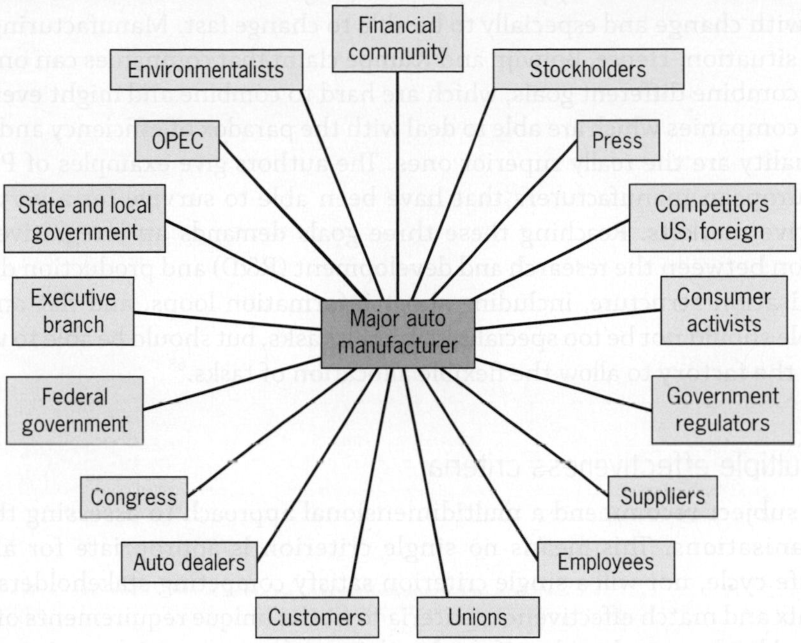

Source: 'The Stakeholder Audit Goes Public', by N. C. Roberts et al., *Organizational Dynamics*, Winter 1989 © 1989, American Management Association International, New York. Reprinted by permission of the American Management Association International, New York, NY. All rights reserved. www.amanet.org.

most likely disagree with a union's demand for a wage increase. Strategic constituents can be identified systematically through a **stakeholder audit** (see the example in Figure 11.5).[61] Conflicting interests and relative satisfaction among the listed stakeholders can then be dealt with.

A never-ending challenge for management is to strike a workable balance between strategic constituencies so as to achieve at least minimal satisfaction on all fronts. McDonald's is an interesting and compelling case in point. After the smoke had cleared from the riots in south central Los Angeles in April 1992, observers were amazed to find every McDonald's restaurant in the area untouched by arsonists. But that outcome was not surprising to McDonald's which is an organisation based on local ownership of franchises. Edward H. Rensi, then president and chief executive officer (CEO) of McDonald's USA, explained why: 'Our businesses there are owned by African-American entrepreneurs who hired African-American managers who hired African-American employees who served everybody in the community, whether they be Korean, African-American or Caucasian.'[62]

Evidence about effectiveness

An analysis of the goals of several different European manufacturing companies showed distinct changes over time. In the 1960s companies needed to achieve maximum efficiency. Later, in the 1970s, attention shifted towards quality and low cost. There was increased global competition, but at the same time customers became more demanding. In the next phase, around the 1980s, flexibility became an additional goal. Competition was still strong and customers were still demanding but the pace of technological renewal and the search by companies to innovate in order to deal with the increasing competition forced every production company to become more flexible. They needed to be able to cope with change and especially to be able to change fast. Manufacturing companies are still in a similar situation. Hence, Bolwijn and Kumpe claim that companies can only survive when they are able to combine different goals, which are hard to combine and might even be conflicting. However, those companies which are able to deal with the paradox of efficiency and flexibility while keeping high quality are the really superior ones. The authors give examples of Philips, Fiat, and several other European manufacturers that have been able to survive for a very long period in highly competitive markets. Reaching these three goals demands an integrative approach with close co-operation between the research and development (R&D) and production departments and a flexible organisation structure, including short information loops, and flat and decentralised structures. People should not be too specialised in their tasks, but should be able to work at different workstations in the factory to allow the flexible allocation of tasks.[63]

Application: multiple effectiveness criteria

Experts on the subject recommend a multidimensional approach to assessing the effectiveness of modern organisations. This means no single criterion is appropriate for all stages of the organisation's life cycle, nor will a single criterion satisfy competing stakeholders. Well-managed organisations mix and match effectiveness criteria to fit the unique requirements of the situation.[64]

Organisational leaders need to identify and seek input from strategic constituencies. This information, when merged with the organisation's stated mission and philosophy, enables management to derive an appropriate combination of effectiveness criteria. The following guidelines are helpful in this regard:

- The goal accomplishment approach is appropriate when 'goals are clear, consensual, time-bounded, measurable'.[65]
- The resource acquisition approach is appropriate when inputs have a traceable effect on results or output. For example, the amount of money the Red Cross receives through donations dictates the level of services provided.
- The internal processes approach is appropriate when organisational performance is strongly influenced by specific processes (e.g. cross-functional teamwork).
- The strategic constituencies approach is appropriate when powerful stakeholders can significantly benefit or harm the organisation.[66]

The next activity is designed to stimulate your reflection on organisational effectiveness criteria.

Activity

What do you see as organisational effectiveness criteria?

There is no single way to measure organisational effectiveness, as discussed in this chapter. Different stakeholders want organisations to do different and often conflicting things. The purpose of this exercise is to introduce alternative effectiveness criteria and to assess real companies with them.

Each year, *Fortune* magazine publishes a ranking of the Global Most Admired Companies. Some might pass this off as simply a corporate-image popularity contest. But we view it as much more. *Fortune* applies a set of eight attributes that could arguably be called effectiveness criteria. These criteria are:

- Revenues.
- Profits.
- Assets (as indicated on the financial balance sheets).
- Stockholders' equity (sum of all capital stock and reserves on the balance sheets).
- Market value (based on share price).
- Earnings per share (based on the earnings indicated on the income sheets).
- Total return to investors (based on prices appreciation and dividend yield).
- Medians (position of the company based on the median of the seven financial criteria in the full list of companies).

In 2003, the 10 companies in the left column below were ranked as the most globally admired companies. In 2010 and 2012 the list was as shown in the middle and right columns:

Rank	2003	2010	2012
1	Wal-Mart stores	Apple	Apple
2	General Motors	Google	Google
3	Exxon Mobil	Berkshire Hathaway	Amazon.com
4	Royal Dutch Shell Group	Johnson & Johnson	Coca-Cola
5	BP	Amazon	IBM
6	Ford Motor Co	Procter & Gamble	FedEx
7	DaimlerChrysler	Toyota Motor	Berkshire Hathaway
8	Toyota Motors	Goldman Sachs	Starbucks
9	General Electric	Wal-Mart stores	Procter & Gamble
10	Mitsubishi	Coca-Cola	Southwest Airlines

Questions

1. Do you agree that the eight attributes are really organisational effectiveness criteria?
2. Is the list of criteria sufficient or is it in need of additions and/or deletions?
3. Are you surprised by the changes in the group of top-ranked companies?

Keeping these basic concepts of organisational effectiveness in mind, we turn our attention to preventing organisational decline in the next section.

Critical thinking

What is a simple, easy way to obtain an unequivocal measure of organisational success and failure?

11.4 Organisational decline

If you think failure is scary, try success. Time after time, big companies such as Siemens (as we have seen), Fiat, Apple Computers, Marks & Spencer, Ericsson, Nokia, IBM and Boeing have stumbled badly after periods of great success. Indeed, after the financial crisis, several high-profile banks have failed or have been nationalised. Société Générale was almost brought down (or into state ownership), as we saw in Chapter 5, as were the Royal Bank of Scotland and the HSBC in the UK and the Fortis group based in The Netherlands.

OB in Real Life

Lego's second coming

In early 2004, Lego, the Danish toy company was in trouble. The losses for 2003 were more than a billion Danish Kroner (about €130 million) on a turnover of just under €1 billion. Revenues were down 25 per cent from the previous year. Market share was down; the Chief Operating Officer, Peter Plougmann had to go, as well as hundreds of other employees. The decline went on for several years and was reported to have been caused by several wrong strategic and marketing decisions made to keep up with the new trends, but the changes failed to meet customers' needs. The toy market changed, became more competitive and more dependent on temporary trends. Lego wanted to follow that change but focused so much on following the new trends that it lost sight of its core strengths; namely, simple Lego blocks for little children. What was Lego doing selling Harry Potter figures and many other spinoffs?

According to the story outlined so far, Lego had strayed from the core and lost sight of its roots. The core of Lego is plastic building blocks, with which children can build almost anything. However, toy markets changed, and computer games grew vastly. This made traditional Lego boring. By combining Lego with Harry Potter and Star Wars, the company was trying to adapt to the new trends in the toy market. The advice from experts was not very helpful: keep doing what you always did (building blocks) but find something new to do.

Fast forward to the 2012 annual report, which reports record revenues of €3.2 billion as well as record operating profits of more than €130 million. Which products were responsible? The classics, but also product lines such as Lego Star Wars and internally developed lines such as Lego PowerMiners and Lego Creators.

Much of the story behind the ups and downs of Lego is not really about straying from the core, but one of careful management, tight cost control and good marketing – but that is perhaps just boring?

For discussion

Did Lego stray from its core – and if it did, how does this compare to other examples of organisations deciding to do new things?

Source: Based on C. Brown-Humes, 'After the Crash: Lego Picks up the Pieces', *Financial Times*, 2 April 2004; 'Trouble in Toyland', *The Economist*, 23 October 2004, pp. 62–3; Lego annual reports (www.lego.com); and P. Rosenzweig, *The Halo Effect* (New York: The Free Press, 2007).

Note: We return to the story of Lego in Chapter 16.

Researchers call this downward spiral **organisational decline** and define it as 'a decrease in an organisation's resource base'.[67] The term 'resource' is used very broadly in this context, encompassing money, talent, customers, and innovative ideas and products. Managers seeking to maintain organisational effectiveness need to be alert to the problem because experts tell us 'decline is almost unavoidable unless deliberate steps are taken to prevent it'.[68] The first key step is to recognise the early warning signs of organisational decline.

Early-warning signs of decline

Managers who monitor the early warning signs of organisational decline are better able to reorganise in a timely and effective manner.[69] Table 11.3 provides a list of the most important early-warning signs of organisational decline. However, recent research has uncovered a troublesome tendency towards inaccurate perception among entrenched top management teams. In companies where there has been little if any turnover among top executives, there is a tendency to attribute organisational problems to external causes (such as competition, the government, technology shifts); by contrast, internal attributions tend to be made by top management teams which include many new members (see also Chapter 4). Thus, proverbial 'new blood' at the top appears to be a good insurance policy against inaccurately perceiving the early-warning signs of organisational decline.[70]

More important is the question of how managers develop an understanding of what actually is happening in the organisation. A study of 15 000 coaches in the US baseball industry indicated that expert knowledge matters a great deal for success as a leader. The study of coaches was especially clear on who became the most successful leaders 20 years later: those players who had been stars when they were playing the game.[71]

Evidence about organisational decline

Many great companies, for example many of those identified as 'excellent' in the 1980s best-selling business book *In Search of Excellence* by Peters and Waterman, have disappeared or fallen on hard times. In some cases, entire industries have vanished, whether they made steam locomotives or floppy disks or something else. Then there are the scandals and the bankruptcies, including Parmelat (which was in fact restructured), Icelandic banks, certain UK banks (starting with Northern Rock)

Table 11.3 The Early Warning Signs of Organisational Decline

• Excess personnel • Tolerance of incompetence • Cumbersome administrative procedures • Disproportionate staff power (e.g. technical staff specialists politically overpowering line managers, whom they view as unsophisticated and too conventional) • Replacement of substance with form (e.g. the planning process becomes more important than the results achieved) • Scarcity of clear goals and decision benchmarks	• Fear of embarrassment and conflict (e.g. formerly successful executives may resist new ideas for fear of revealing past mistakes) • Loss of effective communication • Outdated organisational structure • Increased scapegoating by leaders • Resistance to change • Low morale • Special interest groups are more vocal • Decreased innovation

Source: K. S. Cameron, D. A. Whetten and M. U. Kim, 'Organizational Dysfunctions of Decline', *Academy of Management Journal*, March 1987, pp. 126–38; D. K. Hurst, *Crisis and Renewal: Meeting the Challenge of Organizational Change* (Boston, MA: Harvard Business School Press, 1995); and V. L. Barker III and P. W. Patterson, Jr, 'Top Management Team Tenure and Top Manager Causal Attributions at Declining Firms Attempting Turnarounds', *Group & Organization Management*, September 1996, pp. 304–36.

and in the USA General Motors and Lehman Brothers, Tyco, WorldCom and Enron, to name just a few prominent examples. Although criminal actions were involved in some of these cases, this is more often than not the case. The bottom line is that organisational decline happens.

As indicated by the Lego case, insufficient attention to day-to-day management can allow costs to grow and revenues to shrivel. A so-called 'shake up' may sometimes address the problems, as happened in Lego's case. Lego hired a chief executive with a background as a McKinsey consultant. Digging a little bit deeper, some of the most interesting evidence about the causes of decline comes from one of the more interesting innovative fields in organisation theory since the 1980s. The organisational ecology or population ecology approach has been mentioned briefly but it is also important for organisational decline and death (in ecology language called 'disbanding').

The important elements in this stream of research are inertia, niche theory, resource partitioning, density dependence and age dependence, as well as carrying capacity of the organisational environment.[72]

Of particular importance for decline and disbanding are the concepts of inertia (which makes change difficult and dangerous), density dependence (where the size or density of the population determines disbanding) and age dependence (risk of decline when organisations are new). Lack of legitimacy occurs when organisations are adolescent (lack of resources) or when they are old (due to internal inefficiencies and obsolete activities and products).

Application: preventing organisational decline

The time to start doing something about organisational decline is when everything is going well. It is during periods of high success that the seeds of decline are sown.[73] Complacency is the number one threat because it breeds overconfidence and inattentiveness.[74] However, the world does change, competitors enter valuable markets, new technologies replace old ones and consumer tastes shift, sometimes significantly. These external forces may ultimately make an organisation irrelevant. None of the organisations that once produced steam locomotives for the railways of the world exist any longer. This and many other industries have been wiped out and very little can change such a trend. Similarly, in many industries, a progression from a great number of firms early on, through a consolidation of these to just a few, can be observed. Again these outcomes are not necessarily the consequence of poor or inattentive management, just inevitable facts of life.

! Critical thinking

When organisations stumble, fall or fail, should they be helped back on their feet or should they be left to disband?

Learning outcomes: Summary of key terms

1 **Organisational fit: open systems, chaos theory and systems theory**

Closed systems, such as a battery-powered clock, are relatively self-sufficient. Open systems, such as the human body, are highly dependent on the environment for survival. Organisations are said to be open systems. Chaos theory sees organisations as operating in a highly turbulent environment creating disorder and unanticipated changes for the organisation. According to the systems theory the organisation is part of a large system, while at the same time the organisation itself consists of many interrelated subsystems.

2 **The contingency approach to organisations**

The contingency approach to organisation design calls for fitting the organisation to the demands of the situation. Contingency factors are: environment, technology, structure, strategy and size. The major benefit is the creation of a harmonious balance in the organisational elements and contingency factors to create an organisation design that is best fitted to the particular environment. One drawback of this view is that it pays little attention to organisational processes, change and environmental determinism. The latter questions the unidirectional impact of the environment on the organisation.

3 **Environmental uncertainty and the organisation**

Environmental uncertainty can be mainly assessed in terms of various combinations of two dimensions: (a) simple or complex and (b) static or dynamic. Uncertainty can also be caused by equivocality, diversity and hostility. Depending on the uncertainty in the environment, the organisation needs to be structured differently.

4 **Major strategy types and their relationship with organisation structure**

Porter differentiates between cost leadership, differentiation and focus. Miles and Snow categorise organisations based on their strategies as defenders, analysers, prospectors and reactors. The more defensive the strategy, the more the structure needs to be oriented towards efficiency. The more innovative the strategy, the more flexible the organisation structure needs to be.

5 **The role of size in the contingency view**

Size is a source of complexity. The larger the size, the more complexity and the more advanced co-ordination mechanisms need to be used and the more differences are observed in the contingency factors of each department. The complexity can cause problems by counterbalancing the economics of scale advantage due to the larger scale. Regarding the optimum size for organisations, the challenge for today's managers is to achieve smallness within bigness by keeping subunits at a manageable size.

6 **Technology as organisational element**

Technology encompasses all means used in the organisation to achieve the organisational goals, such as procedures, work methods, skills, tools and knowledge. Information technology is seen as an important new kind of technology that has both positive and negative effects on working in the organisation.

7 **The effect of technology on the organisation structure**

Woodward explained how mass, piece and flow production lead to different levels of complexity and therefore require different co-ordination mechanisms to deal with the complexity. Thompson identifies four kinds of interdependencies between tasks and the kind of coordination best suited for each of these interdependencies. Perrow describes the complexity of tasks in terms of level of analysability of technology and level of change in relation to different types of work and possibilities for standardisation. Galbraith explains that the complexity of the technology refers to the information needed to co-ordinate the tasks.

8 **Four generic organisational effectiveness criteria**

They are goal accomplishment (satisfying stated objectives), resource acquisition (gathering the necessary productive inputs), internal processes (building and maintaining healthy organisational systems which try to achieve the difficult combination of efficiency, quality, productivity, flexibility and innovativeness) and strategic constituencies satisfaction (achieving at least minimal satisfaction for all key stakeholders).

9 **The resource-based view of organisations**

Organisation success is based on control over unique and hard-to-imitate resources. The effectiveness of organisations is evaluated on the basis of the possession of such resources and how these resources can be applied to create unique competences and capabilities which in turn generate a competitive advantage.

10 **Prevention of organisational decline**

Because complacency is the leading cause of organisational decline, managers need to create a culture of continuous improvement. Decline automatically follows periods of great success, so prevention is needed to avoid the erosion of organisational resources (money, customers, talent and innovative ideas).

Review questions

1 Think about an organisation you know and indicate the points where it interacts most intensely with its environment.
2 Can you give an example of an organisation that fits the environment well and one that does not?
3 What is more important, internal consistency between design elements, or fit between design and contingences?
4 Have the environments that organisations face become different from what they were 20 years ago?
5 Can an organisation (or sub-unit) be too big?
6 How much, if at all, is information technology affecting the design of organisations?
7 How would you respond to a manager who claimed the only way to measure a business's effectiveness is in terms of how much profit it makes?
8 What are the stakeholders of an oil company drilling in deep waters offshore?
9 Is complacency the reason for organisational decline?

Personal awareness and growth exercise

Organisation design field study

Objectives

1 To get out into the field and talk to a practising manager about organisational structure.
2 To broaden your knowledge of contingency design, in terms of organisation–environment fit.
3 To make you understand the different effectiveness criteria.

Introduction

A good way to test the validity of what you have just read about organisation design is to interview a practising manager. (*Note*: If you are a manager, simply complete the questionnaire yourself.)

Instructions

Your objective is to interview a manager about aspects of organisational structure, environmental uncertainty and organisational effectiveness. A manager is defined as anyone who supervises other people in an organisational setting. The organisation may be small or large and for-profit or not-for-profit. Higher-level managers are preferred but middle managers and first-line supervisors are acceptable. If you interview a lower-level manager, be sure to remind him or her that you want a description of the overall organisation, not just an isolated subunit. Your interview will centre on the questionnaire described below.

When conducting your interview, be sure to explain to the manager what you are trying to accomplish. But assure the manager that his or her name will not be mentioned in lecture or group discussions or any written projects. Try to take brief notes during the interview for later reference.

Questionnaire

The following questionnaire will help you determine the contingency factors of the manager's organisation. (Circle one number for each item.)

Characteristics of technology, size, structure and strategy

1	Technology changes:	Rarely	1 2 3 4 5 6 7	Very frequent
2	Technology is very:	Simple	1 2 3 4 5 6 7	Complex
3	Task flexibility is:	Rigid; routine	1 2 3 4 5 6 7	Flexible; varied
4	The organisation is compared to others in the industry:	Small	1 2 3 4 5 6 7	Large
5	Degree of hierarchical control:	High	1 2 3 4 5 6 7	Low (self-control emphasised)
6	Primary communication pattern:	Top-down	1 2 3 4 5 6 7	Lateral (between peers)
7	Primary decision-making style:	Authoritarian	1 2 3 4 5 6 7	Democratic; participative
8	The organisation can be described as very:	Formalised	1 2 3 4 5 6 7	Non-formalised
9	Decision-making power is:	Centralised	1 2 3 4 5 6 7	Decentralised

Question about the organisation's environment

This organisation faces an environment that is (circle one number):

Stable and certain	1 2 3 4 5 6 7 8 9 10	Unstable and uncertain

Question about the organisation's strategy

This organisation has a strategy that can be described as (circle one number):

Stable	1 2 3 4 5 6 7 8 9 10	Innovative
Cost leadership	1 2 3 4 5 6 7 8 9 10	Differentiation or focus

Additional questions about the organisation's effectiveness

1 Profitability (if a profit-seeking business):

Low	1 2 3 4 5 6 7 8 9 10	High

2 Degree of organisation goal accomplishment:

Low	1 2 3 4 5 6 7 8 9 10	High

3 Customer or client satisfaction:

Low 1 2 3 4 5 6 7 8 9 10 High

4 Employee satisfaction:

Low 1 2 3 4 5 6 7 8 9 10 High

Based on the scores on the technology questions (first 3 questions), the size question (question 4), the structure questions (from 5 to 9) and the three other groups of questions, describe the fit factors of this organisation.

Questions for discussion

1 Compare the different fit factors and discuss whether there is a fit among the factors.
2 Is the organisation adapted to its environment?
3 Does the organisation's degree of effectiveness reflect how well it fits its environment? Explain.

Group exercise

Stakeholder audit team

Objectives

1 To continue developing your group interaction and teamwork skills.
2 To engage in open-system thinking.
3 To conduct a stakeholder audit and thus more fully appreciate the competing demands placed on today's managers.
4 To establish priorities and consider trade-offs for modern managers.

Introduction

According to open-system models of organisations, environmental factors – social, political, legal, technological and economic – greatly affect what managers can and cannot do. This exercise gives you an opportunity to engage in open-system thinking within a team setting. It requires a team meeting of about 20 to 25 minutes followed by a general class discussion for 10 to 15 minutes. The total time required for this exercise is about 30 to 40 minutes.

Instructions

Your lecturer will randomly assign you to teams with five to eight members each. Choose one team member to act as record keeper and spokesperson.

Identify an organisation that is familiar to everyone in your team (it can be a local business, your college or university, or a well-known organisation such as McDonald's, Royal Dutch Shell or British Airways).

Next do a stakeholder audit for the organisation in question. This will require a team brainstorming session followed by brief discussion. Your team will need to make reasonable assumptions about the circumstances surrounding your target organisation.

Finally, your team should select the three (or more) high-priority stakeholders on your team's list. Rank them number one, number two, and so on. (Tip: A top-priority stakeholder is one with the greatest short-term impact on the success or failure of your target organisation.) Be prepared to explain to the entire class your rationale for selecting each high-priority stakeholder.

Questions for discussion

1 How does this exercise foster open-system thinking? Give examples.

2 Did this exercise broaden your awareness of the complexity of modern organisational environments? Explain.

3 Why do managers need clear priorities when it comes to dealing with organisational stakeholders?

4 How many trade-offs (meaning one party gains at another's expense) can you detect in your team's list of stakeholders? Specify them.

5 How difficult was it for your team to complete this assignment? Explain.

Online Learning Centre

When you have read this chapter, log on to the Online Learning Centre website at ***www.mcgraw-hill.co.uk/textbooks/sinding*** to access test questions, additional exercises and other related resources.

Notes

1 K. E. Boulding, 'General Systems Theory: The Skeleton of Science', *Management Science*, April 1956, pp. 197–208.

2 S. R. Barley and G. Kunda, 'Bringing Work Back In', *Organization Science*, January–February 2001, pp. 76–95.

3 For updates, see J. M. Pennings, 'Structural Contingency Theory: A Reappraisal', in *Research in Organizational Behavior,* vol. 14 (Greenwich, CT: JAI Press, 1992), pp. 267–309; A. D. Meyer, A. S. Tsui and C. R. Hinings, 'Configurational Approaches to Organizational Analysis', *Academy of Management Journal*, December 1993, pp. 1175–95; and D. H. Doty, W. H. Glick and G. P. Huber, 'Fit, Equifinality, and Organizational Effectiveness: A Test of Two Configurational Theories', *Academy of Management Journal*, December 1993, pp. 1196–1250.

4 See for the main authors that developed the contingency theory: T. Burns and G. M. Stalker, *The Management of Innovation* (London: Tavistock, 1961); A. D. Chandler, *Strategy and Structure* (Cambridge, MA: MIT Press, 1962); J. Woodward, *Industrial Organization: Theory and Practice* (London: Oxford University Press, 1965); J. D. Thompson, *Organizations in Action* (New York: McGraw-Hill, 1967); P. R. Lawrence and J. W. Lorsch, *Organization and Environment* (Boston, MA: Harvard University Press, 1967); D. S. Pugh and C. R. Hinings, *Organizational Structure: Extensions and Replications* (Westmead: Saxon House, 1976); J. R. Galbraith, *Organization Design* (Reading, MA: Addison-Wesley Publishing Company, 1977); and P. N. Khandwalla, *Design of Organizations* (New York: Harcourt Brace Jovanovich, 1977).

5 R. Burton and B. Obel, *Strategic Organizational Diagnosis and Design: Developing Theory for Application* (Boston, MA: Kluwer Academic, 1995).

6 S. R. Barley and G. Kunda, 'Bringing Work Back In', *Organization Science*, January–February 2001, pp. 76–95. An interesting distinction between three types of environmental uncertainty can also be found in F. J. Milliken, 'Three Types of Perceived Uncertainty about the Environment: State, Effect, and Response Uncertainty', *Academy of Management Review*, January 1987, pp. 133–43.

7 R. M. Burton, J. Lauridson and B. Obel, 'Return on Assets Loss from Situational and Contingency Misfits', *Management Science*, November 2002, pp. 1461–86.

8 H. Barth, 'Fit Among Competitive Strategy, Administrative Mechanisms, and Performance: A Comparative Study of Small Firms in Mature and New Industries', *Journal of Small Business Management*, April 2003, pp. 133–48.

[9] W. A. Drago, 'Mintzberg's "Pentagon" and Organization Positioning', *Management Research News*, no. 4/5, 1998, pp. 30–41.

[10] P. R. Lawrence and J. W. Lorsch, *Organization and Environment* (Boston, MA: Harvard University Press, 1967).

[11] P. R. Lawrence and J. W. Lorsch, *Organization and Environment* (Boston, MA: Harvard University Press, 1967).

[12] R. Duncan, 'What Is the Right Organization Structure?', *Organizational Dynamics*, Winter 1979, p. 63.

[13] R. L. Daft and R. H. Lengel, 'Organizational Information Requirements, Media Richness and Structural Design', *Management Science*, May 1986, pp. 554–71.

[14] J. Bourgeois and K. Eisenhardt, 'Strategic Decision Processes in High Velocity Environments: Four Cases in the Microcomputer Industry', *Management Science*, July 1988, pp. 816–35.

[15] H. Mintzberg, *The Structuring of Organizations* (Englewood Cliffs, NJ: Prentice Hall, 1979).

[16] T. Burns and G. M. Stalker, *The Management of Innovation* (London: Tavistock, 1961); P. R. Lawrence and J. W. Lorsch, *Organization and Environment* (Boston, MA: Harvard University Press, 1967); R. B. Duncan, 'Characteristics of Organizational Environments and Perceived Environmental Uncertainty', *Administrative Science Quarterly*, September 1972, pp. 313–27; and H. Mintzberg, *The Structuring of Organizations* (Englewood Cliffs, NJ: Prentice Hall, 1979).

[17] H. Mintzberg, *The Structuring of Organizations* (Englewood Cliffs, NJ: Prentice Hall, 1979).

[18] For more information on the population ecology theory, see M. T. Hannan and J. H. Freeman, 'The Population Ecology of Organizations, March 1977, pp. 929–44; H. Aldrich, *Organizations and Environment* (Englewood Cliffs, NJ: Prentice-Hall, 1979); and H. Kaufman, *Time; Change and Organizations* (Chatham, NJ: Chatham House 1985).

[19] A. D. Chandler, *Strategy and Structure* (Cambridge, MA: MIT Press, 1962).

[20] J. W. Frederickson, 'The Strategic Decision Process and Organization Structure', *Academy of Management Review*, no. 2, 1986, pp. 280–97.

[21] M. Porter, *Competitive Advantage: Creating and Sustaining Superior Performance* (New York: Free Press, 1985).

[22] R. E. Miles and C. C. Snow, *Organizational Strategy, Structure and Process* (New York: McGraw-Hill, 1978).

[23] For authors who further developed the Miles and Snow categories, see D. Miller, 'The Structural and Environmental Correlates of Business Strategy', *Strategic Management Review*, no. 1, 1987, pp. 55–76; and N. Nicholson, A. Rees and A. Brooks-Rooney, 'Strategy, Innovation and Performance', *Journal of Management Studies*, no. 5, 1990, pp. 511–34.

[24] For an alternative model of strategy making, see S. L. Hart, 'An Integrative Framework for Strategy-Making Processes', *Academy of Management Review*, April 1992, pp. 327–51. Also see F. E. Harrison and M. A. Pelletier, 'A Typology of Strategic Choice', *Technological Forecasting and Social Change*, November 1993, pp. 245–63; H. Mintzberg, 'The Rise and Fall of Strategic Planning', *Harvard Business Review*, January–February 1994, pp. 107–14; M. Valle, 'Buy High, Sell Low: Why CEOs Kiss Toads, and How Shareholders Get Warts', *Academy of Management Executive*, May 1998, pp. 97–8; G. R. Weaver, L. K. Trevino and P. L. Cochran, 'Corporate Ethics Programs as Control Systems: Influences of Executive Commitment and Environmental Factors', *Academy of Management Journal*, February 1999, pp. 41–57; and C. McDermott and K. K. Boyer, 'Strategic Consensus: Marching to the Beat of a Different Drummer?', *Business Horizons*, July–August 1999, pp. 21–8.

[25] See A. Bhide, 'How Entrepreneurs Craft Strategies That Work', *Harvard Business Review*, March–April 1994, pp. 150–61; and J. W. Dean, Jr and M. P. Sharfman, 'Does Decision Process Matter? A Study of Strategic Decision-Making Effectiveness', *Academy of Management Journal*, April 1996, pp. 368–96; R. L. Osborne, 'Strategic Values: The Corporate Performance Engine', *Business Horizons*, September–October 1996, pp. 41–7; and B. Ettorre, 'When Patience Is a Corporate Virtue', *Management Review*, November 1996, pp. 28–32.

[26] D. S. Pugh and D. J. Hickson, *Organizational Structure in Its Context, The Aston Programme I, second edition* (Westmead: Saxon House, Teakfield Limited, 1976); D. S. Pugh and C. R. Hinings, *Organizational Structure: Extensions and Replications – The Aston programme II*, 1st edn (Westmead: Saxon House, Teakfield Limited, 1976); and D. S. Pugh and R. L. Payne, *Organizational Behaviour in Its Context – The Aston Programme III*, 1st edn (Westmead: Saxon House, Teakfield Limited, 1977).

[27] See, for example, W. McKinley, 'Decreasing Organizational Size: To Untangle or Not to Untangle?', *Academy of Management Review*, January 1992, pp. 112–23; W. Zellner, 'Go-Go Goliaths', *Business Week*, 13 February 1995, pp. 64–70; T. Brown, 'Manage "BIG!"', *Management Review*, May 1996, pp. 12–17; and E. Shapiro, 'Power, Not Size, Counts', *Management Review*, September 1996, p. 61.

[28] David R. King, Dan R. Dalton, Catherine M. Daily and Jeffrey G. Covin, 'Meta-analyses of post-acquisition performance: indications of unidentified moderators', *Strategic Management Journal*, 25(2), pp. 187–200, 2004.

[29] M. Dickson, 'Companies UK: Icon of Inefficiency', *Financial Times*, 27 April 2004.

[30] See J. Woodward, *Industrial Organization: Theory and Practice* (London: Oxford University Press, 1965); and P. D. Collins and F. Hull, 'Technology and Span of Control: Woodward Revisited', *Journal of Management Studies*, March 1986, pp. 143–64.

[31] C. Perrow, *Organizational Analysis: A Sociological View* (London: Tavistock Publications, 1970).

[32] J. R. Galbraith, *Designing Complex Organizations* (Reading, MA: Addison-Wesley Publishing Company, 1973).

[33] R. M. Burton and B. Obel, *Strategic Organizational Diagnosis and Design* (Boston, MA: Kluwer Academic Publishers, 1998), p. 478.

[34] For critics on the contingency approach, see R. B. Duncan and A. Weiss, 'Organizational Learning: Implications for Organizational Design', in *Research in Organizational Behavior*, vol. 1, ed. B. Staw (Greenwich, CT: JAI Press, 1979), pp. 75–123; B. C. Schoonhoven, 'Problems with Contingency Theory: Testing Assumptions Hidden within the Language of Contingency Theory', *Administrative Science Quarterly*, March 1981, pp. 349–77; C. Gresov, 'Exploring Fit and Misfit with Multiple Contingencies', *Administrative Science Quarterly*, September 1989, pp. 431–53; and S. R. Barley and G. Kunda, 'Bringing Work Back In', *Organization Science*, January–February 2001, pp. 76–95.

[35] R. B. Duncan and A. Weiss, 'Organizational Learning: Implications for Organizational Design', in *Research in Organizational Behavior*, vol. 1, ed. B. Staw (Greenwich, CT: JAI Press, 1979), pp. 75–123.

36 W. G. Astley and A. H. Van de Ven, 'Central Perspectives and Debates in Organization Theory', *Administrative Science Quarterly*, March 1983, pp. 245–73.

37 See J. Pfeffer and G. R. Salancik, *The External Control of Organizations: A Resource Dependency Perspective* (New York: Harper and Row, 1978).

38 See K. Weick, *The Social Psychology of Organizing* (Reading, MA: Addison-Wesley Publishing Company, 1969), p. 121; and L. Smircich and C. Stubbart, 'Strategic Management in An Enacted World', *Academy of Management Review*, no. 1, 1985, pp. 8–15.

39 R. Drazin and A. H. Van De Ven, 'Alternative Forms of Fit in Contingency Theory', *Administrative Science Quarterly*, September 1985, pp. 514–39.

40 J. Birkinshaw, R. Nobel and J. Ridderstrale, 'Knowledge as a Contingency Variable: Do the Characteristics of Knowledge Predict Organization Structure?', *Organization Science*, May–June 2002, pp. 274–89.

41 Details may be found in D. Miller, 'Strategy Making and Structure: Analysis and Implications for Performance', *Academy of Management Journal*, March 1987, pp. 7–32. For more, see T. L. Amburgey and T. Dacin, 'As the Left Foot Follows the Right? The Dynamics of Strategic and Structural Change', *Academy of Management Journal*, December 1994, pp. 1427–52; and M. W. Peng and P. S. Heath, 'The Growth of the Firm in Planned Economies in Transition: Institutions, Organizations, and Strategic Choice', *Academy of Management Review*, April 1996, pp. 492–528.

42 See L. W. Fry, 'Technology-Structure Research: Three Critical Issues', *Academy of Management Journal*, September 1982, pp. 532–52.

43 A. Stinchcombe, 'Social structure and organizations', *Handbook of Organizations*, ed J. March (Chicago: Rand McNally, 1965).

44 In particular, see H. Scarbrough and M. Corbett, *Technology and Organization: Power, Meaning and Design* (London: Routledge, 1992), p. 178; J. Fulk and G. DeSanctis, 'Electronic Communication and Changing Organizational Forms', *Organization Science*, July–August 1995, pp. 337–49; and H. Kolodny, M. Lin, B. Srymne and H. Denis, 'New Technology and the Emerging Organizational Paradigm', *Human Relations*, December 1996, pp. 1457–87.

45 S. Zuboff, *The Age of the Smart Machine* (New York: Basic Books, 1984).

46 G. Nairn, 'Vendors Are Gearing Up for Next Phase CRM', *Financial Times*, 3 March 2004.

47 K. Cameron, 'Critical Questions in Assessing Organizational Effectiveness', *Organizational Dynamics*, Autumn 1980, p. 70. Also see J. Pfeffer, 'When It Comes to "Best Practices" – Why Do Smart Organizations Occasionally Do Dumb Things?', *Organizational Dynamics*, Summer 1996, pp. 33–44; G. N. Powell, 'Reinforcing and Extending Today's Organizations: The Simultaneous Pursuit of Person–Organization Fit and Diversity', *Organizational Dynamics*, Winter 1998, pp. 50–61; R. C. Vergin and M. W. Qoronfleh, 'Corporate Reputation and the Stock Market', *Business Horizons*, January–February 1998, pp. 19–26; K. Gawande and T. Wheeler, 'Measures of Effectiveness for Governmental Organizations', *Management Science*, January 1999, pp. 42–58; and E. V. McIntyre, 'Accounting Choices and EVA', *Business Horizons*, January–February 1999, pp. 66–72.

48 See B. Wysocki Jr, 'Rethinking a Quaint Idea: Profits', *The Wall Street Journal*, 19 May 1999, pp. B1, B6; and J. Collins, 'Turning Goals into Results: The Power of Catalytic Mechanisms', *Harvard Business Review*, July–August 1999, pp. 71–82.

49 See, for example, R. O. Brinkerhoff and D. E. Dressler, *Productivity Measurement: A Guide for Managers and Evaluators* (Newbury Park, CA: Sage Publications, 1990); J. McCune, 'The Productivity Paradox', *Management Review*, March 1998, pp. 38–40; and R. J. Samuelson, 'Cheerleaders vs. The Grumps', *Newsweek*, 26 July 1999, p. 78.

50 See A. Reinhardt, 'Log On, Link Up, Save Big', *Business Week*, 22 June 1998, pp. 132–8; and R. W. Oliver, 'Happy 150th Birthday, Electronic Commerce!', *Management Review*, July–August 1999, pp. 12–13.

51 Data from M. Maynard, 'Toyota Promises Custom Order in 5 Days', *USA Today*, 6 August 1999, p. 1B.

52 Main articles on the resource-based view are E. Penrose, *The Theory of the Growth of The Firm* (Oxford: Blackwell Publishing, 1959); J. B. Barney, 'Organization Culture: Can It Be A Source of Sustained Competitive Advantages?', *Academy of Management Review*, no. 3, 1986, pp. 656–65; J. B. Barney, 'Firm Resources and Sustained Competitive Advantages', *Journal of Management*, no. 1, 1991, pp. 99–120; and J. T. Mahoney, 'A Resource-Based Theory of Sustainable Rents', *Journal of Management*, no. 6, 2001, pp. 651–60.

53 J. B. Barney, 'Firm Resources and Sustained Competitive Advantages', *Journal of Management*, no. 1, 1991, pp. 99–120.

54 R. Sanchez, A. Heene and H. Thomas, 'Introduction: Towards the Theory and Practice of Competence-Based Competition', in *Dynamics of Competence-Based Competition: Theory and Practice in the New Strategic Management*, eds R. Sanchez, A. Heene and H. Thomas (Oxford: Pergamon, 1996), p. 7.

55 Ibid., p. 8.

56 D. J. Teece, G. Pisano and A. Shuen, 'Dynamic Capabilities and Strategic Management', *Strategic Management Journal*, August 1997, pp. 509–33.

57 R. J. Schonberger, 'Total Quality Management Cuts a Broad Swath – Through Manufacturing and Beyond', *Organizational Dynamics*, Spring 1992, p. 18. Also see K. Y. Kim, J. G. Miller and J. Heineke, 'Mastering the Quality Staircase, Step by Step', *Business Horizons*, January–February 1997, pp. 17–21; R. Bell and B. Keys, 'A Conversation with Curt W. Reimann on the Background and Future of the Baldrige Award', *Organizational Dynamics*, Spring 1998, pp. 51–61; and B. Kasanoff, 'Are You Ready for Mass Customization?', *Training*, May 1998, pp. 70–78.

58 Mark Zbaracki, 'The Rhetoric and Reality of Total Quality Management', *Administrative Science Quarterly*, no. 43, pp. 602–36, 1998.

59 K. Cameron, 'Critical Questions in Assessing Organizational Effectiveness', *Organizational Dynamics*, Autumn 1980, p. 67. Also see W. Buxton, 'Growth from Top to Bottom', *Management Review*, July–August 1999, p. 11.

60 See R. K. Mitchell, B. R. Agle and D. J. Wood, 'Toward a Theory of Stakeholder Identification and Salience: Defining the Principle of Who and What Really Counts', *Academy of Management Review*, October 1997, pp. 853–96; W. Beaver, 'Is the

Stakeholder Model Dead?', *Business Horizons*, March–April 1999, pp. 8–12; J. Frooman, 'Stakeholder Influence Strategies', *Academy of Management Review*, April 1999, pp. 191–205; and T. M. Jones and A. C. Wicks, 'Convergent Stakeholder Theory', *Academy of Management Review*, April 1999, pp. 206–21.

61 See N. C. Roberts and P. J. King, 'The Stakeholder Audit Goes Public', *Organizational Dynamics*, Winter 1989, pp. 63–79; and I. Henriques and P. Sadorsky, 'The Relationship between Environmental Commitment and Managerial Perceptions of Stakeholder Importance', *Academy of Management Journal*, February 1999, pp. 87–99.

62 E. M. Reingold, 'America's Hamburger Helper', *Time*, 29 June 1992, p. 66.

63 P. T. Bolwijn and T. Kumpe, 'The Success of Flexible, Low-Cost, Quality Competitors: A European Perspective', *European Management Journal*, no. 2, 1991, pp. 135–45; and P. T. Bolwijn and T. Kumpe, 'Manufacturing in the 1990s – Productivity, Flexibility and Innovation', *Long Range Planning*, August 1990, pp. 44–58.

64 See C. Ostroff and N. Schmitt, 'Configurations of Organizational Effectiveness and Efficiency', *Academy of Management Journal*, December 1993, pp. 1345–61.

65 K. S. Cameron, 'Effectiveness as Paradox: Consensus and Conflict in Conceptions of Organizational Effectiveness', *Management Science*, May 1986, p. 542.

66 Alternative effectiveness criteria are discussed in M. Keeley, 'Impartiality and Participant-Interest Theories of Organizational Effectiveness', *Administrative Science Quarterly*, March 1984, pp. 1–25; K. S. Cameron, 'Effectiveness as Paradox: Consensus and Conflict in Conceptions of Organizational Effectiveness', *Management Science*, May 1986, p. 542; and A. G. Bedeian, 'Organization Theory: Current Controversies, Issues, and Directions', in *International Review of Industrial and Organizational Psychology*, eds C. L. Cooper and I. T. Robertson (New York: John Wiley, 1987), pp. 1–33.

67 M. A. Mone, W. McKinley and V. L. Barker III, 'Organizational Decline and Innovation: A Contingency Framework', *Academy of Management Review*, January 1998, p. 117.

68 P. Lorange and R. T. Nelson, 'How to Recognize – and Avoid – Organizational Decline', *Sloan Management Review*, Spring 1987, p. 47.

69 Excerpted from P. Lorange and R. T. Nelson, 'How to Recognize – and Avoid – Organizational Decline', *Sloan Management Review*, Spring 1987, pp. 43–5. Also see E. E. Lawler III and J. R. Galbraith, 'Avoiding the Corporate Dinosaur Syndrome', *Organizational Dynamics*, Autumn 1994, pp. 5–17; and K. Labich, 'Why Companies Fail', *Fortune*, 14 November 1994, pp. 52–68.

70 For details, see K. S. Cameron, M. U. Kim and D. A. Whetten, 'Organizational Effects of Decline and Turbulence', *Administrative Science Quarterly*, June 1987, pp. 222–40. Also see A. G. Bedeian and A. A. Armenakis, 'The Cesspool Syndrome: How Dreck Floats to the Top of Declining Organizations', *Academy of Management Executive*, February 1998, pp. 58–63.

71 A. Goodall A. J. Oswald, and L. Kahn, 'Why Do Leaders Matter? The Role of Expert Knowledge', June 2008, www2.warwick.ac.uk/fac/soc/economics/staff/academic/oswald/leaderjune08.pdf.

72 This approach is described in detail in M. Hanan and J. Freeman, *Organizational Ecology* (Cambridge, MA: Harvard University Press, 1989); see also G. C. Carroll and M. T. Hannan, *The Demography of Corporations and Industries* (Princeton, NJ: Princeton University Press, 2000). The notion of carrying capacity is introduced in A. Lomi, E. Larsen and J. Freeman J, 'Things Change: Dynamic Resource Constraints and System-Dependent Selection in the Evolution of Organizational Populations', *Management Science*, 2005, 51(6), pp. 882–904.

73 For related reading, see C. R. Eitel, 'The Ten Disciplines of Business Turnaround', *Management Review*, December 1998, p. 13; J. R. Morris, W. F. Cascio and C. E. Young, 'Downsizing After All These Years: Questions and Answers about Who Did It, How Many Did It, and Who Benefited from It', *Organizational Dynamics*, Winter 1999, pp. 78–87; and S. Kuczynski, 'Help! I Shrunk the Company!', *HR Magazine*, June 1999, pp. 40–45.

74 A culture of 'entitlement' also hastens organisational decline. See J. M. Bardwick, *Danger in the Comfort Zone: From Boardroom to Mailroom – How to Break the Entitlement Habit That's Killing American Business* (New York: AMACOM, 1991). Also see D. W. Organ, 'Argue with Success', *Business Horizons*, November–December 1995, pp. 1–2; and J. P. Kotter, 'Kill Complacency', *Fortune*, 5 August 1996, pp. 168–70.

Chapter 12

Organisational and international culture

Learning Outcomes

When you finish studying the material in this chapter, you should be able to:

- ✓ discuss the difference between espoused and enacted values
- ✓ explain the typology of organisational values
- ✓ describe the manifestations of an organisation's culture and the four functions of organisational culture
- ✓ discuss the four general types of organisational culture
- ✓ summarise the methods used by organisations to embed their cultures
- ✓ describe the practical lessons from the Hofstede–Bond stream of research
- ✓ discuss the importance of cross-cultural training relative to the foreign assignment cycle

Opening Case Study: Seoul machine

This is the stuff corporate storytelling is made of. Even today people at Samsung still talk about the 'voluntary incineration' at one of Samsung's biggest plants at Gumi. At that time, Samsung was firmly placed at the low end of the electronics market, but its leader, Kun-hee Lee, had started a process of strategic growth through high-end products and market-leading quality.

However, when Lee sent out the new Samsung phones as a new year's gift in 1995, he was appalled to learn that many of them didn't work, and Lee decided to take drastic action by paying a visit to the Samsung plant in Gumi where the phones were made.

Lee ordered the 2000 employees at the factory to assemble outside on the factory grounds, wearing quality-first headbands. There, $50-million worth of equipment (cellphones and fax machines, mainly) was piled in a big heap under a banner stating: 'quality is my pride'. All the equipment was smashed and thrown on a bonfire until it was all incinerated. Rumour has it that several employees wept.

Ritual purification before a strong leader is a centuries-old tradition in most of Asia, and by tapping into this tradition, Lee sent a very strong signal. From this point on, low quality was not an option at this plant or in the rest of Samsung. Even today, top managers at Samsung are known to personally test new equipment by throwing it out of windows to test their durability.

The bonfire at the Gumi plant was but one example of Lee's dramatic and symbol-laden leadership. During the past few decades, he has often done the opposite of what experts and industry specialists have advised him to do. By investing heavily in plants that can produce newer and market-leading high-end electronics, Lee has consistently put quality first and led Samsung to become one of the greatest electronics companies in the world.

For discussion

Is it necessary to be dramatic (as in the case of the bonfire) in order to create such critical changes in a company's culture?

Sources: Based on: Rose, F. (2005), Seoul machine, *Wired*, Issue 13.05.

Much has been written and said about organisational culture, values and ethics in recent years. As long as people are not confronted with other cultures, they take their own world for granted and simply do not realise that a different culture might be valuable. Cultural differences between countries have shown us the way to other cultural differences: cultural differences between professionals, between men and women, between industrial sectors, and so on. In this chapter, we will focus on two important differences: differences in organisational cultures and differences between countries and regions, as reflected in the so-called 'intercultural differences'. We will discuss culture and organisational behaviour, differences in organisational culture, socialisation and intercultural differences.

12.1 Culture and organisational behaviour

Around the year 2000, the academic study of the concept had reached a stalemate. Organisational culture seemed to be overcharged: it was the concept explaining the link between the workplace and outcomes, such as satisfaction, commitment and productivity.[1] In many cases, the success of a so-called 'cultural change' is a direct result of reducing autonomy, close monitoring and threat of sanctions.[2] Many academics looked at culture as a pure management fad. At exactly the same moment, the numerous and highly visible corporate scandals were explained by 'the tone at the top', the corporate culture. There was an outcry for 'cultures of responsibilities'. The results of some 25 years of researching corporate culture can be arranged on a continuum of academic rigour. At one end of the continuum are simplistic typologies and exaggerated claims about the benefits of imitating successful corporate cultures and values. At the other end of the continuum is a growing body of theory and research with valuable insights, but one plagued by definitional and measurement inconsistencies.[3]

Culture is complex and multilayered

While noting that cultures exist in social units of all sizes (from civilisations through to countries to ethnic groups, organisations and work groups), Edgar Schein defined **culture** as a pattern of basic assumptions – invented, discovered or developed by a given group as it learns to cope with its problems of external adaptation and internal integration – that has worked well enough to be considered valid and, therefore, to be taught to new members as the correct way to perceive, think and feel in relation to those problems.[4]

The word 'taught' needs to be interpreted carefully because it implies formal education or training. While cultural lessons may indeed be taught in schools, religious settings and in the workplace, formal training is secondary. Most cultural lessons are learned by observing and imitating role models as they go about their daily affairs, or from those observed in the media.

Culture is difficult to grasp because it is multilayered. International experts, Fons Trompenaars (from The Netherlands) and Charles Hampden-Turner (from Britain), offer the following instructive analogy in their landmark book, *Riding the Waves of Culture* (see Figure 12.1):

> Culture comes in layers, like an onion. To understand it, you have to unpeel it layer by layer. On the outer layer are the products of culture, like the soaring skyscrapers of Manhattan, pillars of private power, with congested public streets between them. These are expressions

Figure 12.1 A Model of Culture

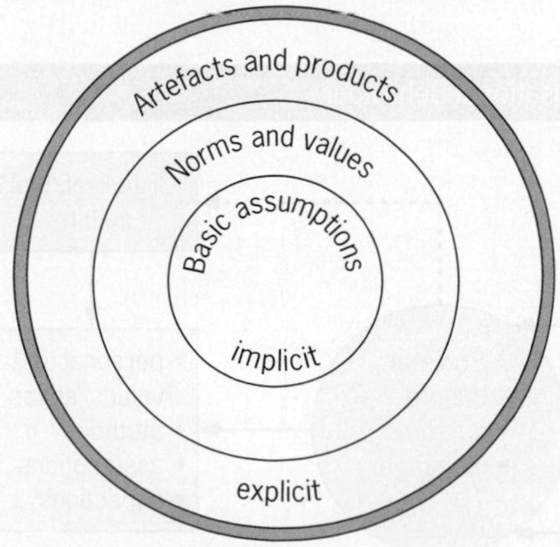

Source: F. Trompenaars, *Riding the Waves of Culture* (London: Nicholas Brealey Publishing, 1994), p. 23.

of deeper values and norms in a society that are not directly visible (values such as upward mobility, 'the more-the-better', status, material success). The layers of values and norms are deeper within the 'onion', and are more difficult to identify.[5]

Culture is a subtle but pervasive force

Culture generally remains below the threshold of conscious awareness because it involves taken-for-granted assumptions about how one should perceive, think, act and feel. Cultural anthropologist Edward T. Hall put it the following way:

> Since much of culture operates outside our awareness, frequently we don't even know what we know. We pick [expectations and assumptions] up in the cradle. We unconsciously learn what to notice and what not to notice, how to divide time and space, how to walk and talk and use our bodies, how to behave as men or women, how to relate to other people, how to handle responsibility, whether experience is seen as whole or fragmented. This applies to all people. The Chinese, Japanese or Arabs are each as unaware of their assumptions as we are of our own. We each assume that they're part of human nature. What we think of as 'mind' is really internalised culture.[6]

A model of societal and organisational cultures

As illustrated in Figure 12.2, culture influences organisational behaviour in two ways. Employees bring their societal culture to work with them in the form of customs and language. Organisational culture, a by-product of societal culture, in turn, affects the individual's values and ethics, attitudes, assumptions and expectations.[7]

The term 'societal culture' is used here instead of national culture because the boundaries of many modern nation states were not drawn along cultural lines. Once inside the organisation's sphere of influence, the individual is further affected by the organisation's culture, which will be explained in the next section. Mixing of societal and organisational cultures can produce interesting dynamics in multinational companies.

For example, with French and American employees working side by side at General Electric's medical imaging production facility in Wisconsin, the French workers witnessed some culture shock, when they found to their surprise that the American parking lots empty out as early as 5 p.m.; the

Figure 12.2 Cultural Influences on Organisational Behaviour

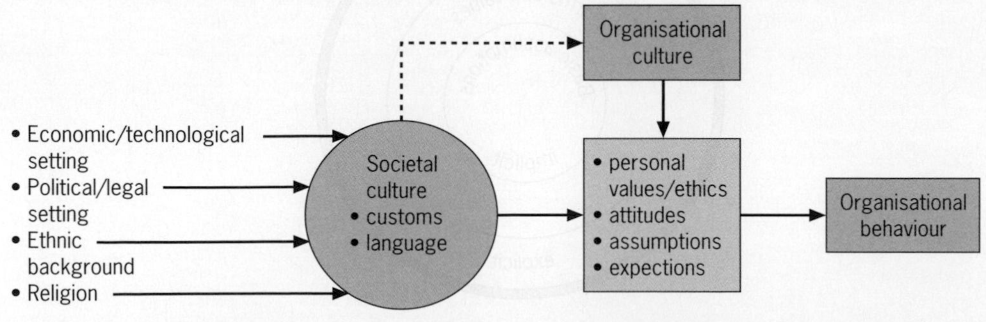

Source: Adapted in part from B. J. Punnett and S. Withane, 'Hofstede's Value Survey Module: To Embrace or Abandon?', in *Advances in International Comparative Management*, vol. 5, ed. S. B. Prasad (Greenwich, CT: JAI Press, 1990), pp. 69–89.

Americans were surprised the French do not start work at 8 a.m. The French are more talkative and candid whereas the Americans have more of a sense of hierarchy and are less likely to criticise.[8] Same company, same company culture, yet GE's French and American co-workers have different attitudes about time, hierarchy and communication. They are the products of different societal cultures.[9]

Influencing people's cultural backgrounds is very difficult as is confirmed by research results from 15 countries. The studies showed that the unique traditions of each country have been maintained in their institutions like families, schools and forms of government and they are also conserved in differences in national cultures in the sense of 'software for the mind': patterns of thinking, feeling and acting that differentiate one country from another and continue to be transferred from generation to generation.[10] Organisational culture will be discussed next. The influence of societal culture will be elaborated on in the section of intercultural differences at the end of this chapter.

12.2 Organisational culture

Organisational culture is 'the set of shared, taken-for-granted implicit assumptions that a group holds and that determines how it perceives, thinks about and reacts to its various environments'.[11] This definition highlights three important characteristics of organisational culture. First, organisational culture is passed on to new employees through the process of socialisation, a topic discussed later in this chapter. Second, organisational culture influences our behaviour at work. Finally, organisational culture operates at two different levels. Each level varies in terms of outward visibility and resistance to change.

At the more visible level, culture represents artefacts. Artefacts consist of the physical manifestation of an organisation's culture. Organisational examples include acronyms, manner of dress, awards, titles, myths and stories told about the organisation, published lists of values, observable rituals and ceremonies, special parking spaces, decorations and so on. This level also includes visible behaviours exhibited by people and groups.

OB in Real Life

Dress codes at Apple

Steve Jobs, founder and chief executive officer (CEO) of Apple, was one of the first of the new generation of managers after the political and cultural upheavals of the late 1960s. After a (spiritual) trip to the Far East, he founded Apple, and from the beginning, the dress code was very relaxed, which at that time was very unusual for a computer company.

Until his death in 2011, when Steve Jobs took the stage at the yearly MacWorld events to present new generations of iPhones, iPads or iMacs, his uniform was completely predictable: Levi 501s *sans* belt, a black mock turtleneck and a pair of trainers.

Other workplaces around the world have eased their strict dress codes to allow for more casual business wear – sometimes coinciding with the need to allow for dress practices from a more diverse workforce.

For discussion

How big a part of an organisational culture is business wear – particularly when worn by the CEO?

Source: Based on Greg Beato, 'Dressed for success in an evolving workplace', *Newsday*, 5 March 2010, pA31.

Artefacts are easier to change than the less visible aspects of organisational culture. At the less visible level, culture reflects the values and beliefs shared by organisational members. These values tend to persist over time and are more resistant to change. Each level of culture influences the other. For example, if a company truly values providing high-quality service, employees are more likely to adopt the behaviour of responding faster to customer complaints. Similarly, causality can flow in the other direction. Employees can come to value high-quality service based on their experiences with customers.

To gain a better understanding of how organisational culture is formed and used by employees, this section begins by discussing organisational values – the foundation of organisational culture. It then reviews the manifestations of organisational culture, a model for interpreting organisational culture, the four functions of organisational culture and research on the subject.

Organisational values

Organisational values and beliefs constitute the foundation of an organisation's culture and also play a key role in influencing ethical behaviour. Whereas the values presented in Chapter 3 were individual, the values described in this chapter are the collective values which:

1. Are concepts or beliefs.
2. Pertain to desirable results or behaviours.
3. Transcend situations.
4. Guide selection or evaluation of behaviour and events.
5. Are ordered by relative importance.[12]

It is important to distinguish between values that are espoused versus those that are enacted.[13]

Espoused values represent the explicitly stated values and norms that are preferred by an organisation. Often, they are referred to as 'corporate glue'. They are generally established by the founder of a new or small company or by the top management team in a larger organisation.

Enacted values, on the other hand, represent the values and norms that are actually exhibited or converted into employee behaviour. Let us consider the difference between these two types of value. A company might embrace the value of integrity. If employees display integrity by following through on their commitments, then, the espoused value is enacted and individual behaviour is influenced by the value of integrity. In contrast, if employees do not follow through on their commitments, then, the value of integrity is simply a 'stated' aspiration that does not influence behaviour. Gareth Jones, a professor of organisation development at Britain's Henley Management College, warns that many companies exert lots of efforts to make their values in all kinds of ways explicit, but very often, they remain a dead letter. What happens most often is that the company sends executives to a number of workshops and seminars to specify the right values; top management tries to sell those values to the rest of the organisation at a kick-off event. And very often, that is as far as it goes. Managers may pay lots of lip service to new values, without ever really practising them or demonstrating how they can benefit the organisation.

When is an organisation's culture most apparent? In addition to the physical artefacts of organisational culture that were previously discussed, cultural assumptions assert themselves through socialisation of new employees, subculture clashes and top management behaviour. Consider these three situations, for example:

- A newcomer who shows up late for an important meeting is told a story about someone who was fired for repeated tardiness.

- Conflict between product design engineers who emphasise a product's function and marketing specialists who demand a more stylish product reveals an underlying clash of subculture values.
- Top managers, through the behaviour they model and the administrative and reward systems they create, prompt a significant improvement in the quality of a company's products.

The gap between espoused and enacted values is important because it can significantly influence an organisation's culture and employee attitudes. A study of 312 British Rail train drivers, supervisors and senior managers revealed that the creation of a safety culture was negatively affected by large gaps between senior management's espoused and enacted values. Employees were more cynical about safety when they believed that senior managers' behaviours were inconsistent with the stated values regarding safety.[14]

It is also important to consider how an organisation's value system influences organisational culture, because companies subscribe to multiple values. An organisation's value system reflects the patterns of conflict and compatibility between values, not the relative importance of each. This definition highlights the point that organisations endorse a constellation of values that contain both conflicting and compatible values. For example, management scholars believe that organisations have two fundamental value systems that naturally conflict with each other. One system relates to the manner in which tasks are accomplished; the other includes values related to maintaining internal cohesion and solidarity. The central issue underlying this value conflict revolves around identifying the main goal being pursued by an organisation. Is the organisation predominantly interested in financial performance, relationships or a combination of the two?[15] To help you understand how organisational values influence organisational culture, we present a typology of organisational values and review some relevant research.

A typology of organisational values

Figure 12.3 presents a typology of organisational values that is based on crossing organisational reward norms and organisation power structures.[16] Organisational reward norms reflect a company's fundamental belief about how rewards should be allocated (see Chapter 6). According to the equitable reward norm, they should be proportionate to contributions. In contrast, an egalitarian-oriented value system calls for rewarding all employees equally, regardless of their comparative contributions. Organisation power structures reflect a company's basic belief about how power and authority should be shared and distributed (see Chapter 14). These beliefs range from the extreme of being completely unequal or centralised to equal or completely decentralised.

Figure 12.3 identifies four types of value systems: elite, meritocratic, leadership and collegial. Each type of value system contains a positive and a negative set of responses to values: some values are reinforced or endorsed by the system while others are seen as inconsistent or discouraged. For example, an elite value system endorses values related to acceptance of authority, high performance and equitable rewards. This value system, however, does not encourage values related to teamwork, participation, commitment or affiliation. In contrast, a collegial value system supports values associated with teamwork, participation, commitment and affiliation while discouraging values of authority, high performance and equitable rewards.

Evidence about organisational values

Organisations subscribe to a constellation of values rather than to simply one and can be profiled according to their values.[17] This, in turn, enables professionals to determine whether an organisation's

Figure 12.3 A Typology of Organisational Values

Organisational reward norms	Organisation power structure: Unequal or centralised power		Organisation power structure: Equal or decentralised power	
Equitable	**Elite**		**Meritocratic**	
	Endorsed values	Discouraged values	Endorsed values	Discouraged values
	Authority Performance rewards	Teamwork Participation Commitment Affiliation	Performance rewards Teamwork Participation Commitment Affiliation	Authority
Egalitarian	**Leadership**		**Collegial**	
	Endorsed values	Discouraged values	Endorsed values	Discouraged values
	Authority Performance rewards Teamwork Commitment Affiliation	Participation	Teamwork Participation Commitment Affiliation	Authority Performance rewards

Source: Adapted from B. Kabanoff and J. Holt, 'Changes in the Espoused Values of Australian Organizations 1986–1990', *Journal of Organizational Behavior*, May 1996, pp. 201–19.

values are consistent and supportive of its corporate goals and initiatives. Organisational change is unlikely to succeed if it is based on a set of values that is highly inconsistent with employees' individual values. Finally, a longitudinal study of 85 Australian organisations revealed four interesting trends about the typology of organisational values, presented in Figure 12.3.

Organisational values were quite stable over four years. This result supports the contention that values are relatively stable and resistant to change.

There was not a universal movement to one type of value system. The 85 organisations represented all four value systems. This finding reinforces the earlier conclusion that there is no 'one best' organisational culture or value system.

Organisations with elite value systems experienced the greatest amount of change over the four-year period. Elite organisations tended to become more collegial.

There was an overall increase in the number of organisations that endorsed the individual value of employee commitment. This trend is consistent with the notion that organisational success is partly dependent on the extent to which employees are committed to their organisations (see Chapter 3).

A model for interpreting organisational culture

A useful model for observing and interpreting organisational culture was developed by Vijay Sathe, a Harvard University researcher (see Figure 12.4). The four general manifestations or evidence of organisational culture in his model are shared things (objects), shared sayings (talk), shared doings (behaviour) and shared feelings (emotion). One can begin collecting cultural information within the organisation by asking, observing, reading and feeling.

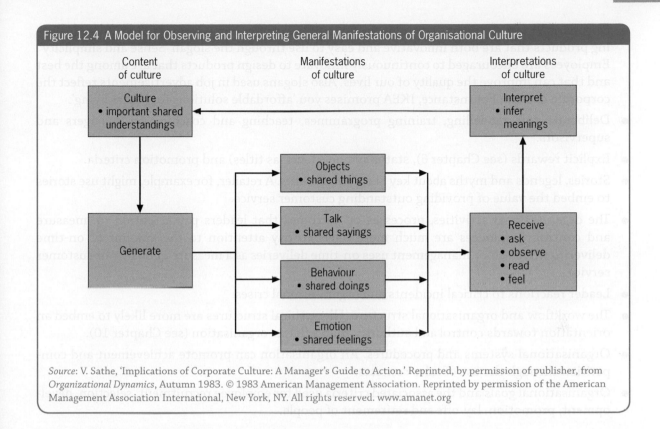

Figure 12.4 A Model for Observing and Interpreting General Manifestations of Organisational Culture

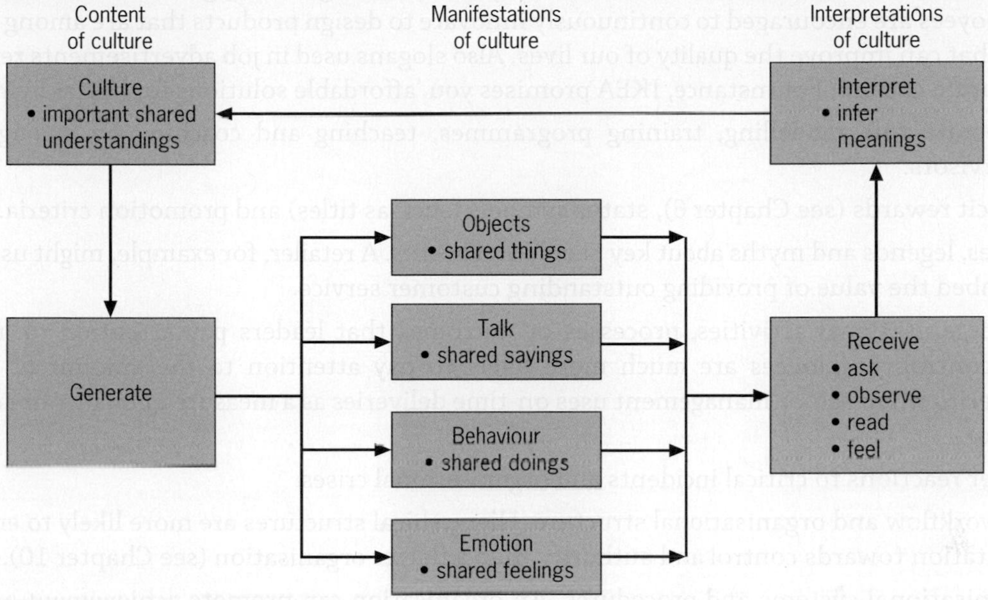

Source: V. Sathe, 'Implications of Corporate Culture: A Manager's Guide to Action.' Reprinted, by permission of publisher, from *Organizational Dynamics*, Autumn 1983. © 1983 American Management Association. Reprinted by permission of the American Management Association International, New York, NY. All rights reserved. www.amanet.org

How cultures are embedded in organisations

An organisation's initial culture is often an outgrowth of the founder's philosophy. For example, an achievement culture is likely to develop if the founder is an achievement-oriented individual driven by success. Over time, the original culture is either embedded or modified to fit the current environmental situation. Edgar Schein notes that embedding a culture involves a teaching process: that is, organisational members teach each other about the organisation's preferred values, beliefs, expectations and behaviours. This is accomplished by using one or more of the following mechanisms:[18]

- Formal statements of organisational philosophy, mission, vision, values and materials used for recruiting, selection and socialisation. Philips, for example, published a list of four corporate values, listed together with some practical ideas on how to put them into everyday practice. The values are: delight customers, deliver great results, develop people and depend on each other.[19]
- The design of physical space, work environments and buildings. Consider the use of a new alternative workplace design called 'hotelling'. As in other shared-office options, 'hotel' work spaces are furnished, equipped and supported with typical office services. Employees may have mobile cubbies, file cabinets or lockers for personal storage; and a computer system routes phone calls and emails as necessary. But 'hotel' work spaces are reserved by the hour, by the day or by the week instead of being permanently assigned. In addition, a 'concierge' may provide employees with travel and logistic support. At its most advanced, 'hotel' work space is customised with the individuals' personal photos and memorabilia, which are stored electronically, retrieved and 'placed' on the occupants' desktops just before they arrive and then removed as soon as they leave.[20]

- Slogans, language, acronyms and sayings. Philips, for example, emphasises its concern for delivering products that are both innovative and easy to use through the slogan 'Sense and simplicity'. Employees are encouraged to continuously innovate to design products that are among the best and that can improve the quality of our lives. Also slogans used in job advertisements reflect the corporate culture. For instance, IKEA promises you 'affordable solutions for better living'.
- Deliberate role modelling, training programmes, teaching and coaching by managers and supervisors.
- Explicit rewards (see Chapter 6), status symbols (such as titles) and promotion criteria.
- Stories, legends and myths about key people and events. A retailer, for example, might use stories to embed the value of providing outstanding customer service.
- The organisational activities, processes or outcomes that leaders pay attention to, measure and control. Employees are much more likely to pay attention to the amount of on-time deliveries when senior management uses on-time deliveries as a measure of quality or customer service.
- Leader reactions to critical incidents and organisational crises.
- The workflow and organisational structure. Hierarchical structures are more likely to embed an orientation towards control and authority than a flatter organisation (see Chapter 10).
- Organisational systems and procedures. An organisation can promote achievement and competition through the use of sales contests.
- Organisational goals and the associated criteria used for employee recruitment, selection, development, promotion, lay-offs and retirement of people.

Types of organisational culture

Researchers have attempted to identify and measure various types of organisational culture in order to study the relationship between types of culture and organisational effectiveness. This pursuit was motivated by the possibility that certain cultures were more effective than others. Unfortunately, research has not uncovered a universal typology of cultural styles that everyone accepts.[21] Just the same, there is value in providing an example of various types of organisational culture. Figure 12.5 represents such an example, based on the competing values framework.

The model is based on two basic dimensions. One contrasts flexibility, change, discretion and freedom with stability, control and direction. The second dimension contrasts internal focus, internal orientation, integration, co-ordination with external focus, external orientation and differentiation. The combination of those two basic dimensions leads to the four quadrants in Figure 12.5. Each quadrant represents a 'pure' or 'generic' type of organisational culture.

In an organisation characterised by an adaptability culture, the organisation constantly redefines itself. The organisation shows a high capacity to change its work methods, objectives and reward systems in response to changing external conditions. Creativity and innovation are highly valued. The organisation rapidly reacts to new needs. It is quick to capture and interpret signals from its environment.

When an organisation is characterised by an external control culture, its focus is on the market. In those organisations, market share, goal achievement and competition are highly valued. The organisation has formulated a clear mission combining economic and non-economic objectives. Those objectives motivate, inspire and direct all organisational members. 'Beating the competition' or 'realising our dream' is the inspiring common theme.

Figure 12.5 Organisational Culture as Competing Values

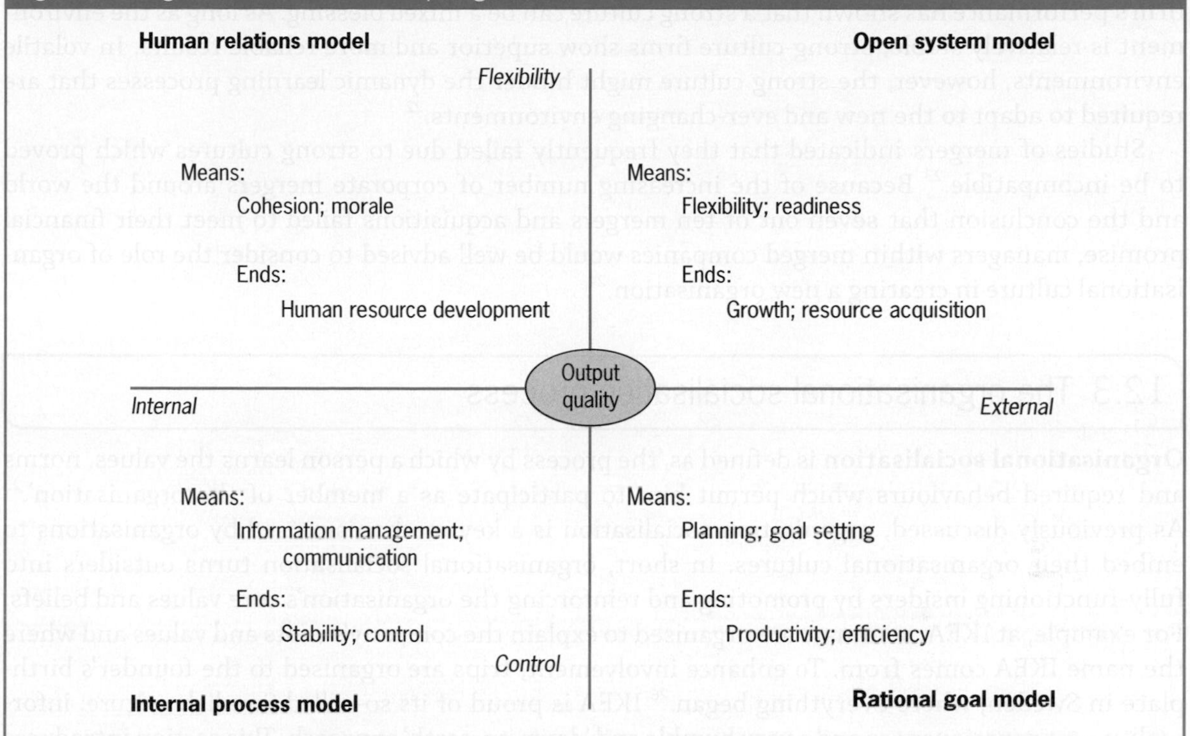

Source: Adapted from R. E. Quinn and J. Rohrbaugh, 'A Spatial Model Of Effectiveness Criteria: Towards A Competing Values Approach To Organizational Analysis', *Management Science*, 29(3), 1983, pp. 363–77.

In a development culture, the emphasis lies on involvement. There is a high sense of belonging and psychological ownership. Levels of morale are very high. Teamwork, mentorship, staff cohesion and participation are highly valued. In those organisations, most collaborators share the belief that the best minute is the minute they invest in other people.

In an internal consistency culture, the organisation is oriented towards efficiency and smooth functioning of the organisation. The ideal organisation is a 'machine organisation' (see Chapter 10) where everything is planned well ahead and is completely under control. Consistency, respect for hierarchy and rules are highly valued.

Although an organisation may predominately represent one cultural type, it can still manifest normative beliefs and characteristics from the others. Research demonstrates that organisations can have functional subcultures, hierarchical subcultures based on one's level in the organisation, geographical subcultures, occupational subcultures based on one's title or position, social subcultures derived from social activities like a tennis or a reading club.

Do strong corporate cultures improve performance?

An organisation's culture may be strong or weak, depending on variables, such as cohesiveness, value consensus and individual commitment to collective goals. Contrary to what one might suspect, a strong culture is not necessarily a good thing. The nature of the culture's central values is more important than its strength. For example, a strong but change-resistant culture may be worse, from the standpoint of profitability and competitiveness, than a weak but innovative culture.

Systematic research on the link between the strength of a corporate culture and the reliability of a firm's performance has shown that a strong culture can be a mixed blessing. As long as the environment is relatively stable, strong-culture firms show superior and more reliable results. In volatile environments, however, the strong culture might hinder the dynamic learning processes that are required to adapt to the new and ever-changing environments.[22]

Studies of mergers indicated that they frequently failed due to strong cultures which proved to be incompatible.[23] Because of the increasing number of corporate mergers around the world and the conclusion that seven out of ten mergers and acquisitions failed to meet their financial promise, managers within merged companies would be well advised to consider the role of organisational culture in creating a new organisation.[24]

12.3 The organisational socialisation process

Organisational socialisation is defined as 'the process by which a person learns the values, norms and required behaviours which permit him to participate as a member of the organisation'.[25] As previously discussed, organisation socialisation is a key mechanism used by organisations to embed their organisational cultures. In short, organisational socialisation turns outsiders into fully-functioning insiders by promoting and reinforcing the organisation's core values and beliefs. For example, at IKEA, seminars are organised to explain the company's roots and values and where the name IKEA comes from. To enhance involvement, trips are organised to the founder's birthplace in Sweden, where everything began.[26] IKEA is proud of its so-called Swedish culture: informality, cost consciousness and a very humble and 'down-to-earth' approach. This section introduces a three-phase model of organisational socialisation and examines the practical application of socialisation research.

A three-phase model of organisational socialisation

One's first year in a complex organisation can be confusing. There is a constant swirl of new faces, strange jargon, conflicting expectations and apparently unrelated events. Some organisations treat new members in a rather haphazard, sink-or-swim manner. More typically, though, the socialisation process is characterised by a sequence of identifiable steps.[27]

Organisational behaviour researcher, Daniel Feldman, has proposed a three-phase model of organisational socialisation that promotes deeper understanding of this important process. As illustrated in Figure 12.6, the three phases are:

- Anticipatory socialisation.
- Encounter.
- Change and acquisition.

Each phase has its associated perceptual and social processes. Feldman's model also specifies behavioural and affective outcomes that can be used to judge how well an individual has been socialised. The entire three-phase sequence may take from a few weeks to a year to complete, depending on individual differences and the complexity of the situation.

Phase 1: Anticipatory socialisation. Organisational socialisation begins before the individual actually joins the organisation. Anticipatory socialisation information comes from many sources. Widely circulated stories about IBM being the 'white shirt' company probably deter from applying those people who would prefer to work in jeans.

Figure 12.6 A Model of Organisational Socialisation

1. Phase: Anticipatory socialisation – learning that occurs prior to joining the organisation

1. Realism about the organisation: A full and accurate picture of what the goals and climate of the organisation are really like.
2. Realism about the job: A full and accurate picture of what the new duties will entail.
3. Congruence of skills and abilities: The appropriate skills and abilities to successfully complete task assignments.
4. Congruence of needs and values: Sharing the values of the new organisation and having personal needs that can be met by the organisation.

2. Phase: Encounter – seeing what the organisation is truly like

1. Management of outside-life conflicts: Progress in dealing with conflicts between personal life and work life (e.g., scheduling, demands on employees' family, amount of preoccupation with work.
2. Management of intergroup role conflicts: Progress in dealing with conflicts between the role demands of one's own group and the demands of other groups in the organisation.
3. Role definition: Clarification of one's own role within the immediate work group, deciding on job duties, priorities, and time allocation for tasks.
4. Initiation to the task: Learning new tasks at work.
5. Initiation to the group: Establishing new interpersonal relationships and learning group norms.

3. Phase: Change and acquisition – mastering the skills, new roles and adjustments to values and norms

1. Resolution of role demands: Agreeing implicitly or explicitly with the workgroup on what tasks to perform and on task priorities and time allocation; also, coming to some mutually acceptable role decisions both to deal with conflicts between personal life and work life and to deal with intergroup role conflicts at work.
2. Task mastery: Learning the tasks of the new job, and also gaining self-confidence and attaining consistently positive performance levels.
3. Adjustment to group norms and values: Coming to feel liked and trusted by peers, understanding the group's norms and values, and making a satisfactory adjustment to the group culture.

Source: Adapted from material in D. C. Feldman, 'The Multiple Socialization of Organization Members', *Academy of Management Review*, April 1981, pp. 309–18.

All this information – whether formal or informal, accurate or inaccurate – helps the individual anticipate organisational realities. Unrealistic expectations about the nature of the work, pay and promotions are often formulated during phase 1. Because employees with unrealistic expectations are more likely to quit their jobs in the future, organisations may want to use realistic job previews.

A **realistic job preview (RJP)** involves giving recruits a realistic idea of what lies ahead by presenting both positive and negative aspects of the job. RJPs may be verbal, in booklet form, audiovisual or hands-on. Research supports the practical benefits of using RJPs. A meta-analysis of 40 studies revealed that RJPs were related to higher performance and to lower attrition from the recruitment process. Results also demonstrated that RJPs lowered the initial expectations of job applicants and led to lower turnover among those who were hired.[28]

A modern trend used in many large organisations to seduce young, recently graduated people is to organise all kinds of flashy events. At these events, the company displays its mastery in its field, but at the same time, potential job applicants get a glimpse of the corporate culture.

Phase 2: Encounter. This second phase begins once the employment contract has been signed. Behavioural scientists warn that **reality shock**, a newcomer's feeling of surprise after experiencing unexpected situations or events, can occur during the encounter phase when the newcomer tries to make sense of unfamiliar territory.

Becoming a member of an organisation will upset the everyday order of even the most well-informed newcomer. Matters concerning such aspects as friendships, time, purpose, demeanour, competence and the expectations the person holds of the immediate and distant future are suddenly made problematic. The newcomer's most pressing task is to build a set of guidelines and interpretations to explain and make the myriad of activities observed in the organisation meaningful.[29]

During the encounter phase, the individual is challenged to resolve any conflicts between the job and outside interests. If the hours prove too long, for example, family duties may require the individual to quit and find a more suitable work schedule. Also, as indicated in Figure 12.6, role conflict stemming from competing demands of different groups needs to be confronted and resolved (also see Chapter 8).

Phase 3: Change and acquisition. Mastery of important tasks and resolution of role conflict signals the beginning of this final phase of the socialisation process. Those who do not make the transition to phase 3 leave voluntarily or involuntarily or become isolated from social networks within the organisation. Senior executives frequently play a direct role in the change and acquisition phase.

Evidence about organisational socialisation

Past research suggests five practical guidelines for managing organisational socialisation.[30]

Professionals should avoid a haphazard, sink-or-swim approach to organisational socialisation because formalised socialisation tactics positively influence new recruits. Formalised socialisation enhanced the manner in which newcomers adjusted to their jobs over a ten-month period and reduced role ambiguity, role conflict, stress symptoms and intentions to quit while simultaneously increasing job satisfaction and organisational commitment for a sample of 295 recently graduated students.[31]

The encounter phase of socialisation is particularly important. Studies of newly hired accountants demonstrated that the frequency and type of information obtained during their first six months of employment significantly affected their job performance, their role clarity, their understanding of the organisational culture and the extent to which they were socially integrated.[32] Managers play a key role during the encounter phase. A study of 205 new college graduates further revealed that their manager's task- and relationship-oriented input during the socialisation process significantly helped them adjust to their new jobs.[33] In summary, managers need to help new recruits become integrated in the organisational culture.

Support for stage models is mixed. Although there are different stages of socialisation, they are not identical in order, length or content for all people or jobs.[34] Organisations are advised to use a contingency approach towards organisational socialisation. In other words, different techniques are appropriate for different people at different times.

HR Practical implications of organisational socialisation

The organisation can benefit by training new employees to use proactive socialisation behaviours. A study of 154 entry-level professionals showed that effectively using proactive socialisation behaviours influenced the newcomers' general anxiety and stress during the first month of employment and their motivation and anxiety six months later.[35]

Organisations should pay attention to the socialisation of diverse employees. Research demonstrated that diverse employees, particularly those with disabilities, experienced more different socialisation activities than other newcomers. In turn, these different experiences affected their long-term success and job satisfaction.[36]

! Critical thinking

Do you perceive any ethical issues in the organisational socialisation process that companies need to take into account?

12.4 Intercultural differences

As mentioned at the beginning of this chapter, the globalising world obliges us to take into account differences between countries and regions, in addition to differences in organisational cultures. It is becoming more frequently recognised that mergers or acquisitions that go beyond national borders multiply the chance of failure. Researchers Fons Trompenaars and Peter Woolliams state in an article on managing change across cultures that: 'it is striking how the Anglo-Saxon model of change has dominated the world of change management. It is based too often on a task-oriented culture and the idea that traditions need to be forgotten as soon as possible.'[37]

One cannot afford to overlook relevant cultural contexts when trying to understand organisational behaviour. In this section, we will look into the following intercultural aspects the future professional will undoubtedly need in this globalising world: ethnocentrism, high- and low-context societal culture, the Hofstede–Bond studies, Trompenaars' insights, time, interpersonal space and foreign assignments.

Ethnocentrism, the belief that one's native country, culture, language and modes of behaviour are superior to all others, has its roots in the dawn of civilisation. First identified as a behavioural science concept in 1906, involving the tendency of groups to reject outsiders,[38] the term 'ethnocentrism' generally has a more encompassing (national or societal) meaning today.

Also, many of today's top leaders are becoming increasingly careful with their international contacts in order to avoid ethnocentrism. Ethnocentrism can be effectively dealt with through education, greater cross-cultural awareness, a conscious effort to value cultural diversity and, of course, international experience. 'You go to America or Asia and you simply learn a whole lot of things you would only read about if you stayed here', says Alison Clarke, head of an Asian division of Shandwick, a British public relations group. 'We like to think that we're the centre of the universe in Britain, but we're not. I find a lot of my colleagues here are way behind in their thinking. The trouble is that they don't realise it.'[39]

Cultural anthropologists believe interesting and valuable lessons can be learned by comparing one culture with another. Many models have been proposed for distinguishing between the world's rich variety of cultures. One general distinction contrasts high- and low-context cultures (see Figure 12.7 and Table 12.1).[40] Professionals in multicultural settings need to know the difference if they are to communicate and interact effectively.

Figure 12.7 Contrasting High- and Low-Context Cultures

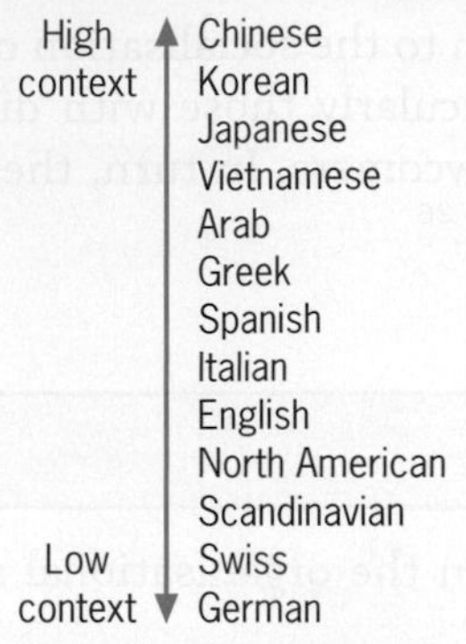

Table 12.1 Characteristics of High- and Low-Context Cultures

High-context culture	Low-context culture
Establish social trust first	Get down to business first
Value personal relations and goodwill	Value expertise and performance
Agreement by general trust	Agreement by specific, legalistic contract
Negotiations slow and ritualistic	Negotiations as efficient as possible

Reading between the lines in high-context cultures

People from **high-context cultures** rely heavily on situational cues for meaning, when perceiving and communicating with another person. Non-verbal cues, such as one's official position or status, conveys messages more powerfully than spoken words. Thus, we come to understand better the ritual of exchanging and reading business cards in Japan. Japanese culture is relatively high-context. One's business card, listing employer and official position, conveys vital silent messages to members of Japan's homogeneous society. An intercultural communications authority explains:

> Nearly all communication in Japan takes place within an elaborate and vertically organised social structure. Everyone has a distinct place within this framework. Rarely do people converse without knowing, or determining, who is above and who is below them. Associates are always older or younger, male or female, subordinate or superior. And these distinctions all carry implications for the form of address, choice of words, physical distance and demeanour. As a result, conversation tends to reflect this formal hierarchy.[41]

Verbal and written communication in high-context cultures, such as China, Korea and Japan, is secondary to taken-for-granted cultural assumptions about other people. In Eastern Europe, business practices are more formal, decision-making is more hierarchical and lengthy, and titles and honorifics are important.

Reading the fine print in low-context cultures

In **low-context cultures**, written and spoken words carry a lot of shared meaning. True, people in low-context cultures read non-verbal messages from body language, dress, status and belongings.

However, they tend to double-check their perceptions and assumptions verbally. To do so in China or Japan would be to gravely insult the other person, thus causing them to 'lose face'.[42] Their positions in Figure 12.7 indicate the German preoccupation with written rules for even the finest details of behaviour and the North American preoccupation with precise legal documents.[43] In high-context cultures, agreements tend to be made on the basis of someone's word or a handshake, after a rather prolonged trust-building period. European-Americans, who have been taught from birth not to take anything for granted, see the handshake as a prelude to demanding a signature on a detailed, lawyer-approved, iron-clad contract.

For example, this distinction between high- and low-context cultures also provides insight into the mechanisms that make negotiations between Western and Asian people so difficult and for us Europeans, often unnecessarily long-winded and boring. The Western negotiator will try to seek a rather fast agreement on the basis of an impersonal set of promises written down in a contract, whereas the Asian party would prefer to explore more fully the nature of the relationship, being distrustful of legalistic approaches to complex problems, before agreeing to commit time and resources to the venture. The Asian will rely more on the trust that grows over time, so that mutual confidence can also grow.[44] A good indicator as to whether a country is high or low context is to check how their meetings are held:[45]

- France: detailed agenda, briefing and co-ordination, interaction between the members through the boss, 15 minutes delay is acceptable.
- Germany: very formal, agenda and minutes, co-ordination and briefing, communication through a senior person, it is very important to be punctual.
- Italy: unstructured and informal, people may come and people may go, difficult to impose an agenda, free for all opinions, delay is accepted.
- The Netherlands: informality of manner but, nevertheless, keep to the basic protocols of keeping an agenda, speaking through the chairman.
- Spain: no meetings culture, only to communicate instructions, delay is endemic.
- UK: most important and time-consuming tool, very serious, unpunctuality is the rule!

Aside from being high- or low-context, cultures stand apart in other ways as well. In the following sections, we will discuss the Hofstede–Bond stream of research, and Trompenaars' forms of relating to other people, time, interpersonal space and communication.

12.5 Hofstede's cultural dimensions

Instructive insights surfaced in the mid-1980s when the results of two very different cross-cultural management studies were merged. The first study was conducted under the guidance of Dutch researcher, Geert Hofstede. The tremendous impact his research had on contemporary cultural thinking is reflected by the fact that Hofstede is one of the world's most cited living author in the entire area of the social sciences. Canadian Michael Harris Bond, at the Chinese University of Hong Kong, was a key researcher in the second study. What follows is a brief overview of each study, a discussion of the combined results and a summary of important practical implications.

Hofstede's study is a classic in the annals of cross-cultural management research.[46] He drew his data for the study from a collection of 116 000 attitude surveys administered to IBM employees worldwide between 1967 and 1973. Respondents to the attitude survey, which also asked questions on cultural values and beliefs, included IBM employees from 72 countries. Fifty-three cultures were

Table 12.2 Key Cultural Dimensions according to Hofstede

Power distance	How much do people expect inequality in social institutions (e.g. family, work organisations, government)?
Individualism–collectivism	How loose or tight is the bond between individuals and societal groups?
Masculinity–femininity	To what extent do people embrace competitive masculine traits (e.g. success, assertiveness and performance) or nurturing feminine traits (e.g. solidarity, personal relationships, service, quality of life)?
Uncertainty avoidance	To what extent do people prefer structured versus unstructured situations?
Long-term versus short-term orientation (Confucian values)	To what extent are people oriented towards the future by saving and being persistent versus being oriented towards the present and past by respecting tradition and meeting social obligations?

Source: Adapted from discussion in G. Hofstede, 'Cultural Constraints in Management Theories', *Academy of Management Executive*, February 1993, pp. 81–94.

eventually analysed and contrasted according to four cultural dimensions. Hofstede's database was unique, not only because of its large size, but also because it allowed him to isolate cultural effects. If his subjects had not performed similar jobs in different countries for the same company, no such control would have been possible. Cross-cultural comparisons were made along the first four dimensions listed in Table 12.2; power distance, individualism–collectivism, masculinity–femininity and uncertainty avoidance.

Bond's study was much smaller, involving a survey of 100 students (50 per cent women) from 22 countries and five continents. The survey instrument was the Chinese Value Survey (CVS), based on the Rokeach Value Survey (see Chapter 3).[47] The CVS also tapped four cultural dimensions. Three corresponded with Hofstede's first three in Table 12.2. Hofstede's fourth cultural dimension, uncertainty avoidance, was not measured by the CVS. Instead, Bond's study isolated the fifth cultural dimension in Table 12.2. It was eventually renamed 'long-term versus short-term orientation' to reflect how strongly a person believes in the long-term thinking promoted by the teachings of the Chinese philosopher Confucius (551–479 BC). According to an update by Hofstede:

> On the long-term side one finds values oriented towards the future, like thrift (saving) and persistence. On the short-term side one finds values rather more oriented towards the past and present, like respect for tradition and fulfilling social obligations.[48]

Interestingly, one may embrace Confucian long-term values without knowing a thing about Confucius.

East meets west

By merging the two studies, a serious flaw in each was corrected. Namely, Hofstede's study had an inherent Anglo-European bias and Bond's study had a built-in Asian bias. How would cultures compare if viewed through the overlapping lenses of the two studies? Hofstede and Bond were able to answer that question because 18 countries in Bond's study overlapped the 53 countries in Hofstede's sample.[49]

Individually and together, the Hofstede and Bond studies yielded the following useful lessons for international collaboration:

- Due to varying cultural values, theories and practices need to be adapted to the local culture. This is particularly true for made-in-America theories (such as Maslow's need hierarchy theory – see Chapter 5) and Japanese practices.[50] There is no 'one best way' to lead people across cultures.

- High long-term orientation was the only one of the five cultural dimensions to correlate positively with national economic growth.
- Industrious cultural values are a necessary but insufficient condition for economic growth. Markets and a supportive political climate are also required to create the right mix.[51]

Cultural arrogance is a luxury individuals and nations can no longer afford in a global economy.

12.6 Fons Trompenaars' cultural dimensions

A competing approach to classify national differences in cultures is presented by Fons Trompenaars. In his study of cultural differences between 28 countries, Fons Trompenaars has developed five relevant dimensions: universalism–particularism, individualism–collectivism, neutral–emotional, specific–diffuse and achievement–ascription[52].

Universalism–particularism

Universalism implies that what is good and right can be applied everywhere (abstract societal codes). Typical rule-based cultures are, for example, Anglo-Saxon and Scandinavian countries like the Netherlands, Germany and Switzerland. Particularist cultures, on the other hand, are more friendship-based. What counts here are relationships and unique circumstances: 'I must protect the people around me, no matter what the rules say.' Typical particularist countries are, for example, Russia, Spain and France. In practice, we will need both judgements. For example, sometimes universalist rules have no answers to particularist problems. Hence, co-operation between people from both cultures will sometimes cause serious problems: universalists will, for example, accuse particularists of corruption when they 'help' a friend or a family member, whereas universalists will be said to be selfish if they refuse to help an acquaintance. A very detailed contract, drawn by a universalist specifying every legal detail, is seen by the particularist as if 'he does not trust me as a business partner'. The particularist will first build a relationship with his business partner. Once mutual trust is established, a particularist considers it is not necessary to draw up a detailed contract: the relationship itself is the guarantee (see Table 12.3).

Individualism–collectivism

Individualist countries, such as the Netherlands and Sweden, are oriented towards one's self. Collectivist countries are fairly group-oriented. Think about the typical family-minded Frenchman.

Table 12.3 Business Areas Affected by Universalism–Particularism

Universalism	Particularism
Focus is more on rules than on relationships	Focus is more on relationships than on rules
Legal contracts are readily drawn up	Legal contracts are readily modified
A trustworthy person is one who honours his or her 'word' or contract	A trustworthy person is the one who honours changing circumstances
There is only one truth or reality, that which has been agreed to	There are several perspectives on reality relative to each participant
A deal is a deal	Relationships evolve

Table 12.4 Business Areas Affected by Individualism–Collectivism

Individualism	Collectivism
More frequent use of 'I' and 'me'	More frequent use of 'we'
In negotiations, decisions typically made on the spot by a representative	Decisions typically referred back by delegate to the organisation
People ideally achieve alone and assume personal responsibility	People ideally achieve in groups which assume joint responsibility
Holidays taken in pairs, or even alone	Holidays taken in organised groups or extended family

Regarding oneself as an individual or as part of a group has serious influences on negotiations, on decision-making and on motivation. Pay-for-performance, for example, is welcomed in the USA, The Netherlands and the UK. More collectivist cultures, such as France, most parts of Asia and Germany, are very reluctant to follow the Anglo-Saxon pay-for-performance systems (see Chapter 6). They take offence at the idea that one's performance is related to another's deficiencies. In negotiations and decision-making collectivists will take no decision without having prior elaborate discussions with the home front. Individualists, however, will usually take a decision on their own without the prior consent of their colleagues or bosses. A Chinese–Dutch study showed that people in collective cultures had more constructive reactions after they had received feedback from their supervisors, compared to people from individualist cultures (see Table 12.4).[53]

Neutral–emotional

Showing or not showing our emotions is culturally embedded. People from countries such as North America, Europe and Japan will hardly express their feelings in a first business contact, whereas people from southern countries like Italy and France are very affective and open. Business contacts between the cultures may frequently result in misunderstandings. Neutral people are considered as having no feelings; emotional people are considered as being out of control (see Table 12.5).

Specific–diffuse

In specific cultures, home and business are strictly separated; contacts are on a contractual basis. In more diffuse cultures, both worlds are interrelated; the entire person is involved. In specific-oriented cultures, the relationship you have with a person depends on the common ground you have with that person at that moment. If you are specialised in a certain area, you will have 'the advantage' in that subject. If, on the other hand, the other person has more knowledge in another

Table 12.5 Business Areas Affected by Neutral–Emotional Relationships

Neutral	Emotional
Opaque emotional state	Show immediate reactions either verbally or non-verbally
Do not readily express what they think or feel	Express face and body signals
Embarrassed or awkward at public displays of emotions	At ease with public displays of emotions
Discomfort with physical contact outside 'private' circle	At ease with physical contact
Subtle in verbal and non-verbal expressions	Raise voice readily

Table 12.6 Business Areas Affected by Specific–Diffuse Relationships

Specific	Diffuse
More 'open' public space, more closed 'private' space	More 'closed' public space but, once in, more 'open' private space
Appears direct, open and extravert	Appears indirect, closed and introvert
'To the point' and often appears abrasive	Often evades issues and 'beats about the bush'
Highly mobile	Low mobility
Separates work and private life	Work and private life are closely linked
Varies approach to fit circumstances especially with use of titles (e.g. Herr Doktor Muller at work is Hans in social environments or in certain business meetings)	Consistent in approach, especially with use of titles (e.g. Herr Doktor Muller remains Herr Doktor Muller in any setting)

area, the roles will be reversed. In diffuse countries like France one's authority permeates each area of life. In such cultures, everything is connected to everything. In negotiations, for example, your business partner may ask for your personal background (see Table 12.6).

Achievement–ascription

In achievement-oriented cultures, such as France, emphasis is put on what you have accomplished; in ascription-oriented cultures, your personality counts. Different countries confer status on individuals in different ways. Anglo-Saxons, for example, will ascribe status to reasons for achievement.

The following situation illustrates the way in which cultural differences can lead to serious misunderstandings in business. A Danish paint manufacturing company wanted a large English firm to represent it in Britain. Having received encouraging signals on a first visit, the Danish managers came over a second time and were surprised by the complete lack of interest. Yet they were still not turned down. The British 'no' was finally received in a telex of three lines after a total of three visits and much wasted advance planning from the Danish end. Why didn't the English say 'no' at the start?[54]

12.7 Cultural perceptions of time, space and communication

In North American and northern European cultures, time seems to be a simple matter. It is linear, relentlessly marching forward, never backward, in standardised chunks. To the German, who received a watch for his or her third birthday, time is like money. It is spent, saved or wasted.[55] Americans are taught to show up ten minutes early for appointments. When working across cultures, however, time becomes a very complex matter.[56] Imagine a Swiss person's chagrin when left in a waiting room for 45 minutes, only to find a Latin-American government official then dealing with him and three other people all at once. The Swiss person resents the lack of prompt and undivided attention. The Latin-American official resents the Swiss person's impatience and apparent self-centredness.[57] This vicious cycle of resentment can be explained by the distinction between **monochronic time**, which is revealed in the ordered, precise, schedule-driven use of public time that typifies and even caricatures efficient northern Europeans and North Americans and **polychronic time**, which is seen in the multiple and cyclical activities and concurrent involvement with different people in the Mediterranean, Latin American and, especially, Arab cultures.[58]

In a European context, we can say that, using our categories, Latins are polychronic whereas Germanics are monochronic. In other words, the first are schedule-independent and the latter schedule-dependent. In Italy, for example, if something intervenes to make you late – a meeting running overtime, a surprise meeting with someone important or an unexpected telephone call – then, it is understandable. While it is impolite to arrive late for a meeting, it is even more impolite to break off the previous one because it is overrunning.[59]

Monochronic and polychronic are relative rather than absolute concepts. Generally, the more things a person tends to do at once, the more polychronic that person is.[60] Thanks to computers and advanced telecommunications systems, highly polychronic managers can engage in 'multitasking'.[61] For instance, it is possible to talk on the telephone, read and respond to email messages (also see Chapter 4), print a report, check a pager message and eat a stale sandwich all at the same time. Unfortunately, this extreme polychronic behaviour is too often not as efficient as hoped and can be very stressful.

What is your attitude towards time? You can find out by completing the polychronic attitude index in the next activity.

Activity

What is your attitude towards time?

Consider how you feel about the following statements. Circle your choice on the scale provided, showing whether you: strongly disagree, disagree, are neutral, agree or strongly agree.

	Strongly disagree	Disagree	Neutral	Agree	Strongly agree
I do not like to juggle several activities at the same time.	5	4	3	2	1
People should not try to do many things at once.	5	4	3	2	1
When I sit down at my desk, I work on one project at a time.	5	4	3	2	1
I am not comfortable doing several things at the same time.	5	4	3	2	1

Add up your points, and divide the total by 4. Then plot your score on the scale below.

1.0 1.5 2.0 2.5 3.0 3.5 4.0 4.5 5.0

Monochronic **Polychronic**

The lower your score (below 3.0), the more monochronic your orientation; and the higher your score (above 3.0), the more polychronic.

Source: A. C. Bluedorn, C. F. Kaufman and P. M. Lane, 'How Many Things Do You Like to Do at Once? An Introduction to Monochronic and Polychronic Time', *Academy of Management Executive*, November 1992, Exhibit 2, p. 20.

Table 12.7 gives some useful tips for dealing with other people's concepts of time.

Table 12.7 Tips for Dealing with Intercultural Concepts of Time

Time concept	Advice for intercultural awareness
Punctuality	Find the basic unit of time: is it 5 minutes, 15 or 30?
Polychronic or monochronic time	In some cultures, the business lunch is devoted to socialising with business partners. It may be hard to figure out what activities can be combined and what cannot
Fast and slow paces of life	A fast pace can lead to stress-related health problems. Social support can lessen these problems
Time as symbol	Time is not money in some cultures and treating it in monetary terms may be considered vulgar
Time efficiency	Speed is not always a virtue. Multicultural teams need more time to achieve their peak performance level; however, they may be more effective after they become comfortable working with each other for some time

Source: Adapted from W. Brislin and E. S. Kim, 'Cultural Diversity in People's Understanding and Uses of Time', *Applied Psychology: An International Review*, June 2003, p. 380.

Interpersonal space

The anthropologist Edward T. Hall noticed a connection between culture and preferred interpersonal distance. People from high-context cultures were observed standing close when talking to someone. Low-context cultures appeared to dictate a greater amount of interpersonal space. Hall applied the term **proxemics** to the study of cultural expectations about interpersonal space.[62] He specified four interpersonal distance zones. Some call them space bubbles. These distances are referred to as:

- Intimate.
- Personal.
- Social.
- Public.

In North America or northern Europe, business conversations are normally conducted at about a metre (three to four feet) distance. A range of approximately a third of a metre (one foot) is common in Latin American and Asian cultures, which is uncomfortably close for northern Europeans and North Americans. Arabs like to get even closer. Mismatches in culturally dictated interpersonal space zones can prove very distracting for the unprepared.

Asian and Middle-Eastern hosts grow weary of seemingly having to chase their low-context guests around at social gatherings to maintain what they feel is proper conversational range. Backing away all evening to keep conversational partners at a proper distance is an awkward experience as well. Awareness of cultural differences, along with skilful accommodation, is essential to productive intercultural business dealings.

Norwegians, by comparison, can be very jealous of their bubbles of space – to an extent that they even astonished an American visitor. 'One of the first things I noticed when I moved to Norway was that Norwegians need a lot of personal space', he remarked to an interviewer.

> Once I went into someone's office for an informal chat and sat down on the edge of his desk, some two metres from him! I had the direct impression that I was on his territory. Also, I have found that if one reaches out to another during a conversation, there will almost immediately be a recoil from the listener.[63]

Critical thinking

Are the intercultural differences getting more or less important, as all aspects of business get more and more globalised?

12.8 The global manager and expatriates

About 80 per cent of all medium-size and large organisations transfer employees to another country.[64] Foreign experience has become a necessary stepping stone in one's career development. As the reach of global companies continues to grow, many opportunities for living and working in foreign countries will arise. For example, one company which, in striving to become a worldwide force, makes increasing use of international assignments is British Airways. 'We knew we had to globalise our company and that centred entirely on how we develop people in the business', says Fran Spencer, former human resources (HR) manager at the airline. 'We will know when we have got there: a third of graduate recruits will be from outside the UK, a quarter of the board will be non-UK nationals; and our own top 100 managers will have spent at least half a year of their working life outside the country.'[65]

Expatriate refers to anyone living or working outside their home country. Hence, they are said to be expatriated when transferred to another country and repatriated when transferred back home. An article described European expatriates strikingly well as 'Euronomads'. According to Kevin Martin, a Scot working in Brussels, 'Euronomads are like mercenaries. They don't have a fixed spot to live; all they need is a decent laptop, the will to wander and a Eurostar schedule.'[66]

As an example, David Best, who works for the pan-European company Motor Care, does business all over Europe. He has been everywhere – to Sweden, Ireland, Germany and France – and has more international than national conversations. He noticed that he is not so much appreciated for his knowledge and his managerial skills as his ability to adapt readily to different European cultures. 'There's a difference between talking French and acting French', he explains. 'The boss needs me, sometimes to play interpreter, sometimes just to inform him about specific sensitivities in certain cultures.'[67]

However, expatriate managers are usually characterised as culturally inept and prone to failure on international assignments. Sadly, research supports this view. A pair of international management experts offer the following assessment:

> Over the past decade, we have studied the management of expatriates at about 750 US, European and Japanese companies. We asked both the expatriates themselves, and the executives who sent them abroad, to evaluate their experiences. In addition, we looked at what happened after expatriates returned home. Overall, the results of our research were alarming. We found that between 10 and 20 per cent of all managers sent abroad returned early because of job dissatisfaction or difficulties in adjusting to a foreign country. Of those who stayed for the duration, nearly a third did not perform up to the expectations of their superiors. And perhaps most problematic, a fourth of those who completed an assignment left their company, often to join a competitor, within a year of repatriation. That turnover rate is double that of managers who did not go abroad.[68]

Because of the high cost of sending employees and their families to foreign countries for extended periods, significant improvement is needed. Research has uncovered specific reasons for the failure of expatriates. Listed in decreasing order of frequency are the following seven most common reasons:

1 The expatriate's spouse cannot adjust to new physical or cultural surroundings.
2 The expatriate cannot adapt to new physical or cultural surroundings.
3 The expatriate has family problems.
4 The expatriate is emotionally immature.
5 The expatriate cannot cope with foreign duties.
6 The expatriate is not technically competent.
7 The expatriate lacks the proper motivation for a foreign assignment.[69]

Collectively, family and personal adjustment problems, not technical competence, provide the main stumbling block for people working in foreign countries. This conclusion is reinforced by the results of a survey that asked 72 HR managers at multinational corporations to identify the most important success factor in a foreign assignment. 'Nearly 35 per cent said cultural adaptability, patience, flexibility and tolerance for others' beliefs. Only 22 per cent of them listed technical and management skills.'[70]

Anticipating failure in expatriate assignments

Finding the right person (usually along with a supportive and adventurous family) for a foreign position is a complex, time-consuming and costly process.[71] Even long before an eventual future expatriate assignment comes up, an assessment can draw a picture of someone's international career planning. Such an assessment can either fuel or extinguish one's international ambitions.[72] This assessment should pay more attention than is the case today to personality traits such as openness to new experiences and friendliness (see also Chapter 2). Both personality traits have proved to be helpful in building relationships with locals, which is important for expatriates' success.[73] Moreover, better selection methods would reduce the enormous costs resulting from failed foreign assignments.[74] In the four-stage process illustrated in Figure 12.8, the first and last stages occur at home. The middle two stages occur in the foreign or host country.

Figure 12.8 The Foreign Assignment Cycle

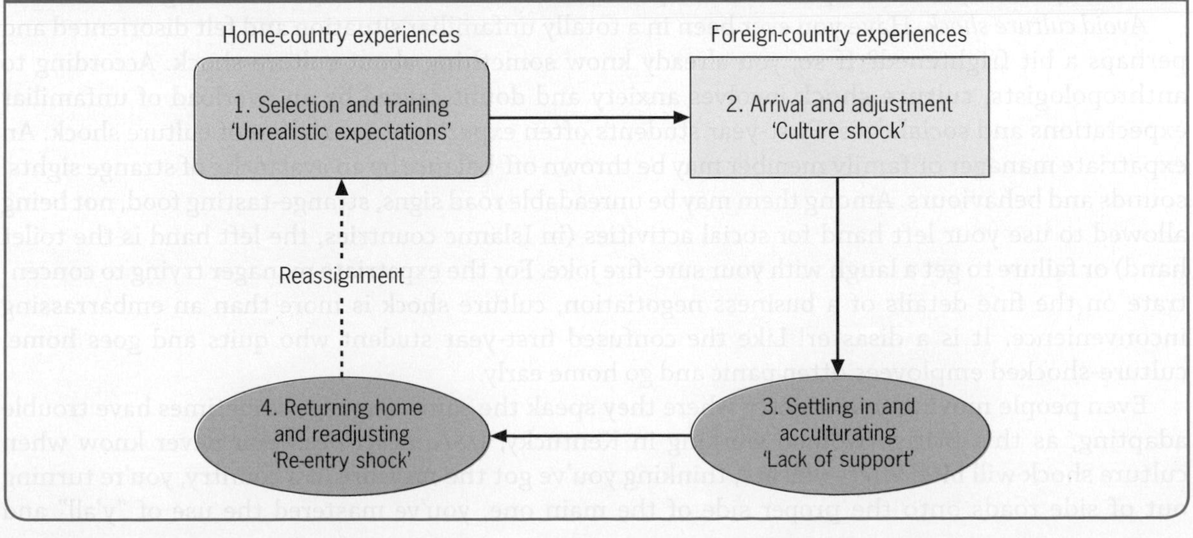

Avoid unrealistic expectations with cross-cultural training. Realistic job previews (RJPs), as predicted earlier, have proved effective at bringing people's unrealistic expectations about a pending job assignment down to earth by providing a realistic balance of good and bad news. People with realistic expectations tend to quit less often and be more satisfied than those with unrealistic expectations. RJPs are a must for future expatriates. In addition, cross-cultural training is required.

Cross-cultural training is any type of structured experience designed to help departing employees adjust to a foreign culture. The trend is towards more such training. Although it is costly, companies wanting to help people adjust believe cross-cultural training is less expensive than failed foreign assignments. Programmes vary widely in type and in rigour.[75] Of course, the greater the difficulty, the greater the time and expense:

- *Easiest:* pre-departure training is limited to informational materials, including books, lectures, films, videos and Internet searches.
- *Moderately difficult:* experiential training is conducted through case studies, role playing, assimilators (simulated intercultural incidents) and introductory language instruction.
- *Most difficult:* departing employees are given some combination of the preceding methods plus comprehensive language instruction and field experience in the target culture.[76]

As an example, when a Dutch manager was assigned to start up a new Philips plant in Skierniewice, Poland, he and his wife went through an intensive 'country information programme'. Some managers, who had formerly worked in Poland, such as the head of Unilever's Eastern Europe division, were invited. At first the couple could ask them some simple practical questions, such as: 'What do I have to do with a drunk employee? Where can I find an interpreter? Why are the rents in Warschau that high? Is it safe to drink tap water?' Then they were taught some basic aspects of behaviour in Poland, such as the do's and don'ts of conversations, meetings and so on and an introduction to the Polish language.[77]

Research has underscored the critical role of spouses' cross-cultural adjustment during international assignments and suggests that companies need to pay closer attention to these issues when selecting and preparing to send expatriates with spouses to another country. At the very least, both expatriates and spouses need to be included in pre-departure training and training on-site.[78] These research findings can only be confirmed by the fact that adjustment problems suffered by the expatriate's spouse are the principal reason for failed expatriate assignments.

Avoid culture shock. Have you ever been in a totally unfamiliar situation and felt disoriented and perhaps a bit frightened? If so, you already know something about culture shock. According to anthropologists, **culture shock** involves anxiety and doubt caused by an overload of unfamiliar expectations and social cues. First-year students often experience a variation of culture shock. An expatriate manager or family member may be thrown off-balance by an avalanche of strange sights, sounds and behaviours. Among them may be unreadable road signs, strange-tasting food, not being allowed to use your left hand for social activities (in Islamic countries, the left hand is the toilet hand) or failure to get a laugh with your sure-fire joke. For the expatriate manager trying to concentrate on the fine details of a business negotiation, culture shock is more than an embarrassing inconvenience. It is a disaster! Like the confused first-year student who quits and goes home, culture-shocked employees often panic and go home early.

Even people moving to a country where they speak the same language sometimes have trouble adapting, as this British woman working in Kentucky, USA, describes: 'You never know when culture shock will bite. There you are, thinking you've got the measure of a country, you're turning out of side roads onto the proper side of the main one, you've mastered the use of "y'all" and learned not to fear doggy bags and suddenly some tiny detail turns everything on its head, reminds you that you are, after all, a stranger in a foreign country.'[79]

The best defence against culture shock is comprehensive cross-cultural training, including intensive language study. Once again, the only way to pick up subtle – yet important – social cues is via the local language.

Support during the foreign assignment. Especially during the first six months, when everything is so new to the expatriate, a support system needs to be in place.[80] The role local people can play in successful expatriate assignments has long been ignored. Researchers and expatriates alike now argue for both local and expatriate support.

Insights resulting from Dutch research among 427 expatriates from 26 countries and posted in 52 countries teach us that close relationships with other expatriates have less influence on expatriates' adaptation than close relationships with locals.[81]

In a foreign country, where even the smallest errand can turn into an utterly exhausting production, a network of expatriates is indispensable as well. Host-country sponsors assigned to individual expatriates and their families can get things done quickly because they know the cultural and geographical territory.

The local staff members who report to the expatriates can also make a large contribution to the expatriates' successful functioning. In many cases, the local staff have a perfect understanding of cross-cultural issues and are well able to point out what training their expatriate bosses need.[82]

Avoid re-entry shock. Strange as it may seem, many otherwise successful expatriate managers encounter their first major difficulty only after their foreign assignment is over. Why? Returning to one's native culture is taken for granted because it seems so routine and ordinary. However, having adjusted to another country's way of doing things for an extended period of time can result in putting one's own culture and surroundings in a strange new light. Three areas for potential re-entry shock are work, social activities and general environment (such as politics, climate, transportation, food).

Lance Richards, senior director of international HR for Kelly Services, states that repatriation must start well before the assignee 'has ever darkened the door of a Boeing 747'. Anyone considering moving their family overseas should ask: 'What happens next?' 'It's amazing how many companies don't have the answer to this simple question. Even worse, sometimes they know the answer, but won't tell the assignee', Richards says.[83]

Overall, the key to a successful foreign assignment is making it a well-integrated link in a career chain rather than treating it as an isolated adventure.

! Critical thinking

Would you expect female managers going abroad as expatriates to have particular challenges?

Learning outcomes: Summary of key terms

1 **Discuss the difference between espoused and enacted values.**

Espoused values represent the explicitly stated values and norms that are preferred by an organisation. Enacted values, in contrast, reflect the values and norms that are actually exhibited or converted into employee behaviour. Employees become cynical when management espouses one set of values and norms and then behaves in an inconsistent fashion.

2 **Explain the typology of organisational values.**

The typology of organisational values identifies four types of organisational value systems. It is based on crossing organisational reward norms and organisation power structures. The types of value systems include elite, meritocratic, leadership and collegial. Each type of value system contains a set of values that are both consistent and inconsistent with the underlying value system.

3 **Describe the manifestations of an organisation's culture and the four functions of organisational culture.**

General manifestations of an organisation's culture are shared objects, talk, behaviour and emotion. Four functions of organisational culture are organisational identity, collective commitment, social-system stability and sense-making devices.

4 **Discuss the four general types of organisational culture.**

Four general types of organisational culture are the result of combining two dimensions. The first dimension contrasts flexibility with stability; the second dimension contrasts internal with external focus. In adaptability culture, creativity and innovation are highly valued. In an external-control culture, goal achievement and competition are the most important values. In a development culture, teamwork and participation are highly appreciated. In an internal-consistency culture, respect for hierarchy and rules is highly valued.

5 **Summarise the methods used by organisations to embed their cultures.**

Embedding a culture amounts to teaching employees about the organisation's preferred values, beliefs, expectations and behaviours. This is accomplished by using one or more of the following 11 mechanisms: (a) formal statements of organisational philosophy, mission, vision, values and materials used for recruiting, selection and socialisation; (b) the design of physical space, work environments and buildings; (c) slogans, language, acronyms and sayings; (d) deliberate role modelling, training programmes, teaching and coaching by managers and supervisors; (e) explicit rewards, status symbols and promotion criteria; (f) stories, legends and myths about key people and events; (g) the organisational activities, processes or outcomes that leaders pay attention to, measure and control; (h) leader reactions to critical incidents and organisational crises; (i) the workflow and organisational structure; (j) organisational systems and procedures; and (k) organisational goals and the associated criteria used for employer recruitment, selection, development, promotion, lay-offs and retirement.

6 **Describe the practical lessons from the Hofstede–Bond stream of research.**

According to the Hofstede–Bond cross-cultural management studies, caution needs to be exercised when transplanting management theories and practices from one culture to another. Also, long-term orientation was the only one of five cultural dimensions in the Hofstede–Bond studies to correlate positively with national economic growth.

7 **Discuss the importance of cross-cultural training relative to the foreign assignment cycle.**
The foreign assignment cycle has four stages: selection and training, arrival and adjustment, settling in and acculturating and returning home and adjusting. Cross-cultural training, preferably combining informational and experiential lessons before departure, can help expatriates avoid two OB trouble spots: unrealistic expectations and culture shock. There are no adequate substitutes for knowing the local language and culture.

Review questions

1 How would you respond to someone who made the following statement: 'Organisational cultures are not important as far as business is concerned'?
2 What type of value system exists within your study group? Provide examples to support your evaluation.
3 Why is socialisation essential to organisational success?
4 Regarding your cultural awareness, how would you describe the prevailing culture in your country to a stranger from another country?
5 Culturally speaking, are you individualistic or collectivist? How does that cultural orientation affect how you run your personal/business affairs?

Personal awareness and growth exercise

How does your current employer socialise employees?

Objective

1 To promote deeper understanding of organisational socialisation processes.
2 To provide you with a useful tool for analysing and comparing organisations.

Introduction

Employees are socialised in many different ways in today's organisations. Some organisations, such as IBM, have made an exact science out of organisational socialisation. Others leave things to chance in the hope that collective goals will somehow be achieved. The questionnaire in this exercise is designed to help you gauge how widespread and systematic the socialisation process is in a particular organisation.

Instructions

If you are presently employed and have a good working knowledge of your organisation, you can complete this questionnaire yourself. If not, identify a manager or professional (such as a corporate lawyer, engineer or nurse) and have that individual complete the questionnaire for his or her organisation.

Respond to the items below as they apply to the handling of professional employees (including managers). On completion, compute the total score by adding up your responses. For comparison, scores for a number of strong, intermediate and weak culture firms are provided.

	Not true of this company				Very true of this company
1 Recruiters receive at least one week of intensive training.	1	2	3	4	5
2 Recruitment forms identify several key traits deemed crucial to the firm's success; traits are defined in concrete terms and the interviewer records specific evidence of each trait.	1	2	3	4	5
3 Recruits are subjected to at least four in-depth interviews.	1	2	3	4	5
4 Company actively facilitates the selection during the recruiting process by revealing minuses as well as pluses.	1	2	3	4	5
5 New recruits work long hours, are exposed to intensive training of considerable difficulty and/or perform relatively menial tasks in the first months.	1	2	3	4	5
6 The intensity of entry-level experience builds cohesiveness among peers in each entering class.	1	2	3	4	5
7 All professional employees in a particular discipline begin in entry-level positions regardless of experience or advanced degrees.	1	2	3	4	5
8 Reward systems and promotion criteria require mastery of a core discipline as a precondition of advancement.	1	2	3	4	5
9 The career path for professional employees is relatively consistent over the first 6–10 years with the company.	1	2	3	4	5
10 Reward systems, performance incentives, promotion criteria and other primary measures of success reflect a high degree of congruence.	1	2	3	4	5
11 Virtually all professional employees can identify and articulate the firm's shared values (i.e. the purpose or mission that ties the firm to society, the customer or its employees).	1	2	3	4	5
12 There are very few instances when the actions of management appear to violate the firm's espoused values.	1	2	3	4	5
13 Employees frequently make personal sacrifices for the firm out of commitment to the firm's shared values.	1	2	3	4	5
14 When confronted with trade-offs between systems measuring short-term results and doing what's best for the company in the long term, the firm usually decides in favour of the long term.	1	2	3	4	5
15 This organisation fosters mentor–protégé(e) relationships.	1	2	3	4	5
16 There is considerable similarity among high potential candidates in each particular discipline.	1	2	3	4	5

Total score = ________________

Comparative norms

55 and 80 = strongly socialised organisation
26 and 54 = moderately socialised organisation
Below 25 = weakly socialised organisation

Questions for discussion

1 How strongly socialised is the organisation in question? What implications does this degree of socialisation have for satisfaction, commitment and turnover?
2 In examining the 16 items in the preceding questionnaire, what evidence of realistic job previews and behaviour modelling can you find? Explain.
3 What does this questionnaire say about how organisational norms are established and enforced? Frame your answer in terms of specific items in the questionnaire.
4 Using this questionnaire as a gauge, would you rather work for a strongly, moderately or weakly socialised organisation?

Group exercise

Assessing the organisational culture at your place of learning

Objectives

- To provide you with a framework for assessing organisational culture.
- To conduct an evaluation of the organisational culture at your place of learning.
- To consider the relationship between organisational culture and organisational effectiveness.

Introduction

Academics and consultants do not agree about the best way to measure an organisation's culture. Some people measure culture with surveys, while others use direct observation or information obtained in interviews/workshops with employees. This exercise uses an informal, group-based approach to assess the three levels of organisational culture discussed in this chapter. This approach has successfully been used to measure organisational culture at a variety of organisations.[84]

Instructions

Your lecturer will divide the class into groups of four to six people. Each group member should then complete the cultural assessment worksheet by themselves. It asks you to identify the artefacts, espoused values and basic assumptions that are present at your current place of learning. When everyone is done, meet as a group and share the information contained on your individual worksheets and discuss what type of culture your place of learning possesses. Strive to reach a consensus. Finally, the group should answer the discussion questions.

Cultural assessment worksheet

Artefacts (physical or visible manifestations of culture; they include jargon, heroes, stories, language, ritual, dress, material objects, mascots, physical arrangements, symbols, traditions, and so forth)	Espoused values (the stated values and norms preferred by the organisation)	Basic assumptions (taken-for-granted beliefs about the organisation that exist on an unconscious level)

Questions for discussion

1. What are the group's consensus artefacts, espoused values and basis assumptions? Are you surprised by anything on this list? Explain.
2. What type of culture does your place of learning possess? Do you like the organisational culture? Discuss why or why not.
3. Do you think the organisational culture identified in question 2 is best suited for maximising your learning? Explain your rationale.
4. Is your place of learning in need of any cultural change? If yes, discuss why and recommend how the leaders might create this change.
5. How would one go about distinguishing national from organisational culture in a particular workplace?

Online
Learning Centre

When you have read this chapter, log on to the Online Learning Centre website at ***www.mcgraw-hill.co.uk/textbooks/sinding*** to access test questions, additional exercises and other related resources.

Notes

1. T. Hallett, 'Symbolic Power and Organizational Culture', *Sociological Theory*, June 2003, pp. 128–49.
2. E. Ogbonna and B. Wilkinson, 'The False Promise of Organizational Culture Change: A Case Study of Middle Managers in Grocery Retailing', *Journal of Management Studies*, July 2003, pp. 1151–78.
3. For a comprehensive review of research, see D. R. Denison, 'What IS the Difference between Organizational Culture and Organizational Climate? A Native's Point of View on a Decade of Paradigm Wars', *Academy of Management Review*, July 1996, pp. 619–54.
4. E. H. Schein, *Organizational Culture and Leadership* (San Francisco, CA: Jossey-Bass, 1985), p. 9. Also see H. H. Baligh, 'Components of Culture: Nature, Interconnections, and Relevance to the Decisions on the Organization Structure', *Management Science*, January 1994, pp. 14–27.
5. F. Trompenaars and C. Hampden-Turner, *Riding the Waves of Culture: Understanding Cultural Diversity in Global Business*, 2nd edn (New York: McGraw-Hill, 1998), pp. 6–7.
6. 'How Cultures Collide', *Psychology Today*, July 1976, p. 69.
7. See M. Mendenhall, 'A Painless Approach to Integrating "International" into OB, HRM, and Management Courses', *Organizational Behavior Teaching Review*, no. 3, 1988–9, pp. 23–7.

[8] J. Main, 'How to Go Global – And Why', *Fortune*, 28 August 1989, p. 73.

[9] An excellent contrast between French and American values can be found in C. Gouttefarde, 'American Values in the French Workplace', *Business Horizons*, March–April 1996, pp. 60–69.

[10] G. Hofstede, C. A. Van Deusen, C. B. Mueller and T. A. Charles, 'What Goals Do Business Leaders Pursue? A Study in Fifteen Countries', *Journal of International Business Studies*, December 2002, pp. 785–803. Also see G. Hofstede, *Software of the Mind* (New York: McGraw-Hill, 1997).

[11] E. H. Schein, 'Culture: The Missing Concept in Organization Studies', *Administrative Science Quarterly*, June 1996, p. 236.

[12] S. H. Schwartz, 'Universals in the Content and Structure of Values: Theoretical Advances and Empirical Tests in 20 Countries', in *Advances in Experimental Social Psychology*, ed. M. P. Zanna (New York: Academic Press, 1992), p. 4.

[13] The discussion between espoused and enacted values is based on E. H. Schein, *Organizational Culture and Leadership* (San Francisco, CA: Jossey-Bass, 1985).

[14] Results can be found in S. Clarke, 'Perceptions of Organizational Safety: Implications for the Development of Safety Culture', *Journal of Organizational Behavior*, March 1999, pp. 185–98.

[15] Excerpted from S. L. Payne, 'Recognizing and Reducing Transcultural Ethical Tension', *Academy of Management Executive*, August 1998, p. 84.

[16] This typology and related discussion was derived from B. Kabanoff and J. Holt, 'Changes in the Espoused Values of Australian Organizations 1986–1990', *Journal of Organizational Behavior*, May 1996, pp. 201–19.

[17] For an example of profiling organisational values, see T. J. Kalliath, A. C. Bluedorn and D. F. Gillespie, 'A Confirmatory Factor Analyses of the Competing Values Instrument', *Educational and Psychological Measurement*, February 1999, pp. 143–58.

[18] The mechanisms were based on material contained in E. H. Schein, 'The Role of the Founder in Creating Organizational Culture', *Organizational Dynamics*, Summer 1983, pp. 13–28.

[19] www.philips.com/about/careers/working_at_philips/how_we_work/our_values.page.

[20] Excerpted from M. Apgar IV, 'The Alternative Workplace: Changing Where and How People Work', *Harvard Business Review*, May–June 1998, p. 123. More examples in D. F. Kuratko, R. D. Ireland, and J. S. Hornsby, 'Improving Firm Performance Through Entrepreneurial Actions: Acordia's Corporate Entrepreneurship Strategy', *Academy of Management Executive*, November 2001, p. 67.

[21] See A. Xenikou and A. Furnham, 'A Correlated and Factor Analytic Study of Four Questionnaire Measures of Organizational Culture', *Human Relations*, March 1996, pp. 349–71; and D. R. Denison, 'What IS the Difference between Organizational Culture and Organizational Climate? A Native's Point of View on a Decade of Paradigm Wars', *Academy of Management Review*, July 1996, pp. 619–54.

[22] J. B. Sonrensen, 'The Strength of Corporate Culture and the Reliability of Firm Performance', *Administrative Science Quarterly*, March 2002, pp. 70–91.

[23] See S. Tully, 'Northwest and KLM: The Alliance from Hell', *Fortune*, 24 June 1996, pp. 64–72; and J. Marren, *Mergers & Acquisitions: A Valuation Handbook* (Homewood, IL: Irwin, 1993).

[24] The success rate of mergers is discussed in R. J. Grossman, 'Irreconcilable Differences', *HR Magazine*, April 1999, pp. 42–8.

[25] J. Van Maanen, 'Breaking In: Socialization to Work', in *Handbook of Work, Organization, and Society*, ed. R. Dubin (Chicago, IL: Rand-McNally, 1976), p. 67.

[26] L. Adent Hoecklin, *Managing Cultural Changes for Competitive Advantage* (London: The Economist Intelligence Unit, 1993).

[27] For an instructive capsule summary of the five different organisational socialisation models, see J. P. Wanous, A. E. Reichers and S. D. Malik, 'Organizational Socialization and Group Development: Toward an Integrative Perspective', *Academy of Management Review*, October 1984, pp. 670–83, Table 1. Also see D. C. Feldman, *Managing Careers in Organizations* (Glenview, IL: Scott, Foresman, 1988), Ch. 5.

[28] Supportive evidence is provided by R. W. Griffeth and P. W. Hom, *Retaining Valued Employees* (Thousand Oaks, CA: Sage Publications, 2001), pp. 46–65. Also see P. W. Hom, R. W. Griffeth, L. E. Palich and J. S. Bracker, 'Revisiting Met Expectations As a Reason Why Realistic Job Previews Work', *Personnel Psychology*, Spring 1999, pp. 97–112.

[29] J. Van Maanen, 'People Processing: Strategies of Organizational Socialization', *Organizational Dynamics*, Summer 1978, p. 21.

[30] For a thorough review of socialisation research, see B. E. Ashforth, *Role Transitions in Organizational Life: An Identity-Based Perspective* (Mahwah, NJ: Lawrence Erlbaum Associates, 2001), pp. 87–108.

[31] Results can be found in H. Klein and N. Weaver, 'The Effectiveness of Organizational-Level Orientation Training Program in Socialization of New Hires', *Personnel Psychology*, Spring 2000, pp. 47–66.

[32] See D. Cable and C. Parsons, 'Socialization Tactics and Person-Organization Fit', *Personnel Psychology*, Spring 2001, pp. 1–23.

[33] See T. N. Bauer and S. G. Green, 'Testing the Combined Effects of Newcomer Information Seeking and Manager Behavior on Socialization', *Journal of Applied Psychology*, February 1998, pp. 72–83.

[34] T. N. Bauer and S. G. Green, 'Testing the Combined Effects of Newcomer Information Seeking and Manager Behavior on Socialization', *Journal of Applied Psychology*, February 1998, pp. 72–83.

[35] See A. M. Saks and B. E. Ashforth, 'Proactive Socialization and Behavioral Self-Management', *Journal of Vocational Behavior*, June 1996, pp. 301–23.

[36] For a thorough review of research on the socialisation of diverse employees with disabilities, see A. Colella, 'Organizational Socialization of Newcomers with Disabilities: A Framework for Future Research', in *Research in Personnel and Human Resources Management*, ed. G. R. Ferris (Greenwich, CT: JAI Press, 1996), pp. 351–417.

37 F. Trompenaars and P. Woolliams, 'A New Framework for Managing Change Across Cultures,' *Journal of Change Management*, May 2003, p. 368.

38 See G. A. Sumner, *Folkways* (New York: Ginn, 1906). Also see J. G. Weber, 'The Nature of Ethnocentric Attribution Bias: Ingroup Protection or Enhancement?', *Journal of Experimental Social Psychology*, September 1994, pp. 482–504.

39 J. Fenby, 'Make That Foreign Posting Your Ticket to the Boardroom', *Management Today*, July 2000, pp. 48–53.

40 See 'How Cultures Collide', *Psychology Today*, July 1976, pp. 66–74, 97; and M. Munter, 'Cross-Cultural Communication for Managers', *Business Horizons*, May–June 1993, pp. 69–78.

41 D. C. Barnlund, 'Public and Private Self in Communicating with Japan', *Business Horizons*, March–April 1989, p. 38.

42 The concept of 'face' and good tips on saving face in Far East Asia are presented in J. A. Reeder, 'When West Meets East: Cultural Aspects of Doing Business in Asia', *Business Horizons*, January–February 1987, pp. 69–74. Also see B. Stout, 'Interviewing in Japan', *HR Magazine*, June 1998, pp. 71–7; and J. A. Quelch and C. M. Dinh-Tan, 'Country Managers in Transitional Economies: The Case of Vietnam', *Business Horizons*, July–August 1998, pp. 34–40.

43 The German management style is discussed in R. Stewart, 'German Management: A Challenge to Anglo-American Managerial Assumptions', *Business Horizons*, May–June 1996, pp. 52–4.

44 M. Cleasby, 'Managing Global Contact', *British Journal of Administrative Management*, March/April 2000, pp. 4–6.

45 Based on J. Mole, *Mind Your Manners* (London: Nicholas Brealey Publishing, 1995).

46 For complete details, see G. Hofstede, 'The Interaction between National and Organizational Value Systems', *Journal of Management Studies*, July 1985, pp. 347–57; G. Hofstede, 'Management Scientists Are Human', *Management Science*, January 1994, pp. 4–13; and G. Hofstede, *Culture's Consequences: Comparing Values, Behaviors, Institutions, and Organizations Across Nations*, 2nd edn (Thousand Oaks, CA: Sage Publications, 2001). Also see V. J. Shackleton and A. H. Ali, 'Work-Related Values of Managers: A Test of the Hofstede Model', *Journal of Cross-Cultural Psychology*, March 1990, pp. 109–18; R. Hodgetts, 'A Conversation with Geert Hofstede', *Organizational Dynamics*, Spring 1993, pp. 53–61; and P. B. Smith, S. Dugan and F. Trompenaars, 'National Culture and the Values of Organizational Employees: A Dimensional Analysis Across 43 Nations', *Journal of Cross-Cultural Psychology*, March 1996, pp. 231–64.

47 See G. Hofstede and M. H. Bond, 'Hofstede's Culture Dimensions: An Independent Validation Using Rokeach's Value Survey', *Journal of Cross-Cultural Psychology*, December 1984, pp. 417–33. Another study using the Chinese Value Survey (CVS) is reported in D. A. Ralston, D. J. Gustafson, P. M. Elsass, F. Cheung and R. H. Terpstra, 'Eastern Values: A Comparison of Managers in the United States, Hong Kong, and the People's Republic of China', *Journal of Applied Psychology*, October 1992, pp. 664–71.

48 G. Hofstede, 'Cultural Constraints in Management Theories', *Academy of Management Executive*, February 1993, p. 90.

49 For complete details, see G. Hofstede and M. H. Bond, 'The Confucius Connection: From Cultural Roots to Economic Growth', *Organizational Dynamics*, Spring 1988, pp. 4–21.

50 See P. M. Rosenzweig, 'When Can Management Science Research Be Generalized Internationally?', *Management Science*, January 1994, pp. 28–39.

51 A follow-up study is J. P. Johnson and T. Lenartowicz, 'Culture, Freedom and Economic Growth: Do Cultural Values Explain Economic Growth?', *Journal of World Business*, Winter 1998, pp. 332–56.

52 Based on F. Trompenaars, *Riding the Waves of Culture* (London: Economist Books, 1994). Also see F. Trompenaars, *Did the Pedestrian Die?* (London: Capstone Publishing, 2003).

53 E. van der Vliert, K. Sanders, K. Shi, Y. Wang and X. Huang, 'Interpretation and Effects of Supervisory Feedback in China and The Netherlands', *Gedrag & Organisatie*, December 2003, pp. 125–39.

54 S. Brittan, 'Economic Viewpoint: The Follies of the Macho Manager', the *Financial Times*, 22 December 1994, p. 14.

55 See, for example, N. R. Mack, 'Taking Apart the Ticking of Time', the *Christian Science Monitor*, 29 August 1991, p. 17.

56 For a comprehensive treatment of time, see J. E. McGrath and J. R. Kelly, *Time and Human Interaction: Toward a Social Psychology of Time* (New York: The Guilford Press, 1986). Also see L. A. Manrai and A. K. Manrai, 'Effects of Cultural-Context, Gender, and Acculturation on Perceptions of Work versus Social/Leisure Time Usage', *Journal of Business Research*, February 1995, pp. 115–28.

57 A good discussion of doing business in Mexico is G. K. Stephens and C. R. Greer, 'Doing Business in Mexico: Understanding Cultural Differences', *Organizational Dynamics*, Summer 1995, pp. 39–55.

58 R. W. Moore, 'Time, Culture, and Comparative Management: A Review and Future Direction', in *Advances in International Comparative Management*, vol. 5, ed. S. B. Prasad (Greenwich, CT: JAI Press, 1990), pp. 7–8.

59 See R. Hill, *We Europeans* (Brussels: Europublications, 1995); and also J. Mole, *Mind Your Manners* (London: Nicholas Brealey Publishing, 1995), p. 59.

60 See A. C. Bluedorn, C. F. Kaufman and P. M. Lane, 'How Many Things Do You Like to Do at Once? An Introduction to Monochronic and Polychronic Time', *Academy of Management Executive*, November 1992, pp. 17–26. Also see F. Trompenaars, *Did the Pedestrian Die?* (London: Capstone Publishing, 2003).

61 'Multitasking' term drawn from S. McCartney, 'The Breaking Point: Multitasking Technology Can Raise Stress and Cripple Productivity', *The Arizona Republic*, 21 May 1995, p. D10.

62 E. T. Hall, *The Hidden Dimension* (Garden City, NY: Doubleday, 1966).

63 R. Hill, *We Europeans* (Brussels: Europublications, 1995), p. 53.

64 P. R. Harris and R. T. Moran, *Managing Cultural Differences*, 4th edn (Houston, TX: Gulf Publishing Company, 1996), p. 23.

65 R. Takeuchi, S. Yun and P. E. Tesluk, 'An Examination of Crossover and Spillover Effects of Spousal and Expatriate Cross-Cultural Adjustment on Expatriate Outcomes', *Journal of Applied Psychology*, August 2002, pp. 655–66.

[66] Adapted and translated from G. Bollen and B. Debeuckelare, 'De euronomaden: Europese elite maakt carrière over de grenzen heen', *Vacature*, 3 December 1999.

[67] G. Bollen and B. Debeuckelare, 'De euronomaden: Europese elite maakt carrière over de grenzen heen', *Vacature*, 3 December 1999.

[68] J. S. Black and H. B. Gregersen, 'The Right Way to Manage Expats', *Harvard Business Review*, March–April 1999, p. 53. A more optimistic picture is presented in R. L. Tung, 'American Expatriates Abroad: From Neophytes to Cosmopolitans', *Journal of World Business*, Summer 1998, pp. 125–44.

[69] Adapted from R. L. Tung, 'Expatriate Assignments: Enhancing Success and Minimizing Failure', *Academy of Management Executive*, May 1987, pp. 117–26.

[70] S. Dallas, 'Rule No. 1: Don't Diss the Locals', *Business Week*, 15 May 1995, p. 8.

[71] An excellent reference book in this area is J. S. Black, H. B. Gregersen, and M. E. Mendenhall, *Global Assignments: Successfully Expatriating and Repatriating International Managers* (San Francisco, CA: Jossey-Bass, 1992). Also see K. Roberts, E. E. Kossek and C. Ozeki, 'Managing the Global Workforce: Challenges and Strategies', *Academy of Management Executive*, November 1998, pp. 93–106.

[72] M. Derksen and A. E. M. van Vianen, 'Aspire to an Expatriate Position: Factors Contributing to International Mobility', *Gedrag & Organisatie*, December 2003, pp. 370–84.

[73] I. E. de Pater, A. E. M. van Vianen and M. Derksen, 'Close Relationships and Cross-Cultural Adaptation of Expatriates: The Role of Personality and Attachment Style', *Gedrag & Organisatie*, December 2003, pp. 89–107.

[74] S. T. Mol, 'Prediction of Expatriate Success as an Industrial/Organizational Psychological Phenomenon: A Theoretical Discourse', *Gedrag & Organisatie*, December 2003, pp. 385–92.

[75] J. S. Black, H. B. Gregersen and M. E. Mendenhall, *Global Assignments: Successfully Expatriating and Repatriating International Managers* (San Francisco, CA: Jossey-Bass, 1992), p. 97.

[76] J. S. Lublin, 'Younger Managers Learn Global Skills', the *Wall Street Journal*, 31 March 1992, p. B1.

[77] Adapted and translated from J. Kroon, 'Leven in het land van de handkus', *NRC Handelsblad*, 18 February 1999.

[78] R. Takeuchi, S. Yun and P. E. Tesluk, 'An Examination of Crossover and Spillover Effects of Spousal and Expatriate Cross-Cultural Adjustment on Expatriate Outcomes', *Journal of Applied Psychology*, August 2002, pp. 655–66.

[79] S. Mackesy, 'I'm Greedy Therefore I Am', *The Independent*, 10 September 2000.

[80] See H. H. Nguyen, L. A. Messe and G. E. Stollak, 'Toward a More Complex Understanding of Acculturation and Adjustment', *Journal of Cross-Cultural Psychology*, January 1999, pp. 5–31.

[81] I. E. de Pater, A. E. M. van Vianen and M. Derksen, 'Close Relationships and Cross-Cultural Adaptation of Expatriates: The Role of Personality and Attachment Style', *Gedrag & Organisatie*, December 2003, pp. 89–107.

[82] P. Prud'homme and F. Trompenaars, 'Invited Reaction: Developing Expatriates for the Asia-Pacific Region', *Human Resource Development Quarterly*, Fall 2000, pp. 237–43.

[83] L. Richards, 'Plan Ahead to Ensure Repatriation Success', *Personnel Today*, 3 February 2004, p. 1.

[84] See E. H. Schein, *The Corporate Culture Survival Guide* (San Francisco, CA: Jossey-Bass, 1999).

Chapter 13

Decision-making

Learning Outcomes

When you finish studying the material in this chapter, you should be able to:

- ✓ compare and contrast the rational model of decision-making, the Carnegie model and the 'garbage can' model
- ✓ discuss the contingency relationships that influence the three primary strategies used to select solutions
- ✓ explain the model of decision-making styles
- ✓ describe the model of escalation of commitment
- ✓ summarise the advantages and disadvantages of involving groups in the decision-making process
- ✓ explain how participative management affects performance
- ✓ compare brainstorming, the nominal group technique, the Delphi technique and computer-aided decision-making
- ✓ describe the stages of the creative process
- ✓ explain the model of organisational creativity and innovation

Opening Case Study: The Gulf of Mexico oil spill

The Macondo Prospect is an area of ocean floor in the Gulf of Mexico, 66 kilometres south-east of the coast of Louisiana. Water depth at the site is around 1500 metres. Drilling rights to the block in which the prospect occurs are owned by a consortium consisting of British Petroleum as operator (65 per cent), Anadarko (25 per cent) and MOEX Offshore (10 per cent). Drilling from the rig *Deepwater Horizon* (owned and operated by Transocean Ltd, a global leader in deepwater drilling rigs) began on 15 February 2010 and ended abruptly on 20 April 2010, when the well blew up, the rig caught fire and, after burning for 36 hours, sank nearby.

After the fire, oil was discovered to be gushing from the damaged borehole on the sea floor. This continued, despite several attempts to cap the well and capture the oil, until a cap was successfully installed on 15 July 2010. Extensive damage to marine life and livelihoods were added to the loss of 11 lives and the rig.

Drilling for oil is extremely costly at any time. Drilling at water depths of around 1500 metres is even more costly, given the scale of the operations. This, however, is not new; the *Deepwater Horizon* had been doing such work ever since it was constructed in 1989.

The cost to the consortium of hiring the rig alone has been estimated at $500 000 per day. To this must be added a further daily operational cost of around $500 000 for crew, supplies, contractors (of which there were many on board) and supply vessels. A rough estimate of the project budget, before things went wrong, is around $65–70 million, based on the number of days drilled and the fact that drilling had essentially already been completed.

However, things did go wrong. The well blew up (or 'out' in oil terminology), 11 workers died and more were injured. The rig sank and oil was gushing into the Gulf of Mexico. BP was blamed for all that went wrong , lawyers converged to bring lawsuits against BP and anyone else they could find. BP worked long and hard to cap the well and finally succeeded. Based on the experience from previous oil disasters, the aftermath would be long and costly.

According to the final report on the accident, a series of risk factors, oversights and mistakes conspired to bypass safety precautions. These are extensive given the high level of risk associated with this activity. The disaster occurred as a result of a series of faulty decisions and management failures on the part of BP, Haliburton (a major contractor involved in the cementing of the well) and Transocean.

For discussion

Was BP's way of making decisions really flawed and if it was, how could decision processes at BP be changed to reduce the risk of accidents?

Source: Based on B. J. Eckhart and A. Faherty, 'The Forensic Anatomy of the Events on the Deepwater Horizon', www.robsonforensic.com/LibraryFiles/Articles/forensic-anatomy-of-deap-water-horizon.pdf; C. Robertson, 'Search Continues After Oil Rig Blast', *New York Times*, 21 April 2010; and 'Deep Water The Gulf Oil Disaster and the Future of Offshore Drilling', Report to the President, National Commission on the BP Deepwater Horizon Oil Spill and Offshore Drilling. January 2011, http://www.oilspillcommission.gov/final-report

Decision-making in the context of organisations is one of the primary responsibilities of all employees. The quality of decisions is important for two reasons. First, the quality of decisions directly affects career opportunities, rewards and job satisfaction. Second, decisions contribute to the success or failure of an organisation. Outside organisations people make decisions all the time, about small matters and big issues: should I eat more cake, invite someone on a date, buy a house, walk the dog etc.?

Decision-making involves identifying and choosing between alternative solutions that lead to a desired state of affairs. The process begins with a problem and ends when a solution has been chosen and sometimes executed – since thinking about execution sometimes feeds back into the thinking leading to the original decision. To gain an understanding of how managers can make better decisions, this chapter focuses on models of decision-making, the dynamics of decision-making, group decision-making and creativity.

13.1 Models of decision-making

There are several models of decision-making. Each is based on a different set of assumptions and offers a unique insight into the decision-making process. This section reviews five key historical models of decision-making. They are:

- The rational model.
- The Carnegie model.
- The incrementalist model.
- The 'garbage can' model.
- The unstructured model.
- The identity-based model.

The sequence of presentation of the models is such that the decision-making process becomes less and less rational as we move along. Actual decisions are unlikely to fit any specific model closely – rather, there can be elements of different models involved in each case.

The rational model

According to the **rational model** people use a rational, four-step sequence when making decisions; they identify the problem, generate alternative solutions, select a solution, and implement and evaluate that solution. Decision-makers are entirely objective and possess all the information they need to make a decision. Despite criticism for being unrealistic, the rational model remains an ideal and a benchmark against which all other models are evaluated. It is important because it analyses the decision-making process and serves as a conceptual anchor for other models.[1]

The first step in the rational model concerns the problem. A **problem** exists when the actual situation and the desired situation differ. For example, when you have to pay rent at the end of the month but do not have enough money. Your problem is not that you have to pay rent. Your problem is obtaining the necessary funds. How do organisations know when a problem exists or will emerge in the near future? One expert proposed that decision-makers use one of three methods to identify problems: historical cues, planning and other people's perceptions:[2]

- Historical cues are used to identify problems on the basis that the recent past is the best indication of what the future will bring. Thus, managers rely on past experience to identify discrepancies (problems) from expected trends. For example, a sales manager may conclude that a problem exists because the first-quarter sales are less than they were a year ago. This method is likely to cause errors because it is highly subjective when it relies on people's judgements alone. However, the field of 'business analytics' is concerned with sifting through data from both outside and inside the organisation in order to provide a better foundation for making decisions.

- The **scenario technique** is used to identify future states, based on a given set of circumstances ('environmental conditions'). Once different scenarios are developed, organisations devise alternative strategies to survive in the various circumstances. This process helps in the creation of contingency plans that reach far into the future.
- A final approach to identifying problems is to rely on the perceptions of others. A restaurant manager may realise that his or her restaurant provides poor service when a large number of customers complain about how long it takes to receive food after placing an order.

After identifying a problem, the next logical step is to generate alternative solutions. For repetitive and routine decisions, such as when to send customers a bill, alternatives are readily available in the form of 'decision rules'. For example, a company might routinely bill customers three days after shipping a product. Where no decision rules exist, however, alternative solutions must be generated and their consequences (costs and benefits in some specification) evaluated.

Ideally, decision-makers want to select the solution which will produce the greatest value. Decision theorists refer to this as maximising the expected utility of an outcome. This is no easy task. First, assigning values to alternatives is complicated and prone to error since they vary according to the preferences of the decision-maker. Research has shown that people vary in their preferences for safety or risk when making decisions. A recent meta-analysis of 150 studies revealed that males displayed more risk-taking than females.[3]

The second step in selecting a solution, that of evaluating alternatives, assumes that each *can* be judged according to set standards or criteria. This further assumes that valid criteria exist, each alternative can be compared against these criteria and that the decision-maker actually uses the criteria. As you know from making your own life decisions, people frequently violate one or more of these assumptions. *Can* in this case essentially means that each alternative solution comes with the same level or quality of information as do the others.

Finally, once a solution is chosen, it needs to be implemented. Before implementing a solution, though, decision-makers need to do their homework. For example, three ineffective managerial tendencies have been observed frequently during the initial stages of implementation (see Table 13.1). Skilful managers try to avoid these. Table 13.1 indicates that to promote necessary understanding, acceptance and motivation, managers should involve implementers in the choice-making step.

After the solution is implemented, the evaluation phase assesses its effectiveness. If the solution is effective, it should reduce the difference between the actual and desired states that created the problem. If the gap is not closed, the implementation was not successful, then the problem was incorrectly identified, or the solution was inappropriate. If the implementation was, indeed, unsuccessful, management can return to the first step, and consider implementing one of the previously identified but untried solutions. This process can continue until all feasible solutions have been tried or the problem has changed.[4]

The rational model is based on the premise that when managers make decisions, they are aiming to solve problems by producing the best possible solution, which is referred to in the literature as **optimising**. This assumes that managers have:

- Knowledge of all possible alternatives.
- Complete knowledge about the consequences that follow each alternative.

Table 13.1 Three Managerial Tendencies Reduce the Effectiveness of Implementing Solutions

Managerial tendency	Recommended solution
Not to ensure that people understand what needs to be done	Involve the implementators in the choice-making step. When this is not possible, a strong and explicit attempt should be made to identify any misunderstanding, perhaps by having the implementor explain what he or she thinks needs to be done and why
Not to ensure the acceptance or motivation for what needs to be done	Once again, involve the implementators in the choice-making step. Attempts should also be made to demonstrate the payoffs for effective implementation and to show how completion of various tasks will lead to successful implementation
Not to provide appropriate resources for what needs to be done	Many implementations are less effective than they could be because adequate resources, such as time, staff or information, were not provided. In particular, the allocations of such resources across departments and tasks are assumed to be appropriate because they were appropriate for implementing the previous plan. These assumptions should be checked

Source: Modified from G. P. Huber, *Managerial Decision Making* (Glenview, IL: Scott, Foresman, 1980), p. 19.

- A well-organised and stable set of preferences for these consequences.
- The computational ability to compare consequences and to determine which one is preferred.[5]

As noted by Herbert Simon (see Chapter 1), 'The assumptions of perfect rationality are contrary to fact. It is not a question of approximation; they do not even remotely describe the processes that human beings use for making decisions in complex situations.'[6] Thus, the rational model is at best an instructional tool. Since decision-makers do not follow these rational procedures, Simon proposed a normative model of decision-making.

The Carnegie model of decision-making

This model takes its name from the Carnegie Institute of Technology, (now Carnegie-Mellon University). This is where Herbert Simon made his fundamental contribution to decision theory. The model attempts to identify the process that managers actually use when making decisions. According to the model, this process is constrained by a decision-maker's bounded rationality. **Bounded rationality** represents the notion that decision-makers are 'bounded' or restricted by a variety of constraints when making decisions. These constraints include any personal or environmental characteristics that reduce rational decision-making. Examples are the limited capacity of the human mind, problem complexity and uncertainty, the amount and timeliness of information at hand, importance of the decision and time demands.[7]

In contrast to the rational model, the Carnegie model suggests that decision-making is characterised by limited information processing, the use of judgemental heuristics and a process that involves 'satisficing' with something short of ideal. The existence of bounded rationality limits information processing by decision-makers. This results in the tendency to acquire manageable rather than optimal amounts of information (see also Chapter 4 with regard to information overload). In turn, this practice makes it difficult for managers to identify all possible alternative solutions. In the long run, the constraints of bounded rationality cause decision-makers to fail to evaluate all potential alternatives.

The second problem in the model is also important. **Judgemental heuristics** represent rules of thumb or short-cuts that people use to reduce information processing demands.[8] Most people use such tricks more or less automatically, without being aware of it. The use of heuristics helps decision-makers to reduce the uncertainty inherent within the decision-making process. Because these short cuts represent knowledge gained from past experience, they can help decision-makers evaluate current problems. They can, however, lead to systematic errors that lower the quality of decisions. There are two common categories of heuristics that are important to consider: the **availability heuristic** and the **prevalence (or representativeness) heuristic**. These and others are examined below in section 13.2.

People 'satisfice' because they do not have the time, information or ability to handle the complexity associated with following a rational process. This is not necessarily undesirable. **Satisficing** consists of choosing a solution that meets some minimum qualifications, one that is 'good enough'. It resolves problems by producing solutions that are satisfactory, as opposed to optimal. Finding a radio station to listen to in your car is a good example of this process. You cannot optimise your choice because it is impossible to listen to all stations at the same time. You thus stop searching for a station when you find one playing a song you like or do not mind hearing.

The final and most important element in the Carnegie model is its solution to the valuation problem of the rational model. The decision is made subject to satisficing and heuristics, by the most powerful coalition in the organisation. The notion of a powerful or dominant coalition means that politics rule as people pursue their individual goals and interests. Unanimity is not required, but those who oppose a particular decision ideally have to accept it with good grace, despite losing out to others.

The Carnegie model is suited to situations with environmental uncertainty, yet it remains rooted to the rational thinking, but modified by a set of constraints.

The incrementalist model

From the ideal but difficult to satisfy demands of the rational model evolved the Carnegie model, with its implicit focus on reducing the volume of information that needs processing for each decision and the emphasis on power and politics. There is, however, an alternative, also developed in the 1950s, by Charles Lindblom.

In the incremental or incrementalist model, managers select only those actions which differ a little from what was previously done. By only making small changes, the risk of making a costly mistake is reduced. If a decision turns out to be wrong, the cost of reversing it is modest. This model is often referred to as 'muddling through', an expression coined by Lindblom in the title of the paper that first introduced the model.[9]

Whereas the Carnegie model provided (or explained) short cuts for decision-makers, the incrementalist model in effect assumes that information is incomplete as soon as we move beyond the immediate future. Managers, in other words, do not have anything approaching perfect foresight. This means that the model is suitable under conditions of moderate and high uncertainty.

The 'garbage can' model

This approach, like the Carnegie model, came about as a response to the rational model's inability to explain how decisions are actually made. It assumes that organisational decision-making is a sloppy and haphazard process. This contrasts sharply with the rational model, which proposed that decision-makers follow a sequential series of steps beginning with a problem and ending with a solution. According to the **'garbage can' model**, decisions result from a complex interaction between four independent streams of events: problems, solutions, participants and choice opportunities.[10]

The interaction of these events creates 'a collection of choices looking for problems, issues and feelings looking for decision situations in which they might be aired, solutions looking for issues to which they might be the answer and decision-makers looking for work'.[11] A similar type of process occurs in a dustbin (or garbage can). We randomly discard our rubbish and it gets thrown together based on chance interactions. Consider, for instance, going to your dustbin and noticing that the used coffee granules are stuck to banana skin. Can you explain how this might occur? The answer is simple: because they were thrown in at about the same time. Just like the process of mixing rubbish in a dustbin, the 'garbage can model' of decision-making assumes that decision-making does not follow an orderly series of steps. Rather, attractive solutions can get matched up with whatever handy problems exist at that time or people get assigned to projects because their workload is low at that moment. This model of decision-making thus attempts to explain how problems, solutions, participants and choice opportunities interact and lead to a decision.

The four streams of events – problems, solutions, participants and choice opportunities – flow in and out of organisational decision situations independently of each other (see Figure 13.1). Because decisions are a function of the interaction between these independent events, the stages of problem identification and problem solution may be unrelated. For instance, a solution may be proposed for a problem that does not exist. Each of the four events in the garbage can model deserves a closer look:

Figure 13.1 'Garbage Can' Model of Organisational Decision-Making

problems
solutions
participants
choice opportunities
A
B
problems
solutions
participants
choice opportunities

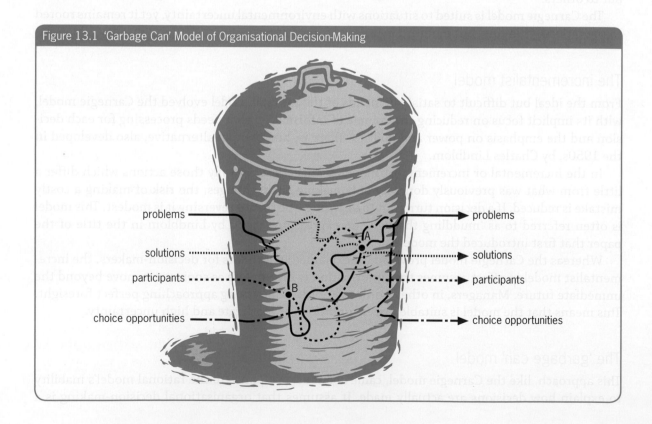

- *Problems* represent a gap between an actual situation and a desired condition. But problems are independent from alternatives and solutions. The problem may or may not lead to a solution.
- *Solutions* are answers looking for questions. They represent ideas constantly flowing through an organisation. Contrary to the classical model, however, solutions are used to formulate problems rather than vice versa. This is predicted to occur because people often do not know what they want until they have some idea of what they can get.
- *Participants* are the organisational members who come and go throughout the organisation. They bring different values, attitudes and experiences, as well as solutions that enter the garbage can with them, to a decision-making situation. Time pressures limit the extent to which participants are involved in decision-making.
- *Choice opportunities* are occasions in which an organisation is expected to make a decision. While some opportunities, such as hiring and promoting employees, occur regularly, others do not because they result from some type of crisis or unique situation.

Because of the independent nature of the streams of events, they interact in a random fashion. This implies that decision-making is more a function of chance encounters than a rational process. Thus, the organisation is characterised as a garbage can (dustbin) in which problems, solutions, participants and choice opportunities are all mixed together. Only when the four streams of events happen to intersect, such as at point A in Figure 13.1, is a decision made. Because these intersections randomly occur within the countless combinations of streams of events, decision quality generally depends on timing. Some might call it 'luck' or coincidence. In other words, decisions, either good or bad, are made when these streams of events interact at the proper time. This explains why problems do not necessarily relate to solutions (point B in Figure 13.1) and why solutions do not always solve problems. In support of the model, one study indicated that decision-making in the textbook publishing industry conformed to it. Moreover, knowledge of the model helped the researchers to identify a variety of best-selling textbooks.[12]

The unstructured model of decision-making

If environments are not stable, a more radical approach is needed. For such situations, Henry Mintzberg and colleagues have proposed the 'unstructured model of decision-making'.[13] Of course, this is anything but unstructured. The essential steps in the model are in fact somewhat similar to the rational model, but with less emphasis on finding optimal solutions. The three stages in the model are *identification*, *development* and *selection*. Identification is about being able to spot changes that will necessitate decisions. Development, where alternatives are sought and developed, is similar to the solutions step in the rational model. Finally, in the selection step, managers mix judgement, negotiation and formal analysis in order to arrive at a final decision.

The unstructured model clearly mixes elements from other models, but it is less programmed and thus better suited to situations with high uncertainty.

Decisions by rule following

An organisation without rules is hard to imagine, and perhaps could never exist. Rules help determine the boundaries, activities and general functioning of any organisation. Thus, it should be no surprise that decisions can be made by following rules. The problem is the origin of rules, They can come from many places: from the rational model, from heuristics, standard practice or norms that have become generally accepted in an organisation.

Before making decisions about what to do, it is part of the model to consider identity. Thus, the first step of a rule-based decision is to identify the situation. Then comes the question of identity: who am I and what would a person like me do in similar circumstances? (Or what can my organisation do in the same circumstances?) The reason this is an extremely important dimension of decision-making is that the three-step model, from defining identity, via assessing the situation to finding a rule that is appropriate is heavily dependent not just upon the individual's identity (as in a sense of who he or she is) but also upon who we have chosen to be that day. Similarly, there may be different rules invoked by the same individual at different times.[14]

Evidence about decision models

The garbage can model of organisational decision-making has four practical implications.[15] The first of these is that many decisions will be made by oversight or the presence of a salient opportunity. Consider Coca-Cola's 1996 decision to hire the world's largest cargo plane to take an 80-ton bottling line out to a new plant in Vladivostok, Russia.

Coca-Cola's decision to use a cargo plane instead of a ship was based on the perceived opportunity to capture more of Russia's soft-drink market. However, while the opportunity seemed attractive at the time, Coca-Cola would perhaps not have made the decision to invest in building bottling plants in Russia had it foreseen the collapse of Russia's economy. Second, political motives frequently guide the process by which participants make decisions. Participants tend to make decisions that promise to increase their status. Third, the process is sensitive to load: that is, as the number of problems increases relative to the amount of time available to solve them, problems are less likely to be solved. Finally, important problems are more likely to be solved than unimportant ones because they are more salient to organisational participants.[16]

HR Application: how to think about decision models

Managers in organisations make great numbers of decisions all the time. Some are more important than others. Some are very much a matter of routine, requiring almost no thought. Conditions vary, from near certainty about input data to the total absence of such data.

The thing for managers to keep in mind is that decisions do not follow one specific model. They may seek to push decision processes in one direction or the other. The choice, also a decision, may be difficult and it is worth keeping in mind that doing nothing can be worse. The point is that apart from a decision that is successful, one that is a failure may still provide important knowledge for next time. The only alternative – of no value – is to do nothing.

! Critical thinking

How aware are managers you know about the pitfalls of 'other than rational' models of decision-making?

13.2 Dynamics of decision-making

Decision-making is part science and part art. The former is informed by data, models and calculations; the latter by experience, feelings and 'hunches' about what is best. However, while it is somewhat

Figure 13.2 A Contingency Model for Selecting a Solution

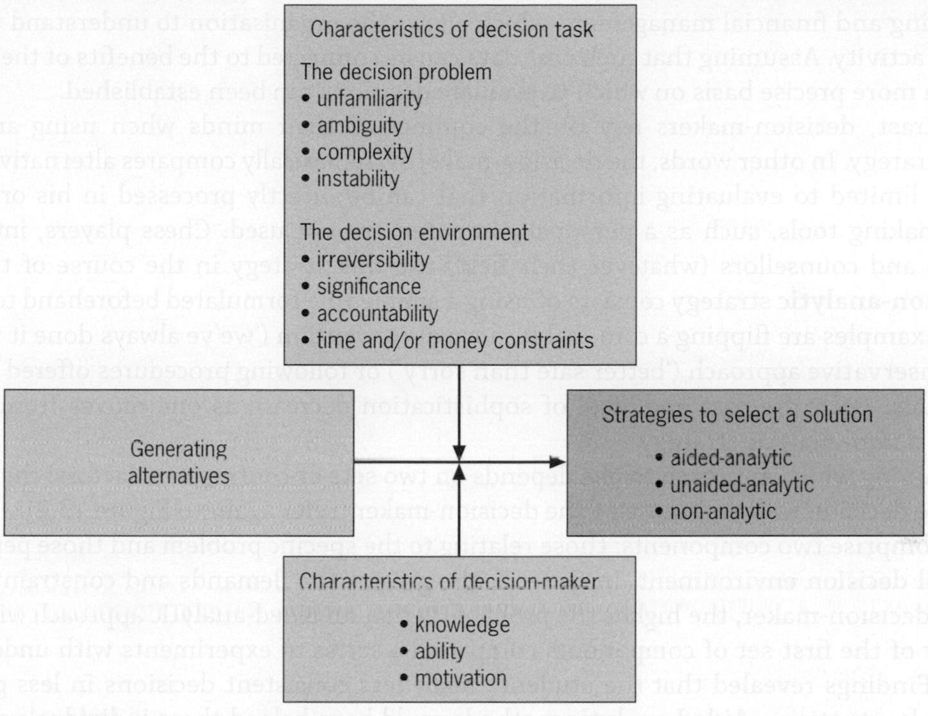

Source: Based on L. R. Beach and T. R. Mitchell, 'A Contingency Model for the Selection of Decision Strategies', *Academy of Management Review*, July 1978, pp. 439–44.

romantic to describe parts of decision-making as 'art', three aspects of the process help demystify the artistic part, at least for those who understand the implications. Three dynamic aspects of decision-making are contingency considerations, decision-making styles and intuitive decision-making; in addition is the problem of decision biases.

Selecting solutions: a contingency perspective

The previous discussion of decision-making models noted that decision-makers typically select solutions that will suffice. However, we did not probe how decision-makers actually evaluate and select solutions. Let us explore the model in Figure 13.2 to understand better how individuals make decisions.

According to the contingency model for selecting decision strategies, one of three approaches can be used: aided-analytic, unaided-analytic and non-analytic.[17] Within the analytic approach, decision-makers systematically use tools such as mathematical equations, calculators or computers to analyse and evaluate alternatives.

Weather forecasters, astronomers and insurance analysts are good examples of people who make decisions by using an **aided-analytic** strategy. This type of professional tends to make decisions by analysing data with complex computer models.[18] In addition to using decision-making tools, organisations may create a decision-making team or hire consultants to conduct a formal study of the problem to hand.

One area where decision-making using this approach interacts with other functions of organisations is when decisions are based (in part) on activity-based costing (or ABC). This is an approach to accounting and financial management which allows the organisation to understand the cost of each small activity. Assuming that such cost data can be connected to the benefits of the activity in question, a more precise basis on which to evaluate decisions can been established.

In contrast, decision-makers rely on the confines of their minds when using an **unaided analytic** strategy. In other words, the decision-maker systematically compares alternatives, but the analysis is limited to evaluating information that can be directly processed in his or her head. Decision-making tools, such as a personal computer, are not used. Chess players, interviewing journalists and counsellors (whatever their field) use this strategy in the course of their work. Finally, a **non-analytic** strategy consists of using a simple rule formulated beforehand to make the decision. Examples are flipping a coin, habit, normal convention ('we've always done it that way'), using a conservative approach ('better safe than sorry') or following procedures offered in instruction manuals. Both the cost and level of sophistication decrease as one moves from an aided-analytic to a non-analytic strategy.

Determining which approach to use depends on two sets of contingency factors: the characteristics of the decision task and those of the decision-maker (refer again to Figure 13.2).

These comprise two components: those relating to the specific problem and those pertaining to the general decision environment. In general, the greater the demands and constraints encountered by a decision-maker, the higher the probability that an aided-analytic approach will be used.

A study of the first set of components comprised a series of experiments with undergraduate students. Findings revealed that the students made less consistent decisions in less predictable and unstable situations. **Aided analytic** methods could have helped these individuals make more consistent decisions. A second study examined the strategic decision-making process within 24 organisations with annual sales ranging from $1.5 million to more than $3 billion. Results demonstrated that more effective decisions were made by managers who collected information and used analytical techniques than by managers who did not.[19]

The environment also restricts the type of analysis used. For instance, a study of 75 MBA students revealed that they purchased and used less information for decision-making as the cost of information increased. In contrast, they purchased and used more information when they were rewarded for making good decisions. These results suggest that both the cost of information and one's accountability for a decision affect the type of analysis used to solve a problem.[20] Moreover, time constraints influence selection of a solution. Poorer decisions are bound to be made in the face of severe time pressure.

The second set of contingency factors relate to the decision-maker. Chapters 2 and 3 highlighted a variety of individual differences that affect employee behaviour and performance. An individual's knowledge, ability and motivation affect the type of analytical procedure used in coming to a decision. In general, research supports the prediction that aided-analytic strategies are more likely to be used by competent and motivated individuals.[21]

The third element in the model is contingency relationships. There are many ways in which characteristics of the task and the decision-maker can interact to influence the strategy used to select a solution. In choosing a strategy, decision-makers must make a compromise between their desire to make correct decisions and the amount of time and effort they put into the decision-making process. Table 13.2 lists contingency relationships that help reconcile these competing demands. As shown in this table, analytic strategies are more likely to be used when the problem is unfamiliar and irreversible. In contrast, non-analytic methods are employed on familiar problems or problems in which the decision can be reversed.

Table 13.2 Contingency Relationships in Decision-Making

1	Analytic strategies are used when the decision problem is unfamiliar, ambiguous, complex or unstable
2	Non-analytic methods are employed when the problem is familiar, straightforward or stable
3	Assuming there are no monetary or time constraints, analytic approaches are used when the solution is irreversible and significant and when the decision-maker is accountable
4	Non-analytic strategies are used when the decision can be reversed and is not very significant or when the decision-maker is not held accountable
5	As the probability of making a correct decision goes down, analytic strategies are used
6	As the probability of making a correct decision goes up, non-analytic strategies are employed
7	Time and money constraints automatically exclude some strategies from being used
8	Analytic strategies are more frequently used by experienced and educated decision-makers
9	Non-analytic approaches are used when the decision-maker lacks knowledge, ability or motivation to make a good decision

Source: Adapted from L. R. Beach and T. R. Mitchell, 'A Contingency Model for the Selection of Decision Strategies', *Academy of Management Review*, July 1978, pp. 439–44.

OB in Real Life

'Put jam in your pockets, you are going to be toast'

In hindsight, what happened at Mount Pinatubo in the Philippines in 1991 was significant. At the time, however, the team involved had only a vague idea about the importance of their decisions. The team were geologists from the United States Geological Survey and from the Philippine Volcanic Institute. They had been assembled in the spring of 1991 as activity seemed to be rising at the hitherto dormant Pinatubo Volcano on Luzon island, some 87 kilometres north-west of Manila.

The core members of the team had considerable experience with the kind of volcanoes that occur both on the US west coast and in the Philippines. These are large mountains capable of causing almost incredible damage. By comparison, the unpronounceable Icelandic Eyjafjallajökull volcano is a minor annoyance, even if it grounded air traffic in Europe for weeks.

The team knew the historical record of explosive volcanoes. Only a few years earlier team members had been involved when another volcano had been considered non-threatening just before it created ash flows and mudslides that killed 20 000 people as they slept. The trouble with these volcanoes is not the lava itself but the so-called fiery clouds consisting of hot gasses and drops of lava suspended within the cloud. These clouds race down the mountain slopes faster than any normal car can drive in a straight line, causing complete devastation in their paths.

The team was based at Clark Air Base, then a US facility. They set up monitoring equipment on the mountain that gave real-time data on earthquakes and ground inclination, both key sources of data for volcano watchers. As they looked at the mountain from helicopters and with their data, they became increasingly worried that a very large eruption might happen with very short notice. The countryside is fertile and hundreds of thousands of people might be in danger. However, even if several levels of alert were available, only a level 3 alert would lead to the large-scale evacuation needed if the mountain erupted in a serious way.

In early June 1991 the team were on the brink of calling a level 3 alert several times, as the volcano rumbled and spewed out minor amounts of ash. The team faced a dilemma. If they increase the alert level to 3 or more, people closest to the mountain would be evacuated. However, if no eruption came, people would begin drifting back to their homes, and be more unlikely to heed a second warning. The minor eruptions grew larger and when the first large explosion occurred on 7 June, people within the 10 and 20 kilometre radius were ordered to evacuate. An Air Force officer asked 'Is this the big one?', to which the geologists replied, still composed, that this was a sort of 'throat clearing' action, signalling that it is going to do 'it'. From 12 June explosions grew in violence, culminating on 15 June, from 14:30 onwards. As if things could not get any worse, the area was hit by the tropical storm Yunya, which converted the hot ash to boiling rivers of mud.

The geologists were jubilant. Not only were they witnessing a spectacular once-in-a-lifetime event, they had also read the signals correctly and had been more or less instrumental in saving the lives of thousands.

For discussion

List the contingencies.

Source: Based on US Geological Survey Fact Sheet 113-97, The Cataclysmic 1991 Eruption of Mount Pinatubo, Philippines, www.pubs.usgs.gov/fs/1997/fs113-97/ (Accessed 2 August 2010).

General decision-making styles

The previous section stressed that individual differences or characteristics of a decision-maker influence the decision-making process. This sub-section expands on this discussion by focusing on how an individual's decision-making style affects his or her approach to decision-making. Remember also the elaboration on cognitive styles (Chapter 2), a rather similar concept.

A **decision-making style** reflects the combination of how an individual perceives and comprehends stimuli and the general manner in which he or she chooses to respond to it.[22] A team of researchers developed a model that is based on the idea that decision-making styles vary along two different dimensions: value orientation and tolerance for ambiguity.[23] Value orientation reflects the extent to which an individual focuses either on task and technical concerns or on people and social concerns when making decisions. Some people are very task focused at work and do not pay much attention to people issues, whereas others are just the opposite. The second dimension reflects a person's tolerance for ambiguity; that is, the extent to which a person needs structure or control in his or her life. Some people desire a lot of structure in their lives (a low tolerance for ambiguity) and find ambiguous situations stressful and psychologically uncomfortable. In contrast, others do not have a strong need for structure and can thrive in uncertain situations. Ambiguous situations can energise people with a high tolerance for ambiguity. When the dimensions of value orientation and tolerance for ambiguity are combined, they form four styles of decision-making (see Figure 13.3): directive, analytical, conceptual and behavioural.

People with a *directive* style are efficient, logical, practical and systematic in their approach to solving problems. People with this style are action-oriented and decisive and like to focus on facts. In their pursuit of speed and results, however, these individuals tend to be autocratic, exercise power and control, and focus on the short run.

The *analytical* style has a much higher tolerance for ambiguity and is characterised by the tendency to analyse a situation too closely. People with this style like to consider more information and alternatives than do directives. They are careful decision-makers who take longer than others

Figure 13.3 Decision-Making Styles

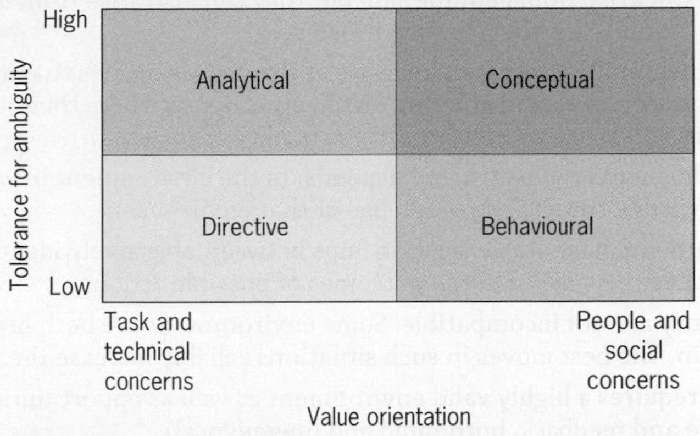

Source: Based on discussion contained in A. J. Rowe and R. O. Mason, *Managing with Style: A Guide to Understanding, Assessing, and Improving Decision Making* (San Francisco, CA: Jossey-Bass, 1987), pp. 1–17.

to make decisions but who can, when necessary, respond well to new or uncertain situations. They can often be autocratic.

People with a *conceptual* style have a high tolerance for ambiguity and tend to focus on the people or social aspects of a work situation. They take a broad perspective to problem-solving and like to consider many options and future possibilities. Conceptual types adopt a long-term perspective and rely on intuition and discussion with others to acquire information. They are willing to take risks and are good at finding creative solutions to problems. On the downside, however, a conceptual style can foster an idealistic and indecisive approach to decision-making.

Of the four styles, the *behavioural* is the one which focuses most on the people aspect of decisions. Individuals with this style work well with others and enjoy social interactions in which opinions are openly exchanged. They are supportive, receptive to suggestions, show warmth, and prefer verbal to written information. Although they like to hold meetings, people with this style have a tendency to avoid conflict and to be too concerned about others. Behavioural types can seem unfocused and have a hard time saying no to others and to have problems making difficult decisions.

Intuition and decisions

Even if the models covered in section 13.1 differ in terms of rationality, they have in common some degree of an informational foundation. Even the unstructured model has a measure of information as it is partly created in the course of the decision-making process.

Sometimes there are no data. At other times getting hold of data seems a complete waste of time, given that the decision-maker knows exactly what to do in a given situation. In these instances it may be a sensible to rely on intuition. However, not all intuition is equally reliable. In Jungian psychology there is even a personality type labelled as intuitive, who acts on the basis of perception rather than rational analysis. Intuition plays a role in a number of areas involving spirituality but most of the writing in these areas is beyond the scope of this text. What is interesting in the context of making decisions is expertise, or the decisions made by experts.

One definition of expert intuition comes from Daniel Kahneman (we will return to his work in the next section): 'Intuitive thinking is perception-like, rapid, effortless. . . . Deliberate thinking is reasoning-like, critical, and analytic; it is also slow, effortful, controlled, and rule-governed.'[24]

Table 13.3 Intuition problems in decision-making

- Intuitive judgements can arise from genuine skill but they can also arise from inappropriate application of rules of thumb (i.e. the heuristic processes).
- People who are genuinely skilled are often unaware of the signals or cues that guide them, whereas those whose intuitions are not skilled are even less likely to know where their judgements come from. Thus confidence about skill is a poor indicator of the quality of intuition.
- Whether intuitive judgements can be trusted depends on the environment in which the judgement is made and on the knowledge the skilled person has of that environment.
- High-validity environments have stable relationships between objectively identifiable cues and subsequent events or between cues and the outcomes of possible actions.
- Validity and uncertainty are not incompatible. Some environments are both highly valid and substantially uncertain. The best moves in such situations reliably increase the potential for success.
- Development of skill requires a highly valid environment as well as opportunities for learning the environment (practice and feedback, both rapid and unequivocal).
- True skill cannot develop in irregular or unpredictable environments, but 'lucky' individuals who make successful decisions by chance may develop an illusion of skill and overconfidence.
- Fractionation of skill is another source of overconfidence. It may occur when an expert in one area is asked to apply that skill in another area where he or she has no real skill. It is difficult for experts and for those observing them to know the boundaries of their true expertise.

Based on D. Kahneman and G. Klein, 'Conditions for intuitive expertise: a failure to disagree', *American Psychologist*, vol. 64, no. 6, September 2009, pp. 515–26.

In the evocatively titled 2005 bestseller *Blink* by Malcolm Gladwell, the benefits of relying on snap judgements and gut feelings was strongly emphasised. While experts can make very quick judgements, it is important to keep a sense of perspective. Table 13.3 lists the challenges facing anyone considering intuition as part of an organisation's decision toolbox.

HR Biases in decision-making

Decisions can, regardless of which model one is using, be affected by the tendency of people to see things in a distorted way when they make decisions. Here we limit ourselves to eight of the most important biases.

The **availability bias** represents a decision-maker's tendency to base decisions on information that is readily available in memory.[25] This can happen when the information involves an event that recently occurred, when it is salient (a plane crash), and when it evokes strong emotions (e.g. a shooting incident). This heuristic is likely to cause people to overestimate the occurrence of unlikely events such as a plane crash or a shooting. This bias also is partially responsible for the recency effect discussed in Chapter 4. A supervisor is more likely to give an employee a positive performance evaluation if the employee exhibited excellent performance over the last few months.

The **representativeness bias** can occur when people estimate the probability of an event occurring. It reflects the tendency to assess the likelihood of an event occurring based on one's impressions about similar occurrences. A recruiter, for example, may hire a graduate from a particular university because the last three people taken on from this university turned out to be good performers. Similarly, an individual may believe that he or she can master a new software package in a short period of time because he or she was previously able to learn how to use a different type of software quickly.

Escalation of commitment refers to the tendency to stick to an ineffective course of action when it is unlikely that the bad situation can be reversed. Personal examples include investing more money into an old or broken car, waiting an extremely long time for a bus when you could have walked there just as easily or trying to save a disruptive personal relationship that has lasted 10 years. Case studies also indicate that escalation of commitment is partially responsible for some of the worst financial losses experienced by organisations. For example, from 1966 to 1989 the Long Island Lighting Company's investment in the Shoreham nuclear power plant in the USA escalated from $65 million to $5 billion, despite a steady flow of negative feedback. The plant was never opened.[26]

Anchoring is a bias that occurs when the decision-maker pays too much attention to the first information he or she receives and not enough attention to information that comes later.[27] For example, if someone advertises a house for sale, the quoted price will influence the final price, even if other later facts indicate that it is all wrong.

The confirmation bias influences decision-making in the phase where we collect information on which to base the decision. However, people are likely to be selective in what bits of information they select: those that support the decision they have already subconsciously made or information which confirms past similar choices. As a result, we overemphasise what confirms existing views and underemphasise information that contradicts them.[28]

After an event, people can come to believe that they have in fact accurately predicted what actually happened. This is called **hindsight**, but many facts and connections between facts only become known later. When someone says that everyone could see the financial crisis coming, they are very likely to be affected by this bias.[29]

How a decision problem is formulated or 'framed' influences how the decision-maker perceives it. The **framing bias** involves the decision-maker valuing a gain more than a loss. Consider a question framed as a choice between two programmes related to an opportunity worth €6 million in total. In programme 1 a net benefit of €2 million will be realised and in programme 2 the probability of gaining the €6 million benefit is one-third and the probability that there will be no benefit at all is two-thirds. The first programme is much more likely to be chosen, even if the outcomes are exactly the same.[30]

When people face difficult questions they are particularly at risk of being hit by the **overconfidence bias**. Give a group of people a factual question and ask them to estimate the probability of them answering correctly, and you will find that they are more confident than the number of correct answers indicated they should be. There are, fortunately, relatively simple solutions. The overconfidence bias is strongest when intellectual and interpersonal abilities are weakest.[31] Apart from being careful about who is asked to make decisions, this indicates that training and practice may be simple solutions.

Evidence about decision-making style and bias

Research shows that very few people have only one dominant decision-making style. Rather, most people have characteristics that fall into two or three styles. Studies also show that decision-making styles vary across occupations, job levels and countries.[32] You can use knowledge of decision-making styles in three ways.

First, knowledge of styles helps you to understand yourself. Awareness of your style assists you in identifying your strengths and weaknesses as a decision-maker and facilitates the potential for self-improvement. (You can assess your decision-making style by completing the 'Personal awareness and growth exercise' located at the end of this chapter.)

Second, you can increase your ability to influence others by being aware of styles. For example, if you are dealing with an analytical person, you should provide as much information as possible to support your ideas. This same approach is more likely to frustrate a directive type.

Finally, knowledge of styles gives you an awareness of how people can take in the same information and yet arrive at different decisions by using a variety of decision-making strategies. Different decision-making styles represent one likely source of interpersonal conflict at work (conflict is discussed in Chapter 14). It is important to conclude with the caveat that there is no one ideal decision-making style applicable to all situations.

HR Application: avoiding biased decisions

Dealing with the eight common biases can be done in a number of ways. The availability and representativeness biases might be countered by formalisation, so that decision-makers are forced to think beyond availability and convenient memories. Minimum targets, rotation of decision-makers and cost awareness mechanisms may help guard against escalation. Anchoring is not always a problem: it can be used to advantage. Otherwise, awareness helps against it. Hindsight harms the ability to learn, since we tend to think we perform better than we actually do. Feedback, precise, timely and objective can alleviate the problem, even if costly to do. Framing problems can be reduced by rethinking and varying the way decision problems are formulated. As for overconfidence, the solution is training and practice.

> **! Critical thinking**
>
> If you could choose a bias that would then disappear, which one would it be?

13.3 Group decision-making and other forms of participation

Groups such as committees, task forces or review panels often play a key role in the decision-making process. Are two or more heads always better than one? Do all employees desire to have a say in the decision-making process? When and how should a manager use group decision-making? This section provides the background for answering these questions, essential for gaining maximum benefits from group decision-making. We discuss the (1) advantages and disadvantages of group-aided decision-making, (2) participative management, (3) when to use groups in decision-making and (4) group problem-solving techniques. A broader examination of group dynamics and groupthink was provided in Chapter 7.

Group-aided decision-making

Including groups in the decision-making process has both advantages and disadvantages (see Table 13.3). On the positive side, groups contain a greater pool of knowledge, provide more varied perspectives, create more comprehension of decisions, increase decision acceptance and create a training ground for inexperienced employees. These advantages must be balanced, however, against the disadvantages listed in Table 13.3. In doing so, managers need to determine the extent to which the advantages and disadvantages apply to the situation facing them. The following three guidelines may then be applied to help decide whether groups should be included in the decision-making process:

- If additional information would increase the quality of the decision, managers should involve those people who can provide the necessary information.

Table 13.3 Advantages and Disadvantages of Group-Aided Decision-Making

Advantages	Disadvantages
1 Greater pool of knowledge. A group can bring much more information and experience to bear on a decision or problem than can an individual acting alone	1 Social pressure. Unwillingness to 'rock the boat' and pressure to conform may combine to stifle the creativity of individual contributors
2 Different perspectives. Individuals with varied experience and interests help the group see decision situations and problems from different angles	2 Domination by a vocal few. Sometimes the quality of group action is reduced when the group gives in to those who talk the loudest and longest
3 Greater comprehension. Those who personally experience the give-and-take of group discussion about alternative courses of action tend to understand the rationale behind the final decision	3 Logrolling. Political wheeling and dealing can displace sound thinking when an individual's pet project or vested interest is at stake
4 Increased acceptance. Those who play an active role in group decision-making and problem-solving tend to view the outcome as 'ours' rather than 'theirs'	4 Goal displacement. Sometimes secondary considerations such as winning an argument, making a point or getting back at a rival displace the primary task of making a sound decision or solving a problem
5 Training ground. Less experienced participants in group action learn how to cope with group dynamics by actually being involved	5 Groupthink. Sometimes cohesive 'in-groups' let the desire for unanimity override sound judgement when generating and evaluating alternative courses of action. (Groupthink is discussed in Chapter 7.)

Source: R. Kreitner, *Management*, 7th edn (Boston, MA: Houghton Mifflin, 1998), p. 234.

- If acceptance is important, managers need to involve those individuals whose acceptance and commitment are important.
- If people's skills can be developed through their participation, managers may want to involve those whose development is most important.[33]

Employee involvement in decision-making

An organisation needs to maximise its workers' potential if it wants to compete successfully in the global economy. Jack Welch, the former CEO of General Electric, noted that:

> Only the most productive companies are going to win. If you can't sell a top quality product at the world's lowest price, you're going to be out of the game. In that environment, 6 per cent annual improvement in productivity may not be good enough anymore; you may need between 8 and 9 per cent.[34]

Employee involvement in decision-making and employee empowerment (which is further discussed in Chapter 14) are frequently suggested methods for meeting this productivity challenge. Interestingly, employees also seem to desire or recognise the need for involvement. A survey of 2408 employees, for example, revealed that almost 66 per cent desired more influence or decision-making power in their jobs.[35]

Advocates of employee involvement claim employee participation increases employee satisfaction, commitment and performance. To gain a greater understanding of how and when **participative management** works, we begin by discussing a model of participative management.

Activity

Assessing participation in group decision-making

Instructions

The following survey measures minority dissent, participation in group decision-making and satisfaction with a group. For each of the items, use the rating scale shown below to circle the answer that best represents your feelings based on a group project you were or currently are involved in. Next, use the scoring key to compute scores for the levels of minority dissent, participation in decision-making and satisfaction with the group.

1 = strongly disagree
2 = disagree
3 = neither agree nor disagree
4 = agree
5 = strongly agree

1	Within my team, individuals disagree with one another.	1 2 3 4 5
2	Within my team, individuals do not go along with majority opinion.	1 2 3 4 5
3	Within my team, individuals voice their disagreement of majority opinion.	1 2 3 4 5
4	Within my team, I am comfortable voicing my disagreement of the majority opinion.	1 2 3 4 5
5	Within my team, individuals do not immediately agree with one another.	1 2 3 4 5
6	As a team member, I have a real say in how work is carried out.	1 2 3 4 5
7	Within my team, most members have a chance to participate in decisions.	1 2 3 4 5
8	My team is designed so that everyone has the opportunity to participate in decisions.	1 2 3 4 5
9	I am satisfied with my group.	1 2 3 4 5
10	I would like to work with this group on another project.	1 2 3 4 5

Scoring key

Minority dissent (add scores for items 1, 2, 3, 4, 5): __________
Participation in decision-making (add scores for items 6, 7, 8): __________
Satisfaction (add scores for items 9, 10): __________

Arbitrary norms

Low minority dissent = 5–15
High minority dissent = 16–25
Low participation in decision-making = 3–8
High participation in decision-making = 9–15
Low satisfaction = 2–5
High satisfaction = 6–10

Source: The items in the survey were developed from C. K. W. De Dreu and M. A. West, 'Minority Dissent and Team Innovation: The Importance of Participation in Decision Making', *Journal of Applied Psychology*, December 2001, pp. 1192–201.

Consistent with both Maslow's need theory and the job characteristics model of job design (see Chapter 5), employee involvement is predicted to increase motivation because it helps employees fulfil three basic needs: autonomy, meaningful work and interpersonal contact. Satisfaction of these needs enhances feelings of acceptance and commitment, security, challenge and satisfaction. In turn, these positive feelings are believed to lead to increased innovation and performance.[36]

Employee involvement does not work in all situations. Three factors influence its effectiveness: the design of work, the level of trust between management and employees, and the employees' competence and readiness to participate. Individual participation in the design of work is counter-productive when employees are highly dependent on each other, as on an assembly line. Employees generally do not have a broad understanding of the entire production process. Also, employee involvement is less likely to succeed when employees mistrust management. Finally, it is more effective when employees are competent, prepared and interested in participating.[37]

Evidence about group decision-making and involvement

Before recommending that managers involve groups in decision-making, it is important to examine whether groups perform better or worse than individuals. After reviewing 61 years of relevant research, a decision-making expert concluded that: 'Group performance was generally qualitatively and quantitatively superior to the performance of the average individual.'[38] Although subsequent research of small-group decision-making generally supported this conclusion, five important issues arose which are important to consider when using groups to make decisions:

- Groups were less efficient than individuals. This suggests that time constraints are an important consideration in determining whether to involve groups in decision-making. A team of Nokia executives, who prize consensus, debated whether or not to license its software for nine months from mid-2000 to early 2001. At eight successive monthly meetings of the company's nine-person executive board, members raised questions and stalled the project.[39] Groups were more confident about their judgements and choices than individuals. Because group confidence does not necessarily guarantee the quality of a decision, this overconfidence can fuel groupthink (see Chapter 7) and a resistance to considering alternative solutions proposed by outsiders.
- Group size affected decision outcomes. Decision quality was negatively related to group size.[40]
- Decision-making accuracy was higher both when groups knew a great deal about the issues at hand and group leaders possessed the ability to evaluate effectively the group members' opinions and judgements. Groups need to give more weight to relevant and accurate judgements while downplaying irrelevant or inaccurate judgements made by its members.[41]
- The composition of a group affects its decision-making processes and ultimately performance. For example, groups of familiar people are more likely to make better decisions when members share a lot of unique information. In contrast, unacquainted group members should outperform groups of friends when most group members possess common knowledge.[42]

Participative management can significantly increase employee job involvement, organisational commitment, creativity and perceptions of procedural justice and personal control.[43] Two meta-analyses provide additional support for the value of participative management. Results from a meta-analysis involving 27 studies and 6732 individuals indicated that employee participation in the performance appraisal process was positively related to an employee's satisfaction with his or her performance review perceived value of the appraisal, motivation to improve performance following a performance review and perceived fairness of the appraisal process.[44] A second metaanalysis of 86 studies involving 18 872 people further demonstrated that participation had a small but significant effect on job performance and a moderate link with job satisfaction.[45] This latter finding questions the widespread conclusion that participative management should be used to increase employee performance. At best, this is one of the many ways to reach this goal.

HR Application of group decision-making and involvement

Additional research suggests that managers should use a contingency approach when determining whether to include others in the decision-making process. Important factors when using others in decision-making are minority dissent, which means the extent to which group members feel comfortable in disagreeing with other group members, and the group's level of participation in decision-making. High levels of minority dissent and participation are important for innovative groups. Take a moment to complete the next Activity. It assesses the amount of minority dissent and participation in group decision-making for a group project you have completed or are currently working on in school or on the job. Is your satisfaction with the group related to minority dissent and participation in decision-making? If not, what might explain this surprising result?

If the decision occurs frequently, such as deciding on promotions or who qualifies for a loan, use groups, as they tend to produce more consistent decisions than do individuals. If there are time constraints, let the most competent individual, rather than a group, make the decision. In the face of 'environmental threats' such as time pressure and the potentially serious effect of a decision, groups use less information and fewer communication channels. This increases the probability of a bad decision.[46] This conclusion underscores a general recommendation that managers should keep in mind, not least because the quality of communication strongly affects a group's productivity. It is essential, therefore, to devise mechanisms to enhance the effectiveness of communication when dealing with complex tasks (see Chapter 4).

What is a manager to do about involvement? We believe that employee involvement is not a quick-fix solution for low productivity and motivation, as some enthusiastic supporters claim. Nonetheless, because involvement is effective in certain situations, managers can increase their chances of obtaining positive results by using the contingency approach.[47] For example, the effectiveness of involvement depends on the type of interactions between managers and employees as they jointly solve problems. Effective involvement requires a constructive interaction that fosters co-operation and respect, as opposed to competition and defensiveness.[48] Managers are advised not to use involvement programmes when they are having destructive interactions with their employees.

Experiences of companies implementing employee involvement programmes suggest three additional practical recommendations. First, supervisors and middle managers tend to resist employee involvement because it reduces their power and authority. It is important to gain the support and commitment of employees who have managerial responsibility. Second, a longitudinal study of Fortune 1000 firms in 1987, 1990 and 1993 indicated that employee involvement was more effective when it was implemented as part of a broader total-quality-management programme[49] (total quality management is discussed in Chapter 11). This study suggests that organisations should use employee involvement as a vehicle to help them meet their strategic and operational goals as opposed to using these techniques as ends in themselves. Third, the process of implementing employee involvement must be monitored and managed by top management.[50]

! Critical thinking

Is employee involvement a tool that can be used independently of structure, leadership and contingencies?

13.4 Group problem-solving and creativity

Using groups to make decisions generally requires that they reach a consensus. A **consensus** is reached when all members can say they either agree with the decision, have had their views heard and everyone agrees to support the outcome.[51] Group members may still disagree with the final decision but are willing to work towards its success.

Groups can come across obstacles as they try to arrive at a consensus decision. For example, groups may not generate all the relevant alternatives to a problem because an individual dominates or intimidates other group members. This can be either overt or subtle, or indeed both. For instance, group members who possess power and authority, such as a CEO, can be intimidating, regardless of interpersonal style, simply by being present in the room. Moreover, shyness inhibits the generation of alternatives. Shy or socially anxious individuals may withhold their input for fear of embarrassment or through lack of confidence.[52] Satisficing (or sufficing) is another barrier to effective group decision-making and is the result of a group having limited time or information, or an inability to handle large amounts of information.[53] A management expert offered the following advice for successfully achieving consensus: groups should use active listening skills, involve as many members as possible, seek out the reasons behind arguments and dig for the facts. At the same time, groups should not 'horse trade' (I'll support you on this decision because you supported me on the last one), vote or agree just to avoid upsetting the process.[54] Voting is not encouraged because it can split the group into winners and losers.[55]

Decision-making experts have developed three group problem-solving techniques – brainstorming, the nominal group technique and the Delphi technique – to reduce the above obstacles.

Brainstorming

Brainstorming was developed by A. F. Osborn, an advertising executive, to increase creativity.[56] It is a technique used to help groups generate multiple ideas and alternatives for solving problems. It is effective because it helps reduce interference, during this early stage, from the critical and judgemental reactions of other group members.

When brainstorming, a group is convened, and the problem at hand is reviewed. Then individual members are asked to silently generate ideas, or alternatives, for solving the problem. Silent idea generation is recommended in preference to having group members randomly shout out their ideas because it leads to a greater number of unique ideas. Next, these ideas are solicited and written on a blackboard or flip chart. A recent study suggests that managers or team leaders may prefer to collect the brainstormed ideas anonymously. Results demonstrated that more controversial ideas and more useful ideas were generated by anonymous brainstorming groups.[57] Finally, a second session is used to check and evaluate the alternatives. Decision-makers are advised to follow four rules for brainstorming:[58]

- Stress quantity over quality. Decision-makers should try to generate and write down as many ideas as possible. Encouraging quantity encourages people to think beyond their favourite (pet) ideas.
- Freewheeling, as in 'thinking without the brakes on', should be encouraged; do not set limits. Group members are advised to offer any and all the ideas they have. The wilder and more outrageous, the better.
- Suspend judgement. Do not criticise during the initial stage of idea generation. Phrases such as 'we've never done it that way', 'it won't work', 'it's too expensive' and 'the boss will never agree' should not be used.

- Ignore seniority. People cannot think or suggest freely when they are trying to impress the boss or when office politics are involved. The facilitator of a brainstorming session should emphasise that everyone has the same rank. No one is given 'veto power' when brainstorming.

Brainstorming is a widely used and sometimes effective technique for generating new ideas and alternatives. It is not appropriate for evaluating alternatives or selecting solutions.

The **nominal group technique** (NGT) helps groups not only to generate ideas but also to evaluate and select solutions. NGT is a structured group meeting that adheres to the following format.[59] A group is convened to discuss a particular problem or issue. After the problem is understood, individuals silently generate ideas in writing. Each individual, in turn, then offers one idea from his or her list. Ideas are recorded on a blackboard or flip chart; they are not discussed at this stage of the process. Once all ideas are elicited, the group discusses them. Anyone may criticise or defend any item. During this step, clarification is provided as well as general agreement or disagreement with the idea. The '30-second soap box' technique, which involves giving each participant a maximum of 30 seconds to argue for or against any of the ideas under consideration, can be used to facilitate this discussion.

Finally, group members vote anonymously for their top choices with weighted votes (e.g. 1st choice = 3 points; 2nd choice = 2 points; 3rd choice = 1 point). The group leader then adds the votes to determine the group's choice. Prior to making a final decision, the group may decide to discuss the top ranked items and conduct a second round of voting.

The nominal group technique reduces the obstacles to group decision-making by separating brainstorming from evaluation, promoting balanced participation between group members and incorporating mathematical voting techniques in order to reach consensus. NGT has been used successfully in many different decision-making situations.

The Delphi technique was originally developed by the Rand Corporation for technological forecasting.[60] Now it is used as a multipurpose planning tool. The **Delphi technique** is a group process that, anonymously, generates ideas or judgements from physically dispersed experts. Unlike the NGT, experts' ideas are obtained from questionnaires or via the Internet rather than by face-to-face group discussion.

A manager begins the Delphi process by identifying the issue or issues to be investigated. For example, a manager might want to inquire about customer demand, customers' future preferences or the effect of locating a plant in a certain region of the country. Next, participants are identified and a questionnaire is developed. The questionnaire is sent to participants and returned to the manager. In today's computer-networked environments, this often means that the questionnaires are emailed to participants. The manager then summarises the responses and sends feedback to the participants. At this stage, participants are asked to:

- Review the feedback.
- Prioritise the issues being considered.
- Return the survey within a specified time period.

This cycle is then repeated until the manager obtains the necessary information.

The Delphi technique is useful in instances when face-to-face discussions are impractical, disagreements and conflict are likely to impair communication, certain individuals might severely dominate group discussion or groupthink is a probable outcome of the group process.[61]

The purpose of **computer-aided decision-making** is to reduce obstacles to consensus while collecting more information in a shorter period of time. There are two types of computer-aided decision-making systems: chauffeur-driven and group-driven.[62] Chauffeur-driven systems ask participants to answer predetermined questions on electronic keypads or dials. Live television audiences on quiz shows such as *Who Wants to Be a Millionaire* are frequently polled for their answers using this system. The computer system tabulates participants' responses in a matter of seconds.

Group-driven meetings are conducted in special facilities equipped with individual computer workstations that are networked to each other. Instead of talking, participants type their input, ideas, comments, reactions or evaluations on their keyboards. The input simultaneously appears on a large projector screen at the front of the room, thereby enabling all participants to see all the input. This computer-driven process reduces obstacles to consensus as the input is anonymous, everyone gets a chance to contribute and no one can dominate the process. Research demonstrated that, for large groups of people, computer-aided decision-making produces a greater quality and quantity of ideas than either traditional brainstorming or the nominal group technique. There were no significant advantages to group-aided decision-making with smaller groups of four to six.[63] Moreover, a recent study demonstrated that computer-aided decision-making produced relatively more ideas as group size increased from five to 10 members. The positive benefits of larger groups, however, were more pronounced for heterogeneous as opposed to homogeneous groups.[64]

Creativity

In the light of today's need for quick decisions, an organisation's ability to stimulate the creativity and innovation of its employees is becoming increasingly important. Although many definitions have been proposed, **creativity** is defined here as the process of using imagination and skill to develop a new or unique product, object, process or thought.[65] It can be as simple as locating a new place to hang your car keys to as complex as developing a smartphone. This definition highlights three broad types of creativity: creating something new (creation); combining or synthesising things (synthesis); and improving or changing things (modification).

Early approaches to explaining creativity were based on differences between the left and right hemispheres of the brain. Researchers thought the right-hand side of the brain was responsible for creativity.

Researchers are not absolutely certain how creativity takes place. Nonetheless, we do know that creativity involves 'making remote associations' between unconnected events, ideas, physical objects or information stored in memory. Consider how remote associations led to a creative idea that ultimately increased revenue for Japan Railways (JR) East, the largest rail carrier in the world. While JR East was building a new train line, water began to cause problems in the tunnel through Mount Tanigawa. As engineers drew up plans to drain it away, some of them were drinking it. One worker thought it tasted so good that he proposed that JR East should sell it as premium mineral water. This was done; a strange but successful bit of creativity for a railway company.[66]

The maintenance worker somehow associated the tunnel water with bottled water, and this led to the idea of marketing the water as a commercial product. Figure 13.4 depicts five stages underlying the creative process.[67]

The preparation stage reflects the notion that creativity starts from a base of knowledge. Experts suggest that creativity involves a convergence between tacit or implied and explicit knowledge.

Figure 13.4 Stages of the Creative Process

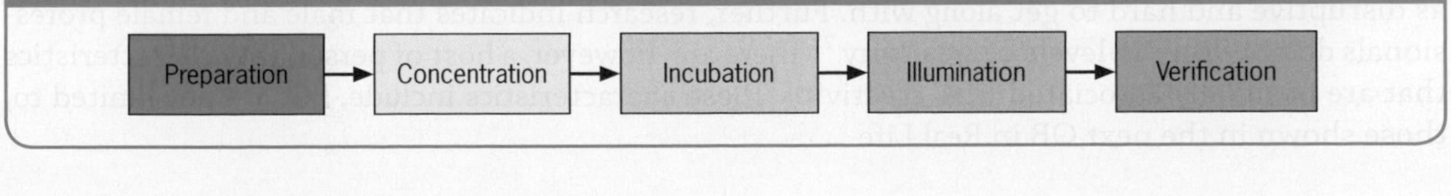

During the concentration stage, an individual focuses on the problem at hand. Interestingly, Japanese companies are noted for encouraging this stage as part of a quality improvement process – more so than Western companies. (Quality is discussed in Chapter 11.) For example, the average number of suggestions per employee for improving quality and productivity is significantly lower in the typical Western company than in comparable Japanese firms.[68]

Incubation is done unconsciously. During this stage, people engage in daily activities while their minds simultaneously mull over information and make remote associations. These associations, ultimately, are generated in the illumination stage. Finally, verification entails going through the entire process to verify, modify or try out the new idea.

One reason why Japanese organisations propose and implement more ideas than Western companies is that Japanese firms have created a management infrastructure that encourages and reinforces creativity. People are taught to identify problems (discontents) on their first day of employment. In turn, these discontents are referred to as 'golden eggs' to reinforce the notion that it is good to identify problems.

These organisations also promoted the stages of incubation, illumination and verification through teamwork and incentives. For example, some companies posted the golden eggs on large wall posters in the work area; employees were then encouraged to interact with each other to execute the final three stages of the creative process. Employees eventually received monetary awards for any suggestions that passed all five phases of this process.[69] This research underscores the conclusion that creativity can be enhanced by effectively managing the creativity process.

HR A model of organisational creativity and innovation

Organisational creativity and innovation are relatively unexplored topics within the field of observational behaviour (OB) despite their importance for organisational success. Rather than focus on group and organisational creativity, researchers had previously examined the predictors of individual creativity. This final section examines a process model for understanding organisational creativity. Knowledge of its linkages can help you to facilitate and contribute to organisational creativity.

Figure 13.5 illustrates the process underlying organisational creativity and innovation. It shows that this creativity is directly influenced by organisational characteristics and the amount of creative behaviour that occurs within work groups. In turn, a group's creative behaviour is influenced both by the group's characteristics and the individuals' creative behaviour. This individual creative behaviour is, in turn, directly affected by a variety of individual characteristics. The double-headed arrows between individual and group characteristics and between group and organisational characteristics indicate that these all influence each other. Let us now consider the model's major components.

Creative people seem to 'march to the beat of a different drummer' by operating differently to others. They are highly motivated individuals who spend considerable time developing both tacit (implied) and explicit knowledge of their field of interest or occupation. Contrary to stereotypes, however, creative people are not necessarily geniuses or studious introverts.[70] In addition, they are not adaptors (also see Chapter 2) 'who . . . prefer to resolve difficulties or make decisions in such a way as to have the least impact upon the assumptions, procedures, and values of the organisation'.[71] In contrast, creative individuals are dissatisfied with the status quo. They look for new and exciting solutions to problems. Because of this, creative organisational members can be perceived as disruptive and hard to get along with. Further, research indicates that male and female professionals do not differ in levels of creativity.[72] There are, however, a host of personality characteristics that are positively associated with creativity. These characteristics include, but are not limited to, those shown in the next OB in Real Life.

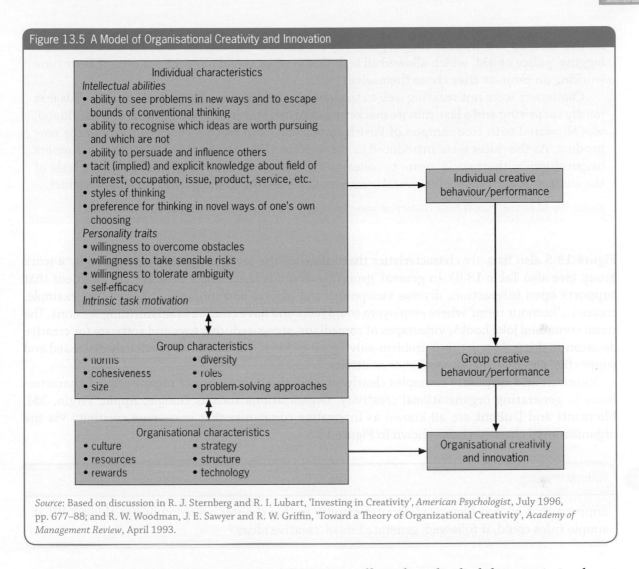

Figure 13.5 A Model of Organisational Creativity and Innovation

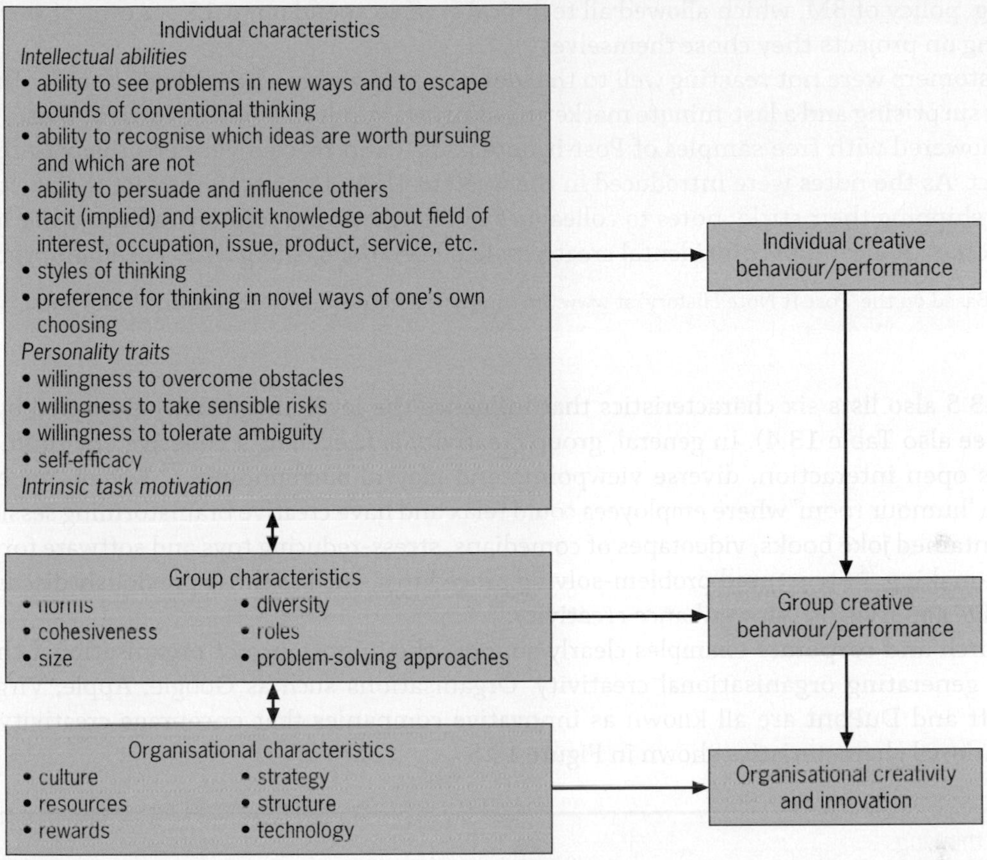

Individual characteristics
Intellectual abilities
• ability to see problems in new ways and to escape bounds of conventional thinking
• ability to recognise which ideas are worth pursuing and which are not
• ability to persuade and influence others
• tacit (implied) and explicit knowledge about field of interest, occupation, issue, product, service, etc.
• styles of thinking
• preference for thinking in novel ways of one's own choosing
Personality traits
• willingness to overcome obstacles
• willingness to take sensible risks
• willingness to tolerate ambiguity
• self-efficacy
Intrinsic task motivation
Individual creative behaviour/performance
Group characteristics
• norms
• cohesiveness
• size
• diversity
• roles
• problem-solving approaches
Group creative behaviour/performance
Organisational characteristics
• culture
• resources
• rewards
• strategy
• structure
• technology
Organisational creativity and innovation

Source: Based on discussion in R. J. Sternberg and R. I. Lubart, 'Investing in Creativity', *American Psychologist*, July 1996, pp. 677–88; and R. W. Woodman, J. E. Sawyer and R. W. Griffin, 'Toward a Theory of Organizational Creativity', *Academy of Management Review*, April 1993.

The Post-it notes story represents a good illustration of how the individual characteristics shown in Figure 13.5 promote creativity. According to the 3M company, which produces the Post-it notes, there are now more than 4000 products related to the Post-It note.

OB in Real Life

Incrementally creating the sticky note

Everybody (almost) knows the little yellow notes that stick, lightly, to various surfaces. They are the Post-it notes, originally developed by the 3M Corporation. This came about through a series of strange events. First, in 1968 Spencer Silver, a chemist at 3M, came up with the adhesive or glue, possibly when experimenting to find a super-strong glue. Silver tried to interest someone in his discovery but only in 1974, when the glue crossed paths with Art Fry, did something happen. Fry sang in a church choir and was always losing the bookmarks in his hymnal. Fry at some point connected Silver's weak adhesive to the idea of making his bookmarks stick.

As this worked just fine for his purpose, Fry set about extending his idea. He used the 'bootlegging' policy of 3M, which allowed all technical staff to spend up to 15 per cent of their time working on projects they chose themselves.

Customers were not reacting well to the idea of a sticky note when asked about it. This was hardly surprising and a last-minute marketing effort was undertaken. The town of Boise, Idaho, was showered with free samples of Post-it note pads – and reacted very positively to the new product. As the notes were introduced in the western USA (11 states), the fact that customers began shipping their sticky notes to colleagues in the rest of the country indicated the scale of the success. A legend in coincidental creativity had been born, along with a brilliant product.

Source: Based on the 'Post-It Note History' at www.3m.com/us/office/postit/pastandpresent/history.htm.

Figure 13.5 also lists six characteristics that influence the level of creativity exhibited by a work group (see also Table 13.4). In general, group creativity is fuelled by a cohesive environment that supports open interaction, diverse viewpoints and playful surroundings.[73] Kodak, for example, created a 'humour room' where employees could relax and have creative brainstorming sessions. The room contained joke books, videotapes of comedians, stress-reducing toys and software for creative decision-making.[74] Structured problem-solving procedures, such as those previously discussed and supportive supervision, also enhance creativity.[75]

Research and corporate examples clearly support the importance of organisational characteristics in generating organisational creativity. Organisations such as Google, Apple, Virgin, 3M, Microsoft and DuPont are all known as innovative companies that encourage creativity via the organisational characteristics shown in Figure 13.5.

! Critical thinking

Suppose that all you have read about creativity in this chapter overcomplicates things? What simple rules could, if followed, generate lots of 'creative ideas'?

Table 13.4 Suggestions for Improving Employee Creativity

- Develop an environment that supports creative behaviour. Try to avoid using an autocratic style of leadership
- Encourage employees to be more open to new ideas and experiences
- Keep in mind that people use different strategies, like walking around or listening to music, to foster their creativity
- Provide employees with stimulating work that creates a sense of personal growth. Allow employees to have fun and play around
- Encourage an open environment that is free from defensive behaviour. Treat errors and mistakes as opportunities for learning
- Let employees occasionally try out their pet ideas. Provide a margin of error
- Avoid using a negative mind-set when an employee approaches you with a new idea. Reward creative behaviour

Source: Adapted from discussion in E. Raudsepp, '101 Ways to Spark Your Employees' Creative Potential', *Office Administration and Automation*, September 1985, pp. 38, 39–43, 56.

Learning outcomes: Summary of key terms

1 **The rational model of decision-making, the Carnegie model and the 'garbage can' model**

The rational decision-making model consists of identifying the problem, generating alternative solutions, selecting a solution, and implementing and evaluating the solution. Research indicates that decision-makers do not follow the series of steps outlined in the rational model. The Carnegie model is guided by a decision-maker's bounded rationality. Bounded rationality means that decision-makers are bounded or restricted by a variety of constraints when making decisions. The Carnegie model suggests that decision-making is characterised by (a) limited information processing, (b) the use of judgemental heuristics and (c) satisficing. The 'garbage can' model of decision-making assumes that decision-making does not follow an orderly series of steps. In this process, decisions result from the interaction among four independent streams of events: problems, solutions, participants and choice opportunities.

2 **Contingency relationships that influence strategies used to select solutions**

Decision-makers use either an aided-analytic, unaided-analytic or non analytic strategy when selecting a solution. The choice of a strategy depends on the characteristics of the decision task and the characteristics of the decision-maker. In general, the greater the demands and constraints faced by a decision-maker, the higher the probability that an aided-analytic approach will be used. Aided analytic strategies are more likely to be used by competent and motivated individuals.

Ultimately, decision-makers must compromise between their desire to make correct decisions and the amount of time and effort they can allow for the decision-making process.

3 **Decision-making styles**

The model of decision-making styles is based on the idea that styles vary along two different dimensions: value orientation and tolerance for ambiguity. When these two dimensions are combined, they form four styles of decision-making: directive, analytical, conceptual and behavioural. People with a directive style have a low tolerance for ambiguity and are oriented towards the task itself and technical concerns. Analytics have a higher tolerance for ambiguity and are characterised by a tendency to overly analyse a situation. People with a conceptual style have a high threshold for ambiguity and tend to focus on the people or social aspects of a work situation. This behavioural style is the most people-oriented of the four styles.

4 **Biases in decision-making**

Escalation of commitment refers to the tendency to stick to an ineffective course of action despite it being unlikely that a bad situation can be reversed. Psychological and social determinants, organisational determinants, project characteristics and contextual determinants cause decision-makers to exhibit this decision-making error.

5 **Involving groups in the decision-making process**

Although research shows that groups typically outperform the average individual, there are five important issues to consider when using groups to make decisions: (a) groups are less efficient than individuals, (b) a group's overconfidence can fuel groupthink, (c) decision quality is negatively related to group size, (d) groups are more accurate when they know a great deal about the issues at hand and when the leader possesses the ability to effectively evaluate the group members' opinions and judgements and (e) the composition of a group affects its decision-making processes and performance. In the final analysis, professionals are encouraged to use a contingency approach when determining whether to include others in the decision-making process.

6 **Employee involvement and performance**

Participative management reflects the extent to which employees participate in setting goals, making decisions, solving problems and making changes in the organisation. Participative management is expected to increase motivation because it helps employees fulfil three basic needs: (a) autonomy; (b) meaningful work; and (c) interpersonal contact. Participative management does not work in all situations. The design of work and the level of trust between management and employees influence the effectiveness of participative management.

7 **Brainstorming, the nominal group technique, the Delphi technique, and computer-aided decision-making**

Group problem-solving techniques facilitate better decision-making within groups. Brainstorming is used to help groups generate multiple ideas and alternatives for solving problems. The nominal group technique assists groups both to generate ideas and to evaluate and select solutions. The Delphi technique is a group process that anonymously generates ideas or judgements from physically dispersed experts. The purpose of computer-aided decision-making is to reduce the obstacles to consensus, while collecting more information in a shorter period of time.

8 **The creative process**

Creativity is defined as the process of using imagination and skill to develop a new or unique product, object, process or thought. It is not adequately explained by differences between the left and right hemispheres of the brain. There are five stages of the creative process: preparation, concentration, incubation, illumination and verification.

9 **The model of organisational creativity and innovation**

Organisational creativity is directly influenced by organisational characteristics and the creative behaviour that occurs within work groups. In turn, a group's creative behaviour is influenced by group characteristics and the individual creative behaviour and performance of its members. Individual creativity is directly affected by a variety of individual characteristics. Finally, individual, group and organisational characteristics all influence each other within this process.

Review questions

1 Can making a decision be dispassionate?
2 How many perfectly rational people do you know – or who comes closest?
3 Can you describe a situation in which you 'satisficed' when making a decision?
4 When did you last encounter the 'garbage can' model – or something that is close to it?
5 When does a decision problem lead to personal conflict?
6 Can you honestly claim that you have never been affected by an escalation of commitment situation?
7 What do you think about solving problems in groups?
8 Given the intuitive appeal of employee involvement, why do you think it fails as often as it succeeds?
9 Can creativity be learned?

Personal awareness and growth exercise

What is your decision-making style?

Objectives

1 To assess your decision-making style.
2 To consider the managerial implications of your decision-making style.

Introduction

Earlier in the chapter we discussed a model of decision-making styles that is based on the idea that styles vary along the dimensions of an individual's value orientation and tolerance for ambiguity. In turn, these dimensions combine to form four styles of decision-making (see Figure 13.3): directive, analytical, conceptual and behavioural. Alan Rowe, an OB researcher, developed an instrument called the Decision Style Inventory to measure these four styles. This exercise provides the opportunity for you to assess and interpret your decision-making style using this measurement device.

Instructions

The Decision Style Inventory consists of 20 questions, each with four responses.[76] You must consider each possible response to a question and then rank them according to how much you prefer each response. There are no right or wrong answers, so respond with what first comes to mind. Although many of the questions are based on how individuals make decisions at work, feel free to use your student role as a frame of reference to answer the questions. For each question, you have four responses, and each should be ranked either 1, 2, 4 or 8; with 8 being for the response that is most like you, 4 for the one moderately like you, 2 for slightly like you, and 1 for least like you. For instance, a question could be answered as follows: [8], [4], [2], [1]. Notice that each number was used only once to answer a question. Do not repeat any number when answering a given question. These numbers should be written in the blank column alongside each response.

Once all of the responses for the 20 questions have been ranked, total the scores in each of the four columns. The total score for column one represents your score for the directive style, column two your analytical style, column three your conceptual style, and column four your behavioural style.

1	My prime objective in life is to:	have a position with status	be the best in whatever I do	be recognised for my work	feel secure in my job
2	I enjoy work that:	is clear and well defined	is varied and challenging	lets me act independently	involves people
3	I expect people to be:	productive	capable	committed	responsive
4	My work lets me:	get things done	find workable approaches	apply new ideas	be truly satisfied
5	I communicate best by:	talking with others	putting things in writing	being open with others	having a group meeting
6	My planning focuses on:	current problems	how best to meet goals	future opportunities	needs of people in the organisation
7	I prefer to solve problems by:	applying rules	using careful analysis	being creative	relying on my feelings

8	I prefer information that is:	simple and direct	complete	broad and informative	easily understood
9	When I'm not sure what to do, I:	rely on my intuition	search for alternatives	try to find a compromise	avoid making a decision
10	Whenever possible, I avoid:	long debates	incomplete work	technical problems	conflict with others
11	I am really good at:	remembering details	finding answers	seeing many options	working with people
12	When time is important, I:	decide and act quickly	apply proven approaches	look for what will work	refuse to be pressurised
13	In social settings, I:	speak to many people	observe what others are doing	contribute to the conversation	want to be part of the discussion
14	I always remember:	people's names	places I have been	people's faces	people's personalities
15	I prefer jobs where I:	receive high rewards	have challenging assignments	can reach my personal goals	am accepted by the group
16	I work best with people who are:	energetic and ambitious	very competent	open-minded	polite and understanding
17	When I am under stress, I:	speak quickly	try to concentrate on the problem	become frustrated	worry about what I should do
18	Others consider me:	aggressive	disciplined	imaginative	supportive
19	My decisions are generally:	realistic and direct	systematic and logical	broad and flexible	sensitive to the other's needs
20	I dislike:	losing control	boring work	following rules	being rejected
	Total score				

Source: © Alan J. Rowe, Professor Emeritus. Revised 18 December 1998. Reprinted by permission.

Questions for discussion

1 In terms of your decision-making profile, which of the four styles represents your decision-making style best (i.e. has the highest score)? Which is the least reflective of your style (has the lowest score)?

2 Do you agree with this assessment? Explain.

3 How do your scores compare with the following norms: directive (75), analytical (90), conceptual (80) and behavioural (55)? What do the differences between your scores and the survey norms suggest about your decision-making style?

4 What are the advantages and disadvantages of your decision-making profile?

5 Which of the other decision-making styles is most inconsistent with your style? How would this difference affect your ability to work with someone who has this style?

Group exercise

Ethical decision-making objectives

1 To apply the rational model of decision-making.

2 To examine the ethical implications of a managerial decision.

Introduction

In this chapter we learned there are four steps in the rational model of decision-making. The third stage involves evaluating alternatives and selecting a solution. Part of this evaluation may entail deciding whether or not a solution is ethical. The purpose of this exercise is to examine the steps in decision-making and to consider the issue of ethical decision-making.

Instructions

Break into groups of five or six people and read the following case. As a group, discuss the decision made by the company and answer the questions for discussion at the end of the case. Before answering questions 4 and 5, however, brainstorm alternative decisions the managers at Telecompros could have made. Finally, the entire class can reconvene and discuss the alternative solutions that were generated.

The case of Telecompros

For large cellular service providers, maintaining their own customer service call centre can be very expensive. Many have found they can save money by outsourcing their customer service calls to outside companies.

Telecompros is one such company. It specialises in cellular phone customer service. Telecompros saves large cellular companies money by eliminating overhead costs associated with building a call centre, installing additional telephone lines, and so forth. Once Telecompros is hired by large cellular service providers, Telecompros employees are trained on the cellular service providers' systems, policies and procedures. Telecompros' income is derived from charging a per hour fee for each employee.

Six months ago, Telecompros acquired a contract with Cell2U, a large cellular service provider serving the western USA. At the beginning of the contract, Cell2U was very pleased. As a call centre, Telecompros has a computer system in place that monitors the number of calls the centre receives and how quickly the calls are answered. When Cell2U received its first report, the system showed that Telecompros was a very productive call centre and it handled the call volume very well. A month later, however, Cell2U launched a nationwide marketing campaign. Suddenly, the call volume increased and Telecompros' customer service reps were unable to keep up. The phone monitoring system showed that some customers were on hold for 45 minutes or longer, and at any given time throughout the day there were as many as 50 customers on hold. It was clear to Cell2U that the original number of customer service reps it had contracted for was not enough. It renegotiated with upper management at Telecompros and hired additional customer service reps. Telecompros was pleased because it was now receiving more money from Cell2U for the extra employees, and Cell2U was happy because the call centre volume was no longer overwhelming and its customers were happy with the attentive customer service.

Three months later though, Telecompros' customer service supervisors noticed a decrease in the number of customer service calls. It seemed that the reps had done such a good job that Cell2U customers had fewer problems. There were too many people and not enough calls. With little to do, some reps were playing computer games or surfing the Internet while waiting for calls to come in.

Knowing that if Cell2U analysed its customer service needs, it would want to decrease the reps to save money, Telecompros' upper management made a decision. Rather than decrease its staff and lose the hourly pay from Cell2U, the upper management told customer service supervisors to call the customer service line. Supervisors called in and spent enough time on the phone with reps to ensure that the computer registered the call and the time it took to 'resolve' the call. Then they would hang up and call the call centre again. Telecompros did not have to decrease its customer service reps, and Cell2U continued to pay for the allotted reps until the end of the contract.

Questions for discussion

1. Was the decision made by Telecompros an ethical one? Why or why not?
2. If you were a manager at Telecompros, what would you have done when your manager asked you to call the customer service line? What are the ramifications of your decision? Discuss.
3. Where did the decision-making process at Telecompros break down? Explain.
4. What alternative solutions to the problem at hand did you identify? What is your recommended solution? Explain why you selected this alternative.
5. Describe in detail how you would implement your preferred solution.

Online Learning Centre

When you have read this chapter, log on to the Online Learning Centre website at ***www.mcgraw-hill.co.uk/textbooks/sinding*** to access test questions, additional exercises and other related resources.

Notes

[1] For a review of research on rational decision-making, see K. E. Stanovich, *Who Is Rational?* (Mahwah, NJ: Lawrence Erlbaum, 1999), pp. 1–31.

[2] See W. F. Pounds, 'The Process of Problem Finding', *Industrial Management Review*, Fall 1969, pp. 1–19.

[3] See B. A. Melers, A. Schwartz and A. D. J. Cooke, 'Judgment and Decision Making', in *Annual Review of Psychology*, eds J. T. Spence, J. M. Darley and D. J. Foss (Palo Alto, CA: Annual Reviews, 1998), pp. 447–77; and E. U. Webber, C. K. Hsee and J. Sokolowska, 'What Folklore Tells Us about Risk and Risk Taking: Cross-Cultural Comparisons of American, German, and Chinese Proverbs', *Organizational Behavior and Human Decision Processes*, August 1998, pp. 170–86. See also J. P. Byrnes, D. C. Miller and W. D. Schafer, 'Gender Differences in Risk Taking: A Meta-Analysis', *Psychological Bulletin*, May 1999, pp. 367–83.

[4] The implementation process and its relationship to decision outcomes is discussed by S. J. Miller, D. J. Hickson and D. C. Wilson, 'Decision-Making in Organizations', in *Handbook of Organization Studies*, eds S. R. Clegg, C. Hardy and W. R. Nord (London: Sage Publications, 1996), pp. 293–312.

[5] For a review of these assumptions, see H. A. Simon, 'A Behavioral Model of Rational Choice', *The Quarterly Journal of Economics*, February 1955, pp. 99–118.

[6] H. A. Simon, 'Rational Decision Making in Business Organizations', *American Economic Review*, September 1979, p. 510.

[7] For a complete discussion of bounded rationality, see H. A. Simon, *Administrative Behavior, second edition* (New York: Free Press, 1957); J. G. March and H. A. Simon, *Organizations* (New York: John Wiley, 1958); H. A. Simon, 'Altruism and Economics', *American Economic Review*, May 1993, pp. 156–61; and R. Nagel, 'A Survey on Experimental Beauty Contest Games: Bounded Rationality and Learning', in *Games and Human Behavior*, eds D. V. Budescu, I. Erev and R. Zwick (Mahwah, NJ: 1999), pp. 105–42. German researcher Gerd Gigerenzer has published a long list of articles on the relevance of bounded rationality; see, for instance, P. M. Todd and G. Gigerenzer, 'Bounding Rationality to the World', *Journal of Economic Psychology*, April 2003, pp. 143–65.

[8] Biases associated with using shortcuts in decision-making are discussed by A. Tversky and D. Kahneman, 'Judgment under Uncertainty: Heuristics and Biases', *Science*, September 1974, pp. 1124–31; and D. Stahlberg, F. Eller, A. Maass and D. Frey, 'We Knew It All Along: Hindsight Bias in Groups', *Organizational Behavior and Human Decision Processes*, July 1995, pp. 46–58.

[9] See C. P. Lindblom, 'The Science of Muddling Through,' *Public Administration Review*, 1959, no. 19, pp. 79–88.

[10] The model is discussed in detail in M. D. Cohen, J. G. March and J. P. Olsen, 'A Garbage Can Model of Organizational Choice', *Administrative Science Quarterly*, March 1971, pp. 1–25; and P. L. Koopman, J. W. Broekhuijsen and A. F. M. Wierdsma,

'Complex-Decision Making in Organizations', in *Handbook of Work and Organizational Psychology, second edition*, eds P. J. D. Drenth and J. Thierry (Hove: Psychology Press, 1998), pp. 357–86.

11 M. D. Cohen, J. G. March and J. P. Olsen, 'A Garbage Can Model of Organizational Choice', *Administrative Science Quarterly*, March 1971, p. 2.

12 Results can be found in B. Levitt and C. Nass, 'The Lid on the Garbage Can: Institutional Constraints on Decision Making in the Technical Core of College-Text Publishers', *Administrative Science Quarterly*, June 1989, pp. 190–207.

13 See H. Mintzberg, D. Raisinghani and A. Theoret, 'The structure of unstructured decision making,' *Administrative Science Quarterly*, no. 21, pp. 246–75.

14 J. G. March, *A primer on decision making: How decisions happen* (New York: The Free Press, 1994).

15 This discussion is based on material presented by J. G. March and R. Weissinger-Baylon, *Ambiguity and Command* (Marshfield, MA: Pitman Publishing, 1986), pp. 11–35.

16 Simulated tests of the garbage can model were conducted by M. Masuch and P. LaPotin, 'Beyond Garbage Cans: An A1 Model of Organizational Choice', *Administrative Science Quarterly*, March 1989, pp. 38–67; and M. B. Mandell, 'The Consequences of Improving Dissemination in Garbage-Can Decision Processes', *Knowledge: Creation, Diffusion, Utilization*, March 1988, pp. 343–61.

17 For a complete discussion, see L. R. Beach and T. R. Mitchell, 'A Contingency Model for the Selection of Decision Strategies', *Academy of Management Review*, July 1978, pp. 439–44.

18 See B. Azar, 'Why Experts Often Disagree', *APA Monitor*, May 1999, p. 13.

19 Results can be found in N. Harvey, 'Why Are Judgments Less Consistent in Less Predictable Task Situations?', *Organizational Behavior and Human Decision Processes*, September 1995, pp. 247–63; and J. W. Dean, Jr and M. P. Sharfman, 'Does Decision Process Matter? A Study of Strategic Decision-Making Effectiveness', *Academy of Management Journal*, April 1996, pp. 368–96.

20 Results from this study can be found in S. W. Gilliland, N. Schmitt and L. Wood, 'Cost-Benefit Determinants of Decision Process and Accuracy', *Organizational Behavior and Human Decision Processes*, November 1993, pp. 308–30.

21 See P. E. Johnson, S. Graziolo, K. Jamal and I. A. Zualkernan, 'Success and Failure in Expert Reasoning', *Organizational Behavior and Human Decision Processes*, November 1992, pp. 173–203.

22 This definition was derived from A. J. Rowe and R. O. Mason, *Managing with Style: A Guide to Understanding, Assessing and Improving Decision Making* (San Francisco, CA: Jossey-Bass, 1987).

23 The discussion of styles was based on material contained in A. J. Rowe and R. O. Mason, *Managing with Style: A Guide to Understanding, Assessing and Improving Decision Making* (San Francisco, CA: Jossey-Bass, 1987).

24 From D. J. Simons and C. F. Chabris, 'The Trouble With Intuition', *The Chronicle of Higher Education*, 30 May 2010, http://chronicle.com/article/The-Trouble-With-Intuition/65674/

25 For a study of the availability heuristic, see L. A. Vaughn, 'Effects of Uncertainty on Use of the Availability of Heuristic for Self-Efficacy Judgments', *European Journal of Social Psychology*, March–May 1999, pp. 407–10.

26 The details of this case are discussed in J. Ross and B. M. Staw, 'Organizational Escalation and Exit: Lessons from the Shoreham Nuclear Power Plant', *Academy of Management Journal*, August 1993, pp. 701–32.

27 The classic on biases is A. Tversky and D. Kahneman, 'Judgement under Uncertainty: Heuristics and Biases', *Science*, September 1974, pp. 1124–131.

28 See R. S. Nickerson, 'Confirmation Bias: A Ubiquitous Phenomenon in Many Guises', *Review of General Psychology*, June 1998, pp. 175–220.

29 R. L. Guilbault, F. B. Bryant, J. H. Brockway and E. J. Posavac, 'A Meta-Analysis of Research on Hindsight Bias', *Basic and Applied Social Psychology*, September 2004, pp. 103–17.

30 Based on an example in M. Bazerman, *Judgement in Decision Making*, London: John Wiley, 6th ed., 2005.

31 This point is made in J. Kruger and D. Dunning, 'Unskilled and Unaware of it: How Difficulties in Recognizing One's Own Incompetence Lead to Inflated Self-assessments', *Journal of Personality and Social Psychology*, November 1999, pp. 1121–134.

32 A. J. Rowe and R. O. Mason, *Managing with Style: A Guide to Understanding, Assessing and Improving Decision Making* (San Francisco, CA: Jossey-Bass, 1987); and M. J. Dollinger and W. Danis, 'Preferred Decision-Making Styles: A Cross-Cultural Comparison', *Psychological Reports*, June 1998, pp. 755–61.

33 These guidelines were derived from G. P. Huber, *Managerial Decision Making* (Glenview, IL: Scott, Foresman, 1980), p. 149.

34 'Jack Welch's Lessons for Success', *Fortune*, 25 January 1993, p. 86.

35 Results are presented in J. T. Delaney, 'Workplace Cooperation: Current Problems, New Approaches', *Journal of Labor Research*, Winter 1996, pp. 45–61.

36 For an extended discussion of this model, see M. Sashkin, 'Participative Management Is an Ethical Imperative', *Organizational Dynamics*, Spring 1984, pp. 4–22.

37 See G. Yukl and P. P. Fu, 'Determinants of Delegation and Consultation by Managers', *Journal of Organizational Behavior*, March 1999, pp. 219–32.

38 G. W. Hill, 'Group versus Individual Performance: Are N+1 Heads Better than One?', *Psychological Bulletin*, May 1982, p. 535.

39 D. Pringle, 'Finnish Line: Facing Big Threat from Microsoft, Nokia Places a Bet', *The Wall Street Journal*, 22 May 2002, p. A16.

40 These conclusions are based on studies from J. H. Davis, 'Some Compelling Intuitions about Group Consensus Decisions, Theoretical and Empirical Research, and Interpersonal Aggregation Phenomena: Selected Examples, 1950–1990', *Organizational Behavior and Human Decision Processes*, June 1992, pp. 3–38; and J. A. Sniezek, 'Groups Under Uncertainty: An

Examination of Confidence in Group Decision Making', *Organizational Behavior and Human Decision Processes*, June 1992, pp. 124–55.

41 Supporting results can be found in J. Hedlund, D. R. Ilgen and J. R. Hollenbeck, 'Decision Accuracy in Computer-Mediated versus Face-to-Face Decision-Making Teams', *Organizational Behavior and Human Decision Processes*, October 1998, pp. 30–47; and J. R. Hollenbeck, D. R. Ilgen, D. J. Sego, J. Hedlund, D. A. Major and J. Phillips, 'Multilevel Theory of Team Decision Making: Decision Performance in Teams Incorporating Distributed Expertise', *Journal of Applied Psychology*, April 1995, pp. 292–316.

42 See J. R. Winquist and J. R. Larson, Jr, 'Information Pooling: When It Impacts Group Decision Making', *Journal of Personality and Social Psychology*, February 1998, pp. 371–7; and D. H. Gruenfeld, E. A. Mannix, K. Y. Williams and M. A. Neale, 'Group Composition and Decision Making: How Member Familiarity and Information Distribution Affect Process and Performance', *Organizational Behavior and Human Decision Processes*, July 1996, pp. 1–15.

43 Supporting results can be found in J. Hunton, T. W. Hall and K. H. Price, 'The Value of Voice in Participative Decision Making', *Journal of Applied Psychology*, October 1998, pp. 788–97; C. R. Leana, R. S. Ahlbrandt and A. J. Murrell, 'The Effects of Employee Involvement Programs on Unionized Workers' Attitudes, Perceptions, and Preferences in Decision Making', *Academy of Management Journal*, October 1992, pp. 861–73; and D. Plunkett, 'The Creative Organization: An Empirical Investigation of the Importance of Participation in Decision Making', *Journal of Creative Behavior*, Second Quarter 1990, pp. 140–48.

44 Results can be found in B. D. Cawley, L. M. Keeping and P. E. Levy, 'Participation in the Performance Appraisal Process and Employee Reactions: A Meta-Analytic Review of Field Investigations', *Journal of Applied Psychology*, August 1998, pp. 615–33.

45 Results are contained in J. A. Wagner III, C. R. Leana, E. A. Locke and D. M. Schweiger, 'Cognitive and Motivational Frameworks in US Research on Participation: A Meta-Analysis of Primary Effects', *Journal of Organizational Behavior*, January 1997, pp. 49–65.

46 See D. L. Gladstein and N. P. Reilly, 'Group Decision Making under Threat: The Tycoon Game', *Academy of Management Journal*, September 1985, pp. 613–27.

47 See E. A. Locke, D. M. Schweiger and G. R. Latham, 'Participation in Decision Making: When Should It Be Used?', *Organizational Dynamics*, Winter 1986, pp. 65–79.

48 A thorough discussion of this issue is provided by W. A. Randolph, 'Navigating the Journey to Empowerment', *Organizational Dynamics*, Spring 1995, pp. 19–32.

49 Results can be found in S. A. Mohrman, E. E. Lawler III and G. E. Ledford, Jr, 'Organizational Effectiveness and the Impact of Employee Involvement and TQM Programs: Do Employee Involvement and TQM Programs Work?', *Journal for Quality and Participation*, January–February 1996, pp. 6–10.

50 See R. Rodgers, J. E. Hunter and D. L. Rogers, 'Influence of Top Management Commitment on Management Program Success', *Journal of Applied Psychology*, February 1993, pp. 151–5.

51 G. M. Parker, *Team Players and Teamwork: The New Competitive Business Strategy* (San Francisco, CA: Jossey-Bass, 1990).

52 Results can be found in L. M. Camacho and P. B. Paulus, 'The Role of Social Anxiousness in Group Brainstorming', *Journal of Personality and Social Psychology*, June 1995, pp. 1071–80.

53 Methods for increasing group consensus were investigated by R. L. Priem, D. A. Harrison and N. K. Muir, 'Structured Conflict and Consensus Outcomes in Group Decision Making', *Journal of Management*, no. 4, 1995, pp. 691–710.

54 These recommendations were obtained from G. M. Parker, *Team Players and Teamwork: The New Competitive Business Strategy* (San Francisco, CA: Jossey-Bass, 1990).

55 Supportive results can be found in S. Mohammed and E. Ringseis, 'Cognitive Diversity and Consensus in Group Decision Making: The Role of Inputs, Processes, and Outcomes', *Organizational Behavior and Human Decision Processes*, July 2001, pp. 310–35.

56 See A. F. Osborn, *Applied Imagination: Principles and Procedures of Creative Thinking, third edition* (New York: Scribners, 1979).

57 See W. H. Cooper, R. Brent Gallupe, S. Pollard and J. Cadsby, 'Some Liberating Effects of Anonymous Electronic Brainstorming', *Small Group Research*, April 1998, pp. 147–78; and P. B. Paulus, T. S. Larey and A. H. Ortega, 'Performance and Perceptions of Brainstormers in an Organizational Setting', *Basic and Applied Social Psychology*, August 1995, pp. 249–65.

58 These recommendations were derived from C. Caggiano, 'The Right Way to Brainstorm', *Inc.*, July 1999, p. 94; and G. McGartland, 'How to Generate More Ideas in Brainstorming Sessions', *Selling Power*, July–August 1999, p. 46.

59 See J. G. Lloyd, S. Fowell and J. G. Bligh, 'The Use of the Nominal Group Technique as an Evaluative Tool in Medical Undergraduate Education', *Medical Education*, January 1999, pp. 8–13; and A. L. Delbecq, A. H. Van de Ven and D. H. Gustafson, *Group Techniques for Program Planning: A Guide to Nominal Group and Delphi Processes* (Glenview, IL: Scott, Foresman, 1975).

60 See N. C. Dalkey, D. L. Rourke, R. Lewis and D. Snyder, *Studies in the Quality of Life: Delphi and Decision Making* (Lexington, MA: Lexington Books, 1972).

61 Benefits of the Delphi technique are discussed by N. I. Whitman, 'The Committee Meeting Alternative: Using the Delphi Technique', *Journal of Nursing Administration*, July–August 1990, pp. 30–36.

62 A thorough description of computer-aided decision-making systems is provided by M. C. Er and A. C. Ng, 'The Anonymity and Proximity Factors in Group Decision Support Systems', *Decision Support Systems*, May 1995, pp. 75–83; and A. LaPlante, 'Brainstorming', *Forbes*, 25 October 1993, pp. 45–61.

63 Supportive results can be found in S. S. Lam and J. Schaubroeck, 'Improving Group Decisions by Better Pooling Information: A Comparative Advantage of Group Decision Support Systems', *Journal of Applied Psychology*, August 2000, pp. 565–73; and

I. Benbasat and J. Lim, 'Information Technology Support for Debiasing Group Judgments: An Empirical Evaluation', *Organizational Behaviour and Human Decision Processes*, September 2000, pp. 167–83.

64 This study was conducted by J. S. Valacich, B. C. Wheeler, B. E. Mennecke and R. Wachter, 'The Effects of Numerical and Logical Group Size on Computer-Mediated Idea Generation', *Organizational Behavior and Human Decision Processes*, June 1995, pp. 318–29.

65 This definition was adapted from one provided by R. K. Scott, 'Creative Employees: A Challenge to Managers', *Journal of Creative Behavior*, First Quarter 1995, pp. 64–71.

66 Excerpted from S. Stern, 'How Companies Can Be More Creative', *HR Magazine*, April 1998, p. 59.

67 These stages are thoroughly discussed by E. Glassman, 'Creative Problem Solving', *Supervisory Management*, January 1989, pp. 21–6.

68 Details of this study can be found in M. Basadur, 'Managing Creativity: A Japanese Model', *Academy of Management Executive*, May 1992, pp. 29–42.

69 M. Basadur, 'Managing Creativity: A Japanese Model', *Academy of Management Executive*, May 1992, pp. 29–42.

70 This discussion is based on research reviewed in M. A. Collins and T. M. Amabile, 'Motivation and Creativity', in *Handbook of Creativity*, eds R. J. Sternberg (Cambridge, UK: Cambridge University Press, 1999), pp. 297–311; G. J. Feist, 'A Meta-Analysis of Personality in Scientific and Artistic Creativity', *Personality and Social Psychology Review*, no. 4, 1998, pp. 290–309; and R. W. Woodman, J. E. Sawyer and R. W. Griffin, 'Toward a Theory of Organizational Creativity', *Academy of Management Review*, April 1993, pp. 292–321.

71 T. A. Matherly and R. E. Goldsmith, 'The Two Faces of Creativity', *Business Horizons*, September–October 1985, p. 9.

72 Personality and creativity were investigated by S. Taggar, 'Individual Creativity and Group Ability to Utilize Individual Creative Resources: A Multilevel Model,' *Academy of Management Journal*, April 2002, pp. 315–30; and J. M. George and J. Zhou, 'When Openness to Experience and Conscientiousness Are Related to Creative Behavior: An Interactional Approach,' *Journal of Applied Psychology*, June 2001, pp. 513–24.

73 See the related discussion in T. M. Amabile, 'How to Kill Creativity', *Harvard Business Review*, September–October 1998, pp. 77–87.

74 See S. Caudron, 'Humor Is Healthy in the Workplace', *Personnel Journal*, June 1992, pp. 63–6.

75 See T. DeSalvo, 'Unleash the Creativity in Your Organization', *HR Magazine*, June 1999, pp. 154–64; and G. R. Oldham and A. Cummings, 'Employee Creativity: Personal and Contextual Factors at Work', *Academy of Management Journal*, June 1996, pp. 607–34.

76 The survey and detailed sources can be found in A. J. Rowe and R. O. Mason, *Managing with Style: A Guide to Understanding, Assessing, and Improving Decision Making* (San Francisco, CA: Jossey-Bass, 1987).

Chapter 14

Power, politics and conflict

Learning Outcomes

When you finish studying the material in this chapter, you should be able to:

- explain the concept of mutuality of interest
- name at least three 'soft' and two 'hard' influence tactics, and summarise the practical lessons from influence research
- identify and briefly describe French and Raven's five bases of power, and discuss the responsible use of power
- understand functional and dysfunctional conflict, and desired conflict outcomes
- recognise stimulation of functional conflict and identify the five conflict-handling styles
- recognise distributive and integrative negotiation, and discuss the concept of added-value negotiation
- explain why delegation is the highest form of empowerment, and discuss the link with delegation, trust and personal initiative
- define organisational politics, and how it is triggered
- distinguish between favourable and unfavourable impression management tactics
- explain how to manage organisational politics

Opening Case Study: The Stanford prison experiment

This psychological experiment was supposed to last for two weeks, but after just six days, it had to be stopped due to concern for the safety of the people involved. Perhaps this fact is the most telling about just how far things went, and how strongly the point of the experiment was driven home. But let us start at the beginning:

In 1971, a psychology professor at Stanford University, Dr Philip Zimbardo, and his team set up an experiment to examine the psychological effects of being either a prison guard or a prisoner. The idea was to get a greater understanding of abusive prison situations and to understand how ordinary people could commit atrocities, such as during the Holocaust, where guards afterwards stated, that they 'were just following orders'.

Participants were recruited among students, who were told that they would participate in a prison simulation lasting two weeks, and after psychological testing the 24 most stable males were selected for the experiment. The participants were then selected to play either the role of guard or prisoner at random. The setting for the experiment was a basement in one of the university buildings that had been converted for the purpose with cells, guard rooms, solitary confinement cells, and so on.

The guards were given uniforms, mirrored sunglasses and batons – although they were instructed not to use the batons to punish prisoners as batons were only to complete the uniform and establish the guards' status. The guards were briefed on their role, including that they were not allowed to physically harm the prisoners.

The participants portraying prisoners were arrested at their homes by local police officers assisting the researchers. They were booked following strict protocol, and moved to the mock prison after a brief stay at the local police station all wearing ill-fitting clothes, a chain around their ankles and just a number by which to identify them.

What happened next baffled everyone, not least the researchers. On the second day of the experiment, a riot broke out in the prison, and the guards immediately teamed up to crush the riot, working extra hours and attacking some prisoners with fire extinguishers. From then on, conditions deteriorated quickly.

Guards forced the prisoners to repeat sentences, such as 'Prisoner 819 did a bad thing' endlessly as punishments and to force their authority on them. Other methods included prolonged and painful exercises as punishment for errors in prisoner identifications, and refusing the prisoners the use of bathrooms or allowing them to empty the sanitation buckets in each cell. As a consequence, sanitary conditions declined rapidly and tension between guards and prisoners rose to critical levels very quickly.

In the last few days, things deteriorated even further, with about a third of the guards exhibiting genuinely sadistic tendencies, forcing some prisoners to sleep on the floor, go naked and carrying out other forms of humiliating punishments. Most of the guards were upset when the experiment concluded after just six days instead of the two weeks originally planned.

In 2007, Dr Philip Zimbardo published the book *The Lucifer Effect: Understanding How Good People Turn Evil* summarising his many years of research on the matter, including drawing parallels between the original experiment and the Abu Ghraib prison scandals in Iraq.

For discussion

Would a similar situation be possible if the experiment was conducted in your class? Why or why not?

Source: Based on C. Haney, C. Banks and P. Zimbardo, 'A Study of Prisoners and Guards in a Simulated Prison', in *Theater in Prison*, ed. M. Balfour (Bristol: Intellect Books, 2004), pp. 19–34.

14.1 Organisational influence

At the very heart of interpersonal dealings in today's work organisations is a constant struggle between individual and collective interests. Preoccupation with self-interest is understandable. After all, each of us was born not as a co-operating organisation member, but as an individual with instincts for self-preservation. It took socialisation in family, school, religious, sports, recreation and employment settings to introduce us to the notion of mutuality of interest. Basically, **mutuality of interest** involves win-win situations in which one's self-interest is served by co-operating actively and creatively with potential adversaries.

How do you get others to carry out your wishes? Do you simply tell them what to do? Or do you prefer a less direct approach, such as promising to return the favour? Whatever approach you use, the core of the issue is social influence. A large measure of interpersonal interaction involves attempts to influence others, including parents, bosses, co-workers, spouses, teachers, friends and children. Even if superiors do not expect to get such dramatic results, they need to sharpen their influence skills. A good starting point is familiarity with the following research insights.

Nine generic influencing tactics

A particularly fruitful stream of research, initiated by David Kipnis and his colleagues in 1980, reveals how people influence each other in organisations. The Kipnis methodology involved asking employees how they managed to get their bosses, co-workers or subordinates to do what they wanted them to do.[1] Statistical refinements and replications by other researchers over a 13-year period eventually yielded nine influence tactics. The nine tactics, ranked in diminishing order of use in the workplace, are:[2]

1 Rational persuasion: trying to convince someone with reason, logic or facts.
2 Inspirational appeals: trying to build enthusiasm by appealing to others' emotions, ideals or values.
3 Consultation: getting others to participate in planning, making decisions and changes.
4 Ingratiation: getting someone in a good mood prior to making a request; being friendly, helpful and using praise or flattery.
5 Personal appeals: referring to friendship and loyalty when making a request.
6 Exchange: making expressed or implied promises and trading favours.
7 Coalition tactics: getting others to support your effort to persuade someone.
8 Pressure: demanding compliance or using intimidation or threats.
9 Legitimating tactics: basing a request on one's authority or right, organisational rules or policies, or express or implied support from superiors.

These approaches can be considered generic influence tactics because they characterise social influence in all directions. Researchers have found this ranking to be fairly consistent regardless of whether the direction of influence is downward, upward or lateral.[3]

Some call the first five influence tactics 'soft' tactics because they are friendlier and not as coercive as the last four tactics. The latter tactics accordingly are called 'hard' tactics because they involve more overt pressure.

Three possible influence outcomes

Put yourself in this familiar situation. It is Wednesday and a big project you have been working on for your project team is due Friday. You are behind on the preparation of your computer graphics for your final report and presentation. You catch a friend who is great at computer graphics as he is heading out of the office at home time. You try this exchange tactic to get your friend to help you out: 'I'm way behind. I need your help. If you could come back in for two to three hours tonight and help me with these graphics, I'll complete those spreadsheets you've been complaining about.' According to researchers, your friend will engage in one of three possible influence outcomes:

- Commitment: your friend enthusiastically agrees and will demonstrate initiative and persistence while completing the assignment.
- Compliance: your friend grudgingly complies and will need prodding to satisfy minimum requirements.
- Resistance: your friend will say no, make excuses, stall or put up an argument.[4]

The best outcome is commitment because the target person's intrinsic motivation (see Chapter 6) will energise good performance. However, professionals often have to settle for compliance in today's hectic workplace. Resistance means a failed influence attempt.

Evidence about influence tactics

Laboratory and field studies have taught us useful lessons about the relative effectiveness of influence tactics along with other instructive insights:

- Commitment is more likely when people rely on consultation, strong rational persuasion and inspirational appeals and do not rely on pressure and coalition tactics.[5] Interestingly, in one study, supervisors were not very effective at downward influence. They relied most heavily on inspiration (an effective tactic), ingratiation (a moderately effective tactic) and pressure (an ineffective tactic).[6]
- A meta-analysis of 69 studies suggests ingratiation (making the boss feel good) can slightly improve your performance appraisal results and make your boss like you significantly more.[7]
- Commitment is more likely when the influence attempt involves something important and enjoyable and is based on a friendly relationship.[8]
- In a survey, 214 employed MBA students (55 per cent female) tended to perceive their superiors' 'soft' influence tactics as fair and 'hard' influence tactics as unfair. Unfair influence tactics were associated with greater resistance among employees.[9]
- Another study probed male–female differences in influencing work group members. The researchers had male and female work group leaders engage in either task behaviour (demonstrating ability and task competence) or dominating behaviour (relying on threats). For both women and men, task behaviour was associated with perceived competence and effective influence. Dominating behaviour was not effective. The following conclusion by the researchers has important practical implications for all people who desire to influence others successfully: 'The display of task cues is an effective means to enhance one's status in groups and . . . the attempt to gain influence in task groups through dominance is an ineffective and poorly received strategy for both men and women'.[10]
- Interpersonal influence is culture bound. The foregoing research evidence on influence tactics has a bias in favour of Europeans and North Americans. Much remains to be learned about how to influence others effectively (without unintended insult) in today's diverse labour force and cross-cultural economy.

Table 14.1 Cialdini's Six Principles of Influence and Persuasion

1 Liking	People tend to like those who like them. Learning about another person's likes and dislikes through informal conversations builds friendship bonds. So provide sincere and timely praise, empathy and recognition
2 Reciprocity	The belief that good and bad deeds should be repaid in kind is virtually universal. Superiors who act unethically and treat employees with contempt can expect the same in return. Worse, those employees, in turn, are likely to treat each other and their customers unethically and with contempt. Superiors need to be both positive and constructive role models and fair-minded to benefit from the principle of reciprocity
3 Social proof	People tend to follow the lead of those most like themselves. Role models and peer pressure are powerful cultural forces in social settings. Superiors are advised to build support for workplace changes by first gaining the enthusiastic support of informal leaders who will influence their peers
4 Consistency	People tend to do what they are personally committed to do. A superior who can elicit a verbal commitment from an employee has taken an important step towards influence and persuasion
5 Authority	People tend to defer to and respect credible experts. According to Cialdini, too many superiors and professionals take their expertise for granted
6 Scarcity	People want items, information and opportunities that have limited availability. Special opportunities and privileged information are influence builders for superiors

Source: Adapted from R. B. Cialdini, 'Harnessing the Science of Persuasion', Harvard Business Review, October 2001, pp. 72–9.

Practical implications of influencing and persuasion

Because of a string of corporate scandals and executive misdeeds at the likes of Enron and WorldCom, and the greed of Wall Street bank executives, the trust and credibility gap between management and workers remains sizeable. These incidents make managerial attempts at influence and persuasion more challenging than ever. Skill development in this area is essential.

Practical research-based advice has been offered by Robert C. Cialdini who presents six principles of influence and persuasion (see Table 14.1).[11]

Significantly, Cialdini recommends using these six principles in combination, rather than separately, for maximum impact. Because of the major ethical implications, one's goals need to be worthy and actions need to be sincere and genuine using these six principles.

By demonstrating the rich texture of social influence, the foregoing research evidence and practical advice whet our appetite for learning more about how today's professionals can and do reconcile individual and organisational interests, beginning with social power.

14.2 Organisational conflict

Mention the term 'conflict' and most people envision fights, riots or war. But these extreme situations represent only the most overt and violent expressions of conflict. During the typical workday, people in organisations encounter more subtle and non-violent expressions of conflict. Conflict, like power and organisational politics, is an inevitable and sometimes positive force in modern work organisations. Whether there are more conflicts now than before is debatable. It is, however, safe to claim that conflicts due to employee diversity, globalisation, electronic communication and greater reliance on teams are different from earlier sources of conflict (not that these have necessarily disappeared). Indeed, one observer notes that 'change begets conflict, conflict begets change'[12] and challenges us to do better in a world full of dreadful stories of alienation, abuse, violence and disagreement.

Defining conflict

A comprehensive review of the conflict literature yielded this consensus definition: '**Conflict** is a process in which one party perceives that its interests are being opposed or negatively affected by another party.'[13] The word 'perceives' reminds us that sources of conflict and issues can be real or imagined, depending on information and it's presentation. The resulting conflict is the same. Conflict can escalate (strengthen) or de-escalate (weaken) over time. Further, a conflict process unfolds in a context, and whenever it occurs, those involved – or third parties – can attempt to manage it in some way.[14] To be able to do so, employees and managers need to understand the dynamics of conflict and know how to handle it effectively.

Ideas about managing conflict underwent an interesting evolution during the twentieth century. Initially, scientific management experts such as Frederick Taylor believed all conflict ultimately threatened management's authority and thus had to be avoided or quickly resolved. Later, researchers in the human relations tradition recognised the inevitability of conflict and advised managers to learn to live with it. Taylor's approach and the human relations view are discussed in Chapter 1. Emphasis remained on resolving conflict whenever possible, however. Beginning in the 1970s, organisational behaviour (OB) specialists realised conflict had both positive and negative outcomes, depending on its nature and intensity. This perspective introduced the revolutionary idea that organisations could suffer from too little conflict. Figure 14.1 illustrates the relationship between conflict intensity and outcomes.

Work groups, departments or organisations that experience too little conflict tend to be plagued by apathy, lack of creativity, indecision and missed deadlines. Excessive conflict, on the other hand, can erode organisational performance because of political infighting, dissatisfaction, lack of teamwork and turnover. Workplace aggression and violence can be manifestations of excessive

Figure 14.1 The Relationship Between Conflict Intensity and Outcomes

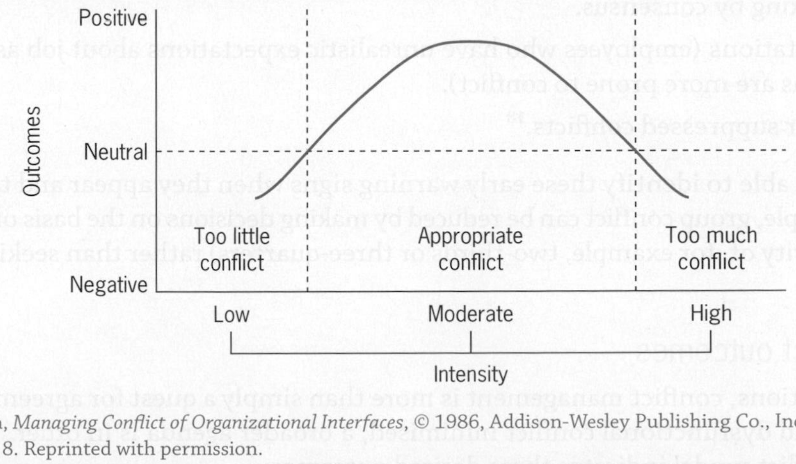

Source: L. D. Brown, *Managing Conflict of Organizational Interfaces*, © 1986, Addison-Wesley Publishing Co., Inc., Reading, MA. Figure 1.1 on page 8. Reprinted with permission.

conflict (see Chapter 3).[15] In contrast, appropriate types and levels of conflict energise people in constructive directions.[16]

Conflict at the individual level is often related to people's personalities. As discussed in Chapter 2, these are stable traits and characteristics and as we are all different, conflicts between people are likely to occur. Personality conflicts occur when people oppose one another because they dislike each other, disagree or use different styles when going about their work.

Two distinctions are useful where conflict is concerned, between personality conflicts on the one hand and intergroup conflict on the other, and between functional and dysfunctional conflict. The first distinction concerns the causes or origins of conflict (which may overlap) whereas the second distinction concerns the outcomes of conflict. The distinction between **functional conflict** and **dysfunctional conflict** depends on whether the organisation's interests are served. Functional conflict is commonly referred to in management circles as 'constructive' or 'co-operative' conflict.[17] Dysfunctional conflict is none of these things.

HR Certain situations produce more conflict than others. By knowing the factors that appear before or signal the appearance of conflict, organisations may be better able to anticipate conflict and take steps to resolve it if it becomes dysfunctional. Among the situations that tend to produce either functional or dysfunctional conflict are:

- Incompatible personalities or value systems.
- Overlapping or unclear job boundaries.
- Competition for (limited) resources.
- Competition between groups and departments.
- Poor or inadequate communication.
- Interdependent tasks (e.g. one person cannot complete his or her assignment until others have completed their work).
- Organisational complexity (conflict tends to increase as the number of hierarchical layers and specialised tasks increase).
- Unreasonable or unclear policies, standards or rules.
- Unreasonable deadlines or extreme time pressure.
- Collective decision-making (the greater the number of people participating in a decision, the greater the potential for conflict).
- Decision-making by consensus.
- Unmet expectations (employees who have unrealistic expectations about job assignments, pay or promotions are more prone to conflict).
- Unresolved or suppressed conflicts.[18]

Some people are able to identify these early warning signs when they appear and take appropriate action. For example, group conflict can be reduced by making decisions on the basis of a majority vote (or a supermajority of, for example, two-thirds or three-quarters) rather than seeking a consensus.

HR Desired conflict outcomes

Within organisations, conflict management is more than simply a quest for agreement. If progress is to be made and dysfunctional conflict minimised, a broader agenda is in order. Dean Tjosvold's cooperative conflict model indicates three desired outcomes:

- *Agreement*: but at what cost? Equitable and fair agreements are best. An agreement that leaves one party feeling exploited or defeated will tend to breed resentment and subsequent conflict.
- *Stronger relationships*: good agreements enable conflicting parties to build bridges of goodwill and trust for future use. Moreover, conflicting parties who trust each other are more likely to keep their end of the bargain.
- *Learning*: functional conflict can promote greater self-awareness and creative problem-solving. Like the practice of management itself, successful conflict handling is learned primarily by doing. Knowledge of the concepts and techniques in this section is a necessary first step, but there is no substitute for hands-on practice. In a contentious world, there are plenty of opportunities to practise conflict management.[19]

Critical thinking

Discuss this conflict model using the distinction between distributive and integrative negotiation.

HR Personal and personality conflict

Conflict at the individual level is often related to people's personalities. As discussed in Chapter 2, these are stable traits and characteristics and as we are all different, conflicts between people are likely to occur. Personality conflicts occur when people oppose one another because they dislike each other, disagree or use different styles when going about their work. Just think about someone who annoys you by their mere presence and an example is at hand.

Addressing conflicts that arise out of personal factors (not just personality but also seemingly trivial characteristics such as a person's way of smiling or the way a person speaks) is far from simple. First of all, personalities are stable and different from one person to the next. In addition, personal factors as well as behaviours can be influenced by a great number of factors that are hard to change. Some are related to some form of psychological condition (several hundred different diagnoses exist), while others can sometimes be changed.

Personal conflicts can to some extent be dealt with by emphasising problem-solving and objectives ('focus on the job, not the person'), others need help from third parties from within or without the organisation. Managers affected should (and often will without prompting), when conflict levels grow, protect themselves and their organisation, by documenting the nature of the conflict and by calling for help when needed.

OB in Real Life

Ferdinand and Wolfgang – and Wendelin

The names sound as if they come from a fairytale. It is no tale but a story of family conflict – and managerial conflict as well. Ferdinand Piëch was named 'Auto Executive of the Century' in 1999. He is a man who displays few emotions, even when winning the battle which decided the future for the iconic German car manufacturers Volkswagen and Porsche. Indeed, Mr Piëch is described as a cool, unemotional strategic thinker, one who never counts the managers he has forced out of companies he has run over the years. Wolfgang Porsche is, like Mr Piëch, one of the grandsons of the renowned engineer, Ferdinand Porsche, who designed the VW Beetle for Adolf Hitler and later created the sports car brand of Porsche. Mr Porsche prefers to avoid conflict and never speaks in meetings.

The Porsche Company was almost bankrupt in the early 1990s when it hired the colourful Wendelin Wiedeking, its production manager, as chief executive. Mr Wiedeking turned Porsche into the most profitable of car manufacturers by phasing out unprofitable models, launching new models and relaunching classics. While Mr Wiedeking has emphasised positive management and attacked those who always look for the negatives, he also brought Porsche back almost to where he started, on the brink of bankruptcy. This had come about just as Mr Wiedeking had gained control of 51 per cent of the shares in Volkswagen. Unfortunately, this strategy was financed by debt and the timing was poor, coinciding with the arrival of the financial crisis in late 2008 and early 2009. In the event, Porsche's takeover of Volkswagen became a merger – and Mr Wiedeking lost his job.

Source: Based on D. Schäffer, 'Wiedeking: Pugnacious Style Brought Enemies', *Financial Times*, 23 July 2009.

Intergroup conflict

Conflict among work groups, teams and departments is a common threat to organisational competitiveness. As we discussed in previous chapters, cohesiveness – a 'we-feeling' binding group members together – can be a good or bad thing (see Chapters 7 and 8). A certain amount of cohesiveness can turn a group of individuals into a smooth-running team. Too much cohesiveness, however, can breed groupthink because a desire to get along pushes aside critical thinking. The study of **in-groups** has revealed a whole package of changes associated with increased group cohesiveness. Specifically:

- Members of in-groups view themselves as a collection of unique individuals, while they stereotype members of other groups as being 'all alike'.
- In-group members see themselves positively and as morally correct, while they view members of other groups negatively and as immoral.
- In-groups view outsiders as a threat.
- In-group members exaggerate the differences between their group and other groups. This typically involves a distorted perception of reality.[20]

Avid sports fans who simply cannot imagine how someone would support the opposing team exemplify one form of in-group thinking. Also, this pattern of behaviour is a form of ethnocentrism (see Chapter 12). Reflect for a moment on evidence of in-group behaviour in your own life. Does your circle of friends make fun of others because of their ethnic origin, gender, nationality, sexual preference, diploma or occupation? In-group thinking is one more fact of organisational life that virtually guarantees conflict. Managers cannot eliminate in-group thinking, but they certainly should not ignore it when handling intergroup conflicts.

In an increasingly globalised world, conflicts that involve people of different cultural backgrounds will grow – and the potential volume of conflicts is vast. For example, Dutch businessmen operating in an Arabic context may find that doing business under these conditions is not in itself very different. However Arabic businessmen behave very differently from Dutch ones, who are very forthright and like to say things exactly as they are, even bluntly. This is likely to be an immediate source of conflict, as Arabic businessmen's sensibilities will be offended. Getting past problems of this kind requires a focus on history, sensibility to others (in general, but to strangers and strange customs in particular) and a co-operation focus.

Evidence about conflict and how to avoid it

Sociologists have long recommended the contact hypothesis for reducing intergroup conflict. According to the contact hypothesis, the more the members of different groups interact, the less intergroup conflict they will experience. Those interested in improving race, international and union–management relations typically encourage cross-group interaction. The hope is that any type of interaction, short of actual conflict, will reduce stereotyping and combat in-group thinking. But recent research has shown this approach to be naive and limited. For example, a study of 83 health centre employees (83 per cent female) probed the specific nature of intergroup relations and concluded that negative relationships were significantly related to higher perceptions of intergroup conflict. It seems that negative relationships are more important, overwhelming any possible positive effects from friendship links across groups.[21]

Intergroup friendships are still desirable, as documented in many studies,[22] but they are easily overpowered by negative intergroup interactions. Thus, priority number one for people faced with intergroup conflict is to identify and root out specific negative linkages among groups. A single personality conflict, for instance, may contaminate the entire intergroup experience. The same goes for an employee who voices negative opinions or spreads negative rumours about another group. The contact model in Figure 14.2 is based on this and other research insights, such as the need to foster positive attitudes toward other groups.[23] Also, notice how conflict within the group and negative gossip from third parties are threats that need to be neutralised if intergroup conflict is to be minimised.

Figure 14.2 The Contact Model for Minimising Intergroup Conflict

Level of perceived intergroup conflict tends to increase when:

- conflict within the group is high
- there are negative interactions between groups (or between members of those groups)
- influential third-party gossip about other group is negative

→

Recommended actions:

- work to eliminate *specific negative* interaction between groups (and members)
- conduct team building to reduce conflict *within* the group and prepare employees for cross-functional teamwork
- encourage personal friendships and good working relationships across groups and departments
- foster positive attitudes towards members of other groups (empathy, compassion, sympathy)
- avoid or neutralise negative gossip across groups or departments

Source: Based on research evidence in G. Labianca, D. J. Brass and B. Gray, 'Social Networks and Perceptions of Intergroup Conflict: The Role of Negative Relationships and Third Parties', *Academy of Management Journal*, February 1998, pp. 55–67; C. D. Batson *et al.*, 'Empathy and Attitudes: Can Feeling for a Member of a Stigmatized Group Improve Feelings Toward the Group?', *Journal of Personality and Social Psychology*, January 1997, pp. 105–18; and S. C. Wright *et al.*, 'The Extended Contact Effect: Knowledge of Cross-Group Friendships and Prejudice', *Journal of Personality and Social Psychology*, July 1997, pp. 73–90.

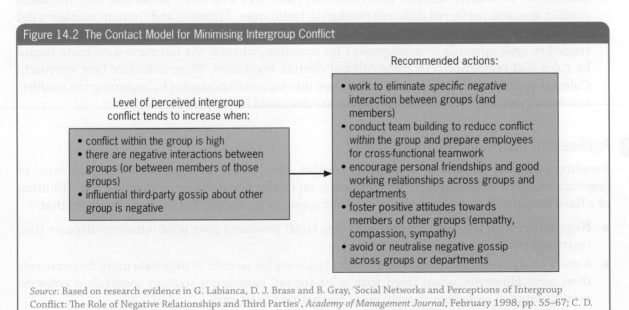

Evidence from laboratory studies, relying on college students as subjects, uncovered the following insights about organisational conflict:

- People with a high need for affiliation tended to rely on a smoothing (obliging) style while avoiding a forcing (dominating) style.[24] Thus, personality traits affect how people handle conflict (see Chapter 2).
- Disagreement expressed in an arrogant and demeaning manner produced significantly more negative effects than the same sort of disagreement expressed in a reasonable manner.[25] In other words, how you disagree with someone is very important in conflict situations.
- Threats and punishment, by one party in a disagreement, tended to produce intensifying threats and punishment from the other party.[26] In short, aggression breeds aggression.
- As conflict increased, group satisfaction decreased. An integrative style of handling conflict led to higher group satisfaction than an avoidance style.[27]

Similarly, evidence from field studies involving managers and real organisations have given further insights:

- Both intradepartmental and interdepartmental conflict decreased as goal difficulty and goal clarity increased. Thus, challenging and clear goals can defuse conflict. Goal setting is discussed in Chapter 5.
- Higher levels of conflict tended to erode job satisfaction and internal work motivation.[28]
- Men and women at the same managerial level tended to handle conflict similarly. In short, there was no gender effect.[29]
- Conflict tended to move around the organisation.[30] Thus, managers need to be alerted to the fact that conflict often originates in one area or level and becomes evident somewhere else. Conflict needs to be traced back to its source if there is to be lasting improvement.
- Samples of Japanese, German and American managers who were presented with the same conflict scenario preferred different resolution techniques. Japanese and German managers did not share the Americans' enthusiasm for integrating the interests of all parties. The Japanese tended to look upwards to management for direction, whereas the Germans were more bound by rules and regulations. In cross-cultural conflict resolution, there is no one best approach. Cultural-specific preferences need to be taken into consideration prior to beginning the conflict-resolution process.[31] Cross-cultural issues are discussed in Chapter 12.

HR Application: handling and using conflict

Avoiding potential conflict or addressing conflict once it has emerged involves some form of negotiation. Such negotiation is far from easy, especially when the issue involves redistribution of a fixed amount of resources, which will leave someone worse off. The evidence suggests that:

- Negotiators with fixed-pie expectations (see later) produced poor joint outcomes because they restricted and mismanaged information.
- A meta-analysis of 62 studies found a slight tendency for women to negotiate more cooperatively than men. However, when faced with a 'tit-for-tat' bargaining strategy (equivalent counter-moves), women were significantly more competitive than men.
- Personality characteristics can affect negotiating success. Negotiators who scored high on the Big Five personality dimensions of extraversion and agreeableness (see Chapter 2) tended to do poorly with distributive (fixed-pie; win–lose) negotiations.

- Good and bad moods can have positive and negative effects, respectively, on negotiators' plans and outcomes. So wait until both you and your boss are in a good mood before you ask for a rise (see Chapter 3).
- Studies of negotiations between Japanese, between Americans, and between Japanese and Americans found less productive joint outcomes across cultures than within cultures. Less understanding of the other party makes cross-cultural negotiation more difficult than negotiations at home.

Three realities dictate how organisational conflict should be managed. First, various types of conflict are inevitable because they are triggered by a wide variety of factors and events. Second, too little conflict may be as counterproductive as too much. Third, there is no single best way of avoiding or resolving conflict. Consequently, conflict specialists recommend a contingency approach to managing conflict. Factors that lead to conflict and actual conflict need to be monitored. If signs of too little conflict such as apathy or lack of creativity appear, then functional conflict may have to be stimulated. This can be done by nurturing factors that generate conflict and/or by programming conflict with techniques such as devil's advocacy and the dialectic method. On the other hand, when conflict becomes dysfunctional, the appropriate conflict-handling style needs to be applied. Realistic training involving role-playing can prepare managers to try alternative conflict resolution styles.

Managers can keep from getting too deeply embroiled in conflict by applying four lessons from recent research: (1) establish challenging and clear goals, (2) disagree in a constructive and reasonable manner, (3) do not get caught up in conflict triangles and (4) refuse to get caught in the aggression-breeds-aggression spiral.

! Critical thinking

Could it just be possible that each organisation needs to have – and keep – one (and only one) really unpleasant, conflict-generating person, just to keep everybody else focused on how not to behave.

HR Managing conflict

Conflict has many faces and is a constant challenge for managers who are responsible for reaching organisational goals. Our attention now turns to the active management of both functional and dysfunctional conflict.

Stimulating functional conflict is sometimes a good idea when committees and decision-making groups become so bogged down in details and procedures that nothing of value is accomplished. Carefully monitored functional conflict can help get the creative juices flowing once again. People in organisations wishing to use this approach basically have two options. They can fan the fires of naturally occurring conflict – but this approach can be unreliable and slow. Alternatively, they can resort to programmed conflict.

Experts in the field define **programmed conflict** as 'conflict that raises different opinions regardless of the personal feelings of the managers'.[32] The trick is to get contributors to either defend or criticise ideas based on relevant facts rather than on the basis of personal preference or political interests. This requires disciplined role-playing. Two programmed conflict techniques with proven track records are devil's advocacy and the dialectic method. Let us explore these two ways of stimulating functional conflict. Note, though, that these two approaches could equally well be considered part of decision-making processes (Chapter 13).

The **devil's advocacy** technique gets its name from a traditional practice within the Roman Catholic Church. When someone's name came before the College of Cardinals for elevation to sainthood, it was absolutely essential to ensure that he or she had a spotless record. Consequently, one individual was assigned the role of devil's advocate to uncover and air all possible objections to the person's canonisation. In accordance with this practice, devil's advocacy in today's organisations involves assigning someone the role of critic.[33] Recall from Chapter 7 how Irving Janis recommended the devil's advocate role for preventing groupthink.

In the left half of Figure 14.3, note how devil's advocacy alters the usual decision-making process in steps 2 and 3. This approach to programmed conflict is intended to generate critical thinking and reality testing.[34] It is a good idea to rotate the job of devil's advocate so not one person

Figure 14.3 Techniques for Stimulating Functional Conflict: Devil's Advocacy and the Dialectic Method

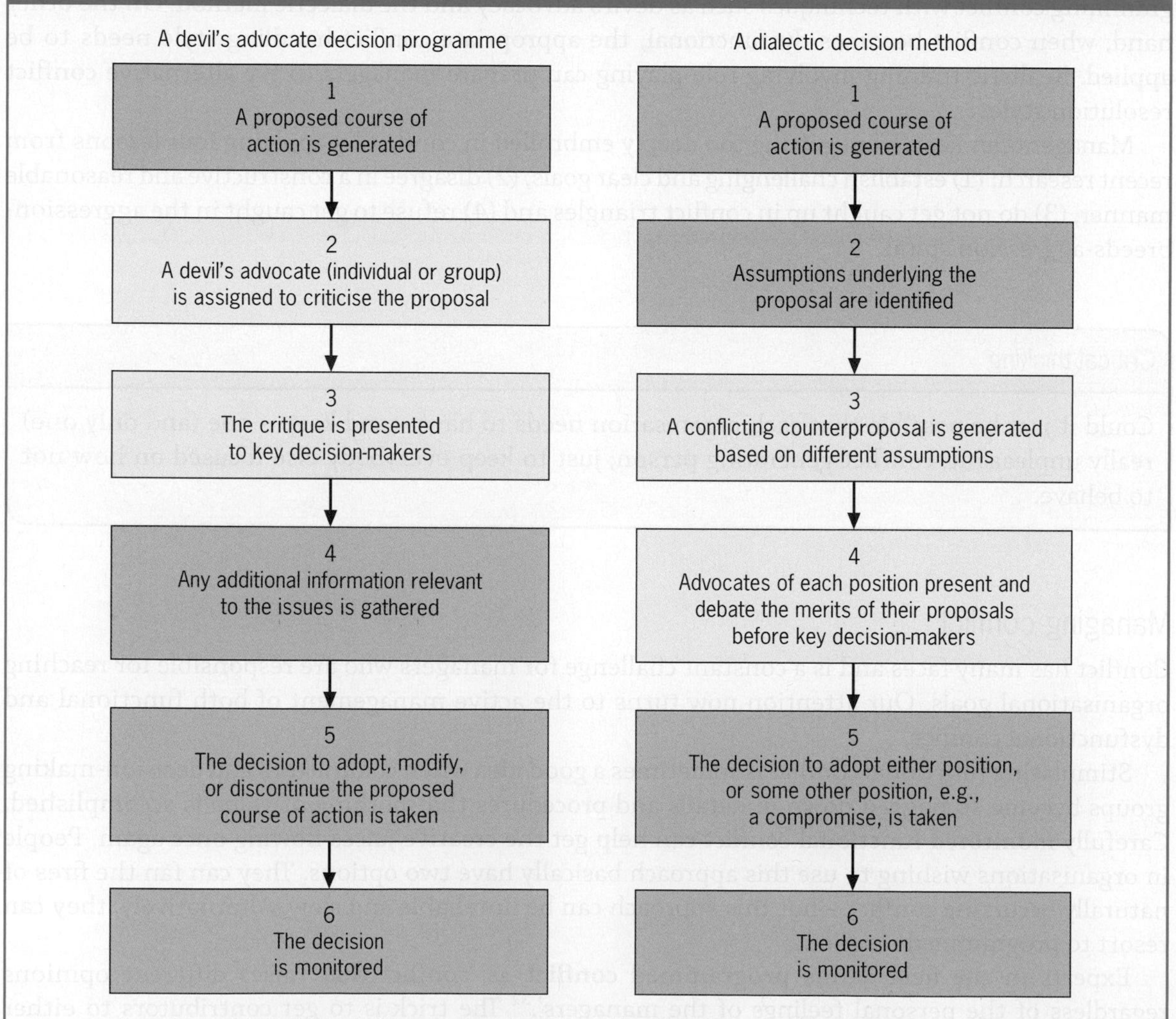
A devil's advocate decision programme
1 A proposed course of action is generated
2 A devil's advocate (individual or group) is assigned to criticise the proposal
3 The critique is presented to key decision-makers
4 Any additional information relevant to the issues is gathered
5 The decision to adopt, modify, or discontinue the proposed course of action is taken
6 The decision is monitored
A dialectic decision method
1 A proposed course of action is generated
2 Assumptions underlying the proposal are identified
3 A conflicting counterproposal is generated based on different assumptions
4 Advocates of each position present and debate the merits of their proposals before key decision-makers
5 The decision to adopt either position, or some other position, e.g., a compromise, is taken
6 The decision is monitored

Source: R. A. Coslier and C. R. Schwenk, 'Agreement and Thinking Alike: Ingredients for Poor Decisions', *Academy of Management Executive*, February 1990, pp. 72–3. Used with permission.

or group develops a strictly negative reputation. Moreover, periodic devil's advocacy role-playing is good training for developing analytical and communication skills.

Like devil's advocacy, **the dialectic method** is a time-honoured practice. This particular approach to programmed conflict dates back to the dialectic school of philosophy in ancient Greece. Plato and his followers attempted to synthesise truths by exploring opposite positions (called thesis and antithesis). Court systems in the USA and elsewhere rely on directly opposing points of view for determining guilt or innocence. Accordingly, today's Dialectic method calls for professionals to foster a structured debate of opposing viewpoints prior to making a decision.[35] Steps 3 and 4 in the right half of Figure 14.3 set the dialectic approach apart from the normal decision-making process.

A major drawback of the dialectic method is that 'winning the debate' may overshadow the issue at hand. Also, the dialectic method requires more skill training than does devil's advocacy. Regarding the comparative effectiveness of these two approaches to stimulating functional conflict, however, a laboratory study ended in a tie. Compared with groups that strived to reach a consensus, decision-making groups using either devil's advocacy or the dialectic method yielded higher-quality decisions to the same degree.[36] However, in a more recent laboratory study, groups using devil's advocacy produced more potential solutions and made better recommendations for a case problem than groups using the dialectic method.[37] In light of this mixed evidence, professionals have some latitude in using either devil's advocacy or the dialectic method for pumping creative life back into stalled deliberations. Personal preference and the role-players' experience may well be the deciding factors in choosing one approach over the other. The important thing is to actively stimulate functional conflict when necessary (e.g. when the risk of blind conformity or groupthink is high).

HR Handling dysfunctional conflict

People tend to handle negative conflict in patterned ways referred to as 'styles'. Several conflict styles have been categorised over the years. According to conflict specialist Afzalur Rahim's model, five different conflict-handling styles can be plotted on a 2 × 2 grid. Low to high concern for self is found on the horizontal axis of the grid while low to high concern for others forms the vertical axis (see Figure 14.4). Various combinations of these variables produce the five different conflict-handling styles: integrating, obliging, dominating, avoiding and compromising.[38] There is no single best style; each has strengths and limitations and is subject to situational constraints.

In the *integrating or problem-solving style*, interested parties confront the issue and cooperatively identify the problem, generate and weigh alternative solutions and select a solution. Integrating is appropriate for complex issues plagued by misunderstanding. Its primary strength is its longer-lasting impact because it deals with the underlying problem rather than merely with symptoms. The primary weakness of this style is that it is very time-consuming.

The *obliging or smoothing style* involves playing down differences while emphasising commonalities. 'An obliging person neglects his or her own concern to satisfy the concern of the other party.'[39] Obliging may be an appropriate conflict-handling strategy when it is possible eventually to get something in return. But it is inappropriate for complex or worsening problems. Its primary strength is that it encourages co-operation. Its main weakness is that it is a temporary fix that fails to confront the underlying problem.

The *dominating or forcing style* is essentially a matter of having high concern for self and low concern for others. This encourages 'I win, you lose' tactics. The other party's needs are largely ignored. This style is often called 'forcing' because it relies on formal authority to force compliance.

Figure 14.4 Five Conflict-Handling Styles

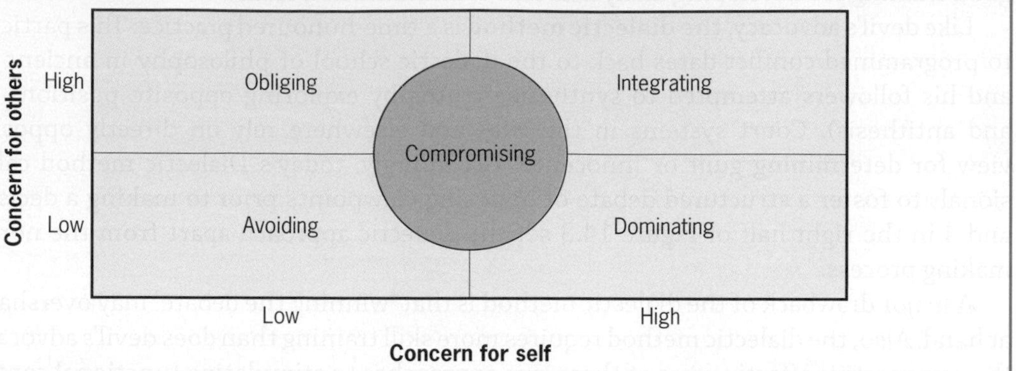

Source: M. A. Rahim, 'A Strategy for Managing Conflict in Complex Organizations, *Human Relations*, January 1985, p. 84. Used with permission of Plenum Publishing.

It is sometimes also called the 'Dirty Harry' method, calling to mind the persuasiveness of the fictional policeman Harry Callaghan and his very large handgun. Dominating is appropriate when an unpopular solution must be implemented, the issue is minor or a deadline is near. It is inappropriate in an open and participative climate. Speed is its primary strength. The primary weakness of this domineering style is that it often breeds resentment.

The *avoiding tactic* may involve either passive withdrawal from the problem or active suppression of the issue. Avoidance is appropriate for trivial issues or when the costs of confrontation outweigh the benefits of resolving the conflict. It is inappropriate for difficult and worsening problems. The main strength of this style is that it buys time in unfolding or ambiguous situations. The primary weakness is that the tactic provides a temporary fix that sidesteps the underlying problem.

Compromising is a give-and-take approach involving moderate concern for both self and others. Compromise is appropriate when parties have opposite goals or possess equal power. But compromise is inappropriate when overuse would lead to inconclusive action (e.g. failure to meet production deadlines). The primary strength of this tactic is that the democratic process has no losers, but it is a temporary fix that can stifle creative problem-solving.

OB in Real Life

Nasty people at work

When is a colleague (or a boss or even a customer) being nasty – and what can you do about it? These simple questions were asked by Bob Sutton in a short piece in the *Harvard Business Review* in 2004. They, and others that they generated, have elevated Professor Sutton to the highest levels of guru fame.

In common language, we can call these bosses 'tyrants', 'bullies', 'jerks' or 'destructive narcissists'. A clinical definition might be that such people engage in 'the sustained display of hostile verbal and nonverbal behaviours, excluding physical contact'.

The problem is that we all have our own inner jerk wanting to get out. Bob Sutton argues that two tests are helpful for identifying someone as one of these nasty individuals. The first is to ask whether people consistently finds themselves oppressed and belittled, as well as feeling dramatically worse about themselves after talking to someone who might be a bully. The second test is whether the supposed bully consistently directs his or her nastiness towards those who are powerless in the organisation – and never towards those who have power.

Those on the receiving end of this kind of abuse cannot always ignore the experience. There are few statistics which illustrate the magnitude of the problem. However, stories of the damage inflicted by nasty bosses and other people abound. Here are two examples:

> Marianne worked for an internet portal called Jubii. She often put in 20 hours per day and was either praised or belittled. She was humiliated, mocked and subjected to sexual harassment. She ended up suffering from severe depression and debilitating stress. It is unclear if she will ever work again. Her boss seemed unable to send a mail to his staff without including some form of sexual suggestion. Marianne's union took the employer to court, but after two days, the lawyers gave up trying to defend the employer. Marianne accepted a settlement worth around €20,000.

This case was reported from Denmark, a country where the courts rarely award large compensations for anything. Had the case been tried in the USA, it is likely that the settlement would have been vastly greater.

Another story comes from a totally different environment, the game of softball, as told by Dave and reported by Bob Sutton:

> A few years ago I was an umpire for a local softball organisation. During the third inning in one game I blew a call at second base. The coach for the negatively impacted team immediately got in my face and spontaneously hit a full-blown [. . . .] rage. I called time-out and sent both teams to their respective dugouts and asked the coach to join me in centerfield. His rage continued until I told him to shut-up or the game was over. Once I had quiet, I told the coach that he was right, I had blown the call and I was not going to reverse it. However, my mistake did not cost his team any runs and earlier in the game his shortstop had made two fielding errors that has cost his team three runs. I now want to know why is it okay for him to get in my face [. . . .] based on my error, but he never said a word to his shortstop when the errors had cost his team runs. The coach was speechless. I then told him he had two choices: 1) Shut the [. . . .] up and play the game with no further incident, or 2) If the yelling at the umpire continued I would forfeit the game to other team taking his team out of contention for the league championship. Needless, to say the game was finished without further incident.

In this case, Dave was fully within his rights, in terms of having the power to give the game victory to the other team.

For discussion

How would you deal with nasty people at work (hint: there is only one really effective solution)? For further reflection: what kinds of costs do nasty people generate?

Source: See Robert I. Sutton, 'More Trouble than they are Worth', *Harvard Business Review*, February 2004, pp. 19–20. For further information on Bob Suttons work, see bobsutton.typepad.com. Marianne's case is detailed on www.hk.dk/aktuelt/nyhedsarkiv/oktober_2006/jubii_betaler_for_elendigt_psykisk_arbejdsmiljoe.

Negotiation and third-party intervention

Although the conflict-handling styles just discussed can be used for all types of conflict, the model primarily targets interpersonal conflict. But what about intergroup conflict that is increasingly common in today's team- and project-oriented organisations? And what about inter-organisational conflict often encountered in today's world of organisational alliances and partnerships? Negotiation and third-party intervention can be helpful in these areas.

Formally defined, **negotiation** is a give-and-take decision-making process involving interdependent parties with different preferences.[40] Common examples include labour–management negotiations over wages, hours and working conditions and negotiations between supply-chain specialists and vendors involving price, delivery schedules and credit terms. Self-managed work teams (Chapter 8) with overlapping task boundaries also need to rely on negotiated agreements.[41] Thus negotiating skills are more important than ever today.[42]

Negotiation experts distinguish between two types of negotiation – **distributive** and **integrative**. When the negotiation concerns the sharing of a fixed amount, negotiation is purely distributive. Any change affects everyone; more to one means less to others, a situation sometimes described as the 'fixed-pie problem'. In real life, however, conflicts are often more complex, involving many dimensions. Under such conditions the 'fixed-pie' analogy may no longer hold. Integrative negotiation goes beyond the win–lose type of thinking, which characterises distributive negotiation, by introducing the notion that if more is available for sharing, some or all can benefit, while nobody needs to lose anything.[43]

Distributive negotiation involves traditional win–lose thinking. Integrative negotiation calls for a progressive win-win strategy,[44] such as the one in Figure 14.5. In a laboratory study of

Figure 14.5 An Integrative Approach: Added-Value Negotiation

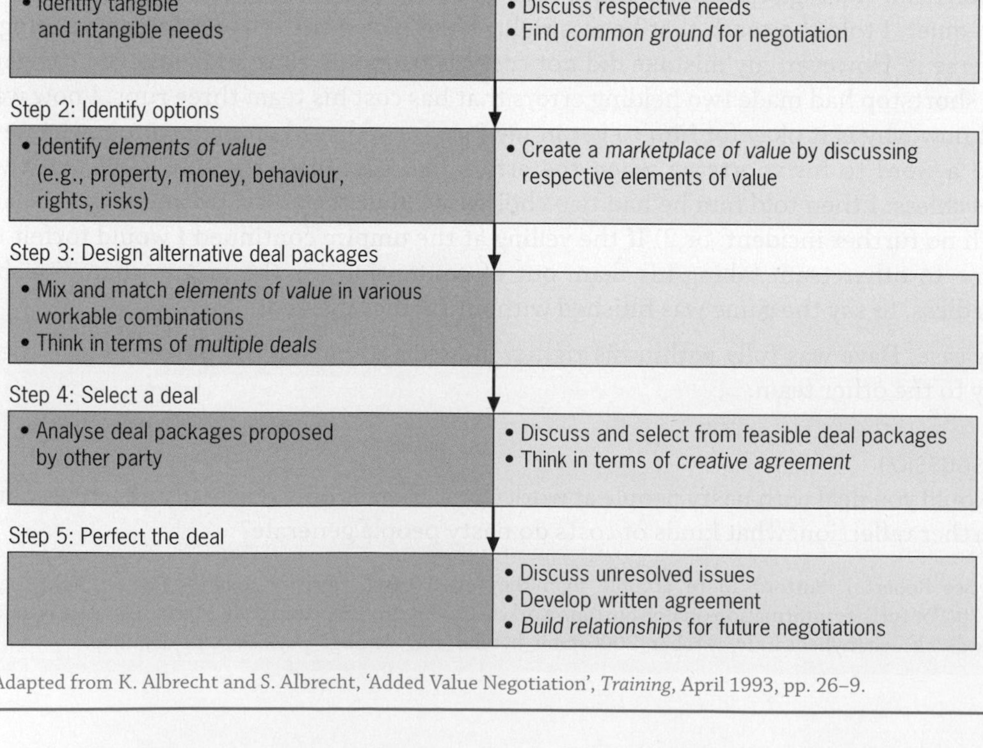
Separately
Jointly
Step 1: Clarify interests
• Identify tangible and intangible needs
• Discuss respective needs
• Find *common ground* for negotiation
Step 2: Identify options
• Identify *elements of value* (e.g., property, money, behaviour, rights, risks)
• Create a *marketplace of value* by discussing respective elements of value
Step 3: Design alternative deal packages
• Mix and match *elements of value* in various workable combinations
• Think in terms of *multiple deals*
Step 4: Select a deal
• Analyse deal packages proposed by other party
• Discuss and select from feasible deal packages
• Think in terms of *creative agreement*
Step 5: Perfect the deal
• Discuss unresolved issues
• Develop written agreement
• *Build relationships* for future negotiations

Source: Adapted from K. Albrecht and S. Albrecht, 'Added Value Negotiation', *Training*, April 1993, pp. 26–9.

joint-venture negotiations, teams trained in integrative tactics achieved better outcomes for both sides than untrained teams.[45] However, another study involving 700 employees from 11 cultures discovered that the integrative (or problem-solving) approach to negotiation was not equally effective across cultures.[46] North American negotiators generally are too short-term oriented and poor relationship builders when negotiating in Asia, Latin America and the Middle East.[47]

The success of integrative negotiation, such as added-value negotiation, hinges to a large extent on the quality of information exchanged, as researchers have recently documented.[48] Telling lies, hiding key facts and engaging in the other potentially unethical tactics listed in Table 14.2 erode trust and goodwill, both vital in win-win negotiations.[49] An awareness of these dirty tricks can keep good faith bargainers from being unfairly exploited.[50]

Third-party interventions are necessary when conflicting parties are unwilling and/or unable to engage in conflict resolution or integrative negotiation. Integrative or added-value negotiation is most appropriate for inter-group and inter-organisational conflict. The key is to get the conflicting parties to abandon traditional fixed-pie thinking and their win–lose expectations.

Table 14.2 Questionable/Unethical Tactics in Negotiation

Tactic	Description/clarification/range
Lies	Subject matter for lies can include limits, alternatives, the negotiator's intent, authority to bargain, other commitments, acceptability of the opponent's offers, time pressures and available resources
Puffery	Among the items that can be puffed up are the value of one's payoffs to the opponent, the negotiator's own alternatives, the costs of what one is giving up or is prepared to yield, importance of issues and attributes of the products or services
Deception	Acts and statements may include promises or threats, excessive initial demands, careless misstatements of facts or asking for concessions not wanted
Weakening the opponent	The negotiator here may cut off or eliminate some of the opponent's alternatives, blame the opponent for his own actions, use personally abrasive statements to or about the opponent or undermine the opponent's alliances
Strengthening one's own position	This tactic includes building one's own resources, including expertise, finances and alliances. It also includes presentations of persuasive rationales to the opponent or third parties (e.g. the public, the media) or getting mandates for one's position
Non-disclosure	Includes partial disclosure of facts, failure to disclose a hidden fact, failure to correct the opponents' misperceptions or ignorance and concealment of the negotiator's own position or circumstances
Information exploitation	Information provided by the opponent can be used to exploit weaknesses, close off alternatives, generate demands or weaken alliances
Change of mind	Includes accepting offers one had claimed one would not accept, changing demands, withdrawing promised offers and making threats one promised would not be made. Also includes the failure to behave as predicted
Distraction	These acts or statements can be as simple as providing excessive information to the opponent, asking many questions, evading questions or burying the issue. Or they can be more complex, such as feigning weakness in one area so that the opponent concentrates on it and ignores another
Maximisation	Includes demanding the opponent make concessions that result in the negotiator's gain and the opponent's equal or greater loss. Also entails converting a win-win situation into win-lose

Source: H. J. Reitz, J. A. Wall, Jr, and M. S. Love, 'Ethics in Negotiation: Oil and Water or Good Lubrication?' Reprinted with the *permission of Business Horizons*, May–June 1998, p. 6. Copyright © 1998 by the Board of Trustees at Indiana University, Kelley School of Business.

Too often, disputes between employees, between employees and their employer and between companies end up in lengthy and costly court battles. A more constructive, less expensive approach called 'alternative dispute resolution' has enjoyed enthusiastic growth in recent years.[51] **Alternative dispute resolution** (ADR) is a quicker, more user-friendly method of dispute resolution than an adversarial approach.[52] The four ADR techniques described in Table 14.3 represent a progression of steps third parties can take to resolve organisational conflicts.[53] They are ordered from easiest and least expensive to most difficult and costly. A growing number of organisations have formal ADR policies involving an established sequence of various combinations of these techniques.

Table 14.3 Alternative Dispute Resolution Techniques

Facilitation. A third party, usually a manager, informally urges disputing parties to deal directly with each other in a positive and constructive way.
Conciliation. A neutral third party informally acts as a communication conduit between disputing parties. This is appropriate when conflicting parties refuse to meet face-to-face. The immediate goal is to establish direct communication, with the broader aim of finding a common ground and constructive solution.
Peer review. A panel of trustworthy co-workers, selected for their ability to remain objective, hears both sides of the dispute in an informal and confidential meeting. Any decision by the review panel may or may not be binding, depending on the company's ADR policy. Membership on the peer review panel often is rotated among employees.
Ombuds(wo)man. Someone who works for the organisation, and is widely respected and trusted by his or her co-workers, hears grievances on a confidential basis and attempts to arrange a solution. This approach, which is more common in European than in North American companies, permits someone to get help without relying on the formal hierarchy chain.
Mediation. 'The mediator – a trained, third-party neutral – actively guides the disputing parties in exploring innovative solutions to the conflict. Although some companies have in-house mediators who have received ADR training, most also use external mediators who have no ties to the company.'[54] Unlike an arbitrator, a mediator does not render a decision. It is up to the disputants to reach a mutually acceptable decision.
Arbitration. Disputing parties agree ahead of time to accept the decision of a neutral arbitrator in a formal court-like setting, often complete with evidence and witnesses. Participation in this form of ADR can be voluntary or mandatory, depending upon company policy or union contracts.[55] Statements are confidential. Decisions are based on legal merits.

14.3 Social power

The term 'power' evokes mixed and often passionate reactions. Citing recent instances of government corruption and corporate misconduct, many observers view power as a sinister force. To these sceptics, Lord Acton's time-honoured statement that 'power corrupts and absolute power corrupts absolutely' is as true as ever. However, observational behaviour (OB) specialists remind us that, like it or not, power is a fact of life in modern organisations. According to one writer:

> Power must be used because managers must influence those they depend on. Power also is crucial in the development of managers' self-confidence and willingness to support subordinates. From this perspective, power should be accepted as a natural part of any organisation. Managers should recognise and develop their own power to co-ordinate and support the work of subordinates; it is powerlessness, not power, that undermines organisational effectiveness.[56]

Thus, power is a necessary and generally positive force in organisations. As the term is used here, **social power** is defined as 'the ability to marshal the human, informational and material resources to get something done'.[57]

While power may be an elusive concept to the casual observer, social scientists view power as having reasonably clear dimensions. Because this need is learned and not innate, the need for power has been extensively studied. Two dimensions of power that deserve our attention are: (1) the two types of power (socialised and personalised) and (2) the five bases of power.

Two types of power

Behavioural scientists, such as David McClelland, contend that one of the basic human needs is the need for power (see Chapter 5). Based on his research, he has drawn a distinction between personalised power and socialised power. **Personalised power** is directed toward seeking to win out over others, because conflicts are seen as a 'zero-sum game' where 'if you win, I lose'. The **socialised power** is fuelled by the idea of exercising power for the benefit of others.[58]

This distinction between socialised and personalised power helps explain why power has a negative connotation for many people.[59] Employees who pursue personalised power for their own selfish ends give power a bad name.

Five bases of power

A popular classification scheme for social power goes 40 years back to the work of John French and Bertram Raven. They proposed that power arises from five different bases: reward power, coercive power, legitimate power, expert power and referent power. Many researchers have studied these five power bases and searched for others. For the most part, French and Raven's list remains intact.[60] Each power base involves a different approach to influencing others:

- *Reward power*: a manager has **reward power** to the extent that he or she obtains compliance by promising or granting rewards.
- *Coercive power*: threats of punishment and actual punishment give an individual **coercive power**. A sales manager who threatens to fire any salesperson who uses a company car for family vacations is relying on coercive power.
- *Legitimate power*: this base of power is anchored to one's formal position or authority. Thus, individuals who obtain compliance primarily because of their formal authority to make decisions have **legitimate power**. Legitimate power may express itself in either a positive or negative manner in managing people. Positive legitimate power focuses constructively on job performance. Negative legitimate power tends to be threatening and demeaning to those being influenced.
- *Expert power*: valued knowledge or information gives an individual **expert power** over those who need such knowledge or information. The power of supervisors is enhanced because they know about work schedules and assignments before their employees do. Skilful use of expert power played a key role in the effectiveness of team leaders in a study of three physician medical diagnosis teams.[61] Knowledge is power in today's high-tech workplaces (see Chapter 16).
- *Referent power*: also called 'charisma', **referent power** comes into play when one's personality becomes the reason for compliance. Role models have referent power over those who identify closely with them.[62] From Martin Luther King to Steve Jobs, almost every well-known leader used or uses referent power to influence his or her followers.

To enhance your understanding of these five bases of power and to assess your self-perceived power, please take a moment to complete the next activity. Think of your present job or your most recent job when responding to the various items. What is your power profile? Finally, as power is strongly linked to leadership, we also suggest that you look at Chapter 15 to find out more about this topic.

Evidence about power

In one study a sample of 94 male and 84 female non-managerial and professional employees completed tests that showed that male and female employees had similar needs for power and personalised power. But the women had a significantly higher need for socialised power than did their male counterparts.[63]

Critical thinking

In what circumstances would one group (e.g. men) be willing to give up some of their power to another group (e.g. women)?

Activity

What is your self-perceived power?

Instructions

Score your various bases of power for your current (or former) job, using the following scale:
1 = strongly disagree
2 = disagree
3 = slightly agree
4 = agree
5 = strongly agree

Reward power

1	I can reward individuals at lower levels.	1 2 3 4 5
2	My review actions affect the rewards gained at lower levels.	1 2 3 4 5
3	Based on my decisions, lower-level personnel may receive a bonus.	1 2 3 4 5

Score________

Coercive power

1	I can punish employees at lower levels.	1 2 3 4 5
2	My work is a check on lower-level employees.	1 2 3 4 5
3	My diligence reduces error.	1 2 3 4 5

Score________

Legitimate power

1	My position gives me a great deal of authority.	1	2	3	4	5
2	The decisions made at my level are of critical importance.	1	2	3	4	5
3	Employees look to me for guidance.	1	2	3	4	5

Score________

Expert power

1	I am an expert in this job.	1	2	3	4	5
2	My ability gives me an advantage in this job.	1	2	3	4	5
3	Given some time, I could improve the methods used on this job.	1	2	3	4	5

Score________

Referent power

1	I attempt to set a good example for other employees.	1	2	3	4	5
2	My personality allows me to work well in this job.	1	2	3	4	5
3	My fellow employees look to me as their informal leader.	1	2	3	4	5

Score________

Scoring key and norms

Arbitrary norms for each of the five bases of power are:

3–6 = weak power base
7–11 = moderate power base
12–15 = strong power base

Source: Adapted and excerpted in part from D. L. Dieterly and B. Schneider, 'The Effect of Organizational Environment on Perceived Power and Climate: A Laboratory Study', *Organizational Behavior and Human Performance*, June 1974, pp. 316–37.

A re-analysis of 18 field studies that measured French and Raven's five bases of power uncovered 'severe methodological shortcomings'.[64] After correcting for these problems, the researchers identified the following relationships between power bases and work outcomes, such as job performance, job satisfaction and turnover:

- Expert and referent power had a generally positive impact.
- Reward and legitimate power had a slightly positive impact.
- Coercive power had a slightly negative impact.

The same researcher, in a 1990 follow-up study involving 251 employed business seniors, looked at the relationship between influence styles and bases of power. Employee perceptions of managerial influence and power were examined and rational persuasion was found to be a highly acceptable managerial influence tactic. Why? Because employees perceived it to be associated with the three bases of power they viewed positively: legitimate, expert and referent.[65]

HR In summary, expert and referent power appear to get the best combination of results and favourable reactions from lower-level employees.[66]

14.4 Organisational politics

Most students of OB find the study of organisational politics intriguing. Perhaps, this topic owes its appeal to the antics of certain movies, picturing corporate villains who get their way by stepping on anyone and everyone. As we will see, however, organisational politics includes, but is not limited to, dirty dealing. Organisational politics is an ever-present and sometimes annoying feature of modern work life. For example, a survey showed that internal office politics are holding back the growth of the UK's electronic economy. It was found that 25 per cent of information technology (IT) directors believe politics is to blame for the brakes being put on e-business projects.[67] On the other hand, organisational politics is often a positive force in modern work organisations. Skilful and well-timed politics can help you get your point across, neutralise resistance to a key project or get a choice job assignment.

David Butcher, from Cranfield Management School, UK, puts things in perspective by observing the following:

> The idea that business and politics don't mix is one of management's most deeply ingrained myths. When people say of a corporation or a hospital that 'it's a very political organisation', it's not meant as a compliment. In the same way, 'he or she plays politics' is a damning assessment of a person. But the ideal of a company as a politics-free zone is getting harder and harder to sustain. It was born of an era where rationality and control were the paramount values, and hierarchy and bureaucracy the logical management expressions of them. Unfortunately the world is no longer predictable and stable, but chaotic and volatile, so the simplistic vision of management as an exercise in machine-like rationality doesn't wash any more. (. . .) Large organisations are hotbeds of political intrigue. Senior managers have competing agendas. It was ever thus. Management works that way. If you ask managers what they do, they say that politics is part of their job. It's a purely notional view that says otherwise. It's time we recognise that fact. Once you accept that a company is a political system, you can begin to make things happen.[68]

We explore this important and interesting area by: (1) defining the term 'organisational politics', (2) identifying three levels of political action, (3) discussing eight specific political tactics, (4) considering a related area called impression management and (5) examining relevant research and practical implications.

Definition and domain of organisational politics

'Organisational politics involves intentional acts of influence to enhance or protect the self-interest of individuals or groups.'[69] An emphasis on self-interest distinguishes this form of social influence. Managers are endlessly challenged to achieve a workable balance between employees' self-interests and organisational interests. When a proper balance exists, the pursuit of self-interest may serve the organisation's interests. Political behaviour becomes a negative force when self-interests erode or defeat organisational interests. For example, researchers have documented the political tactic of filtering and distorting information flowing up to the boss. This self-serving practice puts the reporting employees in the best possible light.[70]

Political manoeuvring is triggered primarily by uncertainty and changes. Four common sources of uncertainty within organisations are:

- Unclear objectives.
- Vague performance measures.
- Ill-defined decision processes.
- Strong individual or group competition.[71]

Regarding this last source of uncertainty, organisation development specialist Anthony Raia noted: 'Whatever we attempt to change, the political subsystem becomes active. Vested interests are almost always at stake and the distribution of power is challenged.'[72]

Thus, we would expect a field sales representative, striving to achieve an assigned quota, to be less political than a management trainee working on a variety of projects. While some management trainees stake their career success on hard work, competence and a bit of luck, many do not. These people attempt to gain a competitive edge through some combination of the political tactics discussed below. Meanwhile, the salesperson's performance is measured in actual sales, not in terms of being friends with the boss or taking credit for others' work. Thus, the management trainee would tend to be more political than the field salesperson because of greater uncertainty about management's expectations. Because employees generally experience greater uncertainty during the earlier stages of their careers, it has also been found that junior employees are more political than more senior ones.[73]

Three levels of political action

Although much political manoeuvring occurs at the individual level, it can also involve group or collective action. Figure 14.6 illustrates three different levels of political action: the individual level, the coalition level and the network level.[74] Each level has its distinguishing characteristics. At the individual level, personal self-interests are pursued by the individual. The political aspects of coalitions and networks are not so obvious, however.

People with a common interest can become a political coalition by fitting the following definition. In an organisational context, a **coalition** is an informal group bound together by the active pursuit of a single issue. Coalitions may or may not coincide with formal group membership (also see Chapter 7). When the target issue is resolved, the coalition disbands. Experts note that political coalitions have 'fuzzy boundaries', meaning they are fluid in membership, flexible in structure and temporary in duration.[75]

Figure 14.6 Levels of Political Action in Organisations

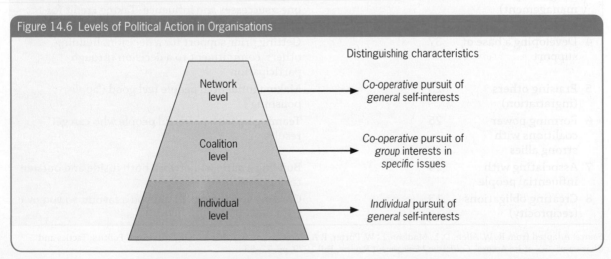

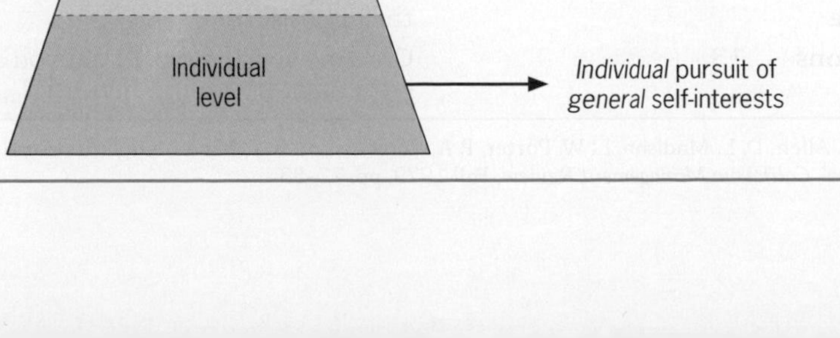

A third level of political action involves networks.[76] Unlike coalitions, which pivot on specific issues, networks are loose associations of individuals seeking social support for their general self-interests. Politically, networks are people-oriented, while coalitions are issue-oriented. Networks have broader and longer-term agendas than coalitions.

Political tactics

Anyone who has worked in an organisation has first-hand knowledge of blatant politicking. Blaming someone else for your mistake is an obvious political ploy. But other political tactics are more subtle. Researchers have identified a range of political behaviour.

One landmark study, involving in-depth interviews with 87 managers from 30 electronics companies, identified eight political tactics. Top-, middle- and low-level managers were represented about equally in the sample. According to the researchers: 'Respondents were asked to describe organisational political tactics and personal characteristics of effective political actors based upon their accumulated experience in all organisations in which they had worked'.[77] The eight political tactics that emerged are listed in descending order in the first column of Table 14.4.[78]

Table 14.4 Eight Common Political Tactics in Organisations

Political tactic	Percentage of managers mentioning tactic	Brief description of tactic
1 Attacking or blaming others	54	Used to avoid or minimise association with failure. Reactive when scapegoating is involved. Proactive when goal is to reduce competition for limited resources
2 Using information as a political tool	54	Involves the purposeful withholding or distortion of information. Obscuring an unfavourable situation by overwhelming superiors with information
3 Creating a favourable image (impression management)	53	Dressing/grooming for success. Adhering to organisational norms and drawing attention to one's successes and influence. Taking credit for others' accomplishments
4 Developing a base of support	37	Getting prior support for a decision. Building others' commitment to a decision through participation
5 Praising others (ingratiation)	25	Making influential people feel good ('apple polishing')
6 Forming power coalitions with strong allies	25	Teaming up with powerful people who can get results
7 Associating with influential people	24	Building a support network both inside and outside the organisation
8 Creating obligations (reciprocity)	13	Creating social debts ('I did you a favour, so you owe me a favour')

Source: Adapted from R. W. Allen, D. L. Madison, L. W. Porter, P. A. Renwick and B. T. Mayes, 'Organizational Politics: Tactics and Characteristics of Its Actors', *California Management Review*, Fall 1979, pp. 77–83.

Activity

Your political tendencies

What is your attitude towards organisational politics? How often do you rely on the various tactics in Table 14.4? You can get a general indication of your political tendencies by comparing your behaviour with the characteristics in Table 14.5. Would you characterise yourself as politically naive, politically sensible or a political shark? How do you think others view your political actions? What are the career, friendship and ethical implications of your political tendencies?[79]

Table 14.5 Are You Politically Naive, Politically Sensible or a Political Shark?

Characteristics	Naïve	Sensible	Shark
Underlying attitude	Politics is unpleasant	Politics is necessary	Politics is an opportunity
Intent	Avoid at all costs	Further departmental goals	Self-serving and predatory
Techniques	Tell it like it is	Network; expand connections; use system to give and receive favours	Manipulate; use fraud and deceit when necessary
Favourite tactics	None – the truth will win out	Negotiate, bargain	Bully; misuse information; cultivate and use 'friends' and other contacts

Source: Reprinted with permission from J. K. Pinto and O. P. Kharbanda, 'Lessons for an Accidental Profession', *Business Horizons*, March–April 1995, p. 45. Copyright © 1998 by the Indiana University Board of Trustees at Indiana University, Kelley School of Business.

14.5 Impression management

Impression management is defined as 'the process by which people attempt to control or manipulate the reactions of others to images of themselves or their ideas.'[80] This encompasses how one talks, behaves and looks. Most impression management attempts are directed at making a good impression on relevant others. But, as we will see, some employees strive to make a bad impression. For purposes of conceptual clarity, we will focus on upward impression management (trying to impress one's immediate supervisor) because it is most relevant for managers. Still, it is good to remember that anyone can be the intended target of impression management. Parents, teachers, peers, employees and customers are all fair game when it comes to managing the impressions of others. At an organisational level, impression management can be used as a tool to differentiate the organisation's image for competitor companies.

A conceptual crossroad

Impression management is an interesting theoretical concept involving self-monitoring, attribution theory and organisational politics.[81] Remember that high self-monitoring employees ('chameleons' who adjust to their surroundings) are likely to be more inclined to engage in impression management than low self-monitors (see Chapter 2). Impression management also involves the systematic manipulation of attributions (see Chapter 4). For example, a bank president will look good if the board of directors is encouraged to attribute organisational successes to his or her efforts and attribute problems and failures to factors beyond his or her control. Impression management definitely fits into the realm of organisational politics because of an overriding focus on furthering one's self-interests.

Making a good impression

If you 'dress for success', project an upbeat attitude at all times and avoid offending others, you are engaging in favourable impression management – particularly so if your motive is to improve your chances of getting what you want in life.[82] Former British Airways chairman, Lord King, admitted he had underestimated his casually dressed rival (Richard Branson, Virgin chairman). 'If Branson had worn a pair of steel-rimmed shoes, a double-breasted suit and shaved off his beard, I would have taken him seriously. As it was, I couldn't. I underestimated him.'[83] On the lighter side, the trend towards more casual dress codes has working men and women rethinking what it means to dress for success.

A statistical factor analysis of the influence attempts reported by a sample of 84 bank employees (including 74 women) identified three categories of favourable upward impression management tactics.[84] As labelled in the next activity, favourable upward impression management tactics can be job-focused (manipulating information about one's job performance), supervisor-focused (praising and doing favours for one's supervisor) and self-focused (presenting oneself as a polite and nice person).

A moderate amount of upward impression management is a necessity for the average employee today. Too little, and busy managers are liable to overlook some of your valuable contributions when they make job assignment, pay and promotion decisions. Too much, and you run the risk of being branded a 'schmoozer', a 'phoney' and other unflattering things by your co-workers.[85] Excessive flattery and ingratiation can backfire by embarrassing the target person and damaging one's credibility.

Also, the risk of unintended insult is very high when impression management tactics cross gender, racial, ethnic and cultural lines.[86] International management experts warn:

> The impression management tactic is only as effective as its correlation to accepted norms about behavioural presentation. In other words, slapping a Japanese subordinate on the back with a rousing 'Good work, Hiro!' will not create the desired impression in Hiro's mind that the expatriate intended. In fact, the behaviour will likely create the opposite impression.[87]

Making a poor impression

At first glance, the idea of consciously trying to make a bad impression in the workplace seems absurd. But an interesting new line of impression management research has uncovered both motives and tactics for making oneself look bad. In a survey of the work experiences of business students at a large north-western US university, more than half 'reported witnessing a case of someone intentionally looking bad at work'.[88] Why?

Four motives came out of the study:

- Avoidance: employee seeks to avoid additional work, stress, burnout or an unwanted transfer or promotion.
- Obtain concrete rewards: employee seeks to obtain a pay rise or a desired transfer, promotion or demotion.
- Exit: employee seeks to get laid off, fired or suspended, and perhaps also to collect unemployment or workers' compensation.
- Power: employee seeks to control, manipulate or intimidate others, get revenge, or make someone else look bad.[89]

Activity

How much do you rely on upward impression management tactics?

Instructions

Rate yourself on each item according to how you behave on your current (or most recent) job. Add your circled responses to calculate a total score. Compare your score with our arbitrary norms.

Job-focused tactics	**Rarely**				**Very often**
1 I exaggerate the value of my positive work results and make my supervisor aware of them.	1	2	3	4	5
2 I try to make my work appear better than it is.	1	2	3	4	5
3 I try to take responsibility for positive results, even when I'm not solely responsible for achieving them.	1	2	3	4	5
4 I try to make my negative results less severe than they initially appear, when informing my supervisor.	1	2	3	4	5
5 I arrive at work early and/or work late to show my supervisor I am a hard worker.	1	2	3	4	5
Supervisor-focused tactics					
6 I show an interest in my supervisor's personal life.	1	2	3	4	5
7 I praise my supervisor about his/her accomplishments.	1	2	3	4	5
8 I do personal favours for my supervisor that I'm not required to do.	1	2	3	4	5
9 I compliment my supervisor on her/his dress or appearance.	1	2	3	4	5
10 I agree with my supervisor's major suggestions and ideas.	1	2	3	4	5
Self-focused tactics					
11 I am very friendly and polite in the presence of my supervisor.	1	2	3	4	5
12 I try to act as a model employee in the presence of my supervisor.	1	2	3	4	5
13 I work harder when I know my supervisor will see the results.	1	2	3	4	5

Total score = ___________

Arbitrary norms

13–26 Free agent

27–51 Better safe than sorry

52–65 Hello, Hollywood!

Source: Adapted from S. J. Wayne and G. R. Ferris, 'Influence Tactics, Affect, and Exchange Quality in Supervisor-Subordinate Interactions: A Laboratory Experiment and Field Study', *Journal of Applied Psychology*, October 1990, pp. 487–99.

Within the context of these motives, unfavourable upward impression management makes sense. Five unfavourable upward impression management tactics identified by the researchers are as follows:

- Decreasing performance: restricting productivity, making more mistakes than usual, lowering quality, neglecting tasks.
- Not working to potential: pretending ignorance, having unused capabilities.
- Withdrawing: being tardy, taking excessive breaks, faking illness.
- Displaying a bad attitude: complaining, getting upset and angry, acting strangely, and not getting along with co-workers.
- Broadcasting limitations: letting co-workers know about one's physical problems and mistakes (both verbally and non-verbally).[90]

Recommended ways to manage employees who try to make a bad impression can be found throughout this book. They include, for instance, more challenging work, greater autonomy, better feedback, supportive leadership, clear and reasonable goals, and a less stressful work setting.[91]

Research findings and practical implications

Field research involving employees in real organisations rather than students in contrived laboratory settings has yielded these useful insights.

In a study of 514 non-academic university employees in the south-western USA, white men had a greater understanding of organisational politics than racial and ethnic minorities and white women. The researchers endorsed the practice of using mentors to help women and minorities develop their political skills.[92]

Another study of 68 women and 84 men employed by five different service and industrial companies in the USA uncovered significant gender-based insights about organisational politics. In what might be termed the battle of the sexes:

> It was found that political behaviour was perceived more favourably when it was performed against a target of the opposite gender. . . . Thus subjects of both sexes tend to relate to gender as a meaningful affiliation group. This finding presents a different picture from the one suggesting that women tend to accept male superiority at work and generally agree with sex stereotypes which are commonly discriminatory in nature.[93]

Impression management attempts can either positively or negatively impact one's performance appraisal results.[94] The researchers in one study of 67 manager–employee pairs concluded: 'Subordinates who were friendly and reasonable were perceived as amiable and favourably evaluated.'[95] However, subordinates who relied on ingratiation (making the boss feel good) did not get better performance appraisals.[96]

Organisational politics cannot be eliminated. A manager would be naive to expect such an outcome. But political manoeuvring can and should be managed to keep it constructive and within reasonable bounds. Harvard's Abraham Zaleznik put the issue this way: 'People can focus their attention on only so many things. The more it lands on politics, the less energy – emotional and intellectual – is available to attend to the problems that fall under the heading of real work.'[97]

An individual's degree of 'politicalness' is a matter of personal values, ethics and temperament. People who are either strictly non-political or highly political generally pay a price for their behaviour. The former may experience slow promotions and feel left out, while the latter may run the risk of being called self-serving and lose their credibility. People at both ends of the political spectrum may be considered poor team players. A moderate amount of prudent political behaviour generally is considered a survival tool in complex organisations.

HR With this perspective in mind, the following are practical steps:[98]

- Screen out overly political individuals at hiring time.
- Create an open-book management system.
- Make sure every employee knows how the business works and has a personal line of sight to key results with corresponding measureable objectives for individual accountability.
- Have non-financial people interpret periodic financial and accounting statements for all employees.
- Establish formal conflict resolution and grievance processes.
- As an ethics filter, do only what you would feel comfortable doing on national television.
- Publicly recognise and reward people who get real results without political games.

> **Critical thinking**
>
> Isn't there a paradox in that it would take a degree of experience of office politics to be able to spot it and fight it? How could a manager fight office politics without being involved in it?

14.6 Empowerment

If leaders are to use their various bases of power effectively and ethically, they need to strive for commitment rather than mere compliance and understand the difference between power sharing and power distribution.

From compliance to commitment

Responsible leaders strive for socialised power while avoiding personalised power. In fact, in a survey, organisational commitment (see Chapter 3) was higher among executives whose superiors exercised socialised power than among colleagues with 'power-hungry' bosses.[99]

How does this relate to the five bases of power? As with influence tactics, managerial power has three possible outcomes: commitment, compliance or resistance. Reward, coercive and negative legitimate power tend to produce compliance (and sometimes, resistance). On the other hand, positive legitimate, expert and referent power tend to foster commitment. Once again, commitment is superior to compliance because it is driven by internal or intrinsic motivation (see Chapters 5 and 6).[100]

Employees who merely comply require frequent 'jolts' of power from the boss to keep them headed in a productive direction. Committed employees tend to be self-starters who do not require close supervision – a key success factor in today's flatter, team-oriented organisations (see Chapter 10).

According to research cited earlier, expert and referent power have the greatest potential for improving job performance and satisfaction and reducing turnover. Formal education, training and self-development can build a manager's expert power.

Empowerment: from power sharing to power distribution

An exciting trend in today's organisations focuses on giving employees a greater say in the workplace. This trend wears various labels, including 'participative management' and 'open-book management'. Regardless of the label one prefers, it is all about **empowerment**, which has been defined as 'a practice, or set of practices involving the delegation of responsibility down the hierarchy so as to give employees increased decision-making authority in respect to the execution of their primary work tasks'.[101] Thus, a core component of this process is pushing decision-making authority down to progressively lower levels and there are parallel ideas in the concepts of job enrichment (Chapter 5), self-managed teams and autonomous work groups (Chapter 8).

No information sharing, no empowerment

Open-book management breaks down the traditional organisational caste system made up of information 'haves' and information 'have-nots'. Superiors historically were afraid to tell their employees about innovations, company finances and strategic plans for fear of giving the advantage to unions and competitors. To varying extents, those threats persist today. Nonetheless, in the larger scheme of things, organisations with unified and adequately informed employees have a significant competitive advantage.

OB in Real Life

Being social at work

While many companies struggle to get their employees to use their intranets and knowledge-sharing platform, it seems that people are taking matters into their own hands using a number of social media, such as LinkedIn, Twitter and Facebook. A study in the UK has shown that the personal use of Twitter, Facebook and other such social network services during the working day was costing the British economy almost £1.4 billion a year in lost productivity, posing a threat to corporate profits. Of course, some would find other ways of procrastinating, if they did not spend their time on those online social networks.

But does it even make sense to try to stop this development? As new generations enter the workforce, more and more are completely immersed in these new technologies and are completely at ease with sharing and collaborating both privately and professionally. Therefore, they take for granted that their workplaces are built on an open, networked and collaborative platform too. This contrasts with the reality of larger and larger global companies where collaboration can be difficult at best.

An increasing number of managers have started to see the potential benefits of implementing some of these social networking platforms. Most of these systems allow a degree of control and have analytical tools built into them, which offer a vast number of interesting data that can be used by human resources (HR) or for marketing purposes.

One of the most important points is that people have no problem sharing information as long as it is done within the frameworks of a set of social norms and rules and that it is easy to use. Therefore, we are likely to see many more companies taking action on these social networks – whether banning them or integrating them into their businesses somehow.

Source: Inspired by Julian Carter, 'Yammering Away at the Office', *The Economist*, 30 January 2010 (US edition).

The problematic question then becomes: how much information sharing is enough (or too much)? As demonstrated in the adjacent 'OB in Real Life', there is no exact answer. Empowering managers need to learn from experience to be careful in what they share and let employees know when certain information requires secrecy. Empowerment through open-book management carries some risk of betrayal, like any act of trust (also see Chapter 8). Advocates of empowerment believe the rewards (more teamwork and greater competitiveness) outweigh the risks.

A matter of degree

The concept of empowerment requires some adjustments in traditional thinking. First, power is not a zero-sum situation where one person's gain is another's loss. Authoritarian managers who view employee empowerment as a threat to their personal power are missing the point because of their win–lose thinking.[102]

The second adjustment to traditional thinking involves seeing empowerment as a matter of degree, not as an either-or proposition.[103] Figure 14.7 illustrates how power can be shifted to the hands of non-managers step by step. The overriding goal is to increase productivity and competitiveness in leaner organisations. Each step in this evolution increases the power of organisational contributors who traditionally had little or no legitimate power.

Evidence about empowerment

Like most other popular management techniques, empowerment has its fair share of critics and suffers from unrealistic expectations.[104] Research about the actual results to date are mixed:

- According to a field study of 26 insurance claims supervisors, employees who enjoyed a greater degree of delegation processed more insurance claims at lower cost.[105]
- A study of 297 service employees led the researchers to conclude: 'Empowerment may contribute to an employee's job satisfaction, but not as profoundly shape work effort and performance.'[106]

Figure 14.7 The Evolution of Power: From Domination to Delegation

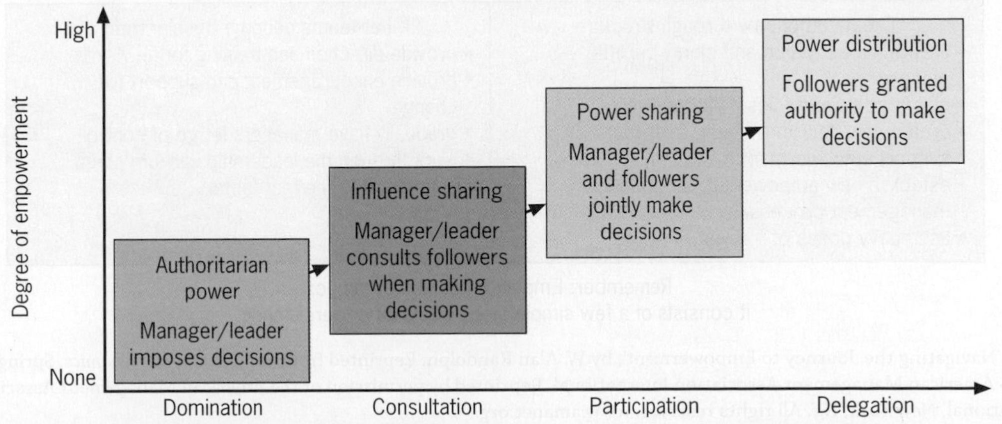

- A study of 24 growing companies by Centre Entreprise at Cambridge University, UK, showed that delegation is fundamental in order to expand a company. While the leaders of the companies examined were all highly motivated and ambitious, some achieved much faster and more consistent growth than others. These high achievers were characterised by their ability to recruit a team of senior managers at an early stage and by their willingness to cede a high degree of control and responsibility to them.[107]
- When the job performance of 81 empowered employees at the home office of a Canadian life insurance company was compared with a control group of 90 employees, the researchers found 'minimal support' for empowerment.[108]
- Factors associated with perceived empowerment were studied at a US hospital. Among 612 nurses, skilled professionals and administrators (21 per cent male), higher perceived empowerment was associated with higher rank, longer tenure with the organisation, approachable leaders, effective and worthwhile task groups, higher job satisfaction and lower propensity to quit. No gender or race effects were found.[109]

Practical implications of empowerment

We believe empowerment has good promise if superiors go about it properly. Managers committed to the idea of employee empowerment need to follow the path of continuous improvement, learning from their successes and failures. Eight years of research with 10 'empowered' companies led consultant W. Alan Randolph to formulate the three-pronged empowerment plan in Figure 14.8. Notice how open-book management and active information sharing are needed to build the necessary foundation of trust. Beyond that, clear goals and lots of relevant training are needed.

Figure 14.8 Randolph's Empowerment Plan

Share information
- share company performance information
- help people understand the business
- build trust through sharing sensitive information
- create self-monitoring possibilities

Create autonomy through structure
- create a clear vision and clarify the little pictures
- clarify goals and roles collaboratively
- create new decision-making rules that support empowerment
- establish new empowering performance management processes
- use heavy doses of training

Let teams become the hierarchy
- provide direction and training for new skills
- provide encouragement and support for change
- gradually have managers let go of control
- work through the leadership vacuum stage
- acknowledge the fear factor

Remember: Empowerment is not magic;
it consists of a few simple steps and a lot of persistence.

Source: 'Navigating the Journey to Empowerment', by W. Alan Randolph. Reprinted from *Organizational Dynamics*, Spring 1995. 1995 American Management Association International. Reprinted by permission of the American Management Association International, New York, NY. All rights reserved. www.amanet.org.

While noting that the empowerment process can take several years to unfold, Randolph offered this perspective:

> While the keys to empowerment may be easy to understand, they are hard to implement. It takes tremendous courage to start sharing sensitive information. It takes true strength to build more structure just at the point when people want more freedom of action. It takes real growth to allow teams to take over the management decision-making process. And above all, it takes perseverance to complete the empowerment process.[110]

14.7 Delegation, trust and personal initiative

The highest degree of empowerment is **delegation**, the process of granting decision-making authority to lower-level employees. This amounts to power distribution. Delegation has long been the recommended way to lighten the busy manager's load while, at the same time, developing employees' abilities. Importantly, delegation gives non-managerial employees more than simply a voice in decisions. It empowers them to make their own decisions.

OB in Real Life

Winning movers

'I used to be a genuine control freak. I was working from 5 a.m. and getting back home after my children had gone to bed – but I still had to examine every letter that left the office, and change something, even if the letter was perfect', Bishop tells. His company had grown rapidly, passing the 1 million turnover mark within three years. His diary was crammed, his desk overflowing, and there were never enough hours in the day to complete the many projects he started. He only realised there was a problem when his employees criticised communication within the company in a staff survey. 'I knew we wouldn't grow further unless I relaxed my grip on others', he says. 'I had to learn to empower the people around me.' Bishop acted fast. He forced himself to 'butt out' of group meetings where he was answering questions on behalf of others. He evolved a system whereby top-line goals for the company were set collectively but responsibility for how best to achieve them was delegated to the individuals involved. It worked. Bishop is now getting home to see his kids and he is clearly pleased that his employees are keen to take on more responsibility and improve their skills and that they appear more motivated.[111]

Delegation is easy to talk about, but many superiors find it hard to actually do. A concerted effort to overcome the following common barriers to delegation needs to be made:

- Belief in the fallacy 'if you want it done right, do it yourself'.
- Lack of confidence and trust in lower-level employees.
- Low self-confidence.
- Fear of being called lazy.
- Vague job definition.
- Fear of competition from those below.

- Reluctance to take the risks involved in depending on others.
- Lack of controls that provide early warning of problems with delegated duties.
- Poor example set by bosses who do not delegate.[112]

Researchers at the State University of New York at Albany surveyed pairs of managers and employees and did follow-up interviews with the managers concerning their delegation habits. Their results confirmed some important common-sense notions about delegation. Greater delegation was associated with the following factors:

- Competent employees.
- Employee shared manager's task objectives.
- Manager had a long-standing and positive relationship with employee.
- The lower-level person was also a supervisor.[113]

This delegation scenario boils down to one pivotal factor, trust.[114]

Superiors prefer to delegate important tasks and decisions to the people they trust. As discussed in Chapters 7 and 8, it takes time and favourable experience to build trust. Of course, trust is fragile; it can be destroyed by a single remark, act or omission. Ironically, superiors cannot learn to trust someone without, initially at least, running the risk of betrayal. This is why empowerment in Figure 14.7 evolves towards trust: from consultation, over participation to delegation. In other words, superiors need to start small and work up the empowerment ladder. They need to delegate small tasks and decisions and scale up as competence, confidence and trust grow. Employees need to work on their side of the trust equation as well. One of the best ways to earn a superior's trust is to show initiative (see Figure 14.9).

Figure 14.9 Personal Initiative: The Other Side of Delegation

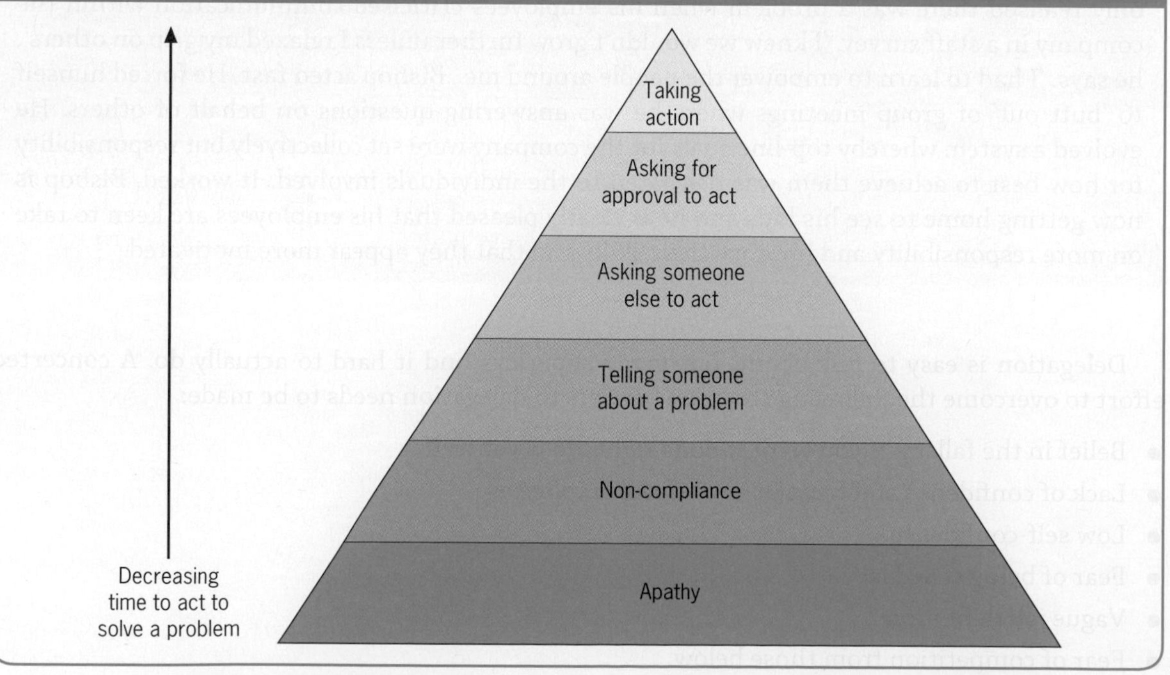

Researchers in the area offer this instructive definition and characterisation: **personal initiative** is a behaviour syndrome resulting in an individual's taking an active and self-starting approach to work and going beyond what is formally required in a given job. More specifically, personal initiative is characterised by the following aspects: it (1) is consistent with the organisation's mission, (2) has a long-term focus, (3) is goal-directed and action-oriented, (4) is persistent in the face of barriers and setbacks, and (5) is self-starting and proactive.[115]

! Critical thinking

In what instances would you recommend a manager not to implement empowerment?

Learning outcomes: Summary of key terms

1 **Explain the concept of mutuality of interest**

Managers are constantly challenged to foster mutuality of interest (a win-win situation) between individual and organisational interests. Organisation members need to actively co-operate with actual and potential adversaries for the common good.

2 **Name at least three 'soft' and two 'hard' influence tactics, and summarise the practical lessons from influence research**

Five soft influence tactics are rational persuasion, inspirational appeals, consultation, ingratiation and personal appeals. They are friendlier and less coercive than the four hard influence tactics: exchange, coalition tactics, pressure and legitimating tactics. According to research, soft tactics are better for generating commitment and are perceived as fairer than hard tactics. Ingratiation – making the boss feel good through compliments and being helpful – can slightly improve performance appraisal results and make the boss like you a lot more. Influence through domination is a poor strategy for both men and women. Influence is a complicated and situational process that needs to be undertaken with care, especially across cultures.

3 **Identify and briefly describe French and Raven's five bases of power, and discuss the responsible use of power**

French and Raven's five bases of power are reward power (rewarding compliance), coercive power (punishing non-compliance), legitimate power (relying on formal authority), expert power (providing needed information) and referent power (relying on personal attraction). Responsible and ethical managers strive to use socialised power (primary concern is for others) rather than personalised power (primary concern for self). Research found higher organisational commitment among employees with bosses who used uplifting power than among those with power-hungry bosses who relied on dominating power.

4 **Understand functional and dysfunctional conflict and desired conflict outcomes**

Conflict is a process in which one party perceives that its interests are being opposed or negatively affected by another party. It is inevitable and not necessarily destructive. Too little conflict, as evidenced by apathy or lack of creativity, can be as great a problem as too much conflict. Functional conflict enhances organisational interests while dysfunctional conflict is counterproductive. Three desired conflict outcomes are agreement, stronger relationships and learning.

5 **Recognise stimulation of functional conflict and identify conflict-handling styles**

There are many antecedents of conflict – including incompatible personalities, competition for limited resources and unrealised expectations – that need to be monitored. Functional conflict can be stimulated by permitting antecedents of conflict to persist and/or programming conflict during decision-making with devil's advocates or the dialectic method. The five conflict-handling styles are integrating (problem-solving), obliging (smoothing), dominating (forcing), avoiding and compromising. There is no single best style.

6 **Recognise distributive and integrative negotiation and discuss the concept of added-value negotiation**

Distributive negotiation involves fixed-pie and win–lose thinking. Integrative negotiation is a win-win approach to better results for both parties. The five steps in added value negotiation are as follows: Step 1, clarify interests; Step 2, identify options; Step 3, design alternative deal packages; Step 4, select a deal; and Step 5, perfect the deal. Elements of value, multiple deals and creative agreement are central to this approach.

7 **Explain why delegation is the highest form of empowerment and discuss the link with delegation, trust and personal initiative**

Delegation gives employees more than a participatory role in decision-making. It allows them to make their own work-related decisions. Managers tend to delegate to employees they trust. Employees can get managers to trust them by demonstrating personal initiative (going beyond formal job requirements and being self-starters).

8 **Define organisational politics and how it is triggered**

Organisational politics is defined as intentional acts of influence to enhance or protect the self-interests of individuals or groups. Uncertainty triggers most politicking in organisations. Political action occurs at individual, coalition and network levels. Coalitions are informal, temporary and single-issue alliances.

9 **Distinguish between favourable and unfavourable impression management tactics**

Favourable upward impression management can be job-focused (manipulating information about one's job performance), supervisor-focused (praising or doing favours for the boss) or self-focused (being polite and nice). Unfavourable upward impression management tactics include decreasing performance, not working to potential, withdrawing, displaying a bad attitude and broadcasting one's limitations.

10 **Explain how to manage organisational politics**

Since organisational politics cannot be eliminated, managers need to learn to deal with it. Uncertainty can be reduced by evaluating performance and linking rewards to performance. Measurable objectives are key. Participative management also helps.

Review questions

1 Of the nine generic influence tactics, which do you use the most when dealing with friends, parents, your boss or your professors? Would other tactics be more effective?
2 Describe conflicts you have witnessed.
3 What is the most common cause of conflict in today's workplaces?
4 What is your own best response to conflict-handling?
5 Will empowerment turn out to be just another management fad? Explain the rationale behind your answer.
6 What are the main advantages and drawbacks of the trend towards increased delegation?
7 Why do you think organisational politics is triggered primarily by uncertainty?
8 How much impression management do you see in your classroom and/or workplace today? Citing specific examples, are those tactics effective?

Personal awareness and growth exercise

What is your primary conflict-handling style?

Objectives

1 To continue building your self-awareness.
2 To assess your approach to conflict.
3 To provide a springboard for handling conflicts more effectively.

Introduction

Professor Afzalur Rahim, developer of the five-style conflict model, created an assessment instruction on which the one in this exercise is based. The original instrument was validated through a factor analysis of responses from 1219 managers from across the USA.[116]

Instructions

For each of the 15 items, indicate how often you rely on that tactic by circling the appropriate number. After you have responded to all 15 items, complete the scoring key below.

Conflict-handling tactics	**Rarely**				**Always**
1 I argue my case with my colleagues to show the merits of my position.	1	2	3	4	5
2 I negotiate with my colleagues, so that a compromise can be reached.	1	2	3	4	5
3 I try to satisfy the expectations of my colleagues.	1	2	3	4	5
4 I try to investigate an issue with my colleagues to find a solution acceptable to us.	1	2	3	4	5
5 I am firm in pursuing my side of the issue.	1	2	3	4	5
6 I attempt to avoid being 'put on the spot' and try to keep my conflict with my colleagues to myself.	1	2	3	4	5

Conflict-handling tactics	Rarely				Always
7 I hold on to my solution to a problem.	1	2	3	4	5
8 I use 'give and take', so that a compromise can be made.	1	2	3	4	5
9 I exchange accurate information with my colleagues to solve a problem together.	1	2	3	4	5
10 I avoid open discussion of my differences with my colleagues.	1	2	3	4	5
11 I accommodate the wishes of my colleagues.	1	2	3	4	5
12 I try to bring all our concerns out in the open, so that the issues can be resolved in the best possible way.	1	2	3	4	5
13 I propose a middle ground for breaking deadlocks.	1	2	3	4	5
14 I go along with the suggestions of my colleagues.	1	2	3	4	5
15 I try to keep my disagreements with my colleagues to myself in order to avoid hard feelings.	1	2	3	4	5

Integrating	Obliging	Dominating	Avoiding	Compromising
Item score	Item score	Item score	Item score	Item score
4 ________	3 ________	1 ________	6 ________	2 ________
9 ________	11 ________	5 ________	10 ________	8 ________
12 ________	14 ________	7 ________	15 ________	13 ________
Total = ________	Total = ________	Total = ________	Total = ________	Total = ________

Your primary conflict-handling style is:
(The category with the highest total.)
Your back-up conflict-handling style is:
(The category with the second highest total.)

Group exercise

Bangkok blowup (a role-playing exercise)

Objectives

1 To further your knowledge of interpersonal conflict and conflict-handling styles.

2 To give you a first-hand opportunity to try the various styles of handling conflict.

Introduction

This is a role-playing exercise intended to develop your ability to handle conflict. There is no single best way to resolve the conflict in this exercise. One style might work for one person, while another gets the job done for someone else.

Instructions

Read the following short case 'Can Larry fit in?' Pair up with someone else and decide which of you will play the role of Larry and which will play the role of Melissa, the office manager. Pick up the action from where the case leaves off. Try to be realistic and true to the characters in the case. The manager is primarily responsible for resolving this conflict situation. Whoever plays Larry should resist any unreasonable requests or demands and co-operate with any personally workable solution. *Note:* To conserve time, try to resolve this situation in less than 15 minutes.

Case: 'Can Larry fit in?'[117]

Melissa, office manager

You are the manager of an auditing team sent to Bangkok, Thailand, to represent a major international accounting firm headquartered in New York. You and Larry, one of your auditors, were sent to Bangkok to set up an auditing operation. Larry is about seven years older than you and has had five more years with the firm. Your relationship has become very strained since you were recently appointed as the office manager. You feel you were given the promotion because you have established an excellent working relationship with the Thai staff as well as a broad range of international clients. In contrast, Larry has told other members of the staff that your promotion simply reflects the firm's heavy emphasis on affirmative action. He has tried to isolate you from the all-male accounting staff by focusing discussions on sports, local night spots and so on.

You are sitting in your office reading some complicated new reporting procedures that have just arrived from the home office. Your concentration is suddenly interrupted by a loud knock on your door. Without waiting for an invitation to enter, Larry bursts into your office. He is obviously very upset, and it is not difficult for you to surmise why he is in such a nasty mood.

You have recently posted the audit assignments for the coming month, and you scheduled Larry for a job you knew he would not like. Larry is one of your senior auditors, and the company norm is that they get the choice assignments. This particular job will require him to spend two weeks away from Bangkok in a remote town, working with a company whose records are notoriously messy.

Unfortunately, you have had to assign several of these less desirable audits to Larry recently because you are short of personnel. But that is not the only reason. You have received several complaints from the junior staff (all Thais) recently that Larry treats them in a condescending manner. They feel he is always looking for an opportunity to boss them around, as if he were their supervisor instead of an experienced, supportive mentor. As a result, your whole operation works more smoothly when you can send Larry out of town on a solo project for several days. It keeps him from coming into your office and telling you how to do your job, and the morale of the rest of the auditing staff is significantly higher.

Larry slams the door and proceeds to express his anger over this assignment.

Larry, senior auditor

You are really annoyed! Melissa is deliberately trying to undermine your status in the office. She knows that the company norm is that senior auditors get the better jobs. You have paid your dues and now expect to be treated with respect. And this is not the first time this has happened. Since she was made the office manager, she has tried to keep you out of the office as much as possible. It is as if she does not want her rival for leadership around the office. When you were asked to go to Bangkok, you assumed that you would be made the office manager because of your seniority in the firm. You are certain that the decision to pick Melissa is yet another indication of reverse discrimination against white males.

In staff meetings, Melissa has talked about the need to be sensitive to the feelings of the office staff as well as the clients in this multicultural setting. 'Who is she to preach about sensitivity! What about my feelings, for heaven's sake?' you wonder. This is nothing more than a straightforward power play. She is probably feeling insecure about being the only female accountant in the office and being promoted over someone with more experience. 'Sending me out of town', you decide, 'is a clear case of "out of sight, out of mind".' Well, it is not going to happen that easily. You are not going to let her treat you unfairly. It is time for a showdown. If she does not agree to change this assignment and apologise for the way she has been treating you, you are going to register a formal complaint with her boss in the New York office. You are prepared to submit your resignation if the situation does not improve.

Questions for discussion

1 What antecedents of conflict appear to be present in this situation? What can be done about them?

2 Having heard how others handled this conflict, did one particular style seem to work better than the others?

Online Learning Centre

When you have read this chapter, log on to the Online Learning Centre website at ***www.mcgraw-hill.co.uk/textbooks/sinding*** to access test questions, additional exercises and other related resources.

Notes

[1] See D. Kipnis, S. M. Schmidt and I. Wilkinson, 'Intraorganizational Influence Tactics: Explorations in Getting One's Way', *Journal of Applied Psychology*, August 1980, pp. 440–52; C. A. Schriesheim and T. R. Hinkin, 'Influence Tactics Used by Subordinates: A Theoretical and Empirical Analysis and Refinement of the Kipnis, Schmidt and Wilkinson Subscales', *Journal of Applied Psychology*, June 1990, pp. 246–57; and G. Yukl and C. M. Falbe, 'Influence Tactics and Objectives in Upward, Downward and Lateral Influence Attempts', *Journal of Applied Psychology*, April 1990, pp. 132–40.

[2] Based on Table 1 in G. Yukl, C. M. Falbe and J. Y. Youn, 'Patterns of Influence Behavior for Managers', *Group & Organization Management*, March 1993, pp. 5–28.

[3] For related reading, see M. Lippitt, 'How to Influence Leaders', *Training & Development*, March 1999, pp. 18–22; and L. Schlesinger, 'I've Got Three Words for You: Suck It Up', *Fast Company*, April 1999, p. 104.

[4] Based on discussion in G. Yukl, H. Kim and C. M. Falbe, 'Antecedents of Influence Outcomes', *Journal of Applied Psychology*, June 1996, pp. 309–17.

[5] Data from G. Yukl, H. Kim and C. M. Falbe, 'Antecedents of Influence Outcomes', *Journal of Applied Psychology*, June 1996, pp. 309–17.

[6] Data from G. Yukl and J. B. Tracey, 'Consequences of Influence Tactics Used with Subordinates, Peers, and the Boss', *Journal of Applied Psychology*, August 1992, pp. 525–35. Also see C. M. Falbe and G. Yukl, 'Consequences for Managers of Using Single Influence Tactics and Combinations of Tactics', *Academy of Management Journal*, August 1992, pp. 638–52; C. A. Higgins, T. A. Judge, and G. R. Ferris, 'Influence Tactics and Work Outcomes: A Meta-Analysis', *Journal of Organizational Behavior*, February 2003, pp. 89–106; and D. M. Cable and T. A. Judge, 'Managers' Upward Influence Tactic Strategies: The Role of Manager Personality and Supervisor Leadership Style', *Journal of Organizational Behavior*, March 2003, pp. 197–214.

[7] Data from R. A. Gordon, 'Impact of Ingratiation on Judgments and Evaluations: A Meta-Analytic Investigation', *Journal of Personality and Social Psychology*, July 1996, pp. 54–70. Also see S. J. Wayne, R. C. Liden and R. T. Sparrowe, 'Developing Leader-Member Exchanges', *American Behavioral Scientist*, March 1994, pp. 697–714; A. Oldenburg, 'These Days, Hostile Is Fitting for Takeovers Only', *USA Today*, 22 July 1996, pp. 8B, 10B; and J. H. Dulebohn and G. R. Ferris, 'The Role of Influence Tactics in Perceptions of Performance Evaluations' Fairness', *Academy of Management Journal*, June 1999, pp. 288–303.

[8] Data from G. Yukl, H. Kim and C. M. Falbe, 'Antecedents of Influence Outcomes', *Journal of Applied Psychology*, June 1996, pp. 309–17.

[9] Data from B. J. Tepper, R. J. Eisenbach, S. L. Kirby and P. W. Potter, 'Test of a Justice-Based Model of Subordinates' Resistance to Downward Influence Attempts', *Group & Organization Management*, June 1998, pp. 144–60. Also see A. Somech and A. Drach-Zahavy, 'Relative Power and Influence Strategy: The Effects of Agent/Target Organizational Power on Superiors' Choices of Influence Strategies', *Journal of Organizational Behavior*, March 2002, pp. 167–79.

[10] J. E. Driskell, B. Olmstead and E. Salas, 'Task Cues, Dominance Cues, and Influence in Task Groups', *Journal of Applied Psychology*, February 1993, p. 51. No gender bias was found in H. Aguinis and S. K. R. Adams, 'Social-Role versus Structural

Models of Gender and Influence Use in Organizations: A Strong Inference Approach', *Group & Organization Management*, December 1998, pp. 414–46.

11 Adapted from R. B. Cialdini, 'Harnessing the Science of Persuasion', *Harvard Business Review*, October 2001, pp. 72–9. Also see J. A. Conger, 'The Necessary Art of Persuasion', *Harvard Business Review*, May 1998, pp. 84–95; M. Watkins, 'Principles of Persuasion', *Negotiation Journal*, April 2001, pp. 115–37; and G. A. Williams and R. B. Miller, 'Change the Way You Persuade', *Harvard Business Review*, May 2002, pp. 64–73.

12 D. Tjosvold, *Learning to Manage Conflict: Getting People to Work Together Productively* (New York: Lexington Books, 1993), p. xi.

13 J. A. Wall, Jr and R. Robert Callister, 'Conflict and Its Management', *Journal of Management*, no. 3, 1995, p. 517.

14 Ibid, p. 544.

15 See A. M. O'Leary-Kelly, R. W. Griffin and D. J. Glew, 'Organization-Motivated Aggression: A Research Framework', *Academy of Management Review*, January 1996, pp. 225–53; D. Bencivenga, 'Dealing with the Dark Side', *HR Magazine*, January 1999, pp. 50–58; K. Dobbs, 'The Lucrative Menace of Workplace Violence', *Training*, March 2000, pp. 54–62; S. C. Douglas and M. J. Martinko, 'Exploring the Role of Individual Differences in the Prediction of Workplace Aggression', *Journal of Applied Psychology*, August 2001, pp. 547–59; and K. Tyler, 'Afraid to Fly, and It Shows', *HR Magazine*, September 2001, pp. 64–74.

16 See S. Alper, D. Tjosvold and K. S. Law, 'Interdependence and Controversy in Group Decision Making: Antecedents to Effective Self-Managing Teams', *Organizational Behavior and Human Decision Processes*, April 1998, pp. 33–52.

17 Co-operative conflict is discussed in D. Tjosvold, *Learning to Manage Conflict: Getting People to Work Together Productively* (New York: Lexington Books, 1993). Also see A. C. Amason, 'Distinguishing the Effects of Functional and Dysfunctional Conflict on Strategic Decision Making: Resolving a Paradox for Top Management Teams', *Academy of Management Journal*, February 1996, pp. 123–48.

18 Adapted in part from discussion in A. C. Filley, *Interpersonal Conflict Resolution* (Glenview, IL: Scott, Foresman, 1975), pp. 9–12; and B. Fortado, 'The Accumulation of Grievance Conflict', *Journal of Management Inquiry*, December 1992, pp. 288–303. Also see D. Tjosvold and M. Poon, 'Dealing with Scarce Resources: Open-Minded Interaction for Resolving Budget Conflicts', *Group & Organization Management*, September 1998, pp. 237–55.

19 Adapted from discussion in D. Tjosvold, *Learning to Manage Conflict: Getting People to Work Together Productively* (New York: Lexington Books, 1993), pp. 12–13.

20 Based on discussion in G. Labianca, D. J. Brass and B. Gray, 'Social Networks and Perceptions of Intergroup Conflict: The Role of Negative Relationships and Third Parties', *Academy of Management Journal*, February 1998, pp. 55–67. Also see C. Gomez, B. L. Kirkman and D. L. Shapiro, 'The Impact of Collectivism and In-Group/Out-Group Membership on the Evaluation Generosity of Team Members', *Academy of Management Journal*, December 2000, pp. 1097–106; J. M. Twenge, R. F. Baumeister, D. M. Tice and T. S. Stucke, 'If You Can't Join Them, Beat Them: Effects of Social Exclusion of Aggressive Behavior', *Journal of Personality and Social Psychology*, December 2001, pp. 1058–69; T. Kessler and A. Mummendey, 'Is There Any Scapegoat Around? Determinants of Intergroup Conflicts at Different Categorization Levels', *Journal of Personality and Social Psychology*, December 2001, pp. 1090–102; and T. Kessler and A. Mummendey, 'Sequential or Parallel? A Longitudinal Field Study Concerning Determinants of Identity-Management Strategies', *Journal of Personality and Social Psychology*, January 2002, pp. 75–88.

21 G. Labianca, D. J. Brass and B. Gray, 'Social Networks and Perceptions of Intergroup Conflict: The Role of Negative Relationships and Third Parties', *Academy of Management Journal*, February 1998, p. 63.

22 For example, see S. C. Wright, A. Aron, T. McLaughlin-Volpe and S. A. Ropp, 'The Extended Contact Effect: Knowledge of Cross-Group Friendships and Prejudice', *Journal of Personality and Social Psychology*, July 1997, pp. 73–90.

23 See C. D. Batson, M. P. Polycarpou, E. Harmon-Jones, H. J. Imhoff, E. C. Mitchener, L. L. Bednar, T. R. Klein and L. Highberger, 'Empathy and Attitudes: Can Feeling for a Member of a Stigmatized Group Improve Feelings Toward the Group?', *Journal of Personality and Social Psychology*, January 1997, pp. 105–18. Evidence that it pays to ignore interpersonal conflicts in teams is reported in C. K. W. De Dreu and A. E. M. Vianen, 'Managing Relationship Conflict and the Effectiveness of Organizational Teams', *Journal of Organizational Behavior*, May 2001, pp. 309–28.

24 See R. E. Jones and B. H. Melcher, 'Personality and the Preference for Modes of Conflict Resolution', *Human Relations*, August 1982, pp. 649–58.

25 See R. A. Baron, 'Reducing Organizational Conflict: An Incompatible Response Approach', *Journal of Applied Psychology*, May 1984, pp. 272–9.

26 See G. A. Youngs, Jr, 'Patterns of Threat and Punishment Reciprocity in a Conflict Setting', *Journal of Personality and Social Psychology*, September 1986, pp. 541–6.

27 For more details, see V. D. Wall, Jr and L. L. Nolan, 'Small Group Conflict: A Look at Equity, Satisfaction and Styles of Conflict Management', *Small Group Behavior*, May 1987, pp. 188–211. Also see S. M. Farmer and J. Roth, 'Conflict-Handling Behavior in Work Groups: Effects of Group Structure, Decision Processes, and Time', *Small Group Research*, December 1998, pp. 669–713.

28 See M. E. Schnake and D. S. Cochran, 'Effect of Two Goal-Setting Dimensions on Perceived Intraorganizational Conflict', *Group & Organization Studies*, June 1985, pp. 168–83. Also see O. Janssen, E. Van De Vliert, and C. Veenstra, 'How Task and Person Conflict Shape the Role of Positive Interdependence in Management Teams', *Journal of Management*, no. 2, 1999, pp. 117–42.

29 Drawn from L. H. Chusmir and J. Mills, 'Gender Differences in Conflict Resolution Styles of Managers: At Work and at Home', *Sex Roles*, February 1989, pp. 149–63.

30 See K. K. Smith, 'The Movement of Conflict in Organizations: The Joint Dynamics of Splitting and Triangulation', *Administrative Science Quarterly*, March 1989, pp. 1–20. Also see J. B. Olson-Buchanan, F. Drasgow, P. J. Moberg, A. D. Mead, P. A. Keenan and M. A. Donovan, 'Interactive Video Assessment of Conflict Resolution Skills', *Personnel Psychology*, Spring 1998, pp. 1–24; and D. E. Conlon and D. P. Sullivan, 'Examining the Actions of Organizations in Conflict: Evidence from the Delaware Court of Chancery', *Academy of Management Journal*, June 1999, pp. 319–29.

[31] Based on C. Tinsley, 'Models of Conflict Resolution in Japanese, German, and American Cultures', *Journal of Applied Psychology*, April 1998, pp. 316–23; and S. M. Adams, 'Settling Cross-Cultural Disagreements Begins with "Where" Not "How"', *Academy of Management Executive*, February 1999, pp. 109–10. Also see K. Ohbuchi, O. Fukushima and J. T. Tedeschi, 'Cultural Values in Conflict Management: Goal Orientation, Goal Attainment, and Tactical Decision', *Journal of Cross-Cultural Psychology*, January 1999, pp. 51–71; and R. Cropanzano, H. Aguinis, M. Schminke and D. L. Denham, 'Disputant Reactions to Managerial Conflict Resolution Tactics: A Comparison among Argentina, The Dominican Republic, Mexico, and the United States', *Group & Organization Management*, June 1999, pp. 124–54.

[32] R. A. Cosier and C. R. Schwenk, 'Agreement and Thinking Alike: Ingredients for Poor Decisions', *Academy of Management Executive*, February 1990, p. 71. Also see J. P. Kotter, 'Kill Complacency', *Fortune*, 5 August 1996, pp. 168–70; and S. Caudron, 'Keeping Team Conflict Alive', *Training & Development*, September 1998, pp. 48–52.

[33] For example, see 'Facilitators as Devil's Advocates', *Training*, September 1993, p. 10. Also see K. L. Woodward, 'Sainthood for a Pope?', *Newsweek*, 21 June 1999, p. 65.

[34] Good background reading on devil's advocacy can be found in C. R. Schwenk, 'Devil's Advocacy in Managerial Decision Making', *Journal of Management Studies*, April 1984, pp. 153–68.

[35] See G. Katzenstein, 'The Debate on Structured Debate: Toward a Unified Theory', *Organizational Behavior and Human Decision Processes*, June 1996, pp. 316–32.

[36] See D. M. Schweiger, W. R. Sandberg and P. L. Rechner, 'Experiential Effects of Dialectical Inquiry, Devil's Advocacy, and Consensus Approaches to Strategic Decision Making', *Academy of Management Journal*, December 1989, pp. 745–72.

[37] See J. S. Valacich and C. Schwenk, 'Devil's Advocacy and Dialectical Inquiry Effects on Face-to-Face and Computer-Mediated Group Decision Making', *Organizational Behavior and Human Decision Processes*, August 1995, pp. 158–73. Other techniques are presented in K. Cloke and J. Goldsmith, *Resolving Conflicts at Work: A Complete Guide for Everyone on the Job* (San Francisco, CA: Jossey-Bass, 2000), pp. 229–35.

[38] A recent statistical validation for this model can be found in M. A. Rahim and N. R. Magner, 'Confirmatory Factor Analysis of the Styles of Handling Interpersonal Conflict: First-Order Factor Model and Its Invariance Across Groups', *Journal of Applied Psychology*, February 1995, pp. 122–32. Also see C. K. W. De Dreu, A. Evers, B. Beersma, E. S. Kluwer and A. Nauta, 'A Theory-Based Measure of Conflict Management Strategies in the Workplace', *Journal of Organizational Behavior*, September 2001, pp. 645–68; and M. A. Rahim, *Managing Conflict in Organizations* (Westport, CT: Greenwood Publishing Group, 2001).

[39] M. A. Rahim, 'A Strategy for Managing Conflict in Complex Organizations', *Human Relations*, January 1985, p. 84.

[40] Based on a definition in M. A. Neale and M. H. Bazerman, 'Negotiating Rationally: The Power and Impact of the Negotiator's Frame', *Academy of Management Executive*, August 1992, pp. 42–51.

[41] See L. Thompson, E. Peterson and S. E. Brodt, 'Team Negotiation: An Examination of Integrative and Distributive Bargaining', *Journal of Personality and Social Psychology*, January 1996, pp. 66–78.

[42] See D. A. Whetten and K. S. Cameron, *Developing Management Skills*, 3rd edn (New York: HarperCollins, 1995), pp. 425–30. Also see C. Joinson, 'Talking Dollars: How to Negotiate Salaries with New Hires', *HR Magazine*, July 1998, pp. 73–8; 'Negotiation Is Not War', *Fortune*, 12 October 1998, pp. 160–64; A. Davis, 'For Dueling Lawyers, the Internet Is Unlikely Referee', the *Wall Street Journal*, 12 May 1999, pp. B1, B4; R. Shell, 'Negotiator, Know Thyself', *Inc.*, May 1999, pp. 106–7; and J. K. Sebenius, 'Six Habits of Merely Effective Negotiators', *Harvard Business Review*, April 2001, pp. 87–95.

[43] M. H. Bazerman and M. A. Neale, *Negotiating Rationally* (New York: The Free Press, 1992), p. 16. Also see J. F. Brett, G. B. Northcraft and R. L. Pinkley, 'Stairways to Heaven: An Interlocking Self-Regulation Model of Negotiation', *Academy of Management Review*, July 1999, pp. 435–51.

[44] Good win-win negotiation strategies can be found in R. Fisher and W. Ury, *Getting to YES: Negotiating Agreement without Giving In* (Boston, MA: Houghton Mifflin, 1981); R. R. Reck and B. G. Long, *The Win-Win Negotiator: How to Negotiate Favorable Agreements That Last* (New York: Pocket Books, 1987); and R. Fisher and D. Ertel, *Getting Ready to Negotiate: The Getting to YES Workbook* (New York: Penguin Books, 1995). Also see D. M. Kolb and J. Williams, 'Breakthrough Bargaining', *Harvard Business Review*, February 2001, pp. 88–97; and K. A. Wade-Benzoni, A. J. Hoffman, L. L. Thompson, D. A. Moore, J. J. Gillespie and M. H. Bazerman, 'Barriers to Resolution in Ideologically Based Negotiations: The Role of Values and Institutions', *Academy of Management Review*, January 2002, pp. 41–57.

[45] See L. R. Weingart, E. B. Hyder and M. J. Prietula, 'Knowledge Matters: The Effect of Tactical Descriptions on Negotiation Behavior and Outcome', *Journal of Personality and Social Psychology*, June 1996, pp. 1205–17.

[46] Data from J. L. Graham, A. T. Mintu and W. Rodgers, 'Explorations of Negotiation Behaviors in Ten Foreign Cultures Using a Model Developed in the United States', *Management Science*, January 1994, pp. 72–95.

[47] For practical advice, see K. Kelley Reardon and R. E. Spekman, 'Starting Out Right: Negotiation Lessons for Domestic and Cross-Cultural Business Alliances', *Business Horizons*, January–February 1994, pp. 71–9. For more, see C. H. Tinsley, 'How Negotiatiors Get to Yes: Predicting the Constellation of Strategies Used across Cultures to Negotiate Conflict', *Journal of Applied Psychology*, August 2001, pp. 583–93; and P. Ghauri and T. Fang, 'Negotiating with the Chinese: A Socio-Cultural Analysis', *Journal of World Business*, Fall 2001, pp. 303–25.

[48] For supporting evidence, see J. K. Butler, Jr, 'Trust Expectations, Information Sharing, Climate of Trust, and Negotiation Effectiveness and Efficiency', *Group & Organization Management*, June 1999, pp. 217–38.

[49] See H. J. Reitz, J. A. Wall, Jr and M. S. Love, 'Ethics in Negotiation: Oil and Water or Good Lubrication?', *Business Horizons*, May–June 1998, pp. 5–14; M. E. Schweitzer and J. L. Kerr, 'Bargaining under the Influence: The Role of Alcohol in Negotiations', *Academy of Management Executive*, May 2000, pp. 47–57; and A. M. Burr, 'Ethics in Negotiation: Does Getting to Yes Require Candor?', *Dispute Resolution Journal*, May–July 2001, pp. 8–15.

[50] For related research, see A. E. Tenbrunsel, 'Misrepresentation and Expectations of Misrepresentation in an Ethical Dilemma: The Role of Incentives and Temptation', *Academy of Management Journal*, June 1998, pp. 330–39.

[51] For background, see D. L. Jacobs, 'First, Fire All the Lawyers', *Inc.*, January 1999, pp. 84–5; and P. S. Nugent, 'Managing Conflict: Third-Party Interventions for Managers', *Academy of Management Executive*, February 2002, pp. 139–54.

[52] B. Morrow and L. M. Bernardi, 'Resolving Workplace Disputes', *Canadian Manager*, Spring 1999, p. 17.

[53] Adapted from discussion in K. O. Wilburn, 'Employment Disputes: Solving Them Out of Court', *Management Review*, March 1998, pp. 17–21; B. Morrow and L. M. Bernardi, 'Resolving Workplace Disputes', *Canadian Manager*, Spring 1999, pp. 17–19, 27. Also see W. H. Ross and D. E. Conlon, 'Hybrid Forms of Third-Party Dispute Resolution: Theoretical Implications of Combining Mediation and Arbitration', *Academy of Management Review*, April 2000, pp. 416–27.

[54] K. O. Wilburn, 'Employment Disputes: Solving Them Out of Court', *Management Review*, March 1998, p. 19. Also see B. P. Sunoo, 'Hot Disputes Cool Down in Online Mediation', *Workforce*, January 2001, pp. 48–52.

[55] For background on this contentious issue, see T. J. Heinsz, 'The Revised Uniform Arbitration Act: An Overview', *Dispute Resolution Journal*, May–July 2001, pp. 28–39; C. Hirschman, 'Order in the Hearing!', *HR Magazine*, July 2001, pp. 58–64; and J. D. Wetchler, 'Agreements to Arbitrate', *HR Magazine*, August 2001, pp. 127–34.

[56] D. Tjosvold, 'The Dynamics of Positive Power', *Training and Development Journal*, June 1984, p. 72. Also see T. A. Stewart, 'Get with the New Power Game', *Fortune*, 13 January 1997, pp. 58–62; and 'The Exercise of Power', *Harvard Business Review*, May 2002, p. 136.

[57] M. W. McCall, Jr, *Power, Influence, and Authority: The Hazards Carrying a Sword*, Technical Report No. 10 (Greensboro, NC: Center for Creative Leadership, 1978), p. 5. For an excellent update on power, see E. P. Hollander and L. R. Offermann, 'Power and Leadership in Organizations', *American Psychologist*, February 1990, pp. 179–89. Also see R. Greene, *The 48 Laws of Power* (New York: Viking, 1998); and N. B. Kurland and L. H. Pelled, 'Passing the Word: Toward a Model of Gossip and Power in the Workplace', *Academy of Management Review*, April 2002, pp. 428–38.

[58] D. C. McClelland, 'The Two Faces of Power', *Journal of International Affairs*, vol. 24, no. 1, p. 29.

[59] See B. Lloyd, 'The Paradox of Power', *The Futurist*, May–June 1996, p. 60; and R. Lubit, 'The Long-Term Organizational Impact of Destructively Narcissistic Managers', *Academy of Management Executive*, April 2001, pp. 127–38.

[60] See J. R. P. French and B. Raven, 'The Bases of Social Power', in *Studies in Social Power*, ed. D. Cartwright (Ann Arbor, MI: University of Michigan Press, 1959), pp. 150–67. Also see P. Podsakoff and C. Schreisheim, 'Field Studies of French and Raven's Bases of Power: Critique, Analysis, and Suggestions for Future Research', *Psychological Bulletin*, May 1985, pp. 387–411; B. H. Raven, 'A Power/Interaction Model of Interpersonal Influence: French and Raven Thirty Years Later', *Journal of Social Behavior and Personality*, no. 2, 1992, pp. 217–44; B. J. Raven, 'The Bases of Power: Origins and Recent Developments', *Journal of Social Issues*, no. 4, 1993, pp. 227–51; P. P. Carson and K. D. Carson, 'Social Power Bases: A Meta-Analytic Examination of Interrelationships and Outcomes', *Journal of Applied Social Psychology*, July 1993, pp. 1150–69; J. M. Whitmeyer, 'Interest-Network Structures in Exchange Networks', *Sociological Perspectives*, Spring 1999, pp. 23–47; and C. M. Fiol, E. J. O'Connor and H. Anguinis, 'All for One and One for All? The Development and Transfer of Power across Organizational Levels', *Academy of Management Review*, April 2001, pp. 224–42.

[61] Data from J. R. Larson, Jr, C. Christensen, A. S. Abbott and T. M. Franz, 'Diagnosing Groups: Charting the Flow of Information in Medical Decision-Making Teams', *Journal of Personality and Social Psychology*, August 1996, pp. 315–30.

[62] See D. A. Morand, 'Forms of Address and Status Leveling in Organizations', *Business Horizons*, November–December 1995, pp. 34–9; and H. Lancaster, 'A Father's Character, Not His Success, Shapes Kids' Careers', *The Wall Street Journal*, 27 February 1996, p. B1.

[63] Details may be found in L. H. Chusmir, 'Personalized versus Socialized Power Needs among Working Women and Men', *Human Relations*, February 1986, pp. 149–59. For a review of research on individual differences in the need for power, see R. J. House, 'Power and Personality in Complex Organizations', in *Research in Organizational Behavior*, eds B. M. Staw and L. L. Cummings (Greenwich, CT: JAI Press, 1988), pp. 305–57.

[64] P. M. Podsakoff and C. A. Schriesheim, 'Field Studies of French and Raven's Bases of Power: Critique, Reanalysis, and Suggestions for Future Research', *Psychological Bulletin*, May 1985, p. 388. Also see D. Tjosvold, 'Power and Social Context in Superior-Subordinate Interaction', *Organizational Behavior and Human Decision Processes*, June 1985, pp. 281–93; M. A. Rahim and G. F. Buntzman, 'Supervisory Power Bases, Styles of Handling Conflict with Subordinates, and Subordinate Compliance and Satisfaction', *Journal of Psychology*, March 1989, pp. 195–210; and C. A. Schriesheim, T. R. Hinkin and P. M. Podsakoff, 'Can Ipsative and Single-Item Measures Produce Erroneous Results in Field Studies of French and Raven's (1950) Five Bases of Power? An Empirical Investigation', *Journal of Applied Psychology*, February 1991, pp. 106–14.

[65] See T. R. Hinkin and C. A. Schriesheim, 'Relationships between Subordinate Perceptions and Supervisor Influence Tactics and Attributed Bases of Supervisory Power', *Human Relations*, March 1990, pp. 221–37. Also see D. J. Brass and M. E. Burkhardt, 'Potential Power and Power Use: An Investigation of Structure and Behavior', *Academy of Management Journal*, June 1993, pp. 441–70; and K. W. Mossholder, N. Bennett, E. R. Kemery and M. A. Wesolowski, 'Relationships between Bases of Power and Work Reactions: The Mediational Role of Procedural Justice', *Journal of Management*, no. 4, 1998, pp. 533–52.

[66] See H. E. Baker III, '"Wax On – Wax Off": French and Raven at the Movies', *Journal of Management Education*, November 1993, pp. 517–19.

[67] C. Hirst, 'Boardroom Battles Slow E-Business Advance', *The Independent*, 3 December 2000.

[68] Adapted from S. Caulkin, 'Political? Be Proud of It', *The Observer*, 3 September 2000; and D. Dearlove, 'Power Games Play Off', *The Times*, 11 November 1999.

[69] R. W. Allen, D. L. Madison, L. W. Porter, P. A. Renwick and B. T. Mayes, 'Organizational Politics: Tactics and Characteristics of Its Actors', *California Management Review*, Fall 1979, p. 77. A comprehensive update can be found in K. M. Kacmar and R. A. Baron, 'Organizational Politics: The State of the Field, Links to Related Processes, and an Agenda for Future Research', in *Research in Personnel and Human Resources Management, vol. 17*, ed. G. R. Ferris (Stamford, CT: JAI Press, 1999), pp. 1–39. Also see K. M. Kacmar and G. R. Ferris, 'Politics at Work: Sharpening the Focus of Political Behavior in Organizations',

Business Horizons, July–August 1993, pp. 70–74; and M. C. Andrews and K. M. Kacmar, 'Discriminating among Organizational Politics, Justice, and Support', *Journal of Organizational Behavior*, June 2001, pp. 347–66.

70 See P. M. Fandt and G. R. Ferris, 'The Management of Information and Impressions: When Employees Behave Opportunistically', *Organizational Behavior and Human Decision Processes*, February 1990, pp. 140–58.

71 D. R. Beeman and T. W. Sharkey, 'The Use and Abuse of Corporate Politics', *Business Horizons*, March–April 1987, pp. 26–30.

72 A. Raia, 'Power, Politics, and the Human Resource Professional', *Human Resource Planning*, no. 4, 1985, p. 203.

73 A. J. DuBrin, 'Career Maturity, Organizational Rank, and Political Behavioral Tendencies: A Correlational Analysis of Organizational Politics and Career Experience', *Psychological Reports*, October 1988, p. 535.

74 This three-level distinction comes from A. T. Cobb, 'Political Diagnosis: Applications in Organizational Development', *Academy of Management Review*, July 1986, pp. 482–96.

75 An excellent historical and theoretical perspective of coalitions can be found in W. B. Stevenson, J. L. Pearce and L. W. Porter, 'The Concept of "Coalition" in Organization Theory and Research', *Academy of Management Review*, April 1985, pp. 256–68.

76 See K. G. Provan and J. G. Sebastian, 'Networks within Networks: Service Link Overlap, Organizational Cliques, and Network Effectiveness', *Academy of Management Journal*, August 1998, pp. 453–63.

77 R. W. Allen, D. L. Madison, L. W. Porter, P. A. Renwick and B. T. Mayes, 'Organizational Politics: Tactics and Characteristics of Its Actors', *California Management Review*, Fall 1979, p. 77.

78 See W. L. Gardner III, 'Lessons in Organizational Dramaturgy: The Art of Impression Management', *Organizational Dynamics*, Summer 1992, pp. 33–46.

79 For more on political behaviour, see A. Nierenberg, 'Masterful Networking', *Training & Development*, February 1999, pp. 51–3; J. Barbian, 'It's Who You Know', *Training*, December 2001, p. 22; and S. Bing, 'Throwing the Elephant: Zen and the Art of Managing Up', *Fortune*, 18 March 2002, pp. 115–16.

80 A. Rao, S. M. Schmidt and L. H. Murray, 'Upward Impression Management: Goals, Influence Strategies, and Consequences', *Human Relations*, February 1995, p. 147.

81 See P. M. Fandt and G. R. Ferris, 'The Management of Information and Impressions: When Employees Behave Opportunistically', *Organizational Behavior and Human Decision Processes*, February 1990, pp. 140–58; W. L. Gardner and B. J. Avolio, 'The Charismatic Relationship: A Dramaturgical Perspective', *Academy of Management Review*, January 1998, pp. 32–58; L. Wah, 'Managing – Manipulating? – Your Reputation', *Management Review*, October 1998, pp. 46–50; M. C. Bolino, 'Citizenship and Impression Management: Good Soldiers or Good Actors?', *Academy of Management Review*, January 1999, pp. 82–98; and W. H. Turnley and M. C. Bolino, 'Achieving Desired Images While Avoiding Undesired Images: Exploring the Role of Self-Monitoring in Impression Management', *Journal of Applied Psychology*, April 2001, pp. 351–60.

82 For related research, see M. G. Pratt and A. Rafaeli, 'Organizational Dress as a Symbol of Multilayered Social Identities', *Academy of Management Journal*, August 1997, pp. 862–98.

83 A. Arkin, 'Tailoring Clothes to Suit the Image', *People Management*, 24 August 1995.

84 See S. J. Wayne and G. R. Ferris, 'Influence Tactics, Affect, and Exchange Quality in Supervisor-Subordinate Interactions: A Laboratory Experiment and Field Study', *Journal of Applied Psychology*, October 1990, pp. 487–99. For another version, see Table 1 (p. 246) in S. J. Wayne and R. C. Liden, 'Effects of Impression Management on Performance Ratings: A Longitudinal Study', *Academy of Management Journal*, February 1995, pp. 232–60.

85 See R. Vonk, 'The Slime Effect: Suspicion and Dislike of Likeable Behavior toward Superiors', *Journal of Personality and Social Psychology*, April 1998, pp. 849–64; and M. Wells, 'How to Schmooze Like the Best of Them', *USA Today*, 18 May 1999, p. 14E.

86 See P. Rosenfeld, R. A. Giacalone and C. A. Riordan, 'Impression Management Theory and Diversity: Lessons for Organizational Behavior', *American Behavioral Scientist*, March 1994, pp. 601–04; R. A. Giacalone and J. W. Beard, 'Impression Management, Diversity, and International Management', *American Behavioral Scientist*, March 1994, pp. 621–36; and A. Montagliani and R. A. Giacalone, 'Impression Management and Cross-Cultural Adaptation', *The Journal of Social Psychology*, October 1998, pp. 598–608.

87 M. E. Mendenhall and C. Wiley, 'Strangers in a Strange Land: The Relationship between Expatriate Adjustment and Impression Management', *American Behavioral Scientist*, March 1994, pp. 605–20.

88 T. E. Becker and S. L. Martin, 'Trying to Look Bad at Work: Methods and Motives for Managing Poor Impressions in Organizations', *Academy of Management Journal*, February 1995, p. 191.

89 T. E. Becker and S. L. Martin, 'Trying to Look Bad at Work: Methods and Motives for Managing Poor Impressions in Organizations', *Academy of Management Journal*, February 1995, p. 181. Also see M. K. Duffy, D. C. Ganster and M. Pagon, 'Social Undermining in the Workplace', *Academy of Management Journal*, April 2002, pp. 331–51.

90 Adapted from T. E. Becker and S. L. Martin, 'Trying to Look Bad at Work: Methods and Motives for Managing Poor Impressions in Organizations', *Academy of Management Journal*, February 1995, pp. 180–81.

91 Based on discussion in T. E. Becker and S. L. Martin, 'Trying to Look Bad at Work: Methods and Motives for Managing Poor Impressions in Organizations', *Academy of Management Journal*, February 1995, pp. 192–3.

92 Data from G. R. Ferris, D. D. Frink, D. P. S. Bhawuk, J. Zhou and D. C. Gilmore, 'Reactions of Diverse Groups to Politics in the Workplace', *Journal of Management*, no. 1, 1996, pp. 23–44. For other findings from the same database, see G. R. Ferris, D. D. Frink, M. C. Galang, J. Zhou, K. M. Kacmar and J. L. Howard, 'Perceptions of Organizational Politics: Prediction, Stress-Related Implications, and Outcomes', *Human Relations*, February 1996, pp. 233–66.

93 A. Drory and D. Beaty, 'Gender Differences in the Perception of Organizational Influence Tactics', *Journal of Organizational Behavior*, May 1991, pp. 256–7. Also see L. A. Rudman, 'Self-Promotion as a Risk Factor for Women: The Costs and Benefits of Counter-stereotypical Impression Management', *Journal of Personality and Social Psychology*, March 1998, pp. 629–45; and J. Tata, 'The Influence of Gender on the Use and Effectiveness of Managerial Accounts', *Group & Organization Management*, September 1998, pp. 267–88.

[94] See S. J. Wayne and R. C. Liden, 'Effects of Impression Management on Performance Ratings: A Longitudinal Study', *Academy of Management Journal*, February 1995, pp. 232–60. Also see M. L. Randall, R. Cropanzano, C. A. Bormann and A. Birjulin, 'Organizational Politics and Organizational Support as Predictors of Work Attitudes, Job Performance, and Organizational Citizenship Behavior', *Journal of Organizational Behavior*, March 1999, pp. 159–74.

[95] A. Rao, S. M. Schmidt and L. H. Murray, 'Upward Impression Management: Goals, Influence Strategies, and Consequences', *Human Relations*, February 1995, p. 165.

[96] Also see A. Tziner, G. P. Latham, B. S. Price and R. Haccoun, 'Development and Validation of a Questionnaire for Measuring Perceived Political Considerations in Performance Appraisal', *Journal of Organizational Behavior*, March 1996, pp. 179–90.

[97] A. Zaleznik, 'Real Work', *Harvard Business Review*, January–February 1989, p. 60.

[98] L. B. MacGregor Server, *The End of Office Politics as Usual* (New York: American Management Association, 2002), pp. 184–99.

[99] Based on P. A. Wilson, 'The Effects of Politics and Power on the Organizational Commitment of Federal Executives', *Journal of Management*, Spring 1995, pp. 101–18. For related research, see J. B. Arthur, 'Effects of Human Resource Systems on Manufacturing Performance and Turnover', *Academy of Management Journal*, June 1994, pp. 670–87.

[100] For related research, see L. G. Pelletier and R. J. Vallerand, 'Supervisors' Beliefs and Subordinates' Intrinsic Motivation: A Behavioral Confirmation Analysis', *Journal of Personality and Social Psychology*, August 1996, pp. 331–40.

[101] D. J. Leach, T. D. Wall and P. R. Jackson, 'The Effect Of Empowerment On Job Knowledge: An Empirical Test Involving Operators Of Complex Technology', *Journal Of Occupational And Organizational Psychology*, vol. 76, 2003, p. 27. Also see R. C. Liden and S. Arad, 'A Power Perspective of Empowerment and Work Groups: Implications for Human Resources Management Research', in *Research in Personnel and Human Resources Management*, vol. 14, ed. G. R. Ferris (Greenwich, CT: JAI Press, 1996), pp. 205–51.

[102] For related discussion, see M. M. Broadwell, 'Why Command & Control Won't Go Away', *Training*, September 1995, pp. 62–8; R. E. Quinn and G. M. Spreitzer, 'The Road to Empowerment: Seven Questions Every Leader Should Consider', *Organizational Dynamics*, Autumn 1997, pp. 37–49; and I. Cunningham and L. Honold, 'Everyone Can Be a Coach', *HR Magazine*, June 1998, pp. 63–6.

[103] R. C. Ford and M. D. Fottler, 'Empowerment: A Matter of Degree', *Academy of Management Executive*, August 1995, pp. 21–31.

[104] See J. A. Belasco and R. C. Stayer, 'Why Empowerment Doesn't Empower: The Bankruptcy of Current Para digms', *Business Horizons*, March–April 1994, pp. 29–41; and W. A. Randolph, 'Re-Thinking Empowerment: Why Is It So Hard to Achieve?', *Organizational Dynamics*, Fall 2000, pp. 94–107.

[105] For complete details, see C. R. Leana, 'Power Relinquishment versus Power Sharing: Theoretical Clarification and Empirical Comparison of Delegation and Participation', *Journal of Applied Psychology*, May 1987, pp. 228–33.

[106] M. D. Fulford and C. A. Enz, 'The Impact of Empowerment on Service Employees', *Journal of Managerial Issues*, Summer 1995, p. 172.

[107] M. Jansen, 'Delegation Is the Key to Effective Growth', *The Times*, 26 October 1999.

[108] Data from A. J. H. Thorlakson and R. P. Murray, 'An Empirical Study of Empowerment in the Workplace', *Group & Organization Management*, March 1996, pp. 67–83.

[109] Data from C. S. Koberg, R. W. Boss, J. C. Senjem and E. A. Goodman, 'Antecedents and Outcomes of Empowerment: Empirical Evidence from the Health Care Industry', *Group & Organization Management*, March 1999, pp. 71–91. Also see K. Aquino, S. L. Grover, M. Bradfield and D. G. Allen, 'The Effects of Negative Affectivity, Hierarchical Status, and Self-Determination on Workplace Victimization', *Academy of Management Journal*, June 1999, pp. 260–72; and J. P. Guthrie, 'High-Involvement Work Practices, Turnover, and Productivity: Evidence from New Zealand', *Academy of Management Journal*, February 2001, pp. 180–90.

[110] W. A. Randolph, 'Navigating the Journey to Empowerment', *Organizational Dynamics*, Spring 1995, p. 31.

[111] S. Gracie, 'Delegate, Don't Abdicate', *Management Today*, March 1999. For more on delegation, see L. Bossidy, 'The Job No CEO Should Delegate', *Harvard Business Review*, March 2001, pp. 46–9; and S. Gazda, 'The Art of Delegating', *HR Magazine*, January 2002, pp. 75–8.

[112] R. Kreitner, *Management*, 8th edn (Boston, MA: Houghton Mifflin, 2001), p. 315. Also see K. Dover, 'Avoiding Empowerment Traps', *Management Review*, January 1999, pp. 51–5; and C. A. Walker, 'Saving Your Rookie Managers from Themselves', *Harvard Business Review*, April 2002, pp. 97–102.

[113] Drawn from G. Yukl and P. P. Fu, 'Determinants of Delegation and Consultation by Managers', *Journal of Organizational Behavior*, March 1999, pp. 219–32. Also see C. A. Schriesheim, L. L. Neider and T. A. Scandura, 'Delegation and Leader-Member Exchange: Main Effects, Moderators, and Measurement Issues', *Academy of Management Journal*, June 1998, pp. 298–318.

[114] See G. M. Spreitzer and A. K. Mishra, 'Giving Up without Losing Control: Trust and Its Substitutes' Effects on Managers' Involving Employees in Decision Making', *Group & Organization Management*, June 1999, pp. 155–87.

[115] M. Frese, W. Kring, A. Soose and J. Zempel, 'Personal Initiative at Work: Differences between East and West Germany', *Academy of Management Journal*, February 1996, p. 38. For comprehensive updates, see D. J. Campbell, 'The Proactive Employee: Managing Workplace Initiative', *Academy of Management Executive*, August 2000, pp. 52–66; and M. Frese and D. Fay, 'Personal Initiative: An Active Performance Concept for Work in the 21st Century', in *Research in Organizational Behavior, vol. 23*, eds B. M. Staw and R. I. Sutton (New York: JAI Press, 2001), pp. 133–87.

[116] The complete instrument may be found in M. A. Rahim, 'A Measure of Styles of Handling Interpersonal Conflict', *Academy of Management Journal*, June 1983, pp. 368–76. A validation study of Rahim's instrument may be found in E. Van De Vliert and B. Kabanoff, 'Toward Theory-Based Measures of Conflict Management', *Academy of Management Journal*, March 1990, pp. 199–209.

[117] D. A. Whetten and K. S. Cameron, *Developing Management Skills* (Glenview, IL: Scott, Foresman and Company, 1984).

Chapter 15

Leadership

Learning Outcomes

When you finish studying the material in this chapter, you should be able to:

- ✓ define the term ‘leadership’, and explain the difference between leading and managing
- ✓ review the research on trait theory and discuss the idea of one best style of leadership, using the Ohio State studies and the Leadership Grid® as points of reference
- ✓ explain, according to Fiedler’s contingency model, how leadership style interacts with situational control
- ✓ discuss Hersey and Blanchard’s situational leadership theory
- ✓ define and differentiate between transactional and charismatic leadership
- ✓ explain how charismatic leadership transforms followers and work groups
- ✓ describe the substitutes for leadership and explain how they substitute for, neutralise or enhance the effects of leadership
- ✓ describe servant-leadership and coaching

Opening Case Study: Sweaty feet – with style, no stink

It all started in 1992 with a hike in the hot Nevada desert. The 57-year-old Italian entrepreneur, Mario Moretti Polegato, was tired of having hot feet and cut holes in the soles of his trainers with a Swiss army knife, and was impressed with how much cooler the shoes felt.

Once back home in north-east Italy, where there's a long and proud tradition of shoemaking, he immediately went to work on a prototype shoe, researching how he could keep the air-conditioning holes while at the same time keeping out water. This led to his first patent, that he was certain would interest all the big footwear giants – but to his surprise they rejected the idea.

'I don't get it, because my idea was different and original. From my viewpoint, it was easy to see the problem with traditional rubber soles, and my idea seemed logical. When I explain it today, people get it instantly, but back then, nobody got it. But I guess that's just my luck', says Mr Polegato.

Rejected, he set up Geox in 1995, a company that 15 years later employed more than 30 000 employees and surpassing a number of well-established shoe companies became the second largest 'brown shoe' brand in the world, after Britain's Clarks, and now operates a retail arm that already has 940 Geox shops worldwide.

After starting the production of his own shoes under the brand name Geox, Mario Moretti Polegato was in 2009 placed as number 468 on Forbes' list of the world's most wealthy. But it does not stop there: his ambition is to be the No. 1 shoemaker in the world.

The Geox chairman gets to work sometime after 8 a.m., walking around the offices and discussing day-to-day issues with staff before having the daily meeting with top managers. In 2002, he handed over the day-to-day control and now focuses his attention on innovation and brand promotion. Therefore, Polegato is often seen in the Geox laboratories monitoring progress and researching new materials.

For discussion

Is it sustainable for a chief executive officer (CEO) of such a large company to spend so much of his time in the laboratory focusing on the technology instead of in the executive meeting rooms?

Source: Based on A. Davidson, 'No Sweat for the Shoe Maestro', *The Sunday Times*, 29 March 2009; and C. Wendt Jensen, 'Kongen af den varme luft,' *Børsen*, 12 March 2010.

Someone once observed that a leader is a person who finds out which way the parade is going, jumps in front of it, and yells 'Follow me!' The plain fact is that this approach of leadership has little chance of working in today's rapidly changing world. Admired leaders, such as Nelson Mandela, Mahatma Gandhi, Body Shop's Anita Roddick, John Kennedy, Charles de Gaulle and Virgin's Richard Branson, led people in bold new directions. They envisioned how things could be improved, rallied followers and refused to accept failure. In short, successful leaders are those individuals who can make a noticeable difference. But how much of a difference can leaders make in modern organisations?

One study, for example, tracked the relationship between net profit and leadership in 167 companies from 13 industries. It also covered a time span of 20 years. Higher net profits were earned by companies with effective leaders.[1] Successful organisational change is highly dependent upon effective leadership throughout an organisation. In a carefully controlled study of Icelandic fishing ships, it was found that differences in skippers accounted for a third to a half of the catch.[2] Leadership can make a difference.

But even the research data are not very conclusive. Peter Wright, a British OB specialist, offers the following view in his book on managerial leadership:

> Most research findings, even when significant, account for a relatively small amount of the variance in subordinates' work performance and satisfaction. Similarly, there are a great many alternative approaches to leadership theory, the different theories within any one approach often contradict each other, and none is without flaws or limitations.[3]

Leadership is culturally bound. Americans are the only people who talk so openly – sometimes obsessively – about the very notion of leadership. In the USA, leadership has become something of a cult concept. The French, tellingly, have no adequate word of their own for it. Germans have perfectly good words for leader and leadership, but historical events have rendered some of them politically incorrect. The situation is even more extreme in the Netherlands or the Scandinavian countries, where leaders do not behave like leaders at all, at least not in the way described in American textbooks (see Chapter 12 on cultural differences).

This culturally bound phenomenon is not only restricted to charismatic leaders or to top management. Figure 15.1 shows how the private management consultants, Management Research Group, have found differences between different countries, compared to the USA.

Figure 15.1 Leadership Differences Between the USA and 25 countries (Larger bars Indicate Greater Differences)

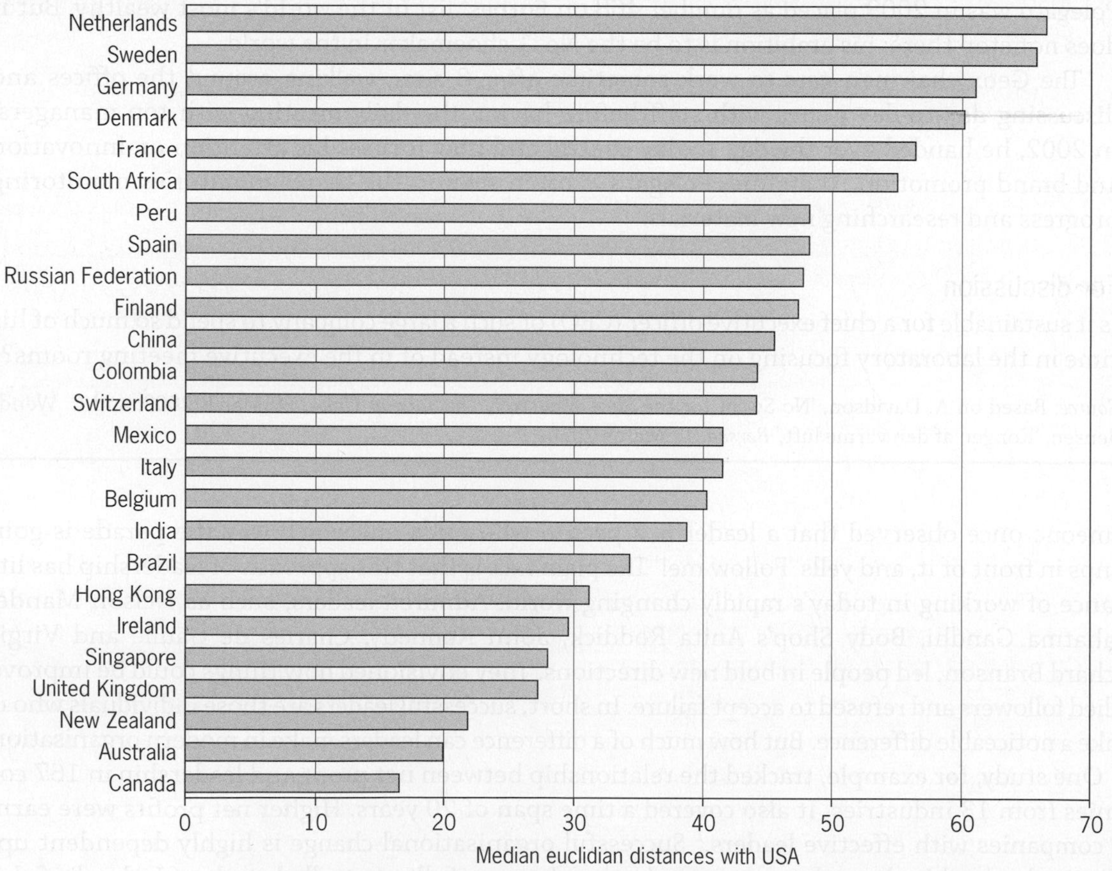

Source: Leading Across Boundaries – Country Differences in Leadership and Why It Matters, Management Research Group, 2013, http://www.mrg.com/education-resources/articles-findings/

Concepts of leadership also differ between clusters of European countries. North-western European countries, and in particular, the Nordic countries, score very highly on a dimension called 'interpersonal directness and proximity'. In these countries, successful business leaders are seen as enthusiastic, encouraging, sincere, informal, trustworthy and inspirational. In countries such as Georgia, Poland, Turkey and Slovenia, successful leaders are seen as self-interested, non-participative, asocial, very administrative, well organised, face-saving and indirect. The Germanic cluster (Germany, Austria, Switzerland) and the Czech Republic score very highly on the dimension called 'autonomy': successful leaders are seen as independent, autonomous, unique and even self-sacrificing. The Latin cluster (Portugal, Spain, Italy) is situated on the other end of this dimension: middle management in those countries see successful leaders as visionary, team integrators and status conscious.[4]

Leadership, and especially its most pronounced form, charismatic leadership, is a mixed blessing. Most American scholars tend to emphasise the beneficial aspects of leadership. Europeans are much more sceptical. It comes as no surprise that the most influential European writer on leadership, Manfred Kets de Vries, who teaches leadership at INSEAD, near Paris, has built a world reputation through his highly critical writings on the subject. He often describes leaders as neurotic and especially as narcissistic.

After formally defining the term 'leadership', this chapter focuses on the following areas: trait and behavioural approaches to leadership; alternative situational theories of leadership; charismatic leadership; and additional perspectives on leadership. Because there are so many different leadership theories within each of these areas, it is impossible to discuss them all.

15.1 What is leadership?

The topic of leadership has fascinated people for centuries, and many classic texts such as Sun Tzu's *The Art of War* (from around 500 BC) and Machiavelli's *The Prince* (1513) can be seen as textbooks on leadership in the contexts of war and statesmanship respectively. However, it was only with the Industrial Revolution that the topic of management and leadership in organisations became a topic in itself (see Chapter 1).

Disagreement about the definition of leadership stems from the fact that it involves a complex interaction between the leader, followers and situation. For example, some researchers define leadership in terms of personality and physical traits, while others believe leadership is represented by a set of prescribed behaviours. In contrast, other researchers believe that leadership is a temporary role that can be filled by anyone. There is a common thread, however, among the different definitions of leadership. The common thread is social influence.

For the purpose of this chapter, **leadership** is defined as: 'a social influence process in which the leader seeks the voluntary participation of subordinates in an effort to reach organisational goals'.[5] An even more formal definition is given by the Globe research group as: 'the ability of an individual to influence, motivate and enable others to contribute toward the effectiveness and success of organisations of which they are members'.[6]

Note that both definitions are definitions of organisational leadership, not leadership in general. As you can see from this definition, leadership clearly entails more than wielding power and exercising authority, and is exhibited on different levels. At the individual level, for example, leadership involves mentoring, coaching, inspiring and motivating. Leaders build teams, create cohesion and resolve conflicts at the group level. Finally, leaders build culture and create change at the organisational level.[7]

Figure 15.2 A Conceptual Framework for Understanding Leadership

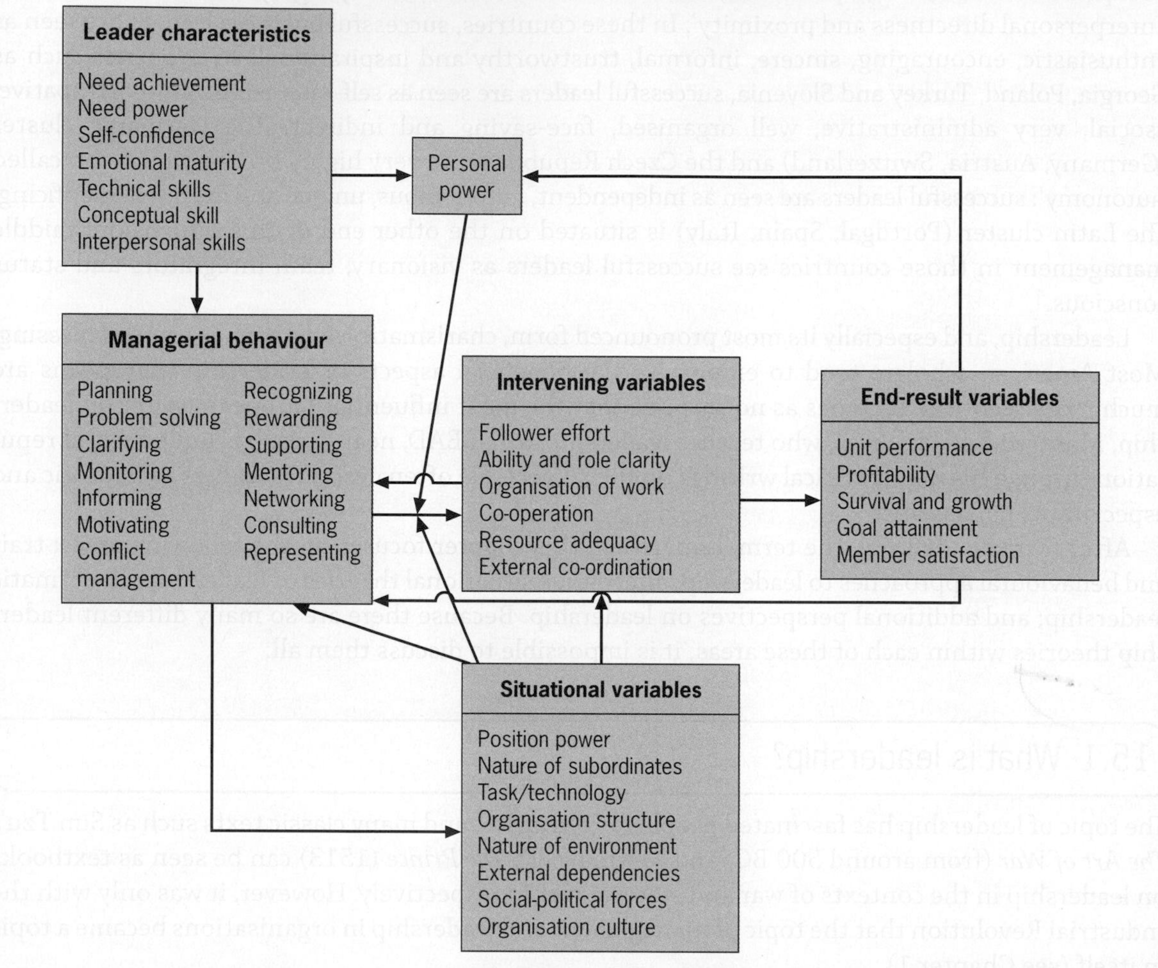

Source: G. Yukl, 'Managerial Leadership: A Review of Theory and Research', *Journal of Management*, June 1989, p. 274.

Figure 15.2 provides a conceptual framework for understanding leadership. It was created by integrating components of the different theories and models discussed in this chapter and indicates that certain leader characteristics or traits are the foundation of effective leadership. In turn, these characteristics affect an individual's ability to employ managerial behaviour and roles. Effective leadership also depends on various situational variables. These variables are important components of the contingency leadership theories discussed later in this chapter. Finally, leadership is result-oriented.

Leading versus managing

It is important to appreciate the difference between leadership and management in order to fully understand what leadership is all about. Bernard Bass, a leadership expert, concluded that: 'Leaders manage and managers lead but the two activities are not synonymous.'[8] Bass tells us that although leadership and management overlap, each entails a unique set of activities or functions. Broadly speaking, managers typically perform functions associated with planning, investigating, organising and controlling, while leaders deal with the interpersonal aspects of a manager's job. Leaders inspire others, provide emotional support and try to get employees to rally around a common goal. Management is about coping with complexity. As Harvard-specialist John Kotter has stressed over and over again: 'Leadership is about coping with change.'[9] The most often cited difference has been formulated by management and leadership gurus like Peter Drucker and Warren Bennis: 'Management is doing things right; leadership is doing the right things.'[10]

It has become a fad to exaggerate the difference between managers and leaders. More and more observers of the world of OB will use John Kotter's words: 'Most corporations today are overly managed and underled.' Table 15.1 summarises the contrast between 'weak' managers and 'real' leaders.

The distinction between management and leadership is more or less ideological. It is very often a distinction between 'bad' and 'good', where management stands for the cold, static, bureaucratic or non-inspiring and leadership for the dynamic, future-oriented or inspiring. This distinction, however, is purely artificial: there is nothing good or bad about management or leadership as such. To illustrate our point of view, take a look at Table 15.2.

Table 15.1 The Supposed Differences between 'Weak' Managers and 'Real' Leaders

Managers . . .	Leaders . . .
Wait until it happens	Are pro-active
Are happy with the status quo	Challenge the status quo
Are pursuing objectives	Have a vision
Are experts of the past	Are experts of the future
Do the things right	Do the right things
Follow their job description	Change their job description
Respect budgets	Create value
Avoid mistakes	Seek learning opportunities
See information as power	Share information
Are myopic	Take the broad view
Are difficult to reach	Are approachable
Adore status symbols	Want the best for all
Use reward and punishment	Inspire and motivate

Source: M. Buelens, 'The Informal Organization: Leading for Performance', in *Integrated Performance Management: A Guide to Strategy Implementation*, eds K. Verweire and L. A. A. Van den Berghe, (London: Sage Publications, 2004), pp. 167–79.

Table 15.2 The Difference between 'Sick' Leaders and 'Dedicated' Managers

Managers . . .	Leaders . . .
Remain humble	Are megalomaniac
Behave like a good citizen	Spend too much money on pet projects
Listen to collaborators	Listen to themselves
Keep balance	Become psychopaths
Think before they act	Have big, hairy, audacious goals
End with a golden watch	End in prison or mental hospitals
Remain in the background	Are on the front cover
Follow realistic strategies	Follow wish-driven strategies

Source: M. Buelens, 'The Informal Organization: Leading for Performance', in *Integrated Performance Management: A Guide to Strategy Implementation*, eds K. Verweire and L. A. A. Van den Berghe, (London: Sage Publications, 2004), pp. 167–79.

Critical thinking

Try and think of a number of great leaders you know of. Do they all have a negative or potentially dangerous side to them?

15.2 Trait theories of leadership

This section examines the two earliest approaches used to explain leadership. Trait theories focused on identifying the personal traits that differentiated leaders from followers. Behavioural theorists examined leadership from a different perspective. They tried to uncover the different kinds of leader behaviour that resulted in higher work group performance.

Before the Second World War, the prevailing belief was that leaders were born, not made. Selected people were thought to possess inborn traits that made them successful leaders; hence, the idea of a **leader trait**.

Before the Second World War, hundreds of studies were conducted to pinpoint the traits of successful leaders. Dozens of leadership traits were identified. During the post-war period, however, enthusiasm was replaced by widespread criticism. Studies conducted by Ralph Stogdill in 1948 and by Richard Mann in 1959, which sought to summarise the impact of traits on leadership, caused the trait approach to fall into disfavour.

Stogdill's and Mann's findings

Based on his review, Stogdill concluded that five traits tended to differentiate leaders from average followers: (1) intelligence, (2) dominance, (3) self-confidence, (4) level of energy and activity, and (5) task-relevant knowledge.[11] Jack Welch, former chief executive officer of General Electric, has been one of the most highly regarded managers in the world.

Consider the leadership traits that Welch indicated he was looking for in his replacement during an interview with *Fortune*:

> Vision. Courage. The four E's: energy, ability to energise others, the edge to make tough decisions and execution, which is key because you can't just decide but have got to follow up in 19 ways. Judgement. The self-confidence to always hire someone who's better than you. Are they growing things? Do they add new insights to the businesses they run? Do they like to nurture small businesses? And one more: an insatiable appetite for accomplishment. Too many CEOs, Welch once said, believe that the high point comes the day they land the job. Not Welch, who says, 'I'm 63 and finally getting smart.'[12]

Although Welch was looking for some of the same traits as those identified by Ralph Stogdill, research revealed that these five traits did not accurately predict which individuals became leaders in organisations.

Mann's review was similarly disappointing for the trait theorists. Among the seven categories of personality traits he examined, Mann found intelligence was the best predictor of leadership.

However, Mann warned that all observed positive relationships between traits and leadership were weak (correlations averaged about 0.15).[13]

Together, Stogdill's and Mann's findings nearly dealt a death blow to the trait approach. But now, decades later, leadership traits are once again receiving serious research attention.

Evidence about leadership trait

A 1986 meta-analysis by Robert Lord and his associates remedied a methodological shortcoming of previous trait data analyses. Based on a re-analysis of Mann's data and subsequent studies, Lord concluded that people have leadership prototypes that affect our perceptions of who is and who is not an effective leader. Your **leadership prototype** is a mental representation of the traits and behaviours that you believe are possessed by leaders. We, thus, tend to perceive that someone is a leader when he or she exhibits traits or types of behaviour that are consistent with our prototypes.[14] Lord's research demonstrated that people are perceived as being leaders when they exhibit the traits associated with intelligence, masculinity and dominance. Another study of 200 students also confirmed the idea that leadership prototypes influence leadership perceptions. People who were more behaviourally flexible were perceived to be more like a leader.[15] A study of 6052 middle-level managers from 22 European countries revealed that leadership prototypes are culturally based. In other words, leadership prototypes are influenced by national cultural values.[16]

Another pair of leadership researchers attempted to identify key leadership traits by asking the following open-ended question to more than 20 000 people around the world: 'What values (personal traits or characteristics) do you look for and admire in your superiors?' The top four traits included honesty, forward-lookingness, inspiration and competence.[17] The researchers concluded that these four traits constitute a leader's credibility. This research suggests that people want their leaders to be credible and to have a sense of direction. This conclusion is consistent with concerns regarding ethical and legal lapses at companies, such as Enron.

In 1998, Daniel Goleman wrote an influential article in *Harvard Business Review*, in which he applied principles of emotional intelligence to leadership.[18] Since then, more and more articles and books quote his (unproven) basic insights: understanding your own and other people's emotions well helps you to move people in the direction of accomplishing desired goals. In practice, this means that all leaders have to understand their emotions (self-awareness), have to control disruptive impulses and moods and understand the emotional make-up of others. In this approach, the most important traits are self-knowledge, self-control, empathy and social intelligence (see also Chapter 3).

Even tried and tested findings, specifically that extroversion (see Chapter 2) is the best predictor of leadership, has been shown to be more complex. It turns out that only if the group being led is passive, will the extrovert manager perform better – if the group is active, it performs better under an introvert manager.[19]

> **Critical thinking**
>
> Research has shown that tall people are seen as better leaders[20] (and earn more). Are individual traits just as important as ever?

Gender as a leadership trait

The increase in the number of women in the workforce has generated much interest in understanding the similarities and differences between female and male leaders. Important issues concern whether women and men assume varying leadership roles within work groups, use different leadership styles, are more or less effective in leadership roles and whether there are situational differences that produce gender differences in leadership effectiveness. Three meta-analyses were conducted to summarise research pertaining to these issues.

The first meta-analysis demonstrated that men and women differed in the type of leadership roles they assumed within work groups. Men were seen as displaying more overall leadership and task leadership. In contrast, women were perceived as displaying more social leadership.[21] Results from the second meta-analysis revealed that leadership styles varied by gender. Women used a more democratic or participative style than men. Men employed a more autocratic and directive style than women.[22] Finally, a meta-analysis of more than 75 studies uncovered three key findings:

- Female and male leaders were rated as equally effective. This is a very positive outcome because it suggests that despite barriers and possible negative stereotypes towards female leaders, female and male leaders were equally effective.
- Men were rated as more effective leaders than women when their roles were defined in more masculine terms, and women were more effective than men in roles defined in less masculine terms.
- Gender differences in leadership effectiveness were associated with the percentage of male leaders and male subordinates. Specifically, male leaders were seen as more effective than females when there was a greater percentage of male leaders and male subordinates. Interestingly, a similar positive bias in leadership effectiveness was not found for women.[23]

As a research tool, ratings have limitations and it is sometimes helpful to add findings obtained in other ways, for example through experiments, either natural, where behaviour is observed and is unaffected by the observation, or controlled, where participants are aware that they form part of an investigation. The study on power, gender and volubility mentioned in the 'OB in Real Life' in section 4.8 also has leadership implications. Women with political power, for example, are not just powerful. To attain their power they have to be leaders. However, the observed tendency to speak less was related to differences in how men and women are perceived as leaders. Because women do not want to stand out, they talk less. Part of the confirmatory experiment in this study involved respondents rating men and women as CEO candidates. Men who talked more were rated higher than men who did not, whereas women who talked more were rated less suitable as CEO material than those who kept their opinions to themselves.[24]

Women also differ in terms of another trait, portability. This refers to the observation, by Boris Groysberg and colleagues, that male business star performers who are headhunted to other organisations tend to underperform after their move. In contrast, women who are headhunted show no decline in terms of performance. This finding is explained by women relying more on external relations and generally on the skill of building relationships. Another reason for this outcome is that women are more careful before they change jobs, looking at items such as cultural fit, values, and managerial style before choosing a new organisation to work for.[25]

In conclusion, it is perhaps most safe to assume that the measured differences between female and male managers depend on the measurement tools, and hence can be made either larger or smaller, depending on which aspects of the complex concept of leadership is under analysis.[26]

15.3 Behavioural and styles theories

This phase of leadership research began during the Second World War as part of an effort to develop better military leaders. It was a response to the seeming inability of trait theory to explain leadership effectiveness and to the human relations movement, an offshoot of the Hawthorne studies (in Chapter 1). The thrust of early behavioural leadership theory was to focus on leader behaviour instead of on personality traits. It was believed that leader behaviour directly influenced the effectiveness of the work group. This led researchers to identify patterns of behaviour (called leadership styles) that enabled leaders to influence others effectively.

The Ohio State studies

Researchers at Ohio State University began by generating a list of the types of behaviour exhibited by leaders. At one point, the list contained 1800 statements describing nine categories. Ultimately, the Ohio State researchers concluded there were only two independent dimensions to describe the behaviour of a leader: consideration and initiating structure. **Consideration**, involving a focus on a concern for group members' needs and desires, is well illustrated by the leadership style of Penny Hughes, the former president of Coca-Cola Company Great Britain and Ireland. According to a close colleague of hers:

> Penny is really excellent at establishing rapport with people and encouraging them to be more open, more challenging. To an unusual and refreshing degree she genuinely values people and is totally fair with them. She often walks around the office, sits on the back of a chair and shares a joke with us. There is always lots of laughter![27]

Initiating structure is leader behaviour that organises and defines what group members should be doing to maximise output. These two dimensions of leader behaviour were oriented at right angles to yield four behavioural styles of leadership (see Figure 15.3).

Initially, it was hypothesised that a high-structure, high-consideration style would be the one best style of leadership. Over the years, the effectiveness of this style has been tested many times. Overall, results have been mixed. Researchers, thus, concluded that there is not one best style of leadership.[28] Rather, it is argued that effectiveness of a given leadership style depends on situational factors.

University of Michigan studies

As in the Ohio State studies, this research sought to identify behavioural differences between effective and ineffective leaders. Researchers identified two different styles of leadership: one was centred on the employee, the other on the job. These behavioural styles parallel the consideration

Figure 15.3 Four Leadership Styles Derived from the Ohio State Studies

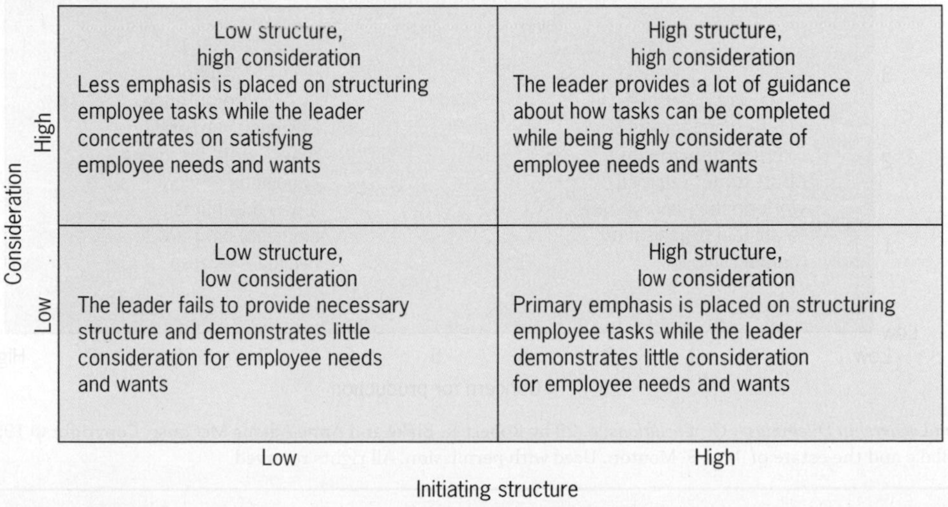
Low structure, high consideration
Less emphasis is placed on structuring employee tasks while the leader concentrates on satisfying employee needs and wants
High structure, high consideration
The leader provides a lot of guidance about how tasks can be completed while being highly considerate of employee needs and wants
Low structure, low consideration
The leader fails to provide necessary structure and demonstrates little consideration for employee needs and wants
High structure, low consideration
Primary emphasis is placed on structuring employee tasks while the leader demonstrates little consideration for employee needs and wants
Consideration
High
Low
Low
High
Initiating structure

and initiating-structure styles identified by the Ohio State group. In summarising the results of these studies, one management expert concluded that effective leaders:

- Tend to have supportive or employee-centred relationships with employees.
- Use group rather than individual methods of supervision.
- Set high performance goals.[29]

Blake and Mouton's Managerial/Leadership Grid®

Perhaps, the most widely known behavioural styles model of leadership is the Managerial Grid® developed by Robert Blake and Jane Srygley.[30] They use it to demonstrate that there is one best style of leadership. Blake and Mouton's Managerial Grid® (renamed the **Leadership Grid** in 1991) is a matrix formed by the intersection of two dimensions of leader behaviour (see Figure 15.4). On the horizontal axis is 'concern for production'. 'Concern for people' is on the vertical axis.

Figure 15.4 The Leadership Grid

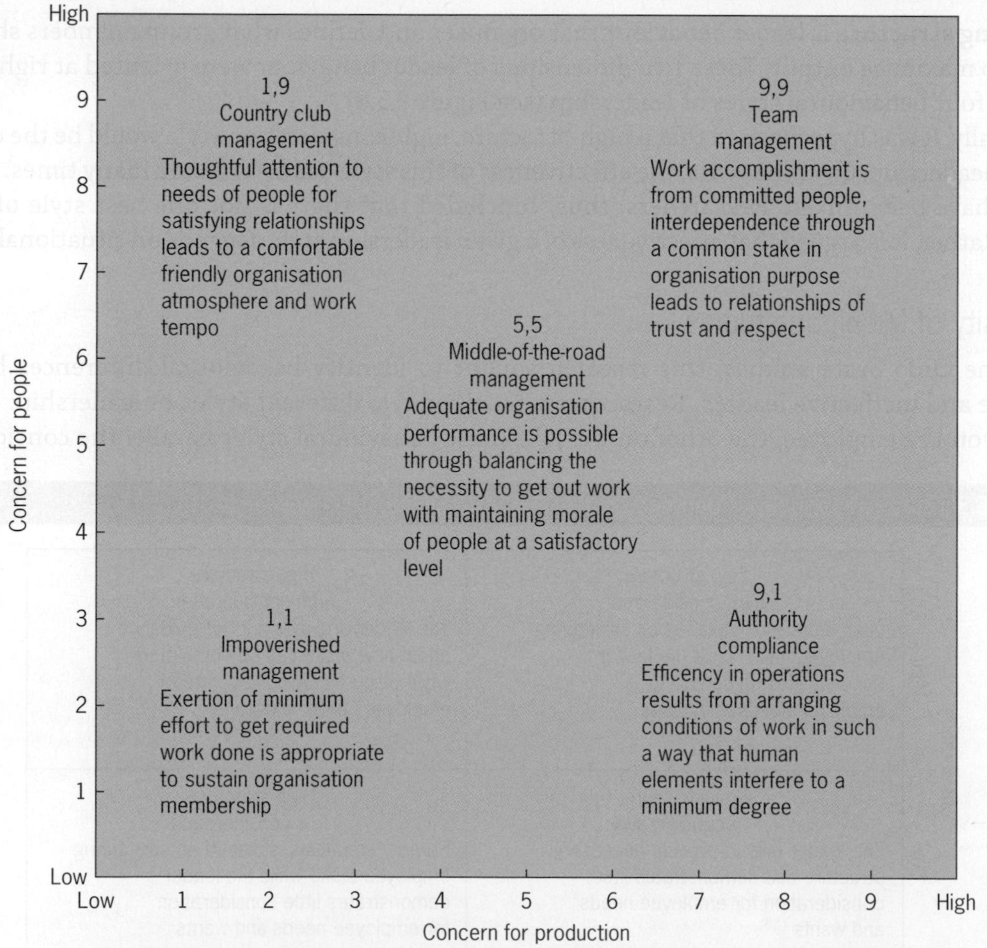

Source: *From Leadership Dilemmas – Grid Solutions*, p. 29 by Robert R. Blake and Anne Adams McCanse. Copyright © 1991 by Robert R. Blake and the estate of Jane S. Mouton. Used with permission. All rights reserved.

Blake and Mouton point out that 'the variables of the Managerial Grid are attitudinal and conceptual, with behaviour descriptions derived from and connected with the thinking that lies behind action'.[31] In other words, concern for production and concern for people involve attitudes and patterns of thinking, as well as specific types of behaviour. By scaling each axis of the grid from 1 to 9, Blake and Mouton were able to plot five leadership styles. Because it emphasises teamwork and interdependence, the 9,9 style is considered by Blake and Mouton to be the best, regardless of the situation. Please note that these two dimensions are again somewhat analogous to the dimensions 'consideration' and 'initiating structure' mentioned above.

In support of the 9,9 style, Blake and Mouton cite the results of a study in which 100 experienced managers were asked to select the best way of handling 12 managerial situations. Between 72 and 90 per cent of the managers selected the 9,9 style for each of the 12 situations.[32] Moreover, Blake and Mouton report, 'The 9,9, orientation . . . leads to productivity, satisfaction, creativity and health.'[33] Critics point out that Blake and Mouton's research may be self-serving. At issue is the grid's extensive use as a training and consulting tool for diagnosing and correcting organisational problems.

Behavioural styles theory in perspective

By emphasising the behaviour of leaders, something that is learned, the behavioural style approach makes it clear that leaders are made, not born. This is the opposite of the traditional assumption of the trait theorists. Given what we know about behaviour shaping and model-based training, the behaviour of a leader can be systematically improved and developed.

OB in Real Life

Ernst & Young

Consider, for example, how Steve Sitek, director of performance development and training at Ernst & Young's Finance, Technology and Administration Division, was striving to grow and develop leadership talent within the organisation:

> Sitek oversees a senior development programme that helps executives gain feedback on how they measure up against 11 critical leadership characteristics. Internal studies have shown a direct correlation between executive performance and the 11 characteristics, which include being innovative, excited, persuasive and strategic. In one-to-one encounters with superiors, managers discuss their assessments to identify characteristics that need strengthening and are charged with structuring their own development plans. Managers are encouraged to work on the characteristics they need to grow incrementally over a multi-year period. Sitek produces specific training geared to each characteristic. 'I have a training programme for each one', he says. 'For example, the No. 1 development gap that we discovered was the characteristic of persuasiveness. I offer a one-day programme on this characteristic.'[34]

Behavioural styles research also revealed that there is no one best style of leadership. The effectiveness of a particular leadership style depends on the situation at hand. For instance, employees prefer structure over consideration when faced with role ambiguity.[35] Finally, research also reveals that it is important to consider the difference between how frequently and how effectively managers exhibit various types of leadership behaviour. For example, a manager might ineffectively display a lot of considerate leader behaviours. Such a style is likely to frustrate employees and possibly result in lowered job satisfaction and performance. Because the frequency of exhibiting leadership behaviours is secondary in importance to effectiveness, managers are encouraged to concentrate on improving the effective execution of their leader behaviours.[36] Take a moment to complete the next Activity on assessing leadership style.

The exercise gives you the opportunity to test the behavioural styles theory by assessing your lecturer's leadership style and your associated class satisfaction and role clarity. Are you satisfied with this class? If yes, the behavioural styles approach is supported if your tutor displayed both high consideration and initiating structure. In contrast, the behavioural style approach is not supported if you are satisfied with this class and your teacher exhibits something other than the standard high-high style. Do your results support the proposition that there is one best style of leadership? Are your results consistent with past research that showed leadership behaviour depends on the situation at hand? The answer is 'yes' if, when faced with high role ambiguity, you prefer initiating structure over consideration. The answer is also 'yes' if, when role ambiguity is low, you prefer consideration over structure. We now turn our attention to discussing alternative situational theories of leadership.

Activity

Assessing the tutor's leadership style, study group satisfaction and student role clarity

Instructions

A team of researchers converted a set of leadership measures for application in a student setting. For each of the items shown here, use the following rating scale to circle the answer that best represents your feelings. Next, use the scoring key to calculate the scores for your lecturer's leadership style, your study group satisfaction and student role clarity.

1 = strongly disagree
2 = disagree
3 = neither agree nor disagree
4 = agree
5 = strongly agree

1	My tutor behaves in a manner which is thoughtful of my personal needs.	1 2 3 4 5
2	My tutor maintains a friendly working relationship with me.	1 2 3 4 5
3	My tutor looks out for my personal welfare.	1 2 3 4 5
4	My tutor gives clear explanations of what is expected of me.	1 2 3 4 5
5	My tutor tells me the performance goals for the class.	1 2 3 4 5
6	My tutor explains the level of performance that is expected of me.	1 2 3 4 5
7	I am satisfied with the variety of study group assignments.	1 2 3 4 5
8	I am satisfied with the way my tutor handles the students.	1 2 3 4 5
9	I am satisfied with the spirit of co-operation among my fellow students.	1 2 3 4 5
10	I know exactly what my responsibilities are.	1 2 3 4 5
11	I am given clear explanations of what has to be done.	1 2 3 4 5

Scoring key

Tutor consideration (1, 2, 3) ________

Tutor initiating structure (4, 5, 6) ________

Study group satisfaction (7, 8, 9) ________

Role clarity (10, 11) ________

Arbitrary norms

Low consideration = 3–8

High consideration = 9–15

Low structure = 3–8

High structure = 9–15

Low satisfaction = 3–8

High satisfaction = 9–15

Low role clarity = 2–5

High role clarity = 6–10

Source: The survey was adapted from A. J. Kinicki and C. A. Schriesheim, 'Teachers as Leaders: A Moderator Variable Approach', *Journal of Educational Psychology*, 1978, pp. 928–35.

15.4 Situational and contingency theories

Situational leadership theories came about as a result of an attempt to explain the inconsistent findings about traits and styles. **Situational theories** propose that the effectiveness of a particular style of leader behaviour depends on the situation. As situations change, different styles become appropriate. This directly challenges the idea of one best style of leadership. Let us closely examine three alternative situational theories of leadership.

Fiedler's contingency model

Fred Fiedler, an OB scholar, developed a situational model of leadership. It is the oldest and one of the most widely known models of leadership. Fiedler's model is based on the following assumption:

> The performance of a leader depends on two interrelated factors: the degree to which the situation gives the leader control and influence – that is, the likelihood that [the leader] can successfully accomplish the job; and the leader's basic motivation – that is, whether [the leader's] self-esteem depends primarily on accomplishing the task or on having close supportive relations with others.[37]

With respect to a leader's basic motivation, Fiedler believes that leaders are either task-motivated or relationship-motivated. These basic motivations are similar to initiating structure/concern for production and consideration/concern for people.

OB in Real Life

Hewlett-Packard

Consider the basic leadership motivation possessed by Cynthia Danaher, general manager of Hewlett-Packard's Medical Products Group:

'Once a manager is in charge of thousands of employees, the ability to set the direction and delegate is more vital than team-building and coaching', she believes . . . When Ms Danaher changed her top management team and restructured the Medical Products Group, moving out of slow-growth businesses to focus on more profitable clinical equipment, she had to relinquish her need for approval. 'Change is painful, and someone has to be the bad guy', she says. Suddenly employees she considered friends avoided her and told her she was ruining the group. 'I wasn't used to tolerating that, and I'd try to explain over and over why change had to occur', she says. Over time, she has learned to simply 'charge ahead', accepting that not everyone will follow and that some won't survive.[38]

Clearly, Danaher has used a task-motivated style of leadership to create organisational change within Hewlett-Packard.

Fiedler's theory is also based on the premise that leaders have one dominant leadership style that is resistant to change. He suggests that leaders must learn to manipulate or influence the leadership situation in order to create a 'match' between their leadership style and the amount of control within the situation at hand. After discussing the components of situational control and the leadership matching process, we review relevant research and some practical implications.[39]

Situational control refers to the amount of control and influence the leader has in his or her immediate work environment. Situational control ranges from high to low. High control implies that the leader's decisions will produce predictable results because the leader has the ability to influence work outcomes. Low control implies that the leader's decisions may not influence work outcomes because the leader has very little influence. There are three dimensions of situational control: leader–member relations, task structure and position power. These dimensions vary independently, forming eight combinations of situational control (see Figure 15.5).

Figure 15.5 Representation of Fiedler's Contingency Model

Situational control	High control situations			Moderate control situations			Low control situations	
Leader–member relations Task structure Position power	Good High Strong	Good High Weak	Good Low Strong	Good Low Weak	Poor High Strong	Poor High Weak	Poor Low Strong	Poor Low Weak
Situation	I	II	III	IV	V	VI	VII	VIII
Optimal leadership style	Task-motivated leadership			Relationship-motivated leadership			Task-motivated leadership	

Source: Adapted from F. E. Fiedler, 'Situational Control and a Dynamic Theory of Leadership', in *Managerial Control and Organizational Democracy*, eds B. King, S. Streufert and F. E. Fiedler (New York: John Wiley & Sons, 1978), p. 114.

The three dimensions of situational control are as follows:

- **Leader–member relations** is the most important component of situational control. Good leader–member relations suggest that the leader can depend on the group, thus ensuring that the work group will try to meet the leader's goals and objectives.
- **Task structure** is the amount of structure contained within work tasks and is the second most important component of situational control. A managerial job, for example, contains less structure than that of a bank teller. Because structured tasks have guidelines for how the job should be completed, the leader has more control and influence over employees performing such tasks.
- The final component, **position power**, covers the leader's formal power to reward, punish or otherwise obtain compliance from employees.[40]

Linking leadership motivation and situational control

Fiedler's complete contingency model is presented in Figure 15.5. The last row under the situational control column shows that there are eight different leadership situations. Each situation represents a unique combination of leader–member relations, task structure and position power. Situations I, II, and III represent high control situations. The figure also shows that task-motivated leaders are expected to be the most effective in situations of high control. Under conditions of moderate control (situations IV, V and VI), relationship-motivated leaders are thought to be the most effective. Finally, the results orientation of task-motivated leaders is predicted to be more effective under conditions of low control (situations VII and VIII).

Evidence about Fiedler's contingency model

The overall accuracy of Fiedler's contingency model was tested by means of a meta-analysis of 35 studies containing 137 leader-style performance relations. The researchers found the following to be true:

- The contingency theory was correctly deduced from studies on which it was based.
- In laboratory studies testing the model, the theory was supported for all leadership situations except situation II.
- In field studies testing the model, three of the eight situations (IV, V and VII) produced completely supportive results, while partial support was obtained for situations I, II, III, VI and VIII.

A meta-analysis of data obtained from 1282 groups also provided mixed support for the contingency model.[41] These findings suggest that Fiedler's model needs theoretical refinement.[42]

The major contribution of Fiedler's model is that it prompted others to examine the contingency nature of leadership. This research, in turn, reinforced the notion that there is no one best style of leadership. Leaders are advised to alter their task and relationship orientation to fit the demands of the situation at hand.

! Critical thinking

Should you try to fit the managerial style of the individual manager to fit the situation or find a manager with the appropriate style to fit the situation?

Path–goal theory

Path–goal theory is based on the expectancy theory of motivation discussed previously in Chapter 6. Expectancy theory proposes that motivation to exert effort increases as one's effort → performance → outcome expectations improve. Path–goal theory focuses on how leaders influence followers' expectations.

According to the path–goal model, behaviour of a leader is acceptable when employees view it as a source of satisfaction or as paving the way to future satisfaction. In addition, it is motivational to the extent that it clears the obstacles to goal accomplishment, provides the guidance and support needed by employees and ties meaningful rewards to goal accomplishment. Because the model deals with pathways to goals and rewards, it is called the 'path–goal' theory of leadership.

Roubert House, an Ohio State University graduate, sees the leader's main job as helping employees to keep to the right paths to reach challenging goals and valued rewards. This approach has a very intuitive appeal. Leaders are always interested in changing people's behaviour, so that they produce more, better or other results. This theory suggests that, in most cases, you begin better by telling them clearly what results you are looking for. Then you discuss how to get those results and you have them experience the rewards once they have obtained the results. If this experience is too far away (e.g. promotion), you visualise the way from efforts to results and from results to rewards.

House believes leaders can exhibit more than one leadership style. This contrasts with Fiedler, who proposes that leaders have only one dominant style. The four leadership styles identified by House are as follows:

- *Directive leadership*. Providing guidance to employees about what should be done and how to do it, scheduling work and maintaining standards of performance.
- *Supportive leadership*. Showing concern for the well-being and needs of employees, being friendly and approachable, and treating workers as equals.
- *Participative leadership*. Consulting with employees and seriously considering their ideas when making decisions.
- *Achievement-oriented leadership*. Encouraging employees to perform at their highest level by setting challenging goals, emphasising excellence and demonstrating confidence in employee abilities.[43]

Research evidence supports the idea that leaders exhibit more than one leadership style.[44] Descriptions of business leaders reinforce these findings. In the 1980s and early 1990s, Percy Barnevik, the then CEO of the Swedish-Swiss group Asea Brown Boveri, was one of the most admired business leaders in Europe. He used multiple leadership styles. When he introduced a matrix organisation and seriously reduced staff numbers, he preferred to communicate directly with the 206 000 staff members: 'You cannot hide up there in an ivory tower. You have to be out there.' Although he prefers a persuasive approach when dealing with conflicts, he had to adopt a severe approach when he was faced with stubborn unions in the 1980s. It was only by issuing an ultimatum that Barnevik achieved the cuts he wanted.[45]

Contingency factors

Contingency factors affect expectancy or path–goal perceptions. **Contingency factors** are situational factors that cause one style of leadership to be more effective than another. This model has two groups of contingency variables. They are employee characteristics and environmental factors. Five important employee characteristics are their locus of control, task ability, need for achievement, experience, and need for clarity. Three relevant environmental factors are the employee's task, authority system and work group. All these factors have the potential for hindering or motivating employees.

There have been about 50 studies testing various predictions derived from House's original model. Results have been mixed, with some studies supporting the theory and others not. House, thus, proposed a new version of his theory.[46] Among other changes, he places more emphasis on the need for leaders to foster intrinsic motivation (see Chapters 5 and 6) through empowerment (see Chapter 14). The most important change deals with 'shared leadership'. An employee does not have to be a supervisor or manager to engage in leader behaviour. Leadership can be shared among many employees within an organisation.

Hersey and Blanchard's situational leadership theory

Situational leadership theory (SLT) was developed by management writers Paul Hersey and Kenneth Blanchard.[47] According to their theory, effective leadership behaviour depends on the level of readiness on the part of a leader's followers. **Readiness** is defined as the extent to which a follower possesses the ability and willingness to complete a task. Willingness is a combination of confidence, commitment and motivation.

The SLT model is summarised in Figure 15.6. The appropriate leadership style is found by cross-referencing follower readiness (which varies from low to high) with one of four leadership styles. The

Figure 15.6 Situational Leadership Model

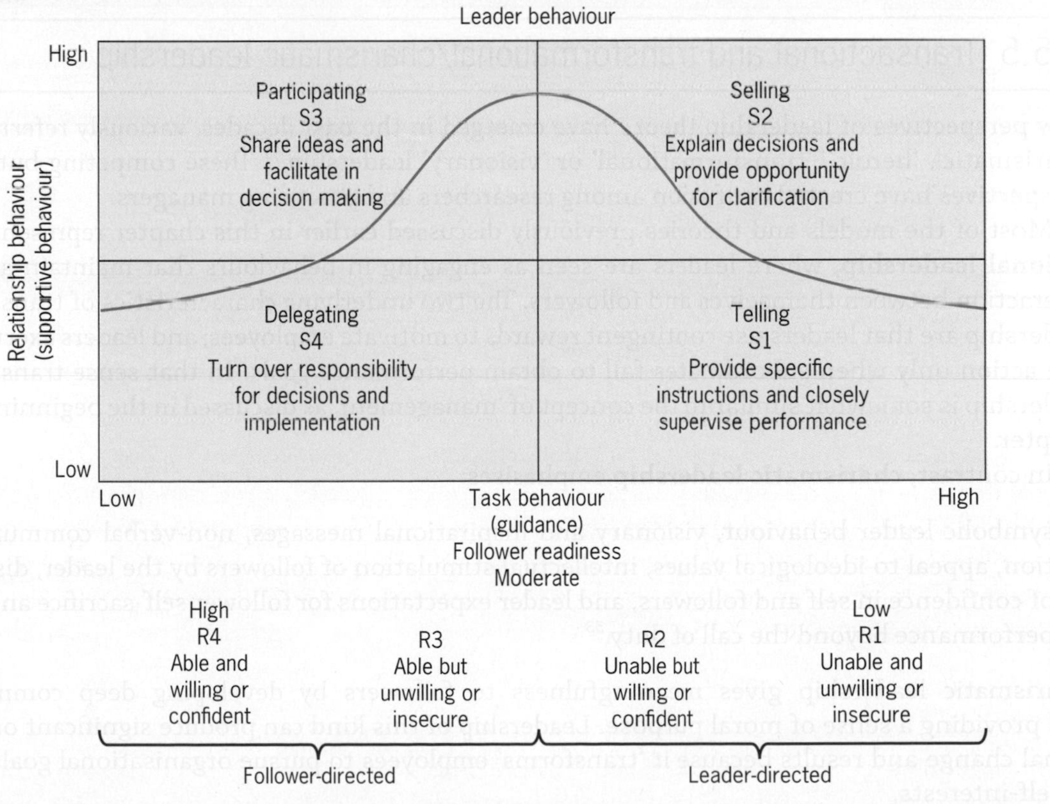

Source: Reprinted with permission from Dr Paul Hersey (1984). *The Management of Organizational: Utilizing Human Resources.* The Center for Leadership Studies, Escondido, CA. All rights reserved.

four leadership styles represent combinations of task- and relationship-oriented leader behaviours (S1 to S4). Leaders are encouraged to use a 'telling style' (directive) for followers with low readiness. This style combines high task-oriented leader behaviours, such as providing instructions, with low relationship-oriented behaviours, such as close supervision (see Figure 15.6). As follower readiness increases, leaders are advised to gradually move from a telling to a selling style, then on to a participating and, ultimately, a delegating style. The four leadership styles depicted in Figure 15.6 are referred to as telling or directing (S1), persuading or coaching (S2), participating or supporting (S3), and delegating (S4).[48]

Evidence about situational leadership theory

Although SLT is widely used as a training tool, it is not strongly supported by scientific research. For instance, leadership effectiveness was not attributable to the predicted interaction between follower readiness and leadership style in a study of 459 salespeople.[49] Moreover, a study of 303 teachers indicated that SLT was accurate only for employees with low readiness. This finding is consistent with a survey of 57 chief nurse executives in California. These executives did not delegate in accordance with SLT.[50] Finally, researchers have concluded that the self-assessment instrument used to measure leadership style and follower readiness is inaccurate and should be used with caution.[51] In summary, managers should exercise discretion when using prescriptions from SLT.

15.5 Transactional and transformational/charismatic leadership

New perspectives of leadership theory have emerged in the past decades, variously referred to as 'charismatic', 'heroic', 'transformational' or 'visionary' leadership.[52] These competing but related perspectives have created confusion among researchers and practising managers.

Most of the models and theories previously discussed earlier in this chapter represent **transactional leadership**, where leaders are seen as engaging in behaviours that maintain a quality interaction between themselves and followers. The two underlying characteristics of transactional leadership are that leaders use contingent rewards to motivate employees; and leaders exert corrective action only when subordinates fail to obtain performance goals. In that sense transactional leadership is somewhat similar to the concept of 'management' as discussed in the beginning of the chapter.

In contrast, **charismatic leadership** emphasises:

> symbolic leader behaviour, visionary and inspirational messages, non-verbal communication, appeal to ideological values, intellectual stimulation of followers by the leader, display of confidence in self and followers, and leader expectations for follower self-sacrifice and for performance beyond the call of duty.[53]

Charismatic leadership gives meaningfulness to followers by developing deep commitment and providing a sense of moral purpose. Leadership of this kind can produce significant organisational change and results because it 'transforms' employees to pursue organisational goals in lieu of self-interests.

Richard Branson, chief operating officer of the Virgin group, is a good example of a charismatic leader.

OB in Real Life

Richard Branson

Richard did not breeze through school. It was not just a challenge for him, it was a nightmare. His dyslexia embarrassed him as he had to memorise and recite word for word in public. He was sure he did terribly on the standard IQ tests . . . these are tests that measure abilities where he is weak. In the end, it was the tests that failed. They totally missed his ability and passion for sports. They had no means to identify ambition, the fire inside that drives people to find a path to success that zigzags around the maze of standard doors that will not open. They never identified the most important talent of all. It is the ability to connect with people, mind to mind, soul to soul. It is that rare power to energise the ambitions of others, so that they, too, rise to the level of their dreams.[54]

How does charismatic leadership transform followers?

Charismatic leaders transform followers by creating changes in their goals, values, needs, beliefs and aspirations. They accomplish this transformation by appealing to followers' self-concepts – namely, their values and personal identity. Figure 15.7 presents a model of how charismatic leadership accomplishes this transformation process.

Figure 15.7 shows that organisational culture is a key precursor of charismatic leadership. Organisations with adaptive cultures anticipate and adapt to environmental changes and focus on leadership that emphasises the importance of service to customers, stockholders and employees. This type of management orientation involves the use of charismatic leadership. Organisational culture is discussed in Chapter 12.

Charismatic leaders first engage in three key sets of leader behaviour. If done effectively, this behaviour positively affects individual followers and their work groups. These positive effects, in turn, influence a variety of outcomes. Before discussing the model of charismatic leadership in more detail, it is important to note two general conclusions about charismatic leadership.[55] First, the two-headed arrow between organisational culture and leader behaviour in Figure 15.7 reveals that individuals with charismatic behavioural tendencies are able to influence culture. This implies that charismatic leadership reinforces the core values of an adaptive culture and helps to change the dysfunctional aspects of an organisation's culture that develop over time. Second, charismatic leadership has an effect on multiple levels within an organisation. For example, Figure 15.7 shows that charismatic leadership can positively influence individual outcomes (e.g. motivation), group outcomes (e.g. group cohesion) and organisational outcomes (e.g. financial performance). You can see that the potential for positive benefits from charismatic leadership is quite widespread.

Charismatic leader behaviour

The first set of charismatic leader behaviours involves establishing a common vision of the future. A vision is 'a realistic, credible, attractive future for your organisation'.[56] According to Burt Nanus, a leadership expert, the 'right' vision unleashes human potential because it serves as a beacon of hope and common purpose. It does this by attracting commitment, energising workers, creating meaning in employees' lives, establishing a standard of excellence, promoting high ideals, and

Figure 15.7 A Charismatic Model of Leadership

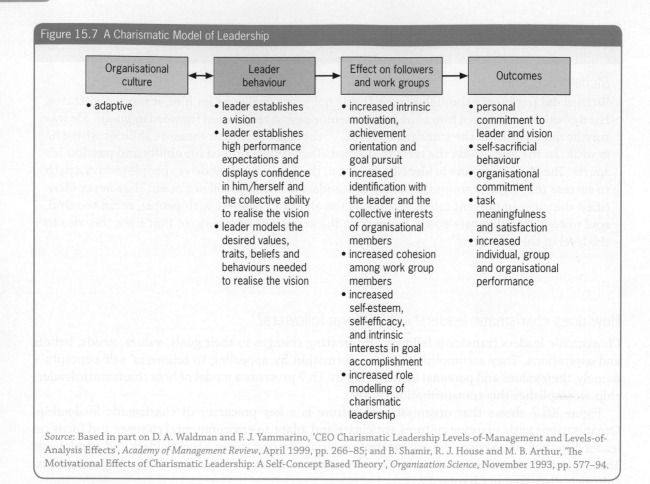

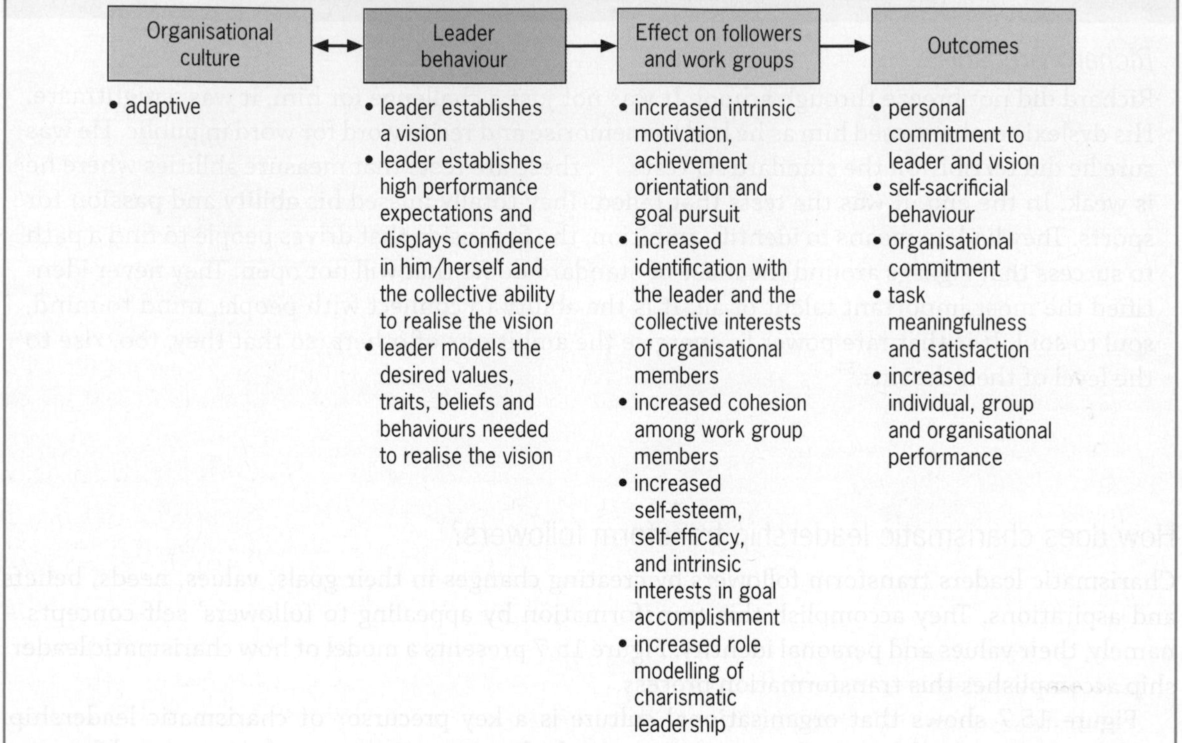
Organisational culture
Leader behaviour
Effect on followers and work groups
Outcomes
• adaptive
• leader establishes a vision
• leader establishes high performance expectations and displays confidence in him/herself and the collective ability to realise the vision
• leader models the desired values, traits, beliefs and behaviours needed to realise the vision
• increased intrinsic motivation, achievement orientation and goal pursuit
• increased identification with the leader and the collective interests of organisational members
• increased cohesion among work group members
• increased self-esteem, self-efficacy, and intrinsic interests in goal accomplishment
• increased role modelling of charismatic leadership
• personal commitment to leader and vision
• self-sacrificial behaviour
• organisational commitment
• task meaningfulness and satisfaction
• increased individual, group and organisational performance

Source: Based in part on D. A. Waldman and F. J. Yammarino, 'CEO Charismatic Leadership Levels-of-Management and Levels-of-Analysis Effects', *Academy of Management Review*, April 1999, pp. 266–85; and B. Shamir, R. J. House and M. B. Arthur, 'The Motivational Effects of Charismatic Leadership: A Self-Concept Based Theory', *Organization Science*, November 1993, pp. 577–94.

bridging the gap between an organisation's present problems and its future goals and aspirations.[57] In contrast, the 'wrong' vision can be very damaging to an organisation. Consider what happened to the UK's Saatchi & Saatchi, once the world's most famous publicity agency, in the following 'OB in Real Life'.

OB in Real Life

Saatchi & Saatchi

Strengthened by successive successful publicity campaigns, including Margaret Thatcher's in the eighties, Maurice Saatchi's unrestrained ambition pulled down the entire business. Thanks to a positive evolution on the stock market, he suddenly had an enormous budget at his disposal which prompted him to buy publicity agencies, marketing companies, public relations agencies and publishing houses. He was game for anything. His wild buying binge led to pure megalomania as, in 1987, he decided to take over Hill Samuel to be followed by one of Britain's biggest banks, the Midland Bank. Mismanagement and disorganisation, followed by a crash resulted in the company's breakdown.[58]

As you can see, Maurice Saatchi's vision produced disastrous results. This highlights the fact that charismatic leaders do more than simply establish a vision. They must also gain input from others in developing an effective implementation plan.

Evidence about charismatic/transformational leadership

The charismatic model of leadership presented in Figure 15.7 is strongly supported by research. A study of 134 mid-level managers from a large Brazilian company found that leadership effectiveness is a direct function of a leader's transformational behaviours (influenced by experience, intelligence and conscientiousness).

However, charisma can clearly be a source of negative outcomes. These narcissistic leaders have been described in much detail by Manfred Kets de Vries.[59] They surround themselves with uncritical subordinates. They know what is best, and do not need advice. They undertake over-ambitious, grandiose projects to glorify themselves. When the first signals are sent that the projects might not be as simple as expected, they ignore those signals, thereby missing the opportunity to correct the situation in time. When the project finally completely fails, they are the only person not to blame. They simple refuse to take any responsibility and they search for scapegoats.

Many critical studies of leadership have not only questioned the value of charisma, but even the concept of leadership itself. In the light of the many corporate scandals in the world (e.g. Enron in the USA, Ahold in the Netherlands, Swissair in Switzerland, Parmalat in Italy), many writers have warned against the 'self-serving' leader and have pointed to the dangers of 'larger than life' leaders, or have described 'the curse of the superstar'.[60] In almost all cases of corporate fraud or clear abuse of corporate resources, a 'strong' leader could be identified who was beyond control of colleagues or supervisory boards.

> **Critical thinking**
>
> There are a number of companies that are almost synonymous with their very charismatic founders/CEOs. How can these CEOs prepare the organisations for the time when they are no longer in charge?

15.6 Additional perspectives on leadership

This section examines three additional approaches to leadership: substitutes for leadership, servant-leadership and coaching.

Virtually all leadership theories assume that some sort of formal leadership is necessary, whatever the circumstances. But this basic assumption is questioned by this model of leadership. Specifically, some OB scholars propose that there are a variety of situational variables that can act as **substitutes for leadership** increasing or diminishing a leader's ability to influence the work group.[61] For example, leader behaviour that initiates structure would tend to be resisted by independent-minded employees with high ability and vast experience. Consequently, such employees would be guided more by their own initiative than by managerial directives.

Kerr and Jermier's substitutes for leadership model

According to Steven Kerr and John Jermier, the OB researchers who developed this model, the key to improving leadership effectiveness is to identify the substitutes for leadership (see Table 15.3). Characteristics of the subordinate, the task and the organisation can act as substitutes for traditional hierarchical leadership. Further, different characteristics are predicted to negate different types of leader behaviour.

For example, tasks that provide feedback concerning accomplishment, such as taking a test, tend to negate task-oriented but not relationship-oriented leader behaviour (see Table 15.3). Although the list in Table 15.3 is not all inclusive, it shows that there are more substitutes for task-oriented leadership than for relationship-oriented leadership.

Two different approaches have been used to test this model. The first is based on the idea that substitutes for leadership are contingency variables that moderate the relationship between leader behaviour and employee attitudes and behaviour.[62] A summary of this research revealed that only 318 of the 3741 (9 per cent) contingency relationships tested supported the model.[63] This demonstrates that substitutes for leadership do not moderate the effect of a leader's behaviour as

Table 15.3 Substitutes for Leadership

Characteristic	Relationship-oriented or considerate leader behaviour is unnecessary	Task-oriented or initiating structure leader behaviour is unnecessary
Of the subordinate		
1 Ability, experience, training, knowledge		x
2 Need for independence	x	x
3 'Professional' orientation	x	x
4 Indifference towards organisational rewards	x	x
Of the task		
5 Unambiguous and routine		x
6 Methodologically invariant		x
7 Provides its own feedback concerning accomplishment		x
8 Intrinsically satisfying	x	
Of the organisation		
9 Formalisation (explicit plans, goals and areas of responsibility)		x
10 Inflexibility (rigid, unbending rules and procedures)		x
11 Highly specified and active advisory and staff functions		x
12 Closely knit, cohesive work groups	x	x
13 Organisational rewards not within the leader's control	x	x
14 Spatial distance between superior and subordinates	x	x

Source: Adapted from S. Kerr and J. M. Jermier, 'Substitutes for Leadership: Their Meaning and Measurement', *Organizational Behavior and Human Performance*, December 1978, pp. 375–403.

suggested by Steve Kerr and John Jermier. The second approach to test the substitutes model examined whether substitutes for leadership have a direct effect on employee attitudes and behaviours. A meta-analysis of 36 different samples revealed that the combination of substitute variables and leader behaviours significantly explained a variety of employee attitudes and behaviours. Interestingly, the substitutes for leadership were more important than leader behaviours in accounting for employee attitudes and behaviours.[64]

Servant-leadership

Servant-leadership is more a philosophy of managing than a testable theory. Robert Greenleaf coined the term **servant-leadership** to highlight that great leaders act as servants, putting the needs of others, including employees, customers and community, as their first priority. Servant-leadership focuses on increased service to others rather than to oneself.[65] Servant-leadership is not a quick-fix approach to leadership. Rather, it is a long-term, transformational approach to life and work. Table 15.4 presents 10 characteristics possessed by servant-leaders. One can hardly go wrong by trying to adopt these characteristics.

Table 15.4 Characteristics of the Servant-Leader

Servant-leadership characteristics	Description
1 Listening	Servant-leaders focus on listening to identify and clarify the needs and desires of a group
2 Empathy	Servant-leaders try to empathise with others' feelings and emotions. An individual's good intentions are assumed even when he or she performs poorly
3 Healing	Servant-leaders strive to make themselves and others whole in the face of failure or suffering
4 Awareness	Servant-leaders are very self-aware of their strengths and limitations
5 Persuasion	Servant-leaders rely more on persuasion than positional authority when making decisions and trying to influence others
6 Conceptualisation	Servant leaders take the time and effort to develop broader-based conceptual thinking. Servant-leaders seek an appropriate balance between a short-term, day-to-day focus and a long-term, conceptual orientation
7 Foresight	Servant-leaders have the ability to foresee future outcomes associated with a current course of action or situation
8 Stewardship	Servant-leaders assume that they are stewards of the people and resources they manage
9 Commitment to the growth of people	Servant-leaders are committed to people beyond their immediate work role. They commit to fostering an environment that encourages personal, professional and spiritual growth
10 Building community	Servant-leaders strive to create a sense of community both within and outside the work organisation

Source: These characteristics and descriptions were derived from L. C. Spears, 'Introduction: Servant-Leadership and the Greenleaf Legacy', in *Reflections on Leadership: How Robert K. Greenleaf's Theory of Servant-Leadership Influenced Today's Top Management Thinkers*, ed. L. C. Spears (New York: John Wiley & Sons, 1995), pp. 1–14.

Coaching

Modern management thinking is no longer characterised by dominant and authoritarian leadership but by coaching.[66] A good coach is able to offer commitment and support, build skills and teams, and to focus on results.

Commitment. A manager directs from a distance, whereas a coach acts directly with his or her players. A coach is present on the field to support the team. He or she is present at the moment of action, which he or she experiences actively. The coach is not engrossed in files or participating in long-lasting meetings. Action happens in the field. A real coach is not afraid 'to put his or her shoulder to the wheel' and help when it is needed. The rational, cool and distant manager has to make place for the enthusiastic coach, who trusts his or her subordinates and knows them personally. The coach is conscious of their weaknesses and is capable of getting the best out of them. Day after day, he or she tries to improve team members' performance and possibilities.

Skill building. The coach invests much effort into his or her employees' skill building. He or she is aware of the fact that they are the driving force of his organisation. He or she will see to it that they improve their professional skills, can organise their work themselves and are directed towards a common goal.

Support. The coach will principally support his or her team to enable it to show results.

Team builder. The coach is a team builder who brings people together with different skills, interests and backgrounds to create a solid team. A struggle for power and political conflict has to be replaced by mutual respect. The coach is successful in transforming internal into external competition, directed towards the real competitors.

Result-oriented. The coach's efforts are not aimed at creating a cosy environment; he or she wants to see results.

Learning outcomes: Summary of key terms

1 **Define the term 'leadership', and explain the difference between leading and managing**

Leadership is defined as a process of social influence in which the leader tries to obtain the voluntary participation of employees in an effort to reach organisational objectives. Leadership entails more than having authority and power. Although leadership and management overlap, each entails a unique set of activities or functions. Managers typically perform functions associated with planning, investigating, organising and control, while leaders deal with the interpersonal aspects of a manager's job.

2 **Review the research on trait theory and discuss the idea of one best style of leadership, using the Ohio State studies and the Leadership Grid® as points of reference**

Previous leadership research did not support the notion that effective leaders possessed unique traits to those of their followers. However, teams of researchers analysed this historical data again, this time using modern-day statistical procedures. Results revealed that individuals tend to be perceived as leaders when they possess one or more of the following traits: intelligence, dominance and masculinity. Another study further demonstrated that employees value credible leaders. Credible leaders are honest, forward-looking, inspiring and competent. Research also examined the relationship between gender and leadership. Results demonstrated that: (a) men and women differed in the type of leadership roles they assume; (b) leadership styles varied by gender; and (c) gender differences in ratings of leadership effectiveness were associated with the percentage of male leaders and male subordinates. The Ohio State studies revealed that there were two key independent dimensions of leadership behaviour: consideration and initiating structure. Authors of the Leadership Grid® proposed that leaders should adopt a style that demonstrates high concern for production and people. Research did not support the premise that there is one best style of leadership.

3 **Explain, according to Fiedler's contingency model, how leadership style interacts with situational control**

Fiedler believes the effectiveness of a leader depends on an appropriate match between leadership style and situational control. Leaders are either task-motivated or relationship-motivated. Situation control is composed of leader–member relations, task structure and position power. Task-motivated leaders are effective under situations of both high and low control. Relationship-motivated leaders are more effective when they have moderate situational control.

4 **Discuss Hersey and Blanchard's situational leadership theory**

According to situational leadership theory (SLT), effective leader behaviour depends on the readiness level of a leader's followers. As follower readiness increases, leaders are advised to gradually move from a telling to a selling to a participating and, finally, to a delegating style. Research does not support SLT.

5 **Define and differentiate between transactional and charismatic leadership**

There is an important difference between transactional and charismatic leadership. Transactional leaders focus on the interpersonal transactions between managers and employees. Charismatic leaders motivate employees to pursue organisational goals above their own self-interests. Both forms of leadership are important for organisational success.

6 **Explain how charismatic leadership transforms followers and work groups**

Organisational culture is a key precursor of charismatic leadership, which is composed of three sets of leader behaviour. These sets, in turn, positively affect followers' and work groups' goals, values, beliefs, aspirations and motivation. These positive effects are then associated with a host of preferred outcomes.

7 **Describe the substitutes for leadership and explain how they substitute for, neutralise, or enhance the effects of leadership**

There are 14 substitutes for leadership (see Table 15.3) that can substitute for, neutralise or enhance the effects of leadership. These substitutes contain characteristics of the subordinates, the task and the organisation. Research shows that substitutes directly influence employee attitudes and performance.

8 **Describe servant-leadership and coaching**

Servant-leadership is more a philosophy than a testable theory. It is based on the premise that great leaders act as servants, putting the needs of others, including employees, customers, and community, as their first priority. A good coach has the following characteristics: commitment, support, an ability to build skills and teams, and an ability to focus on results.

Review questions

1 Is everyone cut out to be a leader? Explain.
2 Has your education helped you to develop any of the traits that characterise leaders?
3 Should organisations change anything in response to research pertaining to gender and leadership? If yes, describe your recommendations.
4 What leadership traits and behavioural styles are possessed by your prime minister?
5 Does it make more sense to change a person's leadership style or the situation? How would Fred Fiedler and Robert House answer this question?
6 Describe how a lecturer might use House's path–goal theory to clarify student's path–goal perceptions.
7 Identify three charismatic leaders and describe their leadership traits and behavioural styles.
8 Have you ever worked for a charismatic leader? Describe how he or she transformed followers.
9 In your view, which leadership theory has the greatest practical application? Why?

Personal awareness and growth exercise

How ready are you to assume the leadership role?

Objective

1 To assess your readiness for the leadership role.
2 To consider the implications of the gap between your career goals and your readiness to lead.

Introduction

Leaders assume multiple roles. Roles represent the expectations that others have of occupants of a position. It is important for potential leaders to consider whether they are ready for the leadership role because mismatches in expectations or skills can derail a leader's effectiveness. This exercise assesses your readiness to assume the leadership role.

Instructions

For each statement, indicate the extent to which you agree or disagree with it by selecting one number from the scale provided. Circle your response for each statement.

Remember, there are no right or wrong answers. After completing the survey, add your total score for the 20 items, then record it in the space provided.

1 = strongly disagree
2 = disagree
3 = neither agree nor disagree
4 = agree
5 = strongly agree

1	It is enjoyable having people rely on me for ideas and suggestions.	1 2 3 4 5
2	It would be accurate to say that I have inspired other people.	1 2 3 4 5
3	It is a good practice to ask people provocative questions about their work.	1 2 3 4 5
4	It is easy for me to compliment others.	1 2 3 4 5
5	I like to cheer people up even when my own spirits are down.	1 2 3 4 5
6	What my team accomplishes is more important than my personal glory.	1 2 3 4 5
7	Many people imitate my ideas.	1 2 3 4 5
8	Building team spirit is important to me.	1 2 3 4 5
9	I would enjoy coaching other members of the team.	1 2 3 4 5
10	It is important to me to recognise others for their accomplishments.	1 2 3 4 5
11	I would enjoy entertaining visitors to my firm even if it interfered with my completing a report.	1 2 3 4 5
12	It would be fun for me to represent my team at gatherings outside our department.	1 2 3 4 5
13	The problems of my team mates are my problems too.	1 2 3 4 5
14	Resolving conflict is an activity I enjoy.	1 2 3 4 5
15	I would co-operate with another unit in the organisation even if I disagreed with the position taken by its members.	1 2 3 4 5
16	I am an idea generator on the job.	1 2 3 4 5
17	It is fun for me to bargain whenever I have the opportunity.	1 2 3 4 5
18	Team members listen to me when I speak.	1 2 3 4 5
19	People have asked me to assume the leadership of an activity several times in my life.	1 2 3 4 5
20	I have always been a convincing person.	1 2 3 4 5

Total score: ___________

Norms for interpreting the total score[67]

90–100 = high readiness for the leadership role
60–89 = moderate readiness for the leadership role
40–59 = some uneasiness with the leadership role
39 or less = low readiness for the leadership role

Questions for discussion

1. Do you agree with the interpretation of your readiness to assume the leadership role? Explain why or why not.
2. If you scored below 60 and desire to become a leader, what might you do to increase your readiness to lead? To answer this question, we suggest that you study the statements carefully – particularly those with low responses – to determine how you might change either an attitude or a behaviour so that you can realistically answer more questions with a response of 'agree' or 'strongly agree'.
3. How might this evaluation instrument help you to become a more effective leader?

Group exercise

Exhibiting leadership within the context of running a meeting[68]

Objectives

1 To consider the types of problems that can occur when running a meeting.

2 To identify the types of leadership behaviour that can be used to handle problems that occur in meetings.

Introduction

Managers often find themselves playing the role of formal or informal leader when participating in a planned meeting (e.g. committees, work groups, task forces). As leaders, individuals must often handle a number of interpersonal situations that have the potential of reducing the group's productivity. For example, if an individual has important information that is not shared with the group, the meeting will be less productive. Similarly, two or more individuals who engage in conversational asides could disrupt the normal functioning of the group. Finally, the group's productivity will also be threatened by two or more individuals who argue or engage in personal attacks on one another during a meeting. This exercise is designed to help you practise some of the behaviour necessary to overcome these problems and at the same time share in the responsibility of leading a productive group.[69]

Instructions

Your tutor will divide the class into groups of four to six. Once the group is assembled, briefly summarise the types of problem that can occur when running a meeting – start with the material presented in the preceding introduction. Write your final list on a piece of paper. Next, for each problem on the group's list, the group should brainstorm a list of appropriate leader behaviours that can be used to handle the problem. Use the guidelines for brainstorming discussed in Chapter 13. Try to arrive at an agreed list.

Questions for discussion

1 What type of problems that occur during meetings is most difficult to handle? Explain.

2 Are there any particular leader behaviours that can be used to solve multiple problems during meetings? Discuss your rationale.

3 Was there a lot of agreement about which leader behaviours were useful for dealing with specific problems encountered in meetings? Explain.

Online
Learning Centre

When you have read this chapter, log on to the Online Learning Centre website at ***www.mcgraw-hill.co.uk/textbooks/sinding*** to access test questions, additional exercises and other related resources.

Notes

1 See S. Lieberson and J. F. O'Connor, 'Leadership and Organizational Performance: A Study of Large Corporations', *American Sociological Review*, April 1972, pp. 117–30.

2 T. Thorlindson, *The Skipper Effect in Icelandic Herring Fishing* (Reykjavik: University of Iceland, 1987); and M. Smith and C. Cooper, 'Leadership and Stress', *Leadership and Organization Development Journal*, no. 2, 1994, pp. 3–7.

3 P. Wright, *Managerial Leadership* (London: Routledge, 1996).

4 R. J. House, N. S. Wright and R. N. Aditiya, 'Cross-Cultural Research on Organizational Leadership: A Critical Analysis and a Proposed Theory', in *New Perspectives in International Industrial Organizational Psychology*, eds P. C. Earley and M. Erez (San Francisco, CA: New Lexington, 1997), pp. 535–625.

5 C. A. Schriesheim, J. M. Tolliver and O. C. Behling, 'Leadership Theory: Some Implications for Managers', *MSU Business Topics*, Summer 1978, p. 35.

6 R. J. House, N. S. Wright and R. N. Aditiya, 'Cross-Cultural Research on Organizational Leadership: A Critical Analysis and a Proposed Theory', in *New Perspectives in International Industrial Organizational Psychology*, eds P. C. Earley and M. Erez (San Francisco, CA: New Lexington, 1997), pp. 535–625.

7 The multiple levels of leadership are discussed by F. J. Yammarino, F. Dansereau and C. J. Kennedy, 'A Multi-Level Multidimensional Approach to Leadership: Viewing Leadership through an Elephant's Eye', *Organizational Dynamics*, Winter 2001, pp. 149–63. Also see H. Mintzberg, 'Covert Leadership: Notes on Managing Professionals', *Harvard Business Review*, November–December 1998, pp. 140–47.

8 B. M. Bass, *Bass & Stogdill's Handbook of Leadership: Theory, Research, and Managerial Applications, third edition* (New York: Free Press, 1990), p. 383.

9 J. P. Kotter, *A Force for Change: How Leadership Differs from Management* (New York: Free Press, 1990); J. P. Kotter, *Leading Change* (Boston, MA: Harvard Business School Press, 1996); and J. P. Kotter, *John Kotter on What Leaders Really Do* (Boston, MA: Harvard Business School Press, 1999).

10 For a thorough discussion about the differences between leading and managing, see G. Weathersby, 'Leading vs. Management', *Management Review*, March 1999, p. 5; R. J. House and R. N. Aditya, "The Social Scientific Study of Leadership: Quo Vadis?', *Journal of Management*, no. 3, 1997, pp. 409–73; and A. Zalesnik, 'Managers and Leaders: Are They Different?' *Harvard Business Review*, May–June 1977, pp. 67–78.

11 For complete details, see R. M. Stogdill, 'Personal Factors Associated with Leadership: A Survey of the Literature', *Journal of Psychology*, 1948, pp. 35–71; and R. M. Stogdill, *Handbook of Leadership* (New York: Free Press, 1974).

12 Excerpted from T. A. Stewart, 'The Contest for Welch's Throne Begins: Who Will Run GE?', *Fortune*, 11 January 1999, p. 27.

13 See R. D. Mann, 'A Review of the Relationships between Personality and Performance in Small Groups', *Psychological Bulletin*, July 1959, pp. 241–70.

14 Perceptions of leadership were examined by R. F. Martell and A. L. DeSmet, 'A Diagnostic-Ratio Approach to Measuring Beliefs about the Leadership Abilities of Male and Female Managers', *Journal of Applied Psychology*, December 2001, pp. 1223–31; and R. A. Baron, G. D. Markman, and A. Hirsa, 'Perceptions of Women and Men as Entrepreneurs: Evidence for Differential Effects of Attributional Augmenting', *Journal of Applied Psychology*, October 2001, pp. 923–9.

15 See R. J. Hall, J. W. Workman and C. A. Marchioro, 'Sex, Task, and Behavioral Flexibility Effects on Leadership Perceptions', *Organizational Behavior and Human Decision Processes*, April 1998, pp. 1–32; and R. G. Lord, C. L. De Vader and G. M. Alliger, 'A Meta-Analysis of the Relation between Personality Traits and Leadership Perceptions: An Application of Validity Generalization Procedures', *Journal of Applied Psychology*, August 1986, p. 407.

16 Results from this study can be found in F. C. Brodbeck et al., 'Cultural Variation of Leadership Prototypes across 22 European Countries,' *Journal of Occupational and Organizational Psychology*, March 2000, pp. 1–29.

17 Results can be found in J. M. Kouzes and B. Z. Posner, *The Leadership Challenge* (San Francisco, CA: Jossey-Bass, 1995).

18 See D. Goleman, 'What Makes a Leader?', *Harvard Business Review*, November–December 1998, pp. 92–102.

19 A. M. Grant, F. Gino and D. A. Hofmann, 'Reversing the Extraverted Leadership Advantage: The role of Employee Proactivity', *The Academy of Management Journal*, vol. 54, no. 3, 2011, pp. 528–50.

20 Judge, T. A. and Cable, D. M. 2004. 'The Effect of Physical Height on Workplace Success and Income: Preliminary Test of a Theoretical Model', *Journal of Applied Psychology*, 89(3): 428–41.

21 Gender and the emergence of leaders was examined in A. H. Eagly and S. J. Karau, 'Gender and the Emergence of Leaders: A Meta-Analysis', *Journal of Personality and Social Psychology*, May 1991, pp. 685–710; and R. K. Shelly and P. T. Munroe, 'Do Women Engage in Less Task Behavior Than Men?', *Sociological Perspectives*, Spring 1999, pp. 49–67.

22 See A. H. Eagly, S. J. Karau and B. T. Johnson, 'Gender and Leadership Style among School Principals: A Meta-Analysis', *Educational Administration Quarterly*, February 1992, pp. 76–102.

23 Results can be found in A. H. Eagly, S. J. Karau and M. G. Makhijani, 'Gender and the Effectiveness of Leaders: A Meta-Analysis', *Psychological Bulletin*, January 1995, pp. 125–45.

24 V. L. Brescoll, 'Who Takes the Floor and Why: Gender, Power, and Volubility in Organizations', *Administrative Science Quarterly*, vol. 56, no. 4, pp. 622–41.

25 B. Groysberg, 'How STAR WOMEN Build Portable Skills', *Harvard Business Review*, vol. 86, no. 2, pp. 74–81.

26 I. M. Snaebjornsson and I. R. Edvardsson, 'Gender, Nationality and Leadership Style: A Literature Review', *International Journal of Business and Management*, vol. 8, no. 1, pp. 89–103.

27 R. Tait, *Roads to the Top: Career Decisions and Development of 18 Business Leaders* (Basingstoke: Macmillan, 1995), p. 21.

28 This research is summarised and critiqued by E. A. Fleishman, 'Consideration and Structure: Another Look at Their Role in Leadership Research', in *Leadership: The Multiple-Level Approaches*, eds F. Dansereau and F. J. Yammarino (Stamford, CT: JAI Press, 1998), pp. 51–60; and B. M. Bass, *Bass & Stogdill's Handbook of Leadership: Theory, Research, and Managerial Applications, third edition* (New York: Free Press, 1990), Ch. 24.

29 See V. H. Vroom, 'Leadership', in *Handbook of Industrial and Organizational Psychology*, ed. M. D. Dunnette (Chicago: Rand McNally, 1976).

30 Even the way Blake and Mouton cite research that contradicts their theory as supportive is sometimes highly questionable.

31 R. R. Blake and J. S. Mouton, 'A Comparative Analysis of Situationalism and 9,9 Management by Principle', *Organizational Dynamics*, Spring 1982, p. 23.

32 R. R. Blake and J. S. Mouton, 'A Comparative Analysis of Situationalism and 9,9 Management by Principle', *Organizational Dynamics*, Spring 1982, pp. 28–9. Also see R. R. Blake and J. S. Mouton, 'Management by Grid Principles or Situationalism: Which?', *Group & Organization Studies*, December 1981, pp. 439–55.

33 R. R. Blake and J. S. Mouton, 'A Comparative Analysis of Situationalism and 9,9 Management by Principle', *Organizational Dynamics*, Spring 1982, p. 21.

34 Excerpted from R. J. Grossman, 'Heirs Unapparent', *HR Magazine*, February 1999, p. 39.

35 See B. M. Bass, *Bass & Stogdill's Handbook of Leadership: Theory, Research, and Managerial Applications*, 3rd edn (New York: Free Press, 1990), ch. 20–25.

36 The relationships between the frequency and mastery of leader behaviour and various outcomes were investigated in F. Shipper and C. S. White, 'Mastery, Frequency, and Interaction of Managerial Behaviors Relative to Subunit Effectiveness', *Human Relations*, January 1999, pp. 49–66.

37 F. E. Fiedler, 'Job Engineering for Effective Leadership: A New Approach', *Management Review*, September 1977, p. 29.

38 Excerpted from C. Hymowitz, 'In the Lead: How Cynthia Danaher Learned to Stop Sharing and Start Leading', *The Wall Street Journal*, 16 March 1999, p. B1.

39 For more on this theory, see F. E. Fiedler, 'A Contingency Model of Leadership Effectiveness', in *Advances in Experimental Social Psychology*, vol. 1, ed. L. Berkowitz (New York: Academic Press, 1964); and F. E. Fiedler, *A Theory of Leadership Effectiveness* (New York: McGraw-Hill, 1967).

40 Additional information on situational control is contained in F. E. Fiedler, 'The Leadership Situation and the Black Box in Contingency Theories', in *Leadership Theory and Research: Perspectives and Directions*, eds M. M. Chemers and R. Ayman (New York: Academic Press, 1993), pp. 2–28.

41 See L. H. Peters, D. D. Hartke and J. T. Pohlmann, 'Fiedler's Contingency Theory of Leadership: An Application of the Meta-Analyses Procedures of Schmidt and Hunter', *Psychological Bulletin*, March 1985, pp. 274–85. The metaanalysis was conducted by C. A. Schriesheim, B. J. Tepper and L. A. Tetrault, 'Least Preferred Co-Worker Score, Situational Control, and Leadership Effectiveness: A Meta-Analysis of Contingency Model Performance Predictions', *Journal of Applied Psychology*, August 1994, pp. 561–73.

42 A review of the contingency theory and suggestions for future theoretical development is provided by R. Ayman, M. M. Chemers and F. Fiedler, 'The Contingency Model of Leadership Effectiveness: Its Levels of Analysis', in *Leadership: The Multiple-Level Approaches*, eds F. Dansereau and F. J. Yammarino (Stamford, CT: JAI Press, 1998), pp. 73–94; and R. P. Vecchio, 'Some Continuing Challenges for the Contingency Model of Leadership', in *Leadership: The Multiple-Level Approaches*, eds F. Dansereau and F. J. Yammarino (Stamford, CT: JAI Press, 1998), pp. 115–24.

43 Adapted from R. J. House and T. R. Mitchell, 'Path–Goal Theory of Leadership', *Journal of Contemporary Business*, Autumn 1974, p. 83. For more detail on this theory, see R. J. House, 'A Path–Goal Theory of Leader Effectiveness', *Administrative Science Quarterly*, September 1971, pp. 321–38.

44 See R. Hooijberg, 'A Multidirectional Approach toward Leadership: An Extension of the Concept of Behavioral Complexity', *Human Relations*, July 1996, pp. 917–46.

45 Based on A. Brown, 'Top of the Bosses', *International Management*, April 1994, pp. 26–31.

46 R. J. House, 'Path–Goal Theory of Leadership: Lessons, Legacy, and a Reformulated Theory', *Leadership Quarterly*, Autumn 1996, pp. 323–52.

47 A thorough discussion of this theory is provided by P. Hersey and K. H. Blanchard, *Management of Organizational Behavior: Utilizing Human Resources* 5th edn (Englewood Cliffs, NJ: Prentice-Hall, 1988).

48 A comparison of the original theory and its latent version is provided by P. Hersey and K. Blanchard, 'Great Ideas Revisited', *Training & Development*, January 1996, pp. 42–7.

49 Results can be found in J. R. Goodson, G. W. McGee and J. F. Cashman, 'Situational Leadership Theory', *Group & Organization Studies*, December 1989, pp. 446–61.

50 The first study was conducted by R. P. Vecchio, 'Situational Leadership Theory: An Examination of a Prescriptive Theory', *Journal of Applied Psychology*, August 1987, pp. 444–51. Results from the study of nurse executives can be found in C. Adams, 'Leadership Behavior of Chief Nurse Executives', *Nursing Management*, August 1990, pp. 36–9.

51 See D. C. Lueder, 'Don't Be Misled by LEAD', *Journal of Applied Behavioral Science*, May 1985, pp. 143–54; and C. L. Graeff, 'The Situational Leadership Theory: A Critical View', *Academy of Management Review*, April 1983, pp. 285–91.

52 For details on these different theories, see J. McGregor Burns, *Leadership* (New York: Harper & Row, 1978); N. M. Tichy and M. A. Devanna, *The Transformational Leader* (New York: John Wiley & Sons, 1986); J. M. Kouzes and B. Z. Posner, *The Leadership Challenge: How to Get Extraordinary Things Done in Organizations* (San Francisco, CA: Jossey-Bass, 1990); B. Nanus, *Visionary Leadership* (San Francisco, CA: Jossey-Bass, 1992); B. Bass and B. J. Avolio, 'Transformational Leadership: A Response to Critiques', in *Leadership Theory and Research: Perspectives and Directions*, eds M. M. Chemers and R. Ayman

(New York: Academic Press, 1993), pp. 49–80; B. Shamir, R. J. House and M. B. Arthur, 'The Motivational Effects of Charismatic Leadership: A Self-Concept Based Theory', *Organization Science*, November 1993, pp. 577–94; and H. B. Jones, 'Magic, Meaning and Leadership: Weber's Model and the Empirical Literature', *Human Relations*, June 2001, pp. 753–71.

53 B. Shamir, R. J. House and M. B. Arthur, 'The Motivational Effects of Charismatic Leadership: A Self-Concept Based Theory', *Organization Science*, November 1993, p. 578.

54 See www.execpc.com/~shepler/branson.

55 This discussion is based on D. A. Waldman and F. J. Yammarino, 'CEO Charismatic Leadership: Levels-of-Management and Levels-of-Analysis Effects', *Academy of Management Review*, April 1999, pp. 266–85.

56 B. Nanus, *Visionary Leadership* (San Francisco, CA: Jossey-Bass, 1992), p. 8.

57 See B. Nanus, *Visionary Leadership* (San Francisco, CA: Jossey-Bass, 1992); and W. L. Gardner and B. J. Avolio, 'The Charismatic Relationship: A Dramaturgical Perspective', *Academy of Management Review*, January 1998, pp. 32–58.

58 Based on and translated from J. Grobben, 'Tien voor twee', *Knack*, 2 February 1995, pp. 40–42.

59 See M. Kets de Vries, *The Leadership Mystique* (London: Financial Times–Prentice Hall, 2001).

60 See R. Khurana, 'The Curse of the Superstar CEO', *Harvard Business Review*, September 2002, pp. 60–66.

61 For an expanded discussion of this model, see S. Kerr and J. Jermier, 'Substitutes for Leadership: Their Meaning and Measurement', *Organizational Behavior and Human Performance*, December 1978, pp. 375–403.

62 See J. P. Howell, P. W. Dorfman and S. Kerr, 'Moderator Variables in Leadership Research', *Academy of Management Review*, January 1986, pp. 88–102.

63 Results can be found in P. M. Podsakoff, S. B. MacKenzie, M. Ahearne and W. H. Bommer, 'Searching for a Needle in a Haystack: Trying to Identify the Illusive Moderators of Leadership Behaviors', *Journal of Management*, no. 3, 1995, pp. 423–70.

64 For details of this study, see P. M. Podsakoff, S. B. MacKenzie and W. H. Bommer, 'Meta-Analysis of the Relationship between Kerr and Jermier's Substitutes for Leadership and Employee Job Attitudes, Role Perceptions, and Performance', *Journal of Applied Psychology*, August 1996, pp. 380–99.

65 An overall summary of servant leadership is provided by L. C. Spears, *Reflections on Leadership: How Robert K. Greenleaf's Theory of Servant-Leadership Influenced Today's Top Management Thinkers* (New York: John Wiley & Sons, 1995).

66 Based on T. Peters and N. Austin, *A Passion for Excellence* (Glasgow: Collins, 1985); C. D. Orth, H. E. Wilkinson and R. C. Benfari, 'The Manager's Role as Coach and Mentor', *Organizational Dynamics*, Spring 1987, pp. 66–74; R. D. Evered and J. C. Selman, 'Coaching and the Art of Management', *Organizational Dynamics*, Autumn 1989, pp. 16–32.

67 The scale used to assess readiness to assume the leadership role was taken from A. J. DuBrin, *Leadership: Research Findings, Practice, and Skills* (Boston, MA: Houghton Mifflin Company, 1995), pp. 10–11.

68 This exercise was based on an exercise in L. W. Mealiea, *Skills for Managers in Organizations* (Burr Ridge, IL: Irwin, 1994), pp. 96–7.

69 The introduction was quoted from L. W. Mealiea, *Skills for Managers in Organizations* (Burr Ridge, IL: Irwin, 1994), p. 96.

Chapter 16

Diagnosing and changing organisations

Learning Outcomes

When you finish studying the material in this chapter, you should be able to:

- ✓ discuss the external and internal forces that create the need for organisational change
- ✓ diagnose organisational problems and challenges
- ✓ describe Lewin's change model
- ✓ discuss Theory E and Theory O in the six dimensions of change
- ✓ demonstrate your familiarity with the four identifying characteristics of organisation development (OD)
- ✓ discuss the 10 reasons employees resist change
- ✓ identify alternative strategies for overcoming resistance to change

Opening Case Study: Oh, no! First place

When Jørgen Vig Knudstorp, the chief executive (CEO) of Lego, one of the world's leading toy manufacturers, was informed that Lego had regained first place in the annual analysis of Danish top corporate brands in 2010, his reaction was not as positive as you might think. Of course he thought it was great news, and that it was very well deserved of all the hard-working employees at Lego – but he was just not sure it would be good for the company. He was worried that it would make them rest on their laurels.

It was a rather surprising reaction from a company that took up the position as the top brand in toys almost by default for much of the 1990s. This position might have contributed to making the company complacent and stop listening to customers and fans of Lego products. The resulting crisis, starting in 2002, with deficits in the billions was very severe for the company and led to a change of management and a tough turn-around.

CEO Jørgen Vig Knudstorp said: 'To survive, the company needed to halt a sales decline, reduce debt, and focus on cash flow. It was a classic turnaround, and it required tight fiscal control and top-down management. At the same time, I had to build credibility. You can make a lot of things happen if you are viewed without suspicion, so I made sure I was approachable. In Danish, we have an expression that literally translates as "managing at eye level," but it means being able to talk to people on the factory floor, to engineers, to marketers – being at home with everyone. Once the company had regained the freedom to live and have a strategy, the management team set out to optimise the firm's value. In order to do that, we had to ask: Why does Lego Group exist? Ultimately, we determined the answer: to offer our core products, whose unique design helps children learn systematic, creative problem-solving – a crucial twenty-first-century skill. We also decided that we wanted to compete not by being the biggest but by being the best. Implementing a strategy of niche differentiation and excellence required a looser structure and a relaxation of the top-down management style we had imposed during the turnaround because the company needed empowered managers. For example, I stopped participating in weekly sales-management and capacity allocation choices and pushed decisions as far down the hierarchy as possible.

'Now we're in a third phase, pursuing organic growth. We are growing quite strongly across the world, but to continue building sales volume, we need to change the leadership style yet again, because the company's management became quite risk averse while focusing on survival. Now it needs to become opportunity driven, which requires taking greater calculated risks. In every phase of strategy change, we have been paving the way by moving leaders within the company and altering organisational structures and ways of working. For example, we set up a business area dedicated to direct-to-consumer sales, which is all about education and collaborative networks and is fundamentally different from selling to retailers, which is all about efficiency.'

After a few really tough years, the company was back on track, and has since regained not only its self-confidence but market share. Lego has in fact managed to defy the financial crisis in a significant manner. Profitability was restored in 2005 and sales slowly started growing. In 2009 the goals were 7 per cent annual growth over the next 15 years, and a doubling of capacity. The company has far outperformed these goals, doubling sales between 2009 and 2012, while at the same time increasing its net profit margin and only with a slight decrease in the return on equity, which was down to 66 per cent in 2012. Lego's operating margin has been rising throughout the financial crisis, from around 20 per cent to 34 per cent in 2012.

For discussion

Is it necessary for a company to experience crisis in order to change and survive in the long run?

Sources: Based on A. O'Connell, 'Lego CEO Jørgen Vig Knudstorp on Leading Through Survival and Growth', *Harvard Business Review*, 2009, vol. 87, no 1; K. Henriksen, 'Ny rolle som vækstgeneral', *Børsen*, 30 September 2009; T. Otkjær, 'Åh nej! Førstepladsen', *Berlingske Nyhedsmagasin*, 7 May 2009, p. 14; and Lego annual reports.

The story of Lego is about toys, strategies and money. The turnaround after 2002 has been little short of spectacular. Some commentators had argued that Lego had lost its way in a strategic sense (see the Lego case in chapter 11). There is little to support this assertion. If anything, Lego may have lost control over costs, but then regained it.

This story seems taken from the classic account of corporate growth developed by Larry Greiner in 1972. This is eminently readable to this day, but in brief, the idea proposed by Greiner is that as organisations grow larger they experience growing pains.[1] Figure 16.1 illustrates the idea in a very linear fashion. Phases of evolution alternate with phases of revolution. The recurring challenge for the growing organisation is to find a balance between control and autonomy. As an organisation grows it also tends to outgrow the control and management mechanisms put in place earlier. One thing to note about the Greiner model is that in real life the overall growth trajectory over time in not necessarily the straight upward sloping line in Figure 16.1, nor are the phases of crisis or revolution always of limited duration or impact.

This book would be mostly irrelevant if organisations did not change. The only use for it would be to make existing organisations perfect. Once perfect and assuming that the outside world also never changes, there would be very little left for managers to do. Fortunately, for textbook authors as well as managers, everything changes all the time, in small ways as well as on the large scale. Change outside the organisation is endemic and unavoidable. Whether the organisation chooses to respond to external change by adopting internal change will determine its survival.

The world outside the organisations front door is dynamic; change happens all the time and all over the place. Markets change, politicians come and go, technology advances, leaders have more or less bright ideas and managers do old things in new ways. These are just a few of the reasons why an organisation may contemplate change.

There are different reasons for doing exactly nothing. The outside events may not be lasting, making change risky. The people inside may not want change and managers or leaders may not have the courage to fight the opponents of the proposed change. Whether the opponents have a valid argument against change is a different story.

Even if outside events suggest that change is a sensible course of action, the organisation and its leaders still have to determine which change is appropriate given the situation. A direction has to be identified, its consequences mapped out, a decision made and then implemented. Part of implementation involves overcoming the inescapable resistance to change. Some leaders and managers manage to finish (to the extent that the process ever finishes) the change process by reflecting upon how it played out.

Understanding context, assessing the current organisational situation, identifying problems, challenges or whatever we choose to call situations that suggest a need for change is an important part of this chapter (and builds on the contingency approach proposed in Chapter 11). We start by describing the practices and structures of an organisation as an unfinished 'prototype', a notion

Figure 16.1 Growing Pains as Organisations Increase in Size

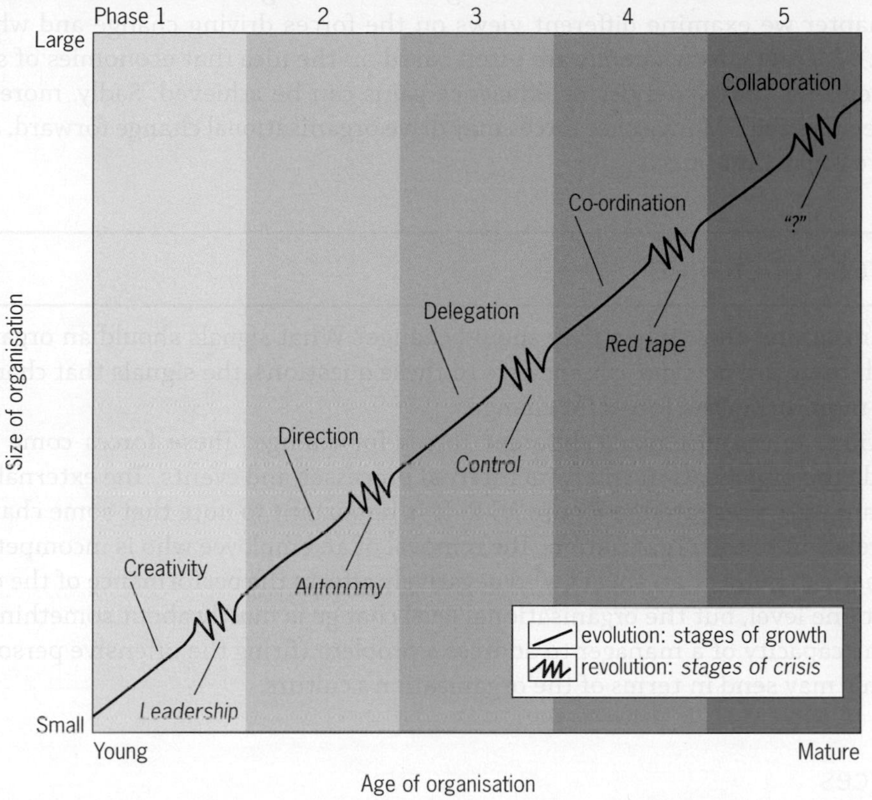

Source: Adapted from L. E. Greiner, 'Evolution and revolution as organizations grow', *Harvard Business Review*, July–August 1972, pp. 37–46.

proposed by Jeff Pfeffer and Bob Sutton. Their point is that finding optimal solutions through extensive analysis and argument is too time consuming and advocate using available knowledge to develop a series of quick and cheap prototypes. Build one, test it, assess performance, tweak the design if test results are poor, revise, test again, etc.[2]

An iterative approach to change is great but it still has to rely on information – obtained through diagnosis. The different aspects of diagnosis begin in the respective chapters of this book. Even if the prototype metaphor is appealing, it is not always possible to create the initial prototype, nor is it possible to modify it without some analysis. If a manager or leader realises that something is wrong in the organisation it needs investigation to establish the nature of the problem. The chapter headings in this book are a useful starting point. Is it a problem with a person, someone's values or attitudes? What about the organisation's communication patterns and culture, teams and so on?

Diagnosing these issues is no trivial matter. For example, the diagnosis may be that incentives in an organisation are perverse. On one level this is a perfectly fine diagnosis. What it may fail to do (in the case of incentives) is asking why perverse incentives remain in place despite being identified as bad.[3]

Once the diagnosis has identified what the problem is, the manager-leader can think about change processes. There are many models designed to facilitate change, some more complicated than others, some also more rough at the edges. We deal with the models in section 16.3 and with the challenges of employing them; section 16.4 covers the dangers involved in the change process; and section 16.5 shows how resistance to change can be managed and overcome.

In this chapter we examine different views on the forces driving change and why they occur (section 16.1). Mergers, for example, are often based on the idea that economies of scale or scope can be realised – or that synergies or efficiency gains can be achieved. Sadly, more than half of all mergers seem to fail.[4] Many other forces may drive organisational change forward, and we introduce the more important ones.

16.1 Forces of change

How do organisations know when they should change? What signals should an organisation look for? Although there are no clear-cut answers to these questions, the signals that change is needed are found by monitoring the forces for change.

Organisations encounter many different forces for change. These forces come from change events outside the organisation and from internal processes and events. The external and internal forces for change are presented in Figure 16.2. It is important to note that some changes are only marginal in relation to the organisation. The removal of an employee who is incompetent or otherwise problematic (a bully or an abuser who negatively affects the performance of the organisation) is a change at one level, but the organisational level change is mostly about something else, in this case about the capacity of a manager to address a problem (firing the offensive person) and about the signals this may send in terms of the organisation's culture.

External forces

Since **external forces for change** originate outside the organisation and have global effects, they may cause an organisation to question the essence of what business it is in and the process by which products and services are produced. There are four key external forces for change: demographic characteristics, technological advancements, market changes, and social and political pressures.

Demographic characteristics, including the age, gender, educational qualifications and location of the population, play an important role in driving change. These factors determine if it is possible to find the people an organisation needs to sustain itself or grow – or even change the focus of its activities.

Several trends are important from a European point of view. The average age of the European population is increasing, partly because people live longer and partly because birth rates are very low in some European countries. There is some degree of immigration into European countries leading to a more diverse workforce. More diversity is transmitted into the pool of current and potential employees and this needs to be taken into account when selecting organisational practices (see Chapter 9 on diversity). A third trend is that educational qualifications are increasing generally. This change, however, may take a long time to be reflected in the pool of employees. Clearly, the opportunity to replace existing, less-well-qualified staff with some that are more qualified and more productive (or that may be the assumption) is a force of change. Whether it is wise to be guided by this force is another matter.

Technological advances occurs when manufacturing and service organisations increasingly using technology as a means to improve productivity and market competitiveness. Manufacturing companies, for instance, have automated their operations with robotics; computerised numerical

Figure 16.2 External and Internal Forces for Change

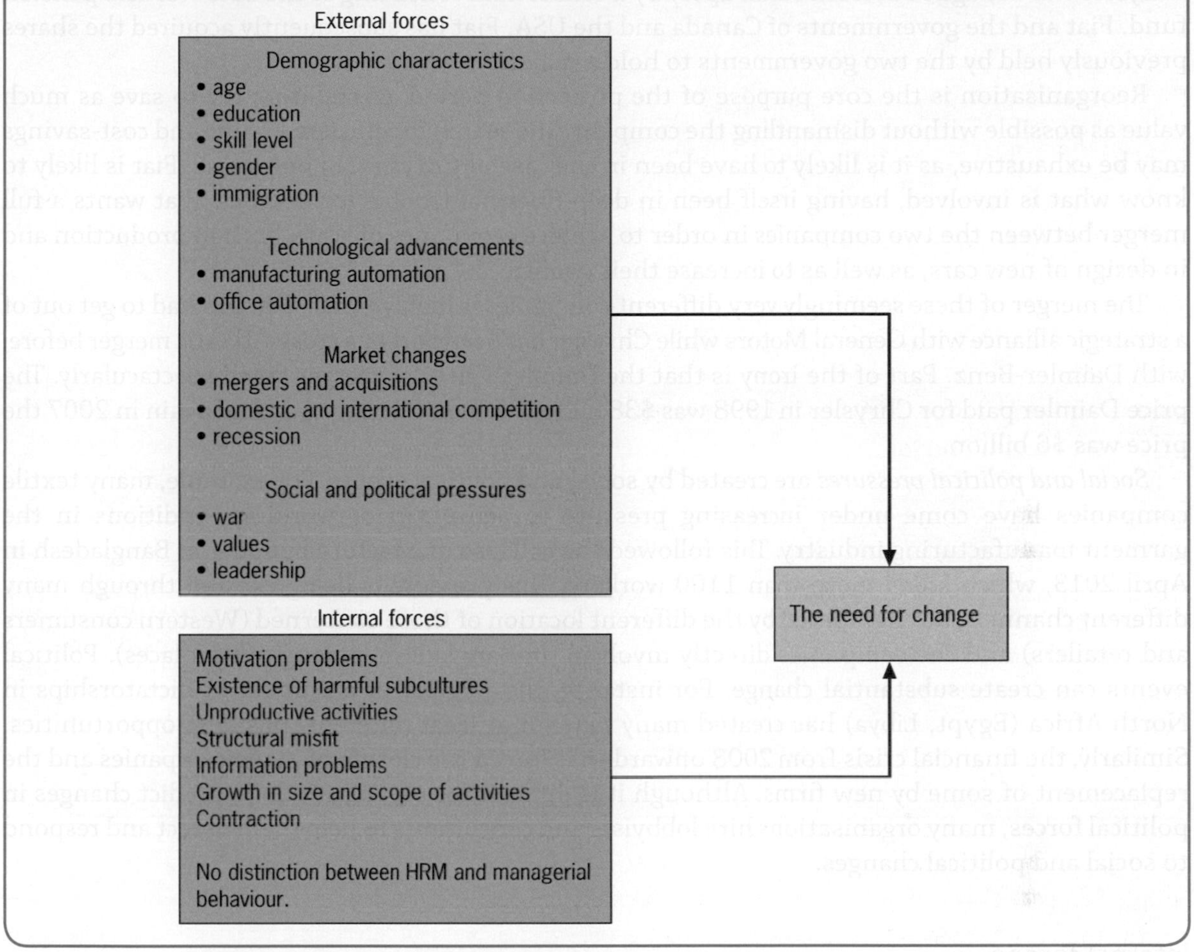

control (CNC), which is used for many manufacturing operations, and computer-aided design (CAD). CAD is a computerised process for designing and engineering products. Companies also use computer-integrated manufacturing (CIM). This highly technical process integrates product design with product planning, control and operations. In contrast to these manufacturing technologies, the service sector is using office automation. Office automation consists of a host of computerised technologies that are used to obtain, store, analyse, retrieve and communicate information.

IT-driven change feeds back into demographics, in the sense that traditional skills become less attractive unless they are matched by improved IT-skills. More generally, IT changes organisations because business models, marketing methods, service practices, sales channels and manufacturing operations all change.

Market changes and the emergence of a global economy is forcing companies to change the way they do business. For example, many Japanese companies have been forced to discontinue their jobs-for-life philosophy because of increased international competition.

The financial crisis since 2008 effectively bankrupted two of the big three US automakers, General Motors and Chrysler. The US taxpayers stepped in and both companies have since emerged from the special protection that exists in US bankruptcy law, known as 'chapter 11' protection. Chrysler was brought out from bankruptcy by a consortium consisting of the auto workers pension fund, Fiat and the governments of Canada and the USA. Fiat has subsequently acquired the shares previously held by the two governments to hold a majority.

Reorganisation is the core purpose of the protection period, as creditors try to save as much value as possible without dismantling the company. The search for efficiency gains and cost-savings may be exhaustive, as it is likely to have been in the case of Chrysler. In one sense, Fiat is likely to know what is involved, having itself been in deep financial trouble for decades. Fiat wants a full merger between the two companies in order to achieve economies of scale, both in production and in design of new cars, as well as to increase their quality.

The merger of these seemingly very different companies is highly ironic. Fiat has had to get out of a strategic alliance with General Motors while Chrysler has been part of a cross-Atlantic merger before, with Daimler-Benz. Part of the irony is that the Daimler-Chrysler merger failed spectacularly. The price Daimler paid for Chrysler in 1998 was $38 billion.[5] When Chrysler was sold again in 2007 the price was $6 billion.

Social and political pressures are created by social and political events. For example, many textile companies have come under increasing pressure to address poor working conditions in the garment manufacturing industry. This followed the collapse of a factory building in Bangladesh in April 2013, which killed more than 1100 workers. This pressure is being exerted through many different channels, but hampered by the different location of those concerned (Western consumers and retailers) and the companies directly involved (in Bangladesh, among other places). Political events can create substantial change. For instance, the collapse of a number of dictatorships in North Africa (Egypt, Libya) has created many new (or at least different) business opportunities. Similarly, the financial crisis from 2008 onwards has forced the closure of many companies and the replacement of some by new firms. Although it is difficult for organisations to predict changes in political forces, many organisations hire lobbyists and consultants to help them detect and respond to social and political changes.

Internal forces

Internal forces for change originate within the organisation and may be subtle. It is, however, easy to mix up forces and symptoms of the forces at work. Low job satisfaction, for example, may be caused by poor leadership, inappropriate structure or unreasonable demands, just to name a few. The outward signs are manifested in low productivity and conflict.

Size changes occur whenever an organisation grows or contracts in size; the forces for change are automatically activated. Whether it is the various crises that accompany growth, as detailed in Larry Greiner's organisational life cycle model above, or the reorganisations needed to keep an organisation efficient while it simultaneously shrinks in size, change will invariably be required. It can be structural or it can be about culture, motivating teams etc.

Human resource (HR) problems and prospects stem from employee perceptions of how they are treated at work and the match between individual and organisation needs and desires. Chapter 3 highlighted the relationship between an employee's unmet needs and job dissatisfaction. Dissatisfaction is a symptom of an underlying employee problem that should be addressed. Unusual or high levels of absenteeism and staff turnover also represent forces for change. Organisations might respond to these problems by reducing employees' role conflict, overload and ambiguity and also by removing the different stressors discussed in Chapter 9. Prospects for positive change stem from employee participation and suggestions. Managerial behaviour and decisions can cause excessive interpersonal conflict between managers and subordinates as discussed in Chapter 14. Both the manager and the employee may need interpersonal skills training or the two individuals may simply need to be separated. For example, one of the parties might be transferred to another department. Finally, inappropriate behaviour shown by leaders, such as inadequate direction or support, harassment or bullying, may require drastic measures.

16.2 Diagnosing the need for change

Momentous external events clearly warrant change. However, even though an external event is quickly identified as something that will require some form of response, the exact nature of that response may be far less clear. Suppose national wage levels have been creeping up. Higher wages erode international competitiveness and the natural managerial response is to look for cost savings. Telling employees to work harder and produce more is a possible solution. But lower costs may also be obtained by smarter organising. In both cases some degree of change is involved, but lower costs do not necessarily follow – at least not immediately.

Simply calling for cost cutting is equivalent to shooting fish in a barrel. As a short-term policy it may have quick effects. These may be overstated, however, as the assumptions and consequences become clear. Making people work harder in the short term, for example, may affect the working climate and overall productivity.

Rather than simply acknowledging that forces of change are in operation we propose a diagnostic approach as a prerequisite to organisational change. This is not necessarily the same as the over-analysis we noted at the beginning of this chapter, but an evidence-based approach to organisational change. The notion of an organisation as a prototype still holds but the diagnostic approach provides evidence for the iterations of the prototype and may help identify where the prototype is so broken that a new organisation may be a viable alternative.

For consistency we follow the sequence of chapters in the book and outline diagnostic approaches in the core areas of each chapter. For some topics we cover diagnosis in one section, e.g. for motivation (Chapters 5 and 6), for groups and teams (Chapters 7 and 8), and for structure and design (Chapters 10 and 11). In some instances diagnosis is about very simple checklists, in others it relies on distinct models, as in the case of teams (Chapters 7 and 8) and culture (Chapter 12).

Individual level analysis

Referring to the material covered in Chapters 2 and 3, diagnosis at the level of the individual may be initiated by demographics (age, gender, personal details, experience with company and elsewhere), job title and tasks assigned. Other items relevant for a diagnosis might be employee record (of attendance/absenteeism, success, failure, compliance, assistance, criticism, whistle blowing). Terms such as behaviour, attitudes and orientations can be used but they are very broad and not well specified.

These items may be useful for assessing an employee. They are highly personal and extremely sensitive as the process involves putting labels on people. These labels may be quite subjective and also highly selective. If they are put in writing, self-censorship is likely; if they are kept locked up in the minds of managers then selectivity is a risk. The reason they are even mentioned as part of a diagnosis is that it is important to keep in mind that this knowledge exists, regardless of whether it is accurate or complete, or indeed fair to the employee.

At the individual level, part of a diagnosis may also include the effectiveness and well-being of the individual employee. Effectiveness is about how the employee performs his or her assigned tasks. Echoing the discussion in Chapter 5 and 6 on motivation, this is straightforward for simple tasks but increasingly difficult as tasks become more complex and as one person's performance comes to depend on that of others, for example when working in a team. Some of the tools noted in the feedback section of Chapter 6, including information from 360-degree feedback, can contribute to an overall picture of individual job performance.

Some of the information a manager holds about an employee may come from regular 'performance reviews', whatever their worth. In the course of such interviews a manager may obtain valuable information about the employee. However, sharing of details is determined by trust between manager and employee. Written notes may be used, but their value depends on accuracy. It is possible that performance review notes may be more accurate if they are signed off by both parties to the review. As for their value, one has to keep in mind the scepticism of Sam Culbert, who thinks these reviews are a waste of time.[6]

Information flow diagnosis

Perception and communication are two sides of the same coin (see Chapter 4). Communication sends off signals and these are perceived by recipients. A diagnosis would seem simple: look at how people perceive, attribute and communicate internally and on whether outgoing signals are received and understood in the manner they were intended. Linked to such an analysis could be one that took stock of information asymmetries and the scope in the organisation for strategic behaviour (moral hazard and adverse selection).

Diagnosing perception, information processing and attributions has very limited precedent and we cannot offer a large body of supporting research that tells us how to do it. What an organisation might do is conduct experiments to see what happens. These might very well take place directly in the organisation. While not at all comparable in terms of the information focus in this section, Gary Latham' seminal paper on simple interventions that reduced employee theft from $1 million to zero (at 2000 employees equivalent to $500 per employee on average), shows how an experiment could be designed and implemented.[7]

Should anyone wish to set up a diagnostic experiment it might involve presenting or injecting the organisation with ambiguous information and then watching how it filters through the organisation, for example by tracking emails. There is, naturally, an ethical issue involved, if the objective or the consequence is that people reveal behaviour that has negative consequences for them. In other words, it is important not to use experiments as entrapment mechanisms. Needless to say, this also requires employees skilled in this type of laboratory work.

Diagnosing motivation problems

Motivation is a cornerstone of any manger's effort to do his or her job, or it ought to be. However, despite what we know about motivational instruments, managers frequently ignore the evidence and instead choose unsuitable incentives. The problem of unsuitable incentives has long been known. The classic argument in Steve Kerr's 1975 article is that an organisation gets exactly what it pays for.[8]

Going through all the many motivation models identified in Chapter 5 and 6 for the purpose of identifying where an organisation makes a mistake is extremely cumbersome and of limited practical value. With this approach ruled out, we propose that a suitable starting point for a motivational diagnosis is the identification of four 'bad' incentive systems, as discussed by Joe Magee and colleagues.[9] While their point is an exploration of why bad incentives are adopted, their identification of the four 'bad' ones is a good starting point for diagnosing motivation.

Overemphasis on financial incentives is based on the idea of an extrinsic incentive bias that leads managers to overemphasise pay, promotions and job security, and to underemphasise freedom, respect, opportunities for learning new information and the development of new skills.[10] Together these elements serve to undermine intrinsic motivation factors.

If extrinsic motivation instruments must be used (it could be an industry norm, for example, and hard to avoid), then there is a risk of ending up with too weak incentives, possibly in an effort to manage the worst side-effects of bad extrinsic incentives. This is expectancy theory (Chapter 6) in action. The outcome of incentives depend both on their efficacy (belief that tasks can be accomplished) and value (reward may be more or less valued by the employee). Only when both are high and not undermined by contingency (the outcome to reward coupling) will an extrinsic incentive work.

Organisations sometimes manage to create perverse incentives. The power company executive rewarded based on how much power sold gets a perverse incentive, since nothing he or she does in the short-term influences sales. The weather does have an influence, but executives have little control in that area. Similarly, if the great football player Lionel Messi was punished financially for every pass that ended up with an opponent, it is likely that he would make fewer passes.

The final type of problematic incentives identified by Magee and colleagues involves incentives clashing with organisational culture (see Chapter 12). The culture in an organisation may be very carefully cultivated, for example to favour teamwork or innovation. However, incentives based on individual performance may work to render most or all of the effort put into culture more or less irrelevant.

A broad overview of all remuneration practices, with details of who gets exactly what in terms of pay, bonuses and benefits (company cars, golf club membership etc.) and the criteria upon which each element is given will provide roughly one-third of a diagnosis. The second third is an equally detailed statement of intrinsic motivation efforts. Some may be documented in the organisation's HR practice, but only as far as line managers are bound to such formalities. If they are not, this may have to be discovered through interviews and surveys. The final third of a diagnosis in the motivation area is an assessment of the information gathered, asking the sometimes awkward question 'Are the practices employed conducive to motivation?' Sometimes the norms in an industry might give very little room for alternative thinking.

Groups and teams

To address the need for change thinking we argue that the team diagnostic survey (TDS) developed by Wageman, Hackman and Lehman in 2005 is a very useful tool. Their survey builds on the research of J. Richard Hackman and his model of team effectiveness. In this model, teams are evolving social systems that are partly autonomous and with results of varying effectiveness.[11] The model identifies five conditions that increase the likelihood of good performance, even though there is no guarantee of this outcome (see Chapter 8 for a summary of the model).

The finished TDS contains 10 sections. Two are descriptive (of the team and its members), two are about the team's effectiveness and six cover the five conditions for team performance. Items are mixed so that they do not follow the sequence given here. Most items use a five-point scale, from highly inaccurate to highly accurate, occasionally reverse scored.[12]

Using the TDS is not simple. It is a fully fledged survey instrument and it can only be applied if the resources to do so are present. This is not just a matter of administering an instrument that comes off a shelf. The data must be collected and analysed. Even though the instrument is available free and online, using it requires disclosure of the users' identities.[13]

Table 16.1 A Sample of Individual and Group Level Conflict Diagnostic Questions[15]

1	How much relationship tension is there in your work group?
2	How often do people get angry while working in your work group?
3	How much emotional conflict is there in your work group?
4	How much conflict of ideas is there in your work group?
5	How frequently do you have disagreements within your work group about the task of the project you are working on?
6	How often do people in your work group have conflicting opinions about the project you are working on?
7	How often are there disagreements about who should do what in your work group?
8	How much conflict is there in your work group about task responsibilities?
9	How often do you disagree about resource allocation in your work group?

What the TDS does not do is examine conflict in groups and teams. It might well capture some existing conflicts but that is not its primary purpose. However, given the ideas about constructive and destructive conflict discussed in Chapter 9, looking at levels of conflict in teams might contribute to team diagnosis.[14] The point about Karen Jehn's conflict model is that it distinguishes between three dimensions of group conflict: relationship, task and process. Despite the fact that the survey involved in Jehn's work is designed for research, a selection of its questions gives an idea about the types of diagnostic questions that might be developed for an applied survey instrument (see Table 16.1).

Organisational climate

The heading 'organisational climate' is used to cover not just the idea of climate but also conflict, diversity, stress and burnout. In one sense, however, these are highly diverse items and up to a point they should be diagnosed individually, not least because they each have their own literature attached.

Diagnosis of organisational climate can be based on the eight dimensions identified in Table 9.1.[16] These were distilled from a much longer list of dimensions found in the literature, some 80 in total. The distillation included removal of all objective dimensions such as absenteeism, disputes and productivity. Similarly dimensions referring to structure and evaluation were removed. The result was eight dimensions, which were then tested and validated by a double survey using a 40-question survey instrument, all of which are listed in the paper by Koys and DeCotiis. This type of survey could be a generally useful overview of what the climate is like in any given organisation.

Some minimal level of conflict is held to be good, as indicated in section 9.2. The challenge is to keep it in the range where the conflict is appropriate and the outcomes positive. The general climate survey items can give an initial idea about conflict (items such as autonomy, cohesion, trust, pressure and fairness). Other sources of data on areas of conflict can be records of grievance held by the personnel/HR department and similar records pertaining to diversity and stress.

Relying on archival data for documentation of climate will, however, only produce a diagnosis as good as the original data. The assumption that all relevant data on conflict, diversity, stress and burnout are accurately recorded may need to be tested in some way. Recorded incidents could be followed up and investigated and the parties interviewed. Even here, however, data may be a problem. If there is no archival starting point, then there can be no follow-up. Indeed, if follow-up is careful and methodical and has consequences for anyone in the organisation, victims may be discouraged from using formal systems.

Critical thinking

Can conflicts, negative stereotyping, stress and burnout pass under the managerial radar?

Structure and design

Diagnosing whether the organisational structure is in need of change raises the diagnosis to a higher level, not least because structure is connected to everything else, and not just to the inside of the organisation. It is connected to its environment through the nature of that environment and through the strategies pursued. For diagnosis we suggest that a thorough description of the structure, technology, strategy and environment is the best starting point. All other aspects can in principle be included in the diagnosis, notwithstanding the various sections above. Such a very structured approach has been devised by Richard Burton and Børge Obel in a series of books and supported by an expert system that can provide indications of whether or not there are misfits between various elements in the organisation.[17] This approach has as one of its most valuable elements a rigid and long list of diagnostic questions that must all be answered for the system to produce a report on misfits. One of the great advantages of this system (which is computer-based and bears the name 'OrgCon') is that it asks the same detailed questions about any organisation. Even if the questions are sometimes annoyingly hard to answer when an organisation is viewed from outside, the benefit is that the questions are rigorous and their number minimised to keep the model simple.

Diagnostic questions for structure and design may also simply plod through the various elements identified in Chapters 10 and 11, starting with the basics, the hierarchy of authority, the coordination of effort, the division of labour and the common goal. What exactly describes the hierarchy, the chain of command and the distribution of decision rights (who is allowed to do what?). Similarly, diagnostic questions can draw out how co-ordination happens (or is supposed to happen) by looking at formalisation, standardisation (of work, output, skills and norms), and differentiation (horizontal and vertical).

The organisational form and type needs to be identified. There is sometimes confusion about the different terms in the literature, for example the relationship between a divisional organisation and the organisational types of Henry Mintzberg (see Chapter 10). Apart from the four classic forms (simple, functional, divisional and matrix), type may be indicated by key parameters such as the degree of formalisation and of centralisation. It may also be possible to use these parameters to get an idea about which of the seven of Mintzberg's types is in front of us.

At this point we are still mostly interested in describing the organisation. The diagnosis of fit comes next, but it requires more answers. Diagnosis of the environment requires answers to questions about the number of different factors characterising the environment as well as the rate at which they change. Diagnosis of strategy is similarly important. Trying to understand an organisation's strategy may, at least from a diagnostic point of view, be aided by comparing an organisations claims and actions to one or more strategic archetypes. Several authors have developed these. Michael Porter distinguishes between 'cost leaders', 'differentiators' and 'focus', while Miles and Snow proposed 'defenders', 'analysers', 'prospectors' and 'reactors'.

There are many similarities between a cost leader and a defender, primarily a strong focus on cost control and efficiency. The challenge is to determine which type of strategy any given organisation is following. For this, diagnostic questions about technology might help. While not directly comparable, the three technology models presented in Chapter 11 lead directly to diagnostic questions about the nature of the technology in use (for example, how does co-ordination take place), and about the fit between the actual and ideal organisational design, insofar as one can be identified.

Culture

The problem with organisational culture is that it is invisible, not just in a physical sense but also in terms of any recordable communication within the organisation or coming from it. This is the reason most models of culture in organisations place the culture itself as somehow shielded from inquisitive eyes, in the middle of something that looks like an onion, or at the bottom of a floating iceberg.

The most widely used diagnosis of organisational culture is based on the competing values framework presented in Chapter 12. Originally developed in the early 1980s by Robert Quinn and colleagues, the procedure for using the associated survey instrument is firmly established.[18] Using six items with four alternative answers, respondents must allocate a total of 100 points (or per cent) to the four alternatives. For the second item, for example, on organisational leadership, the second option is: 'The leadership in the organisation is generally considered to exemplify entrepreneurship, innovation and risk taking'.

The net result is scores on four axes, which in turn separate the four distinct cultural types of the model, each in its own quadrant in the two-axis diagram that is widely used to present the model. The model is very simple to apply.[19]

There are many alternatives to the competing values framework. One overview counted 48 different instruments, but remained unsure about the degree of overlap between them.[20] The same analysis also suggested that the situation might well determine which approach was used. For educational and training purposes, however, we argue that the competing values framework is well suited.

16.3 Models and dynamics of planned change

The diagnostic approach is part of a change sequence that has been labelled 'ANALYSE-THINK-CHANGE'.[21] Despite the clear implication of the previous section that diagnosis is very possible, there are limits to what can be analysed in terms of information availability, cost and analytical capacity within an organisation. When that limit is reached, more reliance may have to be placed on the prototype-tinkering mentioned at the beginning of this chapter. Partly related to limits of an analytical approach is the idea that instead of 'ANALYSE-THINK-CHANGE', we need 'SEE-FEEL-CHANGE'.[22] As proposed by John Kotter and Dan Cohen, the key to successful change is emotions. Even if 'analyse-think' is less 'emotional' than 'see-feel', the essential point about diagnosis is that it helps provide not just the facts but also evidence so compelling that an emotional response is triggered. Managing this process has long been seen as one of the main challenges of organisational change. Researchers and managers alike have tried to identify effective ways to manage the change process. This section sheds light on their insights. After discussing Lewin's change model, we review different types of organisational change and Kotter's eight stages for leading organisational change.

Lewin's change model

Most theories of organisational change originated from the landmark work of social psychologist Kurt Lewin. Lewin developed a three-stage model of planned change which explained how to initiate, manage and stabilise the change process.[23] The three stages are unfreezing, changing and refreezing. Before reviewing each stage, it is important to highlight the assumptions that underlie this model:[24]

- The change process involves learning something new, as well as discontinuing some current attitudes, behaviours and organisational practices.
- Change will not occur unless there is motivation to change. This is often the most difficult part of the change process.
- People are the hub of all organisational changes. Any change, whether in terms of structure, group processes, reward systems or job design, requires individuals to change.
- Resistance to change is found even when the goals of change are highly desirable.
- Effective change requires reinforcing new types of behaviour, attitudes and organisational practices.

Stage 1: Unfreezing. The focus of this stage is to create the motivation to change. In so doing, individuals are encouraged to replace old behaviours and attitudes with those desired by management. Professionals can begin the unfreezing process by disconfirming the usefulness or appropriateness of employees' present behaviours or attitudes. In other words, employees need to become dissatisfied with the old way of doing things (they may already be dissatisfied).

Benchmarking is a process by which a company compares its performance with that of high-performing organisations and can be used to help 'unfreeze' an organisation. Benchmarking describes the overall process by which a company compares its performance with that of other companies, then learns by the strongest-performing process how companies achieve their results.[25] For example, one company discovered through its benchmarking that their costs to develop a computer system were twice as high compared to the best companies in the industry, and the time it took to get a new product to market was four times longer than the benchmarked organisations. These data about performing organisations were ultimately used to unfreeze employees' attitudes and motivate people to change the organisation's internal processes in order to remain competitive.[26] Organisations also need to devise ways to reduce the barriers to change during this stage.

Stage 2: Changing. Because change involves learning, this stage entails providing employees with new information, new behavioural models or new ways of looking at things. The purpose is to help employees learn new concepts or points of view. Role models, mentors, experts, benchmarking results and training are all useful mechanisms to facilitate change. Experts recommend that it is best to convey the idea that change is a continuous learning process rather than a one-off event.

Stage 3: Refreezing. Change is stabilised during refreezing by helping employees to integrate the changed behaviour or attitude into their normal way of doing things. This is accomplished by first giving employees the chance to exhibit the new types of behaviour or attitudes. Once exhibited, positive reinforcement is used. Additional coaching and modelling are used at this point to reinforce the stability of the change.[27]

Critical thinking

If change is more or less the only constant, as many OB scholars have stated, how can you still make use of the framework proposed by Lewin?

Complexity, cost and uncertainty

A useful three-way typology of change is displayed in Figure 16.3.[28] This typology is generic because it relates to all sorts of change, including both administrative and technological changes. Adaptive

Figure 16.3 A Generic Typology of Organisational Change

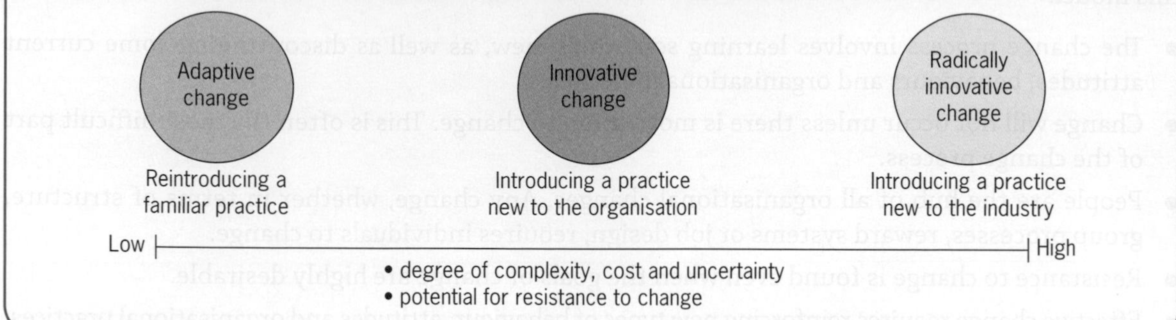

change is lowest in complexity, cost and uncertainty. It involves repeating the implementation of a change in the same organisational unit later on or imitating a change that was implemented by a different unit. For example, an adaptive change for a supermarket would be to introduce two shifts as a response to an external regulation of opening hours. The supermarket's central accounting department might already use longer working hours during end-of-year preparation of the annual report. Adaptive changes are not particularly threatening to employees because they are familiar and occur at regular intervals.

Innovative changes fall midway on the continuum of complexity, cost and uncertainty. An experiment with flexible work schedules by a farm supply warehouse qualifies as an innovative change if it entails modifying the way other firms in the industry already use it. Unfamiliarity, greater uncertainty, makes fear of change a problem with innovative changes.

At the high end of the continuum of complexity, cost and uncertainty are the radically innovative changes. Changes of this sort are the most difficult to implement and tend to be the most threatening to managerial trust and employee job security. They can tear the fabric of an organisation's culture. Resistance to change tends to increase as changes go from adaptive to innovative to radically innovative.

Dimensions of change

Another way of distinguishing different types of change is to consider how change methods are implemented. Michael Beer and Nitin Nohria call these different approaches Theory E and Theory O of change.[29] These approaches are guided by very different assumptions about the purpose of and means for change. Theory E stands for economic value. The creation of economic value is the main purpose. The focus of theory E is on formal structure and systems. Change is driven from the top and consultants play a major role in the process. Financial incentives are important. Change is planned and programmatic.

In Theory O, change is based on organisational capability. The goal is to develop organisational culture through individual and organisational learning. Its focus is on the development of a high-commitment culture. Consultants and financial incentives are not important in the change. The process is not planned, but emergent.

Table 16.2 summarises the E and O approaches to organisational change. Theory E and O differ from each other according to six dimensions: goals, leadership, focus, process, reward system and use of consultants. Beer and Nohria argue that both theories have validity, but that they also have costs, often unintended. Theory E is more able to capture attention and focus the change on a

Table 16.2 Dimensions of Change

Dimensions of change	Theory E	Theory O	Theories E and O combined
Goals	Maximise shareholder value	Develop organisational capabilities	Explicitly confront the tension between economic value and organisational capability
Leadership	Manage change from the top down	Encourage participation from the bottom-up	Set direction from the top and engage people below
Focus	Emphasise structure and systems	Build up corporate culture: employees' behaviour and attitudes	Focus simultaneously on the hard (structures and systems) and the soft (corporate culture)
Process	Plan and establish programmes	Experiment and evolve	Plan for spontaneity
Reward system	Motivate through financial incentives	Motivate through commitment – use pay as fair exchange	Use incentives to reinforce change but not drive it
Use of consultants	Consultants analyse problems and shape solutions	Consultants support management in shaping their own solutions	Consultants are expert resources who empower employees

Source: Reprinted by permission of *Harvard Business Review*. Exhibit from 'Cracking the Code of Change', by M. Beer and N. Nohria, May–June 2000, Copyright © 2000 by the Harvard Business School Publishing Corporation; all rights reserved.

single direction. It is usually aligned with the distribution of power in the organisation.[30] It can be fast and, therefore, it is appropriate in times of crisis. Theory E has, however, several drawbacks. One of the most important is that top management may ignorant of why things are organised in certain ways and of the capabilities and resources at the front line, where the impacts of changes are felt. This may create large short-term losses that are difficult to recover.

Theory O is more sensitive to local contingencies. It is suitable for online experimentation and learning. It is more likely to satisfy needs for autonomy and control. A major cost of Theory O is the slowness of the implementation process. The pre-existing culture and technology may limit the implementation process as well. Theory O is not well suited for strategic or corporate change. It can be insufficiently bold or visionary.

As Theory E and O both have their advantages and liabilities, it is the challenge to resolve the tension between E and O in a way the benefits are optimised and the liabilities limited (see Table 16.2).

OB in Real Life

Asda

One company that exemplifies the reconciliation of the hard and soft approaches is Asda, the UK grocery chain that CEO Archie Norman took over in 1991, when the retailer was nearly bankrupt. Norman laid off employees, flattened the hierarchy, and sold unprofitable businesses. Yet, during his tenure, Asda also became famous for its atmosphere of trust and openness. Consider the way in which Norman dealt with the tension between E and O for two of the six dimensions of change:

Leadership. From day one, Norman declared Asda would adopt a low-pricing strategy, and Norman unilaterally determined that change would begin by having two experimental store formats up and running within six months. He decided to shift power from the headquarters to the stores, declaring: 'I want everyone to be close to the stores. We must love the stores to death; that is our business.' But even from the start, there was an O quality to Norman's leadership style. As he put in his first speech: 'First, I am forthright, and I like to argue. Second, I want to discuss issues as colleagues. I am looking for your advice and your agreement.' Norman encouraged dialogue with employees and customers through colleague and customer circles. He set up a 'Tell Archie' programme, so that people could voice their concerns and ideas.

Making way for opposite leadership styles was also an essential ingredient to Norman's – and Asda's – success. This was most clear in Norman's willingness to hire Allan Leighton shortly after he took over. Leighton eventually became deputy chief executive. Norman and Leighton shared the same E and O values, but they had completely different personalities and styles. Norman, cool and reserved, impressed people with the power of his mind – his intelligence and business acumen. Leighton, who is warmer and more people-oriented, worked on employees' emotions with the power of his personality. As one employee told us, 'People respect Archie, but they love Allan.' Norman was the first to credit Leighton with having helped create emotional commitment to the new Asda. While it might be possible for a single individual to embrace opposite leadership styles, accepting an equal partner with a very different personality makes it easier to capitalise on those styles. Leighton certainly helped Norman reach out to the organisation. Together, they held quarterly meetings with store managers to hear their ideas, and they supplemented those meetings with impromptu talks.

Focus. Norman's immediate actions followed both the E goal of increasing economic value and the O goal of transforming culture. On the E side, Norman focused on structure. He removed layers of hierarchy at the top of the organisation, fired the financial officer who had been part of Asda's disastrous policies, and decreed a wage freeze for everyone – management and workers alike. But from the start, the O strategy was an equal part of Norman's plan. He bought time for all this change by warning the markets that financial recovery would take three years. Norman later said he spent 75 per cent of his early months at Asda as the company's human resource director, making the organisation less hierarchical, more egalitarian and more transparent. Both Norman and Leighton were keenly aware that they had to win hearts and minds. As Norman put it to workers: 'We need to make Asda a great place for everyone to work.'[31]

For discussion

Much has changed since the days of Archie Norman. He has been in and out of the House of Commons and in 2009 was appointed chairman of ITV and in 2013 also became non-executive chairman of Lazard London. Asda was acquired by Wal-Mart in 1999 and has since had both ups and downs, including an involvement with certain products that turned out to have a high horsemeat, rather than beef, content. Track the changes and classify them.

Design and development approach

The typology of Theory E and O resembles the distinction between the design approach and the organisation development approach. Management methods such as business process reengineering, total quality management (Chapter 11), lean production and balanced score-card are typical design methods.[32] They are driven from the top; they are based on a clear-cut model that is implemented according to a plan. Organisation development methods, like teamwork and participative management, focus on a bottom-up approach. Members of the organisation are involved in the change process. There are no standardised solutions. Several perspectives are possible and the direction of the change evolves along the change process.

Kotter's design approach for leading organisational change

John Kotter, a guru in the field of leadership and change management, believes that organisational change typically fails because senior management commit one or more of the following errors. They:[33]

- Fail to establish a sense of urgency about the need for change.
- Fail to create a powerful enough guiding coalition that is responsible for leading and managing the change process.
- Fail to establish a vision that guides the change process.
- Fail to effectively communicate the new vision.
- Fail to remove obstacles that impede the accomplishment of the new vision.
- Fail to systematically plan for and create short-term wins. Short-term wins represent the achievement of important results or goals.
- Declare victory too soon. This derails the long-term changes in infrastructure that are frequently needed to achieve a vision.
- Fail to anchor the changes in the organisation's culture. It takes years for long-term changes to become embedded within an organisation's culture.

Kotter recommends that organisations should follow eight sequential steps to overcome these problems (see Table 16.3).

Each of the steps shown in Table 16.3 is associated with one of the **fundamental errors** just discussed. These steps also subsume Lewin's model of change. The first four steps represent Lewin's 'unfreezing' stage. Steps 5, 6 and 7 represent 'changing' and step 8 corresponds to 'refreezing'. Kotter's research underscores that it is ineffective to skip steps and that successful organisational change is 70 to 90 per cent leadership and only 10 to 30 per cent management. Senior managers are, thus, advised to focus on leading rather than managing change (also see Chapter 15).[34]

The presentation of Kotter's eight steps gives the impression that change is always a logical, step-by-step process that can be managed with a rational programme. This approach is based on assumptions that are very similar to the design approach of change or the Theory E perspective. Change is not always a simple and linear process. It is often messy, going through periods of ebb and flow that repeat themselves.[35] Organisational politics often interfere and can disturb the change profoundly (see Chapter 14). Therefore, the stepwise approach of J. P. Kotter oversimplifies the complex nature of change. Anyone working with change must realise that:

- Change can be emergent, evolving through a series of ongoing adaptations and alterations. Without deliberate dramatic interventions, the accommodations and experiments can result, over time, in striking organisational changes.
- Even when change takes place according to a deliberate, top-driven orchestration like the design approach or Theory E, change can still be iterative, politicised, going backwards and forward. Every change is different and every organisation has its own idiosyncrasies.

Table 16.3 Sequential Steps to Leading Organisational Change

Step	Description
1 Establish a sense of urgency	Unfreeze the organisation by creating a compelling reason for why change is needed
2 Create the guiding coalition	Create a cross-functional, cross-level group of people with enough power to lead the change
3 Develop a vision and strategy	Create a vision and strategic plan to guide the change process
4 Communicate the change vision	Create and implement a communication strategy that consistently communicates the new vision and strategic plan
5 Empower broad-based action	Eliminate barriers to change and use target elements of change to transform the organisation. Encourage risk taking and creative problem solving
6 Generate short-term wins	Plan for and create short-term 'wins' or improvements. Recognise and reward people who contribute to the wins
7 Consolidate gains and produce more change	The guiding coalition uses credibility from short-term wins to create more change. Additional people are brought into the change process as change cascades throughout the organisation. Attempts are made to reinvigorate the change process
8 Anchor new approaches in the culture	Reinforce the changes by highlighting connections between new behaviours and processes and organisational success. Develop methods to ensure leadership development and succession

Source: Based on J. P. Kotter, *Leading Change* (Boston, MA: Harvard Business School Press, 1996).

Nevertheless, Kotter's eight-step approach is based on a multitude of typical design-oriented organisational changes. It provides a useful set of points of attention that professionals can take into account when they introduce a top-driven change.

> **!** Critical thinking
>
> Can you think of a situation where the very generic eight-step change model proposed by Kotter would not be applicable?

16.4 Danger: Change in progress!

The study of change involves more than the different approaches of organisational change, like the design approach or organisation development methods. The field of organisational change is far from mature in understanding dynamics and effects of process, content and context. Many organisational studies often analyse change from one of these perspectives, which gives only a partial view of the complex processes that organisational change involves.[36] Because of the complex nature and dynamic of change, generalisations are hard to sustain over time. Pettigrew, Woodman and Cameron[37] discern several interconnected analytical issues in which the study of organisational change remains underdeveloped.

To understand the nature of change, it is important to notice the context in which the change takes place. Innovations in the IT industry may be much faster than the rate and trajectory of change in health care. Change also involves different levels of analysis. These range from the individual level, through group and organisational level (the inner context) to the industry level, national level and the global level (the outer context). To understand fully those processes, it is important to investigate the terrain around the stream that shapes these processes, which is, in turn, shaped by these processes. The culture of an organisation (see Chapter 12) and its competitive environment are but two of the many important contextual characteristics that influence the way in which change processes are implemented.

Time, history, change and outcomes

Organisational changes should also be studied on a longitudinal basis. Recommendations on how to manage change depend partly on the change history of an organisation. Mergers and acquisitions can have important effects on the way in which future changes are perceived by the remaining employees. Successful or unsuccessful track records can influence the implementation of new changes. Historical investigation of industrial or institutional change can provide valuable information about evolutions in industrial sectors and organisational settings.

Although many studies have tried to answer what makes change successful, the link between change capacity and organisational performance is rarely made. It is not because a change is successful that it contributes substantially to the performance of the organisation. Measuring organisational performance is also a tricky enterprise. The business literature's tendency to focus on a small sample of high performers at a single point in time is a dangerous way of looking at performance. What is a successful company today can be a failing organisation tomorrow. One of the rare studies that have attempted to link change practices to firm performance is a European study by Pettigrew and Whipp[38] that examined the process of managing strategic and operational change in four mature industry and service sectors of the UK economy. The scholars chose a pair of firms in each of the four sectors. Each pair was made up of a higher and a lower performer in the same market. From a 30-year time series study, Pettigrew and Whipp were able to identify in what way the high performers were different from the lesser performers. The high performers:

- Conducted environmental assessment more intensely.
- Led change.
- Linked strategic and operational change.
- Managed their human resources as assets and liabilities.
- Managed coherence in the overall process of competition and change.

Episodic or continuous change

There are a number of important but difficult questions related to the temporal character of change. Where does a change agent begin a given change initiative? What pace of change is appropriate in different settings to meet local objectives? How can you keep the organisation receptive to change, knowing that transformations demand a lot of energy and often result in change fatigue? The answer to these questions is important in order to contribute to the theory and practice of change receptivity, customisation, sequencing and pacing.

In addition, the difference between episodic and continuous change is important.[39] **Episodic change** refers to change initiatives that are infrequent, discontinuous and intentional. Change is an occasional interruption or divergence from equilibrium. It is seen as a failure of the organisation to adapt its deep structure to a changing environment. This is the classic approach of many change studies. But there is another important type of change, **continuous change**, where organisations are emergent and self-organising. Change is constant, evolving and cumulative. Change is a pattern of endless modifications in work processes and social practice. Numerous small accommodations cumulate and amplify. Continuous change is studied far less than episodic change. The study of continuous change is difficult and time-consuming. However, continuous change is a major phenomenon in transformations that needs our attention as much as episodic change. Sometimes, it is argued that an ideal form of change is a combination of episodic and continuous change.

Finally, Pettigrew, Woodman and Cameron also refer to the investigation of international and cross-cultural comparisons in research on organisational change and to the engagement between academics and practitioners as important challenges for future research in organisational change.

It is clear that the complexity of organisational change is too high to summarise the essentials in one or two typologies of change or a few how-to-do checklists. There still remain a large number of questions to be answered as to the nature, the context and the generalisability of change patterns. The challenges discussed in this section map the guidelines of which scholars and practitioners alike should be aware when they address change issues.

16.5 Managing resistance to change

We are all creatures of habit. It is difficult for people to try new ways of doing things. It is precisely because of this basic human characteristic that most employees do not have enthusiasm for change in the workplace. Rare is the professional who does not have several stories about carefully cultivated changes that 'died on the vine' because of resistance to change. It is important for organisations to learn to manage resistance because failed change efforts are costly. Costs include decreased employee loyalty, lowered probability of achieving corporate goals, a waste of money and resources and difficulty in fixing the failed change effort. This section examines employee resistance to change, relevant research and practical ways of dealing with the problem.

Why people resist change in the workplace

No matter how technically or administratively perfect a proposed change may be, people make or break it. Individual and group behaviour following an organisational change can take many forms (see Figure 16.4). The extremes range from acceptance to **resistance to change**, which is emotional/behavioural response to real or imagined work changes. Many targets or victims of change are cynical about its motives, relevance and processes. Cynicism about organisational change combines pessimism about the likelihood of successful change with blame; with those responsible for change being seen as incompetent, uncaring or simply lazy.[40] A change-management programme in a large Spanish savings bank was intended to facilitate changes in managers' values, competences and practices by providing them with relevant feedback from subordinates. However, the change programme was perceived as political and part of a power game, causing negative emotional reactions, such as fear, suspicion and discomfort.[41]

Figure 16.4 shows that resistance can be as subtle as passive resignation and as overt as deliberate sabotage. Professionals need to learn to recognise the manifestations of resistance, both in themselves and others, if they want to be more effective in creating and supporting change. For example,

Figure 16.4 The Continuum of Resistance to Change

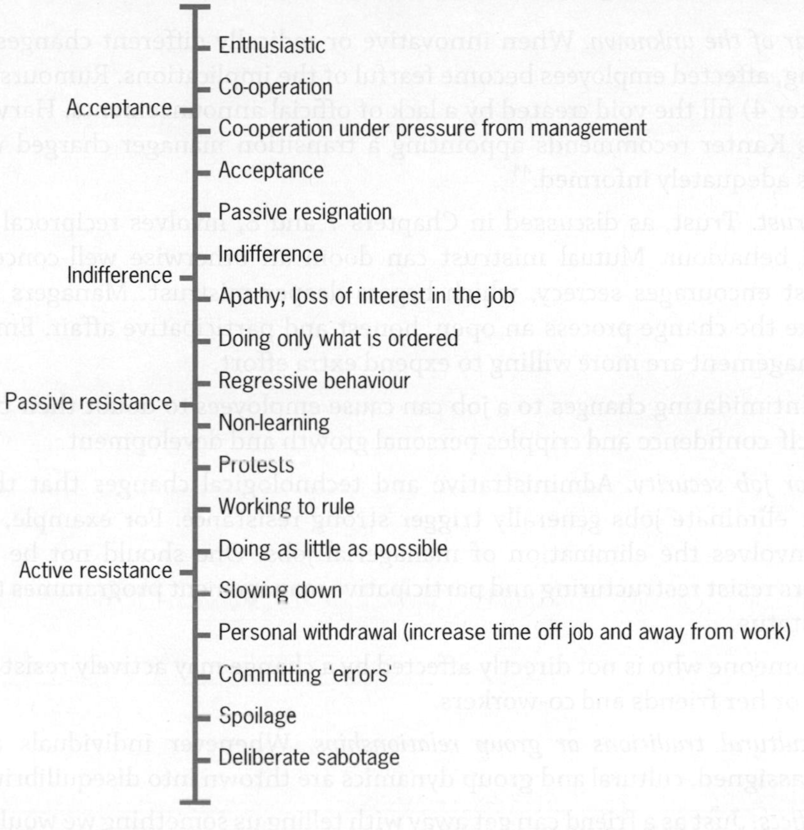

Source: A. S. Judson, *Changing Behavior in Organizations: Minimizing Resistance to Change* (Cambridge, MA: Basil Blackwell, Inc., 1991), p. 48. Used with permission.

organisations can use the list in Figure 16.4 to prepare answers and tactics to combat the various forms of resistance.

Now that we have examined the manifestations of resistance to change, let us consider the reasons employees resist change in the first place. Ten of the leading reasons are elaborated here.[42]

An individual's predisposition towards change

This predisposition is highly personal and deeply ingrained. It is an offshoot of how one learns to handle change and ambiguity as a child. Consider the hypothetical examples of Sandy and Carl. Sandy's parents were patient, flexible and understanding, and Sandy was taught that there were positive compensations for the loss of immediate gratification. She learned that love and approval were associated with making changes. In contrast, Carl's parents were unreasonable, unyielding and forced him to comply with their wishes. They forced him to take piano lessons even though he hated them. Changes were demands for compliance. This taught Carl to be distrustful and suspicious of change. These learned predispositions ultimately affect how Sandy and Carl handle change as adults.[43]

Dell Computer Corporation recognises how important an individual's predisposition towards change can be and tries to hire people with positive predispositions:

Surprise and fear of the unknown. When innovative or radically different changes are introduced without warning, affected employees become fearful of the implications. Rumours from the grapevine (see Chapter 4) fill the void created by a lack of official announcements. Harvard University's Rosabeth Moss Kanter recommends appointing a transition manager charged with keeping all relevant parties adequately informed.[44]

Climate of mistrust. Trust, as discussed in Chapters 7 and 8, involves reciprocal faith in others' intentions and behaviour. Mutual mistrust can doom an otherwise well-conceived change to failure. Mistrust encourages secrecy, which begets deeper mistrust. Managers who trust their employees make the change process an open, honest and participative affair. Employees who, in turn, trust management are more willing to expend extra effort.

Fear of failure. Intimidating changes to a job can cause employees to doubt their capabilities. Self-doubt erodes self-confidence and cripples personal growth and development.

Loss of status or job security. Administrative and technological changes that threaten to alter power bases or eliminate jobs generally trigger strong resistance. For example, most corporate restructuring involves the elimination of managerial jobs. One should not be surprised when middle managers resist restructuring and participative management programmes that reduce their authority and status.

Peer pressure. Someone who is not directly affected by a change may actively resist it to protect the interests of his or her friends and co-workers.

Disruption of cultural traditions or group relationships. Whenever individuals are transferred, promoted or reassigned, cultural and group dynamics are thrown into disequilibrium.

Personality conflicts. Just as a friend can get away with telling us something we would resent hearing from an adversary, the personalities of change agents can breed resistance (see Chapter 2).

Lack of tact or poor timing. Undue resistance can occur because changes are introduced in an insensitive manner or at an awkward time.

Non-reinforcing reward systems. Individuals resist when they do not foresee positive rewards for changing (see Chapter 6). For example, an employee is unlikely to support a change that is perceived as requiring them to work longer and under more pressure.

Evidence about change resistance

In a survey among 90 British managers (almost half of whom were working in the public sector), the following themes emerged:

- Continuing change is much higher on the agenda than managing discrete projects.
- There is evidence of 'initiative fatigue' (most people want to see the pace of change relaxed for a while), information overload and even cynicism.
- Major concerns exist over the lack of effective stress management (see Chapter 9).
- Negotiating, persuading and influencing skills are critical (see Chapter 14).
- Fear of the unknown is a major source of resistance to change but commitment to communication is instrumental rather than value-driven.
- A third of the managers enjoy the politics game, a third do not and a third are neutral.[45]

The classic study of resistance to change was reported in 1948 by Lester Coch and John R. P. French. They observed the introduction of a new work procedure in a garment factory. The change was introduced in three different ways to separate groups of workers. In the 'no participation' group, the garment makers were simply told about the new procedure. Members of a second group, called the 'representative' group, were introduced to the change by a trained co-worker. Employees in the 'total participation' group learned of the new work procedure through a graphic presentation of its cost-saving potential. Mixed results were recorded for the representative group. The 'no participation' and 'total participation' groups, meanwhile, went in opposite directions. Output dropped sharply for the 'no participation' group, while grievances and staff turnover climbed. After a small dip in performance, the 'total participation' group achieved record-high output levels while experiencing no staff turnover.[46] Since the Coch and French study, participation has been the recommended approach to overcoming resistance to change.[47]

Empirical research uncovered five additional personal characteristics related to resistance to change. A recent study of 514 employees from six organisations headquartered in four different continents (North America, Europe, Asia and Australia) revealed that personal dispositions pertaining to having a 'positive self-concept' and 'tolerance for risk' were positively related to coping with change. That is, people with a positive self-concept and a tolerance for risk handled organisational change better than those without these dispositions.[48]

A second study also found that high self-efficacy and an internal locus of control were negatively associated with resistance to change.[49] Finally, a study of 305 college students and 15 university staff members revealed that attitudes towards a specific change were positively related to the respondents' general attitudes towards change and content within their 'change schema' (you may recall from Chapter 4 that a change schema relates to various perceptions, thoughts and feelings that people have when they encounter organisational change).[50]

The preceding research is based on the assumption that individuals directly or consciously resist change. Some experts contend that this is not the case. Rather, there is a growing belief that resistance to change represents, instead, employees' responses to obstacles in the organisation that prevent them from changing.[51] For example, John Kotter, the researcher who developed the eight steps for leading organisational change discussed earlier in this chapter, studied more than 100 companies and concluded that employees generally wanted to change but were unable to do so because of obstacles that prevented execution. He noted that obstacles in the organisation structure or in a 'performance appraisal system [that] makes people choose between the new vision and their own self-interests' impeded change more than an individual's direct resistance.[52] This new perspective implies that a systems model should be used to determine the causes of failed change. Such an approach would most likely reveal that ineffective organisational change is due to faulty organisational processes and systems rather than to employees' direct resistance.[53] In conclusion, a systems perspective suggests that people do not resist change, per se, but rather that individuals' 'anti-change' behaviour and attitudes are caused by obstacles within the work environment.

Alternative strategies for overcoming resistance to change

Before recommending specific approaches for overcoming resistance, there are four key conclusions that should be kept in mind. First, an organisation must be ready for change.

OB in Real Life

Boehringer Ingelheim

Boehringer Ingelheim, a German pharmaceuticals manufacturer of more than 100 years' standing, is one of the few remaining privately owned companies in the pharmaceutical industry. Until the 1980s, its culture reflected a traditional, hierarchical management structure and a strong paternalistic value system. At its UK subsidiary, management identified some of the natural risk-takers who could become role models for other employees. After looking for volunteers, they ended up with a network comprising one change agent for every 50 employees. This network provided the crucial element of bottom-up and sideways-driven change facilitation to complement the more traditional top-down directives.[54]

Just as a table must be set before you can eat, so must an organisation be ready for change before it can be effective.[55] The next Activity contains a survey that assesses an organisation's readiness for change. Use the survey to evaluate a company that you worked for or are familiar with that undertook change. To what extent was the company ready for change and how did this relate, in turn, to the success of the effort to change?

A Dutch study of more than 600 managers from both profit and non-profit sectors indicated that the readiness to change of managers is influenced in order of importance by the emotions the change arouses with the manager, the experience with previous changes and the consequences of the change for the manager's future work.[56] The emotional evaluation is of more importance than the cognitive evaluation for the attitude of a manager towards a change.

Second, organisational change is less successful when top management fails to keep employees informed about the process of change. Third, do not assume that people are resisting change consciously. Managers are encouraged to use a systems model of change, in which transforming one element of change creates changes in other elements, to identify the obstacles that are affecting the implementation process. Fourth, employees' perceptions or interpretations of a change affect resistance significantly. Employees are less likely to resist when they perceive that the benefits of a change overshadow the personal costs. As a minimum, therefore, managers are advised to:

- Provide as much information as possible to employees about the change.
- Inform employees about the reasons/rationale for the change.
- Conduct meetings to address employees' questions regarding the change.
- Provide employees with the opportunity to discuss how the proposed change might affect them.[57]

Activity

Assessing an organisation's readiness for change

Instructions

Circle the number that best represents your opinions about the company being evaluated.

3 = yes
2 = somewhat
1 = no

1	Is the change effort being sponsored by a senior-level executive (MD, CEO, COO)?	3 2 1
2	Are all levels of management committed to the change?	3 2 1
3	Does the organisation culture encourage risk taking?	3 2 1
4	Does the organisation culture encourage and reward continuous improvement?	3 2 1
5	Has senior management clearly articulated the need for change?	3 2 1
6	Has senior management presented a clear vision of a positive future?	3 2 1
7	Does the organisation use specific measures to assess business performance?	3 2 1
8	Does the change effort support other major activities going on in the organisation?	3 2 1
9	Has the organisation benchmarked itself against world-class companies?	3 2 1
10	Do all employees understand the customers' needs?	3 2 1
11	Does the organisation reward individuals and/or teams for being innovative and for looking for root causes of organisational problems?	3 2 1
12	Is the organisation flexible and co-operative?	3 2 1
13	Does management effectively communicate with all levels of the organisation?	3 2 1
14	Has the organisation successfully implemented other change programmes?	3 2 1
15	Do employees take personal responsibility for their behaviour?	3 2 1
16	Does the organisation make decisions quickly?	3 2 1

Total score = ________

Arbitrary norms
40–48 = high readiness for change
24–39 = moderate readiness for change
16–23 = low readiness for change

Source: Based on the discussion contained in T. A. Stewart, 'Rate Your Readiness to Change', *Fortune*, 7 February 1994, pp. 106–10.

These recommendations underscore the importance of communicating with employees throughout the process of change.

In addition to communication, employee participation in the change process is another generic approach for reducing resistance. Consider how George Bauer, president of the US affiliate of Mercedes-Benz Credit Corp., used participation and employee involvement to re-engineer operations and downsize the workforce.

In spite of positive results like those found by Bauer, organisational change experts have, nonetheless, criticised the tendency to treat participation as a cure-all for resistance to change. They prefer a contingency approach because resistance can take many forms and, furthermore, because situational factors vary (see Table 16.4). Participation + involvement does, as shown in Table 16.4, have its place, but it takes time that is not always available. Also indicated is how each of the other five methods has its own situational niche, advantages and drawbacks. In short, there is no universal strategy for overcoming resistance to change. Professionals need a complete repertoire of change strategies.[58]

Table 16.4 Six Strategies for Overcoming Resistance to Change

Approach	Commonly used in situations	Advantages	Drawbacks
Education + communication	Where there is a lack of information or inaccurate information and analysis	Once persuaded, people will often help with the implementation of the change	Can be very time-consuming if lots of people are involved
Participation + involvement	Where the initiators do not have all the information they need to design the change and where others have considerable power to resist	People who participate will be committed to implementing change, and any relevant information they have will be integrated into the change plan	Can be very time-consuming if participators design an inappropriate change
Facilitation + support	Where people are resisting because of adjustment problems	No other approach works as well with adjustment problems	Can be time-consuming, expensive and still fail
Negotiation + agreement	Where someone or some group will clearly lose out in a change and where that group has considerable power to resist	Sometimes it is a relatively easy way to avoid major resistance	Can be too expensive in many cases if it alerts others to negotiate for compliance
Manipulation + co-optation	Where other tactics will not work or are too expensive	It can be a relatively quick and inexpensive solution to resistance problems	Can lead to future problems if people feel manipulated
Explicit + implicit coercion	Where speed is essential and where the change initiators possess considerable power	It is speedy and can overcome any kind of resistance	Can be risky if it leaves people annoyed with the initiators

Source: Reprinted by permission of the *Harvard Business Review*. An exhibit from 'Choosing Strategies for Change' by J. P. Kotter and L. A. Schlesinger (March/April 1979).

16.6 Ongoing change or organisation development

Organisation development (OD) is an applied field of study and practice. Organisation development can be defined as a set of techniques or tools that are used to implement organisational change through commitment, co-ordination and competence.

In an attempt to identify the key dependent variables of OD, seven experienced OD experts reviewed 27 definitions of OD.[59] The experts reached consensus in describing the following categories as representative of 10 key dependent variables of OD:

- Advance organisational renewal.
- Engage organisation culture change.
- Enhance profitability and competitiveness.
- Ensure health and well-being of organisations and employees.

- Facilitate learning and development.
- Improve problem-solving.
- Increase effectiveness.
- Initiate and/or manage change.
- Strengthen system and process improvement.
- Support adaptation to change.

OD and profound change

Change agents using OD generally desire deep and long-lasting improvement. OD consultant Warner Burke, for example, who strives for fundamental cultural change, wrote: 'By fundamental change, as opposed to fixing a problem or improving a procedure, I mean that some significant aspect of an organisation's culture will never be the same.'[60]

OD is value-loaded

Owing to the fact that OD is partly rooted in humanistic psychology, many OD consultants carry certain values or biases into the client organisation. They prefer co-operation over conflict, self-control over institutional control, and democratic and participative management over autocratic management. In addition to OD being driven by a consultant's values, some OD practitioners now believe that there is a broader 'value perspective' that should underlie any organisational change. Specifically, OD should always be customer-focused. This approach implies that organisational interventions should be aimed at helping to satisfy customers' needs and thereby provide enhanced value to an organisation's products and services. Consider the case of B&O:

OB in Real Life

Bang & Olufsen

When the world was hit by the financial crisis in 2008, luxury electronics were hit hard, and the Danish producer of high-tech, high-fidelity audio-visual systems and other related products, Bang & Olufsen (B&O) suffered tremendous losses. A new series of layoffs and cuts were initiated, a lot of new product development was discontinued and a back-to-the-core strategy was implemented. Positive signs are now appearing and some of the new products, such as car hi-fi for luxury brands, have taken off nicely. Whether or not that is enough to help the company through this crisis, only time will tell.

This is not the first time the company has been in turmoil, however. Since its beginning, the company had been at the forefront of design innovation, a philosophy promoted by the two founders of the company. However, that original philosophy stressing product design – which had earned the company much acclaim – carried within it the seeds of failure. The sanctity of the design function came to reign over everything else, particularly cost and customer considerations. Saying 'no' to a new product from the design department was taboo, an action that would not even occur to anyone hoping to stay for long in the organisation. Unfortunately, even though the company won one design prize after another, financially, it was anything but a winner. The balance sheet had been tottering in and out of the red for 22 years, an unheard-of period of time.

Despite the dismal financial figures, not many at B&O seemed to be seriously worried. Most employees were used to the fact that the company was not making a profit, but they never had serious doubts about its survival. Employment security had always been an implicit part of their contract. If ever a doubt surfaced in anybody's mind about the company's future, top management's strong and confident statements reassured them. In the words of the present CEO, 'Every year when we had some problems, it was not our fault. It was the outside world that was so evil to poor Bang & Olufsen.'

Finally, when it became clear that the accounting period of 1990–91 would bring a deficit of €18.25 million, the company's dismal situation could no longer be ignored. The Supervisory Board decided to pull the plug, replacing the CEO who for 10 years had been allowed to run the company at his own discretion, with Anders Knutsen. Knutsen had learned the business of B&O by starting out as a brand manager and working his way through different positions in production and product development until finally ending up as technical director.

His first step was an analysis of the company's cultural values, prepared by B&O's top executives, which centred on an intensive evaluation of the company's critical situation. In particular, the way in which the process of new-product acceptance was treated as sacrosanct was placed under the microscope.

What followed was, as one B&O employee described it, 'an atmosphere of chaos and upheaval'. People were shocked and disoriented, uncertain how the future – theirs and the company's – would look. The shock therapy seemed to achieve the desired effect, however. Participants, trying to impose order on the prevailing chaos, threw themselves wholeheartedly into the activities of the seminar. Despite the risks, they experienced for the first time the power to do something about their own company. They were asked to engage in a strategic dialogue with top management to help restructure and refocus the company. Participating in the design for the future made for motivation, commitment and a sense of ownership. No longer was job security the main pillar of the contract. Instead, that pillar had become accountability and performance.

The distance between top management and the shop floor was cut by reducing the overall number of executives and by slashing two management layers entirely; a total of 712 people were dismissed. As accountability was pushed deep down the lines, employees were expected to develop a sense of ownership and personal responsibility for the company.

To internationalise the company, a new International Sales and Marketing Head Office was opened in Brussels. Product acceptance – the old Achilles' heel of the company (previously almost everything submitted by product design was accepted) – became much more selective. This proved to be the most disturbing 'culture shock' experienced during the transformation, as it clearly signalled management's intent to change the company.

On 29 October 1993, the chairman of the board of B&O could, for the first time after years of losses, predict a profit of €17 million for the financial year 1993–94. The company's share price had risen spectacularly, from €43 million in 1990–91 to €1450 million in 1994–95. These figures indicated a dramatic turnaround of a long-tottering company. After a two-year period, B&O moved from a deficit that seriously threatened the existence of the company to a surplus that exceeded all expectations. The first part of the change process had come to a successful end.

Fast-forward to 2013. The company had a decent streak of years after 2000 but fell on hard times when the financial crisis made designer audio gear less important and Smartphones with streaming content challenged the company's business model. The company has now decided to outsource its manufacturing.[61]

OD is a cycle of diagnosis and prescription

OD theorists and practitioners have long adhered to a medical model of organisation. Like medical doctors, internal and external OD consultants approach the 'sick' organisation, 'diagnose' its ills, 'prescribe' and implement an intervention and 'monitor' progress.[62]

OD is process-oriented

Ideally, OD consultants focus on the form and not the content of behavioural and administrative dealings. For example, product design engineers and market researchers might be coached on how to communicate more effectively with one another without the consultant knowing the technical details of their conversations. In addition to communication, OD specialists focus on other processes, including those of solving problems, making decisions, handling conflict, trust, sharing power and developing careers.

Evidence about organisational change and development

Before discussing OD research, it is important to note that many of the topics contained in this book are used during OD interventions. For example, team building is commonly used to improve the functioning of work teams and was reviewed in Chapter 8. OD research, therefore, has practical implications for a variety of OB applications. OD-related interventions produced the following insights:

- A meta-analysis of 18 studies indicated that employee satisfaction with change was higher when top management was highly committed to the change effort.[63]
- A meta-analysis of 52 studies provided support for a systems model of organisational change. Specifically, varying one target element of change created changes in other target elements. Also, there was a positive relationship between individual behaviour change and organisational-level change.[64]
- A meta-analysis of 126 studies demonstrated that multifaceted interventions, using more than one OD technique, were more effective in changing job attitudes and work attitudes than interventions that relied on only one human-process or technostructural approach.[65]

Practical implications

There are three practical implications to be derived from this research. First, planned organisation change works. However, management and change agents are advised to rely on multifaceted interventions. As indicated elsewhere in this book, goal setting, feedback, recognition and rewards, training, participation, and challenging job design have good track records for improving performance and satisfaction. Second, change programmes are more successful when they are geared towards meeting both short- and long-term results. Professionals should not engage in organisational change for the sake of it. Change efforts should produce positive results.[66] Finally, organisational change is more likely to succeed when top management is truly committed to the change process and the desired goals of the change programme. This is particularly true when organisations pursue large-scale transformation.[67]

Learning outcomes: Summary of key terms

1 **Discuss the external and internal forces that create the need for organisational change**

Organisations encounter both external and internal forces for change. There are four key external forces for change: demographic characteristics, technological advancements, market changes, and social and political pressures. Internal forces for change come from both human resource problems and managerial behaviour/decisions.

2 **Diagnose organisational problems and challenges**

Discuss the diagnostic approaches and tools needed to determine if change is needed and what it should involve.

3 **Describe Lewin's change model**

Lewin developed a three-stage model of planned change that explained how to initiate, manage and stabilise the change process. The three states were unfreezing, which entails creating the motivation to change, changing and stabilising change through refreezing.

4 **Identify alternative strategies for overcoming resistance to change**

Organisations must be ready for change. Assuming an organisation is ready for change, the alternative strategies for overcoming resistance to change are education + communication, participation + involvement, facilitation + support, negotiation + agreement, manipulation + co-optation and explicit + implicit coercion. Each has its situational appropriateness, advantages and drawbacks.

5 **Discuss Theory E and O in the six dimensions of change**

Theory E is oriented towards maximising shareholder value. It is a top-driven approach that focuses on the organisational structures and systems. At the beginning of the change, plans are drawn up to direct the change in a specific way. Change is motivated through financial incentives and consultants play a major role in analysing the problems. The goal of Theory O is to develop organisational capabilities. It encourages participation from the bottom-up and it is focused at employees' behaviour and attitudes. Financial incentives are an unimportant driver of the change and the consultants' contribution is limited to supporting management in shaping their own solutions.

6 **Discuss the 10 reasons employees resist change**

Resistance to change is an emotional/behavioural response to real or imagined threats to an established work routine. Ten reasons employees resist change are (a) an individual's predisposition towards change, (b) surprise and fear of the unknown, (c) climate of mistrust, (d) fear of failure, (e) loss of status or job security, (f) peer pressure, (g) disruption of cultural traditions and/or group relationships, (h) personality conflicts, (i) lack of tact or poor timing and (j) non-reinforcing reward systems.

7 **Demonstrate your familiarity with the four identifying characteristics of organisation development (OD)**

The identifying characteristics of OD are that it involves profound change, is value loaded, is a cycle of diagnosis and prescription and is process-oriented.

Review questions

1 Which of the external forces for change do you believe will prompt the greatest change between now and the year 2020?

2 Have you worked in an organisation where internal forces created change? Describe the situation and the resulting change.

3 How would you respond to a manager who made the following statement: 'Unfreezing is not important, employees will follow my directives'?

4 What are some useful methods that can be used to refreeze an organisational change?

5 Give examples of the way in which Theory E and O can be combined for each of the six dimensions of change.

6 Have you ever resisted a change at work? Explain the circumstances and your thinking at the time.

7 Which source of resistance to change do you think is the most common? Which is the most difficult for management to deal with?

9 Which of the three reasons for organisations' natural resistance to learning is the most powerful? Explain.

Personal awareness and growth exercise

Does your commitment to a change initiative predict your behavioural support for the change?

Objectives

A recent series of studies showed that an employee's commitment to change was a significant and positive predictor of behavioural support for a change initiative. In order to bring this concept to life, we would like you to complete a shortened version of a commitment to change instrument.[68]

Instructions

First, think of a time in which a previous or current employer was undergoing a change initiative that required you to learn something new or to discontinue an attitude, behaviour or organisational practice. Next, evaluate your commitment to this change effort by indicating the extent to which you agree with the following survey items (use the rating scale shown below). Finally, assess your behavioural support for the change.[69]

1 = strongly disagree
2 = disagree
3 = neither agree nor disagree
4 = agree
5 = strongly agree

1	I believe in the value of this change.	1 2 3 4 5
2	This change serves an important purpose.	1 2 3 4 5
3	This change is a good strategy for the organisation.	1 2 3 4 5
4	I have no choice than to go along with this change.	1 2 3 4 5
5	It would be risky to speak out against this change.	1 2 3 4 5
6	It would be too costly for me to resist this change.	1 2 3 4 5
7	I feel a sense of duty to work towards this change.	1 2 3 4 5
8	It would be irresponsible of me to resist this change.	1 2 3 4 5
9	I feel obliged to support this change.	1 2 3 4 5

Total score__________

Arbitrary norms

9 = 18 low commitment
19 = 35 moderate commitment
36 = 45 high commitment

Behavioural support for the change

Overall, I modified my attitudes and behaviour in line with what management was trying to accomplish.
1 2 3 4 5

Questions for discussion

1 Were you committed to the change? Why or why not?
2 Did this level of commitment affect your behavioural support for what management was trying to accomplish?

Group exercise

Creating personal change through a force-field analysis

Objectives

1 To apply force-field analysis to a behaviour or situation you would like to change.
2 To receive feedback on your strategies for bringing about change.

Introduction

The theory of force-field analysis is based on the premise that people resist change because of counteracting positive and negative forces. Positive forces for change are called *thrusters*. They propel people to accept change and modify their behaviour. In contrast, *counterthrusters* or *resistors* are negative forces that motivate an individual to maintain the status quo. People frequently fail to change because they experience equal amounts of positive and negative forces to change.

Force-field analysis is a technique used to facilitate change by first identifying the thrusters and resistors that exist in a specific situation. To minimise resistance to change, it is generally recommended to first reduce or remove the negative forces to change. Removing counterthrusters should create increased pressure for an individual to change in the desired direction. Managers can also further increase motivation to change by following up the reduction of resistors with an increase in the number of positive thrusters of change.

Instructions

Your lecturer will pair you up with another student. The two of you will serve as a team that evaluates the completeness of each other's force-field analysis and recommendations. Once the team is assembled, each individual should independently complete the force-field analysis form below. Once both of you complete this activity, one team member should present results from steps 2 to 5 from the five-step force-field analysis form. The partner should then evaluate the results by considering the following questions with his or her team member.

1 Are there any additional thrusters and counterthrusters that should be listed? Add them to the list.
2 Do you agree with the 'strength' evaluations of thrusters and counterthrusters in step 4? Ask your partner to share his or her rationale for the ratings. Modify the ratings as needed.
3 Examine the specific recommendations for change listed in step 5, and evaluate whether you think they will produce the desired changes. Be sure to consider whether the focal person has the ability to eliminate, reduce or increase each thruster and counterthruster that forms the basis of a specific recommendation. Are there any alternative strategies you can think of?
4 What is your overall evaluation of your partner's intervention strategy?

Force-field analysis form

Step 1

In the space provided, please identify a number of personal problems you would like to solve or aspects of your life you would like to change. Be as imaginative as possible. You are not limited to academic situations. For example, you may want to consider your work environment if you are currently employed, family situation, interpersonal relationships, club situations, and so forth. It is important that you select some aspects of your life that you would like to change but until now have made no effort to.

Step 2

Review in your mind the problems or aspects listed in step 1. Now select one that you would really like to change and which you believe lends itself easily to force-field analysis. Select one that you will feel comfortable talking about to other people.

Step 3

On the form following step 4, indicate existing forces that are pushing you in the direction of change. Thrusters may be forces internal to you (pride, regret, fear) or they may be external to yourself (friends, the boss, a lecturer). Also list existing forces that are preventing you from changing. Again, the counterthruster may be internal to yourself (uncertainty, fear) or external (poor instruction, limited resources, lack of support mechanisms).

Step 4

In the space to the right of your list of thrusters and counterthrusters indicate their relative strength. For consistency, use a scale of 1 to 10, with 1 indicating a weak force and 10 indicating a high force.

Thrusters	Strength

Counterthrusters	Strength

Step 5

Analyse your thrusters and counterthrusters, and develop a strategy for bringing about the desired change. Remember that it is possible to produce the desired result by strengthening existing thrusters, introducing new thrusters, weakening or removing counterthrusters, or some combination of these. Consider the impact of your change strategy on the system's internal stress (i.e. on yourself and others), the likelihood of success, the availability of resources, and the long-term consequences of planned changes. Be prepared to discuss your recommendations with the partner in your group.

Questions for discussion

1 What was your reaction to doing a force-field analysis? Was it insightful and helpful?
2 Was it valuable to receive feedback about your force-field analysis from a partner? Explain.
3 How would you assess the probability of effectively implementing your recommendations?

Online Learning Centre

When you have read this chapter, log on to the Online Learning Centre website at ***www.mcgraw-hill.co.uk/textbooks/sinding*** to access test questions, additional exercises and other related resources.

Notes

1 L. E. Greiner 'Evolution and Revolution as Organizations Grow', *Harvard Business Review*, vol. 50, 1972, pp. 37–46.
2 J. Pfeffer and R. I. Sutton, *Hard Facts, Dangerous Half-Truths, And Total Nonsense: Profiting From Evidence-Based Management* (Cambridge: Harvard Business School Press, 2006).
3 The idea of bad incentives is covered in J. C. Magee, G. J. Kilduff and C. Heath, 'On the Folly of Principal's Power: Managerial Psychology as a Cause of Bad Incentives', *Research in Organizational Behavior*, vol. 31, 2011, pp. 25–41.

[4] D. R. King, D. R. Dalton, C. M. Daily and J. G. Covin, 'Meta-Analyses of Post-Acquisition Performance: Indications of Unidentified Moderators', *Strategic Management Journal*, vol. 25, no. 2, pp. 187–200.

[5] G. Bowley, 'Daimler and Chrysler Set to Link: German and US Groups Discuss Merger Deal Worth almost $40bn.', *Financial Times*, 7 May 1998.

[6] S. Culbert, 'Get Rid of the Performance Review!', *Wall Street Journal*, 21 June 2012.

[7] G. P. Latham, 'The Importance Of Understanding And Changing Employee Outcome Expectancies For Gaining Commitment To An Organizational Goal', *Personnel Psychology*, vol. 54, no. 3, 2001, pp. 707–16.

[8] S. Kerr, 'On the Folly of Rewarding A, While Hoping for B', *Academy of Management Journal*, vol. 18, no. 4, pp. 769–83.

[9] J. C. Magee, G. J. Kilduff and C. Heath, 'On the Folly of Principal's Power: Managerial Psychology as a Cause of Bad Incentives', *Research in Organizational Behavior*, vol. 31, 2011, pp. 25–41.

[10] C. Heath, 'On the Social Psychology of Agency Relationships: Lay Theories of Motivation Overemphasize Extrinsic Incentives', *Organizational Behavior and Human Decision Processes*, vol. 78, no. 1, 1999, pp. 25–62.

[11] The best introduction to Hackman's body of work on teams is his 2002 book: J. R. Hackman, *Leading Teams* (Boston: Harvard Business School Press, 2002).

[12] R. Wageman, J. R. Hackman and E. Lehman (2005) 'Team Diagnostic Survey: Development of an Instrument', *The Journal of Applied Behavioral Science*, vol. 41, no. 4, pp. 373–98.

[13] The Team Diagnostic Survey instrument can be accessed at https://research.wjh.harvard.edu/TDS/

[14] K. A. Jehn, 'A Qualitative Analysis of Conflict Types and Dimensions in Organizational Groups', *Administrative Science Quarterly*, vol. 42, no. 3, pp. 530–57.

[15] Questions are taken from K. A. Jehn and E. A. Mannix, 'The Dynamic Nature of Conflict: A Longitudinal Study of Intragroup Conflict and Group Performance', *The Academy of Management Journal*, vol. 44, no. 2, 2001, pp. 238–51.

[16] D. J. Koys and T. A. DeCotiis, 'Inductive Measures of Psychological Climate', *Human Relations*, vol. 44, no. 3, 1991, pp. 265–85.

[17] R. M. Burton, B. Obel and G. DeSanctis, *Organisational Design* (Cambridge: Cambridge University Press, 2011).

[18] K.S. Cameron and R. E. Quinn, *Diagnosing and Changing Organizational Culture: Based on the Competing Values Framework* (San Francisco: Jossey-Bass, 2006).

[19] Ibid.

[20] T. Jung, T. Scott, H. T. O. Davies, P. Bower, D. Whalley, R. McNally, *et al.*, 'Instruments for Exploring Organizational Culture: A Review of the Literature', *Public Administration Review*, vol. 69, no. 6, 2009, pp. 1087–96.

[21] C. Heath and D. Heath, *Switch: How to change things when change is hard* (New York: Random House, 2010).

[22] Ibid.

[23] For a thorough discussion of the model, see K. Lewin, *Field Theory in Social Science* (New York: Harper & Row, 1951).

[24] These assumptions are discussed in E. H. Schein, *Organizational Psychology, third edition* (Englewood Cliffs, NJ: Prentice-Hall, 1980).

[25] C. Goldwasser, 'Benchmarking: People Make the Process', *Management Review*, June 1995, p. 40.

[26] Benchmark data for 'America's Best Plants' can be found in J. H. Sheridan, 'Lessons from the Best', *Industry Week*, February 1996, pp. 13–20.

[27] Top management's role in implementing change according to Lewin's model is discussed by E. H. Schein, 'The Role of the CEO in the Management of Change: The Case of Information Technology', in *Transforming Organizations*, eds T. A. Kochan and M. Useem (New York: Oxford University Press, 1992), pp. 80–95.

[28] This three-way typology of change was adapted from discussion in P. C. Nutt, 'Tactics of Implementation', *Academy of Management Journal*, June 1986, pp. 230–61.

[29] M. Beer and N. Nohria, *Breaking the Code of Change* (Boston, MA: Harvard Business School Press, 2000).

[30] K. Weick, 'Emergent Change as a Universal in Organisations', in *Breaking the Code of Change*, eds M. Beer and N. Nohria (Boston, MA: Harvard Business School Press, 2000).

[31] Exerpted from M. Beer and N. Nohria, 'Cracking the Code of Change', *Harvard Business Review*, May–June 2000, pp. 133–41.

[32] J. J. Boonstra, *Lopen Over Water* (Amsterdam: Vossiuspers AUP, 2000).

[33] These errors are discussed by J. P. Kotter, 'Leading Change: The Eight Steps to Transformation', in *The Leader's Change Handbook*, eds J. A. Conger, G. M. Spreitzer and E. E. Lawler III (San Francisco, CA: Jossey-Bass Business and Management Series 1999), pp. 87–99.

[34] The type of leadership needed during organisational change is discussed by J. P. Kotter, *Leading Change* (Boston, MA: Harvard Business School Press, 1996); and B. Ettorre, 'Making Change', *Management Review*, January 1996, pp. 13–18.

[35] K. Weick, 'Emergent Change as a Universal in Organizations', in *Breaking the Code of Change*, eds M. Beer and N. Nohria (Boston, MA: Harvard Business School Press, 2000).

[36] A. A. Armenakis and A. G. Bedeian, 'Organizational Change: A Review of Theory and Research in the 1990s', *Journal of Management*, no. 3, 1999, pp. 293–315.

[37] A. M. Pettigrew, R. W. Woodman and K. S. Cameron, 'Studying Organizational Change and Development: Challenges for Future Research', *Academy of Management Journal*, August 2001, pp. 697–713.

[38] A. M. Pettigrew and R. Whipp, *Managing Change for Competitive Success* (Oxford: Blackwell Publishing, 1999).

[39] K. E. Weick and R. E. Quinn, 'Organizational Change and Development', in *Annual Review of Psychology*, eds J. T. Spence, J. M. Darley and D. J. Foss (Palo Alto, CA: Annual Reviews, 1999), pp. 361–86.

40 J. P. Wanous, A. E. Reichers and J. T. Austin, 'Cynicism about Organizational Change. Measurements, Antecedents and Correlates', *Group and Organization Management*, June 2000, pp. 132–53.

41 J. M. Peiro, V. Gonzalez-Roma and J. Canero, 'Survey Feedback as a Tool Changing Managerial Culture: Focusing on Users' Interpretations – A Case Study', *European Journal of Work and Organizational Psychology*, no. 4, 1999, pp. 537–50.

42 Adapted in part from B. W. Armentrout, 'Have Your Plans for Change Had a Change of Plan?', *HR FOCUS*, January 1996, p. 19; and A. S. Judson, *Changing Behavior in Organizations: Minimizing Resistance to Change* (Oxford: Blackwell Publishing, 1991).

43 See Basic Behavioral Science Task Force of the National Advisory Mental Health Council, 'Basic Behavioral Science Research for Mental Health: Vulnerability and Resilience', *American Psychologist*, January 1996, pp. 22–8.

44 See R. Moss Kanter, 'Managing Traumatic Change: Avoiding the "Unlucky 13"', *Management Review*, May 1987, pp. 23–4.

45 D. Buchanan, T. Claydon and M. Doyle. 'Organization Development and Change: The Legacy of the Nineties', *Human Resource Management Journal*, no. 2, 1999, pp. 20–38.

46 See L. Coch and J. R. P. French, Jr, 'Overcoming Resistance to Change', *Human Relations*, 1948, pp. 512–32.

47 For a thorough review of the role of participation in organisational change, see W. A. Pasmore and M. R. Fagans, 'Participation, Individual Development, and Organizational Change: A Review and Synthesis', *Journal of Management*, June 1992, pp. 375–97.

48 Results from this study can be found in T. A. Judge, C. J. Thoresen, V. Pucik and T. W. Welbourne, 'Managerial Coping with Organisational Change: A Dispositional Perspective', *Journal of Applied Psychology*, February 1999, pp. 107–22.

49 L. Morris, 'Research Capsules', *Training and Development*, April 1992, pp. 74–6; and T. Hill, N. D. Smith and M. F. Mann, 'Role of Efficacy Expectations in Predicting the Decision to Use Advanced Technologies: The Case of Computers', *Journal of Applied Psychology*, May 1987, pp. 307–14.

50 Results can be found in C.-M. Lau and R. W. Woodman, 'Understanding Organizational Change: A Schematic Perspective', *Academy of Management Journal*, April 1995, pp. 537–54.

51 See the related discussion in E. B. Dent and S. G. Goldberg, 'Challenging "Resistance to Change"', *Journal of Applied Behavioral Science*, March 1999, pp. 25–41.

52 J. P. Kotter, 'Leading Change: Why Transformation Efforts Fail', *Harvard Business Review*, 1995, p. 64.

53 See E. B. Dent and S. G. Goldberg, 'Challenging "Resistance to Change"', *Journal of Applied Behavioral Science*, March 1999, pp. 25–41; J. Krantz, 'Comment on "Challenging Resistance to Change"', *Journal of Applied Behavioral Science*, March 1999, pp. 42–4; and E. B. Dent and S. G. Goldberg, '"Resistance to Change": A Limiting Perspective', *Journal of Applied Behavioral Science*, March 1999, pp. 45–7.

54 G. Tregunno, 'Changing Routes at Boehringer Ingelheim', *People Management*, 8 April 1999.

55 Readiness for change is discussed by B. Trahant and W. W. Burke, 'Traveling through Transitions', *Training and Development*, February 1996, pp. 37–41.

56 E. E. Metselaar, *Assessing the Willingness to Change; Construction and Validation of the DINAMO* (Amsterdam: Vrije Universiteit Amsterdam, 1997).

57 For a discussion of how managers can reduce resistance to change by providing different explanations for an organisational change, see D. M. Rousseau and S. A. Tijoriwala, 'What's a Good Reason to Change? Motivated Reasoning and Social Accounts in Promoting Organizational Change', *Journal of Applied Psychology*, August 1999, pp. 514–28.

58 Additional strategies for managing resistance are discussed by T. J. Galpin, *The Human Side of Change: A Practical Guide to Organizational Redesign* (San Francisco, CA: Jossey-Bass, 1996); and D. May and M. Kettelhut, 'Managing Human Issues in Reengineering Projects', *Journal of Systems Management*, January–February 1996, pp. 4–11.

59 T. M. Egan, 'Organization Development: An Examination of Definitions and Dependent Variables', *Organization Development Journal*, Summer 2002, pp. 59–69.

60 W. W. Burke, *Organization Development: A Normative View* (Reading, MA: Addison-Wesley Publishing, 1987), p. 9.

61 M. F. Kets De Vries and K. Balazs, 'Transforming the Mind-Set of the Organization: A Clinical Perspective', *Administration and Society*, January 1999, pp. 640–75.

62 M. F. Kets De Vries and K. Balazs, 'Transforming the Mind-Set of the Organization: A Clinical Perspective', *Administration and Society*, January 1999, pp. 640–75.

63 See R. Rodgers, J. E. Hunter and D. L. Rogers, 'Influence of Top Management Commitment on Management Program Success', *Journal of Applied Psychology*, February 1993, pp. 151–5.

64 Results can be found in P. J. Robertson, D. R. Roberts and J. I. Porras, 'Dynamics of Planned Organizational Change: Assessing Empirical Support for a Theoretical Model', *Academy of Management Journal*, June 1993, pp. 619–34.

65 Results from the meta-analysis can be found in G. A. Neuman, J. E. Edwards and N. S. Raju, 'Organizational Development Interventions: A Meta-Analysis of Their Effects on Satisfaction and Other Attitudes', *Personnel Psychology*, Autumn 1989, pp. 461–90.

66 The importance of results-oriented change efforts is discussed by R. J. Schaffer and H. A. Thomson, 'Successful Change Programs Begin with Results', *Harvard Business Review*, January–February 1992, pp. 80–89.

67 See the related discussion in D. M. Schneider and C. Goldwasser, 'Be a Model Leader of Change: Here's How to Get the Results You Want from the Change You're Leading', *Management Review*, March 1998, pp. 41–5.

68 Survey items were obtained from L. Herscovitch and J. P. Meyer, 'Commitment to Organizational Change: Extension of a Three-Component Model', *Journal of Applied Psychology*, June 2002, p. 477.

69 Based on a group exercise in L. W. Mealiea, *Skills for Managers in Organizations* (Burr Ridge, IL: Irwin, 1994), pp. 198–201.

Glossary

A

Ability Stable characteristic responsible for a person's maximum physical or mental performance.

Accommodator Learning style preferring learning through doing and feeling.

Accountability practices Focus on treating diverse employees fairly.

Actor–observer effect An actor assesses his or her behaviour in comparison to his or her reactions in different situations, while an observer sees the actor's behaviour and relates to his or her dispositions.

Adaptor Cognitive style characterised by doing things better.

Adverse selection An instance of hidden information occurring before an agreement is reached.

Affective component of an attitude Feelings, moods and emotions a person has about something or someone.

Aggressive style Expressive and self-enhancing but takes unfair advantage of others.

Agreeableness Personality dimension referring to a person's ability to get along with others.

Aided-analytic Using tools to make decisions.

Alternative dispute resolution Avoiding costly lawsuits by resolving conflicts informally or through conciliation, mediation or arbitration.

Analytic Cognitive style characterised by processing information into its component parts.

Anchoring A decision bias linked to the primacy effect, where initial information colours all subsequent information.

Asch effect Giving in to a unanimous but wrong opposition.

Assertive style Expressive and self-enhancing but does not take advantage of others.

Assimilator Learning style preferring learning through watching and thinking.

Attention Being consciously aware of something or someone.

Attitude Beliefs and feelings people have about specific ideas, situations and people, which influence their behaviour.

Attributions Inferred causes of perceived behaviour, actions or events.

Autonomy The extent to which the job enables an individual to experience freedom, independence and discretion in both scheduling and determining the procedures used in completing the job.

Availability bias A decision-maker's tendency to base decisions on information that is readily available in memory.

Availability heuristic Tendency to base decisions on information readily available in memory.

B

Behavioural component of an attitude How a person intends or expects to act towards something or someone.

Benchmarking Process by which a company compares its performance with that of high-performing organisations.

Big Five Five dimensions largely representing human personality.

Boundaries The distinction between activities inside and outside the legal definition of a firm.

Bounded rationality Constraints that restrict decision making.

Brainstorming Process to generate a quantity of ideas.

Buffers Resources or administrative changes that reduce burnout.

Bureaucracy Max Weber's idea of the most rationally efficient form of organisation.

Burnout A condition of emotional exhaustion and negative attitudes.

Business ethics theory Is about carefully thought-out rules of business organisational conduct that guide decision making.

C

Case study In-depth study of a single person, group or organisation.

Centralisation The concentration of decision-making power at the level of the top management team.

Charismatic leadership Transforms employees to pursue organisational goals over self-interests.

Climate The situation, feelings, reflections and behaviours experienced by people in the organisation.

Closed system A relatively self-sufficient entity.

Closure Tendency to perceive objects as a constant overall form.

Coercive power Obtaining compliance through threatened or actual punishment.

Cognitions A person's knowledge, opinions or beliefs.

Cognitive appraisal An individual's overall perception or evaluation of a situation or stressor.

Cognitive categories Mental depositories for storing information.

Cognitive component of an attitude Beliefs, opinions, cognitions and knowledge someone has about a certain object, situation or person.

Cognitive dissonance Refers to situations of incompatibility between different attitudes or between attitudes and behaviour.

Cognitive style An individual's preferred way of processing information.

Communication Interpersonal exchange of information and understanding.

Communication competence Ability to use the appropriate communication behaviour effectively in a given context.

Communication distortion Purposely modifying the content of a message.

Competence Any individual characteristic that is related to effective and superior performance.

Computer-aided decision-making Decision participants interact through a computer interface.

Confirmation bias tendency Tendency to seek and interpret information that verifies existing beliefs.

Conflict theory Social structures and relationships in organisations are based on conflicts between groups and social classes.

Conflict One party perceives its interests are being opposed or set back by another party.

Conscientiousness Personality dimension referring to the extent a person is organised, careful, responsible and self-disciplined.

Consensus Presenting opinions and gaining agreement to support a decision.

Consideration Creating mutual respect and trust between leader and followers.

Content level 'What' is communicated.

Content theories Theories regarding what motivates people.

Contingency approach to organisation design Creating an effective organisation–environment fit.

Contingency approach Using tools and techniques in a situationally appropriate manner; avoiding the one-best-way mentality.

Contingency factors Situational variables that influence the appropriateness of a leadership style.

Continuity Tendency to perceive objects as continuous patterns.

Continuous change Perceives change as constant, evolving and cumulative.

Contrast effect Tendency to perceive stimuli that differ from expectations as being even more different than they really are.

Control strategy Coping strategy that directly confronts or solves problems.

Converger Learning style preferring learning through thinking and doing.

Co-ordination Tuning the activities to reach a common goal by exchanging information.

Coping Process of managing stress.

Coping strategies Specific behaviours and cognitions used to cope with a situation.

Core job dimensions Job characteristics found to various degrees in all jobs.

Correspondent inference theory An attribution theory which describes how a perceiver infers another's intentions and personal dispositions from that person's behaviour.

Covariation principle Principle of attribution theory holding that people attribute behaviour to factors that are present when a behaviour occurs and absent when it does not.

Creativity Process of developing something new or unique.

Critical theory Criticism of the rational, functionalistic, managerial and capitalistic views on organisations.

Cross-cultural training Structured experiences to help people adjust to a new culture or country.

Culture Socially derived, taken-for-granted assumptions about how to think and act.

Culture shock Anxiety and doubt caused by an overload of new expectations and cues.

D

Decentralisation The dispersion of decision-making power in the organisation.

Decision-making style A combination of how individuals perceive and respond to information.

Decoding (4.384) Translating verbal, oral or visual aspects of a message into a form that can be interpreted.

Delegation Granting decision-making authority to people at lower levels.

Delphi technique Group process that anonymously generates ideas from physically dispersed experts.

Development practices Focus on preparing diverse employees for greater responsibility and advancement.

Devil's advocacy Assigning someone the role of critic.

Dialectic method Fostering a debate of opposing viewpoints to better understand an issue.

Differentiation Division of labour and specialisation that cause people to think and act differently.

Displayed emotion Organisationally desirable and appropriate emotion in a given job or situation.

Distributive negotiation Negotiation that concerns the sharing of a fixed amount.

Diverger Learning style preferring learning through feeling and watching.

Diversity management Enabling people to perform up to their maximum potential regardless of background.

Diversified organisation Large organisation with headquarters and semi-autonomous units.

Division of labour The allocation of tasks and responsibilities to the members of the organisation.

Divisional organisation An independently operating business unit not sharing services with other units (ideally).

Dysfunctional conflict Threatens organisation's interests.

E

Ecological approach An approach to organisations that views each organisation of a certain group/activity as a member of a distinct population (e.g. Italian savings banks).

Efficiency Realising a certain output with a minimum amount of input.

Emotional contagion Emotional influencing process, by which people catch the feelings of others.

Emotional dissonance Conflict between felt/actual and displayed/required emotions.

Emotional intelligence Ability to manage your own emotions and those of others in mature and constructive ways.

Emotional labour The effort, planning and control that is needed to express organisationally desired emotions during interpersonal interactions.

Emotional stability Personality dimension referring to the extent a person can cope with stress situations and experiences positive emotional states.

Emotions Complex human reactions to personal achievements and setbacks.

Empowerment Sharing varying degrees of power with lower-level employees to tap their full potential.

Enacted values The values and norms that are exhibited by employees.

Encoding A process to interpret and evaluate the observer's environment and transfer it into a format that can be communicated somewhere.

Entrepreneurial organisation A simple organisation strongly built on and driven by a leader.

Episodic change Refers to change initiatives that are infrequent, discontinuous and intentional.

Equality Providing the same opportunities to all in an organisation, often mandated by national or supranational laws.

Equity theory Holds that motivation is a function of fairness in social exchanges.

Escalation of commitment Sticking to an ineffective course of action too long.

Escape strategy Coping strategy that avoids or ignores stressors and problems.

Espoused values The stated values and norms preferred by an organisation.

Ethnocentrism Belief that one's native country, culture, language and behaviour are superior.

Eustress Stress that is good or produces a positive outcome.

Event memory Memories that describe sequences of events in well-known situations.

Existence needs The concern with basic material-existence requirements.

Expatriate Anyone living or working in a foreign country.

Expectancy theory Holds that people are motivated to behave in ways that produce valued outcomes.

Expectancy Belief that effort leads to a specific level of performance.

Experienced meaningfulness Feeling that one's job is important and worthwhile.

Experienced responsibility Believing that one is accountable for work outcomes.

Expert power Obtaining compliance through one's knowledge or information.

External factors Environmental characteristics that cause behaviour.

External forces for change Originate outside the organisation.

External locus of control Attributing outcomes to circumstances beyond one's control.

Extra-organisational stressors Stressors caused by factors outside the organisation.

Extroversion Personality dimension referring to a person's comfort level with relationships.

Extrovert Preference for directing perception and judgement outwardly.

Extrinsic motivation Being motivated by extrinsic rewards.

Extrinsic rewards Financial, material or social rewards from the environment.

F

Feedback Objective information about performance.

Feeling Preference for judging based on a subjective and personal process.

Felt emotion A person's actual or true emotion.

Field study Examination of variables in real-life settings.

Fight-or-flight response To either confront stressors or try to avoid them.

Flow A psychological state in which a person feels simultaneously cognitively efficient, motivated and happy.
Formal group Group formed by the organisation.
Formalisation The extent to which rights and duties of organisational members are determined.
Framing bias This occurs when the decision-maker values change expressed in terms of a gain more than the same change expressed in terms of a loss.
Frustration-regression hypothesis When the gratification of a higher-order need is being blocked, the desire to satisfy a lower-level need increases.
Functional conflict Serves organisation's interests.
Functional social support Support sources that buffer stress in specific situations.
Fundamental attribution error Same as the fundamental error, but operating in groups and teams.
Fundamental error Tendency to attribute other's success to external factors and other's failure to internal factors.

G

'Garbage can' model Holds that decision making is sloppy and haphazard.
Gender stereotype Stereotype based on gender (e.g. 'all men are chauvinists').
Genderflex Temporarily using communication behaviours typical of the other gender.
Glass ceiling Invisible barrier blocking women and minorities from top management positions.
Global social support The total amount of social support available.
Goal What an individual is trying to accomplish.
Goal commitment Amount of commitment to achieving a goal.
Goal conflict Degree to which people feel their multiple goals are incompatible.
Goal difficulty The amount of effort required to meet a goal.
Goal specificity Quantifiability of a goal.
Grapevine Unofficial communication system of the informal organisation.
Group Two or more freely interacting people with shared norms and goals and a common identity.
Group-level stressors Stress factors caused by group dynamics and by managerial action or inaction in relation to group and team activities.
Groupthink Janis's term for a cohesive in-group's unwillingness to realistically view alternatives.

H

Hierarchical communication Exchange of information between superiors and employees.
High-context cultures Primary meaning derived from non-verbal situational cues.
Horizontal integration The extent to which a business firm seeks to control the market for one narrowly defined product or component of input (e.g. laptop batteries).
Horizontal organisation Organisations with few hierarchical levels, built around core processes.
Horizontal specialisation The degree to which an employee can do few or many things within his or her job. It is high if an employee can only do one single job and low if the employee is able to fill many positions.
Hourglass organisation An organisation with a very limited number of middle managers.
Hygiene factors Job characteristics associated with job dissatisfaction.

I

Imager Cognitive style characterised by representing information in mental pictures.
Implicit personality theories Network of assumptions that we hold about relationships among various types of people, traits and behaviours.

Impression management Getting others to see us in a certain manner.
Individual-level stressors Stress factors directly associated with a person's work responsibilities.
Informal group Group formed by friends.
Informal structure An organisational structure with few or no formal structures, lines of authority and hierarchy levels.
Information overload When the information we have to work with exceeds our processing capacity.
Information richness Information-carrying capacity of data.
In-group The common feeling of cohesion among members of groups relative to the outsiders.
Initiating structure Organising and defining what group members should be doing.
Innovative organisation Often young and flexible organisation oriented towards innovation.
Innovator Cognitive style characterised by doing things differently.
Instrumental cohesiveness Sense of togetherness based on the mutual dependency required to get the job done.
Instrumental values Represent desirable ways or modes of conduct to achieve one's terminal goals.
Instrumentality Belief that performance leads to a specific outcome or reward.
Integration Co-operation among specialists to achieve common goals.
Integrative negotiation The opposite of distributional negotiation. Concerns the opportunities for finding a solution that increases the total value of an agreement.
Intelligence Capacity for constructive thinking, reasoning and problem solving.
Internal factors Personal characteristics that cause behaviour.
Internal forces for change Originate inside the organisation.
Internal locus of control Attributing outcomes to one's own actions.
Internal motivation Motivation caused by positive internal feelings.
Intrinsic aspects of work These are aspects such as achievement, recognition, characteristics of the work, responsibility and advancement, all related to outcomes associated with the content of the task being performed.
Intrinsic motivation Being motivated by intrinsic rewards.
Intrinsic rewards Self-granted, psychic rewards.
Introvert Preference for basing perception and judgement upon one's own ideas.

J

Job enrichment Enriching a job through vertical loading.
Job involvement The extent to which one is personally involved with one's work role.
Job satisfaction General attitude one has towards one's job.
Judgemental heuristic Rules-of-thumb or shortcuts that people use to reduce information-processing demands.
Judging Preference for making quick decisions.

K

Knowledge of results Feedback about work outcomes.

L

Laboratory study Manipulation and measurement of variables in contrived situations.
Leader trait Personal characteristic that differentiates a leader from a follower.
Leader–member relations Extent to which leader has the support, loyalty and trust of work group.
Leadership Influencing employees to voluntarily pursue organisational goals.
Leadership Grid® Represents four leadership styles found by crossing concern for production and concern for people.
Leadership prototype Mental representation of the traits and behaviours possessed by leaders.

Learned helplessness Debilitating lack of faith in one's ability to control the situation.

Learning style An individual's preferred use of learning abilities.

Legitimate power Obtaining compliance through formal authority.

Liaison individuals Consistently pass grapevine information along to others.

Linguistic style A person's typical speaking pattern.

Listening Actively decoding and interpreting verbal messages.

Locus of control Degree to which a person takes responsibility for his/her behaviour and its consequences.

Low-context cultures Primary meaning derived from written and spoken words.

M

Machine organisation Well-structured, often bureaucratic organisation oriented towards efficiency.

Maintenance roles Relationship-building group behaviour.

Make-or-buy decision The decision about whether to manufacture an item or service inside the organisation, using employee time and corporate resources.

Management by objectives Management system incorporating participation in decision making, goal setting and feedback.

Mechanistic organisations Rigid, command-and-control bureaucracies.

Media The method and mechanism through which communication is transmitted. E-mails, notes, newspapers, handbooks are all distinct media.

Media richness The medium's ability to carry volumes of information. Face-to-face is a very rich medium, binary code is not.

Meta-analysis Pools the results of many studies through statistical procedure.

Missionary organisation An organisation bound together by a clear mission and strong shared values among its members.

Monochronic time Preference for doing one thing at a time because time is limited, precisely segmented and schedule driven.

Moral hazard The information asymmetry that occurs after a contract is signed and one party takes advantage and behaves in selfish ways which the other party cannot observe.

Motivating potential score The amount of internal work motivation associated with a specific job.

Motivation Psychological processes that arouse and direct goal-directed behaviour.

Motivators Job characteristics associated with job satisfaction.

Mutuality of interest Balancing individual and organisational interests through win-win co-operation.

N

Need for achievement Desire to accomplish something difficult.

Need for affiliation Desire to spend time in social relationships and activities.

Need for power Desire to influence, coach, teach or encourage others to achieve.

Needs Physiological or psychological deficiencies that arouse behaviour.

Negative affectivity Tendency to experience negative emotional states.

Negative inequity Comparison in which another person receives greater outcomes for similar inputs.

Negotiation Give-and-take process between conflicting interdependent parties.

Network organisation An organisation structured around reciprocal communication patterns between groups of people.

Noise Interference with the transmission and understanding of a message.

Nominal group technique Process to generate ideas and evaluate solutions.

Non-analytic Using rules, formulated beforehand, to make decisions.

Non-assertive style Timid and self-denying behaviour.

Non-verbal communication Messages sent that are neither written nor spoken.

Norms Shared attitudes, opinions, feelings or actions that guide social behaviour.

O

Organisational stressors Organisational level events, structures and processes, including culture and climate that act in stressful ways.

Open system Organism that must constantly interact with its environment to survive.

Openness to experience Personality dimension referring to the extent a person is open for new experiences.

Optimising Choosing the best possible solution.

Oral communication Verbal communication that is spoken.

Organic organisations Fluid and flexible network of multi-talented people.

Organisation System of consciously co-ordinated activities of two or more people.

Organisation chart Graphic illustration of boxes and lines showing chain of formal authority and division of labour.

Organisation development A set of techniques or tools that are used to implement organisational change.

Organisational behaviour Interdisciplinary field dedicated to better understanding of management of people at work.

Organisational commitment The extent to which one identifies oneself with an organisation and is committed to its goals.

Organisational culture Shared values and beliefs that underlie a company's identity.

Organisational decline Decrease in organisation's resource base (money, customers, talent, innovations).

Organisational moles Use the grapevine to enhance their power and status.

Organisational socialisation Process by which employees learn the organisation's values, norms and required behaviours.

Overconfidence bias When asked to assign probabilities that their answers are correct, most people are more confident than their replies suggest is justified.

P

Participative management Involving employees in various forms of decision making.

Pay-for-performance Monetary incentives tied to one's results or accomplishments.

Perceived stress An individual's overall perception about how various stressors are affecting her or his life.

Perceiving Preference for gathering a lot of information before making decisions.

Perception Cognitive process that enables us to interpret and understand our environment.

Perceptual grouping Cognitive process to form individual stimuli into meaningful patterns.

Perceptual model of communication Consecutively linked elements within the communication process.

Persistence Extent to which effort is expended on a task over time.

Personal initiative Going beyond formal job requirements and being an active self-starter.

Personalised power Directed at helping oneself.

Personality Stable physical and mental characteristics responsible for a person's identity.

Personality type Personality description based on common patterns of characteristics of people.

Platform organisation Combines the new flexible types with the more classic organisation types.

Political organisation An organisation in which power is illegitimate, resulting in disintegration and conflict.

Polychronic time Preference for doing more than one thing at a time because time is flexible and multidimensional.

Position power Degree to which leader has formal power.

Positive affectivity Tendency to experience positive emotional states.

Positive inequity Comparison in which another person receives lesser outcomes for similar inputs.

Postmodernism A very subjective and situational view on the world around us making it impossible to develop general applicable theories of this world.

Prevalence (or representativeness) heuristic Tendency to assess the likelihood of an event occurring based on impressions about similar occurrences.

Primacy effect Effect by which the information first received often continues to colour later perceptions of individuals.

Problem Gap between an actual and desired situation.

Process theories Theories regarding how people get motivated.

Process-style listeners Like to discuss issues in detail.

Productivity Realising the highest possible output with a specific amount of input.

Professional organisation Decentralised organisation with professionals doing highly skilled work.

Profit centre An organisational unit with its own accounts to measure only that unit's performance and profit.

Programmed conflict Encourages different opinions without protecting management's personal feelings.

Project organisation An organisation consisting of temporarily semiautonomous project groups.

Propensity to trust A personality trait involving one's general willingness to trust others.

Proxemics Hall's term for the cultural expectations about interpersonal space.

Proximity Tendency to group elements based upon their nearness.

Q

Quality circles Small teams of volunteers who strive to solve quality-related problems.

R

Rational model Logical four-step approach to decision-making.

Readiness Follower's ability and willingness to complete a task.

Realistic job preview Presents both positive and negative aspects of a job.

Reality shock A newcomer's feeling of surprise after experiencing unexpected situations or events.

Reasons-style listeners Interested in hearing the rationale behind a message.

Recruitment practices Attempts to attract qualified, diverse employees at all levels.

Referent power Obtaining compliance through charisma or personal attraction.

Relatedness needs The need to maintain significant relations.

Relationship level How the relationship between sender and receiver is communicated.

Representative bias The tendency to assess the likelihood of an event occurring based on one's impressions about similar occurrences.

Resistance to change Emotional/behavioural response to real or imagined work changes.

Resource view Growth and competitive advantages of organisations are based on the presence of rare and immobile resources under control of the organisation.

Reward equality norm Everyone should get the same rewards.

Reward equity norm Rewards should be tied to contributions.

Reward power Obtaining compliance with promised or actual rewards.

Role ambiguity Others' expectations are unknown.

Role conflict Others have conflicting or inconsistent expectations.

Role episode A snapshot of the ongoing interaction between two people, a role sender and a focal person who is expected to act out the role.

Role overload Others' expectations exceed one's ability.

Roles Expected behaviours for a given position.

S

Sample survey Questionnaire responses from a sample of people.

Satisficing Choosing a solution that meets a minimum standard of acceptance.

Scenario technique Speculative forecasting method.

Schema Mental picture of an event or object.

Scientific management A scientific approach to management in which all tasks in organisations are in-depth analysed, routinised, divided and standardised, instead of using rules-of-thumb.

Self-concept A person's self-perception as a physical, social, spiritual being.

Self-efficacy Belief in one's ability to accomplish a task successfully.

Self-esteem Belief about one's own self-worth based on overall self-evaluation.

Self-fulfilling prophecy People's expectations determine behaviour and performance.

Self-managed teams Groups of employees granted administrative oversight for their work.

Self-management leadership Process of leading others to lead themselves.

Self-monitoring The extent to which a person adapts his/her behaviour to the situation.

Self-serving bias Tendency to attribute one's success to internal factors and one's failure to external factors.

Semantic barrier Barriers caused by lack of understanding of the meaning of words and concepts.

Servant-leadership Focuses on increased service to others rather than to oneself.

Set-up-to-fail syndrome Creating and reinforcing a dynamic that essentially sets up perceived weaker performers to fail.

Similarity Tendency to group objects, people and events that look alike.

Situational factors Environmental characteristics that affect how people interpret stress factors.

Situational theories Propose that leader styles should match the situation at hand.

Skill Specific capacity to manipulate objects.

Skill variety The number of different skills mastered by an individual.

Social network Social entities (individuals, groups, organisations, etc.) and the relations (or lack thereof) between them.

Social network analysis The systematic and quantifiable collection and analysis of social relations.

Social perception Process by which people come to understand one another.

Social power Ability to get things done using human, informational and material resources.

Social support Amount of helpfulness derived from social relationships.

Socialised power Directed at helping others.

Socio-emotional cohesiveness Sense of togetherness based on emotional satisfaction.

Span of control The number of people reporting directly to a given manager.

Staff personnel Provide research, advice and recommendations to line managers.

Stakeholder audit Systematic identification of all parties likely to be affected by the organisation.

Standardisation The creation of uniform ways of working, usually codified in some way within the organisation.

Stereotype Beliefs about the characteristics of a group.

Strategic constituency Any group of people with a stake in the organisation's operation or success.

Stress Behavioural, physical or psychological response to stressors.

Stress intervention Interventions and actions taken to reduce stress.

Stressful life events Life events that disrupt daily routines and social relationships.

Stressors Environmental factors that produce stress.

Stress-reduction programmes Systematic efforts to identify and reduce or eliminated stress factors.

Style A preferred way or habitual pattern of doing something.

Sub-optimisation Pursuing outcomes that are optimal for an organisational unit but not necessarily for the organisation as a whole.

Substitutes for leadership Situational variables that can substitute for, neutralise or enhance the effects of leadership.

Symbolic interactionism Subjective interpretation of the world around us through interacting in this world.

Symptom management strategy Coping strategy that focuses on reducing the symptoms of stress.

Systems theory Every element is a subsystem of a larger system and every system is composed of subsystems, depending on each other and on the whole.

T

Task identity The extent to which the job requires an individual to perform a whole or completely identifiable piece of work.

Task roles Task-oriented group behaviour.

Task significance The extent to which the job affects the lives of other people within or outside the organisation.

Task structure Amount of structure contained within work tasks.

Team Small group with complementary skills who hold themselves mutually accountable for common purpose, goals and approach.

Team building Experiential learning aimed at better internal functioning of teams.

Team viability Team members' satisfaction and willingness to contribute.

Terminal values Represent desirable goals or end-states of existence a person wants to reach during his or her life.

Theory A story defining key terms, providing a conceptual framework and explaining why something occurs.

Theory Y McGregor's modern and positive assumptions about employees being responsible and creative.

Thinking Preference for judging based on a logical, objective and impersonal process.

Total quality management An organisational culture dedicated to training, continuous improvement and customer satisfaction.

Transaction cost The total cost of undertaking a transaction, including finding the item, appraising it, paying the price and monitoring later on.

Transactional leadership Focuses on interpersonal interactions between managers and employees.

Trust Reciprocal faith in other's intentions and behaviour.

U

Unaided-analytic Analysis is limited to processing information in one's mind.

Unity of command Each employee should report to a single manager.

Upward feedback Subordinates evaluate their boss.

V

Valence The value of a reward or outcome.

Value system A ranking of a person's values according to their intensity or importance.

Values Standards or criteria for choosing goals and guiding actions that are relatively enduring and stable over time.

Verbaliser Cognitive style characterised by representing information through verbal thinking.

Vertical integration The degree to which firms covers different stages in the chain of activities involved in producing an item.

Vertical specialisation Determines who takes responsibility and who has decision-making power in the organisation.

Virtual organisation Geographically dispersed people accomplishing tasks together thanks to modern information technology.

Virtual team Information technology allows team members in different locations to conduct business.

W

Wholist Cognitive style characterised by processing information in a whole.

Withdrawal cognitions Overall thoughts and feelings about quitting a job.

Work values Refer to what a person wants out of work in general.

Written communication Verbal communication that is written.

16 PF model 16 traits or factors representing personality according to Cattell.

360-degree feedback Comparison of anonymous feedback from one's superior, subordinates and peers, with one's self-perceptions.

Index

Page numbers for key terms are followed by 'KT'